Oil and Governance

National oil companies (NOCs) play an important role in the world economy. They produce most of the world's oil and bankroll governments across the globe. Although NOCs superficially resemble private-sector companies, they often behave in very different ways. *Oil and Governance* explains the variation in performance and strategy for NOCs and provides fresh insights into the future of the oil industry as well as the politics of the oil-rich countries where NOCs dominate. It comprises fifteen case studies, each following a common research design, of NOCs based in the Middle East, Africa, Asia, Latin America, and Europe. The book also includes cross-cutting pieces on the industrial structure of the oil industry and the politics and administration of NOCs. This book is the largest and most systematic analysis of NOCs to date and is suitable for audiences from industry and academia, as well as policymakers.

DAVID G. VICTOR is a professor at the School of International Relations and Pacific Studies at the University of California, San Diego, where he also leads the Laboratory on International Law and Regulation.

DAVID R. HULTS is a research affiliate at the Program on Energy and Sustainable Development (PESD) at Stanford University.

MARK C. THURBER is associate director at the Program on Energy and Sustainable Development (PESD) at Stanford University.

D1571319

Oil and Governance

State-Owned Enterprises and the World Energy Supply

DAVID G. VICTOR

DAVID R. HULTS

MARK C. THURBER

CAMBRIDGE
UNIVERSITY PRESS

CAMBRIDGE
UNIVERSITY PRESS

University Printing House, Cambridge CB2 8BS, United Kingdom

Cambridge University Press is part of the University of Cambridge.

It furthers the University's mission by disseminating knowledge in the pursuit of education, learning and research at the highest international levels of excellence.

www.cambridge.org
Information on this title: www.cambridge.org/9781107438965

First published 2012
First paperback edition 2014

A catalogue record for this publication is available from the British Library

Library of Congress Cataloguing in Publication data
   Oil and governance : state-owned enterprises and the world energy supply / [edited by] David R. Hults, Mark C. Thurber, David G. Victor.
      p.   cm.
   Includes bibliographical references and index.
   ISBN 978-1-107-00442-9 (hardback)
   1. Petroleum industry and trade – History.   2. Petroleum industry and trade – Government policy.   3. Corporations, Government.   I. Hults, David R.   II. Thurber, Mark C.   III. Victor, David G.
   HD9560.5.O3654   2011
   338.2´7282–dc23
   2011037726

ISBN 978-1-107-00442-9 Hardback
ISBN 978-1-107-43896-5 Paperback

Contents

List of figures	*page* viii
List of tables	xiv
List of boxes	xvi
List of contributors	xvii
Acknowledgements	xviii

Part I Introduction — 1

1 Introduction and overview — 3
DAVID G. VICTOR, DAVID R. HULTS, AND
MARK C. THURBER

Part II Thematic studies of national oil companies — 33

2 The political economy of expropriation and
privatization in the oil sector — 35
CHRISTOPHER WARSHAW

3 Hybrid governance: state management of national
oil companies — 62
DAVID R. HULTS

4 On the state's choice of oil company: risk management
and the frontier of the petroleum industry — 121
PETER A. NOLAN AND MARK C. THURBER

Part III National oil company case studies — 171

5 Saudi Aramco: the jewel in the crown — 173
PAUL STEVENS

6   Oil, monarchy, revolution, and theocracy: a study
    on the National Iranian Oil Company (NIOC)   234
    PAASHA MAHDAVI

7   Handcuffed: an assessment of Pemex's performance
    and strategy   280
    OGNEN STOJANOVSKI

8   Kuwait Petroleum Corporation (KPC): an enterprise
    in gridlock   334
    PAUL STEVENS

9   China National Petroleum Corporation (CNPC):
    a balancing act between enterprise and government   379
    BINBIN JIANG

10 Petróleos de Venezuela, S.A. (PDVSA): from
    independence to subservience   418
    DAVID R. HULTS

11 Awakening giant: strategy and performance
    of the Abu Dhabi National Oil Company (ADNOC)   478
    VARUN RAI AND DAVID G. VICTOR

12 Brazil's Petrobras: strategy and performance   515
    ADILSON DE OLIVEIRA

13 Sonatrach: the political economy of an Algerian
    state institution   557
    JOHN P. ENTELIS

14 Norway's evolving champion: Statoil and the
    politics of state enterprise   599
    MARK C. THURBER AND BENEDICTE TANGEN ISTAD

15 Gazprom: the struggle for power   655
    NADEJDA VICTOR AND INNA SAYFER

16 NNPC and Nigeria's oil patronage ecosystem   701
    MARK C. THURBER, IFEYINWA M. EMELIFE,
    AND PATRICK R. P. HELLER

17 Fading star: explaining the evolution of India's ONGC   753
    VARUN RAI

18   Petronas: reconciling tensions between company
     and state   809
     LESLIE LOPEZ

19   Angola's Sonangol: dexterous right hand of the state   836
     PATRICK R. P. HELLER

Part IV   Conclusions and implications   885

20   Major conclusions and implications for the future
     of the oil industry   887
     DAVID G. VICTOR, DAVID R. HULTS, AND
     MARK C. THURBER

Part V   Appendices   929

Appendix A: our assessments of NOC performance   931
     DAVID G. VICTOR, DAVID R. HULTS, AND
     MARK C. THURBER

Appendix B: assessing NOC performance and the
     role of depletion policy   940
     PAUL STEVENS

References   946
Index   1000

Figures

1.1 Schematic for this study   *page* 21
1.2a Liquids reserves on working interest basis as of
     October 2009   25
1.2b 2008 liquids production on working interest basis   25
1.3a Gas reserves on working interest basis as of
     October 2009   26
1.3b 2008 gas production on working interest basis   26
2.1 Number of countries expropriating assets in the
     oil sector   44
2.2 Number of countries privatizing national
     oil companies   45
2.3 Marginal effect of executive constraints on
     predicted probability of expropriation   51
3.1 Select elements of NOC governance systems   64
3.2 Sample NOC governance system as part of the
     principal–agent relationship   69
3.3 NOC performance and organization of state actors
     having authority over an NOC   80
3.4 NOC performance and mix of NOC oversight
     mechanisms   84
3.5 NOC performance and reliance on law-based
     mechanisms   86
4.1 The central idea: Petroleum risk and the state's
     capacity for risk can constrain state choice of
     hydrocarbon agent   123
4.2 Relative risk of petroleum investments (illustrative)   127
4.3 Investment risk as a function of petroleum province
     maturity (illustrative)   130
4.4 The choice of operating company and state
     participation when the state desires direct
     control   144

4.5 Water depth of the ninetieth percentile offshore
exploration well worldwide that was spudded in
the given year   155
4.6 Average fraction of exploration wells operated by
home NOC as a function of water depth relative
to the frontier, 1970–1989   159
4.7 Average fraction of exploration wells operated
by NOCs from 1970 through 2008, plotted alongside
oil price   161
5.1 Map of major oil and gas fields in Saudi Arabia   175
5.2 Golden quadrant idea   185
5.3 Oil revenues contribution to government revenue   194
5.4 Oil GDP contribution to total GDP   195
5.5 Oil contribution to merchandise export, 2003–2007 195
5.6 Saudi Arabian and world oil output, 1940–2008   210
6.1 Map of major oil and gas fields in Iran   238
6.2 Organizational chart of NIOC and its subsidiaries 245
6.3 Government revenue from oil and gas sales,
1955–2009   248
6.4 Oil within the Iranian political system   254
6.5 Iranian oil and gas production, 1937–2007   260
6.6 NIOC and OPEC   261
7.1 Map of major oil and gas fields in Mexico   285
7.2 Mexican liquid hydrocarbon production, 1965–2010   288
7.3 Pemex crude oil production by field (1997–2010)   288
7.4 Pemex capex, 1980–2010   303
8.1 Map of major oil and gas fields in Kuwait   338
8.2 Organizational structure of the Kuwait
petroleum sector   342
8.3 Kuwaiti oil production, 1965–2006   356
9.1 Evolution of the Chinese oil industry   381
9.2 Map of major oil and gas fields in China   383
9.3 Oil production and oil consumption by product
group, 1965–2007   386
9.4 Chinese oil production and consumption,
1965–2007   391
9.5 Top CNPC leadership employment history   399
9.6 Technology development at CNPC, 2003–2007   411
10.1 Map of major oil and gas fields in Venezuela   422

10.2 Distribution of Venezuelan proven liquid reserves by
      type, 2007   438
10.3 Selected PDVSA operational data, 1987–2002   456
10.4 PDVSA liquids production, 1999–2007   462
11.1 Map of major oil and gas fields in UAE   483
11.2 UAE total oil production along with
      OPEC allocations   485
11.3 Destination of crude oil production in 2007 from
      ADMA-OPCO's lower Zakum fields   488
11.4 Top-level organizational structure of ADMA-OPCO   503
11.5 Overall facilities block diagram of GASCO's "Ruwais
      3rd NGL Project," including OGD-III/AGD-II   504
11.6 ADNOC's gas flaring, 1996–2007   505
11.7 ADNOC's oil spills per year, 1996–2007   506
11.8 UAE's gas production and consumption,
      1980–2008   508
12.1 Map of major oil and gas fields in Brazil   519
12.2 Brazilian oil production, consumption, and refinery
      capacity, 1955–1965   524
12.3 Petrobras investments, 1954–1980   526
12.4 Petrobras investments, 1975–1995   529
12.5 Increasing water depth of pathbreaking
      Petrobras wells over time   530
12.6 Deficit in the oil account, 1981–1992   532
12.7 Oil price and Petrobras production, 1975–1995   534
12.8 Number of licensed blocks   538
12.9 Petrobras key financial ratios, 1999–2008   539
12.10 Oil price and Petrobras production, 1990–2008   540
12.11 Natural gas production, 1954–2008   541
12.12 Exploration costs and oil prices, 1999–2008   541
12.13 Oil production per upstream employee, 1998–2008   542
12.14 Capacity utilization of refineries, 1997–2008   542
12.15 Refined oil per downstream employee, 1998–2008   543
12.16 Government revenues from oil exploration and
      production, 1998–2007   544
13.1 Map of major oil and gas fields in Algeria   560
13.2 Algeria's petroleum reserves, 1980–2008   565
13.3 Hydrocarbon export value, total export value,
      and GDP for Algeria   565

13.4 The 1998 institutional and energy policy
     framework and Sonatrach's new corporate structure   570
13.5 Algeria's crude oil production, 1980–2007   584
14.1 Map of major oil and gas fields in Norway   606
14.2 Equity share of NCS production held by
     different companies over time   607
14.3 Share of NCS production operated by different
     companies over time   608
14.4 NCS production by hydrocarbon type and field   609
14.5 Oil and gas sector percentage contribution to GNP
     and state revenue, 1971–2008   615
14.6 Market value of Government Pension Fund – Global,
     1996–2008   617
14.7 Degree of success in achieving Norway's
     "Action Rule"   617
14.8 Statoil annual net income, compared against
     Brent crude oil spot price and Statoil NYSE
     share price   630
14.9 Statoil's domestic (NCS) hydrocarbon entitlement
     production by type, 1999–2008   631
14.10 Statoil's international hydrocarbon entitlement
     production by type   631
14.11 Statoil's reserves-to-production ratio, 1999–2008   632
14.12 Relative contribution of domestic and international
     hydrocarbons to Statoil production, reserves,
     and net operating income   633
14.13 Sources of Statoil international equity production
     in 2008   633
14.14 Production costs on the NCS: Statoil, Norsk Hydro,
     and StatoilHydro, with BP global production cost
     as a benchmark   635
14.15 Production costs internationally: Statoil, Norsk Hydro,
     and StatoilHydro, with BP global production
     cost as a benchmark   636
15.1 Russia: GDP growth and crude oil prices, 1966–2008   666
15.2 Russia: total export revenues versus crude
     oil prices, 1966–2008, and GDP versus oil price,
     1994–2008   667
15.3 Global conventional gas reserves by country in 2008 668

15.4 Russia: natural gas production, export, and
      consumption, historical data, 1985–2008   670
15.5 Major Russian natural gas fields production from
      West Siberia   671
15.6 Gazprom organization as of 2004   676
15.7 Map of major oil and gas fields and pipelines in Russia   687
16.1 Map of major oil and gas fields in Nigeria   705
16.2 History of Nigerian oil and natural gas production,
      showing annual petroleum export value as well as
      the type of government in power   709
16.3 Nigerian oil production by business arrangement,
      2005–2007   721
16.4 Amount and sources of Nigerian government oil
      and gas revenue, 2004–2006   724
17.1 Map of major oil and gas fields in India   757
17.2 Crude oil imports and production in India, 1970–2006   769
17.3 Crude oil production by ONGC, 1960–2007   770
17.4 Natural gas production by ONGC, 1980–2007   770
17.5 Hydrocarbon reserves of ONGC (proven reserves),
      2001–2009   771
17.6 Ultimate reserves accretion by ONGC   773
17.7 Financial performance of ONGC, 1995–2007   775
17.8 ONGC's return on assets and sales, 1995–2007   775
17.9 Distribution of pre-NELP and NELP acreage by
      winning bidder   783
17.10 Concessions given by ONGC to downstream
      companies   793
17.11 Distribution of ONGC's working capital into loans
      and advances, and cash and bank balances   795
17.12 ONGC's current ratio (net current assets divided by
      current liability) and debt-equity ratio   796
17.13 Multilayered principal–agent structure of ONGC
      ownership and management   798
17.14 Impact of GoI's monitoring mechanism on
      ONGC's performance   801
18.1 Map of major oil and gas fields in Malaysia   817
18.2 Sources of Petronas revenues   817
18.3 Petronas group oil and gas reserves   819
19.1 Map of major oil and gas fields in Angola   850

19.2 Increasing production amid conflict and instability   853
19.3 Proved reserves   854
20.1 Schematic for this study   888
20.2 The spread of NOCs over time   893
20.3a Functions characteristically undertaken by
      NOCs in sample   897
20.3b Composite hydrocarbon performance
      of NOCs in sample   898
20.3c Non-oil burdens on NOCs in sample   899
20.4 The impact of non-hydrocarbon
      functions on performance   902
20.5 Partnerships and NOC strategy   916
20.6 Geography and NOC strategy   918
20.7 Goals and administration of the hydrocarbon
      sector   922
20.8 Supply curves by type of hydrocarbon politics   923
20.9 Allocation of world oil production by type of
      hydrocarbon politics   925
 B.1 The depletion choices   941

Tables

1.1 NOCs sample, ordered by rank in working interest
   liquids production in 2008   *page* 24
2.1 Effect of executive constraints on expropriations   49
2.2 Effect of executive constraints on privatizations   52
2.3 PESD case study universe   53
3.1 Frequency of state actors having significant authority
   over an NOC   78
3.2 Frequency of various oversight mechanisms in governing
   NOCs   .   82
3.3 Frequency of formal and informal mechanisms
   in governing NOCs   85
4.1 Effect of "frontier" character (water depth,
   previous discoveries) and oil price on NOC
   prevalence in exploration   157
4.2 Effect of "frontier" character (water depth,
   previous discoveries) and oil price on NOC
   prevalence in exploration, this time excluding
   Brazil and Norway   162
5.1 Saudi Arabia – membership of oil governance institutions   189
6.1 Oil revenues in the fiscal budget (Iran)   249
7.1 Key financial indicators for 2000–2010   290
7.2 Allocation of capex (in % total capex) by Pemex
   operating subsidiary   303
8.1 Production costs in Kuwait   349
9.1a External decision-making governmental bodies
   related to CNPC before March 2008   400
9.1b External decision-making governmental bodies
   related to CNPC after March 2008   400
9.2 Petroleum industry extra profit tax collection rate   406

9.3 Comparison of key ratios for CNPC, PetroChina, and ExxonMobil, 2007   408

10.1 Venezuelan presidents, 1959–present   425

10.2 PDVSA payments to government budget, 2003–2008   448

10.3 PDVSA extra-budgetary obligations, 2003–2008   449

10.4 State control of PDVSA revenues, 2003–2008   458

10.5 Total PDVSA investment, and investment in exploration and production, 2003–2008   459

10.6 Estimated actual and planned PDVSA investment, 2003–2008   461

11.1 ADNOC's crude oil production expansion plans to meet its 2015 target   493

13.1 Key players – Algerian hydrocarbons sector   572

15.1 Russian oil and gas export, and total export revenues   667

15.2 Gazprom gas production in Russia by region   669

15.3 Gazprom's revenues, 2003–2008   678

16.1 Significant joint ventures with NNPC, with 2008 liquids production for each   711

17.1 Capital outlay allocated for ONGC in five-year plans between 1975 and 1990   764

17.2 External assistance received by ONGC for development of the Mumbai High fields   764

17.3 Declining crude oil production in early 1990s   765

17.4 Projected and actual oil production from ONGC's Neelam fields   766

17.5 ONGC's reserves replacement ratio   774

17.6 Blocks offered, bids received, and contracts signed for exploration blocks during pre-NELP rounds   780

17.7 Fields offered under joint venture development rounds   782

17.8 CSR expenditure by ONGC   790

19.1 Reported government receipts (Angola)   859

Boxes

1.1	What's in a name?	*page* 4
4.1	Frontier exploration uncertainties	129
4.2	Frontier development uncertainties	131
4.3	Managing exploration risk	135
4.4	Managing development risk	136
5.1	The attempted opening of the upstream in Saudi Arabia	189
6.1	The constitution of Iran	247
6.2	Iran's Oil Stabilization Fund and the rent collection process	250
13.1	Chakib Khelil	578
15.1	Sample of Gazprom's international activities	681
15.2	Major Gazprom projects	686
16.1	Most significant divisions and subsidiaries of NNPC	702
19.1	Some key Sonangol subsidiaries and joint ventures	862

Contributors

Adilson de Oliveira, Federal University of Rio de Janeiro
Ifeyinwa M. Emelife, Stanford University
John P. Entelis, Fordham University
Patrick R. P. Heller, Revenue Watch Institute
David R. Hults, Stanford University
Benedicte Tangen Istad, Petroleum Resource Group AS
BinBin Jiang, Yale University
Leslie Lopez, *The Straits Times* (Singapore)
Paasha Mahdavi, University of California, Los Angeles
Peter A. Nolan, Stanford University
Varun Rai, University of Texas at Austin
Inna Sayfer, Stanford University
Paul Stevens, Chatham House
Ognen Stojanovski, Attorney
Mark C. Thurber, Stanford University
David G. Victor, University of California, San Diego
Nadejda Victor, US Department of Energy
Christopher Warshaw, Stanford University

Acknowledgements

We began this project in 2007 during a period of growing speculation about the future of the oil industry and the national oil companies (NOCs) that are the industry's dominant actors. Our research
group, the Program on Energy and Sustainable Development (PESD)
at Stanford University, had just completed two major studies – one of
the globalization of gas supplies and one of the experiences with power
sector reform around the world. Both those studies pointed to the fact
that politicians had a very hard time managing the political fallout from
volatile energy prices, and the single most important factor explaining
most energy prices was the behavior of the oil market. There was no
shortage of economic models that purported to explain oil prices, but
our team at PESD thought that the most important factors at work in
the oil industry were just as likely to be political as economic. And the
political forces that mattered most were likely to concentrate on NOCs
since they controlled most of the world's oil reserves and production.

When we began this study, most of the existing research spoke
of NOCs as a monolithic block and usually in pejorative terms.
Analysts assumed that competitive, privately owned oil companies would always perform better than state enterprises. We weren't
sure that claim was always correct. And in any case we didn't think
that approach was useful. NOCs would not soon disappear from the
scene – in fact, many analysts suggested the world was in the midst of
a swing back to national control of key industries.

Our starting point was that NOCs weren't monolithic. There was
huge variation in their behavior and performance. We were mindful
that there was no shortage of hypotheses that claimed to explain why
NOCs might vary, but there wasn't much systematic analysis that actually tested such ideas. This book is an effort – the largest and most systematic independent analysis of NOCs – to explain why they varied.

We developed our research methods in stages, and we are particularly grateful to colleagues who helped us test and refine those

methods on the early case studies. Those included many students at Stanford Law School and Paul Stevens who was involved with a similar study at Chatham House. Howard Harris at McKinsey and many colleagues at BP patiently helped us understand the industry. Field visits and interviews in Abu Dhabi, Brazil, Mexico, and Norway were especially formative – thanks to the many people who helped arrange those and the follow up discussions, notably Michael Ohadi in Abu Dhabi; Adilson de Oliveira and Rogerio Manso in Brazil; Pedro Aspe and Andres Rozental in Mexico; and Ivar Tangen in Norway. We also benefited from the insights of Thomas Heller, professor at Stanford Law School, and Francisco Monaldi, who was in residence at Stanford's Hoover Institution for a time during this project and has been a source of wisdom about the political economy of NOCs.

Early in 2008 we held a two week "winter seminar" at Stanford on NOCs. Many of the case study authors attended the sessions along with outside experts who offered invaluable advice – Jeff Colgan, Howard Harris, Christine Jojarth, Saad Rahim, and Edgard Habib. A special thanks to Christian Wolf for sharing his econometric research on NOC performance.

Each chapter in this book has undergone individual peer review, and those reviewers are thanked in those chapters. In addition to the people already thanked, we are grateful to Valérie Marcel for reviewing multiple chapters and sharing her insights from having studied the Gulf region NOCs so carefully.

The project benefitted from terrific administrative and editorial support. Kathy Lung led a team at PESD that included Tonya McPherrin, Rose Kontak, Aranzazu Lascurain, Valerie Wang, Emily Wang, and Joyce Thomas. David Victor moved to UC San Diego near the end of this project and thanks Amanda Brainerd for administrative help and Linda Wong for keeping track of all the references. PESD is grateful, as always, for the ongoing support of BP, plc, and the Electric Power Research Institute (EPRI).

At Cambridge University Press thanks to the team of Chris Harrison and Philip Good, who have guided this project from the early days. Rob Wilkinson and Penny Harper were also of great help in the production process.

David G. Victor
David R. Hults
Mark C. Thurber

PART I

Introduction

1 | *Introduction and overview*

DAVID G. VICTOR, DAVID R. HULTS, AND
MARK C. THURBER

1 Introduction

An array of state-owned[1] entities – known as "national oil companies"
(NOCs) – dominate the world's oil and gas industry. Concentrated in
the Middle East but also based in Africa, Europe, Latin America,
and other parts of Asia, NOCs own 73% of the world's oil reserves
and 61% of production.[2] (Their dominance in gas is similar – 68% of
reserves and 52% of production.) In most segments of the world economy, state-owned enterprises (SOEs) have waned in influence, often
due to government policies that favor privatization and competition.
But in oil and gas (together known as "hydrocarbons") the role of
state enterprises is stronger than ever. This book looks at the origins
and operations of NOCs, which are a major part of our global energy
portfolio and a significant presence in the world economy.[3] Our analysis of NOCs thus has important implications for global oil and gas
markets and the shifting balance between market and state.

Despite the common name, "NOCs" play many different roles (see
Box 1.1). A few are commercially minded entities little different from
their private sector international oil company (IOC) counterparts.
These NOCs, like Saudi Arabia's Saudi Aramco or Norway's Statoil,
are highly profitable and in some cases worldwide operators themselves.
Other NOCs carry many political and social functions alongside their
commercial missions. These include Russia's Gazprom – the world's largest gas company and the Kremlin's instrument of choice in the 2000s
"gas wars" with the Ukraine – and Venezuela's Petróleos de Venezuela,
S.A. (PDVSA), which under President Hugo Chávez is the government's primary agent for providing social services and nationalizing the
domestic economy. Some NOCs perform functions that are normally
left to government. Angola's Sonangol, for example, is foremost a highly
effective regulator of IOC operations within the country; its role as an
oil producer is secondary.

Box 1.1 What's in a name?

For decades, industry and academia have referred to state-controlled oil and natural gas entities that carry out at least some commercial operations as "national oil companies." Yet in practice these entities are often not national, not focused on oil, and not even necessarily companies. The word "national" masks the fact that private interests own a large share of several NOCs, including Brazil's Petrobras and Norway's Statoil; also, some of these firms carry out a large share of activities beyond national borders. "Oil" isn't the only quarry of these NOCs; Russia's Gazprom is predominantly a gas producer, and many NOCs are struggling to produce larger quantities of gas. Many "companies" in the sector also have few commercial functions or other hallmarks of a company. Nigeria's NNPC, for example, has limited financial autonomy and capacity to perform oil and gas operations, and its managers are frequently unable to exert meaningful control over the many individual actors within the enterprise. Until a better acronym comes along – we hunted long and hard for one – we bow to convention rather than clarity and stick with the term "national oil company."

This volume peers beyond the differences among NOCs to find common threads. Using methods of social science, our aim is to explain the variation in strategy and performance of NOCs. We define "strategy" as an NOC's means of achieving long-term objectives. We define "performance," in turn, as an NOC's economic efficiency in finding, developing, and delivering hydrocarbon resources.

In this opening chapter we offer background and lay out our approach in the chapters that follow. We first put NOCs into broad historical context and then describe our research methods. Briefly, our approach rests on a set of hypotheses, drawn from existing research, which purport to explain why some NOCs perform well and others falter. Those hypotheses cover factors such as the relationship between the NOC and its political masters in the government and the types of geology NOCs encounter as they try to find and produce oil and gas. We then test those hypotheses in two ways. First, we look across the whole industry with three cross-cutting studies (see Part II); then we look in-depth at fifteen case studies of major NOCs and their host governments (see Part III). At the end of this chapter we introduce some broader themes that a large, systematic study such as this one can illuminate. In the Conclusion we revisit those themes.

2 NOCs in history

NOCs first arose sporadically in the early twentieth century. States, mostly in the industrialized world, justified their initial intervention in oil as part of efforts to control the "commanding heights" of their economies (Grayson 1981; Wolf 2009). Austria established the first NOC in 1908 to process crude oil and develop downstream markets for petroleum products (Heller 1980). Next in line was Argentina, which established Yacimientos Petrolíferos Fiscales (YPF) in 1922 (van der Linde 2000; McPherson 2003).[4] Other NOCs subsequently developed in states with strong corporatist traditions, such as France, which established the Compagnie Française del Pétroles (CFP) in 1924, and Italy's Azienda Generale Italiana Petroli (AGIP, now part of Eni) founded in 1926.

Over the next three decades, a handful of other governments established their own NOCs, but this time in the developing world. In 1938, Mexico expropriated US and Dutch commercial interests to form Petróleos Mexicanos (Pemex), the first major NOC formed via nationalization (see Chapter 7). Governments established several more NOCs following World War II as part of their economic growth strategies that relied on leadership through state enterprises. These NOCs include Iran's National Iranian Oil Company (NIOC, formed 1948), Brazil's Petrobras (1953), and India's Oil and Natural Gas Corporation Limited (ONGC, founded in 1956). Few of these early NOCs had much global influence on energy supplies and prices because they arose in countries that, at the time, barely produced or consumed any oil or gas. There was essentially no international trade in gas, and these new NOCs generally had little leverage over international trade in oil. For much of the early to mid twentieth century, a small number of vertically integrated, privately managed companies – the so-called "Seven Sisters"[5] – exerted near-total control.

The tide turned in the 1960s and 1970s, when the developing countries that were home to most of the world's oil and natural gas supplies took on a more assertive role. Fueled by resource nationalism, then-popular state-led economic development theories, and the hope for cartelization of the world oil market through the Organization of the Petroleum Exporting Countries (OPEC), these countries established NOCs en masse (Bentham and Smith 1987; Wolf 2009). Even countries such as Saudi Arabia that disfavored full-blown nationalization of oil assets were caught in the strong nationalistic currents flowing against foreign ownership (see Chapter 5). Most of the NOCs under study here date from this time period: Sonatrach (1963), Saudi Aramco (nationalized in three stages between 1973 and 1980), Statoil (1972),[6] Petronas (1974), PDVSA (1975), Kuwait Oil Company (later part of Kuwait Petroleum Corporation, or KPC, in 1975), Sonangol (1976), and Nigerian National Petroleum Corporation (NNPC) (1977).[7] Almost without exception, these states created their NOCs by nationalizing the operations of IOCs.[8] Indeed, nationalization of the oil sector was far more common than of other sectors of the economy (Kobrin 1984). Not all NOCs arose through nationalizations – Petrobras is among the few exceptions – but most find their origins in nationalist sentiment that remains popular today. Mexico's date of nationalization is still commemorated as a civic holiday more than seven decades after the event.

The NOCs formed from these nationalizations radically upended the structure of the energy markets. In 1970, IOCs had full access to 85% of the world's oil reserves; NOCs barely had access to 1% (Diwan 2007). By 1980, the situation had nearly reversed. IOCs had full access to only 12% of the world's oil reserves, and NOCs could access 59% (Diwan 2007). Most of the same governments that had been active in nationalization also used their state controls to influence oil price, at least over the short term: OPEC-coordinated supply restrictions in 1973 (following the Arab-Israeli war that year) and an Iranian production drop in 1979 (resulting from the Iranian Revolution) sent oil prices soaring twice that decade. For periods since the 1970s OPEC has played a central role in influencing prices.[9] During periods when the oil cartel has been strong, the fact that most OPEC production was controlled by state enterprises probably made it easier for governments to pull the levers needed to keep oil off the world market.

After the initial wave of NOC nationalizations, the pace of new NOC formation slackened, in part because there was little left to nationalize. A few oil-importing states (e.g., Germany), shaken by oil crises, established NOCs in the 1970s to promote security of supply.

And in the late 1980s through early 1990s, several states that were formerly part of the Soviet Union founded their own NOCs, including Gazprom (1989) – which was not nationalized but merely recognized as a distinct entity that, previously, had been a government ministry. Generally, however, the list of NOCs today is much the same as it was during the late 1970s.

During the 1980s, oil prices declined, and NOCs pursued divergent strategies to cope with falling revenues. Some NOCs, like PDVSA or Petronas, became vertically integrated and made inroads into international markets, ostensibly to secure downstream markets and compete with IOCs (Stevens 2005). Between 1983 and 1989, PDVSA, for instance, acquired significant equity interests in eleven European and American refineries and took ownership of a large US distributor, CITGO (see Chapter 10). This growth did not come without controversy, however. Critics accused the globalizing NOCs of seeking to avoid payment of taxes in their home country and, more generally, of acting like "states within a state" without regard for broader national objectives that originally inspired governments to create NOCs (Philip 1982; Boué 1993).[10] Other NOCs, such as Algeria's Sonatrach, stayed largely at home and spent much of the 1980s seeking to attract foreign oil investment to generate badly needed new revenues (Fattouh 2008).

During the 1990s, state control over oil waned. Low oil prices stripped government revenues and created an impetus for change; the ideas behind the "Washington Consensus" favoring economic liberalization and a shrinking of the state offered a ready remedy. Liberalization particularly took hold in Latin America: Argentina privatized its NOC, YPF, in 1992, and both Pemex and PDVSA lobbied their governments for greater private sector involvement (Howell 2007; Chapter 10). Other states, including China and India, allowed private investors to take minority shares in their NOCs. Russia also sold off much of its oil sector to private investors, though in most cases these new owners kept close links to the country's political masters (Aslund 1999; Chapter 15). Liberalization in the Middle East lagged by comparison, but even there some reforms occurred (Stevens 2008a). Nevertheless, hydrocarbons saw less liberalization on the whole than other infrastructure sectors like telecommunications or electricity (Kikeri and Solo 2005).

When oil prices rose again in the early 2000s governments responded in many different ways. Some sought a greater role for state ownership in the newly lucrative sector. Many added new social obligations for their NOCs, such as procurement requirements, domestic gasoline subsidies, and sometimes quite significant extrabudgetary spending programs. Many states invited or pushed their NOCs to become, in effect, quasi-governments.[11] Still others have kept an interest in reforms. For example, Abu Dhabi's ADNOC has welcomed a few new private sector projects into the country.

This brief account raises the question of why states with large NOCs have fluctuated so markedly in their approach to private oil companies over time. While there are many confounding factors at work, it appears that price has been a key factor (Manzano and Monaldi 2008; Stevens 2008a).[12] Prices have a particularly large effect on hydrocarbons, relative to other economic sectors, because hydrocarbons projects have high: 1) excess returns, or *rents*; 2) non-recoverable costs of investment, or *sunk costs*; and 3) risk. (See Manzano and Monaldi, 2008, for discussion.) These factors give governments an incentive to seek out private investment when prices are low and renegotiate private sector arrangements when prices are high. In Chapter 4, Nolan and Thurber consider in more detail how price may affect the NOC–IOC balance in hydrocarbon activities.

Looking to the future, forecasts are for NOCs to become even more dominant. The International Energy Agency projects that almost 80 percent of the increase in global oil and gas output to 2030 will come from NOCs (IEA 2008). NOCs have proved to be a durable and important form of enterprise.

3 Surveying the scholarship on NOCs

NOCs are hardly a new topic for scholarly research. Here we briefly sketch some of the major questions that previous studies have examined, engaging a wide range of disciplines, including political science, public administration, and economics. We look not only at studies that focus on NOCs but also scholarship from the much larger literature on state-owned enterprises (SOEs).

3.1 Why form an NOC?

Various studies, drawn mostly from political science, consider the rationales for forming NOCs and other SOEs.[13] One of the more common explanations for SOE creation is that left-leaning governments worldwide adopted statist ideologies between the 1950s and 1970s.[14] According to this view, SOEs reflected the belief that state ownership would better allow governments to promote and control economic development, redistribute income, and advance national pride; this model is contrasted with private ownership and redistribution through taxation (Toninelli 2000). Similar explanations have proven popular among NOC scholars (Jaidah 1980; Auty 1990). Another theory is that governments, particularly in the developing world, created SOEs principally as a tool for marshaling popular support (Smith and Trebilcock 2001). From this perspective SOEs such as state oil companies were seen as convenient political instruments that offered large reservoirs of jobs for dispensation to favored groups as well as other useful products and services that governments could readily control for political purposes (Peltzman 1989; Eller *et al.* 2007). A third rationale – rooted in early views about the "principal–agent problem" in public administration and applied with vigor to NOCs – is that governments found it hard to control foreign oil firms as their agents for developing the country's oil and gas resources. These foreign firms had their own interests and vastly greater amounts of information about a nation's hydrocarbon resources and the sources of value in the world market. Many governments feared that foreign ownership would result in lost rents, lost control over the pace of resource extraction, and – in a more nefarious variant – threats to the security of their rule. NOCs, it was often thought, would be comparatively easier to tame (Grayson 1981; van der Linde 2000).

3.2 Why maintain an NOC?

Scholars have wrestled with the question of why NOCs have thrived even as SOEs in other areas of economic activity have proved less resilient. Some of the key factors initially underpinning state control of NOCs were vestigial statist ideologies and the fact that NOCs remained convenient for political patronage (Auty 1990). Many of the same factors also applied to SOEs generally (Werenfels 2002). By the 1980s and 1990s, however, the storylines for NOCs and other SOEs began diverging. Highly industrialized countries privatized the bulk of their SOEs in the 1980s, and many developing countries followed suit, albeit more unevenly, in the 1990s.[15]

One explanation is that SOEs were often big money losers and thus a drain on public budgets – a factor at work, for example, in the electric power industry that saw broad efforts at restructuring and privatization across the developing world in the 1990s (Victor and Heller 2007).[16] NOCs, by contrast, often generated huge profits that made them more sustainable, though sporadic privatizations nevertheless occurred.[17]

This explanation for NOC survival, while suggestive, assumes that political leaders would be content to maintain an NOC so long as it generated some profit. However, the explanation becomes less satisfying because evidence suggests that an alternative form of organization – i.e., a privately managed oil company – could generate even greater profits over time. Theoretical studies find NOCs tend to underperform relative to their private sector counterparts in hydrocarbons operations (Hartley and Medlock 2008).[18] Empirical research points in the same direction, though NOC variation is substantial and comparisons across NOCs are difficult (Eller *et al.* 2007; Victor 2007; Wolf 2009).[19]

Thus there is a puzzle as to why NOCs endure. It may be that NOCs provide political elites with rents that are easier to capture and non-core services that are difficult to replicate.[20] Or NOCs may be more resistant to change than other entities because of their deep political connections and healthy revenue streams. One of the goals of this study is to assess whether these or other explanations for NOC survival make sense.

3.3 How do governments and NOCs interact?

The interests of NOCs and their host states are not identical, and another thinner line of scholarship has examined how these interests clash as well as how governments and their NOCs interact. Some NOCs, such as 1970s Pemex or 1990s Gazprom, became known as "states within a state" for their independence from government control and, on occasion, for their ability to politically undermine a government's standing. Studies have probed the reasons why this phenomenon occurs and have found that politically powerful NOCs often form in large, organized resource sectors over which the state bureaucracy has little knowledge or regulatory control (Philip 1982; Mommer 2002).[21]

One implication of this research is that the creation of NOCs, generally, did not solve the principal–agent problem plaguing governance of the resource sector. Rather, the emergence of NOCs has merely shifted the information asymmetry between governments and IOCs to the government and the NOC.[22] In some cases, the new insular NOCs seemed harder to control than the original foreign firms they replaced. Where foreign companies were kept at arm's length and competed to provide information and revenues to host governments they plausibly were more reliable agents than NOCs that concentrated their political talents on building their own political foundations and insulating themselves from government. Over time, some states and NOCs managed to find ways to align their interests; others, by contrast, remain at cross-purposes.

We view this as a central puzzle that must be explained. Why have some governments been able to create incentives that encourage good performance and reliable agency by powerful, durable NOCs while other governments have struggled to find effective systems of administration? This volume will offer some answers.

3.4 *What explains the variation among NOCs?*

To sort out the differences among NOCs, previous research has relied mostly on case studies. This work falls into two general camps: those studies looking at particular NOCs in isolation and those offering structured comparisons across a small group of companies. The literature on individual NOCs is huge and highly variable in quality and methods; the individual case studies in Part III of this volume review much of that literature where it is relevant.

Though the questions and methods differ, both types of case studies shed light on the fine-grained details that may have significant effect in explaining the origins, functioning, and performance of NOCs. Detailed studies have also allowed for analysis of how different causal factors interact. For example, in an analysis of Saudi Arabia, Hertog (2008) looks at how government–IOC relationships at the time of nationalization and the degree of political insulation of the resulting NOC may influence the NOC's economic efficiency.[23] Such detailed treatments are invaluable, although the focus and methods of individual case studies usually vary widely and comparisons across cases have proved difficult.

More structured comparisons across detailed cases are rare. A broader study by Marcel (2006) of five NOCs in North Africa and the Middle East reveals, among other things, why NOCs from that region may thrive even though they are unlikely to internationalize (given their large domestic resource base) or privatize (given the many ways in which states remain dependent on them).[24] An even larger study by Jaffe (2007) and a team at Rice University, looking at NOCs in twelve countries – as well as several cross-cutting studies – examines, among other things, the range of private sector institutional tools (company vertical integration, autonomous boards of directors, private minority stakes) used to balance political and commercial goals. Neither of those studies was designed, however, to trace how these causal factors influence performance.

The largest comparison of NOCs in the openly published literature is probably the study sponsored by the World Bank (2008). Because the sample of NOCs was so large and critical data so scarce, that the study arrived at important general observations about NOCs but, by design, did not delve into the detailed factors that explained the cause-and-effect relationships between major factors at work and the performance of NOCs. The World Bank study did suggest a composite 'value creation' indicator that might be used to measure performance, although many of the chief elements of that indicator require data that many NOCs do not report (World Bank 2008, Part A, p. 31). The study also noted that NOCs engage in a wide array of non-commercial activities but noted the difficulty in obtaining systematic information on those obligations. (Our research will show that those non-commercial activities are one of the chief reasons why so many NOCs perform poorly.) Despite difficulties in obtaining data, the study looked at clusters of variables, but relatively few tight relationships between individual variables emerged. The World Bank study also suggested some broad rankings of NOCs based on performance, but the rankings relied on indicators for which data was available and yielded results radically different from those presented in this book (see World Bank 2008, Part A, table 5). For example, Saudi Aramco and Pemex are ranked within 10 percent of each other in performance, while we rank the former much higher and the latter lower. The World Bank study gives some of its lowest rankings to ADNOC and Sonangol – both of which we rank much higher. And it gives an average ranking to Nigeria's NOC, which we find (along with Iran's NIOC and Kuwait's KPC) to be among the poorer performers.

4 This study

The existing literature is rich in its analysis of SOEs but much thinner in applying those insights to NOCs. Detailed empirical studies of NOCs are surprisingly rare and few have been designed scientifically with the aim of testing hypotheses about the factors that explain why NOCs persist and how these firms behave and function. From our review, two gaps in the literature loom especially large. One is the inability to explain why NOCs seem to vary so widely in their performance and business strategies. The other gap – the lack of a theory to explain how NOCs interact with their host governments – could help explain why performance and strategy vary and perhaps why NOCs endure. The central goal of this study is to help fill those gaps.

NOCs are extremely difficult to investigate. Studies that look at the entire oil and gas industry offer the hope of gleaning insights that are relevant to understanding any NOC. Such studies that take a cross-cutting look at the whole industry, including all NOCs, are difficult to utilize on their own. The factors that need analysis are too complex and poorly understood; local details that vary in every NOC are too important. The view from 30,000 feet, on its own, is too broad. An alternative is in-depth case studies. But earlier case study research has been too anecdotal and unstructured to yield conclusions that are "generalizeable" – that is, past case study research has not been designed so that findings from one case study offer insights into other cases.

Our approach is a hybrid of these two broad research methods. At the core of this book lie fifteen case studies. As we shall show, case study research is prone to many flaws because such research usually sacrifices systematic, scientific analysis for the richness of local details and anecdotes. And case study research is usually prone to biases that arise when selecting cases. Yet such an approach is unavoidable because the local details matter; NOCs are so complex and the factors that explain their behavior so poorly understood that in-depth treatment is essential.

In designing our case studies we adopted the standard methods from social science research. Prior to beginning this research we identified our "dependent variables" – that is, the performance and business strategy of NOCs that we are trying to explain. We also identified the major "independent variables" – that is, the factors we thought, based on a careful review of the literature, might plausibly explain the variation in performance and strategy. Those independent variables included factors such as the goals of host governments, geology, and especially the interplay between host governments and their NOCs. Finally, we selected a sample of NOCs that displayed variation along each of these independent variables. By looking at NOCs that operated under widely different circumstances we sought to trace how those circumstances affected performance. We call this approach "structured case studies." By structuring the analysis to look at the same factors in every case study – along with the many important local details – such research makes it easier to draw comparisons between cases and, ultimately, offer insights that are more general rather than tied solely to each individual case.[25]

Even if our case studies were highly successful we knew that they would still face the difficulties that plague most case study research. Richness in case detail nearly always weakens the systematic comparisons between cases. We were particularly worried about that problem because our "dependent" and "independent" variables were necessarily fuzzy. They were hard to describe with precision; there was little prior, systematic research that we could use as a starting point for our study. Some NOCs are so secretive that the factors we were most keen to analyze were often hidden. Yet the strength of the case study approach – its flexibility to allow each study to focus on the relevant details – risked becoming its chief weakness. Thus the other part of our hybrid: we commissioned three cross-cutting studies to look in-depth at crucial aspects of the research. Each looked at independent variables that we expected would be pivotal to the study and which we knew, at the outset, were poorly understood.

For both approaches – case studies and cross-cutting analyses – we have solicited studies from a mix of established and rising scholars. The studies were current in late 2009 and most have been updated since. In each case study the authors began with a highly structured analysis that was organized around the research design which we outline in the rest of this chapter. Many of these first drafts were long and packed with detail and thus we published them separately as working papers. For the versions that appear in this book we dismantled some of the analytical superstructure and edited for length to make the final stories more felicitous for the reader. The rest of this chapter offers more detail on our case study methods and also describes how the cross-cutting studies fit with the detailed case analysis.

4.1 The "dependent variables": what we seek to explain

Our central goal is to explain "performance." There are many standard metrics for performance, such as the cost and employment per barrel produced or refined as well as orthodox financial measures of performance (e.g., return on capital employed). Studies by Wolf (2009) and Victor (2007) looked at such metrics and found that most NOCs probably perform worse than IOCs. At the same time, these studies wrestled with some of the limitations of strictly quantitative approaches in assessing NOC performance. Aside from basic parameters like reserves and production, standard quantitative data is incomplete for many of the key NOCs. Many report full data only to their government shareholders but not the external world. (In some cases high-quality data on operations does not even exist within the NOC; within our sample, NNPC is the most pronounced such case.) Even metrics that are visible to the outside world can be suspect or difficult to compare among companies, with reserves figures being a case in point. More importantly, both geological endowments and policy decisions by host governments appear to have a huge impact on performance measurements. For example, government policies on the rate of allowable depletion of hydrocarbon resources necessarily have a large impact on a company's output. (For more on depletion rates and their importance as well as the possible biases in reported reserves figures, see the detailed treatment in Appendix B.) Yet another complication is that most NOCs commingle their oil and gas operations with a wide array of other functions – such as social programs – that may not deliver direct economic benefits to the company yet are intrinsic to their existence as a state-owned enterprise. The lesson from our review of the empirical studies was that a single, quantitative measure of performance is crude and ill-suited to comparisons across NOCs.

Given the limitations of strictly quantitative treatments and the rich detail available from our large sample of case studies, we developed a four-level qualitative scoring system to rank relative performance of each of the fifteen NOCs. Where available, the authors look at stand-ard metrics for performance focusing on the "upstream" production of oil and gas. They also assess how each NOC performs against an "ideal" efficient firm that operates under the same policy constraints and geological opportunities. The comparison with an ideal firm is a thought experiment that is difficult to perform in practice, and thus where possible each author also looks at performance goals that the NOC and its host government set. Those goals are often a reliable indicator of performance levels that are achievable, and when firms consistently fail to meet them it is often a sign of poor performance. In Appendix A we provide more detail on this four-level scoring sys-tem and also describe the scoring for each of the fifteen NOCs.

We also assess in the case studies the strategy that NOC managers adopt, both as an intervening variable that may affect performance and as a dependent variable in its own right. While strategic choices take many forms, here are four types of decisions that we examine in detail:

1) Operatorship. Does the NOC operate its own fields, and when it shares operations what roles does it assign to itself and its partners?
2) Resources. Does it focus on established low-risk resources or does the NOC invest in developing frontier oil and gas?
3) Geography. Does the NOC work solely at home, or does it have oper-ations overseas? Where NOCs move overseas how do they establish and maintain a competitive advantage?
4) Political. How does the NOC create the political assets it needs to sustain its position at home? Does it embrace or avoid non-core missions, and does it contribute to other state objectives?

Our interest in strategy stems from the observation that NOC strat-egy may directly affect a country's politics, environment, and level of socio-economic development.[26] NOCs are often the largest busi-nesses in their home countries and thus have important policy as well as commercial roles.[27] Governments often mandate that NOCs carry out wide-ranging non-core missions such as programmatic pub-lic works projects (e.g., highways, schools) and political patronage schemes (e.g., discounted oil sales to favored constituencies).[28] We look to NOC strategy to understand how managers mediate these wide-ranging non-commercial obligations as well as their commercial goals. Firm managers may accommodate such obligations or use them to enhance political careers;[29] others may pay lip-service to the state but deflect non-commercial demands as much as possible; and yet a third group of managers might express outright hostility towards state political projects. By capturing the variation in these strategic choices, we seek to better understand how non-commercial policy objectives translate into actual results.

4.2 The "independent variables": factors that may explain performance and strategy

Our study is a contribution to social science. Our aim is not to paint histories of NOCs for the sake of rich historical detail. Rather, we begin with a series of plausible hypotheses about the factors that may explain NOC performance and then use the historical analysis in each case study to examine whether those factors actually play a role in explaining strategy and performance. Then, looking across the fifteen case studies in totality, we test whether each hypothesis withstands the scrutiny of evidence.

Our hypotheses are informed by the literature that we reviewed earlier in this chapter. In part we have looked at hypotheses that cluster into two types. One type of hypothesis relates to factors largely (but not entirely) *external* to the NOC that nonetheless might explain the variation in firm performance at any given point in time. That list is long, but we have concentrated on three that the literature suggests will be most important. One is the goals of the state. Those goals are determined by governments (or elites that control governments) and can vary in many ways. A government may, for example, mandate that its NOC comply with OPEC production quotas; it might set depletion rates that influence the speed at which the NOC can extract resources. Some governments make explicit policy decisions to give their NOCs autonomy and seek only to maximize the revenues that the NOC provides for state activities. Others demand that NOCs take on an array of social projects that drain resources from core oil and gas operations. Or governments may lean on NOCs, as the most competent or powerful institutions in the country, to supply administrative functions such as regulation.

State goals must influence the performance of NOCs, but the origins and nature of state goals is very complex. We commissioned a cross-cutting study that draws from political science theory to identify how state goals arise and might influence NOCs and NOC formation (and privatization) (see Chapter 2). It is clear from this analysis that state goals do not emerge from a vacuum; they are intimately related to political and structural factors within the state. Political systems with long time horizons and leaders chosen by a broad electorate – characteristics often associated with robust institutional checks and balances – tend to produce state goals focused on maximizing benefits to society ("public goods") over the long term. State goals in systems without effective checks and balances are more likely to be short term in nature and to focus on delivering benefits to a narrower group of elites ("private goods"). Further affecting state goals are various structural conditions, ranging from the quality of a state's institutions (further discussed below) to its dependence on hydrocarbons revenues to its level of economic development.

Each of the case studies describes the goals of the state and explores the two political attributes discussed above – the time horizon of the state and the types of benefits leaders seek to channel from the NOC. In turn, these insights plausibly lead to differences in performance. Governments with long time horizons and few threats may foster NOCs that can adopt a patient strategy for allocating investment resources. By contrast, governments under strong pressure from elites or the public to deliver large prompt benefits may put pressure on NOCs to provide these functions rather than concentrate investment on the efficient long-term production of oil and gas. In the Conclusion (Chapter 20) we will revisit this question and explore how these political attributes help explain the size and type of burdens that governments place on their NOCs.

A second external factor is the quality of institutions within the state. Some state bureaucracies possess high levels of professionalism and technical knowledge of hydrocarbon resources; others are plagued by ignorance, inexperience, and corruption. We posit that institutional quality may influence how NOCs develop and perform. The quality of state institutions may also influence the content of state goals and how they are pursued. And state institutions, like state goals, are affected by economic development levels, political regime, and other factors.

To better understand state institutions, we commissioned a cross-cutting study to analyze the many policy tools that governments might utilize to control their NOCs. Those tools include classic instruments of regulation as well as public administration, finance, and corporate governance. That study, presented in Chapter 3, posits that a state's administrative capacity (in tandem with state goals) affects NOC performance by determining the methods that the state uses to control the NOC. The easy cases are states with well-defined goals and highly developed state institutions. In these cases, the state has many options for control. Few of the cases in this book are of that type – examples include Norway and now Brazil. Most of the cases concern states that, despite owning their NOCs, have limited mechanisms for exerting control.

A third external factor is the nature of resources underground. Some countries are blessed with "easy" oil while others face much larger geological challenges. Most governments focus their NOCs on oil, but a growing number now expect their NOCs to manage and produce large amounts of gas. One in our sample, Gazprom, focuses mainly on gas. (All else equal, gas is usually much harder to produce and market than oil. The roles of infrastructure and pricing are much more subtle and complicated in gas, and the time horizons are usually longer as well.) Previous research on NOCs has long recognized that the type of geological challenges and resources matter, but so far there has been no straightforward and systematic way to explain how such factors matter. That is a huge gap in the literature since the type of geology, plausibly, will determine the range of strategies available to the NOC and the success of different efforts to find and produce hydrocarbons.

We commissioned a cross-cutting study that offers a framework for studying how geological resources might affect strategy and performance. The study, presented in Chapter 4, looks at the life cycle of an oil province – from the earliest stages when risks are extremely high through initial production when risks plummet to the final stages of maturity when risks rise again due to the need for complex management of aging fields and enhanced oil recovery (EOR). At the earliest stages firms can manage risks with a portfolio, which usually favors IOCs as the mode of industrial organization. Once risks plummet, NOCs can dominate production without much consequence for economic efficiency. As risks rise again the technical resources and risk-management skills of an IOC may once again lead to better performance. This theory does not explain every facet of an oil or gas province development, but it offers a parsimonious starting point that can explain the strategic choices of NOCs and their implications for performance.

Each of the case studies, mindful of the insights from Chapter 4, describes the types of geological challenges faced by the NOC and then traces how that geology has influenced strategy and performance. Each study also considers the degree of geological difficulty when ranking the NOC's performance.

Our list of three factors external to the NOC is far from exhaustive.[30] Importantly, we note that oil prices may have a sizable effect on NOC performance and strategy. In times of high oil prices, cash-flush NOCs may be more likely to invest in operations or advance ambitious projects; NOCs in times of low prices may opt to retrench. We note that crude oil prices are more or less uniform worldwide whereas our goal is to explain variation among NOCs. Changes in oil prices can help tease out how other factors influence NOC performance and strategy.

In addition, we have looked at factors *internal* to the NOC. A sharp line between internal and external factors is hard to assign; by "internal" we mean those factors over which an NOC has some control. Internal factors include practices entirely within the firm, such as the procedures for project management. Also, at least partly internal are contracting arrangements between NOCs and IOCs. The literature, however, suggests that central factors at work here relate to the interplay between the government and the NOC. That interplay depends, of course, on the government's goals, the administrative capacity of the state, and the geological resources constraining the choices of both state and NOC. Shaping that interplay is one of the most important functions that NOC managers perform. The case studies in all their rich detail will help us assess whether NOC managers influence strategy and performance in this way or if fundamental, external factors play a more dominant role.

Figure 1.1 shows a schematic view of some of the main causal factors that we think explain NOC strategic choices and, in turn, performance. We show the three broad external factors on the left; the central questions surrounding interactions between the state and its NOC in the middle; and our dependent variables on the right. Each of the boxes and arrows is, of course, highly stylized; within each

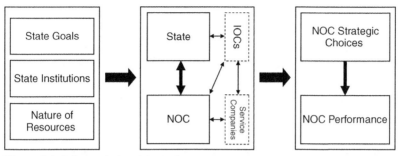

Figure 1.1 Schematic for this study.

Three external factors (shown on the left of the figure) lead to choices about the organization of a country's oil sector. That organization sets the mission and functions of the NOC, including how the NOC interacts with the state and with other firms (shown in the middle). In turn, the organization of the country's oil industry – in particular, the interactions between the state and its NOC – helps define the strategy and performance of the NOC (shown on the right). Three cross-cutting studies look at particular issues in detail – notably the goals of the state (Chapter 2), the ways that states administer, regulate, and govern their NOCs (Chapter 3), and the influence of geological resources on whether states choose NOCs or other forms of organization for their oil industry (Chapter 4). Fifteen case studies then examine how all of these factors work in concert for particular NOCs and their host governments (Chapters 5–19).

many details arise. The task of the case studies is to delve into those details in a way that helps us revisit this model in the Conclusion and assess which factors actually explain strategy and performance (and how).[31]

4.3 Units of analysis and case selection

Our aim is to explain NOC behavior, but we treat the state as the unit of analysis. We are interested in understanding how the state organizes its hydrocarbon sector, and in nearly all of our cases the state has created a singular NOC as part of that organization. (Some exceptions arise when governments create separate state companies to handle downstream activities such as refining, marketing, and petrochemicals; in a very few cases – notably, China, India, and for a brief period Saudi Arabia – the state has also allowed more than one NOC to engage in upstream activities.) Except where the distinction is important, we will use "state" and "NOC" interchangeably in describing the cases that we have selected.

The universe of possible cases for study are states that have a state-owned firm that plays a substantial role in the country's hydrocarbon production. By "state-owned" we mean an enterprise (firm) in which the government has a controlling interest – 100 percent in some cases, but in a few cases as low as perhaps 20 percent if other shares are held widely or the state has a special ownership arrangement (e.g., a golden share) that gives it de facto control over key decisions.

To select our sample we compiled a long list of all significant state-owned oil companies and their attributes (published in PESD 2006). From that list we then selected a sample of fifteen NOCs that span the range of the world's experience with the explanatory factors ("independent variables") identified above.[32] Our sample thus includes cases where the state exerts near complete control over revenues and capital expenditure (e.g., Mexico) and those where such authorities are extensively delegated to the NOC (e.g., Saudi Arabia). It includes cases where the sector is exposed to competition (e.g., Norway), monopoly (e.g., Kuwait), and stylized competition (e.g., Russia). We have selected a sample that varies in geological difficulty and in the stage of development of the geological resources. Most of our cases involve NOCs that operate significant production, but our sample also includes NOCs that principally manage IOC operators and have no significant operational responsibility themselves (e.g., Nigeria). Our cases allow a close historical look at how NOCs have evolved from managerial to operational roles (e.g., Abu Dhabi) as the NOCs have sought to incorporate technical expertise from IOCs.

Our sample also spans a range of state goals. Some of the countries we examine are led by durable governments with long time horizons; others, by contrast, are much less stable and face large political uncertainties. (Some, such as Kuwait and Venezuela, have seen big shifts in governing institutions and state goals over time.) Some governments demand that their NOCs provide broad-based, populist goods and services, as PDVSA has in Venezuela under Chávez, or the large fuel subsidies that PDVSA, NIOC, and many other NOCs supply to local customers. Others concentrate the flow of rents from oil operations to narrower groups of elites, such as in Angola or Nigeria. Lastly, our sample covers the spectrum of state administrative capacities. We consider countries with some of the most professional, technically capable bureaucracies in the world (Norway) and others that struggle for institutional continuity and coherence (as in much of Nigeria).

We are mindful that any study of this type – with broad categories of important variables and hypotheses rather than a laser-like focus on a particular narrow factor – will be vulnerable to concerns about bias in the selection of cases. Thus we have erred on the side of selecting companies that are intrinsically important so that our sample was not only scientifically valid but also obviously relevant for the largest companies and host countries.[33]

Table 1.1 shows our sample of fifteen NOCs. Figures 1.2 and 1.3 show the share of global reserves and production accounted for by the companies in our sample in oil and natural gas, respectively.

5 The rest of this book

NOCs are political creations. Governments created them in an effort to take more control over the development of their oil and gas resources and retain more of the revenues from those activities for themselves. They have proved remarkably resilient and seem likely to be durable features of the world oil market for the foreseeable future. In this study we therefore turn from the question of why NOCs exist and look at how they perform. We have some initial, broad hypotheses that may explain why some NOCs perform much better than others. The rest of this book sets to the task of fleshing out those hypotheses in more detail, which we do through three cross-cutting chapters presented in Part II. Then we turn, in Part III, to a detailed examination of fifteen case studies that cover the world's largest NOCs while also spanning the range of the main factors that we think explain performance and strategy. Finally, in the Conclusion, we revisit our hypotheses.

Before turning to the full analysis, we note that a study such as this one can generate insights of two types. One type of insight comes from the highly structured hypothesis testing for which this study is designed. The other type is much more speculative. It looks to the future and extends the patterns we have observed historically to paint a picture of how the world oil market may unfold.

The Conclusion to this book includes some of that speculation, and here we signal three of the areas we will revisit. First, some analysts have speculated that NOCs will wane in influence because they will inevitably face technical challenges they can't master. Private

Table 1.1. NOCs sample, ordered by rank in working interest liquids
production in 2008

Company	Country	Liquids prod. (000 bpd)	Gas prod. (mmcfd)	Total reserves (bboe)
Saudi Aramco	Saudi Arabia	10,669	6,677	280
NIOC	Iran	3,694	7,840	237
Pemex	Mexico	3,257	3,953	27
KPC	Kuwait	2,832	1,166	47
CNPC (includes PetroChina)	China	2,694	5,354	33
PDVSA	Venezuela	2,275	876	268
ADNOC	United Arab Emirates	1,993	3,523	83
Petrobras	Brazil	1,921	1,713	30
Sonatrach	Algeria	1,201	6,658	21
Statoil	Norway	1,199	4,647	21
Gazprom	Russia	1,124	51,818	270
NNPC	Nigeria	862	1,842	26
ONGC	India	696	2,231	11
Petronas	Malaysia	534	4,076	12
Sonangol	Sonangol	270	0	3
		Working interest, 2008	*Working interest, 2008*	*Working interest, as of October 2009*

Note: "Working interest" refers to an entitlement to a share of production from
the property, usually subject to a royalty. Reserves figures are based on Wood
Mackenzie definition of commercial plus technical reserves.
Data source: Wood Mackenzie (2009a).

firms – notably the IOCs and the service companies – will, according to this perspective, become indispensible as the world tries to tap
increasingly complex, difficult oil and gas resources. We find very little evidence to support that view, and we speculate about a future that
sees a continued dominance by NOCs. This dominance arises not simply because NOCs and their host governments control access to most
of the world's most lucrative hydrocarbon resources. It also reflects
the fact that many NOCs have undergone enormous innovation in the

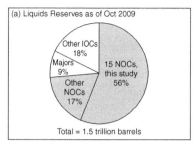

Figure 1.2a Liquids reserves on working interest basis as of October 2009, per Wood Mackenzie definition of commercial plus technical reserves.

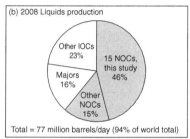

Figure 1.2b 2008 liquids production on working interest basis.
Notes: Majors are here defined to be BP, Chevron, ConocoPhillips, ExxonMobil, Shell, and Total. Data includes top 1,460 petroleum companies in the world.
Data source: Wood Mackenzie (2009a).

last three decades. Some are among the world's top performers independent of ownership; many (perhaps most) have found ways to perform well enough to get by. Most are aggressively looking for ways to incorporate the lessons and best practices of the oil and gas industry. Overall, we will speculate that the ability of many of these firms to incorporate those lessons is keeping pace with the rising complexity and difficulties of managing the world's frontier fields.

Second, we also find little evidence supporting prophecies for the end of IOCs. There is no doubt that IOCs do not dominate like their former (pre-1970s) selves. But the removal of IOCs from production in most of the easiest oil fields over the last four decades has forced these firms to focus to a much greater degree on where they provide special value. That has drawn them into much more complex oil fields and especially into natural gas. There is little evidence that these frontiers

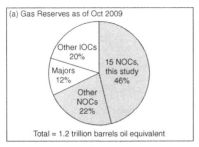

Figure 1.3a Gas reserves on working interest basis as of October 2009, per Wood Mackenzie definition of commercial plus technical reserves.

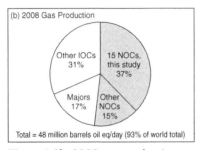

Figure 1.3b 2008 gas production on working interest basis.
Notes: Majors are here defined to be BP, Chevron, ConocoPhillips, ExxonMobil, Shell, and Total. Data includes top 1,460 petroleum companies in the world.
Data source: Wood Mackenzie (2009a).

are closing or that the price of oil will decline to such a degree that such high-cost activities become unprofitable.

Third, our study allows some speculation on the shape of oil supply curves. About three-quarters of the world's oil reserves are under management by NOCs, and our study will allow for a systematic assessment of how the NOCs perform. Looking to the future one of the pivotal questions is how these NOCs and their host governments will respond as oil prices change. In conventional industries, higher prices lead to higher supplies. For most NOCs, we speculate that the nature of the interactions between host governments and their NOCs leads, in most cases, to the opposite behavior. When prices are high, governments with short time horizons and many pressures to deliver benefits to stay in office will extract ever more rents from their oil companies – making it harder for those companies to invest for the long term. And when prices are high, governments with long time horizons may bet that oil will be more valuable if kept in the ground. By these logics, supplies decline and prices rise.

The Conclusion will entertain these and other speculations in more detail. Until then, however, we focus on the more systematic and historical goals of our study.

Notes

1 By "state" we refer to a sovereign political unit. A "government" is the political leadership within a state. Thus, governments can come and go; states tend to endure.

2 Oil and gas reserves and production ownership figures are for 2008, derived from Wood Mackenzie (2009a) – see Figures 1.2 and 1.3.

3 On April 20, 2010, as we were editing this book, the Deepwater Horizon drilling platform exploded in the Gulf of Mexico near Louisiana, killing eleven people and causing the largest offshore oil spill in US history. NOCs were not involved in the Deepwater Horizon disaster. Nevertheless, we are cognizant that NOC activities have significant effects on water pollution, air pollution, land use, and global climate change. Although this book is not, primarily, about the (deeply important) environmental consequences of oil, several of our case studies address the environmental effects of particular NOCs.

4 YPF later merged with an IOC to form today's Repsol YPF. Another early oil company with majority state control was British Petroleum (now BP), but the British state never managed British Petroleum. The British government and Bank of England took a combined 51 percent share of British Petroleum starting in 1914 (Grayson 1981; Stevens 2003b). By agreement, however, the British state appointed only two independent directors to British Petroleum, and the company operated independently before being completely privatized in 1995 (Bamberg 1994, 2000).

5 The Seven Sisters were Exxon, Royal-Dutch/Shell, Texaco, Mobil, Standard of California, Gulf, and British Petroleum. All but one of these companies, British Petroleum, was privately owned at the outset.

6 Norway, unlike the other countries listed here, was not a developing country at the time it established an NOC.

7 Several of these countries had previous failed experiments with home-grown NOCs. Venezuela founded the Corporación Venezolana del Petróleo (CVP) in 1960 but it failed to produce significant amounts of oil; upon its formation, PDVSA absorbed CVP. Saudi Arabia established Petromin in 1962 and it became a minor player in the Saudi oil

industry before eventually dissolving in 2005. NNPC's precursor, the Nigerian National Oil Company (NNOC) was established in 1971.

8 The nationalizations were effectively forced sales in which the original owners – generally hailing from among the Seven Sisters – generally received only partial compensation for their assets.

9 Over the long term, however, OPEC's power to control oil prices did not last. Consumer behavior changes and the failure of OPEC members to adhere to their quotas led to a significant price decline. Reacting to these long-term changes, Saudi Arabia would later use its influence as the most powerful player within OPEC to modulate oil prices, with the goal of reducing alienation among developed countries and disincentivizing investments in alternative energies (Rutledge 2005).

10 For further discussion of the state within a state phenomenon, see Randall (1987) and Szabo (2000).

11 Precursors of this trend include PDVSA's 1990s negotiations with the IMF on behalf of the Venezuelan government (see Chapter 10). But these precursors reflected government weakness; NOC actions today often reflect government capture of NOC objectives.

12 At a global level, the cycles of expropriation and investment are more significant than those of nationalization and privatization (Manzano and Monaldi 2008; Hogan and Struzenegger 2010).

13 The rationales for forming SOEs generally and NOCs specifically are strikingly similar, in part because the NOCs formed in the 1970s were the intellectual progeny of SOEs created in wealthier states during the 1950s and 1960s.

14 This ideology was rooted in then-popular socialist and/or communist thought, structuralist economic theory focused on market, rather than government, failures, and – especially among developing countries – nationalism.

15 Scholars attribute this reversal to a dramatic shift in state ideology (and, perhaps, to voters demanding such a shift) towards market-led "Washington Consensus" economic policies as the Cold War came to an end (Shirley and Walsh 2001).

16 Other studies attribute these privatizations to one-off financial benefits, particularly among indebted countries (Bortolotti *et al.* 2003), and political calculations (Banerjee and Munger 2004).

17 The reasoning is that market-led ideologies are more likely to induce privatization if privatization is seen as important to the company's profitability. State-owned extractive industries, including NOCs, may remain profitable even if they are less efficient than their private sector counterparts.

18 Theory similarly suggests that private companies tend to outperform SOEs generally in most contexts. Some of the most-commonly cited

reasons for reduced SOE performance include: cumbersome control mechanisms (instead of competition and price signals); assignment of multiple, competing goals (rather than the singular goal of profit maximization); narrow, politically motivated time horizons (instead of long-term profit goals); limited performance incentives (instead of stock options or profit sharing); and soft budgetary constraints rather than the discipline of bankruptcy (Laffont and Tirole 1991; González-Páramo and Hernández De Cos 2005). These effects may work at cross-purposes; the soft budget constraint of SOEs induces managers to take on more risk whereas the diffuse state goals may lead to risk-averse behavior. Standard fare theories of market failure suggest some limitations. State ownership may improve economic welfare in markets characterized by lack of competition (e.g., natural monopoly), the possible provision of large-scale public goods such as infrastructure or job training, or extreme uncertainty. Even in these contexts, however, state ownership is rarely the only means of achieving efficient outcomes. Other options include regulation or serial bidding for monopoly franchises and restructuring of industries to remove or isolate the elements that lead to natural monopoly.

19 Empirical studies of SOEs generally reach similar conclusions, although there are severe difficulties in separating the effects of public ownership from other factors. The most common findings are that state-owned enterprises and mixed enterprises (where both the state and private capital hold significant company shares) perform worse than private companies (e.g., Boardman and Vining 1989; Gónzalez-Páramo and Hernández De Cos 2005). A few other studies, however, reach a contrary conclusion, finding that state ownership does not necessarily reduce SOE performance (Martin and Parker 1995; Kole and Mulherin 1997). Some authors seeking to reconcile these findings with economic theory conclude that competition and well-functioning markets, rather than ownership, are the primary determinants of SOE performance (Caves and Christensen 1980; Kay and Thompson 1986; Feng *et al.* 2004). Echoing the view that ownership type per se is not the most important factor affecting performance, Vernon-Wortzel and Wortzel (1989) find that performance problems for SOEs are most often related to lack of clarity in company goals and limited organizational capacity to achieve those goals (which are often but not necessarily tied to state ownership).

20 Regressions reveal the "shadow cost" of these obligations (Wolf 2009). (These shadow costs include both the direct cost of carrying out social programs and the indirect inefficiencies from imposing social obligations on a commercially minded company, state monitoring of that

company, and the like.) Recognizing the methodological challenges in NOC–IOC comparisons, Wainberg and Foss (2007) at the University of Texas's Center for Energy Economics proposed a draft framework for taking account of broader state goals for NOCs.

21 For further analysis, see Randall (1987) and Boué (1993).

22 For more, see Dam (1976).

23 For more NOC case studies, see, e.g., Boué (1993) and Baena (1999a).

24 An earlier multicountry NOC study is Grayson (1981), which looked at NOCs in six industrialized European states.

25 Inevitably, such research must be only partially structured at the outset because the case studies reveal important factors at work that require later adjustment and iteration. Nonetheless, a careful structuring is essential from the earliest stages, as are efforts to minimize iteration since every new adjustment of the research method undermines the extent to which the data from the case studies is a true, independent test of hypotheses. For our first iteration see PESD (2006).

26 We recognize that NOCs also – and perhaps primarily – affect their home countries through their performance in core hydrocarbon functions. (Higher-performing NOCs, for example, may send more monies to their home country treasuries, which in turn could increase those countries' level of development.) We consider NOC strategy in part to understand the effects of NOCs' non-core activities.

27 Victor and Heller (2007) discuss the concept of a "dual firm" with both commercial and political competence.

28 McPherson (2003) catalogs some of these non-commercial objectives for NOCs.

29 In many countries, the ties between senior leadership in the NOC and the state are very close. See, for example, Ernesto Geisel (former president of both Petrobras and Brazil) and Dmitry Medvedev (former chairman of the board for Gazprom and current president of Russia). At the time this book went to press, Sonangol CEO Manuel Vicente was being mentioned as a possible successor to Angolan president José Eduardo dos Santos.

30 These factors listed above are not entirely separate from an NOC's existence. NOCs are large, politically powerful entities that may have the ability to influence a state's political objectives, quality of institutions, and perhaps even its geological make-up (at least at a given moment in time). Thus, we acknowledge that our independent variables, like independent variables in many social science studies, are subject to some feedback effects. We also acknowledge the possibility of more distant, foundational independent variables (e.g., economic prosperity generally), while noting that such variables might also be prone to feedback effects. We chose the independent variables here on the premises that:

1) such feedback effects are often not determinative (though we test for such effects in our case studies); and 2) that the independent variables chosen provide for a close-knit causal chain that is more amenable to the case study format.

31 At the outset of this study we did not know which factors would be most important, so we identified four categories of factors that probably explain NOC performance and partnerships and then began our research with an initial sample of six case studies. Those four categories are: 1) state goals, capabilities, and relationships with the oil sector; 2) management; 3) technology and geology; and 4) state structure. Through the preliminary research we realized that those categories did not map well onto the real lines of influence over how NOCs perform because nearly all of our preliminary research pointed to state influence as the central factor with which other factors interacted. For example, state structure, notably the dependence on hydrocarbon revenues, also explained why some states seemed more compelled to interject themselves directly into the NOC's operations.

32 Though our sample includes NOCs involved in all parts of the hydrocarbons industry, we have been particularly attentive to selecting NOCs with "upstream" operations (i.e., exploration and production) – by far the most profitable segment of the hydrocarbons value chain.

33 We note that geography – having little connection to the literature on NOC performance and strategy – is not one of our case study selection criteria. Therefore, some regions of the world (such as Central Asia) are underrepresented in our case study sample. The Middle East, by contrast, is overrepresented, principally because it is home to many of the world's largest NOCs. Because our case study selection is rooted in those factors considered most important for explaining NOCs, we believe that our study has broad applicability.

PART II

Thematic studies of national oil companies

2 The political economy of expropriation and privatization in the oil sector

CHRISTOPHER WARSHAW

1 Introduction

With more than 70 percent of the world's oil reserves, national oil companies (NOCs) dominate world oil markets (see Chapter 1). Fourteen of the top twenty oil companies in the world are NOCs or newly privatized NOCs. Moreover, NOCs appear to be increasing their control over global oil reserves (Kretzschmar *et al.* 2009). Due to their increasing pre-eminence in world energy markets, NOCs have recently been the focus of a cottage industry of academic studies. A number of studies have found profound differences between the performance of NOCs and independent, private oil companies. Eller *et al.* (2007), Victor (2007), and Wolf (2009) all find that NOCs are dramatically less efficient than their private counterparts.[1] Moreover, Wolf and Pollitt (2008) find that NOC performance improves dramatically following privatization. However, NOC performance is far from monolithic. Some NOCs are able to perform as well as major private companies, while others fall significantly short (Victor 2007). Indeed, this entire volume explores how NOCs perform and how they differ from private enterprise.

These findings raise two interlocking puzzles about the structure of the global petroleum industry. First, if private oil companies usually perform so much better than nationalized companies, why have so many countries nationalized private oil companies' assets and established state-owned petroleum companies? Second, why do so many

Ph.D./J.D. Candidate, Stanford Department of Political Science and Stanford Law School; Research Fellow, Program on Energy and Sustainable Development (PESD).

I am grateful for comments on previous versions of this paper from David Victor, Witold Henisz, Francisco Monaldi, Mark Thurber, David Hults, Christian Wolf, Peter Nolan, Aila Matanock, Rachel Stein, Danielle Harlan, Nicholai Lidow, and Carolyn Snyder. All mistakes are, of course, my own.

countries continue to maintain nationalized oil companies in the face of strong evidence of weak performance?

In this chapter, I provide a new theory and evidence to explain these puzzles. I use a perspective grounded in political economy to analyze how the incentives and constraints on state leaders affect their strategic decisions in the petroleum industry. There is a large literature on expropriation and privatization.[2] But few scholars have focused on the energy industry.[3] Much of the research on regulatory expropriation has focused on the telecommunications and electricity industries – two areas notable for their costly infrastructures that are ripe for expropriation and where governments have adopted substantial regulatory reforms over the last two decades in an effort to entice private investors. No extant study has analyzed state decisions to nationalize and privatize petroleum industries, using a unified framework. This gap in the extant literature is odd given the normative importance of the energy industry in the global economy. The petroleum industry dominates the economy of many developing countries. Moreover, the structure of the petroleum industry may have consequences for democratization, economic development, and the world economy.

The foundation of my analysis is that the primary goal of state leaders is to retain power (Bueno de Mesquita *et al.* 2003). In democracies, loss of power can mean a return to parliament or private life, while loss of power in autocracies can mean a swift flight to Switzerland or a bullet in the back of the head (Haber 2006). This implies that state leaders make strategic decisions in the petroleum industry in order to enhance their ability to retain power. Moreover, these decisions are likely to be structured by leaders' political incentives (i.e., retaining power) and constraints (i.e., checks and balances on their decision-making authority).

I find that states respond rationally to their political incentives and constraints. In particular, fewer checks and balances make states more likely to expropriate investors by nationalizing their oil industry. However, this relationship is concentrated in the period prior to 1980. After 1980, there is no significant relationship between checks and balances and expropriation. This is likely due to the fact that almost every single oil-rich state with weak checks and balances had expropriated the bulk of the privately held oil assets in their country by 1980. I also find that democracies with strong checks and balances are more likely to privatize their national oil companies than autocracies with weak checks and balances. Taken as a whole, these findings highlight the crucial role of political institutions for influencing states' strategic choices in the oil sector.[4]

I proceed as follows. In section 2, I discuss previous literature. Then I develop, in section 3, a new theory that ties the incentives and constraints on state leaders to the strategic decisions of states in the oil sector. In section 4, I discuss my data and research design, and in section 5, I discuss my primary findings. In section 6, I apply my findings to the case studies discussed elsewhere in this volume and then conclude.

2 Previous literature on expropriation and privatization

There is a large, well-developed literature on factors that affect countries' decisions to expropriate private industry and privatize state-owned industry. In this section, I summarize these literatures and discuss their implications for the oil industry.

2.1 Why do countries expropriate private industry?

Previous studies have found that states' decisions to expropriate foreign investors in the petroleum industry are affected primarily by two sets of factors.[5] The first set of factors focuses on the incentives for expropriation – the net benefits that state leaders expect from expropriation compared with leaving investments in private hands (see, e.g., Thomas and Worrall 1994; Banerjee and Munger 2004; Li 2009). The second set of factors focuses on the institutional constraints on state leaders.

2.1.1 Incentives for expropriation

In many cases, state leaders can expect to derive substantial benefits from expropriating independent oil companies' assets and establishing an NOC (e.g., Kobrin 1980, 1984; Lipson 1985; Thomas and Worrall 1994; Guriev *et al.* 2011). The ability to control management decisions at the NOC gives state leaders greater autonomy in pursuing favored political goals, such as channeling investment into favored projects (Peltzman 1989; Li 2009). State ownership may also give governments the ability to assert stricter regulation over the oil sector, such as by gaining information on the real costs of oil operations, which can help assuage the fear that private "agents" operating in the oil sector are operating for their own benefit rather than the benefit of the host country (see Chapter 3). Establishing an NOC can enable governments to provide employment to political allies (Eller *et al.* 2007), as well as develop local commercial and technical capacity, forward and backward linkages into other sectors of the economy, income redistribution through subsidized prices, assistance in state borrowing, and the provision of social and other infrastructure (Nore 1980; Grayson 1981; Horn 1995; McPherson 2003; Stevens 2003b). The nationalization of oil production can also increase national pride, which may bolster the political position of elites. For instance, Domíguez (1982) argues that "business nationalism" contributed to expropriations in Latin America during the 1970s. Some governments, such as in conservative Saudi Arabia, may have nationalized their NOC at the same time that many others did in the 1970s because they feared a nationalist backlash if they did not follow such popular trends of the time. Leaders may also favor nationalization when that makes it easier for governments to engage in collective action; the manipulation of production levels, as required by membership in OPEC, may be easier when states have direct control over production methods (Adelman 1995). Above all, expropriation transfers output and physical asset ownership from the private oil company to the host government. This onetime transfer often creates a significant financial windfall for the current state leaders (see, e.g., Kobrin 1980, 1984; Lipson 1985; Thomas and Worrall 1994).

Of course, this windfall is likely to be larger when the flow of resources through the oil industry is high, which creates strong incentives for countries to nationalize during such periods of high prices.[6] Indeed, a variety of studies have found strong evidence for a link between high prices and expropriation. Duncan (2006) analyzes eight developing countries that export a significant amount of minerals. He finds that price booms are strongly correlated with expropriations. Similarly, Guriev *et al.* (2011) finds that expropriations in the petroleum industry are significantly more likely when oil prices are high.

States may also see benefits, however, from forgoing expropriations. Due to their economies of scale and better use of human capital, private oil companies tend to be more efficient and profitable than NOCs

(Wolf 2009). As a result, over the long term, private oil companies are likely to generate a larger stream of revenue and, arguably, more technology spillovers and economic rents. In addition, the state gains reputational benefits from refraining from expropriation, which can lower its cost of debt and increase foreign investment (see, e.g., Tomz and Wright 2008). Thus, states with longer time horizons, such as industrialized democracies, may see more benefits from policies that encourage private enterprise than policies favoring expropriation (see Olson 1993).

2.1.2 Constraints on expropriation

In order to adopt a potentially controversial decision to nationalize oil companies, a state leader must overcome the political constraints of his office (Li 2009). The leader's ability to change the status quo policy is constrained by the number of veto players in the regime and the preference homogeneity among them (North and Weingast 1989; Tsebelis 1995, 2002; Henisz and Zelner 2001; Stasavage 2003). All things being equal, when there are more veto points with divergent preferences, it is likely to be more difficult for state leaders to expropriate the property of privately owned companies. There also may be fewer benefits associated with the short-term windfall from expropriation in countries with a higher level of checks and balances that constrain the state leader's ability to use the windfall to stay in office.

2.2 Why do countries privatize nationally owned companies?

While no recent study has examined why states choose to privatize NOCs, there is a large literature on the political economy of privatization in other industries (Clarkson 1989; Adams and Mengistu 2008). Various studies argue that countries privatize when the benefits of privatization are larger than the costs. Banerjee and Munger (2004) and Clarke and Cull (2005) focus on the political benefits of privatization and argue that countries privatize state-owned companies when the net political benefits are high. Similarly, Bortolotti *et al.* (2001) find that the political orientation of the political parties in power exerts a strong influence on privatization processes in forty-nine countries for the period 1977–1996. In Dinç and Gupta (2011) it is argued that variation in the importance of a state-owned company for patronage helps explain privatization decisions, finding that privatization in India is more likely in areas with less political competition because patronage is not as important in these areas. Finally, a study by Banerjee and Munger (2004) argues that countries with longer time horizons are more likely to privatize.

Economic factors also affect the benefits associated with privatization. Bortolotti *et al.* (2003) focus on the economic benefits of privatization and argue that countries with a large public debt are more likely to privatize in order to raise money to reduce their debt. Nolan and Thurber (Chapter 4) suggest that the economic risk associated with oil field development may affect the timing of nationalization and privatization. It is also possible that countries privatize their oil industries during low-price regimes when there is a greater need for the industry to operate efficiently (or conversely, during high-price regimes when they can get a greater price for the NOC).

Another large category of studies looks at the effects of institutional checks and balances on the credibility of privatization decisions. Crucially, a greater number of veto players enhances the credibility of governments' promises not to expropriate (North and Weingast 1989). It also enhances the credibility of governments' monetary policies (e.g., Lohmann 1998; Keefer and Stasavage 2002). The ability of governments to make credible commitments is likely to increase the price investors are willing to pay during the privatization process, which makes privatization more likely.[7] In other industries, several studies find that the presence of checks and balances is correlated with privatization decisions. For instance, according to Bortolotti *et al.* (2003) wealthy democracies with strong checks and balances are often the first to privatize.[8]

2.3 Unanswered questions

The extant literature leaves unanswered a number of important questions about the political economy of expropriation and privatization in the oil sector. First, how do political incentives and constraints affect the probability of expropriation and privatization in the oil sector? Second, do the same factors affect both expropriation and privatization decisions? Third, do the factors that affect these decisions vary over time? Finally, how is the political economy of expropriation and privatization in the oil sector different from other industries? In the remainder of this chapter, I seek to answer the first three of these questions and leave the final question for future work.

3 Theory

I build my theoretical framework using a perspective grounded in the political calculus facing individual state leaders. My theory relies on several premises. First, state leaders are able to make choices regarding the level of state involvement in the oil sector. If there are independent companies operating in their oil sector, in each time period state leaders can decide to expropriate investors and establish an NOC. If they choose to establish an NOC, in subsequent periods, they have the choice of partially or fully privatizing the NOC. Second, leaders want to stay in office. Third, leaders will often act strategically in the oil sector to help achieve their goal of staying in office.[9] Based on these premises, I develop clear theoretical predictions for how variation in the incentives and constraints facing state leaders will alter their strategic choices in the oil sector.[10]

3.1 Expropriation and nationalization decisions

My theory begins by looking at the impact of political checks and balances on a government's decision to expropriate or nationalize private oil companies. In most cases, autocracies controlled by a single individual, or just a small group of leaders, have fewer checks and balances than democracies. But the level of checks and balances varies within the simple typologies of "autocratic" and "democratic" regimes. In democracies, there may be few checks and balances where the same party always wins the elections (e.g., Mexico under the PRI (Institutional Revolutionary Party)). In autocracies, even without democratic institutions, leaders depend on the support of domestic groups to survive (Haber 2006; Weeks 2008). Thus, autocracies with a strong party apparatus that can remove the autocratic leader generally have stronger checks and balances than autocracies controlled by a personalist dictator (Besley and Kudamatsu 2008; Gehlbach and Keefer 2008).

The level of checks and balances affects leaders' expropriation decisions in three ways. First, the level of checks and balances on state leaders has an important effect on leaders' ability to change the status quo policies (North and Weingast 1989; Stasavage 2003; Li 2009). All things being equal, when there are more veto points with divergent preferences, it is likely to be more difficult for states to pass policies expropriating private oil companies (Tsebelis 1995, 2002).

Second, in countries with fewer checks and balances, on average, a narrower selectorate will be represented (Bueno de Mesquita *et al.* 2003).[11] By contrast, when there are stronger checks and balances, it is easier for new and underrepresented groups or constituencies to express their voices. This mechanism further enhances the likelihood that higher levels of checks and balances will be associated with fewer nationalizations and expropriations, since expropriations tend to favor narrower particularistic interests.

Third, there are likely to be fewer benefits associated with the short-term windfall from expropriation in countries with a higher level of checks and balances, since these checks and balances are likely to constrain the state leader's ability to use the windfall to stay in office.

Thus, I hypothesize that governments are more likely to expropriate private oil companies and increase their ownership over national oil production when there are few checks and balances on government leaders (Guriev *et al.* 2011).

Hypothesis 1: Fewer veto points (checks and balances) make states more likely to nationalize their oil extraction industry.

3.2 Privatization decisions

Similar influences may also affect the decision to privatize an existing NOC. Stronger checks and balances increase the benefits countries derive from privatizing their NOCs, with the influences working in three ways. First, checks and balances enhance the credibility of state leaders' promises to refrain from future expropriation. Indeed, a large body of literature has found that checks and balances are crucially important for governments to credibly commit that they will refrain from policies that have the effect of expropriating privately held assets (North and Weingast 1989). By reducing the threat of expropriation, the presence of checks and balances raises the price that investors are willing to pay for privatized state assets. This increases the benefits of privatization for the government and makes the decision more attractive.

Second, governments with stronger checks and balances also tend to have longer time horizons (Geddes 2003; Gandhi and Przeworski

2007; Hadenius and Teorell 2007; Magaloni 2008; Wright 2008). This enables them to benefit from the greater long-term efficiency of private oil companies compared to NOCs (see Wolf 2009). Indeed, the benefits associated with privatizations are likely to accumulate over time (Li 2009).

Finally, privatized oil companies may be more efficient when strong checks and balances enable countries to make credible commitments to investors.[12] This means that investors will be willing to pay higher prices for privatized assets and the host countries have larger potential gains from privatization due to higher royalty and tax revenues that can be extracted from more efficient oil industry operations. Together, all these factors imply that privatization is more likely when countries have a greater level of checks and balances.

> *Hypothesis 2: States are more likely to privatize their national oil companies when they have greater checks and balances.*

4 Research design: data and methods

I test these hypotheses using a sample of all forty-nine major oil-producing countries from 1965 to 2006.[13] I focus on oil-producing countries because these are the countries most likely to derive significant rents from their oil industries. Each of the fifteen countries discussed in this volume is among the forty-nine countries in my analysis. Indeed, forty-seven of the forty-nine countries in my sample had an NOC at some point between 1965 and 2006. (The United States and Australia are the only exceptions.) Most countries established their NOC during the 1970s, with a handful establishing NOCs during the 1980s and 1990s.

4.1 Data

4.1.1 Dependent variables
I test my hypotheses regarding expropriations and nationalization using data on forced divestments of foreign-owned oil extraction facilities from Guriev *et al.* (2011). This data set includes all expropriations of foreign property in four categories: 1) formal nationalization; 2) intervention; 3) forced sale; and 4) contract renegotiation.[14] Thus, our measure of expropriation includes both outright expropriations with no compensation for the previous asset owners, as well

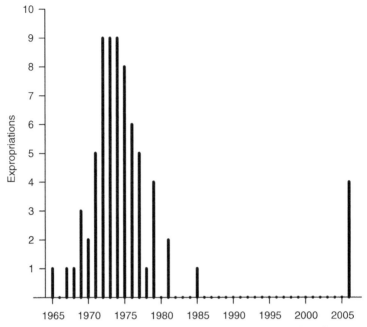

Figure 2.1 Number of countries expropriating assets in the oil sector.

as expropriations where countries nominally bought out the existing owners with pricing and terms that are far less attractive than would be available in a fair market. A given country-year is given a value of 1 if Guriev *et al.*'s data set includes an expropriation event in the country and 0 otherwise.[15] My measure of expropriations is designed to count multiple expropriation events in a given country over a period of years as separate events each year rather than as a single event.

Between 1965 and 2006, there were seventy-one expropriations in the countries in my data set. Twenty-three different countries expropriated assets in their oil extraction industries at some point during this period. The bulk of the expropriations were concentrated in the first half of the 1970s (Figure 2.1). There were almost no expropriations in the 1980s and none at all between 1990 and 2005. However, there was a surge of expropriations in 2006.

I test my hypotheses regarding privatization with data on NOC privatization events collected from Wolf and Pollitt (2008), news reports, and company reports. A given country-year is given a value of 1 if the government's ownership share in its NOC declined during that year

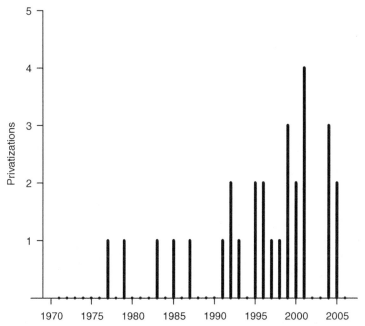

Figure 2.2 Number of countries privatizing national oil companies.

and 0 otherwise.[16] There were twenty-nine privatization events in eleven countries in my data set between 1971 and 2006 (Figure 2.2).[17] The bulk of the privatization events took place during the 1990s.

4.1.2 Explanatory variables

I examine two general categories of explanatory variables. First, I use regime type as a simple proxy for checks and balances, and examine whether democracies have fewer expropriations, and more privatizations, than autocracies. I code whether a country is a democracy or an autocracy using its Combined Polity 2 score from the Polity IV data set. The Combined Polity 2 score is an index that measures the competitiveness of political participation, the openness and competitiveness of executive recruitment, and constraints on the chief executive (Marshall and Jaggers 2000). The Polity Score is measured for each country in the world going back to its first year of independence, through 2006. I normalize these scores to run from 0 (complete autocracy) to 100 (complete democracy). In each year, I classify a country as a democracy if its normalized Polity Score is greater than or equal to 85 (Haber and Menaldo 2011).

As I discuss above, a regime-type typology does not perfectly capture variation in checks and balances across states. Thus, it is necessary to go beyond a simple typology of countries into "democracies" and "autocracies," and explicitly examine the effect of checks and balances. In this analysis, I use two measures for the checks and balances on state leaders in each country-year. As my primary measure, I use the executive constraints measure in the Polity IV data set (Marshall and Jaggers 2000). This variable ranges from 1 to 7 and refers to the amount of institutionalized constraints on the decision-making powers of state leaders. These constraints may be imposed by courts or legislatures in democracies, the ruling party in a one-party autocracy, or councils of nobles in monarchies.

As a robustness check on my primary measure of checks and balances, I use Henisz's (2002) PolCon data on veto points.[18] This measure is based on: 1) the number of independent branches of government with veto power over policy change (including the executive branch and the lower and upper legislative chambers); 2) the degree of alignment across branches of government based on the party composition of each branch; and 3) the degree of preference heterogeneity within each legislative branch.

4.1.3 Control variables
The potential one-time windfall from an expropriation of private industry increases in periods when there are higher short-term profits associated with oil production. As a result, higher oil prices are likely to lead to a greater reward for expropriations (Guriev *et al.* 2011). Oil price shocks could also affect the rewards associated with investment and privatization, although there is less agreement over which way the cause-effect relationship works (Duncan 2006; Guriev *et al.* 2011). Thus, I include an estimate of "oil price shocks" based on the model presented in Guriev *et al.* (2011) in my regression models.[19] I also include the level of oil production in a country and a lagged dependent variable in the full models.[20] In addition, I include a linear time trend in some of the models to control for time trends in countries' propensity to expropriate.

I also include a control to account for the possibility that diffusion between countries plays a role in states' decisions to expropriate or privatize the oil sector. Scholars have long argued that both expropriation and privatization decisions can "spread" between countries (e.g., Murillo 2002). The diffusion between countries could be the result of imitation between oil-producing governments, exogenous pressures from international actors, waves of ideology, or some combination of these forces. For instance, Kobrin (1985) finds that oil nationalization decisions between 1960 and 1980 were strongly spatially correlated with each other. In particular, he argues that Libya's oil nationalization in 1970 and 1971 led to a "ripple effect" that spread to "more militant oil producers like Iraq and then to the conservative regimes like Saudi Arabia" because it reduced uncertainty about the potential costs of nationalization.

There is also strong evidence that diffusion affects countries' privatization decisions. A large study of the timing of countries' privatization decisions across a range of industries finds that countries have grown more likely to privatize over time (Kogut and Macpherson 2008). This upward trend in privatization decisions appears to be largely due to international forces (Henisz *et al.* 2005), such as pressure on countries to liberalize their economies from the World Bank and the International Monetary Fund (IMF) (Brune *et al.* 2004; Kogut and Macpherson 2008), and the influence of market-oriented economists (Kogut and Macpherson 2008).

To control for the effects of diffusion on countries' expropriation decisions, I include a lagged variable in my econometric analysis of the average number of expropriations in the world (excluding the events within each observation country). This variable accounts for the possibility that countries are responding to expropriation decisions in other countries rather than changes in their internal political dynamics.

4.2 Methods

I test each of my hypotheses using a combination of descriptive analysis, regression-based econometric analysis, and qualitative case studies. In the econometric analysis, I use logit models with fixed effects for each country. This approach allows me to examine the effect of changes in the explanatory variables *within each country* on the dependent variables. This approach also allows me to control for unobserved heterogeneity between countries.

5 Empirical findings

In this section, I present my quantitative analysis of the relationship between checks and balances, and expropriations and privatizations in the oil sector.

5.1 Expropriations in the oil sector

I find strong support for hypothesis 1 that the level of checks and balances in a country is correlated with the probability that a country will expropriate private companies in its oil extraction industry. First, I examine the bivariate correlation between regime type and expropriations. I find that autocracies tend to expropriate private assets in their oil industries far more often than other regime types. Among oil-producing countries, there have been only fourteen expropriations in democracies since 1965, while fifty-seven expropriations have occurred in autocracies. In any given year between 1965 and 2006, autocracies were nearly 2.5 times as likely as democracies to expropriate private assets in their oil extraction industries.

The strong relationship between regime type and expropriations suggests that countries with weak checks and balances are more likely to expropriate oil assets. I use an econometric model to examine this hypothesis more directly. I find that countries with weak checks and balances are far more likely to expropriate their oil sector than countries with strong checks and balances. Countries with the lowest levels of executive constraint in the Polity IV data set have an 8.4 percent probability of expropriating assets in their oil industry in any given year, while countries with the highest levels of executive constraint have just a 1.6 percent probability of expropriations in any given year.

My regression results further support hypothesis 1 that the level of checks and balances in a country has a significant effect on the probability of expropriation. The results in models 1 and 2 (Table 2.1) are broadly similar to the results obtained by Guriev *et al.* (2011). Most importantly, I find that an increase in executive constraints decreases the probability that a country will expropriate, even after controlling for oil shocks, oil production, and a country's lagged expropriation (model 2). As Figure 2.1 shows, however, there is a strong time trend in my data, with the probability of expropriation falling dramatically

Table 2.1. *Effect of executive constraints on expropriations*

	(1)	(2)	(3)	(4)	(5)
Executive constraints	-0.327***	-0.235**	-0.029	-0.380**	-0.330*
	(0.115)	(0.119)	(0.126)	(0.182)	(0.202)
Oil shock		1.49***	1.391***	1.44***	0.550
		(0.396)	(0.380)	(0.387)	(0.452)
Oil production		0.0002	0.0005**	0.0006**	0.0006**
		(0.0002)	(0.0002)	(0.0003)	(0.0003)
Time counter			-0.138***	-0.228***	-0.241***
			(0.021)	(0.045)	(0.057)
Time counter x executive constraints				0.024***	0.031***
				(0.009)	(0.011)
Number of other countries that have expropriated in t-1					0.300***
					(0.057)
Lagged expropriation		1.355***	0.563*	0.507	-0.090
		(0.315)	(0.329)	(0.334)	(0.360)
Log likelihood	-194.56	-170.18	-136.18	-132.63	-117.59
Observations	875	813	813	813	813

All models include fixed effects for country.

Standard errors in parentheses.

*** Significant at 0.01 level, ** significant at 0.05 level, * significant at 0.1 level.

Oil price shock is the deviation of the log real price of oil from its fifty-year trend.

over time. Thus, unlike Guriev *et al.* (2011), I add a time counter to the model to control for common time trends across countries. I find that the addition of a time trend makes the effect of executive constraints on the probability of expropriation become insignificant (Table 2.1, model 3). It is possible that the effect of time could be contingent on a country's level of executive constraints since those constraints influence the time horizon of decision makers. Thus, in model 4, I interact executive constraints with time to examine whether the effect of time may vary as a country's level of executive constraints changes. I find that executive constraints, time, and the new interactive variable are all significant at the 0.05 level. Figure 2.3 shows that the effect of executive constraints is highly contingent on time. In particular, autocracies with low levels of executive constraints were much more likely than democracies to expropriate in the 1960s and 1970s, but by the 1980s and 1990s autocracies were no more likely to expropriate than democracies.[21]

Finally, in model 5, I examine the effect of expropriations in other countries on a country's decision to expropriate. In this model, executive constraints continue to exert a strong influence on the probability of expropriation. However, I find that a country's decision to expropriate is also strongly correlated with expropriation decisions in other countries. The results provide support for the notion that diffusion between countries affects expropriation decisions. For instance, it could be that countries often expropriate foreign investors and nationalize their NOC at the same time as many others because they fear a nationalist backlash if they fail to follow such popular trends of the time. It is also possible that an increase in the number of expropriations around the world lowers the reputational risk associated with expropriation. The precise causal mechanism for the strong and significant relationship I observe between countries' expropriation decisions and the expropriation decisions in other countries in the previous year is worthy of further study.

5.2 NOC privatization

I also find strong support for hypothesis 2 that the level of checks and balances in a country is correlated with the probability that a country will privatize its oil industry. First, I examine the bivariate correlation between regime type and privatizations. Democracies tend to

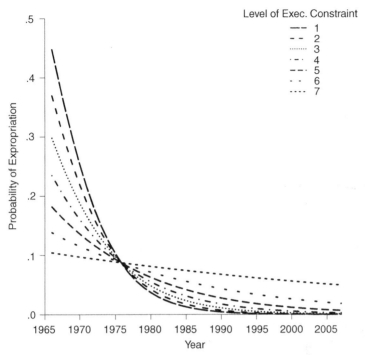

Level of Exec. Constraint
—– 1
– – 2
...... 3
·–· 4
—–· 5
· · 6
···· 7

Figure 2.3 Marginal effect of executive constraints on predicted probability of expropriation.

privatize their NOCs far more often than autocracies. At a descriptive level, there have been twenty-seven NOC privatizations in nine different democracies and just three privatizations in autocracies.[22] There is a 6.3 percent chance that a democracy with a national oil company will privatize its NOC during any given year, while there is just a 0.4 percent chance that an autocracy will privatize its NOC in any given year.

The strong relationship between regime type and privatization suggests that countries with strong checks and balances are more likely to privatize their oil industries. When I break down countries by their level of executive constraints, I find further support for hypothesis 2 that executive constraints are correlated with a country's likelihood of privatization. Oil-producing countries with the lowest level of executive constraints have never privatized an NOC, while countries with the highest level of executive constraints have a 7.3 percent chance of privatizing their NOCs in any given year.

Table 2.2. *Effect of executive constraints on privatizations*

	(1)
Executive constraints	0.387*
	(0.237)
Observations	310

Standard errors in parentheses
*** Significant at 0.01 level, ** significant at
0.05 level, * significant at 0.1 level.

There is not enough data on privatizations to conduct a full multi-variate regression analysis on the relationship between executive constraints and privatization. In a simple fixed effects model with no controls, however, I find that stronger checks and balances make countries far more likely to privatize their NOCs (Table 2.2). Indeed, a shift from an autocracy with the lowest level of executive constraints to a democracy with the highest level of executive constraints makes countries twelve times more likely to privatize their NOCs (i.e., it is correlated with an increase from a 0.01 to 0.12 probability of privatization).[23]

6 Case studies

6.1 Expropriation

Ten of the countries in the case study sample discussed elsewhere in this volume have expropriated assets in their oil industry at least once since 1965 (Table 2.3). My brief qualitative analysis of these cases strongly supports my quantitative regression results. Virtually all of the countries in the case study sample that expropriated investors were autocracies with weak checks and balances when they undertook the expropriations. Here I briefly explore three cases that reveal the pattern.

Although Algeria's NOC Sonatrach was founded in 1963, it refrained from expropriations until Houari Boumédienne deposed the constitutional government in a military *coup d'état.* Boumédienne ruled as a personalist dictator from 1965 to 1978.

Table 2.3. *PESD case study universe*

	At least one expropriation (1965–2006)	Partially privatized NOC
Algeria	Yes	
Angola	Yes	
Brazil		Yes
China		Yes
India	Yes	Yes
Iran	Yes	
Kuwait	Yes	
Malaysia		
Mexico		
Nigeria	Yes	
Norway		Yes
Russian Federation	Yes	Yes
Saudi Arabia	Yes	
United Arab Emirates	Yes	
Venezuela	Yes	

During this period, Algeria undertook repeated expropriations of foreign investors (1967, 1970, 1971, 1974, and 1976). By the mid 1970s, Algeria had nationalized most of the country's oil production (see Chapter 13). As predicted by my theory, the expropriations took place during a military dictatorship with few checks and balances. After the death of Boumédienne in 1978 new leaders faced more checks and balances – some formally established and some informal because none of the new leaders were as singularly powerful as Boumédienne.

Iran nationalized its oil sector in a series of steps between 1974 and 1979. The final expropriation of foreign oil companies and nationalization of their assets occurred in 1979 following the Islamic Revolution (see Chapter 6). While many causal factors were at work in the 1979 nationalization, it is clear that the expropriations occurred during the initial days of the Islamic regime when it was uncertain how long the regime would last, there were virtually no checks and balances on the revolutionary council, and the new government was keen to appropriate any assets it could to hold on to power.

Most recently, the expropriation of foreign investors in Venezuela's oil sector in 2006 and 2007 closely followed the weakening of checks and balances constraining President Hugo Chávez (see Chapter 10). In 2005, Chávez's party secured all 167 seats in the National Assembly after the political opposition boycotted the parliamentary election. Controlling the Assembly gave Chávez enormous freedom of action for policy reforms of all types, including changes to the Constitution. Following this election, Chávez moved quickly to renegotiate contracts with foreign oil companies. In 2006 and 2007, the Venezuelan Energy Ministry mandated renegotiation of contract terms with higher taxes and majority PDVSA control – a form of expropriation that did not actually involve formal nationalization (see Chapter 10).

6.2 Privatization

Five of the countries in this volume's case study sample have privatized oil assets at some point. These are Brazil, China, India, Norway, and Russia (Table 2.3). Here I briefly look at all five. All of these countries had relatively strong checks and balances when they privatized their NOCs. Moreover, most were democracies or in the midst of democratization.

Brazil was ruled as a military dictatorship from 1964 to 1985. During this period Petrobras remained a firm state monopoly; Brazil was not thought to have large oil resources and was largely ignored by major foreign oil companies who, in any case, feared expropriation of their assets if they invested heavily in the country (see Chapter 12). While Petrobras developed substantial capabilities during this period, the country's military rulers had few options for organization of the sector since they were unable to make credible commitments to private investors due to the lack of checks and balances on the regime and a history of expropriation in several sectors of the economy, including oil. As my theory predicts, it was not until the state's return to civilian rule in 1985 that early steps toward privatization of Petrobras were taken (Lavelle 2004, 97). After a few years of instability, Brazil transitioned to a full democracy in 1992. During this period, the government put in place a system of regulation that helped private investors feel confident that markets were open and free to competition (see Chapter 12). It also put in place new rules that encouraged private firms to enter the country's oil industry. These commitments facilitated further privatization of Petrobras.

Russia partially privatized Gazprom in a multi-stage process during the 1990s (see Chapter 15). After the breakup of the Soviet Union in 1991, the Russian federal government gained jurisdiction over the major oil fields in Russia. However, it quickly moved to partially privatize Gazprom in 1993 and 1994 through voucher auctions to workers and Russian citizens. The privatization was inspired by many pressures, but prominent among these was the government's need for cash so it could deliver benefits that could help incumbent leaders stay in office. This auction reduced the government's stake in Gazprom to just 40 percent. The government reduced its ownership stake by a further 5 percent in 1999. As my theory predicts, all these auctions followed the transition of Russia to democracy. The 1999 auction occurred as Russia's checks and balances appeared to be strengthening, taking the form not only of stronger political institutions (marked by the peaceful transition from Yeltsin to Putin) but also the promise of more independent regulation. Russia's democratization was erratic, of course, and thus the investors who ended up with these shares were those that were best positioned to manage the risk associated with a fledgling democracy's ability to make credible long-term commitments. The privatization process ended (and reversed) as the Russian state reasserted more authority under Putin, which undermined its ability to make credible promises to private investors.

Norway did not have any major changes in its level of checks and balances prior to privatization. Norway appears to have privatized due to several context-specific factors: Oil prices were low, putting a premium on efficiency; the industry was restructuring around the world, with private ownership on the upswing; and the Norwegian Continental Shelf (NCS) was nearing its peak in oil production (see Chapter 14). More generally, having adapted over time to being a major oil-producing state, Norway was by this point able to relax its initial concern about maintaining complete control over oil operations.

India followed a similar path, aided by a broad set of market-oriented reforms and administrative reforms that reduced the role of state-owned enterprises and regulatory intervention in the economy. India opened its economy to international trade and investment, deregulated many of its industries, and initiated privatization across a variety of sectors. These reforms made privatization efforts in each sector of the economy, including oil and gas, more credible. They also facilitated the development of market-supporting institutions. Following these reforms, India sold public offerings of ONGC in 1999 and again in 2004.

China partially privatized its NOC CNPC in 2000 (Chapter 9). At first glance, it is surprising that China was able to partially privatize CNPC. As a single-party autocracy, it had far lower levels of checks and balances than India and Norway. But the internal apparatus of the Communist Party imposes significant checks and balances on China's leaders (Besley and Kudamatsu 2008). These checks and balances helped enable China to credibly commit to investors that it would refrain from future expropriations, which makes China's partial privatization of CNPC less surprising. It is also relevant that China did not fully privatize CNPC – rather, it offered a small fraction of the firm to local stock markets (where there were few other options for investors) and to outside oil firms that were desperate to gain a toehold in China.

7 Conclusion

In this chapter, I provide answers to two interlocking puzzles. First, I investigate why so many countries have expropriated private oil companies' assets and established state-owned petroleum companies. I find that states respond rationally to their political incentives and constraints. In particular, the amount of checks and balances that constrain opportunistic state leaders is an important determinant of whether states decide to nationalize their oil industries. Similarly to Guriev *et al.* (2011), I find that lower levels of checks and balances increase the probability that states will expropriate investors and nationalize their oil industry. However, unlike Guriev *et al.* I find that the relationship between checks and balances and the probability of expropriations is contingent on time. Prior to 1980, a country's level of executive constraints is strongly correlated with its probability of expropriation. Indeed, a shift from the lowest level of checks and balances to the highest level of checks and balances makes a country more than three times more likely to expropriate. After 1980, however, I find no significant relationship between a country's level of checks and balances and expropriation. It is possible that the weak relationship between executive constraints and expropriations after 1980 is due to the fact that most of the countries with weak checks and balances had expropriated the bulk of the privately held oil assets in their countries by 1980. While I do not have sufficient data to test this hypothesis, this appears to be a fertile area for future research.

Second, I investigate why some states decide to privatize their NOCs. My most significant finding is that democracies with strong checks and balances are far more likely to privatize their NOCs than autocracies with weak checks and balances. One implication of this result is that future studies on the effect of privatization on NOC efficiency should control for changes in political institutions, since institutions may be jointly determining countries' privatization decisions as well as the ultimate level of efficiency of the country's oil industry. Future studies should also further investigate the factors that make democracies more likely to privatize.

One limitation of my research is that I treat all privatization events the same. I do not explore why some countries choose to fully privatize their NOCs, while others choose to partially privatize them. However, the degree of privatization may very well influence the strategy and performance of NOCs. Therefore, it would be extremely valuable for future research to explore why some states choose to completely privatize their NOCs while others choose to only partially privatize them.

My findings support the growing focus in the political economy literature on the role of political institutions in determining the benefits and constraints for state leaders. By shaping the political calculus of state leaders, institutions not only affect crucial decisions of war and peace but also the involvement of the state in specific industries. While political institutions are clearly not the only important factor affecting the structure of the world oil industry (see Chapter 4), I find strong evidence that political institutions affect the decisions of state leaders about whether to seize control over their nation's oil industries.

This implies that the extant literature on NOCs has erred by ignoring the political processes that lead countries to decide whether to maintain NOCs. Taken as a whole, my findings provide strong support for the idea that autocracies with weak checks and balances are systematically more likely to nationalize their oil industries than democracies – and less likely to privatize them following nationalization. Thus, variation in political institutions has an important effect on the structure of the oil industry around the world.

Appendix

Privatization events (1965–2006)	
Argentina, 1993	Italy, 1997
Argentina, 1999	Italy, 1998
Brazil, 1985	Italy, 2001
Brazil, 1992	Norway, 2001
Brazil, 2000	Norway, 2004
Brazil, 2001	Norway, 2005
Canada, 1991	Romania, 2004
Canada, 1992	Russian Federation, 1994
Canada, 1995	Russian Federation, 1999
Canada, 2005	Thailand, 2001
China, 2000	United Kingdom, 1977
India, 1999	United Kingdom, 1979
India, 2004	United Kingdom, 1983
Italy, 1995	United Kingdom, 1987
Italy, 1996	United Kingdom, 1996

Expropriation events (1965–2006)

Algeria, 1967	Iran, 1979	Peru, 1985
Algeria, 1970	Iraq, 1972	Qatar, 1972
Algeria, 1971	Iraq, 1973	Qatar, 1974
Algeria, 1974	Iraq, 1975	Qatar, 1976
Algeria, 1976	Iraq, 1977	Qatar, 1977
Angola, 1976	Kuwait, 1972	Rep. of Congo, 1974
Angola, 1977	Kuwait, 1973	Rep. of Congo, 1975
Angola, 1978	Kuwait, 1974	Russian Federation, 2006
Chad, 2006	Kuwait, 1975	Saudi Arabia, 1972
Colombia, 1972	Kuwait, 1977	Saudi Arabia, 1974
Ecuador, 1969	Libya, 1969	Saudi Arabia, 1975
Ecuador, 1972	Libya, 1970	Trinidad & Tobago, 1969
Ecuador, 1973	Libya, 1971	Trinidad & Tobago, 1975
Ecuador, 1974	Libya, 1972	Trinidad & Tobago, 1979
Ecuador, 1976	Libya, 1973	Trinidad & Tobago, 1981
Ecuador, 1977	Libya, 1974	United Arab Emirates, 1971
Ecuador, 1979	Malaysia, 1973	United Arab Emirates, 1972
Ecuador, 2006	Nigeria, 1971	United Arab Emirates, 1973
Gabon, 1973	Nigeria, 1973	United Arab Emirates, 1974
Gabon, 1976	Nigeria, 1974	United Arab Emirates, 1975
India, 1975	Nigeria, 1976	Venezuela, 1971
India, 1981	Nigeria, 1979	Venezuela, 1975
Indonesia, 1965	Oman, 1972	Venezuela, 2006
Iran, 1973	Peru, 1968	

Notes

1 These studies fit within a broader research agenda in the economics literature on the effects of privatization of state-owned companies. In a comprehensive meta-analysis across a variety of industries, Megginson (2005) finds
evidence for significant efficiency gains associated with privatization.

2 Scholars have long studied expropriation through nationalization of foreign
assets (e.g., Vernon 1971). More recently, scholars have looked at a wider
array of mechanisms, such as regulation and tax policy, that governments
use to appropriate rents even without complete nationalization and how the
dangers of such regulatory expropriation affect patterns of foreign investment (e.g., Levy and Spiller 1994; Henisz and Zelner 2001; Woodhouse
2006; Manzano and Monaldi 2008).

3 Kobrin (1984, 1985) are obvious exceptions to this generalization. More recently, Guriev *et al.* (2011) analyze expropriation decisions in the oil sector.

4 Political institutions are clearly not the only important factor affecting the structure of the world oil industry. Other factors, such as changing risk profiles of oil fields (see Chapter 4) and long-term trends in oil prices also affect countries' incentives to expropriate or privatize their oil industries.

5 In this article, I refer to the processes of "expropriation" and "nationalization" interchangeably. However, they could be viewed as two distinct processes. Indeed, almost all expropriations involve the nationalization of foreign investors' assets. But in some cases, nationalization may not require expropriation. For instance, countries could nationalize control over future oil discoveries without necessarily expropriating foreign investors (see Manzano and Monaldi 2008).

6 In theory, countries could tax private companies to appropriate the windfalls from price booms. But Manzano and Monaldi (2008) find that the tax structure in many developing countries enables much of the windfall from price booms to be appropriated by private firms.

7 I assume that the greater price for privatization due to the ability of the government to make credible commitments more than offsets the status quo bias caused by the presence of multiple veto points.

8 The array of important institutions is not just those that make and implement political choices. The ability to mobilize and apply private capital also matters. For example, countries with deep and liquid stock markets are more likely to privatize state-owned companies than countries with smaller stock exchanges (Bortolotti *et al.* 2003; Banerjee and Munger 2004).

9 In this chapter, I do not explore the difference between acting strategically through ownership of the sector and acting strategically through regulation.

10 Similarly to the approach in Guriev *et al.* (2011), I do not distinguish between ownership and control in my analysis.

11 I am grateful to Witold Henisz for suggesting this mechanism.

12 In the absence of a credible commitment from their host country to refrain from expropriation, oil companies are more likely to inefficiently extract oil in order to maximize short-term profits.

13 The sample includes all oil-producing countries reported in the 2009 BP Statistical Review of World Energy (BP 2009a).

14 Formal nationalization events take place in accordance with local law. Intervention is an extralegal forced transfer of ownership by either public or private actors. Contract renegotiation is a revision of contractual

agreements involving the coercive power of the government, resulting in an effective transfer of ownership (Guriev *et al.* 2011).

15 I use data on forced divestments to measure nationalization rather than the establishment of state-owned oil companies because the establishment of an NOC may or may not be correlated with control over a country's oil resources. Indeed, NOCs were often established prior to the actual expropriation of foreign investors and the subsequent formal nationalization of countries' oil industries.

16 Of course, NOC "ownership" is a complex phenomenon and I do not, in this chapter, delve into the details. Instead, my focus is on the incentives for leaders to own (or sell) NOCs when what the leaders want are rents and control. Ownership is a proxy – indeed, the best single proxy – for that, but control can be obtained in many ways that do not require full ownership.

17 An alternative way to define privatization might be to use a survival model where an NOC is counted as privatized after the first partial privatization or, perhaps, once the government's ownership level declines below some threshold. However, this approach would force me to discard data from the multiple partial privatizations in many countries. Moreover, I believe that each privatization event was a discrete decision that required governments to be able to make credible commitments to investors.

18 This measure is correlated with my primary measure of checks and balances at 0.83.

19 I use data on real crude oil prices from BP Statistical Review of World Energy (BP 2009a). I adapt the model from Guriev *et al.* (2011) to estimate long-term oil price behavior: $\ln(p_t) = a + b * \ln(p_{t-1}) + c*t + d*t^2 + \varepsilon$. For each year t between 1965 and 2006, I estimate this equation and then use the residual as our estimate for oil price shocks.

20 It is possible that expropriation and privatization decisions could be a function of oil *exports* rather than absolute production levels. My results, however, were not sensitive to whether I used absolute levels of oil production or oil exports.

21 To check the robustness of our results, I also reran our models using Henisz's (2002) political constraints variable ("polcon"). The statistical significance of some of my results declines somewhat, but the substantive results are all robust to the inclusion of Henisz's measure of executive constraints rather than Polity's measure of executive constraints.

22 These privatizations took place in China and the Russian Federation.

23 To check the robustness of my results, I also reran the model using Henisz's (2002) political constraints variable ("polcon"). In this analysis, I replicated my primary results: political constraints are strongly correlated with privatizations.

3 | Hybrid governance: state management of national oil companies

DAVID R. HULTS

1 Introduction

In this chapter, I analyze how states govern national oil companies (NOCs) – typically their chief sources of revenue and technocratic expertise. Some governance systems set clearly defined lines of authority, separating policymaker, regulator, and operator responsibilities,[1] whereas others blur those lines almost completely. States differ in their control over NOC budgets, appointments, investments, and contracting arrangements with international oil companies (IOCs).

Despite these differences, a common thread exists: Most NOC governance systems are a hybrid of corporate governance, public administration, and regulation. Many NOCs' founding laws and organizational by-laws mimic private sector corporate governance models. NOCs typically have a board of directors, hold annual shareholder meetings (with the state as the only or more important shareholder), and pay dividends. Many states also subject their NOCs to the same public administration tools that states use to control government agencies, like legislative budget approvals. And several states use regulatory powers to indirectly control their NOCs, with some also commandeering their NOCs as energy regulators. NOC governance reflects this hybrid blend because of the special challenges posed by managing oil companies. NOCs are almost invariably the leading state-owned enterprise (SOE) and often the largest domestic company, public or private, in the domestic economy.[2] And unlike the perennial problem in many SOEs, which lose money, NOCs usually produce copious rents.[3]

I thank Tarun Khanna and Valérie Marcel for their careful reviews. David Victor, Mark Thurber, Pete Nolan, and my wife Rachel also provided invaluable feedback. Any errors are my own.

Previous research has mined key questions of NOC governance.[4] One thread considers state oversight of both NOCs and IOCs: Representative works include Mommer (2002), which reviews oil sector governance since the commercialization of oil, and Eifert *et al.* (2003), which suggests links between five regime typologies and oil sector governance.[5] Other scholarship takes a narrower perspective by exploring the formal administrative structures for controlling NOCs. In this vein are Khan (1985), evaluating the legal form, structure, and financing arrangements for NOCs, and Bentham and Smith (1986), cataloguing various aspects of NOC founding laws for seventeen countries.[6] Another branch of literature consists of case studies, which are highly dependent on case selection and analyst focus. For example, Al-Kasim (2006) discusses the "Norwegian model" of governance, and Boshcheck (2007) employs an intricate checklist to analyze NOC governance in Nigeria, Norway, and Saudi Arabia.[7] And some work is explicitly policy-oriented, typically with the aim of detailing best practices and other reforms that NOCs might adopt – such as the studies by Myers and Lahn (2006) and Lahn *et al.* (2007).[8]

Although this research derives important implications, little of it tests the links between governance and the performance of NOCs.[9] This gap in the NOC literature is surprising because scholars have developed useful theories on the performance of large organizations (such as bureaucracies and corporations)[10] and because NOCs, as a result of their economic predominance and complexity, present an interesting opportunity to apply and contribute to those theories.

To help fill this gap, I investigate the relationship between specific aspects of NOC governance and performance. I draw upon organizational theory to devolve NOC governance into three essential, widely studied forms. These forms are as follows. First, the *rule setting*, or institutional context in which the rule is made, ranges from highly unified (frequently with the head of state or oil ministry wielding near-total control) to fragmented (control being distributed across such players as the head of state, executive agencies, and legislature). Second the *rule function*, or the way in which the state uses a rule to exert control, spans *ex ante* procedures (giving the state authority to approve or make NOC decisions in advance) and *ex post* monitoring (giving the state greater authority to track those decisions after the fact).[11] Third, the *rule form*, or the concreteness of the rule, ranges from highly law-based (legal frameworks channeling

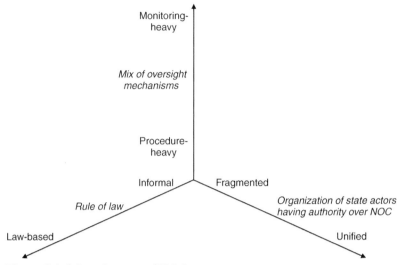

Figure 3.1 Select elements of NOC governance systems.

and constraining governance decisions) to personalistic and informal (social ties between state and NOC leadership mediating those decisions). Figure 3.1 depicts these three elements of NOC governance.[12] This chapter explores the interactions among these elements[13] and tests their links to NOC performance.[14]

I offer the following three hypotheses on the relationships between these governance elements and NOC performance:

1) NOCs perform better in states that have unified control over the companies and worse in states that have fragmented control;
2) NOC performance is positively related to monitoring-heavy oversight systems and negatively related to procedure-heavy systems; and
3) NOCs perform better when their home states primarily rely on law-based mechanisms to administer them and worse when states depend mostly on informal mechanisms.

By carrying out simple but revealing tests of these hypotheses for the fifteen NOCs in this volume,[15] I reach these four findings:

First, in support of hypothesis 1, NOCs are generally higher performing when state institutions exercise power over the company through a centralized government authority. I explain this finding in part by noting that state institutions commonly hold multiple, complex, and shifting NOC objectives (e.g., generating profits, employing workers, advancing foreign policy through oil diplomacy). When state institutions speak with one voice to the NOC, policy becomes coherent. As a result, NOCs juggle a smaller number of competing goals, can make long-term investments in furtherance of those goals, and function more effectively.[16] All of the best performing NOCs in this volume are governed by states that have consolidated authority over the companies. This finding comes with an important caveat, however. Some states with unified control have poor-performing NOCs because the leader in charge sets inefficient objectives (e.g., saddling the NOC with widespread social responsibilities or patronage goals).

Second, backing hypothesis 2, NOCs tend to succeed in oversight systems that monitor company decisions after the fact (through, e.g., annual audits, occasional inspections, robust price signaling) but exert little advance approval of those decisions. Indeed, not one of the high-performing NOCs in this volume operates in a procedure-heavy environment. One explanation for this result is that monitoring-heavy systems give greater company flexibility to adopt mechanisms conducive to high performance. Not all forms of monitoring are essential, however. Competition for equity or upstream projects are often cited as useful tools for gauging company performance. But some countries that do not permit competition have highly successful NOCs because they delegate managerial control to the companies and use other forms of benchmarking aggressively.

Third, lending slight support to hypothesis 3, NOCs are a bit more likely to thrive when states rely on law-based mechanisms to govern the companies. This relationship is modest at best, however. It is possible that NOCs perform better in highly formal environments because laws, when enforced, limit political masters' opportunities to place ad hoc demands upon the company. But this pattern is fraught with many exceptions. In several instances, laws enshrine deeply inefficient governance systems (e.g., government approval of NOC procurement decisions). And elsewhere well-defined informal constraints (e.g., tight social networks) effectively substitute for the law, at least in the short term. One possible reason for these exceptions is that the links between rule of law and company performance are highly attenuated.

Fourth, in decomposing NOC governance into its central functions, this study shows how particular institutional arrangements affect government choice and capacity to carry out that choice. Many states that have fragmented control over their NOCs, for example, govern the company through *ex ante* procedures rather than through *ex post* monitoring mechanisms because each procedure gives a state actor its own lever of authority over the company (e.g., a head of state may control NOC appointment power, a legislature may approve the NOC budget).[17] Particular institutional arrangements may also have a lasting legacy effect. For example, some governments still rely on procedures rather than monitoring because constitutional constraints, founding laws, or NOC political resistance prevent the introduction of competition (and its attendant monitoring benefits) into the oil sector. (A recent example is Mexico, where constitutional constraints on domestic foreign competition in the oil sector diluted government efforts at reform. See Chapter 7.)

I proceed as follows. In section 2, I provide background. I first frame NOC governance within the widely applied principal–agent model and then add context by comparing NOC governance with three other forms of administration: corporate governance, public administration, and regulation. In section 3, I test the NOC governance-performance relationship for the fifteen NOCs in this volume across three dimensions of governance: 1) organization of state actors with significant authority over the NOC; 2) mix of oversight mechanisms; and 3) obedience to the rule of law. Section 4 discusses some implications based on this analysis, both for NOCs and for broader theories of organization. Section 5 concludes. Closing the chapter is an appendix detailing the data sources and empirical assessments.

2 Background on NOC governance

2.1 NOC governance within the principal–agent model

To provide a simplifying framework for analysis, I situate NOC governance systems within the principal–agent model.[18] (Many of the ideas in this model motivated policymakers to establish NOCs in the 1970s. For more, see Chapter 1.) At their foundation, NOC governance systems function as a type of contract between state and NOC in which the state has authority over the NOC.[19] The state, acting as *principal*, relies on its governance system to direct the NOC, serving as *agent*, to fulfill state objectives or "national missions" (generating profits, securing employment, etc.) (Marcel 2006).[20] (Other work in this volume explores these objectives in greater detail. See Chapter 2.)

Because of its day-to-day expertise, the NOC has greater information than the state about NOC activities, particularly in countries with weak administrative systems (Mommer 2002). NOC managers also have distinct interests from the state, including political advancement, reputation enhancement, and self-enrichment. The state's challenge is thus to motivate the NOC to do the state's bidding despite differing interests and incomplete information.[21] To surmount this challenge, states rely on a combination of tools that form the core of NOC governance.[22]

The NOC governance toolkit varies, among other respects, by rule function and form. Two key functional approaches are: 1) *ex ante* procedures to approve or mandate NOC decisions (contract partners, employee salaries, etc.); and 2) *ex post* monitoring to track those decisions[23] (audits, investigations, price signals).[24] States use *ex ante* procedures to dictate NOC decision making and thereby overcome the differing incentives of the agent in the principal–agent relationship. States use *ex post* monitoring, in turn, to reduce some of the information asymmetries inherent in the principal–agent relationship. The form of NOC governance ranges, among other ways, from: 1) formal, de jure instruments embedded in the state's legal framework and NOC organizational by-laws; to 2) informal, de facto instruments that embody the interpersonal ties and power relationships between state and NOC. A particular governance instrument can serve as an informal procedure (e.g., energy ministry blessing of NOC foreign investment decisions to ensure those decisions have political cover), formal monitoring (mandatory NOC annual reports), or any combination therein. Some governance instruments defy easy categorization; periodic government inspections of NOC operations, for example, are a form of company monitoring that also functions as procedure.

The state and NOC rely on governance and "counter-governance" tools, respectively, to advance their own interests. As a state uses procedures and monitoring to incentivize NOCs, an NOC lobbies the state, both directly and indirectly, to secure certain advantages (e.g., preferences in domestic bidding for hydrocarbon projects).[25] Some NOCs also try to blunt the force of the state by adopting wall-building strategies that move the bulk of company activities abroad and therefore outside the state's direct reach. (In the 1980s, PDVSA aggressively adopted these strategies by acquiring significant downstream assets overseas. For more, see Chapter 10.) Because of its hierarchical supremacy, the state probably has more power to influence an NOC than the reverse, but prominent exceptions exist. These include NOCs that had become powerful enough to acquire the moniker of "states within a state" (Stevens 2008a), such as 1990s Gazprom and PDVSA (see Chapter 15 and Chapter 10, respectively).[26]

Within both state and NOC are various self-interested players. For the purposes of this chapter, the most significant players are the state's multiple principals,[27] including the national leader, legislature, and government agencies. In many NOC governance systems, each of these principals has separate authority over, and objectives for, the NOC. The state's leader, for example, may hold authority to name senior management to the NOC and prioritize NOC profit generation (so that the leader can capture those profits for his or her own purposes).[28] A legislature, by contrast, may have separate power to approve the NOC's annual budget and seek localized NOC projects in different legislative districts (so that individual legislators benefit politically from company activities). Each of the principals' objectives may shift depending on the principals' political, rent-seeking, and ideological motivations. As I argue below, the interaction among multiple principals and their objectives substantially affects the administration of NOCs.

Pulling these points together, Figure 3.2 illustrates NOC governance within the context of the principal–agent relationship. This model helps clarify the ways in which state actors manage their NOCs. The model also provides a useful framework for testing the governance-performance relationship, which I analyze in section 3.

Note that this simple principal–agent model suffers from some inadequacies. For one, it suggests a clean division between state and NOC even though the distinctions may be faint at best. For example, the Iranian government's relationship with the National Iranian Oil Company (NIOC) is so deeply intertwined that it is often difficult to separate government and company (see Chapter 6). Moreover, this basic model is static. A more dynamic approach would account for the frictions between underlying interest group incentives (which spur changes in the governance system) and institutional rigidities (which impede those changes).[29] In reality, government and NOC participate in a repeated game of back-and-forth that evolves in context- and history-specific ways. Therefore, the "game" that is most conducive to NOC performance in one country may not be replicable or even desirable in another. My analysis below brings out some of these complexities.

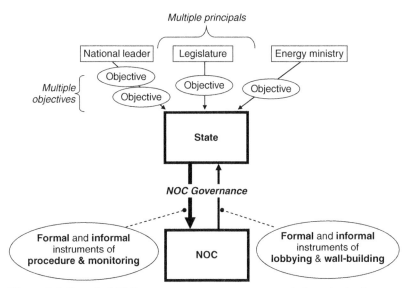

Figure 3.2 Sample NOC governance system as part of the principal–agent relationship.

Despite some shortcomings, the principal–agent framework is a useful starting point for understanding NOC governance systems. I now review the nuts and bolts of these systems by reference to three governance models: corporate governance, public administration, and regulation. I describe these models in a stylized way – recognizing that particular cases may deviate considerably – to illustrate broad linkages. In general, nearly all NOC governance systems reflect the veneer of corporate governance, though some more closely resemble public administration and, to a lesser extent, regulation.[30] Corporate governance is my initial point of departure for illustration.

2.2 NOC governance as corporate governance

NOC governance mirrors corporate governance because of superficial similarities between NOCs and private companies and because the corporate model is a deeply influential form of administration. (In states that created their NOCs via nationalization, NOC governance may also derive from the governance models of their private company predecessors.) In both NOC governance and corporate governance,

principals typically share at least one common objective for their company agent: profit generation.[31] Over its history, corporate governance
has developed a broadly shared set of formal practices for governing
large organizations concerned with profit generation (informal practices diverge, however; see Khanna *et al.* 2006).[32] NOC governance
echoes many of these practices.

The most direct links between NOC governance and corporate
governance systems are in their common legal structures. Since the
1980s, most NOCs have, like their private sector counterparts,
taken the form of corporations[33] that are legally separate from
the state.[34] Incorporation confers a range of formal powers and
responsibilities upon NOCs, ostensibly buffering them from state
influence – and the state from politically controversial company
decisions (Lucas 1985). Most significantly, incorporated NOCs are
typically subject to commercial – rather than administrative – law,
exempt from most state privileges and immunities, formally free
from state employment requirements, and legally under state control only through a state's authority as shareholder. (The controlling and often sole shareholder of the NOC is the state or state
representative, however.)[35]

The shareholder relationship between an NOC and its parent
state is, in turn, associated with a set of corporate governance-style
authorities over the company. Overseeing many NOCs is a board of
directors that has responsibility for hiring and firing senior management, reviewing company strategy, and approving major investment
decisions. (Because of the state's position as controlling shareholder,
many NOC boards are stocked with government members or appointees, and the board's power may be perfunctory.)[36] In addition to this
managerial role, boards also monitor NOCs through audits and
other forms of information-gathering.[37] The board then reports to
shareholder(s) – including, most importantly, the state – at annual
or special shareholder meetings. NOC shareholder(s) have the power
to name members of the board, approve major corporate transformations, and propose resolutions affecting the company. In addition,
most NOCs are, like their private sector brethren, subject to some
financial disclosure, often to satisfy external creditor expectations.[38]
These assorted controls color the relationship between states and
NOCs, though other factors, discussed below, sometimes outweigh
them in importance.[39]

In a select few states, the parallels between NOC and corporate governance run deeper. Like private companies, NOCs compete for the domestic right to exploit and develop hydrocarbons in Brazil, India, Norway, Russia, and (partially) China; their home states use competition, among other purposes, as a benchmarking and external discipline tool.[40] (China straddles the line by restricting outside competition but owning multiple NOCs and permitting some competition between them; see Chapter 9.)[41] The degree of competition is often watered down, however, because these NOCs lobby and exploit home market knowledge to secure large stakes in most domestic projects.[42] Some NOCs also compete internationally for upstream projects, especially if they hail from states in which domestic hydrocarbon resources are or were once perceived to be scarce, like China, Malaysia, Norway, or Brazil. Moreover, NOCs in Brazil, India, Norway, Russia, and (in part) China compete for minority equity investment on stock market exchanges;[43] their home states use stock price listings to assess the capital market performance of the companies.[44] Stock price listings have limited value, however, because NOCs are immune from the threats of takeover or bankruptcy – which serve as major external controls on privately owned companies (Vives 2000).

Though the superficial similarities are considerable, NOC governance and corporate governance sometimes sharply diverge. To explain these differences, I turn to the issue of public administration.

2.3 NOC governance as public administration

For several reasons, the substantive work in NOC governance sometimes follows from public administration rather than corporate governance.[45] The multiple principals (leader, legislature, etc.) and wide-ranging objectives (energy subsidization, employment generation, etc.) affecting many NOCs more closely matches the principal–agent dynamics of public agencies than of privately owned companies. (By contrast, owners of publicly traded companies tend to hold few objectives and employ few mechanisms of authority, due to the mediating effect of capital markets.)[46] States also use public administration tools to manage NOCs because it is, for them, a familiar form of governance.

Thus numerous states supplement or bypass board of director formalities and, as in traditional public administration (Batley and Larbi

2004), exert a complex web of authorities over NOC decision making.[47] Many states hold a tight grip on NOC budgets; in Mexico, the legislature approves Pemex's budget each year. (Other NOC budgeting processes, like Nigeria's, remain cloaked in uncertainty. See Chapter 16.) States also affect NOC planning by reviewing major investment decisions at the legislative or executive level, as in China or India, or by informally directing their companies to make strategic investments on the state's behalf, as in Angola, Malaysia, Russia, and Venezuela. Even day-to-day operational decision making comes under scrutiny: Kuwait, India, and Mexico empower anti-corruption watchdog agencies to review government-wide procurement and employment decisions, including those made by their NOCs.

Public administration and corporate governance explain much, but not all, of NOC governance. States also administer their NOCs as objects and agents of regulation. I address this last angle below.

2.4 NOC governance as regulation

Even when a state lacks express authority over NOC decisions, its principals can indirectly coax agent compliance through command-and-control[48] or economic incentive regulation (Morgan and Yeung 2007).[49] OPEC states set production limits to domestically enforce quotas issued by their cartel. Several countries regulate licensing or tax their NOCs to control the pace of petroleum development and resource extraction (as in Norway and Saudi Arabia). And bureaucratic agencies in Norway and Mexico, among others, promulgate health, safety, and environmental regulations to substantially modify NOC behavior. (In many NOC home states these regulatory safeguards remain weak.)

In addition to being subject to regulation, many NOCs act as state regulators and policymakers – to a greater degree than do most other SOEs. On the downstream side, NOCs frequently serve as de facto domestic energy regulators by overseeing gasoline subsidies, refinery supply arrangements, and other instruments.[50] NOC roles on the upstream side are more uneven, but in some states – including modern-day Angola and Malaysia – the NOC stands in for the state in negotiating contracts with IOCs. This arrangement may create conflicts between the NOC's regulatory and commercial functions.

3 Testing links between NOC governance and performance

Building upon this overview of NOC governance systems, I now evaluate the relationship between those systems and company performance for the fifteen NOCs in this volume. I first explain my methodology and then conduct basic tests across each of the three governance dimensions: 1) organization of state actors with authority over the NOC; 2) mix of oversight mechanisms; and 3) reliance on rule of law. In the appendix to this chapter, I elaborate on my assessments.

3.1 Research methods

Taking advantage of its rich qualitative data, I use the fifteen NOCs in this volume as my sample set. As elaborated in Chapter 1, one basis for selecting NOCs in this volume was their variation in governance. Although a sample of this size inevitably misses some differences, it is nevertheless large and diverse enough to yield a roughly accurate representation of the world's most important NOC governance systems.

I carry out cross-sectional, rather than time-series, analysis. In accord with institutional theories of "stickiness" (North 1990; Boettke *et al.* 2008), I argue that NOC governance systems are often slow to change because of the high transactional cost of reform.[51] (Exceptions occur; I address those below.) As a consequence, I analyze the performance–governance relationship by holding time constant at present, i.e., considering current-day NOC performance and governance systems.

To test the NOC performance–governance relationship, I rely on the holistic measure of company performance detailed in Appendix A to this volume. This measure sorts overall NOC performance into four categories: high, upper middle, lower middle, and low.

I adopt a similar method to determine the three dimensions of NOC governance evaluated here. Because these dimensions aggregate many factors and my data is mostly qualitative, I make general, rather than fine-grained, comparisons across NOCs. My comparisons work as follows: for each of the three dimensions, I classify NOC governance systems into one of three categories. With respect to the mix of NOC oversight mechanisms, for example, I score each governance system as either monitoring-heavy, varied, or rules-heavy. These categories are approximate and do not have strict boundaries between them. Because of coding complications and my limited sample size, I draw findings cautiously.

For much the same reasons, I do not explicitly control for economic, political, and cultural variation in NOC operating environments – though these factors differ extensively. (Consider, for example, the dissimilarities in NNPC's and Statoil's home states.) In all likelihood, the relationship between NOC governance and performance is entangled with other variables, like economic development and political regime (as these variables are linked to one another). But these linkages are complex. With respect to NOC performance, high-performing NOCs crop up in states that are wealthy and democratic (Norway), semi-wealthy and authoritarian (Saudi Arabia), and even poor and authoritarian (Angola). (See Chapter 2 for more discussion of the effects of political regimes on NOCs.) And as for NOC governance, economic and political conditions bear little obvious relationship to the number of NOC principals,[52] mix of oversight mechanisms,[53] and – to a lesser extent – rule of law.[54] As a result of this variance, I make no claims about the relevance of specific government regimes or economic conditions to my findings.

Similarly, governance accounts for only part of the variation in NOC performance. Other potential factors include level of state ownership, degree of upstream or downstream internationalization, political regimes, and economic development. See Appendix A for more discussion.

A final methodological comment before continuing: in two groups of countries, major changes in either NOC governance systems or performance have occurred recently. First, Russia and Venezuela tightened control over NOC governance between 2000 and 2010, and the performance of those companies has suffered.[55] (See Chapter 15 and Chapter 10, respectively.) Second, Brazil and Norway have freed their NOCs from some government requirements during the late 1990s, though Brazil may now be undergoing a partial policy reversal; the performance of both of these companies has remained high. (See Chapter 12 and Chapter 14, respectively.) To simplify matters, I focus on the current-day conditions of these four countries (and their NOCs) in this section. I discuss changes over time in section 5.

Having laid out my methodological approach, I explain my hypotheses for each of the three selected NOC governance dimensions.

3.2 Hypotheses

First, I consider the effect of multiple principals on public agencies.[56] In a seminal work on the economic theory of organizations in US bureaucracy, Moe (1984) proposes that multiple principals compete for control over an agent by putting restraints on one another to preserve each principal's unique interests. This coordination problem among competing principals leads to greater agent independence.[57] Dixit (1997) formalizes a similar intuition in a model showing that multiple principals decrease a public agent's incentives to comply with its political masters.[58] Shifting from autonomy to performance, Whitford (2005) argues that multiple principals' sequential efforts to control agencies lead to a damaging "whiplash" effect. Similarly, Estrin (1998) claims that multiple principles' layered, shifting objectives subvert the performance of SOEs.[59]

In accord with Whitford (2005) and Estrin (1998), I hypothesize that centralization of authority leads to greater clarity in governance roles. And as suggested by Moe (1984), I further hypothesize that fragmented authority may lead to greater NOC autonomy and that this autonomy may in some contexts be beneficial, too. On balance, I propose that the advantages of policy coherence outweigh those from NOC autonomy based on the theory that higher autonomy does not necessarily result in better performance. I thus offer this hypothesis:

1) NOCs *perform better in states that have unified control over the companies and worse in states that have fragmented control.*

Second, I evaluate the links between *ex ante* procedures, *ex post* monitoring, and public agent performance. Thompson and Jones (1986) and Vining and Weimer (1990) suggest that procedure-heavy systems may work better when state missions are fuzzy because rules limit an agent's opportunity to profit from ambiguity and greater knowledge about its own activities. When objectives are vague, Estrin (1998) argues that direct management of a public agent (itself a form of *ex ante* administration) may reduce the risk of that agent carrying out hidden actions (mismanagement, graft). Procedure-heavy systems may thus reduce agent opportunities for waste. However, these systems also reduce efficiency. They impose administrative costs, invite petty corruption over procedural compliance, and limit a public agent's managerial discretion to internally motivate good work (through salary raises, overtime, and personal perks) (Vining and Weimer 1990).[60] Monitoring-heavy systems, for their part, function more effectively when national missions are concrete because these systems measure mission achievement accurately (Vining and Weimer 1990). Nevertheless, *ex post* monitoring of agent activities carries administrative costs of its own (Macey 2008).

In line with the work of Vining and Weimer (1990), I propose that the efficiency costs of procedure-heavy systems outweigh their potential benefits in reducing waste. Following the same theory, I also propose that monitoring-heavy systems are on balance better for performance because they give principals (or the NOC managers delegated with oversight authority) the ability to monitor NOC performance and to remedy it, as necessary, through sanction powers. I thus offer the following hypothesis:

2) *NOCs' performance is positively related to monitoring-heavy oversight systems and negatively related to procedure-heavy systems.*

Moving lastly from rule function to form, I consider the relationship between NOC performance and a state's reliance on law-based mechanisms in administering those companies.[61] Rule of law correlates strongly with "veto points" (Andrews and Montinola 2004) although the former embeds the idea of "legal culture," or norms, constraining individual behavior.[62] Building on the scholarship of Williamson (1985) and Barzel (1997), Haggard *et al.* (2008) propose a logic in which rule of law – acting through well-enforced contracts and property rights – incentivizes individuals to invest and carry out mutually beneficial trades. Increased investment and trade, in turn, foster economic growth. At the macro level, Rigobon and Rodrik (2004) find a robust causal relationship between rule of law and personal income. At the firm level, several law and finance scholars (Johnson *et al.* 2000; La Porta *et al.* 2002; Lemmon and Lins 2003) find positive correlations between rule of law and a corporation's performance. This finding has narrow applicability to NOCs, however, because it is rooted in legal protections for minority shareholders (often absent in the NOC universe). Research on the rule of law's importance for SOEs, including for NOCs, is scant.[63]

Applying the work above to the world of NOCs, I propose that strong rule of law has benefits – in particular, protecting an NOC from unpredictable government predation. These benefits outweigh any negative effects (e.g., codifying inefficient rules as law that become resistant to change). My last hypothesis is thus as follows:

3) *NOCs are higher-performing when their home states primarily rely on law-based mechanisms to administer them and worse when states depend mostly on informal mechanisms.*

I test each of these three hypotheses in turn.

3.3 Analysis

First, I consider the organization of state actors exercising control over NOCs.[64] Looking descriptively at my data sample, a recurring group of state actors emerge. National leaders, energy ministries, or specialized NOC governing bodies[65] are typically the most influential.[66] However, these entities rarely share power with one another; leaders tend to overshadow institutional bodies (as in Chávez-era Venezuela) or delegate most authority to them (as in Norway).[67] The finance ministry or, in less institutional regimes, a ruling clan may separately exercise policymaking control through positions on an NOC board. Administrative agencies may also affect NOC decision making because of their power to review procurement, contracting, and regulatory compliance. Outside the executive branch, the legislature sometimes has power to approve NOC budgets and major investment decisions; informal influence also occurs.[68] And in a few states, subnational institutions shape NOC plans by lobbying for operations in their home jurisdictions. Judiciaries across all countries wield relatively little direct power. Reflecting the case studies in this volume, Table 3.1 shows how commonly different principals exert authority over an NOC.

Across my data sample, the following NOCs operate in states with centralized authority: ADNOC, Gazprom, PDVSA, Petrobras, Petronas, Saudi Aramco, Sonangol, and Statoil. As suggested above, the locus of NOC authority in these states tends to be national leaders, energy ministries, or specialized oil authorities. National leaders typically control NOC governance in states that are oil dependent economically and highly consolidated politically (Angola, Malaysia, Putin-era Russia, Saudi Arabia, Chávez-era Venezuela after 2003).[69] In some leader-dominant regimes, such as

Table 3.1. *Frequency of state actors having significant authority^a over an NOC^b*

State actors with authority over NOC	Near universal	Common	Occasional	Infrequent	Very rare
State leader		X			
Leader's family network			X		
Energy ministry		X			
Specialized state oil authority		X			
Finance ministry			X		
Other ministries				X	
Non-policy executive agencies			X		
Legislature			X		
Subnational institutions				X	
Judiciary					X

[a] I use the words "significant authority" as shorthand to describe consistent, major decision-making power in NOC governance. This power may be formal or informal.

[b] I code these categories as follows: 1) "Near universal," in which the category applies to nearly all states with NOCs; 2) "Common," in which the category applies to most states with NOCs; 3) "Occasional," in which the category applies to some states with NOCs; 4) "Infrequent," in which the category applies to a few states with NOCs; and 5) "Very rare," in which the category applies to almost no states with NOCs.

Source: NOC case studies in this volume.

current-day Russia and Venezuela, national leaders or their advisers closely oversee NOC decision making. In others, like Malaysia, leaders exercise control selectively and entrust authority to trusted allies within the company. Similarly, specialized oil authorities tend to occur in states, like Abu Dhabi, that reach consensus arrangements between senior NOC leadership and national leaders. (See Chapter 11.) Energy ministries, by contrast, predominate in states that have a multiplicity of interests but have reached institutional agreements among those interests to give the ministry primary NOC governance control (as in Brazil and Norway).[70] (NOCs, for their part, often capitalize on their personal ties with the political establishment to secure advantages for the companies. Sonangol's leadership, for example, enjoys direct lines of communication with Angola's president and uses that access to preserve company independence. See Chapter 19.

By contrast, the NOCs within my data set operating in fragmented governance systems are as follows: KPC, NIOC, NNPC, ONGC, and Pemex. Many of these states have competing interests in the executive and legislative branches.[71] Each interest maintains separate lines of NOC authority and, in some cases, wrestles with one another over oil policy.[72]

Based on this data sample, I test hypothesis 1 that low company performance is related to fragmented authority and high company performance is tied to unified authority. Figure 3.3 compares individual NOC performance against the relationship among principals governing the companies.[73]

Consistent with hypothesis 1, I find a positive relationship between performance and centralization of authority over the company. Most of the NOCs in this sample closely conform to this relationship. Two notable exceptions are current-day Gazprom and PDVSA, which struggle despite operating in single-principal environments. I offer an account for these exceptions and discuss some implications in section 5.

Second, I analyze the mix of oversight mechanisms for NOCs. Across my sample, most states have a common set of oversight mechanisms. This common set embodies the corporate governance template and includes board of director power to discipline senior NOC leadership;[74] approve annual budgets; review major investment decisions, strategies, and goals; and receive (public or non-public)[75] audits

80 David R. Hults

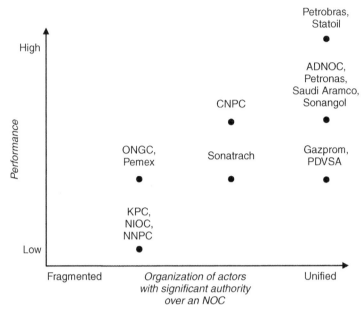

Figure 3.3 NOC performance and organization of state actors having authority over an NOC.

Note: The points on the graph are for rough comparisons only; the corresponding companies for each point are labeled alphabetically above.

Sources: For more information on the performance assessments, see Appendix A; for assessments of the actors having authority over the NOC, see the appendix to this chapter specifically.

and financial disclosures.[76] Virtually all states also have some ability to observe NOCs' general reputation and aggregate production, though production-based monitoring is of little use because NOC cost structures differ. Beyond these boilerplate (and often perfunctory)[77] powers, the mix of NOC oversight mechanisms deviates, with some states implementing invasive public administration-style controls and others taking a hands-off approach. Table 3.2 depicts this mix across the fifteen NOCs in this volume.

Within the data sample, several governance systems rely mostly on *ex ante* procedures; the corresponding NOCs are KPC, NIOC, NNPC, PDVSA, and Pemex. Procedure-heavy systems frequently impose a thicket of requirements, empower institutions to approve company decision making in advance, and vest decision-making authority in the institutions themselves. By contrast, few of these systems expose their NOCs to competition or conduct robust comparative assessments. Most of these systems occur in states with warring multiple principals (as in KPC, NNPC, Pemex), each of which holds distinct objectives and mechanisms of authority. In PDVSA's governance system, a single principal (President Hugo Chávez) dominates NOC governance and has assigned the company a long list of company objectives (see Chapter 10).

By contrast, four NOCs – ADNOC, Petrobras, Petronas, and Statoil – operate in monitoring-heavy systems. Unlike procedure-heavy systems, monitoring-heavy systems grant NOCs wide decision-making power but empower state institutions to review those decisions after the fact. These institutions typically monitor company performance through professional-style audits and at least some exposure to competition in upstream or equity markets. (Petronas, for example, faces tough competition in international markets even as it retains some monopoly privileges at home (see Chapter 18). Following a performance review, states may exercise their sanction powers to reward or punish NOC decisions. State review of NOC performance is not a technocratic exercise, however. At least two NOCs in monitoring-heavy systems, Petrobras and Statoil, have at times used their political influence to at least partially circumvent state oversight bodies. See Chapter 12 and Chapter 14, respectively.

I use this data sample to test hypothesis 2: high NOC performance is associated with monitoring-heavy systems and low performance is associated with procedure-heavy systems. Figure 3.4 compares the performance of individual NOCs against the composition of oversight mechanisms for the NOCs in this volume.

Supporting hypothesis 2, I find that procedure-heavy oversight mechanisms and poor performance go hand in hand. All of the worst-performing NOCs in this sample operate in procedure-heavy or mixed environments. Moreover, all of the monitoring-heavy systems have high- or above-average-performing NOCs. Slight outliers occur, including Gazprom and ONGC (both relatively poor-performing despite some competition) and Saudi Aramco, Sonangol, and Petronas (relatively high-performing though no competition occurs). I discuss these findings further in section 5.

Third, I examine the effect of rule of law on NOC performance. In reviewing the data sample, I note that states employ an array of

Table 3.2. *Frequency of various oversight mechanisms in governing NOCs[a]*

Type of oversight mechanism (whether formal or informal)	Near universal	Common	Occasional	Infrequent	Very rare
Ex ante procedure					
Authority over senior NOC leadership positions					
Board power	X				
State power		X			
Authority over annual budgets					
Board approval power	X				
State power to approve/set		X			
Authority over NOC expenditures					
Board approval of major expenditures	X				
Board approval of minor expenditures					X
Board decision making on expenditures					X
State approval of major expenditures		X			
State approval of minor expenditures			X		
State decision making on expenditures				X	
Approval of procurement		X			
Approval of contracting			X		

Approval of employment		X
Ex post monitoring		
General NOC reputation	X	
Performance contracts	X	
Regulatory investigations of company financial practices	X	
Regulatory investigations of health, safety, and environment practices	X	
Legislative investigations of company practices	X	
Annual audits/company reports	X	
Competition for bonds	X	
Competition for capital (minority capital investment)		X
Competition for right to exploit/develop hydrocarbons		X

[a] Government taxation also acts as a surrogate form of control.

Source: NOC case studies in this volume.

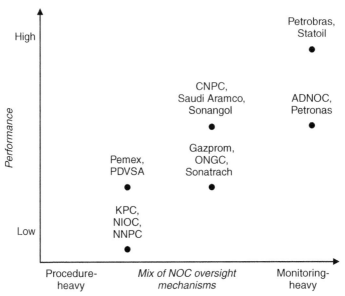

Figure 3.4 NOC performance and mix of NOC oversight mechanisms.

Note: The points on the graph are for rough comparisons only; the corresponding companies for each point are labeled alphabetically above.

Sources: For more information on the performance assessments, see Appendix A; for assessments of the actors having authority over the NOC, see the appendix to this chapter specifically.

formal and informal mechanisms to govern the companies.[78] Nearly all states have laws or law-like instruments on the books governing NOCs. The latter instruments include executive decrees, oil sector regulations, and NOC organizational by-laws carrying the force of law. Also common are government policy guidelines, which tend to be more amorphous than laws but which also shape company behavior. In some states, these formal and semi-formal mechanisms effectively set rules of the game for NOC governance. In others, however, these mechanisms are "ink on paper" (Li and Xia 2007) with little practical significance. Informal tools reign instead. These informal tools include implicit signaling of policy preferences, public political pressure, interpersonal ties, and strong-armed political influence. (Even states committed to the rule of law make use of informal tools, though probably to lesser effect. See Chapter 14, for the Norwegian account.) And lurking in the background of all governance systems are norms

Table 3.3. *Frequency of formal and informal mechanisms in governing NOCs*

Formal/ informal governance mechanisms	Near-universal	Common	Occasional	Infrequent	Very rare
Formal laws and executive decrees			X		
Oil sector regulations			X		
NOC organizational by-laws			X		
Oil sector policies		X			
Policy "signaling"		X			
Public pressure			X		
Interpersonal ties	X				
Direct political influence			X		
Oil sector norms	X				

Source: NOC case studies in this volume.

that establish expectations for state and company behavior. Gleaned from the sample in this volume, Table 3.3 depicts how often states use these formal and informal tools to govern their NOCs.

Several governance systems in this volume are strongly law-based: The corresponding NOCs are ONGC, Petrobras, Pemex, and Statoil. In general, law-based systems occur in states that have a vibrant separation of powers (and that may or may not have reached institutional agreements over the allocation of oil sector governance roles). In these otherwise dissimilar states, the law acts as an effective channel and constraint; state actors use legal mechanisms to manage NOCs and have limited capacity, at least in the short term, to act outside those mechanisms.[79]

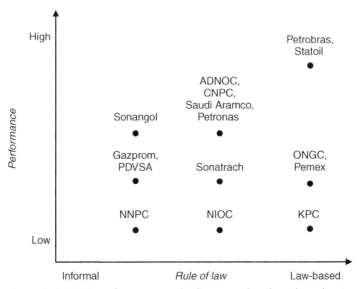

Figure 3.5 NOC performance and reliance on law-based mechanisms.
Note: The points on the graph are for rough comparisons only; the corresponding companies for each point are labeled alphabetically above.
Sources: For more information on the performance assessments, see Appendix A; for assessments of the actors having authority over the NOC, see the appendix to this chapter specifically.

By contrast, many NOCs operate in informal governance systems, including Gazprom, NNPC, PDVSA, and Sonangol. Many of these NOCs are found in states that have relatively low per capita incomes (as in the case of NNPC or Sonangol), politically unstable environments (as in the case of PDVSA and again NNPC), or stable environments based on family rule (Sonangol).[80] Some of the states, like Nigeria, codify their NOC governance systems in law but rely on informal ties to do the actual substance of governance;[81] the law thus functions as a backdrop to informal decision making. Other states, like Chávez-era Venezuela, pay so little regard to laws on the books that they arguably violate them, at least in the short term (as perhaps occurred when Chávez fired PDVSA's board in 2002; see Chapter 10); these countries govern instead through intimate ties and political suasion.

I apply this data to test hypothesis 3 that rule of law is positively associated with NOC performance. Figure 3.5 compares the performance of individual NOCs against their home states' adherence to the rule of law. (One proxy for reliance on law-based mechanisms is the World Bank governance data. The data there is not NOC-specific, however. My assessments reflect a combination of general trends and case-specific insights.)

Based on the sample in this volume, I find a slightly positive but probably insignificant relationship between rule of law and NOC performance.[82] Fitting the hypothesis are high-flyers like Petrobras and Statoil and poor performers like NNPC. But many exceptions exist. Sonangol operates in a relatively informal environment but nevertheless performs fairly well. Conversely, Mexico's Pemex struggles despite operating within a scrupulously followed law-based framework. I discuss the implications of this relationship below.

4 Implications

Having presented my research findings for the three elements of NOC governance, I turn to possible inferences from those findings. I address these inferences sequentially.

4.1 Organization of state actors having significant authority over the NOC

First, in finding a positive relationship between corporate performance and centralized authority, my work applies existing scholarship on multiple principals to the context of NOCs. Consistent with Whitford (2005) and Estrin (1998), NOCs may respond to multiple principals by inconclusively lurching between state objectives or by pursuing interests of their own (e.g., self-enrichment). However, the existence of multiple principals does not necessarily increase the independence of the NOCs. Rather, competing principals seem to affect NOCs in two main ways, only the first of which is autonomy-enhancing: 1) shielding the NOC from other principals to preserve their particular interests (or in response to lobbying from the NOC); and 2) actively interfering in the NOC to further those interests (especially the interest in rent collection). Perhaps because of the large rents at stake, active inference seems more common than political shielding.[83] (Exceptions may occur when the future of those rents is on the line. But even then, political shielding may remain weak. Consider, for example, Mexico. Although consistent decreases in Pemex's production spurred governance reforms in late 2008, those reforms were tepid. See Chapter 7.)

One reason that principals may interfere in NOC operations but insulate other institutions from meddling is because NOC rents are comparatively direct. A government patent agency, for example, can give intellectual property protections to favored political constituencies, but those rents are oblique and accrue over the long term. An NOC, by contrast, can deliver rents to principals directly (by, e.g., giving the principal cash, over or under the table). The immediacy of NOC rents creates a sort of coordination problem within the principal itself, above and beyond the commonly studied coordination problem *across* multiple principals. Institutional "principals" are aggregations of numerous, shifting actors (e.g., legislatures with changing legislators, public agencies with turnover of bureaucrats). These institutions may be unable to internally agree on a long-term political insulation strategy when an NOC could provide immediate rents instead. By contrast, institutions may be better able to coordinate internally – and thus protect the public agent politically – when the only way to secure rents from the agent is by protecting it from micro-management. Further work, particularly in game theory, may shed light on these issues.[84]

My work also suggests that some NOCs suffer even in single-principal environments (Russia, Venezuela). One rationale for this result – consistent with the work of Bueno de Mesquita *et al.* (2003) and Acemoglu and Johnson (2005) – is that single principals with an insecure grasp on power may press their NOCs for short-term political gains.[85] (For example, Venezuelan President Chávez obligates PDVSA to spend its proceeds on patronage in part because he fears the strength of the political opposition – which ousted him from power in a short-lived 2002 coup. See Chapter 10.) Another explanation is that some principals rely on clientelism to maintain power. This explanation partly applies to Russia, Venezuela, and a poor-performing NOC outside this sample: Indonesia's Pertamina, when President Suharto was in power (Hertzmark 2007). By contrast, single principals seem to take a longer-term perspective in states with iron-clad rule (Angola, Saudi Arabia) or highly institutionalized environments (Brazil, Norway).[86] This explanation is mostly conjecture, however, because I do not test for it specifically. (See Chapter 2, for rigorous tests of the effect of leaders' time horizons on major oil sector decisions.)

Although my research did not uncover instances of NOCs thriving in multiple principal settings, I suspect that such cases indeed occur. Examples of this phenomenon might include the more extreme "states within a state," like pre-Chávez PDVSA. These NOCs, presumably small in number, prosper in part by taking advantage of political infighting to create autonomy for themselves (in conformity with Moe 1984). These companies may eventually lose their autonomy if the political factions coalesce or one faction wins out.[87]

4.2 Mix of NOC oversight mechanisms

Second, in showing a link between a monitoring-heavy system and positive NOC performance, I reinforce theoretical arguments favoring monitoring (Vining and Weimer 1990) and add an element of state choice. In an idealized, politics-free world, states would set highly measurable NOC objectives, institute monitoring-heavy oversight systems to track those objectives, and reap the resulting performance benefits. I offer several reasons why many states follow a different script. First and most obviously, some state actors desire goals beyond performance; a leader teetering on the edge of political survival, for example, may prefer immediate employment generation instead. Second, NOCs may lobby the government to maintain their domestic preferences and thereby deprive the states of the benefits from monitoring (as arguably occurred when Saudi Aramco squelched its government's 1998 plans to spur domestic upstream competition; see Chapter 5). And third, state actors may resist greater monitoring because it could come at the expense of short-term rent extraction. A state could monitor its NOC better by allowing company shares to float on a stock exchange, for example, but doing so would require the state to share NOC profits with private shareholders.[88] Similarly, a state could acquire greater knowledge about an NOC by conducting public audits, but doing so could reveal corruption that the state prefers to hide.

In a similar vein, my analysis offers some reasons procedure-based systems endure. Most importantly, state principals jealously guard their own NOC oversight mechanisms – and in the process, cloud the governance system with procedures – because the procedures serve as vehicles for rent appropriation, both explicit and implicit (i.e., graft). Moreover, state actors may retain procedures to rein in NOCs that had become, from the government's perspective, "states within a state" (e.g., as in Venezuela). The institutional legacy of existing rules (e.g., constitutional provisions or founding laws) may also impede reform (as in Mexico or Kuwait, respectively).

More speculatively, my work hints that competition, while useful, is not the sine qua non of NOC success. Several NOCs flourish even though they do not compete for hydrocarbon projects domestically or invite equity investment (as is true for Petronas, Saudi Aramco, and Sonangol). In limited circumstances, entrenched corporate cultures may compensate for a lack of competition, particularly when the state maintains close ties with senior NOC management, as is true for Saudi Aramco (see Chapter 5). Moreover, protection from competition may nurture the early growth of an NOC, as arguably is the case for infant industries generally (Ranis 2003) (though the political dynamic for removing protection at a later stage may prove difficult). Key examples include Statoil and, in particular, Petrobras before the late 1990s (see Chapter 14 and Chapter 12, respectively). Similarly, competition does not necessarily alleviate an NOC of its ills. A few NOCs struggle despite being subject to some competition (as is the case with Gazprom and ONGC). Though my sample is small and I did not test this matter explicitly, competition may offer limited benefits if it remains accompanied by a bevy of procedures and a soft budget constraint.

Lastly, on the issue of oversight, my research speculatively suggests that another type of NOC monitoring – transparency – may have limited benefits for performance. External transparency seems to matter most when the public partly (or indirectly) owns the NOC, as in the cases of Petrobras or Statoil. In these cases, large private investors and the state use publicly available financial information, stock prices, and other signals to supervise corporate performance effectively. But when the state holds sole ownership of the NOC, internal transparency may suffice; at least one highly successful NOC, Saudi Aramco, gives the state benchmarking data but divulges little of it to the public at large (see Chapter 5). Public NOC transparency programs – including the Extractive Industries

Transparency Initiative (EITI) – may therefore bolster civil society or governmental accountability, but their effects on NOC performance may be highly case-dependent. At least some NOCs that have opened up their books, like Pemex, remain poor-performing.

4.3 Rule of law in NOC governance

Lastly, I am unable to draw many implications from state adherence to the rule of law because my findings on that issue are tenuous. Respect for the rule of law may improve NOC performance by shaping and checking state actors' behavior, but my research methods are too coarse to detect much of a relationship. Alternatively, rule of law may have little to no relationship with NOC performance at all. Future studies may reveal the potential links.

One explanation for the weak relationship between rule of law and NOC performance is that formal and informal mechanisms effectively substitute for one another in NOC governance. Because several NOCs prosper in semi-formal or informal environments, interpersonal ties and political pressure may serve as effective governance tools. (Less clear, however, is whether informal mechanisms sustain their efficacy over the long term.[89]) As a result – in line with the cautions of Haggard *et al.* (2008) – externally imposed rule of law reforms may have narrow effects on NOC governance. The Nigerian oil sector, for example, has undergone frequent and sometimes far-reaching legal reforms – often at the prodding of international developmental institutions – but the underlying, entrenched informal mechanisms remain much the same (see Chapter 16). More promising, albeit tentative, legal reforms have occurred in Angola and Kazakhstan, where the governments have used their NOCs, Sonangol and KazMunaiGas respectively, as instruments to formalize and modernize their oil sectors (Chapter 19; Olcutt 2007). But even in these cases, rule of law reform seems like a consequence, rather than cause, of NOC success.

5 Conclusion

This chapter explores the deep, abiding connections between NOC governance and company performance. Based on the fifteen NOCs in this volume, my research indicates that NOCs tend to thrive in centralized, monitoring-heavy systems. NOCs usually suffer, by contrast, in systems beset by a dispersed system of authority and bevy of procedures. My work suggests a weak nexus between NOC performance and state reliance on the rule of law.

Though I test here for correlation only, the causal links between NOC governance and performance probably flow in both directions. NOC governance almost certainly affects company performance (through, inter alia, shifts in national missions, the accumulation of state-mandated procedures, and the absence or presence of competition). And company performance also shapes governance, though the links here are less clear. In response to high NOC performance, for example, some states may relax regulations in the hope of creating rents for the long haul (as arguably occurred in 1990s Brazil and Norway). Others may respond to high performance by setting new rules to cash in on the company's rents (though examples here are scant).[90] Some NOCs may also use their lobbying power to push through reforms themselves (in the 1990s, PDVSA instigated an opening in the Venezuelan upstream sector). Further work may help tease out these causal chains.

More generally, NOC governance mechanisms reflect interest group struggles and broad, structural factors. Interest groups – which line up behind particular institutions or factions within those institutions – affect how states settle on particular governance mechanisms. Once these interest groups reach an equilibrium, either through formal agreements or de facto working arrangements, the broad contours of that equilibrium may persist for long periods of time (as in Kuwait and Mexico). In this institutional inertia, minor shifts in underlying interests yield little change. However, abrupt shocks may destabilize the system. I mention four such shocks here: changes in 1) oil and natural gas prices (Chang *et al.* 2009), such as the oil price rise from 2000 to 2008 and the decline during 2008 and 2009;[91] 2) investment cycles (Chapter 4); 3) political regime (Chapter 2), such as the transition from democratic to semi-autocratic rule in Venezuela from 1999 to 2009; and 4) resource endowment, as may be occurring in Brazil today with the discovery of large subsalt fields offshore (see Chapter 12). Depending on their direction, these changes may induce pro-performance measures or policy backsliding (as in Algeria's 2006 partial reversal of its 2005 pro-liberalization hydrocarbons law; see Chapter 13).

Given the importance of interest groups and extrinsic factors, my work invites caution for NOC policy reform. Although some governance systems seem more likely to improve NOC performance than others, implementing a reform agenda is challenging, unless the external shocks referenced above come into play. Leading state actors are likely to resist shifting from a procedure-based to monitoring-based system, for example, because the existing system better provides for their narrow interests. Even if policymakers introduce formal governance reforms, countervailing changes in informal governance may occur – such as greater reliance on personal connections and political persuasion. And when NOC governance undergoes real change, the triggers for change often lie outside policymakers' control. In this context, policymakers are far from impotent; but their prospects for success remain highly contingent on other factors.

Appendix: detailed research findings

Assessments of NOC performance

NOC (home country)	Performance	Source for assessment
ADNOC (Abu Dhabi)	Upper middle	Appendix A; Chapter 11
CNPC (China)	Upper middle	Appendix A; Chapter 9
Gazprom (Russia)	Lower middle	Appendix A; Chapter 15
KPC (Kuwait)	Low	Appendix A; Chapter 8
NIOC (Iran)	Low	Appendix A; Chapter 6
NNPC (Nigeria)	Low	Appendix A; Chapter 16
ONGC (India)	Lower middle	Appendix A; Chapter 17
Pemex (Mexico)	Lower middle	Appendix A; Chapter 7
Petrobras (Brazil)	High	Appendix A; Chapter 12
PDVSA (Venezuela)	Lower middle	Appendix A; Chapter 10
Petronas (Malaysia)	Upper middle	Appendix A; Chapter 18
Saudi Aramco (Saudi Arabia)	Upper middle	Appendix A; Chapter 5
Sonangol (Angola)	Upper middle	Appendix A; Chapter 19
Sonatrach (Algeria)	Lower middle	Appendix A; Chapter 13
Statoil (Norway)	High	Appendix A; Chapter 14

Assessment of state actors with authority over NOCs

NOC (home country)	Organization of state actors with authority over NOC	Source for assessment	List of relevant state actors
ADNOC (Abu Dhabi)	Unified	Chapter 11	Controlling ADNOC is the Supreme Petroleum Council (SPC), which is led by the ruling family and a few members of closely allied families.
CNPC (China)	Mixed	Chapter 9	Although some recentralization has occurred, state authority remains split between the State Energy Commission (former Office of the National Energy Leading Group) and the National Energy Administration. The state council has influence over key company positions.
Gazprom (Russia)	Unified	Chapter 15	Putin has installed allies on Gazprom's board (at least eleven of eighteen total as of 2008) and exercises tight control over the company.

Assessment of state actors with authority over NOCs (cont.)

NOC (home country)	Organization of state actors with authority over NOC	Source for assessment	List of relevant state actors
KPC (Kuwait)	Fragmented	Chapter 8	KPC control is divided between the legislature (National Assembly), government (particularly oil ministry), and state shareholder representative (Supreme Petroleum Council). Also significant are various state regulatory agencies (particularly the State Audit Bureau for procurement).
NIOC (Iran)	Fragmented	Chapter 6	Although the Ayatollah and president wield significant control, power is shared with the parliament (Majlis) and petroleum ministry (which itself blurs functions with the company).
NNPC (Nigeria)	Fragmented	Chapter 16	The president wields most power but shares it with National Assembly (legislature) in budget and NNPC policymaking; lower-level officials also exert influence through their ability to approve minor company decisions.

Company			
ONGC (India)	Fragmented	Chapter 17	Although the Ministry of Petroleum and Natural Gas has primary authority, both parliament and multiple oversight agencies – the Central Vigilance Commission (CVC) and Comptroller and Auditor General (CAG) – exert considerable influence over the company.
Pemex (Mexico)	Fragmented	Chapter 7	Mexican presidents once held close company control, but since 1995 the legislature, oil ministry, and finance ministry (Hacienda) compete for power. Also influential are a myriad of anti-corruption and regulatory agencies (especially the Ministry of Public Functions, or SFP).
Petrobras (Brazil)	Unified	Chapter 12	Brazilian government exerts control over Petrobras through its majority voting shares and positions on the board of directors.
PDVSA (Venezuela)	Unified	Chapter 10	Chávez and his immediate confidants exert near-total control over company; government ministries and legislature have little independent authority.

Assessment of state actors with authority over NOCs (cont.)

NOC (home country)	Organization of state actors with authority over NOC	Source for assessment	List of relevant state actors
Petronas (Malaysia)	Unified	Chapter 18	Petronas answers primarily to the prime minister; the government has not established an intermediary oil ministry. Exerting lesser influence are the treasury and Malaysia's powerful Economic Coordination Unit.
Saudi Aramco (Saudi Arabia)	Unified	Chapter 5	Senior members of Saudi royal family make major decisions and protect the company from most political interference. At the formal level, the Supreme Council for Petroleum and Mineral Affairs (SCPMA) typically exercises a light supervisory role. The Ministry of Petroleum and Natural Resources has become virtually indistinguishable from the company.

Sonangol (Angola)	Unified	Chapter 19	With backing from a few Futungo families, the president has primary authority over the company, though he delegates most decision making to the company itself. The Ministry of Finance has become increasingly prominent, however.
Sonatrach (Algeria)	Mixed	Chapter 13	Although the president exercises ultimate authority over the company, rival clans within the military elite and various ministries hold influence.
Statoil (Norway)	Unified	Chapter 14	The Ministry of Petroleum and Energy is the center of state authority; exerting lesser control are technical/regulatory agencies (Norwegian Petroleum Directorate, Petroleum Safety Agency), the state investment vehicle (Petoro), and legislature (Storting). The prime minister occasionally plays an informal role.

Assessment of mix of oversight mechanisms for governing NOCs

NOC (home country)	Mix of oversight mechanisms	Source for assessment	Description of oversight mechanisms
ADNOC (Abu Dhabi)	Monitoring-heavy	Chapter 11	SPC provides broad directives to ADNOC but imposes few procedural requirements. Although ADNOC is subject to little direct competition, it has long worked in partnership with IOCs, exposing the company to some benchmarking.
CNPC (China)	Varied	Chapter 9	State reviews major overseas decisions and affects employment decisions. Budget accounting emulates Western companies. CNPC competes with fellow Chinese NOC Sinopec domestically, and its PetroChina subsidiary competes abroad. PetroChina also receives minority equity investment. There are domestic bond issuances.
Gazprom (Russia)	Varied	Chapter 15	Gazprom has nominal power over investment decisions, but the state frequently uses its informal authority to control decision making. Company formally competes for domestic projects but is a de facto near monopolist. Private minority capital investment occurs, though some of it is linked to the Kremlin. State conducts professional audits (though beset by scandal) and some investigations.

KPC (Kuwait)	Procedure-heavy	Chapter 8	Though there are some *ex post* checks (in particular, audits), the bulk of controls involve procedures. Company is subject to onerous requirements on salaries (set by Civil Service Commission), procurement, budget (under SPC), and strategy (requiring more than thirty approvals). KPC's operator subsidiary, KOC, is also under tight control, though other subsidiaries have greater flexibility. The state does not subject company to competition for equity investment or for domestic upstream projects (despite "Project Kuwait" efforts at reform).
NIOC (Iran)	Procedure-heavy	Chapter 6	The state primarily governs through Five Year Development Plans (FYDPs), which set budgets, operations, and investments. FYDP revisions frequently occur, setting new rules for the company. No competition occurs for equity investment or for domestic upstream projects and there is little investment abroad.
NNPC (Nigeria)	Procedure-heavy	Chapter 16	The executive exerts tight scrutiny over company investment and partnership decisions and frequently turns over NNPC leadership. Budget is subject to detailed presidential and legislative review. Employment is also subject to government rules. Nigeria conducts some monitoring of monetary flows through the Extractive Industries Transparency Initiative.

Assessment of mix of oversight mechanisms for governing NOCs (*cont.*)

NOC (home country)	Mix of oversight mechanisms	Source for assessment	Description of oversight mechanisms
ONGC (India)	Varied	Chapter 17	State has highly restrictive employment rules, though 1999 reforms created somewhat more flexibility. State authority over senior leadership is tight. Budgeting, investment, and partnerships have become more independent. Since 1998, ONGC competes for domestic upstream projects, but level of competition is weak. Multiple agencies audit and investigate company.
Pemex (Mexico)	Procedure-heavy	Chapter 7	Congress and financial ministry (Hacienda) exercise tight budgetary controls, with Hacienda also setting rules on domestic pricing. SFP imposes inflexible regulations on employment, salaries, and organization. The company is subject to detailed, professional audits and frequent investigations. There is effectively no competition for equity or domestic upstream projects (IOCs do have service contracts). The company has little overseas presence. The 2008 reforms should give the company slightly greater independence.

Petrobras (Brazil)	Monitoring-heavy	Chapter 12	The government sets few explicit requirements for Petrobras, apart from limited social corporate social responsibility and other projects. However, Petrobras is subject to significant competition, both for investment and licensing blocks. (Brazil's National Petroleum Agency administers licensing programs.) Petrobras also is benchmarked through annual reports.
PDVSA (Venezuela)	Procedure-heavy	Chapter 10	Formal rules are sparse, but Chávez-era state imposes informal controls on spending, contracting, and employment. Recently, the state has professionalized audits, but other forms of company monitoring are rare. The company does partner with IOCs on domestic projects and issue bonds, providing some opportunity for benchmarking
Petronas (Malaysia)	Monitoring-heavy	Chapter 18	The state imposes few formal controls on company decision making, but it has informally compelled Petronas to make financial bailouts and fund pet projects. The company remains fully state-owned and has automatic partnership rights in domestic IOC operations. Petronas is exposed to heavy competition internationally.

Assessment of mix of oversight mechanisms for governing NOCs (cont.)

NOC (home country)	Mix of oversight mechanisms	Source for assessment	Description of oversight mechanisms
Saudi Aramco (Saudi Arabia)	Varied	Chapter 5	SPCMA sets five-year company plans, though they have limited practical effect. SPCMA and semi-independent board of directors also have corporate governance-style controls (e.g., audits, chairman appointments, chairman salaries, capital stock levels). State-imposed rules are few, though the company has extensive internal controls. Company provides non-public benchmarking data to SPCMA. There is no competition for equity capital and limited competition in the upstream sector.
Sonangol (Angola)	Varied	Chapter 19	State sets few rules for Sonangol behavior, relying instead on IOC relations and auctions to gauge company performance. Listing of company shares is possible in the future.

Sonatrach (Algeria)	Varied	Chapter 13	Although Sonatrach formally preserves a formal corporate-style relationship with the state, the state informally reviews many company decisions. Under recent legislation, Sonatrach competes with IOCs for upstream contracts, though it can assert a minority stake in any development.
Statoil (Norway)	Monitoring-heavy	Chapter 14	To govern the company, the state mostly relies on competition, audits, and periodic investigations, rather than prescriptive rules. The company is subject to competition for domestic upstream projects and minority capital investment; it also has extensive international interests.

Assessment of reliance on rule of law in governing NOCs

NOC (home country)	Reliance on rule of law	Source for assessment[a]	Characterization of rule of law
ADNOC (Abu Dhabi)	Varied	Chapter 11; Kaufmann *et al.* (1999–2009)	The state – which includes several emirates – has above-average rule of law scores. The SPC exercises control through formal channels, but the ruling family has important informal influence.
CNPC (China)	Varied	Chapter 9; Kaufmann *et al.* (1999–2009)	State officials have exerted informal influence over the company but formal rules matter, too. State has average to slightly below-average rule of law scores.
Gazprom (Russia)	Informal	Chapter 15; Kaufmann *et al.* (1999–2009)	The Kremlin mostly relies on interpersonal relationships and political pressure to govern Gazprom; the law often acts as a cover. State has low World Bank rule of law scores.
KPC (Kuwait)	Law-based	Chapter 8; Kaufmann *et al.* (1999–2009)	Although the judiciary is not independent and the legislature is subordinate to the emir, the state has above-average World Bank rule of law scores, and the oil sector is relatively formalized. The company's founding law has proven resistant to change.
NIOC (Iran)	Varied	Chapter 6; Kaufmann *et al.* (1999–2009)	Routine policy and financial matters follow formal procedures, but the Ayatollah, Guardian Council, or president will bypass those formalities for major decisions. The state has low World Bank rule of law scores.

NNPC (Nigeria)	Informal	Chapter 16; Kaufmann *et al.* (1999–2009)	Informal relationships strongly color NOC governance, although the state publicly touts its laws in the oil sector. The state suffers from consistently very low World Bank rule of law scores.
ONGC (India)	Law-based	Chapter 17; Kaufmann *et al.* (1999–2009)	Oil sector governance is highly formalized, with the state establishing mandatory policies for the company. State has average to above-average World Bank rule of law scores.
Pemex (Mexico)	Law-based	Chapter 7; Kaufmann *et al.* (1999–2009)	The state has average to below-average World Bank rule of law scores generally, but the oil sector is highly formalized. Both the Mexican constitution and legislative laws play important roles.
Petrobras (Brazil)	Law-based	Chapter 12; Kaufmann *et al.* (1999–2009)	The state has average World Bank rule of law scores, but relies mostly on its formal corporate powers to govern the company. Recent politicization has occurred, however.
PDVSA (Venezuela)	Informal	Chapter 10; Kaufmann *et al.* (1999–2009)	Chávez's informal decision making is by far the most important channel for PDVSA governance. In fact, these informal decisions sometimes contravene legal mechanisms in place for the oil sector (e.g., *apertura*-era contracts). During Chávez's tenure, World Bank rule of law scores have declined from below-average to among the lowest in the world.

Assessment of reliance on rule of law in governing NOCs (*cont.*)

NOC (home country)	Reliance on rule of law	Source for assessment[a]	Characterization of rule of law
Petronas (Malaysia)	Varied	Chapter 18; Kaufmann *et al.* (1999–2009)	The state has above-average World Bank rule of law scores generally. In the oil sector, however, both formal and informal tools matter. The state respects the formal framework but the national leader uses informal mechanisms with Petronas leadership to push through many strategic decisions.
Saudi Aramco (Saudi Arabia)	Varied	Chapter 5; Kaufmann *et al.* (1999–2009)	The company's formal, corporate governance-style controls buffer most outside influence. Saudi royals tend to exercise control over the company (to the extent they do so) through informal relationships rather than through the formal SPCMA channel. In practice, the company governs itself on most matters. The state has average to above-average World Bank rule of law scores.
Sonangol (Angola)	Informal	Chapter 19; Kaufmann *et al.* (1999–2009)	Although Sonangol mostly respects the legal framework in dealing with IOCs, Angola's president governs Sonangol by using his personal ties and trust in senior company management. State has very low World Bank rule of law scores.

| Sonatrach (Algeria) | Varied | Chapter 13; Kaufmann *et al.* (1999–2009) | State has below-average World Bank rule of law scores generally, but the oil sector is more formalized, as illustrated by debates over the 2005 hydrocarbons law. Nevertheless, the president's informal influence strongly affects NOC governance. |
| Statoil (Norway) | Law-based | Chapter 14; Kaufmann *et al.* (1999–2009) | Laws clearly establish the governance relationships in petroleum, though the content of those laws is sparse and non-prescriptive; state actors have considerable discretion to act within the confines of those laws. The state has long enjoyed among the highest World Bank rule of law scores in the world. |

[1] I do not rely on Knack and Keefer (1995) as an additional robustness check because its data is too dated for this exercise.

Summary table of performance and governance data for the fifteen NOCs in this volume

NOC (home country)	Performance	Organization of state actors with authority over NOC	Mix of oversight mechanisms	Reliance on rule of law
ADNOC (Abu Dhabi)	Upper middle	Unified	Monitoring-heavy	Varied
CNPC (China)	Upper middle	Mixed	Varied	Varied
Gazprom (Russia)	Lower middle	Unified	Varied	Informal
KPC (Kuwait)	Low	Fragmented	Procedure-heavy	Law-based
NIOC (Iran)	Low	Fragmented	Procedure-heavy	Varied
NNPC (Nigeria)	Low	Fragmented	Procedure-heavy	Informal
ONGC (India)	Lower middle	Fragmented	Varied	Law-based
Pemex (Mexico)	Lower middle	Fragmented	Procedure-heavy	Law-based
Petrobras (Brazil)	High	Unified	Monitoring-heavy	Law-based
PDVSA (Venezuela)	Lower middle	Unified	Procedure-heavy	Informal
Petronas (Malaysia)	Upper middle	Unified	Monitoring-heavy	Varied
Saudi Aramco (Saudi Arabia)	Upper middle	Unified	Varied	Varied
Sonangol (Angola)	Upper middle	Unified	Varied	Informal
Sonatrach (Algeria)	Lower middle	Mixed	Varied	Varied
Statoil (Norway)	High	Unified	Monitoring-heavy	Law-based

Notes

1 This separation of functions is sometimes known as the "Norwegian model" (Al-Kasim (2006)). Emulating this model are several other states – most notably Brazil (see Chapter 12).

2 As elsewhere in this volume, this chapter mostly focuses on the large, profitable NOCs in oil- and gas-exporting states. Nevertheless, I also consider several NOCs in states that import hydrocarbons (China, India).

3 SOEs are common in sectors that involve natural monopolies (air and rail transport, electricity, gas and water supply), network industries (broadcasting, telecommunications), and the financial sector (banking, insurance). For an overview of SOEs, see World Bank (2006b).

4 McPherson (2003) provides a more general overview of NOC governance.

5 Stevens (2003c, 2008a) frames state-company relations (with respect to both IOCs and NOCs) within principal–agent analysis as part of a broad overview of NOCs.

6 See also Lucas (1985) for a discussion focused on Canada's (since-lapsed) NOC experience.

7 Using the lens of institutional economics, Boshcheck's checklist covers state decision making on, inter alia, NOC missions, oversight, and operational scope. Coming from a similar perspective, Kalyuzhnova and Nygaard (2008) introduce a dynamic model of oil sector governance for resource-rich transition countries in which NOCs emerge as an important form.

8 See World Bank (2006b) for best practices for SOEs generally.

9 Other scholars have analyzed the relationship between company governance and performance for SOEs generally. Chong and Lopez-de-Silanes (2003) argue that privatization of Latin American SOEs is in part successful because the private sector corporate governance framework – including increased disclosures and better accounting standards – allows privatized firms to access capital at lower costs.

10 See, e.g., Moe (1984) and Vining and Weimer (1990) for analysis of the organizational efficiency of public organizations and Macey (2008) for discussion of corporations.

11 The procedure/monitoring division in this chapter broadly corresponds with the one proposed by Thompson and Jones (1986) and Vining and Weimer (1990).

12 These three axes of NOC governance highly correlate with one another. See discussion below.

13 I make no claim about the primary, or necessarily most foundational, lenses through which to view NOC governance. It is possible that "rule form" is a function of institutional settings and that institutional settings, in turn, follow from cultural, economic, and/or political structures. My

claim here is more modest. These elements form an important part of the theory underlying the performance of large organizations, which I test here.

14 Throughout this chapter, I use the generic term "performance" to refer to hydrocarbons performance as defined in Appendix A. I acknowledge that some states highly value an NOC's non-hydrocarbons performance. This chapter nevertheless focuses on hydrocarbons performance; see again Appendix A for discussion. To the extent non-hydrocarbon NOC goals are linked to certain governance elements (e.g., an NOC may be more likely to have non-core goals if it operates in a fragmented governance system), my focus on hydrocarbons performance provides some rudimentary sense of the cost of those non-hydrocarbon goals.

15 The NOCs are ADNOC (Abu Dhabi), CNPC (China), Gazprom (Russia), KPC (Kuwait), NIOC (Iran), NNPC (Nigeria), ONGC (India), Pemex (Mexico), Petrobras (Brazil), Petronas (Malaysia), PDVSA (Venezuela), Saudi Aramco (Saudi Arabia), Sonangol (Angola), Sonatrach (Algeria), and Statoil (Norway). As discussed in the Introduction, these NOCs operate in states that have significantly different levels of economic development and political organization.

16 Multiple objectives impose two costs of NOC performance: a direct opportunity cost (as resources are diverted toward achievement of those objectives) and an indirect inefficiency cost (as corporate management strains to juggle those objectives).

17 Note separately that causation may run in the other direction; i.e., the existence of a monitoring-heavy governance system may induce the legislature, executive, etc. to change its control over the company.

18 The literature on the principal–agent relationship is extensive. See, e.g., Spence and Zeckhauser (1971); Ross (1973); and Jensen (1983). I employ this model for its simplicity and do not suggest that it provides a complete explanation of NOC governance. For a critique of the principal–agent relationship focused on bureaucracy, see Waterman and Meier (1998).

19 For purposes of the principal–agent model, the state need not have an ownership interest in the NOC.

20 The principal–agent relationship between state and NOC is part of a longer chain. In democratic states, this chain begins with the relationship between the citizenry, as principal, and the government, as agent. It also includes the relationship between state and NOC, NOC leadership and NOC junior personnel, and so forth. At some points in this chapter, I address other links in this chain, but for the sake of economy I focus mostly on the state–NOC relationship here. For more on the different links in the principal–agent relationship within states, see Moe (1984).

21 Other factors also matter in principal–agent dynamics, including company history, corporate culture, and organizational dynamics. I omit those factors here for reasons of parsimony. Other academics have suggested ways of incorporating additional assumptions into the principal–agent model. For a review, see, e.g., Lane (2005).

22 See, e.g., Tollison (1982) for a discussion of the differences in principal–agent dynamics among public and private agents.

23 Audits and investigations roughly correspond to McCubbins and Schwartz's (1984) distinction between police patrols and fire alarms, respectively.

24 Scholars have categorized governance tools across a wide array of functional approaches. In the context of corporate governance, Vives (2000) divides governance into passive and active controls. McCubbins *et al.* (1987) suggest a tripartite division of governance tools for US administrative agencies: monitoring, sanctions, and administrative procedures. I use the simpler division of *ex ante* procedures and *ex post* monitoring because sanctions and procedures overlap heavily in the governance of NOCs. For more on the rules/monitoring division, see, e.g., Vining and Weimer (1990).

25 As of 2009, Petrobras was lobbying the Brazilian state for preferential access to the country's lucrative subsalt fields. See Chapter 12.

26 In the public bureaucracy setting, Nikansen (1971, 1975) argues that bureaucrats in some contexts have greater influence on politicians than politicians do over bureaucrats.

27 Moe (1984) points out some problems in modeling public bureaus as single agents. Bureaucratic superiors face widespread problems in monitoring bureaucratic performance because goals are opaque and wide-ranging. Therefore, they cannot easily coax compliance from their inferiors. As a consequence, principal–agent models premised on a single agent representation of a public bureau may not accurately reflect the behavior of that bureau. I argue that this problem is less prevalent in an NOC because monitoring of a subordinate entity in an NOC is often quite feasible (in some cases, approximating that of monitoring within a corporation). In particular, NOC heads often receive some reward for good performance – reputation, a share of profits (regardless of whether those profits are disclosed to the state) – that induce bosses to effectively monitor their subordinates. For this reason and reasons of economy, I omit further discussion of the multiple agents within NOCs here.

28 State principals are in part stand-ins for different private interests (e.g., organized interest groups).

29 These institutional rigidities include state constitutional provisions limiting NOC activities (as in Mexico; see Chapter 7) or entrenched corporate cultures within the NOCs (as in Saudi Aramco; see Chapter 5).

30 NOC governance systems broadly mirror the systems for other SOEs, with some exceptions. Because NOCs compete with other companies, they are at least conceptually more amenable to benchmarking than SOEs operating in natural monopoly environments. On the other hand, the enormous rents generated from NOCs create temptations for closer administration than for other SOEs. And the large size of NOCs makes them particularly useful vehicles, relative to other SOEs, for regulating the economy.

31 State actors value profit generation to achieve various self-interested goals, including (money-bought) political power and/or personal enrichment. In corporate governance, profits serve a different function; private investor principals value them because of their effect on stock prices and, less commonly, dividends. In some civil law corporate governance systems, shareholder profit maximization may be inferior to broader *stakeholder* goals, like worker protection or support for strategic enterprises (Macey 2008).

32 Gilson (2001), among others, explores how corporate governance arrangements differ and function (the latter involving differing formal arrangements to achieve much the same functional result). See also Moore and Stewart (1998) for a discussion of corporate governance norms for nongovernmental organizations.

33 This pattern holds for SOEs generally. SOEs in OECD countries are most commonly private liability companies, followed by joint stock companies (OECD 2005). Several decades ago, many public firms took the form of "trading departments" that were a part of the state, but that phenomenon has partly died out (Lane 2005). Still, a range of SOE legal structures exist (World Bank 2006b).

34 See Khan (1985) for more discussion. NOCs in Spanish- and Portuguese-speaking countries are typically classified as "anonymous societies," which is the equivalent of a limited company. NOCs in the English-speaking world are typically classified simply as corporations.

35 In this sense, NOC governance more closely resembles corporate governance of closely held corporations than the governance of publicly traded corporations. When reformers call for greater independence in an NOC board, they typically desire greater independence from the company *and* the state.

36 NOC corporate governance more closely follows the "control block" model prevalent in some parts of Asia and Europe (in which ownership is concentrated in a small number of stockholders) (Macey 2008). Note that a few NOCs have outside board members. The board of Norway's Statoil has no direct state participation, although shareholders – in which Norway holds a controlling stake – elect twelve of the eighteen members of the board. (Statoil employees elect the other six members.) See Chapter 14. In Saudi Aramco, retired CEOs sit on the board (Marcel 2006; Chapter 5).

And in late 2008, Mexico passed a law establishing that four of the company's fifteen directors are independent of the state, company, and union; see Chapter 7.

37 The dual powers of management and monitoring create some conflicts for boards of directors, both in common-law corporate governance (Macey 2008) and NOC governance. Civil law corporate governance, by contrast, often employs a dual governance structure separating managerial and monitoring roles.

38 See Marcel (2009) for more discussion.

39 Another common strain among most NOCs is that, like privately owned companies, they are often exposed to some level of private creditor discipline. Unlike private companies, however, NOCs may also benefit from issuance of public debt on their behalf.

40 Many NOCs probably benefited from state protection in the early years of their development.

41 Algeria also proposed opening up its hydrocarbons sector in 2005 but has since backed away from that policy. See Chapter 13.

42 The same lack of competition may occur for private companies operating in monopolistic or oligopolistic markets.

43 Partially fitting within the group is China, which allows private shareholder investment in an NOC subsidiary. For several of these NOCs, both private investors and government-linked institutions (pension funds, state-affiliated banks, etc.) own part of the company.

44 States also choose to place their NOCs on stock markets for reasons other than assessing capital market performance. These reasons include windfall gains from the sale of shares and increasing financial autonomy for the NOC.

45 See Christensen and Laegreid (2006) for more discussion.

46 One possible parallel is with socially conscious investors, who hold a broader range of company objectives. For a discussion of the effects of the socially minded investors on corporate governance, see Aguilera *et al.* (2006).

47 Rigid procedural rules are a hallmark of traditional public administration. Vining and Weimer (1990) provide a theoretical basis for why governments use complex sets rules to control public agencies. For more on the traditional public administration approach, see Caiden (1991), Hughes (1998), and Flynn (2002). Since the early 1980s, OECD countries have reformed many of their traditional practices to incorporate private sector approaches. These reforms, known as new public administration (NPM), involve organizational restructuring toward decentralized management; increasing use of market-like mechanisms; and increasing emphasis on performance (Batley and Larbi 2004).

48 Command-and-control regulations set specific standards for various actions.
49 A state may regulate, inter alia, to amass power, to umpire among competing factions, or to fulfill other goals. Scholars debate the extent to which regulation embodies public interest, private interest, or institutional concerns. For a review, see Morgan and Yeung (2007).
50 NOCs plan for expected hydrocarbons demand and may have an interest in regulating demand so that it better coordinates with their supply.
51 Research on the links between the variables chosen and particular governance indicators has found mixed results in other contexts. See Haggard *et al.* (2008) for a discussion in the context of the rule of law. For more on the lasting effect of institutional frameworks on state agencies, see, e.g., McCubbins *et al.* (1987).
52 The links between centralization of NOC governance, political regime, and economic development are complex. Unified NOC governance systems exist in both a wealthy democracy (Norway) and a middle-income semi-authoritarian state (Venezuela). Fragmented NOC governance systems exist in a middle-income, maturing democracy (Mexico) and a poor, fragile democracy (Nigeria).
53 The procedures and monitoring in NOC governance interact with political and economic institutions in complex ways. Procedure-heavy systems occur in a wealthy monarchy (Kuwait) and a poor, fragile democracy (Nigeria); there are monitoring-heavy systems in a wealthy democracy (Norway) and a maturing middle-income democracy (Brazil).
54 Formalized systems of NOC governance tend to occur more often in wealthy, democratic states. But this tendency has exceptions. There are formalized systems in a wealthy democracy (Norway), poor democracy (India), and wealthy monarchy (Kuwait). There are also informal systems in a poor, fragile democracy (Nigeria) and middle-income semi-authoritarian state (Russia).
55 I do not claim a causal relationship between NOC governance and performance in Russia and Venezuela; I merely note that significant changes in both governance and performance occurred.
56 Multiple principals resemble the political science concept of "veto points" in that each principal can check the power of other principals to carry out actions. Importantly, however, principals have the power to both veto and approve.
57 For further discussion of multiple principals within the US government, see, e.g., Whitford (2005).
58 For further discussion in the corporate context, see, e.g., Jensen (2000).

59 These problems are known in the SOE literature as *complex agency chain* (referring to the complications created by multiple levels of government influencing SOE governance) and *common agency* (referencing the different interests among principals within government) (World Bank 2006b).

60 One *ex ante* procedure is a prohibition of fringe benefits. The state may wish to prohibit fringe benefits out of concern they provide avenues for corruption.

61 One metric related to the rule of law is the number of veto points, as measured by, e.g., Henisz (2000) and Keefer (2002), which assesses the ability of actors within a political system to change the policy status quo. Andrews and Montinola (2004) find a positive relationship between rule of law and veto points in emerging democracies. I focus here on rule of law rather than on veto points for several reasons. First, my data sources, primarily case studies of individual NOCs, more frequently address adherence to the rule of law than the power of other institutions to reject those rules (a feature of veto points). Second, previous scholarship has found a positive relationship between corporate performance and rule of law (Johnson *et al.* 2000; La Porta *et al.* 2002; Lemmon and Lins 2003). Third, my sample includes many non-democracies. Andrews and Montinola (2004) suggest a relationship between veto points and the rule of law, but that finding is limited to emerging democracies.

62 For more discussion, see, e.g., Torke (2001); Licht *et al.* (2007); Benton (2009).

63 Li and Xia (2007) find that weak rule of law in China incentivizes private firms to avoid investments with long time horizons. Weak rule of law has less of an effect on SOEs because of agency problems and because their political masters may reward long-term investments.

64 I note that non-state actors – those lacking any direct authority within the state – may also play important roles. Unions, in particular, have proven influential in NOCs in Algeria, Mexico, and other states. I thank Valerie Marcel for raising this point.

65 In a number of states, specialized governmental bodies, such as Abu Dhabi's Supreme Petroleum Council or China's energy administration, effectively take the place of an energy ministry. (See Chapters 9 and 11.) NOC boards of directors may also fill this role. As discussed above, however, NOC boards often play superficial roles and do not have a significant mediating effect on governance.

66 "Energy ministry" includes ministries with different names but equivalent functions, e.g., oil ministries.

67 Note that some states, particularly democracies, have multiple principals exercising independent control over government *generally* but few such principals in the oil sector specifically. Institutional agreements among the principals delegate authority over to the oil sector to a small number of principals. My focus here is on the oil sector specifically.

68 In the 1980s, PDVSA became embroiled in a conflict with the Venezuelan legislature over the latter's power to review company actions affecting the national interest. See Chapter 10.

69 In countries where the national leader takes the lead in NOC governance, the oil/energy ministry usually plays a supporting role.

70 Other state actors exert influence even in states in which energy ministries dominate NOC governance. For example, legislators in Brazil frequently hold hearings to investigate corruption within Petrobras. See Chapter 12. In most cases, however, these incidents have little effect on the NOC.

71 Regulatory agencies here may engage in mission creep or, in less institutionalized regimes, be absent altogether.

72 A state's oil or energy minister is usually chair of an NOC's board of directors, but other ministers – particularly the finance minister – often have seats on the board, too. (In Mexico, the board has seats for five ministers in addition to the chief of the president's office. See Chapter 7.

73 I base my performance assessments on the individual case study conclusions in this volume. Because those assessments are broad, I group performance into three simple categories: low, moderate, and high.

74 Some states maintain the tradition of naming persons experienced in the oil industry (as in Venezuela before Chávez) and/or keeping leadership in its position for a predetermined tenure.

75 Saudi Aramco provides non-public benchmarking data to the state. See Chapter 5.

76 Note that the state may use these tools for various reasons; e.g., a state may allow an NOC to compete for minority private capital investment both to monitor the NOC's performance and to secure on-off gains from a sale of NOC shares.

77 See Macey (2008) for a discussion of how managers capture boards of directors in many corporate governance settings.

78 I refer to "rule of law" or "reliance of law-based mechanisms" in the procedural sense. States that follow the rule of law incorporate: 1) values of fair process (transparency, predictability, enforceability, stability); 2) capable institutions (independence, accountability); and 3) legitimacy. This list is derived from Trebilcock and Daniels (2008). I rely on a procedural notion of rule of law because it provides a simple basis for comparison across NOC governance systems. Other scholars advocate "thicker," substantive notions

of the rule of law that incorporate, inter alia, various individual rights. See Trebilcock and Daniels (2008) for more discussion. My focus is specifically on the rule of law in NOC governance. Other scholars have assessed rule of law across countries generally (Kaufmann *et al.* 1999–2009), and those assessments are instructive for NOC governance. As discussed below, some states rely more on law-based mechanisms in NOC governance than they do generally, and other states rely less on those mechanisms.

79 The law does not always act as a check on the behavior of state actors. In countries with well-functioning legal systems, laws are followed because both civil society (which lobbies and files citizen suits) and the press act as checks against non-compliance with the law. For more, see Bell (2005).

80 I thank Valerie Marcel for suggesting this last category.

81 For discussion in the USSR and environmental contexts, see Schwarzchild (1986) and Bell (2005), respectively.

82 For a discussion of legal formalism – particularly in developing countries – see Bell (2005).

83 Both active inference and political shielding may lead to greater rent collection. A state actor may appropriate rents from an NOC by directly interfering with its revenue disbursement. That same actor may also appropriate rents by constraining other actors and thereby secure greater rents for itself.

84 In line with the work of Karl (1997), it is possible that principals have greater incentives to interfere in NOCs because taxes levied on NOCs result in less political blowback than other taxation methods. This finding, however, depends on the political power of NOCs, the freedom of press in the country, and other factors.

85 For research in this vein, see Bueno de Mesquita *et al.* (2003) and Acemoglu and Johnson (2005).

86 This speculation is consistent with Haggard and Kaufmann's (1995) discussion of the role of strong executives (authoritarian or democratic) in initiating economic reforms in transition countries. For further discussion on the effect of strong executives, see, e.g., Hallerberg and Marier (2004).

87 In Venezuela, pre-Chávez PDVSA reduced political influence by developing a reputation for technocratic excellence and by investing a significant proportion of assets overseas – and thus outside the immediate ambit of the state. Venezuelan state actors, for their part, remained too weak to exert much influence. This situation changed radically when Chávez came into power and consolidated command over the company. See Chapter 10.

88 In 2008 and 2009, the Brazilian government became concerned that private investors would enjoy too many of the profits from Petrobras's discovery of lucrative offshore oil fields. See Chapter 12.

89 See Dixit (2004) for analysis of informal governance in other contexts.
90 President Chávez imposed increasingly heavy off-budget taxes on PDVSA between 2003 and 2008, but the impetus for those taxes was higher oil prices, not higher company performance.
91 As discussed in Chapter 10, the oil price rise may have facilitated the changes in PDVSA's governance structure by creating incentives for Chávez to more deeply intervene in the company.

4 | On the state's choice of oil company: risk management and the frontier of the petroleum industry

PETER A. NOLAN AND MARK C. THURBER

1 Introduction

The record of events that describe the petroleum industry (Yergin 1991; Parra 2004) and the analysis of these events (Jacoby 1974; Kobrin 1984b; Adelman 1995) provide a context from which to draw observations about the drivers and evolution of the structure of the industry. Private operating companies are seen to have been employed in the great majority of instances for the exploration and early development of a new "frontier" petroleum province, yet governments have often revisited those choices in favor of nationalization and the transfer of petroleum assets to a state operating company. Most notably, in the early 1970s, nationalizations in a host of countries, including all of the major developing world oil producers, left three-quarters of the world's oil reserves in the hands of state-owned companies. Control of a major part of the oil industry – decisions on oil price, production, and investment in reserves replacement – passed from private enterprise to a small group of producer countries.

Conventional wisdom holds that nationalizations are rooted in political motives of the petroleum states, which perceive value in the direct control of resource development though a state enterprise. State motives are inarguably important and are considered in detail throughout this book, including in the introductory and concluding chapters, in Chapter 2 by Chris Warshaw on drivers of states' expropriation and privatization behavior, and in all of the individual NOC case studies. At the same time, the argument presented in this chapter is that this motive to nationalize, whatever its cause, is in fact severely constrained by both the significant risks associated with the creation of petroleum reserves and the capacity of the petroleum state to take these risks.

We argue that constraints of risk significantly affect a state's choice of which agent to employ to find, develop, and produce its hydrocarbons. Implicit in much current debate is the idea that private, international oil companies (IOCs) and the state-controlled, national oil companies (NOCs) are direct competitors, and that the former may face threats to their very existence in an era of increased state control. In fact, IOCs and NOCs characteristically supply very different functions to governments when it comes to managing risk. For reasons we will discuss, IOCs excel at managing risk while NOCs typically do not. A third type of player, the oil service company (OSC), does not take on the risk of oil exploration and development, but instead supplies needed technology to both IOCs and NOCs. IOCs, NOCs, and OSCs will all continue to exist because their distinct talents are needed by states seeking to realize the value of their petroleum resources. However, the relative positions of these different players have changed substantially over time, and will continue to do so, in response to the shifting needs of oil-rich states.

Our hypotheses about the role of risk in shaping a state's choice of agent in hydrocarbon activities are summarized in the decision tree of Figure 4.1. This diagram is a stylized representation of how a rational state should choose its agent – private or state – under different conditions; it does not, of course, imply that all states will actually make rational choices. Private operating companies unsurprisingly are employed where oil-rich states perceive no motive for direct control through a state enterprise (A). In the more interesting (and common) cases where states do feel the need for direct control, private companies may nevertheless thrive at the industry frontier, where risks are extreme and the state's capacity to shoulder these risks is low (B). State operating companies are principally found (C) in proven and more mature petroleum provinces where the risks associated with the extraction of petroleum from developed fields are relatively small. However, they can also thrive where the petroleum state has significant capacity to absorb risk (risk tolerance), or in the rare cases where characteristics of the state–NOC relationship allow the NOC to develop appreciable risk management capabilities.

Outcomes A and C in the decision tree are relatively stable, but outcome B creates an inherent tension between the state's desire for direct control and dependence on IOCs to manage risk. In this situation, a significant alteration in either petroleum risk or in the state's capacity for risk can herald change. Over the multi-decade life of petroleum ventures, risks and state capacity for risk do change quite profoundly,

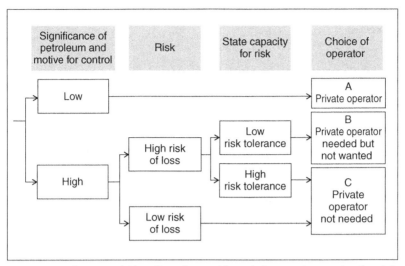

Figure 4.1 The central idea: Petroleum risk and the state's capacity for risk can constrain state choice of hydrocarbon agent.

prompting corresponding changes in the state's choice of hydrocarbon agent. In some countries this has happened only once, in others multiple times – in some cases resulting in "serial" nationalizations.

In the next section of this chapter we develop in more detail the hypotheses expressed in Figure 4.1, exploring the nature and sources of risk in the petroleum industry, how these risks change over time, the task of managing petroleum risks, and the variable capacity of state and private companies to manage them. In section 3, we apply qualitative and quantitative approaches to test the idea that risk significantly affects the state's choice of which agent to use for petroleum operations. First, we review the events leading to the cluster of nationalizations that occurred in the early 1970s and assess whether they were significantly affected by considerations of risk. Second, we explore how well variation in risk and state capacity for risk can explain changing ownership over time within a particular oil province – the UK and Norwegian zones of the North Sea. Third, we use data from energy research and consulting firm Wood Mackenzie to quantitatively test our hypothesis about the key role of risk, looking in particular at the case of oil and gas company exploration behavior. Finally, in section 4, we assess our theory about the role of risk in light of the results of section 3 and speculate about the roles for both private and state operating companies in the oil industry going forward.

2 The constraint of risk

In this section we elaborate on the idea of Figure 4.1 that considerations of risk significantly constrain a state's options for using a state-owned entity to find, develop, and produce hydrocarbons, even when motives of control militate in favor of such an approach. The term "risk" has been used by different people to mean different things, which has sometimes introduced ambiguity into discussions around the concept. Therefore, we begin this section by presenting the definitions of risk and the related notion of uncertainty that will be used in this chapter before we proceed step-by-step through the logical flow of Figure 4.1.

2.1 Defining risk

We define uncertainty to be a state in which outcomes are not known. Uncertainty can also be discussed in terms of degree, with uncertainty being smaller where more accurate estimates of outcomes are possible. Risk exists where some of the possible, uncertain outcomes involve a loss. Risk is higher when either negative outcomes are more probable or the losses associated with these outcomes are higher. (Figure 4.2 illustrates this for petroleum investments.)

The simplest type of risk-weighting for an investment simply multiplies the gain or loss associated with a given outcome by the estimated probability of that outcome and then sums over all possible outcomes (Megill 1988); in other words, it computes the expected value of an investment's profitability. However, two investments with the same expected value of profitability can have widely different variances, with some investments being much more exposed to large losses (or gains). For this reason, more sophisticated risk-weighting approaches incorporate measures of an investor's ability to tolerate a loss of a given size (Lerche and MacKay 1999). Our discussion of petroleum risks in this chapter is not quantitative, but it incorporates the fundamental concepts above: that risk encapsulates both uncertain outcomes and capital exposed to these uncertain outcomes; and that risk tolerance is a key determinant of who can take on particular kinds of investments.

Risk can be managed in several main ways: by reducing one's stake in any one investment, by taking on a diverse portfolio of projects to reduce the variance of overall return on investment, and by using knowledge and experience to improve measurement of uncertainty, arriving at better determinations of the probabilities of different outcomes. This last idea merits further unpacking. In his seminal work *Risk, Uncertainty, and Profit*, Frank Knight (1921) divides probability estimates into those "where the distribution of the outcome in a group of instances is known (either through calculation *a priori* or from statistics of past experience)" and those "where this is not true, the reason being in general that it is impossible to form a group of instances, because the situation is in a high degree unique"[1] (Knight 1921, p. 233). As Knight concedes, real-world probability determinations always lie somewhere on a continuum between these idealized extremes of, on the one hand, a fully characterized distribution of possible outcomes derived from perfect analogues to the present situation (what Knight calls "homogeneous classes") and, on the other, a completely unknowable distribution associated with the absence of any analogues whatsoever that can provide guidance.[2] A key part of skillful risk management is developing the most accurate possible estimates of probability even for relatively unique and unprecedented cases. Models of the workings of physical phenomena – derived from accumulated experience and informed by targeted data collection for the case at hand – can be important tools for refining probability estimates even in the absence of proximate analogues.

2.2 *Petroleum state motives and choices*

In the stylized decision tree of Figure 4.1, we concede as a starting point that political considerations around resource control set the basic context that is then modulated by factors related to risk. As mentioned previously, the desire for national control over oil resources and their revenues is a complex issue that is addressed in detail elsewhere in this book, including in the introductory and concluding chapters, in Chapter 2, on drivers of expropriation and privatization behavior, and in all of the individual NOC case studies. For the purposes of this chapter, we make the following two principal observations about state choices and state motives.

First, there is significant variation in how governments choose to involve themselves in their respective oil sectors. Many petroleum states never seek to control their petroleum industry through a state company. Others have periods of state intervention through NOC but at some point revert to control through regulation of private companies (e.g., the UK). In contrast, other petroleum states seek to nationalize their petroleum industry as soon as they can achieve it and still others are "serial nationalizers," inviting private companies to invest in exploration and field development, then expropriating developed resources, and, at a later date, repeating the cycle.

Second, governments that depend heavily on petroleum revenues typically express a strong desire for direct control over their respective petroleum sectors. These states are prone to seek mastery over all the key variables that affect their petroleum revenues: the pace of investment, the rate of resource development, the government share of revenues, and of course the price of oil. This mastery has often been pursued through the selection of a state operating company. However, control of the factors that determine state revenue from petroleum does not demand a state company. Licensing and contracts with private firms offer a means to control the pace of investment and rate of development of resources. And, as Adelman (1995) points out, setting a price floor through an excise tax supported by a collective production limit by a producer cartel could influence oil price without the need for a state operating company.

Whatever the real, or perceived, value of direct control through a state operating company, the motive for control among the majority of the larger oil producer-states appears paramount. This motive is, however, constrained by the inherent risks of exercising direct control, as will be discussed in section 2.3. The capacity of a state to absorb hydrocarbon risk – its risk tolerance – is essentially a question of how affected the government and the economy would be by a shortfall in oil revenues relative to expectations or potential. For example, Angola's MPLA government from 1976 through 2002 critically depended on oil revenues to prosecute a civil war; the government had very little ability to accept risk that these revenues would fall short of potential (see Chapter 19). Countries like Kuwait (see Chapter 8) with small populations and substantial budgetary surpluses, on the other hand, are relatively more able to tolerate the risk of underperformance.

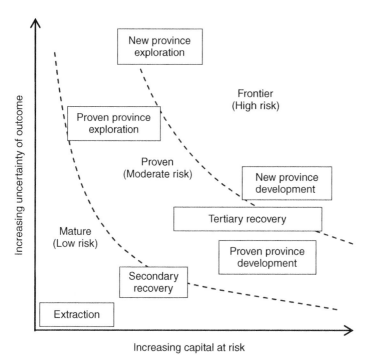

Figure 4.2 Relative risk of petroleum investments (illustrative).

2.3 The nature of petroleum risks

Uncertainty and risk are everywhere in the petroleum industry. In line with the discussion in section 2.1, petroleum investment risks vary in magnitude as a function of both uncertainty and capital invested (Figure 4.2). Exploration risks tend to be high because of their geological uncertainty despite modest capital exposure. In contrast, field development risk is high because despite reduced uncertainty – oil has been discovered – field development requires significantly greater capital. The magnitude of risk is also a function of the maturity of the exploration and production program, with uncertainty decreasing as knowledge and experience are acquired over time and as unproven (frontier) petroleum provinces are proven commercially and eventually become mature.

Relevant uncertainties are not only geological but also related to future market conditions. At the time of competition for hydrocarbon licenses, when future values are being estimated, investors must also make judgments about future costs and future prices for oil and gas produced. For the vast majority of oil today there is little or no risk associated with connecting oil with a consumer, as most oil can be sold at the wellhead into a global spot market. However, when this is not the case, investment in field development carries the additional commercial risk that demand may not materialize or that necessary infrastructure to connect supply to demand will not be available. We call this risk that hydrocarbons will not be able to find or access customers "market availability risk." Even today, despite the existence of spot markets for liquefied natural gas (LNG), gas developments can still face appreciable market availability risk, particularly because they require expensive infrastructure and risky investments throughout the value chain. This risk can be especially pronounced in cross-border projects. A converse market risk, "supply risk," refers to the uncertainty that a downstream investment, for example in a refinery, will receive a sufficient input stream of hydrocarbons to run at capacity over a long period of time as needed to recover costs.

Frontier petroleum activities by definition are those characterized by the highest risk. These can be conceptual oil and gas "plays" yet to be discovered and proved commercial – in other words, cases where only very imperfect analogues are available. The frontier can also include hydrocarbons known to exist but which remain undeveloped because of the significant risk involved in bringing these resources to market (e.g., shale oil and stranded gas). Over many decades, the industry has seen the frontier progress from exploration and development of onshore sedimentary basins through shallow offshore basins and into deep and ultra-deep water basins today. Recent frontiers have included the challenge of deep water as well as that of hydrocarbon activities in the former Soviet Union as it tentatively opened to private investment. Emerging frontiers include the challenge of commercializing vast resources of unconventional oils and gas, known to exist yet plagued by environmental and technical uncertainties and high capital requirements. Another emerging frontier is presented by the world's large but aging oil fields, which require major new investments for their redevelopment through tertiary recovery. The high-risk frontier always exists, but the nature of its challenges changes over time.

As illustrated in Figure 4.3, risks change in a characteristic way over the lifetime of a petroleum province. Frontier exploration is characterized by extreme uncertainty. The key ingredients of success are poorly known (Box 4.1); probability estimates are likely to have significant

---

Box 4.1 Frontier exploration uncertainties

A geological province is a large area, often of several thousand square kilometres, with a common geological history. It becomes a petroleum province when a working petroleum system is discovered. A commercial petroleum system (or "play") has several major components: a source rock that has a rich carbon content and that has spent sufficient time at temperatures required to convert its organic carbon to petroleum; a sedimentary reservoir rock with sufficient pore space to hold significant volumes of petroleum and sufficient permeability to allow petroleum to flow to a well bore; a non-porous sedimentary rock that can be an effective barrier to petroleum migration; a structural trapping mechanism that can combine a reservoir rock and associated barrier/seal rock in a trap to capture and retain petroleum; and fortuitous geological timing such that that trap formation preceded the migration of petroleum. Combinations of these variables that result in the trapping of significant petroleum are rare. This is well illustrated by the USGS World Petroleum Assessment (USGS 2000) which identified 937 geological provinces across the globe. Petroleum has been found in just 406 of these provinces. According to the report, approximately 78 percent of the petroleum outside the US was found in just twenty geological provinces, with about 50 percent in just five.

---

error. Each exploration well carries not only the uncertainty associated with the specific prospect being drilled but also the uncertainty of the regional petroleum system. A high probability of failure means that many wells might be drilled before success is achieved or the attempt abandoned, and frontier wells can be expensive (a single deep water well today can cost more than $100 million).

The discovery of a petroleum field begins a process of appraisal and development. Appraisal of a discovery involves drilling many new wells to confirm the extent and properties of the reservoirs and fluids and also to determine whether the range of possible outcomes can be attractive enough to warrant the much larger investment needed to develop the field. The development of the initial fields in a new

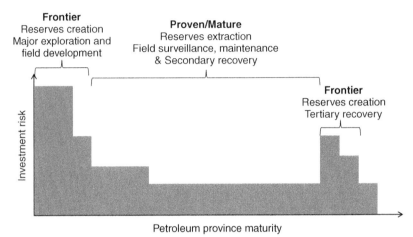

Figure 4.3 Investment risk as a function of petroleum province maturity (illustrative).

province is replete with technical uncertainties that will affect the ultimate volume of oil that can be recovered and commercial uncertainties that will affect the value of recovered oil (Box 4.2).

With the development of one or more commercial fields a frontier becomes "proven." Subsequent investments in proven provinces benefit from the data and knowledge acquired during the frontier exploration and development phase. Uncertainty about the presence of hydrocarbons and their character is much reduced, and accurate probability estimates are more easily arrived at due to the existence of analogues from the same geological system that can inform subsequent exploration or development activities. The associated reduction in risk often prompts an influx of new entrant companies that were deterred when risks to entry were high but are more able to invest in a lower risk environment. These new entrants can include both state companies and smaller, "independent" private companies.

Finally, as a proven petroleum province is further developed, knowledge continues to grow and uncertainty associated with these hydrocarbon activities is reduced still further. Risks shrink accordingly, and a proven province becomes "mature."

After substantial oil or gas has been extracted from mature fields, they can benefit from investment in redevelopment. Two phases of redevelopment carry very different risks. The first, "secondary

Box 4.2 Frontier development uncertainties

Field development at the frontier faces significant technical uncertainties. These include the properties of reservoir rock, the fluids it contains, and the fluid dynamics within the rock. The reservoir rock's porosity, its permeability, its homogeneity, its structure at field and pore scale all contribute to uncertainty of both ultimate recovery and production rates. The reservoir at one location might be vertically or horizontally connected to the fluids in the reservoir at another location. A reservoir might be a single layer of sandstone at one location but made up of many more or less connected layers at another location. Faults at a large or microscopic scale might significantly affect the fluid dynamics of the reservoir. Fractures and pore space might be mineralized, restricting flow to a greater or lesser extent or not at all.

Fluids in a reservoir might be oil or gas or a complex mixture of both. The oil will vary in its API (specific gravity) and also its viscosity. Both oils and gases may contain many impurities (nitrogen, carbon dioxide, and hydrogen sulfide are common). The pressure and temperature of the reservoir fluids will depend on the depth of the reservoir, and this can affect mobility of hydrocarbons. Temperature and pressure change as fluids are produced to the surface, which can cause the complex mixture of petroleum to separate into liquids and gases, often resulting in there being significantly less fluid at the surface than in the reservoir. Oil may have a gas "cap" above it in the reservoir, which may provide valuable energy for pushing oil to the surface. An aquifer at the base of the reservoir might also serve as a key source of energy (pressure) to move oil to the surface. Uncertainties around each of these field variables translate into uncertainty in ultimate recovery volumes; peak production from the field; the life of the field; well flow rates; the density of wells required; required capacities of production, storage, and export systems; and when secondary and perhaps tertiary recovery might ultimately be appropriate. Adding in the uncertainty of future costs and future prices of oil or gas, the distribution of possible financial outcomes can be quite large.

recovery," involves drilling additional producing wells and injecting water or gas to maintain reservoir pressures if pressures have been depleted as oil is extracted. Secondary recovery carries only moderate investment risk: new well positioning is informed by the extensive reservoir and fluid information gathered during the field's production history, and the supply of water (or sometimes gas) for injection is often low cost. Investment in "tertiary recovery," on the other hand, is potentially higher risk. Increased recovery is achieved by injecting a stimulant to oil mobility in the form of chemicals or heat into the reservoir. Tertiary recovery, like other frontier activities, requires the investment of significant amounts of capital and, in contrast to secondary recovery, often has much more uncertain outcomes. Increased knowledge from path-breaking tertiary recovery projects will help reduce uncertainty and risk associated with similar projects in the future.

Figure 4.3 emphasizes the extent to which risk in the petroleum industry is associated with the "creation of the reserves" – the relatively short time period required to find and develop and where necessary create a market for produced products. By contrast, the capital requirements and risks associated with the extraction of the field's petroleum are quite low and the time required can span many decades. This dramatic shift in risk once major exploration and development have been completed can alter the bargaining positions of the petroleum state and any private operating company it employs in these initial phases. No longer needing the risk management abilities of private operators, governments may review their options and seek to increase their share of revenues and degree of control over hydrocarbon resources. As Vernon (1971) put it in his study of petroleum nationalization, the original bargain has become obsolete. (The threat in such cases of contract renegotiation or in extreme cases outright expropriation represents a formidable risk for private oil companies; however, this type of "political risk" falls outside of the scope of this chapter because our analysis focuses on the risks faced by a petroleum state and how they shape its choice of petroleum agents, rather than on the risks faced by private investors.)

While hydrocarbon activities retain a frontier character, incentives to reduce uncertainty and costs are enormous because such actions translate directly into value. By contrast, there is much less leverage on value through efforts to reduce costs in mature operations where costs are low relative to oil price. It is therefore unsurprising that petroleum states with developed resources, which are characterized by low production costs, seek to maximize their revenue by raising oil price rather than reducing cost, as even Herculean efforts to improve project performance will have comparatively minor impact.

Together, these observations about the sources of risk and their change with time suggest the following two expectations. First, agents that are able to most effectively manage risk – typically private companies, as we will discuss in section 2.5 – will provide more value to resource-holding governments in frontier activities than in mature operations, as the frontier is where costs are more significant relative to oil price. Even at the frontier, governments can choose to employ an agent that might be less able to manage risks, like NOC, but only at a potential cost to future revenues. Second, decreases in oil price put a premium on risk minimization in a wider range of hydrocarbon activities, effectively expanding the range of activities that are at the "frontier"; oil prices increases have the opposite effect. One might therefore expect to see oil-price-dependent cycles in the degree to which governments employ the private companies who are best able to manage risk. In sections 2.4 and 2.5 below, we further explore the ways in which oil companies can minimize risk as well as how capable the different types of companies – IOCs, NOCs, and OSCs – are of performing this function.

2.4 The task of risk management in petroleum

Managing risk for a petroleum investor, be it a state or a private company, is about not only maximizing the expected value of net revenue across all investments but also containing its variance – in particular, one's exposure to losses. Accomplishing this can be achieved by: 1) choosing projects with lower uncertainty; 2) investing in a portfolio of projects so that uncertainties (if well estimated) will average out; 3) measuring uncertainty better both to identify projects with lower uncertainty and to provide confidence that revenue from a portfolio of projects will converge to the expected value; and 4) reducing the capital exposed to projects with high uncertainty.

Measuring uncertainty as accurately as possible, and progressively refining one's estimates, is a central function of a petroleum operating company and one source of its competitive advantage. Where the distribution of possible outcomes is well understood due to the availability of plentiful data from close geological analogues – the type of situation referred to by Knight (1921) as "statistical probability" – the measurement of uncertainty is straightforward and a variety of players can function adequately. Where a petroleum operating company truly distinguishes itself, by contrast, is in developing the best possible probability estimates when close analogues are not available. As described in Boxes 4.3 and 4.4, quantifying uncertainty in such cases requires investment in information (most often seismic and well data) and skills in predictive modeling derived from study of geological processes around the world and over many years. Predictive modeling integrates sampled data – informed by global analogues and a deep understanding of the geological processes at work – to predict a probabilistic distribution of hydrocarbons in place at all scales from a petroleum province to a specific field. This process of predictive statistical modeling has become the essence of both province-scale petroleum exploration (Lerche 1997) and reservoir development.

The uncertainty estimates produced by statistical models allow determination of the expected monetary value (EMV) of each investment (Rose 2001) and ranking of investments by attractiveness. Assembling a portfolio of investments allows further reduction of risk through diversification. To the extent that model predictions match the distributions of outcomes that are actually observed in these investments, the net revenue from the portfolio will converge to the overall expected value even though individual investments have highly uncertain returns.[3] However, if major gaps in geological understanding lead to systematic errors in these models that are reflected in investment choices, diversification will not guarantee the expected overall return. The portfolio approach thus offers more risk management value to petroleum operators with superior knowledge, providing yet another motivation for companies to continually work at refining their geological understanding.

Mechanisms to directly reduce capital investment exposed to loss are also important. One strategy is to take a less than 100 percent working interest in a project, sharing risk among partners. States have sometimes reduced capital exposed to uncertain exploration outcomes by mandating that they receive a carried interest in exploration ventures (see, for example, the case of Norway as described in Chapter 14).

Box 4.3 Managing exploration risk

Exploring for a new petroleum province, or a new "play" within this province, is essentially the process of predicting the presence, characteristics, and location of the key elements needed to form a petroleum province. Success in exploration depends on both geological observations (the data samples) and the ability to construct geological models that incorporate all observations and make useful and accurate predictions about both what might be found and the probability of finding it.

This process of observation, modeling, and prediction of what cannot be observed directly has always been at the center of the exploration business. Well and seismic data are two of the more important inputs that inform exploration. Cuttings from the drilling of wells provide rock samples that offer information on the sedimentary formations penetrated and can provide micro-fossils useful for correlation between wells and even across sedimentary basins. The use of remote tools in wells that can measure the electrical resistivity of fluids in penetrated formations and measure the natural radioactivity of the rocks in the well can provide clues to rock types and the fluids they contain. Cores of rock from wells can provide the opportunity for direct rock measurements. Recording and processing of reflected seismic (sound) waves enables the creation of maps of seismically reflective surfaces which in turn can provide clues as to the depositional environment of the sediments, rock types, and geological structure at depth. Stratigraphic data on rocks and their relationship with each other that is obtained from even a limited number of wells can be combined with seismic information to make extrapolations to a much larger area under the ground.

Geological models can be constructed that predict favorable combinations of source, reservoir, and sealing rocks in the subsurface and that consider the timing of trap formation relative to the timing of petroleum generation and migration.

Under such an arrangement, states are not required to front any of the capital for exploration activities but are given the option to take a share in an oil and gas field after the presence of commercial reserves has been established.

Box 4.4 Managing development risk

Managing field development risk is once again about sampling and prediction, this time at a reservoir rather than province scale and in the context of a specific development scheme. The objective at this stage is to quantify and reduce uncertainties about the ultimate volume of recoverable petroleum and the rate of flow from the field over time. Physical sampling technologies include the drilling of appraisal wells to confirm the presence of petroleum at several reservoir locations, the sampling of both rock and fluid properties at each of these locations, and the testing of wells to determine the flow of oil or gas from the reservoir given local reservoir conditions. Seismic data, collected and processed to provide a very high resolution three-dimensional image of the subsurface, is calibrated to well data. In parallel with data collection a detailed predictive model of the reservoir is gradually built and refined as new information becomes available to include the entire range of variables that might have any material effect on the volume of recoverable petroleum or its rate of production. It is a model with many dimensions and where the majority of variables, despite the high density of well and seismic data, still carry considerable uncertainty. Analogous reservoir/fluid combinations from development projects around the world will once again aid and constrain the predictive modeling of the data. The remaining uncertainty that cannot be eliminated manifests itself in the form of changes to estimates of recoverable reserves over the productive life of a field. Increasing computer capacity has enabled ever more sophisticated simulations of the range of possible behaviors of the modeled fluids within their reservoirs. These models can be applied to a variety of possible development well configurations to investigate individual well productivity and longevity as petroleum migrates through the reservoir pore space into hypothetical well bores cut either vertically or horizontally through the reservoir. A development plan will be constructed based on a statistical reservoir model that predicts a range of ultimate recoverable reserves and a range of potential production rates. Wells will be designed and sited to recover the petroleum in the most economically efficient manner given proper regard for safety and environmental considerations.

If uncertainties remain high because of irreducible complexity in the reservoir, then these uncertainties will be reflected in the options built into the development plan, for example the provision for expensive extra space on an offshore production platform that might or might not be required.

Another way to reduce the capital exposed to loss is through engineering innovation that drives cost reduction. Petroleum states focused on reducing risk create incentives for innovation and cost reduction on the part of their petroleum agents. Such incentives can be created by competitive bidding, benchmarking of performance, progress bonuses, variable royalty structures, and other means. Mechanisms through which a producer state (the principal) can manage its agents are explored in more detail in Chapter 3.

2.5 Company type and capacity to manage risk

We have discussed the nature of the risks associated with creating and extracting petroleum reserves and considered approaches for managing them that can be employed by companies and governments. In this section we consider how the distinctive characteristics of state and private companies with respect to risk management offer governments a choice.

Governments can employ three broad categories of company: privately owned IOCs, state-owned (or state-controlled) NOCs, and the various OSCs that provide technical services. While we are centrally interested in the choice between IOCs and NOCs as operating companies, we will also consider the OSCs to highlight both their key role as technology providers and their inability to absorb risk for a petroleum state.

An important point to make at the outset of this discussion is that any company is theoretically capable of pursuing any risk management strategy. Just like an IOC, an NOC would be free in principle to manage risk for its government by building a global portfolio of investments around the world or by hiring or developing experts with outstanding capability to quantify geological uncertainty. Indeed, as we will discuss later, a few atypical NOCs do just this.

However, our point in this section is that the fact of being controlled by a state rather than driven principally by profits characteristically causes an NOC *not* to develop risk management skills on par with IOCs. In the case of OSCs, the salient point is that these specialized companies occupy a particular, profitable market niche that involves providing technology rather than managing hydrocarbon risk.

2.5.1 The international oil companies

Unlike NOCs, which can have a range of motivations and responsibilities depending on state goals, IOCs are focused exclusively on profit maximization. The IOC's particular talent for managing risk stems from this basic orientation. To maximize profits, an IOC must succeed in competition with other oil operators across the globe. A private firm has to compete for the opportunity to invest, compete to attract and retain intellectual capital, and compete for risk capital. To win an opportunity to invest in exploration or development a company must essentially promise value to the petroleum state that exceeds that offered by its competitors. These promises are reflected in bids that are made more attractive to the state through various mechanisms, such as non-refundable cash payments or the commitment to a larger minimum work program, which if successful promises economic growth and other benefits to the state.[4] To create a more attractive bid without sacrificing profitability, a company must be able to predict more value than any other bidder and ultimately to be capable of delivering this value. A company must effectively "see" value that its competitors cannot, such as more in-place petroleum, greater recovery potential, or even the potential of future technologies to reduce costs. A company must get its predictions right more often than it gets them wrong to achieve the long-term performance that enables the private firm to attract risk capital and skills and, critically, to underwrite its promise of higher value to the state.

The skills that a private operating company must develop to survive in the marketplace thus naturally make it ideally capable of managing risk for a resource-rich government. First, an IOC is driven by commercial incentives to refine its ability to predict uncertain outcomes through application of the geosciences. Second, the company can increase its profits by innovating engineering solutions that reduce capital placed at risk. Third, because it is inherently driven to seek out the best opportunities all over the world, a large IOC tends to develop a global portfolio of ventures. As long as project outcomes are uncorrelated and the company's uncertainty characterizations are good, this portfolio approach dramatically reduces the variance in the expected overall profitability for the IOC, allowing it to tolerate below-average financial outcomes, or even a total loss, in a particular project. By shouldering all of the investment risk on such projects, IOCs can transform even frontier projects from ventures that hold enormous risk for host governments into ones that are nearly risk-free for the state.

IOCs have traditionally offered another crucial risk management function to resource-rich governments: the ability to mitigate market availability risk by creating a bridge to sources of demand for products that cannot be internationally traded. Investing upstream without a market commitment or investing in the creation of a market without assured supply would carry enormous risk. The development of stranded gas and its liquefaction for shipment to dedicated international markets is one example. A private company's willingness to invest private capital in development of oil or gas provides assurance to the resource-holding government that the market is "safe" and to the market that supply can be relied upon.

There is no reason in principle why NOCs could not also attract private capital to projects that require cultivating a demand market, and indeed, a small number do. However, there are several reasons why IOCs are typically better positioned to do this. First, the market-driven track record of IOCs in maximizing returns helps more easily convince private capital that IOCs can deliver in developing profitable markets for stranded oil or gas. Second, connecting supply to demand around the globe requires a truly international focus that is almost inevitably precluded to a greater or lesser degree by home country political constraints faced by NOCs. Even Norway's Statoil, among the most international and market-driven of NOCs, faces domestic pressures that can distract from its international activities (see Chapter 14).

2.5.2 The national oil companies

The characteristic feature of an NOC is its need to respond to government goals aside from pure profit maximization. The exact shape and function of an NOC can thus vary widely depending on how the government wants to control and benefit from the oil sector. Some IOCs serve regulatory functions in the oil sector (see, for example, the case of Sonangol in Chapter 19), some become broader development agencies (as in the case of PDVSA), and some play the role of administrative vehicles for state participation in oil (NNPC has this character to a large extent). Many NOCs have operational activities of some kind, but very few are pure hydrocarbon operators. As tools of government, NOCs invariably have a soft budget constraint to some extent – they are never exposed to the risk of takeover or bankruptcy that would threaten a private enterprise that makes unsuccessful investments. On the other hand, NOCs are exposed to political pressures to a greater degree than their privately owned brethren. These basic conditions under which NOCs operate have fundamental implications for their ability to manage risk as hydrocarbon operators.

First, the close linkages between an NOC and its government can impede the NOC's ability to raise risk capital or execute other transactions to manage risk, although such obstacles can sometimes be overcome. Full state ownership precludes equity swaps that might allow an NOC to manage risk by diversifying its assets abroad, but partial privatization can be perceived by governments as weakening their control over the oil sector. Companies funded entirely from government budgetary allocations can face legal constraints on their ability to raise debt on international markets – Pemex was in this situation until the Pidiregas scheme was developed to allow it to raise risk capital against the strength of Mexico's sovereign debt rating (see Chapter 7). Most NOCs remain dependent on their own cash flow or government balance sheets to finance their exploration and development projects. This means that an NOC is putting state rather than private capital at risk; thus risks that the NOC incurs are, in effect, risks to the state.

Second, the relative absence of competitive pressures on the NOC reduces its incentives to develop the strong risk management capabilities that would be essential to survival in a more competitive environment. NOCs generally have a soft budget constraint and are granted special advantages in their home territory, commonly including a preferential position in the upstream or a monopoly over product sales at home. Lacking strong commercial incentives to do so, NOCs can therefore lag both in development of capability to make accurate geological predictions and in innovation (technological or organizational) that would reduce cost and thus capital at risk. In some cases, the lack of competitive pressures can actively *encourage* NOCs to take technology risks that IOCs might avoid as imprudent. For example, its monopoly position at home and soft budget constraint probably encouraged Petrobras to be more aggressive at investing in technology-intensive offshore exploration and development than it would have been if the state were not implicitly underwriting these efforts (see Chapter 12). Risk *taking* does not imply risk management on behalf of the state.

Third, both political pressures and their privileged domestic position tend to encourage NOCs to stay at home rather than diversifying abroad to reduce overall risk. Petrobras's initial partnerships with IOCs and efforts overseas were not politically popular in Brazil (see Chapter 12). Norway's political leadership would probably not have been amenable to an overseas role for Statoil before the 1990s, and the NOC must still weather periodic criticism at home for its activities abroad (see Chapter 14). A more significant factor in most cases, though, is the simple fact that, as long as plentiful domestic resources remain available, an NOC has every incentive to operate on its home turf where it is not exposed to full competition. This is the main reason why only a minority of NOCs have developed any substantial international portfolio (see Figure 20.6 for a picture of the extent to which NOCs in our sample have internationalized). Those that have internationalized in the face of declining domestic resources – such as ONGC, CNPC, and Petronas – are employed by host governments that in any case no longer have as pivotal a need for managing the risks associated with extraction of domestic hydrocarbons.

As discussed above and elsewhere in this volume, governments have many goals beyond managing their exposure to petroleum development risks, and it is the real or perceived ability of NOCs to serve these goals that explains their existence despite characteristically weak risk management capabilities. An NOC in theory offers the state more direct control over resources, including the ability to pursue a depletion policy (rate of production target) that would be in conflict with maximizing return on investment. An NOC can be used to furnish a wide array of public or private goods, such as employment, financial benefits for elites, fuel subsidies, or development services. Host governments might encourage their NOCs to operate overseas if that yields projects and supplies that are thought to improve the country's energy security.

At the same time, recognizing the weaknesses of their NOCs at risk management and the sparse inherent incentives for improvement, states do pursue various strategies to try to squeeze more performance out of their state oil companies. These strategies, which are treated in detail in Chapter 3, can include the introduction of some competition in the home market to benchmark performance.

2.5.3 The oil service companies

A closer examination of what a third entity, the oil service company (OSC), does can help clarify the frequently misunderstood distinction between technology and risk management functions in the petroleum industry. OSCs design and provide the physical equipment that IOCs and NOCs alike use to explore, develop, and produce oil and gas. They are essential vendors, but their roles are focused and limited. The role of the oil company, whether state or private, is to know where to explore and what to develop; the role of the OSC is to provide the technologies that will be used to explore and develop. An oil company might, for example, predict the location of a potential reservoir, but it is the drilling equipment provided by the OSCs that physically tests the prediction. Unlike operating companies, OSCs do not make predictions or promises about the outcome of an exploration or production venture and do not invest shareholders' capital in highly uncertain outcomes. The OSCs supply technology but do not assume risk on behalf of a hydrocarbon state.

While the major oil companies formerly developed and owned significant oil exploration and development equipment, today most such technology functions are outsourced because oil companies gain little competitive advantage from keeping them in-house. IOCs compete by convincing oil-rich states of their ability to manage risk, whereas OSCs compete by convincing IOCs and NOCs that they offer better tools to enable the oil industry to take on the next frontier challenge – to go farther and to do it at a lower cost.

As long as resource-rich countries remained dependent on IOCs for both risk management *and* technology services, they had little prospect of developing state-controlled operating companies. OSCs have played a key role in enabling the development of NOCs by making state-of-the-art technology available to any prospective operating company, even though IOCs retain their advantage in managing risks at the frontier.

2.6 Risk and the state's choice of agent

Returning to the basic thesis expressed in Figure 4.1, we expect that the differences discussed above in the characteristic abilities of different hydrocarbon companies to manage risk will constrain a rational state's choice of agent. In Figure 4.4, we represent this idea as a set of outcomes according to risk and the state's capacity for risk, considering only the case of states that have a strong motivation for direct control over hydrocarbons.

For high-risk ("frontier") ventures in countries with low risk tolerance, the expected agent in petroleum is a private operating company (IOC), as shown in the lower right quadrant of Figure 4.4. In the most risky frontier activities like exploration, IOCs will most likely bear all of the risk for the state. Once the basic commerciality of a frontier play has been established, states might choose to participate on an equity basis in its development, with the IOC's willingness to risk private capital providing an important signal to the state that development risks are acceptable and the investment is a good one.

For high-risk ventures in a state that that can tolerate risk (upper right quadrant of Figure 4.4), for example because state revenues are diversified or the government already has a substantial budget surplus, the outcome is often a sector where NOCs dominate as operators and the state takes all of the investment risk. China and several of the large Middle East producer states fall into this category.

Once reserves are created, markets are available, and risks are low, then NOCs can thrive as operators (left half of Figure 4.4). This situation is characteristic of mature provinces where extraction and maintenance activities dominate. Even so, there may remain cases with significant IOC involvement – for example where institutional weakness and a dearth of technical capability in a country preclude development even of a rudimentary operational NOC that can competently contract technology functions to OSCs. The result might be an NOC that has no operational role but instead seeks technical service agreements with private companies.

As discussed in section 2.3, oil price can play an important role in shifting the boundary between high-risk and low-risk ventures for

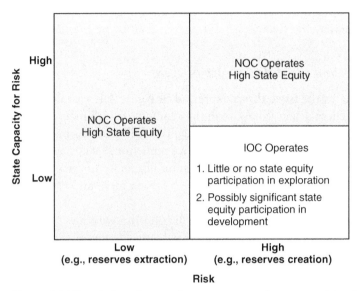

Figure 4.4 The choice of operating company and state participation when the state desires direct control.

resource-rich states. When oil prices rise, minimization of uncertainty and cost becomes a less important part of assuring the desired revenue collection, and resource-rich governments also tend to be more flush with cash that they can pour back into oil (and non-oil) activities. Under these circumstances, a government's desire for direct control of hydrocarbons is less constrained by considerations of risk and an NOC is more likely to be the agent of choice. When oil prices drop, on the other hand, governments wishing to maximize revenues will be more likely to need the risk-minimizing talents of IOCs, which in general can offer lower costs and improved odds of success in resource development. As discussed further in Chapter 20, such a dynamic could in theory lead to a kind of "backward-bending supply curve" for oil, in which higher oil prices actually decrease the rate at which hydrocarbons are found and extracted worldwide.

3 Testing the idea that risk constrains state choice of oil company

This section of the chapter uses three complementary approaches to test the proposition that risk is a significant constraint on state choice of agent in oil. First, we take a high-level look at the most important structural change the industry has seen – the widespread nationalizations of the early 1970s – to see if changes in risk over time had an important influence on events. Second, we examine the effect of risk on state choices of operating company for the particular case of the North Sea, where within one province the behavior of two different countries can be compared. Third, we use exploration well data from Wood Mackenzie to statistically test whether specific frontiers are preferentially explored by private companies as would be expected according to our hypothesis. In particular, we consider exploration in deep water and in zones that have not had a previous discovery. We also use the same data to test for the expected effect of price – that higher prices result in more use of NOCs and lower prices in more use of private companies.

In none of these cases do we expect to find a deterministic effect of risk on outcomes; as we have discussed before, there are simply too many different factors that can affect the state's choice of agent. However, we do expect to see risk emerge as an observable constraint on state choices in hydrocarbons.

3.1 The nationalizations of the early 1970s

In the early 1970s several countries, including all the major producing countries in the developing world, chose to fully or partly nationalize their oil industries and replace private oil companies with national operating companies. Unlike earlier and more isolated nationalizations of private company oil positions – notably in Bolivia in 1937 and Mexico in 1938 – which had only a modest impact on the industry as a whole, the events of the early 1970s marked a transformation of the structure of the international oil industry. To examine how the constraint of risk influenced these events, we need to look at several factors: the risk characteristics of the emerging international oil industry as World War II drew to a close; the players in the industry and the tools they used to manage these risks; the consequences for the petroleum producer states; and the actions these states took to seize control. Our analysis draws upon the excellent documentation and interpretation of these events by Jacoby (1974), Kobrin (1984b), Yergin (1991), Adelman (1995), and Parra (2004).

As oil began to emerge as a key fuel, the United States, Russia, and China were able to transition from indigenous coal to indigenous oil. However, the major industrial countries of Europe and the Far East were faced with the need to import virtually all of their oil. At the same time, virtually no indigenous markets were available to absorb the oil that was being discovered in the Middle East and elsewhere. This mismatch created a pressing need to connect emerging oil provinces with markets abroad. Risks were high not only in oil exploration and development but also in bringing this oil to new consumers. At this stage, no one knew what hydrocarbons might be found, where they would be found, or what it would take to build the infrastructure to transport oil produced in the Middle East, Venezuela, Indonesia, or other oil provinces to markets in Europe or Japan. Market risks ran in both directions: upstream development was extremely risky without a stable long-term market, and market development was risky in the absence of assured supply.

For all the appeal of potential oil revenue, oil-rich countries had low capacity to accept the massive geological and market availability risks in the nascent oil industry. They did not in general have the financial capacity to put the requisite capital at risk themselves, nor did they possess sufficient domestic technical capacity to form a state-owned agent that could manage geological risk. (The few countries that eventually developed NOCs with some risk management talents, notably Norway and Brazil, focused early in their petroleum eras on building indigenous technical capability in oil.) As a result, all of these new producer states chose to employ private companies to take on the risks of exploration, initial development, and, critically, the creation of markets for their petroleum. Only a few major international corporations had the know-how and financial risk tolerance required for such an undertaking: American companies Chevron, Exxon, Gulf, Mobil, and Texaco; Britain's BP; Anglo-Dutch company Shell; and France's CFP. These companies faced the challenge of finding and developing sufficient petroleum in the Middle East, and later Africa, to support and underwrite vast investments aimed at meeting the rapid growth in demand for petroleum products from Europe and the Far East. Refineries, petrochemical plants, distribution systems, and retail outlets as well as ports, infrastructure, and tanker fleets had to be financed.

The major IOCs evolved several strategies for managing the considerable risks of investment in this cross-border oil business: concessions, upstream joint ventures, and vertical integration from supply to consumers. Very large and very long-term concession agreements with producer states, which were to persist until the early 1970s, reduced risk by aggregating geological opportunities and allowing cost recovery over a long period. Joint ventures between oil companies helped spread the political risks of having concessions in a few politically unstable countries. Vertical integration helped keep upstream and downstream investments in harmony, infrastructure at capacity, and consumers content and growing in number. The massive downstream investments required to build refineries and oil transport infrastructure, which were significantly more capital-intensive even than upstream exploration and development, made vertical integration particularly important at this stage of industry development. Without being able to ensure oil supply sufficient to run downstream infrastructure at full capacity, the oil companies would not have been confident in their ability to achieve an adequate return on their downstream investments. Although the major companies were not a cartel in any formal sense, vertical integration and shared upstream JV positions ensured that they shared knowledge and in effect made upstream decisions with a common interest, further reducing their risk. None of these risk management tools were available to the producer states at this phase of oil industry development.

The risk management strategies of the private oil majors were successful: the necessary investments were made in developing oil supply and delivering it to consumers, and the international oil business grew at an unprecedented rate. However, the producer states perceived this to be somewhat at their expense. Private companies were making all the decisions about investment in exploration, whether and when to develop a discovery, and what production levels to take from each field. The producer states were left with no strategic control over critical factors – including the rate of investment and rate of production – that affected the revenues upon which they increasingly depended. They could increase taxes but only on what was produced. These states therefore had a strong motive to wrest control of the decisions affecting oil revenues from the private companies. However, they were constained in their ability to do this by their limited capacity to accept risk or to apply the risk management strategies being used by the private oil companies.

The risks of oil operations began to decline as the industry developed. By the late 1950s the big fields had been found and developed in the key Middle Eastern countries (Iran, Iraq, Kuwait, and Saudi Arabia), significantly reducing upstream risk. Transport and refining infrastructure was in place, and the market for petroleum products was growing rapidly. However, the major oil companies still controlled access to customers, creating a residual market availability risk that still precluded effective nationalization by producer states. The inability of Iran, despite formal nationalization of its oil sector in 1951, to gain de facto control over its hydrocarbons illustrated how this market availability risk still gave the major oil companies the upper hand in their negotiations with oil states.

It was the entry of new companies into the international oil business that ultimately helped provide competitive access to oil markets, reducing market availability risks sufficiently for nationalization of a country's oil sector to be feasible. The rapid growth and profit potential of the international oil industry proved a strong attraction to new entrants, especially once exploration and development risks had fallen and solid demand for oil had been established. More than 300 private companies and 50 state-controlled companies entered or significantly expanded their activities in the international oil business between 1953 and 1972 (Jacoby 1974). These included American "oil independents" in search of lower-cost oil supplies for their downstream positions in the United States as well as companies owned by oil-consuming states that wanted security of supply (Parra 2004). The new entrants pursued oil exploration and development in the already-established provinces of the Middle East and also in new areas in Africa, helping supply stay ahead of demand even in a rapidly growing market. Import controls imposed by the United States after 1957 meant that the US-based independents had to find alternative markets in Europe and the Far East for their crude. As a result, they contributed substantially to the rapid growth of refining capacity in industrial countries of Europe and the Far East and began to create an open market for the trading of crude oil. With infrastructure in place, increasingly open markets, and a multiplicity of both suppliers and consumers – what Jacoby (1974) called an "effective market" for oil – upstream investments carried reduced market availability risk and downstream investments carried reduced supply risk. In theory, the risk management role of the major oil companies had become less important.

Our simple model in Figure 4.1 predicts that nationalizations could have been expected as soon as geological and especially market availability risks had declined in this way by the early to mid 1960s. However, in reality there was some delay before widespread nationalization actually occurred. The nationalizing trend of the 1970s was indeed enabled by reduced geological uncertainty and the ready availability of markets, but its exact timing was affected by other factors. In particular, we speculate that the declining oil prices in the 1960s, themselves the result of increased competition in the oil industry, may have had a role in affecting state perceptions of risk and redirecting state focus temporarily away from nationalization. As discussed in section 2.3, lower oil prices effectively increased the risk that overall revenue would fall short of government targets, placing a greater premium on minimizing hydrocarbon and market availability risks by employing IOCs. At the same time, these states turned to cartelization as their own means of reducing the risk to their revenues. The OPEC cartel was formed in 1960 and made progressively stronger efforts to control price through coordination. At the outset the OPEC states remained reliant on the major oil companies to set the price of oil. By 1971 their bargaining position had improved to the point where they were sharing decisions on price with the major companies. By 1973 their position was sufficiently strong that they could unilaterally set prices above what would be sustainable in a free market, supported by the coordinated withholding of production (Adelman 1995). Nationalization before an effective cartel agreement on production restraint would have opened the door to competition between producer states and depressed crude prices further. However, once an effective cartel was in place to deal with the price risk to state revenues, nationalization could follow.

3.2 The North Sea

The North Sea provides an opportunity to examine how two countries, the UK and Norway, chose their hydrocarbon agents to manage risks within essentially the same petroleum province. The evolution of hydrocarbon policy in these two countries over the course of North Sea petroleum development is well documented by Noreng (1980), Bowen (1991), and Nelsen (1991). Much of that history is consistent with what our theory would predict about how risk constrains government actions. At the same time, differences in the British and Norwegian approaches at particular junctures illustrate that risk is not the only factor that influences government decisions on hydrocarbon development.

Until 1959, with the discovery of the very large Groningen gas field in the Netherlands, there had been very few discoveries of hydrocarbons of commercial value in onshore Europe. Once Groningen was known to exist, the major oil companies began lobbying to open the North Sea for exploration on the theory that the Groningen-like formations might extend offshore. Norway and the UK had a classic frontier province on their hands: The geology of the North Sea was promising but it remained highly uncertain whether commercially viable reserves would be found. Because massive investments in exploration would be needed to prove out the province, this uncertainty translated into substantial risk.

As Figures 4.1 and 4.4 would predict, both the British and Norwegian governments avoided equity or operational participation in the early exploration and development of the North Sea. Instead, after a process of demarcating political boundaries and putting in place requisite legislation in their respective countries, the British and Norwegian governments sought to entice the private oil industry to take on the risks of establishing the new province. Both governments allowed private companies to bid for exploration and production licenses. In the UK, the licenses on offer covered not only the southern basin of the North Sea, which was believed to offer the potential for gas in Groningen-like formations, but also extended into the main areas of the North Sea.[5] Both countries took a remarkably similar approach to exploration licensing, with nearly identical license sizes, incentives for exploration of the more frontier areas, relinquishment requirements, work programs, and commercial terms (Nelsen 1991). (We note that, since the Norwegian civil servants in charge of petroleum explicitly sought to learn from their British counterparts, as discussed in Chapter 14, this similarity of approach was to some extent the result of deliberate imitation.[6])

The results of this initial exploration licensing round emphasized the central role of risk in several ways. First, exploration blocks perceived to have less uncertainty regarding the presence of hydrocarbons were, unsurprisingly, more likely to receive bids. The vast majority of the blocks near the known gas formation of Groningen were licensed, whereas few of the blocks in the more remote Central North Sea and none of the blocks in the more remote Northern North

Sea were bid for. Second, companies shared risk by bidding in consortia. For example, over half of the initial licenses issued by Norway were awarded to partnerships of more than one company (Norwegian Petroleum Directorate 2010). Third, licenses were concentrated among the most established oil companies, reflecting their superior ability to manage the risks of frontier exploration. In this case these frontier risks were associated with both geological uncertainty and uncertainty that suitable technologies for offshore operations in harsh conditions could be developed.

Uncertainty was gradually reduced over time as discoveries followed the early license rounds in both Norway and the UK. In 1965 the West Sole gas field was discovered, which confirmed expectations that the Groningen-like gas extended into the southern basin under the North Sea. The pace of exploration was slower in the more frontier areas of the Central North Sea and the Northern North Sea. In total fourteen wells were drilled in the UK sector of the Central North Sea before the first modest oil discovery, the Montrose field, was made by Amoco in December 1969. The first major oil find (Ekofisk) in the Central North Sea was made in Norwegian waters by Phillips in December 1969, although its size was not appreciated at the time because of the field's geological complexity. The discovery of the giant Forties Field by BP in December 1970, however, left no doubt as to the commercial potential of oil in the North Sea. Just a few months later, in June 1971, another exploration well operated by Shell discovered the Brent field in the far north of the province. These three large oil discoveries, once established to be commercial, essentially proved a major new oil province and significantly reduced the risks associated with any further exploration and development in the central and northern parts of the North Sea system.

These decreasing risks were reflected in the fourth UK license round, held in June 1971, which attracted a great deal of competitive attention from exploration companies. Four times more companies made applications than in any of the first three license rounds. The high level of exploration commitments made in these next bidding rounds, which reflected rising confidence and falling risks, yielded a string of significant discoveries in both the Central North Sea and Northern North Sea areas. In just a few years, by 1977, the discovery rate (measured in barrels found per well drilled) was already in decline in UK waters (Bowen 1991). The province was entering a more mature phase characterized by much higher activity levels and reduced volumes discovered per well.

As expected according to Figure 4.4, both countries shifted to a more participatory approach to hydrocarbon development as risks declined. Increased state involvement was intended to provide the government with more information about operations and greater influence over key operational decisions. In Norway's second license round in 1969, state participation was mandated, in a number of cases in the form of a "carried interest" in exploration blocks. Carried interest meant that the state held an option to participate in development and production activities in the event of a discovery that was determined to be commercially viable. As discussed earlier, this kind of provision meant that the state took none of the risk of failure from exploration or appraisal wells and only participated in development where remaining risks were effectively underwritten by the willingness of the operating company to invest private capital in the project.

During the 1970s, as risks continued to fall, both countries expanded their direct involvement in hydrocarbon activities through the creation of NOCs – initially, to manage the state's equity share in development investments, and later, to take on operatorship of new exploration, development, and production licenses. Norway led the way in nationalizing resource holdings, creating NOC Statoil in 1972, not long after the size and commercial viability of the Ekofisk field had been established. The company initially served as the investment vehicle for state participation in petroleum, and by 1974 it was being given a minimum 50 percent carried interest in all new exploration blocks. The government also increasingly took steps to help Statoil develop into an operator, reserving highly prospective blocks for the NOC as well as granting licenses to experienced international companies with the provision that they relinquish operatorship to Statoil a specified number of years after the commencement of production (see Chapter 14).

Britain moved more slowly than Norway but eventually followed suit in creating an NOC. A 1974 white paper announced the government's determination to build up production as quickly as possible and assert greater public control over national hydrocarbon interests, using carried interest provisions to avoid government exposure to exploration and appraisal risks. The vehicle for this new state interest was the British NOC BNOC, which was formed in 1975 and given the right to acquire up to 51 percent of produced petroleum at market prices.

After tracking each other from the outset of North Sea petroleum activities through the 1970s, British and Norwegian policy clearly diverged in the early 1980s. Britain ended its state participation in oil field developments and began the process of full privatization of both the NOC (BNOC) and the national gas company (BGC). Norway made no such reversal of policy and continued to assert state control of the oil sector through its NOC.

The ideas about risk presented here cannot entirely explain why Britain reversed course and privatized its state industry, emphasizing that risk is far from the only determinant of outcomes. The UK's larger economy and population made oil and gas a relatively less disruptive force and, in line with Figure 4.1, may have reduced the perceived imperative to exert direct control over petroleum development. However, it is also likely that other factors internal to Britain's politics during those years were important. The UK may simply have had a lower political tolerance for government intervention in the economy. Britain had dithered on whether to create an NOC in the first place, remaining content with the initial licensing system well into the 1970s. However, OPEC's success in dramatically raising oil prices in 1973 and the perception that oil companies were reaping extranormal profits had generated political impetus towards nationalization. Additional momentum in favor of creating a British NOC was generated by Labour's election victory in 1974, which ousted a more market-oriented conservative government. However, the political will behind direct national control over hydrocarbons could not be sustained when oil prices tumbled in the 1980s, and Britain privatized BNOC and BGC and reverted to the model that had existed until the early 1970s: government regulation of competing private firms. Even in Norway, political factors – notably including the accession of a Labour government in 1971 – had important influence over the exact timing of Statoil's creation, the form it took as a 100 percent state-owned enterprise, and its eventual partial privatization in 2001 (see Chapter 14).

3.3 Global patterns of oil and gas exploration, 1970–2008

Data on exploration wells around the world from energy research and consulting firm Wood Mackenzie provides an ideal means of testing the hypothesis that risk is an important driver of industry structure. We examined two possible frontiers: exploration in deep water, which is characterized by massive capital requirements and significant technological uncertainty, and exploration in areas where there have been no previous discoveries, for which capital requirements may be lower but geological uncertainty is high. We also tested the possibility, proposed in section 2.3, that oil price might be an important determinant of whether NOCs or private firms predominate in hydrocarbon activities.

The specific hypotheses that we tested were the following:

Hypothesis 1: Governments are more likely to employ national oil companies for exploration in high price environments, where risk minimization is less important.

Hypothesis 2: Governments are less likely to employ national oil companies for exploration in deep water, where risks are higher than onshore or in shallow water.

Hypothesis 3: Governments are less likely to employ national oil companies for exploration in territories (classified in this analysis into "zones"[7]) where no previous discoveries have been made and risks are therefore higher.

We used the following linear regression model to simultaneously test these three hypotheses:

$$NOCFRACTION_{ijt} = \beta_0 + \beta_1 * PRICE_t + \beta_2 * NOFINDS_{jt} + \beta_3 * WATERDEPTH_{jt} \tag{Eq. 4.1}$$

Where:

$NOCFRACTION_{ijt}$ = Fraction of exploration wells[8] spudded in country i and zone j in year t which are operated by the NOC of country i.

$PRICE_t$ = Average of Brent oil price (2008 \$) for five years prior to year t, normalized by highest price during entire time period (1970–2008).

$NOFINDS_{jt}$ = 0 if a commercial discovery has been made in zone j prior to year t; 1 if no commercial discovery has been made in zone j prior to year t.

$WATERDEPTH_{jt}$ = Average water depth of wells completed in zone j in year t and two prior years, normalized by the ninetieth percentile water depth of offshore wells drilled in that year worldwide. The ninetieth percentile water depth frontier is shown in Figure 4.5; however,

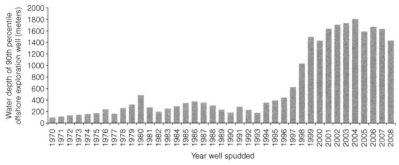

Figure 4.5 Water depth of the ninetieth percentile offshore exploration well worldwide that was spudded in the given year. (In other words, 90 percent of offshore exploration wells were in shallower water.)
Data source: Wood Mackenzie (2009b).

note that for the purposes of the regression model, the frontier value used for normalization is not allowed to decline below the previous high, as the "frontier" depth is intended to reflect knowledge about deep water operations accumulated up to that point.

The basic logic of this model is that *NOCFRACTION* – the fraction of wells in a given zone operated by the home country's NOC – is a proxy for the state's choice of whether to employ an NOC or IOCs. Clearly, there are many factors besides an explicit state choice that could influence this fraction. A state may not have an NOC, for example, or a state may desire to employ an IOC to explore in a given area but find that IOCs are not interested. However, our assumption is that over the long run states can put in place policies (including the establishment of an NOC) and create incentive structures that will favor either NOC or IOC exploration activity. Thus, the value of *NOCFRACTION* should at least implicitly reflect state choices. Because we are focusing on the degree of risk a state is willing to accept, we chose to examine the fraction of wells *operated* by the home NOC. The decision to employ the home NOC as an operator entails more risk (but may also be perceived to afford more control) than simply taking an equity share in an IOC-operated exploration well.

Oil price expectations were represented in a simple-minded way by averaging the Brent benchmark price for the previous five years.[9] Averages of one and three years were also tried; they unsurprisingly showed similar (though noisier) regression results compared with those presented in Tables 4.1 and 4.2.

NOFINDS is a dummy variable that in a coarse way groups exploration areas into putative geological frontiers – those with no previous commercial discoveries as classified by Wood Mackenzie[10] – and areas that should have lower geological uncertainty because a previous commercial discovery has been made in the specified zone. A sophisticated case-by-case analysis of the geological uncertainty faced by each exploration well along with its potential upside would have been a superior approach to characterizing risk, but such an approach was not feasible for this kind of large-sample regression.

WATERDEPTH is intended to capture the challenge and risk posed by the characteristic water depth in a given zone. Because the frontier has advanced over time as shown in Figure 4.5, this variable is normalized by a measure of the "frontier" water depth in a given year.

Our analysis data set included all exploration wells in Wood Mackenzie's PathFinder database, except those in China and Russia,[11] that were spudded between 1970 and 2008. China and Russia were specifically excluded because of known data gaps for these countries which could introduce systematic error, for example because wells with international participation were more likely to be recorded than those without international participation. With these two nations removed, a total of eighty-nine countries were covered by the sample.

The full data table for 1970 through 2008 had a total of 8,602 observations, with each observation representing a zone in a given country in a given year. As part of creating the data table, it was necessary to classify every company operating a well over the sample period as either an IOC or an NOC in each year, and also to identify the home country of a given NOC in order to distinguish its operations at home from those abroad.[12] This classification was performed based on a variety of sources, including the case studies in this volume, the World Bank's 2008 survey of NOCs (World Bank 2008), and company websites. Companies with majority state ownership were considered to be NOCs, as were those for which the government was a minority shareholder but retained control through special shareholding arrangements. Operating companies that were partnerships between the home NOC and other private companies or foreign NOCs were generally *not* classified as home NOCs, with the rationale that the other companies could be providing all of the expertise in risk management for the partnership.

Table 4.1. Effect of "frontier" character (water depth, previous discoveries) and oil price on NOC prevalence in exploration (see equation 4.1)

	(1)	(2)	(3)	(4)	(5)
	1970–2008	1970–1979	1980–1989	1990–1999	2000–2008
Average oil price, Brent (2008 $), norm. – previous five yrs	0.065***	0.089	-0.019	0.696***	-0.086
	(0.018)	(0.054)	(0.053)	(0.189)	(0.082)
No previous finds (1 = no previous discoveries in zone)	0.008	0.011	-0.024	-0.088**	-0.020
	(0.017)	(0.024)	(0.032)	(0.041)	(0.088)
Water depth, normalized	-0.136***	-0.286***	-0.210***	-0.045	0.005
	(0.016)	(0.027)	(0.037)	(0.035)	(0.033)
Constant	0.218***	0.296***	0.317***	-0.022	0.182***
	(0.010)	(0.019)	(0.043)	(0.068)	(0.034)
Observations	8,602	2,145	2,384	2,233	1,628

Robust standard errors in parentheses.
*** Significant at 0.01 level, ** significant at 0.05 level, * significant at 0.1 level.

To test the three hypotheses above, an ordinary least squares regression was performed on the data, using robust standard errors to account for heteroskedasticity. Results are shown in Table 4.1, first for the entire sample period (model 1) and then for the periods 1970–1979, 1980–1989, 1990–1999, and 2000–2008 in models 2–5, respectively. Interpretation is simplified by the fact that price has been normalized to 1 at its highest value in the sample period (in 1984) and water depth is normalized to 1 at the "frontier" in a given year, as measured by the ninetieth percentile water depth worldwide. Thus, for example, the constant term in Table 4.1 (e.g., 0.218 for model 1) represents the expected fraction of NOC-operated wells at zero price and zero water depth (e.g., an onshore zone), for an exploration province that has already seen a commercial discovery. If the average price for the last five years is at its maximum value, on the other hand, model 1 predicts the fraction of NOC-operated wells will be 0.065 higher. If the water depth of wells drilled in the region over the past three years (including the current year) is exactly at the ninetieth percentile "frontier" for the current year, model 1 predicts the fraction of NOC-operated wells will be 0.136 lower.

Model 1, covering the entire period from 1970 through 2008, supports hypothesis 1 (higher oil price increases the likelihood that states will use NOCs for exploration) and hypothesis 2 (states tend to use their NOCs to a lesser degree for exploration in deeper water). The coefficient for *NOFINDS* in model 1, on the other hand, is not statistically significant, meaning that overall there is no support either positive or negative for hypothesis 3 that states are less likely to employ NOCs in territories where no previous discoveries have been made.

The breakdown by time periods in models 2–5 reveals a more complicated picture. The hypothesis that states will preferentially employ companies other than their NOCs in deeper water is strongly borne out for the period from 1970 through 1989, but the effect disappears for the later periods. All of the price effect for the period from 1970 through 2008 is accounted for by a large price coefficient from 1990 to 1999. We will discuss each of these findings in turn.

The finding that states were less likely to employ NOCs relative to other players as operators for deeper water wells between 1970 and 1989 is the most unambiguous and strongly supported by our regression. Figure 4.6, which plots the average fraction of wells operated by

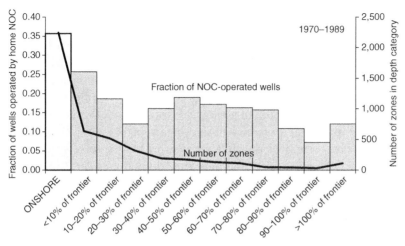

Figure 4.6 Average fraction of exploration wells operated by home NOC as a function of water depth relative to the frontier, 1970–1989.

Note: The fraction of home-NOC-operated exploration wells in a given zone in a given year represents a single observation; all of the observations are grouped into depth bins and averaged for each bin (columns: "Fraction of NOC-operated wells"). The total number of observations in each depth bin is also shown (line: "Number of zones"). Since the frontier is defined as the ninetieth percentile water depth in a given year, depths of greater than 100 percent of the frontier are observed.

Data source: Wood Mackenzie (2009b).

NOCs at different depths relative to the frontier in the time period from 1970 to 1989, clearly illustrates this effect.

Further analysis (including inspection of the raw data table) suggests that the disappearance of the deep water effect on NOC vs. IOC operatorship since 1990 is due almost entirely to the influence on the results of Petrobras (see Chapter 12) and Statoil (see Chapter 14) – two NOCs that have developed substantial skill at operating and managing risks in deep water. In Table 4.2, we rerun the same regression models as in Table 4.1, but removing Brazil and Norway from the data set. When we do this, the strong preference against NOCs in deeper water is roughly consistent across all four time periods. This result suggests that Petrobras and Statoil have truly become "IOC-like" in their ability to operate and shoulder risks for their respective governments in deep water, which is not a surprise in light of the findings of the case studies on these respective NOCs.

Considering all the evidence in Tables 4.1 and 4.2 together, it is difficult to find any support either positive or negative for the idea that states might preferentially use IOCs to explore regions that have not seen previous commercial discoveries and are therefore riskier. Several explanations for this are possible. First, it may be that the presence or absence of a prior commercial discovery in a zone is simply too coarse and imperfect a measure of geological risk. Second, this measure says nothing about the potential upside of a territory with no previous discoveries – it may be that IOCs stay away from a zone with no previous discoveries precisely because they do not consider it to be very prospective. Third, a countervailing factor that could cause NOCs to explore virgin territory even if there have been no previous discoveries is the simple fact that it is on their home turf. (As will be discussed further in section 4.1, NOCs in some cases might have incentive to pursue local exploration *precisely because* the state is shouldering the risk.) Fourth, even if the region is not highly prospective and uncertainties are high, capital outlays can be relatively low in the case of onshore exploration wells, meaning that the risk might be tolerable for certain states.

At first glance, the price effect in model 1 of Table 4.1 seemed to confirm our hypothesis that high oil prices effectively reduce state risk and the need to employ IOCs. However, further inspection reveals that the price effect is almost entirely associated with the period from 1990 to 1999, although when Brazil and Norway are excluded in the analysis of Table 4.2, a statistically significant though smaller effect is also observed between 1970 and 1979. Figure 4.7 suggests that the strong price effect in the 1990s might actually come from the correlated decrease in the overall fraction of NOC-operated exploration wells and the oil price over this period. Because this correlation could be coincidental, we view the implications of the analysis for hypothesis 1 as inconclusive. At the same time, one could plausibly make the broader argument that the flurry of privatizations in the 1990s (see Chapter 2) was related in part to the decrease in oil prices and price expectations – in line with our argument about risk effectively being higher in low price periods.

While our statistical analysis was unable to conclusively demonstrate a price effect on states' preferences for NOCs or IOCs, and it also failed to discern an effect based on our simplistically defined "frontier" of territories without previous discoveries, it did find clear

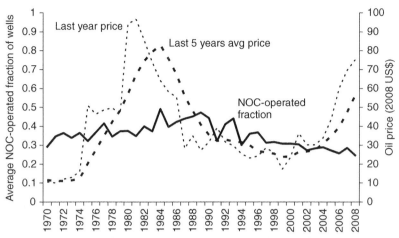

Figure 4.7 Average fraction of exploration wells operated by NOCs from 1970 through 2008, plotted alongside the Brent benchmark oil price for both the previous year and for the average of the previous five years.
Data sources: Brent oil prices from BP (2009a); NOC-operated fraction of wells derived from Wood Mackenzie (2009b).

support for the thesis about risk and state choices in patterns of exploration as a function of water depth. At the same time, we note that the simple model of equation 4.1 only explains a relatively small percentage of the overall variation in the state's choice of an NOC or IOC.[13] This reflects both the coarseness of our ability to assess risk in this simple model and the fact that risk is but one constraint on the choices of the state. The regression model in this section did not attempt to characterize the other major dimensions in the framework of Figure 4.1 – the state's relative desire to control petroleum and the capacity of a given state to take on risk. In addition, there are likely to be other significant drivers of state choices including the characteristics of different political systems as explored in Chapter 2.

4 Conclusion

The central argument in this chapter is that industrial structure, defined by a state's choice of private or state operating company, is shaped in an important way by three variables: the petroleum state's motive for direct control through a state company, the inherent risks of doing so, and the capacity of the state to take on these risks. Both

Table 4.2. *Effect of "frontier" character (water depth, previous discoveries) and oil price on NOC prevalence in exploration (see equation 4.1), this time excluding Brazil and Norway*

Excluding Brazil and Norway	(1) 1970–2008	(2) 1970–1979	(3) 1980–1989	(4) 1990–1999	(5) 2000–2008
Average oil price, Brent (2008 $), norm. – previous five yrs	0.062***	0.123**	–0.035	0.789***	–0.068
	(0.018)	(0.054)	(0.053)	(0.179)	(0.076)
No previous finds (1 = no previous discoveries in zone)	0.028*	0.019	–0.036	–0.050	0.019
	(0.017)	(0.024)	(0.032)	(0.038)	(0.087)
Water depth, normalized	–0.215***	–0.283***	–0.273***	–0.213***	–0.150***
	(0.014)	(0.028)	(0.037)	(0.024)	(0.016)
Constant	0.192***	0.253***	0.302***	–0.080	0.154***
	(0.010)	(0.019)	(0.043)	(0.064)	(0.032)
Observations	7,922	1,994	2,184	2,054	1,496

Robust standard errors in parentheses.

*** Significant at 0.01 level, ** significant at 0.05 level, * significant at 0.1 level.

state-owned and private companies can in theory manage risks for the state, but the very nature of the state-owned company as a tool for government goals beyond the commercial tends to make it a poorer risk manager than its private counterparts. Governments thus have strong incentives to employ private companies in cases involving high risks or in situations where they have little or no desire for direct control of the sector and can achieve state goals through industrial regulation. But these latter settings are rare in the major petroleum provinces; more common is an acute interest in control with a highly varied exposure to risk and equally variable capacity to manage it.

In section 3, we considered the success of this basic model in predicting how the agents most commonly employed by hydrocarbon states shifted as the oil and gas industry developed; which kinds of companies Norway and the UK chose to find and extract North Sea oil and gas; and whether different kinds of exploration frontiers (deep water and virgin territory) would be preferentially occupied by state or private companies. Broadly, the outcomes in these cases supported our thesis that private companies play a central role as risk managers at the frontier; however, other factors also emerged as having some bearing on the state choice of hydrocarbon agent.

4.1 The influence of non-risk factors on agent choice

Political factors can play a particularly important role in what kind of company the state employs in oil and gas and the exact timing of when the state involves itself directly. For example, this factor appears to be relevant in explaining why the UK privatized its national oil company BNOC relatively quickly after its formation whereas Norway preserved Statoil as a fully state-owned company for much longer and has left it as a majority state-owned entity to the present day. In some cases, NOCs may be difficult to privatize or dismantle even after the risk environment has changed such that an IOC would be a more logical choice for a state. Leaders may value the ability of an NOC to provide private benefits to elites or broader public benefits that help them retain their legitimacy among the population. In Chapter 2, Chris Warshaw considers in more detail the political factors influencing nationalization and privatization decisions.

Political considerations and the non-hydrocarbon benefits of NOCs likely explain many "mistakes" in which states persist in employing a state operating company even when it is unable to adequately assess or manage the risks the state will be exposed to. Mexico and Venezuela today are two countries that retain state companies in the face of mounting risks to state investment intended to open new frontiers in these countries. Other "mistakes" may instead be cases in which the state is able to tolerate the risks involved in frontier activities, at least for the time being. For example, India's national oil company ONGC compiled a woeful performance record in exploration activities (see Chapter 17), but these failed investments may not have loomed as large in a diversified economy like India's as they would have in a state like Nigeria in which oil revenues are critically needed to close the state budget. (And in any event, the Indian government in recent years has attempted to benchmark and improve ONGC's performance, including through the introduction of competition.)

The Indian example may also reflect the ironic outcome that NOCs can end up taking on significant risks, even if not prepared to adequately manage them, precisely because they are gambling with state money. This is likely part of the explanation for why IOCs did not systematically emerge in section 3.3 as the dominant explorers in hydrocarbon basins without previous discoveries. As discussed in section 2.5.2, Petrobras was likely more aggressive in taking on the technological risks of offshore development than it would otherwise have been because the state was shouldering the risk of failure. Similarly, Statoil was free to take a more long-term approach to research and development than commercial players because of its implicit support from the state. As Statoil has progressively separated from the state, notably through partial privatization in 2001, it has appeared to move toward a more commercial mode of managing technology development and risk (see Chapter 14).

As the Petrobras and Statoil cases demonstrate, state support for capability development within NOCs can in rare instances lead to long-term benefits for the state, even if it does result in suboptimal risk management in the short term. It can also lead to NOCs eventually developing some risk management skills themselves. As suggested by the results of section 3.3, Petrobras and Statoil by the 1990s were able to play an IOC-like role for their respective governments in taking on the risks of deep water exploration. The development of risk management capabilities within these NOCs was facilitated by the atypically limited demands of their host states for non-hydrocarbon functions.

A final factor that emerged as a qualification to the basic framework of state agent choice was the effect of oil price. By altering the relative contribution of produced quantity, production cost, and selling price to net revenue for the state, price changes effectively shift the location of the frontier by making particular resources more or less economic. We expect lower price environments to place a greater premium on the risk management skills that IOCs bring to the table. As discussed in section 3.3, decreasing oil prices in the 1990s did broadly track a decrease in the use of NOCs in exploration, although further work would be needed to confirm a causal connection. Another way of thinking about price fluctuations is as an independent source of revenue risk to the state that private companies are not able manage on its behalf. The significance of price risk may help explain the observation in section 3.1 that oil-rich states turned to cartelization before nationalization, even after the geological and market availability risks of the oil industry had been substantially reduced.

4.2 *Industry structure and the next frontier*

With such a large share of the world's petroleum reserves under the control of state companies today, it is often suggested that the days of the private operating company are over, and that state companies and oil service companies will increasingly control oil in the future. Based on the theory of risk and the structure of the petroleum industry that we have described here, we are skeptical of such arguments, for several principal reasons. First, the oil service companies do not compete with private operating companies. Rather, they perform fundamentally different roles, with only the private operating companies managing risk as a fundamental part of their business models. Second, most state companies are not well equipped to manage extreme risks on behalf of their respective governments. Because of a lack of competitive pressures at home, their responsiveness to government goals beyond the commercial, and other domestic political factors, only the rare NOC can accumulate the necessary elements of risk management such as strong geosciences capability, the ability to innovate while holding down costs, and a global portfolio of investments. Third, there will remain a new high-risk frontier to be conquered as long as there is a petroleum industry. That being said, the changing nature of the frontier will have implications for what particular opportunities are available to private operating companies going forward.

Previous frontiers have largely been about exploration and development in new geographies, and the private operating companies, of all sizes, have become skillful at managing these risks. We can see that major new exploration geography is limited: the industry has already explored accessible onshore basins, offshore basins, and now deep water basins. Today's frontier opportunities mostly do not involve new geography per se, but like all frontiers they are characterized by high uncertainty and massive capital requirements. Today's frontiers encompass vast volumes of unconventional oils (for example, tar sands, only 20 percent of which can be extracted with today's surface mining technology) as well as unconventional gas in tight sands, in tight shale source rocks, as coal bed methane, and in hydrates. Even conventional natural gas development can retain a high-risk character due to the capital intensity of gas transport infrastructure, the complex and frequently cross-border value chains associated with gas, and the requirement that reliable demand be established at prices that can enable cost recovery. For this reason, IOCs continue to dominate in the gas arena. Other frontiers include exploration in ultra-deep waters, particularly where mobile salt provides a substantial obstacle to the identification and mapping of drillable prospects, as well as exploration of the remote Arctic with its challenges of both static and mobile ice.

Success at these frontiers will depend, as always, on the ability to manage risk through the development of increasingly accurate measurements of uncertainty. It will require the use of innovative data collection methods and accumulated geological knowledge to make skillful predictions of exploration or development outcomes even when an absence of precedent makes these outcomes seem unknowable. It will also demand continual innovation to reduce capital cost. Several broad uncertainties exacerbate the risks of today's frontiers, notably those around climate policy and the direction of future oil prices – the latter being a function in part of how large resource (and spare capacity) holders like Saudi Arabia might try to use production rates to influence oil price so as to undercut any emerging threats to petroleum's dominance.

Because of this ongoing need for risk management at the frontier, the role for private operating companies in the petroleum industry will not disappear; of course, there is no guarantee that these companies will be able to maintain or expand their current share of the market. More certainty in both climate policy and oil price – the latter created, for example, by taxation to create oil price floors in consuming countries – might help in reducing the market risks that private companies are unable to manage themselves, and thereby assist these companies in venturing out more aggressively into new frontiers.

State companies will continue to thrive where there are low-risk and low-cost hydrocarbons to manage. Whenever risks become higher or cost performance becomes more critical to state revenues, their dominance is likely to wane at least for the moment. One high-risk activity on the horizon for oil-rich governments with maturing resources is the redevelopment of large maturing fields through tertiary recovery. Other frontiers that are closed today for political reasons may open as a result of political change, as has occurred in Iraq, or when the true risks of investment and the limited ability of the state to absorb risk are better understood, as in the case of Mexico deep water or Venezuela extra-heavy oil.

It may be that more NOCs over time will follow the lead of Statoil and Petrobras in starting to develop a global portfolio and competitive risk management capabilities. However, in most cases this only seems to happen when an NOC's domestic resources begin to dwindle; until this point, governments tend to ask NOCs to fulfill too many ancillary goals, while NOCs find themselves too comfortably sheltered at home to become truly competitive at managing risk.

Notes

1 Knight suggests that these two canonical types of probability be referred to as "risk" and "uncertainty," respectively. However, we deliberately eschew Knight's use of the terms "risk" and "uncertainty" in this specialized way, believing it to be at odds with the common usage of these words and thus more confusing than helpful. (Some authors resolve this dilemma by adding the modifier "Knightian" to indicate these

specialized meanings – for example, "Knightian uncertainty" refers to the case where the distribution of outcomes is unknowable.)

2 Knight (1921) writes on pp. 225–226: "There are all gradations from a perfectly homogeneous group of life or fire hazards at one extreme to an absolutely unique exercise of judgment at the other. All gradations, we should say, except the ideal extremes themselves; for as we can never in practice secure completely homogeneous classes in the one case, so in the other it probably never happens that there is *no* basis of comparison for determining the probability of error in a judgment."

3 As Knight (1921) writes on pp. 233–234 of *Risk, Uncertainty, and Profit*, "Now if the distribution of the different possible outcomes in a group of instances is known, it is possible to get rid of any real uncertainty by the expedient of grouping or 'consolidating instances'."

4 Which elements of a bid a host government prefers most depends on factors that are outside the scope of this chapter but discussed in more detail in Chapters 1 and 20 and in the NOC case studies. Some governments might prefer cash or direct payments to favored elites; others might seek visible work programs that create jobs and votes.

5 This first round of UK licenses covered virtually the whole of the offshore continental shelf from the Dover Strait to the northern limits of the Shetland Islands (Bowen 1991).

6 This example implicitly points to a driver of government policy that falls outside of our simple theory about risk and desire for control: the way that governments can be influenced by the actions of other countries.

7 A zone is defined in our analysis as a unique combination of a basin, which is a geological depression that could contain hydrocarbons, with a sector, which is defined by the Wood Mackenzie PathFinder database based on other distinctions like whether an exploration area is onshore or offshore. The logic is that each zone will tend to have distinctive characteristics when it comes to exploration risk. Our analysis dataset includes a total of 400 such zones.

8 The Wood Mackenzie classification of a well as an exploration well (as distinct, for example, from an appraisal well) reflects the risk and objective of the well, and incorporates post-drilling evaluation and reassessments of the well status, rather than simply documenting the well type reported at the time of the drilling application. Because well operators may have incentives to report wells as being of an exploration rather than appraisal character, for example to meet work program requirements, we expect that this independent assessment by Wood Mackenzie should provide a more accurate indication of a well's true character than well type as directly reported by operators.

9 A futures price might have been more appropriate in theory, but the oil derivatives market did not develop until the 1980s. We are doubtful in any case that the use of a futures price would have added significant value to the analysis.

10 Note that the assessment we use from Wood Mackenzie (2009b) of whether a previous discovery in a zone was commercial is based on a *current* perspective on the economics of extracting hydrocarbons from the field in question, taking into account today's technologies and oil price outlook. Ideally, it would have been better to characterize commerciality of previous discoveries in the zone as viewed *at the time* a new exploration well was drilled, but such an assessment is not readily available. We do not expect that this use of present-day commerciality assessments will substantially bias our results, as in most cases these present-day characterizations will still correlate in a relative sense to how promising hydrocarbon deposits were considered to be at the time, even though technological advancement and higher oil prices may have increased the fraction of previously discovered fields that are considered commercially viable today.

11 The exclusion of Russia and China turned out to have only a minor effect on regression results.

12 In a study that is focused on measuring the effect of state ownership per se on company performance, it might make more sense to distinguish only between majority state-owned and majority privately owned companies, irrespective of where the company is operating. In this work, however, we are focusing on a state's choice of whether to use its own NOC to develop domestic resources or to rely on outside companies, be they private or owned by other states. Therefore, it was more logical to draw the line between the home NOC and any other operator.

13 Our simple regression model showed the most explanatory power for the period from 1970 to 1979, with an R^2 of about 0.05.

PART III

National oil company case studies

5 | Saudi Aramco: the jewel in the crown

PAUL STEVENS

1 Introduction and overview

Saudi Aramco was never intended to be the national oil company (NOC) of Saudi Arabia. Instead, that outcome was an accident of history. In the early 1970s the government of Saudi Arabia was caught in the rising tide of Arab nationalism and had little choice but to nationalize the Western-owned oil assets across most of the country. The company it intended as its national firm performed badly, and that left Aramco to fill the void. Aramco was the Western-operated oil company whose owners were formally changing with nationalization but whose operations were barely affected. It was the most competent institution in the country and attracted the best talent. Among NOCs today, Saudi Aramco's governance and performance appear to be stellar. Yet it is difficult to compare Aramco with other NOCs because its sheer size and importance to the world oil market are unlike any of its peers. And comparisons are also clouded by Aramco's (and Saudi Arabia's) intense secrecy.

This chapter explores the origins and operations of Aramco (section 2) and focuses on the firm's governance and strategy (section 3), relationship to the government (section 4), and performance (section 5). It makes four broad arguments.

First, it is extremely difficult to judge Aramco's strategy and performance because the company's operations are shrouded in secrecy.[1] Mindful of that caveat, the company's performance appears to be high. That performance is rooted in the fact that as Aramco became Saudi Arabia's NOC it experienced minimal disruption in its operations. It has endured none of the wrenching experiences that other NOCs experienced (such as in Venezuela or Iran) that emptied them of talent and caused managers to lose focus on their mission of finding and extracting oil.

Second, Saudi Aramco provides a convincing example of how an NOC, run by technocrats and to a great extent insulated from political interference, can produce what appears to be a first-rate corporate performance. What particularly emerges is the importance of the governance of the oil sector. This involves the clarity of roles and responsibilities within the sector; the importance of enablement to allow the actors to carry out the roles assigned; and the importance of accountability of decision making and performance. The Saudi government is strong and stable with clearly defined goals; those attributes allow Saudi Aramco to adopt a long-term perspective. Because the firm – more by accident than design – has a Western-style corporate culture and invests heavily in education and technology it has used the opportunity of a long-term perspective to develop and pursue clear strategic goals.

Third, while it is clear that transparency within Saudi Arabia – in particular, between the NOC and the government owner – is important for corporate performance, *external* transparency appears not to be a necessary condition for success. Internal transparency makes it easier for Aramco's owner to oversee and control its operations, but the lack of external transparency makes it difficult for other owners to close the information gap through comparisons between Aramco and other firms. That gap is a critical element of the principal–agent relationship that exists between NOCs and their regulators and has proved so difficult for many countries to manage.

Fourth, Saudi Arabia is blessed by rich geology, which has meant that the company has not struggled much with the need to invest in extremely complex frontier projects. As existing large fields deplete and the need for such investments arises, differences between the company's mission (producing oil as a monopolist) and the country's mission (revenue and other benefits for the Saudi people) may arise. So far, the company's strategy reflects its obedience to the Saudi state although the state's and the company's strategies have sometimes clashed, most obviously over a state initiative in 1998 to open portions of exploration and production to Western companies. Had oil prices stayed low that initiative would have remained a major source of tension, but with the relatively higher prices that have prevailed since 2001 there has been little pressure on the government to seek more competition in its oil sector. It is also important to remember that the company retains the trust of the government and this is central to its role in the oil sector.

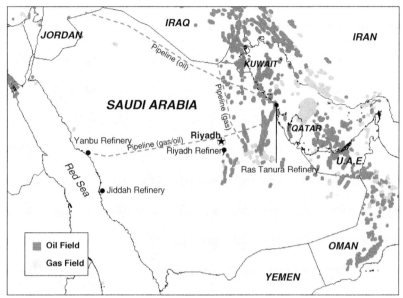

Figure 5.1 Map of major oil and gas fields in Saudi Arabia.
Source for oil and gas field data: Wood Mackenzie (2009b).

2 The accidental NOC

Other studies have explored Saudi Aramco's history in more detail.[2] Here I examine the highlights and focus on a central observation: Saudi Aramco's deep private sector legacy and the government's respect for that legacy are crucial to understanding the company's story and its performance today.

The company began as a traditional "old-style concession agreement" typical of the relationship established between Western major oil companies and the state.[3] The first agreement was signed in 1933 between Standard Oil of California (SOCAL) – which assigned its rights to the wholly owned subsidiary California Arabian Standard Oil Company (CASOC) – and the Kingdom of Saudi Arabia, a newly created state in 1932.[4] The agreement had a life of sixty years and covered most of the kingdom (617,000 square miles of Saudi Arabia's total 860,000-square-mile territory). While the contract included a clause allowing for the company to relinquish the territory to the government, this was entirely at the discretion of SOCAL.[5] It was not until 1948 that the company – by then called Aramco – agreed on a program of relinquishment. By 1963, Aramco had relinquished 75 percent of its original concession.[6]

The terms, similar to those signed in Kuwait, Iran, and Iraq, granted SOCAL exclusive rights to explore for and exploit oil. It also created a firm separation between Saudi Arabia's political sphere and SOCAL's commercial operations. The company, for example, agreed not to interfere with "administrative, political, or religious affairs within Saudi Arabia" (Article 36) while the kingdom granted SOCAL complete managerial freedom in its operations. The financial terms involved upfront loans to the government and a royalty of four gold shillings per ton.[7] The government agreed to forgo its right to impose taxes for all time (Article 21) while also suggesting some social obligations for the firm. For example, "as far as practicable" SOCAL would employ "Saudi Arab nationals" (Article 23).

CASOC spudded its first well in April 1935 and by 1938 had found oil in large, commercial quantities. Indeed, as the huge size of the discovery became apparent there was growing concern that such a large amount of oil would seriously destabilize international oil markets.[8] An existing pricing agreement (dating from 1928) would in theory govern this kind of eventuality, but the find was so large it was unclear if that agreement would hold.[9] In addition, SOCAL faced a serious practical problem: it lacked the outlets to handle such large amounts of oil. At the same time, the Texas Oil Company (Texaco) was increasing its global product sales but had no foreign sources of crude. Thus in July 1936, SOCAL and Texaco converted CASOC into a fifty-fifty joint venture – they married SOCAL's Saudi supply with Texaco's downstream markets.

World War II froze any further developments and also hurt the finances of the Saudi Kingdom, not least because the government's other main source of revenue – pilgrims visiting Mecca – also dried up during the war. CASOC stepped in (with some assistance from the US government) with loans in advance of royalties. The outcome was even more positive relations between the company and the king.

In 1944 CASOC changed its name to the Arabian American Oil Company (Aramco).[10] Still mindful of just how much oil Aramco was sitting on and the difficulty of securing markets for the crude, negotiations began with Exxon and Mobil (using their modern names). By 1948 Aramco was owned by SOCAL (30 percent), Texaco (30 percent), Exxon (30 percent), and Mobil (10 percent).

In 1947, Aramco produced 90,000 b/d. By 1951, production had risen to 278,000 b/d and by 1960 to 480,000 b/d or about 5.7 percent of the world's oil output (Darmstadter 1971). The Saudi government earned dramatically higher fees over the period. In 1947 revenues were $18 million; by 1960, this had risen to $334 million, in large part because of the introduction of a fifty-fifty profits tax in December 1950. Saudi Arabia was in fact the first Middle East producer to introduce a profits tax, following from Venezuela's introduction of such a tax in 1943.[11]

During the 1950s the Persian Gulf rapidly became a politically volatile region. Of particular importance was the Iranian nationalization of the Anglo-Iranian Oil Company in 1951. This presaged a period of growing dissatisfaction of producer governments in the Middle East with the terms of the "old-style concessions." Four issues dominated (Stevens 2008a). First was the very long life of the original concessions; in Iran, Iraq, Kuwait, and Saudi Arabia the average life was eighty-two years. The original sixty-year Saudi concession was extended about the time that Aramco added Exxon and Mobil to its members, with the logic that there was so much oil that a longer period would be needed for marketing.

Second, the areas covered by the agreements were huge. In the four main countries, 88 percent of the national area was covered including all of Iraq and Kuwait. Furthermore there were no required relinquishment clauses. The companies could simply sit on acreage, including commercial discoveries, without yielding revenue and other local benefits.

Third, there was growing dissatisfaction with the fiscal terms. While profit taxes rapidly spread in the Middle East after Saudi Arabia led the way, still more disputes arose over the setting of posted prices used to compute revenue and other factors that affected the benefits that host governments gained from their oil production. Indeed, once the host governments started focusing on the fiscal terms of the concessions, they became wary that the Western firms that controlled the concessions were providing accurate information about real costs and opportunities.

The final and main source of dispute was that the concession gave the majors total managerial freedom within their concession areas. Given the size of these areas, this freedom effectively gave them the power of being a state within a state able to make decisions unilaterally on exploration, development, and production – decisions normally vested in the state itself.

As the 1950s and 1960s progressed, these dissatisfactions yielded a string of disputes that often soured relations between the producer governments and the major Western firms that operated the oil fields. Aramco, however, was different; disputes arose but they were muted. This was especially true after the rather radical Saudi oil minister Abdullah Tariki[12] was replaced in 1962 by the more amenable young lawyer Ahmed Zaki Yamani. While Yamani was certainly no pushover for the Aramco partners and negotiated fiercely over issues of importance to Saudi Arabia, he was at pains to keep politics out of such discussions. The discussions and negotiations were based much more on technical, engineering, and commercial considerations than gesture politics. King Faisal encouraged this approach and left Yamani to oversee its implementation.

This different history for Saudi Arabia in comparison with other oil-rich countries of the region reflected, in part, a quite different political context. In other countries the drivers to change concession agreements included factors such as post-colonial desires (especially evident in Algeria, Iran, Iraq, and Kuwait[13]) that created pressure on governments to demonstrate independence. Those same pressures inspired the rise of the concept of "permanent sovereignty" over natural resources. In 1952, the UN General Assembly passed its first resolution on this issue; in 1962, a UN resolution recognized the rights of a country to dispose of its natural wealth in accordance with its national interests; in 1966, UN Resolution 2158 was even more explicit and host countries were advised to secure maximum exploitation of natural resources by the accelerated acquisition of full control over production operations, management, and marketing.

Saudi Arabia's colonial past did not generate the same popular resentment as elsewhere. Although the regional elements that made up the kingdom had been part of the Ottoman Empire, this had been an extremely loose and undemanding relationship since the middle of the nineteenth century. Furthermore, the Aramco partners were all American and therefore relatively untainted by the colonial footprint of Britain and France. Indeed the US stand over the Suez fiasco in 1956 endeared the United States to Arab popular opinion. This was reinforced by the special relationship that developed between the Al Saud ruling family and various US administrations over many years, starting notably with the US role in orchestrating financial assistance that helped Ibn Saud's political survival. The Saudi population was small and relatively unpoliticized. There were few popular demonstrations in Saudi Arabia where the ruling family was securely in power, even as such demonstrations became commonplace in other parts of the Arab world.[14] In addition to this, Aramco by virtue of the funds and services it made available to the Saudi government[15] built strong support for its continuing operations.

The fallout from the Iranian nationalization of 1951 also left the American management of Aramco shocked and disturbed by the deep and bitter hatred that the Iranian population displayed toward the Anglo-Iranian oil company. It took this as a salutary lesson of the dangers of arrogant British management that made no effort to integrate its company into the Iranian economy, employed Iranians only for menial work, and saw its only local responsibility as payment of taxes to the Iranian government. For Aramco's management, the lesson led to considerable efforts to integrate the company into Saudi Arabia while still staying removed from Saudi politics.[16] Heeding this lesson proved difficult in part because the Eastern Province of the kingdom (where most of Aramco's oil operations concentrated) had no infrastructure apart from a few limited port facilities and some airstrips, let alone any productive economic activities.[17] Effectively in such circumstances the company had no choice but to take on a number of state functions.

And so, over the 1950s the corporate culture within Aramco shifted. The company sought to maximize the employment of Saudi nationals at all levels in the company. (In this respect, the Saudi and Venezuelan pre-nationalization experiences were similar. See Chapter 10.) Given the total lack of any formal education system in the kingdom, this required investing in Saudi capabilities with a very long-term perspective. Thus young Saudi nationals who held junior, unskilled posts were selected for further education and training; the best were sent abroad for school. One legacy of this investment was a rising number of Saudis employed in increasingly higher-level positions as well as an enormous *esprit de corps* among the Saudi employees. To be an "Aramcan" became a major badge of pride for the Saudi employees and opened doors that would have been unthinkable in other oil companies in the region.[18] Many of Aramco's Saudi employees became American corporate animals through and through.

These efforts were epitomized by the project undertaken by Aramco in the early 1950s called "Operation Bultiste" (Coon 1955). At that time, Aramco management realized that for every dollar spent producing oil, twice as much was being spent on basic support services because virtually everything had to be flown in from outside suppliers at high cost. The result was an active effort to persuade some of the brightest young Saudi employees to leave the company and start – with Aramco-backed credit, training, and contracts – private sector companies to produce the services and input required by a modern oil sector. This was effectively the birth of the industrial and commercial development of the Eastern Province and indeed the whole of the kingdom. Both these efforts, inside Aramco and through the creation of an industrial network in tandem, plus its supply of funds and services, put an indelible mark on the company that largely explains its good performance and political durability.

Outside Saudi Arabia the story was quite different, and pressures on Arab governments to nationalize the Western-owned oil companies grew during the 1960s. Rulers, however, were reluctant to oblige. They remembered that the last leader to nationalize had been Iran's Dr. Mossadegh – who overthrew the ruling Pahlavi dynasty in a short-lived coup and found himself sentenced to death when he lost power in the wake of an Anglo-US inspired coup that returned the Pahlavi dynasty to power in 1953. (Mossadegh died in 1967 still under house arrest.) Second, there was a growing concern that oil sales by NOCs outside of established contracts were beginning to undermine the international crude oil pricing structure that the major Western oil companies had created and defended. Further nationalization of the Western-owned oil companies would further reduce those companies' control over the oil market and greatly aggravate this process.

The Six-Day War of June 1967 brought popular demands in the Arab World for nationalization to a peak. To try to defuse this and also to seek greater control over the Western-controlled operating companies such as Aramco, Zaki Yamani came up with the idea of "participation." Producer governments would take an increasing equity share in their operating companies over time. At the same time, the governments would also take equity shares in the downstream operations of the majors. Yamani described participation as a "Catholic marriage" between government and majors, designed to be impossible to dissolve. It also sought to squeeze out the newly arrived small independent oil companies that were undermining the price structure[19] and to send a credible signal to other possible nationalists to avoid upsetting the stable industry organization that had served the large incumbents well. The result of Yamani's efforts was the October 1972 General Agreement on Participation.[20] This gave the governments an initial 25 percent equity that was scheduled to rise to 51 percent in January 1982.

Events on the ground fanned still hotter flames of nationalization and (in nearly all governments except Saudi Arabia) eclipsed Yamani's vision for an orderly shift in participation. In 1971–1972, Algeria and Iraq nationalized their operating companies. Iran withdrew from the final negotiations on "participation" on the grounds that it already "owned" the operating company following the 1951 nationalization. Libya in 1973 announced much better terms from its participation negotiations including an immediate 51 percent equity share. And finally, the Kuwait National Assembly demanded and obtained even higher levels of equity participation, soon reaching 100 percent in 1976. Despite these developments, there was little appetite in Saudi Arabia to speed up the terms of the 1972 agreement because, unlike in most other countries in the region, there was little public mobilization on the streets and most elites believed that continued ownership by the US majors would be more lucrative to the kingdom than outright nationalization. In a context where the company was run on commercial lines and was increasingly employing Saudis and helping the domestic development process, there seemed few benefits from pursuing full control. However, in a region as politically competitive as the Middle East the Al Saud could not be seen to be lagging behind.[21] In February 1974, rumors began to circulate that Saudi Arabia was looking to take over 100% of Aramco (Stevens 1975). Once Kuwait announced (in 1974) it would fully nationalize 100% of its oil company a political "bidding war" emerged; no government wanted to look softer on outsiders than the other. By 1976 Aramco became a de facto 100% Saudi-owned oil company, although the precise dating is uncertain because of the complicated legal status of Aramco as a company incorporated in Delaware.[22]

In many ways, nationalization had little impact on Aramco. Not even the name on the door had changed. (Again, the comparison with Venezuela remains strong. See Chapter 10.) However, over this same period the Saudi government adopted a sweeping series of changes in the organization and structure of its oil sector: a process that had already been under way since 1962 when King Faisal took control over the country and the government sought to create an NOC. It looked not to Aramco but instead to a newly created government body, the General Organization of Petroleum and Minerals (Petromin).[23]

The plan was to turn Petromin into the NOC in waiting with the function of replacing Aramco when the time came. With that aspiration in mind, Petromin's wide mandate covered all exploration, refining, and distribution for oil, gas, and minerals outside the areas controlled by Aramco. It was to be financed from transfers from the central government's budget. During the 1960s, it became the main vehicle for industrialization in the kingdom. It was involved in various mineral projects, exploration, distribution of gas and oil domestically, and also created an oil shipping company. It planned heavy industry joint ventures (with Petromin holding at least 50 percent of the equity), but most of these ambitions were beyond Petromin's capabilities and sank without a trace. By 1970 it employed more than 3,000 but the view was that the employees were underqualified not least because Petromin's governor "didn't like subordinates who were too smart" (Hertog 2008, p. 11). The governor kept strong central control yet the organization's administrative structure remained confused.

After the first oil shock of 1973, Petromin's ambitions strengthened. It announced a series of major export refinery and petrochemical joint ventures with Mitsubishi, Shell, Dow, and Mobil; steel mills with BHP and Marcona; and a major gas-gathering program. Petromin also took on the marketing of the crude oil the government obtained from the new participation agreement. In January 1975, Petromin announced a five-year investment program of $13 billion. To put this in perspective, in that year, the gross fixed capital formation for the country totaled $8 billion. Petromin was clearly trying to dominate the oil sector.

In parallel with Petromin, the government also created the Central Planning Organization with the goal of overseeing economic development of the kingdom. Hisham Nazer, an archrival of Petromin's boss, was selected as president, and when it started its first five-year plan in 1970, it was clear that this new organization was at odds with Petromin's own vision for itself.

The fate of these rival organizations, and most others in the kingdom, hinged on the jockeying for power that occurred after 1975 when Faisal was assassinated and Khalid came to the throne and Prince Fahd became crown prince. Khalid gave Fahd a free hand to oversee Saudi economic development. (By the early 1970s Prince Fahd had already become the effective driver of economic policy and sought rapid industrialization. In 1973 he was named chairman of the Supreme Petroleum Council (SPC), the apparent controller of the oil sector.[24]) In October 1975, the Central Planning Organization became a ministry and Hisham Nazer joined the cabinet as minister of planning. Quickly, Petromin's rival organization dismantled its key projects. The various petrochemical projects were handed over to the ministry, which subsequently created SABIC (Saudi Basic Industries Corporation) in 1976 to oversee their development. This also coincided with the creation of the Royal Commission for Jubail and Yanbu,[25] which further undermined Petromin's position. Significantly, 30 percent of SABIC was sold off to the public and some saw this as a clear indication that the kingdom was moving away from the statist approach characterized by Petromin to a more market orientation (Hertog 2008). This in a way should have been no surprise given that the majority of the younger Saudis making the decisions had all been through American universities that emphasized the advantages of markets over state interference. Petromin was left with just refining and marketing and distribution activities.[26]

Petromin's troubles were not just political but also managerial as the enterprise was increasingly seen as inefficient and ineffective. By the late 1970s Petromin was responsible for selling 1.5–2 million b/d of oil that the country obtained through the participation agreement but as a result began to get a bad reputation for "large-scale improbity" (Hertog 2008, p. 20). In 1979 there was a huge scandal over an Eni deal whereby the Italian company paid a $115 million commission for an oil supply contract. Half went to Italian politicians and the other half to various Saudis. By the early 1980s the refinery projects that Petromin still controlled were in trouble; from 1970 to 1984 Petromin's output of refined product had increased only from 226,000 b/d to 349,000 b/d despite huge inflows of capital. It had grown to a "bureaucratic behemoth planning to employ a further 12,000 staff by 1985." It was losing money and its refinery projects were seriously delayed.[27] As Petromin faltered the government reorganized itself around a new NOC.

In November 1988 a royal decree created Saudi Aramco with Hisham Nazer as chairman to take control of all of Aramco's assets.[28] The SPC, which was supposed to set petroleum policy for the kingdom, was given the official function of approving the company's five-year plans and annual report. It was also tasked with appointing Saudi Aramco's president (upon advice from the main board). In reality, as will be explained below, its actual function was little more than a rubber stamp. Petromin's assets were eventually stripped and reassigned. The lube companies were consolidated by the Ministry of Petroleum and Minerals into Petrolube and Luberef. Its refinery operations were transferred to a new company (the Saudi Arabian Marketing and Refining Company, or Samarec) that was more independent than Petromin. By 1992 Samarec was effectively bankrupt and in June 1993 it was dissolved and its assets taken over by Saudi Aramco.[29] By October 2005 the process was fully complete and Petromin was formally dissolved and its remaining assets handed over to Saudi Aramco. The outcome was a victory for commercialization, markets versus statist options, and for a more performance-driven culture. I was visiting Saudi Arabia at the time of the Samarec takeover in 1993. After a long day of meetings between the Saudi Aramco management and Samarec to discuss the way forward, the Saudi Aramco chair of one meeting suggested reconvening in the morning at 7.00 a.m. When some of the Samarec management objected to such an early start the reply was "Seven o'clock sharp. You are working for Saudi Aramco now!"

3 Saudi Aramco's relationship with the government

Saudi Aramco has always had two objectives. The first is to be a highly successful commercial oil company; later I explore how it achieves that goal. But the second objective is even more vital to its survival: be the supporter of the Saudi national mission. This dual strategy is best expressed in the so-called "golden quadrant idea" (Figure 5.2).[30] All projects can be evaluated on commercial and social terms. Saudi Aramco's managers attempt to locate projects that score well on both dimensions (that is, those in the top right hand corner of Figure 5.2). Appealing in theory, this practice has often yielded tension since the government is particularly keen for Aramco to maximize the social benefit, even at the expense of commercial probity. Determining

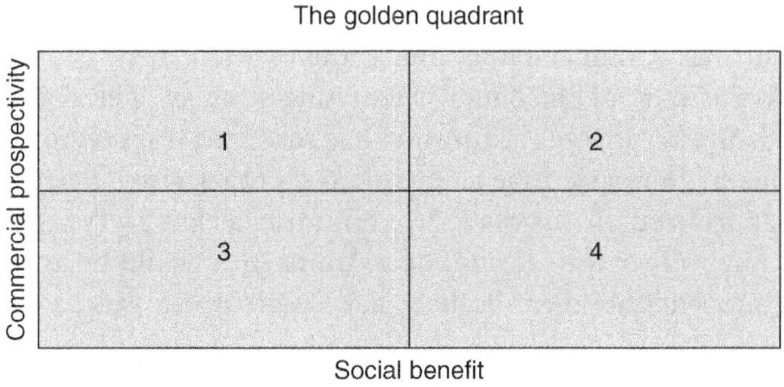

The golden quadrant

Figure 5.2 Golden quadrant idea.

which projects are prized for their social benefits and how the government gets Aramco to pursue them requires looking more closely at the relationship between the enterprise and the state, which is the task of this section.

In 1976 at the time of the takeover of Aramco by the Saudi state, the government's objectives were threefold. First and foremost was survival of the Al Saud ruling family. Saudi Arabia, the country, to all intents and purposes is a family firm. It was created by Abdul Aziz Ibn Saud in 1932 for the benefit of the Al Saud, and the family's prime objective is survival and retention of power and control.[31] All policy objectives in the kingdom are subordinated to that central objective. Most large oil exporters pursue a similar goal, with the result that the NOC is organized to maximize its contributions to the national mission in ways that ensure the popularity of the ruling elite and provide sufficient resources to contain dissent. (For more on government goals see Chapter 2.) In the case of Saudi Arabia, that commonplace goal is combined with the country's unique position in the international oil market due to its large producing capacity and unique ability to carry spare producing capacity. This added a further dimension: Since much of Saudi Arabia's foreign policy revolves around management of the oil market and a lot of the oil market revolves around Saudi oil, Saudi Aramco became an instrument of Saudi foreign policy.[32] However, it remains dangerous to assume linkages between Saudi Aramco's commercial operations and the government's foreign policy on an a priori basis. An example illustrates. Just after the Iraqi invasion of Kuwait in 1990, the Saudi government was negotiating the US troop buildup in response to the invasion. At the time, Saudi Aramco notified its crude customers that there would be a sharp reduction in supplies for the September liftings. Commentators linked the two together asserting the cutback was part of the Saudi negotiating strategy. The reality was that the ministry before the invasion had made the decision to cut back. No one had informed the company to do otherwise. Once the problem was realized all customers were informed that every effort was under way to increase output and extra barrels would be available. The commentators then decided that Saudi Arabia was caving into US pressure!

Second, the Saudi government seeks economic prosperity, which is a necessary (and perhaps also sufficient) condition for survival of the regime and political stability. Thus policy in the petroleum sector has always been closely aligned with the broader development policy objectives of the Saudi government. In practice, the government has struggled to create prosperity outside the oil sector. The eighth five-year plan was launched in December 2005 and contains twelve objectives that are perennial features of earlier plans. They include diversification of the economy and increasing employment for nationals. In turn, these objectives inspire twenty-one "strategies." This plan also claimed to be different from its seven predecessors with its long-term focus to 2024.

Third, the government has sought control of the oil and gas sector to provide financial levers to confirm its legitimacy. Ever since the state's origins, access to funds has been essential for government to assert legitimacy.[33] Firm control over the sector also allows the government to more readily achieve its other goals. However, the state's capacity to regulate the sector – let alone actually operate oil projects – was weak. Therefore it made sense to leave management of most oil issues to Saudi Aramco once the government agreed on the broad strategy. As the government's own capabilities have grown, it has asserted more authority.[34]

Many other NOCs in this book display a divergence between the goals of the state and the behavior of the NOC as its agent. The NOCs become "states within a state" and pursue rents for their own purposes. Saudi Aramco is different because its corporate culture is ingrained with Saudi objectives; the firm's top managers see themselves as guardians of the country's patrimony. Given that the survival of the regime requires strong economic development within the kingdom and that this in turn requires a strong performance from Saudi

Aramco, it is not clear that the objectives of the state and the corporation conflict. This theory, however, was rarely tested until the government attempted to open the upstream in 1998, which appeared to reveal (for a moment) a deep divergence in goals and strategy between the government and its NOC.

3.1 Regulating the oil sector

The system for regulating the oil sector reflects the government's central goals. The ruling family has ultimate control, but as a practical matter it delegates authority to a well-developed system of public administration. The keystone to the formal system is the Supreme Petroleum Council (SPC, renamed in 2000 the Supreme Council on Petroleum and Mineral Affairs, SCPMA). The SPC was supposed to be the effective overseer of the oil sector, allowing other ministries to have some say over how the oil sector operates. Specifically it endorses Saudi Aramco's five-year operating and investment plan and reviews the annual report and accounts of Saudi Aramco and appoints its CEO. In practice the SPC was a means of having a select group of Saudi private citizens, the royal family members, and other ministers play a role in the process. As indicated earlier, in reality its role was minimal and it was the ministry that acted as the government's overseer of the company.[35] For most of the time the SPC simply approved whatever was presented by the board of Saudi Aramco. It has never acted to stop any program of the company or direct any of its activities. The ministry acts as a conduit between the king and his small group of advisors who pass onto the ministry questions or directions. The ministry then directs Saudi Aramco to take whatever action is required.[36]

This closed system of administration minimizing outside interference is crucial to Aramco's success as an NOC because it makes the government goals for the firm clear and generally stable. It creates a protective wall around Saudi Aramco and helps the enterprise avoid the whims of bureaucrats or interest groups whose potential demands could pull Aramco in many directions and extract rents from the enterprise. The experience in neighboring Kuwait is a warning about the outcomes when no such protective wall is in place (see Chapter 8). The tight relationship benefits from clear lines of authority and a particularly close relationship between the company and the Ministry of Petroleum and Natural Resources. As will be developed below, the two institutions in practice are virtually indistinguishable despite their separate functions not least because of the constant exchange of personnel and the fact that the minister since 1995 is a product of Aramco training and corporate culture.[37]

Since the de facto accession of King Abdullah in 1999, the government has reformed its decision-making processes reflecting a concern that the old system had become ineffective and unnecessarily complex as it simply grew with new functions grafted as needed rather than following any overall strategy.[38] Of particular importance was the creation in August 1999 of the (now) thirteen-member Supreme Economic Council, charged with setting strategy for the future development of the kingdom. Because of its overwhelming importance, decisions in the oil sector are the result of attempts at consensus among the senior family members (Obaid 2000), a process informed by expertise drawn mainly from Saudi Aramco and the oil ministry.[39] Abdullah was particularly interested in creating opportunities for the private sector as part of the perennial effort to diversify the economy; a more visible role for the private sector was particularly important to securing entry into the WTO. To signal the shift, in January 2000, Abdullah reformed the SPC by creating the SCPMA – both kept their earlier tasks (i.e., at a de jure level governing Saudi Aramco) along with the new mandate to boost the role of the private sector.[40]

Table 5.1 summarizes the membership of the SCPMA and the Saudi Aramco board. The SCPMA membership is typical of NOC oversight bodies, but the board membership is unusual among NOCs because there are several outside members selected by virtue of their expertise rather than any official position. Indeed, the Saudi Aramco board is not unlike any IOC board containing non-executive directors.

In theory, SCPMA serves as the regulator for the national oil sector and oversees the activities of Saudi Aramco.[41] In practice, Saudi Aramco is virtually self-regulating and SCPMA provides only light supervision, largely endorsing decisions taken by Saudi Aramco. On occasions, however, SCPMA takes a more proactive role, particularly when the issues are more political (such as the gas initiative, discussed later and in Box 5.1). The reason for this "light-touch" regulatory approach is that the SCPMA is dominated by members who believe that Saudi Aramco knows what it is doing and can be

Table 5.1. *Saudi Arabia – membership of oil governance institutions*

Supreme Council on Petroleum and Mineral Affairs SCPMA	Chair = Prime Minister (King) Deputy Chair = Deputy Prime Minister (Crown Prince) Eight Ministers CEO of Saudi Aramco
Saudi Aramco Board	Chair = Minister of Petroleum and Natural Resources Governor of the Capital Market Authority (CMA) Minister of Finance and National Economy President of King Abdulaziz City of Science and Technology (KACST) Head of Saudi Aramco plus three Vice Presidents Retired Presidents Marathon and Texaco; Former Vice Chairman of JP Morgan

Box 5.1 The attempted opening of the upstream in Saudi Arabia

In 1998 then Crown Prince Abdullah took the decision to try to open the upstream to IOCs. The subsequent events proved to be extremely instructive in terms of understanding how the Saudi petroleum sector works and Saudi Aramco's role in it and they are worth considering at some length.[42]

This decision to open the upstream (oil and gas) in principle was taken in the summer of 1998 when the government considered a new position paper prepared by Ministry of Foreign Affairs. This paper was intended to map out a series of major economic reforms to develop the Saudi economy to meet the challenge of growing unemployment (especially among the younger population). The opening was intended to achieve several objectives. First, it was seen as a way to secure support from industrialized countries at a time of an oil price collapse when it was thought the kingdom's purchase of large amounts of military hardware would be increasingly restricted. Second, the resulting investment was to be orientated to providing large numbers of jobs for young Saudis. Third, there were increasing questions within the government, especially in the Ministry of Finance, regarding the performance of Saudi Aramco. Allowing some foreign investment in the petroleum sector was perceived as a mechanism to provide benchmarking and eventually competition.

The rollout of this upstream sector opening was rocky. Crown Prince Abdullah held a meeting in Washington at which the king invited the CEOs of US private oil majors to submit bids to the kingdom. The nature of the bids was deliberately left imprecise but the bids were supposed to present mutually beneficial opportunities for the IOCs and the kingdom. However, there seems to have been limited consultation with Saudi Aramco and the Ministry of Oil on the details of the process. Indeed it was said that while the CEOs of the IOCs were amazed by the offer as it emerged in the meeting, Minister Naimi was even more amazed although there were apparently rumors circulating before the meeting that such an offer might be on the table and so this may not have been the case. There was a serious absence of detail provided to the IOCs that would be needed to allow them to make sensible bids.[43]

It was noticeable that the committee responsible for assessing the projects (created in September 1999) was poorly managed. It did little while its chairman, the Saudi Foreign Minister Prince Faisal, was absent due to illness. Only on his return in early 2000 did things begin to move but even so negotiations were painfully slow. The committee structured the talks in a way that made it very difficult for them to succeed. Thus the competing companies were forced into consortiums for each project preventing them from bidding against each other. The projects involved both upstream and downstream operations without any clear idea of how to structure such agreements. For example, the issue of how gas would be priced and how the tariffs for gas transportation and electricity and water produced from the projects would be set were part of the negotiations. Thus in effect the companies were forced to bid on projects whose economics were unknowable until the agreement was reached. The result was that the consortiums had no competitors and simply demanded a set rate of return on investment equal to the targets for all upstream operations. Yet most of the capital expenditure flowed from the (relatively low risk) utilities that made up the downstream elements of the projects.

Eventually it became clear to the IOCs that upstream oil was not to be on the agenda and attention regarding the opening therefore turned to gas. However, in this case the discussions came up against the completely unrealistic pricing system for gas in the kingdom of 75 cents per million BTU. At such a price the projects were simply not commercially viable even if the units to be fuelled were right on the gas field. In reality they were hundreds of miles away on the coast. On top of this of course was the obvious fact that Saudi Aramco was the only source of expertise competent to assess the IOC proposals and was very hostile to the idea of IOC involvement in the upstream in the kingdom. In December 2000, three core ventures in the Natural Gas Initiative were identified and ten IOCs were invited to bid. However, as indicated, the downstream gas projects being suggested were not highly attractive to the IOCs. They were mainly seeking involvement in the hope that the oil upstream would be opened at some point in the future. In any event, the outcome has been relatively disappointing. Four agreements were signed: SRAK (Shell 40%, Total 30%); Luksar (Lukoil 80%); Sino-Saudi Gas (Sinopec 80%); and a fourth consortium (Eni 50%, Repsol YPF 30%). After three dry wells, Total withdrew from SRAK and the general view is that "tough contract terms combined with surging upstream costs are making it difficult for ... foreign-led consortia that have made discoveries to convert their finds into commercially viable projects" (MEES 51:30, 1).

These events were a rare instance in which the government created hydrocarbon sector policy from above. Previously, it was Saudi Aramco and the Ministry of Oil that laid out plans and strategies for approval by the government. The "opening initiative" came from the government and was perceived by the oil sector as being imposed upon the oil technocrats much to their dismay. It took some time for the sector to reassert its dominance, but ultimately it was successful at doing so because of natural information asymmetries that advantaged operational firms in general and Aramco in particular.

trusted to implement an overall strategy that aligns with the goals of the country. Indeed, there has long been a culture of self-assessment of performance within Saudi Aramco. Aramco's internal governance is marked by clear reporting lines and responsibility. However, the lack of independent assessment makes external observers raise concerns about the company's performance. As is evident in most of the case studies in this book, there are large information asymmetries between the government and the NOC, and they offer many opportunities for rent seeking by the NOC. The extent of such rent seeking is unknown, however.

Thus, as a practical matter, SCPMA relies on the Ministry of Petroleum and Saudi Aramco, and Saudi Aramco relies on its internal procedures for performance assessment that are based on benchmarking exercises that are not transparent even within the company.[44] While benchmarking can be quite effective in the downstream since the laws of physics and chemistry are the same the world over and the relevant technologies relatively mature, in the upstream significant differences in geology raise doubts about its usefulness; Saudi geology provides for very low costs of exploration and production.

The one exception to the rule that SCPMA is unable to exert much oversight, at least in theory, is finances, which are highly transparent to the government and available to SCPMA. However, this information, which includes independently audited financial accounts, is not available outside of the SCPMA for the rest of society or indeed any other part of the government (aside from the eight ministers that are members of the SCPMA).[45] In effect, there is a degree of internal transparency of Saudi Aramco's operations within the Saudi government but extreme opacity outside that small bubble. However, even within that small bubble there are limitations on transparency. The government gets detailed operating reports but these are just descriptions of what each unit has done under the plan but no detailed data is available even within the company. Government auditors only see the overall accounts and do not get business and operations data so they have to accept everything as being done correctly. This system appears on the surface to work well and raises doubts about one of the standard pieces of conventional wisdom offered by outside experts: that public disclosure of performance and other data is a requirement for effective operation. However, because of the lack of transparency it is not clear how much "working well" is simply because of the scale economies of very large fields rather than the company's skills and technology. With fully built-up costs of crude production of around \$2 per barrel[46] a few cents here or there simply becomes "noise."

Thus Saudi Aramco is left, largely, to regulate itself. Apart from production capacity levels (which are set by the government in the context of the kingdom's special role in the world oil market) and a few other decisions, Saudi Aramco sets its own objectives and priorities.[47] (Capacity decisions lie mainly with the ministry, which manages relations with the Organization of Petroleum Exporting Countries (OPEC) and prepares estimates on global supply and demand.) The vehicle for those choices is Aramco's five-year rolling plan that is approved by the board and endorsed by the SCPMA through a process that at least in the past appears to have been largely a formality.

Unlike many other NOCs, which are integrated into the government's financial structure, Saudi Aramco operates on a corporatized basis (Marcel 2006). It is allowed to keep its revenue from crude and product sales and then pays royalties and dividends equivalent to 93 percent of its profits.[48] Sales of crude oil to its own domestic refineries are charged at long-run marginal cost, which is contrary to Western accounting practices but not regarded by the government as a subsidy.[49] This corporate structure allows the company sufficient fiscal predictability to mobilize the capital and operating funds needed to fulfill its objectives. In certain cases involving very large investment projects, the company gets extra funding from the national budget overseen by the Ministry of Finance. When retained earnings are not sufficient, the company can enter the international capital markets to borrow to supplement its access to capital. It has only done this once: in 1996 in order to increase the capacity of its tanker fleet. However, even then it effectively prepaid the loan to avoid the necessity of financial disclosure normal in such transactions.

The company covers its operating costs after the payment of royalties but before paying dividends.[50] This approach leaves Aramco to manage its daily operations with little external interference and a strong incentive to manage costs. Unlike many other NOCs, rumors of corruption in Saudi Aramco's operations are relatively few and far between.[51] It is interesting to reflect why this might be given that Saudi Arabia itself and many of the ruling family are infamous in terms of corrupt practices.[52] Part of the explanation lies in the enterprise's

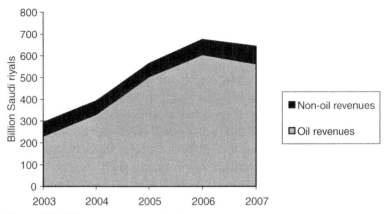

Figure 5.3 Oil revenues contribution to government revenue.
Source: SAMA Annual Report 2008.

own oversight of procurement and managerial processes: a legacy of its former Western partners, notably Exxon, which is famous in the industry for excellence in cost management.

As already indicated, Saudi Aramco's financial relations with the government are based upon a corporatized model. Thus it simply pays royalties, taxes, and dividends to the government in the same way that it did when it was a privately owned company. Unfortunately few details are available. Government accounts include only the line "oil revenues" with no further elaboration. Obviously, that line includes very large numbers, as shown in Figure 5.3 (total government revenue), Figure 5.4 (GDP), and Figure 5.5 (merchandise exports). Oil dominates all, especially government revenue and foreign exchange earnings. And the relatively low oil contribution to GDP is misleading because a significant part of GDP is created by government spending (and thus stems mainly from oil).[53] Based on official reports, in 2008 31% of Saudi GDP was oil, but that fraction excluded the 22% of real GDP that came from the government sector funded largely by oil revenues. Thus the effective contribution of oil to GDP was much higher than 31%. Accounting is also complicated by the use of oil for barter, such as the Al-Yamamah[54] deal whereby Britain sold Tornado aircraft in return for crude oil.

From these numbers, it is perfectly clear that the oil sector and Saudi Aramco's performance are crucial to the well-being of the kingdom.

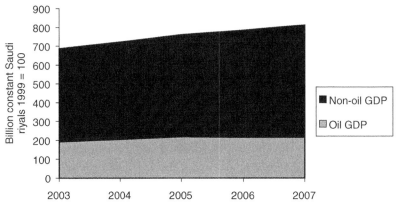

Figure 5.4 Oil GDP contribution to total GDP.
Note: At constant 1999 prices.
Source: SAMA Annual Report 2008.

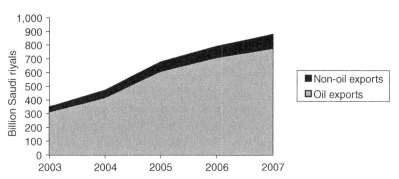

Figure 5.5 Oil contribution to merchandise export, 2003–2007.
Source: SAMA Annual Report 2008.

4 Governance and strategy

The concept of corporate governance is difficult to pin down for
state enterprises since state ownership often leads to corporate
goals and practices that are different from conventional commercial firms. A group of NOCs recently attempted to outline their
views of this question in the Chatham House Document "Good
Governance of the National Petroleum Sector" (Lahn *et al.* 2007).[55]
Its conclusions reveal that NOC managers worry about most of

the same factors that concern managers of commercial firms, such as the need for clarity in goals; freedom and ability of managers to perform assigned tasks; accountability for decision making; and transparency. By nearly all the principles identified in that document – except external transparency – Saudi Aramco scores well. We have already seen the reasons for this secrecy. Saudi Arabia is by nature a secretive society.[56] It is also a very patriarchal society based upon "client-patron" relationships, which tends not to be conducive to the sharing of information. Consultation between rulers and ruled tends to occur at the level of individuals rather than collectively and is not governed by general procedures. As one Saudi Aramco manager remarked when challenged on the lack of external transparency "what right do people have to know when they pay no taxes and when the government provides all needed services" (Marcel 2006, p. 143).

Saudi Aramco's organizational chart will be familiar in most other NOCs and commercial firms. The firm is headed by a president and CEO. Operations are divided into six areas (most important being exploration and production) each led by a senior vice president. Overall governance of the firm is shared between the president and CEO and the corporate management committee. This committee, which reviews all major operational decisions, dates to the 1940s when Aramco needed an institution for discussing strategy and aligning the interests of the Aramco partners. In 1950, Saudi representatives were included (Brown 1999). After the Saudi state fully took over the company in 1976 the committee continued. During the reign of Ali Naimi, the first Saudi CEO under full Saudi ownership, it consisted of the six senior VPs for the various business lines – with the accession of Jum'ah in 1995, the number of senior executives on the committee was increased and decision making became more based on a consensus approach. In 2009, Khalid Al Falih was appointed president and CEO as Jum'ah retired.[57]

4.1 Human capital

A crucial part of the Saudi Aramco story is the fact that the company, unlike so many other NOCs, has been able to maintain control of its hiring and promotion decisions. It is under pressure to hire Saudis, to be sure, but that pressure is general and chronic throughout the kingdom; particular employment decisions reside almost entirely within the company and are made through merit processes that are evident at some other well-performing NOCs such as Petrobras (see Chapter 12). Thus the management, unlike many other NOCs in the region, has been able to avoid being saddled with poorly performing staff. There is rumored to exist in Dhahran (Marcel 2006) an office block where poorly performing staff are given an office and then basically ignored and allowed to do whatever they want thereby preventing them from interfering with the operations of the company.[58] (Firing such staff members is not a viable option in Saudi culture and in any case is restricted by law.) Saudi Aramco is very proud of the fact that it has developed a cadre of highly professional Saudis to run the company and this is very apparent from standard company documents that devote considerable attention to the issue. The company "seeks to be the best, to surpass other NOCs; it gives special emphasis to professionalism and technology" (Marcel 2006, p. 54). While promotion traditionally has been based upon merit, there is concern among senior management that this is weakening and that political loyalties are gaining influence.

Aramco and then Saudi Aramco adopted a mentoring system whereby potential senior management material effectively shadowed senior staff as part of their learning experience. This was particularly prevalent when the expatriate management was much larger than in recent years.

Executives come through the ranks and through an extremely thorough education and career development. It has been estimated that Saudi Aramco spends around $500 million per year on human resource development (Marcel 2008). The company runs the Industrial Training Centre in Dhahran. Employees spend an initial year there and if they pass they are then given full scholarship to use in overseas universities up to Ph.D. level. Since 1994, 4,800 Saudi nationals have succeeded in completing university degrees (Jaffe and Elass 2007). In 2009, the new CEO announced two new training initiatives – the Saudi Technical Petroleum Services Institute in Dammam and the General Organization for Technical Educational and Vocational Training located in Al Hasa. Both will provide technical education for Saudi Aramco employees but also for some from other local employers.

In August 2007 there was a major shakeup in the senior management. The main thrust was bringing in a younger generation of executives.[59] An important point is that these were products of Saudi Aramco as an NOC, whereas those being replaced had grown up within an Aramco dominated by the personnel of the Aramco partners. Thus the new generation has an imperative to modernize the company as well as a more global view than previous generations. For example, Abdullah Jum'ah, CEO for fourteen years, was with the company forty years and was trained by Aramco's Western managers. The new CEO, Khalid Al Falih, joined the company only after the Saudi government had taken full ownership of the enterprise. He is an engineer (Juma'ah was a political scientist by education) and is expected to play a more hands-on role within the company (MEES 51:45[60]). He has a reputation for hard work and as a very tough negotiator.[61] It is widely expected that many contracts will face the prospects of renegotiation.

The CEO leads a company that incorporates two distinct cultures uneasily. The first is the culture of a large American multinational corporation. The language of the company is English and thirty years' service is rewarded with a gold watch! It also continues to operate within a closed compound that is certainly physically separated from the immediate surroundings and is arguably also psychologically separated. Saudi women can drive within the walls of the compound.[62] It has also been suggested that there exists a "fortress culture" that makes Saudi Aramco removed from Saudi society and realities (Marcel 2006).

The second dimension of Saudi Aramco's culture is Saudi.[63] Saudi society is very tightly controlled and is extremely formal and hierarchical. While Saudi Aramco is actually "less formal and hierarchical" (Marcel 2006, p. 62), inevitably there are elements of a mirror image. Individual initiative is not particularly encouraged and group loyalty is seen as extremely important, which is why employees are seldom critical, especially to outsiders.[64] Indeed it is a noticeable trait of Saudi Aramco employees that they tend to avoid talking publicly. Managers tend to micromanage because "they are concerned about any wrongdoings or inefficiencies being uncovered on their watch" (Marcel 2006, p. 68). And the fortress culture described above may make the management resistant to change (Marcel 2006, p. 63).

These two cultures – Western corporate and Saudi – coexist. And much effort has gone into trying to formalize the company's management culture. The most visible aspects of this make the company look like a normal, commercial firm – with the same slogans and goals. The Saudi element is more elusive and difficult to formalize.[65]

Saudi Aramco appears to be a leading investor among NOCs in research and development. These investments include the massive contribution to human capital, including overseas training for the most promising employees, already discussed. In addition, there are dedicated research and development institutions. The most important is the Exploration and Petroleum Engineering Center (EXPEC), inaugurated in May 1983 to be responsible for R&D in the upstream. By 1993 it had become one of the largest upstream earth science and engineering centers in the industry. As a result, the company "has essentially eliminated its dependence on upstream technological support from other oil firms and now provides technical expertise and special services in-house in all facets of engineering and producing operations" (Saddad Al Husseini, quoted in *Saudi Aramco World*, September/October 1993).[66] It is through EXPEC that Saudi Aramco has introduced a great many new technologies to the kingdom, ranging from advanced three-dimensional seismic surveying to horizontal drilling and geosteering. EXPEC has also spawned other institutions, such as the Advanced Research Center (EXPEC ARC) and a linked EXPEC Computer Center (ECC). ECC is responsible for seismic processing, interpretation, and modeling; reservoir simulation and description; graphic display and information management. Early in 2007 an external advisory council was created composed of five renowned international scientists and charged with ensuring that EXPEC did not become too inwardly focused (Amin H. Nasser, vice president, petroleum engineering and development, as reported by *Saudi Aramco Week*, February 26, 2007).[67]

4.2 Strategy and investment choices

Ultimately, these factors – the company's organization, its investment in human capital, and its culture – inform its choices in the context of operations and investments. Here we examine those choices, with a special focus on Saudi Aramco's strategy.

In broad terms, as outlined earlier the company has three broad goals that drive its overall strategy. First, it sees itself as the guardian of the country's patrimony, which influences the way in which it manages the hydrocarbon resources. Second, it sees itself as the main agent in executing the state's objectives. Third, controversially it can be said that it seeks to protect and develop the position of the company within the Saudi oil sector.[68] Given this context the company has developed strategies that for oil relate to recovery rates on the fields, capacity levels, production levels, marketing, and downstream issues and for gas relate to the nature of developments and the deployment of the gas resources. Each will be considered in turn.

4.2.1 Oil
4.2.1.1 Recovery rates and reserves
A long-standing and long-term objective has been to maximize recovery on the fields. Following this approach, Saudi Aramco has maintained a maximum annual depletion of 2–3 percent of the remaining reserves, which corresponds with a notional reserve life of thirty years from 2009.[69] In a June 2008 speech, Amin Nasser explained that Saudi Aramco would not put any field into development without a minimum thirty-year plateau (MEES 51:26). The average recovery factor on the Saudi fields has been 50%, compared with an industry average of 35%; the target is to increase this level to 70%, which would be the equivalent of 80 billion barrels of extra reserves.[70]

Regarding exploration, the official objective is to replace every barrel produced. Amin Nasser in his June 2008 speech argued that "a sense of stewardship and long-term sustainability run though the company" (MEES 51:26, 2). Higher production would require greater reserves. Thus in recent years the strategy has also been to create a considerable expansion in Saudi Aramco's exploration efforts.[71] The official target (MEES 51:26) is to increase original oil in place from the current (2008) level of 735 billion barrels to 900 within 20 years. Saudi Aramco does not include probable or possible reserves in its estimates. This makes its reserve estimates among the most conservative in the industry.

4.2.1.2 Production capacity
Since the early 1970s, Aramco and the government had been in discussion to determine the basis for a long-term plan for capacity expansion. Figures were mooted of 20 million b/d by the early 1980s but this was lowered to 16 million b/d as demand slowed following

the first oil shock (Parra 2004).[72] There was also concern that high production levels would produce a peak scenario (of 16 million b/d, which the company could not maintain for more than fifteen years). Under this scheme, investment in the necessary infrastructure would be unlikely to produce an acceptable return. As a result, the government imposed a ceiling of 8.5 million b/d in early 1978 just before the second oil shock.[73]

Following the change in oil policy in mid 1985, a central plank of the Saudi oil strategy that has developed was to maintain a cushion of spare capacity to allow the kingdom to manage the international oil market. In particular, the aim was to limit price spikes in the event of any outage of crude oil production in the international markets. This was a key part of the strategy to maintain low and stable prices to try to reverse the moves away from oil as a primary energy source to the world, which resulted from the oil price shocks of the 1970s. While this role of developing and maintaining spare crude producing capacity was a major target for Saudi Aramco, it was in fact imposed by their government.

The stated objective was to maintain a cushion of spare capacity amounting to 1.5–2 million b/d to act as a stabilizing force for the global oil market.[74] In 2005, the official capacity target was 12.5 million b/d by 2009,[75] which appears to have been achieved. There was talk around 2004–2005 about expanding this to 15 million b/d (MEES 51:26). However, following growing concerns about future oil demand in 2007 this target although not being completely ruled out was being quietly dropped. It reemerged briefly in June 2008 at the producer–consumer meeting in Jiddah, where Saudi Arabia came under pressure from the major oil consumers to "do more" to mute the apparently inexorable rise in oil prices. However, the collapse in prices after July and the looming economic recession/depression following the collapse of Lehman Brothers in September 2008 has meant that such targets appear at least for the moment off the agenda.

4.2.1.3 Production
The actual production strategy has been, since 1985, to try to balance the international oil market to achieve the desired oil price target. Since 1985, the term "swing producer" became very much a dirty word in the Saudi oil sector given the pain incurred by this

role between 1982 and 1985 (described below). However, playing such a role is effectively what the kingdom does, trying as OPEC's leading producer to balance the market. The trading strategy behind this will be explained below. What the price target is and how much is needed to achieve this target is an oil ministry decision (ultimately approved by the king) although as already explained, Saudi Aramco has an important input in terms of information into these decisions.

4.2.1.4 Marketing
The strategy with respect to crude marketing has been driven by the need to bring stability to the markets, defend a price that does not destroy long-term demand, and secure the maximum revenue possible within the overall price target. Two features characterize the crude marketing strategy: no spot sales of crude and destination clauses in the crude lifting contracts.

The crude is sold on three monthly rolling contracts based on three spot crude prices that have a clear and relatively transparent market. Deliveries to the United States are based on WTI;[76] deliveries to Europe on Brent; and finally deliveries to Asia are based on an average of Dubai and Omani crude. For each formula price there are "adjustment factors" applied. However, the basis for this has never been made explicit, and the adjustments are made by Saudi Aramco without explanation. In the words of a well-respected observer of the industry this process was described as "a little monthly ad hoc finagling, the details of which are not published and not generally known" (Frank Parra, MEES 45:38, D3). In addition to this "fiddling" with the formulae there was also a freight adjustment factor for West of Suez destinations (i.e., the United States and Europe) although deliveries to the Far East faced no such freight adjustment.[77]

These prices are announced at the start of the month based on market conditions in the previous month and are applicable to the following month. Such conditions relate to things such as sweet and sour differentials, the level of refining margins, and the implicit netback value of the crude. However, as indicated the process lacks any transparency. Put very simply, the prices are set based on what the Saudis believe the market will bear. The significance of this price-setting process is that other OPEC prices tend to "pretty much follow" these Saudi formulae prices.

Saudi Aramco's international strategy has been related to the crude export trade and the downstream. The company decided early on that investing in the upstream outside of the kingdom made little sense because it would divert Saudi national resources toward creating a cash cow for another government to milk and to compete in OPEC's markets. This strategy contrasts with that of other NOCs operating in countries with poor domestic prospects (Petronas) or with exportable technical skills (Statoil and Petrobras). Since domestic prospects for further development of reserves within the kingdom are so large, upstream operations abroad were unnecessary.[78]

A key part of Saudi Aramco's downstream strategy has been to create its own tanker capacity to ensure sufficient capacity to be able to carry the crude exports. In January 2006, it was announced that VELA, the tanker company, a wholly owned subsidiary of Saudi Aramco, had ordered six 318,000 dwt tankers to add to its existing fleet of twenty-three tankers.

4.2.1.5 Downstream – domestic

It was clear from the way in which Yamani crafted his proposals on "participation" in 1968 that he and the Saudi leadership had strategic ambitions to extend Saudi Arabia's operations downstream into refining, marketing, and distribution. This downstream strategy was rooted in several aspects of the aftermath of the initial oil shock in 1973–1974. First, the dramatic increase in prices had significantly increased government revenue giving great scope for investment – indeed, the higher revenues created a necessity to find new places to invest these new profits. Second, the process of nationalization meant that the NOCs could no longer readily rely on the majors to plan refinery investments to dispose of crude in the largest markets.[79] Finally, in the economic development literature there was a growing strand of what became called the "unbalanced growth" argument. This idea had come as a reaction to the "balanced growth" approach of the 1950s, which argued a developing economy should grow all sectors smoothly in a coordinated way to avoid wasteful surpluses and shortages (Hirschman 1958). Unbalanced growth maintained that if a country could fine-tune its growth in such a balanced way, it would not be a developing country in the first place. Thus the real barrier to economic development was a shortage of managerial decision making, and in practice this argued for the concentration of talent in a leading development sector, which would shock the moribund economy into action by making extremely obvious the various bottlenecks such that even the poorest decision makers could see what was needed.[80] For the oil-producing economies this sector would obviously be oil in all its dimensions, rather than just production of the commodity with other firms and countries gaining the value from upgrading the commodity to a final product.[81] However, to promote development the economies had to reduce dependence on exporting crude oil.

Given these factors, Saudi Arabia announced four projects to build export refineries in the kingdom. In October 1975 in Damascus, a meeting of the Organization of Arab Petroleum Exporting Companies (OAPEC) was convened so members could compare their downstream plans. When the full extent of the plans emerged from the meeting, virtually all of the attendees scuttled back to their capitals and cancelled the projects. The reason was simple. In 1975, refinery capacity outside of the Soviet Union was operating only at 70 percent (BP 2008) following the slowdown in oil demand after the first oil shock. This event had devastated refinery profitability and the prospect of even further unused capacity was extremely unattractive. The exception was Saudi Arabia, which decided to go ahead with its plans.[82] However, the decision was made by the ministry that this new domestic refinery capacity would be based on joint ventures with IOCs.

The reasons for choosing the joint venture route to develop the domestic refineries were complex. First, there was the fact that Aramco had been an upstream company. Saudi Aramco was short of national technical and managerial experience in building and operating refineries.[83] To be sure, it could learn but the company was still struggling to manage the upstream operations over which it had taken full control in 1976.[84] It was partly for this reason that Petromin had initial responsibility for developing the domestically located export refineries. Petromin in fact had very little experience in anything and foreign partners were essential. Second, there was the obvious point that these were export refineries whose output was to be marketed abroad. Therefore, having foreign partners with an existing downstream marketing capability made a great deal of sense.

More recently, Saudi Aramco's downstream strategy has been linked into its wider international strategy as explained below. However, in domestic terms it has been simply to ensure that the kingdom has sufficient domestic refining capacity to meet domestic demand for oil products. This has been comfortably achieved. It also sees owned refinery capacity as providing security of demand for its crude oil exports and there is an informal target to create enough refinery capacity at home and abroad to process 50 percent of crude output (Al-Moneef 1998).

In November 2006, it was announced that Saudi Arabia's domestic refinery capacity would be increased from 1.9 million b/d to 3 million b/d by 2010. While some of this expansion would come from Saudi Aramco's refineries, there was also a stated intention to involve private sector investment.[85]

4.2.1.6 Downstream – abroad

Downstream plans abroad have been at the center of Saudi Aramco's strategy for some considerable time.[86] Part of the logic for this comes from the aftermath of the first oil shock of 1973 with its consequent access to revenues on a grand scale and ideas of a leading development sector outlined earlier. However, there were other reasons. There was what might be termed a cultural legacy. The Aramco partners had all been operationally vertically integrated IOCs working in many countries. Thus if Saudi Aramco was to be a serious player, it too had to follow suit. There was also the concept of locking in export markets. During the dark days of the defense of price between 1982 and 1985[87] there was a growing realization among the OPEC countries that they were competing with non-OPEC producers for market share and that they were losing since non-OPEC countries could simply shave prices to make their crude more attractive. As demand security became a growing issue, an obvious solution was to secure crude markets by owning the refineries.[88] A particularly important experience in this regard for Saudi Arabia was in the early 1980s when the former Aramco partners refused to lift Saudi crude because of the relatively high government official sales prices.[89] Memories of this event persuaded Ali Naimi and others within Saudi Aramco that they needed a wider, more diversified customer base and also needed to take greater control of crude marketing. This helped drive plans to expand the downstream.

Finally, there was a realization that operating abroad gave the company much greater freedom from interference by its own government. As many of the other case studies have shown, this was derived from ideas associated with principal–agent analysis. Thus

locating downstream activities abroad, especially using operational vertical integration, deepened the information asymmetries
between principal (the controlling ministry) and agent (the NOC
management). This allowed the NOC management to pursue extensive rent seeking. However, the relevance of this as a driver in the
case of Saudi Aramco is not obvious. As this case study is indicating, the corporate culture within the company was such that there
was a sense of responsibility and pride among the Saudi Aramco
management as "guardians of the country's patrimony." While it
is easy to be cynical about such grand statements, it would suggest
that rent seeking was much less in Saudi Aramco than in other
NOCs. However, providing hard evidence to support such a view is
extremely difficult.[90]

Saudi Aramco began to develop its downstream operations abroad
in 1988 by creating a joint venture – Star Enterprise. This allowed
Saudi Aramco to acquire a 50 percent stake in Texaco's three refineries at Delaware City, Louisiana, and Port Arthur. However, the
strategy was in many ways different from that of PDVSA or KPC.[91]
As already explained, the domestic refinery expansion in the 1970s
had been done through the process of joint ventures with a large
number of foreign companies. It was therefore no surprise that the
same model was used when downstream assets were being developed. Furthermore, KPC's experience buying poor assets made
Saudi Aramco very wary of buying other companies' "cast-offs" (see
Chapter 8). Thus the process was developed at a much slower pace.[92]
A key reason for the joint venture approach was that Saudi Aramco,
at least before the takeover of Samarec in 1993, had no experience
of selling oil products internationally. The experience and infrastructure of the foreign partners were essential for the commercial success
of the ventures.

The move downstream abroad was also complicated because while
Saudi Aramco was looking for commercial advantages, in particular to secure market outlets for its crude, the government of Saudi
Arabia also had its own agendas in the field of foreign policy. A
good example of how politics and commerce intermix is the Star
Enterprise joint venture based upon Texaco's refinery at Port Arthur
cited above. Saudi Aramco, under instructions from its government,
insisted on supplying the refinery with Saudi crude despite the fact
that Texaco argued it would have been much better to have run

Venezuelan crude through the refinery. The additional cost was born by Saudi Aramco because the Saudi government wanted to be a crude supplier into the United States to strengthen political links between the two countries.[93]

4.2.2 Gas

The willingness and ability to deliver natural gas domestically has been a major part of the development story in Saudi Arabia and the government has long taken a proactive approach with respect to gas. In 1975, the oil ministry decided that the extensive flaring of associated gas should cease. This for some time had been a bone of contention between the Aramco partners and the government given the poor economics of gathering and processing gas. However, the government saw the associated gas as an integral part of the country's natural resource base and felt simply flaring it was inappropriate. To that end the master gas system (MGS) was planned and executed by Saudi Aramco.[94] As well as supplying gas for Saudi Aramco's own operations the MGS supplies fifty-four other companies including power and desalination plants plus twenty-one large petrochemicals plants, eighteen owned by SABIC and three owned by private sector interests.

However, it is clear that up to the late 1990s some parts of the government believed the company was not paying enough attention to gas (Marcel 2006). This view that gas was being neglected was to some extent reflected in the upstream opening process described above. It also explains the apparently greater emphasis on gas within Saudi Aramco in recent years. The MGS currently is undergoing further expansion to manage 9.3 billion cubic feet per day (bcfd) of gas and produce 7 bcfd of sales gas. This was in part to catch up but also designed to preempt opposition in Riyadh.

The role of gas as a domestic fuel is a controversial subject. The conventional wisdom argues that for an oil exporter it makes sense to replace domestic oil consumption with gas in order to free up oil for export, which has greater value for the country. However, for Saudi Arabia this is a doubtful argument. It assumes that there is some form of constraint upon the capacity to export crude that can be relieved by substituting gas for oil in domestic consumption. However, Saudi Arabia's export constraint is not an inability to increase production. It is only related to the fact that if the kingdom exports more oil, it threatens the global pricing structure, which will reduce revenues. Thus the decision of what to burn domestically should revolve only around the cost of supplying the fuel. Gas tends to be more expensive than oil to produce and certainly to transport. Thus the benefits of using gas instead of oil are far from clear-cut.[95]

5 Saudi Aramco's performance

To achieve the strategic objectives described above, the company must undertake and operate projects, which requires investment, construction, and operations. The company has been described as a "patient investor" (Marcel 2006, p. 73) and "in the game for the long term" (Marcel 2006, p. 162). Investment plans are drawn up within the context of the five-year rolling plan. The company uses a variable hurdle rate that any project must pass before it is then considered in greater detail. The hurdle rate tends to change with market conditions but is relatively high reflecting management's conservative investment strategy. Generally the approach and methodologies used in the project appraisals are those used by any large IOC. However, the golden quadrant is always present as a consideration to allow inclusion of national mission elements in the decision process.

Unfortunately as already discussed at length, there is little public information available on the details of these processes.[96] Thus details regarding how risk is regarded and managed, who makes the final decisions, etc., are simply not known.[97] Based on my casual observations over the years, however, the impression is gained that the company operates on the basis of striving to achieve a consensus based on sound analysis both in terms of economics and engineering considerations. As for judging performance, as indicated earlier, great attention is paid internally to the use of benchmarking techniques to provide bases for comparison.[98]

This section is an attempt to assess the performance of Saudi Aramco despite these problems. Performance is hard to measure, but the impressionistic conclusion advanced here is that Aramco's performance is good when measured against its strategic objectives and its operational context in terms of capacity and production levels as determined by the government. This conclusion is based on its record on project delivery and its contribution to the "national mission." What follows tries to give some justification for this assertion.

Typically, one would measure performance of an oil company by focusing on the size and return on capital employed; finding, development, and production costs; and many other typical corporate metrics used to assess the performance of any company (Stevens 2008c). However, these are difficult to muster and evaluate in the case of Saudi Aramco because as indicated the data is not available in the public domain. As is rare among NOCs, the shareholder (the Saudi government) has access to complete and high-quality data about the enterprise's performance in terms of the overall finances. NOCs that become "states within a state" are usually opaque to all outsiders, including government owners. For Aramco, a measure of transparency exists within the government's inner circle even while those outside of the government see an opaque operation.[99]

The tension created by external opacity was evident when questions arose about the quality of Aramco's legendary oil reserves. In 2005 Matt Simmons produced an article – subsequently a book (Simmons 2005b) – that argued that the Saudi reserves were grossly overstated. He also claimed that Ghawar, the biggest Saudi oil field that accounts for half the enterprise's output, was being badly managed and faced steep declines in production. In response, Saudi Aramco gave a public presentation at the CSIS (Center for Strategic and International Studies) in Washington refuting Simmons' claims and presenting more data than ever before explaining part of the basis of the reserve estimates. The debate continues to rumble on. In June 2008, the company claimed that the water cut in Ghawar (which is the fraction of produced liquid that is water, rather than oil, and one indicator of a field's maturity) is 28 percent (and falling) compared with an industry norm of 80 percent (MEES 51:26). However, Simmons has seeded a tempest. And further doubts arose when Saddad Husseini, the former head of exploration and production in Saudi Aramco, publicly began to doubt some of the claims being made for possible capacity expansions. By implication, the enterprise was performing poorly.

The problem with that approach to assessing performance is that reserves are so large that particular reserve announcements do not necessarily have any bearing on what the firm can produce. Moreover, even looking at output is a poor measure of performance because production levels are political choices rooted in efforts by the government to manage the oil markets. From 1945 until the early 1970s, Saudi output rose steadily (Figure 5.6).

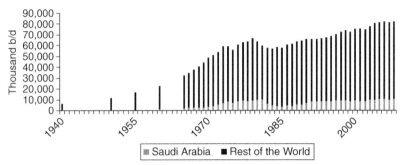

Figure 5.6 Saudi Arabian and world oil output, 1940–2008.
Sources: 1940–1960 – Darmstadter (1971); OPEC Statistical Bulletin 2008; 1965–2008 – BP Statistical Review of World Energy 2009.

However, this steady growth hides important elements of the story. Up to 1960, Aramco's production to some extent was constrained by the joint venture system that dominated production from the Middle East (Blair 1976). This system was designed to manage the potential oversupply from the region by restricting output to what could be refined and resold reliably, which constrained the ability of the majors to increase capacity. In particular, the "average programme quantity" (APQ) system in Iran[100] meant "the Aramco partners have been in a position to exert a downward influence on Iranian output" (Blair 1976, p. 105). Also, Aramco itself had a mechanism to penalize any partner wishing to produce above its equity share.[101] During the 1960s, these control mechanisms began to fray around the edges as new players entered Eastern Hemisphere oil markets and as the majors themselves began to develop capacity outside of the Middle East and its control mechanisms. However, growth in global oil demand as a result of the "OECD economic miracle" disguised this erosion of control (Stevens 2008a).

Figure 5.6 shows Saudi Arabia's oil production in the context of global oil production. After the first oil shock of 1973–1974 a clear pattern emerges with Aramco's (and then Saudi Aramco's) production. In effect, Saudi Aramco becomes the swing producer and so global supply follows closely what Saudi Arabia decides to produce.[102]

The function of the swing producer was to manage prices and in particular to defend particular prices. The decision to take up this role, and the way in which the role was played, was entirely a political decision with the oil ministry acting as the prime mover. After 1973–1974 and until 1978 Saudi acted as swing producer. This was a deliberate policy to manage OPEC but also because it could swing given the fall in oil demand following the first oil shock. The same story is true between 1982 and 1985. It was only in 1985 that, as described earlier, spare capacity became an explicit policy. Before then it had simply happened by accident.[103] Saudi Aramco's role (apart from producing what was required) was twofold. The first was to provide the information necessary to allow the ministry to decide what would and what would not balance the market. The second was to maintain a cushion of spare capacity so that Saudi Arabia could reliably play this swing role under any circumstance. By August 1985 output had fallen to 2.34 million b/d (from 10.5 mbd in 1980) as the government tried to protect prices.[104] As this policy emerged, it became increasingly difficult to measure Aramco's performance just by looking at output.[105] The willingness of the Saudi government to take on this role of controller and stabilizer of the market is rooted in many obscure factors (Stevens 2008a). Fundamentally, no other country could play this role, and some semblance of order in the market – an order previously supplied by the Western majors who controlled access to oil users – was in the interests of the government and Saudi Aramco.

Given the difficulty of using standard metrics for performance, this study will adopt a different approach and explore two other metrics: performance against self-declared targets and contributions to Saudi state mission.[106] The former offers a window on what the leaders of the enterprise think is feasible and achievable. The latter allows exploration of whether and how the enterprise meets the goals of its masters.

Self-declared (within Saudi Aramco) targets concern whether projects come in on time and on budget. In general the company prides itself on its ability to do precisely that and most of the projects certainly have come in on time. By this metric, Aramco has performed extremely well. Only in the period of high prices around 2008, when there were serious shortages in the supply of upstream services, has there been some slippage but this is in a context where such constraints have generally caused delays on projects everywhere. For example, in September 2008 the Khursaniyah field development came onstream after originally being scheduled to be ready for the

end of 2007 (MEES 51:36). It is however a huge project aimed at producing 500,000 b/d, 580 mcfd of gas and 290,000 b/d of NGLs. The
reason given for the delay was late delivery of equipment. In a similar
vein it was announced in July 2008 that utility contracts had been
awarded for the 900,000 b/d offshore Manifa project. It was expected
that these would have been awarded at the start of 2008 but were
delayed "at the request of contractors" amid growing concern about
cost escalations (MEES 51:27). The project was supposed to come
onstream in 2011 and the delays have prompted speculation that the
project might be behind schedule, but Saudi Aramco has expressed
confidence it will deliver according to plan although the field is not
expected to be at capacity until 2012.[107] In a presentation in June
2008, Amin Nasser, the senior VP for exploration and development,
denied delays to the capacity expansion plans to 12.5 million b/d and
claimed they would come in on schedule (MEES 51:26).[108]

As for keeping to budget, the absence of financial data makes it
impossible to assess whether this has been the case. In some projects,
costs have probably been high because of the need for haste. A classic example was in 1995 when the company hurriedly developed the
Shaybah fields with a capacity of 0.5 million b/d. The speed of this
development, it was rumored, led to much higher costs than normal.[109] However, it is not clear that cost control is the highest issue on
the company's agenda. More important is getting a project done well
and on time although cost issues can arise if prices are relatively low.

As for the Saudi state mission, this is central to Saudi Aramco's operations. Assessing the national mission of an NOC is difficult and controversial – in assessing the right missions for evaluation and in measuring
performance (Stevens 2008c). Conventionally it can be defined using
Albert Hirschman's approach of examining three kinds of "linkages":
fiscal, forward, and backward (Hirschman 1981). Fiscal linkages refer
to how much revenue the company generates for the government. We
have already examined those linkages, which are massive.

Forward linkages refer to the provision of inputs (energy) for the
rest of the economy together with the provision of skilled manpower
and good business practices being fed into the rest of the economy.
The oil sector is, not surprisingly, an active supplier of oil and gas. Oil
and gas are priced for local consumption at long-run marginal production costs rather than international prices, explaining why final
product prices in Saudi Arabia are far lower than the world price and

why Aramco's refining division nonetheless posts a profit.[110] Despite very low prices, there is no evidence of shortages (unlike in Iran, for example, where low pricing is not married with integrated control over supply chains and the much larger local population leads to much greater overconsumption; see Chapter 6). Indeed, Saudi Aramco's downstream strategy has entailed building surplus refining capacity; about one-third of its local refining is exported at world prices. There can be little doubt that in terms of supplying oil products to the domestic economy – a goal set by the Saudi government – Saudi Aramco has been a success (although given its very high production levels this has been an easy target to meet). Whether this is good public policy is another matter, since average cost pricing in a low-cost country leads to prices far below international levels although technically they are not subsidized. In the negotiations for Saudi Arabia's accession to the WTO, the government managed (amazingly) to persuade the WTO that Saudi Aramco was not actually a state-controlled enterprise but could be treated as a commercial entity. Therefore low feedstock prices based on actual long-run marginal cost rather than border prices were accepted as not being a subsidy. This decision by the WTO was crucial for Saudi Arabia's future role in international petrochemical markets.

A consequence of these low prices is that domestic energy consumption in the kingdom has grown extremely rapidly and energy intensities are extremely high. In 2009, for the first time, elements within the oil techno-structure have begun to suggest that domestic oil product prices should be moved closer to international prices to encourage more efficient usage.[111]

In addition to forward linkages of energy, Saudi Aramco has also supplied skilled manpower to other parts of the Saudi economy. The most spectacular example was Operation Bultiste (mentioned above). It has also been important in spreading good modern business practices and governance to the rest of the economy. It is not surprising that the recent plans by King Abdullah to create a new university and a major energy "think tank" within the kingdom have been given to Saudi Aramco to execute. Quite simply it is regarded as the best managerial institution in the country, and when the Saudi government needs a vital project performed, it often turns to Saudi Aramco.

Backward linkages are the effects of the enterprise on supply chains that, in turn, can help to develop the rest of the economy. Aramco and then Saudi Aramco have been central to the economic development of the Eastern Province and have always gone to considerable lengths to maximize the backward linkages to the rest of the economy to encourage the availability of local factor inputs. However, attempts to maximize local input have always been done on a commercial basis with no regulatory requirements. Efforts to increase local content have taken many forms. There has been a long history of Saudi Aramco creating joint ventures with private sector companies, teaching them skills, and then selling its shares to the private sector companies. In terms of purchasing, Saudi Aramco claims that in 2000, 86 percent of their purchases were from "Saudi factories or Saudi imports" and that the factories supplied more than $330 million of their purchases.[112] Such data is released only sporadically and is generally scarce, so it is hard to assess just how Aramco has performed in deepening the company's backward linkages.

The company has a "new business development" unit (NBD) whose function is to commercialize the intellectual properties emerging from the enterprise's R&D efforts. In turn, NBD created a local enterprise development division (LEDD) to further encourage local suppliers. More recently, the company has been devising strategies to encourage local firms that are too small to bid on some of the mega-projects to form consortia. In 2005, two contracts for project management were awarded to two consortia based on local engineering companies. To be sure, there is a trade off in this strategy – of using local content on an economic basis while also containing costs. In recent years it has been suggested that Saudi Aramco is trying to "move away from spending" (Marcel 2006, p. 131) on general infrastructure. This is possibly because the company sees the potential of becoming too distracted from commercial operations, as the government desperately tries to encourage broader economic development in the kingdom.

Another area of backward linkages where there is growing concern is in the context of employing Saudi nationals. For many years the government of Saudi Arabia – like governments in nearly all oil-rich countries – has been pursuing a Saudiization program in a desperate effort to find employment for the growing labor force in the face of awesome demographics. Based upon the Saudi Statistical Year Book 2006, 37 percent of the country's population is under the age of

14 and this population bulge will be soon seeking employment. Saudi Aramco employs predominantly Saudis and over the years the number of expatriates has reduced significantly. In 2005, Saudi Aramco's staff of 51,843 was 87 percent Saudi.[113] (In 1995 a staff of comparable size was 80 percent Saudi.[114]) Saudi Aramco has carried on the Aramco tradition and continues to develop extensive training programs for nationals.

The problem with success in Saudiization is that the government increasingly sees the petroleum sector as a source of new jobs for the bulging population. Despite twenty years of government effort at Saudiization, the national program has failed to keep up with the growing population. Moreover, fewer than 10 percent of employees in the Saudi private sector are nationals.[115] This basic number puts growing pressure on the company to play a greater role in employing Saudi nationals, both directly and through possible investments in downstream activities. While the company welcomes the national mission – and the highly visible role of employment – it fears hiring unskilled workers that could dilute the managerial competence of the company. This problem is particularly serious for the sector since the capital-intensive nature of the industry severely restricts its ability to create durable and meaningful jobs.[116] There is concern that pressure to increase employment of Saudis could undermine the effectiveness of the sector if pushed too hard, too quickly. Nonetheless, the pressure to create jobs does not abate, and if IOCs were ever allowed back in the country, they would face similar pressures: under the gas initiative, Saudi Aramco indicated that it would stipulate local employment quotas for IOCs. As is typical, the pressure for local employment extends not only to jobs but also contracts. It has been reported (MEES 51:46) that there is some resentment among Saudi industrialists who claim the company is reluctant to give work to local firms. While the official line with Saudi Aramco is that Saudi firms will get preference in contracts, this promise is generally honored only when those firms meet international standards. When Saudi Aramco's current CEO, Khalid Al Falih, was senior VP for industrial relations, he developed a reputation for being extremely tough on maintaining specification standards on inputs. Nonetheless, the enterprise usually has some initiative under way to help expand the array of viable contractors in the country.[117]

6 Conclusion and the future of Saudi Aramco

There are certain elements of context that are central to understanding the Saudi Aramco story contained in this chapter.

The company was never designed to be the NOC for Saudi Arabia. The result was that the company, which emerged after the de facto takeover in 1976, came from a culture more aligned to an IOC than an NOC. This meant that it had in place clarity in goals, freedom and ability of managers to perform assigned tasks, and accountability for decision making together with internal transparency: all of the characteristics that are required if good governance is to be achieved (Lahn *et al.* 2007). It also meant there existed an overwhelming corporate culture of pride in the company, central to the Saudi Aramco story. Both factors made a major contribution to limiting the extent of rent seeking within the company that differentiates it from so many other NOCs.

Because of the extent of the "technological strangeness" prevalent in Saudi Arabia from the time of the early discoveries of oil, both Aramco as a private company and Saudi Aramco as an NOC were faced with a much greater role in terms of the "national mission" compared with many other oil-producing countries.

Successive kings and their governments protected the company from undue political interference in its day-to-day operations. This was especially true after it effectively became the NOC. It was also a crucial part of the story of effective technical and managerial competence, given that Saudi society was extremely hierarchical based on extensive networks of client–patron relationships. Without that insulation the company would have quickly fallen foul of internal political wrangling, seriously inhibiting its capacity to operate. Instead it was able to operate on an essentially technocratic basis with decisions being made on the basis of commercial, economic, and technical criteria.

Oil became a central plank in Saudi Arabia's foreign policy during the 1960s and remained key to the pursuit of that policy. Given the kingdom's huge reserves and producing capacity this inevitably meant that Saudi Aramco had to consider much wider issues than any other NOC. Its decisions would have huge influence on international oil markets, and international oil markets would create huge constraints on the corporation's freedom of action.

Within this context, Saudi Aramco had three strategic objectives. It was the guardian of the country's patrimony and therefore responsible for the optimal management of the kingdom's hydrocarbon resources. It was the servant of the Saudi state. Finally, it had strong interests to protect and develop its central role in the country's hydrocarbon sector. It is these three objectives that provide the criteria by which to judge the performance of the corporation.

A major problem with assessing Saudi Aramco's performance is the almost complete absence of external transparency. While internal transparency within the corporation and between the corporation and the shareholder (i.e., the government) is good, the government has consistently refused to make public greater detail.[118] This chapter has therefore struggled to measure performance in any detailed or consistent way. That said the overall conclusion is that Saudi Aramco has succeeded in achieving its three strategic objectives. Also, based on the view taken of its record on achieving projects on time, at an operational level it has also been effective.[119]

Of particular note in the story is the extent to which, over the years, Saudi Aramco has developed and nurtured a very high-quality labor force. It is this pool of human capital that has made the company stand out both within the kingdom and among many of its brother NOCs. At the moment, the company is coming under intense pressure to do more to help relieve the growing problems of youth unemployment within the kingdom. This pressure has two directions. One is simply to employ more nationals in what is essentially a capital-intensive rather than labor-intensive industry. The other is to do more to extend the "national mission" thereby increasing job opportunities in other sectors. There are two potential dangers here. One is that employing more within the company for the sake of employing more may well dilute the company's managerial and technical excellence. The other is that putting excessive resources into pursuing the "national mission" will dilute managerial attention away from the core business of managing the country's hydrocarbon resources.

As to the future of Saudi Aramco, this depends very much on what happens to the politics within the kingdom over the next few years. The real danger is that whoever controls the kingdom after Abdullah might allow Saudi domestic politics to increasingly intrude into the day-to-day operations of the company. If external rent seeking intrudes on the company it is difficult to see why a management that has previously restrained itself from excessive rent seeking should not join in any feeding frenzy that may result.

Notes

1 Indeed, this case study faced two major problems in its preparation and writing. First Saudi Aramco is notorious for its lack of transparency to the external world. There are no published annual reports in any meaningful sense or accounts. There is an Annual Review that contains fairly anodyne information and other occasional documents, press releases, interviews in the trade press, etc. There are no data sources that offer consistent time series apart from a few rather obvious operational numbers. As will be cited throughout this case study, there is a very large body of literature on Saudi Aramco (notably Abir 1988; Nawwab *et al.* 1995; Obaid 2000, Marcel 2006; Jaffe and Elass 2007; Vitalis 2007; Hertog 2008), but this suffers from the same problem of a lack of data regarding the usual corporate metrics used to assess oil companies (Stevens 2008c). I draw from sources where they are available as well as my involvement with Aramco and then Saudi Aramco since 1969 providing consultancy, seminars, professional training, and other matters. The second problem is that Saudi Aramco is the central player in the oil sector of Saudi Arabia, which has a uniquely important role in world oil markets. As such it is a policy instrument of the Saudi government as it pursues its state interests. Because of Saudi Arabia's very large proven reserves and exports, Saudi Arabia is above all a price maker and thus strategic decisions play a key role in the state of oil markets and the determination of oil prices.

2 Much of the history presented here has been taken from Longrigg (1961); Hirst (1966); Mikdashi *et al.* (1970); Stocking (1970); Stevens (1975, 2008a); Seymour (1980); Keating (2006). See also the references in note 1.

3 This term is used to describe a concession agreement signed between governments and the so-called "Seven Sisters" who together with the French company CFP became known in the literature of the 1950s and 1960s as "the Majors." Most of the main old-style concession agreements were signed before the 1950s. The term is used to distinguish such agreements from joint ventures, production sharing agreements, and service agreements that came to dominate the oil upstream after the 1970s (Stevens 1975).

4 There was very strong competition between SOCAL and the other majors trying to secure access to exploration acreage following the end of World War I. This competition was further complicated because there was significant involvement by the British, French, and US governments.

5 It should be pointed out that similarly generous terms applied in other Middle Eastern countries at the time.

6 Interestingly, the government of Saudi Arabia published the text of the concession in the official newspaper *Umm Al-Qura* a week after the king signed Royal Decree No. 1135 granting that concession. However, in a move that was to set important precedents that have dogged the company up to today in terms of information and transparency, SOCAL refused to make the text public in English (regarding it as commercially confidential). Indeed, in a US court case in 1947 it refused to provide details of the agreement despite the fact it had been published in Arabic fourteen years previously (Stocking 1970). American courts readily accepted that argument!

7 This was equivalent to eleven US cents per barrel.

8 Those fears were well founded, and the firm quickly shot to the top of producers. By the end of 1945, when CASOC's operations were in full form, the company produced over 21 million barrels (57,000 b/d) loading thirty-eight tankers, nearly three times the total in 1944. By the end of 1949 production was up to 500,000 b/d (Nawwab *et al.* 1995).

9 The "As-Is" agreement of 1928 had created a pricing mechanism – the Gulf Plus Basing Point System – to manage unexpected changes in volume, but finds of this type were not envisioned when that agreement was crafted.

10 There is no hard evidence as to why the name was changed but given CASOC was about to negotiate with Exxon and Mobil both of which were offshoots of the Standard Oil Trust the change of name may well have been to try to distance the company from this connection.

11 See Chapter 11. The reason for Saudi Arabia's being first to move on this issue in the region, according to Stocking (1970), was that "the king was impelled not so much by the poverty of his people as by his own and his royal family's prodigal and conspicuous consumption. This had quickly adapted itself to expanding revenue" (page 145). However, other countries in the region followed rapidly to move to profit tax.

12 Tariki had become director general of petroleum and mineral resources in 1954, the precursor of the Saudi Ministry of Oil.

13 De jure, Iran and Kuwait were never "colonies." However, de facto they were.

14 In May 1956 there were demonstrations in Dhahran demanding the phasing out of the American military base and the nationalization of Aramco. This was followed by a strike within Aramco in June. However, this "was quickly and brutally suppressed … by the governor of the

Eastern Province" (Abir 1988). A royal decree then forbade strikes and demonstrations of any kind.

15 In Aramco this was referred to as the Saudi Arab Government (SAG).

16 There are differing views on this. For example Vitalis (2007) tells a very different story whereby the American parent companies created a "Jim Crow" system in the Dhahran oil camps. While the workers challenged this racial hierarchy in the 1950s and 1960s, they were suppressed by the Saudi state as indicated in footnote 14.

17 Casual stories told to me in the late 1960s suggest that the management of Aramco was more culturally aware than its European (certainly British) counterparts in the rest of the region. They went to greater lengths to accommodate Arab cultural mores and attitudes. A good example was the introduction of what became known as the "son of a bitch regulation" within Aramco in the 1950s. This forbade Americans using the term to Saudis. In US culture such a label is not a big deal and can often be used humorously but in Arab culture calling someone an "Ibn Sharmutta" is extremely offensive.

18 Perhaps the most famous example is the current oil minister, Ali Naimi. He joined Aramco as little more than a tea boy in 1947 aged 12. His abilities were quickly spotted and he was put through the education process. I have been told that when Naimi was informed he was to be sent the US for university training, he was asked what he would like to study. He apparently replied, "What degree does the current CEO of Aramco have?" When told he was a geologist, Naimi replied that that is what he wanted to study. He eventually became president and CEO of Saudi Aramco in 1983.

19 These included a number of US independents ranging from Occidental, Phillips, and Amoco and some of the NOCs of the importing countries such as Eni. It also included a number of NOCs from producers who by virtues of their production sharing agreements and joint ventures had become crude sellers as part of the fiscal terms of the agreements (Stevens 1975).

20 The idea was that this "general agreement" would set the broad terms of "participation." It was then left to the individual signatory countries to negotiate with their own IOCs to finalize the specifics and the details.

21 For a variety of historical reasons competition between the ruling elites in Saudi Arabia and Kuwait was particularly intense. King Faisal once remarked that all the problems of the world stemmed from the fact there were three super-powers "the United States, the Soviet Union, and Kuwait!"

22 In the event only Abu Dhabi managed to resist the pressure for full nationalization and stopped at 60 percent equity because it "lacked the

manpower and technology to be able to dispense with the companies" (Stevens 1975, p. 148).

23 In March 1962, the new king appointed Ahmed Zaki Yamani as the minister of petroleum and mineral affairs with Hisham Nazer as his deputy. Previously this had been the directorate of petroleum and mineral affairs with a director general who had been Abdullah Tariki but had been upgraded to a minister in 1960. In November 1962 Petromin was created and Abdullah Taher, one of Yamani's protégés, was appointed as governor. It has been suggested that Taher was disappointed with the appointment since he had wanted Hisham Nazer's job. This was to lead to significant rivalry between the two, which was important for the future development of the sector (Hertog 2008).

24 In reality, before the late 1990s, the SPC was not particularly important in the control of the oil sector. The author has been told that the board minutes of Saudi Aramco would be translated into Arabic and sent to the SPC but in most years there was no return correspondence.

25 This was a government-created organization intended to manage the new industrial cities of Yanbu and Jubail.

26 Personalities surely played important roles in this shake-up and the eclipse of Petromin. It was alleged that Fahd regarded Yamani, who had always been seen as "Faisal's man," as being too powerful. Yamani had been one of the architects of Petromin, and his deputy was named Petromin's president. Under Faisal these were valuable political assets; under Khalid and Fahd they were liabilities.

27 Meanwhile the antagonism between Taher and Nazer intensified and many of the senior Saudis in Aramco "evolved to be the most committed anti-Petromin group in the Kingdom" (Hertog 2008, p. 19). In July 1978, Taher was given ministerial status. However, in 1986, Nazer effectively became Taher's boss and in December he was sacked.

28 In fact various conversations with former Aramco partners suggest that since 1976, they had treated the company as a wholly owned Saudi company.

29 In 1996 Aramco also got full control over Luberef and Petrolube. In 1997, Petromin's mineral projects were given to a new government-owned mining company MAADEN which in 2007 sold 30 percent of its shares to the public.

30 In fact there are three dimensions to the golden quadrant with the third being the supply of international markets.

31 To be fair, such an objective is central to the objectives of most ruling elites in most countries. Also it is not necessarily as cynical as it may sound at first sight. It is a fundamental assumption in the "economic theory of politics" that politicians seek to maximize power. While this

has attracted debate and discussion, it is a viable working assumption. However, this does not preclude the possibility that the politicians seek power to improve the lot of their people. It is interesting to consider whether this is a desire for its own sake because it is a "good thing" or simply to cling on to power. It is also interesting to consider whether the motive makes any difference to the outcome?

32 Among other things, this has created a positive cottage-industry, inventing conspiracy theories regarding the relationship between the Al Saud and various US administrations.

33 Saudi Arabia was a state created by military conquest between the taking of Riyadh in 1902 and the destruction of the Ikhwan in 1929. The Al Saud rule by the consent of the population as represented by the various tribes, religious leaders, and other interest groups. Even the most cursory reading of the history of the kingdom shows just how important was (and is) this issue of legitimacy.

34 It is interesting to note that even today, if the king has "pet projects" that he wants to see emerging, it is often Saudi Aramco that is given the task of creating and managing the project. A good example is the recent development of the new technical university KAUST at Thuwal near Jiddah and the creation of an energy think tank (KAPSARC) described below.

35 The ministry was also responsible for international relations in the context of the oil sector, most obviously within OPEC.

36 Clearly, such a system would feed those in the Ministry of Finance who believe in principal–agent analysis and see the oil ministry as having been "captured" by the NOC allowing extensive rent seeking.

37 However, it is interesting to note that often when questions regarding key policy issues are asked of Saudi Aramco executives, they are referred to the ministry. However, this is almost certainly related to their reluctance to enter what are essentially political discussions (Marcel 2006).

38 There is an extensive discussion of these changes in the *Gulf States Newsletter* Volume 32 Issue 835, September 1, 2008.

39 Each senior member of the family tends to have his own "oil experts" to provide advice.

40 The 2000 reform set SCPMA's official responsibilities as follows: 1) endorsing the company's five-year plan including its program to produce crude oil and its program for exploration for new reserves of hydrocarbon materials and developing them; 2) endorsing the company's five-year program for capital future investments; 3) appointing the company's chairman upon a nomination by the board of directors; 4) appointing an auditor and fixing his financial compensations;

5) reviewing the auditor's report and endorsing the company's budget and profit and loss accounts; 6) accrediting the annual report of the board of directors and acquitting the board of directors for the year in question; 7) deciding whether to increase, decrease the capital of the company, or allow others to contribute in it; 8) fixing the salaries of the chairman and members of the board of directors; and 9) appropriating any increase in the net value of the rights and assets of the company either to increase its capital or transfer it to the company's reserves.

41 An offshoot has been created to regulate the gas opening described below.

42 What follows is taken directly from ESMAP (2007), which was written by the author in 2006.

43 Shortly after the meeting the invitation to tender was extended to some non-US IOCs.

44 Unfortunately for those studying the company from outside, the results of these benchmarking exercises remain within the company. This of course is normal corporate practice but it is not clear to what extent they are disseminated within the company itself.

45 It is interesting to speculate how far these ministers reveal the details of Saudi Aramco's finances within their own ministries.

46 Before the service company cost escalation that has occurred since around 2002–2003, this was the average number used by Saudi Aramco as the long-run average cost of production of crude under normal circumstances.

47 Of course, even on capacity levels the Saudi Aramco corporate planners have a significant input.

48 Saudi Aramco takes its operating costs "after the receipt of royalties but before sending dividends" (Marcel 2006, p. 140).

49 For crude oil, until the recent rise in costs as a result of service industry constraints and the higher cost of steel this was set at $2 per barrel. This very low cost is of course the result of the large prolific fields with which Saudi Arabia has been blessed and as with other NOCs cannot be viewed necessarily as a reflection of the company's performance.

50 This might reduce the incentive to cut operating costs but this neglects the very strong corporate culture within Saudi Aramco of keeping costs low. For example, the argument has been made (Marcel 2006) that the management wants to minimize costs because it feels this helps retain the trust of the government. It is interesting to observe that the attempted opening of the kingdom's upstream to IOCs in 1998 caused huge resentment within Saudi Aramco precisely because it felt it was effectively a vote of no confidence in the management.

51 In 1977–1978 there was a corruption scandal in Aramco over the gas gathering project. However, such events were seen "as an exception" (Hertog 2008, p. 21).

52 Transparency International on its website lists Saudi Arabia as 80 out of 180 on its Corruption Perception Index 2008 compared with 46 out of 133 in 2003. In its Bribe Payments Index Saudi is 22 out of 30 for 2006. See also Lacey (1981); Abir (1988).

53 This arises from the normal practice in national income accounting of including oil revenues as part of national income. This in reality is quite misleading given that oil is a depletable resource. Revenue from selling oil is not income. It is simply a reshuffling of the nation's asset portfolio from oil below ground to dollars above ground (Stevens and Mitchell 2008).

54 In Arabic, Yamamah simply means dove, which is an interesting name for a deal involving sophisticated warplanes!

55 For details of the project and the workshops and papers that underlie the document, see www.chathamhouse.org.uk/research/eedp/current_projects/good_governance/.

56 This statement of course begs an important question as to what constitutes a "secretive" society versus a "transparent" one and how this can be measured. Certainly Transparency International tends to link a lack of transparency to higher levels of corruption and does attempt to measure this – see note 52. Clearly there is a danger of stereotyping and accusations of prejudice. Ultimately such views are subjective and lack scientific rigor. However, this does not necessarily invalidate such views.

57 He joined Saudi Aramco in 1979 and so is the first CEO of the generation that joined the company after the takeover by the government.

58 These employees used to be described as "low-motivated Saudi employees" (LMSEs). It still apparently remains a problem. In particular, following massive spending on education there is an overhang in qualified but low-performing engineers. It is compounded because there is pressure to advance all members of a "class" i.e., those who joined the company at the same time. However, this inevitably results in a blockage because of the natural reduction in openings as one moves up the ladder. The losers in such a process tend to blame their lack of progress on poor connections and lose motivation. The result has been an expansion of jobs for mid-level managers and excessive staffing in many business lines.

59 Interestingly many of this new generation were actually children of former Aramco employees.

60 The Middle East Economic Survey (MEES) is cited throughout this report. For each citation, the volume and issue number are given.

61 An in-company joke suggests that the worst job in Saudi Aramco is being Mr. Falih's personal assistant!

62 There is however an undoubted glass ceiling for women within the company although to be fair this is very common in most countries. However, there has also been, at least in the past, a glass ceiling for Shi'a reflecting the anti-Shi'a feeling that is a key characteristic of Wahhabi Saudi society. This may be changing and under Falih a Shi'a was promoted to a senior vice president position.

63 Experience has taught me that generalizations about national culture can be an extremely dangerous pastime. Nonetheless some comments are needed to provide a view of context. See also note 56 for comments on this issue.

64 To be fair, this trait is also true of large corporations more generally.

65 Its broader objectives are encapsulated in Corporate Values, which is a list of the corporation's attitudes and resembles the corporate culture of an IOC. An illustrative list taken from the corporate website is as follows: "We pursue excellence in everything we do. We encourage continuous learning and strive to develop our people to their highest potential. We strive for fairness and adhere to the highest ethical standards. We support each other and work together to achieve our business objectives successfully. We strive to maintain the highest levels of safety, security, health, and environmental standards. We are responsive to the expectations of the government and our customers. We place authority where responsibility lies. We are accountable for our actions. We support our communities and serve as a role model for others."

66 However, Saudi Aramco remains very dependent on the oil service companies; it's a relationship that goes back to the 1950s and 1960s.

67 Other centers include the Research and Development Center inaugurated early in 2001 and charged with providing corporate-wide research. While it focuses on upstream research (reservoir – production) and thus duplicates EXPEC's activities, it also covers downstream research (gas plants – refineries), material sciences, and environmental research. Technical support and troubleshooting are also provided. In addition there are advanced laboratory services to provide company-wide advanced analytical support to proponents such as exploration, producing, manufacturing, engineering, and operations services, and area laboratories. It carries out research and program coordination with academic institutions both in-kingdom and out-of-kingdom. It also holds an annual technical exchange meeting and sponsors membership in scientific societies. At full strength some 400 technologists and scientists are employed. In June 2009 it

was given the ISO 29001 standard covering basic activities in R&D in the oil industry, the first center in the Middle East to receive this accolade.

68 This view is controversial because it implies, based upon principal–agent analysis, that the management may be more interested in its own positions than necessarily what is good for the kingdom.

69 This goes some way to explain why Matt Simmons' accusations of mismanagement of Ghawar provoked an unheard-of public response by Saudi Aramco to refute the claims.

70 It is important to be careful when comparing recovery factors since they are very dependent on the geology, which is a gift of nature and cannot necessarily be assumed to be the result of good oil field management.

71 As with so much of Saudi Aramco's operations this assertion is based upon hearsay. The only data available (OAPEC, various years) suggest that seismic activity between 1999 and 2003 increased from 60 crew/months to 120 in 2002 falling to 108 in 2003 while exploration and development wells completed rose steadily from 224 in 1999 to 290 in 2003. The company claims in its website a "60 percent success rate on oil and gas wells." However, the same source gives proven oil reserves constant at 259 billion barrels from 2003 to 2007.

72 It has been suggested that these figures came out of a General Accounting Office study in the late 1970s and were never seen within the kingdom as serious targets.

73 The background to these discussions over capacity levels can be found in United States Congress (1979).

74 The objective set in September 2006 was to increase crude producing capacity from 11.3 million b/d to 12.5 million b/d by 2009 with the possibility of a further 0.9 million b/d of Arab heavy from the Manifa field by 2011 to augment capacity. Up to 2009, the increment was to be 2.35 million b/d from 7 fields of which 1.5 would be net additions, predominantly of lighter crude. As already mentioned, underlying these targets there is an explicit objective to protect the fields and maximize recovery rates. In July 2008, it was announced (MEES 51:30) that Saudi Aramco's plans for 2009–2013 were to double development drilling expenditure to $22 billion compared with the plans for 2008–2012. This has been driven by the desire to increase the booked reserves in a number of operations including Manifa and Karan but also by the increase in well costs reflecting a general increase in global costs. The 2009–2013 budget also shows a $1 billion increase in exploration expenditure to $4 billion. Finally, the maintain production potential well work-over expenditure is to increase by $1.5 billion to $6 billion.

75 This also included 300,000 b/d from the Neutral Zone.

76 In October 2009 Saudi Aramco announced that it was dropping WTI (West Texas Intermediate) as the basing point and using instead a composite crude price that better reflected the quality of export crude from Saudi Arabia. The reason was that in recent years, WTI had become increasingly disconnected from international oil prices.

77 This system leads to what has become called the Asian premium. This is the observed fact that crude prices in Asia regularly exceed those in the Atlantic Basin. The Asian Premium exists because Saudi Arabia sets the formula prices for Asia at a higher level than for the United States or Europe. It is allowed to continue because the destination clauses prevent arbitrage of Saudi crude between the Atlantic Basin and Asia.

78 Somewhat belatedly, KPC has also begun to realize the wisdom of this view (Stevens 2008b).

79 Since 1945 the IOCs had chosen to expand their refinery capacity on the markets in Europe and Japan. Prior to World War II, refineries for the most part had been located on the oil fields (Stevens 2000).

80 Examples from history that were widely quoted at the time were textiles for Britain in the eighteenth century and railroads for the United States in the nineteenth century.

81 At this time (1973–1974) I was teaching at the American University of Beirut and in this period all of the debate in the region among Arab economists was around these issues. I attended a lecture by a prominent oil minister (not Zaki Yamani!) who actually advocated building lots of oil refineries for when the oil ran out.

82 Three export refineries resulted, all joint ventures: Rabigh Refinery with a capacity of 325,000 b/d was a joint venture with the Latsis-owned Greek company Petrola, although in 1995 Saudi Aramco became the sole owner; Jubail Refinery with a capacity of 300,000 b/d with Shell; and Yanbu Refinery with a capacity of 320,000 b/d with Mobil.

83 In the mid 1940s, Aramco had built a 50,000 b/d refinery at Ras Tanura. By 1947 it had been expanded to 100,000 b/d and in the early 1970s to 500,000 b/d (Nawwab *et al.* 1995).

84 The author believes that a major reason for Yamani's ideas for a gradual takeover of the upstream through "participation" was because he realized that there was a danger of stretching the management capabilities of nationals over operations too quickly.

85 Arabian Industrial Development Corporation (NAMA) submitted a bid to build a privately owned 400,000 b/d refinery at Jizan in partnership with Petronas. NAMA is a private consortium of some 300 Saudis and

other GCC nationals created to invest in petrochemicals in which the Saudi Arabian Basic Industries Corporation (SABIC) has a 10 percent stake. In addition two newly planned refineries to process the heavy sour crude from the 900,000 b/d Manifa project have been announced. The one at Yanbu with ConocoPhillips for a 400,000 b/d plant is in question with rumors that cost escalation (currently standing at $13 billion) has killed it (MEES 51:29). It was announced on November 6, 2008, that the bidding process for the project was postponed. The one at Jubail is with Total. This is a $15 billion project due onstream at the end of 2012. Of the project costs, 25 percent is to be financed by an IPO for Saudi nationals. Both projects were on a lump sum turnkey basis. There are also plans to upgrade the (now) 400,000 b/d Samref plant at Yanbu, which is now a joint venture with ExxonMobil following Exxon's merger with Mobil.

86 The author has been challenged on this assertion by one source, who argued that the decision to move downstream abroad was taken by the government and had little support among senior Saudi Aramco management.

87 This was when OPEC began its struggle as a cartel to defend price by cutting back production. This proved painful since governments were losing revenue as prices fell and volumes fell.

88 This argument became especially powerful for PDVSA and KPC, who were the first to develop a downstream capability abroad because both were producing heavy sour crudes, which given required refinery configurations were especially difficult to sell.

89 It was a time when government official sales prices were consistently out of line with actual spot prices in the market. This refusal to lift was particularly annoying to the Saudis since the same companies had been making significant profits by virtue of the "Aramco advantage" during the second oil shock triggered by the events in Iran during 1978–1979. It rather brought home to the Saudis in quite a brutal way that there is no such thing as sentiment or indeed customer loyalty in business unless there is commercial advantage to be had.

90 Certainly from private conversations, within the Ministry of Finance (which could be regarded as the key "principal" to Saudi Aramco) there is a suspicion that the company does indulge in rent-seeking behavior. This explains as indicated above why the finance ministry strongly supported Abdallah's proposed opening of the upstream in 1998. It saw this as a mechanism to provide more accurate benchmarking by which to assess Saudi Aramco's performance.

91 Van der Linde (2000) argued that these two companies and Saudi Aramco vertically integrated abroad "with the objective of guaranteeing

markets and long-term economic rents" (p. 79). However, this neglects the principal–agent motivation for the decision.

92 A good example is the attempted joint venture refinery with China. Negotiations with the Chinese began in mid 1994 but stalled over two issues. One was their insistence that at least 70 percent of the output should be exported, which would compete directly with Saudi Aramco's own export refineries. The other was the huge social and corporate spending required by the Chinese on non-core refining activities for the employees. However, eventually agreements began to emerge and in mid 2005 work started on the $3.5bn Fujian refining/ ethylene project in Quanzhou, a project jointly supported by Saudi Aramco and ExxonMobil. The refinery expansion and upgrade will allow the plant to handle Saudi crude and was due for completion in late 2008 (MEES 48:29). However, talks are still under way between with China Petroleum and Chemical Corp (Sinopec) on a proposed $1.2bn refinery near the city of Qingdao in Shandong province.

93 Despite the view of very close links between the two countries in terms of oil, oil imports from Saudi Arabia into the United States have always been relatively minor. According to the US EIA in 1987 only around 9 percent of total US imports came from Saudi Arabia. By 2005 this had risen to some 12 percent.

94 This system gathered the associated wet gas, stripped out the liquids (which are particularly valuable and sold in markets that work in tandem with the crude oil market), and then delivered the dry gas to consumers. The MGS began full-scale operations in 1980. In 1984, the plants were revamped to allow them to process non-associated gas. In 1996, the MGS capacity was increased and in 2000 gas supplies were provided to Riyadh for the first time. At this point the system had the capacity to process 7.5 billion standard cubic feet per day (bcfd) producing 5.8 bcfd of sales gas and processing 1.1 million b/d of natural gas liquids.

95 Against this argument there is the argument that into the future, if Saudi production is constrained and reaches some sort of technical plateau, then domestic oil consumption will eat into the oil surplus available for export (Mitchell and Stevens 2008).

96 To be fair to Saudi Aramco this is also true of a great many other NOCs (and IOCs). However, what is frustrating for the researcher is that unlike many NOCs, in the case of Saudi Aramco, the detail is available. It is just that the government chooses not to put the information into the public domain.

97 It might be argued that this is the same for any company where the ultimate decision comes from "the shareholder" where the identity of that entity is uncertain.

98 The Saudi Aramco financial system is an extremely efficient and complex system with great internal transparency and accountability. It is a
system of which any large IOC would be proud. The explanation for
this is that it created the system in the first place when the company
was owned and controlled by the Aramco partners. That system was
continued after nationalization and developed as accounting systems,
both hardware and software, improved. The data (financial and operational) is collected and audited internally. The usual large international
accountancy firms then audit the financial data externally. An annual
report and accounts are prepared, as is typical for listed companies.
However, as already indicated, the key difference is that there is only
one shareholder – the government of Saudi Arabia – and it chooses not
to make the report public.

99 This still raises a key question in the context of principal–agent analysis
as to the ability of the government to be able to interpret the data.

100 This was the arrangement whereby each year the partners within the
Iranian Consortium would decide how much oil would be produced and
how that production would be allocated between them.

101 Lifting above that warranted by equity share meant that their dividends
from Aramco declined (Blair 1976).

102 Between 1958 and 1972, the Iraq Petroleum Company (IPC) was the
swing producer with the majors who owned the IPC, using disputes with
the Iraqi government to reduce Iraqi output and then "conceding" points
to the government to increase supply (Stevens 2008a).

103 This strategic decision came out of the turmoil within the kingdom in
1985 described earlier. Since OPEC had tried to introduce pro-rationing
via a quota system in March 1982, the system had suffered from the classic problem of cheating but also from error. Under that system, OPEC
estimated global demand and the volume of non-OPEC supply; the difference was the "call on OPEC," which was then divided between the
members by means of their quota. The problem was that the underlying data on supply and demand was terrible, which meant that the "call
on OPEC" was at best ill-informed guesswork. However, overestimat-
ing the "call" was convenient because it eased the persistent squabbling
over quotas, and thus there was a noticeable tendency for OPEC to over-
produce. Along with persistent cheating, overproduction threatened a
price structure that was already showing signs of weakness. Saudi Arabia
therefore took upon itself to absorb this overproduction by reducing its
own production.

104 This is an average estimated from six trade press sources.

105 This steep drop in output reflected two sources of pressure on the government. First, it was apparent to everyone in the kingdom that falling

production meant falling revenues, which, in turn, meant a collapse in spending on projects. That outcome was catastrophic for their incomes, which hinged on "commissions" from the allocation of such projects. Second, the oil techno-structure, which included both the ministry and elements within Saudi Aramco, argued the policy of withholding supplies to maintain the high prices that had prevailed after the Iranian revolution was misplaced. High prices destroyed demand by making oil uncompetitive with rival fuels and by encouraging users to become too efficient. Given the kingdom's huge reserves, a lower (and stable) price was preferable to encourage energy consumers to move back to oil. Ultimately, the policy was changed in the summer of 1985. Saudi Arabia would no longer act as the "swing" producer. It would produce to quota and it also introduced netback pricing in place of government-administered prices. A key part of this new strategy was to maintain a cushion of spare capacity to ensure that in the event of outages elsewhere, Saudi production could fill the gap thereby limiting subsequent price spikes. It was hoped this promised stability would give confidence to energy consumers to move back to oil. This has remained a central plank of Saudi oil policy ever since albeit without netback pricing, and as will be developed below since 2004 Saudi Aramco has been working extremely hard to restore a cushion of around 2 million b/d. Although the carrying of spare capacity is a political decision at the highest level, it also makes sense from a commercial standpoint, as Saudi Aramco management will admit privately. Thus when there is an international outage and Saudi increases crude sales, it is selling at very much higher prices. A business case for the strategy of spare capacity can easily be made.

106 Much of what follows comes from ESMAP (2007, chapter 4.2).

107 This links to downstream plans. The Manifa crude is heavy and sour and Saudi Aramco was planning two 400,000 b/d export refineries in Yanbu and Jubail explicitly to handle this crude.

108 The increments are 250,000 b/d additional to Shaybah by December 2008; 100,000 b/d Arab Super Light Nuayyim project due in 2009; 1.2 million b/d from Khurais due in June 2009 and Manifa.

109 The reason for the speed of development is an interesting story, albeit controversial, reflecting issues related to "national missions" to be discussed below. In June 1995, the Middle East Economic Survey published the secret 1974 agreement that settled the border dispute between Saudi Arabia and the UAE in which Sheik Zayed ceded to Saudi Arabia the Shaybah field. This publication led to a considerable outcry in Abu Dhabi and there was a fear that once Sheik Zayed died, his successors would raise the issue of ownership of the reserves. Given "possession is nine-tenths of the law" the strategy appeared to be to develop the field (at any cost)

before Sheik Zayed died. Against this rather exciting and exotic story it has been suggested to me that the plans to develop Shaybah were actually begun in the late 1980s, at a time when there was low upstream investment generally, which resulted in very low rates for oil field services.

110 In 2006, OPEC reported Saudi domestic prices at 16 to 20 cents per liter for premium gasoline, 9.9 cents per liter for gas, oil, and diesel, and 9.3 cents per liter for jet fuel. These are significantly below the domestic prices charged in Kuwait.

111 In a paper presented to a meeting of OAPEC on March 28, 2009, Ibrahim Al Muhanna, one of the senior advisors to Minister Naimi, explicitly suggests this as a future option. (Reported by Kate Dourian of Platts on March 30, 2009.)

112 To put this percentage into perspective, a number of countries including Nigeria, Iran, and Libya all aspire to having 60 percent local content and in most cases this number is regarded in the industry as hopelessly unrealistic.

113 It seems likely that the company's policy is not to strive for 100 percent Saudi employees.

114 Interestingly, in 1972 of the 10,353 workforce, 8,630 were Saudi nationals: 83 percent. Thus between then and 1995 the Saudi component actually fell.

115 The reasons for the failure are many and varied. The Saudi education system, for the most part, fails to equip student for work in a modern economy. Once hired, Saudi nationals are expensive, often have negative attitudes to certain types of jobs, and are difficult to get rid of. Finally, expatriate workers from the Asian subcontinent are plentiful, productive, cheap, and very easy to get rid of.

116 For example, MEES has reported that the PetroRabigh joint venture conversion of the refinery into a fully integrated petrochemical complex will generate only 1,400 direct jobs, although it was claimed that three times this number would also be created indirectly in related "industrial, maintenance and support activities." The total cost of the project is estimated at $9.8 billion, reflecting the high capital intensity of the petroleum sector.

117 In 2006, the Ministry of Oil developed the "Saudi industrial cluster strategy" to create secondary industries around a refining-petrochemical hub in order to create jobs. This was as part of a general industrial cluster strategy. Five clusters have been selected for development and will be initiated through 2006–2011. These include automotive; construction; metals processing; plastic packaging; and consumer appliances. The cluster strategy was adopted as a national program under the auspices of the Ministry of Commerce.

118 Given the positive view taken of Saudi Aramco's performance in this chapter and by others who have explored the corporation, such reticence by the government is extremely puzzling. As a clear success story one might have expected much greater exposure.

119 It might be argued that the exception to this was in gas until it was pushed to do so by the gas initiative.

6 | Oil, *monarchy, revolution, and theocracy: a study on the National Iranian Oil Company (NIOC)*

PAASHA MAHDAVI

1 Introduction

The symbol of Iran's independence is not the magnificent Azadi Tower that marks the formal entrance to Tehran, but the rather humble stone building on the corner of Taleghani and Hafez avenues, the headquarters of the National Iranian Oil Company. In 1951 Iran's oil company, more commonly referred to as NIOC, was the second major oil company to be nationalized (after Pemex). Unlike the swift nationalizations of the early 1970s that created most of today's national oil companies (NOCs), NIOC's nationalization began much earlier with a series of failed and quasi-nationalizations before it became fully nationalized in the period 1974–1979. Since its founding, NIOC has been the center of the country's economy, providing more than 45 percent of Iran's exports in the 1950s and peaking at 97 percent of exports at the height of the great oil shock of 1973–1974 (CBI 1980/1981–2008/2009; Karshenas 1990). In addition, NIOC supplies politically visible goods and services, including a costly but very popular subsidy for gasoline that makes retail energy in Iran nearly free.[1] Nearly all politics in Iran is at some level connected with NIOC and the hydrocarbon industry. Despite successful efforts to partly diversify the economy, the country remains in some respects heavily dependent on hydrocarbons: For the 2006–2008 period, oil and gas sales made up 80% of total exports and 50% of government revenue (though only accounting for 15% of GDP) (CBI 2008/2009; World Bank 2009).[2]

Previous studies on NIOC have focused on the fact that while the NOC has vast oil and gas reserves at its disposal the enterprise performs poorly. Some studies have addressed Iran's "resource curse,"[3] finding that increased government revenue from oil sales has damaged the country's economy and hindered democracy (Fardmanesh

234

1991; Khajedpour 2001). Some blame the petroleum industry's shortcomings on the structure of the Iranian government as a "rentier state"[4] that overtaxes the oil industry (rather than broader economic activity) to sustain government expenditures (Mahdavy 1970; Katouzian 1981; Skocpol 1982). More recently, two studies focus on the company itself, analyzing its organizational structure, the relationship between the company and the state (decision-making processes, financial flows), and the company's world-views (Marcel 2006; Brumberg and Ahram 2007). Despite keen interest in NIOC's operations, however, it has proved extremely difficult to unravel and assess the deep-rooted bureaucracies of Iran's government and petroleum sector. The present study aims to provide more clarity by focusing, especially, on how NIOC's structure and operations are integrated with the Iranian state and the company's political masters.

In assessing the inner workings of one of the most secretive and mysterious oil companies in the world, I make four main arguments. First, NIOC has weathered substantial shocks, such as the 1979 revolution, the Iran–Iraq War, the enactment of economic sanctions, and the frequent periods of organizational reshuffling, most recently completed by the Ahmadinejad administration. These factors – in effect, perennial chaos and uncertainty in the oil sector – have periodically resulted in drastic production shortfalls and the inability to develop new fields. In particular, I find that the war with Iraq and the enactment of sanctions have had the largest impacts on NIOC's production levels when compared with other factors. Moreover, the regimes governing foreign investment in the oil sector have made it difficult to attract IOCs as partners, and the arrival of sanctions has narrowed the prospects for foreign participation even further. As a result NIOC's performance as an oil and gas company (and that of the sector overall) has been terrible, particularly since 2005.

Second, explaining NIOC's structure, organization, and performance requires looking far beyond its role as a producer, refiner, and marketer of hydrocarbons. A thorough analysis of the company's strategy involves its handling of government demands. In making this analysis, I find that NIOC's strategy has been one of compliance under the Shah to autonomy after the revolution and back to compliance in the Ahmadinejad era. This dynamic strategy explains NIOC's organization with its many subsidiaries, its relationship with the government, and most importantly its performance – strong before the revolution, weak during the early period of the Islamic Republic, moderately successful in the 1990s, and inefficient during the Ahmadinejad era.

Third, NIOC's poor performance reflects not just political uncertainty but also the fact that NIOC, itself, is not really an oil company. Rather, it is a confederation of partially independent enterprises – each responsible for different functions and none integrated around a common strategy. This fact (along with Iranian policies that make it exceptionally difficult for NIOC to engage outside firms as well as sanctions in recent years that make it hard for outside firms to operate in Iran) explains why the company has particularly poor performance in complex areas of operation. This is evident in the country's newest oil fields, which are too challenging for NIOC to operate on its own. And it is evident, more generally, in offshore operations and in natural gas. NIOC's offshore subsidiary produces only 18 percent of the country's oil despite sitting on two-thirds of its official reserves. And Iran, despite having the world's second-largest gas reserves, lags far behind world leaders such as Qatar, Algeria, Indonesia, and Australia in mustering LNG technology.

Fourth, when focusing on the company's performance as an oil company, in keeping with my second finding I suggest that the root cause of NIOC's troubles is its lack of autonomy from the government. Shortly after full nationalization (in 1974) until the revolution in 1979, NIOC enjoyed a golden age when it assumed the competence and assets of the foreign firms and continued to expand output. The revolution (which included many purges from NIOC's ranks) and the Iraq war (1980–1988) were especially debilitating for NIOC. While the company was able to carve out some autonomy from the late 1980s to the mid 2000s, it could never attract the investment capital or expertise needed to regain its former production levels, let alone expand into technically more complex areas. (Since 2005, the company has suffered another purge and has lost all of its carefully crafted autonomy.) The revolution and the Iraq war were severe shocks that tested the NOC to a degree greater than any other NOC examined in this book, and the enterprise failed to rebuild from those tests. Famously, the company adopted a "buyback" scheme for engaging outside firms that was unattractive to most foreign players; however, while others have consistently expressed their frustration with buyback contracts, I contend that buybacks have actually been a blessing to NIOC in as much as the buyback scheme allows the company to reengage with foreign firms after a long period of isolation. Yet the performance failures of that scheme lie less with NIOC than with the political compromises needed to get any kind of foreign participation in a political climate that was usually hostile to outsiders. External sanctions, especially the 1996 Iran–Libya Sanctions Act, dealt a final blow. Today, NIOC is able to elicit outside participation from only a small number of firms willing to risk pariah status, such as Chinese, Indian, and Russian oil companies. The turmoil today has made it even harder for NIOC to perform, although most of the company's problems were fully evident before the present political troubles began.

The remainder of this chapter is divided into three sections: section 2, the history of NIOC and the Iranian petroleum sector; section 3, the organization of and the relationship between NIOC and government institutions; and section 4, NIOC's historical performance and its causes, some of which are external to the company (e.g., the destruction of war) and some internal to its strategy and relationships to the Iranian government. Methodologically, I rely on previous scholarly work on NIOC and Iran, statistical evidence from the Ministry of Petroleum and the Central Bank, and anecdotal evidence from interviews conducted in August–September 2008 and July 2009.[5]

2 History and background of Iranian oil and gas

As of 2009, NIOC sits on 138 billion barrels of oil reserves and 994 trillion cubic feet of gas reserves (second only to Russia in terms of global gas reserves). Oil in Iran is primarily found between the southwestern ridges of the Zagros mountain range and the Persian Gulf coastline, as indicated in Figure 6.1. As for its chemical nature, Iranian crude is generally medium in sulfur content and notably heavy; in 2008, "heavy" crude (API gravity less than 31 degrees) made up 62.1 percent of exports (EIA 2008b).[6] Over time, the country has tapped its "easy" oil, and newly found structures have created large challenges for development. For example, the southern Azadegan oil field discovered in 1999 holds estimated reserves of 26 billion barrels of medium-sour crude. The field was considered too geologically complex for NIOC to develop on its own and development contracts were signed with Japan's Inpex in 2004 but terminated in 2007.[7] Yet bringing new fields online is essential, as Iran's

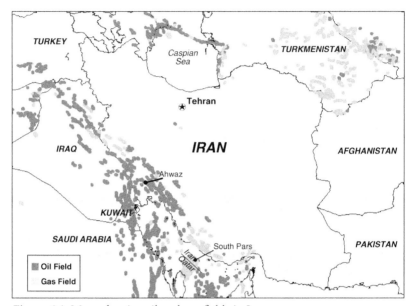

Figure 6.1 Map of major oil and gas fields in Iran.
Source for oil and gas field data: Wood Mackenzie (2009b).

existing oil fields have been declining at roughly 8 percent per year
since 2006 (Stern 2007).[8]

Even as Iran struggles to produce hydrocarbons, it has faced still
larger difficulties in refining and marketing of oil products and
building an effective infrastructure for delivery of natural gas. Most
of Iran's gas resources are located far from its urban consumption
centers in the north, in cities like Tehran, Mashhad, Tabriz, and in
the urban cluster along the Caspian coast. As such, plans to add
capacity to Iran's gas pipeline network are constantly under consideration,[9] but the infrastructure has lagged far behind demand.
As for oil, most politicians and energy advisers have found it more
cost effective to simply import refined products from Iran's northern neighbors and export its own crude from ports on the Persian
Gulf. Lack of expertise and investment explains why Iran, itself,
is largely unable to refine heavier and more sour Iranian crudes
to petroleum products for domestic consumption; there is a planning deficiency in the country's oil sector strategy that fails to take
advantage of the fact that heavier crudes fetch much lower prices

when exported and thus an orderly strategy would utilize more of that crude at home (V. Marcel personal correspondence 2009). The country relies on a large number of swaps in both gas and oil. This has been the case since the Shah first decided to build a gas pipeline to Azerbaijan (known as IGAT-I) in the 1960s. These "swap" arrangements became politically popular again in the 1990s (after the dissolution of the USSR and the restoration of Azeri, Turkmen, and Kazakh sovereignty) with the construction of a pipeline from the Caspian port city of Neka to Tehran allowing 350,000 barrels per day in oil swaps between Kazakhstan and Turkmenistan,[10] as well as the gas pipeline connecting Turkmenistan and Iran, which has been heavily politicized in recent years due to price disputes (Entessar 1999).

Iran's refining capacity has been steadily increasing since the end of the Iran–Iraq war. However, the technology employed in refineries has not kept pace with global best practice, primarily due to the harshness of outside sanctions that prevent Iran from obtaining foreign-made parts and machinery. Aside from sanctions problems, Iranian upper-level politicians, such as those in the office of the ayatollah or the presidency, have been wary about foreign participation in national energy projects; similarly, foreign contractors have not been interested in refining projects given the low-margin nature of refining, coupled with the high cost of doing business in Iran given the presence of sanctions. As of 2008, Iran carried a refining capacity of 1,566,000 barrels per day, with refineries at nine major sites.[11]

As for the history of natural gas in Iran, prior to the 1990s Iran's production was below 20 billion cubic meters (bcm) per year and had been chiefly directed toward modest domestic use. The discovery of gas in the massive offshore South Pars field (the northern section of a large field that across the dividing line of resource sovereignty to the south becomes Qatar's North field) dramatically changed NIOC's outlook for its gas strategy by offering the prospect of lucrative exports.[12] Yet South Pars has not yielded much production so far; only the first five of the planned total twenty-four phases have come online, accounting for roughly 10 bcm per year of gas (MEES 51:8 2008). The ongoing difficulties in developing South Pars as an export project, which requires LNG technologies, reflect the country's many setbacks in foreign contracting and partnerships.

2.1 The history of hydrocarbons in Iran[13]

All of Iran's modern history is comingled with oil.[14] The first permit agreement for oil exploration in Persia to the Western countries was given and signed by Nasseredin Shah of the Qajar dynasty and Baron Julius Reuter of the United Kingdom in 1872. Reuter proceeded by exploring the areas around Kazeroun and Gheshm Island, but after twenty-one years of largely dry holes Reuter finally quit in 1893. Further exploration by Westerners was similarly unsuccessful, until W. K. D'Arcy – working under the famous D'Arcy Oil Concession that gave Russian firms control over oil exploration in the northern provinces while D'Arcy reigned in the south – struck a major discovery in 1908 at the Masjed-e-Suleyman No. 1 well. Shortly after that find, in 1925 the Pahlavi dynasty consolidated its control over Persia. (The term Iran, coined by the Pahlavis, did not supplant Persia as the country's name until 1935.) And in 1932 the government of Iran – now led by the charismatic Pahlavi monarch, Reza Khan Shah – unilaterally canceled its contracts with all foreign companies. It is rumored that the Shah's lavish lifestyle combined with low oil revenues in 1932 had emptied the government coffers: To amend this situation, the Shah sought a new contract that would aid in replenishing the national treasury.[15]

A year later, the Iranian government negotiated a new contract (known as the 1933 agreement) with the newly minted Anglo-Iranian Oil Company (AIOC), a UK-backed firm that had been built upon D'Arcy's enterprise. Despite increasing government revenue, the new contract did not give the Iranians sovereignty over oil, and as a result AIOC had more benefits and rights to oil concessions than before. Under this contract (which has been referred to by Iran scholars as Reza Shah's "historic betrayal"[16]) intended to fuel the British war machine from the late 1930s, AIOC developed vast oil fields and refineries at Abadan, the area in the southwest corner of the country along the Iraq border that still houses Iran's largest refinery and much of today's oil industry. After the war, Iranian public sentiment toward British extraction of Iran's oil greatly worsened; news had spread to the cities of terrible working conditions in the oil fields for Iranians[17] while British employees had "rose beds, tennis courts, and swimming pools," which fueled images of the British as nineteenth-century imperialists (Farmanfarmaian and Farmanfarmaian 1997,

p. 185). Beyond public aggression toward AIOC, there was also growing concern in the Majlis (the Iranian parliament) that AIOC was earning an excessive share of oil revenue.[18] Out of this charged disagreement emerged Dr. Mohammad Mossadeq, who prompted the creation of an NOC.

In the 1940s, Mossadeq was a prominent figure in Iranian politics – serving various roles in the Majlis as an MP and also as a provincial governor – and was known in the public sphere for his opposition to the monarchy's close relationships with foreign governments. When Mossadeq began to make public the revenue disparities between Iran and Britain, his nationalist party – the Jebhi Melli – grew in popularity. With his newfound political strength, Mossadeq sought to nationalize AIOC in 1949 but did not have enough power to impose that outcome; instead, he compromised and signed a "supplemental agreement" that only slightly increased the Iranian government's take but also forced AIOC to improve working conditions. When in November 1950 the Majlis rejected the new agreement, Jebhi Melli led the Majlis in March 1951 to legislatively nationalize British assets and operations in Iran. Concurrently, Ali Razmara, the Shah's appointed prime minister who was put in place to impede the political surge of Jebhi Melli, was found dead outside a mosque in Tehran.[19] Faced with a power vacuum, the Majlis overwhelmingly supported Mossadeq to be the new prime minister by a vote of seventy-nine to twelve; three days later, on May 1, 1951, Mossadeq had canceled AIOC's prior oil concession and fully expropriated its assets. Thus, NIOC came to be nationalized, for the sake of creating revenue for the government and protecting Iran's oil from foreign development.[20]

Western powers, along with AIOC (which had changed its name to BP in 1954), saw their interests threatened and successfully mobilized against Mossadeq – who had all but physically replaced the Shah[21] – and restored the Shah to power in 1953. New laws promptly followed and Western oil companies resumed an active role in the Iranian oil sector in 1954: The Majlis approved the establishment of an "international consortium" in order to make room for non-British companies to explore, produce, refine, and distribute Iranian oil. The consortium, which was made up of members of the Seven Sisters,[22] entered a fifty-fifty contract to split profits from the sale of oil with NIOC.[23] The nationalization process in 1951 actually allocated reserve rights to NIOC alone whereas the consortium was granted exploration and production rights but not full ownership.[24]

Between 1957 and 1974, the Shah's new IOC-friendly arrangement brought the monarchy into closer contact with the United States – in particular companies like Standard Oil of New Jersey (now Exxon). During this period, while NIOC did not fully control either upstream or downstream activities, based on the terms of the consortium, it was able to negotiate its own contracts. One such contract grabbed the attention of the international oil market: In 1957 Enrico Mattei of the Italian firm Eni broke the internationally recognized fifty-fifty production-sharing framework and offered NIOC 75 percent of the profits from its fields (Maugeri 2006). In parallel, NIOC entered into contracts with a number of Japanese, Dutch, Korean, and Soviet companies to establish its foray into petrochemicals, refining, marketing, and natural gas production.

Only in 1974 did NIOC gain monopoly control over exploration, production, and operations of Iranian oil fields. Riding a wave of nationalizations in the region, the Petroleum Act of 1974 reiterated national ownership of petroleum resources and specifically prohibited foreign companies from investing in production or in downstream activities. NIOC took full control over operations in the consortium area and was barred from using the then-standard production sharing agreements (PSAs) with foreign companies, which allowed outsiders to invest in oil operations while earning a return through a variable share of the produced oil. Instead of PSAs, NIOC was obliged to engage foreign services through a service contract mechanism. (In this respect, NIOC followed the lead of Petróleos Mexicanos; Kuwait's NOC has also relied on similar arrangements as a way to keep control over the sector while encouraging, albeit haltingly, the participation of outside firms. See Chapters 7 and 8, respectively.) Whenever a foreign company struck oil, by law it had to hand it over to NIOC; on the other hand, if its efforts resulted in dry wells, then the foreign firm had to bear the costs on its own. By contrast, under the earlier Mossadeq "nationalization," foreign companies could still participate in Iran's oil sector – under contract through NIOC – in ways that created equity-like incentives to find oil. As with many companies in the region, such as in Saudi Arabia, the period up to nationalization saw many local NIOC employees working alongside members of the consortium. Thus by 1974 when the consortium quickly unraveled,

NIOC workers had gained the requisite technical skills for handling operations on their own – along with the benefits of Shah-funded engineering universities in Tehran and Ahwaz – and several Iranians promptly took over operational positions that previously belonged to AIOC British employees (Takin 2009).

Everything changed yet again in 1978–1979. The Islamic Revolution in Iran dramatically altered the way Iran and the rest of the world viewed each other. The new government abolished the monarchy and established a parliamentary theocracy, led by the Grand Ayatollah[25] or supreme leader and his cabinet and councils (the Guardian and Expediency Councils), a bi-cameral parliament (the Majlis) where the upper house is fully appointed while the lower house is elected by popular vote, and an appointed judicial council (the judiciary). As far as NIOC was concerned, one of the changes brought about by the revolutionary government was the abandonment of pre-revolution foreign oil contracts.

Perhaps the most drastic change brought about by the revolution was the establishment of the Ministry of Petroleum. Before 1979, there were ministers or viziers of oil but never a stand-alone ministry: the Shah merely appointed people to his cabinet who were in charge of the oil industry. After the revolution, the existence of a Ministry of Petroleum has made it easier for NIOC to communicate with different levels of government, specifically the Majlis and the executive, especially since in practice the ministry is fused with and not separate from NIOC.[26] In terms of the oil sector itself, the purpose of the ministry was to manage hydrocarbon operations by overseeing the new division of Iran's four state-owned hydrocarbon enterprises: NIOC, the National Iranian Gas Company (NIGC), the National Petrochemical Company (NPC), and the National Iranian Oil Refining and Distribution Company (NIORDC). These different enterprises were remnants of the Shah's era where various hydrocarbon operations were entrusted to different organizations. Unlike other countries where such groups were subsidiary to a central NOC, in practice these units were more like partners for NIOC rather than subordinate units.[27]

After the revolution and the concomitant flight of foreign oil companies from Iran due to the annulment of foreign contracts, NIOC finally took all the reins of the country's oil operations. With the departure of foreign companies from drilling sites, NIOC was forced

to operate some twenty-seven oil rigs that had been abandoned in this
exodus. Already burdened with the task of managing all upstream
and downstream activities, NIOC decided to establish a subsidiary
specifically designed to handle all drilling operations. Indeed, in later
periods when NIOC would temporarily gain more independence
from the government, it would establish still more para-statal or semi-
private companies – a pattern (especially evident in the 1990s) that is
discussed in more detail later.

3 Relationships between NIOC and the Iranian state

In order to understand the nature of state–NOC relations in Iran, it
is helpful to discuss, first, NIOC's organizational structure and then,
second, the structure of the Iranian political system. I then turn to
a detailed analysis of the relationship between the company and the
government in terms of NIOC's avenues of communication with various state actors and institutions, and in terms of what the government
expects and demands from its NOC.

Outsiders regularly criticize NIOC as opaque, inward looking,
and overly bureaucratic; similarly from the inside, NIOC employees,
despite their strong sense of company loyalty and pride, emphasize
the opacity at the upper levels of the organization. While the organization is notably lacking in transparency, in fact the organizational
structure itself is comprehensible. On paper, NIOC oversees a number of semi-independent state enterprises that provide operational
functions such as drilling, production, and refining. Within this
organizational chart, shown in Figure 6.2, NIOC's function is less
as an oil company and more as an overseer of its many subsidiaries. It works with the Majlis to develop policies that are incorporated in the nation's five-year development plans; in turn, NIOC
embeds those plans into the operational plans that the subsidiaries
implement.[28]

The National Iranian Offshore Oil Company (NIOOC), the major
offshore subsidiary, controls production on a reserves base of 91 billion barrels of oil (two-thirds of the national total) and 173 trillion
cubic feet of gas (18% of the total) (APRC 2008). Despite this huge
base, as of 2008, NIOOC produced only 16% of Iran's oil and a tiny
fraction of the nation's gas. The largest subsidiary – measured by production levels – is the National Iranian South Oil Company, which

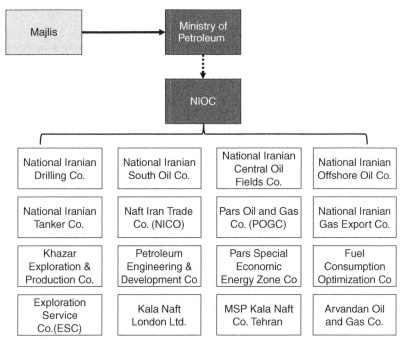

Figure 6.2 Organizational chart of NIOC and its subsidiaries.

Note: The dotted line between the Ministry of Petroleum and NIOC represents the notion that they are largely the same entity, as I have pointed out in the main text. Several members of NIOC's board also work for the ministry and vice versa. As such, NIOC officials communicate directly with the Majlis given that they are part of the Ministry of Petroleum as well.

produced 3.3 million barrels per day (81% of Iran's total production) and 97.4 mcm per day of gas (22% of total gas production) in 2008. Most of the balance of Iran's gas is produced by the National Iranian Central Oilfields Company – which despite its name is predominantly a gas operator – that accounts for 271 mcm per day or 62% of total gas production (Islamic Republic of Iran Ministry of Petroleum 2008).[29] In addition to these production enterprises, NIOC oversees the Oil Exploration Operations Company, which is primarily a service company engaged in geologic surveying.

Before examining the relationships between NIOC and the Iranian state, it is essential to discuss the nature of the political system. *Velayat-e-faqih* is the Persian term that sums up Iran's political structure and can be loosely translated as "the Rule of the Jurisprudent."

It refers to the top level of the theocracy: the ayatollah and his control over all of Iranian politics. After the revolution, Ayatollah Ruhollah Musavi Khomeini established the *velayat-e-faqih* system as a completely top-down government where the supreme leader (the title that Khomeini bestowed on himself and that was given to the current Ayatollah Ali Khamene'i after Khomeini's death) is the ultimate head of state and is mandated to rule according to Islamic Law. The supreme leader has final say over the actions and decisions of the Majlis (the legislative branch that approves presidential appointments and drafts the country's laws), the Office of the President, and the ever-mysterious Assembly of Experts, which is in charge of the selection of successive supreme leaders. Aside from these three branches of government, the supreme leader also oversees three bodies that essentially run the entire country: the Guardian Council, the Expediency Council, and the judiciary.[30] The Guardian Council vets presidential candidates and has veto power over legislative decisions made in the Majlis. With a more opaque role in the government, the Expediency Council is responsible for settling disputes between the Guardian Council and the Majlis, but also serves as an advisory board for the supreme leader. Lastly, the judiciary enforces rule of law, nominates candidates for the Guardian Council, and is appointed and completely controlled by the supreme leader. In practice, the *velayat-e-faqih* also bestows upon the supreme leader direct control over the armed forces, the intelligence ministry, the judicial system, the national broadcast network, and the selection of the government's top officials (Naji 2008). When the *velayat-e-faqih* system was set up in 1979, Khomeini also rewrote the constitution of Iran to impose severe restrictions on the ability of foreign oil companies to own hydrocarbon assets, thus finalizing the process of nationalization of the oil sector. (For more detail, see Box 6.1.)

Thus in theory, all power flows from the supreme leader. In practice, Iran's system of administration is extremely complicated and the ability of the many arms of government to understand and administer the society – including the country's oil industry – is highly variable. Periodically, the government has been wracked by financial crises linked to its extreme dependence on oil revenues, shown in Figure 6.3, which are highly variable with the price of oil and over the long term the capability of the oil sector to yield exports. From the inception of NIOC in 1951, the government budget became increasingly reliant

---

Box 6.1 The constitution of Iran

One of the obvious themes in Iran's constitution is the drive towards nationalization and a state-controlled economy. Fear of foreign "colonialism" drove the Revolutionaries who authored the constitution to design a system that would ensure the security of Iran's natural resources. This is reflected in Article 3.5 – one of the state goals of the new Islamic Republic is "the complete elimination of imperialism and the prevention of foreign influence" – and Article 43.8 where one of the principles of the Iranian economy is the "prevention of foreign economic domination over the country's economy" (Islamic Republic of Iran 1979). To protect the oil sector, the authors of the new constitution mandated that foreign companies be prohibited from owning equity stakes in hydrocarbon projects. Unsurprisingly, the constitution acts as a constraint on the oil sector. World Bank researchers Audinet, Stevens, and Streifel note that the burdensome constitution "tends to act as a rather blunt instrument when it comes to the sector's operations" (World Bank 2007, p. v). In practice, over time Iran has tried to relax those restrictions. Article 44 was amended in 2006 to allow an increasing role of foreign companies in Iran. The amendments specifically allow for the sale of state-owned enterprises and properties, excluding of course NIOC and its assets, but including downstream assets of NIOC's three sister organizations (NIGC, NPC, and NIORDC).

---

on oil revenues up until the 1979 revolution. After the revolution and during the war with Iraq, declining oil revenues significantly damaged the government budget while at the same time the budget began to rely more on income taxes (CBI multiple years). Dependence on oil revenues in the 1990s was largely responsible for the budget crisis in 1996–1998, as the government relied on oil and gas revenues for 55 percent of the budget between 1996 and 2001: As a result of crashing oil prices in the mid to late 1990s, Iranian government revenue fell from 62.6 billion rials in 1997 to 53.6 billion rials in 1998, but with a boost in oil prices by 2000, total government revenues dramatically increased to 104.6 billion rials (CBI 2000/2001).

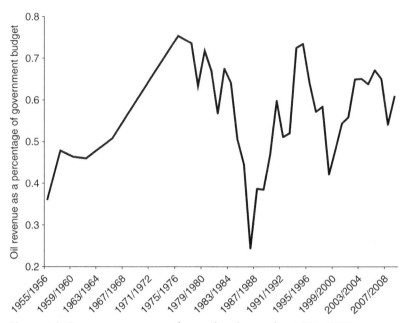

Figure 6.3 Government revenue from oil and gas sales, 1955–2009.
Sources: CBI multiple years; Karshenas (1990); author's calculations.

To help reduce this volatility, Iran followed a practice widely used in oil-rich countries and established an Oil Stabilization Fund (OSF) in 2000. Table 6.1 gives a snapshot of the reliance on oil revenue since the inception of the OSF. NIOC now sends funds both to the government directly and the OSF. As detailed in Box 6.2, the government uses the OSF to smooth budgetary spending, notably for social programs as well as filling in gaps in the government balance sheet (CBI 1998–2008; IMF 2008).

OSF rules allowed the government – through the Central Bank and the Ministry of Economic and Financial Affairs – to borrow against the fund and thus create the risk of uncontrolled debts (if oil prices stayed low in the long term), as OSF extractions would exceed contributions (Davis *et al.* 2003).[31] Unlike other wealth funds, Iran's OSF has a special role in reinvestment in the nation's oil industry because investment in oil operations is, like the OSF, integrated into the government budget. During the first Ahmadinejad administration (2005–2009), the amount of money reinvested in

Table 6.1. *Oil revenues in the fiscal budget*

(In billions of Iranian rials)	2000–01	2001–02	2002–03	2003–04	2004–05	2005–06	2006–07	2007–08	2008–09
Total government revenue	109,407	128,860	213,148	263,375	335,694	470,990	574,989	639,109	814,235
Revenue from oil sales and taxes	59,449	71,957	102,553	128,154	150,413	186,342	181,881	173,519	215,650
Injection from Oil Stabilization Fund	—	—	35,876	43,290	63,752	69,383	142,573	116,494	184,224
Oil as a percent of total revenue	54%	56%	65%	65%	64%	67%	65%	54%	61%

Note: Starting in 2005 new funds emerged through which the government collects additional oil revenue.
Sources: MEES, based on data from IMF, CBI multiple years.

Box 6.2 Iran's Oil Stabilization Fund and the rent collection process

Initially established as a means to control fluctuating oil revenues, the OSF quickly became a "piggy bank" that the government periodically raids.[32] The OSF was set up in 2000 as a foreign currency account to hold oil revenues, at a time when oil prices hovered around $16/barrel; the idea was to dampen the effect of volatile oil prices and stabilize the government's annual budgets while providing a financial means for commercial banks to invest in projects prioritized by the government's five-year plans. Article 60 of the Third Five-Year Development Plan (TFYDP 2000–2004) mandated that the difference between projected and actual oil revenues be contributed to the OSF. For example, the TFYDP predicted that in 2003/2004 fiscal oil revenue would be $11.1 billion, when in fact the actual fiscal oil revenue was $18.5 billion; thus in theory the difference of $7.4 billion would be allocated to the OSF (IMF 2008). Yet in reality, only $5.8 billion actually made it into the fund.[33] As for government withdrawals from the fund, the TFYDP and Fourth Five-Year Development Plan (FFYDP 2005–2009) limited the withdrawals to periods when the government's oil export receipts could not cover the budgeted amount for that period. As an addendum, the five-year plans also allowed for the withdrawal of funds for the purposes of lending to priority private entrepreneurs.

Control of the OSF was in the hands of a seven-member Board of Trustees, the majority of whom were appointed by the president, up until May 2008, when oversight of the OSF was given to the Government Economic Committee (a Majlis subcommittee). In theory, the Majlis has the authority to approve OSF transactions by using forecasted figures from five-year plans. The parliamentary body also has the power to cap OSF lending to domestic companies. Yet in reality, OSF transactions are made without parliamentary oversight. A 2008 report by the IMF found that certain OSF operations are left out of the central government's budget documents, shielding these transactions from parliamentary scrutiny (IMF 2008, p. 39). The World Bank notes that government withdrawals from the OSF have increased dramatically, with the government drawing an estimated 70 percent of oil revenue in the OSF during the 2002–2006 period (World Bank 2006a, pp. 29–30).

The net contributions and withdrawals of the OSF have considerably fluctuated since the fund's establishment in 2000: the yearly balances have ranged from $0.4 billion in 2003/2004 to -$1.1 billion in 2006/2007 to $12.1 billion in 2007/2008. The current balance reflects total inflows of $34.3 billion from oil revenues and loan payments and total outflows of $24.7 billion, with the government taking the lion's share of $20.3 billion while domestic firms only received $4.3 billion in loans (CBI 2008/2009; IMF 2008). The savings policy has been criticized heavily by those who favor more loans to domestic firms to support the struggling Iranian economy. As former Deputy Oil Minister for International Affairs, Hadi Nejad-Hosseinian points out, "Instead of using the money to extend loans to the private and public sectors, the funds are being used to make up for budget deficits ... A major challenge to the economy at present is that the government is competing with the people to control the economy" (MEES 48:21 2008). However, one of the major deficiencies of the OSF is its lack of transparency. The Sovereign Wealth Fund Institute, a watchdog institute monitoring resource funds globally, has rated Iran's OSF as one of the least transparent resource funds in the world: The fund received a 1 out of a possible 10 points on the SWF Linaburg-Maduell Transparency Index.[34] As such, the above figures on the monetary contents of the OSF are merely estimates, as the true value of OSF transactions is unknown.

the oil industry suggests that the government had money to spare: in 2006/2007, the government allowed NIOC to spend $12 billion on oil and gas projects and in 2007/2008, $16 billion (Taghavi 2008). Furthermore, while total oil and gas revenue was $82 billion for 2008/2009, the actual total is most likely much higher if one includes a generous estimate of $32 billion that was deposited (net contributions) into the OSF (CBI 2008/2009; IMF 2008). Yet the reality is that not even members of parliament know how much is actually in the OSF, and some analysts put the oil fund figure as low as $7 billion.[35] What is clear is that the fund remains very small compared with stabilization funds elsewhere in the Gulf, such as in Saudi Arabia and Abu Dhabi, and that it is small in comparison with the annual government budget and the annual investment needs of Iran's oil and gas sector. While it is possible in theory to raise substantial funds for oil projects by linking them to future revenues, in practice most of Iran's budget administration is focused on short-term issues and is not well organized to manage the financial risks that would accompany a large investment program. As such, money that could be going into reinvestment in the oil sector is instead channeled to the OSF. As a former IOC employee explained, "Iran does have the financial capacity to take risks in oil, but perhaps the political motivations prevent such risk."[36]

The government's actual ability to administer policy depends not only on its complicated lines of control but also on the stability and strength of the theocracy. When asked about how the revolution changed the nature of the oil industry, one former NIOC director remarked, "[In post-revolution Iran] all oil ventures are driven by politics and not by commercial reasoning."[37] With the advent of the theocracy, all executive and legislative decisions regarding NIOC became highly politicized, in the effort to use Iran's oil to build effective political alliances to counter growing political pressure from the West. Those political efforts hinge on the stability of the theocracy because that affects the time horizon of the country's political masters – long time horizons allow for more patient investment and broad-based social programs, but short ones lead to patronage and expropriation, including in the oil sector (see Chapter 2). The question of the stability of the Islamic Republic is hard to assess, especially at this writing. While instability is apparent, such as the rioting in the aftermath of the June 2009 elections, so far there has been no real and successful challenge to the current regime. Riots against a long-overdue policy to raise gasoline prices were quelled when the government changed the rationing system, indicating that while the government has command over the population, it still compromises when the stakes reach an appropriate threshold.[38] Indeed, the regime has proved quite resilient. And unlike the Shah (who could flee the country) the current elite has few options outside Iran and is likely to persist as long as possible. Thus, for the oil sector, NIOC's leaders know that they must be compliant to the government structure. The enterprise is thus wedded to instability, the lack of long-term incentives to undertake oil development projects, and the inability to offer much to attract external expertise.

While Iran has, in theory, a centralized system of institutions, the reality is that institutional controls are much more fragmented. Iran's institutional framework is a multifarious, scattered web of semi-private organizations (referred to in Iran as *bonyads*), some as massive as the *Bonyad-e Mostazafen va Janbazan* (The Foundation for the Oppressed and Disabled), which by some accounts employs 200,000 people and essentially runs the industrial, tourism, and services sectors (Saeidi 2004). Such institutions, which have become fiefdoms, are both a drain on the government budget – although exact costs are hard to pin down – and a constraint on political decisions regarding the domestic economy.[39] These institutions are responsible for many costly flagship state projects, such as the massive reconstruction effort in the Imam Reza shrine in Mashhad. In times of privatization, *bonyads* and other politically connected individuals are first in line for underpriced purchases of public assets through mostly rigged or preferential auctions, which siphons resources away from the state (Thaler *et al.* 2010). The *bonyads* have also increased their presence in upstream oil and gas operation ventures, which NIOC has tried to prevent in the past.[40] In theory, budget controls would impose discipline on *bonyads* and other fiscal termites in the system. But the weakest link in this network of institutions is the Central Bank of Iran (CBI). Principally operating under Islamic anti-usury laws,[41] the CBI has done a poor job of creating incentives to price risk. Thus the bank has allowed more risky lending practices that promote heavy borrowing against the OSF, creating the illusion that the government has large resources at its disposal with little attention to the cost of using them – allowing actors such as the *bonyads* to siphon what they can.

In this way, the convoluted nature of Iran's political structure presents many challenges to NIOC. The government's goals are hard to discern; lines of control are convoluted; and the ponderous institutions create many checks and balances that favor gridlock. If NIOC were to strictly follow legal guidelines, every trivial operational decision would be subject to scrutiny by the Majlis, the Guardian Council, the Economic Board of Governors, and countless other bureaucracies. Figure 6.4 traces the major NIOC connections to the government. NIOC's relationship with each of these institutions is one of tiptoeing

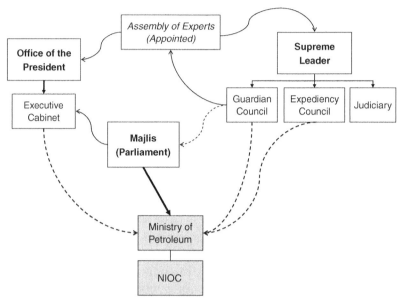

Figure 6.4 Oil within the Iranian political system.

Note: Dotted lines represent informal connections, whereas solid lines represent de jure links; arrows indicate the direction of influence. For instance, the Guardian Council appoints the Assembly of Experts, while the Assembly of Experts determines the list of candidates who can run in elections. The Guardian Council also has an indirect connection with the Ministry of Petroleum, between the chairman of the council and the minister.

Sources: World Bank (2005); Gonzalez (2007); BBC News (2009a); author's interviews.

around overly bureaucratic lines and pursuing indirect or sometimes informal channels with specific government agencies.

Formally, the energy sector is overseen by the Supreme Energy Council, which includes the Iranian president and his cabinet, the Minister of Petroleum, and others.[42] Before July 2007, oil and gas projects were first approved by Iran's Management and Planning Organization (MPO) then by the High Economic Council (HEC), whose approval was necessary primarily for large projects and contracts with foreign oil companies. After July 2007 President Ahmadinejad dissolved the MPO and created a new council (the Supreme Energy Council) in which decisions are based on orders directly from the executive, at times without any consultation with NIOC.[43] Prior to 2007, NIOC could pursue its own priorities by navigating through the chaos in public administration; after 2007 it was forced to be more compliant under stricter direct control from the president. In some other countries, executive control is mediated by a strong ministry that sets policy for the sector, but in Iran the ministry is indistinguishable from NIOC and thus is largely impotent as an independent force. One former IOC manager stated that "some people held two cards – one for NIOC and one for the ministry ... I haven't seen a national oil company that has such an intermingle between political influences – the Majlis and the Ministry of Foreign Affairs, to name a few – and operating people."[44]

Indeed, since NIOC's inception the oil minister and NIOC's managing director have held very close ties and before 2001 were in fact the same person. Before 2001, the oil minister had always been the managing director of NIOC. This approach is rare but evident in a few other countries, such as Venezuela since 2004 (see Chapter 10). This pattern ended when Bijan Zanganeh, former oil minister (and former energy minister), handed over NIOC's reins to Seyed Mehdi Mir-Moezi. Seemingly, this decision was made to change NIOC's image in the global oil market into a more independent, less politically charged oil company; however, few outsiders believed that much had actually changed, as reported in a leading news source at the time: "while the government has indicated that it is in theory not opposed to separating NIOC from the ministry, Mr. Zanganeh is understood to be determined to retain control of Iran's oil and gas industry" (MEES 44:45 2001).[45]

The overarching goal of Iran's leaders is survival. Under this main goal, four particular goals guide most efforts by the government to manage NIOC: rent collection, job creation, freedom from foreign interference, and meeting domestic energy demands.

Aside from the financial importance of oil revenues in the government budget, which I have discussed above, the funding of social programs is vital to the stability of the Islamic government. During the times of relatively low oil prices in the period 2000–2004, when the reformist President Khatami was still in office, social spending was low. Since then, net lending to social programs has increased from $2.1 billion in 2005–2006 to $4.3 billion in 2007–2008. Through oil revenue redistribution, populists within the political system – led by President Ahmadinejad – have solidified their constituencies in impoverished areas of Iran. These social programs are vital to Ahmadinejad's survival as he has drawn electoral strength from his base in rural Iran by promising the expansion of educational, health, and religious programs with oil money during his "provincial tours" (Naji 2008, pp. 216). Though Ahmadinejad's extreme populism is viewed critically by both reformers and hard-line conservatives, these kinds of social programs are not new to the theocracy, as evident in the long-standing role of the *bonyads*. While the government directs funds to social programs through the state budget, the *bonyads* are the operational arm of the public sector, overseen by the supreme leader, and are predominantly tax-exempt; as such, NIOC and its affiliates must foot the bill for these foundations.

The government also uses petrodollars to finance its own political stability by investing heavily in defense and in the state police. A particular beneficiary of this spending is the Revolutionary Guard, whose primary objective is to protect the Islamic Republic and maintain peace and stability in the country. As a former NIOC mid-level manager explained, "Ahmadinejad has been taking a lot out [of the OSF] for various projects of his, not in a corrupt way, but it is going to things like the Revolutionary Guard."[46] Furthermore, the guard has been steadily taking control of downstream assets through clerical appointments to oversee the *bonyads*.[47] As one Iran scholar puts it, "It is certainly a sign of muscling their way into oil, but the *bonyad* is not an official part of the Revolutionary Guard ... [The guard] has been involved in the oil and gas sector heavily, building pipelines and ports, etc."[48] The guard involves itself in the oil sector not only through *bonyads* but also through the guard's many economic subsidiaries, which have invested in several downstream projects and, some believe, at least one upstream project.[49]

In Iran, like most of the other countries rich in petroleum, the government uses prodigious oil resources for job creation. The state sees itself as *the* provider of jobs in the country, especially for college graduates, as the public sector employs 84 percent of eligible workers with at least a bachelor's degree (Salehi-Isfahani 2009); yet unemployment is still rampant, where 21 percent of eligible workers under 29 are without a job (CBI 2008/2009). Yet unlike many other countries, which saddle the NOC with the task of creating jobs, the signals in Iran are more mixed. The government has not strongly encouraged NIOC to increase its employment – in 2008 the company had 140,000 employees with 40,000 more employed as contractors, which are small numbers in a populous country – as the state institutions (e.g., Majlis and Economic Board of Governors) have focused instead on improving the quality of employee training at NIOC.[50] This suggests that the burden of state employment rests more on other institutions that the state controls more directly, namely the *bonyads* involved in the agricultural, metals, and manufacturing sectors (CBI 2008/2009; Thaler *et al.* 2010). The goal of job creation has waned a bit as a priority, given recent growth in the private oil sector (a topic I discuss more below) and employment opportunities outside the realm of the public oil sector (Takin 2009). Compared with other NOCs, NIOC faces some of the same employment challenges that Sonatrach has been adapting to in the past few years, as the Algerian government has been discouraging the oil company from creating more jobs in an attempt to replace the goal of job creation with increased rent collection (Marcel 2006, pp. 130; Chapter 13). This is quite contrary to what we normally expect from an NOC, though as Marcel points out, "more sophisticated human resources policies are increasingly the norm."[51] NIOC has not filled its organization with nearly "useless" employees, as we have seen with other NOCs such as in India and China (see Chapters 17 and 9, respectively.)

Another central goal of the Iranian state is protection of the country's oil wealth from foreign interference. Iranians have long held the perception that Iranian oil is theirs and theirs alone: As one NIOC former employee stressed, "[We] wanted recognition of Iran's sovereignty over foreign agents ... and the main goal [of nationalization] was this recognition of sovereignty. The oil was Iran's and not England's."[52] Out of this sentiment, NIOC was initially created as the protectorate of oil supplies to maintain sovereignty against "foreign imperialists," along with its more traditional role of generating revenue for the government. (Mexico's oil sector was nationalized on the same logic. See Chapter 7.) The executive and the higher-ups in the theocracy also use NIOC to build up partnerships with other NOCs, whom the government views as more trustworthy partners than Western IOCs. (Recently, the Venezuelan state has followed a similar path, and Brazil may be headed in the same direction with its rich new oil finds. See Chapters 10 and 12, respectively.) Given its precarious position vis-à-vis the Western world, Iran has pursued

a strategy of attracting countries that are prone to avoiding or skirt-
ing Western sanctions for involvement in the country's oil and gas
fields. Most notably, Iran has strengthened its alliances with Russia
(through Gazprom), China (through CNPC), and Venezuela (through
work in the Orinoco oil belt via NIOC's subsidiary PetroPars). One
former NIOC director and OPEC diplomat stressed that NIOC
"always wanted to become an international company ... Even during the period of the Shah, they had [projects] in South Korea, South
Africa, and India ... But now the employees who are in Venezuela are
there for completely political reasons and not economic [reasons]."[53]
The theocracy does not necessarily push for increased profitability
in the oil sector but would seemingly rather use NIOC and its sister
affiliates as political tools to strengthen Iran's position in the region
and in the world.

Finally, since the time of the Shah, it has always been the government's goal to provide the domestic market with cheap energy drawn
from Iran's wealth of natural resources. As a practical matter, this
has required addressing the troubling lack of natural gas infrastructure (discussed above). And it has especially centered on securing the
supply of gasoline, whose consumption is growing rapidly. During the
period 2000–2008, Iran imported roughly 40 percent of its gasoline
due to capacity constraints in the refining sector.[54] Since the OSF was
established in 2000, the government has been forced to withdraw
money from the fund to finance gasoline imports at a rate of $5 bil-
lion per year (MEES 49:42 2006; MEES 51:25 2008), as the government – through NIORDC – must pay global market prices to import
gasoline while heavily subsidizing gasoline for domestic usage at 10
cents per liter or roughly 37 cents per gallon (CBI 2008/2009). Iran's
domestic use of oil and gas resources has been in a dangerous position
ever since former Minister of Oil Bijan Zanganeh (1997–2005) made
the decision to rely on imports of gasoline to account for the shortfall
in refining capacity instead of installing new refineries. (The lack of
refining capacity is and has been due to poor investment strategies
and, more significantly, damage done to hydrocarbon infrastructure
during the brutal Iran–Iraq War in the 1980s.) As demand for energy
in Iran continued to grow unfettered in the late 1990s and 2000s,
the gap between gasoline production and domestic demand has wid-
ened. Asked why refining capacity has not kept pace with growing
demand, one interviewee agreed that "[Zanganeh] was not in favor

of building refineries, even though people criticized him widely for it. His argument really was that it is cheaper to import than it is to build new [refineries]. But the main reason for shortage now [and increasing domestic demand] is the cheap price of gasoline."[55] (At the time of writing this chapter, NIORDC has attempted to alleviate this problem by upgrading and expanding current refining capacity by as much as 266,000 barrels per day by 2013.[56])

Fixing the gasoline problem through price reforms has proved politically difficult, and fiscal troubles ripple through the oil sector. Like other NOCs, NIOC is used to satisfy the government's promise to the people for cheap energy, despite the growing concerns within Iran about the country's rapidly increasing energy demand.[57] Much to its detriment, NIOC must supply refining companies[58] with crude oil that is priced well below global prices to ensure that refineries and distributors can provide consumers with gasoline and diesel at $0.10 per gallon and $0.03 per gallon, respectively.[59] If this subsidy were not present, NIOC would be able to sell crude at market prices and reap the profits.

Thus NIOC, like many NOCs, actually faces many objectives. In the next section I turn to the question of how well it performs in meeting them.

4 NIOC's performance and strategy

Oil analysts repeatedly point to Iran's failure to achieve its pre-revolution production levels of 6 million barrels per day as the prime indicator of the inefficiencies and shortcomings of NIOC. Previous scholars explain this failure by telling the story of the Iran–Iraq War and the heavy damage the oil sector incurred as a result of Iraqi bombings in southwestern Iran, the traditional center of the country's oil industry (Brumberg and Ahram 2007; Takin 2009). Others point to factors that are internal to Iran, notably Ahmadinejad's efforts to steer the country toward a statist and populist economy, which has seen government budgets swell and dependence on oil earnings grow as well as direct intervention to assert greater (and more debilitating) control over NIOC (Naji 2008). Political scientists have pointed to the rentier effect and its impacts on the oil industry (Mahdavy 1970; Katouzian 1981; Skocpol 1982). NIOC has particularly suffered from increased state budgets (see Table 6.1) because it has been unable to invest in

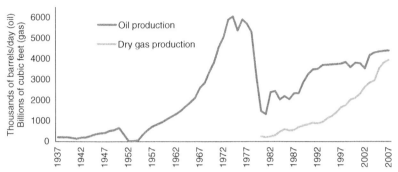

Figure 6.5 Iranian oil and gas production, 1937–2007.
Sources: OPEC (2004–2007); BP (2009a).

new capacity. But NIOC's troubles are more profound: Even when the government has allocated large sums of money for reinvestment into the oil economy, the enterprise has not been able to spend those resources. Some of the difficulty stems from international sanctions, which constrain foreign investment (Esfahani and Pesaran 2009). Here I explore these factors, and I begin by focusing on NIOC's performance as an oil and gas producer.

4.1 Explaining NIOC's poor performance

Iran's oil output has been highly variable (Figure 6.5) and today struggles far below its potential. In this section I focus on oil, although the country is also a poor performer in gas.[60] In the period before 1974, oil and gas production was largely in the hands of foreign companies (under the consortium agreement) and NIOC played a less active role in operations. Between 1974 and the 1979 revolution, NIOC was able to slightly boost production during a time when IOCs were forced to leave the sector and the company was asked to play a larger role.

Iran's oil performance is broadly the result of four forces at work. One is foreign policy – notably Iran's participation in OPEC. A second factor is NIOC's organization as an enterprise – that is, its ability to mobilize external assistance where needed and to plan and execute a coherent strategy (which has been heavily influenced by two major waves of reorganization: the 1979 revolution and the post-2005 reshuffling by Ahmadinejad). The third factor is the damaging effect

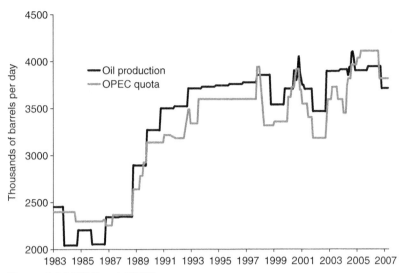

Figure 6.6 NIOC and OPEC.
Sources: MEES; OPEC (2004–2007).

of major external shocks, notably the 1980–1988 war with Iraq, and the periodic enactment of international sanctions since 1979. In terms of impact on oil volumes, these external factors have had the largest impact on NIOC. This destruction is the principal cause of NIOC's inability to achieve pre-revolution production levels, which exceeded 6 million barrels per day. And a fourth factor is the relationship between the oil company and the government, which has at times strained NIOC's ability to perform at its optimal level. In the next section I address the first three factors, which I consider to be external factors with respect to NIOC. In the subsequent section I explore the fourth, more complicated factor of NIOC's relationship with the government: NIOC's strategy in managing state demands, in particular, which will fill out the picture of underperformance.

4.2 Explaining NIOC's poor performance: external factors

The first of these factors – OPEC – is relatively easy to dismiss. For other case studies in this volume, notably Saudi Arabia, OPEC constraints have had a major impact on output and it has been difficult to disentangle the performance of the state oil company from the policy decision to restrict output (see Chapter 5). For Iran, it is much easier to disentangle the forces. It is possible that OPEC quotas were a binding constraint on NIOC during the late 1980s and early 1990s when the enterprise had excess production capacity, but more recently, NIOC has failed to reach its quotas. Figure 6.6 shows post-revolution Iranian oil production alongside Iran's OPEC quotas. Since 2005, NIOC has produced roughly 250,000 barrels per day short of its allotted OPEC production levels. This shortfall has little to do with OPEC and is mainly a sign of NIOC's recent poor performance combined with external shocks.

The second of these factors – NIOC's organizational troubles – is best explained by looking at two critical events in NIOC's history. The first is the 1979 revolution; the second is the 2005 elections. Before the revolution, NIOC's performance was markedly improving every year with the aid of foreign operators and a reasonably high level of reinvestment into the oil industry. With the Shah's exile and eventual deposition in 1979, NIOC tremendously suffered with the flight of many of the oil industry's top officials and their replacement with inexperienced revolutionaries who were appointed by the theocracy. Production dropped to 3.2 million barrels per day in 1979 and by 1980 to 1.5 million barrels per day (BP 2008). Understandably, these personnel changes wreaked havoc on NIOC and the oil industry. A former NIOC director notes, "Since the revolution, appointments came down to the lower levels, and these political appointees didn't have the experience ... They tried to act as politicians and not in the interest of the company. Competent employees under these new managers left and some even tried to play the game and became more political and 'grew beards and tried to become Islamic'. "[61] These "politicized" replacements made it difficult to establish credible ties among NIOC workers and their managers, and as a result NIOC saw much of its staff resign out of frustration toward new managers or because of disagreements with their new managers' political stances (Takin 2009). The same process occurred again in 2005 when Ahmadinejad was elected president and promised to rid the country of the "oil mafia." The organizational changes in 2005 have also seen the replacement of experienced and technically knowledgeable senior staff with inexperienced "cronies" of the Ahmadinejad administration. The fact that NIOC has twice been stirred up by the state, only to be left with technically inexperienced management, has undoubtedly taken its toll on NIOC's ability to make sound investment and production decisions.

The two major reorganizations of NIOC – one after the revolution and the second under President Ahmadinejad – are probably the single most important factors in explaining why NIOC has performed poorly. External shocks, the third factor driving Iran's oil performance, have amplified the harmful effects of these reorganizations and have been studied in depth by a number of scholars. Historians have pointed to the Iran–Iraq War as a cause for the slow recovery of Iranian oil production following the revolution (Elm 1992; Brumberg and Ahram 2007; Takin 2009). Economists have argued that the costs of American-imposed sanctions are crippling for the oil and gas sector (Amuzegar 1997; Torbat 2005). In truth, these explanations are defensible and have some merit in analyzing the performance troubles of the Iranian oil industry.

With casualty figures for both sides estimated at 1 million soldiers, paramilitaries, and civilians, the Iran–Iraq War was the deadliest in Iran's 5,000-year history and the eight-year war cost both states an estimated $150 billion (Mearsheimer and Walt 2003). NIOC was not spared from the conflict, unlike NOCs such as Sonangol, whose oil assets were located far from Angola's civil war zone (see Chapter 19). Saddam Hussein's military, along with US airstrikes, heavily damaged Iran's coastal oil infrastructure, destroying oil platforms, terminals, and tankers (Segal 1988). The particularly vital Kharg Island export facility was severely damaged by persistent and effective Iraqi air raids, and its destruction hampered foreign shipping and reduced NIOC's export capacity. The production difficulties that NIOC faced are evident, as during the war NIOC never broke the 2.5 million barrel-per-day mark (see Figure 6.5). Further, the war prevented large reinvestment even in fields that were not physically hit by the Iraqis. These fields, notably the massive Khuzestan fields in the southwest, began their natural decline during the war period and needed investment for enhanced oil recovery, but the money needed for reinvestment was being used to fund the war.[62] Even after the 1988 ceasefire agreement, the war had lasting effects on the economy and on the oil industry. Massive reconstruction efforts required funding at a time when oil prices were low, leaving few resources for NIOC's own reinvestment. Gradually, oil output grew but had barely reached

two-thirds the peak level of the late 1970s before revolution and war
disrupted the sector.

The implementation of economic sanctions by the United States,
and more recently by the United Nations, has damaged NIOC's capacity to reinvest into the oil industry as well as attract technically
competent foreign operators for the production of its natural gas
fields. Before 1995, the United States had applied targeted sanctions
on Iran in response to the revolution and the hostage crisis, but these
were relatively minor as they only affected US-Iranian trade.[63] In theory, those sanctions should not have had much impact on NIOC,
although during most of that period the Iran–Iraq War (in which the
United States informally participated on the Iraqi side) proved highly
distracting and debilitating for NIOC. With the passage of the Iran–
Libya Sanctions Act (ILSA) in 1995–1996, the United States targeted
any company that invested in Iran's petroleum industry, both domestic
and foreign companies and states. Any firm or agency investing more
than $40 million in the Iranian oil sector in a given year became sub-
ject to a series of economic punishments by the United States targeted
at the defiant firm or agency (Katzman 2007). ILSA and its aftermath
have had a much larger impact on NIOC. Total's abandonment of its
contract to develop South Pars in 2006–2007 was at the request of the
French government, which did not want to suffer the political consequences of violating the ILSA (MEES 50:40 2007). Similarly, NIOC's
ambitions to develop Caspian oil and gas fields with Azerbaijan were
denied when the United States pressured the Azeri government to
exclude NIOC from its operations (Entessar 1999). As one Iranian
oil executive explained, "The current low production levels in Iran
are [driven] by a failure of NIOC to increase exploration and production due to limited domestic capital, technology, manpower, and
management resources and the lack of proper financial incentives for
foreign investment. Of course the enforcement of US-led sanctions on
outside investments by the largest Western companies is [a] significant impediment."[64] Multilateral sanctions have had an even stronger
impact: the enactment of UN Security Council Resolutions 1736 (in
2006) and 1747 (in 2007) focused on Iran's nuclear ambitions and
its state-sponsoring terrorism activities by targeting (among others)
the Iranian banking system. As such, both UNSCR 1736 and 1747
have made it even more difficult for NIOC to obtain enough financial
backing from the Central Bank of Iran for large-scale projects.[65]

4.3 Explaining NIOC's poor performance: internal factors

The complex relationship between NIOC and the state makes it unduly difficult to separate out the strategy of the oil company from the goals and demands imposed on it by the government. Historically, the oil company's strategy was one of compliance with the monarchy and the demands of the consortium. In the formative years of NIOC's operations, between the 1950s and the revolution, the company was largely compliant with the state's demands for the oil sector. NIOC's role was mainly to oversee the foreign IOCs while gaining valuable technical knowledge from consortium employees and facilities. Thus the early period for NIOC was not one in which it had a conscious strategy but instead followed the wishes of the Shah and the oil viziers that the Shah had appointed to manage the oil industry. The central goal was to maximize the revenues for the state, and NIOC – as regulator rather than operator – performed that goal well.

Following the Petroleum Act of 1974 and the institutional changes of the revolution, NIOC was given unrivaled control over the oil and gas sector with the departure of the consortium and other foreign IOCs. Within the context of the new revolutionary political system, NIOC was able to work with the government to create new channels of communication with the state and new ways to shape oil policy. In particular, the creation of an executive branch and the assignment of greater power to the Majlis allowed for two such avenues of communication between NIOC and the government (as Figure 6.2 shows). Such communication was not possible prior to the revolution, as the Shah had absolute authority over any and all oil matters. But the strain of the Iran–Iraq War soon forced the company to adopt a new strategy – one focused on constant repairs and partial reconstruction of damaged facilities. Thus NIOC was not able to benefit from its relative autonomy until the war was over in the late 1980s. In the midst of postwar massive reconstruction efforts at sites that had been heavily shelled by the Iraqi military, NIOC was able to assert control over setting the political and regulatory agenda for the oil industry. Taking advantage of a weak state hampered by the war and by sanctions following the revolution, NIOC reclaimed for itself a much greater influence over oil policies in the drafting of five-year development plans by the Majlis. As discussed earlier, the de jure separation of the Ministry of Petroleum and NIOC was, in practice, a fusion of the two based on the overlap in personnel. Thus, the company's position with the Majlis vis-à-vis the Ministry of Petroleum was essentially a direct channel for NIOC to influence legislation. Ultimately, the war made NIOC much stronger in setting oil policy and much weaker in actually producing oil.

From 1985 to 1997, Minister of Petroleum and NIOC MD Gholam Reza Aghazadeh worked to improve NIOC's operating capabilities in a challenging war and postwar environment. In effect, he created a more autonomous NOC and laid the groundwork for the company to be able to rebuild capacity – which it did slowly, constrained by the massive loss of talented personnel and the strict fiscal environment that made it hard to obtain funding for investment projects. His efforts are seen as a success story, as production figures rose from 2.4 million barrels per day in 1988 to 3.7 million barrels per day by 1993 (Dadwal 1998; BP 2008). Furthermore, the number of active rotary oil rigs in that same period increased from eighteen to forty-five (Baker Hughes 2008). Aghazadeh's efforts to make NIOC into a functioning oil company, independent from the political turmoil of the state at the time, culminated with the selection of his successor to the Ministry of Petroleum.

Aghazadeh's departure led to the appointment of Bijan Zanganeh as minister of petroleum and MD of NIOC, who held power over the oil sector from 1997 to 2005. The policy of allowing NIOC to operate semi-autonomously continued. Fundamental to his political strength, Zanganeh had favorable connections with President Rafsanjani (1989–1997) – some have even called him a "pragmatist and protégé of Rafsanjani" – whose ideals of economic liberalization coincided with Zanganeh's (APS 56:16 2001). Even when the Rafsanjani administration ended, Zanganeh was able to seek out greater autonomy for NIOC, as he also enjoyed strong ties to President Khatami (1997–2005).[66] Even as Iran took a harder line politically, its oil sector continued to enjoy a measure of autonomy. As a sign of NIOC's autonomy in pursuing its profit-seeking strategy, in 1997 Zanganeh proclaimed, "I support decentralization and autonomy for various companies and better performance. I believe that all units of NIOC … should operate strictly on economic and commercial terms. They should also make profit on their own" (MEES 40:49 1997). This was quite a departure from prior oil ministers, who while they believed in Zanganeh's message, were still bound to satisfy the theocracy's desires for the oil sector (APS 56:16 2001).[67]

One sign of NIOC's growing autonomy was the nature of the "buyback" contract system, which was in large part designed by Zanganeh as a strategic compromise between full autonomy and total compliance with the state. Between 1979 and 1997, foreign oil companies were largely absent from operations in the Iranian oil sector except in a small number of projects, including failed operations with Gazprom in the Caspian and Persian Gulf operations with Total (Brumberg and Ahram 2007). Furthermore, the presence of new American-backed sanctions in 1995 and 1996 made it even harder for foreign operators to do business in Iran. In this isolated position, NIOC needed to find foreign assistance – especially for complex projects such as operating the extraction of difficult heavy oils and essentially all operations offshore. Mindful of the framework for analyzing NOC and IOC choices (presented in Chapter 4), NIOC was barely able to operate fields that were already in production and required only mature technologies and practices; the frontier was far beyond its reach and NIOC's managers knew that. The trick was to find a means of engaging foreigners while not running afoul of the conservative forces inside Iran's government – those same forces had led the revolution and, with unfavorable scrutiny, could squash the independence that NIOC had carefully carved for itself since the mid 1980s. As one IOC manager pointed out, "By and large, NIOC would have liked to be more involved with the IOCs. They saw their role as a recipient of technological transfer, general and performance management, strategy and development, business planning, and info management skills. They saw the IOCs as being very knowledgeable and wanted to learn from them."[68]

Desperate for foreign investment in the oil sector, NIOC pressed the state for an amendment to the constitution or at least a preferential clause that would allow NIOC to create incentives to bring foreign operators back to the oil industry. Out of these negotiations between NIOC and the state came the "buyback" system, which replaced the existing framework for foreign operators in the Iranian oil sector. Instead of a thirty-year period for IOCs to explore, develop, and operate a field (as is common for most PSAs), the government implemented a unique contract service mechanism: The buyback system only allowed for a five- to seven-year exploration and operation period (until 2004 when the time length was increased to twenty-five years), after which the operation of the field would be given to NIOC and the initial investment would be returned.[69] The government knew that this arrangement would be unattractive to IOCs that had options in other countries, so it fixed the return on investment at a 15–17 percent profit margin. The thinking among government planners was that a fixed return would reduce risk and attract more foreign operators, although in practice this is not how foreign operators evaluate risk. Moreover, the IOCs following the adoption of the buyback scheme have regularly complained that the government changed the buyback terms, thus making an investment proposition that was barely attractive to begin with into one that included much more risk in practice.[70]

Despite its many flaws, the buybacks did provide incentives for the return of some IOCs into the Iranian hydrocarbon sector. New contracts were negotiated in 2001 with Inpex for the Azadegan oil fields, in 1997 with Total for South Pars phases two and three,[71] and in 1999 with Shell for the offshore Soroush/Nowruz fields (*APS Review Gas Market Trends* 68:14 2007; MEES 42:47 1999). Essentially all of Iran's 1 million barrel-per-day expansion in oil production capacity from 1998 to 2005 can be traced to the benefits of the buybacks (MEES 48:32 2005). That the buyback system was approved by the Majlis and the upper levels of the state was a strategic success for NIOC and Zanganeh. Though NIOC was not fully successful in opening the oil industry to IOCs – given the state-favoring clauses of the buyback – the buybacks still confirmed NIOC's growing influence over key oil decisions. Crucially, the buybacks offered a politically viable way for NIOC to reengage with the outside world of more expert operators.

Whatever nascent autonomy NIOC had been gaining through slow and halting efforts since the late 1980s was reversed with Ahmadinejad's presidential victory.[72] One of his priorities as president was to purge the oil industry of any officials he thought were cronies of Rafsanjani and Khatami and thus, in his mind, linked to corruption. His first act pertaining to the oil industry was to sack Zanganeh and replace him with a more reliable ally. It took three tries before the Majlis approved an oil minister: Nearly five months after Zanganeh was removed from his post the Majlis finally approved Vaziri-Hamaneh. From this first key replacement, Ahmadinejad has since removed hundreds of senior ministry and NIOC staff and replaced them with more loyal officials. The process of purging the company partly resembles Chávez's purge of PDVSA. (Chávez ousted a much larger number of people, but PDVSA was much stronger as a company going into the purge and many of the key relationships with outside firms were left largely intact; see Chapter 10.)

With this change in the organizational structure of NIOC, the oil company returned to its strategy of compliance with the state. Both of the oil ministers after Zanganeh and many of the new senior NIOC officials have at times voiced their criticism of the state's interference with the oil sector but have largely directed NIOC to comply with the Ahmadinejad administration's goals.[73] In particular, upon Vaziri-Hamaneh's resignation as oil minister in 2007, Ahmadinejad was able to exert even more control over the oil sector with the appointment of Gholam-Hossein Nozari, a former NIOC MD with conservative-leaning politics (MEES 50:34 2007).[74] At this point in time, it is widely believed that Ahmadinejad has tightened his grip over the oil sector and has a strong influence over oil decisions given his network of loyalists placed in strategic appointments across the political system and across the oil sector (Hen-Tov 2007; Thaler *et al.* 2010). Thus, the post-2005 political landscape has organizationally changed NIOC and has driven the company to pursue its pre-revolutionary strategy of complete compliance with the state.

5 Conclusion

NIOC has been shaped by a unique confluence of historical events, geologic circumstances, and the changing political winds of Iran. Before the revolution, NIOC was seen as a success story by historians (Katouzian 1981; Zabih 1982). Its success reflected, in part, that it was not truly in charge of the oil industry; it regulated foreign oil companies that, in large measure, set the strategy for Iran's oil sector. The experienced presence of foreign operators in the Iranian oil sector allowed the newly formed NIOC to gain valuable technical and operational skills during the consortium period of 1954–1974, all the while remaining largely compliant with the Shah's oil policies and goals. When the foreign companies left during the period of 1974–1979, NIOC was able to assert itself as a fully functioning oil company, broadly competent in all aspects of the oil industry, which it had overseen only from an arm's length in the preceding period. Those brief five years were perhaps NIOC's golden age.

Political fallout from the revolution dramatically changed NIOC's internal organization and saw the company stuffed with inexperienced (but politically loyal) managers. Significant damage to the oil industry from the Iran–Iraq War in the 1980s diminished NIOC's capacity to produce at its potential and to reinvest in aging oil fields. Sanctions in the 1990s limited the company's ability to procure badly needed technologies to develop offshore and unconventional oil resources. But with the rise of strong-minded oil ministers in the 1990s, NIOC was able to gain more influence in parliamentary decisions while at the same time bargaining with the conservative isolationists in the upper chambers of government to open up the oil industry once again to foreign investment. However, further restructuring in the 2000s has once again changed NIOC's management. Faced with yet another change in the political landscape in 2005 and with subsequent organizational and managerial changes, whatever autonomy NIOC had was lost with Ahmadinejad's political reshuffling of the "oil mafia." Though NIOC has been steadily improving its production despite its aging and declining oil fields, these events and circumstances have made it incredibly challenging for NIOC to live up to its potential. Despite any temporary improvements in autonomy or changes in strategy, NIOC remains a largely inefficient company. NIOC's failures are marked by its inability to produce Iran's vast natural gas resources and its incapacity to reachieve pre-revolution oil production levels.

However, as Iranian political philosopher Akbar Ganji has eloquently observed, "In Iran there is always plurality." The political system, as I have tried to show, is rife with competing factions with different ideas on how to handle the future of the oil and gas industry. While some in power favor increasing short-term profits over long-term stability, others have pushed for the constancy of the Islamic Republic over many years to come. Similarly, there are stark political divisions over what to do about the country's growing energy demand: many seek to redirect exports to the domestic economy while others clamor for higher government revenues through increased oil and gas exports. Since the Islamic Revolution in 1979, those who are loyal to the permanence of the regime continue to dominate debates over the country's oil and gas strategies and objectives. In Iran's tumultuous political landscape, this may be the only truism that can predict where NIOC and the oil industry are headed in the future.

Notes

Department of Political Science, University of California, Los Angeles. I thank Siamak Adibi, Fereidun Fesharaki, Suzanne Maloney, and Valérie Marcel for helpful comments. Special thanks to David G. Victor, David Hults, and Mark C. Thurber for their assistance throughout the project. I also thank Pardis Mahdavi, Pete Nolan, Paul Stevens and my interviewees (who remain anonymous).

Reference note: I refer to articles from the Middle East Economic Survey (MEES) and the American Petroleum Society (APS) throughout the text by [Journal] [Volume]:[Number] [Year].

1 The state also uses oil revenues to fund subsidies for wheat, milk, cheese, rice, chemical fertilizers and pesticides, medicine, and mass transit in Tehran. In 2006/2007 government subsidies amounted to $6.3 billion (CBI 2006/2007). Note: The Iranian fiscal year corresponds with the Iranian calendar year, which starts March 21 and ends March 20. For example, the 2006/2007 year corresponds to the period March 21, 2006–March 20, 2007.

2 This percentage excludes petroleum products.

3 See Ross (2001) for more information on the resource curse. Simply put, a state dependent on rents from natural resources is less likely to become democratized, is more likely to be involved in transborder conflicts or civil wars, and will not develop economically to its full potential.

4 See Mahdavy (1970) and more recently Shambayati (1994) for a more thorough analysis of the theory of a rentier state as it applies to Iran. Essentially, a rentier state can fund government expenditures using resource rents (or any exogenous source of money, such as development aid) instead of using the more traditional method of constituency taxation. The theory posits that such a state will not be held accountable by its citizens because they are not forced to pay high taxes and thus expect very little from the state.

5 Due to all interviewees' requests for anonymity, every interviewee is given a number according to his/her affiliation. Twelve interviews in total were conducted: six with former NIOC employees (managers, directors, and contractors), coded as NIOC1–NIOC6; three with former IOC contractors working within Iran, coded as IOC1–IOC3; and three with academic experts (in Iran, the United Kingdom, and the United States), coded as IranScholar1–IranScholar 3.

6 Included in this category are the ultra-heavy Foroozan and Sirri blends, with an API gravity in the range 29–31 degrees. Both blends accounted for 165,000 barrels per day of Iran's total oil exports in 2008 (the trend has shifted toward heavier crude than in the past).

7 However, in 2007 these negotiations fell apart and as of the time of writing, NIOC has tentatively found a partner to develop the southern sector of Azadegan, having signed an MOU with CNPC in 2009 (MEES 50:15 2007; MEES 52:40 2009).

8 Similarly, NIOC estimates that the output of existing oil fields is declining at 9 percent or 350,000 barrels per day per annum since 2008 (APRC 2008, p. 138).

9 As of early 2011, construction of the IGAT-8 pipeline – which is set to deliver 100 mcm/day (or roughly 20 percent of Iran's natural gas consumption) from the Persian Gulf to Tehran via Qom – was still incomplete.

10 Despite a 350,000 barrel per day capacity, the actual throughput of the pipeline is roughly 100,000 barrels per day.

11 The largest refinery is located in Abadan, on the border with Iraq in the southwest province of Khuzestan, with roughly 30 percent of Iran's total refining capacity.

12 Discovered in 1991 by the National Iranian Offshore Oil Company (NIOOC), a subsidiary of NIOC, the South Pars fields now account for roughly half of Iran's gas reserves, with an estimated 13,500 bcm of gas and 17 billion barrels of condensate, of which 57 percent or 9.7 billion barrels are recoverable. (APRC 2008, p. 158; S Adibi, personal communication, September 14, 2009).

13 Along with the citations noted in the text, this section also draws from historical accounts found in Ala (1994); Daniel (2001); Keddie (2003); and Naji (2008).

14 "Ever since the discovery and production of oil in Iran, the political, economic, and social developments in our country have each been in a way intermingled with oil," NIOC Managing Director (MD) Seifollah Jashnsaz recounted in 2008 (MEES 51:22 2008).

15 For an excellent discussion of this turn of events, see Afkhami (2009).

16 See Elm (1992) for a discussion on the 1933 Agreement and its critics.

17 British accounts from that period offer a different view: "Not only does [the AIOC] provide steady jobs for some 70,000 Iranians; it provides, too, working conditions and amenities better than any which are obtainable elsewhere in Iran, or in neighboring countries either, for that matter" (AIOC 1951, p. 13).

18 Maugeri (2006) estimates that between 1947 and 1950, the British government collected more than 40 percent of AIOC gross profits, while only 20 percent went to the Iranian government.

19 It is believed that Ali Razmara was killed by a supporter of the pro-oil-nationalization group Fadayan-e Islam after Razmara pushed for a motion within the Majlis to oppose nationalization of AIOC assets. While not directly connected with the Fadayan-e Islam, Mossadeq was sympathetic to the group's goal of oil nationalization but was largely opposed to the use of violence as a means of political expression. (See Elm 1992 for more details on Razmara and his death.)

20 NIOC as a company was created in 1948 but was operating independent of state control until 1951.

21 Mossadeq had been granted full control over the military by the Majlis, who gave the prime minister a six-month term of emergency powers following mass protests in Iran in favor of Mossadeq when the Shah briefly forced him to resign his position as prime minister. By 1953, Mossadeq had been given emergency powers by the Majlis for another year, during which time he significantly weakened the powers of the monarchy and aristocracy by reducing the royal budget and prohibiting all foreign diplomats from relations with the Shah (Zabih 1982).

22 The Seven Sisters consisted of Exxon, Mobil, Texaco, Gulf, Chevron, Shell, and of course BP. Also included in the consortium was the Compagnie Française de Pétroles, which had a smaller share with roughly 6 percent control.

23 The first of these "fifty-fifty" agreements was made by PDVSA in 1948. Venezuela's lead on this producer-favoring contractual framework had a marked impact on how the consortium was set up, allowing Iran much more bargaining power over foreign companies. For a description of the first fifty-fifty agreements, see Chapter 10.

24 In this sense, Iran's oil industry was only partially nationalized in 1951 with the passage of Mossadeq's laws in the Majlis, given the presence of foreign companies controlling the bulk of operations. Full nationalization – what I refer to as "re-nationalization" – did not occur until much later, when in the 1970s the emergence of OPEC as a truly influential market force initiated a wave of nationalizations across oil-producing states around the world. Marcel notes that even after the coup, the foreign companies were acting as contractors to NIOC (Marcel 2006, p. 21). Other notable oil nationalizations in this period include the following: National Oil Corporation (Libya 1970), Saudi Aramco (60 percent government ownership by 1974), Petroleos de Venezuela S.A. (1976), Nigerian National Petroleum Corporation (1977), and Kuwait Petroleum Corporation (1980).

25 Note that the title "Grand Ayatollah" is a political title that is bestowed on the leader of an Islamic Republic, whereas "Ayatollah"

is a religious title that is granted to Islamic priests who have achieved
the highest ranking among Shia clerics, indicative of their expertise
in Islamic jurisprudence, ethics, philosophy, and the interpretation of
the Qur'an.

26 On this relationship, see Marcel (2006, p. 102).

27 This chapter does not discuss the other three enterprises in detail, for
they are outside the scope of this study. These three do not have control over Iran's hydrocarbons, as full operative control of oil and gas
reserves in Iran are legally entitled to NIOC. NIGC is not involved in
exploration and production but only performs the duties of an engineering advisory firm as regards the natural gas sector. NPC regulates
and oversees the petrochemical sector, which is largely made up of private companies. Lastly, NIORDC controls the refining, transporting,
and distributing of petroleum products and also markets and exports
refined products.

28 In essence, the subsidiaries act as operators by taking oil policies from
the government level and applying them in the field. For example, if a
five-year development plan calls for an increase in drilling in a given oil
field, this specific decision would be made by managers and ministry
officials in the NIOC board and the Ministry of Petroleum – which
often are the same people – and would be passed on to the National
Iranian Drilling Company, a NIOC subsidiary. While NIOC is delegating the task to a subsidiary in this case, it is still important to note
NIOC's role in the oil sector, listed on its website: "NIOC's 'Directors'
act primarily in policy making and supervision while subsidiaries act
as their executive arm in coordinating an array of operations such as
exploration, drilling, production and delivery of crude oil and natural
gas, for export and domestic consumption" (Islamic Republic of Iran
Ministry of Petroleum 2008).

29 This will change over time as the offshore South Pars fields begin to
come online, which will not be managed by ICOFC but instead by the
Pars Oil and Gas Company, another NIOC subsidiary.

30 Even though the new revolutionary structure of government gives nearly
ultimate control over the country to the Grand Ayatollah, other positions
in the Iranian government also have powers. It should be noted however that Khamene'i is not officially a Grand Ayatollah on theological
grounds but only on political grounds (thanks to Suzanne Maloney for
clarifying this point). The Grand Ayatollah has unfettered control over
major policy decisions, but others in the political system – notably the
president and the head of the Expediency Council – have influence over
other decisions. The current chair of the Guardian Council and the
Assembly of Experts, Ayatollah Akbar Hashemi Rafsanjani, is widely

believed to have a strong influence on the Majlis and the political success of the executive branch of power. An interviewee, whom I code NIOC2, has even gone so far to say, "The Majlis does not have control. People like Rafsanjani do."

31 MEES estimates that if the price of Iranian crude falls below $37.50/ barrel (in 2009 dollars), the government would be unable to balance its budget if current expenditure trends continue, and would have to continue to pull funds from the OSF to make up the shortfall (MEES 52:4 2009).

32 Iran planned to replace the OSF with the National Development Fund in 2011, which the Central Bank hopes will be a more secure and regulated sovereign wealth fund (MEES 53:3 2010).

33 It is hard to trace down exactly where the missing $1.6 billion went, but most insiders believe the money is being siphoned off by those connected to high-level politicians and ayatollahs. Several former NIOC employees and managers indicated to me in interviews that people like Rafsanjani's son or the son of Ayatollah Khamene'i have been stealing oil money and depositing the funds overseas. Still, these beliefs must be taken with a grain of salt without hard evidence to support them.

34 This report by the Sovereign Wealth Fund Institute can be found here: www.swfinstitute.org/research/transparencyindex.php.

35 Interview with NIOC4, July 16, 2009.

36 Interview with IOC2, September 2009.

37 Interview with NIOC2, September 16, 2008.

38 Interview with IranScholar1, July 22, 2008.

39 Mazerei (1996) notes that despite the widely held belief that *bonyads* are the beneficiaries of large sums of government money, no official figures have been published.

40 Thanks to Suzanne Maloney for clarifying this issue.

41 As Mazerei (1996) indicates, "Islamic banking is, theoretically, an equity-based, profit-sharing system that eliminates fixed-interest deposits and loans in deference to Islamic injunctions against usury. Under Islamic banking the lender and borrower share the profits of enterprise (and hence the associated risk) according to some previously agreed upon share; the actual size of the remuneration to the lender, nevertheless, is determined only after the completion of the project."

42 The Supreme Energy Council also includes the directors of atomic energy, environmental protection, and management and planning, and the ministers of agriculture, economy, energy, mines and industries, and trade.

43 Thanks to Fereidun Fesharaki and Siamak Adibi for this analysis.

44 Interview with IOC1, September 16, 2008.

45 Operations have not drastically changed since the oil minister and NIOC managing director became separate posts. From 2001–2005, Zanganeh still controlled NIOC despite not being its managing director, a notion some attribute to Zanganeh's control over Mir-Moezi (APS 56:16 2001). The post-2001 system allows the oil minister to personally select the MDs of NIOC, NIGC, NPC, and NIORDC; these appointments essentially eliminate the gap between the NIOC director and minister of petroleum, as the minister has a strong incentive to appoint those who will not offer him any resistance on key oil decisions. In fact, the two oil ministers since Zanganeh had served on NIOC's Board of Directors prior to obtaining appointment to the ministry: Kazem Vaziri-Hamaneh had held board positions in NIOC and a number of its subsidiaries and current Minister of Oil Gholamhossein Nozari had been MD of NIOC before his 2007 appointment to the ministry. (In the early months of Ahmadinejad's presidency, he had tried to get three appointees through the Majlis approval process before getting parliamentary approval for Vaziri-Hamaneh. It is commonly believed that the three before Vaziri-Hamaneh were grossly unqualified for the position having little or no experience at all in the oil sector (MEES 48:36 2005).) As a former NIOC manager noted, NIOC and the ministry engage in "shared decision making: The Ministry of Petroleum has to keep a lot of people happy, whereas at NIOC, it's about 'corporate planning' that makes plans with projects, but it gets disrupted by other interests" (Interview with NIOC3, September 16, 2008).

46 Interview with NIOC1, September 17, 2008.

47 It is not clear how the Revolutionary Guard is being appointed to head the *bonyads*, but interviews suggest that the supreme leader himself manages the appointments.

48 Interview with IranScholar1, July 22, 2008.

49 Thanks to Suzanne Maloney for making this clarification.

50 Interview with NIOC3, September 16, 2008.

51 E-mail correspondence with V. Marcel, September 2009.

52 Interview with NIOC3, September 16, 2008.

53 Interview with NIOC1, September 17, 2008.

54 Data on imports drawn from BP (2008).

55 Interview with NIOC1, September 17, 2008.

56 This expansion, coupled with a new refinery project at Bandar Abbas being constructed by the Sinopec Design Institute, will help to nearly eliminate the need for gasoline imports in the short term. Yet the problem of addressing long-term demand remains unsettled: up to 600,000 barrels per day of new refining capacity that are in the planning stages have little chance to be properly financed anytime before

2015 and the detailed plans and budgets have yet to be drawn up (SHANA 2008).

57 One government strategy is to offset oil used for electricity generation (filling the gap with nuclear and natural gas), which has been increasing the recent precipitous increase in electricity demand. Rolling blackouts have been plaguing Iran throughout the summers, as there is currently a shortage of roughly 1 GW of peak capacity. The shortages are a significant political problem for the government, as it is forced to increase the electricity price to effectively curb demand. Deputy Minister of Energy Ahmadian has stated that there is no other way to force Iranians to conserve energy, since the subsidized electricity price of 160 rials/kWh ($0.02/kWh) is too low to encourage any kind of conservation (Fars News 2008). An Iranian scholar also criticized the heavily subsidized prices for creating a disincentive for efficient electricity generation, stating that "there is too much demand [for energy] and the government has not planned enough production because the current generation facilities are run by companies who aren't using [subsidized fuel] efficiently. When you have such cheap fuel to burn, then those who are generating electricity are not going to burn it efficiently" (interview with IranScholar3, July 22, 2008).

58 While NIORDC is the state-sponsored refining and distribution company, there are private refiners in the downstream sector. Some examples are Butane Company, Qeshm Island Oil Refinery, Pars Oil Company, and Samen Oil Projects Management Company.

59 These subsidies have recently come under fire, and as of the time of publication, the Ahmadinejad administration has successfully pushed through parliament a new plan to gradually increase the price of gasoline and diesel for the majority of the population.

60 In terms of natural gas, output is expanding, despite the increase in gas being reinjected into oil fields. Yet Iran is still far short of its production potentials. Iran has never exported large quantities of gas and is unlikely to do so in the near future. Most of Iran's gas production is consumed within the country, reflecting the ever-growing usage of natural gas in Iran's economy as a substitute where oil would otherwise be used. Though Iran has the second-largest gas reserves in the world, it is a stark sign of poor performance that it is a marginal and largely irrelevant player in the international gas market. In particular, NIOC and its subsidiaries have failed to fully develop the South Pars fields, which are getting smaller as time progresses: Qatar shares these fields with Iran, and ongoing Qatari production will deplete the availability of gas resources for Iran to develop. The fact that Iran has failed to do so is one of NIOC's biggest failures, as the window of

opportunity for the company to exploit South Pars's potential is rapidly shrinking.

61 Interview with NIOC1, September 17, 2008.

62 As one Iranian oil executive noted, "War damage was a constraint during and for many years after the Iran–Iraq War and it [didn't] help that the big Khuzestan fields [were] in decline and required extensive and expensive remedial work" (e-mail correspondence with NIOC4, June 4, 2009).

63 These were primarily asset freezes (in 1979), the prohibition of financial aid from the United States to Iran (in 1984), and the ban of all non-oil imports from Iran to the United States (in 1990). For more detail on these sanctions, see Torbat (2005).

64 E-mail correspondence with NIOC4, June 4, 2009.

65 This negative effect may be short-lived. Several scholars have found evidence that sanctions that persist over fifteen years may not have much impact on the Iranian economy, given the self-sufficiency and adaptability of many Iranian industries and sectors. See Torbat (2005) and Amuzegar (1997) for a discussion of these studies.

66 In the early years of the post-revolution Islamic Republic, Zanganeh was the deputy minister of culture and Islamic guidance during Khatami's tenure as minister.

67 To be sure, NIOC was not fully autonomous during this period. In fact, NIOC was not nearly as independent from the state when compared to NOCs such as PDVSA in the 1990s and to a certain extent Sonangol. Still, NIOC during Zanganeh's tenure as oil minister was able to pursue its own interests and influence the legislature on matters of oil and gas policy.

68 Interview with IOC1, September 16, 2008.

69 This description of the buyback scheme is drawn from Ebrahimi *et al.* (2003); Marcel (2006); and van Groenendaal and Mazraati (2006).

70 Interview with IOC1, September 16, 2008.

71 As of 2007, Total was pressured by the French government to leave the South Pars project; the new contract is (as of 2007) under negotiation with Austria's OMV. Also, as mentioned in footnote 8, Inpex has been pressured out and was replaced with CNPC.

72 There is also the belief that Ahmadinejad is not reversing the trend of liberalization but instead focusing only on controlling NIOC and the Ministry of Petroleum, while at the same time privatizing gas and services companies. (Thanks to Valerie Marcel for clarifying this point in an e-mail correspondence.)

73 Interview with NIOC6, July 17, 2009.

74 MEES notes that Ahmadinejad may have gained more control of his appointments by negotiation with Supreme Leader Khamenei over Khamenei's appointment of Rafsanjani, Ahmadinejad's opponent in the presidential elections of 2005, to a high political post in the upper levels of the theocracy (MEES 50:34 2007).

7 | Handcuffed: an assessment of Pemex's performance and strategy

OGNEN STOJANOVSKI

1 Introduction

Petróleos Mexicanos, better known as Pemex, is the oldest of the major NOCs. Mexico nationalized its oil industry in the 1930s, long before countries in the Persian Gulf were inspired to expropriate foreign companies' oil assets. Today, Pemex is a large supplier and a key non-OPEC player on the global oil market. In 2009, as for many years before, Mexico was a chief supplier of oil to the United States. The Mexican government, in turn, depends heavily on the vast oil revenues that the company accrues. Pemex refers to itself, correctly, as "the most important company of the country" (Pemex 2010).

But Pemex is a troubled company. Its economic efficiency does not compare favorably to other NOCs and fares even worse when compared with globally oriented international oil companies (IOCs). Its troubles are the result of a decades-long strategy that focused on maximizing short-term revenues and effectively stripped the company's managers of key decision making. That strategy was initially pursued under pressure from the government, which needed the money to cover holes in the national budget at a time of low oil prices.[1] And it worked by the metrics implied in that mission: Pemex indeed provided loads of money to the Mexican national coffers. The company has had enormous revenues for over a decade and is a Fortune "Global 500" company that has, since 2005, been in and near the top fifty positions in pre-tax revenues of all companies worldwide (*Fortune Magazine* 2008).

This strategy has given rise to many criticisms. According to normal accounting practices, Pemex has been running billions of dollars in *losses* in recent years. The government controls Pemex's finances and has prohibited it from retaining much of its earnings for reinvestment. Its capital expenditure (which since 2003 totals more than $10 billion a year, predominantly destined for production activities) is funded almost entirely by debt that is backed, implicitly, by Mexico's sovereign credit rating.

Worse still, Pemex finds itself in the midst of a decline in oil production because it has been so focused on extraction while (until recently) unable to invest in new exploration. By running faster just to stay in place, Pemex has effectively been depleting its existing fields as fast as possible. New fields are available but tapping them requires technical expertise that the firm does not have at hand. Moreover, the company has failed to invest in its own human capital, making it highly unlikely that it can quickly develop the required capabilities from within even as the Mexican legal landscape makes it virtually impossible to efficiently subcontract or partner with outside firms. Pemex's troubles extend beyond crude production – in refining, natural gas, and petrochemicals it faces looming troubles rooted in a history of neglect. The odds of a major national crisis triggered by a drop in oil revenues (sparked by major drops in oil prices or production, or a combination of both) are rising because Mexico's government is overly dependent on Pemex.

Even as it pursues a crash program to find and develop new fields, Pemex's costs are higher than its better-performing peers. Added to these drains is a high cost base, driven in part by overstaffing and generous benefits and pensions for its workers, who are defended by a union that is exceptionally powerful. A fragmented political system in Mexico impedes reform at a time when new policies are urgently needed.

This chapter aims to document and explain Pemex's strategic choices and their impact on the company's performance over the last three decades – from Mexico's transformation into a major oil exporter up to the wave of Pemex-related reforms now unfolding in the country (which, for the most part, are not detailed or analyzed, as it is still too early to judge their effects on Pemex's performance). I focus on Pemex's relationship with the Mexican government, its finances, internal operations, interactions with other oil companies, and internal technology and human capital in order to advance four main arguments.

First, the financial troubles of the Mexican government are a key barrier to better performance at Pemex. Until recently, the government's strategy for Pemex focused on maximizing short-term revenues. Pemex alone finances almost 40 percent of Mexico's entire

federal budget. Impoverished by excessive taxation, the company was
forced to negotiate its uncertain budget with the Mexican government on an annual basis.

To make matters worse, the Mexican style of public administration
has come to be dominated by well-educated economists with a macroeconomic focus who seem willing to sacrifice Pemex's status as an
energy company and turn it into an instrument for the state's financial
engineering. All of Pemex's capital expenditures are reviewed by the
finance ministry, which has little knowledge about long-term investments in technical and production capabilities in the oil industry and
the need to embed such investments in a risk management framework. The federal budget is simply too dependent on short-term revenues from Pemex to give the company more financial autonomy. This
financial trap would be less troubling if the country would restructure
its overall tax system to diversify the government's sources of revenue. But that simply has not happened for the better part of three
decades. So, despite certain steps undertaken in 2006 and 2008 to
reduce Pemex's tax burden, wider-reaching financial reforms for the
entire country remain the easiest way to "help" Pemex.

Second, Pemex faces tight political constraints that have broad negative practical effects on its strategies and performance. The Mexican
constitution and other laws make Pemex the exclusive oil operator in
the country. That leaves the firm, unlike many other NOCs, unable
to pursue domestic joint ventures or other equity contracts, as these
would be unconstitutional, politically unstable, and vulnerable to
the claim that they threaten Mexico's natural patrimony. Reforms in
2008 gave Pemex slightly greater contracting flexibility, but it is far
from certain that the reforms are enough to improve performance.
The restrictive regulatory framework in which Pemex operates means
that it has a difficult relationship with all branches of the Mexican
federal government with the ultimate effect that Pemex's managers
are effectively stripped of much of the responsibility and accountability that comes with running such a large company. Without either the
capital resources or the autonomy to make intrinsically risky investment decisions on commercial merits, they are unable to pursue an
optimal investment strategy. While that lack of autonomy is shared
in many other NOCs, what distinguishes Pemex is that political fragmentation in Mexico has meant that no single actor or entity in the
Mexican government can actually assert political control or maintain

strategic oversight of the company. Thus, Pemex suffers the worst of both worlds: managers stripped of autonomy by the government and a government that cannot control the company.

Other political constraints abound. Pemex is subjected to debilitating procurement rules, which quash incentives for risk taking and make it hard for the company to follow a wise procurement strategy. Unlike some other NOCs (such as Petrobras or Statoil) Pemex has almost no overseas or domestic strategic partnerships but instead relies on subcontracting as the only means of partnering with other companies operating in the petroleum sector. That means its focus is on field services activities rather than the larger joint ventures that could enable Pemex to learn from its peers and bring whole systems of technology and management into the country. This practice elevates the company's cost base because Pemex lacks the internal expertise (both technological and professional) to manage its own production-related projects; neither is it able to manage its many contractors effectively. In addition, it has led to the "de-skilling" of Pemex itself. The human capital base, for one, has declined markedly: whereas the company used to be the most attractive employer in the country – attracting the best engineering graduates – it no longer holds that position. In contrast with the in-house research and development system at Petrobras, Pemex's own internal R&D system is a shadow of its former self.

Third, Mexico's geology accounts for part of Pemex's current predicament. Ever since the discovery of the Cantarell oil field in the 1970s, Mexico has been able to produce large quantities of crude oil with relative ease. Cantarell proved exceptionally generous and for a full two decades Pemex did not need to invest in new infrastructure or advanced technologies in order to generate large revenues. When production finally started to drop, Pemex needed help to keep the aging oil field productive – it did so with a highly successful secondary recovery program (albeit executed through subcontracting for the work and borrowing for the financing). However, that project only delayed the decline and set the firm up to face an even steeper drop-off in production evident today as the field approaches the end of its life.

Fourth, and finally, Pemex is hindered at attempts to improve its performance – in both strategy and economic efficiency – by a volatile combination of public perception and an extremely powerful workers' union. In 1938, Pemex was the first NOC to be expropriated, and that event has retained its nationalistic salience for seven decades. Mexico stands apart from other countries in this study in the degree to which public opinion against even a partial liberalization is entrenched – a view not universally held, but easily polarized by certain politicians. The durable role of Pemex in Mexican society explains why the public, although generally dissatisfied with the enterprise's day-to-day performance, is also hostile to allowing reforms that may boost performance. Public suspicion is especially aroused by ruminations about joint ventures or even a partial opening up of the sector for fear that these are a pretext for privatization. The workers' union fans these concerns as part of a strategy to maintain the status quo – even though the union, itself, plays a large role in contributing to the company's poor performance though corruption, excessive employment, and overly generous contracts.

2 A short history of Pemex

Mexico was one of the world's first important oil producers. Significant exploration and production in the country began at the turn of the last century and by 1921 Mexico was the world's second leading oil producer, accounting for one-quarter of the planet's output. However, over the next decade, Mexican oil production began to fall off due to the difficulty of developing additional production with the then-available technologies. By 1930, output was only one-fifth of the 1921 levels. Nevertheless, foreign companies continued to invest in Mexico's oil industry and the country produced significant amounts for several decades to come. American and British companies organized and controlled Mexico's oil production.

Starting with the Constitution of 1917, oil and other subsoil wealth were declared to be the property of the nation. Whichever governments were in power (at times during the civil war and subsequent power struggles there was more than one "national" government) granted certain rights to this national property to the foreign oil companies while trying to extract as much oil rent as possible in order to fund military actions and other projects intended to preserve political power. In general, the oil industry did not align with any one of the many competing factions during this turbulent period in Mexico's history.

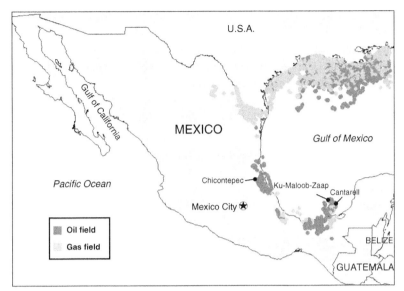

Figure 7.1 Map of major oil and gas fields in Mexico.
Source for oil and gas field data: Wood Mackenzie (2009b).

2.1 Origins and early years (1938–1974)

By the 1930s, Mexican oil production was generally declining while the industry was still controlled by outside companies that operated, in the view of Mexico's president Lázaro Cárdenas, as entities to themselves. In 1937, he stepped in to mediate a conflict between the foreign companies and striking oil workers. After a long series of failed negotiations in which Cárdenas felt the foreigners had insulted and marginalized him, he took the companies by surprise when he followed through on a threat to expropriate the entire industry.[2]

Immediately following expropriation, the government founded two new companies: Pemex Distribution and Pemex Production. In 1940, Pemex Production acquired the other firm and the government's monopolization of the oil industry was complete. The government focused this firm inward and charged it with satisfying domestic demand for oil products. In this respect, Pemex differs from many other NOCs – notably the companies in the countries of the Persian Gulf – in that it did not start out as export focused and was not created in order to be a mass source of revenues for the government. Like Petrobras, Pemex's original focus was domestic (see Chapter 12).

In its early years Pemex survived a gauntlet of challenges. It educated an unskilled labor force and consolidated the properties and activities of the many foreign companies into one state entity. Constant diplomatic pressures and threats of foreign governments, particularly Britain, over the expropriation multiplied the difficulties.[3] True to its orientation to the domestic market, Pemex constructed three new refineries in the 1950s even as crude oil production continued to decline – to a point where in the late 1950s Mexico became a net importer. Facing a crisis sustaining its crude supply, Pemex invited American companies back to Mexico to help search for new oil fields.

During the 1960s, several important new oil fields were discovered and Pemex boosted sagging production with new investments financed by issuing internal debt. The crisis of production abated and the government, once again, prohibited foreign companies from conducting exploration activities in the country. To replace the foreigners and promote national capabilities, the government founded a research arm for Pemex: the Mexican Petroleum Institute (IMP).

It was during this time that Pemex became an elite super-agency the government used to promote a wide range of economic and social objectives related to Mexican development. Pemex, in combination with the electrical utility Comisión Federal de Electricidad (CFE) – another state champion – performed nearly all the interesting engineering and technology-related work in the country. This included not just oil production but also the building of roads, ports, rails, and even company towns and hospitals. While the state oil enterprise was not overly efficient, it was politically effective. And it was the employer of choice for young, competent engineers who could count on steady, well-paid employment and opportunities to do interesting and meaningful work (PESD Interviews).

2.2 *Pemex after 1974*

With encouraging signs from the oil discoveries of the 1960s and the technological development of Pemex and the country, the Mexican government decided in 1974 to restart Pemex's oil export business. This was a time of high worldwide oil prices and the government stood to reap enormous revenues if it could successfully exploit the nation's oil resources. Newly issued external debt and a full 17 percent of federal budget expenditures were dedicated to expanding Pemex's search for oil. With the discovery of the huge Cantarell oil field in 1976 (see Figure 7.1), the country seemed to have struck gold.[4] As the classic story of resource-rich nations goes, there were high hopes for rapid national development and improvement in quality of life thanks to enormous fresh revenues.

Unfortunately, such a story rarely has a happy ending. Mexico's hopes were dashed by two crises in the early 1980s – a macroeconomic shock caused by the global economic recession of 1981 and a collapse in oil prices. Together, they helped spark a foreign debt crisis that by 1985 had put Mexico into an economic spiral. Like much of the rest of Latin America, the 1980s was a "lost decade" for Mexico's economic development. The 1990s saw a partial turnaround in Mexico's fortunes – triggered notably by easier trade with North America – but Pemex remained impoverished because by then the firm had come to play a central role in the Mexican state budget.

From the early 1980s, when the easy to tap Cantarell field fully came online, output stayed roughly flat (Figure 7.2). Pemex operated with aging infrastructure and minimal investments in new production, which eventually contributed heavily to the loss of its engineering talent and saw a shift in the firm's culture away from performance. Low oil prices in the 1990s made Mexico's Ministry of Finance and Public Credit ("Hacienda") wary about allowing investment in new production. But it did not curtail existing production (because of the need to service earlier debt). Hacienda allowed only minimal investments needed to sustain the status quo.

It was not until another pair of crises – the recovery from yet another Mexican financial crisis in the mid 1990s and the looming threat of imminent decline in crude oil production (and therefore government revenues) as the Cantarell field aged – that Hacienda allowed meaningful new investments. In particular, Pemex undertook a large-scale nitrogen injection project at Cantarell that significantly expanded the field's output (Figure 7.3). That decision was taken at a time of low oil prices and, fortuitously for the Mexican budget, allowed the company to carry higher oil production into the run-up of oil prices in the early 2000s. Only in 2003 did the firm make its first significant foray into oil exploration since the 1970s, a difficult task especially since Cantarell finally peaked for good and entered an ongoing decline at the same time. This and Pemex's other performance woes are detailed in the remainder of this chapter.

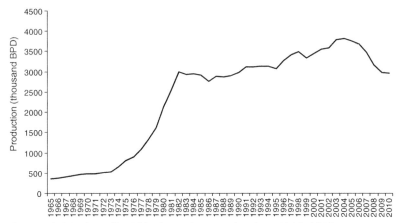

Figure 7.2 Mexican liquid hydrocarbon production, 1965–2010.
Source: BP (2011).

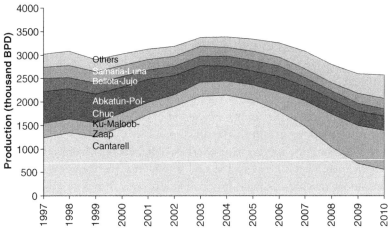

Figure 7.3 Pemex crude oil production by field (1997–2010).
Source: Pemex Statistical Yearbook (2011).

3 Explaining Pemex's strategy and performance

Any conversation about the strategy and performance of Pemex[5] tends to become a broader analysis of the strategy and performance of Mexico, specifically its federal government. The legal environment in which Pemex operates combined with the central role that it has played in national finances for the past three decades make it virtually impossible to evaluate Pemex's performance in and of itself.

Despite these difficulties and keeping in mind the usual caveats that preface a performance analysis of any state-owned enterprise (see Chapter 5, Chang 2008), I come to the conclusion that Pemex is a poorly performing enterprise. Performance, as analyzed in this chapter, consists of two closely related branches that can be compared on a broad level with the other NOCs in this study: First, financial performance using accepted accounting standards, and second, decision making particularly with respect to a long-term strategy.

With respect to finances, the central feature of Pemex's performance is that the company has consistently struggled to break even (Table 7.1). These "bottom-line" figures – which show the company posting low profits and, remarkably enough, losses in recent years – mask Pemex's huge earning potential. Despite other constraints on performance, Pemex is a Fortune "Global 500" company that has, since 2005, been ranked in and near the top fifty positions in pre-tax revenues of all companies worldwide. Its dismal final numbers are due to its heavy tax burden, difficult budgeting process, and corresponding accumulation of mass debt, all of which are explored in detail below. By 2002, oil-related taxes contributed more than a third to the federal budget year after year. Crude oil alone represented 8 percent of the total value of Mexican exports. In the meantime, as of 2006, Pemex had amassed official debts of more than $50 billion, a figure that probably understated the actual debt load. Even after acknowledging that Pemex, as a state-owned entity, does not exist simply to post profits, there is no denying that its financial performance over the last three decades is poor when measured by almost any standard. It was only in 2006 that efforts to relieve the company's tax burden began gathering steam, which led to the enactment of reform legislation in 2007 and 2008, although it will take at least a few more years before any judgments can be made as to their effect on Pemex's performance.

With respect to our other measure of performance, the usual approach for evaluating an enterprise is to reflect on the decisions made by management and analyze how they have paid off, particularly in the long run. But as this chapter will explain, Pemex was for the most part unable to make meaningful decisions over the last thirty years and – to make matters worse – no one from outside the company

Table 7.1. *Key financial indicators for 2000–2010 in millions of Mexican pesos*

YEAR	2000	2001	2002	2003	2004	2005	2006	2007	2008	2009	2010
Total Revenues	473350	450735	481779	628390	784741	940480	1132237	1219055	1526941	1130215	1354072
Domestic Sales	292880	303853	314271	387237	449013	505109	546738	592048	679754	596370	683853
Export Sales	175387	141477	167166	238192	324574	423534	515757	542927	644418	488260	592908
Service Income								1061	4778	5292	5303
Other Revenues	5083	5405	342	2961	11154	11837	69742	83019	197991	40293	72008
Total Operating Costs	192642	206928	204907	257862	318386	429888	481147	545606	757838	661644	736543
Cost of Sales	153060	165315	157802	207118	264106	361177	403106	460666	654032	561135	632290
Transportation and Distribution Expenses	12609	13588	14962	15549	17574	21911	24019	24799	33962	31856	33274
Administrative Expenses	26973	28025	32143	35195	36706	46800	54022	60141	69844	68653	70979
Financing Costs	6652	13104	13773	30742	7048	4479	22983	20047	107512	15308	11969
Associates' Results								5545	−1965	−1291	1118
INCOME BEFORE TAXES AND DUTIES	274056	230703	263099	339786	459307	506113	628107	658947	659626	451972	606678
Total Taxes and Duties	293768	263463	293590	382442	474334	580629	582855	677256	771702	546633	654141
Hydrocarbon extraction and other taxes	224211	168264	179099	288366	419629	560415	582855	677256	771702	546633	654141
IEPS	69557	95199	114491	94076	54705	20214					
NET(LOSS) FOR THE YEAR	−19712	−32760	−30491	−42656	−15027	−74516	45252	−18309	−112076	−94661	−47463

Note: For years 2001, 2003, 2004 and 2005 there are slight inconsistencies in the net "bottom line" figures that we calculated using Pemex's data and the results that Pemex itself reported. Figures are not adjusted for inflation.

Source: Pemex Statistical Yearbook 2011; Pemex Annual Report 2010.

was able to do so either.[6] It is therefore difficult to even develop a coherent concept of "performance" for Pemex in this regard given its inability to develop a long-term strategy, let alone implement it.

My evaluation of Pemex's performance is most easily demonstrated by the precarious state of the company's hydrocarbon reserves and production. In 2009, Pemex suffered large losses due in part to ongoing declines in crude oil output, which slumped to a twenty-year low (Shields 2009; Pemex 2010). According to Pemex, Mexico's total proved hydrocarbon reserves at the beginning of that year were 14.3 billion barrels of oil equivalent. By comparison, proved reserves at the beginning of 1999 were 24.9 billion barrels, or 74% higher than only a decade later (Pemex Statistical Yearbook 1999–2009). Contributing in large part to this rapid decline was the fact that over the six-year period from 1999 through 2005, crude oil production rose 17.2% without any serious corresponding investment in exploration (Smith 2004). Therefore, the alarming decline in hydrocarbon reserves is expected to continue, although Pemex hopes that this negative trend will reverse by 2012 (Fitch Ratings 2009).

The difficult reserves and production situation facing Pemex, as more fully detailed in the appendix to this chapter, is largely the result of a lack of critical decision making and the inability to develop a long-term strategy. The fact that Pemex could not sustain large-scale crude oil production without corresponding investment in exploration was an open secret long before the precipitous recent drop in production (see chapter appendix). Yet Pemex's initial response to the approaching crisis was an expensive program to push for greater short-term production that would hopefully slow the decline. This decision came with a large opportunity cost, as Pemex's focus on boosting the aging Cantarell oil field's short-term production prevented investment in other producing fields, general infrastructure, and, most importantly, new exploration, which did not begin in earnest until late 2003. Between 1996 and 2001, a high proportion of scarce capital and managerial resources at Pemex were devoted to Cantarell as other investment opportunities were neglected or reduced. The resulting rapid depletion of Mexico's proved reserves and corresponding production declines are therefore leading examples of Pemex's poor operational performance.

In the remainder of this chapter, I seek to explain Pemex's poor performance and conclude that the firm had little choice in ending up cash-strapped and making the operational decisions it did.[7] Its performance can be traced back to five closely interrelated forces that hinder the firm in investing in its operations and successfully managing its affairs: 1) the relationship with the Mexican federal government; 2) financing (especially in terms of taxes and investment funding); 3) corporate operations and internal relationships; 4) relations with contractors and IOCs; and 5) human capital. I examine each of these five main factors in turn.

3.1 Relationship with the Mexican government

In the years after the oil industry's nationalization in 1938, Pemex was entrusted with complete and exclusive planning and management of Mexico's hydrocarbon resources. Thus, policy and operations integrated and, by the 1980s, became grafted to the financial planning apparatus of the entire government. The federal government oversees Pemex and has the power to set the company's strategy.[8] When the PRI political party was in control of Mexico's one-party system there was continuity in control over both Pemex and government. As David Hults explores (see Chapter 3) unified control made it easier for the government to set and administer strategy using a variety of mechanisms – including control over budgeting and regulation. Unfortunately for Pemex, Mexico's governments of the last three decades regularly faced financial crises, and the resulting choices they made proved disastrous for the company.

Political liberalization has brought much uncertainty to the government's control over the firm. Following the year 2000 elections, the congress (which tightly monitors and approves Pemex's annual budget) and the presidency (which appoints Pemex's CEO as well as the majority of its directors and also controls the finance ministry, which administers Pemex's budget) were for the first time controlled by rival political parties. At the same time, Pemex was increasingly hamstrung by regulations from several ministries in the vast Mexican bureaucracy. By 2006, the firm faced gridlock, which is why Pemex itself spearheaded the push for major reforms in 2008 – a pattern that is unique among the NOCs in our study.

Pemex remains 100 percent state-owned. Several failed proposals have called for large Mexican institutional investors such as pension funds, and possibly even private Mexican citizens, to be allowed part ownership (Malkin 2004b; Smith 2004). But the idea of even partially privatizing Pemex – especially anything related to its exploration and production of oil – remains tremendously unpopular with the Mexican public (Smith 2004; PESD Interviews).[9]

3.1.1 The executive

As property of "the people" Pemex was set up to be controlled by Mexico's president. Formally, the company is governed by a fifteen-member board that has control over all senior appointments except the CEO, who is appointed directly by the president. Six of the directors are representatives of the state designated by the president. They have overwhelmingly been government ministers that traditionally held a majority on the board (which until 2008 was composed of eleven members).[10] Five other directors are representatives of the Petroleum Workers' Union. The 2008 energy law added four more directors who are supposed to be independent of the state, company, and union.

Traditionally, Mexico's presidents were quite interested in Pemex's operations and they appointed close friends to head the company. In effect, several past presidents including Lázaro Cárdenas, the man who nationalized the oil industry, exercised direct personal control over the firm. However, that has not been the case for most of the last fifteen years – with presidents Ernesto Zedillo (in office 1994–2000) and Vicente Fox (2000–2006) as well as most of their energy ministers – who were perceived as unable to understand and guide Pemex (PESD Interviews). This timing proved unfortunate for Pemex, as the decade from 1995 to 2005 was transformative for the firm and the nation.[11] The current president, Felipe Calderón, may be different. He served as energy minister during the Fox administration and as president is facing the urgent task of replacing lost production as the key Cantarell oil field falters. He has personally insisted on reforms though is still far from achieving the promise of a more agile, flexible Pemex that can have more fruitful relations with other oil companies and suppliers. Like his last two predecessors, Calderón appointed reform-oriented management at Pemex, but these executives have learned that by themselves they have little leverage on the company's performance.

3.1.2 The congress

At the same time that the direct presidential influence over Pemex was waning with Mexico's political fragmentation, the Mexican congress became interested in exerting greater political influence over the company. Prior to 1997, Mexico's PRI-dominated congress did little more than rubber stamp most budgetary and other proposals regarding Pemex that came from the executive branch (PESD Interviews). However, the legislative elections of 1997 marked a milestone in modern Mexican history, as the PRI finally lost its simple majority in the lower house of congress. It remained the largest of the parties in congress, but persistent clashes with the opposition ensured that congress would no longer be a passive branch of government. And with the electoral revolution of 2000 when the PRI lost the presidency and suffered further losses in both chambers of the legislature, congress really came into its own.

In general, the congress opposes any proposed reforms of Pemex, a tradition dating back to the old PRI-dominated congresses. This practice survived throughout the Fox administration, when there were at least a dozen reform initiatives affecting Pemex that never even made it to the floors of congress for a vote (Smith 2001, 2004; PESD Interviews). President Calderón finally succeeded in pushing through reforms in 2008, but even then congress watered them down.

Although the PRI and its allies in congress could agree on what they did not want (privatization), they had no vision for the types of reforms that they would tolerate after 2000. This was probably due to the combination of PRI's nascent role as Mexico's opposition party (which meant it was better at causing trouble than shaping policy) and the one-term limit for legislators (as individuals cannot stay in the same position in government for more than six years).[12] In addition, unlike in the United States, there is no professional committee-based congressional staffing in Mexico. Instead, each member of congress has a relatively small official staff and turnover is high. This leads to a loss of expertise on many matters, which is especially costly to the policymaking process for complicated issues like petroleum governance. Thanks to this lack of knowledge and resources within congress, combined with a divided government, distrust among parties, and an ability to transform nationalistic sentiment over Pemex into votes, PRI's members have simply opposed most reforms for Pemex.

The congress that took power in September 2006 was in a better position to exercise positive power and influence over Pemex than its predecessors. The PAN party dominated both chambers of congress (although it still lacked outright majorities in either) and the new Mexican multiparty political system had a decade to mature and develop in a way that opposition parties were more likely to play constructive roles. Moreover, PAN became more sophisticated in crafting coalitions with like-minded factions within PRI and its control over congress proved instrumental in passing the 2008 Pemex reforms. However, the PRI regained a majority in the 2009 mid-term elections and further reforms are once again on the back burner, in large part because the party was willing and able to mobilize a powerful public nationalistic sentiment against reforming Pemex, in order to gain votes in Mexico's highly competitive political arena regardless of the consequences for Pemex's performance.

While the old habits of opposing reforms are slow to die out, what has changed since 1997 is that congress began to make use of its fiscal powers. While most Mexican congressmen probably do not understand the petroleum industry, they are well aware that it accounts for more than a third of the federal budget in a typical year. Thus, the post-1997 congresses were willing to exercise tight budgetary controls that forced Pemex to beg for every peso it got.

When approving the budget, the Mexican congress gets briefed only on the overall Pemex picture and does not scrutinize individual projects or the allocation of capital expenditures. This macro perspective, along with lack of much knowledge about the sector, means that congress tends to focus on the wrong indicators of performance. And it is prone to fury when Pemex does not deliver quick or expected results. A recent example is congressional anger over the drop in production levels of crude oil despite investments of tens of billions of dollars in the last decade. This decline was entirely foreseeable given Pemex's excessive reliance on the aging Cantarell field, but congressmen can easily claim to have been oblivious of the coming crisis, partially thanks to Pemex's public statements at the time (see chapter appendix). Such episodes feed congressional distrust of the company and sour interest in honoring requests for still more investment funds or managerial autonomy.

3.1.3 The bureaucracy

Even though today's Pemex is vulnerable to political influence from both the president and congress, the most direct government leverage over Pemex in recent history has actually come from the various ministries in Mexico's vast bureaucracy that pursued a myriad of goals – at times operating in conflict. Contradictions were especially glaring on Pemex's board of directors. Ministers sitting on Pemex's board were also charged with regulating the company. The energy ministry monitored all of Pemex's activities and proposals even while the minister was chairman of the board. Hacienda (the finance ministry) is in charge of incorporating Pemex's budget and financing program into the government's annual consolidated budget and also regularly held a seat on the Pemex board. In addition to policy and financial controls, Pemex also faces severe anti-corruption scrutiny of its procurement (discussed below) and increasingly must contend with an array of environmental regulations delegated to no less than five different ministries (environment and natural resources, communications and transportation, health, navy, and energy). Some ministers as board members were vested with approving the same projects and environmental consequences that in their ministerial job they had to regulate (Pemex 2010). Usually, the role of a Pemex board member has been of secondary importance to the government ministers,[13] which does help explain why the Pemex board, in practice, was not really an effective institution for corporate governance, as key decisions usually did not flow through the board.[14]

The central conflict of interest arising from Pemex's governance structure is found in the company's relationship with Hacienda. The impression of Pemex management is that Hacienda is quite concerned about procurement processes and budgeting – issues that are expected to be important to a government regulator – but not nearly as attentive (or informed) about Pemex's technology investments, efficiency, and expansion (PESD Interviews). Yet it is this latter category of issues that is essential to an oil company's long-term health.

Hacienda, in effect, controls all the levers that affect Pemex's finances. It sets the prices Pemex charges domestically, it proposes the taxes Pemex will pay, and it decides on Pemex's budget submitted for congressional approval. However, despite Hacienda's important role, it does not actually provide any strategic oversight for the company (PESD Interviews). Once Pemex submits its annual list of investment needs, it is evaluated by Hacienda's "investment division," which focuses its analysis on the proposed projects' expected cash flows and financial feasibility. Hacienda looks mainly at projects individually for their profitability, rather than in totality for their strategy. It relies entirely on Pemex for geological and technical expertise. After the financial analysis of the investment division, Hacienda's "debt division" looks at the costs of the proposals and the way they fit into Pemex's and the national debt profile. This division then has final say over whether to authorize each project (PESD Interviews). Lost in this division of responsibilities is the fact that no entity – neither Hacienda nor Pemex – develops a portfolio of long-term investment opportunities spread across an array of risks.

Overall, Hacienda – widely perceived as one of the most competent entities in the Mexican government – provides strict financial oversight of the company. But it does not – and cannot – provide strategic and technical oversight. Only Pemex internally has the data necessary to thoroughly evaluate its investments and Hacienda does not employ enough people with energy expertise to keep abreast of Pemex's activities. Ultimately, what matters to Hacienda is whether Pemex will conform to its annual budget, not whether it is using the best technology or has a coherent plan for long-term growth. In other countries this larger portfolio analysis rests with the hydrocarbon regulator and with the ministry that sets energy policy, but in Mexico this function has not been developed with any competent authority.[15]

Perhaps Pemex's most difficult interaction with Mexico's bureaucracy is with the Ministry of Public Administration (known by the acronym SFP). This ministry's regulations influence Pemex's day-to-day operations more directly than any other single entity in government. It was created by President Miguel de la Madrid (in office 1982–1988) under a different name as part of a campaign against corruption, with a mission to ensure external auditing for all public entities, including Pemex. However, over the years, SFP has grown tremendously in size and influence, and the myriad of inflexible regulations it now imposes on public entities have produced a bureaucratic monster, leading other segments of the government to routinely refer to the ministry as "the Inquisitors." This also makes SFP an easy scapegoat and the part of the government that Pemex managers seem to love to hate.

SFP's oversight of Pemex comes in two ways. First, there are internal controllers of Pemex's central corporate operations, as well as controllers for each of the operating subsidiaries. These controllers are actually salaried Pemex employees, but they report directly to SFP. Second, SFP itself employs "commissioners" that are charged with overseeing entire sectors of Mexico's public administration. Traditionally there has been one commissioner who oversees all of Pemex along with the state-owned electricity companies. In practice, it is the internal controllers that scrutinize the actual operations of Pemex. The broader commissioners are much more politically driven and responsive to the political climate (PESD Interviews).

As part of its supervision, the SFP not only appoints Pemex's external auditors but also determines its organizational charts, salaries, and even employment positions – everything from a new managerial position for an important Pemex project to additional low-level union jobs requires the agency's permission. SFP regulations also control all of Pemex's contracting. While the stringent oversight is fitting for a country with a vast bureaucracy that has been prone to corruption and that would be potentially more corrupt and less credible for international bidders if *not* for SFP scrutiny, such oversight also clearly restricts Pemex's autonomy and constrains risk taking that is essential to running a business.[16] Mindful of SFP, Pemex's management has been especially reluctant to engage in creative problem solving or contracting.

At the same time, there is concern in Mexico that SFP is failing in its mission to combat public corruption. Although SFP sees everyone as a potential crook, it may not necessarily be catching the actual crooks, who are innovative and may escape scrutiny. In fact, SFP ultimately loses the large majority of the cases it brings against public servants – although not until after several years of delay and indecision along with high cost and career damage. Thus, public sector employees are afraid of SFP despite the enforcer's poor record in court (PESD Interviews). The result is intensive process-based scrutiny with little impact on corruption (PESD Interviews). The leading example of political corruption – despite SFP oversight – in recent history is the "Pemexgate" scandal of 2001, when funds from the Pemex workers' union were illegally used to support the year 2000 presidential campaign for the then-incumbent PRI political party. The case was not prosecuted vigorously and those claimed responsible were never convicted, although the PRI was fined about $90 million.

Meanwhile, the one ministry with which Pemex should interact most closely, energy, is far too weak to effectively guide the company. In practice, Pemex has traditionally been *the* energy authority in the country. More recently, the energy ministry has experienced tremendous turnover, further hampering its regulatory role. In six years, the Fox administration had four energy ministers (Lajous 2009). Moreover, it is not just the ministers themselves that rotate through the ministry – every time a change occurs all the key decision makers get replaced with a new team (current President Calderón was energy minister under former President Fox only eight months before the cycle was once again repeated). The large state-owned enterprises such as Pemex are "black boxes" whose operations are hard to understand because the ministry lacks the technical expertise and durability of leadership needed to pry open and scrutinize their operations.

The system, in all, provides multiple (and sometimes conflicting) levels of oversight. Yet, none of it is strategic in nature. Pemex insiders and outside observers frequently point out that no one within Pemex will ever advocate the use of more expensive and risky, but potentially much better, petroleum technologies than those currently deployed so long as the company is tethered to conservative capital planning and procurement rules (PESD Interviews). There is simply too much personal risk involved for any Pemex manager pushing for change that would increase managerial discretion, particularly since Pemex managers are not held accountable for performance in the first place. Worse still, even if SFP and Hacienda wanted to move to more advanced approaches, it would be too hard to explain the long-term benefits to an uninformed congress that is prone to focus on immediate and sure yield from Pemex rather than hypothetical benefits from a new approach to risk investment. Indeed, procurement and contracting laws explicitly require that Pemex must always choose the lowest cost option that is arrived at through a scrutinized bidding process. This combination of heavy political interference without actual governmental control is a hallmark of Pemex's troubles and is also evident in Kuwait Petroleum Company and in a few other NOCs (see Chapter 8).

3.2 Finances

For most of Pemex's seven-decade history, its finances have been closely intertwined with Mexico's federal budget. By most accounts, the company's tax payments have accounted for more than a third of the government's annual budget for many years. This has led many observers (including some local politicians) to warn against the serious consequences that may result if oil prices fall or if Pemex's production falters significantly from the recent record high[17] (PESD Interviews).

Indeed, a drop in crude prices helped spark Mexico's foreign-debt crisis in the early 1980s (Smith 2004). Today it can be argued that Pemex's and Mexico's financial situations have returned to where they were before the last major crisis. By the early 1980s, the Mexican government had come to rely on oil revenues. During the presidency of José López Portillo (1976–1982), vast new oil discoveries were announced regularly – chief among them, Cantarell. At the time, despite huge foreign and domestic debt, banks readily lent even more money to Mexico on the expectation that ever larger oil revenues would service the debt. The government's excessive reliance on oil revenues proved disastrous once oil prices fell.

Just as treating Pemex as a cash cow in the early 1980s proved delusional, so too today there is a dangerous overreliance on the firm's revenues. While international banks do not lend huge sums of money to Mexico as readily as they once did, Pemex has nevertheless had little trouble raising more than $100 billion on capital markets in less than a decade. As it once did with Cantarell, Pemex is now actively touting the potential of its (yet unproved) reserves such as offshore in deep water. The central financial relationship between Pemex and Mexico exists on three fronts: taxes, subsidies, and investment financing.

3.2.1 Taxes

Between 2003 and 2009 Pemex paid out at least 60 percent of its total revenues in royalties and taxes.[18] The taxes imposed on Pemex have fallen into three main categories: duties for hydrocarbon extraction and other similar taxes; a so-called "excess gains duty"; and a special tax on gasoline sales known as "IEPS."[19] The largest – by far – of these have been the hydrocarbon duties. Taxes generally rose with revenue, which meant that the effective tax rate on Pemex increased as oil prices rose.[20] This arrangement is common in the industry, but for Pemex it has been especially punishing because the company has been unable to take advantage of the revenues from recent record oil prices for either reinvestment or debt reduction, both of which are critically needed. By contrast, all the best-performing NOCs in this study have been able to set aside at least some of the surplus revenues from higher oil prices for exploration and production activities and other investments.

Starting in January 2006, Mexico took steps to moderately lower Pemex's burden. The major goal of the 2006 reforms was to allow a portion of Pemex's capital expenditure to be funded with internally generated funds rather than constant issues of new debt (Pemex 2010). Pemex's management says it received tax reductions of $1–2 billion for 2006. In 2008, Mexico reduced Pemex's hydrocarbon duty from 79% to 74% and set a schedule for further lowering the duty to 71.5% by 2012 in order to retain more cash for internal investment (Fitch Ratings 2009; Moody's Ratings 2009). The recent reforms have also allowed Pemex for the first time to deduct certain costs from taxes and also provide a special tax regime for the development of certain oil fields seen as key to reversing the recently slumping production.

As a result of these recent changes, Pemex's tax situation has improved moderately. Pemex should be able to post an official profit while also opening up some funds for investment and debt reduction. Nevertheless, the tax burden on Pemex continues to be the highest of Latin American NOCs and among the highest for NOCs worldwide (Fitch Ratings 2009).

In tandem with Pemex-focused reforms, Mexico has also attempted to implement a broader tax reform. For decades, Hacienda was unwilling (and probably unable) to expand Mexico's tax base. The average Mexican consumer and business do not pay any federal taxes. Instead, only a few large entities like Pemex supply the government with an overwhelming majority of its income. A major advantage of the new system is that Pemex corporate, along with the refining, gas, and petrochemicals subsidiaries, will be taxed like "normal" companies with income taxes based on revenues less expenses and costs – a regime that could allow refining, for example, to pay taxes that are rooted in real production costs while also keeping a predictable share of the fruits of better performance.

3.2.2 Subsidies

Unlike many other NOCs, Pemex is not currently saddled with the cost of providing subsidized fuels. During the 1970s and 1980s gasoline was highly subsidized. But that led to large-scale smuggling and crime across the US-Mexican border. Partly as a legacy of that history, today a liter of gasoline tends to cost a little more in Mexico than it does in the United States. The high price of gasoline is in part due to a policy decision allowing for controlled, gradual increases in fuel prices that tend toward market price levels in the United States and partly because Mexico is a net importer of refined products – a large portion of the oil extracted from Mexican soil by Pemex E&P must first be exported to the United States for refining before being reimported by Pemex Refinación for eventual sale to the Mexican market.[21]

Meanwhile, state-owned power company CFE is a major Pemex customer (Carreón-Rodríguez *et al.* 2007). It provides electricity to most Mexicans and operates power plants that run on natural gas and fuel oil purchased exclusively from Pemex. Fuel oil power plants, which are far worse for the environment than natural gas ones and also more costly to operate when fuels are charged at market prices, dominate the Mexican electricity sector today mostly because of the historically tight relationship between Pemex and CFE. Throughout the 1970s and 1980s, Pemex actually sold fuel oil to the power sector at only 30 percent of its opportunity cost, an underpricing that amounted to an implicit subsidy of about $1.5 billion annually. Today, however, it can be argued that it is CFE that subsidizes Pemex because the fuel oil it purchases is essentially a very low-quality non-commercial product that Pemex would be unable to sell for a meaningful price to anyone else at home or abroad[22] (PESD Interviews). In any event, the development of a low-quality fuel oil-based power sector in Mexico has been harmful to Mexico and is one reason that Pemex's gas operations remain "a poor second cousin" to oil production, which continues to dominate all other Pemex activities (Carreón-Rodríguez *et al.* 2007). Fuel oil sales to the power sector accounted for 10 percent of Pemex's 2009 domestic sales – even if at a great cost to the environment and overall efficiency for Pemex and CFE (Pemex 2010).[23]

3.2.3 Investment financing – Pidiregas

For all the onerous taxes that Pemex pays, the firm has steadily and meaningfully increased capital expenditures for fifteen years (see Figure 7.4). Most of this new investment is targeted to exploration and, especially, production (see Table 7.2). Yet Pemex has had no internal funds for long-term investment as it roughly breaks even or runs a loss each year. The tax reforms discussed above are relatively recent and not yet decisive. Pemex, nonetheless, financed an almost $90 billion investment between 1998 and 2008 through a debt mechanism that allowed the company to declare large projects as "Pidiregas."

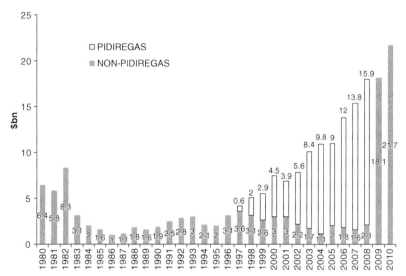

Figure 7.4 Pemex capex, 1980–2010.

Notes: Pidiregas: long-term productive infrastructure projects. Non-Pidiregas: budgetary investments. Includes upstream maintenance expenditures.

Source: Pemex Statistical Yearbook 1999–2011.

Table 7.2. *Allocation of capex (in % total capex) by Pemex operating subsidiary*

	Exploration & production*	Refining	Gas & basic petro-chemicals	Petro-chemicals	Corporate
1998	75%	14%	8%	2%	1%
1999	78%	13%	7%	2%	1%
2000	63%	30%	5%	1%	1%
2001	84%	10%	4%	2%	1%
2002	78%	17%	2%	2%	1%
2003	77.7%	17.5%	2.9%	1.4%	0.5%
2004	92.2%	4.1%	2.0%	1.3%	0.3%
2005	88.9%	7.1%	2.5%	1.2%	0.3%
2006	86.5%	10.1%	2.2%	0.9%	0.2%
2007	87.4%	9.4%	2.4%	0.7%	0.1%
2008	88.3%	8.6%	2.1%	0.8%	0.2%
2009	90.0%	7.4%	1.6%	0.8%	0.2%
2010	89.2%	8.4%	1.4%	0.9%	0.1%

* Includes upstream operations in *both* gas and oil.

Source: Pemex Statistical Yearbook (2011)

Depending on whom you ask, Pidiregas projects were either a disaster waiting to happen (an investment cure that is worse than the disease) or a clever way to work around the complicated Mexican federal fiscal system. The acronym Pidiregas translates as "long-term budget deferred infrastructure projects" that are, at their core, entirely debt-financed projects. For a decade, they were the fashion in Mexican government finance – not just for Pemex. In fact, Pidiregas began being used by the state electrical utility CFE in the early 1990s as a way to move the full cost of debt off the state utility's balance sheet – backed fully by Hacienda, which saw the looming need for investment in the power sector but cash flows that were inadequate to cover the cost (Carreón-Rodríguez *et al.* 2007). Only in 1995 was this practice blessed by congress, as by that time, the use of Pidiregas had caused so many legal inconsistencies and questionable actions by people in important positions that rather than go after the perpetrators, SFP (the public administration ministry discussed earlier in this chapter) had no choice but to recommend that the inconsistencies be elevated to law and the scheme formally legalized.

Pemex in particular enthusiastically adopted the use of Pidiregas. The proportion of Pemex capital expenditures that are Pidiregas (see Figure 7.4) grew steadily from 39 percent in 1998 – the first year that it used the Pidiregas mechanism – to 88 percent in 2008, the last year of Pidiregas. Some of these projects follow a build-lease-transfer (BLT) model, where Pemex contracts a project out to a contractor that is entirely responsible for its financing and completion. Only once the project is complete and handed over to Pemex does the company begin to pay the contractor. The most significant feature of this scheme was that the debt shows up on Pemex's balance sheets only when projects are completed – not during initial approval or years of construction. Even then, an accounting rule permits Pemex to report only the amortization of the project for the current and following fiscal year. Other projects used the Pidiregas mechanism only for construction financing; upon completion, Pemex secures debt from capital markets and pays off the project to the contractor in full.[24] Pemex then amortizes the commercial debt, which shows up in full on the balance sheets as soon as it is amassed according to normal accounting practices (i.e., when Pemex raises it from capital markets) (PESD Interviews).

Some state enterprises were attracted to Pidiregas financing because it allowed them to hide true debt levels. In one sense, Pidiregas is not fooling anyone since the Mexican congress and Pemex's creditors know full well that Pemex (and other state enterprises that rely on the scheme) is indebted well beyond its reported levels. Moreover, there is nothing to suggest that Pemex tried to deceive anyone. For example, the company chose not to take advantage of the BLT accounting rule (reporting only two years' worth of amortization) that would really let it hide debt from its balance sheet. But there does seem to have been a psychological lulling effect in that Pidiregas still makes the situation appear not so dire, especially to those not in the know. In fact, rather than encouraging openness and accurate public debt reporting, the Mexican congress actually promoted the use of BLT-type Pidiregas. It is as if congress, recognizing the need for large-scale investments but unwilling to cut taxes or otherwise reform the system, opted to pull a blindfold over itself.

For Pemex, the major attraction of this scheme was that a project's designation as Pidiregas guaranteed its financing would be immune from budget cuts and other government meddling. These long-term projects were approved as projects and the financing – because it was ultimately reported to (and often secured) from the international markets – was untouchable. This stands in sharp contrast to the rest of Pemex's budget, which was subject to considerable change and uncertainty year to year.

Pemex's management and the government finally had to look for a way out of Pidiregas because the associated debt is difficult to sustain. Any substantial drop in production or oil prices would have drastic consequences for the ability to service the Pidiregas debt. While options such as joint ventures or more flexible contracts remain attractive in theory – although plagued by administrative and constitutional problems – viable alternatives to Pidiregas are yet to emerge, and Pemex funded almost $20 billion in investments despite its already heavy debt in 2009 alone, with every intention of continuing the practice in 2010 (Pemex 2010).

However, alarmism about Pidiregas and other debt may be premature. The credit agencies have not been *that* concerned about Pemex's debt throughout the ramp-up in Pidiregas (Smith 2004; Fitch Ratings 2009).[25] Indeed, in early 2009, debt levels began declining slightly (Fitch Ratings 2009). To date, Pemex has had no trouble raising capital on world markets and at year-end 2009 maintained an investment grade rating with a steady outlook (Moody's Ratings 2009; Standard

& Poor's Ratings 2009). In fact, credit agencies have treated its debt as *pari passu* with Mexican sovereign debt (Fitch Ratings 2009; Moody's Ratings 2009; Standard & Poor's Ratings 2009). The state would never let Pemex become insolvent and everybody knows it.[26] Moreover, there is a sense that the amassed debt is actually doing some good. Every single Pidiregas is explicitly linked to critical infrastructure (by law, the cash earned from the projects must be sufficient to cover at least the cost of the debt and service) and to date, most projects have successfully boosted production. Therefore, servicing Pidiregas debt may not be so difficult after all, precisely because of the increased production and revenues that these projects are meant to bring in the first place.

Nevertheless, most close observers within Mexico and Pemex itself think the government must tame the mounting Pemex debt (PESD Interviews). That is why, as of 2009, Pemex is no longer using Pidiregas to finance new projects, which must now be financed through the federal budget and not by private companies. The already contracted Pidiregas debt, though, is likely to remain a heavy burden on the company for a long time to come.

3.3 Corporate operations and internal relationships

Pemex is a large and fully integrated oil company that also has operations in natural gas and petrochemicals. The core operations are performed by four fully owned subsidiaries, each with its own management team. The oil operations of the firm consist of two of these subsidiaries: Pemex Exploración y Producción (Pemex E&P) which explores, produces, transports, stores, and markets crude oil and natural gas; and Pemex Refinación, which refines, stores, transports, distributes, and markets petroleum products. The other two subsidiaries are Pemex Gas y Petroquímica Básica (processes, stores, transports, distributes, and markets natural gas, natural gas liquids, its derivatives, and basic petrochemicals) and Pemex Petroquímica (which engages in industrial petrochemical processes and stores, distributes, and markets petrochemicals other than basic petrochemicals) (Pemex 2010).

In addition, another subsidiary – P.M.I. Comercio Internacional (PMI) – serves as Pemex's international trading arm. Primarily, it sells Pemex E&P's crude exports but also provides trading, commercial, and administrative services to the other subsidiaries, including the transfer of funds from Pemex's foreign financing vehicles to Pemex corporate. PMI, which was established in 1989 and is tasked with making Pemex more competitive internationally, accounts for virtually all of Pemex's foreign activities. PMI has somewhat more flexibility than the other Pemex subsidiaries and it can enter into some types of contracts that are off limits to the others because it operates offshore and does not actually own any of the oil it markets. In addition, a majority of PMI's workforce is not unionized, which stands in sharp contrast with Pemex's other subsidiaries.

This corporate structure was implemented in 1992 following the "breakup" of operations previously centrally managed directly by Pemex corporate headquarters. The decentralization was intended to lessen the difficulty and increase the efficiency of running such a large company and was part of the strategic shift in the early 1990s to focus on boosting the economic return from investment. As part of the same reforms, Pemex eliminated its bloated and inefficient construction engineering arm.[27] At about the same time, Pemex for the first time established a transfer price mechanism to track and account for the movement and value of goods shifted between the company's different units (PESD Interviews). Prior to 1992, the company was essentially operating blind, as the lack of transfer prices between different units in Pemex eliminated any notion of financial performance outside of end-customer sales (which are far removed from the point where most value is actually added in the oil industry). Pemex managers had no idea which units and projects performed best; nor did they have a system for accurately targeting investment needs. Even well into the mid 1990s, Pemex operated without tracking a portfolio of projects – it was not until 2000 that the company finally started ranking projects by profitability. More recently, the company has begun to keep track of project profitability both before and after tax, signaling that seeing a return on investments is becoming more important (PESD Interviews).

3.3.1 Investment priorities
While more efficient than before, the company still seems to have too much on its plate to be able to operate efficiently. With more than 140,000 employees across its operations, it is difficult for anyone – especially the politically appointed top management – to

effectively manage such a sprawling enterprise. And despite the institutionalization of transfer prices and project portfolios, raising and allocating capital for long-term investment is still proving difficult. Under pressure to maximize revenues, relatively high crude oil prices and the decline at Cantarell have forced Pemex to focus on investment in crude production. The capex allocations of the past few years (see Table 7.2) are consistent with those at other integrated companies – with Pemex E&P getting the lion's share of investments. However, within Pemex E&P, it is *production* that dominates, as exploration has received relatively little attention even while existing fields are running dry (only 10%, roughly, of total E&P investment went to exploration between 2006 and 2010 and this is already a significant improvement over prior periods; Pemex Annual Report 2010).

Even natural gas operations, which could be hugely profitable and easily go hand in hand with the oil side of the business, were traditionally neglected in Pemex's exploration and production activities (PESD Interviews). It is difficult for any oil company to become a gas company, but the entry into the gas business seems to have been particularly challenging for Pemex. An interest in gas operations first materialized in Pemex in the 1960s because of demands from Mexico's chemical industry. This proved to be a false start, however, as meaningful gas operations did not appear until more than thirty years later. Only under external pressure from government and others did Pemex cautiously invest in the gas business in the 1990s. In 1992 and 1995 the Mexican government passed a series of electricity and downstream gas reforms that favored gas for the generation of electricity (it is cleaner and cheaper than the oil-fired power units that have historically dominated Mexico's power sector) and for some industrial applications. In fear of a flood of gas imports, in 1996 Pemex began efforts to develop the Burgos Basin (which was known to have substantial gas reserves). At the time, more than 85 percent of Pemex's gas production was still associated gas.[28] Pemex's total company-wide gas production actually declined for the next several years and it was not until 2004, after the year 2002 opening of the Burgos Basin to private sector development through multiple service contracts (see below), that gas production increased and the effects of the reforms in the mid 1990s were evident. Even so, natural gas represented only 11.3 percent of the value of Pemex domestic sales in 2009, and a much lower percentage of overall sales (Pemex 2010). The company is still underinvesting in its potentially profitable gas operations, as even the insufficient investments in new hydrocarbon exploration tilt heavily toward discovering new crude oil rather than gas.

Operations are even more underdeveloped in refining. Mexico imports around 30 percent of the petroleum products consumed in the country, a market that could be exclusively Pemex's if it could only get its refining capabilities up to speed (Moody's Ratings 2009). The company says it has invested at least $1 billion annually in refining since 1998 but is unable to yield a positive return on the investment. In 2006, it lost more than $3 billion in refining even though the refining sector worldwide had one of its most profitable years (PESD Interviews). But capturing elusive refining profits remains far down the list of priorities given the pressing needs of crude production, and the earliest date that construction could begin on an often-promised new refinery is 2012 (Moody's Ratings 2009).

3.3.2 Internal relationships and the union
The interactions among Pemex management, employees, and the Petroleum Workers' Union are quite troubled. There is a sense that the politically appointed management at the top is disconnected from the career Pemex employees, including other managers. One high-level manager admitted that he "had no idea" who worked four levels below him even though the mid-level managers were "the ones who ran the show" (PESD Interviews). The company also suffers from the impression among the Mexican public that employee corruption and outright theft are rife. However, this perception may, in part, be based on consumers' negative experiences with Pemex gas stations, which are notorious for cutting fuel with water and other scams but which are actually not owned or operated by Pemex despite carrying its brand.[29]

But the single biggest factor that strains internal relations in Pemex is the workers' union – in particular, union leaders. Pemex executives, Mexican government officials, and independent journalists all say that the union has enormous power. Yet almost no one outside the union seems to understand exactly how it wields this power or whether the rank and file really supports its leaders. What seems certain is that the union leaders are virtually untouchable and have de facto veto power over management proposals (PESD Interviews).[30]

The most obvious formal power of the union is that five of the company's eleven board seats are reserved for union representatives. In addition, Pemex managers do not control the hiring of new workers – the union does. The union also decides staffing for particular projects such as well drilling. This "filling of spaces" is one way in which union leaders maintain control over the rank and file and allocate benefits to workers. In turn, Pemex workers support their union leaders because they provide secure, steady jobs that the workers don't want to lose as well as generous benefits in health, housing, and retirement pensions (all widely perceived to be the best among unionized workers in the country). As of 2007, both salaries and pensions were tied one-way to oil prices, meaning that Pemex workers largely benefited from the recent rise in oil prices and did not suffer when prices eventually dropped in 2008. In fact, the union contract then in force (signed in 2004) was seen as so lucrative and favorable to the union by journalists and consultants that it was often cited as the primary reason why former CEO Raul Muñoz had to step down – he was rendered impotent to improve the company's performance after making too many concessions (Malkin 2004a).[31]

Pemex executives place a lot of the blame for Pemex's internal dysfunction on the union; they say that the "system is made for corruption" (PESD Interviews). As an example, one senior executive cites wasteful union employment. In most oil companies, average employment at a refinery that processes 200,000 barrels of oil per day is 800 people (PESD Interviews).[32] But a Pemex refinery of the same size and capacity employs more than 4,000 workers. Of these, half are "unspecialized" (i.e., uneducated or untrained), with no clear job descriptions or duties (PESD Interviews). Thus, management concludes that the real problems with its money-losing refining operations are not finances, old technology, inadequate investment or other inefficiencies, but unnecessary staffing through union-padded payrolls. Whether right or wrong, such opinions highlight the open frustrations and poor relationship between management and the union.

Despite the recent problems, the real struggles between the government and the union leaders were fought out over twenty years ago.

The union saw the climax of its power – and corruption – during the presidency of Miguél de la Madríd in the mid 1980s. At the time, Pemex and its union had essentially become a state within a state. But when Carlos Salinas was elected president of Mexico in 1988, he immediately cracked down on the union. One of his first acts as president was to jail the union leaders for corruption. He then drastically reduced Pemex's bloated unionized workforce from around 220,000 to 120,000. As a result, Salinas's term witnessed almost daily strikes and the company's corporate offices were sometimes closed off by strikers for days on end.[33] During the subsequent presidency of Ernesto Zedillo (1994–2000), the union regained some of its power and influence and even managed to add more than 20,000 workers back into Pemex.[34]

Today, the union remains strong but has changed the way it interacts with Pemex management. For example, it no longer automatically resorts to threats of paralyzing strikes to advance its agenda, which alone distinguishes it from most other unions in Mexico. Instead, union leaders have found new ways to bargain with and profit from Pemex. Most notably, the union has not resisted Pemex's strategic shift to outsourcing and subcontracting many activities over the past decade. Instead, union leaders are involved with, and profit heavily from, many of these contracts. Many service companies such as those that provide transport for Pemex's workers or those that serve food on the oil platforms are actually owned by union leaders. In addition, many of the riskiest and most unsafe jobs at Pemex are now performed not by unionized Pemex workers but by employees of the private companies with which Pemex contracts. The private companies' safety record is worse than Pemex's, but the union leaders tolerate these conditions because they directly profit from the subcontracting (PESD Interviews).[35]

3.3.3 A vocally unhappy management

One of the most remarkable aspects of Pemex's inefficient operations is management's willingness to talk about it. It might be expected that a state-owned company with a long history of political influence would simply align with the government official lines and pretend that nothing is wrong. This is not the case with Pemex. Top executives, it seems, are more than happy to talk about how terribly their company is organized and how badly it is underachieving. And they are quick to place the blame on poor administrative oversight by the Mexican state. Annual reports and other Pemex publications over the past several years are filled with management's complaints about the lack of autonomy and excessive taxation of the firm. While affirming that Pemex exists solely for the benefit of the Mexican nation and that it should not be privatized, Pemex's leadership has voiced concerns that the company is irresponsibly used as a cash machine for too many government programs that benefit neither Pemex nor the country.

Interestingly, while management feels that it has too little control, it also says it feels little accountability to the political forces that control it (PESD Interviews). Managers openly say that because the government is Pemex's owner, manager, and regulator, there is almost no effective oversight of the company.[36] A dissatisfied Pemex leadership is nothing new – management has been making similar complaints for at least the last fifteen years (PESD Interviews).

The managers' ability to at least "complain" to the government has yielded some recent results. As already described, since 1998 the company significantly increased long-term investment, most of it immune from across-the-board budget cuts. Unfortunately, these infrastructure projects are almost entirely debt financed (mostly Pidiregas), which created a whole set of financial problems explored earlier in this chapter. Lobbying by Pemex management also helped spur passage of the latest rounds of tax reforms and the modest 2008 corporate governance reforms.

Managers may also be quick to complain because rather than risking reputational loss and admitting to an inability to deal with (at least some) of Pemex's operational problems, blaming government and the workers' union for their troubles is particularly easy and convenient (PESD Interviews). A case in point is former Pemex CEO Raul Muñoz, who headed DuPont's operations in Mexico before being appointed to lead Pemex. Despite high hopes, Muñoz was unable to achieve any of his stated goals in four years on the job and resigned in frustration (Smith 2004). Two years later, he wrote a book in which he blamed then-president Fox for not having supported Pemex more strongly and for not having installed the right people in the administration, which made Muñoz's job difficult. Muñoz's frustrations seem based, more than anything, on the too many constraints that all Pemex CEOs must manage (Muñoz 2006). The Pemex executives that, like him, come in from successful private businesses may also be particularly unaccustomed to the skills needed for effectiveness in state enterprises, which should give some pause for thought to those who believe installing a board and management with greater private sector experience will directly translate to successful reforms for Pemex.

3.4 Relationships with contractors and IOCs

Pemex has relatively little interaction with the rest of the world's oil majors. Direct competition is minimal since Pemex has exclusive access to its domestic market and virtually no operations abroad. Mexico is the only major Latin American country that doesn't allow foreign oil majors to participate in oil exploration and production (Smith 2004). The only real competition Pemex engages in is the export of crude oil (and some petrochemical products) through PMI, but even that is done through long-term contracts with a limited set of customers rather than on the more competitive spot market.[37] Meanwhile, Pemex's one and only foreign operation is a joint venture refinery in Texas that is operated by Shell, while Pemex takes a largely passive role.

However, Pemex is not isolated from the rest of the global oil industry and has significant relationships with companies that construct infrastructure and perform various field services. Pemex has been unable to develop most infrastructure on its own – especially during the last decade when large new projects came on the heels of two prior decades of minimum investment (and the year 1992 elimination of Pemex's historically huge construction business). Also, the government favored the use of subcontracting because that allowed for full use of Pidiregas financing.

By far the most important project that Pemex contracted out was the nitrogen injection system for the Cantarell oil field. Fifteen years after its discovery in 1976, production from this biggest and most important oil field in Mexico started dropping. In response, Pemex decided to build a large nitrogen separation plant that would inject high-pressure nitrogen into Cantarell to emulsify and push out a larger fraction of the remaining oil. The project began in 1996 and involved several well-known contractors (including Bechtel Corporation and Linde Gas) and the construction of the largest nitrogen production plant of its kind in the world.

While Pemex's heavy recent use of subcontracting has helped it implement projects like the Cantarell injection and invest in many

other projects it could not have built on its own, the exclusively con-
tractor-type relationship Pemex has with other companies is fraught
with problems because Pemex largely lacks the capacity to manage
large and complex contracts. Lack of investment in its own technical
expertise has left the firm unable to understand the technological
frontier in the industry and to negotiate and manage contracts with
industry leaders such as Schlumberger.

There are some faint, recent signs that the company may be starting
to shift strategies when it comes to partnerships, and management is
hoping to move away from the exclusively subcontractor model. In
2001, Pemex signed a deep water technological cooperation agreement with Brazil's NOC Petrobras, recognized experts in deep water
drilling (an area where Pemex has little competence). It has since
signed similar agreements with Chevron, Shell, Exxon Mobil, BP,
and other IOCs. Perhaps as a result of these relationships and other
"conversations" that Pemex says it has had with the world's oil majors
on the topic of deep water, Pemex drilled its first-ever deep water oil
exploration well in late 2004 (Pemex 2010). This was a remarkably
late date for Pemex to be just starting in the deep water business,
especially as the country probably has large deep water resources
(the western Gulf of Mexico – in Mexico's territory – is probably rich
in oil and gas but has barely been explored). But the technological
cooperation agreements, while providing Pemex with valuable knowledge and expertise, still do not offer a way around existing legal
restrictions, and IOCs and other NOCs still cannot participate in
Mexico's oil sector as anything but subcontractors. Nevertheless, the
mere existence of these agreements and the fact that Pemex is now
working with other oil majors rather than its traditional subcontractors (field service companies) may indicate that both sides are looking forward to (or hoping for) the day when they can move away
from pure subcontracting and perhaps share reserves, production,
or revenues.

Another signal of changes in the way that Pemex interacts with
its subcontractors is the multiple service contract (MSC) that Pemex
uses in its gas subsidiary. Following gas and electricity reforms in the
mid 1990s, the company divested most of its gas transportation and
distribution operations. It then used MSCs as a way to outsource the
entire upstream exploration and development of its gas fields because
it lacked internal technological and contract management expertise

thanks to the traditional neglect of the gas business. Rather than sign a series of contracts with several companies for a given project, Pemex could sign one MSC with a single partnering company that would take charge of implementing the entire project. In effect, the MSC would allow Pemex to correct its weak capacity to manage large and complex engineering projects by delegating a larger fraction of the management authority to more competent outsiders. The problem with MSCs, however, was that the partner companies were not allowed to take equity positions in projects, which made the projects unattractive to the most talented outside firms. Instead, the company entering into an MSC with Pemex had to be guaranteed a fixed rate of return – something that is difficult to do for inherently uncertain exploration and production projects. Thus, in practice, the gas MSCs still yielded relationships that were more like those of subcontractors rather than properly risk-incented "partners."

Neither Pemex nor the companies that signed MSCs have been pleased with the arrangement and both sides would have preferred the partners to be able to take an equity risk position in the projects. But the Mexican Constitution does not allow for that. Even without giving away an equity position in the gas projects, the constitutional validity of the MSCs that Pemex signed was called into question. In 2005, Pemex reluctantly suspended MSC tenders following recommendations from the autonomous congressional audit office (Auditoria Superior de la Federación). Moreover, Hacienda (which encouraged Pemex to use these contracts because they offered a novel way to attract outside capital) and Pemex seemingly believed that foreign oil companies would accept any condition for the opportunity to get into upstream Mexican hydrocarbon operations – a view that proved mistaken when very few outsiders bid to develop the blocks of the Burgos Basin (no block received more than two bids) given the unattractive rates of return Pemex offered in its early MSCs (PESD Interviews).

The government, top Pemex management, and independent observers also say that an additional major problem that arises from Pemex's interactions with other companies is extensive corruption by the field service companies, which are accused of illicitly profiting mightily from a system that they profess to dislike (PESD Interviews). The 2008 reforms have given Pemex somewhat greater freedom to enter into incentive-based service contracts. Pemex can now sign

service contracts with outside companies that include incentive
clauses and contract flexibility in case technologies, prices, or other
factors change (Biller 2008). These reforms were aimed at confronting an impending production crisis by attracting investment into deep
water reserves and the Chicontepec oil field (see chapter appendix).
But while welcome, the reforms do not allow for equity participation,
are nevertheless constitutionally suspect, and like the gas MSCs may
prove insufficient to entice IOC participation (Biller 2008; Moody's
Ratings 2009). And they do little to curb contract padding and other
illicit acts by Pemex's "partners."

3.5 Technology and human capital

The main reason Pemex relies heavily on contractors is its poor
internal expertise and engineering capabilities. Earlier in its history
Pemex did invest in a highly competent internal engineering culture
that has since largely evaporated. Some credit this culture as having
come from the IMP (the Mexican Petroleum Institute), an organization
that used to be the company's technology arm in the 1970s (PESD
Interviews). Others say that the IMP never actually became a truly
good research institute but was always an arm for contracting out
projects that Pemex itself could not handle, as well as a place for
employee training (PESD Interviews). My assessment is that the IMP
ensured that Pemex engineers were well trained and supplied the company with fairly advanced (for the time) technologies during the years
that Pemex was engaged in large infrastructure investment from the
1970s through the early 1980s. Today the IMP, while still run by
Pemex, has been reduced to a relic due to budget cuts.

The consensus for the reasons behind Pemex's loss of its engineering
and technology culture are Mexico's foreign debt crisis of the 1980s
and its geology. For more than a decade after the debt crisis, Pemex's
production was kept steady with no new investment in infrastructure
or exploration. It was a cash machine to pay off national debts – an
easy task given Mexico's readily accessible hydrocarbon resources.
But having failed to develop new skills, the firm now has no choice
but to rely heavily on the field service companies and other contractors – the same ones executives often blame for excessive corruption
and Pemex's high cost base – to deliver the technology necessary to
maintain production levels as the easy-to-tap fields run dry.

For now, Pemex's leaders say that they can go to the international market of oil services providers for all their technological needs. In early 2007, they were aiming to put Pemex on a "fast track" to gaining deep water expertise, thanks to its nascent links with Petrobras and other firms, along with massive investments in such fields. Success will be difficult, though. The IMP's budget has not been restored – despite the professed interest by Pemex management in improving the company's technologically sophisticated operations and reducing reliance on contractors (PESD Interviews). And there were no major deep water breakthroughs in the two years after Pemex was supposed to jump on the "fast track" to acquiring new technologies. Even if Pemex manages to improve its technological expertise in exploration and production in the coming years, there is little reason to show similar optimism for its other operating units. Over the years, Pemex's refining, gas, and petrochemical subsidiaries have become even more neglected and outdated than its upstream oil and gas operations.

A common thread that underlies Pemex's other problems is that the enterprise is unable to invest in and deploy human capital efficiently. A senior executive at Pemex E&P stated that what Pemex most needs to learn from its contractors is modern project management, as such managerial skills would be even more important than any technology transfer Pemex could gain from those companies (PESD Interviews). For example, Pemex had the technology to gather real-time data regarding its offshore oil production for years but since it had no way to manage it, the data was solely used for record keeping (von Flatern 2006). It was not until Pemex's recent launch of a large, integrated data center (manned by Pemex but implemented and supervised by multinational giant Schlumburger) that it was able to critically manage the data in real time and raise it "to the level of a daily operational decision-making tool" (von Flatern 2006). So even though Pemex can go to the market for its technological needs, it is much harder to do the same for management capabilities.

These troubles are not new. When the company formed its Texas-based refining joint venture with Shell in the early 1990s, neither Pemex nor the Mexican government showed any interest in learning or transferring skills that would have been readily available through the partnership (PESD Interviews). A proposal to have a regular staff exchange with the refinery received the support of only one board member of the Pemex Refinación subsidiary. The rest of the board (and others within Pemex) thought that such an exchange was irrelevant and were content to leave Shell as the sole operator (PESD Interviews). In recent years, the launch of the data operations center mentioned earlier had to overcome significant cultural barriers, as Pemex engineers in the field initially viewed it as a "punishment tool" and feared for their jobs (von Flatern 2006).

Thus, even if Pemex gets all the fiscal reforms and investment budgets it seeks, it will still have a tough time avoiding a hydrocarbon reserves crisis (see chapter appendix) because the most critical constraint on Pemex these days is not only inadequate investment but also lack of human capital. The company is not simply experiencing a drop in production but also a transition from a company that relied on one super giant field (Cantarell) to a company that now needs to manage a production portfolio of many fields. And the problem is not that individual executives or managers may be poorly trained, lazy, or corrupt, but rather that the company lacks an institutional ability to manage its increasingly complex operations. In early 2007, Pemex claimed it was developing a portfolio with as many as seventy projects just to make up for Cantarell's shortfall (PESD Interviews). In addition, the company drilled an average of over 1,000 wells per year between 2008 and 2010 (up from less than 300 in 2000) so the number of field service contracts has multiplied drastically (Pemex Statistical Yearbook 2011). Such a transition requires that Pemex develop strong specialized skills and management capabilities that it currently simply lacks. It also raises the question of whether continued large-scale investment in Pemex is justified, given that Pemex's recent mission of simply sustaining daily production has forced enormous capex flows toward multiple subcontractors, while neither Pemex nor the government has the capacity to verify whether it is getting its money's worth (PESD Interviews).

4 The prospects for reforms

With crises looming and a company as troubled as Pemex, reforms appear to be the only way ahead, although they could feasibly take different shapes and directions. I briefly propose three kinds: fiscal, sectoral, and regulatory.[38] Fiscal reform depends on further tax decreases, which would free up resources for investment with internal capex to be allocated by management, thus alleviating some of management's autonomy concerns as well as some of the debt problems. Sectoral reform, on the other hand, would be much broader and can address a host of issues such as corporate governance, buildup of human capital, introduction of competition (which may but need not be private, let alone foreign), and development of a coherent policy strategy for the sector. Regulatory reform would change the way that government oversees Pemex's behavior – notably by allowing the company to take more risk and, ideally, reining in the union.

Looking forward, it is clear that proponents of any reforms will have to be extremely vigilant about separating their proposals from the issue of privatization, which lends itself to easy opposition given Mexico's negative experience with the results from some other privatizations (most notably Telmex). If Pemex is to be turned around, the focus of honest debate and reforms must be the company's performance, specifically how to transform Pemex into an effective state-owned enterprise rather than how to maintain certain current benefits it provides or, worse yet, prime it up for eventual privatization (see generally Chang 2008).

Regarding fiscal reform, the tax reductions in 2006, 2007, and 2008 reflect growing awareness that both the country and company are facing a financial crisis. Nevertheless, further tax reform is necessary to wean the Mexican government off Pemex and to transform Pemex into a consistently profitable company.

Sectoral reform is likely to be more difficult to achieve. As the 2008 debate over service contracts reveals, all reform proposals run up against the politically dicey subject of greater private involvement in the sector. While conceptually very different, years of rhetoric make it almost certain that talks of opening up the sector will be followed by accusations of privatization.[39] Pemex's executives are well aware that to sell any reform ideas to the public, they will need to be clear that the reforms will address management, not ownership. For that reason, Pemex's leaders tend to re-frame all reform discussions in the language of corporate governance. As far as they are concerned, since the Mexican people (in theory, owners of the company) are unhappy with their management and the lack of accountability, it is corporate governance that must be the first issue to be fixed before any other sectoral reforms take place.[40] This is why the company's executives lobbied hard for Pemex to have an independent board, strict reporting requirements, and otherwise implement "corporate best practices."[41]

While Pemex's lobbying on this front has, in part, succeeded (managers wanted a fully independent board while the reforms only provided for some independent members), further reforms are likely to be even more challenging.

Sectoral and regulatory reform efforts are also not helped by the fact that Pemex (and Mexico's electricity companies) have cried wolf many times before. For example, electricity companies warned for several years that "the lights will go out by 2005" without any consequence. Pemex itself has a considerable historical track record of surviving despite the odds. One way or the other, no matter how bad things get, Pemex always seems to find ways to keep operating. Even from its earliest days, when Mexican oil was boycotted by the British and Americans, Pemex survived by selling petroleum to Nazi Germany (although it later served the Allies after the Second World War broke out). In the 1960s, it survived a serious production crisis that was abated by new investments and discoveries. More recently, most experts and analysts predicted that the 1997 nitrogen injection project for the Cantarell field would be a total failure and the first step in Pemex's collapse. But, in fact, the project worked largely according to Pemex expectations. Nevertheless, the present indications are that there are real reserves and technology crises in Mexico today.

Yet political fragmentation in Mexico continues and the political constraints on reform are severe, especially since several parties show every sign of continuing the past practice of mobilizing nationalistic sentiments to gain votes. During the 2008 energy reform debates, the PRI fought hard to maintain the constitutional ban on private upstream investment, rejected calls to allow private sector transportation and refining of crude oil, and fought to maintain the privileges of the workers' union (a traditional PRI stronghold). The strategy apparently worked, as President Calderón (who personally lobbied hard for oil reforms in 2008) was dealt a defeat in the July 2009 mid-term elections – with the PRI emerging once again to practically control both houses of congress. The deeply entrenched public opinion surrounding Pemex that PRI is able to exploit sets Mexico apart from other Latin American countries, where presidents have been able to make far-reaching economic reforms even when facing fragmented and highly competitive party systems.

Mexico gave Pemex some breathing space in 2008 and hopefully these changes represent the start rather than endpoint of reforms.

However, they eroded support for President Calderón and have so far not halted the decline in Mexican oil nor achieved the promise of a more agile, flexible Pemex that can have fruitful relations with other oil companies. The timing also proved especially unfortunate, as the recent global financial crises – which hit Mexico hard – hindered the scope and implementation of the reforms and deflated enthusiasm for more.

With no major political party (including Calderón's PAN) apparently willing to push for highly unpopular further reforms, it is unlikely that any significant changes will come before the next presidential elections in July 2012. What remains to be seen is how well Pemex – and the national economy – can manage in the meantime.

Appendix: Pemex's reserves and production – a closer look

Pemex's perilous production and, even more so, reserves situation has been chronicled often over the past few years and was a key impetus to the movement to attempt meaningful reforms for the enterprise in 2008 and 2009. While it is too early to judge the effect of those reforms in terms of replenishing Mexico's hydrocarbon reserves, it is important to understand the situation that Pemex is facing and how it got there.[42]

As mentioned elsewhere in this chapter, for the better part of three decades, Pemex was able to rely on plentiful, easily accessible crude oil flowing from the Cantarell oil field, which at one point was the second-largest productive field in the world and the primary reason that Mexico successfully transformed into a major oil exporter. Unfortunately, this largely served to reinforce the government's financial dependence on Pemex and discourage investment in exploration, new technologies and infrastructure for other producing fields, and human capital.

By the late 1990s, Pemex was busy boosting the country's crude oil production to record levels even as no new meaningful exploration (let alone reserves discoveries) was occurring. This naturally led to the rapid depletion of the country's proved reserves, of which only 68 percent were actually developed for production in the first place (again, largely thanks to Cantarell's plentiful bounty). Cantarell's production peaked in 2003–2004 when its average crude production of more than 2 million barrels per day still represented 60 percent of Pemex's total production.

In the years since, Pemex has not been able to forestall the field's decline any longer, and Cantarell's productivity dramatically decreased (2008 production was less than half that in 2004), forcing the company and the nation to face a potential reserves and production crisis. Yet for the most part, Pemex maintained a surprisingly rosy outlook – at least publicly – on the reserves situation.[43] It was quick to issue a strongly worded optimistic denial of an impending crisis, when internal studies that included some dire reserves and production scenarios were leaked to Mexican media in 2005. And during a conference call in March 2006, the company's CFO even forecast a drastic improvement in the reserves replacement rate between 2006 and 2010, adding a full 77 percent to proved reserves. This vision was based on a planned capital expenditure on *exploration* for the same period of more than $12 billion – a very large sum given that Pemex spent only around $300 million on exploration five years earlier. It did ultimately invest over $9 billion in exploration during that period but did not achieve anywhere close to the envisioned replacement rates. More recently, with Cantarell providing only about 19 percent of total crude production in 2010, the company still clung to an ambitious goal of achieving a 100 percent proved reserves replacement by 2012 (Moody's Ratings 2009; Pemex Annual Report 2010).

But even a successful large-scale exploration program that adds significantly to proved reserves would do little to solve the immediate production problems posed by Cantarell's decline, as it often takes years after a discovery before any oil is pulled from the ground. To make up for the short-term production shortfall, Pemex focused on increased production from other producing oil fields (Figure 7.3). Indeed, it invested more than $40 billion between 2001 and 2005 in developing such fields. In October 2006, the company announced a doubling in production from its Ku-Maloob-Zaap field, which it indeed achieved by 2009 (Pemex Statistical Yearbook 2011).

Pemex also said that it would engage in other development activities that should result in "a significant reclassification of probable reserves to proved reserves" (Pemex 2010). In early 2006, Pemex said that if all went well, it expected crude oil production for 2006 to surpass 3.4 million barrels per day, which would have set a new record high. But, all did not go well, as output from Cantarell had dropped by a full 10 percent in the first half of 2006. By the end of the year,

Pemex's CEO had to at last tell the Senate Energy Committee that output at Cantarell was now expected to decline at an average rate of 14 percent a year between 2007 and 2015 (the actual drops to date have been much steeper).

Independent observers remain highly skeptical of Pemex's optimistic portrayal of its depleted hydrocarbon reserves. Most of the important wells that Pemex says will make up for Cantarell's drop-off in the near term are also old and have peaked. More specifically, there is concern that Pemex may be relying too much on Ku-Maloob-Zaap to make up for Cantarell, as the oil from that field must be mixed with lighter crudes because it is too heavy for most refineries to process (PESD Interviews). The worry is that with Cantarell in steep decline, there will not be enough light crude production to mix with the oil coming from the new heavier fields. Such an outcome would require substantial upgrading of the refineries to handle a fuller stream of heavy crude.

It is also far from certain whether Chicontepec – yet another oil field often mentioned by both Pemex and outsiders as a possible savior to Mexico's reserves and production concerns – will ever become productive. Discovered three decades ago and located onshore, Chicontepec is still untapped, yet it may contain crude reserves that dwarf Cantarell. However, this field is so geologically complex that it would take significant capital, technology, and human expertise, which Pemex lacks, to bring up any oil from the ground.[44] In 2009, Pemex invested around $1.7 billion in developing the field and planned a similar investment in 2010, with ambitious plans to drill between 600 and 800 wells per year (Moody's Ratings 2009). But it is doubtful whether developing Chicontepec will ever be worth the cost, and leaders of Pemex E&P admit that it is a great challenge.

Finally, it is highly probable that Mexico has huge hydrocarbon resources that lie beneath the deep waters of the Gulf of Mexico. But, for the most part, these regions have yet to be carefully explored, let alone developed, in large part because Pemex does not have the required deep water technology to access them. Thus, even if these reserves are ultimately tapped thanks to appropriate investments and reforms, and prove to be the savior to Mexico's long-term oil production problems, this would not occur for years to come. What happens in the near term is highly uncertain and should be a serious concern for all Mexicans.

Notes

I am grateful for interviews conducted for this research (in alphabetical order below). I am also indebted to David Shields for his insightful review of a draft of this chapter, particularly his analysis of recent and potential future reforms of Pemex.

- José Luis Aburto (President, Petrelec Energy Consultants), January 24, 2007, Palo Alto, CA, and March 20, 2007, Mexico City.
- Jose Alberro (consultant; former Director, Pemex Gas y Petroquímica Básica), March 9, 2006, Berkeley, CA.
- Pedro Aspe (CEO, Protego Asesores Financieros; Professor of Economics, ITAM, Mexico City; former Secretary of Finance and Public Credit, Mexico, 1988–1994), March 20, 2007, Mexico City.
- Luis Macias Chapa (New Business Manager, Pemex) May 16, 2006, Mexico City.
- Juan José Suárez Coppel (CFO, Pemex) May 16, 2006, Mexico City.
- Marco Alberto Oviedo Cruz (Director of Financial Planning of Ministry of Finance and Public Credit (Hacienda) Investor Relations Office), March 21, 2007, Mexico City.
- Rafael Diaz (Ministry of Finance and Public Credit; former Mexican congressional aide), May 15, 2006, Mexico City.
- Miguel Tame Domiguez (Director, Pemex Refinación), May 16, 2006, Mexico City.
- Carlos Morales Gil (Director, Pemex E&P), May 16, 2006, and March 21, 2007, Mexico City.
- Ismael Gomez Gordillo (private attorney; former Internal Controller, Pemex; former Undersecretary of Standards and Controls at Ministry of Public Administration – SFP), March 21, 2007, Mexico City.
- Vania Laban (consultant, IPD Latin America), March 20, 2007, Mexico City.
- David Lunhow (*Wall Street Journal* reporter), March 20, 2007, Mexico City.
- Elisabeth Malkin (*The New York Times* Mexico correspondent), May 16, 2006, Mexico City.
- Carlos Mena (Executive Director, MMC; formerly at SEMARNAT), March 20, 2007, Mexico City.
- Gonzalo Monroy (consultant, IPD Latin America), March 20, 2007, Mexico City.
- John Padilla (consultant, IPD Latin America), March 20, 2007, Mexico City.
- Vinicio Suro Perez (VP, Planning and Evaluation, Pemex E&P), March 21, 2007, Mexico City.

- Rafael Alexandri Rionda (Ministry of Energy – SENER), March 21, 2007, Mexico City.
- Geri Smith (*Business Week* Latin America bureau chief), May 15, 2006, Mexico City.

1 Interestingly, Pemex was not always in the business of funding the government. For the first half of its life, Pemex's primary mission was the reliable delivery of hydrocarbon energy to Mexico (whether through selling gasoline to consumers at below market levels or huge subsidies in fuel oil for the electricity sector). Because that mission was a highly political one, Pemex's strategy emphasized the delivery of energy services with minimal participation of outside firms, something that left a lasting effect once Pemex became a financial tool for the government that could have used outside help (PESD Interviews – interviews conducted by Stanford University's Program on Energy and Sustainable Development in 2006 and 2007).

2 One of Pemex's biggest assets throughout its seventy-year history has been its status as a national symbol. The "Expropiación Petrolera" – the date that President Cárdenas stood up to foreign interests and nationalized the oil industry – is a major national holiday in Mexico. While Pemex's nationalistic sheen is wearing off, its national significance remains high and the masses overwhelmingly oppose any privatization or hints of opening up the sector to foreign involvement (PESD Interviews).

3 While US companies like Standard Oil were also outraged by the expropriation and continued to press the US government for action in the years to come, there was generally much more sympathy for the Mexican government's position and actions in the United States than in Britain. The US government at the time was much less sympathetic to the interests of the energy industry and inclined to favor a more state-driven model of economic development.

4 Ironically, this most important of all Mexican oil fields was not discovered by Pemex's large-scale exploration activities of the era. Instead a fisherman accidentally stumbled upon the field by noticing oil bubbling to the surface in the areas he was fishing. He alerted Pemex because the oil was fouling his nets and he assumed the oil company was at fault.

5 The term "Pemex" throughout this chapter refers to the entire organization – Pemex corporate and all its operating subsidiaries. Whenever specific subsidiaries are discussed, they are referred to by their appropriate names.

6 There were exceptions – to be sure – such as Pemex's 1978 reorientation toward exploiting Cantarell and the 1997 decision to inject nitrogen in the field, but such "decisions" tended to be borne of dire necessity and there

was no consistent, long-tern, institutionalized process of decision making across the enterprise.

7 This statement should not be interpreted as absolving anyone in Pemex management, the workers' union or the Mexican government from blame for the company's many problems. Indeed, it would seem that there are many individuals who, over the past three decades, should share the blame for Pemex's performance, but assigning blame for Pemex's ills is not within the scope or intent of this chapter.

8 Mexico, like the United States, is a presidential republic with a bicameral legislature. A popularly elected president is both head of state and the head of a government made up of his appointed secretaries that run the nation's various ministries. All government spending requires the approval of the legislature, known as the Congress, which is divided into two chambers, the Chamber of Senators and the Chamber of Deputies.

9 During a campaign stop in the United States in 2000, then-candidate Vicente Fox hinted that he might try to privatize Pemex (Smith 2001). However, once the predictable public backlash to this statement emerged, Fox backtracked and declared in his inaugural address that Pemex would continue as the exclusive property of the nation. Some analysts think that this promise not to privatize Pemex was unnecessary and amounted to a waste of political capital that made any other reforms for the next six years much more difficult to pass (PESD Interviews).

10 Occasionally, the head of Mexico's state-owned electricity company also served on Pemex's board and vice versa. However, the board seats appointed by the president almost always went to government ministers, with the exact ministries that got a seat varying between administrations.

11 This was the period when, after almost fifteen years of neglect and minimal investment following the oil crisis of 1982, Pemex was reorganized and critical new investments began to be made. Strong presidential guidance could have led to sectoral reforms that would have markedly raised the value of the reorganization and new investments that were undertaken.

12 The term of Congress's deputies is only three years and that of senators is six. An individual can serve first as a deputy and then as a senator (or vice versa) and can then repeat the process, but cannot be reelected to the same position in immediately subsequent terms. In addition, it is rare for congressional deputies to actually repeat terms several times. Thus, most congressional terms are limited and if an individual stays in government longer, they must hold different positions.

13 A notable exception is that of environmental regulations, where Pemex traditionally had enormous influence – inserting escape clauses and

finding other ways to avoid regulatory burdens (PESD Interviews). In addition, environmental laws historically set low penalties – between 2001 and 2005 Pemex paid less than $5 million in penalties, with only one prosecution of an official in connection with negligence, despite numerous accidents and environmental violations over the same period (McKinley and Malkin 2005). It does not help that Pemex's CEOs have traditionally been better connected politically than the environmental ministers and any decision to shut down a major pipeline or halt a refinery would probably have to be made by the president of the nation rather than an environmental minister or prosecutor (McKinley and Malkin 2005; PESD Interviews). It should be noted, however, that while good environmental behavior was never imposed on Pemex from above, the company has nevertheless tried to behave responsibly in recent years. Outside pressures have been mounting and there may have been a generational shift in Pemex's management, with the recent younger managers perhaps seeing environmentalism as a business opportunity, as environmental issues are an increasingly reliable way to get more money from the government at a time when the company is essentially cash starved for projects other than crude oil production infrastructure (PESD Interviews). For example, $5 billion in badly overdue refinery upgrades was secured in recent years in order to bring Pemex in compliance with a new environmental law on the sulfur content of fuels (PESD Interviews).

14 Pemex's subsidiary companies have their own separate boards that appear to be more functional than Pemex's corporate board. Those boards do not have union representation but are nevertheless split fifty-fifty between Pemex insiders and government officials. These boards sometimes face real business decisions and have the discretion to make them. Nevertheless, it appears that whenever difficult issues arise, the government board members usually exert more influence than those that hail from the company (PESD Interviews).

15 It was not until the spring of 2007 that the energy ministry even began to speak of "attempting" to fulfill such a role (PESD Interviews). The reforms that were ultimately enacted in 2009 created a National Hydrocarbons Commission (NHC), an upstream regulator that should, in theory, perform this role. In addition, the laws now say that the energy ministry must consult with the NHC and then define production levels. But some analysts already suggest that in practice Pemex will just continue to produce as high as it can, thanks to the stark geological and operational reality it faces (PESD Interviews).

16 Recent oversight by the SFP has proved even more restrictive. During the 1994–2000 administration, President Zedillo was concerned that

the SFP was failing in its mission to fight corruption and a proposal was made to establish a new, superior corruption-fighting body. A task force assembled to study the idea ultimately resulted in proposed changes to twenty-seven administrative and financial laws. While these reforms did not go through, they did scare SFP leaders into tightening up regulations and oversight (PESD Interviews). This tighter leash nearly immobilized the entire Mexican public sector. No one in government these days wants the personal risk of signing a contract, as the SFP can assault them even for the slightest inconsistencies and mistakes.

17 Interestingly, Pemex did not benefit from the recent high oil prices as much as it did during previous spikes. The high costs of the large quantities of gas and refined products that Pemex imports these days are offsetting gains from high prices in its crude sales. Moreover, Pemex sells mainly a heavy crude that fetches a price much lower than the light, sweet varieties that are the international benchmarks.

18 Some analysts say the "true" figure is as high as 80 percent, depending on the year (PESD Interviews).

19 The IEPS is a so-called "special tax" on domestic sales of gasoline and automotive diesel. It is essentially a gasoline sales tax paid by retail consumers – collected by Pemex at the point of sale and then transferred to Hacienda. However, the amount of tax collected varies constantly because of the way that gasoline prices are set in Mexico. At the start of each year (with subsequent adjustments as it sees fit), Hacienda decides how much consumers are to be charged for gasoline and diesel at retail stations. In general, Hacienda tries to keep this retail price as high as possible – benchmarking its prices mainly against those in the United States (where retail prices float with the market) as the US prices are widely known in Mexico and parity helps to reduce cross-border smuggling (PESD Interviews). In the meantime, the actual revenue that Pemex is allowed to keep from its sales of gasoline and diesel is known as the "estimated production cost." Hacienda calculates this production cost by reference to "an efficient refinery" located in the United States. In other words, the amount Pemex keeps is wholly devoid of any reference to the firm's actual production costs. Thus, the amount of this gasoline sales tax collected by Pemex is constantly shifting. Interestingly, during nine months of 2005 and 2006, the IEPS tax actually went negative. The government owed money to Pemex, which Pemex credited against other taxes it owed during the third quarter of 2006.

The most important result of the IEPS is that Mexico cannot have much higher gasoline sales taxes than the really low retail taxes in the United States (relative to the rest of the world) (PESD Interviews). Hacienda, in effect, indexes the Mexican retail market to the US market. This encourages high consumption of gasoline (because retail prices are relatively low) and forces the government to get revenue through other more pernicious taxes on Pemex itself.

20 Notably, between 1994 and 2005, Pemex paid an "excess gains duty." This tax required Pemex to pay a fixed percentage – determined annually, but usually set relatively high – on all revenues from crude oil sales above Congress's "budget base price," which was always set very conservatively. Thus in 2004, Pemex paid out 39.2 percent on all crude sales above $20/barrel, while in 2005 the excess gain payments were 29.2 percent of crude exports above a $23/barrel threshold. Meanwhile, the actual prices of Mexican crude oil soared above these budget thresholds to over $30 and $40 per barrel for 2004 and 2005 respectively. In the end, the "excess gains" that Pemex was supposedly making from high oil prices actually forced the company to run at multibillion-dollar losses in 2004 and 2005.

   Perhaps recognizing that this tax was proving too costly for Pemex at a time of skyrocketing debt and critical investment needs, Hacienda and Congress eased its burdens (if ever so slightly) during the last two years that the tax was in effect. But rather than significantly reduce the tax directly, Hacienda decided to "refund" some of the taxes that it still considered due so that they could be spent on capital improvements. In 2004, Pemex was refunded the full duty (around $2.5 billion), while in 2005 the refund was significantly reduced and defined as only a 50 percent refund of the tax paid for exports sold above $27 per barrel. Even though these refunds helped somewhat, Hacienda remained firmly in control and retained approval authority for each peso that the company was allowed to keep for capex needs.

21 Nevertheless, despite the lack of customer subsidies, Pemex is not in fact free to pass along all its costs of providing gasoline to customers thanks to the IEPS tax. Hacienda sets the retail price of gasoline, which is the same for all gas stations across the country, except for a special slightly lower price in the north border region (in order to discourage reverse smuggling from the United States into Mexico).

22 Officially, Hacienda allows fuel oil prices to float and CFE is supposed to pay a "market price" for that product, though that notion is somewhat difficult to define when there are essentially no other real customers for Pemex's low-quality fuel oil other than CFE.

23 The last fifteen years have actually witnessed important improvements in Mexico's energy mix, with natural gas making the most significant gains. For example, conventional thermal energy production in the country shifted from using predominantly fuel oil (67.1% in 1993, 47.1% in 2002) to a significant increase in natural gas (15.5% in 1993, 29.8% in 2002). Within a few years, natural gas is expected to represent a majority of total

conventional thermal energy generation. Nevertheless, oil continues to dominate Mexico's overall domestic energy production. In 2001, hydro-carbons still represented 89.4% of primary energy production in Mexico, with crude oil as the main source (70% of the total), followed by natural gas (18%). Electricity, the second most important source of primary energy production, accounted for only 4.6% of overall domestic energy produc-tion, giving a sobering perspective to the natural gas gains in conventional thermal energy generation discussed above. Although it should be noted, once again, that the situation today is not as bleak as it once was and there are some hopeful signs of improvement. Between 1995 and 2001, power generation in Mexico grew almost 52%, as did harmful emissions in abso-lute terms. However, emission *intensity* dropped (3.9% for CO_2, 12% for SO_2, and 10.8% for total suspended particles), as a result of a techno-logical switch from conventional power plants to more efficient combined cycle plants, which also led the power sector to double its consumption of natural gas in the same period (and even begin to drop the consumption of high sulfur fuel oil in 2000).

24 The debt that Pemex takes on under this second Pidiregas scenario can be secured through several special-purpose financing vehicles. "Pemex Finance Ltd," a Cayman Islands vehicle, and the "Pemex Project Funding Master Trust," a Delaware trust, were both established in 1998, the year after Pidiregas first came into use in Pemex. Their purpose is to finance Pidiregas and raise other debt. Pemex Finance operates through the purchase and sale of accounts receivable from Pemex's crude oil sales. Meanwhile, the Master Trust simply funds Pidiregas projects through debt guaranteed by Pemex, as does the "Mexican Trust F/163," a finan-cing vehicle formed in 2003 to fund Pidiregas in domestic currency. It is important to remember that all capex and financing, whether Pidiregas or not, require the approval of Hacienda and Congress.

25 Some of Pemex's credit ratings and associated reports from S&P, Fitch, and Moody's are available on Pemex's website. Pemex's credit ratings were upgraded in 2007, justified by the 2006 tax reforms. But even before those reforms, the credit agencies were not very critical of the situation Pemex operated under and maintained surprisingly positive overall ratings on the company's debt.

26 The "Ley de Concursos Mercantiles" does not allow any state-owned company like Pemex to be declared in bankruptcy. In addition, any signifi-cant debt restructuring for Mexico – past and future – always involves the debt of Pemex.

27 Many of the construction services previously performed by that unit are now contracted "out" to firms closely linked to Pemex and its union, with only questionable savings for the company.

28 The term "associated gas" is used in the industry to refer to gas that naturally occurs in combination with crude oil in reservoirs. Such gas (and any benefits from its capture and sale) is therefore mostly a by-product of an oil firm's exploitation of crude oil reserves. By contrast, non-associated gas is one that occurs separately from crude oil and is targeted, as such, for development by a company.

29 All but a handful of Mexico's 7,000 gas stations, although formally branded "Pemex," are actually concessions managed as private franchises. This arrangement, in place for more than fifty years, is a considerable drag on the company's overall public image. The gas stations are by far the most visible Pemex symbols in Mexico and the most "direct" way that consumers interact with Pemex. In fact, during the NAFTA negotiations, Mexico insisted, for psychological reasons, that Mexico would continue to have only "Pemex" branded gas stations. Unfortunately, these stations are notorious for low-quality gasoline (e.g., diluting it with water or fuel oil) and outright fraud (e.g., giving nine liters of gasoline for every ten charged). In an effort to boost its image, Pemex tried to take away the concessions from a large number of service stations in 2003 only to have a judge rule that the violations of the accused stations were not reason enough to do so. Pemex has also been renegotiating a 1992 contract with its franchisees, insisting on more leeway in verifying retail distribution practices and asking stations to install modern fuel pumps with tamper-proof meters. Federal regulations now actually require that the outdated pumps be upgraded, but the mandate caused an uproar among station operators who claimed they would suffer severe financial harm (Frontera Norte Sur 2006).

30 The common joke about Pemex is that only the union and consultants are constants, with everybody else rotating in and out.

31 In addition, Mr. Muñoz signed the contract without the backing of the Pemex board.

32 Refining is a highly automated operation and some companies achieve those kinds of refining volumes with as few as 200 workers on station – four shifts a day, fifty workers per shift.

33 Salinas had motivations other than economic efficiency and Pemex's performance for attacking the union. The 1988 Mexican elections were corrupt and illegitimate (it is debatable whether Salinas would have won if they had been fair) and the union leader at the time had shown support for Salinas's non-PRI challenger, who was none other than Cuauhtémoc Cárdenas – the leftist son of the Mexican president who created Pemex and was a perennial advocate for unwavering state control over the firm.

34 One analyst says that current employment at Pemex is well over 140,000 and possibly as high as 200,000 because the company does not count a category of "temporary" workers (known formally as "temporary workers who have been with us for over ten years") in its official employment statistics (PESD Interviews).

35 An example is an April 2005 accident that released an estimated 60 liquid tons of ammonia gas that killed six workers and was blamed on a subcontractor cutting into the wrong pipe after a supervising engineer left to check on the location of the correct one. The victims had been employed by the subcontractor for only a few months and had not been provided with protective suits. The total compensation given to all six families was only $74,500 (McKinley and Malkin 2005).

36 "It's just the same guy wearing three different hats. How can he hold himself accountable?" asks one executive.

37 This is, in large part, because Pemex's heavy crude oil requires special refineries and is not as amenable to the fungible commodity status that exists for higher-quality crudes on the oil market.

38 These reform proposals assume that Mexico would like to maintain Pemex as a major crude oil exporter that should become more efficient in funding the government. It is worth noting that a substantial minority in Mexico would likely support a total shift in Pemex's strategy that would focus on its underdeveloped petrochemicals and refining subsidiaries. Prominent Mexican politician Cuauhtémoc Cárdenas (son of Lázaro Cárdenas), for example, has proposed to radically *reduce* crude oil exports and transform Pemex into an exporter of refined products such as fuels and other petrochemicals (Cockrell 2006; Cárdenas 2006). This should not be dismissed as a trivial left-wing argument that comes off as wishful thinking because Mexico is an *importer* of vast amounts of petroleum products, which – like with Iran's NOC – seriously undermines the value the nation is getting from large-scale crude exports.

39 It does not help, either, that the political left in the country wants to further integrate Pemex and tends to focus on jobs creation in the refining and petrochemicals subsidiaries – two of the company's biggest weaknesses, where private sector involvement – or at least some competition – would seem to help the most.

40 Interestingly, management does not exclude the possibility of privatization as one of the "further down the line" reforms after corporate governance. That kind of stance is unproductive and makes it difficult for management to maintain its short-term insistence to separate ownership from management reforms.

41 Ideally, top management would like an independent board that would be responsible for budgeting, procurement rules, nomination of the CEO, and "all the normal functions of a board."

42 Pemex proudly highlights that the company is quite transparent in its evaluation of reserves, as unlike many NOCs, it adopted Western standards for accounting and transparency (including, since 1996, the hiring of external consultants to aid in the reserve calculations and reporting proved reserves in line with regulations from the United States SEC). The move to the widely understood SEC standards for reserves marked an important stroke in the painting of the bleak reserves picture detailed below. Rather than providing support for management's formally optimistic projections, such transparency revealed Mexico's troubled reserves situation to the entire world. One theory is that Pemex management shifted strategy and embraced transparency in order to make the company's troubles highly visible so that, in turn, it would be difficult for the government to cut investment funding.

43 This was somewhat surprising given management's willingness, during the same time period, to openly discuss the enterprise's other shortcomings.

44 Chicontepec is believed to hold about 17.6 billion barrels of recoverable oil. But these are probable, not proved reserves, and the oil is extra heavy crude that requires special refining needs currently considered unviable in Mexico. A 2003 Pemex estimate said it could take total investments of $30 billion over fifteen years to develop oil and gas reserves in Chicontepec – a project that would require drilling 13,500 wells. A March 2006 announcement by former President Fox said that Pemex would invest $37.5 billion US dollars over the next twenty years on the oil fields of Chicontepec, with a goal of producing 1 million barrels per day. Pemex's CEO at the time estimated that 20,000 wells would be drilled in order to exploit the field.

8 | Kuwait Petroleum Corporation (KPC): an enterprise in gridlock

PAUL STEVENS

1 Introduction

The history of oil in Kuwait is riven with political disputes and interference. Lack of trust in international oil companies (IOCs) helped catalyze nationalization of the sector in the 1970s and the creation of Kuwait Petroleum Corporation (KPC), the country's national oil company (NOC). Over its lifetime, KPC has struggled to absorb the many different subsidiaries both in Kuwait and abroad that comprise the nation's oil operations and to assimilate them into a truly functional, integrated company. Nationalization eventually gave KPC ownership of these subsidiaries, but asserting control and consistent and coordinated strategy has been more difficult as the subsidiaries had many different former owners, histories, and corporate cultures.

As is true in many state-owned enterprises, KPC suffers from excessive bureaucracy and extensive political interference. However, of the fifteen countries examined in this book, Kuwait is notable for its particular inability to devise and implement reforms that would improve performance at its oil company. The oil sector as a whole is largely devoid of strategy. The root cause of these troubles is Kuwait's fragmented and dysfunctional political system.[1]

As will be developed in this chapter, since 1991, in particular, Kuwait's oil sector has been in gridlock because political reforms that had been adopted in the wake of the country's liberation from Iraq's invasion have split authority between the government and the National Assembly (parliament). Those reforms sought greater democratic participation in the country, but their main effect is that the National Assembly (which derives authority from popular election) and the government (which is appointed by the emir) are not accountable to each other.[2] Paralysis has been the result because policies face a tortuous process of negotiation and approval; unpopular decisions are easy to veto at many points along the process. As in Mexico, where authority is also divided between the president and the legislature, low accountability makes it hard for Kuwait's political system to see an interest in promoting effective long-term strategy in its NOC (see Chapter 7). Kuwait's National Assembly has been wary of oil sector reforms that might alter the ability of its members to channel valuable benefits, such as jobs, to their constituencies. And the government has been unable to focus on reform due to high turnover – since 2000 there have been six oil ministers, which has been particularly troubling for KPC since the minister controls government policy and also serves as chairman of the company. This high turnover derives from a combination of reluctance by incumbents to be "grilled" by the assembly coupled with frustration generated by the gridlock that characterizes the whole oil sector. In addition to contentious oversight by the government and the National Assembly, KPC is also accountable to its shareholder: the country's Supreme Petroleum Council (SPC), which is part of the government administration yet is distinct and has a majority of private sector appointees.[3] While the SPC has been KPC's most reliable advocate for higher commercial performance, its ability to influence the most constraining of Kuwait's laws and regulations is low.

This chapter aims to explain KPC's performance and strategy. In brief, performance is hard to measure. Unlike many NOCs, KPC and its affiliates produce annual reports with audited accounts; thus, in theory, it is possible to assess the company's financial performance. In practice, however, the efficiency of the operations is difficult to assess. Upstream operational costs appear low but this is normal in the Middle East reflecting the region's favourable geology. This chapter will argue that the performance of the sector is, in fact, quite poor. This is reflected in a succession of missed targets, a string of serious accidents, and the company's inability to deploy capital, people, and other resources strategically. In November 2006, a report from the State Audit Bureau was leaked to the press (MEES 49:49 2006). The report criticized KPC for trying to adjust its targets to make the company's performance look better. Notably, it had pushed back its capacity target of 3 million b/d from 2004–2005 to 2008–2009; it also delayed from 2004 to 2011 the goal of reducing gas flaring to 1 percent because of "technical problems at the gathering stations." In addition, the planned fourth refinery had been postponed due to severe inflation in expected construction costs and an apparent

dispute with Saudi Arabia over the location (MEES 50:8 2009).[4] The
615,000 b/d plant had been due onstream by 2010. In the late 1990s
and early 2000s there were three major accidents in domestic refineries. The reasons for this poor performance are a common theme in
this report.

Assessing strategy requires separating upstream and downstream
operations. In the 1980s KPC pursued a strategy of moving downstream and operating outside of the country. This strategy was partly
the result of financial controls that the government imposes on KPC,
which allow the company to keep profits from downstream operations while the government captures the majority of the earnings
from upstream operations, which account for 94 percent of the state
budget. Thus KPC invested massively (and as will be outlined below,
recklessly) in overseas downstream operations even as its domestic
upstream capabilities languished. Since 1991, this downstream strategy often has come under scrutiny by the National Assembly and even
the company's shareholder (SPC) due to concerns that such overseas
operations allow KPC to disguise its operations from scrutiny within
Kuwait. (Similar fears that the NOC has moved overseas and downstream to evade scrutiny and taxation are also evident in the case
study on Venezuela, for example; see Chapter 10.)

In the upstream, KPC has struggled just to sustain production,
and it faces growing difficulties as its fields mature and become more
complex at a time when the government is setting ever higher targets
for crude output. These problems would be relatively easy to address
with substantial participation by technologically and managerially
more sophisticated outside companies, including the IOCs. However,
the role of outsiders in Kuwait's economy (especially the oil sector)
has always been controversial outside the corridors of KPC and the
Ministry of Oil.[5] Privatization and other schemes to engage outside
investors and operators have been often mooted – notably through
"Project Kuwait," an ambitious plan to rely on outside investment to
expand the country's oil production – but are stalled politically.

This chapter makes three central arguments.

First, the failure of KPC to embrace a coherent strategy and to perform effectively is fundamentally due to Kuwait's dysfunctional political system. One symptom of the lack of accountability between the
government and the National Assembly is that KPC is subjected to an
intrusive and erratic form of administration that makes it particularly

difficult to adopt strategy and implement it efficiently. It also discourages risk taking. Attacking KPC and the oil sector has become a proxy mechanism for the assembly to challenge the government. Notably, government ministers and KPC officials constantly face aggressive scrutiny from the National Assembly; moreover, KPC as a state company must follow onerous procurement rules. (In many respects, KPC's challenges mirror those facing Mexico's oil company; see Chapter 7.) The results are decision-making processes that are complex, cumbersome, unpredictable, and horribly bureaucratic. Strategic choices that need four decision steps in Western companies, for example, must endure a phalanx of thirty-six decisions in Kuwait. In other countries examined in this book – such as Brazil (see Chapter 12) – state oil companies that are exposed to extensive oversight have devised strategies to insulate themselves from meddling. For KPC, however, such an approach is blocked by barriers in Kuwaiti law as well as the high turnover in oil ministers. Because KPC is particularly exposed to the whims of the oil minister, lack of stability in that position has made it hard for the company to cope with an environment that does not seek or reward good performance.

Even when the CEO of KPC (a position where there has been much less turnover) has sought better performance, it has been hard to sustain the external or internal context needed to deliver on that goal. An obviously overdue reform – one that has been discussed widely yet has proved impossible to implement – would separate the two roles of the oil minister (which give the minister two vetoes on KPC's decisions) and allow a more independent board and management at KPC. The SPC is particularly notable for its embrace of initiatives that would allow more autonomy at KPC – such as less onerous procurement rules – but it has found its efforts at reform blocked by the fact that significant changes would require altering the 1980 "Founding Law" that governs KPC. Such legal changes have proved impossible because they require concerted and coordinated action by the government and National Assembly.

Second, while KPC has some excellent senior managers with talent and a deep knowledge of the oil industry, middle-level management in KPC and its subsidiaries is strikingly weak.[6] This appears particularly true in the technical/engineering areas. People are given posts with insufficient experience and knowledge – a reflection of a governance system laden with political interference in the appointment and

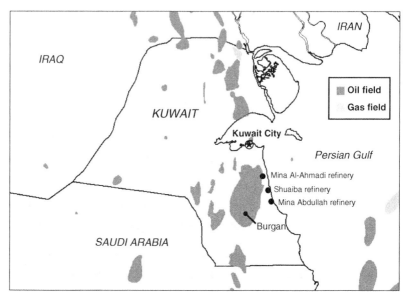

Figure 8.1 Map of major oil and gas fields in Kuwait.
Source for oil and gas field data: Wood Mackenzie (2009b).

promotion of personnel and, increasingly, removed from the frontier of the industry. Efforts to train a new generation of Kuwaitis have not been matched with incentives for them to stay within the country or the oil company.

Third, high oil prices in recent years have masked these fundamental problems. The country's small population and large accumulated reserve funds provide a luxury that could allow these severe problems in the oil sector to persist for a long time before financial crisis besieges the country. Looking to the future, the prospects for the sector are bleak. Political interference will get worse as the National Assembly seeks a greater formal role in the operation of the sector and learns how to exert even greater control over Kuwaiti politics. Fixing this problem will require fundamental reform of the political system, which will be even more difficult to implement than reforms in just the ministry. Moreover, an alternative strategy – opening the sector to outside companies – is equally difficult to adopt. KPC is aware that it lacks the capabilities to manage the growing problems in the upstream, as depletion of easy oil leaves more complex geology, crude that is heavier and more difficult to extract, and sundry problems managing the growing fraction of water that is produced alongside the crude oil. However, as in the Mexican case (see Chapter 7), political gridlock has deterred the entry of IOCs, whose presence is essential if the field problems are to be managed. As "resource nationalism" gains greater support in Kuwait, a pattern that is evident throughout the Middle East, it will become even harder for KPC to get help from IOCs and other non-Kuwaiti firms. KPC has devised some strategies to work around these barriers, but those strategies are generally unattractive to outside companies and also rest on weak legal and political bases.

2 History of KPC

The Kuwait Oil Company (KOC) was created through an old-style concession agreement in 1934 as a joint venture between the Anglo Persian Oil Company (the precursor to today's BP) and Gulf Oil.[7] As in other oil-rich countries of the region, criticism of the agreement began to mount soon after World War II. The concession covered the whole of the land area of Kuwait (except for the Neutral Zone)[8] and its exclusivity prevented any other company, foreign or Kuwaiti, from pursuing oil ventures in the territory. Its ninety-three-year scheduled lifetime included no provision for renegotiation, which made it inflexible in the face of changing circumstances. And apart from a requirement for "good oil field practice" the agreement gave KOC complete managerial control over all operations, decisions on the extent of exploration efforts and the development of discoveries, and the overall level of production. A gathering storm of criticism arose in the 1960s especially among Kuwaitis who were becoming more politicized, as it did against similar agreements across the region. Many began to advocate nationalization as a solution. However, the rulers in the region (remembering the fate of Dr. Mossadegh – who attempted nationalization in Iran, alienated Western powers, and soon found himself out of office[9]) were wary about actually putting such a policy into practice. Instead, as we will see, Kuwait sought to break KOC's monopoly by encouraging an array of new entrants and corporate forms in the sector rather than outright nationalization.

In 1960, the Kuwaiti government created Kuwait National Petroleum Company (KNPC) as the country's NOC that would operate alongside KOC. Unlike all other NOCs formed in the region,

40 percent of the equity was put out to domestic public subscription thus giving a strong private sector flavor to the company. Its remit was to "engage in all phases of the petroleum industry, natural gas and other hydrocarbons, refining, manufacturing, transporting ... and distributing, selling and exporting such substances" (Stocking 1970, p. 440). Among other projects, KNPC built the Shuaiba Refinery; the largest (and one of the most modern) in the world at the time of its construction, it was one of the first refineries built by an NOC in the region. In parallel with the creation of KNPC, several other important players also emerged in Kuwait's oil sector in the late 1950s and early 1960s. The Kuwaiti government created these new companies mainly to deliver more of the oil value chain to Kuwait and reduce KOC's monopoly.[10]

In 1961, Kuwait obtained a limited voluntary relinquishment of acreage from KOC.[11] Kuwait opened acreage for exploration bids and some thirteen potential bidders expressed interest. In the late 1960s the joint venture between KNPC and Hispanoil, the Spanish NOC, won the rights. The private shareholders of KNPC objected strongly to this agreement, which called for the creation of a joint company if oil was found. They felt KNPC should be exploring for oil in its own right without foreign partners. All four of KNPC's private directors resigned in protest.

The 1960s era of pressure for nationalization peaked following the Six-Day Arab Israeli War of 1967. In 1968, Zaki Yamani, Saudi Arabia's oil minister, announced the details of his proposed ideas on "participation" – a scheme that would allow host governments to gradually take control over local oil companies and would, Yamani hoped, forestall a radical nationalization that might alienate Western governments. Over the next few years several governments, including Kuwait, negotiated the General Agreement on Participation signed in October 1972. Kuwait secured an immediate 25 percent of the equity from KOC, with a plan to lift the share to 51 percent by 1982. Kuwait was particularly aggressive in bargaining with the Western companies and thus paid the least for this initial share. Kuwait's compensation was $200 per barrel of capacity. Others paid much more: Saudi Arabia ($351), Abu Dhabi ($580), and Qatar ($592) (Stevens 1975). Nonetheless, the Kuwait National Assembly immediately expressed its dissatisfaction with the process and demanded even more favorable terms, specifically a higher equity share.[12] In June 1973, Kuwait announced that it had negotiated a revision of the terms to 40% with immediate effect; in January 1974 the figure was raised to 60%. By mid 1974, the government announced it would take over 100% of KOC on terms that it never fully revealed. Despite Yamani's hope for gradual and orderly transition to majority state ownership in the region, the fervor of nationalization was hard to contain.

National control was easier to declare than to put into smooth operation. By the end of the 1970s, the Kuwait oil sector was populated by a number of separate companies, all state owned. In an effort to bring coherence and coordination to the sector and integrate the value chain, the government created KPC as a holding company with control over all oil-related subsidiaries in the country. KPC's attempts to control its many subsidiaries – each with different cultures and philosophies – immediately faced problems. For example, the three Kuwaiti refineries that together composed KNPC had three separate owners. It took almost ten years for KNPC to absorb these units into a single refining enterprise. At the same time KOC, which had become accustomed to independent operations, was uncooperative with intrusive KPC management and difficult to control.

The legal instrument for national control was the "founding law" (Law 6 of 1980), which gave KPC the mission of being "a public corporation having economic character and [being an] independent corporate entity." (The full list of KPC's subsidiaries today is shown in Figure 8.2, discussed below.[13]) The founding law also required that an amiri decree establish KPC's board. It also, in effect, appointed as shareholder the SPC – a body that had been created in 1974 to oversee ownership of the wide array of newly acquired state assets.[14]

This form of organization was to cause enormous problems in the future simply because KPC's subsidiary companies were subject to normal Kuwaiti commercial law applicable to any company; thus changes to the companies could simply be agreed by the usual decision process within any company. However, KPC's special founding law is tailored to state ownership and more rigid. (Other countries passed nationalization laws superceding the commercial code, but their laws typically gave the NOC greater flexibility.) Substantial changes to KPC's operations thus require a change in law, which is increasingly difficult to obtain given the political gridlock. Through the 1980s the government avoided rigidities arising from the founding

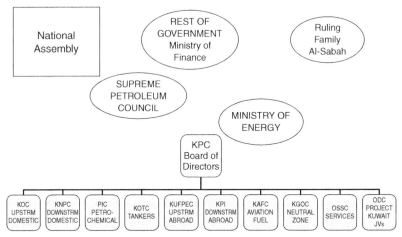

Figure 8.2 Organizational structure of the Kuwait petroleum sector.

law through the use of amiri decrees (as it did in creating KPC's board and in founding the SPC), but this route to law making and regulation has become increasingly controversial as the National Assembly (which has no direct control over amiri decrees) has become more influential and demands a say in the organization of the national petroleum sector. Because each of KPC's new subsidiaries was an independent entity under Kuwait commercial law, each answered to its own board. Throughout the 1980s the sector was highly fragmented because plans and projects decided in the center faced independent review in each operating subsidiary. (This situation contrasts with PDVSA's 1980s experience, in which fragmentation of operations led to intra-firm competition and better performance; see Chapter 10.)

In 1990, Iraq invaded Kuwait. This proved to be a traumatic event for KPC.[15] First, the oil sector lost many of its key managerial personnel when Palestinians and Algerians were declared persona non grata as a result of their governments' support for Saddam. Second, it became very difficult for the government to control or indeed suspend the National Assembly. Before 1991, excessive attempts at interference in policy matters were answered simply by the emir suspending the National Assembly. However, after the liberation from Iraqi occupation, described by some observers unkindly as "making the world safe for feudalism," such behavior was not a realistic option.

This allowed National Assembly members to interfere seriously in the oil sector, a major problem, which is discussed in more detail below.

These problems were compounded in the 1990s as the country's more fragmented political system encouraged the bureaucracy to encroach further on KPC's decision making. During the same era, KPC faced a growing gap in management competence. These challenges, together, slowed KPC decision making and made it increasingly difficult for the enterprise to devise and implement strategy. Far too many small project proposals from the subsidiaries would arrive at KPC headquarters for signoff; KPC would then examine them in great detail and often redo basic project evaluation. Unable to decide on its own strategy and facing little useful oversight by its shareholder and the government, KPC slipped into introspective gridlock. The 1990s were marked by crises that made KPC even less able to encourage initiative and rational risk taking. In 1993–1994 a major public scandal broke over the finances of the KOTC subsidiary, which had been keeping two sets of books – one that allowed senior management to skim off funds. There were also rumors of higher-level involvement in the fraud. The result of this was that in 1998 the government imposed much greater financial controls on all state enterprises, which further encouraged KPC to avoid risks and focus on technical minutia rather than investments or other activities that might draw scrutiny. In the late 1990s and early 2000s there were three major refinery accidents, which fanned outrage and eroded trust in the oil sector, not least within the National Assembly.

Such incidents became symbolic of KPC's poor performance and inspired the government to install new KPC management in 1998, most visibly evident with the appointment of Nader Sultan as CEO of KPC. Sultan's objective was to reorient KPC around commercial goals. Many politicians that might otherwise block such reforms appeared to tolerate this change because KPC's troubles had become highly visible and discussed in the local media and they were concerned further interventions on their part would damage them politically. Poor performance along with prevailing low oil prices created some urgency for reform. The new management was charged with wresting a degree of control away from the politicians both in government and the National Assembly who now feared being held accountable for their decisions in the country's financial crown jewel.

344   *Paul Stevens*

Reforms were pursued throughout the company. KPC employed many consultancy firms to help redesign the company to give the subsidiaries greater autonomy while reducing the number of projects coming to KPC's central decision makers for approval. Thus, from 2004, only "national projects" were referred to KPC headquarters, along with the instruction for the assessors not to "redo the numbers" but rather to assess projects in light of corporate strategy, the track record of the subsidiary company proposing the specific project, and compliance with health, safety, and environment (HSE) goals. The blueprint for reform, formally in force today, is called the Strategic Management Model (Whittington 2001); it pushed many functions to the subsidiaries and separated, completely, the marketing function from KPC.

Reforming KPC would also require reforming the shareholder, the SPC. When created, the SPC had no permanent committees to address major issues on any consistent basis (Al-Atiqi 2005). The government proposed successive, ad hoc technical committees in 1993. An amiri decree in August 1999, inspired by Sultan's reforms, reconstituted the SPC and identified nine non-government members who would help make the SPC more independent and performance-oriented. (As discussed in Chapter 3, this approach differs in some respects from private sector corporate governance arrangements.) In 2000, the government also reorganized the SPC's committee structure to create three specialist subcommittees, on strategy, technical, and financial aspects of the oil sector, to make it easier for SPC to evaluate KPC's performance in each area and to frame a strategic vision for the sector out to 2020. That process, which remains cumbersome and is explored in more detail below, yielded KPC's current strategy, known as Vision 2020. A sign of the efficacy of these reforms is that KPC management soon expressed a certain dread at having to go before the SPC and justify its proposals, with the private sector members of the SPC being notorious for giving the management a "hard time." SPC, as befits a shareholder, became more independent and also better able to assimilate specialized information.

Despite much effort, the oil sector's performance has not improved beyond the glaring troubles that were already evident in the 1980s. The central trouble lies in political interference in KPC's decision-making processes. This interference makes it hard for KPC to implement a strategy and to govern its operations effectively. Political interference has become more severe, notably with the growing role of the National Assembly in the country's governance. The attempts to reform KPC and SPC, while admirable, have not addressed what is most needed – a change to the original founding law – an unlikely proposition given the current fragmented state of Kuwaiti politics. I explore these issues, which lie at the heart of KPC's troubles, below.

3 KPC's current organization, performance, and strategy

By 1980, KPC had been created as a company that would hold the state's ownership of KOC (the country's cash machine) and the many other oil-related subsidiaries. KPC's original architects envisioned a vertically integrated organization that could extract, for the state, the maximum value from the whole chain of activities from crude oil production to final marketing. That strategy was unusual among NOCs that, in general, had been created with a focus on the most lucrative upstream activities rather than vertical integration.[16] Indeed, the two NOCs that were pioneers in moving into the downstream abroad were KPC and PDVSA. (On PDVSA see Chapter 10.) KPC did this in part to lock in market outlets for its crude. To an extent this did make sense given that Kuwait crude was heavy, sour, and generally difficult to refine. However, an additional explanation was to deepen the information asymmetries at the heart of KPC's relationship with the government of Kuwait. Operational integration allowed KPC to capture a greater share of the rent for itself. The government, both the administration and the National Assembly, saw KPC's efforts to remain operationally vertically integrated as an attempt to allow greater rent seeking. Thus, from the very beginning of KPC as a national firm, suspicion of its intentions and strategy has been rife.

Success in vertical integration, however, requires clear strategy. Yet KPC's organizational and governance chart, shown in Figure 8.2, is more of a cloud than a scheme with clear lines of authority. The problems with authority are rooted in two aspects of KPC's founding law and have come to dominate how the company crafts its strategy and how it performs. First, the 1980s founding law split authority over key decisions between KPC and its shareholder, the SPC. Crucially, KPC was empowered only to make recommendations to the SPC on personnel and budget matters; the SPC alone was given the authority to actually set personnel regulations and send the budget to the government and National Assembly. The SPC, although part of the government, remains independent. Thus when the government sets policy for the sector it works, in part, through the SPC and mainly through the various other arms of the government, notably the oil ministry. And the government, itself, shares power between the administration (which is largely controlled by the emir) and the National Assembly, which stands for popular election.

Second, although KPC, itself, is subjected to direct governance by the SPC, its subsidiaries remained governed by standard Kuwaiti commercial law. For KPC to create a new subsidiary requires SPC approval. However, KPC subsidiaries simply need the approval of their own boards to create companies/subsidiaries. In a similar vein, the subsidiary employees are treated as private sector employees while the employees of KPC are in an uncertain limbo between the private and government sectors, with their salaries set by the Civil Service Commission.[17]

The roles of the energy ministry and the National Assembly are difficult to parse. KPC board decisions must be ratified by the minister. The minister also appoints the CEO of KPC and the members of its board. Since the minister is also chairman of KPC, this might be expected to make the ministerial ratification a mere formality (as it is for current-day PDVSA). However, as explained earlier, this is far from the reality and there has been a bizarre history of ministers approving a decision as chairman of the board and then unilaterally rescinding it as minister. In part this reflects the fact that the minister can be held responsible by the National Assembly and frequently leaked decisions of the KPC board can then create political pressure on the minister for a reversal (PESD Interviews). Furthermore this threat of parliamentary sanction tends to make any minister extremely cautious in his decisions. The formally omnipotent yet ambiguous role (along with the constant changing of ministers) presents a serious problem for KPC. As Nader Sultan, then CEO of KPC, said in 2002:

It is crucial that the oil minister stays in his post in a supervisory capacity for as long as possible, because this means continuity of long-term policies. The role of the minister is important and crucial in the interpretation of government policies ... It is important to explain here that every minister needs time to understand the oil sector and to implement government policy. Because of the continual changes of ministers, one should not be surprised that there are substantive or minor ... differences in interpreting public policies. There are also differences in priorities. This, of course, halts the work of KPC. We go ahead, and then we stop ... If you ask any KPC official about this issue, he will tell you that he wants ministers to be stable in their posts. And if they cannot keep ministers in their post, then they have to think of other solutions. (MEES 45:16 2002)

The role of the National Assembly in KPC's decision making adds further complications. It has no formal role in developing strategy for KPC, but it is required to approve KPC's budget and thus, de facto, it can have a large role in assigning spending priorities. (KPC and Pemex's budget approval processes are similar.) Its role has been increasing in recent years, and the senior management in KPC appear to fear ever greater political intervention through the National Assembly. In KPC, trade unions are viewed by some as quite a powerful force, although their role tends to take the form of blocking decisions rather than promoting initiatives (PESD Interviews).[18]

3.1 KPC's performance

KPC and its affiliates, as with many NOCs, produce fairly comprehensive and regular information about financial performance. They deliver annual reports compiled to international standards and undergo internal and external audit. The KPC consolidated accounts simply represent the sum of the accounts of the subsidiaries along with allowances for head office costs. Despite this fairly extensive formal reporting, it has proved extremely difficult to develop a comprehensive picture of the companies' performance.[19] To parse the data, we examine KPC's performance from five angles.

3.1.1 Effects of fiscal system on performance

The Kuwaiti government's fiscal system treats KPC's subsidiaries in different ways, which has a strong effect on the enterprises' investment plans and incentives to perform efficiently. Kuwait's oil sector is organized around a government-controlled budget system for KOC (which generates most of the country's cash) and a less intrusive, commercially oriented approach for the other subsidiaries. KOC receives its capital expenditure allocation in a budget set by the government. This is then spent in developing and maintaining oil fields that produce crude. KOC buys this produced crude oil from the government and deducts its operating expenses (plus 10 percent) from the purchase price. (The 10 percent is a legal reserve required of all Kuwaiti companies and covers possible claims against the company.) A committee consisting of KPC, the Ministry of Oil, and the Ministry of Finance sets the price at which KOC purchases the crude on an annual basis. KOC then sells the oil at prevailing international prices. Along the way, the government removes an additional 10 percent for the Reserve Fund for Future Generations (RFFG) and KOC takes another 50 cents per barrel marketing fee. Alternatively, KOC can transfer the crude to KPC's refinery subsidiary (KNPC), which yields revenue by selling the products and receiving a subsidy from the government for below-market product prices.[20]

Thus KOC is treated as a cost center and faces few incentives to reduce operating costs. Moreover, any difference between the set price at which it purchases the oil and the immediate market price at which it sells (whether negative or positive) falls to KPC. Although normally small, this difference can be large when the oil price is changing quickly. Like most risk-averse firms that are exposed to cost of service regulation, KOC's response is gold plating and rent seeking. Although evidence is sparse, KPC appears to react to price movements for its products with an eye to short-term advantage rather than long-term investment.[21]

KPC's other subsidiaries face less onerous government financial controls and are allowed to earn profits. Thus, by selling the products that it refines itself (and providing an array of other services), KPC can generate earnings that are not immediately stripped away by the government. One obvious consequence of this system is a strong incentive for KPC to maximize its downstream operations, especially those selling into the international market since domestic product prices in Kuwait are regulated at levels below the international market. Not surprisingly, KPC has invested especially heavily in downstream and overseas operations compared with its peers in the region.[22] Kuwait's refineries are relatively sophisticated. Expansion plans were stalled as the expected cost of building a fourth domestic refinery skyrocketed with the global construction boom.[23] However, the fundamental incentives remain in place for the company to be inclined toward large over-investment in downstream capabilities. Refinery capacity utilization is sound although the figures for 2001–2002 were distorted by

Table 8.1. *Production costs in Kuwait*

($ per barrel)	2001/2	2002/3	2003/4	2004/5	2005/6
Average production costs	1.29	1.42	1.42	1.55	1.47

Source: KOC Annual Report 2005–2006.

the loss of refinery capacity following a series of fires. Nevertheless, there are no signs whatsoever of shortages and, according to KNPC's annual reports, the company's refinery operations appear to be financially stable.

There is very little detail given in the central government's budget accounts beyond the heading of "oil revenues." The exact composition of these "revenues" is unknown. However, they are substantial and in 2005/2006 accounted for more than 94 percent of total government revenue.[24]

3.1.2 Operational costs and performance

Other chapters in this book have sought to probe NOC performance by looking at production costs per barrel, which are shown for KOC in Table 8.1. The numbers are extremely low, which reflects the country's relatively easy geology. They are rising, but not by as much as is evident in other areas of the world's oil supply where much more complex geology has exposed producers to the sharp rise (until recently) in the cost of varied oil field services.[25]

With the exception of periodic statements by experts in the sector, the generally low production costs explain why efficiency is usually not high on the list of sectoral priorities. High oil prices since 2002 have also hidden these troubles. Nonetheless, many senior officials in the sector have issued statements underscoring that one of the reasons for Project Kuwait (a scheme that would encourage entry of the IOCs into parts of Kuwait's oil sector) was to reverse rising costs seen as the result of declining efficiency in the sector – notably where more complex geology has been involved, such as in the northern fields. As Nader Sultan, the former CEO of KPC, said in 2002:

[O]ur cost of production is increasing. These costs are divided into three major categories: one third for salaries and employment benefits, and this item is difficult to touch because we can not make our nationals redundant

350   *Paul Stevens*

as IOCs do with their employees; one third for depreciation; and one third for contracts. It is expected that the cost of production will increase in the future because we are moving towards the difficult reservoirs.

(MEES 45:16 2002)

3.1.3 Labor-related performance

One major source of inefficiency already alluded to was the loss of KOC expatriate managers following the Iraqi invasion of 1990. That vacuum, along with steady government pressure anyway to provide more jobs for Kuwaitis,[26] has led KPC to employ a growing number of local workers who quite simply are not competent to perform the job. The political and personal pressure to employ and promote Kuwaitis – (what Marcel 2006, p. 61, calls the "Diwaniya-Wasta culture") – is difficult to counter yet pernicious for efficiency.[27] Nepotism is rife; many are employed and promoted well above their capabilities.

A key problem in promoting Kuwaitis has been finding appropriate places for them when they return from overseas training. Kuwaitis are given scholarships to study in universities both in Kuwait and abroad. However, once they secure a degree, they are often placed into the management structure far above the level their actual experience can justify. This is a process reinforced by political interference in the hiring process within KPC and its subsidiaries. Furthermore, it is very difficult to reverse decisions on managerial appointments once they have been made. In 2002, at a conference in Kuwait at which I was present, Nader Sultan publicly lamented, "How can I be expected to run a major corporation when I cannot sack people?"

Interestingly, managers generally "rise from the ranks" within KPC and its subsidiaries. As with many other firms in the region, there is relatively little lateral movement by managers within the organization, which has impeded development of an integrated oil company.[28] (This problem not only makes it hard for best practices to diffuse through the company but it also leaves KPC with few employees that it can tap when planning strategy for the company as a whole. The SPC and the ministry are also unable to perform this function, and thus the company increasingly operates in a strategic vacuum.) The problems of incompetence are poised to grow as the less competent younger generations are promoted from within.[29]

The pressures to show an increase in the employment of Kuwaiti nationals is evident in nearly all areas of KPC. In 2005, the energy minister decided that security and fire fighting for KPC, which previously had been the responsibility of the military, should be performed by KPC employees. Thus, while in 2004 KPC headquarters employed 800, by 2005 this number had risen to 1,900 – the increase entirely due to these new security personnel who were now on KPC's books at an annual estimated cost of KD 12 million ($41.4 million).[30]

In recent years there have been some efforts to improve managerial performance. For example, senior managers are increasingly offered substantial bonuses (up to 40 percent of final salary) tied to company profits. And throughout KPC and its subsidiaries, a "balanced score card" approach to assessment was introduced using financial; operational; health, safety, and environment; and human resources criteria to assess performance and benchmarking. In tandem with such efforts, the company also introduced in 1998 a capital-tracking methodology together with a project-evaluation process. It is too early to assess whether these reforms are actually improving performance although the "balanced score card" approach is notoriously difficult to implement.

3.1.4 Natural gas performance

Another means of assessing performance is to probe how KPC has confronted new priorities, such as natural gas. As with most countries in the region, Kuwait has used large amounts of domestic oil for purposes that could be achieved much more cheaply (and cleanly) with natural gas, which would free more oil for lucrative export. To date, however, Kuwait's only appreciable natural gas production has been gas associated with oil production.

Slowly, KPC's main production subsidiary, KOC, is implementing plans to develop the country's gas reserves, beyond the associated gas that is produced from the country's oil operations. In March 2006, the government announced a major find by KOC of non-associated gas fields at Umm Niga and Sabriya (MEES 49:11 2006). Working with Schlumberger, KOC is expected to supply 1.3 billion cfd of gas from these fields by 2012 (MEES 50:11 2007). KOC is also negotiating with the IOCs to develop deep horizon gas in the northern fields under technical service agreements. To boost gas supply the government set a goal of reducing flaring of associated gas from 5.2 percent in 2006–2007 to 1 percent by 2010. Overall, there are many reports that gas exploration is being given a higher priority (MEES 50:14

2009); however, KOC's annual reports do not reveal any explicit gas exploration program.

The prospect of being able to produce large volumes of non-associated gas is extremely attractive. Kuwait currently consumes all the gas it is able to produce, and projections put gas consumption in 2010 at 2 billion cfd. Previously it was assumed this could only be managed by importing gas. Initial plans for a subsea pipeline from Qatar were shelved, in part because Qatar had put a moratorium on gas projects while it reassessed its reserves in the North Field, the country's largest gas field and the location of its prodigious export projects. Then it was hoped that gas could be imported from Iraq (35 million cfd per day rising to 200 million cfd) and Iran (300 million cfd). However, continued chaos in Iraq has postponed that option, and negotiations with Iran have proved to be slow and difficult. Meanwhile, there have been suggestions that Kuwait would try to fill the immediate gap by recourse to spot purchases of LNG. This is particularly important because in the summer of 2006, Kuwait experienced an increasingly unreliable power supply system, including several blackouts that provoked considerable political backlash. To forestall future problems it has imported several gas turbines but still lacks gas to fire them. A new governmental focus on gas was partially reflected in a March 2007 reshuffling of the Kuwait cabinet. Responsibility for power and electricity, which in July 2003 had been granted to the oil ministry, was cast off into a separate ministry.[31]

3.1.5 Effect of non-core obligations on performance

As with all the other case studies in this book, I have sought to assess KPC's performance in a way that is mindful of the fact that state oil companies are often required to perform many functions beyond the normal tasks of independent firms. Indeed, as Kuwait's largest supplier of revenue, KPC is often seen as a source that can be tapped for various local benefits. Apart from issues to do with employment, KPC is reticent on the issue of "local content" in the Kuwaiti oil sector. Thus it supplies no data regarding how much of the supply chain comes from Kuwaiti companies. Many observers claim that local vendors get priority in procurement, but it is not clear that much can be supplied from within Kuwait and thus local content is probably quite limited. Given the relatively limited scope of the rest of the Kuwaiti economy such linkages are hardly surprising. Another indication that local content requirements have been a relatively small part of KPC's operations is that the Oil Services Sector Company (KPC's subsidiary aimed at providing construction and security services for the sector) was created only in 2005. An indigenous petrochemical sector has emerged,[32] offering a modicum of local diversification and content, but it thrives mainly due to the availability of cheap feedstock rather than good local suppliers and services. In short, requirements for local linkages appear to be a relatively small drag on KPC's performance; outside of crude oil production and local supply of refined products, KPC has not done much to catalyze broader economic development and it is not much affected (unlike many other NOCs) by such demands. The one exception to this assessment is the preference for Kuwaiti employment, discussed above, which does appear to be a large (but probably not decisive) contributor to the company's poor performance. According to the Government's Annual Statistical Bulletin, while the oil sector accounts for some 50 percent of GDP, it accounts for less than 3 percent of direct employment.

3.1.6 Technological performance

Still another way to evaluate performance is to examine whether and how KPC is able to generate new technologies and to utilize the latest technical advances. When BP and Gulf Oil left in 1976, a later chairman of KOC remarked, "They left the body but took the brains" (PESD Interviews). When the two companies controlled KOC, all of the subsurface work associated with reservoir management was done outside Kuwait. Thus the oil sector has continually struggled with a serious shortage of technically competent management.

KPC headquarters includes an R&D division whose work is driven entirely by the needs of the subsidiaries. However, the activity of this group, based on KPC's annual report, is hard to assess; its main function appears to be providing research projects to other institutions (such as KISR, discussed below) rather than originating its own research. In 2002 a new R&D strategy was approved; it called for a "virtual" R&D center within KPC to meet KPC and its affiliates' technology needs and involved partners within and outside of Kuwait. KPC also established a new affiliate – KPC Energy Venture Inc. (KPC EVI) – capitalized at $100 million to invest in energy ventures based upon oil as the main energy source but with an eye to cleaner energy options.

KPC's subsidiaries have extensive contact with both the IOCs and the service companies and therefore are exposed to the latest technological developments. In addition, there is the Kuwait Institute for Scientific Research (KISR). KISR was formed in 1967 by the Arabian Oil Company (Japan) as part of its concession commitment. In 1981, it was created as an independent public institution. Its focus was on petroleum, desert agriculture, and marine biology. It has a Petroleum Research and Studies Center (PRSC) located in Ahmadi, with the following function:

[T]o be the primary source and focal point of R&D and technical support for the oil-based industry in the country, with the aim of assisting the industry in increasing oil reserves, improving product qualities and optimizing the cost-effectiveness of oil production, refining, petrochemicals and further downstream operations, and generating and maintaining relevant databases for the petroleum and energy industries. (KISR website)

In practice, however, it appears that the country's oil sector relies little on KISR. Many countries in the region are struggling with the task of how to encourage world-class research within their borders and also how to incorporate such research into commercial enterprise.

This section has tried to assess the performance of KPC and its subsidiaries using many different dimensions in the absence of the normal sorts of corporate metrics used to assess company performance. It has described the way in which KOC plans for investment with few incentives for cost control, and while operating costs are low, this is more a reflection of geology than efficiency. It has outlined developments and performance in personnel policies, natural gas, and technology. The general conclusion is that the performance has been poor. Efficiency seems low and much of the management lacks experience.

3.2 KPC's strategy

As with performance, it is hard to assess KPC's strategy in the absence of any broader strategy for the oil sector on the part of the government. KPC and the oil sector in Kuwait are nearly synonymous.

Before the Iraqi invasion, KPC had a clear strategy derived from the vision of Ali Al-Khalifa as minister. The goal was conversion of

KPC into a major IOC that could compete with the IOCs; in practice, however, there were strong incentives to focus "internationalization" on investment in refining – and the financial outcome of that effort as will be developed below was generally disastrous. (KPC's experience in this regard contrasts with PDVSA.) Initially, Ali Al-Khalifa struggled merely to incorporate the various subsidiaries into something resembling a functional IOC. This strategy arose less from a careful analysis and more from the chaos of historical events.

Within a brief period the country had nationalized its oil industry, and it feared that important services that previously had been provided by the IOCs would be lost. At the same time, the newly nationalized company became a basket to hold any and all elements of the industry that the state had found in its hands. The task of integration proved difficult since the various subsidiaries had very different histories and very different cultures – even when they performed similar functions in the value chain. This approach, accumulation without strategy, created a host of immediate managerial problems and little vision for how the company would operate as a synergistic whole.

Ali Al-Khalifa, serving as oil minister and chairman of KPC, devised a strategy that relied on two new efforts. The first was to try to internationalize KPC's activities. This was intended to "diversify the asset base of the company, [develop] new markets for crude, bring in new technology, and maximize the returns for the company" (Marcel 2006, p. 196). In effect, Al-Khalifa wanted KPC to become an IOC. In 1981, he spearheaded the creation of KUFPEC (Kuwait Foreign Petroleum Exploration Company) to manage overseas upstream operations. In 1983 at an OPEC meeting, Al-Khalifa was approached by the CEO of Gulf Oil, who offered to sell to Kuwait Gulf's downstream operations in Netherlands, Belgium, and Luxembourg for $1! The aftermath of the first oil shock saw lower demand even as tranches of new refinery capacity came online, which erased the profitability of refineries – especially in Europe where established refineries protected market share and aggressive efficiency measures killed demand for products. In the mid 1970s, spare refining capacity sat at 30 percent.[33] Many IOCs sought to divest from loss-making downstream operations that tied up large amounts of capital. KPI, a new international arm of KPC, was created in 1983 to manage this acquisition along with additional downstream assets bought from Western majors in Denmark, Italy, and Sweden; still further acquisitions followed. All of these were rebranded under

Figure 8.3 Kuwaiti oil production, 1965–2006.

KPI's trademark: "Q8" (cleverly pronounced "cue weight" to the despair of Arabists concerned over correct pronunciation).

The second element of Ali Al-Khalifa's vision was his effort to contain the fallout from the Iran–Iraq War. By 1982, Kuwaiti crude production had fallen to 862,000 b/d compared with 2,623,000 in 1979 (see Figure 8.3; BP 2008). The central barrier to expanded output was securing tankers willing to move Kuwaiti crude in a war zone. Fixing the problem required KOTC (Kuwait Oil Tanker Company) to get its own tankers.

This two-pronged expansion outside Kuwait's borders was greeted with some skepticism and reservations from within Kuwait. Many saw it as "empire building." The financial state of KPI's downstream operation in Europe was unattractive (as were all downstream operations of its European peers). In particular, Al-Kalifah's critics accused KPC, after its first bargain purchase from Gulf, of paying well above market prices for the further acquisitions – a criticism later confirmed by government auditors (PESD Interviews). As one observer remarked, they "paid top dollar for third-rate assets" (PESD Interviews).

On balance, a measure of diversification was probably wise, especially since the operations within Kuwait were under tight political control. Al-Khalifa and his supporters noted that there was little point in further investing in the Kuwaiti upstream whose production was severely constrained by OPEC quotas after 1983. Investment in non-OPEC countries meant that Kuwait could indirectly increase its production, although much of the financial benefit would accrue to host governments. However, Al-Khalifa's critics found ammunition when allegations appeared of financial impropriety before the 1990 invasion. Such claims eventually led, in 1996, to the conviction of three senior KOTC executives for fraud. A ministerial court dropped related charges against Ali Al-Khalifa for "technical reasons" on two occasions. However, in May 2001, the government announced it was to file fraud charges against him (MEES 44:22 2001).[34]

The country's liberation after 1991 was seen as an opportunity to reconsider the whole of KPC's strategy. However, in the words of one interviewee, "Strategy means vision but in Kuwait it means the vision of one person" (PESD Interviews). The oil minister was central. Given the large number of oil ministers after 1991, it was hardly surprising that the vision kept on shifting. (To be sure, the CEOs of KPC, who turned over relatively infrequently, provided more stable guidance and direction, but CEOs remained at the whim of successive ministers and found it difficult to devise and implement a coherent and consistent strategy.) Vision is particularly important because KPC develops strategy through a tortuous multilevel negotiation – between the company and its varied masters as well as between KPC headquarters and the subsidiaries. What emerges from this is a five-year plan/ budget. Once a version of the five-year plan has been drafted, it must go to the KPC board for approval and then on to the SPC subcommittee responsible for approval of plans. Each of these stages involves still further negotiation. Finally, with the SPC's blessing, the plans go to the State Audit Bureau and the National Assembly. These further stages all involve greater analysis, questioning, and challenges. The process discourages risk taking, rewards the status quo, and is prone to rent seeking along the way – especially when key players threaten to block approval.

The latest installment in this negotiated strategy-making process is "Vision 2020." This plan emerged in 2001 and attempted to set a wider context for the five-year operational plan/budgets. It covers all major aspects of KPC's operations and sets specific strategic targets for key subsidiaries. These include increasing domestic crude producing capacity from 3 mbd in 2005 to 4 mbd by 2020.[35] In the downstream the plan envisaged increasing refinery capacity to 1 mbd (including upgrading kit to convert the heavier ends of the barrel into lighter products) by 2010 and further increasing to 1.5 mbd by 2020.[36] The rest of the subsidiaries have targets expressed as non-quantified aspirations. KPC performed a major revision to the vision in 2005 and is currently undergoing further review.

As noted by senior KPC management, the company is good at producing strategies but poor at actually putting them into practice. As already indicated, the company regularly misses its most important strategic performance targets. Within the Vision 2020 strategy, overseas projects occupy an ambivalent position. Part of the difficulty lies with a new (more favorable) view inside KPC about joint ventures, which are now viewed as a means to strengthen operations and marketing capabilities and also to provide local political support in the operating country (PESD Interviews). After the liberation in 1991 and the positive experience working with IOCs through technical assistance agreements that helped the country with reconstruction, KPC management had a far more positive attitude toward working with the IOCs. In practice, KPC has pursued a triangular approach to its international downstream ventures: KPC supplies feedstock through an IOC (which brings management skills, technology, and risk management) to a local company that can provide market access.

3.3 KPC's relationship with government

Any plans for an oil sector in a country where oil dominates cannot be set in isolation from the wider development strategy of the country. In Kuwait, the process of setting a development agenda has been somewhat haphazard; objectives for the petroleum sector have been similarly erratic. Like KPC, the government is adept at producing strategies; follow-through is more challenging. In 1987, the government created a twenty-six-man Supreme Planning Council, including eight ministers; by 1999 the council had undergone five reformulations.[37] In 1989, it produced a document titled "Long-Term Strategic Development of Kuwait." In 1992, it produced a National Document for Reformation and Development covering the period up to 1995. In February 1994, a five-year plan emerged covering the period 1995–2000; its main objective appeared to be balancing the budget, which had suffered from low oil prices. These documents are laden with aspirations, hopes, and slogans with little by way of specific targets and nothing by way of policy instruments. They had essentially no effect on the policy of government or of KPC.

In March 2004, a new Higher Council for Planning and Development was launched with the aim of producing "goals and development programmes" and was expected to ensure "coherence and harmony" with decisions by the cabinet. The launching speech pointed to the need to develop the oil sector by establishing oil industries that could compete globally and provide Kuwaiti manpower with "productive working opportunities." Little appears to have emerged since the launch and it seems likely that the very high oil revenues experienced since 2002 have eclipsed any fretting about the lack of national strategy.

Putting these ambiguous goals into action – even if the government were actually organized for an earnest effort – would be difficult because Kuwait's divided government ensures that policy directives arrive on the doorsteps of KPC and its subsidiaries from multiple and often conflicting sources ranging from the SPC to the cabinet.

A central trouble in devising strategy is that the Kuwaiti system of government is fragmented; over time, especially since 1991, fragmentation has risen sharply. Senior administrative positions – the prime minister and the ministers who constitute the cabinet – are appointed by the emir. But those positions bear no relationship to the National Assembly. Often, the parties that control government are in the minority in the National Assembly; thus government is unable to assume parliamentary support. One outcome is the periodic spectacle of successive ministers in various portfolios being called to account before the parliament and receiving a televised, vicious criticism by members of the National Assembly.[38] The result has been a policy paralysis of massive proportions in all sectors, which has dominated Kuwaiti politics since the recall of the National Assembly in 1991. Prior to 1991, the emir blunted such troubles by suspending the National Assembly when it became unruly. Since the liberation of Kuwait in 1991, however, power has been more diffused and democratic. Gridlock in oversight, notably for KPC, has become more severe.

A major problem is that the National Assembly, like any rational elected body, plays to popular desires. This is especially prevalent in Kuwait because most National Assembly members serve constituencies that are populated by small numbers of voters. Members are thus particularly concentrated on demanding benefits for their constituents. Yet the logrolling with which most Western governments build coalitions to support policy decisions has proved cumbersome. In Kuwait, one result of this new (democratic) focus on Kuwaiti political life and doling out benefits has been a large backlog of legislation and delay. In March 2007, for example, the assembly faced a logjam of 114 laws awaiting approval, 88 amendments to existing laws, and 26 draft laws to consider (MEES 49:43 2006).

The key government players in determining the strategy of KPC are the minister of oil and the oil ministry more generally. The minister is also the chairman of KPC where he holds effective veto power over any decision taken by the KPC board. Indeed, recent history has seen a number of occasions when the KPC board (with the minister sitting as chair) has made a decision only to have the minister later overturn it using his power as minister. For example, the recent board decision to sell KPI's "refineries"[39] in Europe was reversed by the minister (PESD Interviews). The central role for the minister could help KPC identify and follow an effective strategy if the oil minister had a clear and coherent vision for the sector. However, between 1991 and 2001 there were eight oil ministers; since then, the job has turned over six more times. Often there are "personality clashes" between the minister and the CEO of KPC, which can lead to gridlock. Between 1998 and 2007 there have been only two CEOs of KPC,[40] both of whom managed to secure their own independent political support by promising a better-performing KPC to the government, which has made it harder for the minister to exert his ultimate authority by removing the CEO.[41]

Since 1991, after reformation of the government following the liberation of Kuwait, the ministry's role has been less clear. According to the ministry, its functions include supervising KPC on technical issues (good oil field practice and attention to health, safety, and environment) and financial matters; moreover, the ministry believes its additional role is to suggest policies to the SPC for approval – and then to direct the implementation of these policies after they are approved. Other players in the sector see things differently. KPC thinks that proposing strategy and policy to the SPC is within its purview. Indeed, one senior manager in KPC, when asked, "What is the role of the ministry?" replied, "I have no idea!" (PESD Interviews). The only ministry role over which there is no dispute is the management of relations with international bodies such as OPEC.

Kuwait's ad hoc and tortuous decision-making process is clearly vulnerable to shifting and uncoordinated priorities. It creates a modicum of flexibility, which can empower managers in cases where managers have a clear vision for action; in Kuwait, however, ad hoc decision making has usually created gridlock and indecision. Exemplifying the former, positive effects of flexibility was the response to a series of bad fires in the refineries, which led KPC to adopt a major campaign in health, safety, and environment (HSE). An example of the latter and more regular outcome is KPC's difficulty in internalizing production and performance goals.

The Vision 2020 targets are Kuwait's official policy. Their provenance is uncertain but appears to be rooted in internal discussion. The determination of the crude capacity target illustrates this. According to Marcel, the decision to raise crude producing capacity appeared "to go back and forth between institutions with a degree of confusion for all" (Marcel 2006, p. 80). Thus KPC's Corporate Planning Department projected a possible call on Kuwaiti crude (within the OPEC quota context) of 7 mbd by 2020. KOC indicated that 4 mbd was the maximum sustainable capacity under prevailing conditions. KPC presented this as the target but was overruled by the SPC, which wanted a target of 5 mbd although it is not clear that there was any analytical basis for such a number. In the event, the SPC backed down and reverted to the 4 mbd goal for 2020 (which is the Vision 2020 goal).

In some countries with NOCs, privatization has been a goal. This topic rises and falls on the Kuwaiti agenda; it is abhorred by Kuwait's trade unions, which fear job losses. Two-thirds of Kuwait's gasoline stations have already been privatized, but the proposed privatization of the remaining third was "postponed" by the minister in late 2006 under union pressure via the National Assembly.

3.3.1 Project Kuwait

The single most important strategic decision in the oil sector over the last twenty years concerns the promotion of Project Kuwait. The aftermath of the liberation of Kuwait in 1991 set the stage for Kuwait to adopt a different strategy in the oil sector. With much of the country's producing capacity in flames and KPC facing serious shortages of management at all levels, Kuwait sought (and received) technical assistance from the IOCs. Between 1994 and 1997, five technical service agreements were signed with BP, Chevron, Exxon, Shell, and

Total. The IOCs were willing to do this because they focused on an implied quid pro quo that when things had settled, the Kuwaiti upstream might be opened to those who had assisted. (Many other countries examined in this book have benefited from similar, informal understandings. Mexico, for example, has negotiated memoranda of understanding with most major Western oil companies even though, at present, the Mexican oil sector remains closed to their formal participation. (See Chapter 7.) In 1993 the government decided to extend these arrangements with the IOCs to allow investment in the upstream sector under the terms of "Project Kuwait." A driving force for this initiative was the need to assure postwar military support from the West, which was thought (in Kuwait) to be more reliable if Western nationals were exposed on the front line. There was also a need to secure expertise and technology both in terms of engineering and management to fill the gaps in KPC manpower that remained after the invasion. Maintaining production levels would become increasingly difficult as depletion caused the crude reserves to become heavier and more complex. In particular there was concern over water management in maturing fields. Production of 4 million b/d of crude in 2020 (as Vision 2020 anticipated) would entail handling some 12 million b/d of water. There were also problems with handling extra heavy crude with which KOC had no experience.

Finally, entry of the IOCs might provide a benchmark to allow assessment of KPC's performance. Some in Kuwait believed that KPC had become inefficient and was also engaged in classic rent-seeking behavior. This view was very much supported by Nader Sultan, who had been head of KPI during the company's international expansion to Europe. In 1993 he returned to Kuwait with the perspective that the many firms in Europe created an "intensely competitive" environment that forced companies to be efficient and inhibited rent seeking. Initially, he was made KPC deputy chairman and managing director for planning and projects and then in 1998 was appointed CEO of KPC. His central objective was to make KPC and its subsidiaries more commercial in orientation, which he thought would boost performance culture. The example that illustrated the point was the experience of KPC's petrochemical subsidiary PIC. In 1997, PIC had formed a joint venture operation with Union Carbide. The result was that within two years, PIC had significantly improved its corporate and managerial performance because it had a model (Union Carbide) to follow. Thus, KPC ironically became one of the strongest advocates within Kuwait for involving IOCs. This enthusiasm may also have been intended to forestall the growing calls for privatization, which had risen in volume as low oil prices had brought a focus on the company's poor performance.

Initial proposals from KPC to create Project Kuwait were rejected in 1995 by both the National Assembly and the SPC. A major barrier (faced also by Mexico) was the fact that the Kuwaiti Constitution explicitly rejected the possibility of foreign "ownership" of the oil reserves. According to Article 21: "Natural resources and all revenues therefrom are the property of the State. It shall ensure their preservation and proper exploitation, due regard being given to the requirements of State security and the national economy." Even larger barriers arose in Article 152: "No concession for exploitation of either a natural resource or a public service may be granted except by a law and for a limited period. In this respect, the preparatory measures shall facilitate the operations of prospecting and exploring and ensure publicity and competition."

To get around this problem the concept of an "operating service agreement" was developed whereby the Kuwaiti government retained full ownership and the IOC would be paid a "per barrel" fee, along with allowances for capital recovery and incentive fees for increasing reserves. This workaround was very similar to the multiple service contracts (MSCs) devised in Mexico to circumvent similar restrictions on foreign title to hydrocarbon resources in that country.

During 1998–1999 new details emerged for the terms of these "operating service agreements." Three consortia – involving twelve companies that included a number of Russian, Indian, and Chinese enterprises – were accepted for bids. In November 1999, a major international conference was held to launch the process but effectively this turned into a bitter debate about who inside Kuwait should govern the process. Interestingly, many of the National Assembly opponents did not, in principle, object to IOC involvement, but they had many concerns about the process. At the center of these disputes was an emerging debate over who rules Kuwait, which pitted the National Assembly against the emir's Al-Sabah family. Underlying this debate were lingering concerns over the potential for corruption if the family retained exclusive control over awarding contracts. The National Assembly pressed for a specific law, but it never reached agreement with the emir-controlled government. In January 2001, despairing of progress, KPC sent out initial process protocols to the IOCs, with the hope that the legislative process would fall into place. It also announced that the "data room" (the repository of geological information that the outside companies would need to formulate bids) would open in February 2001. However, without legislation the process was effectively frozen. Since then, despite numerous changes of government and several elections, the situation remains unresolved. In November 2006, the then energy minister publicly stated that he would not be submitting Project Kuwait to the National Assembly unless "appropriate measures" could be agreed upon for preserving Kuwait's oil wealth. Meanwhile, in the shadow of indecision and with the tide turned against foreign involvement, much of the original IOC interest disappeared.

3.3.2 Regulation and competition

The story of the regulation of the oil sector in Kuwait is long and complex and holds the key to understanding why KPC has had difficulties in performing effectively and efficiently. The story begins with Law 19 of 1973: a simple two-page piece of legislation intended to outline the responsibilities of the government (which was represented by the combined Ministry of Finance and Ministry of Oil) with respect to BP and Gulf Oil's control of KOC. The law, which focused on ensuring "good oil field practice," was intended to allow greater government oversight and control in areas where the Western companies had previously largely regulated themselves. However, Law 19 did give the ministry the power to issue regulations, and in 1975 a set of regulations duly appeared (Al-Atiqi 2005). However, it emerged that these regulations were just an Arabic translation of some Canadian regulations with no attempt to adjust them to the context of Kuwait.[42]

When KPC inherited KOC following the nationalization in April 1976, it also inherited this uncertain (and unwelcome) regulatory context. It promptly challenged the legal basis for the ministry's control over KOC's operations – seething at unwelcome intrusions such as the need to obtain ministry approval before drilling wells or developing a field – but the ministry (after a three-year delay) was unwavering although it did relax some of the rules later, in 1989. KPC's efforts to avoid government scrutiny were similar to those that BP and Gulf had made when they controlled the company's operations.

In 2000, the government appointed a new undersecretary in the ministry with the explicit remit to "regain ministry control in terms of supervisory and regulatory roles" (PESD Interviews). This effort to assert greater control arose because both the prime minister and the SPC felt that KPC was "taking them for a ride" (PESD Interviews). New systems to monitor, control, and supervise the sector were needed to tame the NOC, which was seen as a state within a state (as were many others examined in this book, such as Gazprom). The ministry drafted an array of new regulations including new audit control systems. KPC, which had been consulted only minimally, was horrified at the prospect of having all its spending controlled by the ministry. Paralysis set into the sector as a war unfolded between KPC and its ministerial masters. The SPC intervened and brokered a series of secret meetings that led to an uneasy compromise.[43]

In practice, the SPC and the ministry share regulatory oversight. The SPC, as shareholder, is the most effective institution overseeing KPC and has invested heavily to improve its capacity to understand and perform its shareholding function, such as through the creation of specialized subcommittees discussed earlier. Apart from these two institutions, some regulatory functions – those related to HSE – are applied by other national regulators. And the Civil Service Commission provides "back up regulation" in areas where existing regulatory law and practice create a vacuum. In short, there is no clear regulatory strategy and the result is a degree of chaos that inhibits KPC's operational effectiveness.

The area where government regulatory oversight is strongest – and most problematic – is in procurement policy, which involves the State Audit Bureau (SAB) with additional oversight by SPC and the parliament.

Purchases by KPC and its subsidiaries are subject to the rules laid down by the Central Tenders Committee (CTC), which requires a public tender process for any purchase over KD 5,000 (some $17,000, a figure actually set in 1964 and not adjusted since). This is extremely elaborate and can add up to a year to the time required for procurement simply to "buy the pencils" as one KPC observer lamented. (In 1979, the SPC decided that all KPC's subsidiaries must abide by the CTC process, along with KPC itself.) The troubles created by the CTC procurement are widely known, and SPC as shareholder has tried to create flexibility around this rule, along with many other

rigid Kuwaiti laws.[44] In 2005, KPC proposed (to SPC) a reorganization aimed at boosting performance in a variety of ways, including
allowing the subsidiaries much greater autonomy over procurement.
The limit for a referral to the CTC would be raised to KD 1 million.
(Smaller sums would be managed under KPC's own, more flexible
regulations and tender process.) The SPC not only accepted the recommendation but actually proposed raising the threshold to KD 5
million. However, actually implementing this idea would require a
change in the law that, so far, has been impossible. The State Audit
Bureau (SAB), a body that reports directly to the National Assembly
and is charged with post-project review, creates similar bureaucratic
entanglements for KPC. Some expenditures require pre-approval by
the SAB, and the SAB's auditors also "second guess" many of KPC's
decisions, which leads to extreme risk aversion since KPC managers
do not enjoy intensive scrutiny by the National Assembly.

The budget process also creates another layer of oversight and
intervention. The SPC is charged with approving the budgets for
KPC and its subsidiaries. SPC's proposed consolidated budget, however, is reviewed in detail by the budget committee of the National
Assembly. Several years ago this detailed review process would take
two to three weeks, involving the top management of KPC justify-
ing the details of the budget. In 2005, the process stretched to seven
weeks involving twenty-seven meetings. An interesting parallel can be
drawn between this process and a similar one for a typical IOC. In
the case of the IOC, project appraisal is completed before proposals
go to the board for approval or rejection. Upon approval the company springs into action to implement the project. In the case of KPC,
projects are viable only if they are part of a final, approved budget,
which is developed by means of an uncertain and time-consuming
process. Thus, in practice, most detailed project planning occurs only
after the budget proposals are vetted by the board (the SPC) and the
National Assembly. The process has particularly uncertain outcomes
when the National Assembly and KPC are locked in dispute or if the
country is already in political gridlock for other reasons. In 2006,
because of the political stalemate between the government and the
National Assembly, the SPC only met once at the end of the year.
Thus KPC took its budget proposal straight to the National Assembly
without prior approval from the SPC, which slowed and confused the
approval process. In practice, this process means that most projects,

however worthy, face delays because of the inability to obtain reliable access to budget authority (PESD Interviews).

The government and the National Assembly have also uneasily guided efforts to introduce some competition into the oil sector. In the upstream, there is no competition because all the exploration acreage and producing operations (outside of the Neutral Zone) are KOC's exclusive responsibility. (The perennially stalled "Project Kuwait" would have altered that situation.) In the downstream, however, there is competition in the marketing of products due to privatization of gasoline stations (a process that has been drawn out over a decade and is stalled, with one-third of the stations still in government hands), an LPG bottling plant, and an oil lube filling plant.

The rationale for downstream privatization as a vehicle to create competition was rooted in the "Washington Consensus" – the private sector convinced the government of the need to move to a more market orientation, a process also possibly encouraged by Kuwait's Western liberators (PESD Interviews). At the same time, the downstream lacked the political sensitivity of the upstream, which made relaxation of state control feasible. KPC, still recovering from the invasion and its aftermath in 1992 when the privatization decision was made, appeared to offer little or no resistance. However, it is clear that the government had not carefully evaluated the implications of privatizing the downstream in the context of the very low domestic product prices compared with international prices (PESD Interviews). Moreover, the government implemented privatization without any regulatory framework to govern these new (and hopefully competitive) firms. (In fact, just two firms bought most of the newly privatized filling stations.) The government therefore commissioned the World Bank to offer recommendations for the creation of a regulatory body. The bank's proposed approach (which it presented in November 2006) would require implementation by amiri decree. In KPC's view, however, such an approach would violate the Kuwait Constitution. In addition, the National Assembly was unlikely to allow the government to control such a powerful regulator that could affect consumer welfare. These disagreements led the government to postpone the sale of the last third of the filling stations. In particular, the National Assembly demanded scrutiny of the employment implications of selling off the gas stations.[45] The minister duly complied and so further privatization appears to be on hold.

4 Conclusion

KPC has always had a great deal of strategy. What it lacks is consistency in political and regulatory oversight and the ability to deliver on strategic goals. Targets have consistently been missed and recent years have seen a series of accidents in both the upstream and downstream, which reflect on this inability to manage the sector well. There are two prime explanations for this relatively weak performance by KPC and its subsidiaries.

First, KPC is exposed to intense interference from a political system that is deeply dysfunctional. The root of this trouble is divided authority and the absence of accountability. The National Assembly does not appoint the government, with the result that government ministers constantly face scrutiny from a body (the National Assembly) that has only the ability to veto but not initiate major policy decisions. The result is excessive caution and discouragement of vision. Decision-making gridlock, as often occurs in political systems with many veto points, also makes it nearly impossible to obtain necessary change in central laws, such as those that govern procurement. Decision making in the oil sector is complex, cumbersome, unpredictable, and horribly bureaucratic. Insofar as the sector pursues any strategy, it has historically come at the whim of oil ministers who change frequently. An obvious reform would be to separate the roles of chairman of KPC and oil minister, which would restore a degree of control and authority to KPC's board. The SPC, as shareholder, has tried to build its own oversight capabilities and fill this vacuum; that effort, so far, has only been partially successful because SPC, itself, lacks the authority to initiate and deliver needed political and regulatory reforms.

Second, while KPC has some excellent senior managers with talent and a deep knowledge of the oil industry, middle-level management in KPC and its subsidiaries is exceptionally weak. This appears to be particularly true in the technical and engineering areas. People are given posts with insufficient experience and knowledge, a process strongly reinforced by political interference in the appointment of personnel. The root of these personnel troubles is the loss of many of KPC's top talent in the aftermath of the country's liberation in 1991 and the inability of the company to devise a scheme for identifying, training, and promoting the most talented workforce. This is greatly compounded by a Kuwaitization policy that introduced young people with little experience into the company.

KPC faces many other problems as well, such as confusion created as the holding company (KPC) operates on a different legal basis from its subsidiaries. But these problems pale in comparison with the two central barriers to better performance – in particular, the gridlock created by Kuwait's political structure.

Relatively high oil prices in recent years have disguised these problems. In particular, the failure to meet crude producing capacity targets has not resulted in problems for central government revenue. Also the relatively small population and the size of the accumulated reserve funds have allowed the country to avoid the need for scrutiny and redesign of its sector.

Looking to the future, the prospects for the sector are not bright. All the signs suggest that the political interference is likely to get worse as the National Assembly pursues its own interests and seeks a greater formal role in the operation of the oil sector. This is especially evident in the assembly's large and growing role in the approval of KPC's budget as well as its oversight of the audit and procurement policies. These problems are compounded by the lack of a clear administrative framework for the government itself, which leaves many crannies of ambiguity that the National Assembly has filled as it tilts at populist goals and as the feeling grows that the oil enterprise is a state within a state. The only certain solution would be a fundamental reform of the political system whereby the government is appointed by the National Assembly rather than the emir. This would effectively reduce the role of the emir to a constitutional monarch. However, there is a need to consider perhaps less dramatic solutions that can assist KPC to improve its performance.

These political challenges arrive at a time when it is increasingly difficult for KPC to maintain, let alone increase, production of crude oil. This is simply because the geology is becoming more complex, the crude heavier, and the water management problems more demanding. KPC simply does not have the technical capability to manage these growing problems. Furthermore, the political system has effectively stalled the entry of IOCs whose presence is essential if these looming field problems are to be managed. This exclusion of much needed technical help is likely to get worse as resource nationalism gains great support in Kuwait as it has throughout the Middle East.

Thus KPC is hamstrung – by Kuwait and by its own decisions – in managing its response to an array of serious challenges. If oil prices are low for several years – or production costs continue to rise – then Kuwaiti society will find itself accustomed to an expensive lifestyle that it is unable to afford.

Notes

I thank Valérie Marcel and Adnan Shihab-Eldin for detailed comments on an earlier draft and also David Victor, David Hults, and Mark Thurber for much editorial assistance. Any mistakes are of course my own. The chapter is based centrally on detailed conversations with many involved in the Kuwaiti oil sector over a number of years because formal, published studies on KPC and its relationships with the Kuwaiti government are scarce. Most discussions were on the record and cited accordingly, but many were anonymous. A major field trip to Kuwait in February/March 2007 was particularly notable for the large number of anonymous discussions (all cited as "PESD Interviews") with a range of experts and observers (in alphabetical order):

- Abdulaziz E. Al-Attar (Coordinator, Market Research Department (International Marketing), Kuwait Petroleum Corporation).
- Feten Al-Attar (General Manager, SHEMS International).
- Adnan Ahmed Al-Darwish (Board Member, Kuwait Economic Society).
- Kamel A. Al-Harami (Oil Analyst).
- Jamal Al Nouri (MD International Marketing, Kuwait Petroleum Corporation).
- Issa Al Oun (Former Undersecretary, Ministry of Energy (Oil)).
- Nawaf Saud Nasir Al-Sabah (Deputy Managing Director and General Counsel, Kuwait Petroleum Corporation).
- Bader S. Al-Sumait (Deputy Managing Director (Privatization), Kuwait Petroleum Corporation).
- Suhail Y. Bograis (M.D. Planning and Finance, Kuwait Petroleum Corporation).
- Jeremy Cripps (Head of Business and Economics, American University of Kuwait).
- Usameh F. El-Jamali (Organization of Arab Petroleum Exporting Countries (OAPEC)).
- Hashim M. El-Rifaai (Chairman and Managing Director, Oil Development Company).
- Dr. Mohamed Nagy Eltony (Economic Advisor, Economic Department, The Industrial Bank of Kuwait K.S.C.).

- Hani A. Hussain (Chief Executive Officer, Kuwait Petroleum Corporation).
- Mohammad Razak Issa (Journalist, Dar La Watan).
- Ali Muhammad Khuraibet (General Manager, ECO-Environmental Consultants).
- Dr. Amr Mohie-Eldin (Chief Economist, Head of Economic Department, The Industrial Bank of Kuwait K.S.C.).
- Abbas A. Naqi (Undersecretary, Ministry of Energy (Oil)).
- Nader H. Sultan ((former CEO of KPC), Senior Partner, F&N Consultancy).

Academic sources are listed in the bibliography using the standard method; articles in trade periodicals are cited in-text – notably the *Middle East Economic Survey* (MEES) and the *Petroleum Intelligence Weekly* (PIW). For each article, citation is given by date or by volume, issue number, and year. This chapter is based on a longer report published as Stevens (2008b). If anything, the political paralysis that dominates the story has deteriorated further since that report was published.

1 These troubles are not confined to the oil sector but characterize much of the rest of the economy. However, since the oil sector generates most of the funds for the government that allow other sectors to give some semblance of operating, the oil sector needs to be the first to be reformed and protected from the dysfunctional political system otherwise there will come a time when the oil revenues can no longer paper over the cracks.

2 Ideally the government should be accountable to the National Assembly in order to provide some checks and balances to the executive power. While it has some role in this context in terms of approving budgets, votes of no confidence in the government, and providing a general debate of policies and decisions, it is a very imperfect role. One explanation for this is the informal nature of the system without political parties.

3 This of itself has been controversial with a number of National Assembly members demanding that the number of private sector representatives be reduced, especially those with any connection to private oil companies. In October 2009 there were rumors of changes to the personnel on the SPC.

4 This dispute has now been solved and the costs have come down but it is likely that the project will remain stalled since it is unlikely to receive National Assembly support given the worsening relations between the assembly and the government.

5 The actual title of the ministry has changed over time. The terms oil ministry and energy ministry are used interchangeably.

6 This is very concerning since the "excellent" senior management today were good middle managers a decade or so ago. In the future this pool of talent will not be available to produce good top managers.

7 The following section draws heavily upon Stevens (1975) and Marcel (2006). See also Tetreault (1995).

8 The Neutral Zone is a territory that in 1922 at the country's founding was left uncharted and thus shared with Saudi Arabia. A 1966 agreement between the two countries gave the zone a distinct, shared status that allows outside companies to operate even where they are excluded from either Kuwait or Saudi Arabia. The rest of this chapter does not consider the zone further. The presence of many additional players in that zone does not reflect how Kuwait applies fiscal and other controls within Kuwait proper. The Al Kafji and Hout joint operation is a 50 percent joint venture between Kuwait – the Kuwait Gulf Operating Company (KGOC) and the Aramco Gulf Operating Company that took over the Arabian Oil Company's (AOC) operations when its concession ended in 2000. KOGC has a five-year technical service contract with AOC. In January 2006, KGOC also took over Kuwait's interest in the onshore Wafra Field, which was operated by Saudi Arabia Texaco. Throughout the Neutral Zone, KGOC treats its share of the crude produced in the same way as KOC.

9 Actually he was put before a military tribunal and faced a death sentence.

10 In 1963 the government created the Petrochemical Industries Company (PIC) to manage petrochemical and fertilizer plants; initially it worked mainly through a series of joint ventures, principally with BP and Gulf. (All the private sector's equity in the PIC ventures was transferred to the government in 1976.) The Kuwait Oil Tanker Company (KOTC) was formed by private individuals in 1957 to transport crude and products. In 1976, the government decided to get involved and bought 49 percent of the equity and in June 1979 bought the remaining equity to give it 100 percent ownership. The Kuwait Aviation Fuelling Company (KAFCO) was formed in 1963 to supply fuel at Kuwait International Airport. This was a joint venture with BP with KNPC having 51 percent of the shares. In 1977, KNPC bought out BP's shareholding.

11 Relinquishment followed a model pioneered by Iraq, where the government unilaterally forced the Iraq Petroleum Company (a Western-controlled concession similar to KOC) to relinquish acreage. In the wake of that decision, KOC, like many other companies in the region, began to return acreage to the government (Stocking 1970).

12 The details of this story can be found in Al-Sabah (1980). It is an interesting story. An important issue was that of gas flaring and how it
should be handled. This was particularly important for elements within
what was a relatively sophisticated civil society in Kuwait. The story
represents an early example of politics intervening in oil policy.

13 Currently these include KOC; KNPC; PIC; KOTC; KAFCO; the Kuwait
Foreign Petroleum Exploration Company (KUFPEC) established in
1981 responsible for all upstream operations outside of Kuwait; Kuwait
Petroleum International Limited (KPI) established in 1983 responsible
for all overseas downstream operations; and Kuwait Gulf Oil Company
(KGOC) established in 2002 to manage Kuwait's share of upstream
operations in the Neutral Zone.

14 In its early life the SPC had relatively little influence over oil policy.
Responsibility over policymaking rested, formally, with a cabinet committee that consisted of the prime minister and several other ministers
including oil and finance that had neither the time nor the necessary
attention for the strategic requirements of the sector. The result was
that the government expanded the SPC and included a growing number
of private citizens in the hope of making the SPC a more effective controlling body, and it was on this basis that the SPC began to increase
its role (PESD Interviews). This culminated in the SPC being de facto
the sole shareholder of KPC and therefore effectively the controller of
KPC's operations.

15 Obviously it was also painfully traumatic for Kuwait. Apart from anything else, it seriously undermined the political legitimacy of the ruling
family as the majority fled in what can only be described as undignified
panic.

16 Vertical integration has two variants: financial and operational.
Financial integration allows the holding company to control the
cash flow of the affiliates. Operational vertical integration is when
the affiliates supply each other in the form of internal transactions.
The crude producing affiliate supplies the refinery affiliate, etc.
Operational vertical integration requires the presence of financial
vertical integration and is usually pursued when a greater degree of
central control is needed – often when markets do not exist to govern the transactions between independent affiliates. The difference
between these forms of integration has been a central element of the
history of the oil industry (Bindemann 1999; Stevens 2003a). The
major private oil companies, before the second oil shock of 1978–
1981, were both financially and operationally vertically integrated.
Transaction and information costs made operational vertical integration superior to market exchange because markets were non-existent

or highly imperfect. A world market for crude oil, for example, did not exist; the owners of newly nationalized crude oil producer worried that they would not be able to find refiners and markets to buy their output. Operational vertical integration also made it easier for companies to hide information from regulators (and thus reduce tax liabilities) and to deter new entrants from joining the industry. After the second oil shock, the private IOCs moved away from operational vertical integration – in part because they lost control over crude oil supply following the nationalizations of the 1970s and in part because new markets emerged and transaction costs fell. Tax authorities began to constrain transfer pricing. These fundamental patterns lowered the barriers to entry for new independent firms, which led to more liquid and transparent markets. Operational vertical integration among the private IOCs, except in certain specific cases, largely disappeared.

17 This raises the serious possibility of a brain drain from KPC to the affiliates if their "private sector" salaries exceed those set by the Civil Service Commission.

18 The Kuwait Trade Union Federation is the sole national trade union center and was formed in 1968. Only domestic servants (which constitute some 453,000 out of a total workforce of 1.6 million) and maritime employees are not allowed to join. In fact only 80,000 workers are members. Although strikes are legal under certain circumstances, all unresolved disputes are subject to compulsory arbitration (US Department of State 2005). I suspect that those in Kuwait who regard the unions as "quite powerful" do so on grounds of ideology rather than the reality on the ground.

19 This is in part because the production of the data is erratic and often lacks the sort of detail and uniformity associated with oil companies listed on stock exchanges.

20 The government compensates KNPC for losses from domestic sales due to low product prices, but it has proved difficult to obtain details on exactly how this arrangement works. Certainly, domestic oil product prices are below international prices. In 2005, domestic prices for ultra-unleaded were 30.8 cents per liter and for gas oil/diesel 18.8 cents per liter (OAPEC). This compared to the Rotterdam spot prices at the end of 2005 of $1.59 and $1.47 per liter (IEA), respectively, for ultra-unleaded and gas oil/diesel.

21 One consequence of this system is that KPC has a keen interest in getting the "Pricing Committee" to set the internal oil price at a level that is low relative to the world market, which allows KPC to sell more crude (thus increasing marketing fees, which are based on volume) and also

reducing its crude costs for refining (increasing refining margins, which accrue in the part of the company that is allowed to earn a profit).

22 I focus here on refining but throughout KPC's history as an NOC, its managers have pursued a wider array of investments outside core crude oil production within Kuwait. In 1981, as part of KPC's efforts to become a more international company and to obtain access to Western technology, KPC bought the American service company Santa Fe for $2.5 billion. Through this acquisition, Santa Fe obtained the contract for the expansion of the Mina Abdallah refinery and became responsible for all drilling in Kuwait. However, the experience proved costly: Between 1981 and 1990 the company lost a total of $2.89 billion (MEES 43:16 2000) as a result of falling oil and gas prices after 1986. It was reported that Kuwaiti government auditors concluded KPC had overpaid for the company (Myerson 1994). Since 1991 such overseas acquisitions have become much less of a priority since it made little sense for the government to spend national resources to create "cash cows" for other governments to milk (PESD Interviews). Also Santa Fe's expansion plans had been held back by the aftermath of the Iraqi invasion in 1990 (Myerson 1994). As a result KPC gradually sold off its interests although it did retain a percentage of the equity.

23 Some expansion plans appear to be proceeding. In November 2007 the chairman of KNPC announced plans to expand Mina Al Ahmadi and Mina Abdallah with contract dues to be awarded that quarter (MEES 49:49 2007).

24 In 2005, oil exports accounted for 94 percent of total merchandise exports.

25 Clearly also any assessment of the efficiency of the upstream sector, whether qualitative or quantitative, must take account of the necessity to recover from the massive physical destruction on the sector as a result of the Iraqi invasion of 1990 and its aftermath.

26 The government has a *Kuwaitization* policy to encourage greater employment of nationals.

27 The concept of "wasta" is that of the relationship between client and patron with the patron providing wasta or influence for the client in dealing with others. The "diwaniya" process is when the patron effectively holds court often on a weekly basis to anyone who is interested.

28 There is no obvious explanation for this lack of movement across KPC's businesses. Possibly it reflects the fact that managers in the sector expect a "move" to involve a promotion and a raise in salary. However, promotion to a higher level in which the manager has little or no previous experience makes little sense.

29 It appears more recently, the new CEO Saad Al-Shuwaib has instituted lateral movements among the CEOs of the affiliates although what impact this will have is much debated within KPC.

30 At the end of 2002/2003 KPC and its subsidiaries employed 12,963 people; 75.4 percent were Kuwaiti nationals. In 2003/2004, KPC introduced a Five Year Kuwaitization plan. In addition, KPC introduced a requirement that KPC contractors must employ at least 25 percent Kuwaiti nationals. Several years later, KPC had nearly doubled its employment to 20,340 (PIW December 18, 2006). The payroll is bloating mainly due to strong political incentives for local hiring. In part, Project Kuwait to develop the northern oil fields with the help of IOCs was seen as a mechanism to fill the gap in skills in KPC that emerged in the aftermath of the 1990 invasion by Iraq and the 1991 liberation that also ejected many of KPC's best managers. However, Project Kuwait has become mired in internal Kuwaiti politics and looks as far away from fruition as it did ten years ago. It is not hard to comprehend the perennial difficulties pursuing ventures such as Project Kuwait that have the potential to alter employment and other valuable benefits that the government and National Assembly can extract from KPC.

31 It has been suggested to me that combining and separating ministries has more to do with the constitutional limit on the number of cabinet ministers (set at fifteen) rather than anything else.

32 This consists of the Petroleum Industries Company (PIC), a subsidiary of KPC, which has a number of joint venture projects with local and overseas companies. The position of PIC has been thrown into doubt as a result of the dispute with Dow Chemicals after the government allegedly forced PIC to withdraw from a joint venture. The issue, which involves claims for some $7 billion, is currently in arbitration.

33 Based on data from the BP Statistical Review of World Energy in 1975, there was almost 30 percent spare refining capacity in the OECD and the Emerging Market Economies. The high fixed cost component of refinery operations means that profitability requires full capacity operation. Such high levels of unused capacity, which carried on into the 1980s, were a disaster for refinery profitability. In 1982, the year before Gulf's offer, the figure reached a record 47 percent excess capacity.

34 A recent court decision has actually acquitted him of all charges.

35 In 2005/2006 KOC's Annual Report gives actual capacity as 2.337 mbd. Vision 2020 also sets a target for overseas production (KUFPEC), which has been given the goal of boosting overseas production to 100,000 b/d by 2010 and 200,000 b/d by 2020.

36 The KPC report actually says 2010 but this appears to be a typographic error.

37 This reflected a combination of government uncertainty over the role of the SPC and the result of a series of consultancy reports on the sector (PESD Interviews).

38 During the field visit to Kuwait in March 2007 upon which much of this narrative is drawn, the minister of health was due to face such an experience. In the event, the whole government resigned in order to prevent the questioning of the minister.

39 The "inverted commas" reflect that fact that for quite some time these refineries were used only for storage of products rather than actual refining.

40 These were Nader Sultan and Hani Hussein. In 2007, Saad Al-Shuwaib was appointed.

41 The Ministry of Oil is effectively required to act as advisor and secretariat to the oil minister in his role as minister. In practice, the ministry has found it hard to perform these two roles. Ministerial salary scales are significantly below those of KPC and thus it is unable to attract and hold needed talent. At the start of the 1970s, the oil ministry played a major role given its direct contact with the operators. Laws in 1973 and 1975 formalized the functions of the Ministry of Oil; at that time, Sheik Ali Al-Khalifa, who was minister from 1978 to 1990, dominated its activities and offered a clear sector strategy that KPC largely implemented. The earlier period of his control coincided with the huge increase in oil revenues following the second oil shock of 1978–1981, and thus the government had the money to indulge in empire building. Also, his position within the ruling family made him extremely powerful in the Kuwaiti political system. Finally, between 1976 and 1981 and again between 1986 and 1992, the National Assembly was suspended, and Kuwait was governed by amiri decree. Decisions of KPC and the ministry might be questioned within the various diwaniyas (informal local gatherings) held by the (suspended) assembly members, but dissidents had no ability to block decisions.

42 In the regulations, the glossary in Arabic, which normally would be expected to be in alphabetical order, appears random. However, closer inspection reveals that it is in English alphabetical order illustrating the rather limited attention that was paid to formulating these regulations.

43 More detail on the rules and the concerns they engender is in Stevens (2008b).

44 Other examples include the hiring of consultants. Within the Kuwaiti state sector, a practice had emerged that all consultants should be hired

via the Ministry of Planning. In fact, KPC had been hiring via its own subsidiaries. On discovering this, the Ministry of Planning objected and demanded it should be involved in the hiring process. However, when KPC appealed to the SPC to prevent this, the SPC was able to overrule the ministry simply because it could do so without getting alterations to the law.

45 It appears that the gas stations employed some 500 (relatively highly paid) workers while it was estimated that only 200–300 would be required, implying forced redundancies (MEES 46:50 2003).

9 | China National Petroleum Corporation (CNPC): a balancing act between enterprise and government

BINBIN JIANG

1 Introduction

National oil companies (NOCs) are pivotal to the global oil market. They control nearly 90 percent of the world's crude oil reserves and account for two-thirds of the world's crude oil production (EIA 2009b). China's NOCs are especially important due to the role the country plays as a major consumer of oil, but also as an increasingly visible investor in oil producing projects around the world. A previous paper by the Baker Institute at Rice University (S. Lewis 2007) analyzed the Chinese oil industry as a whole, and others (Jakobson and Zha 2006; Ma and Andrews-Speed 2006; Taylor 2006; Downs 2007a, 2007b; Xu 2007) have focused on the overseas activities of the Chinese NOCs. The following study, however, will concentrate on the largest and most important of China's NOCs: China National Petroleum Corporation (CNPC). CNPC has been the central element of the Chinese government's efforts to manage its growing dependence on oil and natural gas, which are essential to China's economy yet China has neither fuel in abundance.

CNPC is often portrayed in extremes. While many Western observers see it as a puppet of the state that schemes to hoard energy resources abroad, the Chinese government has been persistent in characterizing the firm as a transparent and internationalized oil company. The real picture of CNPC is, of course, much more complicated. Its relationship with the state, its financial performance, and the non-financial

I would like to acknowledge the support of David Victor, Mark Thurber, and Kathy Lung from the Program on Energy and Sustainable Development at Stanford University for the completion of this work. In addition, Yuan Ming Dong of the Development Research Center of the State Council provided much of the background information on CNPC. Xiaojie Xu, formerly of CNPC, and Mikkal Herberg, of UCSD, provided valuable comments and insights for improving this report.

aspects of its operations are the result of more than five decades of political upheaval, social change, and economic reforms since the ascent of one-party rule in China. As a result, CNPC is an entity of contradictions and inconsistencies. It is a victim of China's incomplete transition between a planned economy and a free market economy as well as a driver of economic change. It is a forward-thinking and technologically advanced enterprise and one that lacks transparency and accountability in its actions.

In order to understand CNPC as a whole, the enterprise must be understood in its historical context – both in its relationship to the Chinese state and to the outside world. This is explored in section 2 of the chapter. Section 3 examines the relationship between CNPC and the state, with particular attention to three perspectives: 1) the current corporate governance and internal organization of the firm; 2) the overseas expansion of the firm; and 3) the subsidies structure that is supported by CNPC and the government. Section 4 focuses on CNPC's financial performance and compares it with PetroChina and publicly listed Western companies. Section 5 looks at non-financial indicators of firm performance, namely the technical capacity and expertise of CNPC.

This chapter makes three main arguments. First, the financial performance of CNPC represents two realities. One reality is the reported performance of PetroChina, the public arm of CNPC listed on the Hong Kong, Shanghai, and New York stock exchanges, as a financially successful enterprise whose official performance rivals any international oil company (IOC). Another reality is CNPC's financial performance excluding PetroChina's earnings. CNPC without PetroChina is dramatically less efficient than IOCs. The firm's performance is also much more difficult to assess because not all of its activities and financial information are disclosed. As an arm of the Chinese state, CNPC is also preoccupied with state goals that extend far beyond producing oil, such as generating employment and securing particular oil supplies for China. Even though CNPC owns 86 percent of PetroChina's shares and PetroChina is completely controlled by CNPC, the goals of these interwoven, but separate, entities are divergent. PetroChina portrays an NOC that is autonomous, competitive, and modern; CNPC is a conventional NOC that holds the interests of the country as the top priority and acts more like an agency for the government than a business. This divergence reflects the fundamental tension in the relationship between the company and the Chinese government. While CNPC is trying to find ways to earn

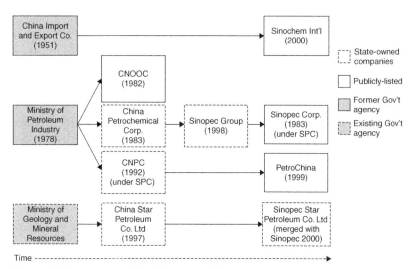

Figure 9.1 Evolution of the Chinese oil industry.
Source: Updated, revised and redrawn from Wang (1999).

its own autonomy, its relationship with the Chinese state is still a balancing act between assuring financial efficacy and the government's efforts to assure social stability and a cheap supply of energy needed for economic growth.[1]

Second, an increasing part of CNPC's operations is overseas. While most analysis has pointed to overt government support for such operations, in fact the Chinese government is increasingly wary about such operations due to their political fallout (e.g., in Sudan). CNPC is not driving overseas with the guidance of the Chinese state; rather, business considerations draw the company overseas where it is able to earn higher profits and enjoy greater autonomy than in its operations on Chinese territory. Moreover, as a state enterprise that accepts a lower rate of return on its risk-adjusted investments than comparable private firms, CNPC has a major competitive advantage in attracting the support of overseas governments. CNPC's initial forays overseas were inspired partly by the Chinese government's goal of assuring energy security, but that is no longer the main reason that the trend has continued and grown.

Third, CNPC is among the few NOCs examined in this book that have built a vast and highly competent research and development and technological capacity. Over its history (and especially since 2003) CNPC has invested in technologies that allow it to better tap the increasingly difficult geology it has at home as well as in technologies that allow it to expand beyond its core competency (onshore exploration and production) into other activities such as refining and offshore operations. However, CNPC is a highly compartmentalized company and expertise developed in certain subsidiaries is often difficult to share with other parts of the company. This mode of organization probably explains why CNPC is relatively good at managing its increasingly complex and aging fields within an existing technological paradigm but is still struggling to develop new business models and competence.

2 Overview and history of the Chinese oil industry

2.1 Overview of the Chinese oil industry

State-owned enterprises (SOEs) comprise a major portion of the economic activity in China. Whereas market-oriented reforms have swept across much of China, SOEs still dominate in critical "pillar" industries – including the petroleum industry, which supplies resources that are seen as essential to the country's economic growth and security (Ma and Andrews-Speed 2006). CNPC is the largest part of the petroleum pillar. As is typical in such industries, the central government oversees most major decisions such as allocation of capital and strategic choices for oil and gas exploration. As part of a broader reorganization of SOEs aimed at boosting performance, the government is partly loosening its grip on the oil industry. Among other initiatives in the sector, CNPC sold shares in its major subsidiary, PetroChina, on the New York Stock Exchange (Ma and Andrews-Speed 2006).

Today, there are five major oil companies in China: China National Petroleum Corporation (CNPC); China National Offshore Oil Corporation (CNOOC); Sinopec; Sinopec Star Petroleum Co. Ltd.; and Sinochem (see Figure 9.1). All China's oil companies trace their roots back to government agencies or government-run organizations: the Ministry of Petroleum Industry (disbanded); Ministry of Geology and Mineral Resources (still existing); China Import and Export Company[2] (disbanded). The Ministry of Petroleum Industry was disbanded in 1978 to create three enterprises: CNPC and China Star Petroleum Co. Ltd., which were responsible for all onshore exploration and production, and CNOOC, which was the dominant player in offshore exploration and production. Sinopec was responsible for

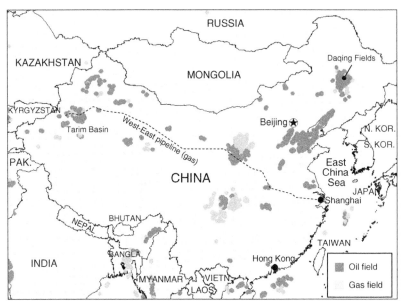

Figure 9.2 Map of major oil and gas fields in China.
Source for oil and gas field data: Wood Mackenzie (2009b).

downstream refining and petrochemical sectors. All oil imports and exports had to be processed through Sinochem.

CNPC, CNOOC, and Sinochem dominated the landscape until 1998 when modern reforms began. However, because the sector is a "pillar" in the economy, reforms mainly have involved reorganizing (and solidifying) state enterprise rather than risking loss of state control. After 1998, the government sought to boost productivity in the sector by creating more vertically integrated NOCs; for example, it forced Sinopec and CNPC to swap some upstream and downstream assets so that both became vertically integrated. (The government also forced CNPC and Sinopec to separate their core and non-core assets so that both would be focused more singularly on the oil industry.) These two large onshore NOCs became, in effect, a duopoly with Sinopec focusing more on the southern and eastern regions of the country and CNPC active in mainly the northern and western regions.

PetroChina, a company listed on both the New York and Hong Kong stock exchanges, is the holding company for CNPC's most attractive and financially viable core assets.[3] Investors bought them eagerly, which offered an opportunity for CNPC to raise funds and to engage more actively in overseas markets. CNPC retained management of all non-core assets, such as hospitals and schools. The firm controls 86 percent of PetroChina's stock, making the state-owned parent therefore, in PetroChina's own words, the "ultimate controller" of the company (PetroChina 2008).

Today, CNPC, Sinopec, and CNOOC together are responsible for 90 percent of China's oil and gas production. While CNOOC's near monopoly of offshore activities allows it to operate in its own world, CNPC and Sinopec have complementary skills and engage in a symbiotic relationship that fosters both cooperation and competition. CNPC has more experience and resources invested in exploration and production (E&P) but is relatively weak in the refining aspects of the industry; indeed, more than 10 percent of CNPC's sale of crude oil and refined oil products is to Sinopec for distribution and retail marketing.

China's NOCs have welcomed the government's goal of maintaining a near monopoly over the oil business. There are strict limitations on private (including foreign) investment, such as in the wholesaling of crude oil and refined oil products as well as in the construction and management of gas stations. In a few areas where the Chinese government is not confident that its NOCs can mobilize the needed investment and technology (such as in some kinds of oil and gas exploration, in the development and application of technologies for increasing recovery rates in mature fields, and in some aspects of oil refining and coking) private investment is allowed, but only when foreign companies work in cooperation with a domestic firm, namely, one of China's NOCs (Shi 2005). Many offshore projects and some gas projects fit into this category, but China's NOCs dominate the bulk of the Chinese oil industry.

2.1.1 Oil production and reserves
CNPC's 1.7 billion tons of recoverable reserves are two-thirds of the country's total and more than three times those of Sinopec and six times the reserves of CNOOC. Eighty percent of its reserves are booked in mature oil fields (such as the Daqing oil fields in northeastern China that are the traditional heart of China's oil industry, see Figure 9.2), and CNPC has developed exceptional competence in managing such fields at relatively low cost. Although independently

verified data does not exist, it is widely thought that total production costs in CNPC's mature oil fields are about $20/barrel – which compare favorably with world-class performance. However, CNPC has not seen the sharp rise in costs during the 2000s that Western companies have experienced because it controls most of its value chain and thus has less exposure to the vagaries of the international market in oil field services (Yuan 2007). Elsewhere in this book Peter Nolan and Mark Thurber (Chapter 4) distinguish oil fields and their operators by risk. CNPC's Daqing fields fit firmly in the category of low-risk mature oil production that most competent NOCs would be able to operate, although some of the aging fields present novel complexities. New developments in exploration are now leading CNPC into territories such as remote deserts and arid plateaus as well as mountainous regions, along with a new focus on smaller and more complex fields; together, these developments are raising the firm's total production costs for new fields to perhaps around $40–50/barrel (Yuan 2007).

Since about 1990, the Chinese government has encouraged greater use of natural gas – in an effort to diversify the energy system and reduce local pollution. Traditionally, the Chinese gas industry has concentrated on the gas fields in the Erdos Basin and also gas associated with oil in the country's maturing fields, notably around Daqing. In the past few years, CNPC has put a higher priority on finding gas, notably in the country's far west (e.g., the Tarim Basin), with favorable results. At the end of 2005, the company held recoverable gas reserves of 1.95 trillion cm (73.3 percent of the nation's total) and its leadership position is likely to remain into the future. CNPC projects that it will find enough new gas that its reserves will be 5.6 trillion cm by 2020 (Yuan 2007) – or about twenty-five years of production at the expected rate of consumption that year (120 bcm per year).

2.1.2 Energy demand and consumption

Since the late 1990s, the demand for petroleum products has rapidly increased, especially for light and middle distillates used to fuel the country's increasing mobility by automobile and truck (see Figure 9.3). At the same time, due to a scarcity of resources and technical limitations, oil production has stagnated. From 1998 to 2005, production grew on average only 1.5 percent while demand soared at 7.5 percent annually (IEA 2008). In 1993 China became a net oil importer. This

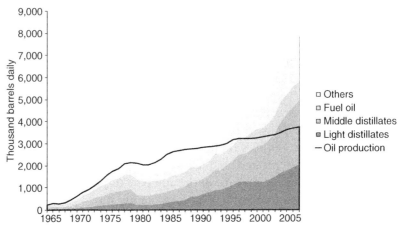

Figure 9.3 Oil production and oil consumption by product group, 1965–2007.
Source: BP (2008).

pattern is expected to continue into the future, although a proper assessment is difficult because Chinese official projections have a history of underestimating demand. Other projections envisioned that about half of China's oil would be imported in 2010, 65 percent by 2020, and three-quarters in 2030 (IEA 2008).

2.2 History of the Chinese oil industry

2.2.1 The beginning

China's oil industry has always been intertwined with the functions of the Chinese government. From the start of Communist rule in 1949 energy was seen as a strategic concern (Zhang 2004). Mao Zedong ordered the 57th Division of the 19th Army of the PLA to be reorganized into an "oil corps" (1st Division of Oil) (Zhang 2004). The unit was charged with the goal of quickly developing areas for exploration and production of oil to allow self-sufficiency; by the early 1960s that goal became urgent as the diplomatic relations disintegrated between China and the Soviet Union, which supplied more than half China's critical refined oil products (Downs 2000).

Communist central planning allowed few exceptions to the rule that the center controlled all resources. The State Planning Commission was ultimately responsible for determining the national plan for the demand

and supply of oil, allocation for processing, and oil imports and exports. To help deploy the plan that the State Planning Commission penned, in 1955 the government created the Ministry of Petroleum Industry (MPI) (Wang 1999). As the headquarters of China's nascent oil industry, MPI was responsible for making investment decisions (e.g., the location and timing of exploration and production projects), coordinating the transportation and distribution of oil products, and allocating oil resources to local-level entities known as Petroleum Administrative Bureaus (PABs). Each of these local agencies managed a particular oil field and was responsible for meeting the production targets that the State Planning Commission set out in the national plan.

The urgent, militarized effort to find local production yielded early successes. China soon started to produce enough oil to become self-sufficient; by 1970 it was a net exporter. During the 1970s, China sold oil (below market price) to Japan in order to decrease Japanese demand for Siberian hydrocarbons and divert cash away from the Soviet Union, which China feared might attack the northeastern part of the country. Starting in the 1980s, the oil fields tapped for the country's surge in production began to mature, and growth in production slowed. At the same time, massive and broader economic reforms led to tremendous economic growth; GNP rose 8.6 percent annually from 1979 to 1991 (Steinfeld 1998). Much of the growth in productivity and employment occurred outside the state sector – notably within township and village enterprises (TVEs) that predominated in southern rural areas; industrial state-owned enterprises, including those that dominated the oil sector, were largely untouched. By 1988, the entire petroleum industry was losing money; its problems included lack of investment in exploration and production of oil as well as mounting debt (Zhang 2004).

In an attempt to improve performance of state enterprises, in 1988 the central government abolished the MPI and assigned its assets and responsibilities to CNPC.[4] (It implemented similar reforms in other sectors, such as coal and nuclear power.) This partial corporatization put CNPC in charge of not only *operations* (onshore and shallow water oil and gas exploration and production; overseas cooperation) but also some *regulation* that MPI had previously overseen, such as setting standards for the petroleum industry.

Through these reforms, CNPC shared with the government the task of planning. In consultation with the State Council, which devised all the country's central economic plans, CNPC was in charge of long-term planning, including control over investment decisions within China and overseas; the planning bureau of CNPC was in charge of business strategy planning and production planning (including regulation of inputs and outputs from the oil industry) in conjunction with the State Planning Commission and State Economic and Trade Commission (SETC). The State Planning Commission's plan also required that CNPC coordinate with Sinopec, the downstream state-owned oil company, to draft the detailed supply and transportation elements that were included in the master plan. Funding for CNPC came from the array of sources that were used to finance operations of most large state-owned enterprises: government budget, state bank loans, domestic bond issues, and overseas sources channeled through the Ministry of Finance and the Bank of China. CNPC, at this point, was not a real business that could reinvest its profits to grow. It required the assistance of the state in order to be operational and it operated with a "soft budget" because many of its loans, for example, were issued with an ambiguous expectation of repayment. Nearly every aspect of the company was interwoven with the state and party apparatus. For example, the State Council and the Chinese Communist Party (CCP) Department of Organization appointed the president and vice presidents of CNPC. A "party committee" within CNPC appointed the rest of the top management team. The structure of CNPC remained almost completely unchanged between 1988 and 1998, although various minor reform policies were implemented to improve performance of the oil industry as a whole.

2.2.2 Reforming CNPC

As the Chinese economy soared in the 1990s, there were many reforms aimed at raising the economic efficiency of the oil industry. These reforms demonstrated the government's recognition of the inherent flaws within the system of state-dependent companies; its reform strategy, in general, sought to give these enterprises greater autonomy as well as exposure to market-like competition. But this strategy was filled with internal contradictions. Notably, the trend toward autonomy had created fiefdoms that made it hard to preserve central planning (still the bedrock of China's economy) and also sowed chaos in the oil industry. In 1998, the government abandoned many of these reforms with a new strategy that recentralized some of CNPC's authority.

One area of particular chaos was the operation of the PABs. Autonomy for the PABs rested on a 1981 government reform called the "big contract" model. While MPI was still nominally in charge of oil fields, it contracted with the central government to hand over 94.5 percent of actual oil output for domestic use but was allowed to keep the rest for export. MPI was also permitted to retain the difference in price between the higher international prices and lower domestic prices – revenues it was supposed to invest in exploration and production. MPI contracted with the PABs to actually produce the oil, and these local agencies also received higher revenues from exceeding quotas, which provided them with a strong incentive to push up production. Each PAB faced a strong, individual incentive to boost output rather than collectively follow the dictates of the central government. This policy, which was seen as a success because it seemingly forestalled decline in production, was renewed in 1991. Under the big contract system, performance indicators were put in place to evaluate the performance of each subordinate enterprise.[5] However, as with most systems that operate on soft budgets, the consequences of failure to meet performance targets were never clear.

PABs were not only allowed to keep a share of profits but there were also reforms that shifted the incentives for local managers of PABs. Known as the "oil company" model of reform, these reforms corporatized the PABs, encouraged them to invest more of their resources in the core elements of the petroleum industry and to contract out the diversified functions needed to support that mission, such as social services, utilities, and the manufacture of drilling machinery. While new oil fields that came online after 1989 certainly followed this organization (for example, the Tarim Basin, which opened that year, was the first region to implement the "oil company" model) it is unclear how much success traditional PABs had with restructuring. In the 1990s, as part of this dalliance with decentralization, CNPC also adopted a policy that gave all its subordinate enterprises "legal person" status. This meant that each enterprise would be responsible for its own profits, losses, and growth – imposing, in theory, hard budget constraints that are often essential to successful market-oriented reforms. For the most successful enterprises, such as China's largest PAB and oil field Daqing, the new status was encouragement to become more than just a regional branch company. It was seen as an opportunity to develop its own business strategy and even to work toward possible listing as a separate company in the future. In the partially reformed planning system – where PABs were encouraged to follow their own instincts yet central planning meant that all parts of the far-flung oil industry were tightly interdependent – this policy of decentralization would later prove disastrous as fragmentation of the oil industry started to cause both financial and management problems for CNPC.

In 1995, the government tried to improve performance of the oil sector by adopting a three-tier oil pricing system that would start to align domestic prices with prevailing international prices. Lower ("grade I") prices were set for transfers from CNPC (which mainly produced crude oil) to Sinopec (which focused on refining); a second price ("grade II") prevailed within the state production plan (*zhi ling xing ji hua*), and anything that the PABs had left over could be sold at international price levels. While the goal of this policy was admirable, its perverse impacts unfolded as the government attempted to regulate similar products at different prices. Sinopec experienced supply shortages. "Oil brokers," who theoretically should not have existed in the planning system, emerged to control key decisions around allocation of effort and rents. They intercepted low-priced oil (intended for use according to government plan) and sold it at a higher rate for the private domestic market. Sinopec was forced to import larger quantities of expensive international oil even as the government subsidized the price difference between "grade I" oil and international market prices.

During the late 1990s, the central government began to abandon the big contract model by adopting a royalty-like approach to revenues from oil production. The new policy would require oil enterprises to "hand over" (*shang jiao*) a negotiated amount that includes the portion of the profits and fees for using the reserves (*chuliang shiyong fei*). As is typical with such reforms, the oil producers (PABs) found themselves in dispute with their regulators (CNPC) over the proper allocation of revenues from their operations – in particular, the size of remittances to the Chinese government. CNPC had little control or knowledge over capital expenditures and thus, as regulator, was poorly equipped to set a royalty fee that encouraged rational production. For example, PABs controlled many more services than just the core functions of oil exploration and production. Despite attempts at reform, these bureaus provided social services such as hospitals, electricity generation, and schools as well as ventures into many diversified businesses that were not on the books at CNPC even though

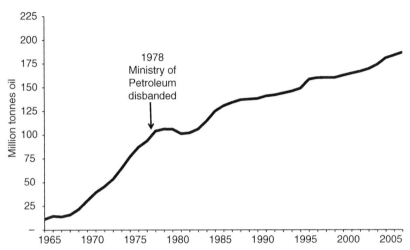

Figure 9.4 Chinese oil production and consumption, 1965–2007.
Source: BP (2008).

CNPC nominally owned and controlled the PABs. Since these ancillary enterprises were under no obligation to achieve a certain return on their investments, they encouraged the PABs to increase spending even when that destroyed value. In practice, however, the reform of the big contract system toward the "hand over" policy did not really affect behavior because the budget constraints remained soft; a portion of the profits from solvent enterprises was remitted to the state while state enterprises that suffered losses were given subsidies using these same funds. Ironically, because the industry had become more decentralized, CNPC was unable to monitor the escalating losses of each PAB, which kept finding new ways to lose money while generating local political benefits.

For a while, the autonomy of the PABs helped to boost the country's overall oil production, but by the 1990s that surge in output had run out of steam (see Figure 9.4).

In 1998, the government ordered sweeping reforms that fundamentally restructured the entire Chinese oil industry. The impetus for change was the government's desire to create a Chinese petroleum industry that would be competitive with IOCs in the global market. In addition, the need for change was also evident in the number of regional oil enterprises that were losing money. Indeed, the cost of oil production was rising above the prevailing domestic level due to the failure to invest in research and long-term planning in the industry. The central government, which owned CNPC, faced steep declines in profit and yet was unable to spur improvements in each of the regional oil enterprises because CNPC had little control over the actions of each region.

The reforms concentrated on three main actions. First, the "legal person" status of the regional enterprises was revoked in an attempt to recentralize decision making in the oil industry. This element of the reform aimed at producing a more coherent strategy for the industry overall and creating stronger incentives for better economic performance, although success on both fronts has so far been elusive.[6] Second, CNPC and Sinopec swapped assets and became regional, vertically integrated companies, making each one a stronger competitor by having access to complementary assets for which they were dependent on one another before.[7] Third, core and non-core assets in each CNPC production unit were separated from each other. The core assets were reconstituted as "branch companies" and were eventually floated as PetroChina. The non-core assets were spun off where possible; where not possible, they were kept together under CNPC's ownership.[8] The CNPC that exists today is the direct descendent of these reforms.

3 The state–CNPC relationship

As a state-owned enterprise, the key to understanding CNPC is in its relationship to the Chinese government. That relationship is not easy to summarize and thus here I examine it through two lenses. First, I examine who really controls CNPC – in particular, its procedures for corporate governance and internal decision making. Second, I examine how CNPC and its listed subsidiary PetroChina have been affected by the various attempts to liberalize the Chinese economy and introduce market-like forces within state enterprises. While some level of competition has been introduced to the industry by reforms introduced in the past couple of decades, wariness about upsetting the political order and completely liberalizing the energy sector has led to policies that explicitly prevent these firms from behaving as truly competitive and efficient enterprises. One by-product of liberalizing reforms has been a stronger incentive for the Chinese oil industry, in particular CNPC, to invest overseas.

3.1 Who controls CNPC?

CNPC's relationship with the Chinese state is mediated by the Communist Party of China (CPC). From the founding of communist China in 1949 until today the CPC has traditionally exercised control over the country's economy. The ultimate priority of such one-party political rule is to retain control of its institutions. In turn, the highest priority for managers within these institutions is to move up the Communist Party's political hierarchy. Thus the heads of state-owned enterprises and other public institutions are, first and foremost, stewards of political ideology and the party line; economic efficiency is secondary.[9] Creating incentives for efficiency has not been easy because it has required disentangling the functions of state enterprises from the political and ideological missions of the state and party. Among those efforts has been corporatization, which has aimed to create the right incentives for managers of state enterprises even as ultimate control over the enterprises has not been divested from the state and the CPC. Below I look at the basic concepts that guide Chinese understanding of corporate governance and then at the managers and decision making within CNPC.

3.1.1 Corporate governance and control over senior managers

The concept of corporate governance came into the consciousness of the Communist Party with the advent of economic liberalization policies in 1978. The idea refers to the institutional forms and mechanisms that govern how managers control the enterprise and allocate risks (McNally 2002). In theory, the embrace of corporate governance reflected a new goal of government in the post-1978 reforms – to maximize efficiency and minimize cost for state-owned enterprises – which was pursued by transforming state enterprises into firms with individual legal status and accountability. In practice, the theory was never so simple and implementation proved to be quite complex. Incentives given to managers were often not strong enough to encourage adequate changes in behavior. Ownership rights were poorly defined, which resulted in a "principal/agent problem" because the people who stood to gain from sound business decisions were not actually the decision makers themselves.

The most important force for change in the management of state enterprises was the problem of losses. Traditionally, state banks covered losses by state enterprises with soft loans. As the financial situation of the SOEs (and their sponsors in the state banking system) worsened, the government began to see corporatization as a way to fix both problems. Not only would reforms clarify ownership and accountability but as the reform movement progressed, it was also thought that public listing would yield an important source of financing for this restructuring and was especially attractive to government masters because it shifted pressure away from state banks to equity markets that were stuffed full of investors that wanted entry into China. The public listing of PetroChina, for example, arose from this logic.

Broadly there were two tracks of market-oriented reform in China. In the first track, which began in the late 1970s and continued into the 1990s, large SOEs were kept under state control although their managers were given more autonomy and responsibilities. By contrast, smaller SOEs were left to fend for themselves.[10] Seemingly, this first track of reform exposed segments of the Chinese industrial sector to elements of market competition although, in practice, the real incentives of a market were blunted. For example, many of the employees that were fired from the smaller SOEs were rehired by larger SOEs that had been only partially reformed. In the oil industry, this approach to reform meant that large, influential companies such as CNPC came under closer scrutiny of the central government, while PABs were left to fend for themselves – at least until the chaos from decentralization led to efforts by the government throughout the 1990s (notably in the 1998 reforms) to reassert authority through CNPC.[11] Nonetheless, today CNPC is probably more efficient as an enterprise due to this legacy of decentralization. Even today, many of CNPC's subsidiaries remain fairly independent (especially regarding their investments in R&D, which are detailed below); moreover, the process of decentralization helped weed out some of the less efficient subsidiaries (at least those that could not secure state resources to sustain their operations) while rewarding the more innovative subsidiaries. These reforms included a new "Company Law," which became effective in 1994 and required that companies create a board of directors and hold meetings of shareholders to elect directors and make major corporate decisions. In addition, limited liability corporations were required to establish a board of supervisors to provide independent oversight and evaluation of the behavior of directors and managers.

In parallel, but on a slower track and thus harder to assess from today's vantage point, the government adopted reforms that would actually enforce accountability in corporate governance and allow the government to become a more effective shareholder. During the late 2000s, the government adopted a new three-tier state asset management system that would align the interests of the owners and those who ultimately managed the companies; organizations on each tier are held accountable to the organizations in the tier above. Traditionally, any single state enterprise might be controlled by several governmental agencies but none would actually own any of the assets or be ultimately accountable. This created incentives for the controlling ministries to act on the behalf of their constituencies rather than the broader public interest or even to serve the government as shareholder. The new system has attempted to align the interests of management with owners by giving government a more singular and decisive voice as shareholder. The first (top) tier of the system includes two new commissions that were created to supervise the state-owned assets and regulate the financial sector: the State-Owned Assets Supervision and Administration Commission (SASAC) and the China Banking Regulatory Commission (CBRC).[12] Under the Company Law, SASAC's main functions include promoting reform of state enterprises as well as promoting better management of SOEs and their integration into the Chinese economy.[13] By some interpretations, SASAC has expansive and extensive control over the jewels of the Chinese state-oriented economy. It implements its obligation at large SOEs – such as CNPC as well as the other major oil companies such as Sinopec and CNOOC – through supervisory panels and by exerting ultimate control over the choice of top executives. Below SASAC is the second tier of the new corporate governance system, which consists of the state holding corporations. The holding company's role is akin to that of an institutional investor for the state that aims to maximize the state's return on its assets. CNPC is the leading example of a holding company in the oil sector. The third tier of the system consists of those SOEs that have been converted to limited liability corporations. Such corporations are owned by holding companies – which appoint the boards of directors and supervisors – although a portion of their shares can be listed.

The goal of the Company Law and the multi-tier system of state-owned asset management was to "clarify property rights, establish

clear powers and responsibilities, separate government and enterprise, and establish a scientific method of management" (Jiang
1995). This complicated structure reflected the conflicting goals of
boosting economic performance while not diminishing the government's hold on strategic industries. Indeed, although top managers
of each corporatized SOE are supposed to be elected via the board of
directors, they are instead usually appointed to the positions by the
Communist Party's Organization Department (Tenev *et al.* 2002).
These managers, in turn, operate according to the incentives in their
career trajectories – they place the political interests of the party
above economic considerations for an enterprise. An additional drag
on performance is that local governments have shielded enterprises
from market forces by diverting money from public funds as subsidies to these organizations. Since SOEs are usually an integral part
of the local economy, it is in the interest of the local government to
scuttle reforms that could cause unemployment or other forms of
social instability.

One interesting aspect of these reforms is that formal governance
and accountability of Chinese SOEs, at least on the surface, now look
a lot like Western companies. For example, CNPC now publishes a
corporate responsibility report every year, in addition to and separate from the annual report, which outlines safety and environmental
measures that the company is taking. In the last few years, CNPC has
adopted a management system focused on health, safety, and environment (HSE) that trains middle- and high-level management on these
goals. This shift reflects an effort to mimic best practice of the West;
however, the actual impact of HSE reporting is hard to ascertain.

These two tracks of reforms have not yet resulted in a fundamental change of the senior leadership in most SOEs, although that pattern is evident even in publicly listed companies. As of the late 1990s,
independent directors on the board of directors with no ties to the
government or the company made up less than one-third of the board
of directors in Chinese SOEs (compared with around 75 percent for
Western private companies) (Mallin and Rong 1998). Today, after the
reforms have been under way for nearly a decade, not much is different. Currently, of PetroChina's twenty-four board members only six
are independent of the government and company.[14]

Heavy insider infiltration of governing boards has produced
all the predictable problems. Notably, it is harder to expel poorly

performing managers and to assure accurate reporting of financial and other performance indicators. Moreover, the performance criteria by which managers are evaluated do not include traditional metrics of stock price, shareholder returns, or economic value added, but rather more subjective measures such as "improving ideological and political work, enhancing Party conduct and anti-corruption campaign" (CNPC 2007). The interpretation of this message is that as long as managers fulfill their roles in keeping the corporation in line with government and party expectations, the managers would not only keep their jobs but also climb up the Chinese SOE ladder (Liu 2006).[15] To be sure, the full range of incentives that affect managers is complicated, but standard shareholder performance plays only a minor role. Top managers receive bonuses that account for a large share of their income, but some bonuses are merely indexed to salaries (and thus not really bonuses). Some are based on performance targets that make sense for the company itself (e.g., net profit, return on capital, and cost savings) and thus partially align with shareholder interest. But shareholder performance (e.g., stock price) or customer satisfaction usually play little role. More importantly, some performance indicators are not financial, but rather political goals such as "eliminating factors causing instability," anti-corruption, "preventing occurrence of mass commotion," and "severe offences against party conducts" (Fan *et al.* 2007). There is no real risk of managers being fired unless a major catastrophe occurs under their leadership. (Such catastrophes usually cause heads to roll for symbolic reasons as they are rarely traced back to the singular decisions of particular managers.) Because of their appointments by the highest levels of government, poor business performance under top management's direction does not warrant a dismissal. Managers also cannot be voted out by the board of directors without the final approval of the State Council – an important part of the government's planning system that itself is steeped in party control.

This system of control for top management positions helps to explain why the population of managers is dominated by middle-aged men with training in either engineering or economics and extensive backgrounds in the oil and gas industry. Based on executive profiles published by the companies, the same people are shuffled between CNPC and PetroChina (see Figure 9.5). Major changes in personnel are usually made on political grounds rather than the performance record of the people involved – the most abrupt changes in leadership are usually crisis-driven and geared toward protecting the reputation of the central government rather than based on what was the best choice for CNPC (Xin 2005). The significant reshuffling of personnel between 2002 and 2003, for example, corresponds with a major natural gas explosion that released a cloud of hydrogen-sulfide gas that killed 243 people over 28 towns in Kaixin County and the suburbs of Chongqing Municipality at the end of 2003. Investigations following the incident pointed to the absence of a critical blowout prevention device in the well due to CNPC's cost-cutting measures (Xu 2004). The president of CNPC at the time, Ma Fucai, was forced to resign, along with lower-level managers, and the six workers who followed improper procedure at the worksite (Hubbell 2004; Jiang 2004). According to CNPC's 2003 annual report, Chen Geng replaced Ma Fucai and more personnel were brought into the top management team. Another disaster followed this incident in November 2005 when CNPC's largest chemical plant, Jilin Petrochemical, contaminated the Songhua River, the main drinking water supply of Harbin, the capital of Heilongjiang Province, and also the Russian city of Khabarovsk. Tap water was turned off for four days and affected 9 million people in two countries (Li and Wang 2008). The president-in-residence once again assumed responsibility and resigned. Heads are sacrificed to garner credibility from the Chinese public, which has been inundated with promises from senior government leaders that such disasters would be averted.

In addition to the fact that reforms have not had much impact on control over senior appointments, those reforms also have not had the expected impact on decision making within CNPC. As already discussed, the reforms starting in the late 1970s decentralized some decision making within the oil industry – notably to the PABs. Even as that control was reasserted by CNPC, the result has been an unusual and fragmented decision-making process that reflects these twin, conflicting pressures for and against central control.

On paper, today's CNPC looks like a highly centralized institution modeled in the tradition of central planning. The CNPC central planning bureau uses market analysis along with mid- to long-term economic and technological projections to devise a five-year plan that optimizes use of the company's resources. Next, each regional office

Name	Former employment	Position within CNPC in 2007	Age	Educational background
Jiang Jiemin	Vice president (CNPC); Vice-governor (Qinghai Province)	President (CNPC), President (PetroChina); Vice Chairman of the Board (PetroChina); Alternate member (17th CPC, Central Committee)	52	M.S., Economics
Zhou Jiping	Vice president (CNPC); Director (PetroChina)	Vice president (CNPC); Director (PetroChina)	56	M.S., Marine geologic structure
Duan Wende	Vice president (CNPC)	Vice president (CNPC); Director (PetroChina)	55	Engineering
Wang Yilin	Vice president (CNPC); Senior Executive (Xinjiang Petroleum Administration Bureau; President (Xinjiang Oil Branch, PetroChina)	Vice president (CNPC); Director (PetroChina)	N/A	Ph.D., Engineering
Zeng Yukang	Assistant president (CNPC)	Vice president (CNPC); Director (PetroChina)	57	B.A., Economics
Wang Fucheng	Vice-president (Petrochina)	Chief of Discipline and Inspection Group (CNPC); Vice president (PetroChina)	58	B.A., Economics
Li Xinhua	Deputy governor (Yunnan Province)	Vice President (CNPC); Director (PetroChina)	N/A	B.S., Chemical Engineering
Liao Yongyuan	Assistant president (CNPC)	Executive director (PetroChina); Safety director (CNPC)	45	M.S., Engineering
Wang Guoliang	CFO (PetroChina)	CFO (CNPC)	N/A	M.A., Accounting
Chen Ming	General manager of the supervisory dept (PetroChina)	Chief of Discipline and Inspection Group (CNPC); Chairman of Supervisors (PetroChina)	N/A	B.A., Economist

Figure 9.5 Top CNPC leadership employment history.

and its subsidiaries submit investment plans to the central office. The central CNPC planning bureau then pieces together this information and creates an integrated plan for the whole company. In turn, it submits this plan to the State Council as well as CNPC's board of directors for approval.[16] In reality, however, the planning process is usually more complicated and less centralized than the official process outlined here. While it is hard to understand the planning process fully by looking from the outside, CNPC's two most prominent accidents, discussed above, have attracted enough scrutiny that they also offer analysts a window on what really happens inside the company. Careful reporting on these accidents usually reveals that CNPC suffers from a lack of standardization in work safety guidelines and inadequate enforcement, especially within operational units not

Table 9.1a. *External decision-making governmental bodies related to CNPC before March 2008*

Ministry	Main function
Office of the National Energy Leading Group	Involved in energy planning and policymaking; creates a strategic and integrated approach to energy
NDRC (Energy Bureau)	Regulation of the petroleum industry, organizational reform; petroleum development planning; strategic petroleum reserves; approval of new projects; set price of petroleum
Ministry of Land and Resources	Approval of exploration and development activities
Ministry of Commerce	Approval of downstream distribution plans
State Environmental Protection Agency	Approval of environmental impacts of projects

Table 9.1b. *External decision-making governmental bodies related to CNPC after March 2008*

Ministry	Main function
State Energy Commission (SEC)	A high-level discussion and coordination body whose specific functions have not yet been determined. Replaces the Office of the National Energy Leading Group.
National Energy Administration (NEA)	Vice-ministerial component of NDRC, successor to the Energy Bureau of the NDRC. Even though this administration has more capability than the Energy Bureau, it still lacks authority for ultimate decision making.
Ministry of Land and Resources	Approval of exploration and development activities
Ministry of Commerce	Approval of downstream distribution plans
State Environmental Protection Agency	Approval of environmental impacts of projects

Source: Yuan (2007).

immediately under the eyes of the CNPC in Beijing. Both of the incidents occurred in areas that are geographically far away from the center, and there was little oversight from the main corporation (Zhang 2004). Another window into company decision making is opened by examining how new technology is devolved through the company. Although CNPC has its own centrally operated R&D centers, many of the important technical innovations in recent years have actually come from individual subsidiaries focused on solving practical problems rather than an overall R&D plan that assigns specific tasks to individual branches of the government. I explore R&D in more detail below.

The most visible evidence of CNPC's efforts to recentralize internal decision making is found in exploration and production. Prior to the 1998 reforms, individual oil field operators (i.e., the PABs) would decide when and where to drill new wells and how to manage the field; currently, those decisions are made by the central CNPC planning offices (Yuan 2007). While field-level decisions are made by CNPC, CNPC does not, itself, fully control its own planning process. Overall production levels for the sector and other long-term strategic decisions are made in consultation with government agencies, such as the ones listed in Table 9.1a and Table 9.1b. The Energy Bureau of the National Development and Reform Committee (NDRC) has an especially important role to play in the process due to its power to set both upstream and downstream conditions by setting the price of petroleum products in the Chinese market. In the next section I explore these many relationships between the enterprise and the government in more detail.

3.2 The state–CNPC relationship as a reflection of the process of economic liberalization in China

A second way to explore the relationship between the state and the NOC is by examining how the process of economic liberalization has altered the relationships between the government and the oil enterprise over time. Here I explore that by focusing on three of the most important aspects of that relationship: 1) the links between CNPC and its major subsidiary PetroChina; 2) the decision to allow and encourage CNPC to invest abroad; and 3) the setting and adjustment of subsidies for oil products.

3.2.1 The relationship between CNPC and PetroChina

CNPC is a holding company that is wholly owned by the government and under the direct control of the State Council; in turn, CNPC controls eighty-seven subsidiary enterprises, most of which specialize in engineering, technical services, and equipment manufacturing (Zhang 2004). Of all CNPC's subsidiaries, PetroChina is the only publicly listed entity. Its shares are listed on the New York Stock Exchange (NYSE), Hong Kong Stock Exchange (HKSE), and the Shanghai Stock Exchange (SSE); thus it must conform to the mandatory laws of the PRC Company Law and the securities laws and regulations of Hong Kong and the United States (PetroChina 2008). Indeed, by meeting these listing requirements, CNPC is able to claim that PetroChina is as open and transparent as Western companies and is therefore better able to gain shareholder trust.

While the governance structure of PetroChina may look similar to other public companies and it must (on paper) conform with stringent listing rules, the actual practice is different. Notably, PetroChina does not vest control over crucial parts of the decision-making process with independent directors. CNPC is able to elect the entire board of directors without practical input of external shareholders; it is also able to dictate the timing and amount of dividend payments (Ewing 2005). The lack of independent directors also means that the top management of PetroChina is reviewed by its peers and associates, people who operate within the same political and social networks – a situation that is rife with conflicts of interest. Moreover, because directors are not obligated to act under a code of ethics required by NYSE and other listing rules (Ewing 2005), they are probably able to escape scrutiny for actions that are not allowed by directors in other companies. Because its operations are still controlled exclusively by CNPC, minority shareholder interests are poorly protected, although such concerns have not urgently arisen because the interests of minority shareholders and CNPC happen to align: the former want growth in share value and the latter needs to demonstrate credibility (for the moment) in Western stock markets.

While CNPC and PetroChina are supposed to be formally separate, in fact there are blurry lines between the enterprises in nearly every aspect of their operations. In 2007, CNPC was the largest supplier and purchaser of products from PetroChina, such as construction and technical services and supply of materials. CNPC and PetroChina also exchange assets, and some analysts believe that such transactions are designed to keep PetroChina attractive to private investors while shuffling less desirable assets to CNPC. In 2007, PetroChina acquired assets of the risk operation service business from CNPC. In addition, CNPC is also a major creditor to PetroChina through its subsidiary CP Finance. In 2006, guarantee of borrowings by CP Finance totaled about 80 percent of the total amount of borrowings for PetroChina. In 2007, CP Finance supplied all of PetroChina's state-backed debt. These loans, backed by a de facto state guarantee, are made on the basis of low interest rates (4.46–7.47 percent). In addition to these activities, PetroChina has also acquired (in 2005) subsidiaries from CNPC, such as the refining and petrochemical business of CNPC, and 50 percent equity interests in an overseas CNPC subsidiary, CNPC Exploration and Development Company Limited (PetroChina 2008). In 2007, PetroChina acquired the risk management services business of CNPC. CNPC and PetroChina are not separate entities; rather, they are more akin to divisions of the same company that are separated by porous technical and legal barriers – with one division listed on stock exchanges mainly for the purpose of raising money.

3.2.2 The decision to "go abroad"

Since CNPC's first overseas service contract – with Peru for the Talahara oil field in 1993 – the company's overseas activities have steadily increased with time. After more than a decade of development, CNPC has established overseas oil and gas operations in Africa, the Asia-Pacific, Central Asia-Russia, the Middle East, and South America. In all, by 2007, CNPC had oil and gas interests in twenty-six countries and provided petroleum engineering and technical services to forty-four countries. Overseas operations produced 60.19 million metric tons of crude oil and 5.36 billion cubic meters of natural gas (Yuan 2007) in total, although the equity-adjusted volume of oil is much lower (less than 40 million metric tons).

Although what motivates CNPC to go abroad is under debate, an important driver of China's overseas oil policy in the past has been the government's concern with energy security. This concept is commonly understood as "the availability of energy at all time[s] in various forms, in sufficient quantities, and at affordable prices" (Xu 2004). Historically – from the time the Chinese Communist Party took over

in 1949 – the Chinese government has struggled to secure the supply of energy. Dependence on Soviet exports through the 1950s and
then the breakdown in Sino-Soviet relations were a stark reminder
of the need for reliable energy supplies; those concerns resurfaced as
production levels started to decline in China's maturing oil fields due
to insufficient levels of investment in exploration and production,
especially in the 1990s as economic reforms caused demand to soar.
The efforts have been on many fronts: alternative energy (e.g., renewable power) and energy efficiency, as well as a global search for oil
resources that China could secure for itself.

Much of China's effort to obtain oil overseas has married state-
owned CNPC with special state resources, notably development
assistance to the host country (Houser 2008). For example, China's
Export-Import Bank extended loans to Angola and other African
nations during Premier Wen Jiabao's African tour in 2006 (Faucon
2006).

In recent years the government has become more hesitant about
overseas investment, while CNPC has become more enthusiastic. In
fact, it is on the topic of overseas investment where we start to see
some of the tension between government and enterprise. Any major
overseas venture requires approval by the central government.[17] The
willingness of the government to offer such approvals is a subject of
great speculation by China scholars within the literature.[18] Some analysts, such as Erica Downs, claim that energy security is the main
driver for China's "going out" strategy – by implication, the government will be keen to offer approvals for overseas operations (Downs
2000). Others, such as Trevor Houser, argue that although Beijing
has encouraged overseas investment in the past, it is less enthusiastic
now due to the small effect such actions have on gaining energy security for the country. Only about 10–20 percent of all the oil that is produced overseas actually makes it back to China (Dirks 2006).[19] The
crude that does make it back is also sour and heavy and thus harder
to refine. The more profitable light, sweet crude tends to be sold in the
international market where profits are higher. Because refining is a
losing business proposition in China due to the artificially low prices
at which the government controls the downstream products, there is
little incentive for the enterprise to bring the crude back to the home
market in China.[20] How much of the different crude types CNPC
brings back for the domestic market is a point of tension between the

Chinese government and CNPC. The exact proportion that is settled on is a negotiation between the government and the company. This situation, however, is in flux. The government raised the market prices of fuel significantly in July 2008 (see below), which helped to reduce the disincentive to bring valuable oil to China for sale. At the time of writing, it is not clear what the future holds.

Our assessment is that CNPC's continued press overseas is a reflection of fundamental forces at work on the enterprise and not simply the Chinese government's effort to secure oil. In fact, government support for CNPC's overseas push is likely to keep waning, not least because of the political troubles that arise in Sudan and other places. Yet the business interest in moving overseas is strong for CNPC. Overseas operations are more profitable (and more autonomous) than those within Chinese territory. And because as a state enterprise CNPC is willing to accept a lower rate of return on its investments, the company is able to outbid many private firms as it competes around the world (Houser 2008). It regularly outbids India's NOC, for example, for CNPC's pockets are much deeper, its political assets such as development assistance are more diverse, and its technical skills more impressive (see Chapter 17). To be sure, development assistance and other sweeteners from the Chinese state have helped to open some markets, but CNPC's business decisions are now the dominant explanation for the push overseas. Energy security might have started out as a main driver for China's going out policy, but in key places such as Kazakhstan, Venezuela, Iran, and elsewhere where there is continuing strong Beijing involvement, it is certainly not the main reason for why the trend has continued and grown.

3.2.3 Subsidies

Even though the industry is now organized in ways that formally reflect the processes that prevail in much of the international oil industry, in practice CNPC (and other Chinese NOCs) are still largely bound by the practices of a planned economy. Inherent conflicts arise because of the dual roles that CNPC is expected to play – as both a competitive (increasingly global) firm and an obedient state entity. These tensions are evident in the role the firm plays as supplier of tax revenue that the Chinese government uses, in part, to subsidize refiners who are required to sell oil products at prices below their full market cost. It plays a central role in the negotiation over the price

Table 9.2. *Petroleum industry extra profit tax collection rate*

Crude price ($/barrel)	Tax rate (percent)
40~45	20
45~50	25
50~55	30
55~60	35
60 and above	40

Source: CNPC (2007).

of domestic oil products; those prices, in turn, determine the level of subsidy the downstream sector will need each year to remain profitable – a burden that CNPC principally bears through cross-subsidies that are financed through heavy taxation of its upstream arm. The amount of tax that is paid is linked to the price of international oil (see Table 9.2), in part because the cost of subsidizing domestic oil products rises with the price of oil. CNPC contributed RMB 198.5 billion in 2007, or 51 percent of total profits, and 0.01 percent of the national GDP.

These downstream subsidies have been difficult to reform because they are popular with the growing urban middle class as well as rural farmers who operate petroleum-fueled equipment. However, there have been some moves toward fuel price and tax reforms. In June 2008, the government moved to increase retail gasoline and diesel prices by 17–18 percent, the first increase in eight months, following months of spreading fuel rationing as refiners cut production to trim deepening losses incurred by record crude costs. Tan and Wolak's careful analysis shows that Chinese prices are now reliably approaching Western prices and the era of subsidies seems to be ending (Tan and Wolak 2009).

4 Financial indicators of firm performance

There is no question that CNPC is a large company. It ranks fifth on *Petroleum Intelligence Weekly*'s Top 50 Oil Companies list. During the feverish interest in Chinese companies from 2006 to 2008 the price of the small fraction (16 percent) of PetroChina's shares that trade publicly implied that PetroChina was the world's largest oil company (Forbes.com 2007).

Looking to the markets, then, CNPC seems to be a highly successful company. But market valuation is hard to parse because so much of CNPC's management of PetroChina seems designed to manipulate the latter's value. Thus I look beyond the markets and attempt to assess the company's performance in four ways.

First, I compare CNPC and PetroChina to see if the latter's listing actually affects its performance. For many indicators, CNPC and PetroChina appear, on paper, as quite similar companies. The big difference is the number of employees: CNPC employs almost twice as many people as PetroChina and therefore it has a lower revenue per full-time laborer. Also, PetroChina has a much lower level of liquidity compared with CNPC, which reflects that PetroChina borrows vast sums of money from its parent company. In effect, CNPC is the financial capital of the enterprise and PetroChina is an operating company that holds most of the profitable assets. Thus, PetroChina has a much higher asset turnover ratio, indicating that it is almost twice as efficient as CNPC in generating revenue (see Table 9.3). This almost certainly reflects the fact that CNPC still holds on to non-core assets that are not financially efficient, while PetroChina is made up of only the best assets from CNPC.

A second way to assess CNPC's performance is to compare it with a "best in class" benchmark, using ExxonMobil and examining measures of liquidity, solvency, profitability, and financial efficiency (as defined in Dobbins *et al.* 2000). In terms of return on equity, ExxonMobil's return is about double that of PetroChina and almost three times the rate of CNPC (see Table 9.3). These comparisons are dominated by oil operations, although all three of these enterprises are increasingly investing in natural gas.[21]

When we compare CNPC and PetroChina with ExxonMobil, there are some striking differences. Most striking, first, is that ExxonMobil's debt/asset ratio is double that of these Chinese companies, even though ExxonMobil is widely seen in the industry as one of the most debt-free companies (see Table 9.3). I interpret this as CNPC/PetroChina keeping its formal debt at a lower rate because it can rely on government as the ultimate backstop and there are strong incentives to finance projects with revenues rather than debt.[22] CNPC's close ties to government create little need to borrow money

Table 9.3. *Comparison of key ratios for CNPC, PetroChina, and ExxonMobil, 2007[a]*

2007	CNPC ($m)	PetroChina ($m)	Exxon Mobil ($m)
Liquidity			
Current ratio	1.4	1.2	1.5
Working capital	22,995	4,726	27,651
Solvency			
Debt/asset ratio	0.28	0.27	0.50
Equity/asset ratio	0.72	0.73	0.50
Debt/asset ratio	0.38	0.37	1.01
Profitability			
Rate of return on assets	0.12	0.18	0.23
Rate of return on equity	0.17	0.25	0.46
Operating profit margin	0.19	0.15	0.15
Net income	16,218	19,432	40,610
Financial effiency			
Asset turnover ratio	0.63	1.22	1.61
Operating expense ratio	0.68	0.49	0.05
Depreciation expense ratio	0.003	0.052	0.031
Interest expense ratio	0.001	0.001	0.001
Net income from operations ratio	0.19	0.15	0.14
Number of employees	760,000	466,502	80,800
Revenue per full-time laborer	0.2	0.4	4.8

[a] Current ratio = current assets/current liabilities; indicator of short-term debt servicing and/or cash flow capacity, extent to which current assets, when liquidated, will cover obligations; Debt to asset ratio = Total liabilities/total assets, proportion of total assets owned by creditors; Asset turnover ratio = Gross revenue/total assets; how efficiently assets generate revenue; Operating expense ratio = (Total operating expenses – depreciation)/Gross revenue; proportion of total revenues absorbed by operating expenses; Depreciation expense ratio = Depreciation expense/gross revenue; Interest expense ratio = total interest/gross revenue; Revenue per full-time laborer = Gross revenue/number of full-time employees (Dobbins *et al.* 2000).
Source: Compiled from CNPC, PetroChina, ExxonMobil 2007 Annual Reports.

from outside sources and (unlike other impoverished NOCs that are heavily relied upon by government for the purpose of raising funds, e.g., KPC, PDVSA, and Pemex discussed in Chapters 8, 10, and 7, respectively) the central government does not depend on CNPC (or

PetroChina) to serve as a fundraising vehicle because the value generated from their oil production is only a tiny part of the Chinese economy. Despite higher debt, ExxonMobil is still a more profitable business – almost twice as profitable as CNPC. The lower return on equity reflects that CNPC/PetroChina is willing to take on projects that have a lower rate of return (see Table 9.3).

Among the striking facts in Table 9.3 is that CNPC's expenses are extremely high. Despite much lower wage levels in China, CNPC has the highest operating expense ratio (PetroChina follows close behind) of the three enterprises examined here because CNPC is saddled with so many non-core operations. Moreover, ExxonMobil's revenue per full-time laborer is about twenty times higher than CNPC and ten times higher than PetroChina. By a very wide margin, Exxon is a much leaner and more efficient operation than CNPC or PetroChina. (Comparisons with other Western companies would yield similar results.) In general, it seems that while both CNPC and PetroChina are financially viable, solvent companies, they are a lot less efficient than the best independent firms. That outcome reflects that the goal of these NOCs is not principally generation of profit: for CNPC a principal goal is employment; for PetroChina a central goal is to look attractive for equity investors. Perhaps the reality of this has set in for some investors as the valuation of CNPC and PetroChina has fallen in the past year.

A third way to assess CNPC's performance is over time – to see if reforms have plausibly changed investment and behavior that could alter performance. For PetroChina and CNPC, absolute income and assets have grown since the first available data came out in 1998 and 2001, respectively. Much more interesting, however, are the changes in financial efficiency over time. The financial efficiency of PetroChina has improved slightly over the last decade, but the financial efficiency of CNPC has not changed much. For example, the operating expense ratio (operating expenses/net sales) for CNPC decreased slightly after 2001 and then actually increased by 2007. This ratio shows that the amount of money spent in operating expenses in relationship with the volume of sales has not improved. This is often seen as an indicator of management efficiency because management usually has greater control over operating expenses than over revenue. PetroChina also has always maintained a much higher operating profit margin than CNPC. This points to the possibility that CNPC's role as a major employer and vessel of the state has not changed much, while PetroChina is increasingly responding to the incentive to become more efficient in the eyes of investors. Notably, revenue per laborer at PetroChina has risen nearly tenfold over the last seven years; some of that improvement probably reflects better performance but most is due to increasingly effective efforts to shed excess workforce (comparable data is not available for CNPC). Much of that shedding appears to have been to CNPC and thus efforts within CNPC to become more efficient have been offset by the need to absorb unwanted elements cast off by PetroChina.

A fourth way to assess performance is to look beyond financial indicators at how the company manages long-term investments. Here I focus on the company's technological capabilities including its investment in human capital and R&D.

Sorting through the list of CNPC's past technological achievements, it is apparent that this firm's expertise lies in working with mature fields as well as building understanding of complex geological formations found in China. Figure 9.6 shows a subset of principal innovations compiled from CNPC's annual reports over five years (2003–2007). Within exploration and production, it is clear that CNPC has invested much time in understanding lithologic and carbonate reservoirs. According to the CNPC Sichuan Petroleum Geophysical Prospecting Company, a subsidiary of CNPC, most of the remaining reservoirs in China are likely to be of this complex geology (CNPC 2005). It has also invested heavily in polymer and chemical flooding as a means of enhanced oil recovery (EOR). And it is investing in techniques to exploit fields with low permeability reservoirs as well as heavy oils. Historically, most of CNPC's investment has been onshore, but it is now concentrating some attention on offshore options. Specifically, the company plans to build two semi-submersible drilling platforms by 2015 and another two by 2020 in the South China Sea (Lei 2008). Among its many other areas of innovation, CNPC is heavily involved in developing high-strength steel materials for oil and gas pipelines – which reflects that PetroChina operates and manages all major pipelines in China. In general, CNPC's technology strategy since 2003 is aimed at developing: 1) technologies that allow CNPC to better adapt to the increasingly difficult geology it must tap, and 2) technologies that allow CNPC to expand beyond its core competency (onshore E&P) into other activities such as refining and offshore operations.

Area of Innovation	2003	2004	2005	2006	2007
Exploration	Lithologic resevoir exploration leading to new reserves; Improvement of seismic data in mountainous and desert areas	Lithologic resevoir exploration leading to new reserves; Geo-East V1.0 integrated seismic data processing and interpretation software	Lithologic resevoir exploration leading to new reserves	Carbonate reservoir exploration	Lithologic resevoir exploration leading to new reserves
Development	Polymer flooding (EOR)	Improved water flooding for high water cut oilfields; Multi well combined thermal recovery techniques for heavy oil wells and steam flooding; Progression development of techniques for extremely low permeable reservoirs; Super high pressure gas producing pipe strings	Polymer flooding and alkai-suractant-polymer (ASP) flooding; ASP-foam flooding; Development of high-pressure condensate fields; Temperature-controlled viscosity acidizing (TCA)	Steam assisted gravity drainage (SAGD)	Integration of development techniques
Drilling	Increase of drilling rate by 50%; Underbalance drilling for high-yield gas flows	Increased drilling rate; Developed under-balanced equipment and mating technology	Increase in drilling speed; 3000 HP rig for ultra-deep wells (9000m+)	Massive application of horizontal drilling; Gas drilling; China geosteering drilling system (CGDS-1)	12000 m drilling rig and matching top drive system
Logging	Array induction image logging techniques	Development of EILog100 w/ capability of open hold well logging and perforation, coring operation; New remote metering system for domestic unitized logging equipment; developed logging data processing and interpretation integrated software LEAD 1.0			Industrial application of prestack seismic reservoir description
Surface Engineering	Rapid synchronous root pass welding (pipes); Pollution treatment of drilling fluid	Product development of X80 high strength steel pipes	Combined oil-gas pipeline system; X80 high-tensile pipeline steel	High-resolution smart magnetic flux leakage (MFL) detector for pipelines	X80 spiral welded steel pipes
Refining and chemical engineering	Two riser catalytic cracking, improve product recovery rate by 1.6%; FCC gasoline alken-reduction series catalyst; Flue gas turbine expander (33,000 kw)	Expansion of use of two riser catalytic cracking; Ionic liquid catalyzer alkylation technique; ABS production technology	LCC-1 high production propylene catalyst and LCC-A aids, LCC-2 catalyst	LIP-100 and LIP-200 catalysts	

Figure 9.6 Technology development at CNPC, 2003–2007.
Source: CNPC Annual Reports 2003–2007; Guo (2006).

According to PetroChina's 2008 interim annual report, the company planned to spend RMB 1,700 million ($243 million) for research and development in 2008 and spent RMB 1,613 million ($230 million) in 2007. This investment, about 1.2 percent of net profit from 2007, is comparable with other IOCs.[23] (BP, for example, is estimated to have spent 1.3 percent of net profit on capital expenditures related to research and development in 2007 (BP 2007).)

CNPC invests in new technologies both through its subsidiaries and through centralized research programs. The highly compartmentalized nature of CNPC's subsidiaries and tight capital controls issued at the central level by CNPC have discouraged subsidiaries from making large technology purchases from outside firms such as field services companies. Thus, CNPC's subsidiaries self-organize to invest heavily in technologies that allow them to be self-reliant. At times, however, CNPC designates a subsidiary to develop a certain technology that would be made more widely available in the company. And for some special projects CNPC creates "heavyweight teams" that operate under special budgetary rules and appear to be an important engine of innovation. These teams are still initiated by subsidiaries, although CNPC headquarters may supervise them. The general manager of the subsidiary is the head of such a team, made up of the best engineers of the organization. The decisions made within this team can be fast-tracked and do not need to follow normal procedures of approval. For example, regular R&D projects need the approval of top management from CNPC headquarters before important decisions can be made, but this step can be bypassed in these cases.

Most engineers within CNPC are assigned to work in one oil field their entire careers. As a result, certain types of geologies are very well understood by CNPC and knowledge of these fields is institutionalized and well documented. It is easy, then, to build upon years of data and experience to develop new ways of developing the same field or other fields of similar geology. This mode of organization probably explains why CNPC is relatively good at managing its aging fields within an existing technological paradigm but it appears to be relatively poor at sharing resources between subsidiaries to foster further breakthrough innovations. For example, in Figure 9.6, we see that almost all of the technologies that have been developed by CNPC from 2003 onward are refinements of existing technologies with a focus on developing existing fields (i.e., development and refining technologies).

5 Conclusion

The story of CNPC reflects China's complex transition from a planned to a more market-oriented economy. CNPC is the largest state enterprise in a sector that China's leaders have long considered as strategically vital to the national well-being. Thus CNPC has been the locus of some reforms – notably the reshuffling of the oil industry in the late 1990s to create a semi-competitive duopoly of CNPC and Sinopec – yet those reforms have never been so dramatic that they might fundamentally alter the mode of operation of the industry. Central leaders perceived reforms in the 1980s that had been intended to boost performance as going awry when regional production units (provincial administrative bureaus, or PABs) started behaving autonomously. Decentralization had been the goal, but when the central government saw rapid changes and chaos from its policies it reasserted control. CNPC reflects an incomplete transition from a planned economy to a market economy. While it is free to emulate Western companies in its internal operations such as formal budget accounting and investment in R&D, CNPC like other state-owned pillar industries is also obligated to work within the framework of a planned economy without liberalized energy prices and markets.

My assessment is that both CNPC and PetroChina are financially viable institutions yet are still highly inefficient relative to the best of the IOCs. While CNPC has technical expertise in particular types of geologies, it is still not able to prosper in many settings that are outside its traditional areas of competence due to compartmentalization of the company and expertise. The company seems to be aware of this problem and is investing – on par with major Western companies – in technology development to become more versatile in the future. However, as evident in many other NOCs, the company still has not built the capacity to meld its internal technical capabilities with the offerings from external firms.

Whether CNPC can become a truly competitive oil company – with operations on the world market – has much to do with the way it is treated by the Chinese state. If the Chinese government continues to support the trend of allowing autonomy and increasing transparency and a role for market forces in the sector, then CNPC is likely to take advantage of new opportunities.

Notes

1 Some CNPC executives will claim that the company is in no way obliged
  to meet the demands of the government and that it is a fully privatized
  entity. During the course of research for this chapter, however, I have
  discovered much more evidence to the contrary.
2 The term "company" is misleading. In actuality, this was a government-
  run organization.
3 Sinopec underwent similar changes. It formed Sinopec Group and within
  that group the China Petroleum & Chemical Corporation (which adopted
  the name "Sinopec") were formed. Sinopec was listed with Sinopec's
  core assets.
4 At this point, CNPC was a wholly state-owned oil company that had
  status as a legal person and was under the direct control of the State
  Council, which is the highest organ of state power in the PRC and is the
  chief administrative authority. The premier chairs this organization and
  is supported by vice-premiers, state councilors, the auditor-general, and
  the secretary general. Heads of each ministry, commission, state administration, bureau, office, and state academic research institution are also
  participants in this body.
5 These indicators included enterprise profit and tax ratio of the industry,
  oil and gas unit cost change ratio (between the beginning and the end of
  the year), net profit/asset ratio, state assets value increase ratio, reserve
  and production ratio, labor productivity, capital expenditure for every
  billion tonnes of recoverable reserves, capital investment of production
  capacity for every million tonnes, debt/asset ratio, and social contribution ratio.
6 These reforms reversed the trend of increasing autonomy of regional
  enterprises. Decentralization could have been part of the solution to
  achieving economic success, but the government (and CNPC) failed
  to simultaneously institute incentives that would guide the enterprises
  toward a common goal of improving economic performance. When "legal
  person" status was revoked, subordinate firms were no longer allowed
  to make investment decisions without the approval of CNPC; nor were
  these local enterprises allowed to sell shares without CNPC approval;
  none was allowed to operate overseas. CNPC also asserted control in
  product pricing, marketing, and procurement. (These new responsibilities created huge demands for information across the dispersed CNPC
  enterprise; the company built an information technology system to help
  it better monitor and manage these individual firms.)
7 The reshuffling of the oil industry required CNPC to transfer twelve
  upstream enterprises engaged in E&P to Sinopec, and Sinopec transferred

nineteen refining units to CNPC. The swap in assets improved Sinopec's supply security while allowing CNPC to have direct access to the market and to build a brand around refined oil products. Integration also led CNPC and Sinopec to share the benefits from government R&D investments in upstream and downstream technologies. Separation and reintegration around two enterprises gave each the freedom to determine its own supply and transportation system for optimizing performance within the enterprise rather than relying on government plans to achieve that goal. This freedom fostered competition between CNPC and Sinopec by putting the two on more equal footing.

8 The core and mostly profitable assets were grouped together and listed in the New York and Hong Kong stock exchanges under a corporation called PetroChina. The goal of the IPO was to raise funds for future business development and also to improve management skills within the corporation by forcing the company to adhere to strict international guidelines and regulations, such as those that govern accounting and reporting of financial and performance data. The government realized that this would be a necessary step to take in order to compete with multinational companies. This was also an essential part of the strategy to recentralize the petroleum industry because external accountability would strengthen the hand of managers at PetroChina. Nonetheless, it was a difficult transition for some of the regional enterprises because previously autonomous organizations now became production units with little control over management, investment, or production targets. The non-core assets had an even more difficult time after the separation because many were already on the brink of bankruptcy before the separation – sustained only by cross-subsidy from the profitable oil production enterprises. Subsidies were provided for these companies for three years, until 2002, after which they were exposed to market competition.

9 One of the most striking ways in which this organizational pattern manifests is through looking at how new products and technologies are developed within the firm (Guo 2006), where local branches and subsidiaries of the company often lead the way in many technical innovations. This will be explored in detail in a later section.

10 At the same time, much of the country's economic growth arose from hybrid companies that were partially private and partially state-owned – often by local governments. Such companies, which my colleagues have also referred to as "dual firms" because they combine both political and commercial elements, have been a major feature of the Chinese economic landscape (Victor and Heller 2007). Classic state enterprises of all sizes lagged behind these dual firms.

11 We focus in this article on the 1998 reforms, but the seeds for stronger corporate control and management were sown in the early 1990s as part of a broader push for economic reform. In 1993, two landmark policy decisions set a foundation for the "modern enterprise system" in China. First, the Central Committee passed its "Decision on Certain Questions in Establishing a Socialist Market Economy Structure," which called for the formation of large enterprises across sectors and regions. This legislation was a part of a recentralization movement that aimed at shifting decision-making power from local enterprises back in the hands of a central authority. (Decentralization had been the watchword in many industries, not just oil, and the effects were widely seen by the central government as not encouraging – especially in heavy industries with large network interdependencies between units, such as electric power and integrated production of oil products.) Second was the new "Company Law," discussed in the main text.

12 CBRC governs all banking institutions in China and works closely with SDRC (State Development and Planning Commission) to determine the total number of shares that should be issued for SOEs.

13 www.sasac.gov.cn/n2963340/n2963393/2965120.html.

14 PetroChina Board of Directors 2008, www.petrochina.com.cn/Ptr/About_PetroChina/Executive_Profiles/.

15 The special role of the party helps explain why leadership in CNPC differs from that of IOCs and even many other NOCs. Such positions seem to be stepping stones to gaining a position in the highest authority within the Communist Party – the Central Committee. The Central Committee has 300 members and normally appoints the Politboro of the Communist Part of China, the primary decision-making body in China. This would be the equivalent of using board positions at Exxon as a pathway to the US Senate or presidency. Looking at Figure 9.5, we can see that five former and current members of the top leadership in CNPC, or 25 percent of all the people who have served in such a position, are affiliated with the Central Committee. CNPC leadership is a governmental position, first and foremost, rather than one that principally seeks industry expertise and shareholder stewardship.

16 Approval of large projects (exploration and development of oil fields that produce above 2 million tons annually, gas fields that exceed 3 billion cubic meters per year, and construction of refineries with an annual capacity larger than 5 million tons) requires direct decisions by the State Council and NDRC (Yuan 2007).

17 According to "Provisions on the Examination and Approval of Investment to Run Enterprises Abroad," the approval of new projects overseas (including establishment of a new enterprise, equity purchases,

mergers and acquisitions, etc.) is obtained from the Ministry of Commerce and officiated by a certificate of approval for overseas investment. In 2004, NDRC announced the "Verification and Approval of Overseas Investment Projects Tentative Administrative Procedures" that stated that exploration investments over $30 million must be directly approved by NDRC. For exploration investments above $200 million and for purchases above $50 million, both the NDRC and the State Council must submit their approval (Yuan 2007).

18 See Downs (2004); Lieberthal and Herberg (2006); Xu (2007) and S. Lewis (2007).

19 The latest estimates have been as high as 20 percent (Mikkal Herberg, private communication).

20 Yan, K. F. Interview with author, April 2007.

21 Over 90 percent of CNPC's revenue comes from exploration, refining, and retail activities. Those same core assets are concentrated within PetroChina. Historically nearly all of these revenues have come from petroleum, but the natural gas segment is now growing the most rapidly at 26 percent per year as the Chinese government is actively promoting the use of natural gas by building infrastructure, such as the West-East pipeline that aims to bring in supplies from western China, Russia, and Kazakhstan to energy demand centers on the eastern coast. Oil production from E&P petroleum is growing much more slowly (annual rate of 6.8 percent) as the domestic production output from very mature oil fields stagnates.

22 Outside of state banks – for which formal accounting of true debt levels is still poor – there are few mechanisms for debt financing of large oil projects inside China. In some countries the government has transformed the NOC for purposes of raising debt on commercial markets – notably Mexico's Pemex (see Chapter 7) – but PetroChina's creation was not inspired with this purpose but rather for the purpose of encouraging equity investment in China's oil sector.

23 While numbers are not available for all of CNPC, the level of funding going to R&D is not likely to change since PetroChina accounts for most (if not all) of the profit.

10 Petróleos de Venezuela, S.A. (PDVSA): from independence to subservience

DAVID R. HULTS

1 Introduction

Venezuela's national oil company (NOC), Petróleos de Venezuela, S.A. (PDVSA), has undergone the most significant recent transformation of the NOCs in this volume. Between its 1976 creation via nationalization and the early 2000s, PDVSA was one of the most capable, forward-thinking, and autonomous NOCs. During 2002 and 2003, however, it launched a series of politically disastrous strikes against President Hugo Chávez. After surviving the strikes, Chávez purged the company in 2003 of (real and perceived) dissidents, converting PDVSA from a commercially oriented firm to one that is less proficient but much more attentive to state objectives. The current version of PDVSA functions simultaneously as an operating company, development agency, political tool, and government cash cow.

Yet in some respects the PDVSA of today remains similar to its pre-Chávez incarnation. PDVSA has maintained its status as one of the world's fifty largest companies and two or three largest NOCs (*Petroleum Intelligence Weekly* 1986–2009). Since the 1980s, the company has held extensive international interests, including major US gasoline chain CITGO. And since the 1990s it has been one of a handful of NOCs to partner with international oil companies (IOCs) in domestic upstream operations (though not without acrimony).

This chapter explains PDVSA's continuity and change. I focus on how the key variables considered in this book – the nature of oil resources, state institutional capacity, and state goals – apply to Venezuela and have affected the relationship between company and state. I then explore how that relationship has shaped PDVSA's performance and strategy.[1]

I advance six main arguments in this chapter.

First, changes in the relationship between the Venezuelan state and PDVSA largely explain why PDVSA's performance has deteriorated and its strategy has shifted since Chávez's 2003 takeover of the company. Unlike many nationalization experiences, Venezuela minimized oil sector disruption by preserving the private sector orientation of the newly formed NOC. Venezuelan politicians maintained a mostly hands-off approach to PDVSA through the late 1990s. Because of its autonomy and private sector heritage, PDVSA became a highly efficient enterprise that insulated itself from the state. When the *Petroleum Economist* conducted three expert polls in the 1990s, each one rated PDVSA as both the best-managed and best financially managed NOC (*Petroleum Economist* 1993, 1995, 1999).[2] Following the 2003 company overhaul, the Venezuelan government became more deeply interventionist. The Chávez administration fired a net 30–40 percent of PDVSA's workforce in the immediate aftermath of its antigovernment strikes (derived from Mares and Altamirano 2007). The government has also levied irregular and heavy financial obligations that annually consume up to 40–50 percent of PDVSA's revenues (roughly \$35–45 billion/year).[3] And it has imposed an ever-changing slate of non-core domestic and foreign policy goals on the company. Partly as a consequence, PDVSA's performance has weakened; current production is likely more than 25 percent off pre-strike levels, despite the Chávez administration's claims otherwise. And PDVSA's strategy has switched from autonomy seeking to accommodation of the many government demands.

Second, while the Chávez administration has been the immediate cause of the changes between PDVSA and state, Chávez's rise to power occurred in the context of broader structural factors. By the late 1990s, PDVSA had become controversial because it grew in influence at a time when the Venezuelan economy declined (partly as a result of an extended period of low oil prices). Many Venezuelans perceived that PDVSA had become, by virtue of its autonomy and sway over government policy, a state within a state. Chávez capitalized on those perceptions in a successful populist campaign to win the 1998 presidential election. Once in power, the Chávez administration slowly but deliberately took steps to assert greater authority over the oil sector, particularly as oil prices rose in the early 2000s. These steps, which included the dismissal of three PDVSA presidents in three years, inspired PDVSA's management to initiate its 2002–2003 antigovernment strikes – a profound misjudgment rooted in management's history of independence and its assumption that the government would back down. The failure of those strikes then set the stage for Chávez's decisive reordering of the company in 2003.

Third, Venezuela's endowment of abundant, heavy and extra-heavy oil[4] has had a formative impact on PDVSA. Heavy and extra-heavy oil are relatively costly, require specialized technologies to produce and upgrade, and pose some environmental threats. PDVSA became one of the world's most vertically integrated NOCs in the 1980s in part to ensure that its heavy and extra-heavy oil could reach downstream markets. Venezuelan oil has become even heavier over time: Today, nearly 60 percent of Venezuelan proven reserves are extra-heavy and another 15–20 percent are heavy (PDVSA 2008). This geological reality is a reason Chávez has maintained PDVSA's operational structure despite making wide-ranging changes to the company in other respects.

Fourth, personal ties substantially color the relationship between PDVSA and the Venezuelan state; institutional arrangements play by contrast a minor role. Before Chávez, PDVSA preserved its autonomy by cultivating links with the political leadership and by capturing the country's weak regulatory institutions and government ministries. (Venezuela has remained among the bottom 50 percent of countries for all six World Bank governance indicators since compilation began in 1995 (Kaufmann *et al*. 1999–2009).) Since Chávez took command of PDVSA in 2003, bureaucrats remain on the sidelines; Chávez relies mostly on trusted allies to manage the company. Institutions have, in fact, become even more ineffective than before.

Fifth, in accord with the arguments above, PDVSA largely conforms to this volume's research design. The three independent variables in the research design – state goals, state capacity, and nature of resources – explain much of the relationship between PDVSA and the Venezuelan state. Shifts in Chávez administration goals for the oil sector caused dramatic changes in the state–PDVSA relationship, but the continuity in Venezuela's heavy oil resources and weak state institutions have ensured that some aspects of that relationship remain intact. This relationship, in turn, accounts for much of PDVSA's performance and strategy. As I discuss below, other factors not explicitly considered in our research design – particularly oil prices – also played critical background roles. Nevertheless, I argue that the research design provides a useful framework for understanding PDVSA.

Sixth and lastly, both doomsayers and stalwart defenders of PDVSA in the Chávez era make a mistake in taking Chávez's pronouncements at face value. Chávez has announced far-reaching plans for PDVSA to bankroll new initiatives, but those imagined plans are often not carried out. Rather, PDVSA and the government usually negotiate practical implementation of the Chávez administration's grand announcements to better reflect commercial realities. There is thus often a gap between pronouncement and policy. PDVSA's new autonomy lies, to some degree, in how it creates and exploits that gap – though the distinctions between government and company strategy are sometimes difficult to parse.

This chapter is structured as follows. Section 2 chronicles the development of the Venezuelan oil sector, from its beginnings in the 1910s through today. Over the course of several decades, foreign oil companies established an entrenched organizational structure and esprit de corps that carried over to PDVSA. Section 3 analyzes several factors affecting the state–PDVSA relationship over time: nature of resources, state capacity, and state goals. In Section 4, I discuss how PDVSA's links to the state have affected the company's strategy and performance. Pre-Chávez governments took a mostly hands-off approach toward PDVSA, and that approach led to high company performance and an autonomy-seeking strategy. Since the 2002–2003 strikes, PDVSA's performance has waned and its strategy has shifted toward managing state demands. Section 5 concludes.

A methodological note before proceeding: After Chávez remade the company in 2003, PDVSA and the Venezuelan government released oil sector data selectively and somewhat haphazardly. More recently, PDVSA has made more information available. Nevertheless, questions abound about the accuracy of PDVSA data and scholarship seeking to debunk that data (Boué 2009). Keeping these questions in mind, I refer to established third-party sources, like BP or *Petroleum Intelligence Weekly*, where available. I also rely in part on PDVSA's own financial reports, though I draw findings based on those reports cautiously.

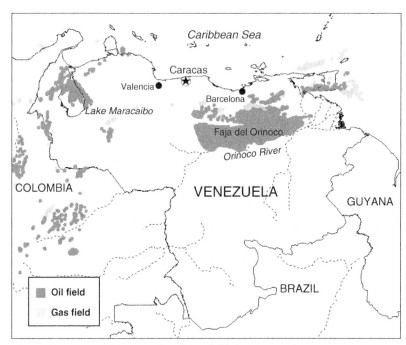

Figure 10.1 Map of major oil and gas fields in Venezuela.
Source for oil and gas field data: Wood Mackenzie (2009b).

2 Historical background on the Venezuelan oil sector

2.1 The foundations of the Venezuelan oil sector (1910–1958)

IOCs turned Venezuela into an early and important oil producer. Commercial development began in 1914, when foreign-owned
Caribbean Petroleum (later acquired by Shell) started producing from
the Mene Grande fields. Major discoveries followed in fields at Las
Cruces (1916) and especially at La Rosa (1922). The Venezuelan
government, controlled by powerful military general Juan Vicente
Gómez, allocated long-term oil concessions to cronies who then resold
them to IOCs. Because of the pro-development taxation framework
in place at the time of concession allocation, the IOCs paid extremely
low royalty (often 3 percent) and subsurface tax rates (Manzano
and Monaldi 2010).[5] The IOCs enjoyed tremendous success under
these conditions and by the late 1920s a sophisticated Venezuelan oil

industry was under way. Venezuela became the world's leading oil exporter and second-largest oil producer (behind the United States). (Around this time, Venezuelan intellectual Arturo Úslar Pietri urged the country to *sembrar el petróleo* – "sow the oil" – by investing oil rents in productive economic sectors. This saying still resonates in Venezuela today.[6])

These initial IOC concessions proved politically unsustainable. Particularly after Vicente Gomez's death in 1935, Venezuela's government began pressing for changes in taxes and concession terms. After protracted negotiations between the government and IOCs, Venezuela set landmark laws in 1943 and 1948 creating a roughly "fifty-fifty" profit split.[7] (Saudi Arabia and Iran later followed Venezuela's lead.) The Venezuelan government and IOCs reached forty-year concession agreements under this taxation framework, and Venezuelan-IOC relations would remain steady for the next fifteen years.

The combination of legal stability, long-term investment horizons, and the country's copious oil resources substantially benefited Venezuela. From 1944 through 1958, Venezuelan oil production increased at an annual rate of 19.5 percent and its capital stock grew by 14.3 percent annually (Monaldi 2001, 2004). Oil sector wealth spilled over to the broader Venezuelan economy. By some estimates, Venezuela had by 1960 become the wealthiest country in Latin America.[8]

2.2 Creeping nationalization (1958–1976)

Although Venezuela prospered under the 1940s hydrocarbon framework, fissures later emerged. Venezuelan politicians challenged military government laws, including the 1940s hydrocarbons legislation, as the country transitioned to (elite-based) democratic rule. Because Venezuela had set low income tax rates for IOCs, it received a decreasing share of revenues as oil prices rose or as costs declined; the government share fell from around 50 percent in 1943 to 40.4 percent by the late 1950s (Manzano and Monaldi 2010). Ironically, just as Venezuela's "fifty-fifty" split arrangement became a model in the Middle East, it no longer accurately described actual revenue sharing in Venezuela.

Starting in the late 1950s, successive Venezuelan governments used a hodgepodge of tools to increase state involvement and capitalize on sunk IOC investments.[9] One front was fiscal: Venezuela's military-civilian regime raised taxes in 1958, shattering the long-established "fifty-fifty" profit split.[10] The democratically elected administrations of Rómulo Betancourt (1959–1964), Raúl Leoni (1964–1969), and Rafael Caldera (1969–1974) later followed suit. (See Table 10.1 for a list of presidential administrations.) Another tack was contractual: in 1963, the government chose not to renew the forty-year concessions awarded twenty years previously, shortening IOC investment plans. Organizational changes also occurred. Through a 1958 law and fee system for foreign workers, Venezuelan governments established local employment preferences for private oil companies (Randall 1987).[11] By the time of nationalization, nearly all Venezuela's oil sector employees, including most top managers and engineers, were Venezuelan. And the Venezuelan government became a pioneer in the world oil cartel: Betancourt's oil minister, Juan Pablo Pérez Alfonzo, and his Saudi counterpart spearheaded OPEC's formation in 1960. (Interestingly, Pérez Alfonzo also referred to oil as *el excremento del diablo* – "the devil's excrement" – and predicted that it eventually would ruin the country.[12]) Venezuela even experimented with the idea of building an NOC from the ground up fifteen years before establishing PDVSA. In 1960, the Betancourt administration founded the Corporación Venezolana del Petróleo (CVP) to learn about the oil industry and catalyze Venezuelan-run oil operations. CVP foundered, however, and PDVSA later absorbed CVP upon nationalization (Mares and Altamirano 2007).

By the 1970s, Venezuelan oil sector interventions had reached a crescendo. A decade-long period of tax and contract changes, combined with the emergence of low-cost alternatives from the Middle East, had hollowed out private sector investment in the sector (Monaldi 2001). To compensate for the private sector retreat, Venezuela – emboldened by rising oil prices and a global tide of resource nationalism – looked to the state. The congress passed a 1970 law mandating reversion of oil sector concessions upon expiration, government approval of IOC changes to operations, prohibitions on movement of assets, and an IOC requirement to post a bond or guarantee. The Caldera administration initially viewed this legislation as overreaching but later, sensing public sentiment, supported it (Matsuda 1997). In this environment, nationalization of the oil sector became the obvious next step.

Table 10.1. *Venezuelan presidents, 1959–present*

Term	President
1959–1964	Rómulo Betancourt
1964–1969	Raúl Leoni
1969–1974	Rafael Caldera
1974–1979	Carlos Andrés Pérez
1979–1984	Luis Herrera Campins
1984–1989	Jaime Lusinchi
1989–1993	Carlos Andrés Pérez (second term)
1993–1993	Octavio Lepage[a]
1993–1994	Ramón José Velásquez[b]
1994–1999	Rafael Caldera (second term)
1999–present	Hugo Chávez

[a] Lepage became Venezuela's interim president after the congress removed Carlos Andrés Pérez from office because of corruption charges.
[b] Velásquez replaced Lepage as interim president until Caldera won elections and entered office in 1994.

Yet PDVSA formed mostly from a peaceful transfer of power rather than from the fires of resource nationalism. Cognizant of Mexico's tumultuous nationalization of Pemex and Venezuela's own experiences creating CVP and nationalizing the iron ore industry,[13] the first Carlos Andrés Pérez administration (1974–1979) structured nationalization to dampen oil sector politicization and smooth large-scale change. (Venezuela's strategy parallels that of Saudi Arabia. See Chapter 5.) To retake policymaking control from the congress, the government formed a presidential commission on nationalization in 1974. Removed from congressional politicization, the commission carried out technical discussions and brokered compromises among different interest groups, easing the path to agreement (Matsuda 1997). Venezuelan oil industry employees – long opposed to nationalization until that outcome was unavoidable – voiced additional concerns through their lobby group, AGROPET (the "*Agrupación de Orientación Petrolera*," or oil association). The Venezuelan government incorporated many of AGROPET's concerns in its final legislation (Coronel 1983). Lastly, the Venezuelan government agreed to substantially compensate private companies for the value of their expropriated assets, paying the equivalent of $1.02 billion over time (Manzano and Monaldi 2010). (PDVSA later would enter into lucrative oil distribution and technical assistance contracts with private companies that offered owners of the nationalized assets still more compensation (Manzano and Monaldi 2010)).[14] With these steps in place, the government introduced, and the congress later passed, a 1975 bill nationalizing the Venezuelan oil sector and providing the nationalized company with fresh state capital. PDVSA subsequently formed as a 100 percent state-owned company on January 1, 1976.

2.3 A private business under government control (1976–1982)

Because of Venezuela's nationalization strategy, the newly minted PDVSA built heavily upon its private sector heritage.[15] Most former Venezuelan IOC employees immediately joined PDVSA, holding virtually the same roles and responsibilities as before – a process aided by the previous "Venezuelization" of the oil sector workforce.[16] Through at least the mid 1980s, some PDVSA managers followed the private sector tradition of holding meetings and writing reports in English (Randall 1987). Moreover, PDVSA adopted a "federal model" in which its formerly private-owned affiliates retained control over operational decisions (the PDVSA holding company, by contrast, at first had authority only over strategic and financial planning). Two of the most important affiliates, Maraven and Lagoven, behaved much like their private sector predecessors, Shell de Venezuela (Shell) and Creole (Exxon), respectively.[17] Befitting their corporate pedigree, Maraven excelled in marketing activities, like Shell; and Lagoven's specialty was exploration and development, the same as Exxon (PESD Interviews). The similarities between PDVSA operating companies and their predecessors even extended to corporate color schemes. Maraven used Shell's yellow and red ensemble, whereas Lagoven chose Exxon's red and blue combination. Nationalization critics would later call PDVSA a "Trojan horse" because of its heavy private sector legacy (D'Leon 2006).[18]

Nationalization also led to few immediate changes in corporate structure. PDVSA initially converted twenty-two private sector concessionaries into thirteen state-run operator subsidiaries; CVP, Venezuela's first failed experiment in state-run oil, became operator subsidiary number 14 (Boué 1993). Because the operator subsidiaries had their own departments of marketing, accounting, etc., they suffered from substantial overlap and duplication. Yet they were also well positioned to compete with one another because they had done so prior to nationalization.

As time passed, PDVSA implemented broader-scale reforms that balanced the benefits of increased economies of scale and intra-firm competition. Between 1976 and 1978, PDVSA cut the number of major operator subsidiaries from fourteen to Maraven, Lagoven, Corpoven, and Meneven.[19] (Meneven became part of Corpoven in 1986.) Even as consolidation occurred, PDVSA took care to promote competition among its operating subsidiaries. Upon merging Corpoven and Meneven, PDVSA transferred part of the refining and production activities to Maraven and the exploratory acreage to Lagoven (Boué 1993). The operator subsidiaries also had the power to negotiate with individual clients over services, delivery, and time (price competition was discouraged, however) (Baena 1999b).

Due in part to these measures, both PDVSA and the Venezuelan state thrived during the late 1970s. Nominal PDVSA investment in exploration and production grew by more than 500 percent and 600 percent, respectively, between 1976 and 1981 (derived from PDVSA various years). Buoyed by PDVSA's growth and an oil price boom, Venezuela became known as "Saudi Venezuela." Wealth conferred many privileges. The country was at that time a leading importer of whisky (and remained among the world's top ten in 2007) (Enright *et al.* 1996; Scotch Whisky Association 2007).

2.4 PDVSA goes abroad (1982–1989)

Beginning in the 1980s, PDVSA launched an internationalization strategy to secure downstream markets for its production and place assets outside direct reach of the state.[20] Brought on by its heavy oil endowment, oil price declines, OPEC domestic production quotas, and periodic government interference, PDVSA's internationalization was the most aggressive of any NOC in the world. KPC carried out a less ambitious version of this same strategy. (See Chapter 8.)[21] Initially, PDVSA entered into joint venture interests for refineries in overseas markets. PDVSA and German counterpart Veba Oel inked the first such contract in 1982.[22] After a three-year pause, PDVSA acquired further refinery interests in Belgium (1),[23] Curaçao (1),[24] Sweden (4),[25] the United Kingdom (2),[26] and the United States (7, including St. Croix).[27] (Later deals reduced this number.) PDVSA also targeted downstream consumers. In 1986, PDVSA purchased – and probably overpaid for[28] – a 50 percent stake in CITGO, which provided a major distribution channel for gasoline products to consumers in the United States.[29] PDVSA acquired CITGO's remaining 50 percent share in 1990. After taking full ownership of CITGO, PDVSA became one of the first developing-country companies to run a major US oil business and among the first foreign companies anywhere to obtain an important piece of the US energy industry (Baena 1999b).

However, the rapid pace of internationalization sowed seeds of conflict between PDVSA and the Venezuelan state. Congress blasted PDVSA for not seeking its approval for overseas acquisitions, especially the 1982 Veba Oel contract[30] and 1990 CITGO purchase. Although these criticisms did not stop – and in fact likely propelled – PDVSA's internationalization, they tapped into an undercurrent of discontent. Academics would later condemn internationalization for its high costs and for depriving Venezuela of tax revenues (Boué 2002; Mommer 2002). This argument would become gospel during the Chávez administration, in which several of those academics have served. (As detailed below, Chávez would nevertheless leave much of the internationalization legacy intact.)[31]

While internationalization was under way, another major development occurred: PDVSA became one of the world's most technologically advanced NOCs. The company created a top-flight research center known as INTEVEP. Much of its early work focused on devising marketable products from Venezuela's extra-heavy oil in the Orinoco Belt. By the mid to late 1980s, INTEVEP research led to "Orimulsion," a patented underboiler fuel substitute made from the Orinoco's extra-heavy oil (Economides *et al.* 2007). Orimulsion subsequently became one of the company's first revenue sources from that region.

While PDVSA continued growing during the 1980s, the Venezuelan economy faltered. Because of low oil prices and the Latin American debt crisis, Venezuelan oil revenues plunged, its access to capital markets dried up, and public spending declined (Baena 1999b; Paris 2006). As a result, Venezuela and its regional counterparts became mired in a deep economic recession known region-wide as the "lost decade." Venezuela's economy shrank 2.6 percent annually per capita during the 1980s, the worst performance in at least sixty years (Hausmann 2003). The disconnect between strong company performance and fading national welfare would generate further conflicts for the company down the road.

2.5 Foreign investors move in (1990–1999)

By the 1990s, PDVSA's strategy shifted emphasis toward Venezuelan upstream operations. Because oil prices remained low, PDVSA had limited monies available for reinvestment. To fill the investment shortfall, increase access to new technologies, and cultivate marketing relationships, PDVSA solicited outside investor participation in a strategy known as *la apertura petrolera* (oil sector opening).[32] Rolled out in three rounds during 1991, 1992, and 1997, the *apertura* gave private companies majority equity interests[33] in development projects with attractive fiscal terms and strict procedural protections.[34] The *apertura* centered on three elements: 1) expanding investment in extra-heavy oil from the Orinoco Belt; 2) developing the country's older, low-producing fields; and, least importantly, 3) increasing production in other high-risk areas through risk exploration and profit-sharing agreements.

The first element – aimed at encouraging investment in the Orinoco Belt, which was Venezuela's largest oil resource yet barely tapped – involved heavy-crude upgrading association agreements (AAs) between PDVSA and outside oil companies. The thirty- to thirty-five-year AAs, four in all (often with multiple companies holding interests), set low royalty (1 percent) and tax (34 percent of income) rates. The combined marginal rates were substantially more advantageous than the rates for traditional projects. AA participants included BP, ConocoPhillips, Chevron, ExxonMobil, Statoil, and Total.

For the second element, PDVSA and outside oil companies entered into operational service agreements (OSAs) to exploit marginal fields. Under these contracts, outside oil companies operated the oil fields; PDVSA paid the companies a fee for their services, with payment structures varying by *apertura* round. Because the OSAs designated outside companies as "operational service providers" rather than as oil producers, those companies paid a lower-than-normal 34 percent income tax (PDVSA 2005b; Manzano and Monaldi 2010).[35] PDVSA ultimately entered into thirty-two OSAs with twenty-two separate companies, including many large IOCs (Manzano and Monaldi 2010).

For the third and final element, PDVSA and outside companies researched risk- and profit-sharing agreements (RPSAs) for investment in high-risk blocks (only a few of which received offers). The thirty-nine-year RPSAs set a baseline 16.67 percent royalty rate and conventional income tax rate of 66.67 percent; contract provisions allowed for a reduction in the royalty depending on the rate of return. PDVSA had the option to purchase up to a 35 percent stake in the project if a company discovered commercial quantities of oil in the exploration phase, but the outside company would retain majority control (EIA 2009a). The RPSAs also included an additional contractual government-take fee.

The *apertura*-era contracts were in many respects successful. Foreign investment in Venezuelan oil skyrocketed from $619 million in 1995 to $4.4 billion in 1999 (Monaldi 2001). Most of this investment was for AAs and OSAs rather than for RPSAs. As Nolan and Thurber (Chapter 4) show, the skills of the IOCs in managing challenging projects created a special interest in high-risk (and high-reward) frontier operations such as in the Orinoco.

Despite their pro-investment effects, the *apertura*-era contracts stoked political controversy much like the internationalization strategy the decade before. Some scholars lambasted the contracts for reducing the share of revenues given to the Venezuelan state (Mommer 2004); these criticisms became particularly biting once oil prices rose in the early 2000s and as technology lowered production costs. Other critiques centered on the legality of the contracts and their effects on Venezuela's (politically framed) oil sovereignty.[36] Chávez would later enshrine these criticisms into his electoral campaign and, eventually, his oil sector policy.

Amid political controversy over PDVSA's links to IOCs, PDVSA became more like an IOC itself. In 1997, PDVSA president Luis Giusti dismantled the company's decades-old multiple operating company framework and began to establish a vertically integrated structure to replace it (Giusti 1999). That same year, Giusti pushed through public sale of shares in PDVSA's petrochemicals affiliate, PEQUIVEN. In

1998, the Venezuelan government – acting with PDVSA's support – opened up domestic distribution and retail of gasoline and other oil products to competition with private companies. These moves were opening salvoes in a long-term PDVSA plan to increase private sector participation in the sector. In 1999 (the same year Chávez took office), PDVSA paid for an advertisement in the Latin American edition of *Time* suggesting that the company's privatization was inevitable (Tinker-Salas 2005). Chávez would later seize upon PDVSA's moves and claim that the company was not acting in the interests of the Venezuelan state.

PDVSA's IOC-friendly stance put it on the losing side of a larger Venezuelan debate over the country's direction. By nearly every estimate, Venezuelan economic growth remained deeply disappointing; its late 1990s per-capita GDP was roughly the same as it had been in 1960.[37] Poverty levels had risen significantly; economic inequalities had compounded. Though many causes were to blame (especially low oil prices, high debt, and an uncompetitive non-oil sector), critics cited Venezuela's "neoliberal" pro-foreign investment economic model,[38] including oil policy,[39] as a principal reason for the country's poor performance.

This economic critique became a leading issue in Venezuela's 1998 presidential campaign. Chávez, a lieutenant colonel in the Venezuelan army and ringleader of a failed 1992 coup (he served two years in jail before being pardoned), ran for president on a platform of ending Venezuela's economic malaise and poverty. Chávez denounced the country's economic model in general and targeted PDVSA as the model's most visible symbol; another target was the country's entrenched, corrupt two-party political system. Thanks to his campaign message and powerful charisma, Chávez won the election with 56 percent of the vote. At his February 1999 inauguration, Chávez called on his citizens to join in a "Bolivarian Revolution" to reshape Venezuelan society (so named in honor of Simón Bolívar, the nineteenth-century South American independence leader and native of what would later become Venezuela).

2.6 Transition to firmer state control (1999–2003)

Despite his aggressive campaign platform, once in power Chávez made few immediate changes to the Venezuelan energy sector. In 1999,

Chávez appointed oil industry expert Robert Mandini as PDVSA president and signed an investment-friendly gas hydrocarbons law. That same year, Chávez lobbied for and won ratification of a new constitution by popular referendum; it entered into effect in December 1999. Although the new constitution significantly strengthened presidential and popular referendum powers, it mostly reaffirmed the preexisting legal regime for the energy sector.[40] In July 2000, Chávez won reelection to a six-year term. (The new constitution not only empowered the president but also lengthened the term and allowed for one-term reelection.) Chávez tinkered with PDVSA to an extent, such as by lobbying for OPEC production cuts and by designating his ally, Hector Ciavaldini, as new PDVSA president in August 1999. (Ciavaldani's tenure was brief and deeply ineffective.) On the whole, however, many observers believed at the time that Chávez would mostly adhere to the policies previously in place (Giusti 1999; Mares and Altamirano 2007).

Then shortly after his 2000 reelection victory, Chávez began asserting greater authority over PDVSA. In October of that year, Chávez named Army Brigadier General Guaicaipuro Lameda as company president – a sharp break in the long-standing tradition of naming oil industry experts to the position. In 2001, Chávez used newly granted authority to decree a controversial hydrocarbons law that required future private investment to take the form of joint ventures with majority PDVSA ownership. These joint ventures carried higher royalty rates (30 percent) but lower income tax rates (50 percent) for oil projects.[41] Although the new law granted PDVSA greater power over the oil industry and actually reduced the aggregate tax burden above \$15–20/barrel,[42] company management feared the tax consequences if oil prices fell and therefore opposed it. Even Lameda, Chávez's pick for PDVSA president, became allied with the company's management and joined in opposition to the new law.

The conflicts between PDVSA and the Chávez administration took place within a context of escalating political polarization throughout Venezuelan society. The 2001 Hydrocarbons Law was one of forty-nine laws enacted by decree that year. Others included the *Ley de Tierras* (Law of the Land), giving the government power to tax and expropriate idle lands for the rural poor, and a new banking law, requiring banks to allocate 15 percent of their lending portfolio to small farmers. Though popular with the Venezuelan left and poor, these initiatives galvanized Chávez's opposition. A one-day antigovernment strike in December 2001, organized by the leading business association, portended future strife.

During early 2002, government-opposition hostilities came to a head. In February, Chávez fired Lameda and the entire PDVSA board (perhaps illegally) and installed political allies. Gastón Parra-Luzardo, an oil industry outsider without management experience, became PDVSA's fourth president in three years. After PDVSA management launched an April strike in objection to the new board, Chávez fired seven top PDVSA executives on his daily television show, *Aló Presidente* (Hello, President). The PDVSA firings and generalized downturn of the Venezuelan economy (itself a product of unrest and policy mistakes) sparked widespread discontent and Chávez's popularity rating slipped to around 30 percent (Whalen 2002). On April 11, some 500,000 anti-Chávez protestors, including many from PDVSA, crowded the Caracas streets. Violent clashes followed between the protestors, police, and Chávez supporters; approximately seventeen people died and more than a hundred were injured. During the night, a faction of the Venezuelan military rebelled against the government, detained Chávez, and installed business leader Pedro Carmona as interim president. The coup was short-lived; on April 12, Chávez supporters rioted and the pro-Chávez presidential guard and some segments of the army retook control without firing a shot. By April 13, Chávez was back in power. His authority, however, remained tenuous.

A second wave of unrest followed in late 2002. A three-day December strike at PDVSA's headquarters turned into a nine-week work stoppage with the goal of securing a February 2003 recall referendum on Chávez's rule.[43] In response, Chávez sent the army to occupy the nation's oil facilities. As the strike wore on, domestic oil production tumbled, falling from 3.3 million barrels/day in November 2002 to an estimated 700,000 barrels/day in January 2003 (EIA 2004). Venezuela's economy was paralyzed. The February 2003 date came and went without a referendum, and the strike faltered. Public sentiment largely blamed the company, rather than the Chávez administration, for the nation's troubles. (Chávez would later face a recall referendum in August 2004 but win it by a 59 to 41 percent vote; the opposition claimed fraud.)

2.7 PDVSA partially transformed (2003–today)

Having outlasted the coup and multiple strikes, Chávez took near-complete command over PDVSA. During early 2003, the government shed more than 18,000 of the company's 33,000 employees. After subsequent rehiring, PDVSA lost a net 30–40 percent of its staff (derived from Mares and Altamirano 2007). The Chávez administration later reshuffled PDVSA's senior management to put closer confidants at the helm. In November 2004, Chávez appointed personal friend and energy minister Rafael Ramírez to become PDVSA president (subsequently changing the company charter to make the appointments legal); Ramírez continues to hold both positions through the present day. (Iran is another country in which the NOC president has simultaneously served as oil minister. See Chapter 6.) Ramírez would later declare in a 2006 speech that the new PDVSA was "*roja, rojita*" (red, red – the color of socialism).[44]

The newly revamped PDVSA has vastly expanded responsibilities to the Venezuelan state. Starting in the run-up to his recall referendum, Chávez mandated that PDVSA fund and manage social programs known as *Misiones Bolivarianas* (Bolivarian Missions). Progressive, varyingly effective, and clientelistic, the *misiones* promote initiatives ranging from literacy training to inner-city health care; some thirty are under way as of early 2010.[45] PDVSA's management responsibilities for its social initiatives have been, in some cases, extensive. Since 2008, for example, PDVSA's subsidiary, *Producción y Distribución Venezolana de Alimentos* (PDVAL) has run a price-controlled food distribution network. The government also siphoned off other PDVSA revenues for a Chávez-controlled fund (known as FONDEN) and politically driven international assistance programs. In total, PDVSA's spending for these non-core obligations rose from $14 *million* in 2002 to nearly $14 *billion* by 2007 (PDVSA 2009).

Moreover, the Chávez administration increased PDVSA's stake in oil operations by rolling back the *apertura*-era contracts. In 2004, the energy ministry demanded higher royalty payments from the Orinoco AAs. Companies eventually complied with the demand, though ExxonMobil initially threatened international arbitration. In 2005, the government announced that OSAs should have paid the 50 percent income tax rate for oil production (set in 2001 for new projects), instead of the lower 34 percent rate that they were paying (because of the *apertura* framework).

The energy ministry then declared OSAs illegal in 2006 and mandated renegotiation of contract terms with higher taxes and majority PDVSA control. In 2007, Chávez decreed the migration of existing AAs and RPSAs to *empresas mixtas* (mixed companies), also with majority PDVSA control. PDVSA offered compensation to the AA contracting parties but based it on book value, rather than the typical market value (which was estimated at $10 billion higher) (Millard 2007). Most companies eventually accepted the government's terms; ExxonMobil and ConocoPhillips opted for arbitration, however. PDVSA took majority control of all projects, including those for which it did not reach agreement, on Venezuelan Labor Day, May 1, 2007. (De facto, however, IOCs continued to play significant roles.)

Yet in the midst of wide-scale change, key parts of PDVSA have remained intact. PDVSA has retained its legacies from the 1980s internationalization era and existing domestic operations infrastructure.[46] In addition, most PDVSA service-related subsidiaries continue to operate largely as before.[47] And because of PDVSA's expansive new role in carrying out state social programs, the Chávez administration has in some ways maintained PDVSA's status as a state within a state.[48]

Chávez's partial transformation of PDVSA reflects his broader consolidation of power across Venezuelan society. Since the 2002–2003 strikes, Chávez has nationalized larger segments of the economy and taken control of the country's supreme court, lower courts, nearly its entire legislature, and armed forces. Though his agenda suffered a setback when Chávez lost a proposed constitutional reform in 2007, he won a pared-down referendum giving him the unlimited right to run for re-election in 2009 and remains popular among a sizable (though variable) segment of society. A key reason for his popularity is the government's extensive social spending, pro-Chávez television stations (Telesur, ViVe), Chavista community organizations (*círculos bolivarianos*, or Bolivarian circles), and frequent political advertising. Chávez's source of funding for these activities has primarily come from PDVSA.

3 Explaining the state–PDVSA relationship

3.1 Natural resources: oil-dependent government, investment-dependent company

Venezuela's hydrocarbon resources have shaped the state–PDVSA relationship in four key ways. First, Venezuela has considerable supplies of oil, relative to both the size of its economy and most other countries. As a result, Venezuela has long been dependent on oil revenue. Second, Venezuelan oil is costly and difficult to produce and refine. This geological fact has caused Venezuelan governments to balance policy goals of maximizing fiscal take with the need to allow PDVSA to make substantial investments and, at times, to encourage outside firms to do the same. Third, Venezuela's oil resources have experienced periodic waves of investment. The country's long history of oil development gave PDVSA a foundation on which to grow and an opportunity for Chávez to forcibly renegotiate IOC contracts between 2004 and 2007. Fourth, Venezuela has substantial, though partially untapped, natural gas reserves. Their underdevelopment helps reveal the forces at work in the country.

3.1.1 Plentiful oil resources

Venezuelan oil reserves have for decades been among the largest in the world. In 1980, Venezuela held the world's ninth-largest oil reserves, at 19.5 billion barrels (BP 2009a). By 2008, Venezuelan oil reserves had grown[49] to the world's sixth-largest – and greatest in the Western Hemisphere – at 99.4 billion barrels (BP 2009a).

In contrast to its resource base, Venezuela's economy is modest and relatively undiversified. Its 2009 gross domestic product of $350.1 billion is the thirty-third largest in the world (CIA 2010a).[50] The non-oil export industry (concentrated in metals and chemicals) has long been weak because of historical path dependencies, rigid labor markets, and weak knowledge dissemination in the export sector (Hausmann and Rodríguez 2006).

As a consequence of Venezuela's large oil endowment and undiversified, medium-sized economy, the country is heavily dependent on oil – particularly oil exports. Since 1950, oil has supplied on average 80–90 percent of Venezuela's export revenues, 50–60 percent of its government revenues, and 20–35 percent of its GDP (Boué 1993; EIA 2009a).[51] In the context of long-standing oil dependence, nearly all Venezuelan governments have viewed the oil sector, fueled by PDVSA, as the key to economic development and government financing. The first Carlos Andrés Pérez administration (1974–1979) devised its nationalization strategy of minimizing oil sector disturbance to ensure the steady flow of government funds.[52] Subsequent administrations usually followed the same tack. (Critically, PDVSA played a leading role in advocating this approach within the Venezuelan government.) Although the Chávez administration's oil sector strategy differs markedly from previous administrations, oil nevertheless remains the government's top priority.[53]

3.1.2 Costly, dirty oil

Venezuelan oil has long been relatively heavy and, as a result, costly to develop. The country's first commercial oil strike yielded heavy oil, and heavy and extra-heavy oil have dominated Venezuela's production profile ever since.[54] Between the 1910s and 1970s, Venezuela drained much of its supply of lower-cost – and higher-profit – light and medium crudes (Boué 1993).[55] (Those light crudes that remain are widely distributed; individual Venezuelan wells produce around 180 barrels per day, compared to 7,000 barrels per day in parts of the Persian Gulf (The Economist 2006).) Venezuela then increasingly shifted to heavier crudes from the Zulia oil fields around Lake Maracaibo and, secondarily, from the Oriental Basin in eastern Venezuela. By the 1990s, however, many of these fields had also become mature, especially in Zulia (EIA 2007).[56] The near-exhaustion of older oil sources has made Venezuelan oil even heavier. By far the most significant remaining source of oil in Venezuela is the extra-heavy oil deposits in the Orinoco Belt, or *Faja del Orinoco*. See Figure 10.2. The Orinoco Belt holds greats promise, as it is the largest such deposit in the world. However, making extra-heavy oil suitable for conventional applications requires expensive, complex upgrading and refining technologies.[57] Extra-heavy oil also can have significant adverse environmental consequences, because it consumes greater water and energy and yields more mineral contaminant and other waste by-products than lighter oil.[58]

Because of the steep cost and technological complexity of Venezuelan oil, Venezuelan governments have historically given PDVSA free rein to formulate an investment strategy and to work with foreign partners. High processing costs underpinned PDVSA's push abroad in the 1980s, though political factors (discussed below) also played a role.[59] That same decade, the technological challenges in developing extra-heavy oil from the Orinoco Belt[60] spurred PDVSA to devise the Orimulsion boiler fuel substitute.[61] And the 1990s *apertura* was rooted in the logic that PDVSA needed IOC investment to fully exploit Venezuela's difficult oil, especially in the

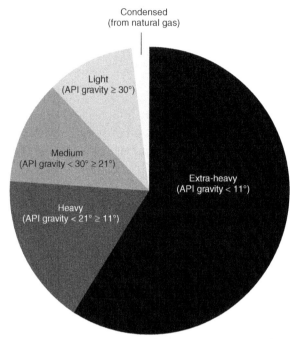

Figure 10.2 Distribution of Venezuelan proven liquid reserves by type, 2007.
Source: Derived from PDVSA (2008).

Orinoco Belt. The Chávez administration has followed a largely different path, though it, too, has been cognizant of the technological hurdles of Venezuelan oil development. The Chávez administration continued to work with IOC partners in the Orinoco Belt even at the height of its nationalistic rhetoric (and has shown greater cooperation of late).

3.1.3 Long investment cycles

As in many other, large oil-exporting countries, oil investment in Venezuela has followed a recurring pattern. First, the government solicits outside investment at highly favorable terms, then steadily modifies those terms to the government's advantage, and finally returns to offering better terms in the hopes of fresh investment. This pattern emerged during the 1920s and 1930s (when the Venezuelan government sought out IOCs under Vicente Gómez and became more assertive towards them once he died) and repeated itself from the

1940s to early 1970s (when Venezuela welcomed IOC investment under the 1940s "fifty-fifty" profit split only to increase intervention in the sector, ultimately culminating in the formation of PDVSA). The reason for this recurring pattern is that oil development projects are mostly front-loaded, especially if the projects concern costly, difficult heavy and extra-heavy oil. Because of this cost structure, government has an incentive to make attractive offers that draw in the large initial investments and then renege on those offers once the investments are "sunk" so as to capture a greater proportion of the rents. The cycle commences again once the initial investments become obsolete. Over time, the cycle of courtship and confrontation becomes a repeated game, and both government and IOCs know how to play it; the role of NOCs, like PDVSA, in this game is dependent on their relationship to the state. (See Chapter 4 for a discussion of this dynamic in greater detail.)

The wild swing in IOC investments between the 1990s *apertura* and the Chávez-era nationalizations conforms to this longer-run pattern. In the 1990s, PDVSA – which was then the de facto Venezuelan oil policymaker – lured IOCs to invest in Venezuela through the *apertura*. By 2004 and 2005, most of those investments were in place. Completion of these investments, along with high oil prices, gave the Chávez administration breathing space to then undo the *apertura* and give the spoils of his nationalizations back to PDVSA (which shifted, over the course of the decade, from top government policymaker to trusted government agent). Thus, the fact that Chávez reversed course of many of the *apertura* policies was less surprising than the speed and rhetoric with which he did it.

Less than three years after the nationalizations of IOC investments, the cycle of Venezuelan oil investment began anew. By 2009, the Chávez administration began a rapprochement toward IOCs by holding a public auction for development projects in the Orinoco Belt. I return to the subject of this rapprochement in section 4.

3.1.4 Off-the-radar natural gas
In contrast to oil, Venezuela's natural gas sector is mostly unexploited, though it offers some opportunity. Venezuela's natural gas reserves, consistently among the world's top ten, grew from 1.26 trillion cubic feet (Tcf) in 1980 to 4.84 Tcf in 2007 (BP 2009a). Roughly 90 percent sits in associated fields with higher-value oil (EIA 2009a). For

that reason, the oil industry absorbs 70 percent of Venezuelan natural gas production and uses a large share of that production for reinjection into oil fields (EIA 2009a). Venezuela's smaller supply of non-associated gas suffers from high carbon dioxide levels, decreasing its energy value and increasing pipeline corrosiveness (Boué 1993). The high proportion of associated gas and the lower quality of non-associated gas have limited the commercial attractiveness of this sector, though it remains important for oil production, domestic consumption, and implementation of any future Venezuelan climate change mitigation strategies.

Because of these geological conditions, Venezuelan governments have embraced a planning-based approach to PDVSA's natural gas development. This approach differs by necessity from the one for oil: instead of inheriting a mature infrastructure upon nationalization (as for oil), Venezuela has, to a much greater extent, built that infrastructure from the ground up.[62] PDVSA discovered major natural gas fields in 1978 (Mejillones 1) and 1980 (Patao 1) (Mallet-Guy Guerra et al. 1993). During the mid 1980s, PDVSA constructed a gas distribution network to free up higher-value oil for export (Boué 1993). And in the late 1980s, PDVSA drew up the "Cristóbal Colón" project to develop and export liquefied natural gas (LNG) from its offshore reserves. Cristóbal Colón marked PDVSA's first effort to give IOCs equity stakes in Venezuelan hydrocarbon operations. (High costs and low natural gas prices ultimately shelved the project, however.)

The relative underdevelopment of Venezuelan natural gas has prompted even the Chávez administration to exempt that sector from heavy political influence.[63] The centerpiece of this policy is its 1999 law giving private operators the right to own a 100 percent stake in non-associated natural gas projects, far greater than for oil. PDVSA may take a 35 percent share of projects that reach a commercial stage, however (EIA 2009a). Results from the law have been mixed thus far – in part because oil is the bigger prize and domestic gas prices are uncertain.[64] One promising development was Spanish IOC Repsol's discovery of a large natural gas find off the coast of Venezuela in late 2009 (Repsol 2009). Less successfully, the government sought to create an ambitious (and unworkable) trans-South American gas pipeline and revive the moribund Cristóbal Colón project by gearing it toward domestic demand.

3.2 State capacity: an oil company fills the state's gaps

As Venezuela's geology has shaped its dealings with PDVSA, so has the state's administrative capacity. I make two points below. First, Venezuelan institutions have been generally ineffective in formulating oil policy. PDVSA stepped into – or, arguably, elbowed its way into – the policymaking gap, dominating oil policy between the 1980s and 1990s. In the process, PDVSA became vulnerable to claims that it was a state within a state, creating an opening for Chávez to assert control over the company. Second, Venezuelan institutions have been unable to implement tax regimes that adjust revenue intake in response to price and cost changes. Partly because of this tax framework, the Venezuelan government has had periodic quarrels with IOCs and PDVSA.

3.2.1 The missing Venezuelan state

Venezuela has historically suffered from weak institutions.[65] Though Venezuela established a two-party democratic system between 1958 and the 1990s that was remarkably stable by Latin American standards, competition within that system was limited[66] and the two political parties relied on oil-fueled patronage to maintain power. (The country was then known as a *partidocracia* (partyocracy) (Buxton 1999).[67]) Partly because of their low accountability, Venezuelan public institutions have been largely ineffective in providing public goods, particularly as real wages fell during the 1980s and 1990s. Evidence of government mismanagement is legion. One academic compiled a three-volume dictionary on Venezuelan corruption in the late 1980s (Diccionario de la corrupción en Venezuela 1989; Philip 1999). Since 1995, Venezuela has remained among the bottom 50 percent of countries for all six World Bank governance indicators (Kaufmann *et al.* 1999–2009).[68]

Like the rest of the Venezuelan administrative apparatus, oil sector institutions perform poorly. The energy ministry, which at one time was populated with capable staff (Matsuda 1997), shriveled in competence after PDVSA's 1976 formation. The Venezuelan government reduced support for the energy ministry on the belief that ownership of PDVSA diminished the need for distinct oil policy (Baena 1999b). As a result, PDVSA sapped the ministry of technical talent (in part by offering higher salaries) and weakened its administrative responsibilities.

The Chávez administration, which took power partially on a pledge to stamp out mismanagement, has made Venezuela's governance worse by entangling political goals with public administration. Since Chávez came into power, four of the six World Bank governance indicators have declined by an amount that is statistically significant (Kaufmann *et al.* 1999–2009).[69] In fact, Venezuela was in the bottom-fifth percentile for most World Bank governance indicators by 2008 (Kaufmann *et al.* 1999–2009).[70] Interviewees report that the Chávez administration has concentrated talent and government resources in a few institutions – including, until recently, Venezuela's tax agency (known as SENIAT) and central bank – at the cost of reduced performance elsewhere and widespread politicization (PESD Interviews). Interestingly, control of corruption has *not* declined significantly under Chávez according to World Bank governance indicators (Kaufmann *et al.* 1999–2009).[71] Nevertheless, corruption remains rife. To cite one instance in which it has likely played a role: So many government officials and favored businesspersons, known as "boli-bourgeois,"[72] purchased Hummer brand sports utility vehicles during the oil price boom of 2007–2008 that Chávez publicly asked, "What kind of a revolution is this? One of Hummers?" (Treewater 2008). Chávez later imposed a luxury tax on the vehicles.

Throughout Venezuela's storied history of government ineffectiveness, PDVSA has remained comparatively efficient. Even during the Chávez administration – a time in which PDVSA's performance has waned – the company has remained probably the most effective institution under control of the Venezuelan government.

The combination of PDVSA's strengths and Venezuela's administrative weaknesses help explain why PDVSA has dictated Venezuela's oil policy. Although Venezuelan law gives the energy ministry wide-ranging formal powers,[73] PDVSA frequently set oil policy as a practical matter before Chávez. Oil sector development priorities, overseas investments, and IOC contract terms were all mainly PDVSA decisions. PDVSA also generally enjoyed the freedom to set its own budget (though ministries had formal oversight powers), make operational decisions, and hire and fire staff. The energy ministry periodically sought to assert greater authority over PDVSA, but those efforts largely failed.[74] Thanks to PDVSA's organizational efficiency and enormous information advantages, the company was, until Chávez, usually able to convince politicians its oil plan was in the best interests of the country.[75] The energy ministry, plagued by institutional failures, typically did not stand a chance.

By the 1990s, PDVSA exerted pervading influence over the Venezuelan state. The government reduced PDVSA's tax burden even though the country was in a fiscal and banking crisis (PESD Interviews). PDVSA loaned economists to other government agencies (Matsuda 1997) and gave frequent economic advice to the government (Philip 1999). At its late 1990s zenith, PDVSA had effectively replaced the finance ministry as principal negotiator with the International Monetary Fund (PESD Interviews). The company's wide-ranging influence helped feed the political blowback during the Chávez era.

Even after Chávez transformed the company in 2003, PDVSA has remained the pillar on which government stands. PDVSA administers most of Chávez's social programs and public works projects because of its competence and large, positive cash flow (which offers an attractive and readily tapped discretionary tool for government finance that is easier to insulate from patronage-seeking legislators and sometimes-corrupt bureaucrats). In fact, PDVSA has actually taken over more administrative functions than its pre-Chávez incarnation. This time, however, Chávez, rather than PDVSA, remains firmly in control of most decision making.

3.2.2 Tax policy in a rudderless policymaking environment

The strength of the oil sector and the weakness in Venezuelan institutions has also limited the country's capacity to appropriate rents from the oil sector. The Venezuelan government, primarily through the energy ministry and secondarily through SENIAT, has long levied a combination of income taxes, royalties, and surcharges on oil companies. (PDVSA and IOCs are generally subject to the same taxes.) In practice, however, Venezuela has relied on easily administered tax schemes that favor royalties rather than information-intensive income taxes (Manzano and Monaldi 2010).[76] These regimes are regressive in nature because they appropriate a decreasing share of rents as prices rise or as costs decline; they may also reduce the financial viability of projects as prices fall or as costs rise (Manzano and Monaldi 2010).

Venezuela's regressive oil tax framework is one reason that Venezuelan governments periodically have come into friction with the oil sector (another reason is the long investment cycles, discussed above). The most explosive of these tensions occurred during the

Chávez administration – when the government introduced the tax framework of the 2001 Hydrocarbons Law[77] and forcibly renegotiated *apertura*-era contracts with IOCs. But these disputes are part of a long-term pattern. Tensions also flared during negotiations over the 1943 Hydrocarbons Law[78] and again during the 1960s and 1970s[79] (Manzano and Monaldi 2010).

3.3 State goals: *major shifts over time*

Probably no factor led to more sweeping changes in the state–PDVSA relationship than Venezuela's state goals. I analyze three phases of time below. First, Venezuelan politicians mostly prized long-term oil sector stability between the late 1970s and 1990s. Only occasionally did short-term political aims preempt this political consensus. Second, state goals shifted during the early years of the Chávez administration, partly because of Chávez's growing appetite for control. By the early 2000s, this shift helped provoke PDVSA's 2002–2003 strikes against the government and Chávez's wide-scale firings. Third, Chávez administration goals for the oil sector have swelled in recent years. This expansion in state goals occurred because of Chávez's increased authority over PDVSA, perceived threats to his rule, and the temptations created by higher oil prices.

3.3.1 Pre-Chávez era: stability reigns (mostly) supreme
Venezuelan politicians initially refrained from interfering in PDVSA because of the justifications behind that company's formation and its early successes. Key among the justifications for nationalization – in Venezuela and elsewhere – was that IOCs had exploited Venezuela's regulatory weaknesses to short-change the state. Nationalization, according to this view, would help reduce asymmetries because a state-owned enterprise would act more faithfully on the state's behalf than would the private sector (Mommer 2002). As a result, Venezuelan politicians initially gave PDVSA wide latitude in which to operate. Moreover, Venezuela's nationalization was regarded as successful because the newly formed PDVSA sustained oil revenues flowing to the government (helped in large part by high oil prices) while it revitalized investment in the sector. As a result, PDVSA enjoyed a "honeymoon" of sorts (Coronel 1983).[80]

Even after the honeymoon faded during the 1980s, Venezuelan governments continued favoring oil sector stability because the political dynamic remained tranquil. Venezuelan presidents set policy at that time in cooperation with a small number of repeat players: leaders of two national political parties (*Acción Democrática* (AD) and *Partido Social Cristiano de Venezuela* (COPEI)) and labor and business interest groups (the legislature, by contrast, was relatively weak). In this setting, policy volatility was low, until low oil prices and new electoral rules fragmented Venezuelan politics in the late 1980s (Monaldi *et al.* 2008).[81]

Further supporting Venezuela's oil policy was its macroeconomic environment and policies. In line with conventional Latin American thinking, Venezuelan governments embraced a policy of "import substitution industrialization" (ISI) to build up domestic manufacturing capacity. To implement ISI, Venezuelan governments relied on a steady stream of oil revenues to prop up state-run petrochemicals, steel, and aluminum industries (Randall 1987). (In accord with *rentista* "rent-based" thinking, policymakers viewed the oil sector mostly as a source of rents rather than as an engine of growth (Espinasa 1996).) Oil sector stability, including limited political interference, became the means to secure reliable oil revenues, even as oil prices declined during the mid to late 1980s. Although Venezuela's ISI policy eventually sputtered[82] as the policy did in other countries,[83] oil dollars gave Venezuelan governments the means to maintain ISI policy for longer than its Latin American counterparts. (Other Latin American countries mostly abandoned the policy during the 1970s oil crises or early 1980s debt crisis.) Not until the second Carlos Andrés Pérez administration (1989–1992) did financial strains force Venezuela to pursue a different strategy.[84]

This story of limited government interference comes with significant caveats, however. First, Venezuelan politicians have for political reasons long sought to channel oil sector wealth directly to the Venezuelan populace. As in other oil-exporting states, this goal has mostly taken the form of domestic gasoline subsidies.[85] Venezuela began subsidizing gasoline in the 1940s and continues to do so heavily through the present day. In fact, Venezuela's 12 cent/gallon price made it the world's least expensive by 2008 – one-fifteenth the price of a liter of bottled water (Wilson 2008).[86] During the 2002–2008 price spike, the opportunity cost of the gasoline subsidy reached $10–20 billion/year (PESD Interviews).

Second, infrequent state interference in the oil sector kept the state–PDVSA relationship off balance. On several occasions, the government raided PDVSA's resources to fill gaping holes in the state budget. Major incursions occurred during the 1982 Latin American debt crisis (when the government compelled PDVSA to transfer around $5 billion of its reinvestment monies to prop up Central Bank reserves)[87] and the early 1990s negotiations with the International Monetary Fund (IMF) (when the government limited a PDVSA expansion plan to meet IMF conditions).[88] Venezuelan politicians, usually hailing from congressional opposition parties, also attempted (less successfully) to score political points by intervening in PDVSA investment decisions. Key instances include PDVSA's 1982 refinery agreement with Veba Oel and, to a lesser extent, its 1990 acquisition of CITGO's remaining 50 percent shares (Baena 1999b). Much rarer, until Chávez, were government attempts at PDVSA micromanagement; the most significant cases occurred during the interventionist Herrera administration (1979–1984).[89]

Venezuela's infrequent meddling and ordinary restraint had a major effect on state management of PDVSA. Because of the mostly arm's-length approach, Venezuelan politicians granted PDVSA broad autonomy. PDVSA's independence came under serious strain, however, when it fell captive to political and economic demands. These demands would escalate under the Chávez administration.

3.3.2 Early Chávez era (1999–2002): transition in state goals

The Chávez administration's early approach to the oil sector was, as noted above, relatively cautious. Though anti-PDVSA ideology helped thrust Chávez into power, Chávez was more practical than ideological[90] and he was mindful of PDVSA's political prowess and its funding of government operations. Chávez also feared making significant changes that would alienate IOC partners during a time in which oil prices were low and investment budgets were tight. As a result, the Chávez administration at the outset took a somewhat conciliatory approach – such as by naming an oil industry expert to head PDVSA and passing an investor-friendly 1999 natural gas law.

Yet as oil prices tipped above late-1990s lows, Chávez began subjecting the oil sector to his whims more freely.[91] Chávez grew disenchanted with PDVSA senior management when it exerted its once (mostly) protected independence from government influence, motivating him to repeatedly appoint and dismiss PDVSA senior management in the early 2000s. Oil sector politicization, mostly an exception for the three decades earlier, became the rule. And the 2001 Hydrocarbons Law further aggravated relations by introducing uncertainty into the oil sector tax regime. These changes put enormous pressure on the state–PDVSA relationship and sparked the company strikes against the government in 2002 and 2003.

3.3.3 Later Chávez era (2003–present): state goals expand
In the aftermath of the 2002–2003 strikes, the Chávez administration's goals for the oil sector proliferated. Ironically, PDVSA's own strikes had galvanized opposition to Chávez's rule, which spurred Chávez's need to use PDVSA monies to stave off political challenges. Chávez thus transformed the company from a threat to his rule into a tool for sustaining it. And rising oil prices gave Chávez the opportunity to use that tool aggressively.

Most notably, the Chávez administration has used PDVSA to bankroll the government far more deeply than ever before. Like most oil-producing states, the Chávez administration relies on a grab bag of tax instruments, but in Chávez's hands those instruments have grown in both number and effect. Royalties, set at 30 percent since the 2001 Hydrocarbons Law, have been by far the single-largest revenue source, reaching around $20 billion annually in 2007 and 2008.[92] Income taxes[93] – set at a 50 percent rate (after costs) since the 2001 law[94] – are also significant. Relatively minor revenues also come from surface taxes, value-added taxes, and consumption taxes on gasoline consumption, among others. In 2006, the Chávez administration added two taxes: 1) an additional 3.33 percent extraction tax that functions as a royalty and 2) a 0.1 percent tax on exports (the latter first implemented in 2007). (An additional off-budget windfall tax, passed in 2008, is discussed below.) Lastly, the Chávez administration has used its position as sole shareholder to receive a portion of PDVSA's net profits through dividends – which PDVSA previously pegged for reinvestment. In total, the Venezuelan government received more than $125 billion in budgetary taxes between 2003 and 2008. A summary is provided in Table 10.2.

Table 10.2. *PDVSA payments to government budget, 2003–2008*[a]

($m)	2003	2004	2005	2006	2007	2008
Royalties	5,945	8,881	11,327	17,505	19,872	20,294
Income tax and related taxes[b]	1,216	1,978	5,069	7,594	5,392	4,872
Dividends	2,326	1,302	1,317	1,317	2,658	2,000
Extraction tax	0	0	0	797	1,720	2,487
Export registration tax	0	0	0	0	76	54
Total budgetary obligations	9,487	12,161	17,713	27,213	29,718	29,707

[a] Precise figures should be interpreted with caution because they come from two different PDVSA sources.

[b] The definition of "other taxes"(treated here as "related taxes") in PDVSA (2008) (used for the 2003–2006 figures) is unclear. Based on the taxation description in that document, it appears this grouping includes the surface tax, the value-added tax, and general consumption tax. PDVSA (2009) includes no such separate category but lists surface taxes, special advantage taxes on *empreses mixtas*, and the "LOPTISCEP" tax. I group these under related taxes for comparability purposes.

Source: PDVSA (2008, 2009).

   In addition to budgetary payments, the Chávez administration has appropriated substantial revenues for off-budget, or extra-budgetary, programs.[95] Among these are the *Fondo de Desarollo Nacional* (National Development Fund, or FONDEN), the *misiones*, and other social programs. Although the process by which the Chávez administration collects extra-budgetary taxes is murky, PDVSA has published some figures on taxation amounts. The single-largest category of extra-budgetary taxes is FONDEN, totaling nearly $28 billion between 2005 and 2008.[96] (The Chávez administration has dedicated FONDEN monies mainly toward infrastructure, defense, and public debt restructuring.) The next largest extra-budgetary tax is for the *misiones*, especially *Misión Barrio Adentro* (low-income health clinics) and *Misión Mercal* (subsidized food). The remaining two types of spending obligations are classified as other social programs (mostly community building and public works projects) and social investment trusts (which hold monies for later social

Table 10.3. *PDVSA extra-budgetary obligations, 2003–2008*

($m)	2003	2004	2005	2006	2007	2008
FONDEN	0	0	1,525	6,855	6,761	12,407
Misiones	141	1,070	2,008	3,101	4,248	340
Social investment trusts	300	3,100	3,200	1,066	2,131	1,315
Other social programs	108	146	554	971	962	671
Total off-budget obligations	549	4,316	7,287	11,993	14,102	14,733

Source: Derived from PDVSA (2008, 2009). By comparison, total extra-budgetary taxes for 2001 and 2002 were $34 million and $14 million, respectively.

spending).[97] These extra-budgetary taxes began rising in 2003 – immediately after the strikes and company restructuring – and swelled through 2008. In 2008, the Chávez administration passed a windfall tax (known as a special contribution) in response to high oil prices, sending $5.730 billion directly to FONDEN that year (out of $12.407 billion total).[98] Table 10.3 summarizes these many extra payments.

The Chávez administration has imposed new obligations on PDVSA in part because the *apertura* taxes were low and oil prices had risen strongly. As a result of the *apertura*, Venezuela's fiscal take declined from 51 percent in the mid 1990s to around 47 percent at the time Chávez came into power (Manzano and Monaldi 2008).[99] (The *apertura*-era contracts also had a major pro-investment effect, but the Chávez administration devalued that effect because the investments were already in place.) The Chávez administration's new budgetary and off-budget obligations reversed this slide in fiscal take. But as I suggest in the next section, the Chávez administration has consumed so many PDVSA resources that it has undercut the company's performance.

Beyond using PDVSA to help finance the government, the Chávez administration has imposed a multiplicity of national missions on PDVSA to further policy goals. Some advance the government's development and related patronage agenda – such as managing (in addition to funding) the government's *misiones*, procuring goods from social cooperatives, and expanding projects in Venezuela's undeveloped interior (PDVSA 2008). Beyond these programmatic projects, the government has obligated PDVSA to construct one-off highways, hospitals, and other public works. Moreover, the government has used PDVSA monies to capture strategic segments of the Venezuelan economy (or potential sources of political opposition); at the government's behest, PDVSA has acquired formerly private-owned cable, electric, and agriculture entities. PDVSA has also become an instrument of Chávez's macroeconomic policy. In late 2009, PDVSA issued bonds in part to shore up the value of the local *bolivar* currency. And the Chávez administration has commandeered PDVSA to serve its expansive foreign policy priorities. Oil has become both a geopolitical carrot – through discounted oil sales programs and PDVSA partnerships with NOCs from Chávez-friendly countries – and a stick – through empty threats of oil sales embargoes to the United States. Because PDVSA is Chávez's most powerful (and now trusted) instrument, the company has become embroiled in the government's foreign policy adventures, such as the 2007 *maletinazo* or *valijagate* (the "suitcase scandal" in which Argentine officials discovered that a businessman flying in from Venezuela, accompanied by PDVSA officials, was carrying a suitcase with nearly $800,000 in undeclared cash). I analyze the effect of these obligations on company performance in section 4.

3.4 Effect of other factors on the state–PDVSA relationship

In discussing Venezuela's state goals, state capacity, and nature of resources, I have referenced other factors affecting the state–PDVSA relationship. Most important among these factors is the price of oil. Low oil prices and the need for new investments have incentivized the Venezuelan government to grant PDVSA autonomy. Conversely, high oil prices and established investments have given Venezuelan governments opportunities to exert greater influence over the company.[100] Here, the Chávez administration has been no exception; his government ratcheted up fiscal pressure on PDVSA as oil prices rose and forcibly renegotiated *apertura*-era contracts after the IOCs had completed many of their initial investments. And since the collapse in world oil prices in late 2008, his government has given PDVSA slightly greater freedom to work with IOC partners.

4 Explaining PDVSA's strategy and performance

4.1 PDVSA strategy: from autonomy to partial accommodation

Because of the changing relationship between PDVSA and the Venezuelan state, PDVSA's strategy has swung from political insulation to subservience. I make two points below. First, PDVSA's strategy from the 1970s to 1990s was to advance commercial interests and secure freedom from intermittent government demands. Second, the Chávez administration has chosen a vastly more invasive approach to PDVSA. After Chávez reshaped the company in 2003, PDVSA developed a strategy to accommodate those interventions and, at times, mitigate them.

4.1.1 Seeking autonomy (1976–2002)

Between the 1970s and early 2000s, Venezuela's approach to PDVSA alternated between (mostly) arm's length and (infrequently) intrusive. Venezuela generally gave PDVSA broad discretion to run its business, though politics occasionally reared its head. As a matter of law and practice, PDVSA's corporate governance system embodied this mostly hands-off approach.

As a matter of law, PDVSA's corporate governance system gave the company considerable managerial independence. PDVSA was subject to the commercial (rather than administrative) code and its formal relationship with the state was through shareholder meetings. Article 3 of the Nationalization Law empowered PDVSA to use the most efficient means to commercialize hydrocarbons. Article 5 of the law gave Venezuela's congress power to review PDVSA actions affecting the national interest, but the article – at least initially – carried little force. Article 6 of the law designated PDVSA's operator subsidiaries under the commercial (rather than administrative) legal code and designated 10 percent of PDVSA's operator net earnings for company reinvestment.[101] And Article 8 of the law exempted PDVSA workers from public employee restrictions. Although these articles at times provoked differing interpretations (particularly Article 5), they nevertheless set rules of the game for state–PDVSA interactions.

PDVSA further insulated itself from government interference as a matter of practice. The energy ministry had de jure authority to approve PDVSA budgets, strategies, and goals (including production levels and capital expenditures) at annual or semi-annual shareholder meetings. De facto, however, PDVSA had considerable influence over approval decisions because of Venezuela's weak state capacity. The law gave Venezuelan presidents the power to name PDVSA's board of directors but before Chávez presidents typically named industry experts rather than politicians to those positions (Matsuda 1997). The net effect of this corporate governance system was to grant PDVSA broad autonomy over the oil sector.

Because of the government's grant of autonomy, PDVSA's strategy initially focused on commercial considerations. (PDVSA's strategy for engaging the Venezuelan government was by comparison undeveloped.)[102] The company's late-1970s highly successful plan to increase exploration and production spending was a business response to decades of decreased investment by IOCs. In the early 1980s, oil price declines motivated PDVSA's first tentative steps overseas. PDVSA's high-cost heavy oil had become less commercially attractive relative to low-cost light crude; in a difficult price environment, PDVSA sought out overseas refining and distribution systems to secure downstream markets for its oil production.

As PDVSA began internationalizing, however, politics intruded on PDVSA's independence.[103] The first major intervention was the Herrera administration's 1982 taking of PDVSA reinvestment monies to relieve Central Bank strains. Later that year, PDVSA's incipient internationalization strategy came under attack. PDVSA's first deal, its 1982 joint venture refinery agreement with Veba Oel,[104] provoked a political firestorm in part because PDVSA did not submit it to congress for Article 5 approval. The opposition-led congress then sought to derail the agreement (Matsuda 1997; Baena 1999b). Caught in the congress–government political crossfire, the agreement remained in question for roughly a year. The controversy finally dissipated once the Lusinchi administration came into power in 1984 and Lusinchi himself intervened to quell the opposition (Baena 1999b).

The combination of political threats and commercial desire for downstream markets spurred PDVSA to deepen its internationalization strategy once the political fallout from the Veba Oel deal died down.[105] PDVSA's 1986–1990 acquisition of overseas refinery interests and its purchase of CITGO helped politically insulate company assets. By selling oil to overseas refineries, PDVSA engaged in transfer pricing that minimized the risk of Venezuelan tax fluctuations, reduced net tax burden, and financed refinery upgrades (Baena 1999b).[106] PDVSA further reduced its payments to the Venezuelan state by investing most dividends from its overseas operations in expansion overseas (Mares and Altamirano 2007).[107]

A similar desire for commercial success and political insulation drove PDVSA's 1990s *apertura* strategy for foreign domestic upstream investment. On the commercial side, domestic upstream investment became critical because of declining conventional oil fields and continued low oil prices. And politically, company management believed that it could protect the oil sector from continued state predations by signing contracts with outside companies that included extensive procedural protections (Manzano and Monaldi 2010).[108] Although the political component of the *apertura* ultimately proved unsuccessful – the Chávez administration eventually rolled back the contracts – it paid off commercially.

4.1.2 Switch to compliance (2003–today)

By the early 2000s, PDVSA's autonomy-seeking strategy backfired. After PDVSA launched strikes against the Chávez administration during 2002–2003, the company created an open conflict between the NOC and the state. Chávez's victory in this conflict opened the door for a fundamental break in state–NOC relations. The Venezuelan state's approach to PDVSA flipped from mostly arm's length to deeply interventionist, and the state implemented a new corporate governance system to reflect this approach. The once-clear separation between state and NOC became blurred.

Since transforming the company, the Chávez administration has governed PDVSA through informal ties at the senior leadership level. Though much of the pre-Chávez legal formalism exists – PDVSA continues holding shareholder meetings with the state – it has become more ceremonial than before.[109] Ramírez (as PDVSA president) submits decisions to *himself* (as energy minister) for shareholder approval. Because managerial and oversight roles overlap, Chávez relies heavily on Ramírez and his coterie of advisers to both formulate and carry out the government's many goals. Personality has thus, in some sense, become the basis for policy.[110]

Because of the interventionist state–PDVSA relationship, company strategy has swung from autonomy seeking to (real and superficial) accommodation of government demands. Though specifics are opaque, it appears that Chávez funnels his directives through Ramírez, and Ramírez, in turn, uses his own influence with Chávez to negotiate their scope (PESD Interviews). The negotiated outcome may be different from stated plans – which are part political theater[111] that neither PDVSA nor Chávez fully believes.

Publicly, PDVSA's plan is named – in a nod to Úslar Pietri's famous saying – *Siembra Petrolera*. Particularly before the late-2009 economic downturn, this plan was deeply infused with politics; its objectives once included socioeconomic development, regional energy integration, and creation of a multipolar international relations system (PDVSA 2008, 2009). In some ways, these objectives materially affect PDVSA's real strategy; in others, however, they function as political window dressing.[112]

Consider PDVSA's policies in the Orinoco Belt.[113] Starting in 2005, PDVSA and foreign companies from Chávez-friendly governments (mostly NOCs) conducted reserves certification in sixteen development regions, or "blocks," within the Orinoco Belt.[114] This partly cosmetic project, known as *Magna Reserva* (Great Reserves), supported Chávez's geopolitical goals for the oil sector.[115] (In a gross overstatement, Chávez called the project the largest "ever envisioned in Latin America and one of the most important projects worldwide" (Otis 2007).) Since 2006, Venezuela has assigned several Orinoco development blocks to Chávez-friendly NOCs, also for political reasons. Despite the grandiosity of the initial announcements, several of these assignations – such as those to NOCs from Belarus and Vietnam – are largely superficial. Others may become significant, though questions remain. PDVSA had agreed to work with Chinese NOCs in the Orinoco's Junin 4 block (though the Chinese lack extra-heavy oil expertise) and with Russian NOCs in the Junin 6 block (though the Russians, for their part, may not have reliable funding for the projects) (Kebede 2009; Parraga 2009).

In the most promising parts of the Orinoco Belt, PDVSA and the Chávez administration have reversed course on years of confrontation by courting IOC interest. In late 2008, PDVSA launched a public auction process for minority interests in several blocks within the Orinoco Belt's highly attractive Carabobo area. After several false starts, two consortiums, led by IOCs Repsol YPF and Chevron, were awarded blocks in early 2010.

As the Orinoco Belt case illustrates, PDVSA's underlying strategy is to marry political and commercial goals where possible (as with the Russian and Chinese NOCs) while quietly working with IOCs as necessary (as occurred in Carabobo). PDVSA's dance of political and commercial objectives in the Orinoco Belt is the most significant element of its strategy, because of that region's production potential. Other goals include developing the natural gas sector (in which political factors remain mostly at bay)[116] and securing new refinery interests to diversify downstream markets (in which political and commercial priorities overlap).[117]

Note that improvization heavily colors PDVSA's strategy. Because of Chávez's impulsive governing style, PDVSA frequently reshuffles its priorities in response to new demands. And this constant retooling has taken a toll on company performance – the issue to which I turn next.

4.2 PDVSA performance: success, then decay

The changes in the state–PDVSA relationship have profoundly affected PDVSA's performance. I argue two points below. First, limited state interference in the oil sector and the legacy assets and talents from IOC operations largely account for PDVSA's tremendous performance between the 1970s and early 2000s. Second, the Chávez administration post-2002 interventions in PDVSA's affairs have stymied the company. The unpredictability and weight of Chávez-imposed obligations have reduced PDVSA's capacity to maintain and invest in operations. Moreover, Chávez's wide-scale firings of PDVSA's workforce have depleted its technical and managerial skill base.

4.2.1 World-class performer (1976–2002)

The hands-off relationship between Venezuelan politicians and PDVSA had a decisive effect on company performance between the 1970s and early 2000s. State interventions were infrequent, and those that did occur rarely affected how PDVSA deployed its capital or labor resources.[118] Because of this autonomy, PDVSA paid its workers attractive salaries[119] and advanced them on a non-discretionary basis (Randall 1987; Philip 1999). (PDVSA's human resource policy was, in fact, called a "meritocracy.") Combined with its extensive intra-firm competition and legacy assets (both physical and human capital), PDVSA fostered professionalism and commercial ambition.

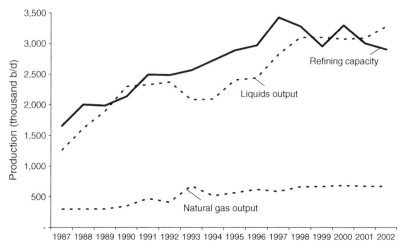

Figure 10.3 Selected PDVSA operational data, 1987–2002.
Source: PIW data, 1987–2002.

In this environment, PDVSA flourished.[120] *Petroleum Economist* conducted three expert polls in 1993, 1995, and 1999, and each one rated PDVSA as both the best-managed and best financially managed NOC (Petroleum Economist 1993, 1995, 1999). The combination of political insulation and a performance-oriented corporate culture transformed PDVSA into a technology leader. The company's research arm, INTEVEP, secured hundreds of patents for its innovations in instruments, substances, and equipment – the most notable of which was Orimulsion (Economides *et al.* 2007). PDVSA's operational data is also indicative (though not dispositive) of its performance: the company's oil production, natural gas production, and refining skyrocketed by more than 100 percent between the late 1980s and late 1990s. (Refining activities were not very profitable, however.) See Figure 10.3.[121]

4.2.2 Transformation brings inefficiency (2003–present)
PDVSA's performance has waned since the Chávez administration overhauled the company in 2003. Most immediately, the firing of 30–40 percent of the company workforce depleted PDVSA's employee skill set. Those fired had an average of fifteen years of experience and

included two-thirds of the company's managers and engineers (APS Review Oil Market Trends 2005; The Economist 2006). In the wake of the purge, PDVSA hired new employees – the payroll now exceeds 100,000 workers, more than twice as many as before the strike (The Economist 2010) – but many of them are inexperienced and their sheer numbers have strained company finances. Though PDVSA remains capable of carrying out most operations (and in this sense the company remains superior to the most dysfunctional NOCs), its talent stock has diminished considerably.

Moreover, Chávez's ever-changing and escalating demands on PDVSA have created uncertainty for the company. Unlike the pre-Chávez era, when Venezuelan politicians advocated a few, mostly complementary objectives, the Chávez-era goals are frequently divergent. Oil sector stability, for example, remains a Chávez administration objective, but that aim is in constant competition with – and has usually lost out to – foreign policy missions, political patronage, and other national goals. And because of Chávez's rash governing style, PDVSA's responsibilities change frequently. As a result, the company has struggled to define what its most important obligations are at any given moment.

The most debilitating of these obligations has been financial. Combining PDVSA's budgetary and extra-budgetary payments (see Tables 10.2 and 10.3), the share of PDVSA's revenues controlled by the government increased, according to its own figures, from 21.5 percent in 2003 to 45.4 percent in 2007. (This share dipped to 35.2 percent in 2008 as company revenues and costs escalated during the early mid-year oil price spike.) The jump in government take occurred even though PDVSA's own revenues rose on the strength of rising oil prices. Furthermore, the government has appropriated between 85 percent and 100 percent of PDVSA's revenues net of costs and expenses since 2006.[122] See Table 10.4 for more information.[123] PDVSA has to some extent compensated for the weight of these obligations through bond issues, but its efforts have been insufficient: Partly as a result of revenue shortfalls, PDVSA has by its own figures failed to invest sufficient resources to maintain production (EIA 2009a).[124] Only in 2007 and early to mid 2008, when high oil prices fueled revenues, did PDVSA's core investment perhaps surpass recommended levels of $3 billion/year.[125] See Table 10.5 above.[126]

Tax uncertainty has further complicated PDVSA's ability to plan and produce hydrocarbons. As suggested in Table 10.4 above, off-

Table 10.4. *State control of PDVSA revenues, 2003–2008*

($m)	2003	2004	2005	2006	2007	2008
A. Obligations to government budget	9,487	12,161	17,713	27,213	29,718	29,707
B. Off-budget obligations	549	4,316	7,287	11,993	14,102	14,733
(A. + B.) Total PDVSA payments controlled by government	10,036	16,477	25,000	39,206	43,820	44,440
C. PDVSA revenues	46,589	63,736	85,730	99,252	96,242	126,364
D. PDVSA costs and expenses, excepting government obligations	33,370	44,074	53,203	60,122	49,702	74,685
(C. – D.) PDVSA revenues, net of commercial costs and expenses	13,219	19,662	32,527	39,130	46,540	51,679
(A. + B.)/C. Percentage of PDVSA's total revenues controlled by government	21.5	25.9	29.2	39.5	45.4	35.2
(A. + B.)/(C. – D.) Percentage of PDVSA's revenues net of commercial costs and expenses controlled by government	75.9	83.8	76.9	100	94.2	86.0

Notes: Amounts differ slightly depending on source. I rely on the most comprehensive sources available.
Where possible, I rely on PDVSA's most recent reports filed with the SEC; 2005–2008 figures are not based on SEC filings.
Source: Derived from PDVSA (2003, 2005a, 2006a, 2007, 2008, 2009). Details on budgetary and extra-budgetary taxes are included in Tables 10.2 and 10.3, respectively.

Table 10.5. *Total PDVSA investment, and investment in exploration and production, 2003–2008*[a]

($m)	2003	2004	2005	2006	2007	2008
Total PDVSA investment[b]	1,969	2,960	3,938	1,748	9,254[c]	11,656[d]
Investment in exploration and production	1,276	1,912	2,077	N/A[e]	4,809	6,986

[a] Note 1: Actual investment refers to "cash used in investment activities" (worldwide) from the most recent PDVSA financial reports in which that data is available. Note 2: Where possible, I rely on PDVSA's most recent reports filed with the SEC.
[b] Total investment excludes investment from third parties, such as *empresas mixtas.*
[c] PDVSA reports actual 2007 investment as $13,187 million, but that figure apparently includes $3,933 million in "Support and Management." I subtracted 3,933 from 13,187 because Support and Management is not found in previous financial reports and includes PDVSA's purchase of electric companies and investments in non-core electric operations.
[d] This figure excludes: 1) $1,175 million in non-PDVSA investment by *empresas mixtas*; 2) $1,258 million in non-PDVSA investment from partners in the Orinoco Belt; and 3) $1,738 million in "other" investment, much of which goes toward non-core activities like PDVSA América, PDV Naval. Because some of PDVSA's "other" investment may go toward core activities, this figure may be a slight underestimate.
[e] Based on the 2007 report, which does not break out 2006 investment in exploration and production. PDVSA's 2006 report lists $4,166 million for investment in exploration and production but that figure is based on $7,205 million in 2006 total investment. Because this figure is inconsistent with the $1,748 million in 2006 total investment reported in 2007 (and on which I rely, following my decision rule above), I have left this figure blank.
Source: Derived from PDVSA (2003, 2005a, 2006a, 2007, 2008, 2009).

budget payments are almost completely unpredictable from year to year because the Chávez administration has enormous discretion to adjust extra-budgetary spending. (The main constraints to this discretion are political, not procedural, because most extra-budgetary tax rates are not enshrined in law.)[127] Even budgetary taxes are erratic; the Chávez administration used its control of the legislature to impose new taxes in 2006 and 2008. As a result of shifting government obligations and state goals, PDVSA's investment fluctuated wildly from less than $2 billion in 2003 and 2006 to more than $11 billion in 2008[128] and likely fell short of planned investment every year between 2003 and 2008.[129] See Table 10.6.

Because of heavy government obligations, PDVSA's workforce turnover, and other factors,[130] PDVSA's oil production has failed to recover to pre-strike levels. Keeping in mind that statistics on production are more contentious than others, PDVSA's production conservatively fell off by 10–15 percent between 2002 and 2007, including its joint ventures with IOCs. See Figure 10.4. Increased IOC production in joint ventures partly masks the decline in PDVSA's production. Excluding those joint ventures – and considering the company's effort only – PDVSA's production conservatively dropped from 2.2 million bbl/d before the strikes to 1.5 million bbl/d in 2007, a more than 30 percent decline (EIA 2009a). The reasons for PDVSA's production fall are complex, but some part of the decline probably indicates weakening performance.

5 Conclusion

In this chapter, I argue that the relationship between the Venezuelan state and PDVSA accounts for much of PDVSA's strategy and performance. From the 1970s to the late 1990s, Venezuela awarded PDVSA broad control over the oil sector, although periodic interventions occurred. In this environment, PDVSA walled itself off from the state and became a highly competent NOC.

After shaking up the company in 2003, the state–PDVSA relationship flipped almost completely. The Chávez administration has taken a much more obtrusive role in oil sector management. As a result, PDVSA's strategy has moved away from autonomy and toward accommodation. In particular, it has taken on many of the goals of the state, including providing a wide array of social services. As an oil company, its efficiency has declined due to the inability of senior managers to focus on oil operations and due to the scarcity of capital for investment – even with high oil prices. The purging of the company's top ranks after disastrous strikes in 2002–2003 has further undercut performance.

Looking ahead, the global economic collapse has pulled PDVSA in competing directions. On the one hand, the late-2008 price drop

Table 10.6. *Estimated actual and planned PDVSA investment,*
2003–2008

($m)	2003	2004	2005	2006	2007	2008
Total PDVSA investment[a]	1,969	2,960	3,939	1,748	9,254[b]	11,656[c]
Planned investment for that year[d]	2,978	6,706	6,607	8,244	11,048[e]	13,422[f]
Difference between actual and planned investment	–1,009	–3,746	–2,668	–6,946	–1,794	–1,766

[a] Total investment excludes investment from third parties, such as *empresas mixtas*.

[b] As above, PDVSA reports actual 2007 investment as $13,187 million, but that figure apparently includes $3,933 million in "Support and Management." I subtracted 3,933 from 13,187 because Support and Management is not found in previous financial reports and includes PDVSA's purchase of electric companies and investments in non-core electric operations.

[c] As above, this figure excludes: 1) $1,175 million in non-PDVSA investment by *empresas mixtas*; 2) $1,258 in non-PDVSA investment from partners in the Orinoco Belt; and 3) $1,738 million in "other" investment, much of which goes toward non-core activities like PDVSA América, PDV Naval. Because some of PDVSA's "other" investment may go toward core activities, this figure may be a slight underestimate.

[d] Planned investment refers to planned capital expenditures (worldwide) *generally based on the financial report that most immediately precedes actual investment.* That is, I rely on PDVSA's 2002 20-F SEC Report (published in October 2003) for 2003 planned investment. Because PDVSA did not publish an SEC report in 2004, I also rely on PDVSA's 2002 SEC Report (published in October 2003) for 2004 planned investment. And I rely on PDVSA's 2003 SEC Report (published a year late in October 2005) for 2005 planned investment, and so forth.

[e] This figure is based on PDVSA's 2004 SEC report (published in 2006) rather than its 2005 financial report because only the 2004 report shows planned 2007 worldwide investment. The 2005 financial report shows domestic investment ($10.070 billion) only.

[f] PDVSA reports planned investment as $15,671 million, but that figure apparently includes $2,249 million in "Support and Management." I subtracted $2,249 million from $15,671 million because Support and Management is not found in previous financial reports and includes PDVSA's purchase of electric companies and investments in PDVSA América, PDV Naval, and other items.

Source: Derived from PDVSA (2003, 2005a, 2006a, 2007, 2008, 2009).

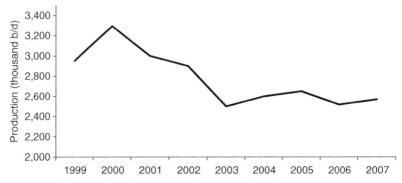

Figure 10.4 PDVSA liquids production, 1999–2007.
Note: Includes PDVSA's interest in various joint venture projects. These interests include the former apertura-era Orinoco Belt Association Agreements (now called joint ventures), Operational Service Agreements (now called Empresas Mixtas), and Risk Exploration Agreements (name remains unchanged).
Source: PIW data, 1999–2008.

dried up PDVSA's (already unstable) investment budget. Partly to fill the investment gap, the Chávez administration has sought outside companies, including many IOCs, to develop the Orinoco Belt. (It has also made its books somewhat more transparent – perhaps to reassure bond creditors and potential IOC partners.) The success of this approach depends on outside company judgments of Venezuela's reserves and its dreadful track record in contract enforcement. At the same time as PDVSA rebuilds IOC relationships, it is straining relationships with oil field service companies. Because of stressed finances (caused by both falling oil prices and government taxation), PDVSA fell nearly $8 billion in arrears to those companies by 2009 (Parraga 2010). The Venezuelan government subsequently nationalized some of their operations later that year and pledged to repay some debts.

I make no argument on whether PDVSA's transformation has benefited Venezuelan society. The Chávez administration has captured a much higher share of PDVSA's revenues relative to previous governments and has redirected some of those revenues toward social spending. Scholars have reached little consensus on the developmental effects of these policies.[131] What is clear, however, is that Chávez's reshaping of PDVSA has come at some cost to company performance and, in all likelihood, future revenues for the Venezuelan people.

Notes

In preparing this chapter, I interviewed eighteen individuals from PDVSA, the Venezuelan government, IOCs, academia, energy consulting groups, and non-governmental organizations (NGOs). Most interviews took place in Caracas, Venezuela during August 2006 and March 2007. A few additional interviews occurred in Palo Alto, California at later dates. To encourage openness during interviews, I have kept the names of interviewees private.

I thank David Victor, Mark Thurber, Peter Nolan, and my wife Rachel for their feedback and Ramón Espinasa and Francisco Monaldi for their incisive, detailed reviews. Thomas Heller, Noah Long, and Rose Kontak participated in and helped arrange visits to Venezuela; their perspectives were very helpful in writing early drafts of this chapter. Any errors are my own.

1 This chapter contributes to a rich literature on PDVSA. Various 1970s and 1980s works examine the Venezuelan oil sector, particularly its nationalization. Among these are Tugwell (1975); Petras *et al.* (1977); Coronel (1983); and Randall (1987). By the 1990s, scholars devoted increasing attention to PDVSA specifically. Key works include Boué (1993); Sosa Pietri (1993, 2000); Espinasa (1996); Baena (1999b); and Mommer (2002). After Chávez took control of PDVSA in 2003, a new wave of scholarship looked at the company's transition period. These works are highly polarized – reflecting the charged political environment of the time. Major research in this vein includes Mommer (2004) and Espinasa (2006). Most recently, Mares and Altamirano (2007) and Bermúdez Romero (2004) provide historical accounts of PDVSA and examined its behavior during the Chávez era. My chapter builds upon this literature by evaluating PDVSA from its inception through the Chávez administration.

2 Answering the polls were senior-level energy specialists from financial institutions, advisers, and accounting and law firms. PDVSA won the poll convincingly in 1993 (KPC and Saudi Aramco were its nearest competitors); beat out Saudi Aramco in 1995; and edged Statoil in 1999.

3 Including the opportunity cost of Venezuela's enormous domestic gasoline subsidy, the proportion of *potential* revenues controlled by the government rose from roughly 30–40 percent in 2003 to 50–55 percent in 2007.

4 The heaviness of oil is gauged by its API gravity, which measures petroleum's weight relative to water. PDVSA classifies extra-heavy oil as having an API of less than 11 degrees; and heavy oil as having an API gravity of less than 21 degrees but greater than or equal to 11 degrees (PDVSA 2008).

5 Taxation rates slowly rose over time but higher rates applied only to new concessions.

6 Úslar Pietri (1936)

7 Actual profit shares between the government and IOCs varied somewhat, however. For more, see Randall (1987) and Mommer (2002).

8 See, e.g., Alesina and Perotti (1996); Jones (1997). See Rodríguez (2006) for a separate analysis of Venezuelan growth figures using different approaches.

9 Note that Venezuelan governments took care not to alienate the private sector. The Betancourt administration was nationalistic, but it did not pursue nationalization and maintained a pragmatic approach toward IOCs (Matsuda 1997). The Leoni administration was more confrontational but backed off its most aggressive proposals after receiving IOC resistance (Matsuda 1997).

10 The civil-military government in power at the time issued the *Decreto Sanabria* raising oil sector income taxes from 28.5 percent to 46.5 percent (Manzano and Monaldi 2010).

11 Shell, however, adopted a policy of employing Venezuelan talent voluntarily (Randall 1987).

12 The term "devil's excrement" has had impressive staying power, being used in popular books on oil dependence (e.g., Karl 1997) and a political blog (Wordpress.com blog www.devilsexcrement.com/).

13 For more on Mexico's nationalization, see Chapter 7. For more on Venezuela's nationalization of the iron ore industry, see Baena (1999b).

14 By providing substantial compensation, the Venezuelan government ousted IOCs "in a gentleman-like way – i.e., asking them to leave and still keep in touch" (Baena 1999b).

15 In some ways, PDVSA's immediate post-nationalization experience mirrors that of Saudi Aramco. See Chapter 5.

16 Again like Saudi Aramco, PDVSA inherited the talent pool and capital stock of its IOC forerunners. See Chapter 5.

17 Post-1986 Corpoven was the merged entity of Corpoven and Meneven. Only the Meneven part of Corpoven came from Mene Grande, but that part dominated the corporate culture.

18 2004–present oil minister and PDVSA president Rafael Ramírez (2006b) would later use the same term to describe PDVSA's 1990s opening to IOCs, known as *la apertura petrolera*.

19 PDVSA also maintained the legal status of other operating subsidiaries, like Bariven and Palmaven (even though those companies were no longer active) because it wanted to preserve flexibility for future corporate changes. PDVSA also established other types of subsidiaries, such as petrochemical subsidiary Pequiven.

20 Unlike some other NOCs, PDVSA never internationalized its upstream exploration and production activities.

21 The strategies of KPC and PDVSA contrast with the more recent upstream acquisitions of many NOCs. See Chapter 12; Chapter 18 and Chapter 14.

22 Through the Ruhr Oel joint venture, PDVSA has held 50 percent interests in four German refineries.

23 PDVSA held a 50 percent interest in a Belgian refinery through joint venture company Nynäs.

24 PDVSA entered into a lease agreement with the Netherlands Antilles for a refinery in Curaçao.

25 Four refineries in Sweden are part of the Nynäs deal.

26 Two refineries in the United Kingdom are part of the Nynäs deal.

27 Venezuela's CITGO subsidiary (discussed immediately below) owns five of the US refineries (after acquiring the Lemont refinery from another PDVSA subsidiary, Midwest Refining, in 2002). Another was owned by LYONDELL-CITGO, in which PDVSA held a 41.25% ownership interest. (PDVSA sold its stake to this refinery in 2006.) Hovensa, a joint venture in which PDVSA holds a 50% interest, owns the St. Croix (US Virgin Islands) refinery. Lastly, Chalmette Refining, a joint venture in which PDVSA holds a 50% interest, owns the Chalmette refinery. Note that ExxonMobil owns the other 50% interest in Chalmette. Although PDVSA and ExxonMobil would enter into a protracted legal battle over interests in Venezuela's Orinoco Belt, their joint interest here – as of mid 2009 – remained intact.

28 PDVSA paid out $120 million in cash and $170 million in crude supplies for the 50 percent stake (Baena 1999b).

29 By 1999, the company had 13,000 CITGO gas stations and controlled more than 10 percent of the US market (Economides *et al.* 2007).

30 The opposition party *Acción Democrática* (AD) led the political fight against this contract.

31 Venezuelan energy minister and PDVSA president Rafael Ramírez claimed in 2006 – in a probable exaggeration – that PDVSA's internationalization strategy transferred $14 billion in taxable assets outside the country (Ramírez 2006a).

32 This strategy was part of a broader Latin American trend toward welcoming foreign investment during the 1990s.

33 These interests took the form of profit-sharing agreements (PSAs) and operational agreements.

34 Most of the contracts gave companies the right to subject disputes under those contracts to international arbitration; the provisions called for arbitration in New York under International Chamber of Commerce

(ICC) rules. These contracts further contained *force majeure* clauses providing for compensatory damages if the state were to act in a discriminatory way (rather than of general applicability) that impeded production. And the contracts exempted the companies from regional and local taxes (Monaldi 2001).

35 However, PDVSA paid the full royalty and oil tax on the oil produced.

36 The OSAs designated companies as "operational service contractors" rather than as oil producers even though the companies were, in fact, producing oil. Because of this classification, the OSAs exempted companies from the 1943 Hydrocarbons Law, which set forth special taxes on oil production (including a higher royalty, special rate of the income tax, and surface tax). The OSA contractual definition of operational service contractors implicated Article 5 of Venezuela's 1975 Nationalization Law, which allowed joint venture foreign participation subject to three conditions: that 1) PDVSA "controls" the joint ventures; 2) the joint ventures are in effect for a limited timeframe; and 3) the Venezuelan congress approves their basic framework. The "control" provision of Article 5 further affected RPSAs and AAs, because those contracts permitted oil companies (which were, in fact, mostly IOCs) to take majority control of the projects.

  PDVSA and the Venezuelan government took creative measures to minimize the impact from, or circumvent, these laws. To work around hydrocarbons law and the nationalization law provisions on "oil production" affecting OSAs, the Venezuelan government convinced the supreme court to interpret the laws so as to uphold the legality of those contracts. And to reduce the effect from the Article 5 Nationalization Law "control" provision on RPSAs and AAs, the Venezuelan congress approved, and the supreme court later upheld, a loose definition of control. PDVSA "controlled" the joint venture according to this interpretation so long as it approved "important" decisions (even though the joint venture could make "regular" decisions by approval of a majority of shareholders) (Mommer 2002).

37 See, e.g., Astorga *et al.* (2005), which shows that Venezuela's Gross Domestic Product per capita grew poorly relative to most Latin American states between 1960 and 2000. The issue of whether Venezuela suffered a "resource curse" is hotly debated. For a skeptical view, see Rodríguez (2006).

38 The neoliberal prescription for economic reform called for, inter alia, reduced government spending, privatization of state enterprise, and trade liberalization. Many Latin American governments adopted neoliberalism in the early 1990s as part of the "Washington Consensus" (Williamson 2002). By the late 1990s, however, neoliberalism became a bogeyman among the Latin American left, including in Venezuela.

39 PDVSA's defenders argued that Venezuela had to shed its *rentista* model of development (using the oil sector to fund the rest of the Venezuelan economy) and instead view the oil sector as the principal engine of growth (Espinasa 1996).

40 One major change was to prohibit, at the constitutional level, PDVSA's privatization. However, the 1999 constitution does not prohibit privatization of PDVSA's operating companies.

41 The Chávez administration decreed this law in part because of long-standing concerns about income taxes in weakly administered states like Venezuela (Mommer 2002). (The concern was that states need company cost data to collect income taxes, which companies could more easily manipulate in weakly administered states.) But in the rising oil price environment of the early 2000s, the 2001 Hydrocarbons Law actually gave the state a smaller proportion of the total take than previously.

42 For a detailed comparison of the changes resulting from the 2001 law, see Espinasa (2001).

43 Ship captains in the state-owned oil fleet and dockworkers later joined in the strike.

44 See www.youtube.com/watch?v=dmXpbT7Fhiw. Ramirez is also vice president of Chávez's political party, the *Partido Socialista Unido de Venezuela* (PSUV). This combination of roles is unprecedented in Venezuela's history.

45 For discussions of the *misiones*, see Penfold-Becerra (2007); Ortega and Rodríguez (2008).

46 PDVSA management contemplated selling off CITGO in 2003 but decided against it. In 2006, PDVSA sold off its Texas-based Lyondell-CITGO refinery; most outside observers believe this sale occurred for business rather than ideological reasons (PESD Interviews).

47 Although some social development-oriented PDVSA subsidiaries have sprouted up, their long-term significance is unclear. These new subsidiaries include PDVSA *Industrial* ("PDVSA Industrial," designed to manufacture consumer products such as shoes and clothing); PDVSA *Agrícola* ("PDVSA Agriculture," aimed at harvesting food); and PDVSA *Desarrollos Urbanos* ("PDVSA Urban Development," designed to assist in home construction).

48 Indeed, PDVSA has become known as an *estado paralelo* (parallel state).

49 Note that the growth in Venezuelan oil reserves is partially illusory. Venezuela discovered some new reserves, mostly in the eastern part of the country during the 1980s, but some of the growth resulted from Venezuelan political decisions to reclassify (and third-party decisions to accept reclassification of) already known supplies. PDVSA and the

Venezuelan government carry a long tradition of reserves overstatement, having done so in the late 1980s and early 1990s (Boué 1993) and again during the Chávez administration. The reasons behind reserves over-statement have been to increase Venezuela's influence within OPEC, financial creditworthiness, and (especially during the late 1980s and 1990s) OPEC production quotas. (Many other oil-exporting govern-ments have engaged in similarly creative reserves accounting.)

50 This figure is based on purchasing power parity (PPP) estimates.

51 Although long-term trends are quite stable, the yearly figures are sub-ject to considerable variation, especially in the case of contribution gov-ernment revenues and GDP.

52 This strategy contrasts with the approach taken by Venezuelan govern-ments between the 1950s and early 1970s, which imposed escalating tax and local content obligations on private companies in the oil sector. By the mid 1970s, these companies mostly expected nationalization to occur.

53 Venezuela's dependence on oil exports has also led the government peri-odically to seek control over oil prices and, as a consequence, oil sec-tor production plans. This desire for control is a principal reason that Venezuela first promoted cartelization among oil exporters in the 1940s and co-founded OPEC in 1960. After that time, however, Middle Eastern countries with larger oil reserves and closer affinities largely overshad-owed Venezuela within OPEC, and Venezuela's enthusiasm for OPEC has often waned. (Further eroding Venezuelan support was the forma-tion of PDVSA – which often disagreed with OPEC policies.) By the early 1990s, PDVSA advocated Venezuelan withdrawal from the organization (Boué 1993; Philip 1999). Venezuela became the second-worst cheating OPEC member between 1992 and 2001 (behind only Qatar, whose oil output was only one-fifth of Venezuela's) (Molchanov 2003).

This situation changed markedly under the Chávez administration. Venezuela – along with Mexico and Saudi Arabia – led efforts to cut OPEC production since 1998 and has remained an OPEC enthusiast and an oil price hawk ever since. Not coincidentally, the Chávez gov-ernment's price hawkishness dovetails with PDVSA's diminished cap-acity to produce oil, which is explored in more detail below.

54 As of 2007, the average API gravity of Venezuelan oil fields was less than 20 degrees, heavy by international standards (EIA 2007).

55 Even during these early years, however, Venezuela was the world's lead-ing heavy oil supplier (Boué 1993).

56 Venezuela has four traditional sedimentary basins for oil production: Zulia; Oriental; Barinas-Apure; and Falcón (these basins do not include the more recently exploited Orinoco Belt). The Barinas Basin is located in the south-central part of the country, in an area historically known

for cattle production. Although the basin showed some promise in the 1990s, its production remained minor – 2.6 percent of total – during the 1990s (PDVSA 2008). The Falcón Basin, near the northwest coast of Venezuela, has minimal production and has very little potential (Boué 1993).

57 The most common production process in Venezuela is "cold" heavy oil production which uses horizontal well and multilateral wells. Estimates of Venezuelan production costs differ because of changing input prices and technological developments. A recent estimate of production costs in Venezuela's extra-heavy Orinoco Belt is $15–20/barrel (Centre for Economics and Management 2007). Production costs for conventional oil projects are, by comparison, somewhat lower but difficult to obtain because a common proxy for production cost – oil company threshold decisions – includes taxes and other considerations.

58 Extra-heavy oil contains several environmental harmful contaminants, including sulfur, nickel, and vanadium, that require treatment and disposal (Neff and Hagemann 2007). Another by-product of upgrading is petroleum coke. Thermal power plants can use petroleum coke for power generation but it is very carbon-intensive. In April 2010, Venezuela reached agreement with China to develop extra-heavy oil in the Orinoco Belt and to build three thermal power plants that would run on petroleum coke (Carlisle 2010).

59 The motives behind PDVSA's 1980s internationalization strategy remain hotly debated. For more on the argument that PDVSA internationalized to secure downstream markets for its heavy oil, see, e.g., Espinasa (2006). Boué (2002), among others, counters that PDVSA could have ensured revenue stability through hedging on capital markets rather than through internationalization and argues that a primary motive behind internationalization was instead to avoid tax liability and Venezuelan government interference.

60 At the time, extra-heavy oil was not easily convertible into conventional oil.

61 This strategy had the side-benefit of circumventing (already partially ignored) OPEC production quotas because Orimulsion was not classified as conventional oil (see EIA 2007).

62 Some pre-nationalization development had occurred, however. Between 1945 and nationalization, IOCs shifted natural gas production from flaring toward reinjection and feedstock use for petrochemicals (Boué 1993). And in the 1960s and 1970s, Venezuela established gas pipelines in the Andean, Central-Western and Eastern regions (Mallet-Guy Guerra *et al.* 1993).

63 Taking over existing oil operations is much less expensive than developing new natural gas operations.

64 Several IOCs bid for exploration blocks auctioned in 2003 but later blocks received less interest. Part of the reason for uncertainty is that the law requires operators to sell some natural gas domestically, but the domestic sales price is uncertain. Note that even in investor-friendly Brazil, it has proved difficult to encourage private exploration and production of gas due to high exposure to local price regulation and long payback times for gas infrastructures (Chapter 12). In addition, the Chávez administration also supported PDVSA's construction of pipelines internally and between Venezuela and Colombia; these pipelines are mostly for natural gas reinjection. The Venezuelan government plans to reverse the course of the Venezuela-Colombia pipeline in the future after it has further developed its natural gas reserves (EIA 2009a).

65 The reasons behind Venezuela's institutional failures are mostly beyond the scope of this chapter. See Karl (1997) for more discussion.

66 See Monaldi *et al.* (2008) for discussion.

67 As Venezuela transitioned from military rule to democracy in 1958, the major Venezuelan political parties agreed on a power-sharing agreement known as the Pact of Punto Fijo (named after a Venezuelan home in Caracas where party leaders met). This pact served as the basis for Venezuelan democracy through the 1990s. Although *puntofijismo* provided stability to the Venezuelan political system, it enshrined a system of clientelism and marginalized third-party competition. See, e.g., Myers (2000); Hellinger (2003) for general discussion. Note that public participation in the Venezuelan political system broadened somewhat in the 1980s because of decentralization reforms (Naim 2001).

68 The six indicators are: 1) voice and accountability; 2) political stability and absence of violence/terrorism; 3) government effectiveness; 4) regulatory quality; 5) rule of law; and 6) control of corruption.

69 These four indicators are: 1) voice and accountability; 2) political stability and absence of violence/terrorism; 3) regulatory quality; and 4) rule of law. The word "significantly" refers here to statistically significant change.

70 In the case of voice and accountability, Venezuela has fallen from the bottom 50 percent to bottom 30 percent of countries.

71 Transparency International statistics buttress the World Bank view of Venezuelan corruption. Venezuela has remained more or less constantly in the bottom 25 percent of countries in the Transparency International Corruption Perceptions Index since the index's inception in 1995 (four years before the Chávez administration took office) (Transparency International and University of Goettingen 1995–1998; Transparency International 1999–2009).

72 They are known as "boli-bourgeois" because of their wealth and at least public commitment to Chávez's Bolivarian revolution.

73 The energy ministry had two types of formal powers to control pre-Chávez PDVSA: 1) to formulate energy policy under the Oil Nationalization Law and 2) to control PDVSA through its authority as state representative in shareholder holdings (in which the state was, of course, the only shareholder). Here, PDVSA lost out in the drafting of the Oil Nationalization Law. AGROPET had advocated giving ministerial rank to the PDVSA president (so that the PDVSA president would answer only to the Venezuelan president) but the law did not incorporate its position (Matsuda 1997). Note that the nationalization process stripped the oil ministry of its pre-nationalization power to serve as sole oil sector supervisor (Baena 1999b).

74 The only real exception to this pattern was in the Herrera administration (1979–1984), when budget pressures and ideology prompted the government to temporarily wrest budget control and administration for itself. That moment did not last.

75 Other factors facilitated PDVSA's pre-Chávez control over oil policymaking. From the time of PDVSA's first president, Rafael Alfonzo Ravard, PDVSA leadership enjoyed close relationships with the Venezuelan executive. These personal relationships – themselves a product of appointment decisions reflecting the importance of PDVSA to the Venezuelan economy – allowed the company to largely circumvent energy ministry interference (Coronel 1983). Partly because of its successful nationalization experience, Venezuela also had a strong political norm of oil industry non-interference, especially between the late 1970s and early 1980s. And legal questions over the limits of government authority also gave PDVSA greater policymaking space.

76 Note that other countries with even fewer institutional resources have had great success in implementing a progressive oil tax system. Perhaps part of the reason of Venezuela's lack of success is a self-ingrained belief in its institutional inabilities.

77 Staffed with critics of the pre-Chávez Venezuelan oil tax structure like Bernard Mommer, the Chávez administration shifted a greater proportion of the tax burden from income taxes to royalties. This shift made the oil tax scheme easier to administer but also less progressive (Manzano and Monaldi 2010).

78 At that time, the Venezuelan government transformed existing oil concessions into new concessions based on a "fifty-fifty" revenue-sharing model.

79 During this time, the government steadily increased its fiscal take.

80 Carlos Andréz Pérez sided with PDVSA, rather than with the energy ministry, in awarding PDVSA jurisdiction to manage the Orinoco Belt. He also gave PDVSA the power to reorganize its newly absorbed petrochemicals industry (Matsuda 1997). Congress was similarly restrained, holding few hearings on the oil sector (Matsuda 1997).

81 These changes include: 1) direct elections for governors and mayors starting in 1989; and 2) a 1993 shift in the legislative electoral system, from pure proportional representation to a mixed-member system of personalized proportional representation (Monaldi *et al.* 2008).

82 State-run enterprises became inefficient and often corrupt; for a brief time, the government operated a dog track (Philip 1999).

83 Possible exceptions include Brazil and Mexico, where large internal markets created more favorable conditions for ISI. See generally Silva (2007).

84 The Lusinchi administration (1984–1989) also faced strains because of falling oil prices but largely maintained spending because it believed low oil prices would recover. By the time Carlos Andrés Pérez (or CAP) came into power, the problems became great enough (as did the need for IMF conditionality requirements for financing) that the government instituted significant economic reforms. Interestingly, CAP had presided over the expansion of the state during his first term and then reduced its size during his second term.

85 This goal differs from the tax-and-redistribute features of ISI policy because the oil sector distributes oil resources directly – mostly to car owners – rather than through the government.

86 In January 2007, Chávez announced that domestic fuel prices would rise, but in April 2007 the legislature decided that the government would not raise prices in the short term.

87 The government then compelled PDVSA to use some of those monies to purchase public bonds from a bankrupt bank.

88 When the Persian Gulf War (1990–1991) created demand for Venezuelan oil, the government and IMF entered into an agreement whereby the government agreed to divert windfall oil revenues in return to IMF financing. However, the government spent much of the oil revenues and ultimately compelled PDVSA to transfer monies to make up the shortfall (Baena 1999b). Further economic troubles during the second Carlos Andrés Pérez administration (1989–1992) prompted the Venezuelan government to significantly cut PDVSA's budget and halt investment plans (Mares and Altamirano 2007).

89 In 1979, the government issued a decree rewriting PDVSA's corporate governance rules to exercise greater control over the company. Then, the government and left-wing politicians put political pressure on

PDVSA to postpone a 1979–1980 Orinoco Belt development plan in which US construction company Bechtel served as technical adviser (the project later ended for unrelated reasons) (Matsuda 1997).

90 Ideology played some role, however. Critiques of PDVSA by Bernard Mommer and other left-wing academics, by this time members of the Chávez administration, also informed Chávez's views.

91 For a detailed account of Chávez's personality and biography, see Marcano and Tyszka (2006). Note that some of Chávez's more public outbursts may in fact be carefully staged.

92 Foreign companies operating in the Orinoco Belt paid a lower rate through 2004.

93 As oil prices rise income taxes have become an increasingly important source of revenue.

94 Extra-heavy oil projects once paid a lower 34 percent rate.

95 These programs are extra-budgetary because the congress does not approve them as part of its formal budget.

96 In March 2009, PDVSA president Ramírez raised eyebrows by claiming that FONDEN had accumulated $57 billion, a number that is almost certainly an exaggeration (Minuto 59 2009).

97 Included in these trusts are monies for the *Fondo para el Desarrollo Económico y Social del País* (National Economic and Social Development Fund, or FONDESPA).

98 The rate of 50 percent applies to the difference between the actual average of the Venezuelan basket and the reference price of $70. If the price goes above $100 the rate applicable to the difference is 60 percent.

99 Mommer (2002) points out that the Venezuelan government suffered a long-term decline in its share of PDVSA oil income between 1981 (when the share was 71 percent) and 2000 (when the share was 39 percent). Although non-regressive tax frameworks are one part of the explanation for the declining share, rising costs (as Venezuelan oil became increasingly heavier) were another important cause. See Dunning (2008) for further discussion of changing fiscal takes in Venezuela over time.

100 Note that this effect is not universal. To some degree when prices were low, e.g., in 1998, the government has put pressure on PDVSA to compensate for lower government revenues. Whereas when revenues were large, e.g., in the early 1980s, PDVSA was able to invest even beyond original plans.

101 The government granted PDVSA permission to keep these export earnings in dollar-denominated accounts overseas. The purpose behind this provision was to give PDVSA greater flexibility to make international payments (Matsuda 1997).

102 In fact, PDVSA managers initially lacked an effective government strategy. Accustomed to working with foreign corporate management, PDVSA at first struggled to communicate effectively with politicians. Matsuda (1997) cites one instance in which politicians asked PDVSA managers not to use graphic presentations in a briefing session because the politicians had difficulty understanding them.

103 PDVSA sometimes carried out internationalization on behalf of (rather than to avoid) the Venezuelan government. One reason that PDVSA entered into its joint venture arrangement on the Caribbean island of Curacao is because the Venezuelan government was concerned about the political stability of the nearby island (Baena 1999b).

104 The 1983 Veba Oel deal took place the year after oil prices fell, creating an incentive for PDVSA to secure markets for its high-cost oil. (The same logic drove PDVSA's later internationalization decisions, too.) However, some scholars reject the argument that PDVSA began its internationalization process for commercial purposes. Mommer (2002) points out that the company's first foreign refinery, in Germany, has never refined extra-heavy crude; it refines instead PDVSA's smaller supplies of light oil, which are more easily marketable.

105 PDVSA's internationalization strategy differs strongly from the strategies of other NOCs seeking to hedge downstream oil market risks. Some, like Pemex, bought oil futures on the open market (Boué 1993). Others, like Saudi Aramco, entered into netback contracts with separately owned refineries (Baena 1999b).

106 Another reason for transfer pricing to the refinery network overseas was to finance the investments required to upgrade and make adequate these refineries to intake larger quantities of the extra-heavy and sour Venezuelan crude. These refineries at the time of purchase were not fit for taking full amounts of Venezuelan crudes.

107 An alternative explanation for why PDVSA did not remit significant dividends to Venezuela for its US subsidiaries is because Venezuela and the United States did not have a double tax treaty (Mares and Altamirano 2007). Note also that oil sales to overseas refineries helped PDVSA evade OPEC-set production quotas (Baena 1999b). OPEC quota evasion was possible because those quota restrictions arguably bound exports rather than production. Under this interpretation, PDVSA refineries could produce from non-Venezuelan sources without regard for quota restrictions. The Oil Ministry, by contrast, argued that OPEC quota restrictions affected all of PDVSA's production (Baena 1999b).

108 PDVSA had previously acted as a protective shield by serving as the link between its operator subsidiaries and the Venezuelan state (Espinasa 2006).

109 Pre-Chávez shareholder meetings were often also for show, but Chávez has erased the fiction of energy ministry supervision.

110 These links have remained strong thus far. Ramírez's power has not threatened Chávez partly because Ramírez presents himself as a technocrat with little political ambition. Long-standing ties between Ramírez and Alí Rodríguez, another Chávez confidant, have helped cement the Ramírez–Chávez friendship (Bodzin 2009).

111 For more on Chávez's use of public pronouncements to enhance his image, see Marcano and Tyszka (2006).

112 For example, the company also has specific growth targets, but like other elements of PDVSA's formal strategy, those targets are probably not credible. In 2008, PDVSA envisioned increasing production from an EIA-estimated 2.7 million barrels in 2007 (1.5 million under direct management) to 5.8 million barrels per day by 2012 (4 million barrels per day under direct management) (PDVSA 2008; EIA 2009a). PDVSA's real strategy is likely more modest.

113 PDVSA's approach to procurement embodies the same differences between government goals and reality. Formally, the company has initiated a program to incentivize procurement from social cooperatives known as *Empresas de Producción Social* (EPS, or social production companies). In accord with Chávez's development and/or patronage goals, the EPS program is designed to democratize oil wealth. Evidence of EPS cooperatives actually carrying out work for PDVSA, however, is minimal. PDVSA continues to rely on traditional suppliers for the vast majority of its contractor services and in early 2009 suffered major disputes with them.

114 The Orinoco Belt consists of twenty-eight total blocks, divided into four areas: Ayacucho, Carabobo, Boyacá, and Junin.

115 These goals include: 1) building ties with NOCs from Chávez-friendly governments; 2) increasing Venezuela's OPEC production quotas (which are based on reserves) and therefore its influence within OPEC; and 3) increasing Venezuela and PDVSA's standing within the financial community by using booked reserves as a measure of creditworthiness. A PDVSA newsletter states that *Magna Reserva* would contribute to the "creation of a multipolar world" (PDVSA 2006b).

116 In keeping with this strategy, PDVSA signed contracts for development of two liquefied natural gas (LNG) plants in March 2009 (Watkins 2009).

117 Government foreign policy objectives have strongly influenced PDVSA's choice of new refinery locations (including Brazil, Cuba, China, Jamaica, and Nicaragua). Announcement of these refineries serve short-term, political needs, but actual project implementation – which depends on hard-nosed commercial calculations by PDVSA – is up in the air.

118 Key exceptions, noted above, were PDVSA's 1982 joint refinery agreement with Veba Oel and its 1990 acquisition of CITGO's remaining shares.

119 Chávez heavily criticized PDVSA's compensation levels during his 1998 presidential campaign. Before the strikes, young executives made $30,000–45,000 per year and top executives took in more than $250,000 per year (Miller 2002). Even after the strikes, however, PDVSA salaries have nevertheless remained attractive by Venezuelan standards.

120 The company remained highly efficient virtually from the time of nationalization until Chávez reshaped it in 2002–2003. External assessments of PDVSA's performance before the 1990s are less available, however.

121 PDVSA also boasted of having lower operating costs than IOCs in the later 1990s (PESD Interviews). Operating costs, however, are only a partial measure of performance, as geologic, geographic, and other factors substantially influence them.

122 An ideal analysis would compare government obligations to PDVSA rents, but the latter figures are not available. Export figures might approximate rents, but exports include some oil production that is refined and other production that is not; therefore I take the rougher approach above.

123 If the estimated opportunity cost of Venezuela's domestic gasoline subsidy is included, this figure rises even higher: the proportion of PDVSA's *potential* revenues (including the subsidy) controlled by the government rose from roughly 30–40 percent in 2003 to 50–55 percent in 2007.

Exact figures are omitted because the confidence in this estimate is low. Venezuela's domestic gasoline subsidy costs PDVSA roughly $10–20 billion/year, but accurate time-series data is not available.

124 One estimate is that PDVSA needs to spend $3 billion/year to maintain production at existing fields (EIA 2009a). This figure is a crude estimate only because it does not reflect changes in costs.

125 Exact 2006 figures are unavailable but must be below $3 billion because total investment was only $1.748 billion.

126 PDVSA's average annual investment for 2003–2007 ($3.882 billion/year) slightly exceeds the previous five-year 1998–2002 average ($3.856 billion/year). The extremely high 2007 investment figure clouds the 2003–2007 average, however. Omitting the 2007 figure, PDVSA 2003–2006 average investment is somewhat lower ($3.039 billion/year) than the previous five-year average (again $3.856 billion/ year).

127 The government directs most of its extra-budgetary funds to specific beneficiaries, who may lobby for continued spending on extra-budgetary programs like the *misiones*. The lobbying power of these beneficiaries is questionable, however, because they are widely dispersed, generally poor, and support the current government.

128 PDVSA's 2007 reported investment is even higher but includes monies used for the purchase of Venezuelan electric companies. PDVSA reports actual 2007 investment as $13,187 million, but that includes $3,933 in "Support and Management." I subtracted 3,933 from 13,187 because Support and Management is not found in previous financial reports and includes PDVSA's purchase of electric companies and investments in non-core electric operations.

129 Part of the reason for this persistent shortfall is that planned investment figures were probably unrealistic even at the time PDVSA made them.

130 Many of Venezuela's fields outside the Orinoco Belt are very mature and therefore declining as part of the ordinary hydrocarbon production process. Moreover, several of Venezuela's fields were damaged because the 2003 PDVSA strikes – because of sabotage by disaffected workers on strike (an argument made by Chávez supporters) and/or improper reactivation by unskilled PDVSA workers in the wake of the strike (an argument of Chávez detractors).

131 For discussions of the *misiones*, see Penfold-Becerra (2007); Ortega and Rodríguez (2008). Note also that these extra-budgetary social programs have reduced the accountability of traditional Venezuelan political institutions.

11 | Awakening giant: strategy and performance of the Abu Dhabi National Oil Company (ADNOC)

VARUN RAI AND DAVID G. VICTOR

1 Introduction

Abu Dhabi sits on the world's fifth-largest oil reserves (after Saudi Arabia, Iran, Iraq, and Kuwait) and is the eighth-largest producer of liquid fuels (after Saudi Arabia, Russia, the US, Iran, China, Mexico, and Canada). Its output, which had been roughly flat at about 2.5 million barrels per day (mbpd) during the 1990s, is now rising. It stood at 2.9 mbpd in 2008 and is poised to grow, perhaps to 4.5 mbpd over the next decade, as the company invests in managing its aging fields better and also in bringing new fields into production. Although its financial indicators are difficult to assess because the company is famously secretive, the Abu Dhabi National Oil Company (ADNOC) appears to be well managed and efficient. Compared with KPC, the Persian Gulf state oil enterprise with reserves comparable in size, ADNOC is a completely different organization. KPC, despite huge reserves, struggles to maintain production and is strikingly inefficient (see Chapter 8). ADNOC, by contrast, sits alongside Aramco among the star performers in the Persian Gulf. But where Aramco's performance stems from having internalized all facets of oil discovery and production, ADNOC's success comes from a blend of internal expertise and heavy reliance on foreign partners.

This chapter explores the history of ADNOC and examines the factors that explain its strategic choices and performance. We make four arguments. First, the company's high performance seems to be

We are grateful to Howard Harris (McKinsey and Company) and Michael M. Ohadi (Petroleum Institute, Abu Dhabi) for detailed comments and discussions on earlier drafts of this chapter and to Mark Thurber and David Hults for discussions. We also thank the senior officials at ADNOC we interviewed, on a confidential basis, for this study. Most of those interviews occurred in October 2008.

478

the result mainly of two factors. One is the relatively late arrival of Abu Dhabi to the league of large world oil producers. When the waves of nationalization overtook the petrostates in the 1970s, Abu Dhabi had little to nationalize because it was just beginning to organize a large oil industry. The emirate was part of a fragile country (United Arab Emirates) that was just three years old on the eve of the first oil shock in October 1973; Abu Dhabi had little internal capacity and many distractions just assuring its national integrity. Those accidents of history yielded the defining feature of Abu Dhabi's oil sector: concessions for exploration and production of oil that are operated through a consortium in which the controlling share (usually 60 percent) rests with the state (ADNOC) but minority shares are allocated among several Western oil companies. Unlike its peers in North Africa and the Persian Gulf, Abu Dhabi didn't fully nationalize its industry because its industry was at a much earlier stage of development; risks were much higher; and the country had little choice but to offer a large role for foreign ownership and operators. The other factor that helps explain ADNOC's high performance relative to its peer NOCs is that the company has used this unique position to build internal management talent through a clever system of corporate governance. ADNOC puts senior managers from the Western oil companies working alongside local employees and continually elicits information and technology from the Western companies. Whereas other studies in this book describe NOCs that have encouraged information and technology on best world practices by opening the oil sector to competition (e.g., Brazil and India), Abu Dhabi has done this within its oil company. In effect, ADNOC serves the dual roles of regulating the oil sector and also governing one of the world's largest oil companies. Not surprisingly, it is the emirate's leading institution for building indigenous talent.

Second, Abu Dhabi's geology has allowed for a leisurely development of the oil sector, and that has probably allowed ADNOC time to build competence while also allowing the state to retain essentially complete control over the oil sector. Abu Dhabi has, to date, faced none of the huge technical hurdles that sent Petrobras and Statoil offshore to deep water and required less capable companies (e.g., Sonangol) to defer a much larger role to outside companies. Until very recently, complex oil and gas fields have been largely set aside as abundant, and relatively easy to tap fields (including one of the world's largest continuous oil fields) have been tapped. Exploration risks have been extremely low, not just because the geology was accommodating but also because the country's largest fields were already mapped by Western companies in the 1960s long before the state assumed more control over the oil sector starting in the 1970s. Today, this is changing rapidly. Driven by depletion of the country's "easy" fields and also the political desire to boost output (and earnings), a new era of complexity and risk has arrived, confronting ADNOC with the need to boost investment in technology and expertise. Costs have risen sharply along with the need for highly skilled technical workers and management, and ADNOC now competes for a small pool of skilled Emirati workers with many other firms at home and abroad. A "race" is on between rising complexity (which creates pressure to defer to outsiders) and ADNOC's continuous efforts to build its internal expertise. That race has spawned a large number of experiments in managing oil and gas operations in the country because it isn't clear to ADNOC or the country's ruling elite which model will work best. Those experiments include redoubling the effort to build ADNOC's internal expertise so the standard 60 percent controlling share approach is more efficient; giving controlling roles to foreign companies for risky small fields; and creating new structures outside ADNOC for operations, such as gas and petrochemicals, that the company has historically neglected.

Third, it is impossible to understand ADNOC's success without reference to Abu Dhabi's political organization and its relationships with the other emirates that, together, constitute the United Arab Emirates (UAE). Abu Dhabi is almost entirely controlled by the ruling Al-Nahyan family along with a small number of other, closely allied families. Two aspects of this political organization have proved to be especially important. One is extremely stable political control, which has allowed the government to make credible, long-term decisions for the oil sector that have greatly eased the management task for ADNOC and also reduced risks for foreign participants. While foreigners confront closed or unattractive markets across nearly the entire Gulf, these lower risks along with explicit provisions for outside companies to play (minority) roles in the oil sector make Abu Dhabi the most enticing of all the region's large oil producers. This fortuitous situation in Abu Dhabi might have been quite different if the emirate's leadership had not been instrumental in creating the UAE in the 1970s. Each of the individual emirates was probably too small to be secure, but in the larger UAE along with settlement of troubling border disputes with Saudi Arabia and Iran, the emirates were more secure. UAE is run as a federation, but Abu Dhabi (which has 94 percent of the country's oil) is the country's dominant player. That has given the emirate (and its oil company) the advantages of a larger state while allowing retention of unitary rule.

Fourth, today ADNOC faces massive challenges. In addition to the rising complexity of its fields, demand for energy is increasing rapidly. Much of that demand is for electricity and natural gas to fire power plants – an area that has historically not been one of ADNOC's points of expertise. This has created a conflict between usage of gas to repressure existing oil fields and for power generation. Solutions, such as shifting to CO_2 injection so that gas could be sold rather than reinjected, are in sight, yet the company has barely any experience in such operations. The first contracts for large non-fossil power plants – notably a Korean supplied nuclear plant – have just been inked in 2010 with delivery much later. And the biggest challenge has been to create indigenous Emirati talent because the population base is small and the system of high school, university, and postgraduate education is weak. ADNOC and the government are aware of all these challenges and investing mightily to address them, but these are very difficult problems to solve. For ADNOC's Western partners, the biggest challenge is the looming expiration (starting in 2014) of the concession agreements that govern the partnerships with ADNOC's operating arms. We doubt that expiration is a major challenge to ADNOC itself since the Western companies have few other places to turn for acreage and ADNOC is already quietly making assurances that concessions will be extended and investments will be honored – assurances that many other governments would find difficult to make credible, but which are a hallmark of the stable and conservative system of governance in Abu Dhabi. But renewing the contracts is a relatively easy step. Much harder challenges, still unsolved, lie with building Emirati talent within the company and creating the capacity to manage the risks associated with highly complex oil and gas operations. So far, the company has not faced the one risk that has been paramount in most other case studies in this book – political instability. However, it is conceivable that such instabilities could arise if transitions in power are handled poorly and as other emirates, notably Dubai, exert larger pressure on the UAE's economic stability.

The rest of this chapter proceeds as follows. First, we begin with an overview of the history of Abu Dhabi and the UAE, with particular attention to the development of the oil sector. Second, we summarize what is known about the strategy and performance of ADNOC relative to its peers. Third, we examine the organization and governance of ADNOC and explore how those factors relate to performance and strategy. Fourth, we briefly examine the relationship between the oil sector and the rest of the government – a discussion that will necessarily be brief since ADNOC is seamlessly integrated into the government's power structure.

2 History

With a concession that covered most of Iraq, a group of international oil companies formed the Iraq Petroleum Company (IPC) in 1928. At the same time, IPC's partners decided that any future concession in other parts of the former Ottoman Empire would have the same ownership structure as the IPC. The Petroleum Development in Trucial Coast Ltd (PDTC) was formed in 1935 with Anglo-Persian Oil (now BP), Shell, Compagnie Française des Pétroles (CFP, now Total), Exxon, and Mobil as the partners. In 1939, the PDTC secured a concession for seventy-five years for the rights to exploration and development of oil in Abu Dhabi. Later, in 1951, Abu Dhabi established that these concessions to PDTC did not include the emirate's offshore territory. The Abu Dhabi Marine Areas Ltd. (ADMA), owned two-thirds by BP and one-thirds by CFP, received the offshore concessions in 1954 (ADNOC 1988, 2010).

Exploration for oil in Abu Dhabi had a slow start as the PDTC partners focused efforts elsewhere in the region, notably Iraq and Qatar. An undeveloped economy and nearly complete lack of roads or other infrastructure made Abu Dhabi particularly unattractive and delayed the process further (ADNOC 2010). Serious exploration began only after 1950, with efforts in onshore (PDTC) and offshore (ADMA) in parallel. After a number of false starts beginning in 1953, oil reserves in the onshore Bab field were proved in 1960. Discovery of the Bu Hasa field followed shortly after, and the first shipment of oil left the borders of Abu Dhabi in 1963. Offshore, the Umm Shaif field was

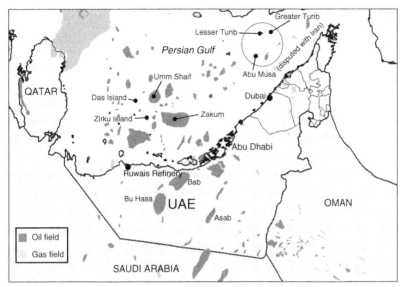

Figure 11.1 Map of major oil and gas fields in UAE.
Source for oil and gas field data: Wood Mackenzie (2009b).

found in 1959 and exports began in 1962. By 1970 production from Abu Dhabi had reached nearly 700,000 bpd – dominated by these three fields. Figure 11.1 shows the country's major oil fields.

2.1 UAE as member of OPEC

Working in concert, Venezuela and Saudi Arabia founded the Organization of Petroleum Exporting Countries (OPEC) in 1960. OPEC had five members at inception: Venezuela, Saudi Arabia, Iran, Iraq, and Kuwait. The guiding principle was to consolidate the market position of the member countries, affording them greater influence on the price of oil (Yergin 1991). The structure of the oil market in the 1960s didn't allow a cartel of suppliers to have much influence, but over time they became more decisive.

UAE joined OPEC in 1967 and has been one of the more reliable members along with Saudi Arabia. With some of the largest oil reserves in the world, these two countries are naturally interested in maintaining "stability" in the oil market. Stability for them is a combination of "fair price" of oil *and* an assured market for oil. The definition of fair price is quite nebulous, but loosely it means prices that will maximize revenues over the lifetime of the entire reserve base. Thus, in May 2004, when oil was at $42/bbl – a price considered high by historical standards – UAE urged OPEC nations to increase production to meet increasing global demand (Associated Press 2004). When oil prices were at all-time highs (reaching $147/bbl in July 2008) Abu Dhabi and ADNOC took pains to underscore that such prices were not sustainable and resisted upward pressure on wages and delayed some projects because they thought contracting costs had risen too rapidly. As the oil price spiraled down from July's heights to less than $60/bbl in early November 2008, UAE was one of the first OPEC countries to meet the production cuts that OPEC decided in October 2008 with a view to preventing a total collapse in oil price (The National 2008). Unlike most OPEC countries, UAE (and Saudi Arabia) largely behaves in accordance with the cartel's declared production and price goals.

2.2 *UAE's unique approach to nationalization*

ADNOC was formed as a fully state-owned company in 1971. In line with other OPEC members, Abu Dhabi began nationalization of its concessions: ADNOC acquired 25 percent stakes in the earlier concessions and moved swiftly to raise its interest in both the onshore and offshore companies to 60 percent by the end of 1974.

Yet, ADNOC stopped short of riding the waves of complete nationalization that had swept most of the Middle East. The main reason for this was Abu Dhabi's complete lack of knowledge, both technical and commercial, of the oil business. With many major discoveries already made and production rising (Figure 11.2), the inherent geological risk was very low in Abu Dhabi. But going solo for ADNOC was very risky for the reasons indicated in Chapter 4 – while geologic risks were declining they were far from zero. The government of Abu Dhabi recognized the limitations in its ability to manage, maintain, and expand such large production levels. It also worried about sustaining access to a market where it could sell its huge oil output. Thus, the decision to retain the IOCs was entirely need-based. In contrast, by the early 1970s, the countries that completely nationalized their industries already had well-established firms (e.g., Libya, Saudi Arabia, and Kuwait); those that nationalized with the least adverse

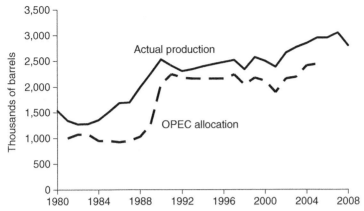

Figure 11.2 UAE total oil production along with OPEC allocations.
Note: Consistent data on OPEC allocations was available only through 2005.
Data source: EIA (2010c) (production data) and OPEC (2007) (allocation data).

consequence on production did it in an orderly way that allowed for a transition in talent (notably Saudi Arabia; see Chapter 5). Abu Dhabi had neither the governmental capacity nor any of the other infrastructures (e.g., a well-educated local talent pool) needed to proceed on its own.

Abu Dhabi's special position is closely related to its political development. A key event was the UK's decision in 1971 to end its stewardship in the Gulf region. Formally, that decision led the UK to end treaties of peace and military cooperation signed in 1853 and 1892 with the "Trucial Sheikdoms" – as the emirates were called before the formation of the UAE. Following this event, the seven emirates, with Abu Dhabi and Dubai in the lead, joined together to form the UAE on December 2, 1971.[1] A decisive force behind the union of the emirates came from Abu Dhabi's Sheikh Zayed bin Sultan Al Nahyan, who became the first president of the UAE in 1971.

Sheikh Zayed rose to prominence slowly. He started as his ruling elder brother Sheikh Shakbut's representative in Al Ain in 1946. But, in 1967, Sheikh Zayed became the ruler of Abu Dhabi, when the ruling Al Nahyan family chose him to succeed his elder brother. He was famously known to be visionary, open, and to act in the interests of his kinsmen. As oil revenues started pouring in from the mid 1960s onwards, Sheikh Zayed used much of the income to build hospitals, schools, and roads, which reinforced his position as a useful leader.

He also donated large sums of money to other emirates and also to other Arab countries (Davidson 2009). For the population of Abu Dhabi and the other emirates, Sheikh Zayed was the most visible and credible political force at the founding of the country. While passionate about all-inclusive growth of the emirates, Sheikh Zayed always acted with caution and restraint when it came to the development of Abu Dhabi's oil reserves. Sheikh Zayed's watchword was stability, which continues largely today long after his death. For the Western oil companies this has offered a relatively attractive island within a region of risk and instability.

3 Operations and management of ADNOC group of companies

Abu Dhabi's oil and gas industry is organized around ADNOC, which provides the main link between the government and the various foreign firms that play central roles in operating the country's oil and gas fields. ADNOC was formed in 1971, in tandem with the creation of the UAE, as a vehicle for an active involvement of the Abu Dhabi government in the emirate's oil and gas industry, for implementing the government's oil and gas policy, and also for holding the government's share in the operating companies and joint ventures. At the time, as in most of the countries examined in this book, there was little effort to distinguish the roles of the NOC as operator, policymaker, and regulator. Only much later did the government attempt to disentangle some of these functions – notably with the creation of the Supreme Petroleum Council (SPC) to set policy for the sector, a key decision that we discuss later.

At present, ADNOC runs most of Abu Dhabi's oil and gas business through a network of fourteen subsidiaries, which are categorized by their position along the value chain of the oil and gas industry (ADNOC 2008a): exploration and production of oil and gas (ADCO, ADMA-OPCO, ZADCO), oil and gas processing (GASCO, ADGAS, TAKREER), refined products distribution (ADNOC Distribution), oil services (NDC, IRSHAD), chemicals and petrochemicals (FERTIL, BOROUGE, ESNAD), and maritime transportation (ADNATCO, NGSCO).[2] In effect, ADNOC is a fully integrated, holding company that has the capacity to understand and manage all operations of its subsidiaries. In recent years it has also made forays into ventures that it controls jointly with foreign firms.[3]

Wholly owned by the Abu Dhabi government, ADNOC is a limited-liability commercial entity under Abu Dhabi law (Suleiman 1988). As legally it is a separate entity from the government, ADNOC has somewhat greater freedom in decision making and conducting its business than the direct arms of the government. Formally, it is not assigned regulatory power or controlling authority over the sector on behalf of the government. But given its central position in Abu Dhabi's oil and gas sector, ADNOC sways enormous influence over government decisions. Thus, like many other national companies, ADNOC is continuously faced with the task of reconciling the interests of the government with those of commercial firms working in the sector. The closest comparison, perhaps, is with Angola's Sonangol that plays a similarly central role in managing that country's oil sector while also conducting some operations itself and importing knowledge from foreign operators through joint ventures (see Chapter 19).

In the upstream part of the oil business ADNOC's subsidiaries are its three operating companies: Abu Dhabi Company for Onshore Oil Operations (ADCO) along with Abu Dhabi Marine Operating Company (ADMA-OPCO) and Zakum Development Company (ZADCO) for offshore. ADNOC owns 60% of ADCO. The other partners in ADCO are BP (9.5%), Shell (9.5%), Total (9.5%), ExxonMobil (9.5%), and Partex (2%). ADNOC owns 60% of ADMA-OPCO, BP 14.67%, Total 13.33%, and Japan Oil Development Company (JODCO) 12%. ADMA-OPCO's main producing fields are Umm Shaif and Lower Zakum – most of the production from these fields is destined for East Asia and Southeast Asia (Figure 11.3). ADCO and ADMA-OPCO are the vestiges of the original onshore and offshore concessions.[4] ZADCO arrived later to the scene. It was established in 1977 as a fifty-fifty joint venture operating company between ADNOC and CFP (the French NOC Compagnie Française des Pétroles) to operate the Upper Zakum field on behalf of ADNOC and JODCO, Japan's overseas oil development company. Japan, like China today, was worried about its ability to sustain growth without reliable sources of oil that it controlled; Abu Dhabi offered an ideal site for Japan to diversify its suppliers. (CFP developed the field and also provided services and personnel for its operations; JODCO's main role was as investor.) Abu Dhabi also had a special interest in a closer relationship with Japan, which became

Lower Zakum Crude Export - 2007

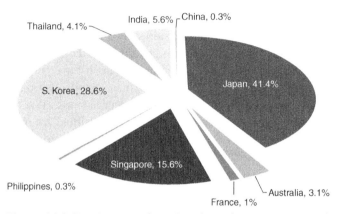

Figure 11.3 Destination of crude oil production in 2007 from ADMA-OPCO's lower Zakum fields.

Note: Crude oil from the Umm Shaif fields is also mostly shipped to East Asian countries: Japan, 78.4%; Philippines, 9.6%; India, 6.3%; Thailand, 5%; and China, 0.7%.

Data source: ADMA-OPCO (2007).

the country's largest customer and, like Abu Dhabi, had a conservative and orderly approach to investing and operating petroleum supply. Japan not only bought Abu Dhabi crude but was also the anchor customer for the country's LNG export project, which sold its gas to Tokyo Electric Power Company (TEPCO). Since then Japan has realized that direct ownership of foreign hydrocarbon resources can be expensive and does not much improve energy security, and the country has dismantled its national oil company, but the legacy of its investment in Abu Dhabi remains.

Abu Dhabi's gas operations have followed a different trajectory than oil. As in most of the oil industry, gas was an afterthought. Until the mid 1970s operators simply flared much of the associated gas. To remedy the wastage of that gas Abu Dhabi established a law in 1976 (Law No. 4) that provides the Abu Dhabi government, through ADNOC, complete control over the exploitation of gas within its territory (Suleiman 1995). Law 4 gives ADNOC the discretion to pursue Abu Dhabi's gas interests alone or through joint ventures where it maintains a minimum of 51 percent stake.

ADNOC's gas strategy has sought to utilize associated gas produced with crude oil and also to develop non-associated natural gas reservoirs, although in practice its interests and abilities align much better with the first approach to gas production. Through its two main gas processing subsidiary joint ventures – Abu Dhabi Gas Liquefaction Company Limited (ADGAS) and Abu Dhabi Gas Industries Limited (GASCO) – ADNOC has developed a number of gas processing plants supported by gas gathering systems and pipeline networks.

The centerpiece of ADGAS's operations is Das Island, which houses gas processing and liquefaction plants. At Das Island ADGAS receives and processes associated gas from ADMA-OPCO's offshore operations in the Umm Shaif and Lower Zakum fields and non-associated gas from the giant Khuff structure under the Abu Al Bukhoosh oil field. The main products of ADGAS's operation in Das Island are LPG and LNG, both of which are mainly shipped to TEPCO. At present, Das Island has an installed capacity for producing 5 million tons per annum of LNG and 800,000 tons of LPG. The Das Island LNG project was conceived in the late 1960s by Japanese companies Mitsui and Bridgestone and the partners of ADMA-OPCO (ADNOC, BP, and Total). ADNOC owned 51 percent of ADGAS until June 1997, when it increased its holding to 70 percent.

GASCO was formed as a joint venture between ADNOC (68%), Total (15%), Shell (15%), and Partex (2%) in 1978 to exploit associated and non-associated gas from onshore fields. Initially formed for thirty years (1978–2008), the joint venture agreement has been renewed for another twenty years (2008–2028). Whereas Das Island is principally oriented for export, GASCO's operations look inward to a larger degree. It has four facilities that process and extract natural gas liquids (NGLs), delivering a range of gas products into the UAE's gas distribution network, where it is used locally, and to the Ruwais plant, where NGLs are fractionated and separated into propane, butane, and pentane – partly for export.

In addition to the five major operations with varying forms of foreign participation discussed above (ADCO, ADMA-OPCO, ZADCO, ADGAS, and GASCO), ADNOC also conducts E&P operations on a sole-risk basis. In 1980 the Abu Dhabi government assigned three offshore and two onshore blocks, totaling 34,750 square kilometers, to ADNOC for exploration and production of hydrocarbons. ADNOC has maintained an aggressive exploration program in these areas, as well as in the joint venture concessions, using cutting-edge technology. The program has resulted in several important discoveries (Oil & Gas Directory 2007). So far, however, sole-risk exploration and production account for a small part of ADNOC's total operations and output.

4 Strategy and performance

When Kuwait increased its reported reserves by one-third in 1984 in an effort to acquire a larger OPEC quota, most other OPEC members followed suit (Red Orbit 2005). ADNOC was no different, and in 1986 it doubled the country's declared reserves to nearly 100 billion barrels. Official reported reserves have remained exactly unchanged for the last twenty-three years despite twenty billion barrels of production over the intervening period and barely any effort at exploration.[5] No reliable information is publicly available for assessing either the actual size of reserves or how the country's reserves might vary with the oil price since recovery rates are higher at elevated prices.

Figure 11.2 shows production for the whole of the UAE over time. Beyond Abu Dhabi, however, the only significant production in the UAE has come from Dubai (< 1 percent of current production), where output is in steep decline.

ADNOC has one of the lowest production-to-reserves ratios in the world (0.011, or 1.1 percent of reported reserves are produced each year). This low output, however, is not an indicator of poor performance. (For more detail on the relationship between depletion and performance see Appendix B.) Rather, the country's extraordinarily low depletion appears to be mainly the result of an explicit policy taken at the formation of the country when production was rising rapidly. Sheikh Zayed famously declared that the country's wealth should be saved for the future and that the "last drop of oil" should be produced from Abu Dhabi. (Saudi rulers made similar pronouncements – see Chapter 5.) Until recently, when the decision was taken to increase output over the coming two decades, there was little discussion in ADNOC about the inability to produce at set targets. (By contrast, Pemex and PDVSA, among others, are beset with troubles in producing at rates that their political masters think should be possible.) Compared with other NOCs examined in this book, ADNOC is one of the better performers – both because it has been able to incorporate technical skills from its partners and because it (and its political masters) have a realistic vision for the targets the firm can actually reach.

Abu Dhabi's low depletion rate is not accidental and stems mainly from three factors.[6] First, as indicated, low depletion was the declared policy at the outset of the UAE's existence. While this policy reflected Zayed's long-term vision for a strong and prosperous country it also reflected, surely, that the young kingdom could not absorb much revenue. The early years of the UAE marked a fragile collection of formerly independent clan emirates; large joint and costly infrastructure projects came later. Roads, ports, and construction projects were few. Nearly all of the revenues stayed within Abu Dhabi itself, which had a tiny population and few needs. Even Dubai's takeoff as a financial capital in the 1980s (partly because it was an attractive place for Iranian businessmen to park their money after the revolution) came mainly on the back of real estate, banking, and other activities that benefited from Abu Dhabi's oil but did not make a huge draw on those financial resources. (Dubai's draw on Abu Dhabi resources has been much larger during the 2008 crash from the real estate boom, although Abu Dhabi's role in helping its fellow emirate recover is probably a one-off event that does not signal a fundamental realignment in the financial roles of the emirates. Most of the oil money comes from Abu Dhabi and is managed by Abu Dhabi.)

Second, the style of leadership in the emirate and the oil company is highly deliberative and conservative. Almost no significant decisions are delegated below the level of a handful of crucial top managers; all major policy decisions are concentrated in the country's main oil policy body, the SPC (discussed later), which is controlled by the ruling family and a few reliable members from other families. Decision making is laden with fear of making mistakes and of becoming dependent on outside advisers and vendors who exploit the country's inexperience. In our interviews, the single most quoted reason for a low depletion rate is fear of "damaging the fields" (also see Marcel 2006). Third, Abu Dhabi sees itself as a reliable member of OPEC. It has reduced output when requested and it looks to OPEC for orderly development of the oil market (Butt 2001). Its decision to increase output over the coming two decades seems to stem from confidence that the country will be able to secure a larger OPEC quota – partly because world demand for oil has continuously risen and mainly because other OPEC members (and aligned countries such as Russia) are struggling to produce. This third factor seems to be the least important of the three, and some studies suggest Abu Dhabi is not so reliable an OPEC member. For most of OPEC's history, OPEC quotas have not imposed a meaningful constraint on ADNOC and compliance with OPEC quotas has arisen mainly from a coincidence of interests rather than Abu Dhabi's decision to put OPEC cohesion above its national priorities (see for example Europa 2004).

Our overall assessment is that ADNOC's performance has been high in light of the low depletion targets that have been set for the company and the relatively "easy" oil that the country has tapped for production. Easy oil has put few demands on the company, which has relied heavily on management and expertise from its partners. Unlike Kuwait, for example, ADNOC has consistently met its internally set targets. (For more on Kuwait see Chapter 8.) Under ADNOC's umbrella, Abu Dhabi has maintained oil production of about 2.5 mbpd despite its major fields being in decline for over a decade now – a record in striking contrast to Mexico's, even after controlling for the difference in the two country's oil geology (on Mexico, see Chapter 7). It has led the development of Abu Dhabi's technologically modern gas industry, almost completely eliminating gas flaring in the process. Through their role in the development of the Das Island LNG project – in tandem with foreign investors and operators – Abu Dhabi and ADNOC were pioneers in the LNG industry. ADNOC has continually upgraded Abu Dhabi's infrastructure to stay competitive in the LNG business, although it is striking that its early lead in this industry has not led to a much larger presence, in contrast with neighbor Qatar. The core of ADNOC's interest and plans for growth lie with oil, not gas. Further, in an effort to seize more of the value from gas and especially oil production, ADNOC (like most NOCs in the region) has sought to expand its petrochemicals business with a view to help diversify Abu Dhabi's economy by developing intermediate industries and also to new employment opportunities for UAE nationals (Al Matroushi 2004; Davidson 2009). ADNOC might have shifted to petrochemicals on its own, but the government has certainly had a keen interest in encouraging the firm to support more value-added enterprises with benefits that spill over to the broader economy.

Throughout, ADNOC has exhibited a remarkable drive to utilize cutting-edge technology and best practices in the industry. As the

Table 11.1. *ADNOC's crude oil production*
expansion plans to meet its 2015 target

(mbpd)	2006	2015	Change
ADCO	1.5	1.8	0.3
ADMA-OPCO	0.6	0.9	0.3
ZADCO	0.5	0.8	0.3
Others	0.1	0.1	—
Total	2.7	3.6	0.9

Note: mbpd – million barrels per day. These numbers include
just crude to which NGL production will be added so that
the 4 mbpd target is reached.
Data source: Oil & Energy Trends 2007.

company reports, it has used state-of-the-art 3D seismic surveys and
special geophysical studies; it employs cutting-edge drilling rigs; it has
embarked on technologically highly complex developmental projects
involving water alternating gas, and sour gas reinjection; and it is
expanding and modernizing its gas processing infrastructure at a
rapid pace (ADNOC 2005).

However, oil production in Abu Dhabi is getting more complicated.
Many fields are entering the decline phase, and it is proving more difficult
to predict their behavior. ADNOC has been surprised on several occasions by the presence of unexpected levels of water from the production
wells. In view of Abu Dhabi's aggressive target of increasing production
to nearly 4 mbpd by 2015 and 5 mbpd by 2030 (Oil & Energy Trends
2007), the company faces the dual challenge of managing more complex fields while bringing many new fields online. Meeting these new
production goals will require an effort spread across the E&P arms of
ADNOC; Table 11.1 indicates how the company plans to meet its production target for 2015. ADNOC plans to increase the production of
ADMA-OPCO, ADCO, and ZADCO by 0.3 mbpd each (Table 11.1).
It is not clear where the additional 1 mpbd production will come to
meet the 2030 production target (Oil & Energy Trends 2007).

One area where ADNOC has met with relative failure is the development of cutting-edge technology for carrying out operations independently. ADNOC has undergone major reorganization of its corporate
structure twice, in 1988 and in 1998. Both the reorganizations were

aimed at making ADNOC more nimble in its response to changing market conditions and technologically more capable. (Both reorganizations occurred in a period of low oil prices and thus worries about revenues from inefficient oil production.) Since its formation in 1971, and notwithstanding the recent organizational changes, ADNOC still struggles to build strong internal technical capabilities; it continues to depend heavily on its partner IOCs and on oil services companies for almost all major technical works. As the technological complexity of operations has increased so has evidence of kinks in ADNOC's otherwise stellar performance. There is also growing concern about bureaucratic decision making and the lack of risk taking in the company – factors that probably have been omnipresent in the company's history but are just more apparent today.[7]

The Introduction asked each case study to comment on the company's strategy – that is, how the company selected, mobilized, and applied the resources needed to achieve its objectives. For most NOCs, the crucial determinant of strategy is the company's objectives. ADNOC is secretive about its goals, but two seem to dominate. First is to be a reliable, controllable source of revenue through the careful (conservative) development of the country's oil resources. That first element has dictated state control over all major parts of the oil sector. (Small projects – such as those pursued by Conoco and Occidental and discussed later – are now being tolerated, but those are marginal activities that do not threaten state control over all the main elements of the hydrocarbons sector.) Given the underlying objective to maintain direct state control of the sector, a wide array of possible alternative strategies for producing revenues – such as privatization or minority shareholding of the state oil company, both of which are evident in Brazil (see Chapter 12) – are simply unthinkable in the Abu Dhabi context. To be sure, there is an element of "satisficing" at work – that is, doing just enough to meet expectations – since revenues have been sufficient for state needs and thus the country's conservative decision-making process has never had to contend with the need for a radical change in strategy. (Indeed, the revenues have made Abu Dhabi's sovereign wealth funds among the largest in the world.) Abu Dhabi has never faced the kind of crisis in oil production that is seen in Mexico (Chapter 7) or crisis in gas supply that Russia will soon face (Chapter 15). Unlike other countries where this first element of strategy to have direct state-controlled development of the oil and gas industry has blended with the need to tap the oil company to provide a far flung array of public services and other non-core activities – such as in Venezuela (Chapter 10) – ADNOC has very few non-core operations. The bulk of its activities focus on oil and gas. The revenues from its operations are given to the government, where they are then invested or spent through other processes, notably the emirate's sovereign wealth funds and domestic investment authorities.

The second element of ADNOC's strategy is the one "non-core" area where the company is active: the creation of a qualified, employable Emirati population. UAE as a whole is marked by a very low population for its economic activity. In 2010 about 4 million expatriates lived alongside only 800,000 Emiratis.[8] The country's birth rate is the highest in the world, as is net migration. While ADNOC has effectively used the technical strengths of its partners through synergetic partnership deals, there is a growing apprehension within the country's most senior leaders that limited technical expertise at home is hindering the country's ability to frame policies and coordinate planning in the long-term interest of the UAE.[9] Such worries are a regular topic of conversation within the SPC, which sets the goals for the oil sector (more on that below) and thus are also internalized at ADNOC. As such, ADNOC puts improvement of the Emirati condition as one of its central goals – put explicitly, the firm "endeavors to maximize the number of UAE Nationals in its workforce" (ADNOC 2008b). ADNOC's strategy to spur Emiratization is based on strengthening in-house technical capability, mostly by preparing Emiratis for technical positions in ADNOC through research and training at the Petroleum Institute (PI) and the ADNOC Technical Institute (ATI). Put differently, ADNOC has sponsored the creation of two Western-style academies – along with feeder institutions such as primary and secondary schools – to raise the supply of qualified Emiratis. ADNOC controls the supply of qualified Emiratis through its support for their education and its control over the higher education pipeline. All Emiratis who graduate from these two ADNOC-sponsored institutions are recruited in the oil and gas industry in Abu Dhabi through ADNOC, which has a complete list of Emiratis who seek such employment.[10]

ADNOC's increased emphasis on Emiratization has been difficult to square with the rising technological complexity of its fields. Emiratization is a chronic problem that requires long-term investments

with uncertain outcomes. The need for much higher technical expertise to manage the country's maturing fields is immediate. Notably,
there is a much greater need for enhanced oil recovery (EOR) techniques, and for that ADNOC will continue to rely on its existing partners (BP, Shell, Total, ExxonMobil). Unlike Petrobras, which built its
technical capabilities from within and augmented them through partnerships with other oil companies (see Chapter 12) from the beginning ADNOC has looked outside for technical expertise. ADNOC
is aware of its dependence, but wants to minimize its vulnerability
to being exploited by foreigners. That partly explains why ADNOC
is trying to maintain confusion around extension of its partnerships
beyond 2014; it has kept existing partners, who are hard pressed for
acreage all over the world, uncertain about their future in the emirates; it has created the specter of competition with new entrants (e.g.,
Occidental). All these efforts have strengthened ADNOC's hand in
negotiating the next generation of partnerships, and it has used that
stronger hand to strengthen its demands for help in training of the
Emirati population. Indeed, some recent contracts concluded between
ADNOC and some IOCs have manpower training as a central component of the agreement. For example, as part of a deal that gave
ExxonMobil a 28 percent stake in the Upper Zakum field (operated
by ZADCO) it was agreed that ExxonMobil would provide support
for training and personnel development, including access to its world-
class training center in Houston. ExxonMobil also agreed to assist
in establishing a specialized R&D facility at the Petroleum Institute
(ADNOC 2006). Similarly, the renewal in 2009 of the GASCO concession – involving Shell, Total, and Partex – through October 2028
was concluded not only on commercial terms less favorable for the
IOCs, but also included technology transfer and training agreements.
It was agreed that the international partners would contribute $100
million over the twenty-year period of the agreement to the Petroleum
Institute to facilitate technological development and R&D that will
make the Institute a much stronger research-oriented body (MEES
2009a).

ADNOC has also learned that it can't rely on the supply of qualified Emiratis entirely for its workforce. The need for a skilled technical workforce made ADNOC extend educational opportunities
such as enrollment at the Petroleum Institute beyond UAE nationals.
In 2005 the Institute allowed entry for highly qualified expatriate

students who in 2010 accounted for 30 percent of the student population. All expatriate students enter with a fellowship that pays for their tuition and fees (including books and lodging). Such initiatives help explain rapid growth at the Petroleum Institute, which is currently graduating 150 students per year and on track to double soon. Nonetheless, ADNOC estimates that its demand for engineering graduates is about three to four times higher than what the Institute is graduating. Somewhat akin to ADNOC's efforts to build partnerships with leaders in the industry, the Petroleum Institute has international academic partners, including Colorado School of Mines, University of Maryland, University of Texas at Austin, Rice University, the China University of Petroleum, and Johannes Kepler University in Austria.[11]

Besides focusing on augmenting production and preparing a technically competent Emirati workforce for the domestic oil industry, another area of more recent strategic interest for ADNOC is downstream value-added activities, especially refining and petrochemicals. The push for refining comes mainly from rapidly increasing local and regional demand for refined products. Nearly all ADNOC's refining operations take place at the Ruwais refinery and the Abu Dhabi refinery, both of which are run by ADNOC subsidiary Abu Dhabi Oil Refining Company (TAKREER). Since the late 1990s ADNOC, through TAKREER, has very aggressively increased refining capacity, while emphasizing the installation of the latest in refining technology. TAKREER refineries produce over 23 million tons per year of products, including LPG, unleaded gasoline (98 and 95 octane), naphtha grades, Jet-A1 grades, and granulated sulfur, for the local and export markets. In 2001–2002 the bulk of TAKREER's gasoline production was converted to unleaded gasoline to enable the "UAE Goes Green" program, which started on January 1, 2003. Increasingly, TAKREER has become a vehicle for meeting local demand, not just of petroleum products but also electricity and water. Located in a relatively remote location 240 kilometers west of Abu Dhabi City, the Ruwais refinery operates a general utilities plant (GUP) to provide reliable power and desalinated water. With the intention of supplying only the Ruwais industrial area, the GUP started with an installed capacity of 90 MW (gas) and 26,000 m³/day of clear water. But since 2001 the GUP has been called upon to assist the Abu Dhabi Water & Electricity Authority (ADWEA) in meeting local electricity and water needs. Following the completion of a major expansion in 2002, the GUP's power capacity has increased to 650 MW (seven gas and two steam turbines), while water production capacity stands at over 60,000 m³/day from five desalination units (TAKREER 2010). The GUP is now interconnected and synchronized with the ADWEA grid affording TAKREER the flexibility to import and export power.

Abu Dhabi is hardly alone in the shift to local production. Most of the NOCs examined in this book are under pressure to provide for the local economy for at least two reasons. One is that linkages with the oil company as a supplier and user of goods and services could catalyze broader economic development and employment. The other is capturing more of the value-added in transforming raw gas and especially oil into useable products such as refined fuels and chemicals. Efforts to capture more value from the supply chain of refined fuels have generally not been successful – as Kuwait, for example, learned when it tried to integrate downstream through purchase of European refineries and retail outlets. But the potential gains from linkages as well as from value-added in petrochemicals are more promising but also more risky since the best petrochemical strategies are often hard to identify. In addition to Abu Dhabi, other countries that are prominently following this strategy and examined in this book include Brazil and Saudi Arabia.

As in other countries, Abu Dhabi has made a strong push for petrochemicals on the theory that a more vibrant industry will spill over to the broader economy and will diversify (at least partly) the emirate's economic base. ADNOC's petrochemical operations include the production of ammonia, urea, and polyethylene. ADNOC subsidiary FERTIL, a joint venture between ADNOC and Total (originally CFP), produces urea and ammonia most of which is geared for export to the Indian subcontinent. ADNOC's latest push in the sector is the Abu Dhabi Polymers Company (Borouge), a joint venture established in 1998 between ADNOC and Borealis. Borealis is one of Europe's leading producers of polyefins and was originally owned by Norway's Statoil, Austria's OMV, and Abu Dhabi's downstream investment arm International Petroleum Investment Company (IPIC; Butt 2001). Borealis is now majority owned and controlled by ADNOC and Abu Dhabi. Borouge uses Borealis's proprietary Borstar technology to produce economical and substantially stronger polyethylene, which is used in making plastic films, molded packaging, high-pressure pipes and other applications (ADNOC 2005). Since its initial commissioning in 2001, the Borogue complex has been expanded in two tranches to utilize surplus ethylene that was being exported and for the production of a range of advanced petrochemicals such as vinyl chloride monomer (VCM) and polyvinyl chloride (PVC). ADNOC and its subsidiaries have not so far invested much in the building blocks for other petrochemical chains, such as propylene and aromatics.

It is still too early to assess Abu Dhabi's petrochemicals industry, which was slow to form due to lack of gas, interest, and capability. Unlike the core oil production industry, ADNOC does not have a guaranteed monopoly in petrochemicals – indeed, other companies are building facilities and are probably more nimble and competent.

5 ADNOC and the state

The pivotal actor in Abu Dhabi's oil and gas sector is the SPC, which is dominated by the ruling family and a few members of closely allied families. The SPC's members also hold key positions in nearly all of Abu Dhabi's important state bodies, including banks, investment authorities, defense, domestic and foreign affairs and so on. Since its creation in 1988, the SPC has consistently acted to consolidate the chain of control and streamline strategic decision making. The SPC makes essentially all decisions on strategy for the sector and then delegates to ADNOC to implement those policies. Its approach has been to coordinate Abu Dhabi- and UAE-level investment and strategic decisions within the SPC. After setting goals and strategy, the SPC passes its decisions to ADNOC for implementation. In effect, the SPC resolves all conflicting issues at the very top level and leaves ADNOC with a relatively clear signal of what needs to be done. Although nearly all key discussion topics in the SPC are proposed by ADNOC and ADNOC is well represented in the SPC – ADNOC's chairman is also the secretary general of the SPC – decisions in the SPC concentrate first and foremost on the central objectives of Abu Dhabi and, through Abu Dhabi's interests, on the cohesion of the UAE. (For example, ADNOC's Emiratization policy stems from SPC decisions and the policy is written to favor any Emirati rather than Abu Dhabians especially.)

The clarity in goals and strategy stemming from the SPC is one of the central reasons why ADNOC has seen such high performance

as a company. Most of the particular strategies that ADNOC has
followed to boost performance – such as through sharing operational responsibilities with foreign firms and the patient process of
Emiratization – have required that the firm make long-term commitments and investments. None of that would have been possible without long-term commitments and guidance from SPC. By contrast,
the poorer-performing operational companies in this book – such as
KPC, Pemex, PDVSA under President Chávez, as well as the NOCs
in Iran and Nigeria – do not have reliable planning guidance from a
credible institution such as the SPC.

The power and legitimacy of the ruling family and close allies in Abu
Dhabi derives from using the oil rents to provide enough broad-based
development across Abu Dhabi (and the UAE) to sustain support and
avoid dissent. The ruling family has shown a consistent preference
and support for political stability through choosing a leader who is
dynamic and capable to ensure their continued dominance (Davidson
2006). With those goals in mind, a well-functioning ADNOC that
operates much like a private corporation and is attentive to managing
costs and boosting performance is expedient for the ruling family.

The creation of the SPC in 1988 reveals how the government has
tried to marry a conservative approach to political change with the
need for good performance from its NOC. Until creation of the SPC,
clear lines of authority in the oil sector were muddied and large strategic decisions were difficult to organize and implement. By creating the SPC the government tried to ensure that Abu Dhabi's oil and
gas operations were efficient yet remained firmly guided by the larger
vision of the ruling masters. The SPC was a reaction to the standard problem for any regulator: how to oversee the agents to whom
responsibilities have been delegated. (For more on the question of
administrative control over delegated agents, see Chapter 3.) In this
case, the delegated agent is ADNOC, and in the mid 1980s the Abu
Dhabi government grew frustrated with ADNOC's performance. The
company had developed a thick bureaucracy, which was too slow to
identify and seize opportunities. Besides, the existence of the government's Department of Petroleum in parallel with ADNOC had led to
a multipolar power struggle in Abu Dhabi's oil and gas industry. That
power struggle was also personal – between Dr. Mana Said Al Otaiba,
who then was chairman of the government's petroleum department
and Sheikh Tahnun Bin Mohammed, Sheikh Zayed's most powerful

cousin who then was chairman of ADNOC's Board of Directors (APS Review Oil Market Trends 1999). These power struggles were unseemly, distracting for the company and the government, and they introduced instabilities within a country that prized itself on stability around the ruling family above all else. With the aim of giving the Government of Abu Dhabi much tighter control over the industry the government abolished both warring factions – the Department of Petroleum and ADNOC's Board of Directors – and replaced them with the SPC. As a sign of this new control, Abu Dhabi's ruler chaired the SPC and ADNOC's CEO served as the SPC's secretary general. In effect, the SPC became ADNOC's board of governors. Control was asserted not just through public administration and regulation but also through complete integration of ADNOC's key decision-making bodies with the government.[12]

Very little is known in the outside about the SPC's decision-making processes or goals, but what is clear is that it has historically been conservative and wary. Historically, conservatism has come from the blessing of huge oil reserves; the (until recently) relatively modest revenue requirements; and the risk-averse ruling style in the emirate. Indeed, one interpretation of the recent decision by the SPC to increase output is that those revenue requirements are rising and the SPC is also convinced that demand for the country's higher output will exist – in part because world demand continues to rise and mainly because other major oil producers are struggling to increase output.[13] In interviews with senior officials we found that special emphasis has been placed on "not damaging" the fields physically, which as a guiding principle has meant slow depletion. In some respects, the SPC has only made one pivotal decision during its tenure – to boost production over the next two decades – because prior to that decision the industry was focused on the strategy, set long ago by Sheikh Zayed, to produce at a pace that kept depletion rates low.

The SPC has delegated to ADNOC most operational decisions – including, notably, management of the company's relationship with other oil companies. Unlike most NOCs in the Gulf, ADNOC has worked very closely with its partners, especially the IOCs, all along. That approach of participation-agreement-based operating joint ventures started in the early 1970s, when Abu Dhabi had very little experience in the oil and gas industry and needed access to the technology, expertise, and best practices of the industry. Like Sonangol, operational partnerships have allowed ADNOC and its sister companies to build internal capability, which they have used in sole-risk projects. However, there is little prospect of a day when these partnerships would not be needed. In Sonangol's case, the partnerships are needed for the high-risk exploration and production offshore. For ADNOC the partnerships are especially crucial to the management of maturing fields that are complex to operate as well as to essentially all major gas operations. This experience follows exactly the logic outlined in Chapter 4 concerning geological risk. For ADNOC, outside partnerships have been needed in the early stages of the country's oil industry because there was very little indigenous capacity to manage risk. Even as risks declined ADNOC was not able to operate its fields – unlike, for example, Saudi Aramco. With depletion of its fields the risks are rising once again, giving rise to the need for external expertise despite the massive effort at Emiratization.

The organizational structure of ADNOC's subsidiaries ensures a seamless integration not only with ADNOC but also with the SPC (Figure 11.4). The highest governing body for each ADNOC subsidiary is the Joint Management Committee (JMC) followed by the Board of Directors (BoD). The JMC formulates long term policies for investment and development while the BoD is responsible for monitoring the technical and financial performance of the company. Power in these institutions is concentrated in the hands of ADNOC's senior officials. There are also roles for each foreign partner. Under the governing structure is the General Manager (GM), who reports to the chairman of the BoD and overseas operations of the subsidiary. (Reflecting Western terminology, as of 2010 most of the GMs are now called Chief Executive Officers – CEOs.) ADNOC is represented in both the JMC and the BoD, and so are the partner companies. For instance, Yousef Omair Bin Yousef (the CEO of ADNOC) and Abdulla Nasser Al Suwaidi (the deputy CEO of ADNOC), both of whom are members of the SPC, are ADNOC representatives on ADCO's JMC and BoD. Thus, the presence of SPC members and the top executives of ADNOC on the governing bodies of the subsidiary companies allows for a clear chain of communication between the policymakers (the SPC) and the operators.

ADNOC and its subsidiaries have shown a remarkable ability to adapt to changing conditions – including the growing list of demands placed on modern oil companies. The management of very complex

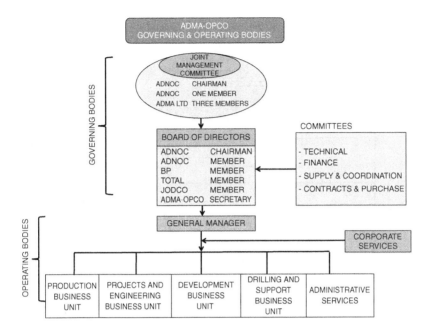

Figure 11.4 Top-level organizational structure of ADMA-OPCO. Other ADNOC subsidiaries have a similar structure.
Source: Adapted from ADMA-OPCO (2007).

oil and gas projects in Abu Dhabi and a strong emphasis on health, safety, and environment (HSE) practices provide good examples. ADNOC has adapted and employed the best project management practices to ensure timely and cost-effective completion of its oil and gas projects. This approach has created an incentive for better performance in tandem with rising size and complexity of projects. Most big new projects have multilayered interactions within the project as well as with existing projects and infrastructure. Figure 11.5 shows, for example, one of GASCO's most complex new undertakings, consisting of three coupled projects.

Indeed, ADNOC has invested heavily in improving project management. It emphasizes effective interface management to ensure timely and efficient completion of different work streams. Responsibilities, interactions, risks, and obligations associated with projects are clearly identified ahead of time and the interaction between the relevant parties is coordinated through a dedicated team. International

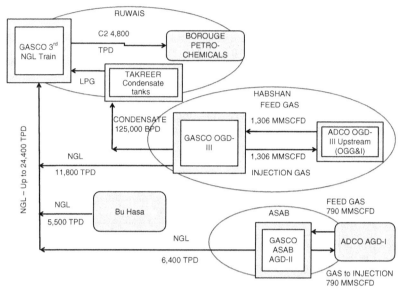

Figure 11.5 Overall facilities block diagram of GASCO's "Ruwais 3rd NGL Project," including OGD-III/AGD-II.
Note: The large ovals represent hydrocarbon complexes. OGD-III and AGD-II recover and process additional quantities of oil and gas from ADCO's Bab and Asab fields respectively. Different parts of this project are owned and operated by GASCO, ADCO, and TAKREER. This project not only exemplifies the complexity of ADNOC's projects, but also the increasingly integrated nature of ADNOC's operations. OGD-III NGL: Natural Gas Liquids; OGD: Onshore Gas Development; AGD: Asab Gas Development; BPD: Barrels Per Day; TPD: Tonnes Per Day.
Source: Adapted from Collins *et al.* (2008).

engineering and consultancy firms are frequently hired as integral parts during the planning and development phases of the projects (Collins *et al.* 2008). This approach is also evident in how ADNOC has fairly easily incorporated rising international concern and awareness, especially among the Western oil industry, for management of HSE impacts from oil and gas operations. Historically, nature conservancy and support for improving the environment have been highly visible goals of the emirate's rulers (Davidson 2009). Yet, a formal HSE program had been missing until the mid 1990s. Mindful of that commitment and keen to strengthen ADNOC's public image, in 1996 ADNOC's CEO Yousef Omair Bin Yousef set a goal for ADNOC to be world class in HSE matters and in the process lead the way for

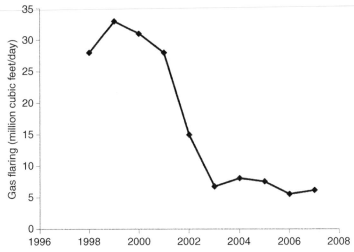

Figure 11.6 ADNOC's gas flaring, 1996–2007.
Data source: ADMA-OPCO (2007).

other UAE institutions (Oil & Gas Directory 2007). The environmental health and safety (EH&S) division was formed to achieve this task and has since pursued a wide array of projects (Al Mansouri *et al.* 1998; ADNOC 2005). Starting in 1998 ADNOC made it compulsory for all new projects to have HSE impact assessments that span the full life cycle of a project, from initial design through operation and decommissioning. Figures 11.6 and 11.7 show results from two of ADNOC's most successful HSE programs – one to cut flaring of gas and the other to reduce wasteful spills. As with many successful HSE programs, both of these aligned the company's commercial goals with advancement of HSE objectives.

In the last two decades ADNOC has seen two major reorganizations. The first reorganization happened in 1988 in an effort to slim ADNOC's bureaucracy, and led to the creation of the SPC. The second wave of reorganization hit ADNOC in 1998. This time around the motive was to reshape ADNOC's management with the aim of enabling future growth and expansion. The number of subsidiaries was increased from nine to fifteen in an effort to make subsidiary operations more transparent (internally).[14] And across all the subsidiaries ADNOC also tried to create stronger incentives for efficiency through the use of performance contracts. Every year all the

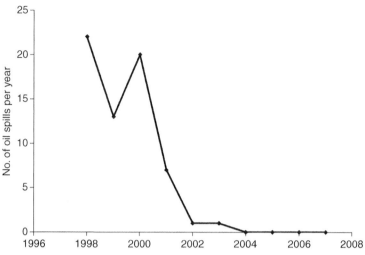

Figure 11.7 ADNOC's oil spills per year, 1996–2007.
Data source: ADMA-OPCO (2007).

subsidiaries propose to shareholders (ADNOC being one of them) performance targets for 'Key Performance Indicators' (KPI). The shareholders review the proposals, and after a few iterations with the subsidiaries the performance contracts are signed. Progress against targets is assessed quarterly by the shareholders. ADNOC relies heavily on the knowledge of its partners (BP, Shell, etc.) during both the proposal and the review periods. This is the quintessential feature of the control structure through the performance contracts, as it enables ADNOC to leverage the knowledge of the outside companies in management.[15]

Salary has been a sore issue. The service companies operating in Abu Dhabi as well as Saudi Aramco and some Qatari companies pay high salaries that compete for the already small manpower pool accessible to ADNOC. Although it has been more resistant to demands for salary increases in the wake of high oil prices in 2007–2008, in the last few years ADNOC has moved swiftly to remedy the highly competitive manpower situation by increasing salaries on several occasions. This is in sharp contrast with some other NOCs – e.g., in India (see Chapter 17) – that have been unable to respond to a more competitive global market for talented local workers and have seen performance suffer accordingly.

5.1 At the margins: projects outside the ADNOC sphere

So far we have concentrated on the core of ADNOC's operations – that is, areas where ADNOC is completely in control. It is useful, in addition, to look at activities in the hydrocarbon sector that have unfolded outside ADNOC's direct control. Here we explore two such activities because they reveal some of the deficiencies in ADNOC's abilities and how the government as well as ADNOC's management has attempted to address them. First we examine the Dolphin project, which brings natural gas to the emirates (and Oman) from Qatar, which has been developed largely outside the ADNOC apparatus. The Dophin project arose through government frustration with ADNOC's lack of interest in gas supply, even though demand for gas in electricity and water supply was rising rapidly. Second we look at how ADNOC has handled fields that its onshore company (ADCO) has been unwilling or unable to pursue – using the example of fields that require complex management of sour gas (awarded to Conoco). But these are not the only examples where ADNOC has been forced to turn to outsiders; others include a cluster of small fields near Abu Dhabi that ADNOC has awarded exclusively to Occidental – fields too small to be of interest to ADCO but enticing to Occidental as a beachhead into the country (Oil Voice 2008).

5.1.1 Dolphin Gas Project

Commissioned in 2007, the Dolphin Gas Project involves the supply of 2 billion cubic feet/day gas produced in Qatar's offshore North Field. (The North Field is the world's largest gas field and the source of nearly all Qatar's prodigious gas export projects.) The gas travels to UAE and then to Oman via dedicated pipeline. The idea for the project dawned as the UAE leadership realized in the late 1990s that UAE's gas demand was growing at a pace that could not be sustained based just on domestic gas supplies (Butt 2001). With its numerous electricity, water desalination, petrochemicals, fertilizer, and aluminum smelting plants, Dubai's demand for gas has been soaring in particular (Figure 11.8). Because most of ADNOC's gas production is destined for exports and local gas supplies were already locked-in under long-term agreements, import of gas became an inevitable choice for a country whose population and economy were growing rapidly. ADNOC itself put very little emphasis on domestic gas supply

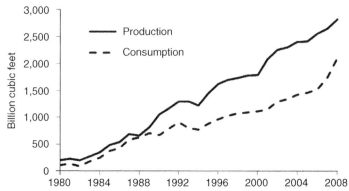

Figure 11.8 UAE's gas production and consumption, 1980–2008. The production data is "gross production", a portion of which is reinjected, exported, or flared. Over the last decade reinjection rates have grown very rapidly: annual reinjection rates were about 250 bcf during 1996–2000, 550 bcf during 2001–2005, and shot up to 817 bcf in 2008. As a result, the domestic production available for consumption has plummeted. At the same time, gas consumption for domestic and industrial usages has increased rapidly. The net effect is that UAE's gas consumption has outstripped its domestic gas production available for consumption.
Note: 1980–1989 production data is for "dry gas" only. All consumption is for "dry gas."
Data source: US Energy Information Administration (EIA 2010c).

and could not credibly meet growing demand through its own operations. If domestic gas supplies faltered then some gas-using applications would be forced to switch to oil, which carried a much higher opportunity cost since oil burned at home would not be available for lucrative export. The frustrations with ADNOC's lack of interest in boosting domestic gas supply were particularly acute at the Abu Dhabi Water and Electricity Authority (ADWEA), which was forced to notify ADNOC whenever it needed new supplies yet was unable to reliably count on the appearance of the needed gas. With a shortage of gas looming and support from the ruling family, a group of people who later were integral to Mubadala launched the Dolphin Project in 1999 and officially incorporated it in May 2002.[16]

The Dolphin Project is a very different kind of deal from ADNOC's skill set because it involves three-nation supply and utilization of gas. As is typical with international gas pipeline projects, the needed skills are a combination of infrastructure engineering and political talent in crafting and sustaining the supply and purchase (offtake) arrangements that underpin any successful project (see Victor *et al.* 2006). Thus, it has proceeded largely outside the ADNOC framework and is dominated by external players. Dolphin's three shareholders are the Mubadala Development Company (MDC, 51%), Total (24.5%), and Occidental (24.5%). Owned wholly by the Abu Dhabi government, Mubadala was founded in 2002 by the present Crown Prince, Sheikh Muhammad bin Zayed Al-Nahyan. It is Abu Dhabi's fourth-largest but fastest-growing sovereign-wealth fund (Davidson 2009). UAE's main role has been in signing long-term offtake agreements through ADWEA, Union Water and Electricity Company, and Dubai Supply Authority; UAE also plays a key role in allowing transit to Oman. The project also supplies gas to power and desalination plants in the eastern emirate of Fujairah, which is mostly inhabited by farmers and inland rural communities. Qatari gas reaches Fujairah through a 240-kilometer-long cross-country pipeline from Taweelah, the initial point on UAE soil where the Qatari gas arrives.

5.1.2 Stranded fields: Conoco enticed to work sulfur gas fields and then abandons the project

As part of its plan to expand domestic gas production for meeting domestic demand ADNOC has initiated the development of the Shah gas field. Abu Dhabi is rich in gas resources with more than 200 trillion cubic feet of known gas reserves. However, most of that gas, including from the Shah field, is sour (i.e., high in hydrogen sulfide, H_2S) and has remained untapped due to the complexity of treatment and handling of H_2S and ADNOC's limited experience with managing such projects (Zawya 2010). The Shah field, for example, has projected H_2S levels of 23 percent.) In 2008 ADNOC selected ConocoPhillips as a partner in the $10 billion Shah project after a closely contested bidding round of over two years between ConocoPhillips, ExxonMobil, Occidental, and Shell. (In the era of rising prices, ConocoPhillips bid aggressively to get the project.) The project, the first of its kind in the Gulf region, involves stripping natural gas liquids (NGL) from 1 billion cubic feet per day (cfd) feed gas to produce about 540–570 million cfd, nearly all of which is planned for reinjection into oil fields for enhanced oil recovery (MEES 2009b). ADNOC and ConocoPhillips entered a 60:40 joint venture and field entry agreement in July 2009.

But the Shah project has faced problems since the beginning. Declining oil prices since the highs of 2008 made the project much less attractive to ConocoPhillips. After several delays, ConocoPhillips pulled out of the project on April 28, 2010 (Daya 2010). Although ConocoPhillips did not provide any specific reason for its exit from the project it is understood that it is part of Conoco's larger decision to focus on short- and medium-term growth; by contrast, the returns from a first-of-a-kind sour gas project in Abu Dhabi would accrue over a long time horizon and through the foothold that the project would offer. It also appears that the ConocoPhillips bid to deliver gas at $5/million cubic feet was too low in light of the complexity and cost of the project (Karrar-Lewsley 2010).

For now, ADNOC seems to be moving forward with the project. On May 1, 2010, only days after Conoco's exit from the Shah project, ADNOC granted contracts worth $5.6 billion to various companies (Trade Arabia 2010), including Italy's Saipem ($3.1 billion) and South Korea's Samsung Engineering ($1.5 billion). But the episode is a reminder that ADNOC's strategy of relying heavily on IOCs as providers of technology and expertise is difficult to implement reliably outside the kinds of projects that the company already knows how to manage. In the past, when the complexity and risk of ADNOC's operations were declining and stable this strategy was relatively easy to follow and looked prescient. But with complexity and risk rising this strategy has become both more important and much harder to manage. It requires a set of skills – such as the ability to evaluate which bids and strategies by foreign partners are most credible and in Abu Dhabi's best interest – that ADNOC has not yet mastered. Today there is much interest by NOCs in the option of "buying" services from vendors when the NOC itself can't perform such functions; the case of ADNOC underscores that even when a firm's goal is to obtain expertise from others it still must have the managerial capacity to manage its partners and vendors.

6 Conclusion

ADNOC is one of the better-performing NOCs examined in this book. Its good performance stems mainly from a host government that is stable and confident and able to offer clear, long-term policy guidance. Such a government does not automatically yield an efficient

NOC. Indeed, by the mid 1980s ADNOC exhibited many of the signs of a faltering NOC – it had become insular and bureaucratic and a state within a state; in-fighting between powerful factions of the Abu Dhabi government threatened to paralyze the company. The ruler of Abu Dhabi reasserted more direct control over the company through his creation of the SPC. The SPC's credibility and stability have allowed ADNOC, unlike many of its peers in OPEC, to focus on long-term strategies. The SPC, backed by a stable ruling family, is the central explanator of ADNOC's good performance.

Other factors that have contributed to ADNOC's good performance include, for most of its history, the country's exceptionally low depletion rate, which stems mainly from Abu Dhabi's small population and modest revenue requirements. Low depletion has allowed the company to gain skills without extreme pressure on production. The country's "easy" geology has played a contributing role. However, that is changing rapidly as the country's fields mature and as the company faces daunting new tasks such as managing sour gas fields.

Unlike countries that fully nationalized their oil operations, Abu Dhabi is one of the few that has sustained a role for IOCs that has been attractive for the host (ADNOC) and the IOCs alike. This contrasts with Saudi Arabia and Kuwait (which rely nearly fully on their NOCs) and Iran (which has unattractive terms for most IOCs). ADNOC has used these arrangements to learn skills and, gradually, assume a larger operational role for its own employees. Ironically, however, even as the company has become more capable the need for foreign participation has grown since the company is working more complex fields today than a decade ago and because the government has sharply raised production goals.

ADNOC's goals have been twofold. One has been to maximize the provision of rents from its oil operations, which has meant running as an efficient oil company. The other has been to play a role in boosting the country's economic development – notably through Emiratization of its workforce, which has occurred not just through employment but also investment in education such as the building of the Petroleum Institute.

We find that it has delivered well on both those goals – in line with reasonable expectations. Looking to the future, however, we caution that the company is under a larger array of stresses today than perhaps at any time in its history. Higher production goals along with more complex operations such as the greater need for domestic gas supply will require a much more capable firm, and the capabilities that are most needed – management of foreign partners internalizing their skills within ADNOC – require highly sophisticated management. The Shah gas project is only one example and is a reminder that the interests of ADNOC and those of foreign partners can easily come out of alignment as the company tries to expand its operations into areas where it has little experience. These concerns arise not just with novel operations, such as in high sulfur gas fields, but also the mainstream operations of the company as all the concessions are due to expire in the next few years. Abu Dhabi's political stability and highly unified control of its oil and gas sector under the SPC do offer the promise that ADNOC will be more adept at maneuvering in the face of these stresses than most other NOCs. Its great attractiveness as a stable, desirable investment destination will likely provide it some leeway not only in negotiating favorable commercial terms with the IOCs in the next round of concessions, but also in tying those concessions to more fundamental ways of improving technological capabilities, such as through increased domestic R&D and manpower training.

ADNOC has made many reforms that point to continued high performance, but the expectations on the firm are rising quickly. So is competition. In the area of Emiratization, for example, the firm must now compete with new industries – such as nuclear power, semiconductors, aerospace manufacturing, renewable energy, and a growing service sector – for a limited talent pool. The firm even sees competition in its core oil and gas operations from new entrants such as Mubadala's Dolphin Project and other activities on the fringe of the hydrocarbon sector that could become more central in the coming years.

Notes

1 The emirate of Ras al-Khaimah joined in early 1972.
2 ADCO: Abu Dhabi Company for Onshore Oil Operations; ADMA-OPCO: Abu Dhabi Marine Operating Company; ZADCO: Zakum Development Company; GASCO: Abu Dhabi Gas Industries Limited; ADGAS: Abu Dhabi Gas Liquefaction Company Limited; TAKREER: Abu Dhabi Oil Refining Company; NDC: National Drilling Company; IRSHAD: Abu Dhabi Petroleum Ports Operating Company; FERTIL: Ruwais Fertilizer Industries; BOROUGE: Abu Dhabi Polymers Company Limited; ADNATCO: Abu Dhabi National Tanker Company; NGSCO: National Gas Shipping Company.

3 For example, in 2007 ADNOC also established the ADNOC-Linde
  Industrial Gases Company (Elixier) to manufacture industrial gases
  used by the oil and gas and petrochemical industries in the Gulf. Its
  production facilities are closely integrated with those of the GASCO.
  Elixier is jointly owned by ADNOC (51 percent) and Linde Group of
  Germany (49 percent).

4 ADCO is the descendant of PDTC, which on January 11, 1939 had
  received a seventy-five-years concession for exploration and production
  for onshore areas in Abu Dhabi. At formation in 1939, PDTC was owned
  by a consortium of IOCs. But following the formation of OPEC, on
  January 1, 1973 the Government of Abu Dhabi acquired a 25% interest
  in PDTC; the government raised its interest to 60% on 1 January 1974.
  ADCO's main (onshore) producing fields are Asab, Bab, Bu Hasa, Sahil,
  and Shah. ADMA was formed in 1954 to exploit Abu Dhabi's offshore oil
  concession areas. In the early 1950s Abu Dhabi established that PDTC's
  concessions did not include its offshore areas, following which D'Arcy
  Exploration Company was granted offshore exploration concession. A
  year later that concession was assigned to ADMA, which at inception was
  owned two-thirds by BP and one-third by CFP (now Total). But, owing
  to changes in ADMA's ownership structure in the early 1970s similar to
  those at ADCO, at present ADNOC owns 60% of ADMA-OPCO, BP
  14.67%, Total 13.33%, and Japan Oil Development Company (JODCO)
  12%. ADMA-OPCO's main producing fields are Umm Shaif and Lower
  Zakum. The Umm Shaif field was discovered in 1958 and Abu Dhabi's
  first oil exports from Das Island came from Umm Shaif in 1962. Zakum,
  one of the world's largest oil fields, was discovered in 1963.

5 Proved reserves and production drawn from BP Statistical Review of
  World Energy (BP 2010).

6 PESD Interviews, November 2008.

7 PESD Interviews, November 2008.

8 Demographic estimates vary and are difficult to reconcile. Some sources
  suggest the expatriate population is much larger (about 7 million). Here
  we use estimates from the CIA (2010b) based on the 2005 census.

9 PESD Interviews, November 2008.

10 PESD Interviews, November 2008. As part of the yearly proposals (discussed later), the subsidiaries also propose manpower requirements.
   ADNOC, then, plays the matchmaker by directing Emiratis to suitable
   positions.

11 We are grateful to Michael Ohadi for information on the Petroleum
   Institute's mission and strategy.

12 Worthy of note is that Sheikh Zayed chaired the SPC, which is now
   chaired by the current ruler, Sheikh Khalifa. Some at the time saw the

514   *Varun Rai and David G. Victor*

move as a part of the settling of accounts within the extended ruling family. Since then, no cousin has held a position of comparable authority, which may reflect that the ruling family has learned that it is crucial to keep power over the oil sector highly consolidated to avoid repeating the pre-SPC experience of confusion.

13 PESD Interviews, November 2008.
14 PESD Interviews, November 2008.
15 PESD Interviews, November 2008.
16 We are particularly grateful to Howard Harris for help in understanding the origins and purpose of the Dolphin Gas Project.

12 | Brazil's Petrobras: strategy and performance

ADILSON DE OLIVEIRA

1 Introduction

Petrobras stands out as a particularly successful national oil company (NOC). One of the world leaders in deep water oil exploration and production, Petrobras has a dominant position in the Brazilian oil and gas market and has a small but growing presence abroad as well. Its dominant position in Brazil and strong performance, along with other factors that the company itself doesn't control such as the high price of oil, explain why its market value grew from $26.4 billion in 2000 to $173.6 billion in August 2009. It is currently Latin America's largest publicly traded company. Among its peers – both NOCs and the international oil companies (IOCs) – the company is widely seen as a well-managed, efficient leader in the industry.

Created in 1954, as a result of a congressional decision in the previous year to create a state monopoly in the Brazilian oil industry, Petrobras started its operations with no meaningful oil reserves or much expertise in producing, refining, and marketing oil or refined products. Unsurprisingly, oil experts were skeptical about the future of the newborn company.

Unlike other NOCs, which were founded amid oil riches, Petrobras was not created to be a source of fiscal resources to the government or to provide politically oriented services such as local employment. Indeed, the company relied on fiscal subsidies for the first twenty years

This chapter is the result of several years of monitoring Petrobras activities. An earlier paper on Petrobras's performance, elaborated by Brian Sandstrom for PESD, was its starting point. I am grateful to several people in Petrobras and to my academic colleagues who helped to shape my understanding of the issues Petrobras faced in its history. I am especially grateful to my friends at PESD who offered me the opportunity to contrast the Petrobras experience with those of the IOCs and other NOCs. I have had the chance of having my drafts closely reviewed by David Hults and especially David Victor, which added much value to the chapter. Any fault is my own, however. Bento Maia and Diego Maciel were helpful in organizing the data and preparing the figures presented in the chapter.

of its existence. While the government gave Petrobras some discretion to spend revenues that it earned from oil production and sales, the scarcity of revenues forced Petrobras to learn how to rationally select projects in order to guarantee the cash flow demanded by its investment program. Successive Brazilian governments gave Petrobras the managerial autonomy needed to deliver on the government's central goal: to save scarce hard currency and provide a competitive, secure fuel supply for the industrialization of Brazil.[1] To achieve these goals, Petrobras was organized vertically and oriented to the exploitation of economies of scale. And while it soon looked for (and found) oil, in the early years the main job of Petrobras was to manage the country's growing oil imports.

The history of Petrobras can be divided into three main periods. Prior to the discovery of oil offshore in the Campos Basin (1974), Petrobras used its monopolistic power to organize the Brazilian downstream. It oversaw the creation of a national infrastructure needed to supply domestic oil products to consumers, and once that infrastructure was in place Petrobras soon found itself short of domestic oil onshore to feed its refineries. The company aggressively hunted for oil at home (onshore and offshore, but only the latter offered large reserves) as well as overseas. When Petrobras discovered the offshore Campos Basin was rich in oil the company was short of financial and technological resources to develop it. To tap these resources the company needed to engage its technological capabilities while at the same time insulating itself from erratic Brazilian macroeconomic policy that rocked the company (and the rest of the Brazilian economy) with hyperinflation and instability.

Petrobras used its monopolistic power over Brazilian oil resources to lower financial and operational risks from testing new technologies that might have deterred competitive companies. First it mastered production from relatively shallow waters and then moved deeper offshore while using the cash flow from shallow water projects to finance the move further offshore. The technological capabilities of Petrobras (as well as its suppliers of equipments and services) were gradually improved using the learning by doing approach. When its domestic monopolistic power was removed in 1997 (as part of broader pro-market reforms of the Brazilian economy), Petrobras nonetheless kept a de facto monopoly in the Brazilian market (upstream and downstream). The company dominated critical technological, logistic, and managerial capabilities to operate in deep offshore.

From 1997 until now, Petrobras's strategy has been centered in increasing production and the preservation of its dominant position in the domestic market both upstream and downstream while searching for opportunities overseas where the company's technological capabilities would give it an edge. Despite the company's dominant position it faces increasing competition, which has induced Petrobras to reorganize its structure and services to improve its operational and financial performance. In addition to internal reforms, Petrobras used its offshore technological capabilities, along with its political connections, to entice IOCs into partnerships. In a few countries, it has also searched overseas for opportunities where Petrobras, as a Brazilian company, might have an advantage through its connection to the Brazilian state – mainly in Latin America where the company might serve as an instrument for continental energy integration. For a time that advantage existed in Bolivia and in the last decade it has been urged by the Brazilian government to foster opportunities in Venezuela. In practice, though, neither Chávez nor Morales foster inviting investment contexts, and in Bolivia (where Petrobras had the most at stake) the company's ventures have proved disastrous.

From the mid 1990s, the government has seen competition as the best strategy for encouraging investment in the country's oil resources. That strategy worked well and by 2008 Brazil reached self-sufficiency in oil and is now a net exporter. The recent discovery of very large oil fields in the deep offshore "pre-salt"[2] of the Brazilian coast opens a new era for Petrobras. As oil imports have faded and are no longer a critical macroeconomic concern for the government, political attention has turned to oil revenues as a future major source of government revenue. In an effort to maximize revenues for itself and increase its control over oil resources, the government is introducing production-sharing agreements and also creating another state oil company – Petrossal, fully owned by the government – to manage these resources. Petrossal will have a dominant position in the managing committee of any consortia organized for the exploration of the pre-salt resources. Petrobras will be the operator of any of these consortia with a minimum investment share of 30 percent. A social fund will be created for the management of the government take of the oil eventually produced in the pre-salt.

It is unambiguous that the government intends to establish a new relationship with Petrobras. This shift is a sign that the government

is wary of Petrobras becoming a state within a state as has happened
in so many other countries with NOCs that dominate the country's
economy and society. Petrossal, the government hopes, will help it
reduce the asymmetry of information between state and NOC and
may also help it gain the information needed to regulate Petrobras
more effectively.[3]

So far these changes in the political context have not manifested
in Petrobras's strategy. Under the present government, the company
intends to remain a de facto monopoly in the domestic downstream and
to build large domestic oil refineries for the supply of oil by-products
overseas. It plans to expand its oil production to 6.4 million barrels
of oil equivalent daily (with only 0.4 mbd from overseas) by 2020;
roughly half this output would be sold in the international oil market.
To achieve its goals, Petrobras intends to invest $224.7 billion in the
next five years, including $11.2 billion overseas (Petrobras 2011).

This chapter describes the rise of Petrobras and explains why the company has been so successful. The central argument is that Petrobras's
success largely results from a collection of strategies oriented to the
minimization of risks, a critical aspect of the oil business (Adelman
1993). In the early years the company's strategy was insulation.
Organized by a group of military officers[4] to operate professionally,[5]
Petrobras was protected from petty political interference so long as it
acted to meet high-level government objectives, notably the minimization of foreign expenditures.[6] As imports rose, the company's risk management strategy shifted and became more commercial. To manage
commercial risks, Petrobras first developed its downstream logistics –
notably refineries, which were expensive but not risky due to the company's monopoly. This made it easier to absorb later the large increase
in output as its upstream operations found and produced more oil.
To minimize its technological risks, Petrobras initially relied heavily
on technological cooperation with other companies while eventually
building its own in-house capabilities. Petrobras also had the blessing
of the gentle topography of the Campos Basin, making it easier for the
company to move progressively along a technological learning curve to
deeper waters as it mastered the shallow ones.

The next section of this chapter offers a review of Petrobras's historical trajectory. Then I examine the company's performance by measuring its activities against the goals that the Brazilian government (the
"principal") had set for its NOC (the "agent"). This "principal–agent"

Figure 12.1 Map of major oil and gas fields in Brazil.
Source for oil and gas field data: Wood Mackenzie (2009b).

framework reflects the insights from David Hults (Chapter 3) who examined the various ways that governments have tried to control and steer their NOCs. This relationship is particularly important to understanding the recent attempts by the government to create, in effect, a new NOC that would manage the pre-salt fields. A final section summarizes the chapter.

2 The strategy for success

2.1 *State monopoly*

Brazil's first oil concessions date from the Imperial period, but the country's interest in the oil business grew stronger as of the early twentieth century. However, a practical focus on oil did not emerge until an alliance of the military and the urban middle class replaced the rural oligarchy in government through the 1930s revolution (Fernandes 1981). The revolution included new financial measures aimed at substituting local production for imports – a popular development strategy at the time (Furtado 1971). The economic model after the 1930s favored industrialization and urbanization, which increased consumption of oil products – essentially all of which were imported – and diminished the availability of foreign currency for other purposes.

After the revolution, the government started to assign property rights on minerals in an effort to encourage and shape the development of these resources. The 1934 Constitution established such property rights for the first time; the 1937 Constitution assigned those rights solely to Brazilian citizens or companies constituted by Brazilians. In 1938, a decree gave the federal government control over the oil supply.

Assigning property rights would not be enough, however. Thus the government also adopted the Service for Promotion of Mineral Production (SFPM) – a scheme designed to promote the search for oil on Brazil's territory. Lacking the expertise to explore sedimentary basins, the SFPM hired oil technicians from the United States to survey and identify potential territories (Penna Marinho 1970). Independently, a local Brazilian oil company demanded that the SFPM provide the drilling machinery to prove that the oil surfacing in Lobato (Bahia) would be economically viable to produce, but the SFPM disagreed and refused to offer its services. This refusal provoked a caustic press campaign against the SFPM and its American technicians with the slogan: "The SFPM was created not to find oil but to avoid anybody finding it." Eventually, the SFPM decided to drill in Lobato and an oil field with commercially viable supplies was found in 1939. Immediately, the government decided to prohibit any exploration by private companies within a radius of 60 km from Lobato. As in many countries, such as Mexico (see Chapter 7) Brazil's search for oil began with an uneasy dependence on external experts who were thought to be essential yet at the same time disposable when their decisions did not align with national ideals.

The SFPM proved to be an unsuccessful experience because the organization's skills were difficult to tie to practical (and risky) decisions to provide investment in commercial-scale oil production projects. In 1938, the government created the National Petroleum Council (CNP) to supervise, regulate, and carry out the oil industry activities previously executed by the SFPM. General Horta Barbosa was named its first president and focused the exploration efforts in the sedimentary basin of Bahia. In 1940, a decree declared that oil by-products, either imported or locally produced, were subject to a single federal tax whose revenues were earmarked exclusively for the development of the oil industry (and thus CNP). The revolutionary government of the time remained extremely suspicious of outsiders and, indeed, of private industry.[7]

When World War II in Europe drew to a close so did the revolutionary government of President Getúlio Vargas. With a new government (led by General Dutra) the pendulum swung in the direction of a greater role for foreign investors. A new constitution allowed international companies to organize operations in Brazil to explore mineral resources, including oil. In 1948, the government sent an oil bill (Estatuto do Petróleo) to the National Congress that would have allowed IOCs to invest in the oil business. This movement opened a public struggle between those who felt that partnerships with IOCs would be the quickest route to the needed technological and financial support and those who adopted a nationalistic approach steeped in mistrust of foreign capital. CNP's General Horta Barbosa stood up for the monopolistic state-owned company, and public lobbying emerged with the slogan "Keep the Brazilian oil for Brazilians" ("*O petróleo é nosso*"), still used by nationalists today. The Dutra government, unable to muster the needed votes, was unable to pass the bill. Brazil's oil strategy found itself in gridlock.

In 1951, Vargas returned to the presidency by popular vote and the political pendulum swung left again. The compromise on oil policy, found in a bill the Vargas administration sent to the congress, was the proposed creation of Petrobras, with no indication that the company would be a monopolistic oil company. The debate between nationalists and their opponents became quite acrimonious but it ended with the opponents outvoted and having little choice but to accept that Petrobras, a state-owned monopoly, should be in charge of exploiting oil resources.

In contrast to the electric power market, where private investors already had a strong position in the Brazilian market, there was limited political resistance to the creation of a national monopoly in the oil industry (Pereira de Melo *et al.* 1994). Local investors professed to have an interest in the oil business, but they lacked the financial and technological capabilities to develop it and did not devote substantial resources to opening the market for their exploits (Cohn 1968). The IOCs had little interest in Brazil since there was plenty of cheap oil elsewhere (Grenon 1972) and the available geological data suggested that the country's onshore oil resources were scarce and costly. Moreover, Brazil's oil consumption was too small to justify risky investments in refineries to supply the future consumption that the government expected would materialize, and IOCs knew that it would be hard to have a large presence in the country without also playing a role in the risky downstream.

Those that wanted to attract IOCs to the Brazilian market had lost much of their political influence while the nationalists used the growing pressure of oil imports on the balance of payments to support their view that the country's financial exposure required a state enterprise to manage the national interest.[8] Eventually, Law 2.400 (1953) laid the foundation of Petrobras, a state-owned monopoly for exploration, production, transportation, and refining of hydrocarbons in the Brazilian market.[9]

2.2 Organizing the downstream (1954–1973)

Unlike many NOCs, Petrobras started with poor oil reserves and insignificant logistic infrastructure to supply oil products to consumers. The company received CNP's oil assets, which consisted of oil fields producing 2,700 bpd and recoverable reserves of 15 million barrels.[10] But for the most part, oil activities in Brazil were limited to transportation, refining, and marketing. The refining capacity under construction would be able to supply only 50 percent of the domestic consumption of oil products; available tankers could transport only 20 percent of the needed imports, which made the country dependent on contracting for tankers in an unreliable market; and the domestic oil production supplied 2.5 percent of the country's consumption.

This situation placed a high premium on frugality and ingenuity in the company. The top managers of Petrobras were drawn from the military and followed a disciplined culture that soon pervaded the company. In time, a system of admission based on competitive national exams was established to select the techno-bureaucracy needed to manage the company. A job in Petrobras became a prized outcome for young graduates, and placement and progress within the company's technical ranks, as in the military, was competitive and based on merit rather than decided through personal connections.[11] Petrobras employees were trained abroad and foreign experts were hired to provide technical advice and instruction. Brazilian universities were encouraged to offer graduate degrees in geology and chemical engineering and thus a pipeline of qualified students for the state company. Following the model of an efficient IOC, the Petrobras top managers organized the company to operate as an integrated oil company, with multiple divisions and a central executive board.

The government set objectives for the new company. Its main goals were to find domestic oil resources and to develop downstream infrastructure needed to supply the growing domestic consumption of oil by-products at internationally competitive prices. A single large vertically integrated company, as was envisioned, would allow purchasing power to be used to promote the domestic supply of equipment and services for its projects.

To achieve these goals the government provided Petrobras with generous financial incentives, such as exemption of import duties and royalties, tax relief on sales of equipment earmarked for Petrobras projects, international parity pricing for oil products (which reduced any subsidy requirement that would have fallen to Petrobras while also fortuitously keeping domestic consumption in check), and a scheme to give Petrobras 80 percent of the foreign currency "saved" by its domestic production of oil (Alveal 1993). The last provision, particularly important when foreign earnings were scarce, allowed Petrobras to squirrel away the cash it would need to fund needed imports.

For the first few years following the company's creation, Petrobras was under continual assault from both sides of the political spectrum. Politicians on the right complained that almost 40 percent of the company's funds stemmed from tax exemptions and earmarked sources of revenue, while 40 percent of profits in the 1950s were the direct result of protection in the refining sector (Philip 1982). Conversely, the left felt that the company was not doing enough to meet national goals.

These tensions escalated in 1958, with an open debate between CNP and Petrobras's business-minded managers over whether the company should allocate more of its resources to meeting government goals (Penna Marinho 1970). The government backed Petrobras. Similar

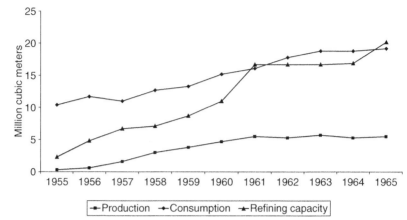

Figure 12.2 Brazilian oil production, consumption, and refinery capacity, 1955–1965.
Source: Petrobras.

debates have happened in the decades since and nearly always the government has aligned with the commercial decisions of the oil company. That has been a durable signal that Petrobras would keep the autonomy needed to focus on being an oil company – a sharp contrast with the later history of the company's peers such as PDVSA and Pemex, which became distracted with other missions (see Chapters 7 and 10).

Petrobras responded to these incentives. Its crude production reached 57,000 b/d in 1958 and by that same year it had built refining capacity sufficient to supply 55.9 percent of the domestic consumption of oil products (Figure 12.2). The foreign currency expenditures for oil imports stabilized at $250 million a year, even though domestic demand for oil products was rising at 6.3 percent a year. Petrobras also began reorganizing its supply chain by negotiating with a Brazilian industrial association to supply capital goods and spare parts for its projects (Macedo e Silva 1985). While the company was becoming more efficient, it still had not found any sizable new oil fields despite a substantial drilling effort.[12]

To improve its prospects for finding oil, Petrobras decided to hire Walter Link, a geologist from Standard Oil, to conduct a geological survey of Brazil. The aim of his study was to gain a better sense of the country's potential oil reserves. Link concluded that Brazil did not have any significant onshore oil reserves, which meant that the plan to hunt for easy oil and make the country self-sufficient would not work. Nationalists were furious about the decision to engage Link – both because it relied on foreign advice and because the answer was inconvenient. All this bad news meant, for a time, that Petrobras would be given even greater control over the sector. The government nationalized the few remaining existing private refineries, authorized Petrobras to distribute oil products to final consumers (an activity up to then mostly in the hands of IOCs) and gave Petrobras the monopoly on oil imports. This trend came to a dramatic halt with the military coup of 1964.

The new military government, divided between internationalists and nationalists (Stepan 1971), sold the nationalized refineries back to the IOCs that previously owned them, removed the Petrobras monopoly over shale oil, and allowed private investments in petrochemicals to please the internationalists who were part of the government's key supporters. However, the Petrobras oil monopoly was preserved. Moreover, the head of the military coup declared that Petrobras's mission was "to find the oil demanded by the economy in such way that the expenditures of foreign currency would not increase" (Petrobras 1965). The hunt for oil was on, and Walter Link suggested it would be a lot tougher than the nationalists originally expected.

Shortly after the military coup, Petrobras stopped revealing much about its internal operations or affairs to the public. A new organizational model redefined responsibilities and the hierarchy, resulting in a vertical structure with four departments[13] and a few support services: the service for the supply of materials (SERMAT), the engineering service (SEGEN), and the innovation center (CENPES). Disgruntled employees were discouraged from airing their grievances outside the company or through the political process. Petrobras operations became marked by a lack of transparency, which limited public oversight (Randall 1993).

In 1968, General Ernesto Geisel, later to become a Brazilian president, agreed to be appointed president of the company but only if the Minister of Mines and Energy refrained from interfering in his management of the company.[14] The enlarged autonomy given to General Geisel allowed him to make a heretical political move. Indeed, at his inaugural speech, he stated that the company mission was to "guarantee the domestic supply of oil products," meaning that oil imports were not considered a critical aspect of the company success. He was

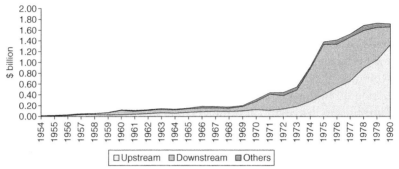

Figure 12.3 Petrobras investments, 1954–1980.
Source: Petrobras.

convinced that the conclusions of the Link report were correct. The search for oil should go where competitive reserves were likely to be found: more likely overseas but possibly in the domestic offshore.[15] While new supplies were the long-term goal, over the short term Geisel thought Petrobras should focus its investments in the downstream (Figure 12.3), taking advantage of the falling international oil prices (Odell 1986) to squeeze economic benefits from crude oil suppliers. Lower crude prices and scale economies in the downstream would lower the oil products prices for consumers.

To diversify and to augment Petrobras operations, Geisel created four new companies, all subsidiaries of Petrobras: 1) Braspetro, to explore for oil overseas; 2) Petrobras Distribuidora, to develop the logistic and marketing infrastructure needed to supply oil products to the areas of little or no interest to private investors (especially in Amazonia); 3) Petrofertil, to develop the domestic supply of fertilizers; and 4) Petroquisa, for the development of the domestic supply of petrochemicals in a tripartite financial arrangement between Petrobras, domestic, and international private investors (Alveal 1993). A reasonable share of the company investments (listed as "others" in Figure 12.3) was oriented to these subsidiaries.

To support the new strategy, the cash flow from domestic oil production and loans from European banks were channeled to an ambitious downstream investment program. To foster the domestic supply of equipment and services needed for the construction of the downstream logistics (pipelines, refineries, terminals, tanks), the National Economic Development Bank (BNDE) made soft loans available to private investors who worked closely with state-owned Petrobras. A special team (Grupo Executivo de Obras Prioritárias – GEOP) was made responsible for the development of the company's key projects. The early technological efforts at the Petrobras research center (CENPES) were oriented to the downstream, and strict quality procedures were adopted for the procurement of equipment and services, forcing domestic suppliers to improve their economic competitiveness.[16] These developments offered political benefits for an unpopular military regime and they improved the legitimacy of Petrobras among the general public; they also expanded Petrobras's presence to virtually all areas of the country and to the most important sectors of the economy.

Geisel's strategy provided room for the verticalization of Petrobras operations, but it came with risks. If Petrobras found oil overseas, the oil self-sufficiency objective could be threatened. If the new domestic oil was more expensive than the oil available in the international market, it would save foreign currency but Petrobras would depend on additional financial incentives from the government to explore for it – none of which could be assured. The risks for Brazil were high but for Petrobras were relatively small. General Geisel used his autonomy to push his policy forward.

2.3 Developing the offshore (1974–1994)

In 1974, General Geisel moved from his job as head of Petrobras to replace General Medici as Brazil's president.[17] Within Petrobras, the company's intense focus on the downstream and much slower effort to boost domestic production meant that crude oil imports reached 80 percent of the domestic consumption. With the oil crisis of 1973 prices escalated and the import bill exploded in size. Taking advantage of petrodollars that needed investment, General Geisel's administration borrowed heavily in the international financial market and ploughed those resources into Brazil's industry. He did for Brazil what he had done at Petrobras by concentrating investment on capital-intensive industrial projects on the theory that those would catalyze the country's broader industrial development. Large incentives were given to domestic suppliers of capital goods and intermediate materials (e.g., petrochemicals, steel, and aluminum) (Castro and Pires de Souza 1985). It was assumed these projects would later save the foreign currency needed to pay their initial loans.

To reduce expenditure on crude oil imports (which had jumped from $1.0 billion to $4.9 billion between 1972 and 1974), the government decided to build nuclear plants (which would reduce the need for oil for future electricity generation); it expanded reliance on hydropower (for the same purpose); and it launched the world's largest fuel ethanol program (de Oliveira 2007). To improve energy efficiency, the taxation of gasoline was substantially increased but taxes were kept relatively low for other oil products (notably diesel fuel) that were more central to the industrialization process (de Araújo and Ghirardi 1987). Costly gasoline and favorable incentives for ethanol, in time, induced a shift to much greater reliance on alcohol fuels (de Oliveira 1991).

In tandem with finding ways to use oil more efficiently and to shift from oil, the government also pushed Petrobras to accelerate its search for domestic oil supplies. Mindful of Link's insight that onshore oil supplies were likely to be modest, the company had started looking offshore. A small field (Guaricema) offshore of the state of Sergipe had been found in 1969, indicating that Brazil's long coastline held the geological potential for much more oil (Grenon 1975). In 1974, the Garoupa and Pargo fields were identified in the Campos Basin, offshore of the state of Rio de Janeiro. While the geological data suggested that Campos would hold sizable oil reserves,[18] Petrobras had little technological capability to operate in the offshore. Cooperation with the IOCs was needed to speed up the development of Campos and there was strong interest by IOCs in the area. However, Petrobras was not keen to share its findings with them.[19]

Aware of this problem, General Geisel made another heretical political move. He demanded in a television announcement, with no legislation to support his decision, that Petrobras sign service contracts with IOCs.[20] Under this new arrangement, the IOCs would absorb the risks associated with finding and developing the oil fields; they would be reimbursed through revenues that would come from a share of the oil and gas if and when produced but earn no return if no oil or gas was found – and Petrobras would be the sole operator of any oil field eventually found. Because the government had no oil expertise, Petrobras was put in charge of setting the conditions for contracting the IOCs and making the choice of blocks to be licensed.

Nationalists left and right strongly criticized Geisel's decision, which recalled the debates a generation earlier over the question of whether to vest control of the oil sector with a state-owned company.

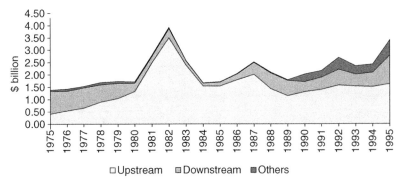

Figure 12.4 Petrobras investments, 1975–1995.
Source: Petrobras.

By the 1970s that company was firmly in place, and Geisel's announcement also engendered resistance among Petrobras technicians who perceived the new arrangement as a threat to its monopolistic position in the Brazilian market. Nevertheless, Geisel was able to quash dissent by making his announcement highly visible. Soon the country licensed 243 blocks to 35 IOCs, covering 1.5 million km² of sedimentary basins.

Afraid it would fall behind the new players that had just been invited into the country's upstream, Petrobras reoriented its investment strategy toward the upstream: by 1979 more than half of all investment was for exploration and production, whereas in the early 1970s only about one-quarter of resources were dedicated to that purpose (Figure 12.3 and Figure 12.4). Taking advantage of its monopolistic power over domestic oil resources and the favorable topography of the Brazilian continental shelf (it gently slopes to deeper water), Petrobras adopted a stepwise approach to the development of the technology and practices needed to exploit the Campos Basin (Figure 12.5).

Progressively moving its projects from shallow to deeper waters, the company introduced several technological innovations which enabled the discovery of increasingly larger reservoirs in the deep offshore. At first the company worked with jack-up rigs in shallow water; then it moved to floating platforms. Success with these technologies did not hinge on any particular, radical innovation; instead, it came through incremental technological changes. It seems unlikely that Petrobras would have developed these resources largely on its own if it did not,

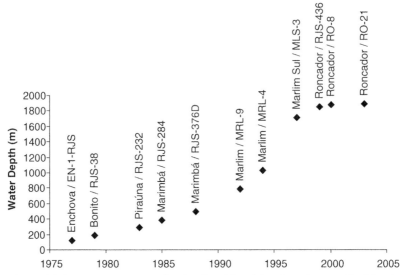

Figure 12.5 Increasing water depth of pathbreaking Petrobras wells (identified by field and well name) over time.
Source: Petrobras.

first, have access to offshore oil close to the coast which yielded the
experience and the cash flow needed to move deeper.

To speed up its cash flow (and consequently increase its ability to
invest) Petrobras decided to start producing oil at the Enchova field
(discovered in 1976) using the then risky concept known as the Early
Production System (SPA) while a conventional Definitive Production
System (SPD) was under construction. A conventional SPD required
four to six years to start production, but the SPA allowed production
of 10,000 bpd from Enchova within two years of its discovery. This
new concept offered the additional benefit of providing geological
information that helped speed development of other fields as well.[21]
With such strategies Petrobras increased its investments from $920.4
million in 1974 to $1,712.6 million in 1980 (Figure 12.3).

To overcome its technological fragility, Petrobras created incentives for its offshore suppliers of services and equipment to innovate and share their new technologies with the company. Consortia of
Brazilian and international engineering companies were structured
by Petrobras to develop the platforms for the Brazilian offshore,
and the learning obtained from these innovations was consolidated

in CENPES.[22] Eventually, the Campos Basin became a gigantic innovation laboratory for offshore oil production.

General Figueiredo replaced General Geisel in the presidency of Brazil in 1979. In tandem, almost immediately, events in the international markets put the country into a long period of economic and political instability. Rising interest rates in the late 1970s, a global economic contraction in the early 1980s, and the Mexican debt default in 1982 all put severe pressure on countries, including Brazil, which had borrowed heavily in the international financial markets. The new government was forced to respond with radical economic measures to maintain the balance of payments (Carneiro 1982).

In 1980, with oil prices at an all-time high, Brazilian oil consumption was 1,107,200 bpd while domestic production totaled only 185,100 bpd. Oil imports needed to be drastically and rapidly reduced to conserve scarce foreign reserves and avoid the risk of a Brazilian default. The government set the objective of producing 500,000 bpd by 1985 and proposed to offer production-sharing agreements to further entice IOCs to invest. However, the military regime was too weak to introduce such politically controversial policies and the proposal died and Petrobras continued as a monopolist.

In total, the IOCs invested $1.2 billion from 1975 to the beginning of the 1980s but they were unable to find much oil.[23] The IOCs blamed this poor outcome on Petrobras, which determined the blocks that would be offered and, in the view of the IOCs, released acreage that had little chance of holding oil. Petrobras claimed that the IOCs lacked the expertise to explore the Brazilian geology that Petrobras had obtained by moving along the learning curve. The reality is that Petrobras offered the blocks with *hard to find oil* to the IOCs, but it is also true that the IOCs needed time to learn the Brazilian geology. Suspicious that they would be dealt an unfair hand, the IOCs were unwilling to make the needed long-term investment (a familiar problem across many areas of high capital investment within regulatory systems that change in unexpected, opaque, and difficult-to-manage ways). Indeed, even after the government removed Petrobras's monopoly and offered IOCs fair access to the Brazilian offshore in the 1990s, the IOCs were still skittish about the risks that attended to long-term investments; partnerships with Petrobras became the preferred IOC strategy in most cases – a topic we revisit in the next section.

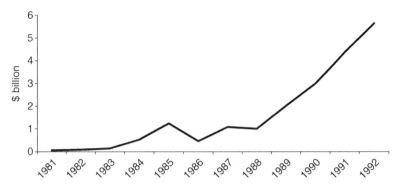

Figure 12.6 Deficit in the oil account, 1981–1992.
Source: Petrobras.

During the 1980s, Brazil was trapped between unsustainable debt payments and macroeconomic choices politically difficult to muster – a situation familiar to many Latin American countries at the time. The government introduced successive economic stabilization plans; all sought to control inflation but all failed (Rego 1986). The Ministry of Finance took control over pricing of crude oil, oil products, and ethanol with the goal of taming inflation while not, at the same time, squelching the country's industrial growth.

Wholesale gasoline sales were taxed more heavily while the prices of the remaining oil products (e.g., diesel) were cross-subsidized and remained below their opportunity cost. Gasoline was seen as a luxury good while other oil products were considered essential to maintaining economic activity. *Reference prices* were adopted for the crude oil processed at Petrobras refineries.[24] Differences between the price that Petrobras actually paid for imported crude oil and the reference price used to determine domestic prices for refined products were accumulated on an "oil account" on the company's balance sheet, which would later be offset by price adjustments or reconciled by the Treasury (Lodi 1993). Eventually, the oil account always ran a deficit (Figure 12.6), which meant that the net effect of the government's pricing policy was to subsidize energy consumers and to force Petrobras to operate with a "soft" budget constraint.

Over time, this pricing policy radically changed the pattern of fuel consumption in the country. During the 1980s gasoline sales plummeted and diesel along with ethanol soared. Unable to adjust the output from its refineries so quickly, Petrobras convinced the government to relax the quality standards of the gasoline and diesel offered to the marketplace so that, at least in total volumes, the company could minimize production of gasoline and augment its output of diesel and other oil products (Fantine 1986). Consumers suffered as fuel efficiency declined with lower-quality fuels; the productivity of Petrobras's refineries decreased and the company eventually became a large exporter of gasoline blendstocks.

Facing high prices when buying imported oil, Petrobras concentrated its investment strategy in the domestic upstream. The risks of this strategy were large but so were the rewards for success. The oil monopoly under the government umbrella offered Petrobras a privileged position to accept these extraordinary technological and financial risks.

Until 1983, Petrobras was able to shield its cash flow from the pricing arrangement introduced by the Ministry of Finance. The dependency on oil imports was a major government concern still, and Petrobras investments in the upstream were crucial to reducing oil imports. This situation drastically changed after 1983, when inflation started to run out of control. The government used its control over the prices of oil products to mitigate inflation, which rapidly increased the deficit in the "oil account" (Figure 12.6). Short of cash, Petrobras was forced to reduce its investments but nonetheless was able to achieve the goal of boosting national oil production to 500,000 bpd for 1985 by operating twenty-two SPAs.[25] Around the same time the company discovered two giant offshore fields – Albacora (1984) and Marlim (1985) – that boosted the company's morale and its public legitimacy during a period when the military regime (which had been the main political protector of Petrobras) was losing public support. But these new fields would require quite different technologies to exploit.

After twenty years of military rule, a civilian government was elected by the National Congress and charged with planning a transition to democracy. The new government introduced still more macroeconomic stabilization plans – all of which failed to tame inflation. Moreover, the collapse in the oil price and the uncertainties of the Brazilian transition to democracy coupled with a period of soft demand and surplus OPEC capacity dampened any interest of the IOCs in the Brazilian oil market. The economic and political risks in Brazil were seen as high, and the IOCs had better investment opportunities elsewhere.

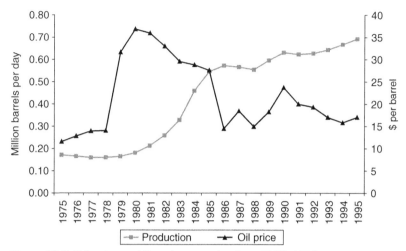

Figure 12.7 Oil price and Petrobras production, 1975–1995.
Source: Petrobras.

But for Petrobras, the domestic oil fields were the best opportunity available, and the country's macroeconomic shocks underscored the need for the company to exert greater control over its cash flow. The company launched an aggressive innovation program (Procap 1000), coordinated by CENPES but including participants from both Brazil and overseas, to develop the two new offshore giant oil fields and other fields that the company soon found in deep waters (Furtado and de Freitas 2000).

In spite of the economic difficulties of the 1970s and the 1980s, Petrobras visibly delivered on the government's central goals of providing a *secure oil supply while saving scarce hard currencies*[26] *and supporting the country's broader industrialization*. Success in boosting the volume of production was largely due to Petrobras's own efforts, but in its fiscal goals the company gained a large boost from the collapse in oil prices in the 1980s. As shown in Figure 12.7, during the 1980s the oil price dropped to half its earlier level while the country's oil production tripled. From 1981 to 1989 foreign currency spending for oil imports dropped from $11.3 billion (55.3 percent of Brazilian imports) to $4.4 billion (24.3 percent of Brazilian imports).[27] Unsurprisingly, the nationalists used this evidence to reaffirm the Petrobras oil monopoly when the country enacted a new constitution in 1988 as part of Brazil's shift to democratic rule. But enshrining the monopoly in the constitution did not end the debate over the proper industrial form for the country's oil sector.

2.4 Deregulation (1995–2008)

The transition to democracy was completed in 1989 with a government elected by popular vote. The new government introduced privatization and liberalization as key elements of its economic policies. The political battle over Petrobras's monopoly started but was tabled when the new president, Fernando Collor de Mello, was impeached by congress in 1991. The battle resumed when President Fernando Henrique Cardoso, elected in 1994, took office in 1995.

Cardoso quickly set out to fix the country's economic situation through market liberalization and privatization policies along with a successful macroeconomic plan ("Plano Real") that, after many earlier plans had failed, actually brought inflation under control (de Oliveira 2007). The privatization of Petrobras and the liberalization of the oil market were envisaged as part of a package of measures to improve its economic efficiency and to unravel the financial stalemate in the country's balance of payments and the government's fiscal accounts. Privatization intended to attract foreign investors and fresh income for the Treasury, while liberalization intended to reduce subsidies and make the economy operate in more transparent ways, which would improve the government's ability to raise tax revenues. To accommodate political pressures from nationalists, the government abandoned the idea of fully privatizing Petrobras but moved forward with the liberalization of the oil market. In 1995 the government ended the Petrobras monopoly over hydrocarbon resources and retained, for itself, the right to allocate concessions (to state or private entities) for the exploration of these resources.[28] Once taxes and levies were paid, the hydrocarbons extracted from reservoirs became the property of the concessionaire. Actually implementing this policy would require further reforms, which came two years later when the government established a modern, sophisticated regulatory regime. The National Petroleum Agency (ANP) was created to manage the auctioning of blocks for exploration, to contract the licensing of exploration with winning bidders, and to regulate both the upstream and the downstream activities across the oil sector. Following standard best practice in the industry, once a company discovers any oil resource, it is required to report its findings along with its development plans to ANP. Any company, including Petrobras, engaged in the extraction and development of the country's hydrocarbon resources is then subject to a clear regime of financial compensation to the government (signature bonuses, royalties, special participation fees, and fees for retention of an area) for subsequent production activities.[29] The aim of these reforms was to expose Petrobras to competition, increase fiscal transparency, and attract IOCs to the Brazilian hydrocarbons market.[30]

These reforms also included efforts to reduce interference in the governance of Petrobras. Shares of the company were sold to private investors (both domestic and overseas) and floated on the New York Stock Exchange. This move was the most sensitive one for the country's nationalists, and to placate them the government maintained a majority of the company's voting shares[31] as well as authority to appoint a majority of the board of directors. Indeed, seven of the nine members of the board of directors are nominated by the central government, whereas two directors are nominated by minority shareholders.[32] Although the government maintained control over Petrobras, an independent shareholder base (along with listing rules, notably in New York) forced much greater transparency on the company and helped reorient its mission to profitability along with other goals of modern, publicly held oil companies such as social and environmental responsibility.

Not all parts of the oil industry were liberalized to a degree that would allow full competition. In those areas the new regulator was charged with preventing anti-competitive activity. Notably, Petrobras was forced to create a subsidiary for the transportation of hydrocarbons (Transpetro) that ANP regulates to ensure that third parties are offered access to its facilities at fair rates and terms. Government-controlled pricing of oil products was gradually removed, and to strengthen Petrobras's ability to compete with IOCs the company was allowed to function without the constraint of a law that compels state-controlled companies to operate under an especially strict open-bidding process for any purchase of equipment and services.[33]

The new regulatory regime for the upstream was intended to establish a fair allocation of risks and benefits between the government and the oil companies, including Petrobras. Recognizing that risks and benefits are hard to estimate before exploration actually starts, the new regulation increased the taxation of the oil companies as their risks diminish and their expected benefits increase. The government used competition over the size of the signature bonus as a preliminary estimate of the risks and benefits associated with each oil block. ANP also tailored special participation fees (on top of royalties) on the basis of information about the actual oil production and costs linked to each field when production started. And it set a fee for area retentions with the goal of keeping oil companies from sitting on potential oil reserves for future exploration instead of prompt production, which would better align with the country's interest.

Petrobras accepted these new policies because they removed the government's control over the pricing of oil products (and thus avoided a repeat of the disastrous experience with the oil account) and because Petrobras correctly judged that the company would preserve a de facto monopoly in the domestic market for a relatively long period of time. Indeed, the government allowed Petrobras to safeguard its existing assets (both upstream and downstream) from privatization. It was required to give back to the government only the exploration blocks where Petrobras was not yet producing oil and where the company anticipated no prospect for finding oil reserves in the near future – an arrangement that allowed the company to cherry pick the country's known oil fields and retain the most attractive acreage for itself. Moreover, in the environment of increasing oil prices of 2002, the new regulatory regime gave the company more autonomy to use its surge in revenues to invest in new production.

The new regime for the upstream proved very attractive for the IOCs as well. It allowed them to take advantage of their ability to manage the geological, technological, financial, and marketing risks of the oil business. Starting in 1999, ANP ran annual licensing rounds and allocated through 2008 roughly 503,600 km^2 to sixty oil companies, both majors and smaller players in the oil business. In principle, these new entrants could have pursued these new projects alone, but in fact they preferred joint ventures with Petrobras – especially for highly risky offshore projects (Figure 12.8). Petrobras's large asset of domestic information (especially geological and political) as well as its access to the network of domestic suppliers of equipment and services offered the easiest way for a successful entry into the Brazilian oil market (de Oliveira 2008b). In smaller and less risky onshore ventures private players were more likely to explore and develop blocks alone (Figure 12.8). In contrast, the theory outlined

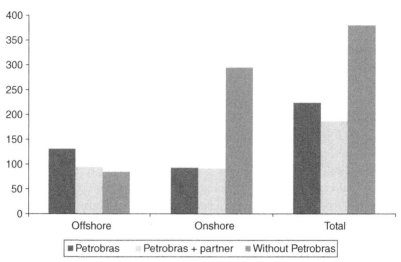

Figure 12.8 Number of licensed blocks.

by Nolan and Thurber in Chapter 4 suggests that states will in general employ NOCs rather than private players where risks are lower. However, Nolan and Thurber's quantitative analysis of exploration activities corroborates the observation here that Brazil in recent years is an exception to this general pattern (as is Norway). The reason that the experience in Brazil has been so different is the special ability of Petrobras to help manage intangible risks (such as regulation, pricing, and access to infrastructures) and its accumulated knowledge of the Brazilian geology.

From the government's point of view, the new regulatory regime guaranteed its control of the exploration and production efforts of the oil companies while also increasing the flow of oil benefits to the Treasury (e.g., signature bonuses, royalties, special participation fees, and fees for retention of an area). Moreover, the new regime reduced the profound asymmetry of information that existed between Petrobras and the government. Over time, the government regulators became quite skilled at using information from bids, such as from the signature bonus, to glean information about the country's oil basins – especially those poorly explored by Petrobras so far.

For government reformers, the de facto monopoly of Petrobras was perceived as a short-lived problem because it was assumed that

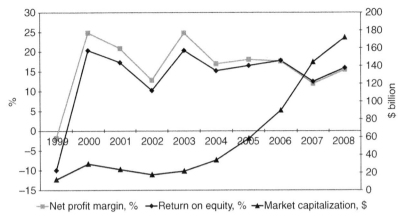

Figure 12.9 Petrobras key financial ratios, 1999–2008.
Source: Elaborated using Petrobras data.

the newcomers would eventually erode Petrobras's dominant position. And Petrobras's decision to abandon its previous opposition to importing gas from Bolivia and to embrace it as a mission was gladly received because integration with neighboring countries was a central foreign policy of the civilian governments of Brazil (de Oliveira 2008a). With hindsight, we can say that the government underestimated the time that would be required to reduce Petrobras's dominant market position and also to achieve regional energy integration. Nowadays, Petrobras remains dominant in the Brazilian market, and a new Bolivian government forced a renegotiation of Petrobras's contracts in the country (de Oliveira 2008a).

The new legal and economic context prompted radical changes in Petrobras, opening a new era for the company. The company promoted (and in some cases hired from outside) commercially minded managers who reorganized the firm to operate in the model of an IOC. The concept of "business unit" was introduced in the company and its managers rewarded according to economic performance of their units. Petrobras set for itself the goal of becoming an international energy corporation with leadership in Latin America. Its financial performance rose along with world oil prices and the increasing ability of Petrobras to fix domestic prices at international parity (Figure 12.9). Financially strong, Petrobras significantly increased its investments to protect its position in the domestic market and to earn positions overseas.

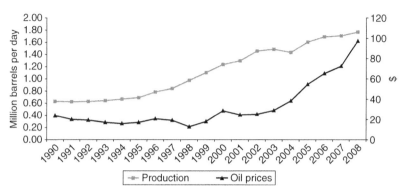

Figure 12.10 Oil price and Petrobras production, 1990–2008.
Source: Petrobras and BP.

This new financial strength inspired the company to adopt a strategic five-year plan to boost domestic oil production to 1.85 million bpd by 2005. This plan also included upgrading the company's
refineries to be able to process the rising fraction of heavy oil in the
company's crude oil production while also meeting more stringent
emissions requirements that required higher-quality fuels. In tandem, Petrobras declared its intention to develop new projects in petrochemicals, renewable energy, and also in the power sector so that
the gas in the country's incipient domestic natural gas market could
be utilized.

Overseas, Petrobras invested in places where the skills it had
developed in Brazil offered a competitive advantage to the company,
especially in deep water operations but in the downstream as well.
Overseas oil production was planned to reach 170,000 bpd by 2005.
A swap of Brazilian assets with Repsol Argentina allowed Petrobras
to secure a strong position in Argentina. Two Bolivian refineries were
acquired as part of a larger deal (brokered by the Brazilian government) to develop Bolivian gas production to feed the pipeline built to
bring gas to the Brazilian market. A 50 percent share in a US refinery
created a beachhead for future access of Brazilian oil and oil products
to the US. The overseas strategy was to sell not only crude oil but also
oil products to final consumers, consolidating the vertically integrated
operations of the company. In 2002, Braspetro – the formerly independent overseas operator – was merged into the general structure of
the company to develop Petrobras's operations overseas.

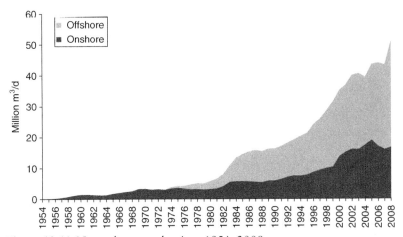

Figure 12.11 Natural gas production, 1954–2008.

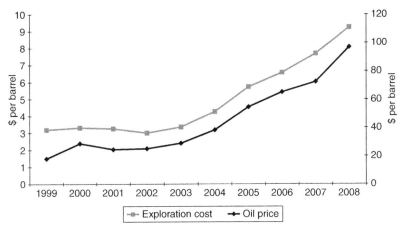

Figure 12.12 Exploration costs and oil prices, 1999–2008.
Source: Elaborated using Petrobras and EIA data.

Petrobras's strategy proved successful. Its oil reserves and production roughly doubled (Figure 12.10) while domestic gas reserves multiplied by seven and gas production roughly quadrupled between 1997 and 2007 (Figure 12.11). Its investments increased from $5 billion in 1997 to $25 billion in the same period. These results, helped by a favorable international oil market, resulted in much better financial and economic performance (Figures 12.12–12.15).

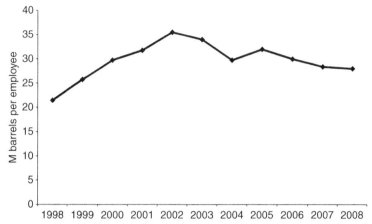

Figure 12.13 Oil production per upstream employee, 1998–2008.
Source: Elaborated using Petrobras data.

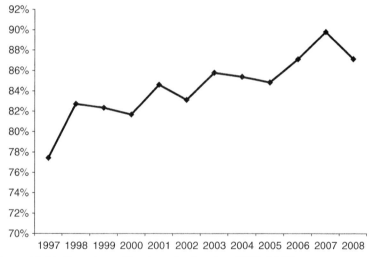

Figure 12.14 Capacity utilization of refineries, 1997–2008.
Source: Elaborated using Petrobras data.

As Petrobras shifted to more complex projects its exploration cost increased from $3.20 to $9.20 per barrel from 1999 to 2008 (Figure 12.12). But more efficient logistics and a sharp rise in the oil price (from $23 to $97 over the same period) generated large amounts of cash. In the downstream, the utilization of refining capacity has

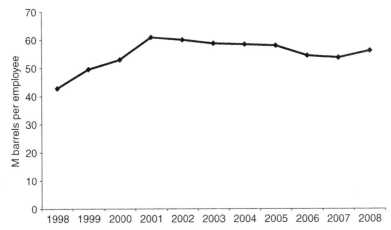

Figure 12.15 Refined oil per downstream employee, 1998–2008.
Source: Elaborated using Petrobras data.

substantially increased from 82.3 percent to 87.1 percent in the same period. The productivity of employees in both upstream and downstream rose as well (Figures 12.13 and 12.15).

Looking across the entire global footprint of Petrobras the push into Latin America is especially evident. Considering the whole oil sector from the perspective of benefits to the government – which we measure as the government's take from oil exploration and development – the results are impressive (Figure 12.16). In the 2000s the country became self-sufficient in oil and eliminated net expenditures associated with oil imports. The original national mission that inspired creation of the NOC had been achieved – not simply by nationalizing production but through a combination of NOC-led oil development and the creation of many complementary roles for other private firms.

At the end of 2002, the opposition won the presidential election and shifted the country's economic policies in a more command and control direction. The domestic acquisition of equipment and services became a stronger criterion for the licensing of oil blocks, but most striking was that the new government made few changes to the oil regulatory framework. Petrobras kept in place the strategy established in the middle of the 1990s until the oil price escalation after 2005, when the government (and in turn Petrobras) changed strategy.

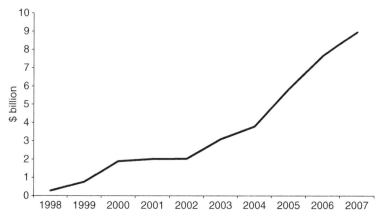

Figure 12.16 Government revenues from oil exploration and production, 1998–2007.
Source: Elaborated using ANP data.

The higher oil price substantially increased the opportunities for oil exploitation in the Brazilian offshore; Petrobras and IOCs alike invested heavily in exploration. In 2007, Petrobras identified a very large oil reservoir in the pre-salt geological layer of the Campos Basin and informed the government that its data indicated that several other giant oil reservoirs were likely to be found in a vast offshore area that stretches from the north of Santa Catarina state to the south of Bahia state.[34] The government immediately decided to stop the licensing of blocks in the pre-salt and ordered a review of the regulatory framework for the development of the pre-salt oil resources. The outcome of that review was an October 2009 proposal the government sent to the congress that would establish a new relationship with the oil companies, Petrobras included. The next section explores the likely effects of this new relationship on the performance of Petrobras by looking at the company's performance in historical context.

3 Explaining Petrobras's performance: the relationship between the state and the NOC

Here I consider the factors that explain Petrobras's performance. My approach is to look at Petrobras from two perspectives – that of the government (the "principal") and also that of the company that the government has centrally authorized to develop the country's resources (the "agent"). My claim is that the performance of Petrobras is best understood by looking closely at this "principal–agent" relationship. The government has struggled over the years to set and enforce goals that encourage Petrobras to behave in different ways. Following the framework discussed in Chapter 3, I use this principal–agent perspective to understand when and how the government has been able to exert leverage over Petrobras and other players in the oil sector. This perspective, I suggest, helps explain the unfolding current policy as the government tries to assert greater control over the "pre-salt" riches.

3.1 The principal's perspective

Oil is a risky but profitable business. Governments expect to take a large share of the benefits from oil to compensate for the depletion of their exhaustible resources. However, these benefits are largely determined by the oil companies' ability to manage the risks of the oil market. Although the government and the oil companies both have full incentives to cooperate for the minimization of the risks involved in the oil business, they have different perceptions when it comes to the evaluation and the division of risks and benefits.

Oil companies are organized to produce financial return for shareholders while governments respond to the demands of politicians. Different from government, the oil companies are not prepared to accept low premiums for high risks or to pay for externalities as commanded by politicians. This asymmetric situation is a major difficulty for finding a fair deal between government, which grants the right to explore the oil resources, and an oil company that is expected to achieve government objectives. As happened in many other countries (Nore and Turner 1980; see also the Introduction), the inability to find a sound solution for this problem was the main reason for the creation of Petrobras as a state-owned NOC.

The government assumed that by owning Petrobras the company would share its set of preferences and it expected that Petrobras would acquire the set of technological and managerial capabilities that any oil company needs to efficiently assess the risks associated with the oil business. In the mindset of the 1950s Brazilian political establishment, Petrobras was thought to be a suitable institutional device for the efficient development of the then infant domestic oil market.

As we have seen, the government was prepared to provide Petrobras with a large set of economic and regulatory incentives to achieve its objectives. Particularly important were the legal oil monopoly and the autonomy granted to Petrobras that were intended to allow the company to use its revenues from selling oil products to develop a vertically integrated professional oil company. The monopoly removed market risks, allowed Petrobras to explore economies of scale, and created room for moving along the technological learning curve, while the financial incentives enhanced Petrobras's capacity to invest.

As expected, Petrobras concentrated its operations where risks were relatively low and financial returns were more immediate: the exploration of the oil reservoirs received from CNP and downstream operations. Within a few years, this strategy contained the pressure of oil imports on the trade balance and Petrobras developed the downstream capacity to satisfy the domestic consumption of oil products in the vast Brazilian territory.

This arrangement worked so long as there were no major shocks to the system and thus the interests of the government and its agent were aligned. But those interests diverged after the fortunate discovery of offshore oil in the Campos Basin in the 1970s. The government wanted to accelerate the development of oil production in the Campos Basin, but Petrobras (operating within its old structure of incentives) was committed to very large investments in the downstream. Moreover, Petrobras had little of the technological expertise needed to operate in the water depths where the oil fields were likely to be found. The government decided to open the Brazilian offshore to the IOCs, in spite of Petrobras's opposition to the policy, with the goal of encouraging IOC investment and especially to change the incentives at work on its agent Petrobras.

Although the Brazilian offshore was attractive for the IOCs, the regulations offered were not. The IOCs abandoned the Brazilian offshore eventually. In the meantime, Petrobras was able to invest to achieve the goal of producing 500,000 bpd by the year 1985 (Figure 12.7). Government anxiety surrounding the oil market diminished after the oil price collapse in 1986, and the nationalists were able to reaffirm and strengthen the oil monopoly in the 1988 Constitution. The agent, it seemed, was back in alignment.

The 1990s marked a radical change in government economic and oil policies. It abandoned the import substitution industrialization policies that had been followed since the 1930s. It removed the Petrobras oil monopoly from the constitution to offer room for the IOCs in the Brazilian oil market. Regulations were changed to give transparency to the flow of oil revenues and to allow competition in the oil industry as well. A regulator (ANP) was created to manage the oil market in line with government oil policies; by reducing the information asymmetry between the government and the oil industry (Petrobras included) the government hoped it could create incentives that would encourage the larger number of agents it had invited into the sector to behave in ways better aligned with the national interest. Indeed, the new institutional arrangement proved very fruitful from the government's point of view – notably evident in the rising government revenues from oil operations (Figure 12.16) as well as rising investment in the sector and more participation by IOCs (Figure 12.8). The principal seemed satisfied with the performance of its agent, an observation underscored by the fact that the new government which took power in 2003 made relatively few changes to the country's single most important economic sector.

The brutal escalations in oil price of the last few years have once again changed the government's preferences concerning the oil business. The prospect of large oil riches – with Brazil perhaps becoming a large oil-exporting country – inspired the government to find a new set of incentives and mechanisms to oversee the existing agents. To increase oil revenues that accrue to the state, the government proposed the replacement of the concession regime by production-sharing agreements in production areas declared "strategic" by the Brazilian government (including the pre-salt).[35] To handle the oil resources in these areas, the government proposed the creation of a new, fully state-owned company (Petrossal) which would not be an oil operator or an oil investor. Petrossal would have the chief role in the development and marketing of the oil resources from these areas, reducing the role of Petrobras in upstream. Indeed, although Petrobras would be the sole operator in these areas, it would have to create a management committee for each block licensed by ANP. The president of each committee, appointed by Petrossal, would have the power to veto committee decisions. Moreover, at least 50 percent of the committee members would be appointed by Petrossal as well. The role of the IOCs in these areas would be limited to participation in consortia with Petrobras for bidding at ANP auctions.

Since every consortium must have Petrobras partnership (30 percent minimum), it is unclear how the bidding process would be carried out. In many respects, Petrossal would perform a role quite similar to that originally envisioned for Petrobras in the 1950s: to oversee and tightly control these resources. This new mechanism would be needed, according to the government's logic, because the existing mechanisms for controlling the oil sector (ANP, in particular) would be unable to focus adequately on the special tasks that arise in these strategic oil areas, especially concerning the industrial backward linkages of the oil business.

Creating a new oversight system would not automatically generate the investment in these new resources. To do that the government sought to increase the capacity of Petrobras to invest by recapitalizing the company with new shares, which the government would fund through borrowing backed by 5 billion barrels of government oil reserves yet to be identified, hopefully in the oil blocks contiguous to the blocks where Petrobras has already identified pre-salt reserves.

The main objective of this new strategy is to shift the behavior of the agents in the oil market in line with the government's new preferences. The government is convinced that the oil supply will play a strategic role in the world economy in the foreseeable future and that oil resources will become increasingly scarce and expensive. Moreover, the government expects a dramatic increase in its oil revenues that can be used to promote political legitimacy which presumably will make incumbent politicians more durable in their elected offices. A social fund is proposed for the promotion of several government programs (to fight poverty, to promote innovation, etc.).[36]

3.2 The agent perspective

Petrobras was created to coordinate the development of the incipient Brazilian oil market.[37] The government offered a substantial set of incentives (regulatory, financial, taxation) to the newborn company to accomplish its central objective of supplying domestic oil consumption with minimal pressure of oil imports on the trade balance. As we have seen, the company responded to the incentives that the government offered. Initially it focused on the least risky activities most aligned with the government's goal, and thus for its first decades Petrobras concentrated on the downstream. Upstream activities were fraught with high risk. Indeed, once the initial optimism for finding domestic oil reserves onshore disappeared, Petrobras moved its oil exploration efforts overseas, where the company had to face political risks but where geological risks were much lower and easier to manage within the incentives that the government applied to its agent.

The oil crisis of the 1970s blew up Petrobras's strategy and generated the first sign of the distance between the set of preferences of the government and of Petrobras. Oil imports reemerged as a major constraint to industrialization, a critical problem for the political legitimacy of the military government. The government responded with a new strategy – notoriously revealed by Geisel's public demand to open the sector to IOCs – and Petrobras as the government's agent responded to the new context with actions of its own. The new, higher oil price generated opportunities to seek oil reserves in the domestic offshore. But Petrobras was unable to develop these resources on its own and had the company followed Geisel's preferred strategy of allowing IOCs unfettered access then Petrobras's monopoly (its key asset) would have been in jeopardy. Petrobras took advantage of its close links to the government at that time[38] to subordinate the IOCs to its lead. Indeed, the government allowed Petrobras to offer the high-risk offshore oil blocks to the IOCs and to select the lower-risk offshore blocks for its own exploration. In effect, the agent had become highly autonomous through its huge informational advantage over the government – it could control which acreage was available to the IOCs and the terms under which the most important fields would be developed. It also ensured that the contracts IOCs signed required them to develop any found resources and to hand over the resources to Petrobras for the oil uplift. These conditions proved unattractive for the IOCs and the military government had neither the information nor the political legitimacy to exert tighter control over its agent. Petrobras had become a state within a state.

The oil monopoly guaranteed that any domestic oil produced by the company, in spite of its cost, would find its way to the refineries that were processing mainly imported oil so far. Thus as Petrobras developed the ability to find and produce oil it had a guaranteed market protected from competition. The company used its monopoly also to encourage foreign suppliers to share the risks and benefits of the development of new technologies in the absence of meaningful competition, moving along the offshore technological learning curve (Furtado and de Freitas 2000). The company organized itself to identify the most promising technologies and to integrate those technologies into the firm.

The first major instance of this new strategy was in the Campos Basin. Fifteen professionals were selected in the company to be part of a special unit to develop these fields. This unit conceived of the SPA-led approach already discussed. The concept was to adapt the temporary floating production system used by Shell in the North Sea to operate for long periods in the more benign environmental conditions of the Campos Basin.[39] As noted earlier, the SPA offered the prospect of advancing the cash flow from these projects, though it also came with substantial risks.[40] These risks, which only a company protected by monopoly could take, put Petrobras on the trajectory to much higher oil production.

In the 1990s, the liberalization of the Brazilian economy opened a new era for Petrobras. Although the oil sector was opened to other companies by changes in the constitution, Petrobras remained a de facto monopolist in the downstream; in addition, it dominated the upstream through its ability to select for itself the blocks where it would hunt for oil. It used its large asymmetry of information (geological, technological, industrial, and political) to compete in the domestic oil market. Even though Petrobras kept a dominant position, the pressure to liberalize changed the incentives at work on the firm. The company responded by reorganizing its structure to operate as business units, each one rewarded on the basis of its performance. It invested in a comprehensive study ("digital cartography") to improve the company's ability to manage geological risks. Building on its earlier investments in technologies to move offshore it invested in a new research program ("Procap 2000") to develop technologies for underwater exploration in the deep offshore (2000m). Innovative solutions were used to convert old oil tankers and semi-submersible units into platform complexes that could accelerate the oil production of the giant oil fields. Eventually, these technological initiatives offered Petrobras a major advantage in competing with the IOCs that were pondering whether and how to enter the Brazilian upstream.

The recent oil price escalation created a completely new context for the oil industry worldwide. Petrobras moved its offshore exploration efforts further into deep waters, finding an extremely promising oil province in the pre-salt. This game-changing development further distanced the set of preferences of government from that of Petrobras. At the same time, Petrobras has been operating overseas where the government, too, is less able to control its behavior.

The government's reaction to these events – especially the discovery of the pre-salt fields – creates large risks for Petrobras. The effort to create Petrossal is an attempt to subordinate Petrobras to the government's policies while making Petrobras responsible for taking on the large financial and operational risks associated with these new fields. In theory, these new arrangements will confer control on Petrossal (which must approve all operational decisions). In practice, Petrobras may use its informational and operational advantage to keep that decision-making authority for itself. This is an unusual institutional and regulatory arrangement for an NOC operation in its domestic market and is radically different from the one under which Petrobras has been operating since its inception in 1954. While it is too early to assess the outcome,[41] I expect Petrobras to use its expertise to fight for the control of the allocation of risks because the new regime would force Petrobras to participate in every bid for oil blocks auctioned by ANP.

4 Conclusion

Petrobras was created in a context of domestic crude oil scarcity in which its preferences were designed to align with those of the government. The government offered substantial incentives for the company, chiefly among them a monopoly over oil, expecting that Petrobras would help meet growing domestic demand while reducing the negative effect of oil imports on the trade balance. Petrobras responded by focusing on the least risky activities that were most aligned with its organizational capabilities.

In the 1970s, when the government decided to invite the IOCs into the Brazilian offshore, Petrobras used its privileged information to subordinate the IOCs to its own interests. The IOCs thus abandoned the Brazilian offshore – an outcome exactly the opposite of what the government had hoped to achieve – while Petrobras adopted the risky "early production system" to speed up the offshore production in the newly discovered Campos Basin. In retrospect, it appears that the process of technological innovation dominated by a single national firm was not necessarily the most efficient economically for the country, but for Petrobras it had the benefit of conferring huge technological resources on the firm. Using an incremental innovation approach, Petrobras became a leading oil company in the deep offshore.

In the 1990s, the Petrobras oil monopoly, which had been critical for its performance up until that point, was removed. In the wake of sustained economic troubles and new ideas about how to organize the national economy the government adopted a radically new approach to all major industries, including the oil sector. The IOCs were offered fair, transparent opportunities to compete with Petrobras in the Brazilian upstream. However, Petrobras preserved a dominant position in the Brazilian market and used that position to generate cash and other resources needed to invest – especially in the lucrative upstream. Petrobras also reorganized its services to operate as an IOC, developing operations overseas (especially in South America). The company's economic performance improved substantially and the revenues collected from the oil business by the government increased as well.

The relationship between government and NOC in Brazil has gone through many periods of stress and stasis. When the company is performing well and government goals are not shifting the relationship is symbiotic and stable. Today that relationship is possibly entering a new period of stress with the discovery of the large pre-salt fields and sustained high oil prices that make those fields potentially very lucrative. Petrossal – a government-appointed administration (not an oil company!) – would enforce the government policy for the oil sector. Petrobras would be limited to being the operational arm of the government in oil and IOCs left as financial partners for those blocks that Petrobras will not be able to finance entirely on its own. This radical new arrangement would remove from Petrobras one of its most valued activities – the evaluation and management of risks in Brazil's oil sector – and will require the company to find new ways to regain that control. Through most of its history Petrobras thrived because it successfully sought autonomy and because it faced a scarcity of capital and other resources. It has kept the government at bay partly through its huge informational advantage and partly by performing well in an environment of scarcity. Today, the perception of oil scarcity has disappeared and the government's appetite for oil revenues has increased spectacularly, moving the set of preferences of the government far away from where it was at the time of Petrobras's founding.

Notes

1 Eventually, Petrobras also played a crucial role in the industrial deepening of the country, particularly in petrochemicals (Evans 1979). But unlike many other NOCs that were created with the goal of establishing "linkages" that benefited the nation's broader industry this was not one of the original goals for Petrobras (see the case study on Saudi Aramco, for example, in Chapter 5).

2 *Agência Brasil, Descobertas no pré-sal levam Petrobras a rever plano de investimentos*, May 2008, www.agenciabrasil.gov.br. The area is called "pre-salt" because it lies underneath a layer of salt.

3 The Petrobras share of the domestic GDP increased from roughly 2 percent to almost 10 percent (ANP 2004).

4 Until 1979, the president of the company was selected among the ranks of the military. The only exception was the period 1962–1964 that anticipated the military *coup d'etat* (see the list of Petrobras presidents and their curricula at www.coopetroleo.com.br).

5 Top management decisions have to be informed by technical committee studies.

6 The annual report of Petrobras activities presents a section on the savings of foreign currency expenditures produced by the company, and oil self-sufficiency has always been presented as a major Petrobras goal.

7 General Horta Barbosa suggested to the government that the oil industry should be managed by a state monopolistic company. Standard Oil reacted to this proposal by sending a confidential document to the government indicating that it was prepared to develop the Brazilian oil industry if modifications were made in the legal framework. General Horta Barbosa refused the proposal and insisted on the monopolistic company. (See Penna Marinho 1970.)

8 Oil consumption moved from 26.1 to 138,700 bpd between 1939 and 1953 (de Oliveira 1977).

9 Private investors were allowed to keep their refineries under operation or under construction. Distribution of oil products to final consumers was not included in the monopolistic power of Petrobras.

10 See Petrobras Investor Relations, Overview, and History available at www2.petrobras.com.br/portal/frame_ri.asp?pagina=/ri/ing/index. asp&lang=en&area=ri.

11 This process generated a strong *esprit de corps* among Petrobras employees that limited political interference in the company.

12 Between 1955 and 1965, Petrobras drilled 1,907 holes. Data assembled at Petrobras, Relatórios Anuais de Atividades from each year.

13 Exploration and Production; Industrial Activities (Refineries and Petrochemicals); Transportation Activities; Marketing.

14 General Geisel's brother was the minister in charge of the army, a key partner in the management of the central government at that time.

15 Link was pessimistic about onshore oil reserves but his report signaled that there might be oil reserves in the offshore.

16 Sarmento and Lamarão (2006).

17 One characteristic of the Brazilian military regime was that the president appointed by the military establishment had a single five-year term in office.

18 Several new fields were found in 1975 (Namorado, Badejo, and Bagre), in 1976 (Enchova), and in 1977 (Cherne, Bonito, and Pampo).

19 Petrole Informations No. 1389, March–April 1976.

20 Only General Geisel could have taken this decision. Indeed, he was the president of Petrobras that could be blamed for the overseas strategy for the upstream and he was the president of Brazil that completely reversed the previous strategy.

21 To maximize the economic recovery of oil resources, reservoir engineering suggests that oil production must start only after full identification of oil reserves and the development of the production facilities. The SPA changed this traditional concept, proposing to start the oil production using exploration wells and facilities while development of the field is in process. Earlier revenues improve the project cash flow and the early geological information gathered reduces the time needed to develop the SPD. Its major shortcoming was that the natural gas produced in the early stages was not useable without logistics (e.g, pipelines) that were not yet in place. Moreover, use of the SPA could lower the recovery factor of the oil reserves since key planning decisions are made without full information of the characteristics of the oil reservoirs.

22 Sarmento and Lamarão (2006).

23 A gas field was found offshore of the state of São Paulo by Shell. This field was sold to Petrobras when gas production started.

24 This was accomplished through Legal Decree No. 1785 of May 13, 1980.

25 Sarmento and Lamarão (2006).

26 "From 1974 on, except for 1986, which saw low world oil prices, it cost less for Brazil to produce crude oil than to import it. By 1981, these savings were so great that they offset the earlier opportunity-cost losses.

By 1990, Petrobras had saved at least $14 billion for Brazil, over its entire history" (Randall 1993).

27 www.mdic.gov.br.

28 Concessionaires under this regime do have to establish themselves under Brazilian laws and operate out of a headquarters located within the country.

29 Royalties are fixed between 5 percent and 10 percent; both fees were set by presidential decree; they can be changed without changing the law.

30 Other liberalization measures taken included the loosening of restrictions on maritime transport that existed prior to that period, which allowed for greater competition in the shipping industry and transport of oil products.

31 Shares in Petrobras are divided into two categories: common shares, which carry voting rights, and preferred shares, which do not. Law 9.478 requires that a majority of the company's voting capital stock be held by the government of Brazil.

32 Two of the five members of the fiscal board are nominated by the private investors and another one by the minority shareholders (Campodonico 2007).

33 The special law (number 8666) forces state-controlled companies to buy at the lowest price irrespective of the ability of the supplier to provide on time with adequate quality.

34 Around 47,000 km² were already licensed.

35 The concession regime will remain for the blocks not considered strategic or in the pre-salt area. This seems to be a compromise that intends to limit the criticism of those who see no need for a radical change in the previous institutional and regulatory arrangement.

36 There are other stated goals as well. The government intends to use the exploration of the pre-salt resources to move industrialization forward. The objective is to create a competitive supply industry oriented to the South Atlantic oil market. Petrossal is designed to play the central role in the new institutional and regulatory arrangements for the oil industry.

37 Firms are created to organize activities that the market is not able to coordinate efficiently (Coase 1990).

38 The president of Brazil (Ernesto Geisel) was the former president of Petrobras.

39 Eventually the FPS proved the technological trajectory that was best suited for operations over 400m deep. They were upgraded to floating production storage and offloading (FPSO) units, largely used in the Brazilian offshore nowadays. It is important to note that the IOCs could hardly use the SPA approach in Brazil without strong political

criticism because any strategy that lowered recoverable reserves could be seen as harmful to Brazilian interests.

40 The SPA approach allowed Petrobras to start commercial oil production in the Campos Basin in August 1977, only two years after the first oil field was identified, and its oil production increased steadily afterward. While the tension leg platform (TLP) concept was developed in the Gulf of Mexico, Petrobras and its partners developed the floating production system (FPS) approach in the Campos Basin. Eventually the Brazilian offshore became the testing area for the economic viability of new technological concepts in the offshore.

41 The bills proposing the new institutional and regulatory arrangement were still under Congressional review when this chapter was prepared.

13 Sonatrach: the political economy of an Algerian state institution

JOHN P. ENTELIS

1 Introduction: overarching themes

The hydrocarbons sector is Algeria's primary source of economic activity and a major source of revenue for the government. As is evident in most other case studies in this book, the authoritarian Algerian government has sought to promote efficiency within its hydrocarbons sector to maximize revenues to the state without relinquishing control over this industry in Algeria. Its strategy has hinged on a national oil company (NOC), Sonatrach, which is involved in virtually every significant oil and natural gas project in the country. Sonatrach participates in joint ventures with other domestic and foreign hydrocarbons companies, owns several subsidiaries, and has recently developed worldwide operations but these operations are still under the control of the government. Sonatrach is a particularly important player in the natural gas market, though its oil production is significant as well.

Across most of the economy, Algeria has pursued a variety of policy reforms aimed at boosting transparency and economic efficiency. Such reforms have encouraged greater competition and have enhanced the performance of the Algerian hydrocarbons industry, but the government's strong desire to retain control over this sector explains why these efforts at liberalization are invariably abandoned when they diminish the state's control over Sonatrach. Despite repeated promises for a more liberalized and market-oriented hydrocarbons industry, the status quo of patronage relationships between Sonatrach and the state usually prevails. To be sure, the relative importance of these pressures – liberalization and control – varies with oil prices and other factors. Moreover, internationalization of the hydrocarbons industry has put pressure on Sonatrach to enhance its efficiency quite apart

Thanks to Eric M. Fischer, Ph.D. student in International Economics at the University of California, Santa Cruz for excellent research assistance; thanks also to Valérie Marcel and to Clement M. Henry for their valuable comments.

557

from particular government policies. Yet the overall strategy and performance of Sonatrach's activities in the hydrocarbons industry in Algeria remain remarkably the same.

This chapter draws upon a range of original, primary, and secondary source materials to provide a comprehensive analysis of Sonatrach in Algeria. Much of the original and primary source material comes from my many years of following the political economy of Algeria and the interviews and conversations I have had with Western and Algerian business executives, Algerian government officials, and other academics studying Algeria. Secondary materials I found particularly useful, and which I refer to frequently throughout this paper, include Ali Aissaoui's book *Algeria: The Political Economy of Oil and Gas* to understand the complicated nature of Algeria's energy sector, Valérie Marcel's book *Oil Titans: National Oil Companies in the Middle East* for its treatment of Sonatrach in the context of other NOCs in the region, and Isabelle Werenfels' *Managing Instability in Algeria: Elites and Political Change since 1995* for an understanding of the interaction between business and state actors in Algeria. I use data and analysis from the Economic Intelligence Unit reports, Business Monitor International, IMF and World Bank statistics for the graphs and tables in this chapter. Drawing upon these various sources, this chapter reaches three main findings.

First, it becomes clear that Sonatrach has endured varying degrees of financial, administrative, and legal control by the Algerian government that indicate the country's hydrocarbons policy is subject to government policy changes. When the price of oil has been low, Algeria has sought to attract investment, to push market reforms, and to improve the efficiency of Sonatrach. However, similar to a pendulum swinging back and forth, when the price of oil has returned to original or even higher price levels, Algeria has sought to block these same reforms and to renegotiate the contracts that it had with foreign firms in favor of its NOC Sonatrach. The events leading to the passage of the Algerian Hydrocarbons Reform Bill of 2005 and the subsequent amendments to this legislation provide just one case study of this type of pendulum swinging.

Second, Algeria's governing elite rely upon Sonatrach for revenue from which they gain power, patronage, and privileges. This patron–client relationship, which is infused with socialist ideology, is deeply rooted in the post-independence period in Algerian history and explains some of the difficulty in streamlining the Algerian government bureaucracy and improving Sonatrach's strategy and performance. The price of oil is, therefore, not the only factor at play in determining the fundamental nature of the Algerian hydrocarbons industry. Because the Algerian government depends heavily on the hydrocarbons sector, which earned nearly $75 billion in 2008 or 97 percent of the country's foreign exchange revenue, and because of the lack of any other realistic economic alternative for providing economic rents, any changes to the status quo are seen as threats to this long history of patron–client relationships.[1] At the top of this patriarchal scheme is the Algerian President Bouteflika, who has managed to maintain and enhance his presidential powers and who has ultimate authority and responsibility for the fate of Sonatrach.

Third, the Algerian government has run into difficulty committing to market reform that would benefit the Algerian economy and enhance Sonatrach's productivity and independence, while balancing the domestic political constraints that characterize Algeria's political landscape. A culture of corruption has gripped the Algerian state for nearly five decades, which has had the effect of making Algerian state institutions weak and subject to central control. According to one UN report, the lack of substantial economic reform has led to Algeria becoming, with the exception of Comoros Islands, the Arab country with the lowest level of physical capital productivity (otherwise known as investment efficiency) (UNIDO 2004). Labor productivity growth was negative throughout the 1990s and is now hovering between 1 percent and 2 percent. At the same time, Algeria has become a major supplier of energy to Europe through pipelines that cross the Mediterranean. Unless there are fundamental and comprehensive changes to Algeria's political-economic system, these three characteristics of Sonatrach's activities in Algeria will likely remain the same into the future.

This chapter consists of six sections. In section 2, I put Sonatrach's historical development into context within the political and economic climate of Algeria and also provide an overview of Algeria's natural resources. Section 3 analyzes the nature of Sonatrach's relationship with the Algerian state by focusing on the organizational structure of the company, Algeria's goals, and the capacity of the Algerian state to administer such a large and important enterprise. Section 4 uses the 2005 Algerian Hydrocarbons Law as an example of the influence the state has over natural resources and how Sonatrach can influence

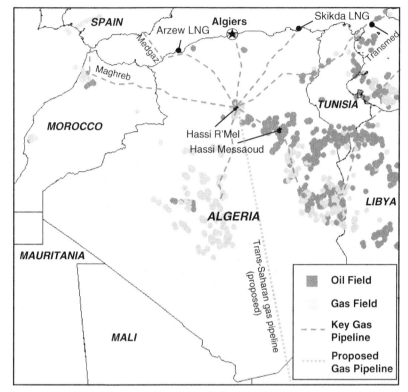

Figure 13.1 Map of major oil and gas fields in Algeria.
Source for oil and gas field data: Wood Mackenzie (2009b).

the actions of the state. It offers proof of the axiom that liberal policy reforms survive so long as they do not disrupt the fundamental controlling relationship between the government and the state oil firm. Section 5 explores how these factors explain Sonatrach's performance and strategy. The chapter concludes with section 6 to provide the lessons learned and the upcoming challenges faced by Sonatrach in Algeria.

2 Historical overview and natural resources: Sonatrach and Algeria

2.1 *Historical overview*

Algeria gained political independence on July 5, 1962, after a bitter war of national liberation against the French, who had colonized the country beginning in 1830.[2] While the country became free, its polity was fractured, its society divided, its culture ruptured, and its economy devastated. Only one sector showed any promise of growth – hydrocarbons. The new leadership in Algiers envisioned exploiting the income, jobs, and other opportunities rooted in this sector to overcome the legacy of political and economic backwardness left by the colonizing power. Independent Algeria's vision, from the beginning, saw oil and gas production as the key to Algeria's position as a future power in the southern Mediterranean region.

Sonatrach was founded in 1963 as a joint stock company that, in theory, allowed the firm some semblance of independence. In reality, Sonatrach was conceived as an instrument by which the state would exert central control over the industry – the very status it has today. At first, Sonatrach was one of several players in major hydrocarbon projects – such as the pipeline project to build a third export pipeline from Hassi Messaoud to the Arzew oil terminal on the Mediterranean in December 1963 or the 1965 revision of the 1962 Evian Accord and adaptation of the Saharan Petroleum Code which stated that Sonatrach would cooperate with French and other foreign companies. Before long, however, Sonatrach became the dominant player in Algeria's hydrocarbons industry; as the government tightened its control over the economy in the 1960s and 1970s Sonatrach was the most readily available instrument for controlling hydrocarbon revenues. Beginning with the first post-independence president, Ahmed Ben Bella (1962–1965), the Algerian government moved toward nationalization. Under the leadership of President Houari Boumediene (1965–1978), in 1971 Algeria fully nationalized the sector.[3] Boumediene also passed a national charter in 1976 that reaffirmed the socialist nature of the regime and strengthened the power of the executive and the existence of a single legitimate party, the National Liberation Front (FLN).

During the Boumediene years, Sonatrach was an extremely large company, responsible not only for oil and gas production, distribution, refining, and processing (petrochemicals production) but also for oil and gas industry engineering and exploration. Sonatrach's size, power, and centralization hampered its efficiency and ability to coordinate with the other economic sectors that it was ultimately meant to serve.

Boumediene's successor, President Chadli Benjedid (1979–1992), ruled during a period of economic chaos and shifting ideas about the best ways to achieve a vibrant, modern economy. The government adopted liberalization policies aimed at radically restructuring large state-owned companies to make them more economically efficient. Initially, Benjedid maneuvered through the apparatus of the FLN to secure control of the main source of income and power. After success on that front he established the National Energy Council (NEC) in 1981, under his direct control, as the highest institution in charge of energy policies and strategies. In this new structure, there were two main tasks for Sonatrach: as producer of oil and gas (in close collaboration with international oil companies (IOCs) that still operated many of the country's most lucrative projects) and as provider of revenue for the government along with direct services needed to satisfy the increasing social needs of a young, restless, and expanding population. The tension in these functions is the same that exists in many other cases examined in this book, such as Chávez-era Venezuela (see Chapter 10). The government saw strict control and centralization as essential to assuring visible benefits from oil and gas to sustain the power and rule of the state, while the firm suffered in its core function from that same control. Algeria responded to this tension by promoting both nationalist *and* liberalization policies in its administration of Sonatrach. The outcome was chaos.

In the early years of Benjedid's presidency this tension between nationalization and liberalization was resolved with the decision that Sonatrach would be decentralized but not denationalized. Several major companies were created from divisions of Sonatrach in April 1980, and others have since been set up in a further process of decentralization.[4]

In its second term (1984–1989), the Benjedid government accelerated its economic restructuring strategy. Benjedid passed a new national charter in 1986 that remained faithful to the conservative nature of the national charter of 1976 while also increasing roles for the private sector. While the hydrocarbons sector remained firmly in the hands of the state, Sonatrach (and other state-owned enterprises) was subjected to de-integration at a time when most other NOCs of the Organization of Petroleum Exporting Countries (OPEC) were being integrated domestically and abroad. (Contrasting cases include KPC and PDVSA. See Chapter 8 and Chapter 10, respectively.) Although deintegration was the watchword in these late-1980s reforms, Sonatrach was sheltered from the full extent of these liberal reforms, which transformed all other state companies into commercial entities with increasing managerial autonomy. The focus was put on Sonatrach's rent-generating export activities, which, as described by the Economist Intelligence Unit, "would be entrusted to a national company specializing in the export of hydrocarbons and derived products, the supervision of which would be set at the suitable political level" (Economist Intelligence Unit 1982, pp. 133, 138). In other words, the government saw no choice but to keep control over essential oil and gas operations in the hands of Sonatrach. Sonatrach underwent alternating phases of "deintegration" and "reintegration" reflecting the country's political struggles during a period of economic liberalization and political democratization that ended with the military *coup d'état* of January 1992.

After a series of short-lived Algerian leaders, Liamine Zeroual (1994–1998) emerged as the army-appointed president who accelerated the liberalization process. Zeroual modernized Sonatrach to make it competitive with the world petroleum industry, which would enable the company to enhance its management skills, improve its business practices, catch up with technological advances, and pursue objectives other than rent maximization. Through a three-stage program known as PROMOS (PROjet de MOdernisation de Sonatrach), Sonatrach was to be transformed into a commercial company with separate subsidiaries with competition under state control. In the first stage (1993–1995), Sonatrach would concentrate and improve its core upstream and downstream business activities. In the second stage (1995–2000), Sonatrach would expand its international operations in the energy and chemical industry. Beginning in 2000, the plan was for Sonatrach to expand its scope from hydrocarbon and energy activities to include mining and other types of services.

Zeroual stepped down as president of Algeria in 1998 and subsequent elections awarded the presidency to Abdelaziz Bouteflika (1999–present). In an increasingly competitive world energy environment and strapped for cash, Algeria launched another "restructuring" phase in September 2000. During this time, Sonatrach managed to escape the Algerian government's direct control over its operations that had been enshrined in the NEC. Indeed, in response to compelling and volatile domestic political changes including a violent civil war that erupted in 1992, the NEC and similar government-headed policy frameworks created uncertainties for Sonatrach because the company could never be sure of gaining adequate government attention or competence for decision making. And some decisions reflected political priorities of the government rather than the best choices for development of oil and gas resources. Yet when Abdelaziz Bouteflika decided to directly appoint all senior managers within Sonatrach in September 2000, Sonatrach was reminded that although the NEC was no longer its master, there was no doubt that the state still set the agenda. Bouteflika appointed Chakib Khelil, who had been working at the World Bank, as his Minister of Energy and Mines (see Box 13.1). Bouteflika was reelected in 2004 and was recently reelected to become president of Algeria for a third term (to 2014), after a change to the constitution.

Sonatrach is the twelfth-largest oil company in the world (as of 2010) and remains under the firm control of an Algerian state that makes empty promises of independence and transparency. Sonatrach now has, in addition to four operational divisions (upstream, downstream, pipelines, and marketing and sales), a petroleum service group and an international holding group. According to its annual report in 2007, Sonatrach employs approximately 41,000 people in its oil and gas operations, all of whom are Algerian and most of whom are permanent workers (Sonatrach 2007). The number of workers rises to 120,000 if one counts all the employees affiliated with Sonatrach.[5]

2.2 *Nature of resources: copious gas, limited oil*

The hydrocarbons industry is a key component to Algeria's economic growth, earning nearly $75 billion in 2008 or 97 percent of its foreign exchange revenue.[6] Its current proven hydrocarbon reserves are estimated to be 14.790 billion barrels of oil equivalent (Figure 13.2). This represents nearly 1 percent (0.9 percent) of the world's crude oil reserves and nearly 3 percent (2.6 percent) of the world's natural gas reserves (Standard & Poor's 2009). The hydrocarbon industry remains an important sector to the Algerian economy, especially as prices have climbed since the late 1990s (Figure 13.3).

This exponential increase in the levels of hydrocarbon exports with relatively constant imports has created a current account surplus for

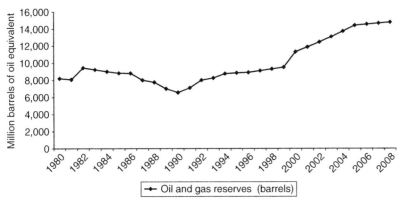

Figure 13.2 Algeria's petroleum reserves, 1980–2008.
Source: Economist Intelligence Unit database (2009).

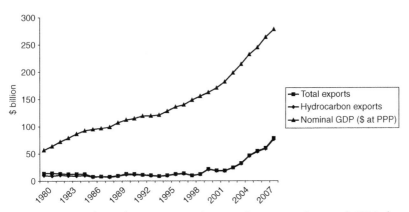

Figure 13.3 Hydrocarbon export value, total export value, and GDP for Algeria.
Note: Note that hydrocarbons constitute the vast majority of exports, so the hydrocarbon export value and total export value lines are indistinguishable over most of the date range considered.
Source: IMF Statistics 2008.

Algeria, which has led to the massive increase in the foreign exchange reserves of the country. According to IMF International Financial Statistics, foreign exchange reserves reached $143.243 billion in 2008. Unlike the largest NOCs, which are predominantly focused on oil, Algeria's industry is based on rich gas deposits as well as liquids. Each is addressed in turn.

2.2.1 Algeria's natural gas industry

Natural gas constitutes about 70 percent of the country's total hydrocarbon reserves (Economist Intelligence Unit 2008). Output of natural gas in Algeria has grown steadily over the years, from 36.5 bcm in 1986 to 49.2 bcm in 1990; to 65.9 bcm in 1996 and to 84 bcm in 2006 (Standard & Poor's 2009). Apart from encouraging foreign oil companies to develop Algeria's gas fields (see below), the government is also promoting the use of natural gas in the domestic market – especially in the industrial sector where plants can easily be converted from fuel oil to gas.

Two-thirds of Algeria's known gas reserves are contained at Hassi R'Mel, in central Algeria, 500 km south of Algiers. Other important fields include Rhourde Nouss, Alrar, Rhourde El Chouff, Rhourde El Adra, Gassi Touil, and Bassin d'Illizi. Four plants at Arzew and Skikda, all owned by Sonatrach, liquefy gas for export (Business Monitor International 2009).

Export of gas is particularly lucrative for the country. Algeria was the world's first large-scale producer of liquefied natural gas (LNG) and at the time of writing is the second-largest exporter of LNG (behind Qatar) with around 17 percent of the world's total. It is by far the largest gas producer in Africa, with roughly twice the capacity of the next largest producer, Egypt. Most of the gas goes to Western Europe where Sonatrach has LNG supply contracts with GDF Suez, Belgium's Distrigaz, Spain's Enagas, Turkey's Botas, Italy's Snam Rete Gas, and Greece's DEPA (Business Monitor International 2009).

In addition to LNG, the country was a pioneer (along with Russia) in the long-distance export of gas by pipeline to Europe (see Victor *et al.* 2006). In total, Algeria accounts for 25 percent of European Union gas imports (Sonatrach 2007). Algeria has built two major gas pipelines to facilitate exports to Europe. The 2,100-km Trans-Mediterranean gas pipeline (TME) to Italy via Sicily, providing throughput capacity of 25 bcm per year to Italy and neighboring markets, was initiated in the 1970s and has recently expanded (Hayes 2006). The $1.3 billion Maghreb-Europe gas pipeline (GME) was completed in November 1996, allowing the transportation of 10 bcm per year to Spain, Portugal, and Morocco. Both pipelines run from Hassi R'Mel through neighboring countries – the TME through Tunisia and the GME through Morocco – before crossing the Mediterranean seabed (Hayes 2006). Although the real prospects for the project are a matter of debate (see Chapter 16), Algeria has plans to build the Trans-Saharan gas pipeline (TSGP) project that would be started in 2015 to build a pipeline to transport hydrocarbons from Nigeria to Algeria via Niger. Sonatrach is also actively engaged in expanding existing pipelines to Europe through an Algeria Sardinia gas pipeline (GALSI) project to be started in 2012 from Algeria to Italy through Sardinia and the Mediterranean gas pipeline (MEDGAZ) from Algeria to Spain that started up in 2011.

Despite gas liquefaction facilities producing below capacity during an extended period of renovation and expansion work, Sonatrach is the world's fifth-biggest gas exporter – after Gazprom, BP, Shell, and Exxon (Standard & Poor's 2009).

In addition to the gas, Algeria is particularly rich in condensates, and the country is one of the world's leading exporters of this resource (at around 400,000 bpd).

2.2.2 Algeria's oil industry

Algeria's oil industry, while smaller than natural gas, remains important. The first major discovery of oil was made in the Sidi Aissa region in 1948, and by 1958 the country's main oil field – Hassi Messaoud – was coming onstream. In 1961, gas production began at Hassi R'Mel. Not surprisingly, these developments led France, the colonial power, to reassess its view of Algeria's future. Shortly before it finally conceded on the issue of full independence, Paris was prepared to give up the three northern departments – previously thought the only part of the vast territory worth economic exploitation ("useful Algeria") – but hoped to hold onto the *territoires du sud* (southern territories), where oil and gas rather than welfare of the native Touareg caught the French imagination. However, these dreams vanished with Algerian independence (1962), and Algerian control of the region was fully consolidated with nationalization of hydrocarbons in 1971.[7]

Today Algeria is one of the major oil-producing countries of Africa, second only to Nigeria in oil production (Business Monitor International 2009). During the 1990s Algeria found more new oil reserves than any other country in Africa, but its oil production has still to be fully and reliably established. In addition to its upstream strength, Algeria has a growing downstream sector that includes refining, distribution, marketing, and chemicals.

There are currently about thirty-five major producing oil fields in the country. The main fields are located in the east-central region of the country at Hassi Messaoud and around In Amenas near the Libyan border. Recently a cluster of new fields with commercial potential has been discovered at Hassi Berkine, east of Hassi Messaoud toward the Tunisian border. Algerian oil fields generally produce light crude oils with a low sulfur content. The principal crudes are Sahara Blend and Zarzaitine. Exports of crude oil and refined products from Algeria increased dramatically in recent years (reflecting the high demand for oil), but they have leveled off because of the downturn in the global economy.

3 Sonatrach and the Algerian state: joined at the hip

The link between Sonatrach and the Algerian state is based on a long history of political, economic, and administrative relationships. This is similar to many other NOCs. Sonatrach generates petroleum rents and serves as an instrument for Algerian state petroleum policy. According to Ali Aissaoui, for Sonatrach this relationship with the Algerian state "clouds the company's corporate governance and undermines its economic performance" (Aissaoui 2001, p. 202). In this section I explore why it has been so difficult to break these relationships between the enterprise and the government. To do this, I will look at the formal relationships, examine the fundamental goals of the Algerian state that include modernization and control, and consider the Algerian state's capacity for change in its policies towards Sonatrach.

3.1 *Organization of the Algerian hydrocarbons sector: blurring the lines between company and state*

The nature of the Algerian hydrocarbons sector cannot be understood without a basic understanding of the fundamental socialist nature of the patron–client relationships in the Algerian political system. Patron–client relationships have existed in Algeria since the revolution up through the post-independence period when the populist idea of the Algerian state was developed in which there was a socialist work order, state-owned public enterprises (SOEs) became symbols of national sovereignty, and these enterprises were viewed as providing their workforce with basic social services (Werenfels 2002; Werenfels 2007). Various attempts at privatization have been met with deep-rooted and more complex forces extant in Algeria's political character including the opaque role of the military and the patron–client networks, clan structures, and regional affiliations that comprise the country's dominant social forces (Werenfels 2002). No enterprise is more immune to potential privatization efforts than the one associated with the hydrocarbons sector. Over time, modernizers have been slightly more influential, but their reforms have been highly incomplete and ultimately unsuccessful. This system of patron–client relations has remained relatively constant since the nationalization of the hydrocarbons industry in 1971.

The structure of the Algerian hydrocarbons sector today reflects the push and pull between modernizers and this system of political patronage that governs the country. The 1998 restructuring of Sonatrach was particularly important; it created five organizational bodies involved with Sonatrach's operations, which remain essentially the same today (see Figure 13.4).

In this organizational structure, the National Energy Council (NEC)[8] receives the reports of the General Assembly. The Ministry of Energy and Mines chairs the General Assembly, nominates Sonatrach's chairman and CEO, and approves the Executive Committee of Sonatrach. The Sonatrach Board of Directors, as is typical for state enterprises in other countries where the state is the sole or dominant shareholder, is populated with individuals from various ministries of the Algerian state and also includes the CEO and four senior Sonatrach managers. The Executive Committee consists of twelve individuals from Sonatrach's senior management. Behind this entire organizational structure the president of Algeria has the final say on Sonatrach's personnel, even in questions of the appointment of managers and vice presidents.

The Algerian political system operates in such a way as to reap maximum benefit from its control over Sonatrach. The operational and legal control of Sonatrach is now embedded within the NEC, which is headed by the president of the country, and includes key government ministers and high-level members of the security establishment. The

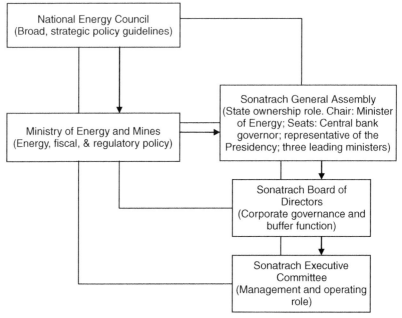

Figure 13.4 The 1998 institutional and energy policy framework and Sonatrach's new corporate structure.
Note: Arrows indicate command lines; straight lines indicate information flow.
Source: Aissaoui (2001).

NEC has been given the authority to oversee the implementation of Sonatrach's multibillion dollar restructuring and development plan discussed above. Yet, while the NEC is responsible for the overall energy policy agenda of the country, it is not involved in the daily operations of Sonatrach. Indeed, the NEC has not been convened as a formal institution since 1998, permitting President Bouteflika, who came to power in 1999, to effectively serve as a one-man decision-making body. In short, Sonatrach is a public company with all its shares owned by the government.

The lines of control established through law, as seen in the diagram in Figure 13.4, show clear roles for the various government actors and for Sonatrach but in reality the situation is much more ambiguous. This ambiguity of the interactions derives mainly from the inability of the government either to define clear lines of accountability or to define the functions that fall under its own role in particular. There is no clear system of checks and balances. The Algerian government is both the sole shareholder of the company as well as regulator of the sector (where the NOC is a dominant player alongside many other companies) and has a broader function of allocating the benefits of hydrocarbon operations such as social functions. In this vacuum, "authority has rested on the personality and capability of singular individuals – notably Sonatrach's president and the minister in charge of its supervision – both of whom are directly appointed by the country's president" (Aissaoui 2001, p. 212). In fact, Chakib Khelil, the current Minister of Energy and Mines, was recruited by President Bouteflika from the World Bank, and so the organizational structure has been used in such a way that the president retains substantial power and authority (see Box 13.1).

The NEC and the Ministry of Energy of Mines also approve and monitor the many other foreign companies that have operations in the country. The Algerian government influences the behavior of these foreign companies, as well as Sonatrach, through financial means such as taxation after royalties. These companies work not only in upstream oil and gas production but also downstream, which is relatively rare in large hydrocarbon provinces where there is a dominant 100 percent state-owned NOC. US-based Anadarko, BHP-Billiton of Australia, UK major BP, Norway's StatoilHydro, Eni of Italy, and Total France are some of the companies with offices and operations in Algeria (see Table 13.1).

3.2 Algerian state goals: the push–pull between modernization and control

There have always been two competing goals on the part of the Algerian government with regard to the overall economy: The first is to make Algerian industry competitive and the second is to maintain control over rent-generating activities. Throughout this time period, the Algerian government has pursued both these goals with many of the companies owned by the government but has given special consideration to Sonatrach because of the size and significance of this particular company in relation to Algeria's economy.

The special relationship between the government and Sonatrach became evident in the 1980s when President Benjedid embarked on his modernization program. In 1988 many state-owned enterprises

Table 13.1. *Key players – Algerian hydrocarbons sector*

Company	2005 Total Sales of Algerian Production (US$mn)	% share of total sales	No. of employees	Year established	Ownership
Sonatrach	24,000	100	120,000	1963	100% state
Anadarko Algeria	1,300	18	na	1991	100% Anadarko Petroleum
Eni Algeria	1,800	1.5	na	1981	100% Eni
BHP Petroleum	1,000	16.5	na	1989	100% BHP Biliton
BP Algeria	900	0.4	156	1956	100% BP
Naftec	na	100	na	na	100% state
Naftel	na	100	na	na	100% state
Sonahess	900	na	na	2000	49% Hess
Cepsa Algeria	2,000	1.5	na	1996	100% Cepsa
StatoilHydro	na	na	na	2003	100% StatoilHydro
Maersk Oil & Gas	1,800	na	na	1990	100% AP Moeler
ConocoPhilips	250	na	na	1993	100% ConocoPhilips
Talsman Algeria	170	na	na	na	100% Talisman Energy
Total Algeria	1,700	1	na	1952	100% Total

Source: Author's source through Anadarko associate.

were transformed into joint stock companies under corporate law and vested in participating funds. When Algeria faced severe economic challenges in the early 1990s, the International Monetary Fund and the World Bank offered assistance in 1994 on the condition that the public sector would be restructured for privatization. The Algerian government agreed that small and medium enterprises would be privatized and the larger ones would, at the time, only be restructured. The larger enterprises would open their capital to equity investors or issue shares on the newly established stock market. However, Sonatrach and a few other state-owned companies, including the country's largest commercial banks, were considered special cases and excluded from this privatization process on the grounds that they represented more strategic assets.

This failure to privatize Sonatrach has led to a complex situation where the Algerian government is involved in formulating both the state policy and company strategy. Interviews conducted by Valérie Marcel were extremely helpful in elucidating these interactions between Sonatrach and the Algerian government. "Oil policy is for the legislature," noted one of Marcel's Algerian sources, "and strategy is for the actors, the practitioners. In reality, there are no borders, no walls between them. The ministry [of energy] participates in strategy because it represents the state as the shareholder of the company and also because the ministry sets out the rules of the game through policy. Sonatrach contributes also to policy because it has the expertise, and it's in the field" (Marcel 2006, p. 78). Another official is more explicit: "There is no difference [between the state's policy-making function and the strategic role of Sonatrach]. Especially now, when the NOC is deeply influenced by the state (*imprégné par l'Etat*). It has no independence" (Marcel 2006, p. 78). It is clear from these and other of Marcel's interviews with officials of the company that "the state intervenes in everything the company does" (Marcel 2006, p. 86).

Algerian policymakers are so connected to Sonatrach that, when Algeria develops a policy directive or drafts a law the Ministry of Energy and Mines "sends it to Sonatrach for review, usually approaching the relevant managers for comments and critiques" (Marcel 2006, p. 79). Behind the scenes, "the company's corporate planning department works closely with the ministry on policy planning in most cases" (Marcel 2006, p. 79). In this way, "on an informal level, there are numerous ties between the ministries and Sonatrach, as many of the ministry people, often including the minister himself, have come from the national oil company" (Marcel 2006, p. 79).

Much of my analysis of the dynamic of Sonatrach's economic relationship with the government draws from Ali Aissaoui's work on this subject (Aissaoui 2001). Aissaoui believes that some of the benefits that Sonatrach management receives from the relationship it has with the government are offset by costs associated with this relationship. Aissaoui characterizes this relationship as one where Sonatrach maximizes its return on investments while the government is concerned with maximizing its share of revenues through royalties and taxes. Aissaoui also believes "Sonatrach has used its tremendous resources to actively pursue patronage and alliances in order to influence government policy decisions or to escape management scrutiny" (Aissaoui 2001, p. 211). Indeed, the Ministry of Energy and Mines, Ministry of Trade, Ministry of Finance, and the Ministry of Foreign Affairs all influence Sonatrach's activities because of its prominent economic and rent-channeling role for various particular interests. As a result, Aissaoui concludes that Sonatrach not only sees a reduction in its share of hydrocarbon revenue as a result of government intervention but is also unable to directly receive hard foreign currency revenues on the international market. Furthermore, Aissaoui notes that when the revenues from Sonatrach's operations are received they go through the Bank of Algeria before being transferred to bank deposits. In this way, the government has control over the foreign exchange reserves and the exchange rate (Aissaoui 2001, p. 212).

The upsurge in foreign direct investment (FDI) in Algeria and Sonatrach's efforts to internationalize has led to opportunities for transparency in Sonatrach's transactions but has yet to fundamentally change the dynamic between Sonatrach and the state. When the Algerian government restructured Sonatrach in the late 1990s, it encouraged much higher levels of foreign investment in the form of joint ventures and overseas alliances with Sonatrach. More recently, in order to maintain operational control over the projects, Sonatrach has sought access to the foreign capital markets to finance its operations so it would not be so dependent on foreign oil and gas companies for capital. These international capital agreements are made in ways that ensure Sonatrach does not negatively impact foreign exchange or diminish the control of the Algerian central bank. This arrangement has allowed Sonatrach to concentrate its foreign relationships where outsiders have an essential role to play – notably in providing access to technology and markets. In other countries confronted with a similar need to encourage more investment, governments have taken a quite different stance – in Brazil, for example, the government (until very recently) opened the sector for full foreign participation and allowed private investors to own shares in the oil company (see Chapter 12). Algeria's strategy reflects the maxim that Algerian leaders are not interested in surrendering their control of Sonatrach.

3.3 Algerian state capacity: fuzzy lines between Sonatrach and the state

Despite efforts to modernize and reform the company, close linkages between Sonatrach and the Algerian state have persisted through changes in legislation, Sonatrach personnel, and formal structures of government petroleum administration. Movements of senior personnel between the government and Sonatrach reflect the fuzzy lines between the NOC and its ostensible masters. For example, Mohamed Meziane, who was appointed chairman and CEO of Sonatrach in September 2003, previously served as director general of hydrocarbons for Algeria's Ministry of Energy and Mines; earlier he had been at Sonatrach.

The shadowy relationships between powerful officials can occasionally erupt into open intra-elite conflicts around the oil sector. The dramatic recent corruption scandal involving Sonatrach may be such a case. In January 2010, Meziane and three of Sonatrach's four vice presidents "were removed from their posts pending the resolution of a judicial enquiry into alleged corruption" (Economist Intelligence Unit 2010). The charges against Meziane and others were "brought in a 20-hour hearing at a tribunal in the capital, Algiers, on January 12th following an investigation carried out by the *Département de renseignement et de sécurité* (DRS) lasting more than two weeks," two local papers, *El Watan* (French-language, Algiers) and *El Khabar* (Arabic-language, Algiers), reported on January 14 (Economist Intelligence Unit 2010). According to reports, "Mr. Meziane has been asked to report to the court on a weekly basis, while Belkacem Boumediene, vice president of the company's upstream division, and Benamar Zenasni, who runs the oil and gas transportation division, have been jailed" (Economist Intelligence Unit 2010). The underlying reasons for what prompted this corruption investigation and the motivation behind these administrative changes remain unclear. However, the incident seems to follow the same historical pattern of state control over Sonatrach reflecting the broader intra-elite struggles that continue to dominate Algerian national politics especially between civilian authorities and the intelligence service.[9]

While several key legal initiatives were introduced that were intended to encourage market-style economic activity, such as the 2005 Hydrocarbons Law, they were never fully implemented because they threatened the power of the ruling elite. Aside from the authoritarian nature of the Algerian government, and underneath the declarations of increased transparency and accountability, there is a culturally profound trend toward an ingrained socialism, which has made it a challenge to modernize Sonatrach. As one example of this socialist atmosphere, the members of parliament in the Algerian National Assembly debated against the privatization of Sonatrach in 2003 (Luxford 2003).

Algeria suffers from weak state institutions. A culture of cronyism has gripped the Algerian state for nearly five decades. The industrial output of public enterprises in the non-hydrocarbons sector, for example, has declined by around 25 percent in the 1990s (Dillman 2000). Most of these enterprises are technically bankrupt, supported by a public banking sector that has become burdened with non-performing loans. Algerian labor productivity growth was negative throughout the 1990s and is now hovering between 1 percent and 2 percent. Finally, problems of corruption pervade Algeria, constituting the most serious barrier to fundamental economic reform. Algeria scored 3.2 out of 10, ranking 92nd out of 180 countries in Transparency International's 2008 Corruption Perceptions Index (compared with 88th out of 133 countries in 2003), putting it just behind Saudi Arabia, Morocco, and Madagascar and placing it among the five countries perceived as the most corrupt in the Middle East and North Africa (MENA) (Transparency International 2008).

The cause of this malaise is multifaceted. First, public enterprises (including public banks) have been viewed as a means of channeling oil revenues around the economy, not as a means of adding value or making profits. Second, this channeling is based largely on cronyism, which compounds the inefficiency of the process. Regime insiders, often members of or persons closely connected to the military, control the public enterprises (without necessarily having technical ownership of them) and staff them with their own supporters. Third, the political "protection" that these firms consequently enjoy has prevented their privatization. Privatization would, in effect, require the reshaping of the entire political economy. This is not something that anyone or any group, from President Bouteflika on down, will likely attempt. While most Algerian administrations talk about such reforms, there has been little movement on this front.

Legal reform has been another area where government needs to act (contract enforcement leaves much to be desired) but has done very little. This was one of the three great reform areas proclaimed by President Bouteflika at the outset of his first term in office in 1999. An initial surge of press interest was followed by a period of preparing "expert" reports, upon which future government action would be based. Yet again, there was no follow-through, and the reports either failed to materialize or were not released – let alone acted upon – by the government. Sonatrach's alternating financial, administrative, and legal status vis-à-vis the state over the last two decades represents the quintessential case study of such government policy changes – a phenomenon that is explored in greater detail in connection with Algeria's 2005 hydrocarbons law.

4 The 2005 hydrocarbons law: a case study of the fractious nature of Algerian state–NOC relations

A relatively recent example of the back and forth between reformers and traditionalists or resource nationalists over Sonatrach was the hydrocarbons law of 2005. This law was passed with the goal of making Algeria more attractive to foreign investors by reducing the level of participation that Sonatrach could require in production-sharing agreements and making Sonatrach a more commercial company. By enacting this legislation, the Ministry of Energy and Mines hoped to attract foreign investors and companies, which have the advanced technology and investment capacity, to explore for new sources of oil and gas. Furthermore, a more commercially oriented hydrocarbons

Box 13.1 Chakib Khelil

Born in 1939 in Frenda in western Algeria, Chakib Khelil spent his early years in Oujda, Morocco, where Abdelaziz Bouteflika was a childhood friend. Khelil became interested in coal mining as a result of the school trips he took to the mines and eventually went on to study petroleum engineering at Ohio State University in the United States; a move he regards as fortuitous since today the coal mines in southwest Algeria are all closed. At Ohio State he met his wife, Najat Arafat Khelil, a Palestinian from the West Bank, who was there to get a doctorate in physics. They both moved to Texas A&M University where Khelil earned his Ph.D. in petroleum engineering. They have two grown sons who are now American citizens.

The family moved back to Algeria in the 1970s where Khelil rose quickly to become an advisor to President Houari Boumediene. He was appointed head of Sonatrach's petroleum engineering department before moving to the presidency where he stayed three years to 1976. When Belkacem Nabi succeeded Sid Ahmed Ghozali as energy minister in the wake of Chadli Benjedid's accession to the presidency following Boumediene's death in 1978, Khelil went to work for the World Bank in Washington DC. He specialized in upstream problems of oil and gas exploration and production and for a while ran the bank's Latin American energy department where he oversaw the privatization of state petroleum concerns in Argentina and Peru.

When Abdelaziz Bouteflika became president of the republic in 1999, he recruited Khelil to leave the World Bank and serve in his government. In that year Khelil was appointed Minister of Energy and Mines; a position he still holds today. He also served as CEO of Sonatrach from 2001 to 2003 and head of OPEC in 2001 and once again in 2008. In all these capacities, Chakib Khelil has gained the respect of diverse individuals and groups as he put forth a radical plan to transform Sonatrach into a major force economically and politically, domestically and abroad.

sector would be more inviting to outside firms, and success on this front would require changing not just the law but Sonatrach's behavior as well. In the end, the series of legal reforms, similar to a pendulum moving back and forth, were amended or overturned by subsequent legislation.

The "pendulum effect" is best understood through an analysis of the infighting within governmental circles and between state and society at the time that a liberal reform bill was introduced. The central problem with reform, such as privatization of state-owned enterprises like Sonatrach, is that it threatens to disrupt the flow of "rents" between various groups and their supporters. Rival groups within the military elite compete with each other for political influence by extending patronage networks deep into public sector firms. That makes particular groups extremely reluctant to see "their" firms sold off. Sonatrach, the crown jewel of rent creators, is particularly likely to spawn such worries. Indeed, all groups within and outside the military would strongly oppose Sonatrach's privatization or near privatization. All agree that to lose the source of their political influence – hydrocarbon rents – would be disastrous. This explains the strong and widespread resistance to the idea, first introduced in 2001/2002, of using the hydrocarbons reform law, drafted by Chakib Khelil, the Minister of Energy and Mining, to privatize Sonatrach. Then Prime Minister Ali Benflis and future premier Ahmed Ouyahia were "totally opposed" to the idea however much President Bouteflika supported Khelil's broader goals of liberalizing the economy via its most vital enterprise.

It originally appeared that Chakib Khelil's close association with President Bouteflika would ensure that his efforts would not be severely challenged. Yet the political priorities of regime elites, fearful of losing their principal source of perks, privileges, and patronage, effectively overturned these reformist efforts leaving Khelil politically exposed and bureaucratically weakened. In any case, given the president's uncertain health and the intra-elite competition endemic to Algerian politics, there was never any guarantee that the liberalization program would succeed. Indeed, the high price of oil, and the ripple effects this had on the rest of the Algerian economy, made it even more difficult for reform to occur.

The main intention of the reform bill was to liberalize the hydrocarbons sector, primarily by relieving Sonatrach of its regulatory role. Thus freed, Sonatrach would focus more intently on winning contracts in competition with foreign firms. At the time, the bill was unique since once passed it would have seen Algeria become the first country in the Middle East and North Africa to adopt global and competitive benchmarks and practices throughout its domestic hydrocarbon industry, by allowing free competition in the upstream, midstream, and downstream sectors through the elimination of de facto monopolies. Yet the bill presented a challenge for Sonatrach since it would require more restructuring or reorganizing. Furthermore, uncertainty existed over how the increasing presence and participation of foreign firms would threaten the flow of rents from Sonatrach to the government.

Chakib Khelil's reformist efforts stalled when the hydrocarbons law was withdrawn from legislative consideration in early 2003. The bill's defeat was a severe blow to the reform process yet one consistent with the existing pattern of intra-elite competition over valued resources necessary to maintain patronage, power, and privilege. In a broader sense, the bill's defeat underlined the malign influence of military powerbrokers in economic decision making. In addition, there was opposition to the law by many members of parliament and even popular demonstrations against the law when President Bouteflika visited the University of Constantine in November 2002. Although the government was able to effect change at the margins of the economy by deregulating the mining and power sectors, for example, it was forced to back away from changes that might threaten the financial, and hence, political, power of the army high command and certain ministers of parliament and various special interest groups. This retreat has called into question the prospects for privatization and banking sector reform, as well as the liberalization of capital flows and exchange rate management. The failure of the hydrocarbons law also underscored the power of the trade unions. Although influenced by the conservatives in the military, the unions are fiercely opposed to the modernization of working practices and the loss of jobs that would come from competing with foreign firms, and they have repeatedly demonstrated their opposition with strikes.

With the apparent support of President Bouteflika, Chakib Khelil persevered and reintroduced the reform initiative in early 2005. As before, the goal was to transform Sonatrach into a purely commercial entity involving the creation of two self-financed agencies to take over the company's regulatory functions, including the award of exploration and development contracts. With the president's unequivocal support, after his 2004 reelection, Khelil went back on the offensive in early 2005 promoting his plan. Bouteflika even removed some twenty-five generals following his reelection in 2004 yet a number of generals remained vocal in their opposition to reform-minded plans. In late January Chakib Khelil replaced Sonatrach's vice president for upstream operations, Rafaa Babaghayou, because he was a vigorous opponent of the bill, with Belkacem Boumediene, an engineer who had previously run the group's production division (Economist Intelligence Unit 2005).

Both houses of parliament finally passed the hydrocarbons reform bill in March 2005. Bouteflika had wanted the law passed during his first term (1999–2004) but was obliged to shelve it in the face of opposition from conservatives in the military and the trade unions, as well as the then Prime Minister, Ali Benflis, who ran a distant second in the 2004 presidential election that Bouteflika won handily. This opposition, which was based on a reluctance to tamper with a "strategic resource," dissipated following the president's overwhelming victory at the polls. Crucial to the law's passage was the support of the main trade union, the Union Générale des Travailleurs Algériens (UGTA) (Petroleum Intelligence Weekly 2005). In a speech to a UGTA rally the day after the law was approved by the cabinet, Bouteflika said that it had "pained" him to have to reform a system of nationalization that he had played a part in creating when he was the foreign minister under the presidency of Houari Boumediene, but it was a response to global "transformations that forced us to adjust." In an effort to reassure the trade unionists, he said that "this law is not the Quran: if we do not succeed with it, we can always review it." The president also emphasized the government had no intention of privatizing Sonatrach – a persistent theme of the law's opponents (Economist Intelligence Unit 2005).

In November 2005, Chakib Khelil appointed the heads of the two new agencies set up according to the 2005 law intended to regulate the oil and gas industry. Sid-Ali Bitata was appointed head of *Agence Nationale pour la Valorisation des Resources en Hydrocarbures* (ALNAFT), responsible for collecting royalties and tax revenue, awarding exploration contracts, and approving development plans. Bitata was previously director of the ministry's department responsible for monitoring the exploitation of oil and gas discoveries and ensuring that such reserves were properly managed. Noureddine Cherouati was appointed head of *Autorité de Régulation des Hydrocarbures* (ARH), which oversees midstream and downstream operations, including access to pipelines and storage facilities. Cherouati was formerly head of the Milan-based Algerian-Italian joint venture that manages the TransMed gas pipeline from Algeria through Tunisia onto Italy. He had earlier worked as secretary general of the energy ministry and as director of NAFTAL, the state-owned petroleum distribution company. Djillali Takherist was appointed head of the mining division of ALNAFT. He was previously head of exploration at Sonatrach.

In all three cases, personnel selections reflect the integrated nature of state-enterprise relations with department heads routinely alternating between government ministries and national companies and back. Such a process seriously undermines claims made by different interested parties about the "autonomous" nature of newly created regulatory bodies and the "separateness" of Sonatrach's status vis-à-vis the state.

In theory, the chief effect of the 2005 law was to separate the regulatory and commercial functions of Sonatrach. The law's supposed purpose was to eliminate the inherent conflict of interest in these dual roles, allowing it to function as a purely commercial entity and improving the operating environment for foreign oil companies. Sonatrach was scheduled to compete for exploration and production contracts on very similar terms to foreign firms but the July 2006 amendments reversed those terms. Article 48 of the 2005 law, for example, gave Sonatrach the option of taking a stake in new ventures but limited the stake to 20–30 percent and required the option to be exercised within thirty days.

The 2005 law represented, formally, the extreme position of the pendulum. Once it reached this position, the pendulum immediately began to swing back. A 2006 amendment law eliminated, for example, the maximum stake and short option period of the 2005 law. Sonatrach continues to dominate the Algerian oil and gas industry by virtue of its existing operations in the country's main producing fields. ALNAFT was scheduled to take over Sonatrach's previous role of collecting the state's share in foreign companies' oil and gas production and transferring the proceeds to the Treasury. ALNAFT was also to be responsible for approving Sonatrach's development plans. The original law made important changes to the role of Sonatrach in production-sharing agreements (PSAs) with foreign companies and provided for foreign firms to invest, without restriction, in pipelines within the country. The main effect of the July 2006 amendment was "to restore Sonatrach's controlling role in both these areas. The company [is] now obliged to take a stake of at least 51% in PSAs, rather than the option to hold 20–30% that was specified in the original law. Sonatrach must also hold a minimum 51% share in pipelines" (Economist Intelligence Unit 2008, p. 36). This majority share of participation gives Sonatrach, and thereby the Algerian state, control of all upstream operations. The 2006 amendment law thus reversed much of the liberalization aspects of the 2005 law (Business Monitor International 2009).

The inability to enact reforms to bring about more independence and transparency in Algeria's oil and gas sector, in a time of global economic downturn, has made it more difficult for Algeria to attract foreign investment. As one example, when Algeria launched its seventh exploration and production licensing round in July 2008, its first since April 2005, Chakib Khelil had stated that sixteen exploration blocks were available and that candidates would be chosen on their ability to support Algeria's goal of boosting its growing upstream sector, technical competitiveness, and technology. An added key factor in determining successful candidates seemed to be the likelihood of possible asset swaps that chosen firms could offer Sonatrach. By December 2008, Algeria announced that during this licensing round it had awarded blocks to Eni, BG Group, E.ON, and Gazprom. Khelil said that when the bidding round was first announced, more than fifty companies had expressed an interest in the acreage on offer but that Algeria received bids on only four of the sixteen blocks put up for tender. Khelil blamed the global financial situation for the low turnout. While surely the downturn in the economy is partially to blame, the lack of substantial hydrocarbons reform (with Algerian control over all PSAs and the windfall tax) increased the risk for foreign companies and scared them from investing in Algeria.

5 Sonatrach performance and strategy

5.1 *Sonatrach performance: muddling through*

The tightly interwoven relationships between the Algerian government and Sonatrach have affected the performance of the company. A

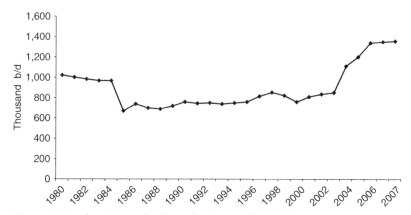

Figure 13.5 Algeria's crude oil production, 1980–2007.

Note: With inclusion of condensates and other natural gas liquids (see section 2.2.1), total Algerian oil liquids production is substantially higher than the crude oil production shown here.

Source: IEA (2008); Economist Intelligence Unit database (2009).

central theme of this analysis has been that the Algerian government has sought to enhance the efficiency and performance of Sonatrach while maintaining its influence and control over the revenue and operations of the company. While these goals resonate at times, most often the efforts to maintain control over Sonatrach (which is the paramount goal) have resulted in red tape and misdirection that undercut the company's performance as an oil and gas enterprise. Furthermore, Sonatrach uses its relationship with the Algerian government in ways that bring benefits to the company but are less than optimal for the Algerian economy in general. Overall, my assessment is that Sonatrach performs passably well; it has too much technical talent and elite support to fail but too little freedom from government intervention to fully succeed. It muddles through.

One indication of company performance is its recent oil production (see Figure 13.5). Algeria on average produced 1.36 million barrels of crude oil per day in 2007; this production is a significant increase on the roughly 800,000 barrels per day produced between the mid 1980s and early 2000s. These production trends reflect Sonatrach's long period of muddling through, followed by some recent improvement.

Sonatrach has achieved its performance through foreign partnerships and the related technology transfers this entails. Since the mid 1980s, the Algerian government has put a high priority on attracting IOCs because it needs their help in order to expand oil and gas exports to get through the economic crisis still facing the country. Sonatrach has fallen far behind in its ability to develop technology and equipment and has been unable to carry out the necessary exploration and production on its own. An important new development in this regard has been the shifting away from contracts negotiated based on subjective criteria to those employing standard international legal and arbitration procedures. Thus, participation has become more attractive to foreign companies as economic reforms continue and Algeria increasingly adopts international business practices.

Few foreign partnerships between Algeria and foreign companies existed before the 1990s because they were not even permitted to operate in the country without encountering prohibitively high barriers to entry. Under Algeria's 1986 petroleum law, Sonatrach continued to enjoy full control over all activities in the hydrocarbons sector. At that time, any foreign company interested in doing business in this sector had to have Sonatrach as a partner. There were two ways for foreign companies to go into the oil business in Algeria: through a production-sharing contract or a participation contract. A third possibility, the service contract, never gained popularity. International arbitration had been introduced in other sectors of Algeria's economy but applying it to the oil and gas sector required changes in the 1986 law – a decision that could be taken only at the highest political levels. Therefore, it was a big deal for foreign companies when the Algerian parliament passed a hydrocarbon investment law on the eve of the military *coup d'état* of January 11, 1992, that made the oil and gas sector more attractive to foreign investment.[10]

Many of these bold reforms to encourage foreign investment were ultimately reversed by the new team that was installed by the ruling army group that came to power through a military coup. And so was a program to restructure Sonatrach, prepared in the first half of 1992 under the government of Ahmed Ghozali – the man who had built up Sonatrach in the 1970s. In July 1992, the premiership was assumed by his former boss, Belaid Abdessalam, a hard-line nationalist-socialist who was the "father" of Algeria's industrializing industries strategy of the 1960s and 1970s. Abdessalam insisted on strong control by the state, imposed tough terms on foreign companies, and reversed the reforms.

The reforms, however, had stimulated foreign interest such that by mid 1992, fifteen companies had bid for eight of the fields with their total investment offers coming to nearly $4 billion. Abdessalam rejected their offers immediately as he came to the premiership, saying they were "below the minimum acceptable" to his government – even though Sonatrach and Nordine Aït Laoussine, until then the energy minister, had worked hard to attract these companies. It seemed at the time that the "political" pricing strategy of the Boumediene years was being reinvoked, to the serious detriment of the country's economy. More accurately, it reflected the kind of inter-elite political struggle over power, patronage, and privilege that had long characterized Algerian decision making whether in the political, military, or economic spheres. Fortunately for the Algerian economy, after Abdessalam was removed from office in 1993, Sonatrach revived its efforts to attract foreign companies and again took up its reform and restructuring program. The time, costs, and opportunities wasted by the diversion were considerable.

Sonatrach's performance is also affected by the strong labor union within the company. The labor unions at Sonatrach are given somewhat more favorable attention by the government than the labor unions of other companies in Algeria and so many of the smaller companies operating in the hydrocarbons field see it in their own interest to somehow find a way to connect with the union at Sonatrach – in other words, these other unions have long campaigned to have the companies regrouped under Sonatrach. The unions fear layoffs that might result from foreign competition and want wage provisions similar to those of Sonatrach. Sonatrach, on the other hand, has strongly opposed the unions' demand and has refused to take back control over the companies. Sonatrach wants to continue to concentrate on its core business to develop oil and gas exploration and production activities.

As the single largest company in Algeria, Sonatrach plays a critical role in the country and receives special attention from the government. This attention is one that often benefits Sonatrach in the short term but does not provide the company with the structure and incentives it needs in order to be competitive in its performance with the other world energy companies. At different times, the government has pursued various strategies for getting Sonatrach the right incentives but ultimately the government has tended to stay on the side of maintaining the final say over the company's operations. Sonatrach has been able to achieve significant growth in both its upstream and downstream activities in Algeria and overseas. The company is not responsible to shareholders since all the shares are held by the government and so its performance is tied to maximizing the rent that the government receives. As long as oil prices remain high, Sonatrach can have free rein concerning its performance, but when the oil prices move down, the government looks for new ways to make Sonatrach more efficient in order to enhance its overall performance.

5.2 Sonatrach strategy: internationalization constrained by government demands

The Algerian government's relationship with Sonatrach not only affects the company's performance but also its continuing operations and strategy. As was described earlier, in the sections on the history of Sonatrach and Algeria as well as the sections on the political economy of Sonatrach, the government is intimately involved in all aspects of Sonatrach's operations and its strategic goals. This involvement is sometimes in the interest of Sonatrach but flows most fundamentally from the interests of the government. So long as Algeria continues to be an authoritarian state that receives the bulk of its rents from oil revenue, Sonatrach will continue to be used as a way to channel funds to those in power.

Algerian government control over Sonatrach's financial activities has a direct impact on the company's strategy. In 1994, for example, at a period when the country was facing a major fiscal and balance of payment crisis, the government decided on a considerable levy on Sonatrach's profits, leaving it with little of the hydrocarbon revenues to finance a rapid expansion program. Sonatrach is denied access to the hard currency it earns on the international market. Indeed, the bulk of Sonatrach's revenues (i.e., receipts from exports) are repatriated and surrendered to the Bank of Algeria (the central bank) before being transferred as bank deposits. This institutional arrangement simplifies the mechanism of intervention by the government to achieve some of its macroeconomic policy objectives, in particular in regulating foreign exchange reserves and the exchange rate. Since the government ultimately controls the cash flow, Sonatrach cannot hide any of its operations and profits from the government.

The chief planks in Sonatrach's current development program are its multibillion dollar strategic alliances formed with overseas operators. Since 1991, IOCs have been allowed to work in or even buy into existing oil fields. By the end of 2006, for example, thirty exploration and production-sharing contracts were in place with eighteen IOCs. The foreign firms involved in Algeria's hydrocarbons sector generally take a long-term view of the political risks, and major investments are under way or planned in all areas of production. To protect foreign installations against attack by Islamic militants, private security arrangements and a strong army presence have been put in place.

In addition to expanding its operations in Algeria, Sonatrach is also expanding its international operations. Sonatrach began its overseas expansion when it purchased a minority stake in Peru's Camisea gas field in 2003. Sonatrach has since expanded to Niger and Mauritania as well as to Nigeria. Sonatrach is already actively involved in upstream ventures and pipeline activities in Latin America and Africa and pipeline transportation in Europe. The Algerian government has put forward a new regime in which firms bidding for exploration contracts in Algeria must offer Sonatrach stakes in foreign oil ventures. This strategy seems to be one that addresses Sonatrach's exposure to risk of supply disruption. According to Khelil, the company will seek to swap upstream assets with IOCs, offering the blocks with the highest potential. The company is looking to expand into new geographical locations or new products, such as petrochemicals, to obtain access to new markets. At the same time, Sonatrach's main sphere of operations will continue to remain in Algeria where it enjoys preferential treatment from the government and is not required to be transparent in its operations.

As revealed earlier, the hydrocarbons reform bill in 2005 ultimately ended up being revised in 2006. These revisions were consistent with Algeria's long-term strategic objectives to control – and exploit to its advantage – the country's principal source of revenue upon which rests the governing elites' power, patronage, and privileges. More immediately, there is little doubt that the real instigator of these essentially populist policy measures was President Bouteflika himself, who wanted to bolster his chances of securing overwhelming support in the 2008 referendum that tailored the constitution to his personal aspirations.

However, Khelil's position is very different. Much of his professional life, as a minister in Algeria and as an energy specialist working on Latin America for the World Bank (see Box 13.1), had been dedicated to the cause of liberalization and privatization. He fought long and hard, in the face of strong opposition from the conservatives in the military and the trade unions, to get his cherished hydrocarbons bill onto the statute books, apparently secure in the knowledge that he had the unwavering support of President Bouteflika. The substantial change in policy betrays the reality of Algerian political life that like most of the ministers in the cabinet he is essentially a civil servant, whose job is to carry out the instructions of his political leader.

Sonatrach's strategy is therefore one that is created, managed, and controlled by the highest level of government because of the key role that Sonatrach plays in the Algerian economy. Furthermore, the strategy that the government makes for Sonatrach and that it creates for the hydrocarbons industry as a whole is oftentimes in the interest of short-term gains but creates long-term problems for the competitiveness and overall efficiency of this industry in Algeria.

6 Conclusion: lessons learned and upcoming challenges

This chapter has sought to demonstrate the deeply integrated nature of Sonatrach, with the country's broader political economy. This analysis has also highlighted the competitive if not conflictual character of intra-elite relations over time that has made it difficult if not impossible for the government to fully denationalize, deconcentrate, or decentralize Sonatrach as it has begun doing in other sectors of the economy. Given this political reality it seems unlikely that the country's "golden goose" from which flows so much power, patronage, and privilege will anytime soon be "democratized."

For more than two decades, Algerian political elites have been aware that for the country to meet the challenge of globalization it would have to accelerate the transition to a market economy and work toward integration into the world economy. In this regard, fear of losing an edge to its immediate neighbors has put pressure on the government to conclude the ongoing negotiations for an association agreement with the European Union and membership into the World

Trade Organization (WTO), both of which are expected to offer new opportunities for greater access to capital, markets, and low-cost supplies as well as the economic benefit of introducing information technology into business. However, even when there has been apparent unanimity in recent years about the appropriate reforms to be undertaken in the non-oil economy, there is still a lack of consensus on when, how, or even if the hydrocarbons sector should be reformed.

The reality of Algerian politics, of course, has made it virtually impossible to undertake serious reforms in this rent-seeking sector without alienating deeply entrenched interests and powerful forces in the military-industrial complex (*le pouvoir*). Since the early 1980s successive "reformist" and "restructuring" initiatives have been undertaken that were intended to clarify the relationship between politics and business as, for example, with the institutional and energy policy framework put in place in 1998. This framework put forward by then President Liamine Zeroual was intended to demarcate the roles and clarify the responsibilities of the president in his capacity as chairman of the National Energy Council (NEC), of the Minister of Energy, and of Sonatrach's new statutory bodies. The resulting arrangements were expected to give the NOC more freedom and provide some separation between politics and business. In reality, no such separation ever occurred, reflecting the fundamental dilemma faced by government reformers in reconciling their commitment to reform with domestic political constraints and realities. Those leaders opposing reform have always voiced concerns about control of a strategic natural resource, fear of losing some element of sovereignty, and the potential dominance of the national economy by foreign interests in the event of liberalization. For their part, budget reformers put forward the view that a constructive debate should move beyond the issue of sovereignty, which no one questions, and focus, instead, on how to substitute genuine productive efforts for rent-seeking behavior. They see liberalization as capable of restraining the power of those who influence the distribution of the rent and discouraging those whose only effort consists of seeking to benefit from this largesse.

The fact that Sonatrach was not going to be "denationalized" or "privatized" anytime soon was made perfectly clear early on in the reformist process when President Bouteflika in 2000 moved to directly appoint all senior managers within Sonatrach. From a managerial point of view, this decision weakened the company's new statutory bodies, undermined efforts to improve its governance, and signaled once again the government's insincerity about reform. In the Algerian context, however, politics has always trumped good management, efficiency, and sound administration when they come at the expense of government control. Following his uncertain and highly controversial election as the republic's president in 1999, Bouteflika was determined to gain control of Sonatrach. The move was meant to deprive the president's opponents within the regime of support within Sonatrach and to neutralize the opposition within the company itself. A similar process occurred in 2005–2006 when the president reversed his support for Sonatrach's incipient "denationalization" in favor of continued control of the goose that lays the golden eggs. In both periods, unexpectedly high oil-generated revenues unleashed intra-elite conflicts over the distribution of the large profits. Interest groups of all stripes lobbied in order to undermine the government's objective of channeling excess budget revenues into a newly established stabilization fund designed as a buffer against future fiscal crises. The resulting tug of war between rent seekers and budget reformers has deflected the government from its intention to tackle the country's pressing socio-economic problems.

The move to squelch any liberalization of Sonatrach is one among many manifestations of the still unsettled struggle for political and economic control. As has been the case since independence, the divisive issues continue to be those of *power* (who will make the key decisions affecting the economy) and of *distribution* (which social groups will be favored by those who hold power). Until this struggle is settled through genuine representative institutions, factional conflict will continue to characterize the pattern of the Algerian transition to democracy and a market economy. As a consequence of the dilatory movements to date, the pace of economic reform has been slow, even protracted. In the hydrocarbons sector, where reforms are more complex and politically sensitive, the already long and laborious process of implementation has virtually halted – as the recent "reintegration" of Sonatrach within the state apparatus has made abundantly clear.

Privatization efforts and IMF-inspired institutional improvements needed to nurture the private sector and create an environment that rewards innovation and growth rather than rent seeking continue to face enormous challenges in the face of Algeria's opaque political system. Despite repeated declarations to the contrary, the emphasis remains very much on rent seeking – hence the desire to protect the main source of rent, Sonatrach, from restructuring and privatization. There is a general fear that full privatization and liberalization would expose the Algerian government to outsiders as corrupt and would fundamentally threaten its ability to control the operations of Sonatrach. Maintaining the status quo, while at the same time vacillating on various reform measures, allows the Algerian government to keep the sizable rent from the hydrocarbons industry coming into state coffers, and preserves the patronage relationships that have developed over time.

Whatever the neoliberal theoretical framework for transforming state-owned enterprises (SOEs) into market-based ones, the specificity of historical, social, political, and cultural contexts provides a more compelling explanation of Algerian state behavior, including its extremely weak record on privatization. This was made evident early in the 1990s when Algeria signed an IMF standby agreement committing itself to privatizing SOEs in a comprehensive way. By 2000, however, the World Bank noted, "Algeria's privatization has not yet resulted in a single complete divestiture of shares of corporatized public enterprises to outside private interests" (Werenfels 2002. p. 1). This resistance to privatization is rooted in deeper and more complex forces extant in Algeria's political character, including the role of the military and the patron–client networks, clan structures, and regional affiliations that define the country's dominant social forces (Werenfels 2002, p. 2). No enterprise is more immune to potential privatization efforts than one associated with the hydrocarbons sector. While a host of factors hinder privatization efforts, Algerian specialist Isabelle Werenfels identifies three principal causes for why privatization of the industrial SOEs in Algeria has been virtually non-existent:

First, because the country has long been dominated by competing military clans, the country lacks two necessary conditions for successful transformation and development: a unified leadership with a coherent economic strategy ... and a bureaucracy which is insulated ... but which [nonetheless] has strong ties to the private sector.

Secondly, privatization of state-owned industries affects the distribution of rents because it undermines the patron–client networks in which these SOEs are embedded.

Thirdly, privatization is hampered by the continuing and powerful remnant of the nationalist, *étatiste* and collectivist ideological foundations on which post-independence Algeria was built. These resulted in a strong mistrust of the private sector and, even more so, of foreign investment. Although this ideology has been significantly attenuated over the years, it remains a powerful instrument in public discourse for groups fighting privatization. Neoliberal goals such as efficiency are further undermined by ... a rentier mentality among the elites – a mentality which results from income not being related to work but to the redistribution of hydrocarbon rents. (Werenfels 2002, p. 2)

These powerful factors help explain the challenges faced by economic reformers seeking to rationalize industrial production through privatization policies. Such policies are almost impossible to implement, however, in the oil and gas sector, where politics trumps economic considerations. "As it has been the backbone of the Algerian economy for decades, privatization of this sector has been an extremely sensitive issue" (Werenfels 2002, p. 7). However much reformers may frame privatization debates in instrumental terms arguing for greater efficiency, rationality, and transparency, the sector's critical role in sustaining regime-accrued revenues makes it almost impossible to escape state control.

In a broader sense, flawed institutions have held back private sector growth. Sound institutions and laws, together with effective law enforcement, improve economic interactions among economic agents and reduce transaction costs. If institutions are not well developed, and in particular if there is a lack of accountability and transparency, the business environment is not conducive to growth. One of the chief criticisms of the Algerian state is its secrecy. The military and its civilian counterparts within *le pouvoir* have an enormous influence on political and economic decisions, but they remain accountable only to themselves. They in turn can influence the bureaucracy and the judiciary, resulting in a situation where only businessmen that are "connected" can prosper. The patronage network linking key groups within the hierarchy of power is dense and widespread, with its tentacles reaching into every key sector of national economic activity, the most important being the hydrocarbons sector.

While ideology and political culture are rarely invoked in explaining otherwise hard-headed business considerations, the case of Algeria is an exception. And while the country's current leadership lacks an explicit political belief system through which it justifies economic policies, there remains a strong ideological residue that still permeates the thinking of all political groups. This is especially the case when referring to the country's natural resources and the industrial production flowing from them whether in the hydrocarbon or non-oil sector. From the time of its revolutionary experience through its post-independence period, the Algerian state enterprise has been, argues Werenfels:

a space around which ... the populist *imaginaire* of the Algerian state [has] crystallized. This *imaginaire* comprised a socialist work order and framed state-owned public enterprises as symbols of national sovereignty and as places of collective efforts rather than individualism. Moreover, there was no separation of the economic production sphere at the enterprise and the social reproduction sphere of its workforce: SOEs nourished, lodged and formed the workers and their families, treated them medically and sent them to their vacation colonies. (Werenfels 2002, p. 12)

To be sure, much of this socialist orientation has lost its immediacy in the wake of successive economic downturns in the 1980s and 1990s. Yet the populist *imaginaire*, which provided the backdrop to a social contract between the regime and the population, "is still part of the national discourse and has been evoked and instrumentalized by opponents of neo-liberal policies" (Werenfels 2002, p. 12). While the professional personnel populating Sonatrach's highest decision-making levels possess business-oriented ethics, they still retain a certain fidelity to the "formerly mandatory populist rhetoric which has not been [fully] replaced by a dominant new capitalist one. The fact that capitalism is not yet a socially embedded ideology explains some of the resistance to privatization and thus contributes to raising political transaction and transition costs (Werenfels 2002, p. 12). In the aftermath of the global financial crisis of 2008–2009 that has raised serious doubts about capitalism's efficacy, it will be even more difficult to fully replace a socialist culture with a capitalist one, even among the business-oriented Western-trained bureaucrats in the hydrocarbons industry.

Many sectors of the once nationalized economy are now being privatized except for one – hydrocarbons. And despite the expansive role being played by scores of foreign oil and gas companies in exploiting Algerian resources, Sonatrach remains state-owned. Indeed, while in the past, historical, ideological, economic, and global considerations were fused to justify maintaining national control of oil and gas production, today's *raison d'être* is pure political economy. In order to remain in power the country's leadership depends heavily on the national rents that oil and gas production provides. In the nearly four decades since Algeria nationalized its hydrocarbon industry, one constant feature has defined the status of Sonatrach in an otherwise turbulent political economic landscape – the primacy of the national oil and gas company as the locomotive of the Algerian state. Despite chronic and often unpredictable circumstances from within and without that have affected prices, strategies, and performances, Sonatrach has remained the determinative instrument of state development, embedded within a complex web of political, personal, and patrimonial relations whose roots are found in the country's tortured history since its independence in 1962. Regardless of the repeated pressures from external actors to "rethink the role of the state, to open up to the world economy, and to embrace global competition" (Aissaoui 2001, p. 3). Algerian decision makers have remained faithful to a set of political principles that prioritize state interests at the expense of reform, efficiency, transparency, and accountability. While the regime has experimented with various forms of private–public arrangements as part of its political economy of development, it is unmistakably clear that Algeria will not, now or in the foreseeable future, "transition from a hydrocarbon-dependent and state-controlled economy to a diversified and private sector led economy" (Aissaoui 2001, p.2).

Notes

1 Data is from the EIU Country Data online databank, which aggregates data from a variety of sources. This particular data originally comes from the *Oil and Gas Journal 2008* and *IMF Statistics 2008*.
2 The most referenced English-language publications concerning Algeria's political history are Quandt (1969); Entelis (1986); Tlemcani (1986); Metz (1994); Ruedy (2005).
3 See *Journal Officiel de la République Algérienne* No. 17 Ordinance 71–8 of February 25, 1971 (www.sonatrach-dz.com/NEW/histoire.html).

4 Companies spun off from Sonatrach in 1980–1981 were the follow-
ing: Entreprise Nationale de Raffinage & de Distribution de Produit
Pétroliers (ERDP); Entreprise Nationale de Grands Travaux Pétroliers
(EGTP); Entreprise Nationale de Plastiques & Caoutchoucs [rubber]
(ENPC); Entreprise Nationale de Forage [drilling] (ENAFOR); Entreprise
Nationale des Travaux aux Puits [wells] (ENTP); Entreprise Nationale
de Géophysique (ENAGEO); Entreprise Nationale de Génie Civil & de
Bâtiment [engineering & construction] (GCB); Entreprise Nationale de
Services aux Puits (ENSP); and Entreprise Nationale de Canalisations
[pipelines] (ENAC).
5 See Sonatrach website (www.sonatrach-dz.com/). The company has dozens of affiliates in joint ventures with foreign companies in the petroleum
industry. The NEC allowed Sonatrach to gain control over NAFTEC,
NAFTAL, and ENIP (refining, distribution, and petrochemical companies) and has a 51 percent stake in petroleum service companies EGTP,
ENAFOR, ENAGEO, ENTP, and ENSP. These Sonatrach acquisitions
were the product of the company's special relationship with the government and its ability to offer better terms for employment and for its
operational activities with the government. As Sonatrach has grown so
has its importance as a rent-generating entity on which the government
relies to sustain itself and Algeria.
6 Data is from the EIU Country Data online databank, which aggregates
data from a variety of sources. This particular data originally comes
from the *Oil and Gas Journal* and *IMF Statistics 2008*.
7 Data is from the EIU Country Data online databank, which aggregates
data from a variety of sources. This particular data originally comes
from the *Oil and Gas Journal* and *IMF Statistics 2008*.
8 See Hayes (2006, p. 42) for further discussion. Increases in export pipeline capacity are necessary for a projected gas export capacity of 75 bcm
a year in the early twenty-first century. There are plans to further boost
the GME's throughput capacity to some 11 bcm a year, and to add a
further 5 bcm capacity to the TME line through the construction of
new compression stations. Other recent projects were expansion of the
Alrar–Hassi R'Mel pipeline, consisting of a gas pipeline 42–48 inches
in diameter with four compression stations; completion of the 42-inch
Hassi R'Mel–Skikda gas pipeline that came online in 1998; and construction of the 521-km In Salah–Hassi R'Mel gas pipeline, with a capacity of 7 million cubic meters per year.
9 Algeria fully nationalized its hydrocarbons industry through a series of
separate ordinances, decrees, and presidential edicts in which foreign territorial rights and resource assets were transferred to Sonatrach, beginning in mid 1970 and ending in early 1971. The most important of these

decrees were Ordinance 70–44 of June 12 1970 Nationalizing CREPS, CPA, SRA & TRAPSA, and Société Shell Petroleum N.V.; Ordinance No. 70–43 of June 12 1970, Nationalizing Rights and Interests of Société Française des Petroles Elwerath (SOFRAPEL); Decree No. 71–98 of April 12 1971, declaring the creation of 51/49 Sonatrach/Private Companies for Each Private Company Nationalized; Presidential [Houari Boumediene] Statement of February 24 1971, Nationalizing French Oil Companies; Decree No. 71–99 of April 12 1971 Declaring the Transfer of the Property Nationalized Under Ordinance No. 71–23 of April 12 1971, to Sonatrach; Ordinance No. 71–10 Dated February 24 1971 Nationalizing the Companies SOPEG, SOTHRA, TRAPES, CREPS, TRAPSA, and Pipelines "PK 66 In Amenas Mediterranée à Ohanet" and "Hassi R'Mel-Haoud El Hamra"; Ordinance No. 71–9 of February 24 1971 Nationalizing Associated Gas; Ordinance 71–8 of February 24 1971 Nationalizing All Interests of the Société d'Exploitation des Hydrocarbures de Hassi R'Mel (SEHR), All Mining Interests Held by All Companies in Nord In Amenas, Tin Fouyem Sud, Alrar Est, Alrer Ouest, Nezla Est, Bridas, Toual, Rhourde Chouff and Rhourde Adra, and Mining Interests Held in Gas Derived from Deposits in Gassi Touil, Rhourde Nouss, Nezla Est, Zarzaitine, and Tiguentourine (Including El Paso, Francarep, and Petropar); Decree No. 71–66 of February 24 1971 Transferring All Concessions Nationalized by Ordinances No. 71–11 to Sonatrach; Decree No. 71–65 of February 24 1971 Transferring All Concessions Nationalized by Ordinance No. 71–10 to Sonatrach; Decree No. 71–64 of February 24 1971 Transferring All Concessions Nationalized by Ordinances Nos. 71–8 and 71–9 to Sonatrach; and Ordinance No. 71–11 Dated February 24 1971 Nationalizing the Companies CFP (A), CREPS, PETROPAR, SNPA, SOFREPAL, COPAREX, OMNIREX, EURAFREP, and FRANCAREP.

10 Conseil National de l'Energie.

11 While the top echelon of the military old guard, long serving as the institutional foundation of *le pouvoir*, has been systematically displaced by Bouteflika since 2000, that has not been the case with the DRS and its powerful leader, General Mohamed "Toufik" Mediene. Indeed, the DRS commander has remained securely ensconced as head of an organization that many consider as a state within a state during a lengthy period that has otherwise witnessed regular turnovers in government personnel and within the army high command. The determinative role of Mediene at the apex of political power was well captured by the Economist Intelligence Unit when it surmised that "although Mr. Bouteflika has been able to develop a more independent power base than many of his predecessors, the support of General Mediene is still

believed to be crucial to his presidency. At a time when popular support for the president is low, he is particularly vulnerable to the influence of the DRS chief, who is seen as the embodiment of Algeria's conservative old guard. In this interpretation, recent events [surrounding the Meziane corruption scandal] could be regarded as undermining Mr. Bouteflika's authority, or at least reminding him of on what it rests" (Economist Intelligence Unit 2010).

12 Law 91–21 of December 4, 1991, amends the 1986 Hydrocarbon Investment Law 86–14 of August 19, 1986. See Middle East Executive Reports (1992). The major features of the 1991 law were as follows: 1) foreign firms were authorized to explore for and develop gas deposits in partnership with Sonatrach, "the state-owned hydrocarbons firm"; 2) foreign firms were authorized to exploit existing oil fields in partnership with Sonatrach; 3) international arbitration was permitted for disputes between foreign firms and Sonatrach; and 4) royalties and petroleum taxes were reduced for oil and gas found in certain remote or otherwise difficult areas of exploration or production.

14 Norway's evolving champion: Statoil and the politics of state enterprise

MARK C. THURBER AND BENEDICTE
TANGEN ISTAD

1 Introduction

Den Norske Stats Oljeselskap AS ("Statoil") was founded in 1972 as the national oil company (NOC) of Norway. Along with Petrobras, Statoil[1] is frequently considered to be among the state-controlled oil companies most similar to an international oil company (IOC) in governance, business strategy, and performance. Partially privately owned since 2001, its formal governance procedures are beyond reproach. The company is a technologically capable producer, having built up expertise in deep water[2] and harsh environments from years of experience on the Norwegian Continental Shelf (NCS).[3] Strategically, it hopes to leverage these home-grown engineering advantages to expand its international production, which now comes principally from Angola and Azerbaijan, with significant contributions from Algeria, Canada, the US Gulf of Mexico, and Venezuela as well.

Statoil's development and performance have been intimately connected to its relationship with the Norwegian government over the years. Norway's approach of separating policy, regulatory, and commercial functions in petroleum has inspired admiration and imitation as the canonical model of good bureaucratic design for a hydrocarbons sector. For example, Nigeria's current oil and gas reform plan envisions reconstituted institutions whose functions and relationships would strikingly parallel those in Norway.[4] Policymakers in Mexico have also looked to Norway's separation-of-functions model as a possible blueprint for improving the country's woeful performance in petroleum. At the same time, other countries have followed quite different paths and yet still performed well (Thurber *et al.* 2011). Angola, for example, has built a productive and fairly efficient petroleum sector with almost no formal separation of policy, regulatory, and commercial roles (see Chapter 19).

The reality is that Norway's comparative success in hydrocarbons development, and that of Statoil, has been about much more than a formula for bureaucratic organization. Belying the notion of a pristine "Norwegian model" that unfolded inexorably from a well-designed template, the actual development of Norway's petroleum sector at times was, and often still is, a messy affair rife with conflict and uncertainty. But Norway had the advantage of entering its oil era with a mature, open democracy as well as bureaucratic institutions with experience regulating other natural resource industries (hydropower generation, fishing, and mining, for example). Thus far, the diverse political and regulatory institutions governing the petroleum sector – and governing the NOC – have collectively proven robust enough to handle the strains of petroleum development and correct the worst imbalances that have arisen. What appears as consensus governance in retrospect was often really a process of accommodation between contending parties in this system. In this case study we closely trace the progression of the state–NOC relationship in Norway over time, and we examine the way that this relationship has shaped the performance and strategy of Statoil. We make the following six principal observations from our research.

First, Norway's policy orientation from the start was focused on maintaining control over the oil sector, as opposed to simply maximizing revenue. Norway began its petroleum era as a country of fewer than 4 million people with well-functioning institutions and favorable economic conditions including very low unemployment. As a result, the country was more concerned with the possible negative ramifications of oil wealth than with any special advantage that could be gained from it. Its policy-making process was thus very cautious, involving among other things voluminous economic studies of the absorptive capacity of the Norwegian economy and the possible impacts of oil and gas wealth on society. To avoid negative impacts of oil, the government sought to moderate the pace of petroleum development and to skillfully regulate the activities of international and domestic oil operators. The latter objective motivated efforts to build up government knowledge and competence in oil and gas. Some politicians believed that formation of an NOC would help in this process.

Second, the principal means through which Norway was able to exert control over domestic petroleum activities was a skillful bureaucracy operating within a mature and open political system. Civil servants gained knowledge of petroleum to regulate the sector through systematic efforts to build up their own independent competence, enabling them to productively steer the political discourse on petroleum management after the first commercial oil discovery was made. The "Norwegian model" of separating commercial, policymaking, and regulatory functions worked in large part because the country's bureaucracy could draw on enough talent and experience to develop into a legitimate counterbalance to the power and ambition of NOC Statoil. Robust contestation between socialist and conservative political parties also helped contribute to a system of oil administration that supported competition (including between multiple Norwegian oil companies as well as international operators) and was able to evolve new checks and balances as needed. A particularly important instance of corrective policy action occurred in 1984, when the government decided to strip more than half of Statoil's assets from its balance sheet to attenuate its cash flow and reduce its influence over NCS resource development decisions.

Third, Statoil did play an important role in contributing to the development of Norwegian industry and technological capability, in large part because it had the freedom to take a long-term approach to technology development. With a strong engineering orientation and few consequences for failure as a fully state-backed company, Statoil developed a culture valuing innovation over development of a lean, commercially oriented organization. It prioritized long-term R&D and tackled projects that were highly ambitious technically. This orientation led to a number of unalloyed triumphs, including the laying of the Statpipe gas pipeline across the Norwegian trench in the 1980s and the pathbreaking development of subsea production systems in the 1980s and 1990s (Knudsen 1997). It also contributed to severe cost overruns and delays in a few pioneering efforts, most of which were ultimately successful but not before attracting severe criticism in Norway for their problems in the development phase. As the most significant employer of domestic oil service companies, Statoil's technology investments helped accelerate the development of the entire Norwegian supply industry in petroleum, turning the North Sea into the "world's technology laboratory." Along the way, oil operations in Norway gained a reputation for incurring higher costs relative to comparable activities across the border in the UK.

However, despite possible implications for government revenue collection in the short term, it is difficult to argue that the country's strategy of pouring money into indigenous technology development by means of Statoil (and other broad-based R&D initiatives) has not been an overall success. It is likely to have yielded significant long-term economic benefits by contributing to the development of a high-value-added domestic industry in oil services.

Fourth, the formal relationship between Statoil and the government has become more arm's length as Norway's resources and oil expertise have matured. Under its first CEO, experienced Labour politician Arve Johnsen, Statoil aggressively flexed its political muscles to gain special advantages in licensing and access to acreage. Politicians at the time (especially but not exclusively in the Labour Party) justified these privileges as necessary support for the fledgling Norwegian enterprise in oil. As domestic resources began to mature, Statoil's leadership (starting with Harald Norvik in 1988, and continuing through the tenures of subsequent CEOs Olav Fjell and Helge Lund) saw the need to forge an independent corporate identity and governance structure that would allow the company to compete effectively abroad.[5] For its part, the government by the 1980s came to worry more about Statoil's excessive dominance than its fragility, leading it to revoke many of the company's special privileges. At the same time, the government over time became increasingly willing to grant Statoil a level of formal corporate autonomy – most notably by allowing it to expand internationally in the 1990s and partially privatize in 2001 – that would not have been politically possible earlier in the development of the Norwegian petroleum sector.

Fifth, notwithstanding changes in their formal relationship, it has remained impossible to sever the close ties between the Norwegian state and a company with the domestic significance of Statoil. These residual ties can manifest in various ways, including: 1) the effect on policy decisions of direct personal connections between Statoil leaders and politicians; 2) persistent "Norway-centric" influences on Statoil's strategy even in the larger context of efforts to internationalize; and 3) public pressure from politicians who continue to see themselves as Statoil's masters. The power of personal links between company leaders and politicians was evident in the approval process for the 2007 merger of Statoil with the oil and gas division of Norwegian competitor Norsk Hydro, which left the merged company controlling a massive 80 percent of NCS production operatorship. Statoil and Norsk Hydro directly and successfully lobbied Prime Minister Jens Stoltenberg in favor of the merger, turning the deal into a foregone conclusion before there was any chance for a broader debate among politicians, regulators, and the public. The merger both revealed and exacerbated Statoil's difficulty in disengaging its strategic focus from Norway. While stated goals of the merger included the realization of cost-saving synergies on the NCS and creation of a unified Norwegian champion that could more effectively compete abroad, it also had the effect of making Statoil much more wedded to the NCS while directly adding few significant international assets.

The existence of a majority state-owned company like Statoil – especially one that is unrivalled in the country in visibility, importance, and historical sense of its being "Norwegian property" – gives politicians and the public the expectation and perception of control over operational questions. Even while direct intervention of the Ministry of Petroleum and Energy in Statoil strategy has mostly disappeared, politicians continue to weigh in as though they were making policy for the company. Statoil's investments in Canada oil sands and operations in poorly governed countries have been particular lightning rods for political criticism, even as the government has declined to insert itself in a formal way into such questions. Minority shareholders, as is often true for partially privatized NOCs, can be confused about who really controls the key decisions. The political potency of the perception of control on the part of politicians – which we believe was largely illusory even when Statoil was fully state-owned – is why the government is likely to retain more than a two-thirds stake in Statoil for the foreseeable future. In a sense, current governance arrangements are ideal for politicians: They remain free to score political points by criticizing Statoil without needing to worry that their invective will adversely affect operational performance. Meanwhile, Statoil will be required to expend resources on managing and responding to political noise on the home front for some time to come.

Sixth, Statoil's experience thus far casts doubt upon the conventional wisdom that NOC–NOC connections provide material benefit in opening resource access around the world. To the extent that such linkages are important, Statoil would seem to be among the best positioned to benefit from them as both a highly competent producer and a company that might be sympathetic to the needs of resource-rich countries. However, there are few instances so far where Statoil's status as an NOC has been an obviously decisive factor in unlocking resources that would otherwise be off-limits. In fact, the company's biggest expansionary efforts in recent years have been through M&A in regions like the US and Canada where resources are allocated through open processes. Arguably the most significant case in which Statoil's NOC status played to its advantage in expanding its international resources was in attracting BP as a partner in the 1990s.

The remainder of this study is organized as follows. Section 2 provides a short history of Norway's resource development from both a hydrocarbon and an institutional perspective. Section 3 describes the goals that Norway formally defined for petroleum development in the years following the Ekofisk find and then the policies and institutional structures – an NOC central among them – that it put in place to achieve them. Section 4 traces the subsequent evolution of state–NOC relations over time. It first examines how the government was forced at various points to counterbalance an ambitious and politically astute young Statoil. The section then explores Statoil's more recent evolution towards a corporate identity distinct from Norway, especially through internationalization of operations and partial privatization. Finally, the section identifies those respects in which Statoil today is relatively free of political entanglements and those in which it continues to influence and be influenced by the political process in Norway. Section 5 assesses Statoil's performance and strategy in its most salient dimensions – focusing on technology development and project execution as well as degree of success in international expansion – and how they have been affected by the company's relationship with the state. Section 6 concludes the study by considering key challenges going forward for both Statoil and the state of Norway.

2 A brief history of Norway's resource development

Norway entered its oil era with the significant advantage of possessing a highly competent bureaucracy with previous experience regulating natural resource industries like hydropower, fishing, and mining. (The country's experience with civil engineering and shipbuilding also proved to be helpful technical background for the nascent petroleum industry.) The ability to adapt the bureaucracy to oil matters even before any major discoveries had been made was central to Norway's

effective stewardship of hydrocarbons. Spurred to action by a peti-
tion in 1962 by Phillips Petroleum to the Norwegian government for
an exclusive concession over the NCS, Jens Evensen at the Ministry
of Foreign Affairs began to assemble a core group of civil servants to
work on petroleum. The first task facing Norwegian bureaucrats was
to secure the most favorable possible boundaries of Norway's resource
sovereignty, which they successfully accomplished in negotiations with
other states bordering the North Sea.[6]

The next main task confronting Norway's still-inexperienced pioneers in petroleum[7] was to set up a framework for licensing exploration blocks to private companies. Evensen was particularly focused
on Denmark's experience as a cautionary tale (Lerøen 2002). That
country ceded all of its oil and gas exploration and production rights
to Danish shipbuilder A. P. Møller in 1962; only later was the concession gradually unraveled by the government after attracting a
storm of controversy amid the high oil prices of the 1970s and early
1980s (Hahn-Pedersen 1999). The young Norwegian civil servants
were given substantial resources to learn everything they could about
how to design effective licensing policy.[8] In April 1965, the work of
the initial group of government employees[9] was codified in a Royal
Decree which opened the first license round and laid down the basic
guidelines for Norway's administration of oil and gas. (A formal law
regulating petroleum was not put in place until 1985, and the broad
outlines of Norway's petroleum governance even today remain largely
unchanged from this initial decree of 1965.) Personnel at the Ministry
of Industry continued to refine their expertise through learning-by-
doing over subsequent licensing rounds.[10]

The initial licensing framework led to Esso spudding the first well
on the NCS in 1966. Gas condensate was found by Phillips in the
Cod Field in 1968, and the first commercially viable oil was discovered in the Ekofisk Field (see Figure 14.1) by Phillips at the very end
of 1969. Only after the discovery of Ekofisk did oil attract significant
interest from politicians and broader Norwegian society. Having built
up their knowledge and capabilities in the five years preceding the
Ekofisk discovery, Ministry of Industry officials were able to steer the
debate over how Norway should manage its newfound oil.[11]

Developing resources on the NCS was technologically challenging from the very start. Ekofisk was in only moderately deep water
(70–75 meters), but creating offshore platforms even at this depth that

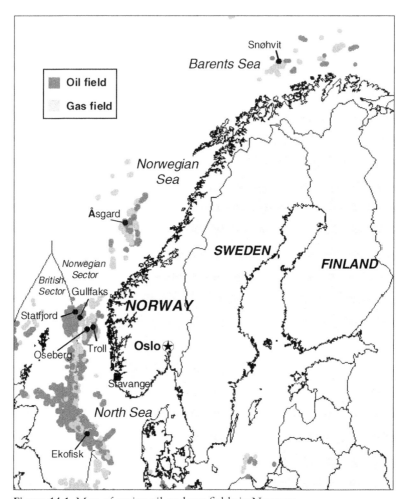

Figure 14.1 Map of major oil and gas fields in Norway.
Source for oil and gas field data: Wood Mackenzie (2009b).

would be stable in the harsh winter conditions of the North Sea required innovations in platform technology. In addition, the oil at Ekofisk was in a chalk reservoir, whose ability to sustain long-term production was poorly understood at the outset (Al-Kasim 2006; Tofte *et al.* 2008). Test production from Ekofisk took place from 1971 to 1974, with full production starting thereafter. As a partner in the Petronord Group which owned a share of Ekofisk,[12] Norsk Hydro became the first Norwegian equity participant in oil and gas production on the

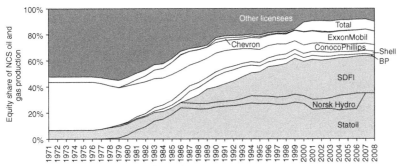

Figure 14.2 Equity share of NCS production held by different companies over time, with production for the year attributed to the equity holder at year end. Companies that later merged are grouped according to their current merged form, with the exception of Statoil and Norsk Hydro. Starting in 1985, the Norwegian government took direct equity interest in oil and gas fields through the State's Direct Financial Interest (see section 4), labeled here as SDFI.
Data source: Norwegian Petroleum Directorate (2009a).

NCS when Ekofisk came online in 1971 – see Figure 14.2. The first natural gas was pumped from Ekofisk in 1977.

Determining that an NOC would be an important tool for resource management, Norway in 1972 formed 100-percent-state-owned oil company Den Norske Stats Oljeselskap AS (the "Norwegian State Oil Company"), shortened to "Statoil." Not long before, the Norwegian government had increased its stake in Norwegian industrial conglomerate and petroleum operator Norsk Hydro to 51 percent.[13] The government also directed the remaining private Norwegian petroleum interests to merge, creating a third Norwegian player in oil and gas, Saga Petroleum. To enhance its ability to monitor and control the petroleum industry, the government established the Norwegian Petroleum Directorate (NPD) in Stavanger[14] to offer independent technical and regulatory expertise to the Ministry of Industry, which set hydrocarbon policy at the time.[15]

On the back of strong advocacy by Statoil's politically adept CEO Arve Johnsen (and also from 1972 to 1974 its forceful chairman Jens Christian Hauge), Statoil was given a 50 percent carried interest in all new exploration blocks by 1974, with an additional "sliding scale" put in place that allowed it to claim up to a full 80 percent interest

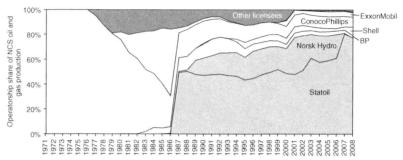

Figure 14.3 Share of NCS production operated by different companies over time, with production for the year attributed to the operator at year end. Companies that later merged are grouped according to their current merged form, with the exception of Statoil and Norsk Hydro.
Data source: Norwegian Petroleum Directorate (2009a).

after a discovery. This meant that Statoil risked no capital in the exploration phase but could then opt in to a dominant equity share of the field once a discovery was made. International partners still operated all fields at that point. To facilitate development of indigenous expertise, the country aimed to provide operatorship opportunities to Norwegian players. A "golden block" expected to harbor lucrative resources was granted to Statoil in 1978; it indeed yielded oil in the Gullfaks field in the northern part of the North Sea, and Statoil took on its first field operatorship at Gullfaks in 1981.

Other fields were initially granted to international operators with the provision that Norwegian companies would have the option to take over operatorship after a certain period of time. The most important early example was the Statfjord field, which was discovered in 1974 and developed by Mobil, with first production in 1979. In taking over the field from Mobil in 1987 and adding Statfjord's volumes to production from Gullfaks which had recently come online, Statoil instantly became the largest operator of production on the NCS (Figure 14.3). Norsk Hydro started producing in 1988 from its own operations at the Oseberg field further south, with volumes becoming significant by 1989. The Statfjord, Gullfaks, and Oseberg fields together produced the lion's share of North Sea oil into the mid 1990s (Figure 14.4), facilitating continued Statoil and Hydro dominance of NCS production.

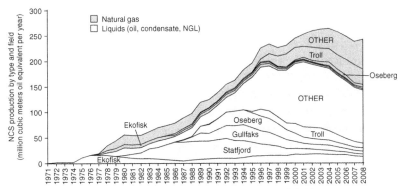

Figure 14.4 NCS production by hydrocarbon type and field.
Data source: Norwegian Petroleum Directorate (2009a).

In the early 1980s, a shift in political alignment, with a Conservative Party government replacing the previous Labour one, spurred moves to check an increasingly powerful Statoil. To stem the company's cash flow, Statoil's balance sheet was split in two in January 1985, with more than half of Statoil's interests in oil and gas fields, pipelines, and other facilities transferred to the newly created State's Direct Financial Interest (SDFI) in petroleum. Statoil's power and influence in government were exposed to further public scrutiny in connection with the severe cost overruns in its Mongstad refinery project.[16] This scandal helped lead to the resignation of CEO Johnsen and his replacement in 1988 with the less political Harald Norvik.

With an eye on Statoil's long-term future beyond the maturing NCS, Norvik set out to build up Statoil's identity as a corporate entity distinct from Norway. Through an alliance with BP from 1990 to 1999, Statoil established some significant international operations, including in Angola and Azerbaijan. Statoil continued its drive towards an independent corporate identity under subsequent CEOs Olav Fjell (1999–2003) and Helge Lund (2004–present). A particularly notable step was the partial privatization of the company. Statoil was listed on the Oslo and New York stock exchanges on June 18, 2001. The state initially sold an 18.3 percent share of the company and then further reduced its shareholding to around 70 percent through subsequent share issues in 2004 and 2005.

A more recent seismic shift in the Norwegian petroleum landscape was the merger of Statoil with the oil and gas division of Norwegian competitor Norsk Hydro in October 2007. A justification for the merger was the need to create a unified Norwegian champion with the cash flow and scale to compete more effectively abroad. At the same, the paradox of the merger was that it created an even more dominant player on the NCS – Statoil at the time of this writing controlled roughly 80 percent of production operatorship – without making significant new international assets available to Statoil.

A characteristic pattern for Statoil over its lifetime has been projects that push the envelope of technology in response to increasingly harsh conditions as developments have moved into deeper water and also further north – first within the North Sea (e.g., Statfjord, Gullfaks, Oseberg, and later major gas field Troll) and then into the Norwegian Sea (e.g., the Åsgard field) and the Barents Sea in the Arctic (e.g., the Snøhvit gas field and associated LNG terminal).

3 State goal: control over petroleum

Following the Ekofisk discovery, the Norwegian parliament (Storting) sought to more formally define both the state's goals for the sector and the instruments it should use to achieve these goals. Norway, with its heritage of transparency and mature democratic institutions, was unusual among oil states in the degree to which it publicly deliberated on these points. Ministry of Industry personnel, with their knowledge accumulated from having managed early activities in the petroleum sector, were able to have a significant influence on the debate. Guiding principles to govern the sector – "The Ten Commandments" (see the appendix to this chapter) – were laid out by the parliament's industry committee in mid 1971 after a new Labour government replaced the previous four-party coalition.

Underlying the oil commandments was Norway's overriding goal of avoiding negative impacts from hydrocarbon development on an economy, political system, and society that were already functioning quite well in the opinion of its citizens. Norway had a population of fewer than 4 million and very low unemployment, and entrenched interests like fisheries or manufacturing that might be negatively affected by a new petroleum industry carried significant political weight. In this respect, Norway's orientation was different from almost all of the other nations that came into petroleum riches, with a balance of risk and reward that tilted more in the direction of avoiding disruption than seeking immediate economic gain. The contrast between how Norway and the UK approached the potential of North Sea petroleum resources highlighted this difference in national needs. As Øystein Noreng (1980) points out: "The British desperately needed an economic miracle while the Norwegians could do without one." Norway's concern about managing the inevitable impacts of large petroleum operations on a small country was expressed in remarkable (and prescient) detail in Parliamentary Report No. 25 from the Ministry of Finance to the Parliament (Norwegian Ministry of Finance 1974). The document considered potential effects of petroleum development on diverse aspects of society, focusing in particular on macroeconomic balance, employment, and industrial structure, but even touching on such fine-grained topics as possible increased commute times for petroleum workers and consequent disruption of social and family life.

Parliamentary Report No. 25 suggested two dimensions of control over the sector that were considered critical to avoiding negative impacts: first, control over the pace of hydrocarbons development, to ensure that petroleum impacts did not outstrip Norway's capacity to adjust; and, second, supervisory control over the operations occurring on the NCS. Maintaining adequate supervisory control was understood to require among other things that Norwegian players develop technological know-how in petroleum "to provide the popularly elected institutions with the necessary insight to enable them to supervise and regulate activities which are due to be started up" (Norwegian Ministry of Finance 1974). An ancillary benefit would be the development of Norwegian technological capability more broadly.[17]

Norwegian politicians and civil servants agreed – though not always for the same reasons – that a state-owned oil company was a necessary tool for achieving the country's objectives in petroleum management. Norway had some existing tradition of managing key industrial efforts by way of SOEs, and policymakers noticed NOCs increasingly becoming the common currency of other oil- and gas-rich nations (PESD Interviews). Some politicians envisioned an NOC as a direct instrument of state control – a company that would plan production in accordance with government dictates and build up expertise that would directly accrue to government regulators to help them control private players (Dam 1976; Grayson 1981).[18]

Ministry personnel, on the other hand, mostly viewed an NOC as an essential administrative strategy to separate government commercial and regulatory functions, rather than as a tool for direct control (PESD Interviews). Civil servants at the Ministry were well aware of the fact that NOCs rarely functioned as pliant agents of government,[19] and they also understood from experience that goals of control could be accomplished through skillful licensing and regulation. Three principal rationales were behind the bureaucrats' perceived need to create a separate commercial agent of government. First, they felt that the government indeed needed to engage in commercial transactions in oil, but that the Ministry itself lacked the proper administrative structures and competence to do this. An incident that highlighted this deficiency for these civil servants was when Conoco in negotiations offered the Norwegian government a petroleum license in the Netherlands. Ministry officials – lacking a suitable commercial vehicle – temporarily vested state participation in this license in Norwegian arms manufacturer Kongsberg Våpenfabrikk until the license could find a more permanent home after the founding of Statoil in 1972 (PESD Interviews).

Second, Ministry personnel believed that separation of the government's regulatory and commercial functions was inherently a logical way of avoiding conflicts of interest that could make Norway a less attractive place in which to do business. All the early Ministry officials we interviewed expressed some variation on the theme that, as Karl-Edwin Manshaus put it, "we realized that we were not businessmen, and that we were sitting on both sides of the table [i.e., as both regulators and competitors]."

Third, the particular sensitivity of Ministry officials to avoiding commercial entanglements[20] had its roots in a mining accident in 1962 that killed twenty-one on the arctic island of Spitsbergen.[21] The mining company responsible was state-owned, and at that time the head of the mining division at the Ministry of Industry also served on the board of the company. Negligence was alleged, and the ensuing scandal brought down the Labour government in power at the time. Since then, no civil servant in Norway has been allowed to serve on the board of any state-owned company, protecting politicians and government officials when state-owned ventures go bad.[22] This is atypical among countries with dominant NOCs. In many countries, in fact, the petroleum minister serves as the chairman of the board of the NOC – see, for example, the cases of Kuwait, Nigeria, Mexico, and Saudi Arabia in this volume. In some cases, such as Iran and Algeria, NOCs and government petroleum ministries can appear so intertwined at times as to be indistinguishable.

While most politicians and civil servants favored creation of some kind of NOC, a series of political compromises had a large impact on the exact form. The center-right government of Per Borten decided to increase the state's share of existing oil player Norsk Hydro to 51 percent in late 1970 with the idea that it could serve as Norway's commercial instrument in oil. However, the Borten government was replaced in 1971 by a Labour government under Trygve Bratteli, leading to the decision to create Statoil in 1972 as a fully state-owned NOC. Around the same time, the government encouraged several private Norwegian players in oil to consolidate to form Saga Petroleum. The Norwegian Petroleum Directorate (NPD) was also established as a regulatory and technical advisory organization reporting to the Ministry of Industry but whose autonomy would in theory be assured by a separate board of directors (Al-Kasim 2006).[23]

These various political compromises in the early 1970s helped set up key checks and balances in several ways. First, the establishment of three principal Norwegian oil companies set the stage for strong domestic competition to emerge later, especially between Statoil and Hydro. Ultimately, the skillful use of licensing policy to balance competition and cooperation among both domestic and foreign players proved to be the single most important regulatory mechanism for the Norwegian government. Second, the simultaneous creation of Statoil and the NPD under the supervision of the Ministry of Industry established the three-part separation of functions – policymaking (Ministry of Industry), technical/regulatory (NPD), and commercial (Statoil) – that is often considered to be the "Norwegian model" for petroleum. Statoil was supposed to execute the state's commercial objectives at arm's length from licensing and regulatory functions to avoid conflicts of interest. The Ministry as representative of the state (the sole shareholder) could exert full control over Statoil, but this control could in theory only be exercised by the Minister acting as the General Assembly[24] to the company in order to enable political oversight by Parliament (Al-Kasim 2006). After 1974, Statoil was also directed by Section 10 of its Articles of Association to publically disclose its outlook and strategic plans on an annual basis for Parliamentary review.

(To some interviewees this was an impressive illustration of government control, to others a largely toothless formality.) The role of the NPD was to offer independent technical advice on petroleum to the Ministry to facilitate control of Statoil and all of the other players on the NCS. The existence of the NPD also would allow the Ministry to focus on policy by relieving it of the all-encompassing portfolio of oil-related activities[25] which it had needed to take on in the early years. The reality of how these formal checks and balances functioned over the course of Norway's petroleum development was imperfect and is discussed in greater detail in section 4.

From the start of its petroleum era, Norway faced the same fiscal policy challenges confronting any resource-rich state: how to maximize government revenue while still achieving the desired rate of development, and how to deploy the revenue for the maximum benefit of the country. What made Norway unusual among oil states was its conscious effort at the outset of petroleum development to reflect in detail on the effects that this new industry might have on Norwegian society and how to steer the development process accordingly. As discussed earlier, this effort was embodied in a visionary document, Parliamentary Report No. 25 of 1973–1974 from the Ministry of Finance,[26] which among other things illustrated the unusually high capacity of the Norwegian civil service. Translating the key qualitative observations of Parliamentary Report No. 25 into tangible petroleum policy, however, was challenging. Different political parties became attached to different petroleum extraction "targets" that were connected in theory to optimal revenue goals. The reality is that government had very little control over revenue, due to fluctuations in the oil price, and not a great deal more over petroleum production. Exploration block allocations could be controlled, but not the eventual production that would flow from them, and Statoil was never really used as an instrument to restrict production rates from developed fields. Furthermore, it was impossible to truly know in advance the actual absorptive capacity of the economy (Al-Kasim 2006). All of these real uncertainties translated into policy that was by necessity somewhat adaptive and ad hoc. Indeed, one of the fundamental strengths of Norwegian oil governance was precisely the combination of a thoughtful and comprehensive initial roadmap (exemplified by Parliamentary Report No. 25) with flexible subsequent policymaking against the background of a diverse political system.

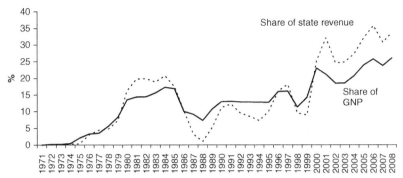

Figure 14.5 Oil and gas sector percentage contribution to GNP and state revenue, 1971–2008.
Source: Nordvik *et al.* (2009).

Noreng (1980) and El Mallakh *et al.* (1984) argue that hydrocarbon development in the 1970s turned out to be more cautious than optimal. A "countercyclical" program of domestic spending intended to subsidize and protect traditional industries combined with delays in petroleum revenues to push Norway to an extremely high level of debt by 1978 – over half of GNP, the highest debt ratio ever recorded in an OECD country to that point (Noreng 1980). In fact, the countercyclical policy degraded the competitiveness of Norwegian non-oil industry by shielding it from change and boosting wages and costs. Rising unemployment suggested that the true capacity of the economy to absorb petroleum revenues was higher than had been anticipated (El Mallakh *et al.* 1984). Showing laudable pragmatism, Norway's policymakers discarded the countercyclical policy in 1978 and accelerated petroleum licensing. With the additional help of an increase in oil prices in 1979–1980, Norway's accounts were back in surplus by 1980. At the same time, these events highlighted the extent to which Norway had already become a hydrocarbon-dependent state by the 1980s (El Mallakh *et al.* 1984), as illustrated in Figure 14.5.

The deep recession in Norway triggered by the oil price drop of 1986 further emphasized the country's exposure to petroleum-related economic fluctuations. (As Klaus Mohn points out, there has been substantial volatility not only in revenues but also in investments on the NCS.) In part as a vehicle to help smooth out these cycles, the government in 1990 created the Government Petroleum Fund (the name was later changed in 2006 to the Government Pension Fund – Global, referred to hereafter as the "Fund"). The net cash flow from petroleum activities each year accrues directly to the Fund, with any non-oil budget deficit plugged by a transfer from the Fund. To avoid "Dutch Disease," in which natural resource revenues cause inflation, affect exchange rates, and make domestic industry uncompetitive, the Fund's capital is invested outside of Norway (as suggested many years before in Parliamentary Report No. 25).

In essence, Norway's Fund serves both as a stabilization fund, designed to smooth economic cycles and insulate government budgets from oil revenue volatility, and as a savings fund, to build up wealth that will support the population even after petroleum resources have been depleted (Davis *et al.* 2003; Skancke 2003). These Fund goals were considered to argue for a cautious and measured use of pet-roleum revenues. The fiscal "Action Rule" was established that the non-oil budget deficit to be covered each year by an injection from the Fund should not exceed the annual real rate of return on the Fund capital. This real rate of return is typically estimated to be 4 per-cent as a long-term guideline, although the Action Rule is not meant to preclude smaller or larger transfers in a given year as needed to respond to economic cycles. Soaring Fund capital (Figure 14.6) and a humming Norwegian economy enabled the 4 percent benchmark to be easily met in recent years (Figure 14.7), although expansionary fiscal policy was planned in 2009 to counter the effects of the world-wide financial crisis.

Røed Larsen (2006) argues that policy mechanisms like the Fund and the Action Rule – in combination with other factors like trans-parency, media scrutiny, and the rule of law – have been helpful in preventing rent seeking and thus maintaining fiscal restraint in Norway's spending of petroleum revenues. Nevertheless, the question still remains as to how Norway has been able to hold together the political consensus around prudence in revenue management, as poli-ticians could presumably win election by promising immediate ben-efits from increased spending. Røed Larsen implicitly suggests that the relative lack of public visibility of petroleum revenues in past years might have played some role. Several of our interviewees concurred with this view, arguing that the public was only distantly aware of the massive money generator offshore until massive budget surpluses surfaced in the late 1990s (PESD Interviews). Røed Larsen goes on

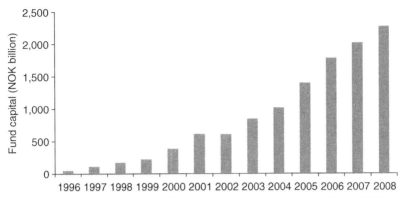

Figure 14.6 Market value of Government Pension Fund – Global, 1996–2008.
Note: Before 2006, the name of the fund was the Government Petroleum Fund.
Source: Norges Bank (2009).

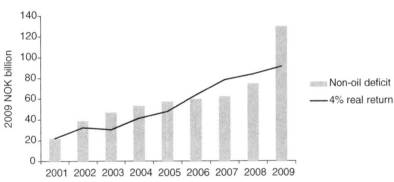

Figure 14.7 Degree of success in achieving Norway's "Action Rule" that the non-oil deficit should be less than the real return (typically estimated at 4 percent) on the Government Pension Fund – Global over the long term.
Source: Norwegian Ministry of Finance (2009).

to express concern that the political will to restrain spending may be eroding in the face of today's highly visible Fund balances, which give the popular impression of unbounded national wealth (Røed Larsen 2006).[27] Indeed, at the time of this writing, the populist Progress Party had been steadily gaining traction in the polls in part by promising to use more oil and gas money to improve Norway's infrastructure.

4 State–NOC relations

The key to understanding Statoil's behavior is understanding its relationship with the Norwegian state. That relationship has existed in two main modes, with an inflection point between them in the mid 1980s. All through the 1970s, the relationship was a highly political struggle for control, with Statoil CEO Arve Johnsen lobbying aggressively for advantages and the bureaucracy trying, with partial success, to check Statoil's rising power. The tide began to turn in the early 1980s, with the political parties (led by the conservatives) and bureaucracy collectively driving measures to contain Statoil by taming its cash flow and removing its licensing advantages. The installation of Harald Norvik in the top post of Statoil in 1988 ushered in a new era of corporate normalization for Statoil and increasingly arm's-length formal relations with the government.[28] This shift was driven in large part by the increasingly evident need for Statoil to unshackle itself from Norway and become commercially competitive abroad in the face of maturing Norwegian resources. At the same time, recent trends – including events surrounding the merger with Norsk Hydro's oil and gas division – have illustrated how difficult it is for Statoil to fully transcend its strong ties to Norway.

Petroleum policymakers and regulators in the government had two principal challenges from 1972 onwards: controlling Statoil and controlling the other players in the oil sector. The latter task proved easier than the former. As soon as Statoil was formed, it immediately began to press its advantage in the petroleum and political arenas. Founding Statoil CEO Arve Johnsen was formerly a deputy minister in the Labour Party, and first chairman Jens Christian Hauge was also a very powerful and prominent Labour figure. Johnsen was a brilliant political tactician who tirelessly pushed claims to the best acreage and the most beneficial terms for Statoil in license groups. With strong early support from Labour and the Ministry of Industry, Statoil was able to increase its carried interest in new exploration blocks from 35 percent at the time of its founding to 50 percent by the time of the licensing round in 1974, with an additional "sliding scale" provision for Statoil to claim an additional share of up to 30 percent after a commercial discovery had been made (Claes 2002). Thus, in effect, Johnsen created an exploration regime that concentrated investment and risk from E&P activities on the foreign players who obtained exploration blocks while appropriating a large (and growing) share of the benefit from those activities for Statoil. Johnsen curried support in Parliament by appealing to regional and popular constituencies. In addition to leveraging direct links to politicians, Johnsen was skillful throughout his tenure as CEO at developing a base of political support among other Norwegian industries by contracting out services – flights, rigs, shipping – where possible rather than supplying them in-house, even when Statoil could have afforded to do so (PESD Interviews).

The Ministry of Industry (and later the Ministry of Petroleum and Energy) had to walk the fine line of both supporting Statoil and containing it. Early Ministry officials in petroleum were aware of the potential for an NOC to become a state within a state, and they were determined to retain the upper hand in the relationship. An early test was presented by Statoil Chairman Hauge, who by 1974 was felt by officials within the Ministry to be meddling inappropriately in the political realm. Despite Hauge's being a larger-than-life figure – a Norwegian resistance leader during World War II and the Minister of Defense in the Labour government elected just after the war – the Ministry held firm and forced him to resign,[29] appointing a new chairman[30] and replacing the entire board.[31]

The Norwegian Petroleum Directorate, which started with few resources and limited knowledge, had to fight to find its role in the sector – neither Statoil nor the Ministry itself were initially all that receptive to its efforts. In addition to cajoling the IOCs and a grudging Statoil to share data and expertise,[32] the NPD increased its knowledge and capability through its own fledgling technical efforts, for example seismic surveying (Al-Kasim 2006). A key step to building capability was the ability of NPD leadership to obtain from the Ministry a separate and more generous salary structure for the NPD, which with its technical orientation was often competing directly with private industry for talent (PESD Interviews).

By the early 1980s, with Norwegian control over petroleum well established but the government's control over Statoil still dubious despite the best efforts of the Ministry and NPD, a larger chorus of voices was coming together to argue that Statoil needed to be further constrained. The group of concerned parties unsurprisingly included IOCs, who argued that Statoil's special preferences and effective veto power on field development due to its minimum

50 percent share in all the license groups was making the Norwegian operating environment unattractive (PESD Interviews). Officials within the Ministry itself were also reaching the conclusion that the government's formal separation of political and commercial roles needed to be strengthened in practice.[33] With the change to a Conservative government in 1981, the heated debate over the subject started to move towards real action; at this point, Labour realized that change was inevitable and came to the table to seek a compromise solution.

The result of the negotiations, implemented as of January 1985, was that Statoil's balance sheet was split into two, with more than half of Statoil's interests in oil and gas fields, pipelines, and other facilities transferred to the newly created State's Direct Financial Interest (SDFI) in petroleum.[34] (These reforms were widely referred to as Statoil's "wing clipping.") All revenues from SDFI shares would now be channeled directly to the state, dampening Statoil's cash flow.[35] Statoil was to continue managing the government's SDFI interests in oil and gas, so there was no direct change in operational structure. However, the company lost its ability to vote the government's shares in a license group, which, combined with some modifications to the licensing rules, eliminated its veto power over field decisions. (With the support of Parliament, the Minister could still in his role as "the General Assembly" instruct Statoil to vote all of the government's shares in a certain way, so Norway retained its control of hydrocarbon development more broadly.) Statoil lost its right to a carried interest in future concessions.

The final nail in the coffin of Statoil's period as an overt political player was the Mongstad debacle, which seemed to expose indiscipline, hubris, and excessive power within Statoil. (The former Conservative prime minister in the government that had originally approved the project, Kåre Willoch, said that Statoil's influence in parliament was so strong that no government would have stopped the project (The Economist 1987).) Recriminations over Mongstad led to Johnsen's resignation in 1988. While the Mongstad debacle provided the immediate pretext for the change, some parties involved in the process said that replacing Johnsen had already been identified by key policymakers as a necessary step towards increasing state control over the company (PESD Interviews). Various interviewees suggested that Johnsen's brilliance, energy, and political savvy were crucial to getting Statoil established but ultimately became an obstacle to the company's further development.

Whereas Statoil's strategy under Johnsen relied on playing the domestic political scene for advantage, the company's strategy starting with Norvik and continuing thereafter aimed increasingly at developing a more arm's-length relationship with the Norwegian state. Several principal factors were behind this shift. First, in a general sense, Norvik and his top managers recognized that the company's long-term survival depended on being able to compete effectively abroad, since Norwegian domestic resources were finite. Second, they believed that a stronger sense of employee identification with the company rather than with the state would improve performance. Third, they had come to feel that the close links to the state which had been useful in establishing the company were now limiting its freedom of action in a procedural sense (for example, through the inability to pursue equity-based acquisitions due to 100 percent state ownership). Fourth, with the Norwegian government now more confident of its ability to manage oil operations and revenues than it had been initially, a window had opened to allow Statoil further formal separation from the state than would have been politically possible in the 1970s. The means through which Statoil's leadership sought to evolve beyond being an arm of the Norwegian state were the development of a stronger corporate culture,[36] diversification of operations abroad (which as an additional benefit would benchmark and improve performance by exposing Statoil to international competition), and the increased deployment of formal techniques of corporate governance.

Norvik sought significant internationalization of upstream operations as one key strategy for creating more breathing room between Statoil and the Norwegian state.[37] There were three main options for Statoil: independently identify and develop positions abroad based on Statoil's geological knowledge; buy international assets from other players while also developing independent projects; or seek an experienced international partner who could share knowledge and investment risk and generally accelerate Statoil's efforts to cut its teeth internationally. After discussions with the Board, Norvik pursued the third route as offering the fastest and lowest-risk path to international operations. He unsuccessfully courted Shell[38] before a partnership with (then struggling) BP developed serendipitously through contacts with BP executive and later CEO David Simon. The addition of BP as a credible, experienced partner made it much easier for Statoil to gain approval from the Ministry for the internation-alization push (PESD Interviews). Conversely, Statoil's NOC status (which made it a complementary partner for BP) and close connection to the Norwegian government probably were advantages in helping convince BP to enter into the alliance.[39]

The Statoil–BP Alliance, which ran from 1990 to 1999, was unam-biguously successful in allowing Statoil to rapidly expand onto the world stage. Together with BP, Statoil went into upstream E&P projects in Kazakhstan, Azerbaijan, Vietnam, China, Angola, and Nigeria, although Statoil was the operator only of the Nigerian venture. Statoil later sold its assets in Kazakhstan and Vietnam, but its operations in Angola and Azerbaijan remain a mainstay for Statoil abroad, and the company's presence in Nigeria is gradually expanding.

Important benefits from the alliance beyond access to acreage included growth in Statoil's confidence to operate internationally as well as the continued refinement of a commercial culture that came from constantly rubbing elbows with an experienced global IOC. And although it was already somewhat exposed to competition on the NCS, international operations gave Statoil the first understanding of what it meant to be truly on a level playing field with the world's international majors.

A second important autonomy-seeking strategy initiated under Norvik was to put in place more formal corporate governance struc-tures, principally by partially privatizing through a share offering on a major stock exchange. On the one hand, Statoil by the late 1990s was already a commercially oriented company, and the state in gen-eral did not interfere significantly in operational decisions. At the same time, exposure in the international arena increasingly convinced Norvik and other executives at Statoil that full state ownership was holding Statoil back in more subtle ways. Listing on a stock exchange could provide full and frequent benchmarking for the company and thus aid in instilling discipline, enhancing management control, and focusing employees on common objectives, in the process furthering the development of a corporate identity distinct from Norway (PESD Interviews). There were also complaints that full state ownership lim-ited Statoil's financial freedom of action relative to international com-petitors (Ramm 2009). Statoil's ability to rapidly mobilize investment for international projects could be compromised by the six months to a year it might take to obtain parliamentary approval to access international capital markets (PESD Interviews). Mergers and acquisitions using equity were impossible as long as the state insisted on 100 percent ownership of the company. Finally, privatization offered Statoil the possibility of putting to rest persistent demands from Parliament for high dividend rates to boost revenue (PESD Interviews).

In the late 1990s, Norvik saw a window of opportunity to push partial privatization of Statoil, and he did, floating the idea at the 1999 Sandefjord Conference. This irked certain Ministry and government officials, who felt that Statoil was out of line to essentially ask for new management. At the same time, several specific factors caused the Labour government to be relatively open at the time to the possibility of partial privatization: oil prices were low, putting a premium on efficiency; the industry was restructuring around the world, with private ownership on the upswing; and the NCS was nearing its peak in oil production (PESD Interviews). More generally, having adapted over time to being a major oil-producing state (and having put in place fiscal policies to preserve the country's wealth when hydrocarbon resources began declining in the future), Norway was by this point able to relax its initial concern about maintaining complete control over oil operations.

The main formal effect of partial privatization on the NOC–government relationship was to place the government on an equal footing with minority shareholders.[40] In addition, Statoil's IPO prompted several other changes in organizational relationships to satisfy the corporate governance requirements of stock exchanges and EU rules,[41] as well as the general Norwegian preoccupation with proper delineation of roles among government entities. Among the most significant changes was the creation of a 100-percent-state-owned, non-operating company – Petoro – to be steward of the state's SDFI assets in oil and gas. (Maximizing the value of these assets for the government was previously the responsibility of a dedicated group within Statoil, but the government felt that continuing this arrangement would be incompatible with its new formal relationship with Statoil following privatization.) Petoro was given no independent income; all of its operating funds came directly from the state budget.[42]

Not all of the detailed arrangements associated with partial privatization were to Statoil's liking, demonstrating that the government (principally through the Ministry of Petroleum and Energy) maintained some degree of control over the process. The company proposed that SDFI be merged back into Statoil at the time of privatization (Ramm 2009). As it turned out, Statoil was only allowed to buy back selected SDFI assets that fortified its natural gas portfolio in order to make it more attractive to potential investors. In addition, Norway shifted control over transmission of natural gas from Statoil to a newly created company, Gassco,[43] in order to establish a framework it viewed as compatible with EU competition rules. Statoil kept the responsibility for marketing and selling the oil and gas owned by the state through the SDFI, with Petoro looking over its shoulder to make sure the selling price was correct.

Government officials and Statoil personnel themselves have usually (though not always) been quite conscientious in living up to the formal obligations of their arm's-length relationship as majority shareholder and publicly traded company. Two recent examples of government–Statoil interactions illustrate the extent of their formal separation. In the first case, the Ministry of Petroleum and Energy on the advice of the NPD ruled in October 2007 to block further development of natural gas by Statoil from the Troll field on the grounds that such activity would likely harm the ultimate oil recovery from the field (Quinlan 2007). Statoil was highly displeased based on commercial considerations[44] but was forced to accede to the Ministry's dictates.[45]

A second recent instance of state–NOC conflict, which might on the surface appear to indicate sectoral dysfunction, in fact provides among the clearest evidence that the government and Statoil are formally isolated from each other. The Norwegian government in April 2008 filed suit against Statoil for recovery of NOK 11 billion (~$2 billion) it believes it is owed by the company in connection with expansion of the Kårstø gas processing terminal between 1997 and 2000 (Platts Oilgram News 2008). As one Ministry official explains it, Statoil managers need to be diligent about not giving minority shareholders the impression they are paying off their main shareholder. For its part, the government is answerable to the State Auditor, and thus has its own obligation not to back down if it feels that it has been shortchanged (PESD Interviews).

For all the success of Statoil and the government in establishing and adhering to corporate governance frameworks that treat the company the same as any international operator, there are a number of respects in which Statoil and Norway remain as stubbornly conjoined as ever.

First, the size of Statoil's Norwegian activities, and its continued difficulty in generating substantial cash flow internationally, keep its focus inescapably on Norway. Second, personal connections within Norwegian politics still give Statoil a special ability to influence significant decisions that affect it, even though it no longer overtly throws its weight around as it did during the Johnsen era. Third, a company that looms as large in a small country as Statoil does cannot escape the influence in return of politics on its own actions, even in the absence of direct government intervention.

The sheer scale of Statoil's petroleum operations on the NCS, particularly since the merger with Norsk Hydro's petroleum division in 2007, is one factor that complicates company efforts to behave as a fully global operator. (As one reflection of this, at the time of this writing there still did not yet exist a completely unified system of ranking domestic and international projects within Statoil (PESD Interviews), although there are methods of cross-comparing investments.[46]) Statoil's international production in 2008 accounted for 24% of total equity oil and gas production (see Figure 14.12) but only 7% of net operating income, compared with 84% of net operating income that comes from domestic upstream activities. The company's massive production activities on the NCS (see Figures 14.2 and 14.3) provide the basic cash flow to fuel its business. This cash flow is on the one hand an advantage for international expansion as it can help to fund mergers and acquisitions activity – for example, Statoil's 2008 acquisition of a significant stake in the Marcellus shale gas project in the US. At the same time, it quite understandably keeps the company's center of attention squarely on Norway. (The Ministry of Petroleum and Energy is eager to diversify production operatorship on the NCS, but Statoil holds significant legacy assets and often ends up being the most compelling license applicant for new blocks, despite somewhat successful efforts by the Ministry since 2002 to involve more players in exploration.[47])

While Statoil's merger with Norsk Hydro's petroleum operations created some potential advantages for expansion abroad, it also illustrated (and in a sense reinforced) Statoil's ties to Norway. One of the rationales for the merger was that the financial resources and human talents of a merged Norwegian champion would enhance its international prospects.[48] This argument has some merit, especially given the deep pockets required to pursue international M&A or pay signature bonuses to win contracts. At the same time, some commentators have questioned why the company did not pursue international assets more directly. The government sold only 18.3 percent of its stake in Statoil in the initial IPO in 2001, with the idea that it could later sell off more to support a strategic alliance or merger that would give Statoil additional international assets. However, Statoil never availed itself of this option, instead pursuing an abortive merger with Norsk Hydro in late 2003/early 2004 before finally consummating a deal in 2007. As Claes pointed out well before either attempt (Claes 2002), an arrangement with Hydro directly offered Statoil few international assets compared with a deal involving an IOC. Ramm (2009) makes a similar point in questioning the wisdom of the 2007 merger with Hydro as a route to international expansion. Such arguments imply that Statoil was preoccupied with swallowing up its Norwegian rival rather than pursuing the best arrangement for international growth. Other commentators, however, think that Statoil was genuinely limited in its other options, including by majority state ownership and domestic political considerations standing in the way of a deal with a major international player (PESD Interviews). What is not in dispute is that the merger with Hydro significantly expanded Statoil's domestic portfolio.

The merger also revealed the extent to which personal and political connections within Norway's tight-knit governing circles can remain a significant factor in oil-related decision making. Having agreed on the merger among themselves, Statoil CEO Helge Lund and Norsk Hydro CEO Eivind Reiten directly cleared the deal with Prime Minister Jens Stoltenberg and a very small group of civil servants (those in the Ministry of Petroleum and Energy and Ministry of Industry and Trade charged with the government's ownership of Statoil and Hydro, respectively). Stoltenberg then promptly announced the merger in public and gave it his unconditional endorsement. Neither the civil servants charged with regulating oil and gas nor the Norwegian Competition Authority[49] were seriously consulted. Government authorities did go through the prescribed formal review process after Stoltenberg's announcement, but by this point his ringing endorsement of the deal had turned it into essentially a foregone conclusion.[50] By only consulting ministry officials in their ownership capacity and preempting the input of regulators, the process certainly did not fulfill the ideal of separation of regulatory and commercial functions embodied by the formal governance structures in the sector.[51]

The reverse side of Statoil's ability to influence government decisions as a "big fish in a small pond" is the way in which its own operations can be negatively influenced by Norwegian politics. These influences can play out as: 1) direct government intervention in Statoil decisions for political reasons; 2) attempts by Statoil to please political constituencies that lead to bad decisions; 3) actions by Statoil in response to government and public sentiment; and 4) political disapproval of Statoil actions that does not directly influence these actions but does create distractions for Statoil. It is important to note that these phenomena can arise around important companies in *any* country. However, Statoil's position as a major strategic player in a small country exacerbates the challenges they pose.

Fortunately for Statoil, the first type of influence – direct meddling by the government in Statoil operational decisions – is rare today, though not unheard of (one arguable example occurred in 2008 when the Minister of Petroleum and Energy pressured Statoil to source power for an oil field from a politically influential area[52]). Calibration of Statoil strategic decisions for political advantage has not been uncommon historically. An interviewee cited Statoil's location of a research center in Trondheim in the early 1990s as one example (PESD Interviews).

Statoil can feel a strong need to respond to implicit government and public pressure. Compensation decisions around the time of the merger were one example. A flurry of public attention to how Norsk Hydro executives had profited (entirely legally) from share options in the run-up to the merger led to new government guidelines on compensation for Norwegian partially or fully state-owned companies. These guidelines caused Statoil to shelve proposed employee stock incentive plans (PESD Interviews). The government's guidelines did not constitute a direct instruction to the Statoil board as a shareholder, but they nevertheless impacted the company's policies. Statoil's engagement in other countries may at times be affected by government and public pressure, although the exact impacts can be difficult to assess. Regulators and the press are certainly quick to seize upon any hint of malfeasance abroad.[53] For example, a 2003 bribery incident in Iran, which led to the departure of Statoil CEO Olav Fjell, might have set back Statoil's efforts at the time to engage with NIOC (PESD Interviews).

Norwegian politics can generate a lot of sound and fury around Statoil activities even when it ultimately has no direct influence on decisions. Statoil's investments in oil sands in Canada have attracted particular ire from politicians and Norway's influential environmental movement. Some members of parliament have forcefully stated that Statoil should not be participating in such projects because of their potential climate change impacts. Such individual views have not yet led to any direct interference in Statoil's commercial choices on this matter – the Ministry of Petroleum and Energy voted down a May 2009 shareholder resolution that would have instructed Statoil not to invest in oil sands. (The Norwegian environmental movement has likely had a more significant effect on Statoil's operations in an indirect way by helping slow the pace at which the government opens new areas on the NCS for exploration.) At the same time, the political cacophony can be confusing to minority shareholders, who may not grasp the distinction between political figures speaking on behalf of the government as Statoil owner and speaking as private citizens. Statoil needs to devote significantly more time and resources to responding to political noise (including to manage staff morale) than its IOC brethren (PESD Interviews), in the process strengthening its ties to Norway even as it needs to focus more energy abroad.

As long as petroleum remains central to Norway's economy, it is difficult to see that the resonance of Statoil as a political issue will diminish significantly. The existence of a dominant NOC with majority state ownership can provide politicians with the satisfying illusion that they control the critical petroleum sector, even when their direct influence over the company's actions is in fact tightly circumscribed by governance rules. One irony is that the merger probably enhanced politicians' perceived control, as Norway's overall stake in NCS operations is now larger, while reducing the government's actual control by diminishing its regulatory leverage, especially its ability to stimulate competition. Nevertheless, the durable political attraction of this perceived sense of control is one reason why the state seems unlikely to significantly reduce its stake in Statoil in the near future.[54]

5 Statoil's performance and strategy

Statoil can be assessed on the one hand as a domestic champion intended to serve broad purposes of Norwegian petroleum and economic development, and on the other hand as a profit-maximizing enterprise in competition with major IOCs and benefiting Norway principally through its tax and dividend payments. As the rest of this study has discussed, the emphasis on how the government sees the company has shifted over time from the former role to the latter role, although elements of both views are still present. Company strategy has shifted accordingly. In the 1970s and 1980s, Statoil took advantage of the government's emphasis on national control of petroleum and industrial development to push for privileged access to NCS resources and chances to "learn by doing" in early operatorship opportunities. As NCS resources began to mature and Norway relaxed into its status as a petroleum state, Statoil increasingly sought to assure its future by becoming competitive on the global stage. Apart from some efforts to leverage its NOC heritage at the margins, Statoil's strategy today appears quite similar to that of a major IOC, albeit one with an out-size domestic footprint.

We start this section by considering the degree to which Statoil has succeeded in becoming a competitive global player as measured by standard hydrocarbon and financial indicators. After that we turn our attention to Statoil's historical performance in the less-easily meas-ured function of national champion – in particular, to the role the company has played in helping to develop Norwegian technological and industrial capability more generally. A theme of our observations is that there has been a trade-off at times between short-run eco-nomic efficiency and actions that have supported the development of the Norwegian oil sector and services industry over the longer term.

In the years following its IPO, Statoil's financial and market per-formance were strong. The company's net income and stock price climbed steadily through 2007 (Figure 14.8) alongside oil prices. The financial crisis and decreasing oil prices hit both in late 2008. Combined equity oil and gas production of Statoil in 2008 was 1.9 million boe per day.

However, Statoil as a company now faces maturing resources on its critical home turf of the NCS (Figure 14.4). The Norwegian Petroleum Directorate (2009b) predicts that overall petroleum production on the NCS will remain steady until around 2020 before declining after that, with the share of gas production steadily increasing. Exploration success rates on the NCS have steadily improved over the years, and exploration activity has increased since 2004, but new petroleum

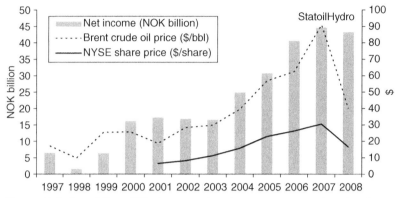

Figure 14.8 Statoil/StatoilHydro annual net income, compared against Brent crude oil spot price (December average) and Statoil NYSE share price (STO, as of December 31). (For comparison, BP net income in 2008 was equivalent to NOK 122 billion; ExxonMobil net income in 2008 was equivalent to NOK 255 billion.)

Source: Statoil/StatoilHydro annual reports (www.statoil.com/en/InvestorCentre/Pages/default.aspx); BP (2009a, 2009b); ExxonMobil (2009).

discoveries have become progressively smaller (Norwegian Petroleum Directorate 2009b). Larger discoveries may still be possible in large tracts of acreage – including parts of the Barents Sea and coastal areas of the Norwegian Sea – that have not yet been opened to exploration by the government in the face of environmental and fisheries opposition.

Mirroring these trends, Statoil's domestic output has reached a plateau, and oil production in particular is in decline (Figure 14.9). International production is generally increasing (Figure 14.10) but struggles to keep pace with falling output on the NCS. International reserves generation through exploration or acquisitions has so far been insufficient to counter the decline in NCS reserves, resulting in a steadily falling reserves-to-production ratio (Figure 14.11). Overall, both Statoil and Hydro struggled on the exploration front leading up to the merger. Statoil's exploration results may be looking up of late with several recent discoveries on the NCS and a partner-operated deep water find in Angola.

Given the finite (though still appreciable) remaining resource base of the NCS, Statoil's efforts to expand internationally take on particular urgency. In 2008, international equity production constituted 24 percent of Statoil's total production, although it was responsible for

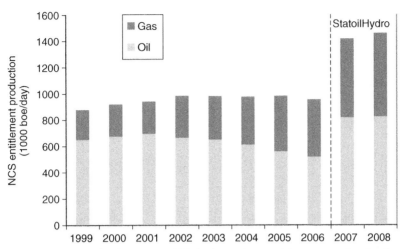

Figure 14.9 Statoil's domestic (NCS) hydrocarbon entitlement production by type, 1999–2008.

Source: Statoil/StatoilHydro annual reports (www.statoil.com/en/InvestorCentre/ Pages/default.aspx).

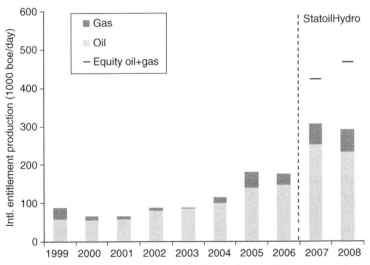

Figure 14.10 Statoil's international hydrocarbon entitlement production by type. Equity production data points (combined oil and gas) are also shown for StatoilHydro in 2007 and 2008.

Source: Statoil/StatoilHydro annual reports (www.statoil.com/en/InvestorCentre/ Pages/default.aspx).

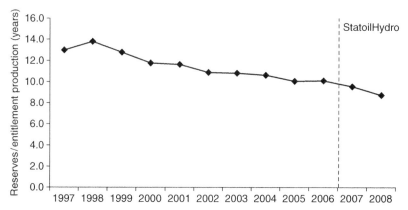

Figure 14.11 Statoil's reserves-to-production ratio (combined oil and gas, uses entitlement figures for production), 1999–2008.
Source: Statoil/StatoilHydro annual reports (www.statoil.com/en/InvestorCentre/Pages/default.aspx).

only 7 percent of net operating income compared with 84 percent of net operating income contributed by NCS production (Figure 14.12). Statoil's results in expanding international production over the last decade have been mixed. The majority of production still comes from operations in Angola and Azerbaijan that date from the BP alliance (Figure 14.13). At the same time, there are good prospects for growth in the coming years on the back of projects in deep water Angola, the US Gulf of Mexico, Brazil, Canada, US onshore, the UK, and Nigeria (Wood Mackenzie 2010).

Statoil's technological competence (see discussion later in this section) and formal autonomy from the government have enabled it to pursue an international growth strategy that looks remarkably like that of the major IOCs. Statoil attempts to compete in international frontiers that play to its strengths (for example, oil sands in Canada, shale gas in the US, heavy oil in Venezuela and Brazil, arctic offshore gas in Russia, deep water in the US Gulf of Mexico and Angola), while managing political relationships along the way to open acreage and keep it open. Since partial privatization, the company has become more coherent in trying to leverage its particular technological strengths to support international expansion. A number of the company's specialties have grown out of the characteristic rigors of

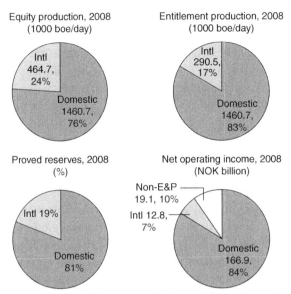

Figure 14.12 Relative contribution of domestic and international hydrocarbons to Statoil production, reserves, and net operating income.
Source: StatoilHydro Annual Report 2008.

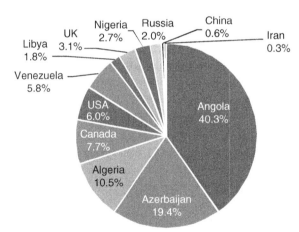

Figure 14.13 Sources of Statoil international equity production in 2008. Total international equity production was 464,300 barrels of oil equivalent per day.
Source: StatoilHydro Annual Report 2008.

operations on the NCS, including its talents in deep water technology (even though NCS resources themselves are no longer considered to be that deep), operations in harsh environments, and integration of complex value chains for natural gas. The company has also developed strong expertise over the years in enhanced oil recovery, which can be a selling point abroad as well as on the maturing NCS. A final area of perceived advantage, producing and refining heavy oil, which is key to the important Peregrino field development in Brazil, developed on the Hydro legacy side from experience with the Grane heavy oil field on the NCS and on the Statoil legacy side from the Sincor partnership in Venezuela which started in the late 1990s. New investments today are scrutinized more carefully against the company's core competencies than were past ones. For example, Statoil's reentry into the Gulf of Mexico in 2005 through the purchase of Encana's deep water assets was more carefully considered than its original foray into the Gulf of Mexico in shallow water developments where it held less of a comparative advantage (PESD Interviews).

Even as it deploys an IOC-like strategy, Statoil has tried where possible to use its NOC heritage to gain a competitive edge abroad. In theory, it should have some advantages in convincing resource-rich governments that it would be a good partner. Statoil has historically shown more willingness than major IOCs to enter into the service contracts and other non-equity arrangements – for example in Iran, Iraq, and Russia – that are often preferred by host countries. Still unclear is the degree to which Statoil can gain access to international acreage by convincing host countries and their NOCs that Norway's successful experience and its own NOC heritage give it a unique ability to understand and help meet the development needs of these countries. According to Willy Olsen, Statoil has, as part of this strategy, engaged in efforts to strengthen and leverage its linkages to Sonatrach, NIOC, Pemex, Petrobras, PDVSA, and Saudi Aramco. However, even if this strategy proves successful in certain instances, it is a difficult one for Statoil to employ on a large scale,[55] especially as more resource-rich countries have moved to using auctions to allocate exploration blocks. Statoil's focus in recent years on acquisitions in the US, including the Encana purchase mentioned above and the 2008 acquisition of a stake in the Marcellus Shale, seem to suggest that it recognizes that strategic investment and project execution are at

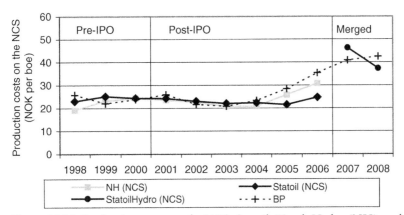

Figure 14.14 Production costs on the NCS: Statoil, Norsk Hydro (NH), and StatoilHydro, with BP global production cost as a benchmark. 2007 data for StatoilHydro includes some significant merger-related costs.
Source: Wolf and Pollitt (2009), based on data from company SFAS 69 disclosures for Statoil and Norsk Hydro; StatoilHydro annual reports (www.statoil.com/en/ InvestorCentre/AnnualReport/Pages/default.aspx).

least as important to its success abroad as efforts to gain preferential resource access by leveraging its NOC status.

Statoil's cost discipline seems to have improved in recent years. The logical benchmark for Statoil's cost performance is that of other international and Norwegian companies operating on the NCS – particularly, before 2007, Norsk Hydro. (Indeed, one of the problems in assessing Statoil's operating efficiency since the merger is the lack of the ideal benchmark formerly provided by Hydro.) As part of a social cost-benefit analysis (SCBA) of the effects of Statoil's partial privatization, Wolf and Pollitt (2009) have done the most detailed analysis of this type. Wolf and Pollitt find that Statoil's production costs (Figure 14.14) and finding and development costs on the NCS pre-IPO were comparable to, or perhaps worse than, Norsk Hydro, but that Statoil's relative performance improved in the run-up to the IPO and beyond. Wolf and Pollitt's analysis implies that Statoil's privatization made the company more efficient. Our interviews anecdotally support the finding that Statoil's partial privatization motivated some strategic decisions in the run-up to the IPO aimed at containing costs, including the sale of Statoil's assets in Kazakhstan, Vietnam, and the Gulf of

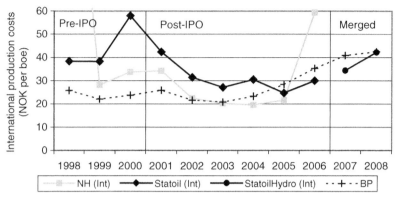

Figure 14.15 Production costs internationally: Statoil, Norsk Hydro (NH), and StatoilHydro, with BP global production cost as a benchmark.
Source: Wolf and Pollitt (2009), based on data from company SFAS 69 disclosures for Statoil and Norsk Hydro; StatoilHydro annual reports (www.statoil.com/en/InvestorCentre/AnnualReport/Pages/default.aspx).

Mexico (PESD Interviews). A drop in Statoil's international production costs around the time of the IPO is evident from Figure 14.15.

We argue that the development of cutting-edge technological capability has over most of Statoil's history been emphasized over cost minimization and the creation of a lean organization. These priorities reflected Statoil's role as a tool for achieving broader government goals for the sector including intensive technology transfer to Norway, high employment, and maximum oil and gas recovery from fields on the NCS. A comparison between Statoil, Norsk Hydro, and Brazil's NOC Petrobras highlights how a company's relationship with the state can affect corporate culture. Norsk Hydro was a preexisting industrial player that was not viewed as a government policy vehicle to the same degree as Statoil, although it did have strong political connections as well. With a long industrial culture that included exposure to the rigors of competition, Hydro was innovative on the NCS but also more focused on the bottom line than Statoil, leading it to be relatively more risk averse (and prudent) in technology development. The development trajectory of Brazil's Petrobras (see Chapter 12), on the other hand, was more similar to that of Statoil. Both Petrobras and Statoil faced domestic resources that were difficult to exploit and took full advantage of their privileged positions as national champions to develop the technological capabilities needed to do so at low risk to themselves. With the advantage of full state backing, neither company developed into a particularly lean organization.

Government support of Statoil certainly helped accelerate its technology learning. One avenue through which the government directly contributed to Statoil's development of technical expertise was by supporting its push for early operatorship on several key fields. In the case of Gullfaks, the government granted Statoil a "golden block" in 1978, in the face of some grumbling by the IOCs; this translated into the company's first production operatorship in 1981. The second critical support for Statoil of this type involved transferring operatorship of Statfjord from Mobil to Statoil in 1987.[56] This handover almost certainly occurred earlier than could have been justified on purely competitive grounds (PESD Interviews). For Statoil, there was no substitute for "learning by doing," and government support thus proved important in accelerating development of the company's technical competence, although at some expense in increased cost. Statoil was partnered with IOCs in almost all license groups, which provided both the opportunity to learn from IOCs and the advantage of mitigating risk.

The government arguably supported Statoil's innovative mentality and long-term outlook to an even greater degree by implicitly granting Statoil nearly full discretion over its cash flow combined with ready access to capital and a soft budget constraint (PESD Interviews). As a fully state-backed enterprise, Statoil never faced the threat of bankruptcy or takeover, and there were relatively limited repercussions to personnel (except perhaps at the CEO and Board level) in the event of failures. These conditions were ideal for encouraging risk taking. Time and again, Statoil attempted projects that were massively ambitious in technology and scope. One result was fast-moving technology development. Statoil's notched pioneering successes, for example, in undersea pipeline development (notably, Statpipe), improved oil recovery (for example, on Gullfaks and Statfjord), subsea installations (for example, on Gullfaks and Norne), and CCS (Sleipner). A side effect of this prodigious appetite for technological risk, however, was costs and timetables that could on occasion spiral out of control. Statoil attracted fierce domestic criticism for several high-profile projects that ultimately pushed technological limits in challenging environments but along the way experienced problems leading to severe cost overruns. The principal examples were the Mongstad refinery in the 1980s, the Åsgard field in the 1990s, and the Snøhvit project in recent years.

It should be noted that cost overruns on the NCS pre-dated Statoil's operation of projects: the Ekofisk, Frigg, and Statfjord fields all ran into cost overrun problems in the 1970s (Al-Kasim 2006). These earlier overruns on IOC-operated projects were generally attributed to the pioneering character of the projects as the first forays into the challenging conditions of the North Sea as well as Norwegian local content preferences which pushed up costs – the so-called "Norwegian Cost Factor."[57] Nevertheless, we believe that some part of the cost and project management problems that occurred on Statoil's watch can legitimately be attributed to the company's prioritization of innovation over a more commercial approach to risk management. Characteristically, the company would favor novel solutions over established ones in these projects,[58] which was terrific for learning but also often the root cause of problems: for instance, the decision to do a major retrofit of a refinery acquired from BP in Mongstad instead of selecting cheaper, safer options in Germany or Sweden; or, in the case of Snøhvit, the use of a relatively untested LNG plant design instead of tried-and-true alternatives.[59] Not all of the fault lay with Statoil's risky choices; the Mongstad case was an example of how political complexities could be layered on top of Statoil's technical decisions. Both Statoil and Hydro were originally asked by the government to consider jointly implementing the Mongstad refinery upgrade, but it would have been more difficult for Statoil to pull out of the project and pursue foreign refining options as Hydro did.

Norsk Hydro saw the same NCS geology as Statoil but developed a different organizational culture in accordance with its different historical relationship to the state. Hydro was also considered to be innovative in petroleum – among its biggest successes was the development of the thin oil layer in the Troll gas field (PESD Interviews) – but in general it was viewed as less bold and also more attentive to managing project costs and execution than Statoil. Hydro's perception of excessive risk was one commercial reason it pulled out of the Mongstad refinery upgrade. Hydro was minority state-owned until the early 1970s, and it had developed a strong industrial engineering orientation through its diverse manufacturing activities (PESD Interviews). Statoil, fully state-owned at birth, did not have the chance to develop an independent business-oriented culture at the outset. Hydro had a significant political base of support, particularly within the Conservative Party though also through linkages of its unions to Labour, but it did not have the same entitled status as Statoil. The combination of its stronger business legacy and the perception that it was less politically protected probably contributed to Hydro's greater prudence in project management.

At the same time, it was precisely Statoil's ability to pursue projects that non-state-backed players might have shied away from that helped it play a key role (though far from the only one[60]) in achieving the government's goal of maximizing domestic benefits from development of a world-leading industry in petroleum, even at the cost of short-term rent collection.[61] Statoil's key role in developing Norwegian gas infrastructure illustrates this point. As Willy Olsen describes, Norway came face-to-face with the threat of limited gas sales options when the British government in 1985 indicated it would refuse gas from the Sleipner East field. Statoil served both to buffer the impact on the Norwegian petroleum industry with a replacement project (a third platform on Gullfaks) and ultimately to provide a dependable route to Norwegian landfall of natural gas through development of the Statpipe gas pipeline (on time and on budget) from Statfjord to Kårstø. IOCs, recounts Olsen, had been unwilling to take on the pipeline project in the face of the technical obstacles posed by crossing the Norwegian trench. Even Statoil's expansion of the Mongstad refinery, for all its problems in development, eventually became a significant asset for Norway.

In the way that it served as a driver of the development of the domestic petroleum industry, Statoil is remarkably similar to Petrobras, another leader in subsea technologies, which similarly benefited from both challenging geology at home and ample government support. Statoil officials themselves cite Petrobras as the company most similar to Statoil in corporate culture. (Probably not coincidentally, in addition to their similar histories as innovators, neither company has traditionally been known for a particularly efficient organizational structure.) Both Statoil and Petrobras created strategic R&D operations to a greater degree than IOCs, which almost always subordinated their R&D efforts within commercially oriented project teams (PESD Interviews). Such long-term R&D was expensive but led to numerous technological breakthroughs as previously described.

Some observers worry that Statoil may be losing its longer-term perspective on technology development as market pressures since partial privatization encourage it to emulate its private competitors in prioritizing R&D more closely in accordance with near-term commercial benefit (PESD Interviews). Such concerns have grown more acute since the merger between Statoil and Norsk Hydro, as technology competition between the former rivals used to play an important role in advancing the state of the art on the NCS. These trends could negatively impact the Norwegian supply industry, which developed its worldwide competitive advantages in part on the back of long-range technology investments by Statoil, aided by a competitive dynamic in which both Statoil and Hydro would partner with distinct suppliers. The supply industry also benefited significantly from explicit local content preferences in early licensing,[62] which according to Storting Report No. 53 increased the Norwegian share of services delivered to petroleum operations from 28 percent in 1975 to 62 percent in 1978 (Al-Kasim 2006). Such high levels of local content persist to this day.

6 Conclusion: the path forward

Statoil and the Norwegian state both face significant challenges moving forward. For Statoil, the key question is how rapidly the company can evolve into a truly global player while continuing to keep domestic production high for as long as possible. This means growing reserves through improved domestic exploration results (ideally helped along by government willingness to open more areas) as well as through both strategic M&A and organic exploration efforts abroad. And of course Statoil must procure financial terms for international operations that allow it to turn production into profits. Statoil's innovative character is one of its great strengths in confronting these challenges but by itself will not be enough to assure the company's global competitiveness. Like its competitors, the company will have to continually find the right ways to meld technological leadership with hard-headed strategic decision making and efficient execution.

The degree to which Statoil's NOC heritage will prove a significant competitive advantage in international operations is still very much an open question. Tellingly, perhaps, much of Statoil's international expansion in recent years has been through strategic M&A activity that does not depend on any privileged position in closed markets, most notably its acquisitions in the deep water US Gulf of Mexico, oil sands in Canada, and shale gas in the US (Wood Mackenzie 2010a). While Statoil has many interactions with other NOCs, especially through cooperative technology agreements (most significantly with Petrobras), there are few cases thus far in which Statoil's privileged relations with other NOCs have proved obviously decisive in enabling it to clinch access to resources. One example where being an NOC might have put Statoil on a privileged track was in Algeria. BP was looking for a joint venture partner, and some interviewees felt that BP chose Statoil without considering other candidates because Statoil's good relations with Sonatrach would make the Algerian NOC's approval of the deal straightforward. On the other hand, one interviewee suggested that Statoil might have overpaid for the deal, and that the relations between Statoil's head of international E&P at the time, an ex-BP employee, and his former company might have been at least as important as the links between Statoil and Sonatrach (PESD Interviews). Other examples are equally ambiguous. Being an NOC could have given Statoil some edge in being elected a partner with Total and Gazprom in the Shtokman project. Statoil may also have benefited from efforts by the respective governments of arctic neighbors Norway and Russia to build relations. (Of course, large oil companies can benefit from their countries' diplomatic efforts whether or not they are NOCs.) At the same time, Statoil's experience with natural gas in harsh, deep water environments made it a logical choice anyway. As in the Algeria case, some argued that the contract terms were not so desirable, although IOC Total proved willing to accept them as well (PESD Interviews).

For Norway, whose petroleum resources are still far from dead, the challenge going forward is fundamentally the same as it has always been: how to maintain control over petroleum resource development and best use the resulting revenues for the benefit of Norwegian society. Norway has demonstrated impressive prudence in managing its petroleum riches so far, but political pressures to do otherwise are perhaps growing and are unlikely to disappear. As for control of the NCS resource itself, the disappearance of Norsk Hydro's presence in petroleum certainly complicates the job of the civil servants who have helped keep Norway's oil administration on an even keel so far. Synergies on the NCS were one valid justification for the merger, but the converse of this potential benefit was the creation of a dominant player that operated around 80 percent of the oil and natural gas

production on the NCS. The three principal Norwegian oil companies of the 1970s, already winnowed to two with the takeover of Saga
Petroleum by Hydro in 1999 (Nore 2003; Ramm 2009), were reduced
by the merger to only one. Competition between Statoil and Hydro on
the NCS, and the accompanying ability of state authorities to compare two distinct Norwegian points of view on oil and gas development solutions, was always the most effective check on the domestic
performance of Statoil. IOC licensees could in theory have played
a similar role but in practice often held back for fear of irritating
politically powerful Statoil; Hydro, with its own domestic political
base, did not have this concern. Now this critical balance has been
removed, which will truly test the ability of Petoro, the NPD, and the
Ministry of Petroleum and Energy to maintain leverage over the sector.[63] Specific concerns include the impact of decreased competition
on the efficiency of Statoil's NCS operations and pace of projects as
well as the effect of Statoil's near-monopsony buyer position on the
vibrancy of the Norwegian supply industry. Possible policy responses
could include efforts to increase the role of IOCs on the NCS to the
extent that is politically feasible and to further incentivize small companies to expand their contribution. Norway has responded creatively
to imbalances on the oil patch before; time will tell how it adapts to
this one.

Appendix: the Ten Commandments for the Norwegian oil sector, authors' translation. Source: Norwegian Parliament 1971

In accordance with the government's view that an oil policy should be
developed with the aim of ensuring that the natural resources on the Norwegian Continental Shelf are exploited for the benefit of the whole society,
the committee prescribes:

1) National management and control of all operations on the NCS be
   ensured.
2) Petroleum discoveries on the NCS be exploited so as to make Norway
   as independent as possible with regards to supply of crude oil.
3) A new industry based on petroleum be developed.
4) The development of a petroleum industry occur with due consideration
   for existing industry and the natural environment.
5) The flaring of gas not be allowed except for short testing periods.

6) Petroleum from the NCS should as a general rule be landed in Norway except in cases where socio-political considerations dictate another solution.

7) The state involve itself at all appropriate levels to coordinate Norwegian interests within the Norwegian petroleum industry and to create an integrated Norwegian oil community.

8) An NOC be established to attend to the government's commercial interests and to facilitate cooperation with domestic and foreign oil interests.

9) Activities north of the sixty-second parallel be compatible with the distinct socio-political conditions in that region of the country.

10) It be understood that Norwegian petroleum discoveries will present new tasks for Norwegian foreign policy.

Notes

The authors wish to specially acknowledge the following people for their extraordinary contributions to the study: Willy Olsen, Hans Henrik Ramm, and Øystein Noreng, for truly heroic and generous work in reviewing this study and providing detailed commentaries based on their own long experiences observing and participating in Norwegian petroleum development; Pål Eitrheim and Ivar Tangen, for their own insightful perspectives as well as invaluable assistance in arranging interviews; Klaus Mohn, for providing several valuable suggestions for improvement; Christian Wolf, for overall feedback on the study and specific suggestions regarding company data; Francisco Monaldi, for helpful ideas about "separation of functions"; Emily Wang, for helping to put together the Norway map; Varun Kishore Kumar, for assistance with NCS data analysis; and David Hults, Pete Nolan, and David Victor, for detailed comments on the text. We also gratefully acknowledge the many people we interviewed for this research (listed in alphabetical order): Mette K. Gravdahl Agerup (Assistant Director General, Oil and Gas Department, Ministry of Petroleum and Energy), June 17, 2009, Oslo, Norway; Farouk Al-Kasim (President, Petroteam AS Resource Management Consultancy; former Director of Resource Management, Norwegian Petroleum Directorate, 1973–1990), August 11, 2008, Stavanger, Norway; Johan Alstad (Deputy Director General, Department for Economic and Administrative Affairs, Ministry of Petroleum and Energy), August 15, 2008, Oslo, Norway; Elisabeth Berge (Permanent Secretary, Ministry of Petroleum and Energy), June 15, 2009, Oslo, Norway; Bjarte Bogsnes (Performance Management, Statoil ASA), August 11, 2008, Stavanger, Norway; Jan Bydevoll (Director, Forecasting Analyses and Data, Norwegian Petroleum Directorate), August

12, 2008, Stavanger, Norway; Pål Eitrheim (Head of CEO's Office, Statoil ASA), August 11, 2008, Stavanger, Norway; Nils-Henrik M. von der Fehr (Professor, University of Oslo; Member of the Board of Petoro AS), June 11, 2009, Oslo, Norway; Nils Gulnes (Attorney, Grette Advokatfirma DA; former Chairman of the Board, Amerada Hess Norge AS, 1999–2003; former Deputy Director General, Oil Department, Ministry of Industry, 1965–1973), August 13, 2008, Oslo, Norway; Gunnar Hognestad (Deputy Director General, Oil and Gas Department, Ministry of Petroleum and Energy), June 17, 2009, Oslo, Norway; Einar Hope (Professor, Norwegian School of Economics and Business Administration; former Director, Norwegian Competition Authority), June 15, 2009, Oslo, Norway; Martine Linge Johnsen (Higher Executive Office, Oil and Gas Department, Ministry of Petroleum and Energy), June 17, 2009, Oslo, Norway; Johannes Kjøde (Director, Production and Operations, Norwegian Petroleum Directorate), August 12, 2008, Stavanger, Norway; Rolf Magne Larsen (Vice President, International Exploration and Production, Statoil ASA), August 13, 2008, Oslo, Norway; Ole Anders Lindseth (Ministry of Petroleum and Energy), August 15, 2008, Oslo, Norway; Per Gunnar Løge (Owner, Løge Resources AS; former CEO, Ener Petroleum ASA; former CEO, OER Oil AS), June 16, 2009, Oslo, Norway; Karl-Edwin Manshaus (Manager Government & Public Affairs Europe and West Africa, ConocoPhillips; former Permanent Secretary, Ministry of Petroleum and Energy), August 14, 2008 and June 17, 2009, Oslo, Norway; A. Bjarne Moe (Director General, Oil and Gas Department, Ministry of Petroleum and Energy), August 15, 2008 and June 15, 2009, Oslo, Norway; Klaus Mohn (Statoil ASA; former Head of CEO's office, Statoil, 2003–2005), August 11, 2008, Stavanger, Norway; Peter Mellbye (Executive Vice President, International Exploration and Production, Statoil ASA), August 12, 2008, Stavanger Norway; Øystein Noreng (Professor, Norwegian School of Management), June 12, 2009, Oslo, Norway; Harald Norvik (Partner, Econ-Pöyry; former CEO, Statoil, 1988–1999), August 14, 2008, Oslo, Norway; Ariwoola Ogbemi (Business Development Manager, Statoil Nigeria), September 19, 2008, Lagos, Nigeria; Willy Olsen (Advisor, INTSOK Norwegian Oil and Gas Partners; former Senior Vice President, Government and Public Affairs, Statoil; former Head of CEO's Office, Statoil; former Managing Director, Statoil-BP Alliance), August 13, 2008 and June 12, 2009, Oslo, Norway; Hans Henrik Ramm (journalist, author, and manager, Ramm Kommunikasjon; former Deputy Minister of Petroleum and Energy, Ministry of Finance; former Political Advisor on Petroleum Issues, Ministry of Finance; former Member of Parliament; former Political Advisor for the Conservative Party's group in Parliament with responsibility for petroleum, energy, and finance), June 11, 2009, Oslo, Norway; Jon Saglie (Assistant Director

General, Oil and Gas Department, Ministry of Petroleum and Energy), June 17, 2009, Oslo, Norway; Tore Sandvold (Chairman, Sandvold Energy AS; former Chairman of the Board, Petoro AS, 2001–2002; formerly held various positions in Ministry of Industry / Ministry of Petroleum and Energy), August 13, 2008, Oslo, Norway; Arild Selvig (Director, New Markets and Business Development, FMC Technologies), June 16, 2009, Asker, Norway; Ivar Tangen (Secretary General, Energy Policy Foundation of Norway), April 14, 2008, Palo Alto, California, USA; Runar Tjersland (Head of Strategy, Natural Gas, Statoil ASA), August 11, 2008, Stavanger, Norway; Johan Nic Vold (Chairman, Gassnova AS; former CEO, Norsk Shell; former executive, Statoil), August 14, 2008, Oslo, Norway. These acknowledgements do not imply any endorsement of our conclusions, and any errors are ours alone.

1 The company became StatoilHydro with its merger with the petroleum operations of Norsk Hydro in 2007 and then reverted to the Statoil moniker in November 2009. We here use the Statoil name to refer to all incarnations of the company, except in cases where we specifically want to distinguish between the company before and right after the merger with Norsk Hydro.

2 Wells offshore of Norway are no longer considered to be at the frontier for water depth, but the years during which they were near the frontier, particularly given the challenging weather to which they were exposed, pushed Norwegian firms to develop leading technologies for the combination of deep water and harsh conditions.

3 The Norwegian Continental Shelf (NCS) constitutes the entire offshore region over which Norway has resource sovereignty. It includes parts of the North Sea, Norwegian Sea, and Barents Sea. As described in section 2, the extent of the NCS was determined through international negotiations to extend to the median line between Norway and other bordering countries in both the North Sea and Norwegian Sea. The exact border with Russia in the Barents Sea was still under dispute at the time of writing.

4 The plan outlined by Nigeria's Oil and Gas Reform Implementation Committee (OGIC) as of 2008 proposed recreating NNPC as a fully commercial entity like Statoil; rolling out a focused policymaking body (the Nigerian Petroleum Directorate) analogous to Norway's Ministry of Petroleum and Energy; empowering an autonomous regulator (the Nigerian Petroleum Inspectorate) that parallels the Norwegian Petroleum Directorate; and even creating a government agency to oversee state investment in the sector (the National Petroleum Assets Management Agency), echoing the role of government-owned company Petoro in Norway.

5 Arve Johnsen in fact had international designs for Statoil from the start, but government resistance did not permit such a strategy during his tenure.

6 The Geneva Convention, which Norway had not yet ratified at that point, defined a nation's resource sovereignty as extending into its adjoining seabed up to the maximum depth at which resource exploitation was feasible, and not further than the median line between countries. Because the Convention defined this maximum depth as 200 meters and the Norwegian Trench cuts through the continental shelf to a depth of more than 700 meters, there was wariness from the Norwegian side that a strict interpretation of the Convention could dramatically restrict the country's area of resource sovereignty. With this in mind, skillful Norwegian negotiators in the Ministry of Foreign Affairs were able to first obtain acceptance of the median-line principle from the UK in March 1965 and then subsequently from Denmark in December of the same year (Al-Kasim 2006). Norway's lack of pressing economic need for hydrocarbon revenues probably put it at a substantial advantage in negotiations with the UK, which was much more anxious to quickly resolve any disputes to enable development to proceed (Noreng 1980).

7 Nils Gulnes was hired out of law school into the Ministry of Industry at the beginning of 1965 as the first government employee dedicated full-time to petroleum. As Gulnes recalls, his recruiters sought someone with a legal background, ability in English, and interest in working with "something called oil" – specific knowledge of petroleum regulation would have to be learned on the job (PESD Interviews).

8 Britain, which had just licensed 374 offshore blocks in September 1964 (Hardman 2003), was an obvious role model right across the North Sea median line. Angus Beckett, Undersecretary at the British Ministry of Power, proved an important mentor to the Norwegians (PESD Interviews). The young Norwegian officials in the Ministry studied the Dutch and German experiences as well; they were also given free rein to travel further afield to understand how other countries managed their petroleum sectors. Petroleum employee No. 5 at the Ministry of Industry, Karl-Edwin Manshaus, who later became Permanent Secretary (the top civil service position) at the Ministry of Petroleum and Energy, recalls trips to Baton Rouge, Houston, Iran, and other parts of the Middle East soon after he started work.

9 This group included key players Carl August Fleischer, Leif Terje Løddesøl, and Nils Gulnes in addition to Evensen.

10 Lessons from each licensing round were incorporated into the design of the next one, and officials showed impressive ingenuity in working

around gaps in their own knowledge until the gaps could be closed. For example, after winners of the 1965 license round were selected, the civil servants managing oil were faced with the challenge of evaluating the work programs of the successful licensees, despite having no independent technical capability to do so. This challenge was overcome by using the number of bids received for a given block as a proxy for the desirability of the block, and then judging the ambition of a proffered work plan in accordance with this metric (Al-Kasim 2006).

11 According to Nils Gulnes, who started at the Ministry of Industry in 1965 as the first employee working full-time on petroleum: "The politicians were not interested at all until Ekofisk. That gave us [early Ministry officials] five years to get it right ... After 1969, people interfered more. The benefit was that we knew so much more [by then]. The parliament asked us to teach. The government asked us to teach" (PESD Interviews).

12 Principal partners in the Petronord Group were Norsk Hydro, Elf Aquitaine, and Total, with several other French companies participating as well. Petronord had acquired its shares in exploration block 2/4, in which Ekofisk was found, through a swap with the Phillips Group (Phillips, Petrofina, and Agip) (Al-Kasim 2006).

13 The decision in late 1970 to boost the state's share in Norsk Hydro made it seem as though that company would become the state's principal commercial tool in petroleum. However, as will be discussed later, the new government that came to power in 1971 decided instead to create an entirely new NOC in the form of Statoil.

14 Stavanger, on the southwest coast of Norway, was the home of Statoil and became a major center for the country's petroleum industry. The NPD's physical separation from the Ministry and the rest of the government in Oslo may have helped contribute to its independence.

15 The Ministry of Petroleum and Energy was created in 1978 to focus solely on petroleum affairs. In 2004, regulatory responsibility for safety was split out from the NPD into a new body, the Petroleum Safety Authority, which reports to the Ministry of Labor and Social Inclusion.

16 The Mongstad incident involved a cost overrun of over NOK 6 billion on a NOK 8 billion project to expand the capacity of the formerly BP-owned refinery. The Norwegian press pounced on the excess spending, computing how the money might otherwise have been allocated, for example on hospital beds (Oil and Gas Journal 1988; The Economist 1989).

17 Parliamentary Report No. 25 expressed this intent, stating: "It is not primarily a question of stimulating industry to undertake deliveries on a large scale, but to ensure that Norwegian industry should engage itself in those sectors where there are possibilities for building-up expertise

and for further development. Importance will be attached to enabling Norwegian industry to join in technological developments, so that the country will be competitive in other fields as well when the era dominated by oil activities in this country has ended" (Norwegian Ministry of Finance 1974).

18 The concern that Norway would struggle to manage its oil sector without knowledge and capability gained from a Norwegian NOC was probably accentuated by the relative lack of even private sector Norwegian expertise in the oil sector – in contrast to the UK, which already had a number of domestic upstream companies (PESD Interviews).

19 In fact, consultancy Arthur D. Little had explicitly recommended that Norway *not* form an NOC due to the difficulty that states typically have in controlling NOCs (PESD Interviews).

20 One official at the Ministry of Petroleum and Energy remarks that some of his counterparts from elsewhere in Western Europe poke fun at the Norwegian insistence on scrupulous separation of commercial and regulatory functions as "almost religious."

21 This incident was cited by a number of interviewees as having had a pivotal role in shaping Norwegian attitudes.

22 It could be argued that the existence of Statoil serves this function in a more general sense as well by providing cover for politicians to loudly criticize and disavow company actions when they are unpopular while simultaneously claiming that they have no direct control over what the company does.

23 The NPD's board was deemed to be superfluous and abolished in 1991. To the extent that the NPD has remained relatively independent of the ministry, this seems to be mainly due to its complementary, more technical skill set. Some interviewees in fact argued that the NPD serves essentially as an extended arm of the ministry and that its autonomy is often overstated.

24 The General Assembly represents the totality of the company's shareholders; in the case of a fully state-owned company, the Minister serves as the representative of the state as the only shareholder. Acting as the General Assembly requires the Minister to follow a formal and visible process when providing direction to the company, as opposed to issuing private instructions that are not transparent.

25 After oil was found, the scope of required regulations expanded markedly; employees at the Ministry found themselves testing helicopters to gain insight into the sizes of helidecks that should be required on offshore platforms (PESD Interviews).

26 The Ministry of Industry produced an analogous document, Report No. 30.

27 One government official expressed to us his personal view that the scale of Norway's petroleum wealth has led to high expectations for services, and in turn contributed to more frequent changes of government when politicians fail to deliver to their citizens' satisfaction (PESD Interviews).

28 Relative to many other countries, of course, Norway had rather arm's-length formal interactions with its NOC from the outset. That it still had a difficult time keeping the NOC from becoming a state within a state shows the extent of the challenge facing governing institutions in oil-rich states.

29 When informed that the Minister planned to replace him, he was reported as saying, "I believe it will be easier to find a new Minister than to find a new Chairman of Statoil" (Hanisch and Nerheim 1992).

30 The new chairman was Finn Lied, who had been the Minister of Industry proposing the establishment of Statoil under Bratteli.

31 The stated goal was the creation of a board that was more "politically diverse."

32 Politicians who had imagined that a government company would strengthen the hand of government regulators by readily sharing its expertise (Dam 1976, p. 64) proved to be mistaken.

33 Two different interviewees who were Ministry officials in the years soon after Statoil's formation suggested that the Ministry at the time sometimes took advantage of its ability to informally call Statoil and signal its desires rather than exposing itself to accountability by using the formal, transparent process of a General Assembly to give instructions to the company as its shareholder. It could be politically convenient, for example, to have Statoil be seen as the entity blocking development of a certain field rather than the Ministry.

34 Although the SDFI reforms were implemented over Statoil's strong objections, oil and gas consultant (and former Statoil executive) Willy Olsen argues that the change ultimately was a well-timed boon to Statoil, whose heavy portfolio of investments from the early 1980s would have weighed it down severely in the low oil-price environment that followed had a large share of the burden not been shifted to SDFI (PESD Interviews).

35 At the same time, negotiators of the compromise that resulted in SDFI were mindful not to cripple Statoil – for example, the company was allowed to retain its 50 percent equity interest in the productive Statfjord field, which at the time was a major source of cash for the company. The state took larger shares of fields like Gullfaks and Troll that had significant long-term potential (PESD Interviews).

36 Statoil after the Mongstad affair was particularly fractious and demoralized; Norvik began to build it back up through an aggressive program of cultural change. Managers were removed and new personnel (including Swedes and Danes who had entered the company through its downstream acquisitions) put in positions of authority. Written materials were put together to express Statoil's vision and principles, and an intensive series of town hall meetings within the company in 1989 and 1990 built cohesiveness while emphasizing the need for change.

37 As Willy Olsen points out, Statoil had pursued a few international activities prior to Norvik, including in Asia (China, Malaysia, and Thailand) and Europe (the UK and Denmark). These failed to take off for a variety of reasons. In an effort to improve Statoil's financial condition in the wake of the Mongstad cost overruns, Norvik in fact sold off some international ventures soon after he became CEO (PESD Interviews).

38 Statoil had existing close ties with Shell, but that company was already far-flung in its operations and did not have a tradition of forming strategic alliances (Lerøen 2002).

39 One particular benefit that BP apparently hoped to gain through the relationship was access to Norwegian natural gas, despite Harald Norvik's insistence that the Norwegian government was *not* likely to be amenable to this (PESD Interviews). On balance, the alliance probably turned out to be less valuable for BP than for Statoil, although likely still a net positive. Despite never achieving its goal of gaining access to Norwegian natural gas through the alliance, BP was able to share with Statoil both the significant risks of the joint international exploration effort and the costs of jointly conducted R&D work.

40 Since privatization, direct dialogue between the Ministry and Statoil on commercial issues has been prohibited so as not to provide material information to one shareholder to the exclusion of others. Meetings with the Ministry of Petroleum and Energy are programmed to be exactly the same as meetings with other investors, down to the particular slides that are shown (PESD Interviews).

41 While Norway rejected entry into the European Community and European Union in referendums in 1972 and 1994, respectively, it did become party to the Agreement on the European Economic Area in 1994, which generally requires it to follow the economic rules of the EU (see www.ec.europa.eu/external_relations/norway/index_en.htm).

42 In a way, the creation of Petoro – a fully state-owned, non-operating company – at the time of Statoil's IPO paralleled an idea for a non-operating NOC that the civil service and Borten government had originally pushed in the early 1970s before Bratteli became prime minister (PESD Interviews).

43 Physical ownership of pipelines on the NCS (as opposed to control over transmission) was consolidated in 2003 into Gassled, a joint venture between all pipeline-owning oil and gas companies in which each company received a share in Gassled proportional to its share of pipeline ownership on the NCS.

44 One observer suggests that divergent prior views between Statoil and Hydro may have played a role in how this situation played out and on what timescale. Because Hydro had previously backed the NPD's position, the interviewee suggests, the government may have been anxious to act on Troll before the legacy Hydro elements lost too much power within the merged company, perhaps making it more likely that the company would contest the government's decision.

45 One long-time participant in the Norwegian petroleum sector cited this case as an example of residual hubris on the part of Statoil. In his opinion, the likelihood that the NPD and Ministry would block the development was well known, but Statoil persisted anyway, thinking it could somehow strong-arm the deal through. Overall, though, he says that the company is behaving more and more like an IOC as time goes on, and that it tries to pull political power plays less and less often (PESD Interviews).

46 The return requirement for Norwegian investments is slightly lower than for international ones due to the different tax regimes to which they are exposed (PESD Interviews).

47 Statoil has deeper knowledge of the region's geology and operational challenges than anyone else from having had a dominant position there for so long. The NCS is also of course far more material to Statoil's financial success than to that of any IOC majors, leading it to devote significant resources to opportunities where the majors have less interest. For these reasons, the Ministry can find itself in the position of choosing Statoil as the desired operator for a new area even though, all other things being equal, it would prefer more diversity. Some Ministry officials speculate that Statoil actually held back in its operatorship applications in the twentieth license round, perhaps sensitive to perceptions that it had become excessively dominant on the NCS since the merger. In fact, there was one case in this license round in which the Ministry asked Statoil to accept operatorship on a block for which no operatorship applications were received.

48 One oft-employed justification for the merger with Norsk Hydro was that it would resolve confusion that could arise among resource-owning countries when they encountered two Norwegian companies with state backing competing against each other; the bidding for participation in Russia's Shtokman field was invariably cited as the principal example of this problem.

49 The argument was made that the Competition Authority had no jurisdiction as the matter had been referred to the EU to review its implications for competition, but the Norwegian government could in fact
have involved the Competition Authority had it chosen to do so (PESD
Interviews). The EU authorities for their part were primarily concerned
with any ability of the merged company to exert market power in oil
and gas marketing outside of Norway, not on the possible effects on
competition within upstream oil and gas operations on the Norwegian
Continental Shelf itself.

50 The merger certainly had some legitimate arguments in its favor, and it
might have been inevitable if Hydro's hydrocarbon prospects had continued to dwindle, especially in a political environment likely hostile
to foreign ownership of Hydro's oil and gas division (or maybe even
to its being a stand-alone company vulnerable to outside investors).
Nevertheless, the short-circuiting of debate about the merger prior to
its approval – and the absence of any steps to reduce the NCS market
share of the new company by forcing it to sell some assets – illustrated
the still-formidable political influence of Statoil and Hydro in Norway,
made virtually unstoppable when the two stood side-by-side.

51 As Ramm (2009) points out, the approval process for the division of
Saga between Norsk Hydro and Statoil in 1999 had some of the same
characteristics.

52 Then Minister of Petroleum and Energy, Åslaug Haga, pressed on
Statoil a particular solution for electrification of the new Gjøa field –
sourcing power from the island of Lutelandet in Fjaler – that played to
political constituencies but was costlier than Statoil's preferred alternative of bringing power from Mongstad. Though the Lutelandet option
was supported by Parliament, it can be argued that the Minister did not
follow the correct formal procedure of instructing Statoil as its majority shareholder, and in any case that the intervention did not represent
proper stewardship of the company's interests. Ultimately a compromise
ise allowed Statoil to get its power from Mongstad but fund significant infrastructure construction on Lutelandet. (*NRK* April 18, 2008,
www.nrk.no/nyheter/distrikt/nrk_sogn_og_fjordane/1.5422221;
Aftenbladet.no July 17, 2008, www.aftenbladet.no/energi/olje/art-
icle669738.ece; *Tecknisk Ukeblad* September 9, 2008, www.tu.no/
energi/article178275.ece).

53 One recent example was the 2007–2008 scandal over suspicious consulting contracts arranged by Saga in Libya in the late 1990s, which
became Norsk Hydro's responsibility when it took over Saga in 1999
and were allegedly not disclosed by certain Hydro employees during the
due diligence for the merger with Statoil.

54 A two-thirds share grants a shareholder full positive control over company by-laws; a mere one-third share would be sufficient to allow the state to veto any company decision to ever move its headquarters out of Norway. One interviewee commented that a further reduction in the state's share of Statoil might not be as unlikely as the conventional wisdom dictates if a Conservative government were to come to power.

55 A Statoil official said that finding situations and ways to take advantage of the company's heritage is "amazingly complicated; there are maybe two to three places in the world at one time where we can use [this strategy]." He cited Norsk Hydro's experience in Angola as an example of how to pursue this strategy, and also of its complexity and uncertain outcome. Hydro gained a privileged position through its offer to help Sonangol develop operational expertise, which it did by pairing Hydro personnel with staff in Sonangol's development organization. In return, Hydro was given the ability to match competitors' bids and was granted joint operatorship of a supposedly "golden block" in Angola. However, the venture was ultimately not a commercial success, as the company drilled only dry wells. And when Norsk Hydro approached Nigeria with the same idea, it found no interest (PESD Interviews).

56 A key later transfer of operatorship was the handover of the Troll gas field from Shell to Statoil in 1996 upon completion of field development.

57 A present day example of how the NCS regulatory environment can push up costs is the "two weeks on, four weeks off" work schedule for personnel on offshore platforms.

58 One current Statoil manager said that the company propagates a guideline internally that a project is not to be considered a success unless there are at least five new things in it.

59 Interestingly, a big part of the ostensible rationale for the new LNG plant design was potential cost savings. One could argue that incentives in the licensing process might implicitly encourage Statoil to make an overly aggressive estimation of costs to get an operator license, with the knowledge that it would be less likely than IOCs to suffer consequences if costs turned out to be higher, though we have no evidence that this actually occurred.

60 Significant technology development in Norway was also spurred by measures not specific to Statoil. As Willy Olsen points out, the ministry required all companies to come up with technology transfer plans as part of the 1979 licensing round, and investment in R&D was made tax-deductible. Another government mechanism for increasing technological capability was the creation of NPD-led R&D initiatives involving broad-based cooperation between IOCs, Norwegian oil companies, and research institutions. Early R&D efforts that played an important

role included the Chalk Research Programme (which drew upon and expanded early efforts by Phillips to understand the characteristics of Ekofisk) as well as an initiative aimed at developing improved oil recovery technologies. Current-day research priorities of the NPD include integrated operations (the use of information technology to connect onshore and offshore activities and make operations more efficient) and carbon capture and storage (CCS).

61 Any increased costs associated with using Statoil as a tool to achieve national hydrocarbon goals would decrease tax revenues and dividends.

62 Article 54 of the Royal Decree of December 8, 1972 specified that: "Licensees shall use Norwegian goods and services in petroleum operations to the extent that these are competitive in terms of quality, service, delivery time and price."

63 The NPD has been allocated more resources by the Ministry to hire staff in order to enhance its ability to keep tabs on Statoil (PESD Interviews). Petoro's counterbalancing role may become more important as well, but mere exhortations from this watchdog company have less bite than direct competition from Norsk Hydro, and the government has made it clear that it does not intend to let Petoro grow into an operating company that would compete toe-to-toe with Statoil. Both Petoro and suppliers have expressed concerns since the merger that some projects are proceeding more slowly than promised. Statoil has explained delays as representing natural post-merger growing pains (PESD Interviews); more recently, the global economic crisis could be having some effect as well.

15 | *Gazprom: the struggle for power*

NADEJDA VICTOR AND INNA SAYFER

1 Introduction

Russia's national oil company (NOC), Gazprom, is a deeply important player in world energy markets. If Gazprom were a country, its combined oil and gas reserves would rank behind only those of Saudi Arabia and Iran. In 2008, Gazprom controlled about 20% of the world's natural gas reserves, 70% of Russia's gas reserves, and 94% of Russia's gas production.

Gazprom is also a major corporate player. Many of Gazprom's shares are freely traded on the stock market where its market capitalization briefly stood above $300 billion before energy prices plunged in the second half of 2008. Gazprom is one of the fifty largest companies in the world and by any reasonable valuation of its assets the largest company in Russia (Fortune Global 500 Rankings 2009). In 2008, Gazprom alone accounted for more than 10 percent of Russia's GDP and provided about 40 percent of its earnings to the federal budget (Gazprom 2009a).

Despite its commercially oriented facade, Gazprom has a long history of tight state control. Gazprom traces its origins to 1965, when the Soviet Union established a gas ministry as a way to develop the national gas industry. Just before the Soviet collapse in 1991, the government transformed Gazprom into a company and in 1993 partly privatized it through a widely criticized sale of state assets. In 2003, Gazprom came under even closer state command. Only when it was confident that the enterprise was unequivocally under its power did the Kremlin – while retaining a controlling share – sell larger stakes to private investors and favored companies in the West.

In this study, we make five central arguments about Gazprom.

First, Gazprom's performance compares poorly with most other firms in this study. This is partly due to the fact that most of these other firms are oil-dominated companies, not gas companies. Gas distribution requires longer time horizons and a much closer physical connection to the customer than is the case with oil. Indeed, Gazprom's oil assets post better performance than its gas assets because the Russian oil market is more fully governed by market economics and the oil network is much less costly to operate. Gazprom's performance is also especially sensitive to the special politics of gas. By tacit agreement with the state, Gazprom provides an enormous supply of cheap gas to the Russian economy. This arrangement saps the company of desperately needed funds for investment in its large new fields. Therein lies the paradox that Western observers always note about Gazprom. On the one hand it controls the world's largest conventional gas resources. On the other hand it faces a looming gas crisis (which was postponed when the global financial crisis dampened demand for energy) because production in its major fields continues to decline and the company fails to invest adequately in new fields.

Second, Gazprom's investment strategy is not entirely irrational from the perspective of its managers. Like many of the NOCs examined in this book, managers are responsive to a wide array of concerns and they do not operate in a competitive market. Managers are convinced that shortfalls in gas supply are not necessarily a disadvantage, to the extent that they keep markets tight. To this end, managers often coordinate supplies from associated gas and independent gas companies to prevent oversupply to the market and are especially attentive to the risk of a decline in gas prices that would accompany an oversupply. Such risks (that became a reality in 2009) make the managers wary of investing resources in large capital-intensive projects. Similar forces explain Gazprom's expansion outside Russia, such as with the purchase of gas distribution companies in Europe that allow the firm to exert more control over the whole supply chain from wellhead to final customer.

Third, by Western standards Gazprom has weak corporate governance. Its managers are accountable to politicians rather than to shareholders, even as privately owned shares have risen to 49 percent of the enterprise. This system reflects Gazprom's insular history as a Soviet ministry and the fact that control over the firm is rooted in the Kremlin rather being based on the successful production of gas (and now oil). Shareholders have tolerated the situation mainly because Gazprom's political connections are seen as the keystone to its viability as an enterprise.

Fourth, Gazprom is an example of the phenomenon of regulatory capture. The Federal Tariff Service, the regulator, has been responsible for setting domestic gas prices with rate setting always done in consultation with Gazprom. Thus, Gazprom is in many ways a quasi-ministry that is partially regulating itself. Until about a decade ago, Gazprom's political strategy was anchored in keeping domestic tariffs low, which made the company indispensible. Now that its political relationships with the Kremlin are more secure, it has been able to raise tariffs, which has given the company more control over financial resources.

Fifth, the 2008 global financial crisis has turned the gas sector upside down. Previously, supplies were tight and energy prices were rising; in the midst of the crisis, demand weakened and so did prices. This shift in demand along with the arrival of large volumes of shale gas in the US (and perhaps soon similar gas sources in Western Europe, Gazprom's most lucrative market) portend a global gas oversupply that will be a disaster for Gazprom. It will erode the company's power over consuming and transit countries, and it will leave the company's LNG ambitions unfulfilled before 2030. This looming gas glut could have major consequences for the structure of gas markets, as Russia could come under pressure to modify pricing terms – moving away from lucrative oil-linked gas contracts to lower prices that will be fetched from gas-on-gas competition.

This study proceeds as follows. Section 2 looks historically at the "yin and yang" of Gazprom's (and its predecessors') interactions with the state. We focus especially on the reasons for early privatization efforts following the demise of the Soviet Union and the "renationalization" of the oil and gas sectors as world oil and gas prices rose. Section 3 provides an overview of the Russian oil and gas sectors, with special attention to Gazprom and its previous incarnation as a Soviet gas ministry – long the key drivers of the industry. Section 4 focuses on Gazprom as an organization today, including its structure, revenues, and its activities within Russia, Western Europe, and overseas. As the study makes clear, Gazprom is far more than the world's largest gas company. It is a monopoly controlled by the Kremlin, serving both economic and political agendas, as well as a multidimensional investment enterprise seeking a larger role on the world stage. Section 5 concludes.

2 A history of state involvement in the oil and gas sectors

In this section, we sketch the history of Russia's long involvement in the oil and gas sectors, focusing particularly on Gazprom and its gas sector predecessors. The relationship between the Russian state and the oil and gas sectors has been changing in two fundamental ways. First, the goals and strategies set by the Kremlin have shifted back and forth, initially from tight control under the Soviet Union then to some liberalization during the 1990s and most recently to a renationalization, so that the company has become as much an instrument of state as a commercial enterprise. Second, the particular tools that the government uses to affect behavior in the sector, including regulation, taxes, and competition, have become more powerful since re-nationalization began.

2.1 Foundations of Gazprom in the Soviet state (pre-1989)

Oil and gas development started in Russia on an industrial scale at the end of the nineteenth century with the financial and technological investment of major foreign investors, notably the Rothschild family and the Nobel brothers. By that time, the major cities in Russia were supplied by a gas network, primarily for lighting, which was the first widespread application of gas. Gas was mainly produced and used locally and Russia did not lay long-distance gas pipelines until well after World War II.[1]

By 1955, the USSR was producing only 9 billion cubic meters (bcm) of gas from fields that were dispersed across the European part of Russia and Ukraine. Communist Party leader Khrushchev set the ambitious goal of catching up with the United States economically within twenty-five years, and along with this vision came new objectives for oil and gas. The desire to develop a gas industry was officially inserted into the sixth Five-Year Plan (1956–1960) and the ambition was stepped up in the seventh Five-Year Plan (crafted starting in 1959 and running 1961–1965).

As the small and dispersed gas fields west of the Urals and close to demand centers became depleted, net production shifted east. Khruschev's eighth Five-Year Plan, which began in 1966, recognized the potential importance of the vast Siberian gas reserves to the east of the Ural Mountains. This plan marked the beginning of the "Siberian period" with the opening of the world-class fields in Urengoi that were discovered in 1966 and first brought into service in 1978.

By the time of the Siberian period, the persistent state sponsorship of oil during the preceding fifteen years had finally paid off, catapulting oil to the top as the Soviet Union's primary energy supply. Gas development, however, was proceeding more slowly, in part because the infrastructure requirements for gas make it harder to handle and in part because gas was not seen as uniquely qualified for any particular industrial application, unlike oil which was used for petrochemicals and transportation.

The oil shock of 1973, however, put a premium on boosting gas production to replace oil, while also lifting the export price of gas that the USSR could use to generate cash. The gas projects that followed through the middle 1980s had two basic goals. Projects for Soviet satellite nations (through the Council for Mutual Economic Assistance, or CMEA) involved the Soviet parent selling gas at depressed prices and through complex barter exchanges to generate political support. The projects for Western nations, by contrast, involved competitive pricing in hard currency financed with concessionary hard currency loans that were secured with the proceeds of a long-term gas purchase agreement. Usually these Western-oriented projects were backed by guarantees from the Soviet and Western governments. In 1980, the Soviet Union was earning about $15 billion per year from gas and oil exports, or more than 62 percent of the Soviet's total hard currency earnings (see Austvik 1991).

The Soviet invasion of Afghanistan in 1979, coupled with Ronald Reagan's assumption of power in the United States in 1980, had the effect of "refreezing" the Cold War and erasing the Western consensus on the acceptance of Soviet oil and gas exports. The United States initiated sanctions to limit access to hard currency that the Soviets could earn through gas exports. It also tried to block the exports of grain and essential high technology from the West to the USSR. From the European perspective, the US objections were rooted in an imagined geopolitical threat. Nevertheless, the risk of US sanctions served to slow numerous projects and led the Soviet Union to develop its own technology, including compressors.

In 1989, during the "perestroika" era, the goals of the Russian state changed because the inefficient planned economy desperately needed reform.[2] At that time, President Gorbachev created Gazprom as a state unit responsible for gas production, distribution, and sales. The relationship between the state and Gazprom began to evolve according to larger institutional changes under way in Russia.

The dissolution of the Soviet bloc in 1990, and the USSR in 1991, had a major impact on the contractual environment for gas exports to the West. In particular, the political changes created transit countries. The routes of all the pipeline projects connecting the European part of Russia to the outside world passed through Belarus and Ukraine. In fact, at the time of the Soviet Union's dissolution, about 90 percent of Russia's exported gas was traveling through Ukraine. Although these new ex-CMEA nations created new uncertainties for gas supply, there were strong incentives for them to avoid disrupting Soviet-era gas export arrangements.

The collapse of the Soviet Union caused economic shock waves that dramatically lowered the demand for gas in Russia, as well as in the ex-CMEA nations. With a shrinking economy, gas consumption in Russia declined more than 16 percent during the 1990s – from 420 billion cubic meters (bcm) in 1990 to 350 bcm in 1997 (BP 2010). Gas exports to the former Soviet countries in the Commonwealth of Independent States (CIS) also declined by 31 percent (from 110 bcm in 1990 to 75.6 bcm in 1998) in part because these countries' economies were intertwined with the Soviet economy and thus also suffered a severe economic recession. In addition, they were now forced to purchase gas at semi-hard export prices, which were higher than the internal Russian price but lower than the price charged for Western exports. Those higher prices discouraged gas consumption and promoted efficiency. However, even as consumption shrank, reported gas production declined only slightly (about 8 percent) from 1992 to 1998 because most of the infrastructure for production from large gas fields and transportation of the gas was already in place and relatively inexpensive to operate. That generated a strong incentive for the Russian gas ministry (and later Gazprom) to export outside the CIS countries. (Russia's total oil production, by contrast, fell nearly 23 percent during the same period.) This large and growing surplus available for export allowed Russia to expand its role as the world's largest exporter of natural gas and to earn additional hard currency for the Russian economy.

2.2 Privatization of the oil and gas sector in Russia (1989–2000)

Following the breakup of the Soviet Union in 1991, the Russian federal government gained jurisdiction over the major oil fields in Russia and control over the transport and export of oil and gas. But oil exports were constrained by the capacity limitations of the old Soviet pipeline system and a lack of investment; the oil fields, too, were aging. The Russian oil sector of the 1990s urgently needed investment and restructuring. Reformers of the newly democratized Russia saw only one way to do it – through privatization. This privatization process occurred in two stages, only the first stage of which was applied specifically to the gas industry.

The first stage of privatization, made possible via a 1992 presidential decree, provided for voucher auctions of formerly state-owned facilities. The decree established Gazprom as a joint stock company focused on gas and also created several oil-focused companies (such as Lukoil, Yukos, Surgutneftegaz, and Rosneft). The government first sold these companies through voucher auctions with ownership limited to workers and Russian citizens. This first stage ended in June 1994, with the requirement that 38–45% of the shares in the companies would remain in government hands for at least three years, after which time the government's share might be reduced. In the case of Gazprom, 40% of its shares were left in government hands for at least three years, and 9% of shares were set aside for foreign ownership.

The second stage of privatization, a shares-for-loans scheme, began in 1995 just as the Russian budget deficit had climbed to 20% of the country's GDP. This scheme auctioned blocks of government shares in certain joint stock companies (including five of Russia's oil giants) to a group of Russian commercial banks for cash.[3] The shares-for-loans stage did not apply to Gazprom because then Prime Minister Viktor Chernomyrdin did not want to introduce new competition that might weaken his control[4] and because internal gas prices were too low to make Gazprom a commercially viable enterprise. Even after the 1998 crisis, when the Russian government was looking for more cash, Russian President Yeltsin approved the sale of only a further 5% stake in Gazprom. Although limits on foreign ownership of Gazprom stock later increased from 9% to 14%, only an additional 2.5% stake was actually sold to Ruhrgas for $660 million (to establish a close liaison with the German company).

For most of the 1990s, Russia's new oil barons and their private money restructured oil operations to become more efficient than their state company equivalents. As part of their strategy, however, the oil barons significantly reduced the taxes they paid to the Russian state and moved large amounts of capital offshore. At the time, oil and gas prices were on the rise, but the Russian federal government's ownership in the oil and gas sector was limited to Rosneft (responsible for 5% of total Russian production) and a small share in Lukoil (about 7.6%). Including regionally controlled companies, the government controlled only about 15% of total oil production. Moreover, the regional governments where the oil was produced were highly independent and their policies often conflicted with federal rules (Treisman 1999). The government thus had to look to gas to provide the much needed revenue.

During the 1990s Gazprom existed as a state within a state. The Russian government was not able to control the gas giant either formally (most of the 38% of state shares were managed by Gazprom itself) or informally (Gazprom was a very successful lobbyist) (Kim 2003). The government – particularly the compliant Ministry of Fuel and Energy – was loyal to the company, and there were few attempts to change the situation. In 1992, the government of Prime Minister Yegor Gaidar tried to open the gas industry to competition, introducing for the first time the idea of establishing independent producing companies to supply gas to the centrally controlled gas transportation system. Gaidar ordered a review of Gazprom's foreign accounts (as the government allowed the company to keep 38 percent of the currency it earned abroad). However, the "tail was smarter." After the audit by Gaidar finished, Gazprom won the support of Chernomyrdin, the Chairman of the Government of the Russian Federation and a powerful political player within Russia, who gave the company monopoly rights to supply gas to the state's foreign contracts. The government also allowed the company to keep 45% of the earnings from these contracts and exempted foreign operations from taxes. In 1993, Gazprom also convinced Boris Yeltsin to let it set up a tax-exempt special stabilization fund into which it could divert up to one-third of the income it derived from the value-added tax on gas to consumers.[5]

Gazprom's defenders pointed to the very high degree of technical integration between the different parts of the industry and the need to use centralized control to optimize the production and transmission of natural gas. (In reality, of course, there was nothing intrinsic in the integration of the gas industry that required monopoly control.) These arguments, together with the gas industry's importance to the Russian economy, ensured the survival of the monopoly.[6]

Gazprom also became politically powerful by providing implicit subsidies to domestic customers. Through these subsidies, Gazprom allowed non-payment of gas bills and charged a higher value than the market price in non-monetary transactions, such as settlements by near money, like barter and mutual netting provided to Gazprom. In the meantime, Gazprom delayed payments to the government budget and to its suppliers. The Russian government tolerated Gazprom's delay in payments in recognition of the gas company's implicit subsidies.

In 1997, Boris Nemtsov became the first deputy prime minister and promised to split up Gazprom. There was some restructuring, but mostly to Gazprom's liking. All drilling enterprises within Gazprom were united under a specialized company, Burgaz, and production and transport companies delegated their sale functions to a limited liability company, Mezhregiongaz. One more attempt to take control away from Gazprom took place in April 1997 when Nemtsov, along with reformer Anatoly Chubais, convinced President Yeltsin to terminate the trust agreement with Rem Vyakhirev, who managed the government's 35% stake in Gazprom (Kim 2003). Boris Yeltsin signed the decree when Prime Minister Chernomyrdin took a two-day holiday. But once he came back from the holiday, the prime minister blocked the decree.

2.3 PetroKremlin: renationalization of the oil and gas sector (2000–present)

When Putin became president in 2000, the government had little command over the oil and gas sector. Oil monies often circumvented the state budget and it was hard for Putin's government to control their flow. In addition, the new oil barons became more involved in politics and saw selling their companies' shares to foreign majors as a means of insulating their business from the Russian bureaucracy. At the same time, world oil and gas prices started to climb, which meant that the stakes in controlling the hydrocarbons industry rose as well. The new administration sought to re-nationalize the sector and opened hunting season on Russia's tycoons (see more on re-nationalization in Locatelli 2006). The first steps consisted of ministerial change.

In May 2000, the government restructured the Ministry of Fuel and Energy and shifted many of its responsibilities to other state institutions.[7] For example, the responsibility for allocating quotas – which ultimately determined which wells were used for production and the revenues their firms earned – shifted to a special commission controlled by the vice prime minister. By March 2004, massive ministerial reforms were complete. All federal ministries came under the direct jurisdiction of the president, and nine federal ministries were placed under the prime minister's jurisdiction, including the former Ministry of Fuel and Energy, which was renamed the Ministry of Industry and Energy.

The Ministry of Industry and Energy became responsible for issuing resolutions and orders that defined policy, but it no longer had the right to make specific decisions such as issuing licenses for a particular activity. Supervisory and control functions passed to the Federal Energy Agency (FEA). Thus, Putin separated the ministerial bureaucrats who determined the "interests of the state" from those in the FEA who implemented these interests. By 2004, the Russian Ministry of Industry and Energy had become a "Queen of England" (only without the money). Direct management of state-owned energy enterprises passed completely to the FEA. And Putin's government kept tight control over the FEA.

In June 2000, in tandem with asserting greater control over hydrocarbon markets and regulation, the Kremlin sought greater control over Gazprom itself. Dmitry Medvedev replaced Gazprom's key ally Chernomyrdin as deputy head of the presidential administration. The following year, Putin chose a new team from his hometown of St. Petersburg, headed by Aleksei Miller, to run Gazprom; Rem Vyakhirev, who had been running the company for ten years, was out.[8] By May 2005 only three out of nineteen members of the earlier management committee remained.

Putin made similar changes across the oil and gas sector between 2004 and 2005. Oil oligarchs and ex-soviet bureaucrats lost power that shifted to new allies of the Kremlin. The government also catalyzed a "merger mania," putting the many regional and private companies under state control. The Kremlin sought to take over Surgutneftegas, Slavneft, at least half of TNK-BP, and the remains of Yukos, using the state giants Rosneft and Gazprom as the vehicles for consolidation. An added benefit from the Kremlin's perspective was that it could more easily control two consolidated oil and gas companies than many regional and private companies.[9] Following "renationalization," the new oil actors, the so-called "St. Petersburg team," controlled almost 60 percent of oil production and nearly all of Russian gas production. After taking Gazprom under state control, Vladimir Putin signed amendments to a federal law allowing the government to have a controlling interest in the gas monopoly, by holding 50 percent plus one share, while controlling the sale of Gazprom's shares to foreign investors.

Thus, since 2000 Gazprom has become a firmly controlled agent of the Kremlin. That agent proved useful as the Kremlin, politically and economically, sought to reestablish Russia's status as a great power. As shown below, the Kremlin's political interests and Gazprom's economic priorities have led to incompatible goals – the government is seeking greater revenue from the energy sector, while at the same time asking Gazprom to carry out social and political aims that distract the company from its commercial aims.

Although the Kremlin has regained control over the company's high-level decisions, the takeover of Gazprom has not been nearly as thorough as, for example, Chávez's takeover of the Venezuelan national oil company (see Chapter 10). Gazprom has used its expertise to exercise influence over lower-level issues. The Federal Tariff Service, as the regulator, has been responsible for setting domestic gas prices and this is always done in consultation with Gazprom. Thus, to a large extent Gazprom remains a quasi-ministry that is regulating itself. Gazprom has obtained not only a monopoly on all gas pipelines and gas exports but also the legal right to be awarded certain exploration licenses without competition. Gazprom has achieved these results by using its political influence and technical knowledge to make the regulatory agency dependent on the company's knowledge and advance the company's priorities. The regulatory agency, in turn, uses formal powers over Gazprom to secure a part of the company's (political and financial) largesse. Therefore, internal and external competition is absent for the benefit of the monopolist and political actors. Gazprom is an example of the phenomenon of regulatory capture.[10]

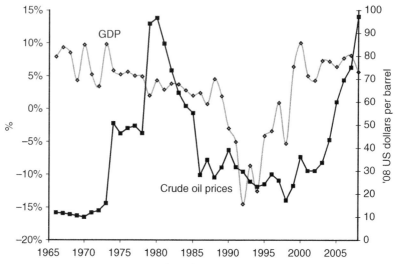

Figure 15.1 Russia: GDP growth and crude oil prices, 1966–2008.
Data source: World Bank 2009 Key Development and Data Statistics (www.data.worldbank.org/topic); BP (2010).

3 Russian gas and oil: capabilities and limits

In this section, we survey the Russian oil and gas industries and Gazprom's role within both. We begin with a discussion of gas and oil's important position in the Russian economy and then provide overviews of the gas and oil industries. We then focus specifically on Gazprom.

3.1 Oil and gas in the Russian economy

The oil and gas industries are of large and growing importance to the Russian economy. The steady increase in world oil and gas prices since 1998 has accelerated Russia's GDP growth (see Figures 15.1 and 15.2). Revenue from oil and gas export equaled about 25 percent of total Russian GDP in 2008 – a significant increase from 6 percent in 1994.

It is hard to estimate the figures for how much the oil and gas sector accounts for of the Russian GDP.[11] However, indirect estimates show that every doubling of oil price has resulted in a GDP increase of 80% (see window in Figure 15.2 and equation). Oil and gas exports accounted for 66% of Russia's total export income in 2008 and in 1998–2008 grew on average 20% a year (see Table 15.1).

Table 15.1. *Russian oil and gas export, and total export revenues*

Year	Oil and oil products $m	% in total export	Natural gas $m	% in total export	Total export $m
1995	18,348	22%	12,122	15%	82,419
2000	36,191	34%	16,644	16%	105,033
2005	117,245	48%	31,671	13%	243,569
2008	241,033	51%	69,107	15%	471,603
2009	148,738	49%	41,971	14%	303,388

Data source: CBR 2009 Balance of Payments (www.cbr.ru/eng/statistics/credit_statistics/); BEA 2009 National Economic Accounts (www.bea.gov/national/index.htm).

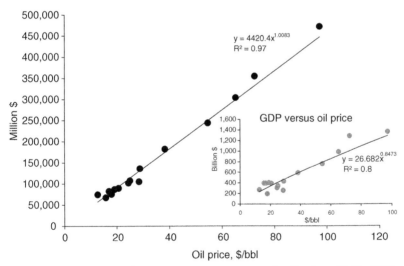

Figure 15.2 Russia: total export revenues versus crude oil prices, 1966–2008. The right-hand window: GDP versus oil price, 1994–2008.
Data source: World Bank 2009 Key Development and Data Statistics (www.data.worldbank.org/topic); BP (2010), CBR 2009 Balance of Payments (www.cbr.ru/eng/statistics/credit_statistics/).

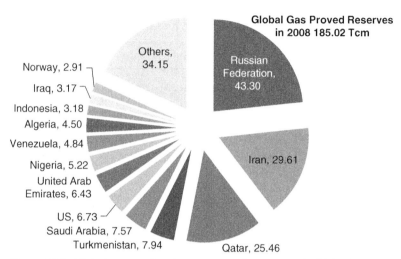

Figure 15.3 Global conventional gas reserves by country in 2008 (Tcm).
Data source: BP (2010).

The relationship between oil prices and total export revenues in Russia is extremely strong: A doubling of oil price results in an increase of export revenues by 101 percent (see Figure 15.2). The growing export revenues now fuel the economy, provide liquidity, and keep the current account in surplus.

Thus, the Russian economy is highly dependent on the international oil and gas markets. Perhaps too dependent, as many analysts agree that Russia has become a country with progressing "Dutch disease" (Egert 2005; Oomes and Kalcheva 2007). The investment climate in Russia will be critical to any effort to foster economic diversification that does not resort to the unsuccessful industrial policies of the past.

3.2 Overview of the Russian gas industry

Russia is by any measure a gas giant. At the end of 2008, Russia accounted for about one-quarter of the world's total gas reserves (BP 2010: see Figure 15.3). About 80 percent of Russian gas reserves are in West Siberia, where the existence of many giant and a few super-giant gas fields has been proven. Currently Gazprom produces about 90 percent of its gas from this region (see Table 15.2). Gas discoveries

Table 15.2. *Gazprom gas production in Russia by region*

Region	Percent of Russian production
The Urals, West Siberia	93.0
Volga Region	3.4
Southern Region	2.5
(East) Siberia	0.6
Northwest	0.5

Source: Gazprom (2009b).

peaked in the early 1970s, although it is expected that more gas will be found offshore in the Arctic.[12] The extremely hostile environment of the Arctic makes exploration for further gas reserves economically unattractive, at least in the near future. There is little incentive to go further since nearly 60 percent of the already known gas reserves are not currently being produced.

Russia is a large producer, but estimates for its future production vary widely. They range from the 2009 Russian Energy Strategy estimates on the high side (800 bcm in 2020 and about 900 bcm in 2030) to IEA mid-level estimates (712 bcm in 2015 and 760 bcm in 2030 according to IEA 2009) to those of the more conservative 2003 Russian Energy Strategy (between 650 and 730 bcm by 2020) (see Figure 15.4). The Russian Cabinet of Ministers projects that Gazprom's production will represent more than 80 percent of the Russian total.[13]

Despite its large size and potential for further growth, the Russian gas sector faces several key uncertainties. First, the steady decline of three major gas fields invites questions about the long-term strategy for the development of new fields. Second, future gas demand is unclear in Russia, CIS, and the EU. Third, Russia may no longer be able to rely on Central Asian states to meet domestic demand for low-cost gas.[14] We discuss these uncertainties below.

The stagnating production of natural gas in Russia is a direct result of the depletion of the Urengoyskoye, Yamburgskoye, and Medvezhye fields – the three major fields in Russia under production in the Urals (see Table 15.2).

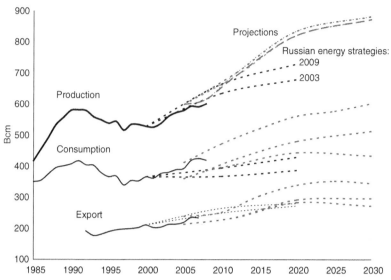

Figure 15.4 Russia: natural gas production, export, and consumption, historical data, 1985–2008.
Source: Russian Energy Strategy (2003, 2009) projections.

The Yamburgskoye field is currently producing only 110–115 bcm per year, compared with the plateau production of 205–207 bcm. The Urengoyskoye field peaked in 1988 at around 300 bcm and is currently in decline; it produces about 135–140 bcm, although total associated production of 260–270 bcm has been maintained by bringing smaller satellite fields online. The Medvezhye field has been in decline since 1985 and has already produced a relatively high percentage of its initially recoverable reserves, though the associated production seems relatively stable. The speed of the decline at both Urengoyskoye and Medvezhye will depend on future investments and additional compression at the fields.

According to our estimations (see equations in Figure 15.5), these old fields will decrease production by about 5 percent annually in 2008–2020, resulting in production levels of roughly 140 bcm by 2020. Many analysts believe that the aging fields' production levels will begin to contract by more than 5 percent a year.[15]

The commissioning of smaller Siberian fields to compensate for declines in production began in the 1990s. However, smaller satellite production is simply a Band-Aid for the maturing super-giant

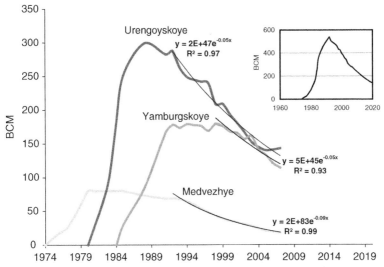

Figure 15.5 Major Russian natural gas fields production from West Siberia. The right-hand side window shows total major Russian natural gas fields production from West Siberia (historical and projections until 2020).
Source: IEA (2002), Stern (2005), Victor (2008), EIA (2009c).

fields. The only large gas field to begin production in recent years is Zapolyarnoye, with total gas reserves of around 3.3 Tcm. It was discovered in 1965 but did not begin production until October 2001. Starting in 2006, Gazprom has been recovering gas from Zapolyarnoye, which currently produces about 110 bcm (see EIA 2009c); this recovery partly masked the decline in the older fields.

Huge investments are needed to replace Russia's dwindling supply of natural gas, and all the options for new production will prove costly and difficult. New fields in the far north and east of the country are distant from most of the Russian population centers and export markets, requiring wholly new transport systems such as pipelines. Moreover, most of these new fields are found in extremely harsh environments where it is technically and financially difficult to operate. Gazprom controls neither the capital nor the technology needed for the task. As discussed below, the state-controlled company is already highly indebted and faces many expensive obligations that drain its coffers.

Second, another major uncertainty is future gas usage. This uncertainty is particularly acute domestically. Although Russia is the

second-largest gas consumer (after the United States) – consuming
more than 420 bcm of gas to support an economy only one-eighth
the size of the US economy (IMF 2010) – the inefficiency of usage
and low price of domestic gas[16] make future predictions of demand
difficult. Russia's energy strategy for the period up to 2030, which in
2009 became a cornerstone of the country's fuel and energy complex,
estimated internal usage for gas at 562 bcm in 2020 and 608 bcm
in 2030.[17] However, these estimates may be off, because more than
90 percent of residential and industrial gas consumers lack meters.
Consumers do not have information on how much gas they are using
and have no control over their own consumption (IEA 2002, 2006a).
There is also no consistent information on the payments for gas consumed or whether consumers pay at all. Also "payment" by consumers in Russia is more loosely defined than in other economies,
with exchange possible via money, barter, or a variety of other instruments. Much of the reason for this inefficiency lies in the fact that gas
is extremely cheap domestically. At the end of 2008, domestic natural
gas prices in Russia were around $52 per thousand cubic meters (or
14 percent higher than in 2006), while the price for Europe hit $450.
Overall, gas is cheaper than coal in Russia – the only large country
where that is true.

There is also uncertainty in future gas demand in the EU. In the
short term, the global recession has hammered Europe's gas consumption, particularly for industrial users. The EU's gas imports in
the first quarter of 2009 declined by about 12 percent compared with
2008. But Russian exports to Europe fell by an even greater margin
(in the first quarter of the year they dropped by 35.3 percent), partly
indicating that Europe has effectively diversified its import structure,
especially via Statoil.[18] Further weakening the position of Russian
gas in the EU was Russia's dispute in 2009 over supplies and transit in Ukraine that led to widespread shortages throughout much of
Europe. And over the long term, the EU's plans for greater energy
efficiency and security (based on nuclear, coal, and renewable energy)
could dent gas demand. The management board of Gazprom seems
to dismiss such concerns and envisions that Gazprom's exports to
Europe will climb to 250 bcm per year by 2020.

Third, despite Russia's copious gas reserves, something of a paradox exists in the Russian gas sector because of a domestic supply
gap. At the root of this gap is Gazprom's desire to export its own

production coupled with Central Asian producers' (which used to be part of the Soviet Union and now are independent countries) lack of access to the Gazprom-controlled pipeline network.[19] Until recently, Russia met this gap through imports of low-cost Central Asian gas to domestic and CIS consumers. Russia has been squeezing geographically isolated Turkmenistan to sell gas to Russia at a deep discount. Because of their dominant presence in Uzbekistan, Gazprom and fellow Russian producer Lukoil also profitably import gas production from that country.

However, recent events have called this strategy into question. Russia can no longer count on Turkmenistan's cheap gas, as it is poised to decline, and a new 7,000 km gas pipeline was inaugurated in December 2009 that will carry mainly Turkmen gas to China across Uzbekistan and Kazakhstan with planned capacity of 40 bcm a year.[20] Moreover, in 2008, Gazprom agreed to pay Central Asian producers European prices for gas in an attempt to block competition for supplies it needed to compensate for declining output at its Siberian fields. And Uzbekistan's friendly attitude toward Russian producers may change in the future. Although Russia has inked some other deals to shore up supplies from Azerbaijan, these deals are either modest[21] or – in the case of its efforts to stop the widely publicized Nabucco pipeline – expensive. Some analysts have reported that Russia has agreed to purchase Azeri natural gas at a record price of $350 per thousand cubic meters to try to make the so-called Nabucco project unfeasible. (The Nabucco project is supposed to transport Caspian and Central Asian gas west across the South Caucasus and Turkey, reducing Europe's reliance on Russian gas.)

Given the uncertainty and rising costs of supplying gas from Central Asia, Russia may look at other options to fill the supply gap. Russian oil companies such as Lukoil and TNK-BP have always produced substantial quantities of gas, both in association with crude oil production and as non-associated gas. The options available to oil companies to dispose of their associated gas are still not attractive because Gazprom restricts their access to gas processing plants and pipelines. By 2010, these companies could produce about 50 bcm in the Nadym-Purtazovsky region's new fields alone. Gazprom is also pulling independent gas suppliers Itera and Novatek into its orbit.[22] Gazprom bought a 19.9 percent stake in Novatek and has taken control of Itera's largest remaining field. Thus, it might be more appropriate to call these companies "Gazprom-dependent" rather than independent.[23] While these actions dilute Gazprom's share of the domestic market they allow the company to shift the risks associated with capital-intensive development of new fields to other players.

Another way to surmount the gas shortage is through a price increase for domestic gas consumers. Since 2008, domestic gas prices have been set to increase as much as 25 percent annually and are expected to double by 2010 to $100 per thousand cubic meters. The government planned to achieve a declared level of equal profitability of sales in both local and export markets by 2011. It is still unclear how equal profitability in both markets can be achieved because the 2011 target for the domestic price is significantly lower than Gazprom's export price for 2007–2008 (see more details and discussions in Pirani 2009).

However, an internal gas price increase would not guarantee the security of the Russian energy system.[24] The future security of gas will be related more to the development of the fields of the Far North and Eastern Siberia, as well as the shelf deposits of northern and Far Eastern seas. A great deal of new capacity has to come online over the next two decades; with lead times of five to seven years to bring large fields into production, development plans need to be set well ahead of time.

While Gazprom is a large gas company it has also benefited from the government's desire to assert tighter control over the oil industry. That is making Gazprom into an oil company as well. In 2005, Gazprom agreed to buy most of Sibneft, the country's fifth-biggest oil firm. It was the biggest takeover in Russian history. Dmitry Medvedev, who is currently Russia's president but was formerly the chairman of Gazprom's board of directors and the first deputy prime minister, said this acquisition was the kind of deal you normally see in the marketplace.

4 Inside Gazprom: profile of the largest company in Russia

In this section, we move beyond Gazprom's production and reserves figures to peer inside the company. Gazprom is an enormous entity that employs 376,300 people (including 221,300 specifically in gas) and even has its own corporate anthem (see Radio Free Europe/Radio

Liberty 2009). To capture a company of this size, we proceed as follows. We first discuss Gazprom's complex corporate structure, then its financing arrangements, followed by its domestic, international, and non-core holdings. We conclude by addressing the company's business strategy.

4.1 Corporate structure

Gazprom's ownership has undergone some reforms, though it remains dominated by the Russian government. In 2005, as a result of state-owned Rosneftegaz's purchase of a 10.74 percent stake in Gazprom, the government's stake in Gazprom increased to 50.1 percent. Other major shareholders include banks and favored Russian firms and one German firm (E.ON Ruhrgas) that is Gazprom's key customer in the West. A "ring fence" that separated Russian and foreign shares was removed late in 2005 as part of the Russian government's efforts to make the country more attractive to investors in the wake of the Russian government's dismantling of Yukos. Removing the ring fence transformed Gazprom from being a reasonably insignificant entity in the international capital markets into one of the most liquid of the emerging market stocks. This economic turn will prove important because the company will need substantial investments in the future to maintain infrastructure and to keep up production levels.[25] Although the company's capitalization has grown substantially – because of its low base and enormous reserves – it has one of the lowest returns on assets in the energy sector.[26]

Since 2001, the company has been in the process of intra-corporate reforms aimed at enhancing business efficiency. The reforms were to be carried out in two stages. During the first stage (2001–2003), the company sought to identify key corporate governance responsibilities, to develop governance rules and regulations, and to improve budget planning. The goal of the second stage (2004–2005) was to improve operating efficiency as a vertically integrated company. The crucial task of this stage was to optimize the business management structure in the various subsidiaries to ensure the transparency of financial flows.[27] These reforms led to changes in the organizational structure, as shown in Figure 15.6 for 2004 (the latest available information).

Reforms continue through the present day. Gazprom's top management instituted another round of two-step reforms between 2006 and

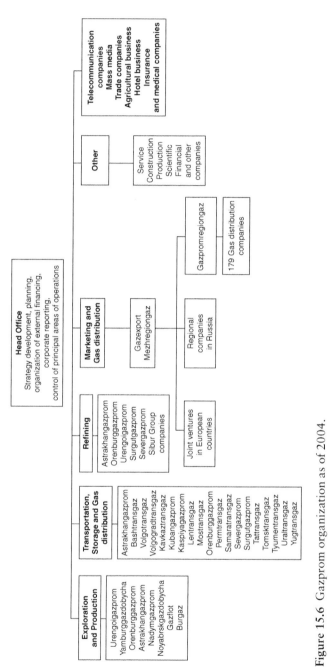

Figure 15.6 Gazprom organization as of 2004.
Source: Victor (2008).

2008. In the first step, the Gazprom subsidiaries, which own or lease about 80 percent of the company's property, singled out their non-core assets into special "buffer" companies. In the second step, the buffer companies merged according to business segment. One company was selected to be the principal company at the core of the segment and the others would be linked to it.[28]

The expected effects of these internal governance reforms are mixed. They will raise corporate administrative spending by $100 million per year or more. At the same time, they will reveal Gazprom's actual expenses, and with such new transparency market capitalization is expected to increase by more than $30 billion since it will make it easier for investors to assess the company's health and risks (see Collins 2006). A successful reorganization should allow the Gazprom management to determine which business units are actually profitable.

4.2 Finances

Gazprom enjoyed strong financial performance between 2004 and 2008, mostly on the strength of (until recently) rising hydrocarbon prices. Total sales revenues in 2008 were about $120 billion, or about 328% higher than in 2003 (see Table 15.3). Net profit climbed more slowly, for 2008 profit was $19.8 billion, an increase of 162% over 2004 levels. However, the company's $46 billion 2008 debts have increased by 160% since 2003 (though they were about the same as in 2007).[29] Gazprom's debt-to-asset indicator is about 22% (Gazprom 2009a), or roughly twice the industry average.[30] Looking ahead, increases in debt,[31] ambitious acquisitions, and a higher share of short-term debt or annual debt maturities could cause Gazprom's financial situation to deteriorate.

The central issue of Gazprom's finances is the company's three distinct sales markets: the home market in Russia; the market in the rest of the former Soviet Union (FSU); and the lucrative Far Abroad Countries (mostly Western Europe). The price of natural gas delivered to Western Europe was about three times higher than the gas price sold to FSU and five times higher than the domestic price. This explains the company's continued interest in expanding exports and its more recent (and successful, if slow) reform of domestic pricing. Since the export market will be difficult to expand significantly, the

Table 15.3. *Gazprom's revenues, 2003–2008*

	2003	2004	2005	2006	2007	2008
Sales revenues						
Far abroad countries						
Net revenue from sales, $m	19,282	21,899	29,535	43,661	47,314	63,495
Sales, bcm	140.6	153.2	156.1	161.5	168.5	184.4
Average price, $/thousand cm	131.6	137.7	192.4	261.9	269.4	312
Former Soviet Union (FSU)						
Net revenue from sales, $m	2,002	3,187	4,565	9,234	11,143	12,989
Sales, bcm	44.1	65.7	76.6	101	96.5	96.85
Average price, $/thousand cm	43.6	46.7	60.7	88.6	110.9	149
Russia						
Net revenue from sales, $m	7,031	9,101	10,818	13,569	16,271	16,304
Sales, bcm	309.1	305.7	307	316.3	307	287
Average price, $/thousand cm	22	29	36	42	51	67
Total gas sales revenue						
Net revenue from gas sales	28,314	34,187	44,918	66,464	74,727	92,788
Sales, bcm	494	525	540	579	572	568
Other sales revenues						
Gas condensate & refineries sales (net VAP, excise, export duties), $m	3,130	4,405	7,535	17,284	21,394	22,207

Crude oil sales (net VAP, export duties), $m	N/A	N/A	1,378	5,758	6,833	7,311
Transportation services (net VAP), $m	958	1,046	870	1,310	1,700	2,404
Other sales (net VAP), $m	1,660	2,092	2,278	3,771	6,551	10,678
Total sales revenues (net VAP, excise, export duties), $m	27,835	35,199	48,073	81,736	98,707	119,681
Sales profit, $m	8,047	10,374	15,640	32,513	30,979	50,767
Net profit, $m	6,984	5,733	9,472	20,664	22,245	19,827
Net debt, $m	17,713	22,255	33,193	41,015	61,534	46,450
Investments, $m	6,935	8,700	12,252	18,444	23,498	27,254

Note: For calculation we used end of period exchange rate of the ruble against the US dollar.

Source: Gazprom 2003–2008 Financial Reports.

single largest leverage point on Gazprom's finances is probably the domestic price of gas.

4.3 Domestic holdings

Gazprom has a wide range of energy possessions within Russia. Many of these holdings reflect its status as a fully vertically integrated hydrocarbons company: It has facilities for domestic exploration, production, sale, and distribution of gas; the production and sale of crude oil and gas condensate; and hydrocarbon refining operations. Gazprom's refining capacities (exclusive of the Sibur Group) include six facilities producing a wide range of products. The refineries are designed to process 52.5 bcm of natural gas and 28.6 million tons of unstable gas condensate as of December 31, 2007 (the latest available information). Gazprom acquired Sibur assets by using a bankruptcy procedure. As a result of the acquisition, Gazprom now owns Russia's largest natural gas processing plant.

Gazprom also owns the largest gas pipeline system in the world. As of December 31, 2008, the total length of the system was approximately 159.5 thousand km. The system includes 219 compressor stations on the pipelines with a total capacity of about 42.0 thousand MW.[32] Future growth in gas-powered generation and downstream gas assets (such as those represented by Britain's Centrica) are possible. As part of its infrastructure, Gazprom owns and operates twenty-five underground gas storage (UGS) facilities on the territory of Russia with total volume of commercial gas amounting to 65.2 bcm. (The idea of splitting transportation from Gazprom's production arm, much discussed by reformers in the 1990s, has been more or less dropped. Gazprom says that it has no incentive to keep independent gas producers out of its transport system, since the more gas is available for sale in Russia, the more gas will be available for Gazprom to export to Western Europe at higher prices. However, lack of transmission capacity has precluded independent producers from gaining access.)

One of the greatest problems facing Gazprom is the age and condition of its infrastructure. About 70 percent of the large diameter transmission lines were commissioned before 1987, and about 40,000 km of pipeline are more than thirty-five years old and will need replacement soon. The investment requirements of the transmission system will increase sharply over the next two decades – as investment will be needed to connect new fields to existing pipelines, as well as to replace and refurbish old lines.

As noted above, Gazprom has also moved more aggressively into oil. In October 2005, Gazprom bought the fifth-largest Russian oil firm, Sibneft, for $13.1 billion. This was an extraordinary deal as the state paid near market price to buy back a firm it had sold for almost nothing in the "loans for shares" auctions a decade ago.

4.4 International activities

To boost its international presence in the gas market, Gazprom has acquired assets in many gas distribution companies throughout Europe. At the end of 2006 Gazprom and Italian Eni signed a new agreement on a strategic partnership that enables Gazprom to supply gas directly to Italy. Gazprom has sealed similar agreements with Gaz de France, E.ON Ruhrgas, OMV, RWE, and BASF and intends to conclude a few more agreements in the future (the list of Gazprom's joint ventures is in Gazprom-Subsidiary Companies[33]). Gazprom's goal is a direct sales strategy to capture the profit margins that go to downstream suppliers (for an excellent examination of this subject, see Finon and Locatelli 2008).

More recently, Gazprom has been in a "shopping mood" and has pushed ahead with an expansion plan and huge ambition, raising questions over its true motives. As of December 31, 2008, Gazprom Group held nineteen licenses for subsoil use that imply hydrocarbon exploration, development, and production abroad, including five geological exploration, development, and production licenses and fourteen geological exploration licenses. In 2008, Gazprom's international activities also extended to oil and gas exploration, production, and marketing (see Box 15.1).

Box 15.1 Sample of Gazprom's international activities

Exploration & production

- In Vietnam (geological exploration work on Block No. 112).
- In India (geological exploration work on Block No. 26 in the northern part of the Bay of Bengal).
- In Libya (geological exploration work in licensed areas Nos. 19 and 64).

- In Venezuela, Gazprom received licenses for research and development of hydrocarbon reserves of Urumaco 1 and Urumaco 2 block deposits.
- In Libya, Gazprom agreed to swap a stake in its Yuzhno-Russkoye gas field in exchange for an interest in Libyan oil concessions.
- In Algeria, Gazprom and Sonatrach signed a Memorandum of Understanding in August 2006 on joint projects for gas exploration and production in Algeria, Russia and other regions.
- In Central Asian countries (in 2008, licenses were received to carry out geologic exploration work at the Kugartskaya area and Vostochny Maylisu IV in Kyrgyzstan, Sarikamash and Zapadny Shaambary in Tajikistan, and Ustyurt region in Uzbekistan).
- In Nigeria, Gazprom has made a new contribution to the global branding blunders: "Nigaz" – the fifty-fifty partnership between Gazprom and NNPC. Nigaz is set to build refineries, pipelines and gas power stations in Nigeria.
- Gazprom Neft is also considering participation in foreign projects; the most promising of which are in Libya, Syria, Iran, Indonesia, Iraq, Venezuela, and Kazakhstan.

Marketing

- In the UK, Gazprom has acquired the retail supply business of Pennine Natural Gas Ltd, and signed a leasing agreement with the Vitol Company providing Gazprom with a five-year access to 50 percent of Humbly Grove UGS in the south of Great Britain.
- In Denmark, Gazprom signed a twenty-year agreement with DONG Energy to deliver 1 bcm of gas to Denmark. Gazprom Marketing & Trading (GM&T, a 100 percent subsidiary of Gazexport) signed a fifteen-year supply agreement with DONG for 0.6 bcm of gas to be sold to the UK beginning in 2007.
- In the US, GM&T registered a LNG and natural gas marketing subsidiary, GM&T USA Inc in Houston.
- In France, GM&T registered a retail marketing subsidiary GM&T France SAS in Paris.
- In Scandanavia, Gazprom signed an SHA with BASF and E.ON confirming mutual involvement in the Northern Europe Gas Pipeline (NEGP) through NEGP Company (Gazprom 51 percent; BASF and E.ON each with 24.5 percent).

- In Hungary, Gazprom agreed to swap stakes in E.ON Hungaria, Foldgaz Storage, and Foldgaz Trade for stakes in Yuzhno-Russkoye.

Transport

- Stakes in SPP in Slovakia and alliances and partnerships in key transit nations to secure deliveries.
- In 2006, Gazprom negotiated the purchase of ArmRosGazprom from the Armenian government, along with a 40-km section of the Iran–Armenia gas pipeline. Gazprom has agreed to supply gas to Armenia at a fixed price of $110 per thousand cubic metres until 2009 in return for control of Armenia's gas pipelines, part of a power station, and a 40km section of a pipeline under construction between Armenia and Iran. Gazprom will participate in the construction of the Iran–Pakistan–India pipeline, and the refurbishing of one or two lines at the Southern Pars deposit.
- Shares in companies owning and operating UGS, namely: ArmRosGazprom Armenia), AO Latvijas Gaze (Latvia), WINGAS GmbH (Germany) and VNG AG (Germany).
- Access to foreign storage sites in Ukraine (17.5 bcm), Latvia (1.9 bcm), and Germany (1.5 bcm). The company plans to refurbish and expand existing sites and to build new ones in several countries in the CIS, Eastern Europe and elsewhere.

4.5 Non-core activities

Gazprom has extensive, poor-performing assets unrelated or only distantly connected to its gas and oil businesses. According to one 2004 estimate, non-core businesses generated a loss of $350 million and accrued staff costs of $1.4 billion.[34] As of 2006, these assets were worth approximately $14 billion and employed 38 percent of the company's employees (Kramer and Myers 2006). More recent figures indicate these assets (along with some core holdings, like gas storage facilities) represent roughly 11 percent of the company's total (Gazprom 2009b).[35] An OECD report noted Gazprom's "seemingly insatiable appetite" for investing in sectors of the Russian economy (OECD 2006).[36] Although Gazprom executives say they intend to drop the company's non-core assets, the company continues to make investments that have an unclear business motive. Following a series of "gas wars" with CIS countries, which has undermined European confidence in Gazprom, the company wants to improve its image abroad. Gazprom was prepared to pay $11 million in 2007 to PR firms headed by the Omnicom Group, a US communications company, for their services.[37] Some analysts think the Gazprom campaign will be just part of a larger campaign by the Kremlin to improve its image in the West (Butrin 2007).

Some of Gazprom's assets span the energy sector generally. Gazprom holds 10% of the largest Russian electricity producer, RAO UES, which supplies 70% of the domestic market, and owns 25% of Mosenergo, the provider of heat and electricity for Moscow.[38] It also has a stake in hydrocarbon spillover industries, particularly petrochemicals, machine tools, and metallurgy.

But many of the company's assets are in the media sector, acquired at least initially to facilitate government influence in that sector. Probably the most impressive is its Gazprom-Media Holding that comprises television, radio, printing press, cinema production, advertising, and movie theaters. Gazprom-Media Holding is one of the largest media holdings in Russia and Europe, posting 2008 revenues of $1.624 billion. In 2005, Gazprom expanded its media holdings with the acquisition of *Izvestia*, and in November 2006 the company purchased *Komsomolskaya Pravda*, Russia's largest circulation newspaper.

In addition to these media holdings, Gazprom has a diverse and quite surprising range of other interests. Many of these assets are financial: Gazprom is the main shareholder of AB Gazprombank (ZAO), which meets most of Russia's domestic banking needs (other than borrowings). It is also the founder of NPF Gazfund, the largest non-government pension fund in Russia, providing pension services to employees of Gazprom. In addition, the company owns an insurance company (Sogaz).

Other interests are more difficult to characterize. Gazprom is also the biggest single owner of agricultural land in Russia and has both a sausage factory and a brewery. It runs twenty-six cultural centers, many sports centers (including a soccer team, Zenit, from Putin's hometown of St. Petersburg), and medical and therapy centers. Gazprom even has its own space projects through a subsidiary,

Gazprom Space Systems, which operates three telecommunication satellites.

Information on Gazprom's international non-core activities is relatively limited. In one of the better-documented cases, in 2001 Gazprom sought to gain control of the plastic maker Borsodchem in Hungary using the privately owned Austrian CE Oil and Gas as a conduit. Countering Gazprom's plan was the MOL Hungarian Oil and Gas Company, another shareholder in Borsodchem. Nevertheless, in 2006, the CEO of Gazprom's banking affiliate in Hungary, General Banking and Trust, managed to increase his personal shareholding in Borsodchem to 18 percent by using his UK-registered family-owned firm Firthlion (see Kalotay 2008).

4.6 Business strategy

Gazprom has a broad strategy of globalizing its operations and becoming more vertically integrated, but this strategy is hostage to Russia's ambitious political interests. One reflection of these competing concerns is its investment strategy: Gazprom had, from 2004 to 2006, invested less in its core extraction and production activities (while increasing investment overall), and directed resources instead into gas transit projects. The heavy investment in transit reflects the company's desire to become a more vertically integrated company and in part to maintain influence and control over transit routes through markets and assets seeking. More recently, Gazprom has invested more in exploration and production – since 2005 its budget for such activities has more than doubled.[39]

Looking ahead, the company's business decisions will shape its future role in the international gas business. It is extremely difficult to predict future European gas demand (see Stern 2009). Gazprom may not be able (or maybe does not need) to increase gas supplies to Europe, at least in the short term. Thus, the looming gas crisis that was supposed to have major implications was suspended by the global financial crisis. Since 2008, reduced consumption in Russia, FSU, and Europe and low spot market prices have given Gazprom excess capacity and reduced its exports. In the first half of 2009, Gazprom's profit was 48 percent lower compared with 2008, while its debt grew by 31 percent. Thus, Gazprom can consider itself lucky that it did not invest heavily in its new gas fields as its current situation would look much worse.

Gazprom has a wide range of priority commercial projects (see Box 15.2), but pursuing these projects simultaneously is likely to prove overly expensive and risky for Gazprom. (Indeed, the onset of the 2008 economic crisis prompted Gazprom to cut its investments by 15.8 percent.)[40] The company's choices will largely depend on the position of the Russian government with respect to reforming the domestic gas market. Increasing gas prices for internal consumers would likely slow down the growth of the domestic market, increase the profitability of domestic gas sales, and therefore reduce Gazprom's dependence on the European market.[41] By contrast, if the government maintains the current policy, Gazprom would continue financing loss-making projects at home, making the European gas market critically important to the financial health of the company. In the long term, Gazprom has no real alternative but to develop the new gas fields to boost supply.

Box 15.2 Major Gazprom projects

Gazprom is involved in a number of wide-ranging field development and pipeline projects designed to increase its production capacity in Europe and Asia (see Figure 15.7).

First discovered in 1988, the Shtokman field is one of the biggest known offshore gas fields in the world and is located more than 600 km from shore, at a depth of 340 m. The field contains 3.8 trillion cubic meters of gas and 37 million tons of gas condensate.[42]

1. Development of the Shtokman field (on the Arctic shelf of the Barents Sea)

Over four phases, development of the Shtokman field is estimated to cost more than $50 billion. A preliminary development scheme envisions the construction of a sea platform above the field, an undersea pipeline, and a liquefied gas plant on the coast. Annual gas production is expected to be 60 bcm and the full development period is projected at fifty years.

After repeated delays and political grandstanding,[43] in 2007 Gazprom and French energy company Total signed a framework agreement, according to which Gazprom and Total will set up Shtokman Development Company to organize the design, financing, construction, and operation of the Shtokman phase

Figure 15.7 Map of major oil and gas fields and pipelines in Russia. *Source for oil and gas field data*: Wood Mackenzie (2009b).

one infrastructure. Later, a similar contract was signed between Gazprom and Statoil. Shtokman Development Company will bear all financial, geological, and technical risks related to the production activities. (Gazprom owns 51% of shares in Shtokman Development Company, while Total has 25% and Statoil 24% of shares).

Gazprom may delay development of the giant Shtokman gas condensate field depending on market conditions. Under Gazprom's original plan, it would produce 23.7 billion cubic meters of natural gas a year starting in 2013 from the first development phase of the field and up to 7.5 million metric tons of LNG a year starting in 2014.

2. Development of Yamal fields

Western Siberia's Yamal[44] has eleven gas and fifteen oil, gas, and condensate fields with approximately 16 Tcm of explored and preliminary estimated gas reserves (ABC1+C2) and nearly 22 Tcm of in-place and forecast gas reserves (C3+D3). Reserves of condensate (ABC1) are estimated at 230.7 million tonnes (mln t) and those of oil at 291.8 mln t. Within this region, Gazprom holds the development licenses for the Bovanenkovskoye, Kharasaveyskoye, Novoportovskoye, Kruzenshternskoye, Severo-Tambeyskoye, Zapadno-Tambeyskoye, Tasiyskoye, and Malyginskoye fields.

The Bovanenkovskoye field is the most significant with 4.9 Tcm of gas. The initial gas reserves of the Kharasaveyskoye, Kruzenshternskoye, and Yuzhno-Tambeyskoye fields amount to about 3.3 Tcm.

Developing the Yamal – with resources predominantly on land – would require less new technology and involve lower risk. Unlike Shtokman, which would require investment and technology from Western companies, Russian companies could develop Yamal by themselves.

In October 2005, Gazprom's management sanctioned the start of the development of the Bovanenkovskoe field. Gazprom planned to pump 8 bcm of gas a year at the Bovanenkovo deposit starting in 2011, eventually increasing production to 115 bcm per year in 2015 (see Gazprom 2010). Long-term gas production is to be increased to 140 bcm a year. In 2008 Gazprom launched the construction of the Bovanenkovo–Ukhta gas trunk line system. However, battered by the 2009 financial crisis and facing competition from LNG coming into Europe (mostly from Qatar), Gazprom has delayed the launch of Bovanenkovo to 2012 (Belton and Gorst 2010).

After some delays, Gazprom had plans to invest RUB 150 billion (more than $5 billion) into the development of Yamal fields in 2010. Now, the first gas is expected to come online in 2016 (Belton and Gorst 2010).

3. Nord Stream pipeline

Nord Stream is a 1,200 km-long offshore natural gas pipeline stretching through the Baltic Sea, from Vyborg, Russia, to Greifswald, Germany. It is designed to be a new route for exporting Russian gas from Yuzhno-Russkoye, Yamal Peninsula, Ob-Taz bay, and Shtokmanovskoye fields. It will link Russia directly to the all-European gas network, bypassing today's transit nations. Nord Stream will carry gas to Germany, from where it can be transported to Denmark, the Netherlands, Belgium, the UK, and France. The length of the sea section of the gas pipeline from Vyborg to Greifswald will be 1,189 km. It will use a 1,067 mm pipe, operating under a pressure of 200 atmospheres. The Shtokman gas and condensate field will be a resource base for gas deliveries via Nord Stream.

Nord Stream is planned to begin operating in 2011 with a transport capacity of around 27.5 bcm of natural gas per year. The second line construction by 2012 is projected to double throughput capacity to 55 bcm. The total investment for the offshore pipeline is estimated to be at least EUR 5 billion (the total cost of the project – including the onshore pipelines – could be around EUR 12 billion). Managing this project is Nord Stream AG, established in 2005. Gazprom holds a 51% interest in the joint venture and as of 2008 the other shareholders are Wintershall Holding, 20%; E. ON, 20%; and N.V. Nederlandse Gasunie, 9%.[45]

The project is controversial because of national security risks and environmental concerns. Environmental concerns include disruption of the seabed, impact on Baltic bird and marine life, and the dislodgement of World War II-era naval mines and toxic materials and other waste dumped in the Baltic Sea in the past decades. Some transit countries are also concerned that a long-term plan is to attempt to exert political influence on them by threatening their gas supply without affecting supplies to Western Europe. The fears are strengthened by the fact that Russia has so far refused to ratify the Energy Charter Treaty. In April 2006, Radosław Sikorski, then Poland's defense minister and currently the foreign minister, compared the project to the pre-World War II Russian-German Molotov–Ribbentrop Pact. According to Gazprom, the direct connection to Germany would decrease risks in the gas transit zones, including the political risk of cutting off Russian gas exports to Western Europe. In late 2009, the Danish, Finnish, and Swedish governments issued construction permits for the project.

4. South Stream pipeline

South Stream is a proposed gas pipeline to transport Russian natural gas under the Black Sea from the Russian coast (Beregovaya compressor station) to the Bulgarian coast and farther to Italy and Austria. The total length of the offshore section would be around 900 km, with a maximum underwater depth of over two km and a full capacity of 63 bcm. Two possible routes are under review for South Stream's onshore section from Bulgaria – one northwestward and the other southwestward. The project could partly replace the planned extension of Blue Stream from Turkey through Bulgaria and Serbia to Hungary and Austria and is seen as a rival to the planned Nabucco pipeline. The new pipeline would expand the country's export capacity to the continent from 47 bcm to 63 bcm of gas per year.

In May 2009, Russia signed initial transit deals with Greece, Bulgaria, Serbia, and Italy. (Gazprom and Italy's Eni have also signed a related agreement.)

As of July 2009, the Nabucco pipeline project staged a comeback, while South Stream seems to be losing. Bulgarians elected Boyko Borisov, and he wants to take Bulgaria out of the South Stream consortium. Without Bulgaria on board, the South Stream project is unlikely to happen. The Nabucco signing ceremony (involving Turkey, Bulgaria, Romania, Hungary, and Austria) signaled that the project is at last gaining traction. Meanwhile, uncertainty surrounding future demand raises the possibility that neither pipeline will ever become a reality.

In addition, the development of the Yamal and Shtokman gas fields on Gazprom's list of priorities and the financial crisis have forced Gazprom to cut back on investment by 26 percent in 2009. The technical and financial challenges facing South Stream will be fully known only after the completion of feasibility studies. Russia is projecting that South Stream will cost about $15 billion.

5. Supplying China

In September 2007, the Russian energy ministry approved a program for an integrated gas production, transportation, and supply system in Eastern Siberia and the Far East, taking into account potential gas exports to China and other Asia-Pacific countries (Eastern Gas Program). Russia is to supply natural gas to China via two Gazprom pipelines from Western Siberia and the offshore Sakhalin fields. The pipelines would be capable of supplying China with 68 bcm of gas annually or 85 percent of the gas China currently consumes. The West Siberian gas route could be operational in 2015, since the main trunk pipelines already exist and only their extension to China is required. However, price has been a particular sticking point, as Russia is seeking a pricing regime that is similar to the one in Europe, and China is seeking a lower-priced scheme. Given the fact that Asian markets are the growth markets, it is likely that at least the West Siberian route will be established sooner or later.

5 Conclusion

Gazprom has grand ambitions to become a global, vertically integrated energy company occupying a leading position in the world market. The company wants to compete with the majors on their own territory by developing upstream and downstream activities overseas.

Gazprom also wants to increase its stock price and market capitalization which, in turn, could allow the company to raise funds for new capital projects. The growth in the company's market value from 2003 to 2008 has been primarily driven by rising gas prices and the low level of Gazprom's initial market value; neither of those factors is any longer at play. Compared with IOCs, Gazprom's capitalization per barrel of proven reserves is extremely low – a reflection of the company's overall poor performance and large risks that arise from its close connection to the Russian state. The current financial crisis is becoming an important variable in Gazprom's future development. With little investment in infrastructure, Gazprom will likely be unable to continue to operate current (mostly mature) fields let alone undertake large new projects.

A supply glut on the scale projected by the IEA (see IEA 2009) would be a U-turn for an industry that braced for shortages in 2008 and be a significant blow to Russia. The projected oversupply would also be a major setback for Gazprom. This glut could have comprehensive consequences for the structure of gas markets. Suppliers could be under pressure to modify pricing terms under long-term contracts and to delink gas prices from oil prices and sell more gas on the spot market to stimulate demand. These new circumstances also lead to speculations that the link between oil and gas prices could be broken (see Stern 2009). In addition, the competitors are increasing their market share. Qatar is bringing on line new LNG supplies facilities, the United States is developing its massive unconventional gas reserves, and Iran has signed a deal to develop the immense South Pars gas field (although its prospects remain uncertain – see Chapter 6).

Where Gazprom as a company ends and Gazprom as a tool of the state begins is a rhetorical question. The Russian government has taken a stand against the European Energy Charter and its Transit Protocol because it will reduce Gazprom's monopoly powers. The export monopoly offers the state a benefit as it guarantees the Kremlin's control over what has become Russia's most powerful foreign policy tool. Gazprom's business decisions often have a political context, including Gazprom's plan to build one or two gas pipelines to China rather than build an LNG plant. The price of oil and gas rarely figures explicitly into the political strategy, but surely it is a very important background force in any political decision. When prices were low in the 1990s, there was less reason to try to control Gazprom, while at the same time there was an urgent need for outside capital and, thus, the government was interested in the production-sharing agreement contracts. It was the combination of Putin's rise to power – with a state-controlled "champions" model of industrial development – and high energy prices – which created the revenues for Russia – that made the strategy of asserting control over Gazprom both feasible and attractive.

The problems currently facing Gazprom are many and significant. Gazprom is trying to deal with new circumstances through its investment strategy (delaying the development of the Bovanenkovo field), turning its attention to new markets (particularly China), relaxing payment conditions for industrial users in Russia (with the hope that this will stimulate domestic demand), and strengthening its position in Europe (partially by reducing its own dependence on Ukraine's transit system). Some of these policies involve higher risks than others.

The future of the company is uncertain, as it depends not only on the company's effort but also on political and economic variables, such as global economic growth, gas demand, world oil and gas prices, the economic and political situation inside Russia, and the government's foreign policy priorities. If the main driving forces for Gazprom's decision making become even more political rather than business oriented, it will be hard for Gazprom to reach its ambitious goals.

Notes

1 This was several decades after the appearance of the first long-distance gas pipelines in the United States. By the early 1930s the Soviet economy

consumed 10–15 million cubic meters annually (mcm), but within a decade, this figure had grown to 3.4 bcm. For comparison, the United States consumed about 50 bcm in 1935.

2 The joke about the State Committee for Planning (Gosplan) explains the economic situation in the USSR – if Gosplan took over the Sahara, there would soon be a sand shortage.

3 The successful bidders were required to hold the shares in trust for a maximum of three years in return for providing loans to the government to reduce its budget deficit. At any time the government could buy back its shares. In a series of auctions, stakes in the companies were transferred into trust accounts and then sold to insider banks for a fraction of their market value. Stakes often went to the very companies organizing the loan tenders for the government, and through the loans-for-shares scheme, the government sold assets estimated at more than $25 billion for just $1.2 billion. The buyers included Mikhail Khodorkovsky of Yukos as well as Boris Berezovsky and Roman Abramovich of Sibneft. (These new oil barons had no prior experience in the industry but, more importantly, they had access to financial capital from private banks [which they owned and controlled] and close political connections to the Russian government.)

4 In 2000, the government owned 38% of Gazprom; the managers' official stake was around 35%, leaving about 20% in other, hidden hands. At least some of the hidden shares were also likely held by Gazprom insiders. Former Gazprom chairman and former Russian Prime Minister Viktor Chernomyrdin is rumored to be a major owner. (See Black *et al.* 2000.)

5 In 1995 Anatoly Chubais, the first deputy minister and a promoter of a strict budget policy, asked for the liquidation of the Gazprom stabilization fund and an investigation of its activities. In 1996 a tax scandal affected the relationship between Gazprom and the government: the accounts of some companies affiliated with Gazprom were frozen for tax arrears. The frozen property of Urengoigazprom amounted to about $14 million.

6 The gas exploration and distribution were handled by subsidiaries of Gazprom, though gas to the end users was distributed by local gas distribution companies. Since most of the local gas distribution companies were controlled by local authorities, it was difficult to suspend gas supply because of unpaid gas bills. Thus, Gazprom provides "hidden subsidies" to customers by allowing non-payment of gas bills.

7 The restructuring also led to a temporary name change from the Ministry of Fuel and Energy to the Ministry of Energy.

8 Rem Vyakhirev's license expired and the Federal Commission on Securities postponed the issue of its prolongation indefinitely.

9 The international majors were merging themselves, downsizing and outsourcing and not investing in new refineries. IOCs knew that production was set to decline and that exploration opportunities were declining as well. These internationals in Russia had "to sing" to the stock market, so their mergers hid the collapse of the weaker companies. On the state's side, Gazprom and Rosneft were getting bigger for the same reasons – to look better to the investors (though not because of lack of reserves as in the IOCs' cases, but to conceal depleting fields and a lack of investment).

10 This theory was set out by Richard Posner and developed by George Stigler. Colloquial characterizations of regulator capture date back even further in time. In 1913, Woodrow Wilson wrote, "If the government is to tell big business men how to run their business, then don't you see that big business men have to get closer to the government even than they are now? Don't you see that they must capture the government, in order not to be restrained too much by it? Must capture the government? They have already captured it." (See Wilson 1913.)

11 A World Bank study published in 2004 raised doubts about the accuracy of official GDP statistics and, in particular, the impact of transfer pricing. Transfer pricing is a common practice whereby oil and gas companies sell their output at a cheap price to a subsidiary located in a low-tax region. The subsidiary – which is registered as a trading, i.e., services company – then sells the oil or gas on at the market price, making large profits in the process. Once this effect is accounted for, the World Bank estimates that the oil and gas sector accounts for 25 percent of GDP (World Bank 2004b, 2005c). The official lower figure (19 percent according to Russian Energy Strategy 8 (www.inreen.org/node/89)) is distorted by questionable accounting practices.

12 Russia plans to step up exploration of the "Russian Arctic." Two-thirds of potential gas reserves are scattered throughout four polar regions, notably the Yuznno-Karsky oil and gas field, the western and eastern parts of the Barents Sea, and Alaska. The Yuznno-Karsky field accounts for 39 percent of the Arctic's unproven gas deposits.

13 The company's plan was to produce 570 bcm in 2010, 610–615 bcm in 2015, and 650–670 bcm in 2020 (Gazprom 2009b). (It actually produced 508.6 bcm of gas in 2010.) The Russian Cabinet of Ministers is predicting that independent producers will have only a 17–18 percent share, despite owning 30 percent of the resource base. Gazprom's latest (summer 2009) plans for the period to 2012 envisaged a one-year delay in the development of the huge Bovanenkoye field (reserves of 4.9 trillion cubic metres) from Q3 2011 to Q3 2012. Delay in Bovanenkoye's

development means that Gazprom's total capital investment is likely to reach 500 billion rubles, around 22 percent less that the 643 billion rubles that it planned to invest in December of 2008. Gazprom claims that its forecast of a 10 percent drop in gas consumption over the next four years is what has delayed the startup of Bovanenkoye. Gazprom is likely to postpone the development of the even more inaccessible and technically difficult Shtokman field (EGM 2009a.)

14 The gas sector has moved from a tight supply and demand balance with extremely high gas prices to an easing one with plummeting prices. Gas markets face enormous uncertainty surrounding the timing, pace, and extent of economic rebound, which affects all prognoses for the future.

15 There has been an average rate of production decline at the three major gas fields of more than 22 bcm per year during the period 1999–2004 (Stern 2005) and that corresponds to annual declines of 5 percent.

16 The inefficiency extends to electricity production as well. In fact, 60% of total internal gas consumption is now used for electricity generation. The country's gas-fired electric generators operate at only 33% efficiency on average, compared with 50–55% for the modern combined-cycle generation plants in Europe.

17 The new energy strategy is urging a stage-by-stage implementation. Three phases are outlined in the strategy: in the period 2010–2013, the consequences of the current crisis are to be overcome; in the period 2015–2022, the fuel-based sector is to be made efficient; and in the period 2022–2030, the economy will be turning toward the use of alternative sources of energy. In order to reach these ambitious goals, a total of RUB 60 trillion (more than $2 trillion) need to be invested in the Russian energy sector with 90 percent of it coming from private investors. From 2013, up to 5.5 percent of the GDP will be spent on the energy fuel sector.

18 While Gazprom's production dropped in 2009, Statoil increased production by 21 percent (Kommersant 2009a). Besides, Statoil has boosted its exports and is now almost as big as Gazprom in the European market. Gazprom's relations with foreign customers are regulated by long-term contracts, where quarterly price adjustments are based on European petroleum prices six to nine months before. Algeria and Nigeria suffered from the same problem and only Norway had increased supplies in 2009, as it had benefited from trades on the spot market for gas, where deals take immediate effect.

19 Few oil companies even bother to look for gas, as they know they cannot deliver what they find to the market. Many companies have no choice but to flare their gas due to a lack of transportation infrastructure.

20 Turkmenistan began focusing on China as a trade partner in April 2009, after an explosion on a pipeline halted Turkmenistan's exports to Russia, and exports have not resumed at the time of this writing. The Russian import stoppage has struck Turkmenistan during the recession-induced low demand, but the halt of gas imports from Turkmenistan has attracted far less international attention than its recent halt of gas exports to Europe.

21 In June 2009 Azerbaijan's state oil company SOCAR signed an agreement to sell gas to Gazprom, beginning with a relatively modest 500 mcm in 2010, with future increases built into that deal.

22 Itera was founded in 1992 as a company trading in consumer goods, oil, and oil products in the former Soviet republics. It entered the gas market in 1994 through the good connections with Turkmenistan (Turkmen companies were unable to pay for goods except with gas). In 2000, Itera sold nearly 80 bcm of gas to customers in CIS countries. OAO Novatek (formally Novafininvest) was founded in 1994 and is currently a rapidly growing independent natural gas producer with upstream operations located in the Yamalo-Nenets Autonomous Region (it holds net estimated reserves of 1.5 Tcm of natural gas). In 2004 Novatek became the biggest independent gas producer and in 2006 the company supplied about 29 bcm of gas to the domestic market (Pirani 2009). In 2008 Novatek produced 30.9 Gm^3, up 7.7 percent from the 2007 level. Novatek has not experienced a decline in production during the financial crisis. This is largely due to competitive prices. Novatek can charge what it likes for gas, while Gazprom has to stick to relatively inflexible regulated prices set by the Federal Tariff Service (FTS). At times of high demand and prices Russian buyers maximize their offtake from Gazprom, but the reverse is true when demand and the free market prices drop (EGM 2009b).

23 Recent reports have indicated that Novatek has been making gains on the domestic market. According to Catherine Belton and Isabel Gorst, it is as yet unclear whether the rise of Novatek – where output grew in volume by more than 11 percent in 2009 even as Gazprom's output fell by 18 percent – is part of the state's strategy to boost competition in order to increase Gazprom's efficiency or a distribution of assets among the groups competing for influence in the Kremlin (Belton and Gorst 2010).

24 The price elasticity for natural gas demand tends to be larger (in absolute value) than that for oil. Domestic natural gas demand can be expected to decline at least by 1 percent for every 10 percent permanent increase in price. It is unclear whether it would happen in Russia: the domestic gas consumption dropped in 2007 some 6 bcm, but that decline was not due to higher prices but due to lower gas demand in the

unusually warm winter. The Russian government hopes that the higher domestic gas prices would encourage independent producers to prod- uce more gas to supply about 50 percent of domestic industrial clients' needs (up from 29 percent now).

25 A proposal by the Russian Federal Property Fund (RFPF) to sell Gazprom's shares to foreign investors through a state organization (not through a stock exchange) was supported by the government. It helped the state to increase its stake in the company (the Russian Trading System (RTS) services are supposed to be paid by the company's shares). In the first three days after the ring fence was lifted, Gazprom's share price increased by 25 percent.

In April 2006, Gazprom applied to the US Securities and Exchange Commission for registration of a new program of F-6 American Depositary Receipts (ADRs). The new ADRs are now traded not only on the London Stock Exchange but also over the counter in the United States. The launch was complemented by an optimistic signal in terms of an ADR split: now one ADR consists of only four local shares (not ten as in the previous case). With this move, the ADR price has been returned to the $30–70 range in the US markets, sending a signal that the stock is likely to continue growing.

26 The average return on assets in the industry is 12–14% while Gazprom expected a 6% return on assets as of December 31, 2008, and a 5% return as of December 31, 2007 (see Gazprom 2008).

27 Gazprom set up specialized units within the subsidiaries that combined gas production and processing with gas transmission and storage. The structural changes were expected to differentiate the financial flows in gas (and liquid hydrocarbon) production from those in transmission, processing, underground storage, and marketing. This would help, for example, to expose gas transmission expenses under regulated gas transmission tariffs.

28 The buffer companies will be consolidated into six new entities man- aging different business segments: Gazprom-PKhG (underground stor- age), Gazprompererabotka (processing), Gazpromseverpodzemremont (northern underground maintenance), Gazpromyugpodzemremont (southern underground maintenance), Gazpromtrans, and Gaz- promtrans-Kuban. The company expects to increase its share in Gazpromtrans to 100 percent.

29 By comparison, the entire combined public and private sector debt com- ing due for India, China, and Brazil in 2009 totals $56 billion (Kramer 2008).

30 The majors currently have a debt-to-assets indicator of about 7% (for Exxon Mobil Corporation it is 3.8%, for Royal Dutch Shell 6%, for

Chevron 7.4%, and for BP 11%). On average, oil and gas companies have an 11% debt-to-assets ratio (Reuters Oil & Gas – Integrated: Company Rankings 2007).

31 In 2004–2008, Gazprom failed to convert an extremely favorable gas price situation into free cash flows that could have been used to reduce debt. Instead, Gazprom's long-term borrowings increased. In 2008, long-term bank borrowings included loans from Credit Suisse International, Salomon, Morgan Stanley and Dresdner Bank, which have been secured by revenue from export sales of gas to Western Europe. Also part of the long-term debt is money lent by the banks in the form of direct payment to equipment suppliers. Another source of borrowing (though with smaller share) is the series Russian bonds. The total amount of loans Gazprom received in 2008 was more than $15 billion (Gazprom 2009a). The borrowing is usually done in Western markets (80–88%) via Eurobonds. Gazprom continues to slash its short-term debt relative to total debt and plans to have 25% in short-term loans soon instead of more than the 30% it has at present. The company will also focus on unsecured loans with the aim of gradually freeing up to 50% of its export revenues from collateralized agreements. At present, Gazprom's exports to Western Europe are almost entirely used as collateral against loans.

32 Gazprom is the only company in Russia legally allowed to sell gas outside of the borders of the former Soviet Union. By Russian law, Gazprom is obligated to allow other producers to use its pipelines for domestic needs (not for foreign exports). However, when pipelines are filled to capacity, it is allowed to refuse to do so and usually does refuse.

33 www.gazprom.com/subsidiaries/subsidiary/.

34 Hermitage Capital Management (www.hermitagefund.com/).

35 Although official figures for non-core activity are not available, in 2008 so-called "other activities assets" that include production and sales of electric and heat energy, construction, and gas storage represented 11 percent of total company assets (Gazprom 2009b).

36 In November 2006, the OECD released a report on the Russian economy that criticized the Russian government for its expansion into key economic sectors. The OECD report expressed alarm that instead of investing in gas production, Gazprom had been expanding its interests in oil, electricity, power generation machinery, and media. Gazprom's investment in developing new gas fields has been minimal and its monopoly over the gas transportation infrastructure has constrained the development of independent gas producers. This strategy is potentially dangerous during a time of growing concern about Russia's ability to sustain and increase its gas production.

37 Most likely, $11 million is a prepayment and the total expenses will be greater. The sum is about 8 percent of Gazprom's 2007 PR budget ($140 million in 2006).

38 Gazprom's entities are organized around profitable firms that take control of non-profitable firms by exchanging debts for shares. Gazprom has established internal artificial transfer prices with respect to the specific funding requirements of the individual subsidiaries within each segment. Thus, stated results don't provide an accurate picture of the segment's financial position or the results of its operations. Generally speaking, internal transfer prices are set below the cost of gas production, so company independence is considerably compromised. Through this mechanism of artificial pricing, Gazprom also keeps the investments centralized.

39 Gazprom 2005–2008 Financial Reports. Note: For calculation we used end of a period exchange rate of the ruble against the dollar.

40 On July 13, 2009, the cabinet approved Gazprom's revised investment program, which was 15.8 percent lower than planned earlier. Gazprom declined to release which specific projects will be suspended, but more likely it will delay the development of the Bovanenkovskoye deposit in Yamal. Furthermore, Gazprom previously planned to pump 550–560 billion cubic meters (bcm) of gas in 2009 but now it aims to produce only 460–510 bcm. Gazprom also decided to cut its Shtokman deposit investment from $184 million down to $45.2 million and spend only one-third on constructing underground gas storage facilities. However, it plans to increase investment in the Nord Stream project by $113 million up to $1.1 billion (Kommersant 2009b). Thus, Gazprom appears to be cutting its major production projects, while still funding selected export programs. Moreover, Gazprom still seemed to have some money to spend on purchasing natural gas that the company apparently does not require: on June 29, 2009, Gazprom and Azerbaijan's state-run energy company SOCAR signed an agreement on Azeri gas supplies to Russia. SOCAR agreed to supply 0.5 bcm annually to Russia's southern regions beginning in January 1, 2010. Gazprom's deal with Azerbaijan was apparently aimed at undermining the Nabucco pipeline project, which would bypass Russia and Ukraine. Despite Gazprom's efforts in Azerbaijan, the Nabucco pipeline deal was signed.

41 Gazprom estimated its losses at the domestic market to have been about RUB 9 billion ($324.09 million) in 2006 and RUB 11 billion ($396.11 million) in 2007.

42 Since the 1990s, a consortium of Conoco (12.5%), Fortum (12.5%), Norsk Hydro (12.5%), and Total (12.5%) headed by Gazprom (50%) had been working on assessment and solutions to technical problems.

In 2001, Gazprom announced its intention to develop the gas field together with Rosneft. In 2002, the license for the field development and recovery was transferred from JSC Rosshelf to Sevmorneftegas. In 2003, Gazprom and Sevmorneftegas prepared for the project of gas field development, based on the analysis of the accumulated data. However, currently Gazprom does not have clear and reliable solutions to the questions of field development, as the company has not gathered enough observations and information.

43 In 2005 representatives of Gazprom stated that foreign partners in the development of Shtokman would be announced in the last quarter of 2005; the decision was delayed and analysts tried to explain the postponement primarily in political terms (including reasoning that Russia was holding Shtokman hostage over the WTO issue). In October 2006 Gazprom announced that the company will develop the Shtokman without Western companies and will no longer send Shtokman gas to the United States by LNG, but rather to Europe by pipeline.

44 Preparations for the Yamal's development started in the 1990s.

45 Originally, BASF and E.ON each held 24.5 percent interests. On June 10, 2008, N.V. Nederlandse Gasunie was added into the Nord Stream AG shareholders, creating the 2008 arrangement.

16 | NNPC and Nigeria's oil patronage ecosystem

MARK C. THURBER, IFEYINWA M.
EMELIFE, AND PATRICK R. P. HELLER

1 Introduction

Any attempt to analyze Nigeria's national oil company (NOC), the Nigerian National Petroleum Corporation (NNPC), must first confront the question of what it really is. Despite its formal organization as a vertically integrated oil company, NNPC is neither a real commercial entity nor a meaningful oil operator. It lacks control over the revenue it generates and thus is unable to set its own strategy. It relies on other firms to perform essentially all the most complex functions that are hallmarks of operating oil companies. Yet unlike some NOCs it also fails to fit the profile of a government agency: its portfolio of activities is too diverse, incoherent, and beyond the reach of government control for it to function as a government policymaking instrument.

Nigeria depends heavily on oil and gas. Hydrocarbon activities provide around 65 percent of total government revenue and 95 percent of export revenues (Nigerian Ministry of Finance and Budget Office of the Federation 2008; EIA 2010a).[1] While Nigeria supplies some LNG to world markets and is starting to export a small amount of gas to Ghana via pipeline, the great majority of the country's hydrocarbon earnings come from oil. In 2008, Nigeria was the fifth-largest oil exporter and tenth-largest holder of proved oil reserves in the world (EIA 2010b).[2]

NNPC sits at the nexus between the many interests in Nigeria that seek a stake in the country's oil riches, the government, and the private companies that operate most oil and gas projects. The best NNPC employees have good expertise in hydrocarbons and genuinely seek the best for the company and the nation, although they often lack the institutional support they need. The worst use their positions principally as a route to graft.

NNPC plays a number of roles in the oil sector through the activities of its manifold divisions and subsidiaries (see Box 16.1).[3] First

Box 16.1 Most significant divisions and subsidiaries of NNPC

Interface with IOCs
NAPIMS   National Petroleum Investment Management
                Services

Crude Oil Buyers and Sellers
COMD   Crude Oil Marketing Division
PPMC   Pipelines and Products Marketing Company
HYSON   Hydrocarbon Services Nigeria (marketing JV with
                Vitol)
Operational (Upstream and Natural Gas)
NPDC   Nigerian Petroleum Development Company
                (exploration & production)
NGC   Nigerian Gas Company (natural gas pipeline
                operation)
NLNG   Nigerian LNG (LNG facility operation, 49%
                NNPC-owned)

Operational (Downstream)
WRPC   Warri Refining & Petrochemical Company
PHRC   Port Harcourt Refining Company
KRPC   Kaduna Refining & Petrochemical Company
EPCL   Eleme Petrochemicals Company Limited

Services
NETCO   National Engineering & Technical Company
                (engineering design)
IDSL   Integrated Data Services Limited (seismic data
                processing)

and foremost, the company is a sector manager and quasi-regulator, using the approval authority of its subsidiary NAPIMS (National Petroleum Investment Management Services) to assert control over the international oil companies (IOCs) operating in Nigeria. Second, NNPC is a buyer and seller of oil and refined petroleum products. Third, NNPC plays an operational role in upstream, downstream, and gas transport activities, though none of its operational ventures is as yet a success.[4] (NNPC also plays a role in LNG operations through its participation in Nigeria LNG, but we treat this company as a special case as it is only 49 percent owned by NNPC.) Fourth, NNPC is a service provider to the Nigerian oil sector.

With isolated exceptions, NNPC is not very effective at performing its various oil sector jobs. It is neither a competent oil company nor an efficient regulator for the sector. Managers of NNPC's constituent units, lacking the ability to reliably fund themselves, are robbed of business autonomy and the chance to develop capability. There are few incentives for NNPC employees to be entrepreneurial for the company's benefit and many incentives for private action and corruption. It is no accident that NNPC operations are disproportionately concentrated on oil marketing and downstream functions (as indicated in a rough way by the breakdown of major divisions and subsidiaries in Box 16.1), which offer the best opportunities for private benefit.[5] The few parts of NNPC that actually add value, like engineering design subsidiary NETCO, tend to be removed from large financial flows and the patronage opportunities they bring. In this study, we make the following principal observations about NNPC and the Nigerian oil sector.

First, NNPC is the centerpiece of a system that performs poorly at the task of maximizing long-term oil revenue for the state. NNPC serves as a mechanism for administering the oil sector and transferring hydrocarbon wealth to the government, most significantly through sales of oil and gas to which NNPC is entitled from its joint ventures (JVs) with IOCs. However, NNPC also imposes massive burdens on the oil sector – it ties oil operators in red tape, which increases costs and uncertainties and deters investment.

Second, NNPC functions well as an instrument of patronage. Each additional transaction generated by its profuse bureaucracy provides an opportunity for well-connected individuals to profit by being the gatekeepers whose approval must be secured, especially in contracting processes. NNPC's role as distributor of licenses for export of crude oil and import of refined products also helps make it a locus for patronage activities. Indeed, the implicit government goal for the oil sector appears to be the maximization of patronage opportunities; government policies have been too inconsistent to allow discernment of any more explicit objectives.[6] Ever since Nigeria's independence in 1960 the country has evolved a host of patronage mechanisms that defuse threats to power and help hold a potentially fractious republic together. NNPC plays an important role in this ecosystem of patronage, though it is hardly the only institution with this function.

Third, the fundamental organization of the Nigerian oil sector has remained surprisingly stable over time despite the country's perennial political turmoil. Foreign oil companies control all operations, revenue flows to the federal government, and there are few independent regulatory checks on the sector. These basic realities have remained unchanged through numerous political realignments, including three transitions from civilian to military rule and three transitions back again. The basic structure of the industry has remained constant even in the face of numerous efforts to "reform" the oil sector, including the original creation of NNPC in 1977 through the merger of its precursor, the Nigerian National Oil Corporation (NNOC), with the federal regulatory authority at the time, the Ministry of Mines and Power. We will argue in this chapter that Nigeria's failures to develop operational, policymaking, and regulatory capability reflect the patronage equilibrium that has entrenched itself in Nigeria's governing institutions.

The remainder of this chapter explores how NNPC's position within Nigeria's broader ecosystem of oil-based patronage affects its organization, functioning, and performance. In section 2, we review Nigerian history relevant to the oil sector, focusing on salient points of both political development and oil industry evolution. In section 3, we examine the most important interactions between the Nigerian government, NNPC, and the IOCs that actually extract Nigeria's oil. In section 4, we consider how NNPC and the Nigerian oil sector more generally perform on various dimensions, including as a means of distributing patronage. Finally, in section 5, we conclude by looking at how corruption, bureaucracy, and non-market pricing reinforce each other in the Nigerian oil sector, and what this implies about the prospects for reform of Nigeria's oil institutions.

2 History of Nigerian oil and institutions

Whether or not one believes that Nigeria was inexorably "cursed" by the discovery of oil within its borders in 1956, there is no doubt that oil-related factors have become interwoven with the country's political development. We explore that history in two parts. First, we

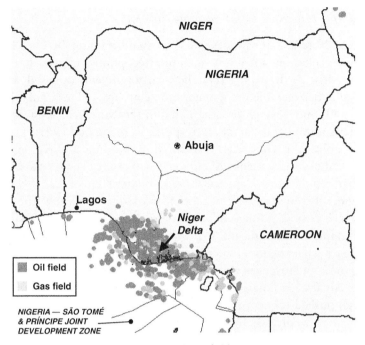

Figure 16.1 Map of major oil and gas fields in Nigeria.
Source for oil and gas field data: Wood Mackenzie (2009b).

examine the country's political development, and in particular the evolution over time of an increasingly sophisticated patronage system fueled by oil revenues. This system has arguably helped to hold the federation together, albeit at a high cost in economic inefficiency and stunted development of political institutions. Second, we trace the development of oil and gas operations in the country, concluding with some discussion of the present-day problems in the oil- and gas-producing region of the Niger Delta (see Figure 16.1). In this discussion of Nigeria's political and hydrocarbon development, NNPC itself is most notable for its lack of direct relevance except as an administrative tool for government revenue collection through its formal role as majority JV partner with IOCs. At the same time, it is impossible to understand the functioning of NNPC in isolation from the broader logic of why the Nigerian oil sector developed as it did and how it works today.

2.1 Oil and Nigeria's political development

At the time Nigeria gained independence from Britain on October 1, 1960, oil revenues remained too small to affect politics in a substantive way. Most of the young republic's early problems centered on the struggles between the three major ethnic groups – Hausa/Fulani, Yoruba, and Igbo – which predominated in the Northern, Western, and Eastern administrative regions, respectively (Diamond 1995). The country's political parties largely mirrored these ethnic and regional origins. Gridlock, disagreement, and a series of political crises caused the civilian republic to collapse in a 1966 military coup.[7]

By 1966, oil-related considerations had started to noticeably affect the country's politics, though oil was far from the only driver of political developments. Significant oil resources were located in the Igbo-dominated Eastern region, which focused attention on the question of how power and revenues would be distributed among regions. Igbo leaders were already nursing grievances against the national government[8] and pushed for secession of the Eastern region – a move that would leave them directly in control of substantial oil revenue in the future.[9] In May 1967, President Gowon – after failed attempts at reconciliation – pushed in the other direction, splitting the four Nigerian states into twelve in an attempt to undercut the dominant regional/ethnic political cleavages by creating jurisdictions heavily populated by other smaller ethnic groups.

Gowon's move was an early use of a tactic that future leaders would often employ when the Nigerian Federation was under threat: the creation of additional state and local jurisdictions.[10] Such jurisdiction creation can function as patronage writ large – a tactic of splintering opposing coalitions by buying off elements within these coalitions with the promise of revenue from the center. From the perspective of control over anticipated future oil revenue, the increase in the number of states placed the Igbos in an even weaker position than under the previous status quo. This economic rationale in conjunction with existing political complaints plausibly played some role in the decision of Igbo leaders in the Eastern Region to secede as Biafra, precipitating a horrific civil war that ran from 1967 to 1970 and ended with an Igbo defeat.[11]

Mindful of the potential for regional and ethnic cleavages to threaten central power, later politicians turned political parties into instruments for redistributing spoils more broadly throughout the country. That approach created powerful vested interests in redistribution. During the civilian Second Republic from 1979 to 1983, the party of President Shehu Shagari (NPN, the National Party of Nigeria[12]) perfected this technique,[13] and the Nigerian political system solidified into its current form as a sophisticated patronage network.[14] Tactics to maintain stability of the system included the creation of more jurisdictions in response to local pressure for revenue, the rotation of the presidency among the three major ethnic groups,[15] and the balancing of the presidential cabinet with two members from each state (Bevan *et al.* 1999). At the same time, the distribution of centrally collected oil windfalls to state and local jurisdictions in fact bred dependence and the endless pursuit of a bigger allocation rather than autonomy. A collection of states that might otherwise have no reason to bind themselves together instead evolved into a relationship of false federalism (Suberu 2001).[16]

Civilian and military governments alike proved incapable of effectively handling windfalls from oil. The quadrupling of oil prices in 1973–1974 resulted in a massive infusion of revenue that Gowon's military government was completely unprepared to manage prudently. As Tom Forrest describes, "economic policy was passive and took the line of least resistance" – taxes were cut, salaries and wages increased, and the naira appreciated against foreign currencies (Forrest 1995). Budgets ballooned,[17] making the government critically dependent on oil almost overnight. By 1974, oil provided 80 percent of government revenue and 95 percent of exports (P. Lewis 2007), figures not too different from those prevailing today. With few effective accounting mechanisms in place, corruption developed on a massive scale, yielding huge rewards for those connected to government[18] (Diamond 1995; Forrest 1995; P. Lewis 2007). Following another oil price spike in 1979, corruption scaled even greater heights, while regulatory bodies inside and outside of the oil sector remained impotent (Diamond 1995).

Following Shagari's reelection at the end of 1983 in a contest marked by significant fraud, the military seized power again in January 1984, gaining popular legitimacy from its promise to stamp out corruption and repair the crumbling economy. A long period of military rule followed, interrupted briefly in 1993 by the interim civilian regime of Ernest Shonekan, which fell in part due to dismay over its effort to raise the heavily subsidized prices of domestic fuel (P. Lewis 2007). Only after General Sani Abacha died of an apparent heart attack in 1998[19] – having allowed the civil service and public enterprises to atrophy as he diverted ever larger sums of money to himself and his cronies (P. Lewis 2007) – did the military itself orchestrate a more durable return to civilian rule. Political parties were re-constituted[20] and elections held during the transitional regime of Abdulsalami Abubakar, with the result that former military leader Olusegun Obasanjo, who had himself turned power over to civilian rule in 1979, returned to power as a civilian president in 1999.

The civilian regime of Olusegun Obasanjo was contradictory, for it pursued substantial reforms, yet in many ways business continued as usual. Perhaps the most significant achievement of the Obasanjo administration was its skillful macroeconomic management. Nigeria eliminated most of its previously massive debt, in part by containing expenditures and utilizing revenues from high oil prices more wisely than past governments. It also followed sound monetary policy and reformed its financial sector (Gillies 2007). With much fanfare, Obasanjo helped establish anti-corruption bodies, including the Economic and Financial Crimes Commission (EFCC) and, for the oil and gas sector, the Nigerian Extractive Industries Transparency Initiative (NEITI). These entities have had some real and impressive positive effect. At the same time, overall progress towards reform has been mixed at best. NEITI has brought heretofore unavailable oil sector data into the light, but it has not yet managed to effect broad changes in governance and accountability.[21] Furthermore, Obasanjo diminished his own anti-corruption credibility both by preserving elements of business as usual that benefited him personally as well as by using some of the new anti-corruption bodies like the EFCC against his political opponents (Gillies 2007).[22] Obasanjo's unsuccessful push for a third term in office and perceived manipulation of the 2007 presidential election was particularly damaging to his reputation as a reformer.

2.2 History of oil operations in Nigeria

Under British rule, a JV between Royal Dutch Shell and British Petroleum[23] dominated petroleum activities, receiving an initial concession in 1938 that covered all of Nigeria (Pearson 1970). Shell-BP

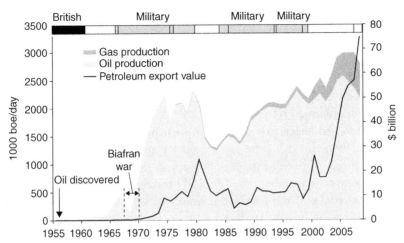

Figure 16.2 History of Nigerian oil and natural gas production, showing annual petroleum export value as well as the type of government in power (black = British colonial rule; white = civilian rule; gray = military rule). *Data sources*: Pearson (1970); BP (2009a); OPEC (2005, 2009).

made a small commercial discovery in 1956 at Oloibiri in the Niger Delta, leading to the first production and exports from Nigeria in 1958. Following Shell's discovery, a number of major foreign companies obtained licenses and began pursuing oil activities in Nigeria. The first offshore oil discoveries were made in 1963 by two companies eventually to become part of Chevron: American Overseas Petroleum (later Texaco Overseas (Nigeria) Petroleum) and Gulf Oil (Chevron 2010). Numerous significant oil fields[24] came online in Nigeria throughout the early and mid 1960s, driving an increase in total production from 20,000 barrels/day in 1960 to 420,000 barrels/day in 1966, as displayed in Figure 16.2. The high quality of Nigerian crude, which was mostly light and sweet (low sulfur), assured a ready market (Ahmad Khan 1994).

The Biafran War curtailed oil output in 1967 and 1968, though with no significant damage to productive capacity.[25] (Biafra extended from the Niger Delta and Niger River east to the Cameroon border, thus spanning a large portion of Nigeria's oil resources.) The more significant long-term impacts of the war on Nigerian oil administration stemmed from the way that it strengthened the victorious central government and encouraged it to assert national control over oil.

The perceived support of France's Safrap for Biafra was a particular spur towards reducing dependence on foreign oil operators (Onoh 1983). The desire to join OPEC may also have encouraged Nigeria's push towards greater state participation in oil – OPEC was at the time pressing member countries to secure robust national control over their resources, including by acquiring at least 51 percent of foreign oil operators (Ahmad Khan 1994). The Petroleum Act of 1969 restricted oil licenses to Nigerians or Nigerian-incorporated companies (Ahmad Khan 1994). In 1971, the government began to acquire IOC assets (including a 35 percent share of Safrap); created an NOC (NNOC)[26]; and became a member of OPEC. Throughout the 1970s the government nationalized increasing shares of foreign oil concessions in Nigeria; as of July 1, 1979 it had increased its stake to 60 percent of all major concessions in the country (Ahmad Khan 1994). These partially nationalized entities became the principal NNPC–IOC JV companies that still dominate production in the country today (see Table 16.1).

Oil production exploded in the early 1970s on the back of exploration and development success. As previously mentioned, oil revenue windfalls followed dramatic price jumps in 1973–1974 and 1979–1980. However, world oil demand contracted sharply in the early 1980s, and unwise policies under President Shagari[27] left Nigeria ill-prepared to adapt, contributing to a precipitous drop in Nigerian oil output in the early 1980s. Output did not recover to near previous levels until the early 1990s.

Development of Nigeria's natural gas resources has been much slower than in comparison countries with similar potential (Shepherd and Ball 2006), largely as a result of the country's unfavorable policy environment. Gas infrastructures (pipelines or LNG facilities) are expensive and their benefits accrue to investors only after many years of reliable operation; they are therefore nearly impossible to build in the absence of markets and a regulatory framework that foster confidence in long-term cost recovery. In Nigeria, controlled domestic prices for gas and for the electricity it can be used to produce have been the principal culprits in discouraging the development of domestic demand and associated gas infrastructure. Helpless to change basic pricing policies, NNPC's gas subsidiary, the NGC, operates existing domestic pipelines but is limited in its ability to significantly expand the domestic market. And only within recent

Table 16.1. *Significant joint ventures with NNPC, with 2008 liquids production for each*

Joint venture	2008 liquids production (thousand b/d)
60% NNPC / 40% ExxonMobil*	512
55% NNPC / 30% Shell* / 10% Total / 5% Agip	354
60% NNPC / 40% Chevron*	347**
60% NNPC / 40% Total*	207
60% NNPC / 20% Agip* / 20% ConocoPhillips	139
60% NNPC / 40% PanOcean*	27

Note: PanOcean is the one Nigerian operator. The Shell, Chevron, and Agip JVs saw the most impact on 2008 production figures from militancy in the Niger Delta.
* Operator.
** Figure includes 12,000 b/d from former NNPC/Texaco joint venture.
Sources: NNPC (www.nnpcgroup.com) and Ariweriokuma (2009) for JV ownership shares; Wood Mackenzie (2009b) for production figures.

years has Nigeria been able to create an investment framework sufficiently inviting to encourage the extremely high investment needed to develop LNG trains for gas export. As will be discussed in section 3, it did this in part by relegating NNPC to a minority stake (49 percent) in the venture.

Because most of Nigeria's gas is associated gas, more than 95 percent of lifted gas was flared in the first two decades of hydrocarbon operations (Ahmad Khan 1994). Flaring has been formally outlawed since 1984, and yet repeated deadlines for ending the practice have passed unmet. The most recent deadline to pass was in 2008, with about 40 percent of gas produced still flared as of November 2008 (Izundu 2009a).[28] As discussed above, insufficient infrastructure exists to collect and use all of the associated gas domestically or for export, and the government for its part has little incentive to shut down revenue-generating oil fields in order to enforce the no-flaring edict.

After three decades of fitful effort, Nigeria finally became a natural gas exporter in 1999 when it delivered its first cargo from the Bonny LNG terminal (Shepherd and Ball 2006). Due to periodic concerns about the strength of the gas market and government vacillation that heightened an already high perception of political risk, the Bonny LNG project fell apart and was relaunched twice (in 1982 and 1993) before finally coming to fruition. Gas production has increased since then, with the opening of a fourth and fifth train at Bonny in 2006 and a sixth one in 2008. Other proposed LNG projects in the country are moving slowly. A Chevron-led pipeline to deliver gas to neighboring Benin, Togo, and Ghana (the West African Gas Pipeline, or WAGP) was originally to have been online by the end of 2006 but was delayed repeatedly, including because of funding disputes and damage to feeder pipelines in Nigeria (Petroleum Economist 2009). Limited quantities of gas had begun flowing to Ghana as of early 2010 (Yusuf 2010).[29] The prospects for a far more ambitious project than the WAGP – the Trans-Sahara Gas Pipeline (TSGP) to deliver Nigerian gas to Algeria and then on to Europe – remain much more nebulous. Some worry that the TSGP is a distraction from the more important goal of increasing domestic gas handling capacity and demand (Brower 2009).

A striking aspect of Nigeria's recent oil sector performance has been the precipitous drop in crude oil production from a peak of around 2.5 million barrels/day in 2005 to a nadir of as low as 1.6 million barrels/day in July 2009, although monthly production appears to have recovered to around 2.0 million barrels/day as of this writing (IEA 2010). The main reason for the decrease was increased strife in the main producing region of the Niger Delta (see Figure 16.1); the EIA (2010a) estimated that Nigerian oil production in 2009 fell at least 30 percent short of capacity as a result of militant attacks on oil infrastructure.[30] The capabilities of militants to disrupt operations through activities like sabotage and hostage taking for ransom have grown in recent years. Militant actions that had previously been largely confined to onshore installations began to touch offshore facilities in early 2006 (Mouawad 2006) and reached their most audacious heights to date with a June 2008 raid on a Shell rig 75 miles offshore (Polgreen 2008). In addition to these direct attacks on oil-producing installations, organized oil theft from pipelines ("bunkering") may divert around 10 percent of production – worth millions of dollars per day – before it reaches IOC tankers (The Economist 2008b; Igbikiowubo and Amaize 2009). Insecurity in the Niger Delta leads not only to lost revenue but also to dramatically increased operating costs,[31] as IOCs are forced to pay more to security providers, oil services companies (many of which have pulled out of onshore operations in Nigeria), and employees.[32] An amnesty deal with Niger Delta militants in August 2009 appears to have eased the security situation somewhat of late and allowed restoration of some lost production, but it is unclear whether the truce will hold over the longer term.

A detailed analysis of the complex causes of the conflict in the Niger Delta (not to mention further discussion of its human toll) is beyond the scope of this paper, but some aspects of the situation in the Delta connect to other themes of this study. The unrest can be viewed through a number of lenses, all of which have some validity and are not mutually exclusive. First, in line with the public proclamations of militant groups in the Delta, the conflict can be seen as the rising up of oppressed and impoverished people who have suffered from environmental degradation and destruction of livelihoods associated with oil extraction but have not shared in its economic benefits. This viewpoint lays primary responsibility for the Niger Delta's woes at the feet of the IOCs, NNPC, and/or the Nigerian government at various levels. The fact that most of those suffering from the despoilment, violence, and anarchy in the Delta belong to minority ethnic groups that have been left out of the principal horse-trading in Nigerian politics between dominant Hausa-Fulani, Yoruba, and Igbo ethnicities layers an ethnic dimension on the basic grievance.

Second, the strife in the Niger Delta can be viewed as the natural flourishing of criminality in an environment in which governing and security institutions and the economy more generally have broken down (DonPedro 2006). A lack of alternative options for productive economic activity – unemployment rates were estimated by one Nigerian study to exceed 80 percent in Rivers and Delta states (Nigerian Institute of Social and Economic Research 2006) – facilitates ready recruitment by militias. And notwithstanding their Robin Hood political rhetoric about increasing the share of oil revenues going to the people of the Niger Delta, there is little evidence that money which armed groups like MEND (Movement for the Emancipation of the Niger Delta) generate from oil theft, kidnapping, and payoffs is used for anything but the enrichment of its leaders (Connors 2009).

Third, the patterns of violent competition in the Delta can be seen as an extension of the dense web of patronage that governs political dealings in Nigeria. The rise of the Delta militia groups has been closely linked to the machinations of key government figures seeking to use patronage networks to capture elected office[33] or a greater share of economic rent. There is widespread speculation that Rivers State Governor Peter Odili was the major patron supporting the rise of Alhaji Mujahid Dokubo-Asari, who later became the leader of MEND (ICG 2006a), and that Odili turned around and funded Asari's rival Ateke Tom when the governor had a falling out with the militia (PESD Interviews). Furthermore, according to government officials and IOC executives who spoke with the authors, certain state and federal government officials are suspected to be receiving income from illegal activities of the militant groups. For example, the diversion of oil from pipelines to unauthorized oil tankers offshore is a technically challenging and highly visible activity that would likely be impossible without high-level support in government.[34]

The problems in the Niger Delta represent an extreme manifestation of a vicious cycle that plagues Nigeria and its oil sector more generally. Government (and militant) activity centers around short-term competition for resources, not on provision of services or establishment of a stable longer-term framework for productive economic activity. In the absence of broad-based, strong institutions, individuals (and companies) seek to advance their interests by tapping into their private networks of people who can get things done. Connections to government officials or, in the Delta, to militant groups, can be particularly effective. Thus, for example, IOCs themselves may knowingly or unknowingly support the very groups that terrorize them through "surveillance contracts" that blur the boundary between protection and extortion (ICG 2006b). In 2008, NNPC's group managing director allegedly stated in congressional testimony that NNPC had paid a substantial "protection fee" to militants in order to assure the security of a pipeline, although the company subsequently claimed that his statement had been taken out of context (Amaize 2008; Hallah and Okeke 2008; Uwugiaren 2008).

Seen in light of this overall dynamic of institutional breakdown, the idea that fulfillment of the leading militant demand – an increase in the percentage of oil revenue that is allocated to state and local governments through the so-called "derivation formula" – will resolve the problems in the Niger Delta seems highly suspect. Spending by subnational governments already accounts for almost half of consolidated government spending in Nigeria, and the accountability mechanisms at state and local levels are virtually non-existent. There is no evidence that existing allocations to states and localities have been effectively translated into development. Increasing these allocations in the absence of improved measures to create jobs and government accountability to citizens seems likely to exacerbate the current problems by raising the stakes in the intense resource competition that already exists in the Delta.

3 State–NOC–IOC relations

3.1 *"Strong" president, weak institutions, and Sisyphean cycles of reform*

The president is the central figure in the Nigerian government and sets the tone for interactions between the state, NNPC, and the IOCs. There have historically been few limits on the president's freedom of action in making government appointments and directing the civil service and public enterprises. Since the return to civilian rule in 1999, there has been some modest strengthening of institutions of civil society like the media and NGOs that counterbalance presidential power. The federal legislative body, the National Assembly, increasingly wields some power through its control over legislative or constitutional changes,[35] although it remains mostly ineffective as a check on the executive branch of government. The best recent demonstration of constraints on the president's power came in 2006, when civil society groups, the media, and the National Assembly, collectively supported by substantial international pressure, joined forces to scuttle Obasanjo's bid for a constitutional amendment that would have allowed him to run for a third term.

Conspicuous by their absence are independent, effective government policymaking or regulatory bodies that could provide continuity in oil policy and a real check on the players in the oil sector. Government policymaking in oil is mostly rudderless and reactive, with IOCs able to have a large influence and domestic interests including NNPC able to block reforms that threaten their positions. Regulatory institutions are unable to exert effective oversight over IOCs, NNPC, or any of the other players in the Nigerian oil sector. As one example, the under-resourced government bodies responsible for collection of taxes and royalties – FIRS (the Federal Inland Revenue Service) and DPR (the Department of Petroleum Resources), respectively – have little capability to question sophisticated IOC accountants and often have difficulty coordinating among themselves (Hart Group 2006b). The result is undercollection of revenues. Equally serious is the inability of DPR, NNPC, or any other regulatory entity to accurately measure flows of petroleum within Nigeria and across its borders. The result is an environment in which both outright oil theft (as discussed in section 2) and shady trading (as discussed later in this section) flourish.

Both overlap of regulatory responsibilities and self-regulation are common, as highlighted by Nwokeji (2007) and Gillies (2009). Notably, while DPR is the formal regulatory body, NNPC often plays the role of de facto regulator through its interactions with IOCs. Conflicts of interest are inevitable. For example, NNPC both regulates local content and in theory can supply it.[36] Also, NNPC is responsible for cost regulation in the JVs while simultaneously serving as the majority partner in these ventures.[37]

Efforts by various presidents to "reform" NNPC and oil administration more generally have frequently involved either splitting out a regulatory and/or policymaking body from the NOC or reincorporating one into it. NNPC was originally formed in 1977 by combining the government's commercial and regulatory arms in oil. Under the later military regimes of Buhari (1983–1985) and Babangida (1985–1993), efforts were made to reestablish regulatory independence. Under Abubakar in 1998, the regulator was again eliminated. Under Obasanjo's civilian regime starting in 1999, the Ministry of Petroleum Resources was restored, but Obasanjo made himself Petroleum Minister and Chairman of NNPC. (Nwokeji (2007) provides an excellent historical review of the institutional changes in the oil sector.)

The historical lack of success in establishing an independent regulator despite outward efforts to do so is part of a pattern of lurching reform that does nothing to sustainably alter the functioning of the petroleum sector. As described in detail by Nwokeji (2007), initiatives to reform NNPC and the oil sector have been put forward by many Nigerian presidents. Such efforts have often been focused on

organizational forms, leaving intact the basic power dynamics, institutional dysfunctions, and deficiencies in human capacity that support
the status quo. Also, because the Nigerian system has lacked adequate
constraints on the president's power, reforms instituted by one leader
have frequently been quashed, intentionally or not, by a subsequent
one. A nascent effort to create an independent NNPC Board under
Babangida, for example, came to nothing when interim President
Shonekan's petroleum minister dissolved the Board because of corruption within NNPC (Nwokeji 2007). More generally, Babangida's
attempts to create organizational clarity and a more commercial
approach within the sector were undone by an Abacha regime that
prioritized the redirection of a huge fraction of oil rents directly to
Abacha himself (P. Lewis 2007).[38]

We suggest that there are two principal ways to think about why
reform and institution-building efforts have failed. First, the failure
of reforms illustrates a fundamental paradox about the Nigerian
political system. On the one hand, the center is "strong," in that
Nigeria's president is able to redraw the contours of government
bodies and decide who sits in important (and lucrative) government
positions.[39] The president's ability to influence NNPC appointments
is a key aspect of this power. On the other hand, the president's ability to fundamentally alter the basic parameters of governance – for
example, to improve institutional capacity, reduce corruption, or
change the relationship between the federal government and the
states – has appeared limited. As described in section 2, the president sits at the top of a pyramid of patronage, with the best ability to
steer benefits towards his associates. However, the fact that the president's power depends on success in delivering patronage can prevent
him from altering the nature of the pyramid that he ascended to
get to where he is. As demonstrated by Nigeria's unstable succession of chief executives, presidents who do not keep their demanding
patronage networks satisfied while at the same time steering clear
enough of national catastrophe to maintain their basic legitimacy
will soon be replaced.[40]

Second, the failure to achieve reform can be seen as representing
a failure of will on the part of politicians to break with the habits
that have gotten them to the top and set aside personal benefit for the
good of the nation. Even presidents who have understood the need
for reform have not wanted to be personally constrained by it. Major

reform efforts under the 1999 to 2007 regime of Olusegun Obasanjo seemed contradictory for just this reason. Obasanjo restored the Ministry of Petroleum Resources and its regulatory branch, the Department of Petroleum Resources. However, he then made himself Petroleum Minister and Chairman of the Board of NNPC,[41] removing any pretense of independence on the part of the ministry and NNPC. In another example, the Obasanjo administration initiated the Oil and Gas Sector Reform Implementation Committee in 2000 but then failed to act on its 2004 recommendations, which included measures to strengthen DPR and make NNPC more autonomous.[42] The feeble resources allocated to DPR[43] (and to Nigerian regulatory and policy bodies historically) support the premise that the appetite of the president for a truly independent regulatory authority is limited (PESD Interviews).

3.2 Government–IOC interactions

The Nigerian government has periodically introduced special incentives to maintain IOC interest in the face of a high government take and challenging operating environment. Such incentives, however, can place even more strain on government oversight capabilities. In the late 1970s, with IOC activity at risk of slowing as a result of rising government taxation, the government offered faster capital write-downs and reduced initial taxes to encourage investment (Wood Mackenzie 2009c). A major change in incentive structures followed the collapse of oil prices in the mid 1980s, in the form of a Memorandum of Understanding (MOU) that guaranteed IOCs in JVs with NNPC a minimum profit margin (Wood Mackenzie 2009c). The MOU allowed IOCs the choice of opting out of the standard petroleum profit tax (PPT) regime and instead paying a revised government take (RGT) based on non-transparent, oil-price-dependent terms in the MOU document (Nigerian Ministry of Finance, Oil and Gas Accounting Unit 2005). The MOU proved successful at generating significant investment (World Bank 2004c),[44] although at some cost to transparency. At the same time, the NEITI financial audit for 2005 suggests that the government has not properly administered the complex regime of the MOU overlaid on top of the PPT, with oil companies in Nigeria able to get away with overly favorable interpretations of the tax rules (Hart Group 2008).

The history of incentives for the development of natural gas shows the limitations of policy inducements in the face of systemic institutional failures. Significant incentives for investment in the upstream gas sector were put in place in the late 1990s, including a zero royalty rate, a reduced tax rate, and a more favorable capital allowance rate and investment tax credit than for oil (Wood Mackenzie 2009c). Unfortunately, these liberal incentives[45] did nothing to address the fundamental deficiencies in the natural gas sector – the lack of adequate systems for transporting the gas and then marketing it at profitable rates – with the result that Nigeria's natural gas production and utilization have continued to fall far short of potential.[46] Gas producers sell most of their gas to NGC, which in turn markets it to domestic end users, the largest of which is the state-owned Power Holding Company of Nigeria (PHCN). Artificially low power prices have stunted the development of the domestic gas market, and NGC has had difficulty collecting payments it is owed by PHCN.[47] As expressed in its Gas Master Plan, the government appears to be aware of some of these problems. However, it has thus far lacked the political will to address the core issues of gas and electricity pricing, even in the face of chronic deficiencies in electricity quantity and quality nationwide.[48] Government actions have instead focused on politically easier solutions that do not address the root problems, like pressuring IOCs to develop gas-fired power plants on an independent power producer (IPP) basis (Ariweriokuma 2009; PESD Interviews).

In a number of ways, the IOCs would seem likely to benefit if the Nigerian government could fix fundamental sectoral dysfunctions rather than simply papering them over with compensating incentives. These companies would see reduced costs and possibly increased development opportunities from a hydrocarbon governance regime that imposed less bureaucracy, uncertainty, and insecurity than Nigeria's does. It is far more straightforward for IOCs to operate within a unified and consistent administrative regime like Angola's (see Chapter 19).

On the other hand, there are potential benefits to IOCs from the current system in Nigeria. First, the failure to develop significant operational capacity within NNPC or other indigenous companies means that IOCs remain central to hydrocarbon activities in Nigeria. Second, the lack of technical expertise within NNPC keeps it from having any real bite in its oversight role through NAPIMS, meaning that IOC "cash call" demands cannot easily be verified and controlled. Third, the lack of strong independent regulation through DPR and FIRS allows IOCs to interpret tax rules in an aggressive manner without being challenged.[49] Fourth, as mentioned above, IOCs are often successful in lobbying for ad hoc incentives to counterbalance unfavorable features of Nigeria's operating environment. Fifth, when IOCs do run into serious conflicts with government bodies including NNPC, they have developed informal channels that allow them to resolve conflicts in a manner satisfactory to them (PESD Interviews).

The net result is what appears to be a conflicted attitude within IOCs towards the possibility of reform. While improvement in the country's oil institutions could in theory make IOC operations in Nigeria more straightforward and profitable, it could also disrupt a system within which IOCs play the dominant role and have learned to operate more or less successfully. Perhaps as a result, IOCs have tended to be quite supportive of reform ideas in their early stages, but increasingly wary as ideas have advanced further towards implementation or actually been put into practice. IOC concerns can be legitimate or self-interested or frequently both. Many IOC executives have expressed concern about possibly unfavorable tax implications of the Petroleum Industry Bill (Izundu 2009b), even though they may approve in principle of other provisions in the bill to correct institutional deficiencies, such as the idea of creating incorporated joint ventures (IJVs) that would control their own revenue streams (PESD Interviews).[50]

3.3 NNPC–IOC interactions

While the president and the National Assembly interact with IOCs at a high level through the creation of legal carrots and sticks, NNPC mediates most of the government's day-to-day functional interaction with IOCs. Historically, the great majority of Nigerian production has come from NNPC–IOC JVs operated by the IOC (see Table 16.1 for a listing of the current JVs). However, as shown in Figure 16.3, the fraction of production governed by standard JV terms has dropped significantly in recent years, largely in response to the government's inability to adequately fund the JVs. Some existing JVs have turned to modified carry agreements (MCAs) whereby the IOCs pay NNPC's

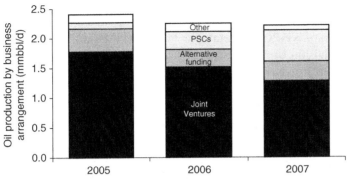

Figure 16.3 Nigerian oil production by business arrangement, 2005–2007.
Data source: Nigerian Ministry of Finance and Budget Office of the Federation (2008).

share of upfront costs on certain fields – this arrangement is also referred to as "alternative funding." All new contracts with foreign companies since the 1990s have taken the form of production-sharing contracts (PSCs), mirroring global trends towards this administrative arrangement. In a PSC, the operating oil company fronts all costs and then reimburses itself from revenues in the event hydrocarbons are discovered and developed. Figure 16.3 highlights the significant growth in production from PSCs in Nigeria between 2005 and 2007. While the PSCs reduce government risk and resolve the funding dilemma, they tend to reduce government take over the longer term according to the Nigerian Ministry of Finance (Nigerian Ministry of Finance and Budget Office of the Federation 2008).[51]

Through its interactions with IOCs, NNPC in effect provides most regulatory functions for the oil sector. In practice, the most important arm of NNPC in discharging this role is its division NAPIMS. NAPIMS serves as the first-line approver of the yearly budgets for the IOC-led JV companies, and then it is the conduit through which the government is supposed to fund its share of each JV in monthly cash calls. NAPIMS also acts as the government's agent under the PSC framework – it is responsible for negotiating and signing a PSC with each company that is awarded a hydrocarbon license. Critically, operating companies must obtain NAPIMS approval for the great majority of contracts tendered.[52] NAPIMS and higher-level NNPC management can strongly disagree at times, causing particular problems when both of their approval is required. At times a given oversight responsibility seems to be explicitly assigned to more than one division of NNPC– for example, both NAPIMS and the Nigerian Content Division of NNPC appear to be charged with maximizing local content in contracting. While the PSC framework removes the chronic problem for IOCs of collecting on cash calls in JVs, one IOC executive pointed out that many of the NNPC approval processes faced by IOCs operating under PSCs are equivalent to those for JVs (PESD Interviews).[53]

For the IOC, the various required interactions with NNPC create a bureaucratic thicket that adds significantly to the cost of doing business in Nigeria. Processes around contracts are particularly problematic, for several reasons. First, the contract approval process is exceedingly slow and bureaucratic. One IOC executive said that it takes at least twelve to eighteen months, and often significantly longer, to put in place a contract of any significance, as compared with three to four months from tender to award in other parts of the world (PESD Interviews). Second, a high percentage of contracts are subjected to a cumbersome sign-off process due to approval thresholds that are very low given the capital intensity of the petroleum industry. NAPIMS approval is required for any contract of greater than $500,000 (Office of the US Trade Representative 2010),[54] which several IOC executives estimated to comprise 80–85 percent of contracts (PESD Interviews). Most contracts additionally require the sign-off of the NNPC Executive Council and the NNPC Board (of which President Obasanjo served as chairman during his tenure). Large tenders are passed for approval to the Federal Executive Council, which is headed by the president (Gillies 2009).[55] Third, NNPC rules favor short-term contracts, typically limiting contract duration to two years or less. This both multiplies the number of contracts that need to be approved and makes it more difficult to attract quality contractors. With the expectation of aggressive bidding on cost and the requirement that contractors develop and employ significant local content, competent and serious firms may decide that they simply cannot make money by participating.

Problems associated with the contracting regime are further exacerbated by bureaucracy in the approval of yearly budgets for the JV operating companies. Significant delays are introduced by the need to obtain approval of the budget from NAPIMS, NNPC corporate, the

Ministry of Finance, and then the National Assembly (Hart Group 2006d). An IOC executive with whom we spoke said that his company's budget for 2008 had still not been finalized as of September of that year, even though the company had already committed significant money by that point. Since government funds are chronically short and authorities generally lack the technical capability to critically evaluate IOC proposals, the process becomes a somewhat aimless one in which the JV's budget allocation is typically lowered at each approval stage (PESD Interviews). IOCs respond by inflating their original budgets. The final government budgetary commitment may fall short of the funding the operator says it requires. In addition, the government may end up paying less than its upfront commitment in the monthly cash calls that are intended to cover NNPC's share of JV costs. Failures to fund the cash calls to the requested levels can delay JV investments in oil operations (Chukwu 2006). The combination of this protracted and capricious budgeting and disbursement process with a regime prohibiting long-term contracts is an especially potent recipe for waste.

3.4 Government–NNPC interactions

The way that money flows between NNPC and the rest of the Nigerian government is a major determinant of how the corporation is organized and functions. In the cash call payments described above, NNPC really only serves as an administrative pass-through from the government to the IOCs. The transactions that most fundamentally shape what NNPC is revolve around sales of crude oil abroad and refined products domestically. As shown in Figure 16.4, crude oil sales supply the majority of government revenue from the petroleum sector, with royalties and petroleum profits tax (PPT) making up the balance. The particulars of crude oil and petroleum product transactions are often highly opaque, but we here outline how they work at a high level following Gillies (2010). NNPC sells the majority of the crude oil it receives from the JVs to marketers for export, remitting the proceeds directly to the Federation of Nigeria's account in the Central Bank of Nigeria. At the same time, the corporation is allowed to "purchase" from the government a portion of crude oil at a below-market rate – this is known as the "domestic crude allocation" and is intended to be processed by the refineries to supply the domestic market. In practice,

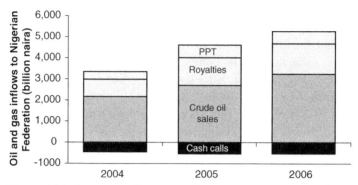

Figure 16.4 Amount and sources of Nigerian government oil and gas revenue, 2004–2006. In 2006, total revenues were ₦5300 billion ($41 billion), with ₦529 billion ($4 billion) paid back out in cash calls to the joint venture operating companies.

Data source: Nigerian Ministry of Finance and Budget Office of the Federation (2007).

the refineries meet at best about 15 percent of domestic demand (EIA 2010a), so NNPC sells the majority of the domestic crude allocation for export and uses the proceeds to help cover the cost of importing refined products at international prices. However, NNPC must then sell refined products to domestic marketers for resale at highly subsidized official pump prices, which were set at ₦65 (around $0.43) per liter as of early 2010 (Ailemen 2010). The loss NNPC takes on the refined products far outweighs its profit on the original sales of crude. The government is supposed to pay back NNPC to fill the yawning gap, but as of February 2010 NNPC claimed it was still owed ₦1.1 trillion ($7 billion) by the Federal Government and thus could not make good on the ₦450 billion ($3 billion) in crude oil proceeds it in turn is said to owe the Federation Account (Ailemen 2010).

The above interactions have a number of profound implications for NNPC and the Nigerian oil sector more generally. First, they suggest that NNPC is structurally insolvent. Crude sales are supposed to pass straight through to the Federation Account; NNPC loses money on refined product sales; other operating divisions (to be discussed later) cannot begin to generate sufficient revenue to fund the company; and there appears to be no other formal allocation to NNPC from the budget of the federal government. Any funding seemingly must come from informal allocations (or from NNPC withholding what it supposedly owes the government).

Second, this condition of perpetual corporate indebtedness helps explain and reinforce the absence of clarity around NNPC's budgeting processes. Several former NNPC executives described a process in which the group executive directors (GEDs) of NNPC's constituent business units would prepare budgets based on their own needs, jointly hash out an overall corporate budget along with the group managing director (GMD), and then submit the results to the NNPC board (with the president as chairman ever since Obasanjo's administration) for approval. Beyond these basics, subsequent approval processes and precise funding sources seemed unclear and changeable. One source said that approval of the National Assembly was not required for NNPC budgets. However, another NNPC executive mentioned that the legislature had become involved in the budget approval process ever since it passed a "transparency" provision in 2007 to help the government look into the high cost of fuel subsidies (PESD Interviews). There was also disagreement among sources as to whether NNPC budgets were really meaningful documents or merely technical exercises. Our supposition is that much of the ambiguity in budgeting processes for NNPC ultimately stems back to the NOC's basic design as a formally commercial entity that in fact can never make money.

Third, the nature of the financial flows between the government and NNPC means that NNPC has no financial autonomy from the government and thus no genuine ability to act as a business. Its formal structure as a diversified, vertically integrated company is only a facade. A striking observation from our conversations with former NNPC executives was how little control they had over the operations of their respective units. Without any ability to reliably allocate funding from the top, GEDs may sometimes find creative solutions that allow them to pursue business goals at the margin (for example, NNPC's upstream arm NPDC was able to fund some of its operations through a partnership with Agip) but are unable to improve unit performance in a more comprehensive way.

Fourth, the same architecture of financial flows that leads to NNPC being formally insolvent provides an ideal opportunity for individuals to extract private gains. Any transaction for which there exists an official price rather than a market-determined one offers the potential for individuals to profit handsomely through arbitrage, and there are many such transactions at the nexus of crude oil sales, refining, and refined product imports and distribution in Nigeria. It is therefore hardly surprising that a disproportionate number of NNPC divisions and personnel are concentrated in these areas (see Box 16.1). The Crude Oil Marketing Division (COMD) is supposed to sell the government's share of crude oil on a term basis, at an official selling price (OSP) set by COMD each month, to international traders and refiners as well as to NNPC's Pipelines and Products Marketing Company (PPMC) to supply NNPC's domestic refineries. When domestic refinery output does not meet demand, which is invariably the case, PPMC can arrange import contracts to bring refined products into the country for domestic sale. Lack of transparency in COMD and PPMC procedures creates significant opportunities for corruption. On the crude oil marketing side, according to the first NEITI audit, "The choice of term buyers is taken at higher levels than COMD, implying NNPC's group managing director and the presidency. Decision making is particularly opaque at these levels" (Hart Group 2006f). Especially given pricing terms that can be favorable to buyers, being awarded a term contract for buying crude oil can be a very lucrative proposition. COMD procedures are also not up to the task of ensuring accurate physical accounting of the crude oil, which opens up another possible pathway for corruption (PESD Interviews). Analogous problems of both physical accounting and vulnerable contracting procedures[56] create corruption risks in the import of refined products (Hart Group 2006f).

Capped official prices for fuel sales to consumers provide ample opportunities for corruption at the retail marketing level. (In addition to selling to marketers, NNPC operates some of its own filling stations.) One characteristic dynamic, described by Ariweriokuma (2009) as having been especially pronounced in the late 1990s, is that low domestic prices drive marketers to divert products to neighboring countries,[57] create scarcity, and stimulate the development of a sizeable black market in Nigeria. Even today, fuel scarcity remains the norm, and sales to consumers often take place at prices above the official ₦65 per liter rate despite periodic government noises about enforcing price directives (Bello 2008). Several interviewees described a process by which "privileged Nigerians" with political connections are able to obtain allocations of petroleum products from NNPC at subsidized prices, which they can then resell at market rates.

The government has moved to open up imports to a larger diversity of major and independent marketers, but Ariweriokuma (2009) notes that fewer marketers than expected have taken advantage of the policy change. This is probably not surprising given that they cannot make a profit unless they develop channels selling at above the official price. As in the markets for natural gas and electricity, no amount of deregulation, privatization, or government mandates will yield satisfactory results while low, centrally planned prices remain in place. This fact is generally recognized by market participants including NNPC personnel with whom we spoke, but fuel price subsidies remain fiercely supported by unions and the broader public on grounds of social equity.[58] Price liberalization seems to be a third rail that is challenged by politicians at their own risk (PESD Interviews).

3.5 NNPC's operational units

As described above, one of the striking features of NNPC is the degree to which buying and selling of oil and refined products is emphasized over operational activities. In some cases, operational weakness may serve to directly strengthen the position of the buyers and sellers, with the area of refining being the most obvious example. NNPC's downstream subsidiaries – which include Warri Refining & Petrochemical Company (WRPC), Port Harcourt Refining Company (PHRC), and Kaduna Refining & Petrochemical Company (KRPC) – have compiled a woeful record as operators of domestic refineries. NEITI found the refinery utilization rate to be 43 percent, less than half of the global average of 85 percent during the audit period (Hart Group 2006e). Low refinery capacity creates massive profit opportunities for crude exporters who can arbitrage between NNPC's domestic crude allocation price and international prices as well as for importers who can sell refined products in Nigeria at well above the official price. NNPC personnel in a position to facilitate and participate in these transactions also stand to benefit.

Meanwhile, NNPC executives who genuinely seek to improve the operational performance of downstream units are undercut in a variety of ways. First and foremost, NNPC refining operations are not embedded in any kind of rational market framework that would allow them to develop into functioning businesses. As the chief executive of an indigenous Nigerian oil company aptly put it, "Being the MD

[managing director] of a refinery [in NNPC] is no job. It's a processing unit where you don't know the price of the input or the price of the
output!" Second, downstream executives have no real business autonomy due to their inability to reliably procure from the government
the resources needed to run the refineries.[59] One former executive of
an NNPC refining subsidiary discussed his shock upon taking the
job at the complete state of neglect of the wastewater treatment system. He soon found himself stymied trying to obtain the money for
the required repairs. The same executive also detailed his struggles
to secure government funding to replace a broken catalyst.[60] When
asked about allegations that some in government might like to keep
refinery utilization factors low to protect their own lucrative import
positions, the former executive responded that such allegations are
"not totally false." At the same time, he said, no one ever told him
not to run his refinery. In practice, though, withholding funding for
ongoing maintenance has the same effect.

What makes the Nigerian refinery situation even more frustrating, as Nwokeji (2007) points out, is that massive sums of money
have been sunk into ambitious initiatives to turn around performance, without lasting positive results. Funsho Kupolokun, NNPC's
GMD at the time, reportedly testified to the Nigerian House of
Representatives in January 2007 that NNPC had spent over $1 bil-
lion on its refineries over the previous eight years (Adelaja 2007; Isine
and Nwankwo 2007). NNPC management reported in February
2010 that the latest turnaround maintenance effort has enabled the
Kaduna and Warri refineries to come back online at a capacity factor of greater than 60 percent (Daily Trust 2010), although these
figures are difficult to verify.[61] In any case, the real acid test will be
whether the willingness to sink massive capital into refinery turnaround contracts, which has never been in short supply,[62] is matched
with an effort to create incentives for running ongoing operations
reliably.

Some argue that the refineries will never run effectively as subsidiaries of NNPC, and that selling them off would benefit both the
refineries and NNPC itself (PESD Interviews). A long-time NNPC
employee and former group executive director in the downstream
described refinery privatization initiatives that began under Babangida
and have proceeded on an on-again, off-again basis ever since. An
attempted sale of the Port Harcourt and Kaduna refineries to private

parties on the eve of President Obasanjo's departure from office was scrapped in 2007 amid charges that the sale was a corrupt handout to the president's cronies (Haruna 2007). Several interviewees pointed to the sale of Eleme Petrochemicals to an Indonesian firm in 2006 (NNPC retained an equity stake) and its subsequent improvement as a sign that privatization can work in the downstream. However, we speculate that the Eleme sale might have succeeded in part because its petrochemicals-oriented business is not exposed to the profound distortions of markets for vehicle fuels.

While downstream operations have been most spectacular in their non-performance, most of NNPC's other operational subsidiaries are also largely ineffectual because of the way they confront distorted markets and/or entrenched rent seeking. In the case of NGC, NNPC's subsidiary charged with developing and operating the nation's gas handling infrastructure, the fundamental problem is the electricity and natural gas pricing policy over which NGC has no control. Now that the West African Gas Pipeline appears to have come online in a limited capacity, NGC is indirectly participating in regional exports by transporting Nigerian gas to the pipeline (Yusuf 2010). Looking forward, this has the potential to create tension between exports through the WAGP and domestic use of gas, particularly as long as the domestic market remains underpriced and undersupplied.

NNPC's upstream oil and gas subsidiary NPDC (Nigerian Petroleum Development Company) has some limited operations. However, in a strong contrast to countries like Norway (see Chapter 14) and Brazil (see Chapter 12) that have focused on developing domestic capability in the upstream, the Nigerian government has historically provided little support for NNPC's own exploration and production activities. Nwokeji (2007) points out that the government in 1985 sold to IOCs all except one of the offshore blocks in which NNPC had discovered oil and in 1990 reassigned other NNPC blocks to IOCs. NPDC's current sole-operated production is probably no more than around 10,000 bpd (Nwokeji 2007), which comes mostly from marginal fields. Including the output of a partnership between NPDC and Agip (the Agip company name is still associated with Eni's operations in Nigeria), production capacity could be as high as 60,000–80,000 bpd (PESD Interviews). At the time of writing, NNPC/NPDC appeared determined to claim operatorship of acreages being sold off by Shell,

Total, and Agip, but Akinosho (2011) argues that private Nigerian operators would be better stewards of the fields than today's weakened NPDC.

Nigeria LNG (NLNG) has been successful as an operator, but this enterprise is a special case unlike any other of NNPC's operational ventures. A condition for IFC financing of Nigeria LNG in the early 1990s was majority private ownership, so NNPC owns only 49 percent of the company (Shepherd and Ball 2006). As a result, government interference has not disrupted the operation in the same way that it has NNPC's majority or wholly owned subsidiaries. It took many years to arrive at an arrangement that could allow LNG exports to go forward in Nigeria, but once the suitable institutional framework of NLNG was finally in place, progress was relatively rapid. The importance of the Nigerian government's not having a majority stake in NLNG was demonstrated in 1997, when Nigerian energy minister Dan Etete attempted to sack the entire board of NLNG, only to realize that he was unable to do this because NNPC owned only 49 percent of the venture (Shepherd and Ball 2006).

NNPC's service-oriented subsidiaries are among the most promising parts of the corporation in part because they offer fairly limited opportunities for private benefit and do not have to contend with badly distorted markets.[63] The principal services subsidiaries of NNPC are NETCO (National Engineering & Technical Company), which focuses on engineering design, and IDSL (Integrated Data Services Limited), which provides seismic data processing services. As services-focused ventures, neither of these organizations is involved with the same kinds of rent streams as are found in the rest of the industry, nor are their operations particularly capital-intensive. These attributes can potentially be a great blessing in limiting the interactions of the Nigerian government with NETCO and IDSL. Their lack of windfall profit opportunities means that NETCO and IDSL attract significantly less interest and interference from NNPC and government officials. Their relatively low funding requirements mean that they are less dependent on the government for resource support and in theory could become financially independent.

NETCO is the only division of NNPC that is significantly self-funded and perhaps even self-sufficient.[64] The operation started in 1989 as an NNPC JV with Bechtel, which sold its stake back to NNPC to make NETCO a fully owned subsidiary in 1997 (www.

netco.com.ng).[65] NETCO's early years under Bechtel's tutelage helped
to instill a strong engineering culture. NETCO contracts today come
from a variety of clients including all of the significant IOCs operating
in Nigeria; NLNG; major service companies like Kellogg, Brown, &
Root; and NNPC itself. While NETCO certainly benefits from local
content preferences in obtaining contracts, it also appears to be genuinely capable[66] and focused on further learning and improvement.[67]
Most IOC executives with whom we spoke (with one exception[68])
were complimentary of NETCO's performance in the contracts it had
executed for them.

4 Strategy and performance of NNPC

Because of the diffuse and heterogeneous character of NNPC and its
lack of control over its own cash flow, corporate strategy for NNPC
does not exist in any conventional sense – as a set of approaches
designed to most effectively accomplish centrally determined goals.
The strategy that seems implicit in NNPC's actual functioning is to
continue to rely on IOCs to do the actual work of hydrocarbon extraction while NNPC functions largely as a tool for patronage.

The performance of NNPC can thus be measured both by its contribution to traditional hydrocarbon goals – maximization of existing
and future production and associated revenues for government, and
development of indigenous capability in oil – and by how well it delivers private goods for patronage. In fact, it is usually possible to explain
the company's shortcomings in the hydrocarbon arena by looking at
how the apparently dysfunctional status quo actually serves goals of
patronage. Often, the performance of NNPC is powerfully shaped by
institutional structures beyond its control.

4.1 *Maximizing government revenue from hydrocarbons*

At first glance, oil sector arrangements in Nigeria seem to do a reasonably good job of maximizing government take, at least in the narrow sense of what percentage of revenue from current oil operations
flows to the government. As discussed in section 3, the government's
take across Nigeria's oil and gas portfolio is usually estimated to average 80 percent or higher. Government take is lower for deep water
(World Bank 2004c) and natural gas operations than it is for onshore

oil in order to incentivize these activities, although some pressures exist within the Nigerian government to roll back these incentives.[69] NNPC contributes to the high government take mainly by serving as an administrative vehicle through which the JVs and PSCs are implemented, rather than through any special skill of its own.

At the same time, there are a number of ways in which NNPC and the broader systems of which NNPC is a part significantly limit government revenue collection. First, the enormous costs that NNPC bureaucracy imposes on oil operations cause the total rents available to the government to be much less than they could be. In a highly capital-intensive business like oil, approval times of over a year for even relatively minor contracts push up costs dramatically, significantly cutting into net government revenue. These costs end up being built in to the cash calls paid out by the government to JVs or the cost oil allocated to PSC operators.

Second, the delays and insufficiencies in cash calls executed through NNPC actively delay hydrocarbon developments, deferring government revenue from these projects. This problem is caused more by government funding limitations and the use of the JV arrangement than by anything NNPC does or does not do. However, NAPIMS and NNPC are deeply enmeshed in the highly bureaucratic process of allocating budgets for the JVs. They also have a say in how to distribute what money there is when the government falls short of its cash call obligations (PESD Interviews). The cash call conundrum has been avoided on new developments through the use of PSCs and will likely be worked out over time on existing projects through conversion of JVs into incorporated JVs or at the very least increased use of "alternative funding."[70]

Third, NAPIMS and NNPC are unable to adequately oversee the cost performance of the IOCs or to ensure that these companies provide good long-term stewardship of Nigeria's resources for the country's benefit. As a NAPIMS manager with whom we spoke freely admitted, IOC staff are better trained, better funded, and have better access to technology than their NAPIMS counterparts.[71] According to the NAPIMS manager, NAPIMS staff review IOC budgets and work programs line by line and request justifications for the technical choices made. They may disagree with a particular choice, arguing, for example, that the operator should drill a different number of wells from what was proposed. However, NAPIMS for the most part lacks the technical expertise, confidence, and backing within the company and government to impose an alternative solution.[72] A more capable sector manager and regulator than NAPIMS might be able to better ensure that costs are being minimized overall and especially that they are not being disproportionately allocated by IOCs to the Nigerian government. NAPIMS staff mentioned to us some attempts to benchmark performance among IOCs, but these efforts appear to be at a very nascent stage. More generally, NAPIMS lacks any internal incentives that would reward staff for skillful regulation of the IOCs.

Fourth, the dreadful performance of NNPC's refineries contributes to a situation in which the corporation and the country take a massive loss subsidizing fuel. However, as we argued in section 3, refinery underperformance is arguably more an effect of subsidized fuel markets and intertwined patronage activities than the root cause of NNPC's and Nigeria's overwhelming fuel subsidy burden.

Analogously, NNPC's gas subsidiary NGC might appear superficially responsible for failing to develop the domestic gas market and the revenue that could flow from it, when the real culprit is distorted markets. Nigeria certainly leaves money on the table by failing to exploit natural gas to a greater degree than it does. In particular, non-associated gas fields are not developed by IOCs due to uncertainty about whether the investment can be recouped, according to one IOC manager whose company holds significant reserves in a non-associated gas field. However, the real root cause of this problem is not NGC but rather the absence of a liberalized gas market that would provide confidence to gas developers that gas could be sold at a reasonable price over a sustained period.

Fifth, as a central cog in the nationwide machinery of oil patronage and organized disorganization, NNPC has contributed significantly to the climate of tension and self-interest that has fueled the Niger Delta conflict. In addition to its direct human cost, the conflict has resulted in significant losses of production, which have dramatically impacted the Nigerian Federation's revenue gains from oil.

4.2 Developing indigenous technological capability

Hydrocarbon-rich countries may seek to build up their technological capability in petroleum as a route to broader industrial development and economic growth, even if this means sacrificing some revenue in the short term. Norway is the most successful demonstration of this strategy in the petroleum sector (see Chapter 14),[73] and developing countries like Trinidad & Tobago have also achieved significant results. The Nigerian government appears to share this ambition. In 2005 it set goals of achieving 45 percent Nigerian content in the oil and gas industry by 2006 and 70 percent by 2010.[74] In April 2010 it passed a law to make local content objectives legally binding and provide for enforcement, including through a Nigerian content development and monitoring board (Shosanya 2010).[75] NNPC has thus far served as the principal agent of government efforts to increase local content; it could also in theory serve as a vehicle of local content development through its own operational activities. As we will discuss below, NNPC has been moderately successful as a driver of private local content and for the most part a failure in developing its own capabilities.

NNPC has pushed the local content agenda through the efforts of NAPIMS as well as its Nigerian Content Division (NCD), which was established in 2005 (Vanguard 2010). The percentage of local content remains well below the 2010 target of 70%; one sector observer estimated local content to have reached 35% as of 2009 (PESD Interviews), as compared with around 5–8% in 2005 (Ariweriokuma 2009). However, most of those we interviewed felt that trends were positive and that NAPIMS and NCD deserved some of the credit for this.

One of the most nettlesome ongoing challenges is how to separate legitimate Nigerian value addition from cases that involve no more than the establishment of a Nigerian middleman. The 2005 auction of exploration blocks, which was intended to inject more transparency into the petroleum licensing process[76] (PESD Interviews; Reed 2006), illustrated this problem, as did the 2006 and 2007 follow-on bidding rounds.[77] An explicit focus on local ownership resulted in the awarding of most contracts to politically connected Nigerian companies with relatively little experience. A significant number of these companies were then unable to pay signature bonuses, leading to speculation that they were pursuing a strategy of operator-as-arbitrageur, wherein they bid amounts they were incapable of paying under the presumption that an international company would come along and both cover the fees and add a profit for the Nigerian seller (PESD Interviews). In part to address these problems with ownership-based local content directives, NNPC has issued twenty-two guidelines to the industry that emphasize domiciliation – the location in Nigeria of activities that add value – rather than just indigenization of ownership (Vanguard 2010).

There are an increasing number of Nigerian companies playing meaningful roles in the oil sector, although their contribution remains small overall. Among indigenous companies, Oando PLC[78] is the most significant player, with successful ventures in the upstream, downstream, services, and gas and power segments (Vanguard 2009). Oando's upstream unit is production operator of two oil blocks and holds equity in a marginal field. Under a program that first awarded acreage in 2003, designated marginal fields with reserves too small to be of interest to IOCs are preferentially offered to Nigerian companies (Ariweriokuma 2009).[79] This program is still a work in progress, with many indigenous companies facing obstacles of both financing and expertise (PESD Interviews), but the marginal field program may help Nigerian companies develop their operational skills. A number of indigenous players (including NETCO) exist in the oil services space, although funding is also a significant challenge for these companies (Ariweriokuma 2009; PESD Interviews).

In contrast to its somewhat successful efforts to foster private local content, NNPC has been largely unsuccessful in improving its own capacities. Particularly remarkable is the degree to which upstream subsidiary NPDC has been neglected and at times actively undermined in its operational activities (see section 3). NNPC has undergone periodic capacity-building initiatives at the corporate level, including the PACE (Positioning, Aligning, Creating and Enabling) program that began in 2004. This was an effort led by Accenture and Shell Manufacturing Systems (SMS) and aimed at increasing professionalism and skills within NNPC (Kupolokun 2006; Ariweriokuma 2009). Several interviewees thought this program achieved some success but that the improvements were hard to maintain through the next politically motivated purge of NNPC leadership that would inevitably come.[80] As discussed in section 3, NNPC's engineering design subsidiary NETCO has achieved some success in capacity development, in part because its functions are somewhat removed from the core concerns of NNPC.

Easy to overlook in the struggle to improve the capacity of Nigerian companies is the fact that Nigeria has developed significant indigenous talent in hydrocarbons within the IOCs themselves.[81] The great majority of IOC employees in Nigeria – one sector observer estimated 90 percent – are Nigerians. The fraction of Nigerians among the ranks of top in-country executives is lower but still significant. Several interviewees reported that the fraction of Nigerians employed by IOCs has been growing in recent years. Unfortunately, it has been difficult so far to translate the overall expansion in Nigerian talent into noticeable improvement in the policymaking and regulatory capability of the government, not to mention the operations of NNPC itself. Some Nigerians who gained experience as IOC executives have moved over to the Ministry of Petroleum Resources, but their ability to change the system for the better has generally been limited, in the opinion of a Nigerian journalist with whom we spoke (PESD Interviews). Development of Nigerian talent within IOCs is not an adequate substitute for the cultivation of independent Nigerian companies, including because the incentives of Nigerians within IOCs are aligned in favor of continued IOC dominance.

4.3 Delivering patronage

Many of the same factors that have made NNPC unsuccessful as a tool for maximizing revenue or developing its own capability in oil have made it ideal as an instrument of patronage. First, the complexity and bureaucracy of NNPC processes provide ample opportunity for distribution of favors, with each approval step representing a transaction that can benefit a gatekeeper or his network of associates. Contracting is the area with the most opportunity for steering benefits to one's connections. As one IOC executive described it, there is no way to entirely avoid questionable contracts when operating in Nigeria. For example, he said, oil operators depend on houseboats to house workers in the Niger Delta, and the only suitable houseboats might be owned by former government officials. As he put it, "You do business with them or you don't do business" (PESD Interviews). NNPC is right in the middle of such contract decisions.

Second, top jobs in NNPC are dispensed to politically favored individuals. Alexandra Gillies cites the implicit rotation of NNPC Board Members, often on a regional basis in line with the regional structure of Nigeria's patronage network (see section 2). The GMD of NNPC changes with each presidential transition, and sometimes more frequently, making it difficult to effect sustained positive change within the organization.[82] Employment at the NNPC staff level is also facilitated by connections, although overall employment rolls within the company appear to be less padded than they once were; according to Nwokeji (2007), NNPC staff size shrank from 17,000 in 2003 to around 9,000 as of the beginning of 2007.

Third, as highlighted by Gillies (2009), the allocation through NNPC of "lifting" licenses for exporting crude oil and importing refined products is opaque and highly discretionary. As discussed at length in section 3, the gap between market prices and subsidized official prices for both crude oil and refined products creates enormous profit opportunities for holders of these licenses. Bello (2008) alleged that NNPC officials in collaboration with politicians distribute such licenses both for individual gain and to buy support of politicians in the legislature, who in turn use the proceeds for patronage among their home constituencies.

Beyond the ways in which it actively serves patronage goals, NNPC's lack of financial autonomy ensures that the corporation cannot become a self-sufficient actor in the oil sector that could threaten existing constituencies which benefit from the status quo. In a similar way, the sparse resources allotted to regulatory agencies prevent these bodies from developing capability and exercising real oversight. Actors that benefit from the status quo only need to perpetuate the disorder that allows them to find profitable niches, while reformers face the much more difficult challenge of building a new order that eliminates such dark corners.

5 Conclusion: prospects for reform

Nigeria's dysfunctional equilibrium in the oil sector will be difficult to dislodge. Our study of NNPC sheds light on how corruption, bureaucracy, and non-market pricing regimes for oil sales reinforce each other – a lesson that is applicable well beyond Nigeria's borders. Bureaucracy facilitates patronage and corruption by multiplying the number of transactions that are required to accomplish anything, with each transaction creating an approver who can extract personal gain. Non-market pricing generates profitable opportunities to arbitrage between controlled and free or black markets, with public officials able to dispense access to these opportunities as a means of patronage. Implementation of controlled pricing regimes is inevitably byzantine and bureaucratic and becomes more so as ad hoc policies are put in place to try to manage the inevitable distortions like fuel shortages. Moreover, an entity like NNPC that operates within a fundamentally non-market framework has little choice but to retreat to bureaucratic behavior, as autonomous commercial operations are not possible. Finally, sustained patronage as has existed in Nigeria creates many entrenched interests that resist moves towards price liberalization and commercialization, which would expose and eliminate their shadowy niches. The few relative success stories within NNPC, like its engineering design subsidiary NETCO, are somewhat removed from the massive capital flows that would make them appealing prey for patronage.

Reforms embodied in the Petroleum Industry Bill (PIB) that was introduced in the National Assembly in 2009 attempt to fix many surface problems in the Nigerian oil sector, but legislation alone is unlikely to be able to address these core dynamics. To address NNPC's lack of financial autonomy and consequent inability to run as a commercial enterprise, the bill intends to turn it into a limited liability corporation, NNPC Ltd., which would control and reinvest its own revenue. NNPC Ltd. would continue to partner with IOCs, but existing partnerships would be formalized into IJVs – presumably allowing them to be freer of bureaucratic encumbrances and raise money independently rather than depending on the capricious cash calls. In an effort to correct Nigeria's lack of capable and independent policymaking and regulatory authority in oil, the bill would create two new bodies, the National Petroleum Directorate (NPD) and the Nigerian Petroleum Inspectorate (NPI). The NPD and NPI would for the most part assume the duties of MPR and DPR, respectively, but with more autonomy, due in part to independent revenue generation capability. The current tension between NNPC's role as sector manager and quasi-regulator of IOCs and its (as yet largely theoretical) role as an operational player in the sector would be resolved through the creation of the National Petroleum Assets Management Agency (NAPAMA). NAPAMA would take over the current functions of NAPIMS as approver of IOC investments and contracts, leaving NNPC free to be more of an actual oil company.

The proposed reforms attempt to fix the problems of the Nigerian oil sector by mimicking the institutional design of a model sector that functions well. The model aspired to seems to be that of Norway (see Chapter 14). NNPC Ltd. maps to Norway's NOC, commercially oriented Statoil. Nigeria's NPD would set policy in the same way as Norway's Ministry of Petroleum and Energy. The NPI would be a quasi-autonomous regulator in the mold of the Norwegian Petroleum Directorate. And finally, NAPAMA would play a role analogous to that of state-owned company Petoro in Norway, which has the responsibility of managing the state's direct financial interests in oil and gas assets.

Unfortunately, declaring that new oil institutions exist and will function in a fundamentally different way from current institutions does not make it so. The failed history of previous oil reform efforts in Nigeria, which for the most part merely shifted organizational functions on paper, urges caution. So too does the recent history of electricity reform in Nigeria, which exhibits disconcerting parallels to the current path of oil reform. Formal privatization of Nigeria's profoundly dysfunctional state power company was accomplished in 2005 with the passage of the Electric Power Sector Reform Bill by the National Assembly (Vanguard 2006), almost four years after a draft bill was first presented to the legislature (Akwaya and Bassey 2004). The idea was that the Power Holding Company of Nigeria (PHCN) would be unbundled into eighteen successor companies (eleven distribution companies, six generation companies, and one transmission company), and that these companies would be bought by private commercial entities which would then improve the nation's electricity generation and delivery (Onwuka 2005; Ahima-Young 2009). In practice, no investors showed interest in the unbundled companies because the unchanged electricity tariff structure would have precluded any profit (Dickson 2008).

As in the electricity reform case, the current oil and gas reforms address apparent causes of sectoral problems – a weak regulator, an NOC that does not function like a true corporate entity – that are in fact manifestations of deeper root causes. The oil regulator is weak because it is to the advantage of powerful interests for it to be so. The implicit rotation of government power among regional and ethnic interests, as described in section 2, means that even groups not currently in power anticipate their turn and want to make sure they are not encumbered by a strong oil sector regulator when their chance to govern arrives.[83] NNPC does not run as a financially autonomous business in part because the current broken system, under which the corporation is nominally commercial but in practice structurally indebted to the government, offers the possibility for many politically connected interests to benefit. Giving NNPC genuine control over its revenue would entail taking this control away from others, and the bill does not even begin to discuss how to do this (Heller 2009).[84]

By simultaneously confronting so many parties with an interest in preserving the status quo, a comprehensive bill like the PIB is likely to consolidate opposition. For example, IOCs might be attracted to certain aspects of the bill, such as measures that try to reduce NNPC bureaucracy, internal conflict, and control over funding. At the same time, they are passionately opposed to provisions in the bill to increase royalty and tax rates on deep water production, which they say will make such projects uneconomic (Petroleum Economist 2009). The excessive sweep of the bill may result in its failure to pass, or, as in the power sector case, the eventual passage after a long delay of a set of "Potemkin" reforms that alter relationships on paper while having only a limited impact on real problems. (Given the high profile of the PIB, we suspect this latter outcome is more likely than outright non-passage.)

As appealing as it may seem to try to fix the Nigerian petroleum sector in one fell swoop, the likelihood is that real positive change will require more incremental effort over a long period of time. Based on the observations of this study, we suggest four principal areas for focus. First, transparency initiatives like NEITI should be supported and continued. The biggest worry on the transparency front is how deep the political commitment to the process really is. In the absence of President Obasanjo, who was the strongest political force behind NEITI, the process seems to have slowed down. The most critical missing piece of transparency efforts so far has been any concerted effort to throw a spotlight on the opaque workings of NNPC, including the awarding of export and import licenses and the flows of funds both within NNPC and to and from the government. Unfortunately, this is also likely to be the area where transparency efforts will meet the most entrenched resistance from those who benefit from opacity.

Second, Nigeria needs to further develop indigenous private companies that can play a productive role in the oil industry. Local content targets have had some real positive effect, but the problem remains that shell companies with connections can vault ahead of genuine productive enterprises in contracting processes. A pre-qualification process for local firms might help, as would greater transparency in the awarding of oil industry subcontracts. Local enterprises also face substantial hurdles in finding funding. Nigeria's new local content law inspires both hope that it can help bring capacity building to another level and fear that it might be exploited as yet another means for "privileged Nigerians" to benefit without adding value to the country's economy. The effort to foster Nigerian enterprises is certainly worthwhile. To the extent that more domestic companies grow and develop as legitimate players in the industry, they can start to provide an alternative route to Nigerian involvement and wealth creation in the oil sector that is less dependent on milking government bureaucracy. Ultimately, such players could help form a constituency for genuine reform.

Third, markets must be fixed through some degree of price rationalization, and NNPC and its business units should be made more commercial and less bureaucratic. The sequencing of these two steps is critical and extremely thorny. As numerous past initiatives in Nigeria have shown, formal privatization in the absence of market reform is likely to fail. Time and again, the government has courted private investment in the provision of energy services – for example, in electricity supply, refinery operation, and import of refined products – but failed to arouse the expected interest because markets were too distorted to allow real commercial operation. Where markets are reasonably unencumbered, on the other hand, Nigerian industries have proven attractive to private investors, as demonstrated by the sale of Eleme Petrochemicals to Indorama.

Reforming Nigeria's energy pricing is both the most important and the most challenging step towards increasing NNPC's commercial orientation, enabling the country to more fully develop its own hydrocarbon resources and capabilities, and finally establishing reliable energy services for Nigerians. One reform strategy that has had success in other developing country contexts is to build up new markets in parallel to established ones in which entrenched interests block reform. Natural gas markets might be a reasonable starting point for price reform in Nigeria, as their underdevelopment means that there are fewer players that benefit from the status quo than in, for example, the vehicle fuel market. The state electricity company is an unreliable customer for gas that itself operates in a non-functional market, but industrial and commercial consumers – who experience massive dissatisfaction with the current dysfunctional system – might be able to form a base for further development of the domestic gas market. As an illustrative example, India's domestic market for natural gas is heavily distorted by subsidies for fertilizer production and electricity generation, but the government satisfied significant unserved demand when it made imported LNG available to industrial consumers at international prices (Jackson 2007). Nigeria could start increasing domestic gas utilization through a similar approach of multi-tiered pricing in which certain applications see higher prices and could thus be supplied profitably, albeit in this case from domestic rather than international gas. Indeed, the Gas Master Plan appears to suggest just such a multi-tiered pricing policy, with prices for industrial and commercial consumers driven by those of competing fuels rather than an arbitrary official price (Yar'adua 2007). Some industries might choose to develop their own captive, gas-fired power to sidestep broken electricity markets. However, pricing reforms will do little to develop the gas market if the government cannot find a way to make pricing promises credible to potential investors.[85]

Vehicle fuel subsidies are most integrally connected to NNPC's dysfunctions and also excruciatingly difficult to unravel. On the one hand, any attempt to increase prices unleashes howls of protest from a Nigerian populace that sees the subsidy as one of the only things the government provides them with of any value. Politicians conclude with some justification that price reform is political suicide. On the other hand, efforts to gain public trust by increasing transparency in the shady transactions around petroleum exports, imports, and marketing are likely to be thwarted by the private interests that benefit richly from them. Nonetheless, tenacious efforts at reform from both ends could help. Genuine improvement in transparency over time might help convince a skeptical public to go along with needed reforms in other areas including pricing.

The fundamental difficulty is that the ailments of Nigeria's energy sector (and broader political system) are all connected. This is one argument of reformers who argue that nothing short of a comprehensive reform will bring sustainable change. However, our own observation is that overly ambitious statutory or executive-led reforms are easily rejected or subverted by Nigeria's resilient ecosystem of patronage. Somehow the basic conditions within which oil activities take place need to shift over time. Patronage transactions, central planning, and bureaucracy need to be gradually replaced by durable and competent public institutions, genuine markets, and productive indigenous enterprises that add value rather than milking government connections. Incremental improvements in each area could over time begin to reinforce each other in a virtuous cycle. The creation of isolated functioning markets, for example in sales of gas to domestic industry, could allow productive Nigerian businesses to develop. Nigerian businesses in turn could start to demand fairer and more transparent treatment from public institutions. Higher-quality institutions could better regulate the oil sector, and so on.

Nigeria has a deep pool of latent talent and entrepreneurial energy. Unfortunately, in the absence of a basic institutional framework that supports productive activity, much of the country's human potential goes untapped or is directed only towards getting ahead in the patronage-based system. Progress would be helped along by the emergence of wise and selfless political leadership that focuses to a greater degree on the long-term good of the country. Unfortunately, the short time horizons created by Nigeria's stage-managed rotation of power make such leadership both rare and difficult to sustain.

Notes

The authors wish to specially acknowledge Alexandra Gillies, G. Ugo Nwokeji, and Willy Olsen, who provided unusually comprehensive and valuable reviews of this study, often with extended commentaries drawn from their own extensive expertise on NNPC and the Nigerian oil sector. These reviews shaped the final study in very significant ways, though they do not imply any endorsement of our conclusions by the reviewers, and any errors remain ours alone. We also express our deep gratitude to the many people inside and outside of Nigeria who took the time to speak candidly and thoughtfully with us about their views and experiences of NNPC and Nigerian oil institutions. Much of this study is based on a set of research interviews conducted in January 2007 (by P. Heller) and September 2008 (by M. Thurber and I. Emelife). A number of interviews were also conducted by phone during the period from 2007 through 2010. In total, more than forty people with knowledge of different aspects of the Nigerian petroleum sector were canvassed. The sample included people who worked (currently or formerly) at different levels for several divisions of NNPC, Nigerian government agencies, private Nigerian oil companies, IOCs and oil service companies operating in Nigeria, private Nigerian businesses (including in finance), aid agencies of foreign governments, international NGOs, Nigerian NGOs, and Nigerian workers' unions. We also spoke with several journalists and academics. Because of the sensitivity of the topics discussed, a large number of those with whom we spoke preferred not to be identified by name. Therefore, in lieu of an interviewee list, we have attempted in the text to identify the general background of the source of particular assertions where useful.

1 Per capita oil export revenues for Nigeria remain low, approximately $214 in 2009 as calculated from figures in the OPEC *Annual Statistical Bulletin* (OPEC 2010).
2 According to the US Energy Information Administration (EIA 2010b), Nigeria in 2008 exported 2.03 million barrels per day of oil and held proved oil reserves of 36.2 billion barrels.
3 While Box 16.1 includes the divisions and subsidiaries that are most material to the functioning of NNPC in our opinion, there are many other corporate divisions that we have not listed. These include, for example, Accounts, Corporate Audit, Corporate Planning and Development, Engineering and Technology, Finance, Human Resources, Information Technology, Investment, Nigerian Content, Renewable Energy, and Research and Technology (Nwokeji 2007).
4 Upstream arm NPDC has only a small share of total oil operations, the refineries have always operated far below design capacity, and gas pipeline operator NGC has not been able to create a viable domestic gas market.
5 We thank Alexandra Gillies for pointing out this relationship.
6 Angola offers a counterexample of a country with similar resource endowments whose government has acted coherently to assure dependable and growing revenues (see Chapter 19). As members of a homogeneous elite under pressure to survive, Angola's leaders were far more unified than Nigeria's as they developed oil, allowing them to focus on creating an attractive investment climate that would most reliably deliver the oil revenues they needed to prosecute a civil war.
7 These crises included an increasingly vicious dispute between regions over census results that would determine ethnic/regional representation in government, as well as some unwanted interventions in Western politics by the East and North (Diamond 1988; Bevan *et al.* 1999). The government of the First Republic had also been generally corrupt and incapable of delivering stability and economic benefits, leading the military coup to be widely welcomed by the populace (Diamond 1995).

8 The January 1966 coup was widely viewed as favoring the Igbos; the July countercoup replacing General Ironsi – an Igbo who had been installed as president after the January coup – with Yakubu Gowon was in turn a major blow to the Igbo elite (Bevan *et al.* 1999).

9 Calculations by Scott Pearson at the time suggested that an independent Eastern region could expect to control more than half of the country's oil revenues by the early 1970s (Pearson 1970).

10 The splitting off of a new Mid-Western region from the Western region in 1963 could be argued to have been the first use of state creation as a political tool, although this earlier instance was not connected to the promise of oil revenues.

11 Estimates vary widely, but at minimum hundreds of thousands died, primarily in the East. Many civilian fatalities were the result of associated famine.

12 Highlighting one difference between the First and Second Republics, the NPN was a truly national party. Accordingly, it sought to stay in power through the development of a truly national patronage network.

13 Tom Forrest commented that the NPN might more aptly have been referred to as the "Party of National Patronage (PNP)" (Forrest 1986).

14 As Bevan *et al.* (1999) point out, a patronage system – which relies on a continual stream of income – inherently creates incentives at odds with sound economic management.

15 This arrangement, which arguably continues to this day, highlights the role of Nigerian elections as complex mechanisms for distributing resources and influence rather than as true referendums on government performance.

16 Comments by Michael Watts at a forum at Stanford University on November 12, 2008 shaped our thinking on the problematic interaction between oil revenues and Nigeria's particular brand of federalism.

17 Government expenditure in this first oil boom gravitated towards infrastructure, grandiose and poorly conceived industrial projects, and a worthwhile but poorly administered drive to improve the educational system (Forrest 1995). State enterprises of all kinds proliferated.

18 An incident that exemplified the excess of the era – including the way that government contracts could be inflated to provide massive rents to everyone involved in a transaction – was when a Ministry of Defence order for a vastly excessive quantity of cement clogged the port of Lagos with ships in 1975 (Forrest 1995). Contracting remains the principal vehicle for corruption in Nigeria today.

19 There were rumors that Abacha's death was engineered from within the military.

20 Many military officers acted to protect their own interests by joining these nascent political parties (P. Lewis 2007).

21 Nicholas Shaxson (2009) offers a detailed critique of NEITI.

22 The most visible example of this occurred in connection with what became a seamy public spat between Obasanjo and his vice president Atiku Abubakar, in which each aired significant dirty laundry on the other. Obasanjo used the EFCC and a handpicked panel to indict Abubakar (Nwokeji 2007). While in general the public believed that Abubakar was indeed guilty (Gillies 2007), the impression left by the whole affair was that Obasanjo was far from untainted himself.

23 The JV was originally known as Shell/D'Arcy Exploration Parties and later renamed the Shell-BP Petroleum Development Company of Nigeria Ltd.

24 One characteristic of Nigeria's geology is that oil has tended to be spread out over a large number of relatively small fields.

25 Most onshore oil and gas facilities were not in Igbo-dominated areas, and the Nigerian government gained control over them early in the conflict (Bevan *et al.* 1999).

26 The establishment of NNOC was part of a larger trend that saw Nigeria create a number of state-owned companies in the 1970s (Forrest 1995).

27 Shagari reversed the previous military government's pragmatic policy of preserving oil production and revenues by letting IOCs lift more oil than their formal equity share when NNPC could not find sufficient customers. This policy change, coupled with a stubborn refusal to adjust price in a timely fashion to respond to plunging world demand, contributed to a precipitous drop in Nigerian output in the early 1980s. Sarah Ahmad Khan points out that this production decrease was not significantly related to either OPEC quotas (which were tightened for Nigeria after a significant output drop had already occurred) or to deficiencies in production capacity (Ahmad Khan 1994).

28 In January 2010 the legislature set a new deadline of December 31, 2012 for ending flaring (Nzeshi 2010).

29 NNPC's Group Managing Director Sanusi Barkindo claimed that the Niger Delta amnesty facilitated the improved gas supply situation (Yusuf 2010).

30 OPEC quotas for Nigeria are currently set near the level of actual production (IEA 2010). However, based on past experience, it seems that the problems in the Niger Delta are a much more real constraint on production than OPEC quotas, and that Nigerian production would increase very substantially if Niger Delta violence were to disappear.

31 We thank Alexandra Gillies for emphasizing this point.

32 Of course, if environmental degradation in the Niger Delta is charged to criminal activities and the difficulty of environmental remediation in a conflict zone, the tally of environmental costs associated with problems in the Delta could be astronomical. IOCs tend to argue that it is these factors more than their own practices that have resulted in the despoliation of the Niger Delta.

33 Historically, it has not been uncommon for politicians in Nigeria to enlist armed militias to prevent opposition voters from reaching the ballot box (Smith 2007).

34 As one oil sector participant described it: "You can see the oil theft, it's blatant. If you fly over the Delta in a helicopter, you can see it with no problem at all. It's everywhere … [Government officials] know the theft is taking place, but they don't do anything to stop it, because it's connected to people high up. The boundaries between politics, criminality, and business are very vague" (PESD Interviews).

35 The president is rarely able to accomplish his legislative goals without extensive consultation, cajoling, and deal making with members of the legislature, even within his own party (CIDCM 2003).

36 Nigeria's new local content law could ease this particular conflict of interest by assigning local content regulatory responsibilities to a dedicated monitoring board, though whether this is successful in practice remains to be seen.

37 We acknowledge our debt to Alexandra Gillies for pointing out both of these examples.

38 While the Nigerian president has traditionally benefited from his control over the oil sector, what distinguished Abacha from other rulers was the degree to which he blatantly siphoned money directly from oil revenues to himself, totally heedless of the damage that this might inflict on the sector (P. Lewis 2007).

39 In the current civilian republic dating from 1999, the president has been slightly more constrained by the legislature in his ability to do this.

40 This fundamental character of Nigerian governance has been largely continuous through both civilian and military rule. Governments, whether civilian or military, that fail to deliver prosperity, are seen to be unusually corrupt, or transgress accepted norms of patronage, are vulnerable to coups. Sani Abacha, for example, dismayed even his own military in his capriciousness, extreme brutality, and concentration of benefits upon his person.

41 Obasanjo dissolved the NNPC Board completely before leaving office.

42 The OGIC recommendations went on to form the basis for the Nigerian Petroleum Industry Bill, which is currently under consideration in the Nigerian legislature.

43 As one example of a critical resource limitation, the NEITI audit for 1999–2004 pointed out deficiencies in information technology at DPR – especially problematic for a regulatory body whose functions require data collection (Hart Group 2006a). One DPR official we spoke with also lamented the inability of the organization to obtain funds to renovate its building after twelve years of trying (PESD Interviews). DPR's funding must be approved by the Ministry, President, and National Assembly. DPR can suffer from its subservience to Ministry bureaucrats; one interviewee with long experience in the sector suggested that DPR's higher pay scales lead to resentment within the Ministry, which in turn translates to lower funding for DPR (PESD Interviews). DPR salaries are on the same scale as those at NNPC (PESD Interviews), though lower than those available in private industry. The rationale (also applied by other countries in their oil sectors) is to limit the extent to which competent personnel at the technical regulator are poached by the NOC or other private players.

44 The MOU was revised in 1991 and 2000 to increase the guaranteed notional profit margin (Wood Mackenzie 2009c).

45 In fact, some efforts have been made to blunt the impact of the incentives, with the rationale that they are overly generous to the oil companies (World Bank 2004c; Nigerian Senate 2006).

46 In the face of basic uncertainty about how to monetize natural gas, IOCs have been particularly reluctant to develop fields that consist entirely of gas, as opposed to fields that have oil with associated gas (PESD Interviews).

47 The NEITI 1999–2004 audit reported that PHCN's precursor, the National Electric Power Authority (NEPA), owed NGC arrears of 6.7 billion naira (about $53 million) (Hart Group 2006c, pp. 16–17).

48 NEPA's power transmission loss in 2004 was estimated at 40 percent, and businesses and households in Nigeria who want reliable power (and can afford it) are forced to run on private generators (World Bank 2004a; Hart Group 2006c).

49 According to petroleum economist Obo Idornigie, who worked at NEITI, FIRS civil servants generally have insufficient training in the particularities of the petroleum industry and the complex calculations used to determine royalties, deductions, and PPT under the MOU framework (see Heller 2007).

50 Even the IJVs might start to look less appealing to the NOCs if they move towards becoming a reality. One potential concern is that they would bind the IOCs uncomfortably tightly to NNPC and the Nigerian government.

51 The contribution of another type of business arrangement, the service contract, remains negligible for the time being (Nigerian Ministry of Finance and Budget Office of the Federation 2008). Only two service contracts, both with Agip, were active at the time of this writing (Wood Mackenzie 2009c).

52 NAPIMS defends its position as gatekeeper zealously and can inflict headaches on IOCs and other parts of NNPC if it feels that this prerogative is not respected (PESD Interviews).

53 Whereas a JV company needs to secure NNPC funding through a cash call, an IOC in a PSC needs to secure approval for the amount of "cost oil" that can be used to reimburse expenses.

54 According to a presentation from NAPIMS, the threshold in PSCs is $250,000.

55 NAPIMS and NNPC employees themselves expressed frustration with some of the bureaucratic hurdles that slowed down project execution – such as the low authority limits for contract approval. However, they said they felt constrained to follow the procedures in place, including by the threat of a potential audit.

56 The NEITI audit cited some improvements in transparency in the tendering of import contracts, including through the introduction of a sealed tender process adjudicated by a committee representing various parts of NNPC, and the imposition of additional requirements on bidding companies including that they demonstrate a good credit rating (Hart Group 2006a). However, the audit conceded that procedures still fall short of "good practice" (Hart Group 2006a).

57 Ariweriokuma described a cycle whereby some marketers would use a portion of profits from diversion of products abroad to construct new filling stations, which would in turn be used as a basis for receiving increased allocations of subsidized petroleum products from PPMC (Ariweriokuma 2009).

58 One specious argument is that many OPEC members have much *more* subsidized fuel prices relative to Nigeria. Fuel subsidies have significant negative effects in these places too (see, for example, the case of Venezuela in Chapter 10), and Nigeria's oil export revenues on a per capita basis are by far the lowest of any OPEC producer (OPEC 2009).

59 Sabotage has also played some role in disrupting refinery options, although NEITI correctly identifies this as a less significant factor than the limited resources allocated to ongoing refinery operations.

60 Difficulties procuring catalysts to run refining operations are legendary. A current NNPC employee described a discussion with a French delegation visiting the Warri refinery, during which the Nigerian group asked

how the French engineers would feel if they had to obtain President Chirac's approval every time they wanted to purchase a new catalyst.

61 One Nigerian observer of the oil sector with whom we spoke criticized NNPC executives for constantly overstating refinery performance figures.

62 Such contracts provide substantial opportunities for private gain.

63 Of course, local content preferences may create some distortions in their favor.

64 IDSL remains more distant than NETCO from the ideal of being an autonomous business. One observer from within NNPC (but with no affiliation with IDSL) argued that the division has the human capacity and knowledge to succeed in the same way NETCO has but has not been given the "right tools" by the corporation and the government (PESD Interviews). One obstacle is a lack of resources to procure the information technology on which it depends for seismic processing.

65 As Nwokeji (2007) notes, NETCO took proactive steps after Bechtel departed to reassure customers who were initially wary of continuing to give contracts to a 100 percent indigenous Nigerian firm.

66 NETCO staff seem proud of their status as the only NNPC subsidiary with ISO certification (PESD Interviews).

67 An engineering manager at NETCO with whom we spoke was refreshingly no-nonsense in his approach to developing Nigerian capability through "learning by doing" – mandating among other things that NETCO engineers spend significant time at the sites for which they will be designing platforms and other equipment (PESD Interviews).

68 This one IOC executive's criticism of NETCO was not that it had done a poor job as a contractor per se, but rather that it still had a bureaucratic mindset as opposed to being a completely commercial company (PESD Interviews).

69 IOCs are concerned about efforts to link an increase in deep water royalty and tax rates to the Petroleum Industry Bill before the National Assembly (Petroleum Economist 2009).

70 While there remain a number of roadblocks to establishment of incorporated JVs (not least IOC concerns about being bound to the Nigerian government in uncomfortable ways), the prospects for resolving the cash call funding problems in some manner are relatively bright because the status quo has little benefit even for patronage purposes.

71 A simple comparison of IOC and NAPIMS offices revealed the vast gulf in facilities and technology between organizations.

72 The NEITI audit diplomatically questions the ability or inclination of NAPIMS to participate as an equal partner in the decision making of JV companies, stating that "it is unclear whether as a co-venturer

it undertakes truly independent technical assessments or economic evaluations of potential opportunities, or relies mainly on the JV/PSC Operators to provide the information that it reviews" (Hart Group 2006d, p. 2).

73 Norwegian oil and gas consultancy INTSOK led a study that characterized progress on local content development in Nigeria and recommended ways to increase the effectiveness of capacity-building efforts.

74 The exact definition of local content and the approach used to quantify it have remained somewhat vague. The term can encompass in-country value addition, use of Nigerian-owned companies, employment of Nigerians, and application of Nigerian material resources.

75 The new legislation seems to have injected significant new uncertainty into the oil sector in recent months as both foreign and indigenous companies wait to see if the law will be applied in ways that will positively or negatively affect their operations.

76 The outcomes of previous rounds depended almost entirely on the discretion of the Nigerian executive.

77 One series of transactions in the 2006 mini-round emphasized the continued potential for personal connections to play a role in contract awards. After DPR offered block OPL291 to India's ONGC, which declined, the license was granted to Transcorp, a local conglomerate with links to President Obasanjo. When Transcorp could not satisfy the terms of the block, OPL291 was passed to Starcrest Nigeria, an apparent shell entity that had been registered as a company the day of the mini-bid round and agreed to pay a $55 million signature bonus. Starcrest Nigeria turned out to be owned by businessmen connected to an Obasanjo aide. Months later, Addax Petroleum bought out a majority stake in OPL291, paying the signature bonus plus an additional $35 million to Starcrest as a finder's fee (Africa Confidential 2006; African Energy 2006). The sequence suggested that open bidding could have netted the state at least a $90 million signature bonus, rather than $55 million paid to the government and $35 million paid as a windfall to private individuals with links to the president.

78 Like NNPC's most successful unit, NETCO, Oando is partially descended from foreign firms – it was born in 1956 as a unit of Exxon, bought by the Nigerian government in 1976, and given its current name following a merger with Agip Nigeria in 2003 (www.oandoplc.com).

79 IOCs took some convincing before they were willing to release marginal fields to Nigerian companies under this program (Oduniyi 2003; Ariweriokuma 2009).

80 For example, one Nigerian working in the finance sector expressed regret at the departure of NNPC GMD Funsho Kupolokun at the

time the presidency passed from Obasanjo to Yar'Adua. He felt that Kupolokun had been a particularly constructive and professionalizing influence within NNPC.

81 We thank both Alexandra Gillies and Willy Olsen for emphasizing this point.

82 Often these changeovers are accompanied by promises of a full investigation of NNPC's past dealings.

83 We are grateful to Alexandra Gillies for highlighting this point.

84 A further concern, if one were actually able to give NNPC control over its revenue, would be how to avoid simply creating a new money grab from within NNPC.

85 The problem of credible commitment is illustrated by a new gas pricing policy introduced in 2010 that would increase natural gas prices from their current $0.20/mmbtu to $1/mmbtu by the end of 2010 and $2/mmbtu by the end of 2013 in an effort to spur investment in domestic gas infrastructure (Alike and Ezeigbo 2010). However, the report quotes Minister of Petroleum Resources Deziani Alison-Madueke as saying that "each price change is triggered only when the gas sector has demonstrated that it has developed sufficient gas to attain a particular threshold of electricity generation." The caveat could be taken to signal the lack of a credible commitment by the government to the new pricing scheme and thus actually deter potential gas developers from making the large investments needed to bring online new gas aimed at the domestic market.

17 Fading star: explaining the evolution of India's ONGC

VARUN RAI

1 Introduction

The national oil company Oil and Natural Gas Corporation Limited (ONGC) is India's largest company devoted to exploration and production (E&P). Founded in 1956, ONGC has seen remarkable growth in the last five decades. In 2007–2008, ONGC group's total production of oil and oil-equivalent gas (O+OEG) was about 60 million metric tonnes per annum (MMTPA) or 1.2 million barrels per day, thus accounting for nearly 80 percent of India's oil and gas production. In 2007 *Energy Intelligence Top 100* ranked ONGC at 31 among global oil and gas companies.

ONGC's evolution is a remarkable story of how state-owned firms respond and adapt to shifts in owner (government) priorities, which in turn are strongly influenced by macroeconomic and political conditions. Historically, ONGC has been the Government of India's (GoI's) trusted custodian of India's oil and gas reserves. As such, ONGC enjoyed a near monopoly in this sector for nearly four decades (1955–1995), during which good luck and easy oil elevated ONGC to stardom. During those years ONGC also functioned as the de facto regulator of the oil and gas sector. The oil ministry (the government ministry in charge of the sector) depended heavily on ONGC for coordinating activities in the sector. But changing economic priorities and soaring domestic demand for oil and gas in India have significantly changed the dynamic of ONGC's relationship with the government in many ways. Through a series of reforms since the mid 1990s, the GoI has increasingly tried to maintain an arm's-length relationship with ONGC. ONGC is exposed to more competition in the sector than ever before and it has also lost its regulatory function, which is now the responsibility of a separate arm within the government.

This chapter attempts to unpack the dynamic of the government–ONGC relationship. Focusing specifically on how government ownership and control have influenced ONGC's performance and strategy, this chapter makes four main arguments.

First, ONGC exists, just as with NOCs in many other countries, because of a legacy of suspicion about outsiders. It performed well when it was tasked with things that were not that difficult and when it had help for the more difficult ventures, such as frontier E&P and development.

Two factors were critical in the Indian government's decision to put a state-owned company (ONGC) in charge of India's oil and gas E&P efforts: the government's socialist bent and fears of opportunism of the international oil companies (IOCs). In the years following India's independence in 1947 a large fraction of India's production was under government ownership, reflecting the strong bias of the GoI for a socialist-like development of India. Additionally, by the mid 1960s GoI's fears of possible opportunistic behavior of the IOCs seemed to be justified, as there was increasing evidence of unfair products pricing internationally by the IOCs. The past baggage of imperial control and fears of opportunistic behavior of the IOCs convinced the GoI to have government ownership of oil and gas E&P.

The GoI set up ONGC in 1956 to lead India's indigenous E&P efforts, but the breakthrough for India's indigenous oil plans and ONGC came from Russia. Russia transferred technology and equipment to kick start ONGC's exploration work. In the 1970s ONGC and its Russian partners began exploration in offshore areas and soon found the giant Mumbai High field in February 1974. The subsequent years from 1975 to 1990 were ONGC's golden era. Production went up from 4.5 MMT (O+OEG) in 1974–1975 to nearly 48 MMT (O+OEG) in 1989–1990. Starting from barely 450 employees at formation in 1956, ONGC swelled to more than 47,000 employees by 1990.

Second, ONGC has run into trouble as it has matured, and the roots of its troubles are mainly in its interactions with the GoI and secondarily in its management.

The years of expanding production masked severe and growing performance problems at ONGC. Among other problems, financial profligacy, organizational and planning difficulties, declining reserves, and the deteriorating health of producing fields brought much flak and negative attention to ONGC in the 1990s. These troubles became more apparent with India's foreign exchange crisis in 1991. The crisis forced a fiscal probity on the Indian government that also required a fresh look at the ownership and management of state enterprises.

ONGC's performance and strategy largely owe to its interactions with the government. The rule-based monitoring and regulated rate-of-return mechanisms (until the late 1990s) that the GoI has employed for ONGC have led to serious financial and corporate culture atrophy at ONGC. The most harmful impact of using indirect and preestablished (*ex ante*) rules to monitor ONGC's performance is the lack of a performance-based incentive structure, which is at the heart of ONGC's inefficiencies.

As a government company ONGC has been exposed to political demands and exigencies to a significant degree. Those demands focus on managing ONGC's free cash flow in an ad hoc and politicized way, but from time to time the government (or powerful individuals in government) attempt to reassert direct government control over ONGC. The government has charged multiple government oversight agencies with auditing ONGC's accounts and verifying the transparency of business dealings of ONGC. The process for selecting ONGC's chairman-cum-managing director (CEO-equivalent) and the board of directors is also prone to political interference. Those demands were more direct and stifling pre-reforms (before the mid 1990s).

As the GoI's preferences and methods of controls have shifted over time, ONGC has adapted its strategy to pacify those demands. For the most part, ONGC's response has been reactive. Working within the incentive structure and constraints that government ownership and control entail, ONGC has tried to adopt strategies that not only serve the GoI's demands but also preserve its (ONGC's) corporate freedom.

Third, a slew of reforms instituted since the mid 1990s have fundamentally changed the landscape of the E&P sector in India and the dynamic of the government–ONGC relationship. Targeted at improving corporate governance, enhancing competition in E&P, and eliminating price controls, those reforms have had a mixed impact on ONGC's performance and strategy. They also highlight the difficulties the GoI has had in encouraging higher efficiencies in ONGC and the oil and gas sector.

In efforts to improve corporate governance of ONGC, in 1999 the GoI accorded ONGC a *Navratna* status, which gave ONGC wide-ranging financial and organizational independence from the government. Subsequently, ONGC's stock-listing in 2004 has also contributed to reducing government influence over and interference with ONGC's corporate affairs.

One of the most important results of the GoI's reform efforts has been the introduction of competition in E&P through the New Exploration and Licensing Policy (NELP). The NELP has certainly weakened ONGC's monopoly status in the upstream sector. By bringing more competition to the sector, the NELP has also enabled the greater use of benchmarks and industry standards for monitoring ONGC's performance.

But the impact of competition on ONGC's performance is significantly diluted by the large free cash flow at ONGC's disposal. High oil prices in the international markets since 2002 and the successful adoption of a market-oriented pricing scheme for crude oil in India have sent ONGC's revenues and profits soaring. Distribution of large dividends and concessions by ONGC seems to be largely influenced by the GoI's motive to take away any extra cash that cannot be productively employed by ONGC. Yet, ONGC is debt free and has significant cash reserves, which gives it enough leeway to employ its own resources in a range of projects without having the need to go through close scrutiny of third parties and the financial markets.

Fourth, given the deep interconnects of the oil and gas sector with India's political economy, fixing the oil and gas sector essentially entails fixing the larger political economy within which the sector is embedded. Uncertain government policies and continued government intervention in politically sensitive matters (such as petroleum pricing) have stymied critical components of the reform process. The situation is exacerbated by insider dealings and favoritism by the government, including with private companies as the beneficiaries. That the GoI's reform efforts have been limited in impact is a manifestation of the fact that those reforms have often tried to address issues specific to the oil and gas sector without also reforming the larger system. By design, such partial reform will fail to enhance the efficiency and performance of the sector.

The rest of the chapter is organized as follows. Section 2 provides an overview of the origins and operations of ONGC. Section 3 discusses how ONGC's relationship and interactions with the government influence ONGC's performance and strategy. Finally, section 4 presents the conclusions of the study and offers some insights for

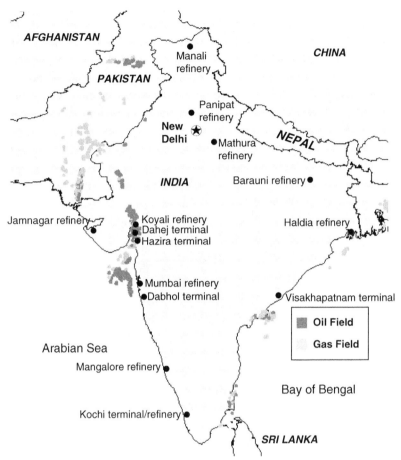

Figure 17.1 Map of major oil and gas fields in India.
Source for oil and gas field data: Wood Mackenzie (2009b).

improving the efficiency and performance of ONGC and also of India's oil and gas sector.

2 The origins and operations of ONGC

2.1 *Formation and initial years of ONGC (1947–1970)*

Two factors were critical in the GoI's decision to assume full control of the oil industry by the end of the 1960s. First, at the time of India's independence in 1947 there was a clear bias in favor of government

ownership of industries of strategic importance. Since India's independence, the energy sector in India – notably oil and gas, coal, and
electricity industries – has largely been organized through SOEs
(state-owned enterprises), which operate (even today) in tightly regulated price regimes. India's first prime minister, Jawaharlal Nehru,
was convinced of the increasingly greater role the state would play
in India's development. Second, there was suspicion about outsiders. The dominant thinking, based on India's past experience, was
that foreign investments end up meddling in national politics and, in
general, are detrimental to the national development. At the time of
independence, the small amount of petroleum products used in the
country was imported from the Abadan Island refinery in Iran, which
was owned by the British Anglo-Iranian Oil Company (AIOC), and
was marketed in India by the American companies Standard Vacuum
and Caltex and the British company Burmah Shell. These three oil-
marketing companies then had monopoly distribution rights. By the
mid 1960s the GoI's fears of possible opportunistic behavior of the
IOCs seemed to be justified, as there was increasing evidence of unfair
products pricing internationally by the IOCs. India's hostile relations with its largest neighbors, China and Pakistan, made GoI very
uncomfortable in leaving so much market power with the IOCs, who
were not averse to using that power to boost profits.

The importance of oil in India was recognized early on. A pre-
independence sub-committee on power and fuel emphasized the
importance of liquid fuel for India's defense and development. When
the Industrial Policy Resolution of 1948 was revised in 1956 to grant
equal status to the private sector vis-à-vis the public sector, mineral
oil was placed in the Schedule A, a list of industries to be exclusively
developed under the state. This was a clear indication that the government considered oil a matter of strategic national importance.

2.1.1 Disappointing results of India's first engagement with the IOCs

Unlike in many other countries that built NOCs by nationalizing
existing operations, in India the logic of state ownership applied to
building new firms, as there wasn't much industry already in place.
But developing oil single-handedly was fraught with huge financial
risks. There was very little, if any, experience within the GoI about
the politics and economics of the oil industry. Despite reservations

about foreign participation in oil exploration and production, the high perceived risks of the oil business pushed the government to engage the IOCs. In the early 1950s the GoI started negotiations with Standard Vacuum (Stanvac) for oil exploration in the Bengal Basin. Preliminary surveys of this area indicated high chances of large quantities of oil, both on the Indian and the East Pakistani sides of the border. The possibility of Pakistan taking the lead on oil exploration in the area hastened the GoI to start oil exploration in the Bengal Basin. The agreement with Stanvac was finalized in December 1953 granting Stanvac exploration rights to 10,000 square miles in the Bengal Basin. The GoI made generous concessions to clinch the exploration agreement. High depreciation rates of 80 percent and higher were permitted for equipment within the first year. Depletion allowances and write-off provisions against the company's oil-marketing business were, as found in later investigations, unjustifiably generous compared with similar agreements elsewhere in the world (Kaul 1991).

The first round of interactions of independent India with the IOCs was disappointing at best. While Indian geologists had assessed the need for two-dozen wells to be drilled by Stanvac in the Bengal Basin, Stanvac drilled only seven wells there between 1953 and 1957. The GoI ended up sharing more than 60 percent of the losses from the operations instead of the 25 percent that was planned at initiation. There was virtually no cost to Stanvac, as it wrote off the losses against its revenue from the marketing business. From Stanvac's perspective there was not much incentive to take unnecessary risks in the Bengal Basin given the cheap oil in West Asia. But this was not in line with the plans of the GoI, which wanted to quickly develop India's domestic resources. The experience with Stanvac underscored that GoI had little ability, on its own, to steer development of the oil industry unless it was more firmly in control.

Mistrust of the IOCs was blowing up also due to increasing evidence of unfair petroleum-products pricing. Investigations by the GoI into products pricing by the IOCs found that to earn higher profits these prices were padded with unreasonable freight and insurance charges linked to the Gulf of Mexico prices even though the crude was imported from the Persian Gulf. Neither did the IOCs take into account the discounts they obtained at the source of supply for the crude oil they purchased. "Tricks" like these allowed the IOCs to sell the imported products at a hefty profit – by using questionable accounting practices the IOCs had managed to earn profits in the high 20s against the initial 7.5 percent that they had sought (Kaul 1991). Moreover, when faced with these allegations the IOCs issued a veiled threat to cut off supply of products, at a time when India was at the brink of war with China around 1960. This progression of events brought GoI's worst fears of IOC opportunism to life and, more than ever, solidified its resolution to bring all aspects of the oil industry under firm state control.

2.1.2 Push for government ownership and Russian help

Amid all this, K. D. Malaviya, first the deputy minister and then the minister of Natural Resources & Scientific Research (NR&SR), was pushing hard for an indigenous oil program. Malaviya strongly supported a state-run oil industry in India.

The breakthrough for Malaviya and India's indigenous oil plans came from Russia. The Russians were very keen not only to help India develop its oil industry but also to develop overall relationships between the two countries. This was hardly surprising given the aura of the Cold War and the Sino-Soviet tensions of that time. In 1956, India bought several rigs from Romania and Russia, a move that further strengthened Indo-Russian ties in oil and also in the heavy engineering industry in general. A unique feature of these purchases was that India was allowed to pay Russia in Indian rupees, which Russia could use to buy Indian products. Thus, in effect a modern barter system came to be employed. This came as a huge relief for India, which was already reeling under the pressure to meet its prior foreign exchange commitments. Interestingly, the Russian assistance also increased the willingness of the West to assist India in the oil industry, but that was limited, in some ways, by how much foreign exchange India could provide. In any case, the arrival of the Russian help was a boon for ONGC: "[I]t broke the monopoly of the big oil companies [for supply of equipment to India] … [and] India got the equipment along with the know-how" (Kaul 1991).

2.1.3 ONGC as a government department: focus on rules and regulations

With the support of two senior geologists at the geological survey of India (GSI), Malaviya succeeded in establishing the oil and natural gas (ONG) division as a department in the NR&SR ministry in

October 1955. The purpose of this department was the exploration and production of oil and the learning and acquisition of the techniques of the oil industry (Kaul 1991). On the recommendations of a high-level Russian team and the revised Industrial Policy Resolution of 1956 the ONG division was raised to the status of a commission in August 1956 and became the Oil and Natural Gas Commission. The commission, though it still had limited financial powers, had a much wider scope of operations including surveying, exploration, and advising to the GoI. This was the beginning of the present day Oil and Natural Gas Corporation (ONGC).

Being a government department also meant that ONGC's activities were subject to burdensome red tape. The government paid all of ONGC's Rs. 343 crores[1] equity capital. Financial requirements of ONGC were met through annual appropriations from the revenues deposited in the treasury (Singh and Singh 2004). Accordingly, government rules, regulations, and procedures were closely followed to monitor financial prudence of ONGC's operations. ONGC was directly responsible to the Parliament for day-to-day operations, and decision-making authority lay with the bureaucrats who ran the department but had limited or no technical knowledge of the oil business. This restricted the flexibility that ONGC needed to develop its operations.

But perhaps the most lasting impression on ONGC of being a government department was on its organizational culture: "Initially, when the ONGC was functioning as a government department, it failed to inculcate work culture and create initiatives among employees, which [is] an essential input for improving efficiency of an organization" (Singh and Singh 2004). Seeing that ONGC was finding it difficult to behave strategically and flexibly, the government reformed the enterprise as a public corporation by the ONGC Act 1959. But in reality ONGC had very limited financial and operational autonomy even as a public corporation. Government advisors and appointees to ONGC often were in conflict with ONGC's governing board. Bureaucrats in the ministry, working with the politicians, ensured that ONGC remained entangled in red tape.

2.1.4 E&P activities

ONGC made its first sizable discovery of oil in 1958 in the (onshore) Cambay Basin in the western state of Gujarat. Through the 1960s ONGC explored mostly in on-land basins and made a string of discoveries in the Cambay Basin (Cambay, Ankleshwar, Kalol, Sanand, North Kadi, etc.) and in the Assam-Arakan Fold Belt in the country's eastern region (Galeki, Lakwa, Rudrasagar, etc.) (ONGC History, www.ongcindia.com/history.asp; Sharma 2002). By 1970 ONGC's crude oil production had reached 3.5 MMTPA.

2.2 Discovery of Mumbai High: ONGC comes of age (1970–1990)

In the 1970s ONGC began exploration in offshore areas. Working with Russian explorers, ONGC discovered the giant Mumbai High field in February 1974, and production from Mumbai High started in 1976.[2] The rapid development of Mumbai High was remarkable even by the international standards of those days. Besides the Russian help in exploration and later in development, two factors contributed to the Mumbai High success. First, the French IOC CFP-Total was also deeply associated with the initial development of Mumbai High. That association imparted much needed technical expertise and training to ONGC. Second, the GoI and the prime minister at that time (Indira Gandhi) fully supported a fast and efficient development of Mumbai High under ONGC. That was largely motivated by the need to reduce pressure on foreign exchange by cutting the oil import bill. The GoI brought in as ONGC's chairman Mr. N. B. Prasad, who was a true technocrat. Previously Prasad had been at India's Atomic Energy Commission, where he was associated with the country's nuclear program. With the GoI's support, during Prasad's tenure best practices in E&P were promoted at ONGC. Further, association with the Russians and CFP-Total charged "ONGCians" with a meticulous technical culture. Under Prasad's leadership ONGC became a focused, goal-oriented company.

The years between 1975 and 1990 were ONGC's golden years. Total oil and oil-equivalent gas production went up from 4.5 MMTPA in 1974–1975 to nearly 48 MMTPA in 1989–1990. Thanks to ONGC's production, India's crude oil import dependency (ratio of imports to consumption) dropped from 65 percent in 1974–1975 to 38 percent in 1989–1990, even as consumption increased nearly threefold over the same period to 55 MMTPA. ONGC also grew dramatically in size. Starting from just 450 employees at formation in 1956, ONGC swelled to more than 47,000 employees by 1990.

ONGC's rapid success during these years was timely for India, as it helped reduce the import bill for oil. Since independence India had embarked on an agenda of self-reliance in economic affairs. This agenda intensified post-1965. Among other policies, the government imposed significant trade barriers, supported a heavily subsidized capital-intensive industry in the public sector, and ran a tight licensing regime for businesses. When the world was hit by spiraling high oil prices starting in 1973 following OPEC's oil embargo, India's economy was nearly in shambles. Per-capita GDP grew at an average of less than 1 percent between 1965 and 1980 and foreign debt and interest payments were dangerously high (Frankel 2005).

Efforts were made on all fronts to manage the tough foreign exchange situation. Reducing imports of crude oil and petroleum products were top on the list, as those imports alone formed 26 percent of the import bill in 1975–1976 (Government of India, Ministry of Finance 1976). Rapid development of Mumbai High and other fields and a greater emphasis on exploration to increase domestic reserves appeared to the GoI as an obvious step in reining in the tough foreign exchange situation.

As the balance of payment and foreign exchange situation of India remained quite poor during 1975–1990, the overarching policy goal remained focused on increasing domestic exploration and production of oil. To support ONGC in rapidly developing Mumbai High the capital outlay in the Fifth Five-Year Plan (1975–1980) was increased to Rs. 1,056 crores as compared with Rs. 420 crores in the Draft Fifth Plan. Subsequent five-year plans also allocated significant capital to finance ONGC's plans (Table 17.1).

Loans from international crediting agencies, particularly the World Bank, were instrumental in financing ONGC's foreign exchange needs, but also in broadly supporting development of oil and gas infrastructure in India. Table 17.2 shows the external assistance that ONGC received for development of the Mumbai High fields. (The Appendix at the end of this chapter presents the fuller picture of external assistance to India's oil and gas sector between 1975 and 1991.)

By the late 1980s ONGC had become the shining star of the public sector. Starting from just a few hundred barrels of oil per day (bopd) production in 1976–1977, at its peak (between 1984–1985 and 1990–1991) production from Mumbai High reached more than 400,000 bopd. Had it not been for ONGC's increasing crude oil production, the foreign exchange situation would have been worse given that oil demand in India grew at nearly 7 percent annually between 1975 and 1990. (Absent ONGC, India's foreign reserves crisis of 1991 might have happened a decade earlier. It is interesting

Table 17.1. *Capital outlay allocated for ONGC in five-year plans between 1975 and 1990*

Plan period	5th plan (1975–1980)	6th plan (1980–1985)	7th plan (1985–1990)
Capital outlay (in Rs. crores)	1,056	2,853.6	8,752.7

Note: 1 crore = 10 million.
Source: Planning Commission, Government of India.

Table 17.2. *External assistance received by ONGC for development of the Mumbai High fields*

Project	Donor	Year of approval	Amount
Bombay High I	World Bank	1977	$150 million
Bombay High II	World Bank	1980	$400 million
Bombay Offshore I	Japan (OECF)	1979	¥6.2 billion
Bombay Offshore II	Japan (OECF)	1979	¥8.6 billion

Source: Asian Development Bank (1991).

to speculate whether that would have ushered in the country's economic reforms earlier, or if the country was not ready for such innovation until other factors were in place in the early 1990s.) Thanks to Mumbai High, ONGC became the role model of an indigenously nurtured, self-reliant government company that was successfully delivering energy security to the nation. And because of the difficulties in opening the country's oil fields to outside bidders, ONGC faced no competition and thus there was no sense of whether the firm actually performed well.

2.3 From spoiled kid to shunned stepchild: crisis and reforms (1991–1998)

2.3.1 ONGC's problems at Mumbai High

Amid adulation from all sides and the pressure to produce as rapidly as possible, ONGC had pushed its luck too far. In 1990 ONGC started

Table 17.3. *Declining crude oil production in early 1990s (million metric tonnes)*

1989–1990	1990–1991	1991–1992	1992–1993	1993–1994
21.71	20.38	18.96	15.75	15.38

Source: www.indiastat.com.

having problems with the Mumbai High field. Flogging (overproduction) of several production wells caused erratic behavior of the hydrocarbon reservoir. In consultation with ONGC and an international consultant, a government committee recommended to immediately stop production from the flogged wells (ninety in total) in order to build reservoir pressure. The problem was so severe that the government accepted the recommendations. The deputy oil minister, Satish Kumar Sharma, stressed that the action was necessary "so that the reservoir is not permanently damaged."[3] The shutdowns resulted in a 30 percent reduction in ONGC's crude oil production, which came down from 21.7 MMT in 1989–1990 to 15.38 MMT in 1993–1994 (Table 17.3).

2.3.2 Neelam fields

ONGC started development of the Neelam fields off India's west coast in 1989. By the time the development project was completed in 1994 reservoir issues similar to Mumbai High had erupted (but not due to flogging). Grossly inaccurate technical planning of the Neelam fields led to a production peak in 1994–1995 instead of ONGC's predictions of a several years long production plateau at 4.5 MMTPA (Table 17.4). An audit report found that despite the availability of 3D data and data processing technology, ONGC had used old 2D seismic data (taken between 1977 and 1984) to prepare the technological scheme for the field development program. Shortly after, 3D data analysis reports completed in March 1991 found that the reservoir was steeper than originally thought, which suggested lesser reserves than predicted by the 2D data (Comptroller and Auditor General of India 2001).

2.3.3 Financial crisis of 1991 and foreign loans: origins of oil sector reforms in India

The problems at Mumbai High coincided with India's foreign exchange crisis of 1991. By the late 1980s India's delicate balance-of-

Table 17.4. *Projected and actual oil production from ONGC's Neelam fields*

Oil rate (MMTPA)	1992–1993	1993–1994	1994–1995	1995–1996	1996–1997	1997–1998
Projected	0.5044	0.379	4.485	4.5	4.5	4.5
Actual	0.54	0.6	3.81	3.54	2.29	1.92

Source: "Avoidable Expenditure on Creation of Excess Capacity," Report by Comptroller and Auditor General of India (2001), www.cag.gov.in/reports/commercial/2001_book4/chapter6.htm.

payment situation had snowballed to disastrous proportions as India came close to defaulting on international debt repayments. Special assistance loans of $150 million each from the World Bank and the Asian Development Bank (ADB) helped India avert the crisis.

The crisis opened the floodgate of reforms in India. Some of these reformist ideas were already in place but they were finally successful because reform-oriented bankers held the country hostage. The oil and gas sector, which at that point was dominated by state-owned companies, was one of the top items that the World Bank and the ADB emphasized for introducing reforms and increasing private participation. The World Bank and the ADB required India to improve economic efficiency through "support for structural reforms, promotion of competition, and private sector participation" (Asian Development Bank 2001) as a precondition for providing the assistance loans and a separate $350 million loan from World Bank for ONGC's gas flaring reduction projects. With no other choice left, the government acquiesced to these demands (Comptroller and Auditor General of India 1996). It was the outside banks that devised the main strategic reforms. With inputs and advice from the banks, the GoI took the lead on implementing the proposed reform measures. It is noteworthy that the GoI has continued its reform efforts in the oil and gas sector even after the engagement of the banks on this issue has waned. That is a manifestation of a pro-reform mindset of the GoI, partly motivated by the tremendous economic benefits of the broader economic reforms in India since 1991. A detailed description of the progress on these reforms is presented in sections 3.1–3.4.

The Hydrocarbon Sector Plan (HSP) loan was approved by ADB in December 1991 with the main objective "to promote accelerated exploration and development of domestic hydrocarbon resources through increased participation of the private sector and enhanced operational efficiency of public sector enterprises" (Asian Development Bank 2001). The program loan of $250 million was planned to be disbursed in two tranches of $125 million each; the first tranche was disbursed by February 1992. The second tranche, planned for closing on June 30, 1995, was canceled when it became clear that the GoI could not meet one of the key covenants of the loan, namely the divestment of 20 percent of the GoI's equity in ONGC.

2.3.4 Oil sector policy changes: new rules of the game
Among other things, pushing for the introduction of the New Exploration and Licensing Policy (NELP) was perhaps one of the most important contributions of the ADB HSP. The NELP envisioned expanding exploration in geologically challenging areas requiring huge risk capital and cutting-edge technologies by increasing competition in the E&P sector and attracting private capital. In the pre-NELP era, India had provisions that allowed private companies to search for oil. But those efforts to attract private capital to the sector were not successful, as the bidding provisions were opaque and covered only small areas. The NELP envisioned changing all that. Under the NELP, which India instituted in 1998, all new exploration acreage is offered only through an open-for-all competitive bidding process. Importantly, the state-owned firms ONGC and OIL (Oil India Limited) are also required to compete for these new exploration areas. The NELP allows 100 percent foreign direct investment (FDI) and offers improved contractual terms to make business in the oil sector attractive in India. Further, under the NELP the Directorate General of Hydrocarbons (DGH, the upstream technical regulator) replaced ONGC as the overseer of the exploration blocks, bids, and the associated exploration work.

Before the first NELP round in 1999, only 15% of the Indian sedimentary basins were moderately or well explored and 50% were unexplored. NELP has contracted 162 blocks via six bidding rounds (NELP-I to NELP-VI) (Government of India, Ministry of Petroleum and Natural Gas, Directorate General of Hydrocarbons 2007). As a result, in 2006–2007 20% of the sedimentary basinal area was moderately or well explored, while exploration has been initiated in 44% of the remaining areas. Participating companies have committed to invest more than $8 billion in these blocks (Rediff India Abroad 2007). During NELP-VII, bidding for which closed in June 2008, the Ministry of Petroleum and Natural Gas (MoPNG) offered another fifty-seven oil and gas blocks. Of those, forty-five blocks received bids and finally contracts were signed for forty-one blocks in December 2008. Overall, the actual investments from NELP-VII auctions are expected to be about $1.5 billion, in contrast with the initial hopes for $3.5 billion (The Hindu 2008).

2.4 Adapting to the new rules (1999–2008)

The wave of reforms and policy changes started in the aftermath of the 1991 economic crisis has significantly changed the conditions under which ONGC was used to operating. Amid rising import bills and import dependency on crude oil, the GoI has been increasingly vocal in asking ONGC to improve performance and production. Further, with the NELP, ONGC has lost its status as the GoI's de facto regulator of the oil and gas sector and has also lost the right to preferential access to acreages.

2.4.1 Pressure from rising imports

Rapidly growing imports have put tremendous pressure on the GoI to increase domestic production. In 2007 India consumed 2.8 million bopd,[4] making it the fifth-largest consumer of oil in the world. It imported more than 76.7 percent of its crude oil requirements in 2006–2007, compared with about 43.4 percent in 1995–1996 and 31.7 percent in 1985–1986. The rapid increase in oil import dependency has occurred because of a dramatic growth in India's oil demand since 1995, while domestic production has remained flat at around 0.66 million bopd (Figure 17.2). More than 70 percent of India's crude oil imports come from Middle East countries, which are geographically close and thus favored suppliers.

Due to both increased demand and prices and a booming domestic refining industry, India spent about $68 billion to import crude oil in 2007–2008 (Government of India, Ministry of Petroleum and Natural Gas, Petroleum Planning and Analysis Cell 2010). Earnings from exported petroleum products – notably naphtha, petrol, and

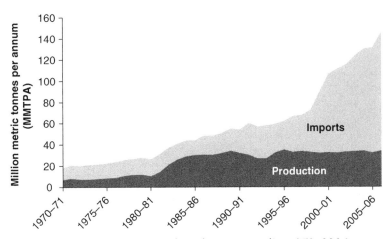

Figure 17.2 Crude oil imports and production in India, 1970–2006.
Note: 1 MMTPA ~ 20,000 bopd.
Source: Petroleum Planning and Analysis Cell (PPAC), Ministry of Petroleum and Natural Gas, Government of India, and www.indiastat.com.

diesel – partly reduced that burden: the *net* oil import bill was about $57 billion in 2007–2008.[5] As in the past, the substantial burden on India's trade position and foreign exchange from crude oil imports is a key reason that the GoI continues to emphasize greater domestic exploration and production.

2.4.2 Production plateau and exploration troubles

But ONGC's E&P record has disappointed the GoI on both fronts. ONGC's yearly domestic oil production has hovered around 25–30 MMTPA since 1990 (Figure 17.3) and its annual gas production too has plateaued near 23 BCM since 1995 (Figure 17.4). That is, ONGC's combined oil and gas production has been stagnant around 50 MMTPA (O+OEG). If ONGC's foreign production is taken in account, between 2000–2001 and 2006–2007 ONGC's O+OEG production increased from 49.08 MMTPA to 60.72 MMTPA.

ONGC's reserves have also remained flat. As shown in Figure 17.5, the combined oil and gas reserves of ONGC stood at 938.8 MMT as of March 31, 2007, increasing somewhat from 857.7 MMT on March 31, 2001. At current levels of production ONGC's reserve life is about 15.5 years. In terms of combined oil and gas reserves in 2004 ONGC ranked 32 among global oil and gas companies. It ranked below most

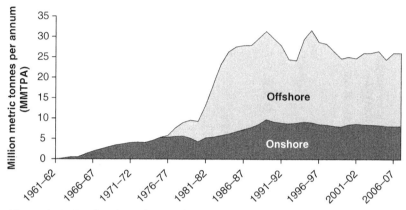

Figure 17.3 Crude oil production by ONGC, 1960–2007.
Source: www.indiastat.com and Ministry of Petroleum and Natural Gas, Government of India.

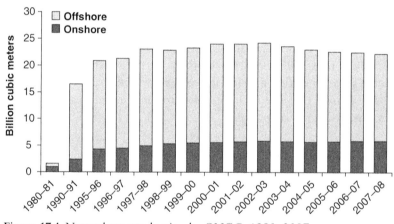

Figure 17.4 Natural gas production by ONGC, 1980–2007.
Source: www.indiastat.com and Ministry of Petroleum and Natural Gas, Government of India.

other major NOCs (among others Pemex, Petrobras, and PetroChina), almost at par with Statoil, and ahead of Sonangol (Victor 2007).

While declining reserves and the deteriorating health of producing fields brought negative attention to ONGC in the 1990s, over the last decade ONGC's biggest performance troubles have revolved around exploration. Much of that flak has been spearheaded by the DGH,

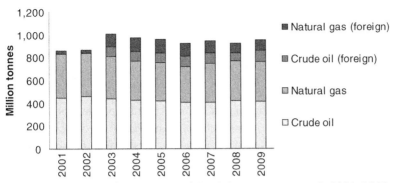

Figure 17.5 Hydrocarbon reserves of ONGC (proven reserves), 2001–2009.
Source: ONGC Annual Reports (www.ongcindia.com).

which has publicly criticized ONGC's poor performance in the recent past (Moneycontrol.com 2006). Until 2000 nearly all of ONGC's exploration work was either on land or in shallow water. Since the initiation of the NELP rounds of competitive bidding for exploration acreage in 1999, India opened up several prospective areas offshore, especially in deep water. ONGC and Reliance (separately) won the bids for most of those deep water blocks. But ONGC's lack of deep water capabilities and poor risk management have significantly impeded ONGC's deep water exploration program. A 2006 report of the DGH showed that of the forty-seven blocks (including on land and offshore) awarded to ONGC at that point, the company had not made any discoveries. All the thirty-two wells that ONGC drilled in those blocks turned out to be dry (Moneycontrol.com 2006). As a result, in a few deep water exploration blocks for which ONGC was the highest bidder, the DGH recommended to the MoPNG to not award them to ONGC in view of ONGC's poor track record in such projects (The Financial Express 2006).

Short-term focus of the top management and a weak R&D program are at the root of ONGC's recent problems in deep water explorations. Although ONGC has more than five decades of experience in exploration, its expertise and capabilities in oil and gas exploration are far behind the international level of exploration geosciences and technologies that most IOCs and some NOCs like Petrobras and StatoilHydro develop and employ (PESD Interviews). During the 1960s and 1970s ONGC received significant E&P help on technology and equipment from the Russians and ran a focused R&D program (PESD Interviews; Sharma 2002). Besides, the major oil and gas discoveries of ONGC (mostly in 1970s and 1980s) were in relatively simple geology, either on land or shallow offshore. ONGC's early success in E&P gave it a substantial oil and gas production base by the early 1980s. As cash flow from those operations was adequate, ONGC did not have to conduct much R&D on exploration sciences to stay in business. In the midst of its much-celebrated E&P success through the 1980s, ONGC's focus had already started shifting toward developing the discovered fields, partly in response to government pressure (see sections 2.2 and 2.3). An intensive focus on developing discovered fields and urgent need to maintain existing production brought ONGC's exploration and associated R&D "almost to a halt" (Modak 2002). More recently, even though ONGC's yearly expenditure on R&D has hovered around 0.3 percent of revenues during 2001 and 2007, its R&D program is poorly managed and not well targeted to its business. Consequently, ONGC's exploration capabilities have significantly eroded since 1990.

2.4.3 E&P strategy

Pressure from the GoI to alleviate the worsening oil supply situation is also evident in ONGC's strategy, both domestically as well as internationally. At a strategy meeting in 2001 ONGC devised a two-pronged approach to enhance production and put its exploration program back on track. Per the strategy, one track would accelerate efforts to find and produce oil at home. The other would intensify the efforts of ONGC Videsh Limited (OVL, ONGC's overseas arm) to find equity oil abroad.

Domestic

Domestically, as new production has not come online in the last few years, ONGC's strategy has been to monetize marginal fields and to invest in the maintenance and redevelopment of its declining fields, particularly Mumbai High. These investments have been obviated by the need to save face domestically amid rising concerns of dropping production. Some of these efforts are paying off, at least in the short term. After a lackluster period in the 1990s, the reserves replacement (RR) record of ONGC has improved since 2000 (see Figure 17.6

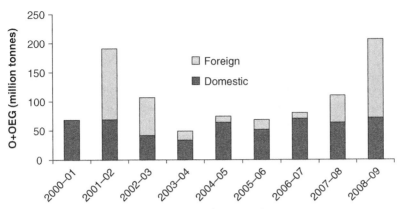

Figure 17.6 Ultimate reserves accretion by ONGC.
Note: 3P reserves: Proved+Probable+Possible.
Source: ONGC Annual Reports (www.ongcindia.com).

and Table 17.5),[6] partly because of reinvigorated exploration efforts at home and partly because of the successful acquisition of overseas assets (discussed in detail later). Interestingly, though ONGC has declared an RR ratio of greater than one in the past several years, that has done little to enhance ONGC's production of oil or gas. That itself raises questions about the methods of reserve assessment as well as managerial issues in translating discoveries to production (PESD Interviews).

Besides domestic redevelopment, new exploration has also received renewed interest from ONGC. Armed with extensive experience in the domestic business environment and geology, and a very strong cash flow situation (discussed in detail later), ONGC has bid aggressively for exploration blocks in all of the seven NELP rounds that have been held so far. As a result, ONGC has won more than half of all the NELP blocks offered so far.

Equity oil and gas abroad: ONGC Videsh Limited (OVL)
In addition to efforts to accelerate domestic E&P, another idea has gathered significant traction within ONGC: obtaining equity oil abroad. The government also believes that oil production owned by Indian companies, whether at home or abroad, enhances energy security by securing supply (Government of India, Planning Commission 2006; Government of India, Ministry of Petroleum and Natural Gas 2008).

Table 17.5. *ONGC's reserves replacement ratio*

2003–2004	2004–2005	2005–2006	2006–2007	2007–2008
0.65	1	1.1	1.35	1.32

Note: Reserves replacement ratio is defined as the ultimate reserves added divided by the production during a year.
Source: ONGC presentation at the ABN Amro Asian Conference, November 2008 www.ongcindia.com/download/ABN_Asian_Conference_London_Newyork.pdf.

Leading this quest for overseas assets is ONGC Videsh Limited (OVL), the overseas arm of ONGC. OVL aims to "tie up" 60 MMPTA (1.2 mbd) oil and gas production overseas by 2025. As of March 31, 2007, OVL's assets had grown to about $4.5 billion – mostly in loans from its parent company, state-owned ONGC – from virtually nothing in 2001. By March 2008 OVL had thirty-eight projects in eighteen countries, giving it a proven reserve base of 194.6 MMT (95.7 MMT oil and 98.9 MMT oil-equivalent gas) and an annual O+OEG production of 8.8 MMT (ONGC 2008).

2.4.4 Finances
Until April 2002 prices of crude oil and petroleum products in India were determined as a weighted average of international prices and the domestic cost of production. But, in line with the HSP's objective of moving toward market-determined prices, since April 2002 the GoI has linked the price of crude oil to international prices. That has been a big boost for ONGC's finances. Like other oil companies with an established production base, high oil prices in the international markets since 2002 have sent ONGC's revenues and profits soaring (Figures 17.7 and 17.8).

2.4.5 Financial efficiency and project management
Amid growing pressure to improve performance and production and a stronger-than-ever financial position, ONGC's financial efficiency continues to be questionable. Its contracting system (for awarding contract work to outsiders) and project management of exploration work for the NELP blocks are good examples of the more general problem of financial inefficiency that Cuts across ONGC's operations.

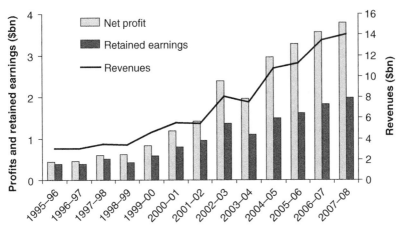

Figure 17.7 Financial performance of ONGC, 1995–2007.
Source: ONGC Annual Reports (www.ongcindia.com).

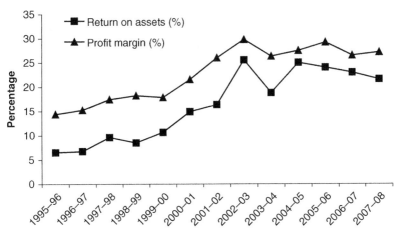

Figure 17.8 ONGC's return on assets and sales, 1995–2007.
Source: ONGC Annual Reports (www.ongcindia.com).

Weak contracting system

ONGC's poor contracting system – including contract tendering, bidding, award and performance appraisal – has enabled contractors to escape with poor equipment and supply deliveries, while leaving the consequent financial risks and losses with ONGC. For example, in one case a contract was awarded to a financially sick party (with prior knowledge of the contractor's weak financial position), eventually leading to the failure of ONGC to meet the minimum work program (MWP) – the exploration work committed in the production-sharing contracts – associated with the contract (Comptroller and Auditor General of India 2008).

Even though there is a standard procedure for awarding contracts (the *L1 process*[7]), that process is thoroughly abused by ONGC personnel and contractors for rent seeking (PESD Interviews). One strategy is particularly well suited to exploit the L1 process. In this gaming strategy, first the contractor bids very low to ensure winning the tender. On grant of the contract, the contractor works in cahoots with ONGC personnel to see that critical steps of the contract for which ONGC is responsible are not completed on time. Sometimes ONGC has to pay the contractor for "delays" that hinder work by the contractor, but often many contracts are renegotiated successfully by contractors after award because they were poorly framed in the first place (PESD Interviews).

The weak contracting system of ONGC is one of the prime causes for significant project delays and cost overruns – it takes away from ONGC the main levers of enforcing risk-abatement strategies that are industry standards.

Poor planning and coordination
One of ONGC's biggest organizational issues relates to overlapping responsibilities between different functional groups (technical, exploration, on land, and offshore). As a result there is no single point of responsibility for core exploration and development activities.

For the period from 2002–2003 to 2006–2007 ONGC committed to drill fifty-one exploration wells, but planned for only thirty-five. This not only highlights internal coordination issues but also suggests aggressive bidding by ONGC. ONGC's aggressive bidding has resulted in a series of shortfalls by ONGC on MWPs in various blocks. In the aftermath ONGC has had to surrender several NELP blocks besides paying fines to both the DGH and the MoPNG (Comptroller and Auditor General of India 2008).

In general, activities needed for the completion of the MWP are not well planned, and clear targets are not set (Comptroller and Auditor General of India 2008). Poor planning and action for chartering and mobilizing of vessels for seismic surveys have led to delays in data acquisition and interpretation in many cases. Under the PSCs for the NELP blocks the contractor needs to begin exploration work within six months of signing the contract. It has taken ONGC nearly two years in many cases, and sometimes up to four years, to begin exploration in NELP blocks. Deep water drilling has also suffered tremendously on account of delays in finalization of hiring contracts. Further, in the last few years when getting rigs has been difficult, ONGC chose to forgo the option of hiring two rigs. That decision has cost it an estimated Rs. 900 crores (~$200 million).

3 Explaining ONGC's performance and strategy

In its five-decades-long history ONGC has had remarkable successes, notably the discovery and development of Mumbai High between 1974 and 1985 (see section 2.2), a string of significant oil and gas discoveries during the late 1970s and 1980s (see section 2.2), and a praiseworthy revival and salvation of Mumbai High since significant reservoir issues surfaced around 1990. Until the late 1980s, ONGC was a huge success story and GoI accorded it a star status.

But since 1990, ONGC has been notorious for serious performance issues. It grossly mismanaged some of its major oil fields, significantly impacting ONGC's production during the mid 1990s. By the time (around 2000) ONGC got its act together to reclaim its production, its poor exploration record and declining reserves became objects of severe criticism by the GoI and the media alike. What has not changed in the last five decades is the question mark over ONGC's financial prudence and efficiency.

ONGC's performance and organizational problems have long been recognized by the GoI. But, despite tremendous economic pressures and a worsening supply-demand situation, the GoI has had a very hard time devising a strategy to encourage higher efficiency in ONGC and the oil and gas sector. Between 1970 and 2000 the GoI set up seven review committees for organizational restructuring of ONGC. Although themes of the individual reviews varied, each of them highlighted that "there is no evidence of cost consciousness or cost effectiveness in the operations in general" (Kaul Committee Report, Government of India 1992). The last major reorganization effort was started in 2001 based on the recommendations of McKinsey & Co. Although ONGC implemented the changes that McKinsey suggested for hierarchical restructuring, it left out McKinsey's core recommendation of establishing a performance-based incentive structure across the hierarchy. Additionally, since the 1991 economic crisis, which also coincided with ONGC's serious technical problems, the GoI has tried to introduce a number of reform measures in the oil and gas sector. Those reforms have been targeted at making the sector more competitive, changing the monitoring mechanisms to incentivize performance, improving corporate governance, and increasing the transparency of pricing and taxation.

Those reforms, while well intended, have been half-hearted and therefore have proved inadequate. In all, the GoI's reform agenda has been punctured by its ad hoc interventions motivated by political exigencies. The result is a complex web of institutional and business actors interacting in a partially reformed system that is a hybrid of market-oriented policies in some parts and strong state intervention and control in others.

Similarly, for the most part ONGC's strategy has been a reactive response to government priorities and demands rather than a proactive agenda ensuing from a long-term vision. Amid shifting priorities and preferences of the GoI, ONGC has adapted its corporate strategy as best suited to pacify the GoI. Further, even as the boundary conditions of GoI–ONGC relations have evolved over time, ONGC's organizational behavior – the way ONGC's managers and other employees approach the conduct of business – has exhibited a remarkable inertia toward organizational slack, rent seeking, and managerial discretion.

While at a first glance ONGC might appear to be the prime actor behind these performance and strategy outcomes, in reality the main determinant of ONGC's technical and financial performance is the interaction between ONGC and the GoI, in particular the incentive structure and constraints that government ownership has entailed for ONGC. In this section I discuss the main elements of this dynamic, while emphasizing how ONGC's long and close associations with the GoI have deeply influenced ONGC's performance and strategy.

3.1 Competition

Although never one of the top items on the GoI's agenda until the late 1990s, making the oil and gas sector more competitive has always been on the GoI's radar. Prior to the NELP, nearly all of the GoI's attempts at increasing competition by bringing in more private participation in the sector have either been unsuccessful or controversial. A heavy reliance on ONGC as the de facto regulator of E&P activities afforded ONGC the opportunity to keep competition at bay. And wherever the GoI has run the show without ONGC's assistance, powerful "dual firms" – private firms with deep political connections and financial clout – have been able to get very favorable contractual terms, thus leaving little benefit to the GoI and the public.

3.1.1 Early attempts to increase competition

Between 1979 and 1991 the government made several unsuccessful attempts at getting private and international companies involved in oil E&P. With the rapid development of Mumbai High being the topmost priority, ONGC's plate was full. The government decided to enlist the services of others for exploring new areas to keep reserves accretion rolling. Four exploration bidding rounds ("pre-NELP" rounds[8]) were launched between 1979 and 1991. But, as shown in Table 17.6, the response was lukewarm at best.

Three factors contributed to the failure of these pre-NELP bidding rounds. First, by the time the first exploration round was held in 1980 international oil markets had begun easing off – partly due to the lower demand that arose from high oil prices and economic recession induced by the oil shocks of the late 1970s, and partly due to large new supplies of oil from non-OPEC countries, particularly Norway and Mexico. By the mid 1980s oil prices had declined further and IOCs were interested only in very prospective areas – India was certainly not one of them. Second, around 1980 China too offered offshore exploration blocks to IOCs, as part of its plan to open up its economy. Chinese blocks were generally considered more promising than the Indian blocks. Third, the bidding process was handled by the Exploration Contract Monitoring Group (EXCOM), which was a part of ONGC. The exploration blocks and associated data packages were formulated mostly under the aegis of ONGC, and in a few instances blocks advertised for bidding were removed later on from the list of available blocks. This lack of transparency created a perception that promising blocks were being held for ONGC or OIL and only high-risk acreage was being offered for bidding.

Table 17.6. *Blocks offered, bids received, and contracts signed for exploration blocks during pre-NELP rounds*

Year	Round	Number of blocks offered			Bids received	Contracts signed		
		Offshore	Onshore	Total		Offshore	Onshore	Total
1980	One	17	15	32	4	1	0	1
1982	Two	42	8	50	0	0	0	0
1986	Three	27	0	27	13	0	0	0
1991	Four	39	33	72	24	2	3	5
1993	Five	29	16	45	15	4	2	6
1993	Six	17	29	46	20	2	3	5
1994	Seven	17	28	45	12	2	3	5
1994	Eight	15	19	34	38	1	3	4
1995	Nine (JV)	10	18	28	22	1	1	2

Source: Review of E&P Licensing Policy, Petroleum Federation of India 2005 www.petrofed.org/19_Sep_05.asp.

3.1.2 Joint venture development of oil fields with private firms

The coincidence of ONGC's troubles with Mumbai High and the reform agenda that was beginning to grab the nation around 1991 provided an entry point for private players. Development of some already discovered fields was held up due to lack of funds and adequate foreign exchange (Comptroller and Auditor General of India 1996): "The issue here is that we just don't have the requisite money to invest in the already discovered fields ... Even in the area of already discovered oil fields we require additional induction of fund[s]"[9] Besides, after being bogged down with the development of Mumbai High during the 1980s, it was clear that Mumbai High's maintenance and redevelopment would keep ONGC busy through the 1990s. Under these circumstances, the idea of opening the oil and gas sector to private players gained traction.

In the spirit of assurances given by the GoI to the World Bank and ADB via the Hydrocarbon Sector Plan (HSP), in 1992 the government offered several medium- and small-sized fields for development by private companies in JVs with ONGC or OIL, the two state-owned companies. These fields were already discovered by ONGC or OIL, and in some cases were also under development. The response to these offers was good, especially for the medium-sized fields. PSCs were executed between October 1994 and December 1994 for five medium-sized fields and thirteen small-sized fields. The government followed up with a second round of offers for joint development in 1993.

Table 17.7 shows the breakdown of fields offered by size, bids received, and contracts signed.

A particular event in the JV rounds illustrates the troubles with bringing private players into the E&P sector. In December 1994 the GoI signed a 25-year production-sharing contract (PSC) for the development and production of the proven Panna, Mukta, and Tapti (PMT) fields with an unincorporated JV between ONGC, Enron Oil and Gas India Ltd (EOGIL),[10] and Reliance Industries Limited (RIL) (Padmanabhan 1998). The PMT fields were discovered and partially developed by ONGC. Per the suggestions of the World Bank, extra capital needed to further develop PMT was sought through the sale of participating interests (PIs) in the fields. The 1994 PSC gave Enron and RIL a 30 percent PI each; the remaining 40 percent was retained by ONGC.

Table 17.7. *Fields offered under joint venture development rounds*

Year	Round	Medium-sized fields		Small-sized fields		Bids received	Contracts signed
		Offshore	Onshore	Offshore	Onshore		
Aug 1992	One	6	6	10	21	117	18
Oct 1993	Two	2	6	4	29	29	12

Source: Review of E&P Licensing Policy, Petroleum Federation of India 2005 www.petrofed.org/19_Sep_05.asp.

Subsequently, the PSC generated a lot of criticism for the GoI and the prudence of the JV PSC was questioned. In 1995 the Comptroller and Auditor General (CAG) of India released a scathing audit report thoroughly criticizing the MoPNG in the award of PSCs for the medium-sized fields (Comptroller and Auditor General of India 1996). The audit found that the bidding process was very opaque and that the parameters on which the selection was made (to maximize the projects' NPV to GoI) were poorly defined. Besides, there was no specific language in the final contracts to hold the contractors accountable to the capital and operating expenditure estimates presented in the bids. The audit found further that the contractors were given several very favorable concessions.

The CAG observations were examined by the Central Bureau of Investigation (CBI) and were also the subject matter of public interest litigation in the Delhi High Court and thereafter in the Supreme Court. The CBI and the Supreme Court ultimately upheld the PSCs awarded in the JV round and the allegations made by the CAG were found to be unsubstantiated. Many of these complaints may actually have resulted from corporate rivalries. Later on, both PMT and the Ravva JVs established far higher reserves and have been able to maintain production at far higher levels than envisaged by ONGC. Over their lives these projects have returned substantial revenues to the government as profit share on top of royalty payments. This episode is not surprising, as ONGC officials have always rankled at the thought of their discovered fields having been divested.

3.1.3 Competition under the NELP

With the introduction of the NELP in 1998 (see section 2.3.4), the GoI's efforts to inject competition into India's oil and gas upstream

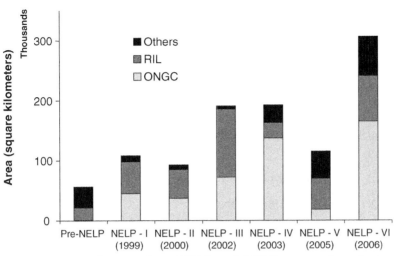

Figure 17.9 Distribution of pre-NELP and NELP acreage by winning bidder.
Source: Annual Report 2006–2007, Directorate General of Hydrocarbons (DGH), Government of India.

(E&P) have finally been successful, albeit only partially. As shown in Figure 17.9 ONGC and RIL have won most of the exploration acreage auctioned through the NELP, but several other NOCs and IOCs have also initiated E&P bases in India. At present, India's E&P is really a duopoly between ONGC and Reliance, with only a few other players. Over the past decade Reliance, India's largest private sector conglomerate, has emerged as ONGC's major competitor in oil and gas E&P. Starting in 2002, Reliance has made a series of discoveries, largely gas, in the eastern offshore Krishna-Godavari (KG) Basin. By 2011–2012 Reliance is projected to become India's largest gas producer (Business Standard 2009).

Reliance's strong emergence on India's oil and gas E&P scene (along with the successes of other companies) has changed ONGC's operating environment and its relationship with the GoI in fundamental ways. By bringing more competition the NELP has enabled benchmarking of performance in the E&P sector in India. As several companies are now engaged in exploration work, the GoI and the upstream regulator (the DGH) have more information about the true costs of oil and gas discovery in India. This has, for the first time, allowed the GoI to start using benchmarks and industry standards for monitoring ONGC's performance.[11] Effects of competition are already showing on ONGC's performance and strategy. ONGC has started forming technology partnerships and joint ventures with IOCs both in exploration and development projects (see, among others, Khanna 2007; Frontier India 2008; ONGC 2009). It is also increasingly using and adopting international best practices in exploration efforts and benchmarking of its technical performance.[12]

3.2 Ownership and corporate governance

3.2.1 Corporatization of ONGC

The undercurrent of reforms that began in 1991, both economy-wide and in the oil sector, signaled a move toward a more competitive E&P scenario in India. That also needed public sector enterprises (PSEs) like ONGC to be nimble in responding to market demands. In that spirit, one of the covenants of the ADB's HSP (see section 2.3.3) was for the government to divest 20% of its equity in ONGC. The main motive of that covenant was to provide flexible decision-making powers (financial and organizational) to ONGC, which so far had been entangled in government red tape.

The rate of divestment has been much slower and the quantity much smaller than envisioned in the HSP, as the GoI has found it hard to let go the reins of ONGC. In line with the HSP, the GoI started divesting in ONGC starting in 1994. In October 1994 the government sold 2% of its ONGC holding, mostly to domestic financial institutions (Asian Development Bank 2001). And in December 1994 shares for about 2% of its ONGC holding were issued to ONGC employees. In 1999 the government sold another 12% of its equity, this time to two other public sector units (PSUs) under a cross-shareholding scheme: Indian Oil Corporation (9.6%) and Gas Authority of India Limited (2.4%). That continued until March 2004 when the government put on sale 10% of its ONGC equity.[13] But even after several rounds of divestment the GoI still owns about 88% of ONGC – 74% directly and 14% through other government companies. There are two main reasons for the GoI's slow divestment in ONGC. First, state ownership of ONGC provides flexibility to the GoI in controlling downstream prices (of petroleum products), which is an issue of paramount political importance. Second, the GoI still views its control of ONGC as a critical factor in pursuing India's energy security agenda. To its surprise, the GoI has found that even with the present 12% divestment, its control over ONGC has waned significantly. The fear of losing further control over ONGC, and consequently of the oil and gas sector more broadly, has also kept forces of further divestment from ONGC at bay.

3.2.2 Impact of corporatization on the GoI's control over ONGC

Post reforms, concomitant with changes in ONGC's ownership structure have been changes in ONGC's corporate governance, which has shown positive signs of improvement generally. The government took a big step in reducing its grip on ONGC and enhancing ONGC's financial and organizational independence when in 1999 it granted the *Navratna* status to ONGC. The board of directors of PSUs with *Navratna* status exercises all powers of capital expenditure, proposal for acquisition of technology, strategic alliances, organizational restructuring, formation of joint ventures, and investment of funds.

But it was not until April 2002 that ONGC received real financial autonomy. Until then ONGC was dependent upon the MoPNG and the Oil Coordination Committee (OCC) for having its costs scrutinized and returns approved. The OCC mechanism was in fact a very detailed *ex ante* mechanism of cost control and monitoring, which enabled the MoPNG to keep a check on ONGC. Thus, even though it became a *Navratna* board as far back as 1999, prior to 2002 ONGC did not have true financial autonomy. After April 2002 crude prices payable to ONGC became independent of the assessments of costs and returns done by the OCC. With ONGC no longer dependent on OCC assessments for its cash flows, April 2002 marked a major turning point in ONGC's financial independence from the GoI.

Public listing too has given ONGC another way of reducing government intervention. As a publicly listed company many individuals of the general public are shareholders of ONGC (~2 percent). This group has a clear interest in ONGC's stock price, which is linked with profitability. In the recent past when ONGC has gone public with its grievances about undue government interference, this interest group (public stockowners) has been vocal in its support for ONGC's independence from the political process. Thus, public listing has served as a potent weapon in ONGC's efforts to dampen government control.

3.3 The GoI's continued intervention in ONGC's corporate matters

While by granting ONGC the *Navratna* status the GoI has handed ONGC near complete autonomy in matters of finances, capital expenditure, strategy, and organizational structure, it continues to exert direct and indirect influence over ONGC through hiring restrictions, monitoring exercises such as audits, and appointment of board members and the chief managing director (CMD, the CEO equivalent at ONGC). Such controls have engendered new challenges for ONGC, particularly in those aspects of the sector that are exposed to greater competition, such as the labor market for skilled personnel.

3.3.1 Multiple vigilance and monitoring bodies

Historically, the GoI has employed *ex ante* procedures – a system with prescribed rules for the conduct of business – for monitoring ONGC's performance. To implement that system the GoI has charged multiple government oversight agencies with auditing ONGC's accounts and verifying the transparency of business dealings of ONGC. This is typical of how governments monitor state-owned companies: "[R]epresentative governments typically give oversight authority or opportunity to more than one official so that public organizations often must respond to conflicting and unstable political demands" (Vining and Weimer 1990). Consequently, ONGC has to regularly encounter inquiries from oversight agencies such as the Central Vigilance Commission (CVC) and CAG. Top ONGC managers, including the CEO, are often summoned by the ministry and various parliamentary committees and are expected to be available on demand (PESD Interviews).

Being a PSE also means that members of the parliament can ask questions (to the petroleum minister) about ONGC's operations. The MoPNG must answer these questions either orally or in writing, and the response is in the public domain. This too is a checks-and-balances measure to ensure transparency of ONGC's operations. Although it could not be firmly established in this study, several interviewees said that to get business information from ONGC "private interests" (private oil and gas companies) get members of the parliament to raise issues in the parliament (PESD Interviews).

3.3.2 Appointment of the board of directors and the CMD

ONGC's fourteen-member board of directors has executive (functional) and non-executive members. The Securities and Exchange Board of India (SEBI) requires publicly traded companies to have at least half of the board members be non-executives. In compliance with this requirement, ONGC usually has a 7–7 split between executive and non-executive board members. Two of the non-executive members are government appointees (*official* directors) – one each from the MoPNG and the Ministry of Finance (ONGC 2007).

Appointment of the non-official directors on ONGC's board is made by the MoPNG based on the recommendations of a search committee composed of: 1) chairman, Public Enterprises Selection Board (PESB); 2) secretary (top bureaucrat) of the MoPNG; and 3) secretary, Department of Public Enterprises (Government of India, Ministry of Heavy Industry and Public Enterprises, Department of Public Enterprises 1997).

A similar selection committee selects ONGC's chairman-cum-managing director (CMD) too.[14] But given the much publicized selection process for CMD, the CMD selection committee usually has more members representing diverse interests.[15] Once the committee makes its selection, the Appointments Committee of Cabinet (ACC), which the prime minister's office (PMO) controls, must also approve of that selection. The CMD's tenure is normally five years. At the end of that period the tenure may be extended by the government, subject to superannuation limits (sixty years of age).

The process for selecting ONGC's CMD and board of directors leaves room open for political interference. Two recent episodes in the CMD/board of directors selection process highlight the nature of political interference involved.

In September 2005 the petroleum minster, Mani Shankar Aiyar, was involved in a public controversy with the then CMD of ONGC, Subir Raha. After Aiyar rejected a list of candidates recommended by the selection committee for non-official, non-executive director posts at ONGC, Raha took the controversy public by discussing the issue openly at ONGC's annual general meeting. In doing so, Raha leveraged the sentiments of ONGC's common shareholders to generate broad support for opposing Aiyar's actions. Subsequently, the selection committee rejected the petroleum minister's nominees and a few nominees withdrew from the process. Partly because of the events that followed this controversy, Raha was denied an extension at ONGC when his term expired in May 2006.

After Raha's extension as CMD was declined in May 2006, R. S. Sharma, then finance director and the senior most official in ONGC, was appointed as the acting director. Based on interviews, a PESB panel selected Sharma as the regular CMD in August 2006. But in February 2007 the ACC scrapped that appointment and set up a wider search committee. This led to outrage and uproar in ONGC. The government portrayed its move as an effort to expand the search for the CMD by also including candidates from the private sector (in the name of energy security!) (Business Standard 2007; Mehdudia 2007a). Apparently much of this political jugglery involved Najeeb Jung, who was formerly the joint secretary (exploration) in the MoPNG. At the time of these events Mr. Jung was serving as director of the Observer Research Foundation, a non-profit think tank backed by Reliance Industries. After interviewing twenty-eight candidates, the reconstituted selection committee reselected Sharma as the top choice, but also indicated that Mr. Jung was its second choice for the post (Mehdudia 2007b). Finally in July 2007 the government too gave its approval to Sharma's appointment as ONGC's CMD with tenure through January 31, 2011.

3.3.3 Hiring constraints and post-reforms changes

Being a public sector enterprise (PSE) ONGC has to follow rules for hiring and compensation guidelines prescribed by the government. The most restrictive limitation faced by ONGC is in compensation of its employees. For all PSEs, salaries are predetermined by the GoI for all job levels; ONGC's employees also receive these salaries. The pay scale for an executive director (E-9), the highest salaried level in ONGC, is only about three times that of an assistant officer (E-0), the lowest technical level in ONGC. Inclusive of perks and additional benefits, the entry-level jobs are comparatively well placed vis-à-vis jobs in the private sector. But the difference is glaring at higher levels, and sometimes salaries at higher levels are over an order of magnitude higher in private sector E&P companies in the domestic private sector and in the Middle East (Katakey 2008).

These salary restrictions were not an issue until 1995 or so, when almost the entire workforce in the oil and gas E&P industry in India was employed by ONGC.[16] But the situation has changed rapidly as labor markets have become more competitive and fluid. With the rapid rise of private companies in the domestic E&P industry and high demand for skilled personnel in the oil and gas (O&G) sector in the Middle East, the opportunity cost of working at ONGC has become high. ONGC has mostly remained a spectator in the job market while its competitors have bid skilled manpower away.

Although even as a *Navratna* PSE ONGC is not free to set salaries of its employees, the post-reforms structure has afforded ONGC enough flexibility to revamp employee perks and benefits. In just five years between 2002 and 2007, ONGC's expenditure on employees nearly tripled to Rs. 60 billion in 2007, while the number of employees declined from more than 39,000 to a little less than 33,000 during the same period. Although it is hard to separate and pinpoint the underlying causes, two factors explain such massive increase in ONGC's manpower costs. First, as discussed above, over the last decade or so the labor market for ONGC has become very competitive. In the face of rapid employee attrition, making the overall compensation package attractive is a practical choice to retain employees. Second, the large free cash flow during these years (discussed in detail later) has provided ONGC with the opportunity to take advantage of the financial flexibility as a *Navratna* PSE for increasing salaries and benefits of its employees.

While compensation of ONGC employees has become attractive post-reforms, not much of that manpower cost increase is linked to performance. Performance evaluation and monitoring methods largely remain the same as in the pre-reforms period (PESD Interviews).

3.3.4 Social spending

The GoI does not require ONGC to spend heavily on social and developmental programs. That is mainly because the GoI has a fully functioning bureaucracy (with its own competences and rent-delivering activities) for most parts of the economy. Thus, unlike many other NOCs, ONGC is left to focus, more or less, on oil operations. As per ONGC's policy, 0.75 percent of net profit is allocated for corporate social responsibility (CSR) activities. Some of ONGC's CSR work involves supporting programs for education of women, local entrepreneurship, health care initiatives, and water management in drought-prone areas (ONGC 2007). One of ONGC's biggest CSR projects is

Table 17.8. *CSR expenditure by ONGC*

($m)	2003–2004	2004–2005	2005–2006
Social expense	4.76	10.11	7.16
Net profit	1,969.18	2,950.68	3,279.73
% of profits	0.24	0.34	0.22

Note: Rs/$=44.
Source: ONGC Annual Reports (www.ongcindia.com/financial_new.
asp).

the Rajiv Gandhi Institute of Petroleum Technology (RGIPT), for which ONGC has committed about $33 million over several years.

Notwithstanding these programs, there is a shortfall in ONGC's CSR expenditure as per the allocation of 0.75 percent of net profit, as shown in Table 17.8 below. CSR expenditure in recent years has hovered around 0.25 percent of net profit, or about a third of the amount planned for this category. This has raised some questions in the parliament.[17] But as the amount involved is relatively small compared with ONGC's profits, the issue of CSR does not pose significant operational difficulties for ONGC.

3.4 Price controls and difficulties for reform

Pricing of crude oil, gas, and petroleum products has always been a thorny issue in India, which has still not been able to develop a coherent policy for price determination.

Until April 1998 oil and gas prices in India were largely determined based on the cost-to-producer principle ("cost plus"). This mechanism is popularly known in India as the administered price mechanism (APM). The guiding principle of APM was to insulate the domestic market from volatility in international oil prices. Under APM, ONGC and OIL were allowed to recover operating cost and a 15 percent post-tax return on the capital employed for production of domestic crude. The refiners were allowed operating costs and return on capital too, but the allowed return was 12 percent for net worth (equity capital plus free reserves) and the rate of interest on borrowings (Government of India, Ministry of Petroleum and Natural Gas 2006). APM was cumbersome, as it involved actual auditing of the cost of domestic production, and pricing of gas was more cumbersome and ad hoc than oil (Joshi and Jung 2008). Further, cross-subsidization under APM to provide subsidies for kerosene, LPG, and naphtha created a complex web of distortions across the entire petroleum industry (Government of India, Ministry of Petroleum and Natural Gas 2006).

For improving efficiency in pricing and market allocation, the ADB's HSP (see section 2.3.3) suggested phased dismantling of APM toward fully market-based prices. Dismantling of APM was also considered necessary for attracting private capital and technology. In 1995 the Strategic Planning Group on Restructuring of the Oil Industry (the "R" Group) recommended the GoI to adopt the suggestions of the HSP. The "R" Group concluded that APM was a breeding ground for inefficiencies across the oil and gas sector, as the cost-plus approach of APM provided little incentive for technological innovation or financial prudence. Also in its view, the APM failed to generate enough financial resources for expanding investments by the companies. Subsequently, phased dismantling of APM was started by GoI in April 1998 and APM stood completely dismantled in April 2002.

3.4.1 Pricing of gas from the PMT fields

One of the first major efforts to break away from the APM was the pricing of gas from the PMT fields (see section 3.1.2 for background information on PMT). But the GoI's ad hoc interventions made this scheme a burden upon ONGC. In 1994 when the PSC for PMT was signed, price for all domestically produced oil and gas was administered by the MoPNG. But given the involvement of private companies with PMT and in the spirit of the ADB's HSP, the price of oil and gas produced from PMT was not administered. Instead, it was linked to international prices (Padmanabhan 1998).

But pricing of gas from PMT was far from market-based. It involved complicated juggling between producer and consumer prices. Based on recommendations of the Shankar Committee, the GoI chose a pricing formula that set consumer prices to 75 percent parity with a basket of fuel oils in 1999–2000, with a ceiling of Rs.2850/mcm, or $1.76/mmbtu (Joshi and Jung 2008). The ceiling in effect fixed the consumer price of gas at $1.76/mmbtu through June 30, 2005, even in the face of dramatically rising gas prices internationally. As per the PSC, the gas price received by the PMT JV was linked to a basket of fuel oils, with a floor of $2.11/mmbtu and a ceiling of $3.11/mmbtu (Joshi and Jung 2008), but mostly on the higher side of the range owing to high prices internationally. Thus, while the PMT gas was being sold at $1.76/mmbtu, the JV was being paid around $3/mmbtu. The balance of somewhere between $1–1.5/mmbtu was being paid for by ONGC.[18] (Quite an expensive price for discovering the fields in the first place!)

Discouraged by this discriminatory treatment by its owner (the GoI), ONGC had little incentive to invest further in gas E&P. At the administered customer price ONGC found the internal rate of return on capital investment in development of new or additional gas to be lower than the Bank Rate (ONGC 2005): "ONGC seeing diminishing and then negative returns from its producing fields saw little, if any, incentive to invest in exploration, development, or improved recovery of domestic gas" (Joshi and Jung 2008).

3.4.2 Concessions to oil marketing companies

Following the dismantling of the APM in April 2002, the pricing of crude oil and petroleum products (at refinery gate) have been fully liberalized by linkage to import parity prices. The refinery-gate prices (the import-parity-based price that oil marketing companies, or OMCs, pay) for petroleum products are high due to a large tax component – about 50 percent of the price of petrol (gasoline) and diesel in India comprises different taxes levied by the central and the state governments (Misra *et al.* 2005). And the retail selling price (RSP) of petroleum products, or the price that consumers pay, is tightly regulated by the government. In the face of high crude oil prices, since 2005 RSP of petrol and diesel has been set by the GoI well below the cost of purchase by the OMCs. Consequently, OMCs in India were losing nearly $60 million a day in 2007 even as the average Indian customer paid some of the highest prices in the world for petroleum products (more than $5 per gallon for gasoline).

But those losses did not reflect on the bottom lines of the OMCs. Indeed, the OMCs made large net profits even as they "lost" money in their marketing operations.[19] Each year the GoI grants oil bonds (government debt) to the OMCs to recoup about two-thirds of their "under-recoveries" – the difference between the RSP and the notional

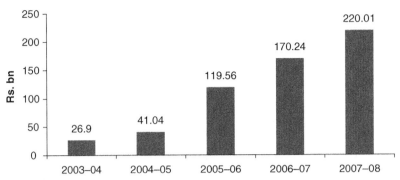

Figure 17.10 Concessions given by ONGC to downstream companies.
Source: "E&P Performance," presentation by ONGC, New Delhi, May 2008.

price of the products the OMCs would have sold them at had not the government fixed prices. For FY 2007–2008, OMCs received over $7 billion in oil bonds. At the behest of GoI, the remaining one-third of the under-recoveries is shared by state-owned upstream companies (ONGC and OIL), mostly ONGC. Figure 17.10 shows the contribution of ONGC in helping OMCs recoup under-recoveries. In 2007–2008 ONGC received on average only $52.9/bbl of oil compared with the $85.54/bbl price of the international benchmark that year. In total ONGC gave concessions of about $5 billion in 2007–2008.[20] Although, in theory, the GoI could ask ONGC to cover a larger share of the oil subsidies, that has not happened. As mentioned in section 2.4.4, ONGC's return on assets and return on sales (profit margin) have hovered around the 25 percent mark despite very volatile international oil prices and the ad hoc oil-subsidy policies of GoI. This suggests that the overall concessions that ONGC is required to provide are tailored so that its financial indicators remain healthy, which is important for ONGC's attractiveness to the capital markets.

3.5 ONGC's free cash flow

A great challenge that the GoI has faced is managing ONGC's free cash flows. Successful dismantling (for the most part) of price controls for crude oil prices and high oil prices since 2002 have resulted in high revenues and profits for ONGC: ONGC's revenues more than doubled to $14 billion between 2001 and 2007. In general, such large free cash flows create a conflicting situation between the owners (shareholders) and the management of a company. While owners want maximum performance (for example, returns on investments or some other criteria), the management of a company may have other motives (for example, maximizing growth of the company) that are at loggerheads with the owner's expectations. If not properly managed, large free cash flows provide the management with the opportunity to engage in potentially wasteful projects. The difficulty for the GoI really has been how much cash to leave with ONGC so as to enhance E&P performance, while also improving financial efficiency.

One way the GoI has tried to manage ONGC's large free cash flow is by having ONGC pay out large dividends. Thus, the government's take from ONGC increased from $2.5 billion in 2000 to about $7 billion in 2007, mostly on account of higher corporate tax (on profit) and dividends paid by ONGC. By reducing free cash flows, high dividend payments are a way of reducing the conflicting situation described above between the owners and the management of a company. Thus, the distribution of large dividends by ONGC seems to be largely influenced by the GoI's motive to take away any extra cash that cannot be productively employed by ONGC.

Notwithstanding, ONGC is still left with huge amounts of cash (Figure 17.11). That has afforded ONGC the opportunity to forgo proper risk assessment and due diligence on its ventures, many of which are quite outside ONGC's core competency in the E&P business. ONGC's working capital (i.e., net current assets) has increased dramatically in the last few years – in 2007–2008 ONGC's working capital was about $8 billion (of which $3.5 billion was in cash); this was less than $1 billion in 1995–1996. With sufficient funds at its own command neutral third-party assessments by financial institutions have not been a requirement and the job has largely been left to in-house teams or financial consultants who themselves have a stake in commitment to a project by ONGC (PESD Interviews).

In the absence of sufficient sound domestic upstream projects, a strong cash position has led ONGC to pursue an aggressive overseas exploration agenda and a range of diversification plans at home. Since 2002 ONGC has tried to enter several unrelated businesses including

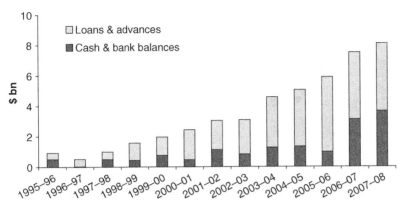

Figure 17.11 Distribution of ONGC's working capital into loans and advances, and cash and bank balances.

Source: ONGC Annual Reports (www.ongcindia.com/financial_new.asp).

compressed natural gas, retailing, petrochemicals, power, and shipping. These diversification attempts have brought ONGC in conflict with downstream state-owned companies as well as the GoI itself. Additionally, ONGC has used its strong financial position to purchase new reserves both at home and abroad and to win a large share of exploration blocks offered under the NELP by bidding aggressively. ONGC has also used its cash flow to pay off most of its debt. At present ONGC is nearly a debt-free company (Figure 17.12). By comparison, the debt-equity ratio of IOCs is significantly higher: in 2006 it was 0.12 for both Chevron and Shell and 0.28 for BP.

3.6 ONGC's overseas operations

ONGC is also spending large sums for acquiring exploration blocks overseas, thus allowing it (at least in the short term) to claim coherent exploration efforts – by 2007–2008 ONGC had extended about a \$4.5 billion interest-free loan to its overseas subsidiary OVL. But OVL's operations provide little evidence of a good E&P business strategy built on strong technical competence. Nearly all of OVL's production comes from properties that were already discovered at the time OVL entered the project or were subsequently discovered by the project operator. Besides having secured a large number

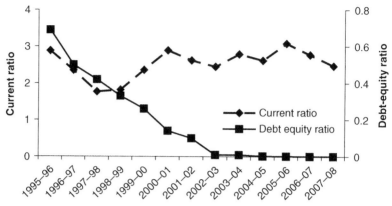

Figure 17.12 ONGC's current ratio (net current assets divided by current liability) and debt-equity ratio. Between 1995 and 1998 ONGC used cash flows to pay back debt (both current and debt-equity ratios decline together). But since 1998–1999, besides paying off the remaining debt, ONGC has also built up significant cash reserves (also see Figure 17.11 above).
Source: ONGC Annual Reports (www.ongcindia.com/financial_new.asp).

of exploration blocks, OVL has had little success in international projects based on its own technical competence.

The two projects that account for most of OVL's proven and producing assets are Sakhalin-I (Russia) and the Great Nile Oil Project (GNOP; Sudan). Both these acquisitions were made early on when OVL was just waking up to the equity-oil-abroad game – OVL acquired a 20 percent stake in Sakhalin-I in February 2001 by buying half of Rosneft's equity (Rosneft is a Russian state-owned company), while contracts were signed in September 2002 for acquiring a 25 percent equity in the GNOP project by taking over the entire stake of Talisman Greater Nile BV (a subsidiary of the Canadian company Talisman Energy) (The Hindu Business Line 2003; Subramanian 2005). When OVL acquired them, at a time when the average crude oil price was around $25/barrel, both these assets had proven reserves. Spiraling crude prices since then have made both these investments profitable for OVL.

ONGC has been selling OVL's overseas ventures to the GoI under the agenda of energy security. But, at present, OVL's operations do not enhance India's energy security by much. OVL's unimpressive technical competence, especially in the international arena, puts severe limits on its ability to run a successful E&P business. Most of OVL's manpower is drawn from ONGC, which has a dubious technical-performance record since the late 1980s even in India, where it has been the main E&P company for more than five decades. Further, in the present era of fiercely competitive bidding for promising prospects (in locations with low political risk; see below), it is doubtful that OVL has the technical competence to assess the risk-reward scenarios well enough to put it in an advantageous situation. Indeed, many of the exploration blocks acquired by OVL are in the "very high risk" category (Sinha and Dadwal 2005). Such a portfolio is particularly poorly matched for OVL's technical skills.

Partly because of ONGC and OVL's desperate need for good technology, ONGC acquired Imperial Energy, a British company with significant hydrocarbon assets in Russia and Kazakhstan. ONGC's acquisition of Imperial was driven not only by Imperial's established and prospective reserves base but also by Imperial's exploration prowess. Thanks to its technological edge, Imperial has been very successful in oil and gas exploration. Thus, it's not surprising that ONGC fought a fierce battle directly with Sinopec and indirectly with Gazprom in order to acquire Imperial. The OVL–Imperial deal was sealed in late 2008 when international crude prices were around $130/barrel. ONGC paid a whopping $1.89 billion to acquire Imperial (Thaindian News 2009).

3.7 Agency costs of monitoring: counterproductive monitoring mechanisms

The choice of government ownership of oil and gas E&P in India through a single dominant firm (ONGC) has had two major implications for the efficiency of the sector. First, the incentive for the MoPNG (the political agent) to effectively monitor ONGC is inherently very low in comparison with monitoring by markets. This arises due to the paramount difference in the incentives and constraints faced by political agents (the MoPNG in India's oil and gas sector) vis-à-vis those faced by market agents (stockowners). Second, ONGC's predominant position in O&G production in India has meant lack of any market benchmark against which ONGC's performance evaluation could be based. Thus, the only choice for the government to monitor ONGC was through indirect and preestablished (*ex ante*) rules. The above

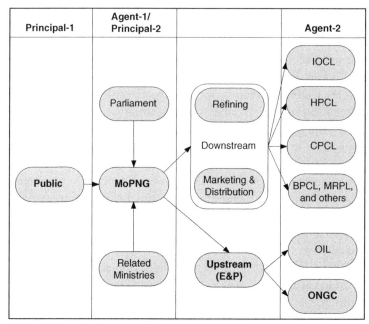

Figure 17.13 Multilayered principal–agent structure of ONGC ownership and management.

two factors, in turn, have meant a lack of an incentive structure to encourage efficiency and performance in ONGC.

3.7.1 Reduced incentives to monitor: GoI–ONGC as a multilayered principal–agent problem

ONGC's ownership and management structure can be best described as a multi-layered principal–agent situation (Figure 17.13). The real owner of majority equity in ONGC is the general public (Principal-1), which in turn has employed the government (the parliament and the MoPNG) as its *agent* (Agent-1) to manage oil and gas production. The government (Principal-2) in turn entrusts ONGC's operations with ONGC's management (Agent-2), while assuming the responsibility to monitor ONGC's functioning.

Principals in the market (stockholders), whose prime motive is profit making, have high incentives to monitor and control costs, as higher costs come at the expense of reduced profitability. But those incentives are significantly weakened in the multilayered principal–agent situation described above.

Political agents (Agent-1) are best described as self-interested actors, whose interests are likely very different from the interests of the public in maximizing the efficiency of a government firm's operations (Vining and Weimer 1990). First, the political agents can themselves not receive directly any benefits (say dividends or bonuses) from the improved efficiency of a government firm. Second, as political agents are normally concerned about maintaining their position in office, they are likely to focus more on politically sensitive issues (like pricing and subsidies) than on mundane day-to-day monitoring of government firms, which is a much more strenuous task. Finally, while in a market principals can easily remove or replace agents (e.g., through firing or takeovers), it is very costly for principals of government firms (voters) to remove political agents (e.g., through elections). The end effect of these vast differences between the incentives of market and political agents is that due to lack of incentives there is limited effective monitoring of government firms (by the government) to ensure operational efficiency.

3.7.2 The lack of a performance-based incentive structure
Another key aspect of the GoI–ONGC relationship is the use of a rule-based oversight system by the government (see section 3.3.1). This choice of oversight system was not intended to make life difficult for ONGC, but it was concomitant with the government's decision to have state-ownership of oil and gas production through ONGC. This is best described by Vining and Weimer (1990):

An oversight system can be thought of as a combination of *ex ante* rules and *ex post* monitoring ... when quality, quantity, and marginal cost are costly to discover, *ex ante* rules tend to be more efficient. Therefore, we expect an efficient oversight system to rely relatively more on *ex ante* rules than *ex post* monitoring when supply is less contestable because less information about marginal cost is conveyed by price.

Indeed the market to which ONGC supplies is not contestable, as ONGC still produces about 80 percent of oil and gas in India. As such, the government has little benchmark from the market against which it could judge ONGC's performance. Hence, the government resorts to other, usually more tortuous and time-consuming (and thus expensive) sources of information such as internal audits and parliamentary committee reviews.

Higher monitoring costs result in greater use of *ex ante* rules to set boundaries for managerial behavior. Examples of such rules include limiting discretion over selection and dismissal of employees or rewards and punishments given to them. The idea is to make it difficult for executives to use the public company's financial residual for personal gains (for example, through selectively favoring subordinates) (Vining and Weimer 1990, p. 14). But such rules usually engender operational inefficiencies throughout the hierarchy by making it harder to respond to dynamic production demands. For example, *ex ante* rules may prohibit transfer of resources between different functions, thus preventing potential efficiency gains that could be possible through such internal transfers.

But perhaps the most harmful impact of using sweeping *ex ante* procedures for nearly all functions at ONGC is the lack of an incentive structure that encourages efficiency. There is extensive evidence in the literature that shows that management needs to be motivated not only to innovate ways of improving efficiency but also to even apply existing knowledge: "[W]here the motivation is weak, firm managements will permit a considerable degree of slack in their operations and not seek cost-improving methods" (Leibenstein 1966). For example, the possibility of receiving a higher bonus or a promotion based on performance acts as a positive motivating factor and helps increase productivity. Thus, incentive structure plays an important role in increasing the efficiency and profitability of a firm.

For ONGC *ex ante* rules have precluded it from leveraging efficiency gains offered by a flexible incentive structure to promote a performance-based work culture. For example, if the incentive structure awards better performance then "managers move to better jobs by superior performance on present jobs" and "managers have incentives to try to gain personal advancement by eliminating 'inefficient' behavior in others connected with the firm's operations" (Furubotn and Pejovich 1972). But, largely as a consequence of *ex ante* rules, managerial promotions at ONGC (and other Indian PSEs) are based less on performance and more on age and years of service (PESD Interviews). Such practices restrict the use of penalty-

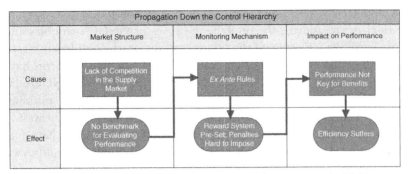

Figure 17.14 Impact of GoI's monitoring mechanism on ONGC's performance.

reward mechanisms by managers at all levels, thereby denying the management one of the most potent methods to improve efficiency. As illustrated in Figure 17.14, the lack of performance-based incentive structure, then, is the root cause of ONGC's inefficiencies.

4 Conclusion

ONGC is India's *fading star*. Its first three decades between 1960 and 1990 were spectacular. But since then financial and operational mismanagement has been rampant at ONGC. Its technological capabilities, especially in exploration for oil and gas, have also eroded significantly over the last two decades. ONGC's strategy has nearly always been a reactive response, either to deal with its troubles or to display action consistent with the shifting demands of its owner, the government. The lack of a coherent long-term strategy but more so ONGC's inability and unwillingness to act on one have meant a continued erosion of ONGC's core capabilities.

The GoI's influence on ONGC is the single most important determinant of ONGC's performance and strategy. In 1956 GoI formed ONGC mainly because of the GoI's socialist bent but more importantly because of fears of opportunism of IOCs. After what appeared to be a glorious success of state-owned business, serious performance troubles emerged in ONGC in the 1990s. Those troubles were a direct consequence of the GoI's largely ineffective oversight of ONGC's operations and a poor incentive structure that government ownership has created for ONGC. That has bred at ONGC a culture of complacency, slack, and rent seeking, which continues even today. In an effort to address the underlying causes of ONGC's troubles and improve the efficiency of the oil and gas sector, the GoI has initiated a number of reforms since the mid 1990s. While those reforms have fundamentally changed the dynamic of the government–ONGC relationship by making ONGC more independent, the GoI still continues to influence ONGC's performance and strategy in important ways.

The GoI's reform efforts to improve ONGC's efficiency have met with mixed results. Among those, the reforms that have addressed the underlying causes of inefficiency, such as the lack of competition and the overlap between ownership, regulation, and operations, have successfully encouraged efficiency gains. But those that are still mired in the larger political economy of ad hoc government intervention have not only failed to achieve their own intended results but have also undercut positive gains elsewhere. In effect, the GoI's hybrid approach of (successful) reforms on one hand and continued intervention and control on the other has failed to unlock the potential efficiency gains in ONGC.

Parts of the GoI's reforms have addressed some key fundamental issues related to ONGC's performance. The GoI's reforms, particularly the policy for empowerment of centrally owned public sector units, have significantly increased ONGC's financial and operational freedom. As a result, government meddling with ONGC's investments, organizational matters, and day-to-day operations has declined significantly. But perhaps the most positive impact of the GoI's reform efforts has come from the competition that the GoI injected in India's oil and gas upstream (E&P) sector since 1998 through the NELP. The competition in E&P is still limited – India's E&P is really a duopoly between ONGC and Reliance, with only a few other small players. Yet, even that limited competition has induced ONGC to increasingly adopt international best practices and to benchmark its technological performance. The NELP has also stripped away nearly all of ONGC's regulatory functions and established the DGH as a largely independent technical regulator. That has not only improved oversight of ONGC's operations but also enhanced the trust and transparency in the oil and gas sector, at least in matters of acreage allocation, bidding, and regulation. Thus, elements of the GoI's reform efforts over the last decade represent substantial positive strides in improving the transparency and efficiency of ONGC's operations.

But three factors have prevented the full potential benefits of the GoI's reform efforts from accruing to India and ONGC. First, the reforms have achieved little in establishing a sound incentive structure at ONGC to encourage efficiency. As the GoI continues to be the majority owner of ONGC many of the problems of multilayered principal–agent interactions discussed in section 3.7 still remain. Second, the GoI's continued intervention in several aspects of ONGC's corporate governance and oil and gas sector policy continues to present challenges to ONGC. Those interventions are largely motivated by the GoI's political exigencies and the desire to maintain control over ONGC. By requiring ONGC to devote corporate resources to dealing with them, such interventions have often been counterproductive for ONGC's performance. Third, ONGC's large free cash flow has acted as a war chest against the pressures that the reforms have impressed upon it. (Ironically, ONGC's large free cash flow owes largely to successful reform in the sector elsewhere, namely in the pricing of crude oil.) As its exploration record has come under GoI and public scrutiny, ONGC has flexed its financial muscles to purchase new reserves and exploration acreage both at home and abroad. ONGC's extremely strong financial position is a major reason for its success in winning a large fraction of NELP exploration blocks, thus suppressing true competition under the NELP. Large free cash flow has also encouraged managerial deviation at ONGC – over the last decade ONGC has forayed into a range of non-core and unproductive national and international ventures.

Addressing the above issues lies at the heart of driving true efficiency improvements at ONGC and hinges around two items. First, the GoI needs to become a better regulator of ONGC's activities and set right the incentive structure at ONGC. Becoming a better regulator involves developing strong independent regulatory bodies (such as the DGH) across the oil and gas sector, a process at which the GoI has only scratched the surface. And providing the right incentives to ONGC involves the increasing use of a performance-based evaluation mechanism (as opposed to rule-based evaluation) both by the GoI to evaluate ONGC's performance and by ONGC internally. As discussed above, the developments over the past decade suggest that

ONGC's performance and the GoI's ability to effectively monitor it are positively correlated with competition. Accordingly, progress on the first item depends on the ability of the GoI to foster more effective competition in the oil and gas sector. Second, ONGC's free cash flow must be tightened. So far the GoI has tried to do that in an ad hoc manner, for example through having ONGC pay out large dividends and provide subsidies to downstream companies. But those measures have been inadequate – as discussed above, there is ample evidence of free-cash-flow-induced managerial deviation at ONGC. Moving forward, the GoI should require ONGC to use more debt from the capital markets such that ONGC's debt-equity ratio is broadly in line with other companies in the industry.

Finally, it is interesting to speculate how further privatization, if possible at all, might impact ONGC's performance. In theory, further privatization of ONGC, say to reduce the GoI's stake down to less than 50 percent, could help both in establishing an effective incentive structure at ONGC and in reining in its free cash flow. As in the case with all publicly traded companies, a high degree of exposure to the equity markets would make ONGC's ownership contestable, which in turn would increase the threat of corporate takeover in the event of persistent poor performance. As corporate upheavals put senior managers' jobs and compensation at serious risk, this structure of ownership provides inherent incentives for the company's top management to enhance performance and efficiency in order to avoid such upheavals. But in practice such a reduction in the GoI's stake in ONGC seems improbable. The GoI continues to regard ONGC as a necessary vehicle for enhancing India's energy security and is nervous about losing further control over the company. ONGC itself is financially stronger than ever, which helps mitigate concerns about performance issues but also enables it to resist calls for further privatization. Besides, with Reliance, ONGC's main competitor, having its plate full with the management of its massive natural gas discoveries, pressure from the private sector for the GoI to further divest in ONGC has waned. Putting all this together, it is likely that the GoI will continue to maintain a high stake in ONGC. In the absence of any major changes to the equity structure of ONGC, then, ONGC's performance and strategy will continue to depend upon the choices and demands of the GoI.

Appendix: external assistance to India's oil and gas sector between 1975 and 1991

Project	Donor	Year of approval	Amount
Bombay High I	World Bank	1977	$150 million
Bombay High II	World Bank	1980	$400 million
Godavari Petroleum Exploration	World Bank	1982	$165.5 million
Refineries Rationalization	World Bank	1982	$200 million
Offshore Gas Development	World Bank	1983	$222.3 million
Cambay Basin Petroleum	World Bank	1984	$242.5 million
Oil India Petroleum	World Bank	1987	S$140 million
Western Gas	World Bank	1988	$295 million
Petroleum Transport	World Bank	1989	$340 million
Gas Flaring Reduction	World Bank	1991	$350 million
Oil and Gas Sector Development	World Bank	1991	$150 million
Special Assistance	ADB	1991	$150 million
Gandhar Field Development	ADB	1991	$267 million
Hydrocarbon Sector Plan	ADB	1991	$250 million
Oil and Gas I, Line of Credit	Canada (CIDA)	1986	C$65 million
Oil and Gas II, Line of Credit	Canada (CIDA)	1987	C$198 million
Oil and Gas III, Line of Credit	Canada (CIDA)	1988	C$75 million
Offshore Supply Vessel	Japan (OECF)	1982	¥2.1 billion
Gas Pipeline I	Japan (OECF)	1984	¥20 billion
Gas Pipeline II	Japan (OECF)	1985	¥15.8 billion
Gas Pipeline III	Japan (OECF)	1986	¥18.9 billion
Bombay Offshore I	Japan (OECF)	1979	¥6.2 billion
Bombay Offshore II	Japan (OECF)	1979	¥8.6 billion
Special Assistance	Japan (OECF)	1991	$150 million
Gas Pipeline	France	1986	FF 624 million

Source: "Report and Recommendation for the Gandhar Field Development Project," Asian Development Bank (1991).

Notes

A list of interviewees (in alphabetical order):

- Swagat Bam, Vice President (Corporate Strategy E&P), Reliance Industries Limited.
- Board of Directors, ONGC (interviewed in a group).
- R. S. Butola, Managing Director, ONGC Videsh Limited.
- Ruchika Chawla, Associate Fellow and Area Convener, The Energy Resources Institute (TERI), New Delhi, India.
- Parag Diwan, Vice Chancellor, University of Petroleum and Energy Studies, India.
- Anurag Gupta, Head of Department (NELP), Directorate General of Hydrocarbons, Government of India.
- Sunjoy Joshi, Senior Fellow, Observer Research Foundation, New Delhi, India.
- Sanjiv Kumar, Chief Manager (Finance and Corporate Planning), ONGC.
- Sudha Mahalingam, Member, Petroleum and Natural Gas Regulatory Board of India.
- Basudev Mahanty, Director, Petroleum Planning and Analysis Cell, Government of India.
- Anshuman Maheshwary, Manager, A. T. Kearny Limited, India.
- Sashi Mukundan, Country Head, BP India.
- R. K. Narang, Ex Chairman, Indian Oil Corporation Limited, Distinguished Fellow, The Energy Resources Institute (TERI), New Delhi, India.
- A. S. Popli, Head of Department (Production), Directorate General of Hydrocarbons, Government of India.
- Subir Raha, Ex Chairman & Managing Director, ONGC.
- Ashish Rana, Energy Resources Group, Reliance Industries Limited, India.
- Udayan Sen, Finance Director (Africa, Middle East, Turkey, and South Asia), BP.
- Pramod Seth, Executive Director (Corporate Planning), ONGC.
- Suresh Chandra Sharma, Planning Commission, Government of India.
- Uma Shankar Sharma, Observer Research Foundation, New Delhi, India.
- Vinod K. Sibal, Director General, Directorate General of Hydrocarbons, Government of India.
- Manak Singhi, Advisor, Department of Economic Affairs, Ministry of Finance, Government of India.

- Ajay Tyagi, Ex Joint Secretary, Petroleum and Natural Gas Regulatory Board of India.

1 1 crore = 10 million.
2 These fields were originally named Bombay High. Later when the city of Bombay was renamed to Mumbai that change was also reflected in the name of the fields. For consistency, throughout this study we use Mumbai High.
3 The Minister of State of the Ministry of Petroleum and Natural Gas, Captain Satish Kumar Sharma during Questions and Answers session to the Parliament of India, November 3, 1993 (www.parliamentofindia.nic.in/ls/lsdeb/ls10/ses6/0111039302.htm).
4 1 million metric tonnes per annum (MMTPA) ~ 20,000 bopd.
5 Close to the Persian Gulf sources of crude, India is well positioned to become a refining hub; some of its refinery infrastructure is already oriented entirely for reexport.
6 Note though that the data in Figure 17.9 and Table 17.5 is based on 3P reserves (proved+probable+possible) and hence is prone to large uncertainty. See for example, Simmons (2005a).
7 In the L1 process bidders must satisfy certain minimum financial and technical criteria. Of the qualifying bidders, the lowest quote (hence L1) bidders win the tender.
8 In 1997 India instituted the New Exploration and Licensing Policy (NELP), a comprehensive policy under which all new blocks were to be offered on competitive bidding. The two government E&P companies, ONGC and OIL, are also required to compete for these blocks. The competitive bidding rounds between 1979 and 1991 that preceded the NELP rounds are commonly referred as the pre-NELP rounds.
9 The Minister of State of the Ministry of Petroleum and Natural Gas, Captain Satish Kumar Sharma during Questions and Answers session to the Parliament of India, November 3, 1993 (www.parliamentofindia.nic.in/ls/lsdeb/ls10/ses6/0111039302.htm).
10 As part of its asset rebalancing, Enron sold its entire PMT stake in 2002 to British Gas (BG).
11 "Among forces that mitigate the manager-stockholder conflict are competitive labor and product markets, managerial compensation plans, the structure of equity ownership, and the threat of corporate takeovers" Mitchell and Lehn (1990).
12 PESD Interviews; in 2008 ONGC conducted a post-drill analysis of 350 wells drilled between 2002–2005. The analysis was done by an international consultant (DeGolyer MacNaughton).

13 Two percent was reserved for ONGC employees and directors. The remainder was sold to domestic and foreign institutional investors (~4%), non-institutional bidders (~2%), and to retail investors (~2%).

14 The chairman-cum-managing director (CMD) is the CEO equivalent.

15 The last selection committee for ONGC CMD constituted in February 2007 comprised the chairman of PESB, two other members of PESB, the secretary of MoPNG, and two non-government persons of distinguished repute.

16 ONGC recruits young engineers in various major disciplines, fresh out of college with little or no industry experience in oil and gas E&P. These "trainees" are then placed in training assignments across the country. Historically, these entry level engineers have stayed on with ONGC, in most cases for the entire span of their careers. Many of these trainees rise through the ranks at ONGC and usually form the top level of ONGC's management.

17 Government of India, Fourteenth Lok Sabha Session 10, Unstarred Question No. 5036 May 10, 2007 (www.loksabha.nic.in/).

18 Author estimates and PESD Interviews.

19 Most OMCs in India are publicly traded and produce independently audited accounts annually.

20 "E&P Performance," presentation by ONGC to media, New Delhi, May 22, 2008.

18 | *Petronas: reconciling tensions between company and state*

L E S L I E   L O P E Z

1 Introduction

Petroliam Nasional Bhd., or Petronas, is a national oil company (NOC) that strives to operate like an international oil company (IOC). Although the company has had great success, its never-ending tight-rope walk of balancing enterprise and politics is generating increasing strains, undermining the corporation's efforts to firmly establish itself as a serious player among second-echelon oil majors.

Starting off as the sole regulator and manager of the country's oil and gas sectors in the early 1970s, Petronas is today a fully integrated oil and gas multinational with interests in more than thirty countries. Consider these numbers: Its international operations contributed to roughly 40 percent of income in 2008 and emerged as the single largest contributor to group revenue. By 2013, more than 60 percent of its oil and gas reserves are projected to be in the form of deposits outside Malaysia.

In a country where state-owned companies are often associated with financial scandals and mismanagement, Petronas is held up as a sure-footed example of an integrated approach to natural resource management. And in a region where oil companies are distinguished for their financial shenanigans, Petronas's transformation from an NOC to one of the world's top ten most profitable energy corporations

This chapter is based on previous articles (Lopez 2003) and on interviews with senior Petronas officials conducted on multiple occasions (in alphabetical order):

- Azizan Zainul Abidin (former Petronas chairman).
- Rastam Hadi (founding management team of Petronas).
- Ananda Krishnan (former director of Petronas).
- Hassan Marican (Petronas CEO).

Other sources include Bowie (2001); von der Mehden and Troner (2007); and Azam (2008).

underscores why the company is often tapped as a partner of choice by IOCs.

Its overseas expansion has not only helped the company build new reserves and revenue streams but has also, to a large extent, shielded the NOC from political interference.

Few, if any, dispute that Petronas represents a solid role model for NOCs to emulate on natural resource management. But the corporation's intimate relations with the government have often exposed it to political meddling over the years, resulting in departures from its core business to finance wanderlust pursuits of its political masters. More worrisome is the prospect that Petronas could be tapped into to dispense patronage, a main characteristic of Malaysian politics.

The thrust of this study will focus on the constant juggling of tensions between the oil corporation and the state and will offer three key observations.

First, Petronas's reputation as one of the world's best-managed NOCs is well deserved and the company can be held out as a strong model for other NOCs looking for templates on how best to manage a nation's natural resource. Petronas continues to successfully leverage its role as regulator – particularly through production-sharing contracts with IOCs operating in Malaysia – to help the country retain a lion's share of the oil profits. Through direct partnerships with IOCs in exploration and production activities in Malaysia, the company has benefited from a high degree of technology transfer. The skillful application of its regulator card has helped spawn a vibrant domestic oil and gas sector, which is today 85 percent controlled by Malaysian groups and which employs more than 400,000 people. Its strict guidelines on employment have over the years forced IOCs to train locals to take on senior positions, including country heads, for their Malaysian subsidiaries. Apart from developing world-class expertise in the LNG (liquefied natural gas) value chain, the company is also establishing itself as a serious deep water player. The company's financial heft – it remains Southeast Asia's sole *Fortune 500* listing – also offers it the luxury of exploring overseas acquisitions to build on its hydrocarbon reserves and fuel downstream expansion plans.

Second, this somewhat rosy picture is clouded by tensions between the NOC and the state. Petronas's nearly three-decade transformation from an NOC to an organization of international repute is a product of management to international standards and the company's deft handling of its relations with the state. Increasingly, however, the state is coming to rely on the NOC to fund national development, turning it into Malaysia's chief fiscal "cash cow."

Moreover, the oil corporation's political masters are becoming worryingly interventionist at a time when Malaysia's boss-patronage political model seeks new cash cows to milk. The face-off between the board and the premier over the appointment of a key aide, which culminated in the untimely departure of CEO and Chairman Hassan Marican, has served only to deepen concerns that the new administration, headed by Najib Razak, intends to play a more interventionist role in the corporation's business affairs.

Third, the main challenge for Petronas going forward is to deliver on its international strategy.

Petronas's frontier acreage – in countries international rivals have shunned or have been barred from entering – is high risk and, apart from Sudan, exploration results have so far been disappointing. The Malaysian oil corporation's push overseas has largely been through mergers and acquisitions – and armed with more than $25 billion in net cash, Petronas is expected to step up its M&A activities to expand its international operations. Here we will examine the company's overseas business profile and its many challenges.

I structure this chapter as follows. In section 2, I offer a historical snapshot of Petronas and how its reputation as one of the world's most capable state oil corporations is well deserved. In section 3, I provide an overview of Petronas's reserves and exploration. In section 4, I offer a quick look at the structure of the Malaysian oil sector before discussing the important issues of the state–Petronas relationship in section 5. In section 6, I discuss the NOC's key strategies and performance. Section 7 concludes.

2 History of Petronas

Hydrocarbon deposits were first discovered in the Borneo region, which is now under Malaysian territory, in the 1870s and commercial production of the resource began in the early 1900s by Shell and later Exxon. The two World Wars hobbled real growth in the sector and it wasn't until the early 1960s that renewed discovery and exploration activities of offshore oil fields expanded to establish Malaysia as a hot spot for IOCs (Petronas 1984).

Foreign oil companies dominated the downstream and upstream sectors and quickly expanded their reach to oil fields in the east coast of Peninsular Malaysia, which secured independence from Britain in 1957. Foreign oil players were largely left to their own devices. As long as they made their regular royalty payments, there was little interference from the relatively young Malaysian government, which was struggling with an increasingly messy political landscape because of the country's multiracial makeup, including Malaysians of Malay, Chinese, and Indian descent.

A keenly contested general election in 1969 led to racial riots in several urban centers and the imposition of a state of emergency. The civil unrest was largely a result of fears among Malaysia's ethnic Malay Muslim elite of the possible loss of political power to the more economically advanced non-Malay groups, particularly the Chinese. With Parliament suspended, the country was governed by the National Operations Council, which crafted the New Economic Policy (NEP) (Kahn and Wah 1992).

Simply put, the NEP, as it is commonly referred to, was an ambitious social engineering experiment that sought to eradicate poverty and positively discriminate in favor of the country's economically backward ethnic Malays by providing them with greater opportunities in education and business. In fact, the NEP was much more than just a program to award ethnic Malays with scholarships and licenses to dominate sectors of the economy.

It effectively signaled the weakening of the alliance between the Malaysian state and private capital, a coexistence where the government had been content to support independent wealth accumulation, both foreign and local, and restrict itself to programs to eradicate poverty and rural discontent. Through the NEP, Malaysia established a new economic model where the state would play an interventionist role, with particular focus on the utilization of national resources to sponsor the ethnic Malay community (Jin 1992).

This burgeoning sense of Malay nationalism in the early 1970s would conspire with global political and economic tumult triggered by the oil crisis to radically alter the Malaysian oil and gas sector and with it the way IOCs operated. The war in the Middle East and the OPEC oil embargo, which raised global oil prices, provided incentives for the Malaysian government to adjust its relationship with foreign oil companies and seek a larger slice of the profits. It was also during this period that many oil-producing countries, such as Abu Dhabi, Egypt, and neighboring Indonesia, were moving away from the concession system in favor of a production-sharing contract arrangement with IOCs.

OPEC's nudging of producing countries to wield greater control over their oil sectors evoked strong sentiments in non-member but commodity-rich Malaysia, which had long felt that the country's wealth from the production of rubber and tin was exploited by its British colonial masters. To ensure that the country's oil and gas sectors wouldn't suffer the same fate, the Malaysian government, under then premier Tun Abdul Razak, decided to establish Petronas in August 1974, making it the sole custodian of the nation's hydrocarbon reserves and regulator of the national oil and gas sector (Bowie 2001).

More like Brazil (Petrobras) than Venezuela (PDVSA), the government of Malaysia did not nationalize IOC assets upon Petronas's creation; it instead called on IOCs to give partial interests in their projects and built Petronas from the ground up. The government also authorized Petronas to act as licensing regulator for the Malaysian oil sector.

A combination of political and economic considerations shaped Petronas's corporate structure, which, looking back, laid the foundations for a strong and independent organization. Keeping in mind the tumultuous Indonesian NOC experience and seeking to safeguard relations with the IOCs operating in Malaysia, the architects of the Malaysian oil corporation demurred from establishing Petronas as a state statutory body. They strongly pushed the government to incorporate the new organization as a commercial entity that would be governed by the country's corporate laws and then nurtured under the umbrella of a civil service mindset (PESD Interviews).

The end product was a hybrid entity, commercial in structure but a statutory enterprise in most other aspects. Petronas was incorporated on August 17, 1974, under the Malaysian Companies Act with the state-owned Ministry of Finance Inc. as its sole shareholder. It was also immediately vested with ownership and control of the nation's petroleum resources under the newly minted Petroleum Development Act of 1974. The Petroleum Development Act comprised ten Articles but it gave Petronas wide-ranging privileges that didn't require it to conform to rules under the country's corporate laws. It isn't required to file annual accounts, which all corporations registered in Malaysia

must do. Like all companies, Petronas has a board of directors, but the
act stipulates that the oil corporation "shall be subject to the control
and direction of the Prime Minister" – an all-important provision,
which will form a major focus of this study. There was also a strong
view at the time Petronas was incorporated that the organization,
which played the role of regulator and operator, needed to present a
business-friendly face to preserve Malaysia's attractiveness, to draw
foreign direct investment into the economy. Petronas retains profits
on its earnings, which has allowed it to fund its expansion program.
And like IOCs operating in Malaysia, Petronas pays royalties, petroleum taxes, and export duties directly to the government. As the corporation's sole shareholder, the Malaysian government also receives
an annual dividend. Capping the novel nature of Petronas's charter
was the decision by the Malaysian government at the time to direct
all funds flowing from the NOC into the government's consolidated
fund, in a bid to ensure parliamentary oversight over the spending of
the executive (PESD Interviews).

Despite all the safeguards to ensure transparency in Petronas's operations, political consideration always shadowed the corporation. The
country's premier at the time, Tun Abdul Razak, recognized the potential of Petronas as a powerful political tool and envisioned the crucial
role it would play as the prime mover to uplift the economic standing of
the country's Malay Muslim community under the NEP. Key pioneers
of Petronas included Rastam Hadi, the country's no-nonsense deputy
governor of the central bank in the early 1970s; Abdullah Salleh, a
chief secretary to the government; and Raja Mohar Raja Badiozaman,
who was the principal economic advisor to premier Tun Abdul Razak.
At Petronas's incorporation, the government's shareholding was held
by the minister of finance, who at the time was an ethnic Chinese. But
in accord with the oil corporation's charter, Razak insisted that the
prime minister have the sole prerogative over the running of the company, a safeguard to ensure that Petronas would remain a vehicle for
the NEP and that successive finance ministers wouldn't be able to use
the oil corporation to undermine the premier (Interview with Azizan
Zainul Abidin, January 2003 in Kuala Lumpur).

Incorporating Petronas was the easy part. Getting IOCs, particularly Shell and Esso, to surrender their concessions in favor of new
production-sharing contracts (PSCs) and coaxing state governments,
which had oil within their territories, to surrender their control over

a portion of their petroleum operations and accept royalty payments proved much more difficult. Political pressure and inducements were applied on oil-producing states such as Sabah and Sarawak on Borneo and Terengganu in the northeast to accept Petronas's monopoly position in return for a share of oil royalties (see Figure 18.1). The IOCs were tough at the bargaining table and Malaysia, which was struggling at the time to secure foreign direct investments, had to be mindful that it couldn't afford to raise the bogey of nationalization. The negotiations broke down several times and it was only after the Malaysian government watered down licensing regulations and agreed to a profit-sharing structure that would allow oil companies to recover part of the exploration costs (often referred to as cost oil) that the IOCs agreed to embrace the PSCs (Bowie 2001).

The first PSCs were signed with Shell in 1976, paving the way for dozens of others over the next decade. The main features of the maiden PSC included a maximum cost recovery of 20% (25% for gas) and the government receiving a 10% royalty. The remaining 70% was broken up into a 70:30 split, with Petronas taking the major share. While the lion's share in the ownership structure of existing concessions at the time was awarded to IOCs under the newly minted fifteen-year tenure PSCs, Petronas took on minority equity interests through its own exploration arm, Petronas Carigali (Bowie 2001).

This structure not only helped the NOC extract a high degree of technology transfer from its foreign partners, but it allowed the company to quickly dominate the oil and gas sector within a short period of time. Under the PSC system introduced in 1976, IOCs retained overall management of the key production areas and grafted on Carigali as minority partner with a stake of between 15 and 25 percent in the concession assets. The arrangement allowed Carigali to secure technology know-how and upon the expiry of the first clutch of PSC pacts, which averaged about fifteen years, Petronas comfortably secured 100 percent ownership of these hugely profitable production fields. Alternatively, it could relicense these acreages to the same foreign oil company, or a completely new player, while retaining a substantially higher equity stake. Until the late 1990s, only a handful of oil and gas companies operated in Malaysia, with Shell and Exxon dominating the landscape in acreage under both exploration and production. But as PSC concessions matured, Petronas was able to wrest away full control of these highly productive oil and gas fields and in many cases renegotiate new partnerships with foreign contractors, under far more favorable terms and higher equity participation for the state.

While Carigali learned the ropes of the exploration and production side of the business, Petronas began plotting a diversification strategy in the late 1970s to exploit the country's massive gas reserves, which were discovered in offshore Sarawak. Nearby energy-hungry Japan was a ready market, and Shell and Mitsubishi were eager to participate in a greenfield LNG plant.

But the plan quickly stumbled because of disagreements over the shareholding structure for the $3.2 billion LNG plant, which at the time ranked as the country's largest infrastructure undertaking.

The skills Petronas's young negotiators picked up during their tough PSC negotiations with Shell and Esso served the NOC well. The two foreign companies, which originally insisted on holding a joint 40 percent interest in the project, settled for a 30 percent interest divided equally, with the remainder held by the Malaysian government. Construction of the plant began in 1979 and the first LNG shipment to Japan was flagged off in 1983. The move to invest in the gas sector has paid huge dividends. More than 40 percent of total hydrocarbon production in Malaysia is made up of gas and LNG, and its LNG plant in Sarawak, which is a joint venture with Shell that began operations in 1983, ranks as the largest such facility in the Asia-Pacific. The strategy has helped the company establish itself as a leading player in large and financially complex long-term LNG-supply deals with Japan, South Korea, and Taiwan. Overall, Petronas's shrewd leverage of its licensing powers over the domestic oil and gas sector has also helped spawn a local oil and gas sector, which is today 85 percent controlled by Malaysian groups that employ more than 400,000 people. Its strict guidelines on employment have over the years forced IOCs to train locals to take on senior positions, including country heads, for their Malaysian subsidiaries (PESD Interviews).

Unlike most state oil companies, Petronas decided to venture overseas to build on its rapidly depleting domestic reserves of oil and gas (see Figure 18.2). The ties Petronas forged with IOCs in its domestic operations provided a tremendous boost for its international expansion, where it today enjoys cooperation agreements with a wide range of other national oil corporations and oil majors.

Petronas also opted, partly at the behest of then premier Mahathir Mohamad, for the risky strategy of venturing into countries its

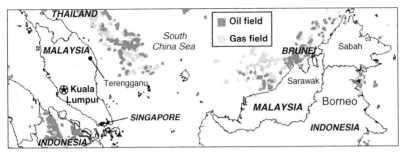

Figure 18.1 Map of major oil and gas fields in Malaysia.
Source for oil and gas field data: Wood Mackenzie (2009b).

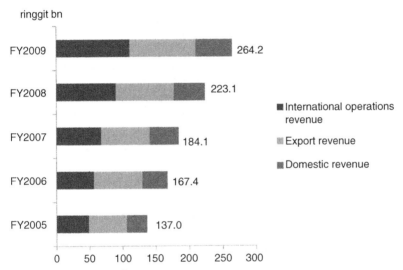

Figure 18.2 Sources of Petronas revenues.
Source: Petronas (2009a).

international rivals had shunned or been barred from entering. The NOC is credited for turning strife-torn and terrorist-ridden Sudan into a net oil-exporting nation. It is also producing oil in Algeria, Myanmar, Chad, Iran, and Turkmenistan. Today, Petronas has emerged as one of the few successful NOCs with a credible international presence. It has operations in thirty countries worldwide that contribute roughly 42% of the group's revenues. Another 37% is derived from exports and 21% from its domestic operations.

3 Malaysia's reserves and E&P profile

3.1 Reserves

The offshore coastal regions of Malaysia fronting the South China Sea
are littered with oil and gas provinces. Malaysia is part of a relatively
energy-rich region made up of more than ten basins with tertiary-
aged petroleum systems that drive economic activity in countries such
as Brunei, Indonesia, the Philippines, and Thailand. Malaysia's oil is
light and sweet and is referred to as "Tapis" in global markets.

Naturally, the region is a hot spot of overlapping territorial claims
and, as I show below, Petronas has used its financial heft and leveraged
on relationships with regional NOCs to pursue joint exploration pacts.
The company dominates the Southeast Asian piped gas market and its
joint-exploration arrangements with neighboring NOCs have helped
Malaysia secure future sources of gas supply.

Total Petronas hydrocarbon reserves stood at 27.02 billion barrels
of oil equivalent at the beginning of 2009, with international reserves
accounting for 25.3 percent of the group's total reserves (see Figure
18.3). Of the oil and gas reserves being discovered a high proportion are
located in geologically complex frontier acreages; about 15 percent of
Malaysia's oil reserves rest in deep water blocks and another 25 percent
of its gas reserves have a high content of carbon dioxide (CO_2). Despite
the increasing maturing of its core domestic legacy oil assets – found
in the east coastal waters of Peninsular Malaysia (bordering Thailand)
and in the East Malaysian states of Sabah and Sarawak (on Borneo)
– Petronas's reserve position remains healthy because the company has
built an impressive upstream portfolio in different regions worldwide.
Its oil and gas assets abroad increased 9.6 percent during 2009 to 6.84
billion boe (barrels of oil equivalent) on the back of significant gas discoveries in Turkmenistan and Mozambique. Gas accounts for close to
three-quarters of Petronas's domestic commercial reserves, while its
oil reserves are held in relatively mature legacy fields. Its international
reserves also are heavily gas-biased (Petronas 2009a).

3.2 Exploration overview

For the past decade, Malaysia's declining oil reserves have been the
chief challenge for Petronas, and the management has responded
to this challenge by sweetening terms for IOCs seeking to explore

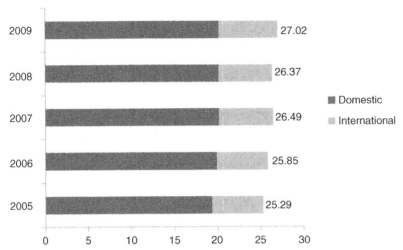

Figure 18.3 Petronas group oil and gas reserves as of January 1, 2009 (billion barrels of oil equivalent).
Source: Petronas (2009a).

oil and gas domestically. It has also moved aggressively to explore on its own overseas. The strategy has worked – making Malaysia a world-class deep water play – and helped this hermetic organization to diversify its reserves portfolio away from its home base. For all its international profile, Malaysia remains a key growth area for Petronas in its exploration strategy. Under the country's production-sharing terms with IOCs, Petronas's exploration arm, Carigali, has a right to a carried interest in any exploration within the 128,000 sq km of net acreage in Malaysia. The interest assigned to Carigali varies between 15 percent and 25 percent, and once a commercial discovery has been made the company automatically becomes a working partner in any development. Since 2002, Petronas and its international partners have made eighteen deep water discoveries, but the volumes haven't been exciting, partly because the company has been forced to move further eastward into underexplored areas. But there could be significant upside in future discoveries once Malaysia settles its boundary dispute with Brunei.

The corporation's regional exploration model has proved to be very successful, particularly in developing its gas business across Southeast Asia. It currently plays a major role in the Southeast Asian gas market through its investments in Indonesia (Java, Natuna Sea, and

Sumatera), the Malaysia–Thailand Joint-Development Area (JDA), Myanmar, and Vietnam. Exploration activity in Indonesia has been high in recent years with thirty-five wells drilled since 2005. But the discoveries have been modest. The company has stakes in three blocks in the Malaysia–Thailand JDA stretching over 3,600 sq km, which promise significant upside. The prospects are also bright in Vietnam, where Petronas is partnering with Chevron in deep water exploration. Moreover, Petronas moved into Australia's LNG sector in 2008 when it acquired a 40 percent stake in Santos's proposed Gladson LNG plant for an initial consideration of $2 billion. The project is among the first LNG developments that will utilize coal seam gas as feedstock and could firmly establish the company as a major LNG player in the Pacific Basin (PESD Interviews; corporate disclosures from Petronas website).

Since the 1990s, Petronas has moved further afield, a strategy that former premier Mahathir Mohamad had wanted the corporation to embark on much earlier but had found difficult to implement because of opposition from the oil corporation's top management, which at the time was packed with strong-willed civil servants. It wasn't until Hassan Marican became CEO in 1995 that the overseas drive moved into overdrive. Slipstreaming on the activist brand of diplomacy promoted by Dr. Mahathir, under Hassan, Petronas first set its sights on Africa in the mid 1990s and gained a foothold in the region through the acquisition in 1996 of a controlling interest in South Africa's Engen.

Today, Petronas has established itself as one of the largest net acreage holders in Africa. The results have been mixed and there are concerns that the company's strategy of venturing into countries largely off-limits to IOCs because of sanctions or political instability (countries such as Sudan and Chad) could make Petronas vulnerable to global campaign groups and also to pressure from the international financial community because its bonds are traded overseas.

Petronas's main success story is Sudan, where the company is the country's largest foreign investor. Petronas has made more than 500 million barrels (mmbbl) of net oil discoveries in this terrorist-ridden region since 2000 and the company sees excellent potential from the more than 126,000 sq km of acreage it owns in the country.

The results haven't been as encouraging elsewhere in Africa. The company has just over 16,000 sq km of acreage in land-locked Chad, but much of it is underexplored, and the situation is the same in Mauritania and Benin. Exploration activities in Morocco, Ethiopia, and Mozambique have also proved to be disappointing. Egypt holds the promise of providing multiple trillion cubit feet (tcf) of gas discoveries. The company owns a 50 percent interest in the Egyptian business of Italy's Edison group. So far, exploration hasn't been encouraging and the Egyptian government's ban on new gas exports until 2010 has complicated Petronas's activities in the country.

Lastly, Petronas has some burgeoning prospects in Central Asia and Russia. The company is a leading player in Turkmenistan, where it is close to nailing down a gas sales deal, and it has embarked on exploration activities in Uzbekistan. In Russia, Petronas invested $1.1 billion in the initial public offering for Rosneft in 2006; this investment is a precursor to exploration and production activities in the country.

4 Structure of the Malaysian oil sector

Malaysia does not have a dedicated petroleum ministry and Petronas, which is organized under a chairman and the company's board of directors, reports directly to the prime minister. The company's board has thirteen members, which includes six independent directors from the private sector. The government has one representative and the company has six of its own representatives on the board, which includes its president and CEO as well as vice presidents from various divisions of the group. The company has four key corporate divisions: Exploration and Production, Gas Business (LNG plants and the Thai–Malaysia joint development region), Oil Business (covering refining, international retail, marketing of oil products), and Petrochemicals. Division heads report to the CEO and the company's chairman, both of whom wield enormous power within the organization. Petronas also has a shipping arm. Through MISC (formerly known as the Malaysian International Shipping Corp. Bhd.), Petronas owns container ships, chemical parcel tankers, LNG vessels, and liquefied petroleum gas carriers (PESD Interviews).

Beyond these formal structures, two men have been chiefly responsible for shaping Petronas into the organization that it is today: Azizan Zainul Abidin, the former chairman of Petronas, and Hassan Marican, the chief executive officer. The soft-spoken Azizan was a distinguished civil servant who served as the secretary general of the powerful Ministry of Home Affairs before moving to Petronas in 1988. He was among the few senior government officials whom former premier Mahathir Mohamad counted on as a trusted lieutenant and that connection put him in a unique position to politely reject several of the government's more outlandish demands on Petronas.

Azizan was assisted by the dour and no-nonsense Hassan, a British-trained accountant who left a high position as partner at local accounting firm Hanafiah, Raslan & Mohamad to join Petronas as its senior vice president of finance in 1989. Characterized by colleagues and senior oil industry executives as more forceful than Azizan, Hassan is widely credited with expanding and institutionalizing Petronas's tough and transparent contract-awarding procedures. Hassan is also credited by foreign oil executives in Malaysia for crafting the pathway forward in Petronas's international push and quietly leading the break from the civil service mindset that dominated Petronas's top management. Hassan was instrumental in pushing the corporation to make public its first set of financial accounts in 1990. In the same year, its accounting systems were fully integrated by SAP, which introduced a new financial discipline and enhanced the company's credentials among IOCs. The structural revamps were part of an overall strategy for Petronas's first international bond issue in 1993.

The Azizan–Hassan partnership presided over the most tumultuous years, which saw the group push aggressively overseas and fend off, but only to a point, overt government intervention into the company's affairs and how the country's oil bounty would be used. After Azizan passed away in 2004, Hassan was appointed executive chairman of Petronas, the first non-civil servant to helm the company. But the enormous confidence he enjoyed with Dr. Mahathir and his successor Abdullah Ahmad Badawi quickly fizzled when Najib Abdul Razak assumed the premiership in April 2008.

The face-off between the Hassan-led board and the new premier over the appointment of a key aide in mid 2009 culminated in Hassan's untimely departure as CEO and chairman of Petronas after the government announced just days before the expiry of his contract that his services were no longer required. The manner in which Hassan was shown the exit (to be discussed later in the chapter) has only served to deepen concerns that the new administration headed by Najib intends to play a more interventionist role in Petronas's business affairs.

The Hassan affair offers a strong case study into the all-important dynamic of the relationship between Petronas and its only boss, Malaysia's prime minister of the day. This relationship will be explored in more detail in the next section. In any case, it adds to concerns that Petronas's political masters are becoming worryingly interventionist at a time when Malaysia's boss-patronage political model seeks new cash cows.

5 The state–Petronas relationship

Few, if any, would argue with the assertion that Petronas represents a solid role model for NOCs to emulate on natural resource management. But its intimate relations with the government have often exposed the corporation to political meddling over the years, resulting in departures from its core business in order to fund bailouts or to finance the pursuits of its political masters or at times to serve as a instrument for inflicting pain on the country's political opposition.

The close political nexus is largely due to the unique charter of Petronas. While the corporation was formed as a commercial entity under the Companies Act, a separate set of laws specially designed to regulate Petronas resulted in the creation of a hybrid entity. Incorporated on August 17, 1974, under the Malaysian Companies Act, Petronas is wholly owned by the government through its investment vehicle, the Ministry of Finance Inc. But unlike other entities incorporated under the Companies Act, Petronas enjoys wide-ranging privileges under the Petroleum Development Act. It isn't required to file annual accounts, which all corporations registered in Malaysia must do. Like all companies, Petronas is represented by a board of directors, which provides direction and manages the company at the highest level. But the act stipulates that the oil corporation "shall be subject to the control and direction of the Prime Minister." To cement the issue of control, the act further states that "not withstanding provisions of the Companies Act 1965, or any other written law to the contrary, the direction so issued shall be binding on" Petronas. Because these directives don't have to be in writing, the power the prime minister wields over Petronas is immense and open to abuse.

The ramifications of Petronas's subservient nature to the Malaysian prime minister are tackled in this section of the chapter, which will show that since the early 1980s those resulting pressures have only intensified.

5.1 The early years – getting established

It wasn't like that in the early years. Conscious of the "resource curse" – so named because countries blessed with natural wealth often end up as basket cases compared with those less endowed – Malaysia's political elite responsible for nurturing Petronas during the 1970s often looked to the example of neighboring Indonesia. On the one hand, Indonesia's Pertamina was held up as a model for the incorporation of Petronas and for how to deal with IOCs. The architects of Petronas borrowed heavily from Pertamina when drawing up terms for production-sharing contracts with IOCs. Pertamina also represented a strong case study on what not to replicate. Flush with cash, Pertamina had become a private plaything for former dictator Suharto and his cronies led by Ibnu Sutowo, who headed the Petronas. Bereft of any oversight and accountability, Pertamina was riddled with mismanagement and corrupt practices, which included the awards of inflated contracts to foreign companies that typically featured massive kickbacks to members of its senior management. At the time when Malaysia was putting the final touches to the incorporation of Petronas in August 1974, massive debts incurred by Pertamina plunged Indonesia into one of its worst economic crises. A four-week interruption in oil exports to Japan severely hit Petronas's cash flow, forcing it to default on a short-term loan to a US bank. Saddled with debts in excess of $10 billion, the company was technically insolvent and had to be bailed out by the government (Vatikiotis 1993). The Pertamina scandal underscored the need to pack Petronas's top management with people of high integrity. They included the likes of Rastam Hadi, the country's no-nonsense deputy governor of the central bank at the time; Abdullah Salleh, a chief secretary to the government; and Raja Mohar Raja Badiozaman, who was the principal economic advisor to the then premier Tun Abdul Razak. This powerful team of technocrats helped lay the foundation of strong managerial integrity.

Their high standing also allowed them to keep meddling politicians from interfering with Petronas's affairs. The government at the time showed no intention of interfering in its affairs. Malaysia never established an oil ministry to oversee Petronas. Instead, the corporation was structured to answer directly to the prime minister, and to this day it has complete autonomy in contract negotiations with IOCs.

There was also little need to interfere. Petronas's first management team quickly showed that it was capable of playing the regulator card of the domestic oil and gas sector effectively. It also quickly put in place building blocks to transform the company into a fully integrated oil corporation. Within the first four years, Petronas had expanded its domestic operations by entering into the manufacturing and distribution of petroleum products, airport refueling operations, a bunkering facility at a port north of Singapore, and a multibillion-dollar LNG plant in a joint venture with Shell and Mitsubishi Corp (Bowie 2001).

In 1982 Carigali, the group's own exploration and production arm, which was set up in 1978, made its first discovery, and in 1983 Petronas's first 30,000 bpd capacity refinery came onstream at about the same time as Petronas was putting the finishing touches to a nationwide gas pipeline project that sourced gas from the offshore fields of the northeastern Terengganu state to power industries.

Petronas's gamble with Carigali offers an insight into the group's risk-taking streak. The group's pioneers decided that to be a good manager Petronas needed to know the business, particularly the complex operations involved in oil explorations. Within three months of its incorporation, Carigali had acquired a concession area in the east coast waters of Peninsular Malaysia held by Conoco. By early 1983 the company had its own jack-up rig, joining five other foreign production-sharing contractors at the time exploring for oil.

A majority of Carigali's personnel were Malaysians who had just returned with their newly minted petroleum engineering degrees. And because of the overlapping nature of oil and gas assets, these Malaysian engineers were often seconded to the platforms of IOCs where they gained valuable experience (Bowie 2001).

5.2 The Mahathir era (1981–2004) – the beginning of interventions

As its profitability soared, Petronas's immunity from political meddling started to come under attack from the government, particularly under the twenty-two-year leadership of premier Mahathir Mohamad.

Many of these interventions were subtle. Consider the so-called Malaysianization of the oil and gas sector. This was brought to bear on the company by the implementation of a government-directed vendor program, which essentially restricts contract-awards for particular segments of the business to the politically dominant ethnic Malay business groups under Malaysia's controversial affirmative action policy. That in turn has led to leakages in its domestic operations. Also little discussed is how the NOC has been central in providing cheap energy to fuel economic growth in the form of subsidies that have benefited industries dominated by businessmen and private companies with strong ties to the government. Gas prices in Malaysia are subsidized by Petronas under a regulated regime introduced in May 1997 and the principal beneficiaries are the country's state-controlled and privately owned electricity power producers. For the financial year that ended March 2009, Petronas incurred gas subsidy liabilities of nearly $5.6 billion. Taken cumulatively, Petronas has incurred subsidies amounting to $28 billion since the regulated price regime was introduced.

5.3 Lender of last resort

Other interventions were more blatant, and it would be a financial crisis in far away Hong Kong in mid 1983 that would deeply fracture the arm's-length relationship between the Malaysian government and Petronas.

Bank Bumiputra, a state-owned financial institution, had lent heavily to one of the island's most aggressive property developers, The Carrian Group. When it collapsed under the weight of its debts, the Malaysian financial institution became technically insolvent and required an urgent bailout to stay in business. The administration under premier Mahathir Mohamad turned to Petronas to play the role of savior by injecting roughly $1 billion into the financial institution.

Bank Bumiputra was established to promote the economic interests of the country's politically dominant ethnic Malay community and because Petronas's charter clearly spelled out its role as a key engine of the nation's socio-economic reengineering, the government at the time defended the controversial bailout on the grounds of national interest. Most other Malaysians saw it differently and to this day a debate rages over Petronas's charter, which gives the prime minister sole prerogative over its affairs and which can turn the corporation into a private banker for the Malaysian prime minister and the ruling government.

The 1984 bailout of Bank Bumiputra would mark the beginning of the NOC's occasional departure from its core business, largely as a result of the wanderlust and adventurism of its political masters, particularly under the "can-do" premiership of Dr. Mahathir. Petronas would be tapped for the second time to bail out scandal-plagued Bank Bumiputra – in 1989 it injected roughly $400 million into the financial institution, again on grounds of national interest. But it was largely private interest when Petronas was directed by the Mahathir government four years earlier to purchase a B747 aircraft from Boeing, which was fitted with a Pratt & Whitney engine. The aircraft was then leased to the national carrier, Malaysia Airlines System or MAS (Lopez 2003).

The deal was designed to prevent any legal dispute between MAS and Rolls Royce, which had entered into an agreement four years earlier that gave the UK engineering concern a monopoly in the supply of aircraft engines. It was also a "sweetheart" transaction because the agency fee for the purchase of the Pratt & Whitney aircraft went to a company controlled by groups linked to Dr. Mahathir's ruling political party.

5.4 Banker of pet projects

Petronas's involvement in non-energy-related projects at the behest of the Malaysian government has long been a magnet for controversy. But company officials have often argued that these diversions were necessities to protect national interests. The bailouts of Bank Bumiputra – now renamed CIMB Bank after a consolidation exercise with another local financial institution – preempted a possible meltdown of the domestic financial sector. Company officials also argue that the NOC recouped most of its investment because many of the financial institution's bad loans were secured by property assets that subsequently soared in value (Lopez 2003).

In any case, Petronas's role as the chief private banker for the government became more pronounced after the mid 1990s, pushing it further away from its core business.

In August 1997, the NOC paid nearly $500 million to acquire a 29 percent interest in Malaysia's largest shipping company, Malaysian Indonesia Shipping Corp., or MISC. The shipper wasn't facing any financial grief, but eight months later, Petronas acquired a debt-laden shipping concern controlled by Dr. Mahathir's eldest son for $226 million and assumed its debts of more than $324 million.

The NOC's move into non-core business did not stop with the bail-out of Dr. Mahathir's son, whose business empire was struggling under a mountain of debt. In March 2000, Petronas was tapped to take a controlling stake in Dr. Mahathir's pet project, national car maker Proton; the transaction was widely criticized as a bailout of a private company closely associated to the government. Petronas would exit Proton thirteen months later.

During the Mahathir premiership, Petronas also took on the role of property developer for the government, spearheading the construction and ownership of the Kuala Lumpur Twin Towers and the administrative capital of Putrajaya. While the iconic Twin Towers (Petronas's headquarters) is widely regarded as a symbol of national pride synonymous with Malaysia and is considered a major tourist attraction, Putrajaya is seen is less glowing terms. Where rubber and palm trees once stood, the Mahathir government directed Petronas to construct an administrative city, comprising office complexes, hotels, mosques, and civil service housing, at an estimated cost of 20 billion ringgit at the height of the regional financial crisis, which struck in the summer of 1997. Because it had Petronas as its chief backer, Putrajaya was able to steamroll financial logjams that bedeviled other large infrastructure undertakings in Malaysia and the region. The chief bugbear about Putrajaya today is the huge cost involved in maintaining the government complexes in the administrative capital. While exact figures aren't available, the financial burden of Putrajaya on the government is connected with a sharp rise in government spending. Federal government operating expenditure doubled to 151 billion ringgit in 2008 from 75.2 billion ringgit in 2003 (Chi-Chang 2009).

Apart from tapping Petronas to fund and bail out projects close to him, Dr. Mahathir wasn't averse to using Petronas as a political tool. When the oil-and gas-rich state of Terengganu in northeastern Peninsular Malaysia fell into opposition hands after the 1999 general election, Dr. Mahathir issued a federal government decree ordering Petronas to cease making oil royalty payments to the state, payments that were due under an agreement signed in 1975. The move underscored the veto powers held by the Malaysian premier over the running of the NOC and raised the prospect with Petronas's own business partners that the government could force the company to rescind contracts in the event of any political fallout (Lopez 2003).

For all the meddling Petronas was subjected to during the Mahathir era, its transformation to an NOC of international repute also took place under his premiership. This was partly because Petronas was a source of huge pride to him. In a country where state agencies are better known for their leaky and corruption-tainted management, Petronas ranked as one of the country's best-run companies. And in an economy dominated by ethnic Chinese, Petronas was staffed largely by ethnic Malays, which endeared the corporation to the can-do former political strongman, Mahathir.

Slipstreaming on Dr. Mahathir's activist brand of diplomacy – which cast Malaysia as a champion of the Third World and exporter of capital and corporate expertise – Petronas first turned to South Africa. The Mahathir administration openly backed Nelson Mandela's bid for the presidency in 1994 and funded the ANC's political campaigns. The gambit worked and the Mandela government backed Petronas in its successful bid to acquire a controlling stake in the African nation's biggest refiner and marketing company: Engen.

The headline-grabbing acquisition was the 30 percent interest for roughly $680 million in South Africa's Engen, which subsequently served as a key platform for Petronas's aggressive expansion into exploration and production in the African continent. Three years later Petronas acquired a 25 percent interest in Premier Oil for $167 million, a deal that helped it establish a toehold in upstream ventures in Myanmar and Natuna Sea.

Petronas's aggressive M&A approach to satisfy its international growth strategy forced the company to shed its NOC image and behave more like an IOC by striking high-profile deals in a more public manner. As it increasingly tapped global bond markets for funding, it was forced to become more transparent in its affairs, a transformation that has helped the management shield Petronas from too much political meddling.

5.5 Najib administration – a heavier state hand

Petronas enjoyed a brief spell of little government interference during the five-year premiership of Mahathir's successor, Abdullah Admah Badawi.

But Najib Razak, who took over from Abdullah in April 2009, hasn't wasted time showing that he intends to have a greater say over the NOC's affairs.[1]

In early May, Najib informed Petronas CEO Hassan Marican that he wanted to appoint a senior political aide, Omar Mustapha, to the board of the NOC. What was supposed to be a simple procedural exercise has mushroomed into an awkward face-off between the NOC's relatively independent board of directors and the premier, underscoring the major challenge of reconciling tensions between the government and Petronas. When Omar's proposed appointment was presented at the NOC's monthly board meeting in May 2009, the four government-nominated directors raised their reservations because of his somewhat tainted past with Petronas; he had failed to settle a scholarship loan he had received from Petronas in the 1990s. Najib was advised of the board's reservations, which stemmed from concerns that Omar's appointment could have adverse effects on staff morale in the corporation where honoring bond commitments is taken seriously.

The prime minister's office saw the rebuff as insubordination on the part of the Hassan-led board. Press reports of the boardroom strife with the premier further strained relations between Petronas and the government – and that according to people close to Najib left him with no choice but to force through Omar's appointment.

Hassan was later informed by government officials that Najib had decided to invoke his powers under the Petronas charter (which gives the prime minister veto power over all affairs of the NOC) and directed him to formalize Omar's appointment in the June board meeting. After some minor opposition, the board ratified the PM's directive. But Najib's decision to flex his muscles and apply the little-used veto power enjoyed by the prime minister over Petronas has raised several issues.

The move to appoint Omar is likely to affect the morale in an organization where a high premium is placed on loyalty to the corporation. A bond-breaker ascending to the lofty position of director of the parent organization is not likely to sit well. The episode also cast a shadow over Hassan's future and began speculation that his contract wouldn't be renewed. Over the years, Hassan has emerged as the international face for Petronas, not only establishing close ties with his counterparts in NOCs and IOCs but also with the international financial community. (Petronas is the country's most trusted bond issuer and has $19 billion worth of bonds issued in the global financial market.)

The flap over Omar's appointment was initially seen as a minor misunderstanding between the strong-willed Hassan and his new boss, Najib. But as it got closer to the end of Hassan's three-year contract, it became clear that Najib viewed the Omar episode as a serious case of insubordination by the Petronas chief. Just days before his term was to expire in early February this year, Hassan was called for a meeting with Najib and was told that his term would not be renewed. He was offered a position as special advisor to the government on energy matters, which he declined. Hassan was replaced by the former chief of Petronas's shipping arm, Shamsul Azhar Abas. Najib's choice of a successor came as a surprise. That's because the government had indicated that Hassan's successor would come from *within* the organization. Shamsul retired in early 2009, clearly suggesting that he wasn't part of Petronas's internal succession plan. Shamsul's return is largely a result of his close ties to Omar, Najib's point man on the Petronas board of directors.

In any case, the somewhat shabby manner in which Hassan's services were terminated served as a reminder of the prime minister's immense power over the NOC. It also reinforced the view that, unlike other premiers, Najib intends to play a more interventionist role in Petronas affairs.

6 Key strategies and performance

The reputation of Petronas as a model for NOCs to emulate is well deserved. The deft leveraging of its role as regulator of the domestic oil and gas sector has helped the country retain a large chunk of its hydrocarbon wealth. Through Malaysia's unique licensing regime, Petronas has built strong relationships with IOCs that helped lay the foundation for its aggressive international expansion.

6.1 Domestic strategy

Petronas dominates Malaysia's upstream sector through the country's unique licensing system and the production-sharing contracts (PSCs) introduced in 1976. Under Malaysia's PSC arrangements, Petronas's exploration arm, Carigali, has rights to a carried interest in any exploration within the country's roughly 128,000 sq km of net acreage set aside for exploration. The interest assigned to Carigali varies between

15 percent and 25 percent and upon discovery Carigali automatically becomes a working partner in the development. Its active participation in key stages of upstream development has made Petronas a major beneficiary of technology transfer and in the process radically altered the makeup of the country's upstream business, which was once dominated by Shell and Exxon. The technology transfer has enabled Petronas to completely take control of a producing field at the expiration of a PSC with several options open to it. It can relicense the area and retain a much larger share of the profits from production by assigning only a smaller stake to its original joint venture partner. The NOC is also forging new relations with smaller IOCs, ones with specialized skill sets such as Murphy Oil and Talisman, to exploit maturing fields.

Through partnerships with IOCs, Petronas has also established itself as a serious player in the LNG business. Its tie-up with Shell in the early 1980s to build Asia-Pacific's largest LNG plants has helped it secure dominant stakes in the Japanese and Korean markets (corporate disclosures from Petronas website; Bowie 2001).

6.2 Overseas strategy

The lifeblood for any oil company is making new discoveries. Barring any major discoveries, Malaysia will become a net importer of oil within the next ten years, and it was on this premise that Petronas began its overseas push to find new business opportunities and bulk up its reserves in the early 1990s.

Nearly 40 percent of Malaysia's hydrocarbon production is made up of gas, and Petronas has leveraged its growing expertise to dominate the regional gas market. The corporation has forged ties with regional NOCs to ensure security of supply of gas to drive Malaysia's economic development. It has a tripartite pact with PetroVietnam and Pertamina to explore acreages in offshore Sarawak; this has met with some measure of success. Petronas also has separate upstream gas projects with Vietnam (in the PM3 offshore block that straddles Malaysian and Vietnamese territory) and Thailand (in the Malaysian–Thai Joint Development Area). These investments will provide future sources of supply for heavily gas-dependent Peninsular Malaysia.

With an already strong presence in the Pacific Basin, Petronas has moved to establish itself as a player in the Atlantic Basin and in Australia through acquisitions in recent years. It owns a 50 percent interest in the

Egyptian gas business of Italy's Edison Group and 40 percent equity in the proposed Gladstone LNG plant in Australia with Santos. The push into Australia represents a big bet for Petronas. The $2 billion investment offers an entry into the still infant coal seam to LNG business. Both these deals demonstrate Petronas's readiness to pursue the path of mergers and acquisitions to expand. The NOC has also relied heavily on political ties to expand overseas. It has established itself as a major player in Africa (benefiting from the active brand of diplomacy pursued by former premier Mahathir) and has ventured into countries (such as Chad and Sudan) largely off-limits to IOCs due to political instability or international sanctions. However, these high-risk bets could make Petronas vulnerable to campaigns by international pressure groups – and that could sully the NOC's image globally and undermine its standing with the international investing community.

Still, its overseas strategy continues to pay dividends. In December, Petronas pulled off a major coup when it, together with Shell, secured rights to develop the giant Manjoon oil field in Iraq at the second auction in the war-ravaged country since the 2003 invasion. The consortium beat out rival bids by France's Total SA and China National Petroleum Corporation for the rights to Manjoon, which has estimated reserves of almost 13 million barrels of oil.

The role of Petronas in the consortium underscored the NOC's standing among IOCs as a partner of choice and a recognizable international brand, able to contribute to a partnership in terms of management and technology.

It controls roughly 2 percent of the global lubricants market, which is valued annually at more than $48 billion, and enjoys sole OEM (original equipment manufacturer) status for Fiat vehicles, underscoring the company's downstream push. It is also the world's largest owner-operator of LNG tankers and its Aframax tankers transport roughly 30 percent of imports by the United States from the Gulf States (PESD Interviews).

Comparing Petronas's performance with other NOCs is difficult. While the company continues to sustain a performance level that is either at par or above that of leading IOCs based on key financial ratios, its peer group benchmarking on areas such as capital expenditure and upstream development investment levels is weak.

A survey provided by Petronas showed that it ranked last among ten NOCs based on upstream development investment levels for 2008 and 2009. Among NOCs such as PetroChina, Statoil, and Petrobras it ranked eighth in estimated capex for the next five years.

But pressure points are becoming apparent. A consultancy report on Petronas in late 2008 argued that Petronas was starting to lose ground to other key players in the global LNG sector and international deep water exploration and production. It also listed the corporation's relative inexperience in the international sector, constraints on human capital, and the involvement in non-core activities as key weaknesses.

6.3 Key challenges at home and overseas

Petronas easily ranks as Malaysia's best-managed state-owned entity. But its success has also increased the state's reliance on the NOC to fund national development and is raising concerns over how well proceeds from this natural resource are being channeled.

Despite lower profits posted by Petronas in 2008, the group's payments to the government in the form of royalties, dividends, taxes, and other duties amounted to $21.14 billion, representing 44.9 percent of federal government revenue for the year. The amounts are more staggering when considering the figures over the last five years, during which time total contributions to the Malaysian government totaled $76.6 billion. Since its incorporation thirty-five years ago, the group paid a total of $135.6 billion to the government, underscoring how heavily the Malaysian government has come to rely on the NOC to fund development.

While payments to the government have more than doubled over the last five years, profit reinvested to fund development amounted to $6.3 billion in 2008, or roughly 21% of total earnings, ranking it among the lowest in the industry. Based on figures provided by Petronas, oil majors reinvested roughly 57% of their profits in 2009, while NOCs on average reinvested just over 70%.

7 Conclusion

As an NOC, Petronas has delivered a sterling performance at home and is playing a major role in fueling economic development in Malaysia. It has leveraged its role as regulator – particularly through production-sharing contracts with IOCs operating in Malaysia – to help the country retain a lion's share of the oil profits. Through direct partnerships with IOCs in exploration and production activities in Malaysia, the company has benefited from a high degree of technology transfer. It can claim credit for creating an oil and gas sector that is today 85 percent controlled by Malaysian groups that employ more than 400,000 people, while its strict guidelines on employment have forced IOCs to train locals for senior positions with their Malaysian subsidiaries.

It is often held up as a sure-footed example for practicing high standards in natural resource management. Petronas's transformation from an NOC to one of the world's top ten most profitable energy corporations underscores why the company is often selected as a partner of choice for many IOCs.

Petronas's international push is less glowing. It has a high-risk and geographically diverse portfolio with large acreages in Africa, Central Asia, and Russia. The exploration results, however, have so far been disappointing and the rapid international expansion has stretched the NOC's human resources. It will need to rationalize and streamline its overseas business if it is to emerge as a serious player among second-echelon oil majors. Petronas's nearly three-decade transformation from strictly an NOC to an organization of international repute has a lot to do with its management's deft handling of relations with the state. The intervention has fluctuated over the last three decades between Dr. Mahathir's heavy hands over the NOC's affairs to a lighter touch during the five-year premiership of Abdullah Ahmad Badawi. Those ties are now becoming more complex to manage as the government increasingly relies on Petronas.

Notes

1 This section is based on my interviews with Malaysian government officials and Petronas executives during 2009 in Kuala Lumpur.

19 | Angola's Sonangol: dexterous right hand of the state

PATRICK R. P. HELLER

1 Introduction

The Sociedade Nacional de Combustíveis de Angola, commonly known as Sonangol, is the dominant institution in Angola's petroleum sector. It has guided the sector through the country's decades-long civil war as well as during a post-conflict boom marked by massive new investments and production streams that have cemented Angola as one of the world's most important oil centers. Growing up in the midst of a bloody and destructive contest for power and operating in a state characterized by low human capital and major physical impediments to production efficiency, Sonangol has developed into a singularly effective agent of the government's interests. To a large degree, Sonangol's evolution into a successful manager of state petroleum-sector policies has taken place *in spite of* these obstacles to a traditional national development path, as the company has had to deftly negotiate dangerous operational terrain and generate investment in an environment seen by most as extraordinarily risky. In another sense, though, Sonangol has reached the lofty position it occupies precisely *because of* these challenges, which have inexorably shaped the company's outlook, competencies, and room to operate within the Angolan political system.

Since throughout most of its history the company devoted relatively little attention to field operation, its performance cannot be fully measured according to the most traditional metrics used to assess the performance of an oil company. However, I will argue that Sonangol should be viewed as a high-performing national oil company (NOC) because it is particularly skilled at providing what its political masters seek. The company's primary responsibilities are fourfold. First, and most obviously, the state has given Sonangol primary responsibility for building a dynamic, dependable domestic oil sector. The company has achieved this primarily by establishing and managing contracts with international companies IOCs charged with the administration of technical operations and the mobilization of investments. Throughout its history, Sonangol has provided the conditions in which operational companies could make technical decisions with confidence that political interference would be minimal, which has encouraged foreign operators to make massive long-lived capital investments. This accomplishment is particularly impressive in light of the country's broader political uncertainty. The company's leadership in this realm was particularly crucial between its founding in 1976 and the end of the civil war in 2002. During this period, when most sophisticated economic activity in Angola was brought to a standstill by the conflict, hostility to non-oil investors, and destructive socialist policies, Sonangol managed to protect the interests of its international partners and maintain a thriving enclave oil economy. The company's stewardship role has evolved in the late-war and post-war periods, as it has granted concessions for and managed the operations of ever more complex deep water production.

Sonangol's second core responsibility is closely connected to the first. Without upsetting the broadly investor-friendly conditions and commitment to high-level technical performance discussed above, the company is charged with maximizing the share of petroleum revenues accruing to the Angolan state. In the absence of a strong legislature or Ministry of Petroleum, Sonangol has taken primary responsibility for policymaking, and it has developed fiscal terms that deliver a sizable take to the government without proving so confiscatory as to discourage private investment. The company is also charged with minimizing the deductible costs of the partners' operations (which serve to reduce taxable income), and the IOC officials consulted for this chapter indicate that Sonangol steers its partners' activities with uncommon strictness as well as deft (and sometimes frustrating) political/administrative maneuvering.

The motivation for the company's final two core duties extends beyond day-to-day revenue generation to the regime's broader survival and state-centric economic management strategies. The third duty is using the oil sector as a tool for steering money and opportunity to the fledgling Angolan "private sector," which is dominated by individuals with personal and business ties to the core of the ruling regime. (Angola has been ruled since independence in 1975 by the Popular Movement for the Liberation of Angola – Party of Labor, or

"MPLA," which survived the long war and has retained firm control over the oil-producing regions throughout Angola's history. The party has continued to solidify its hold on power since the war's end in 2002.) Sonangol has established a huge web of subsidiaries and joint ventures, currently numbering more than thirty and covering both oil services and activities with much more tangential links to the oil industry, such as an airline and an insurance company. It also obliges international oil consortia to accept minority participation from well-connected Angolan companies and steers contracts during operations to non-Sonangol Angolan companies. This focus on "Angolanization" serves to reduce short-term revenue, as these companies are often more expensive or less efficient than comparable international firms. But the strategy serves as a patronage mechanism for the regime's net-work of supporters and is a key to the government's expanding-core economic strategy.

Fourth, as the most competent arm of the Angolan state, the com-pany has been called upon to perform a variety of functions that most countries would traditionally assign to other government agencies. Most notably, Sonangol funded and managed arms purchases as the regime fought for survival during the civil war; it has used its super-ior debt rating to secure loans for the national government; it has formed strategic partnerships with Asian companies linking produc-tion rights to broader aid packages; and it has crafted an ambitious international investment strategy to manage the country's growing wealth and expand Angola's profile in international markets. The company has also performed roles that quite literally helped ensure the survival of the country's elites, including paying their medical bills.

While these core priorities clearly give the company an expansive role within Angola's economy, I argue that Sonangol is most note-worthy among the world's most important NOCs primarily because its founders and subsequent leaders have steadfastly *limited* the scope of its activities. Sonangol's oil-producing subsidiary (Sonangol Pesquisa & Produção) has in recent years sought to expand its opera-tions capacity, but Sonangol has been careful to ensure that its own ambitions did not threaten the international partners who have been the backbone of investment in Angola's oil sector. Amid the fervent international resource nationalism of the 1970s and the MPLA's stated Marxist-Leninist ideology, Sonangol remained focused, recognizing its limitations and its dependence on the international companies for obtaining the maximum benefit of the company's "principal" – that is, the country's ruling elite. (Much of this chapter looks at how Sonangol, as an "agent," behaves in ways that are consistent with the desires of its main "principal." Many studies of corporate governance and regulation use this kind of framework to understand how the incentives that principals create influence the behavior of agents. For more on such theories see Chapter 3.) And though Sonangol has been responsible for carrying several subsidiaries that do not add to its core petroleum-development mission, the company has been able to avoid many other sorts of non-petroleum responsibilities that have strained the resources of other NOCs, such as social services and the provision of large-scale employment as a welfare mechanism.[1]

This limitation of role differentiates Sonangol from most of the large NOCs being analyzed in this volume, but not from its counterpart companies in other African countries, many of which have, in recognition of their limited access to finance and technology, adapted similar regulator/banker models, generally with far less success.[2] In contrast with NNPC (see Chapter 16), Sonangol has become sub-Saharan Africa's most successful NOC, by a wide margin, because of the following factors:

- *Geology.* Though not sufficient on their own to engender success, the country's natural advantages cannot be discounted. During the early days of the Angolan industry, activity focused on the onshore and shallow water fields around the province of Cabinda, where a Gulf Oil/Chevron subsidiary (CABGOC) was able to able to extract relatively "easy" oil despite broader political and economic uncertainty. In the mid 1990s, as new technologies made more complex offshore operations feasible, Angola witnessed the discovery and development of massive new deep water fields. Because Sonangol had demonstrated it was a competent and credible regulator of the earlier, simpler fields, private investors were much more willing to supply the massive capital needed to exploit the new, complex fields. Sonangol and Angola reaped the benefits of these endowments as new production came online during the high-price 2000s.
- *Trust and independence.* Sonangol's leadership has been afforded high levels of latitude to set policy and make day-to-day management decisions, with limited interference from the legislature or the

formal manager of the sector, the Ministry of Petroleum, both of which lack technical skills and political clout. The company has been able to maintain this independence in large part because its CEOs have enjoyed direct communications and high levels of trust with Angola's president, forged in the close-knit wartime decision-making hierarchy and their common place within a tiny ethno-political elite class. In combination with the factor discussed next, its independence has enabled Sonangol to act decisively and avoid the competitive interest-group politics that diminish the efficiency of other NOCs. The government determined that the country could optimize the development of its oil sector by concentrating its limited resources and building capacity within the company, rather than seeking to empower multiple bodies simultaneously. In this manner, Sonangol serves as a counterpoint to the conventional wisdom that NOCs function best when their activities are constrained by oversight from a strong independent regulator, with one important caveat. Sonangol has succeeded at governing the sector efficiently and implementing the wishes of its principal, but whether a stronger independent regulator or more open debate about sector management would have better promoted the long-term development needs of the Angolan populace remains a much-debated question (and one that is largely outside the boundaries of this chapter).

• *Training and competent management.* Independence on its own can prove disastrous when not accompanied by skill. From its first days, Sonangol pursued an ambitious learning agenda, identifying core needs and providing its personnel with high-quality international training to meet them. The company has also relied heavily on private international experts, hiring prominent firms to help design and enforce contracts, conduct audits, and implement management structures to international standards (Soares de Oliveira 2007a).

Given the weakness of the Ministry of Petroleum and Angola's formal legal system, the state has relied mainly on informal mechanisms for controlling Sonangol through most of the company's history. The most important checks on Sonangol's behavior have been the obligatory cooperation with IOCs (which ensures some degree of technical capability and professional decision making) and the conduct of competitive auctions to allot operatorship (which provides the government with a powerful market signal about the value of concession rights and the health of the Angolan industry). The close relationship between the company's leadership and the so-called "Futungo" political elite that controls the country could not be easily replicated in countries without Angola's particular history and social composition, but it has served as a central ingredient in the synergy between principal desires and agent actions.

Sonangol has evolved dramatically in the postwar period. The company has gone international, making large-scale and high-profile investments elsewhere in Africa and throughout the world, and it is investing heavily in developing the operational capability of its exploration and production subsidiary. At the same time, Sonangol retains its primacy as the overseer of the domestic oil sector and the controller of all activities in Angola and off its shores. Having built up its capacity gradually over decades, Sonangol's leadership is pushing the company toward a more mature phase of broader ambitions. In recent years the company and the government have announced several future plans that may serve to increase the independent controls on Sonangol, including an intention to list shares on public exchanges and the transfer of some of the company's concessionary duties back to a beefed-up ministry. It remains to be seen whether these reforms and the widening of the company's horizons will improve the company's performance or disrupt the careful balance and limited focus that have enabled it to succeed.

This chapter will proceed in four additional sections. In section 2, I will lay out the context, detailing the company's history and assessing the political, economic, and geological environment in which it operates. Section 3 elaborates upon my claim that the company should be deemed relatively successful, focusing on the strategies that Sonangol has adopted and on company performance measured by the overall health of the Angolan oil industry, the sizable government take, the company's realization of stated goals, and its increasing skill and professionalism. Section 4 attempts to crystallize the independent variables that have shaped this success, looking specifically at government–company relations and arguing that the company's independence, commitment to non-ideological partnerships, limited agenda, and focused capacity building have been the key determinants of its strategy and performance. Section 5 discusses some of the challenges that the company will face in the future, as the regime's goals and Sonangol's focus continue to evolve.

Before proceeding, it is important to make two qualifying notes. First, Sonangol remains largely averse to information disclosure. A recent World Bank Survey of NOC public reporting indicated that Sonangol releases none of the more than thirty "key operating and performance measurements and ratios" typically used to assess company performance (World Bank 2008, Part A, figure 1). It publishes scant financial data and did not grant a formal interview or statement for this research. As such, my conclusions are based on a combination of not-for-attribution interviews with two current Sonangol officials (one in Luanda and another in one of the company's overseas offices) and additional professionals who have worked for the company or the government in the past; interviews with IOC officials and others with direct experience working with the company; discussions with other Angolan and international experts on the Angolan industry and economy; the data that the company does publish about its activities; public information from other Angolan government agencies; and secondary-source review.

The second caveat is that, like the other case studies in this project, this chapter focuses on analyzing the success of Sonangol *as an agent of the state's intentions* and does not represent a normative evaluation of those intentions. Angola's history has been marked by tragedy and violence, and the "clientelistic" nature of the management of the economy by the state and its political elites has been a major determinant of government policy, both during the war and after its conclusion. This case study analyzes the role that the state's patronage-maintenance goals and its broader political strategy have played in determining the priorities for the company; I do not much delve into the already-rich academic treatment of how the government's priorities have impacted national development or human rights.[3]

2 History and context

Sonangol's structure and priorities have been inexorably shaped by the physical and political context in which the company has evolved. Of paramount importance were the civil war, which started nearly at the moment of independence and continued until 2002; the tight control of the MPLA by a small inner circle of militaristic elites; and the nature of Angola's geological endowments.

2.1 The role of conflict and socio-ethnic identity

Sonangol was established in 1976, the year after the country had formally gained independence from Portugal. Independence did not correspond with nationalist unity; the violent movement against the Portuguese had been conducted on various fronts by three distinct Angolan factions – the Movimento Popular de Libertação de Angola (MPLA), União Nacional para a Independência Total de Angola (UNITA), and Frente Nacional para a Libertação de Angola (FNLA) – with competing visions of post-colonial power. A brokered power-sharing deal between the colonial administration and the three groups never gained traction, and the independence war quickly morphed into a civil war. Before the end of 1975, the MPLA exerted firm control over Luanda and the formal organs of governance, the FNLA had seen its capabilities decimated, and UNITA had returned to its bases of support in the rural periphery, from where it launched ongoing military operations. Notably, the MPLA also established control over the non-contiguous province of Cabinda, the capital of Angola's oil industry, despite continued resistance from the secessionist Frente de Libertação do Estado de Cabinda (FLEC) and other groups.[4]

The MPLA's roots and the composition of its leadership played a central role in shaping its priorities and its behavior during the war and beyond. The Angolan ruling elite has its origins in the mid-twentieth-century marriage of two groups that David Birmingham dubs the "old creoles" and the "new creoles" (Birmingham 1995, pp. 91–92). The old creoles had their roots in the Mbundu-dominated kingdoms around the Luanda highlands and other coastal areas, which intermarried heavily with Portuguese and Dutch settlers beginning in the sixteenth century, creating an elite community that became increasingly influential in the region's politics and economy throughout the sixteenth and seventeenth centuries. These mixed-race families, most of whom carried European names like dos Santos, Dias, and Van-Dunen and came to speak Portuguese as their first language, became privileged, cosmopolitan elites that viewed themselves as the logical leaders of their more rural "indigenous" neighbors, many of whom

worked as slaves or wage-laborers on their plantations. These elites
played a particularly important formal role during the colonial system
of the late nineteenth and early twentieth century, when they occupied many important mid-level posts in the colonial administration.
A shift in Portuguese policy in the early twentieth century removed
the Angolan elites from their formal governing roles in favor of new
migrants from Portugal, though the creole class largely maintained
relatively prosperous living standards (Birmingham 1995; Green
1995; Hodges 2004; Newitt 2008).

The "new creole" class was composed primarily of mission-
educated Angolans from the hinterlands outside Luanda and mixed
race children of more recent Portuguese administrators. Like the old
elites, these new creoles were frustrated by the artificial ceilings placed
on them under Portuguese rule, and together the two groups began
to build the MPLA in the late 1950s. The party was initially dominated by new creoles, but beginning in the late 1970s the old elites
reclaimed their dominant position within the alliance (Birmingham
1995; Green 1995, p. 174).

Though it has been said that the Angolan civil war was not primarily an ethnic conflict, the key players used ethnicity as an organizing
force, to varying degrees, throughout the conflict. UNITA leader Jonas
Savimbi crafted his rebel movement as a struggle by the Ovimbundu
group (the largest in Angola) against the MPLA, which was dominated
by members of the Mbundu ethnicity (Angola's second-largest group).
For its part, the MPLA did not explicitly tie its image to Mbundu
supremacy, but the image it projected of a party-led Angolan nation-
ality was inexorably linked not just to the Mbundu but to the creole
elite that dominated its leadership. It is common to hear Angolans
speak of the "hundred families" (or even the ten or eleven families)
who have dominated all elements of political and economic decision
making in the government since independence (Guimarães 1998,
pp. 25–26; Hodges 2004, pp. 40–41). As Reginald Green notes, the
dominant role played by descendants of the old creole elite through
Angola's post-independence history places the country in a unique
position in African history: "[N]o other 1870/1910 Creole elite has
regained power or now leads a government" (Green 1995, p. 174). As
will be discussed below, this identity has played (among various other
factors) a central role in the evolution of Sonangol, which has been a
product of and a tool for the perpetuation of this elite domination.

2.2 *Wartime, lack of capacity, and the pragmatist priority*

The conflict between the MPLA and UNITA would continue in various forms from 1975 until 2002, when Savimbi's lieutenants surrendered after he was killed by the loyalist army. Though the MPLA held onto Luanda and the formal organs of state power throughout the war, its leaders faced severe challenges, especially during the conflict's early stages. Angola's was one of the most significant proxy wars of the late Cold War. The MPLA received extensive financial and military support from the USSR and Cuba, while UNITA was supported by South Africa and the United States.[5] As the conflict extended into the 1990s and international funding dissipated, UNITA was able to sustain its campaigns through the export of diamonds in violation of international sanctions and of other spoils, including ivory, timber, and coffee.

From independence, the MPLA's leadership recognized the significance that oil could have as a source of income that could support its war efforts and provide the rents necessary to placate its network of clients and keep it in power. Oil had played a growing role in the colonial Angolan economy since the mid 1960s,[6] with most production under the control of the Cabinda Gulf Oil Company (CABGOC), a subsidiary of Gulf Oil, and smaller fields operated by Texaco and Petrofina. As the Portuguese exited and the civil war began, these foreign companies, fearful of violence and instability, as well as the communist affiliations of the new MPLA-dominated government, briefly left the country (Soares de Oliveira 2007a).

Faced with a core decision about how to manage the sector at independence in 1975, the government established the National Commission for the Restructuring of the Petroleum Sector (CNRIP). The commission officially espoused a view of Angolan dominance over the oil sector that resonated with the formal ideological views of the MPLA as well as the resource nationalism that dominated discourse in oil states across the world. But CNRIP members, a small group organized by Percy Freudenthal, a white Angolan businessman with close ties to the political elite (who would become Sonangol's first CEO), recognized that the lack of indigenous expertise meant that a total government takeover of oil operations (which already comprised onshore and offshore fields) could be disastrous for the country's ability to extract oil and generate revenues. Their first order of business was to negotiate the return of Gulf Oil, to ensure that any break in production would be short-lived. Given the domestic and geopolitical contention over the fate of Angola, these negotiations were politically delicate, but the commission's representatives were able to convince the company's representatives that their investment would be protected, both from the threat of expropriation and from violence (Costa 2005; Soares de Oliveira 2007a).

The decision to create an NOC was made in 1976. As described by one official who was involved with the CNRIP's process, the goal was a company that would serve as "an instrument to control activities, and to craft [the state's] own vision about the pace of the industry and how to influence the development of oil in the country." The long-term viability of Angola's reserves was far from certain at the time,

and if there was no entity able to understand what was happening and recommend to the government a broad strategic approach, there was no guarantee that the industry would continue to develop. The [foreign] companies could make suggestions, but without an integrated vision. They all had interest in getting their benefits out of their individual blocks, but had no real incentive to look after the long-term health of the sector as a whole. (Interview with Mangueira 2008)

Rather than starting from scratch, the company was created out of the shell of the Portuguese oil company ANGOL, which the new Angolan regime had nationalized (Soares de Oliveira 2007a, pp. 599–600). The CNRIP, both in its early stages and as it fused into the leadership of the company, remained pragmatic about the company's limited abilities and began to build Sonangol's internal capacity as a sector manager and partner. The company hired the US-based consulting firm Arthur D. Little to advise on company and sector structure and strategy. Inspired by the success of NOCs elsewhere in the developing world – particularly Sonatrach and Petrobras – Sonangol sought to build relationships abroad. Beginning in the late 1970s, the company sought advice from these companies on a variety of high-level decisions and sent the first cadres of Angolan technicians to facilities run by Sonatrach and Italy's Eni for training (Soares de Oliveira 2007a; Interview with Mangueira 2008). This began a tradition within the company that continues to today – investing in long-term internal capacity development while relying on outside expertise to ensure that the oil continues flowing. The company also began what would be a long-standing practice of funding overseas academic scholarships, which served both to begin to build a class of Angolan experts on oil issues and to strengthen the company's (and the country's) overseas ties.

At the same time that Sonangol was being organized, CNRIP also advised the Angolan government on the functioning of the National Petroleum Directorate, which morphed into the Ministry of Petroleum in 1979. This body was formally charged with oversight of the sector, but officials made a strategic decision early on to vest the bulk of the new capacity being developed (and the bulk of decision-making power) in the company, rather than the ministry. The level of human capacity and infrastructure in Angola during the early post-independence years was extremely low, and the MPLA decided to concentrate resources and authority in Sonangol rather than spread it to two administrative organs (Interview with Mangueira 2008). In the law and under formal decrees Sonangol was subject to the supervision of the Ministry of Petroleum,[7] but in reality the ministry was given little ability to drive strategy or constrain Sonangol's actions.[8]

2.3 Evolution of political needs and company goals

As the war progressed, the prerogatives of the ruling elite evolved, causing the government to call upon Sonangol to be flexible and provide a wide and varying range of services. I will go into detail about these services below, but it bears providing a bit of historical narrative here, both to lay the groundwork for what follows and to underscore the importance of the company's broad vision for the sector in enabling it to flourish in an unpredictable setting. Some of the important shifts represented responses to international forces and the actions of UNITA. Others were designed to maintain the complex internal management of the MPLA's patronage network, over which President José Eduardo dos Santos has been able to retain control since coming to power at the death of Agostinho Neto in 1979. The MPLA hewed closely to Soviet-model Marxism-Leninism for the first decade or so after independence, with state control of the economy and a dominant role in political decision making for the formal party apparatus. The party became particularly rigid in its control of the state and its suppression of dissent after the quelling of a coup attempt in 1977. During these early years, first Neto and then dos Santos exercised high levels of control but did so within the MPLA structure and had to maneuver within the party to minimize the influence of rivals and officially link their policies to the vision dictated by the party's formal ideology (Hodges 2004, pp. 49–52; Messiant 2008a, pp. 93–95).

The dominant political paradigm began to shift during the second half of the 1980s, when the clear failure of Soviet-style economic policies and the increasing consolidation of power in the presidency fueled a diminished reliance on Marxist-Leninist ideology. The void was filled by an official commitment to market-oriented reforms that actually resulted in a more focused *clientelism*, whereby powerful political patrons controlled access to virtually all economic opportunities and distributed them to maintain political support. Rents bypassed the formal strictures of the party apparatus and were distributed directly to key figures necessary to preserve the power of the ruling elite. The privatization of businesses, letting of military and public works contracts, and management of the oil sector were increasingly used to lubricate elite patronage networks and consolidate the power of dos Santos's inner circle, commonly identified in Angola as the Futungo elite, in reference to one of Angola's presidential palace complexes, the Futungo de Belas (Hodges 2004, pp. 52–57; Messiant 2008a, pp. 95–97). These developments coincided with the glasnost-era decline in official financial and geopolitical support from the USSR, heightening the need for Angola to further expand internal sources of revenues and rents.

This drive was accelerated in the early 1990s. An internationally brokered peace accord in 1991 led to hopes for multiparty democracy and the conduct of an election in 1992. The prospect that the MPLA might not win the election provided further incentive for the ruling elites to build up a more robust private sector network dominated by their allies. In the end, the MPLA prevailed in the poll, Savimbi refused to accept the result, and UNITA took up arms again. The period that followed was particularly bloody, as the rebels became increasingly isolated from the international community and each side sought to exert maximum suffering on the supporters of the other (Messiant 2008a, pp. 99–102). Subsequent peace deals in 1994 and 1997 brought temporary respites in the violence but ultimately failed to take hold, and intense military campaigns continued until Savimbi's death in 2002.

While remaining engaged with UNITA on the military front, the Futungo elite continued throughout this late-war period to consolidate its domination of the government and the economy and to minimize the influence of civil society, the independent media, and the non-Futungo private sector. The front lines of the war reached Luanda only on a couple of occasions, and challenges to the government's control over Cabinda and the ports necessary to access offshore oil production were similarly rare.

Since the end of the war, the MPLA and its ruling elite have sought to enhance their stature as the stewards of "one Angola," using booms in oil prices and production to fund massive reconstruction programs, repay national debt, and enact macroeconomic reform. Angola's growth rate has been one of the highest in the world – GDP expanded by 20.6% in 2005, 18.6% in 2006, 22.6% in 2007, and 13.8% in 2008 (IMF 2009a, 2009b, 2011).[9] Core government clients have been able to expand their reach and their wealth as oil revenues have increased and new business opportunities in construction, service, and other sectors have appeared. UNITA, meanwhile, has failed to generate large-scale success in its attempts to reinvent itself as a political party, and independent checks on the ruling elite's power (including the legislature, judiciary, media, and civil society) remain weak (Vines *et al.* 2005). International perceptions of Angola's stability have improved significantly since the end of the war – the country's score for "Political Stability" in the World Bank's World Governance Indicators has climbed steadily from -1.41 in 2002 (11th percentile of all countries ranked) to -0.43 in 2008 (30th percentile) – and diplomats and investors in Luanda are almost uniformly confident about Angola's business prospects. The dominance of the MPLA and its core ruling elite was punctuated in September 2008, when the country's first elections since 1992 were conducted in relative peace and order and saw the MPLA gain more than 80 percent of the seats in parliament (BBC News 2008).[10]

2.4 Geology and strategy

Angola's extremely favorable geology has played a central role in the company's success. The country's reserves – measured at 13.5 billion

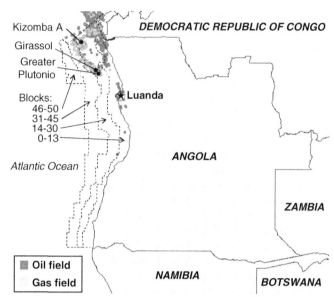

Figure 19.1 Map of major oil and gas fields in Angola.
Source for oil and gas field data: Wood Mackenzie (2009b).

proved barrels at the end of 2010 (with billions more in probable reserves) after decades of heavy production – are the second largest in sub-Saharan Africa (BP 2011). Most of Angola's crude is relatively light and sweet, with API gravity from 32 to 40 and sulfur content from 0.12 to 0.14, and is appropriate for processing in major international refineries (IEA 2006b).

Beyond the sheer quantity and the quality of Angolan crude, the geographic sequencing of discovery and production has influenced Sonangol's development. At the time that the company was founded, CABGOC had already been operating in the areas in and off the coast of Cabinda for nearly twenty years, and heavy exploration had also been conducted in the Congo and Kwanza Basin offshore regions (Sonangol Universo 2006, p. 10). By far the most significant deposit in this area is what came to be known as Block 0, a huge collection of fields that has been operated by Gulf Oil and its successor Chevron since the 1950s, with production reaching more than 600,000 bpd in the 2000s (Wood Mackenzie 2002; Bermúdez-Lugo 2004). While not without their technical challenges, these highly endowed, onshore/ shallow water fields presented relatively easy oil for the operators to extract. This combined with the heavy level of surveying that had been done before independence (and the concomitant confidence in the quality of likely discoveries) provided a crucial incentive for Gulf/ Chevron and the other operating partners to return to Angola and remain there (and accept Sonangol majority ownership) during the uncertain early independence period.

As the Angolan oil sector matured, exploration and production expanded further offshore, as technological improvements, promising finds, and increasing investor confidence expanded the country's production horizons. The licensing of rights to shallow water blocks (up to 200 meters) all the way down the Angolan coast began in 1978 and was followed in the 1990s by another round that licensed a roughly parallel row of blocks in deeper waters (Novaes 2006). Interest in these deep water fields was heavy, but production projections truly exploded with the discovery by Elf (now part of Total) of the Girassol field, a 1,400 meter deep deposit in Block 17, about 150 km offshore, with production capacity of 250,000 bpd. Similarly promising finds were made in deep water blocks operated by ExxonMobil and BP. Subsequent licensing rounds have built on this success, attracting substantial interest and massive signature bonuses from major IOCs and NOCs for relinquished portions of existing blocks and license areas that venture further offshore into ultra-deep waters of up to 2,500 meters (Offshore Technology 2005; EIA 2008a).

The timing of the sector's offshore expansion has aided the company's development and the government's ability to exercise its will. The gradual move into more technically challenging deep fields gave the company time to increase its capacity for the more complex oversight that such fields require. The large deep water discoveries of the mid to late 1990s stimulated a much-needed jolt of investment at a time when international weariness with the long war might otherwise have proliferated. And those deep water fields came online one by one beginning with Girassol in 2001, providing an infusion of revenue that fueled the MPLA's consolidation and Sonangol's expansion at the end of the war and the immediate postwar period. This production expansion coincided beginning in 2004 with a worldwide boom in oil prices, deepening its impact on government coffers and the company's reach.

The fact that most of Angola's large oil deposits are offshore also helped the government isolate the industry from violence within the country (only once, in 1993, did UNITA occupy and destroy oil facilities) and limited visible health or environmental impacts on Angolan communities, which minimized the risk of the sort of widespread oil-inspired violence that has beset countries like Nigeria (Clarke 2000, p. 216; Hodges 2004, p. 151).[11]

3 Company strategy and performance

Sonangol has largely succeeded as an agent of the government's goals. It has provided strategic and financial oversight for technical operations led by experienced multinationals, presiding over a sector that has continually expanded amid a long war and various physical and monetary obstacles. In so doing, it has supplied the MPLA elite with the funding to win a war, manage complex patronage networks, and during the postwar oil boom fund large-scale reconstruction. It has served as a tool for international relations and has catalyzed the creation of a network of companies that dominates the Angolan economy.

Sonangol's macro-strategy can be summarized relatively simply. Throughout its history, the company has acted as a *manager* of the oil sector and a *transmitter* of the benefits of production from international partners to the state/ruling elite. Pragmatism has ruled from the company's founding; its leaders have focused on oversight and relationships, not on the brass ring of becoming a traditional integrated company. In a country characterized by poor infrastructure and violence, Sonangol has focused on developing and maintaining relationships of trust and mutual obligations, both between the government and international companies and within the Futungo patrimonial elite. In practice, Sonangol's strategy has focused on playing four roles – and it has succeeded in each.

3.1 Predictable partner for international operators

Once the CNRIP made the broad decision to let IOCs continue to play a dominant technical role in the Angolan sector, Sonangol was charged with generating the standards and predictability that would enable them to function in the country at a high level of productivity. This task was far from simple. As was noted above, Angola's was a communist regime with close ties to the Soviet Union, one

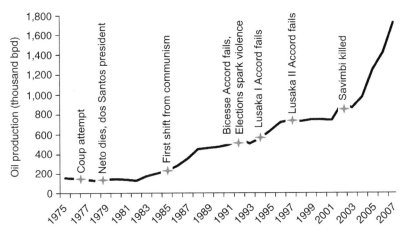

Figure 19.2 Increasing production amid conflict and instability.
Source: Hodges (2004); BP (2008).

whose government the United States was actively trying to unseat through its support of UNITA. Yet throughout the tensest episodes of Cold War geopolitical wrangling, Sonangol maintained close relationships and secured billions of dollars worth of investments in high-risk operations from major Western companies, including US giants Gulf, Chevron, and Texaco. That is why, despite Angola's creaky infrastructure, low administrative capacity, and endemic corruption, IOCs nonetheless have been able to mount highly complex operations at the frontier of deep water (Interview with Gazel 2008; Transparency International 2008).

As Figure 19.2 illustrates, Sonangol and its partners maintained Angolan production levels in the early years of independence despite the departure of Portugal and intra-MPLA shifts. Production expanded steadily throughout the violence-wracked 1980s and 1990s and then increased sharply in the 2000s, as the end of the war, the rise in price levels, and the coming online of the massive deep water fields all coincided. Figure 19.3 illustrates that the sector was largely able to maintain booked reserve levels through most of the conflict and to increase them sharply with the deep water discoveries.

Sonangol has been able to facilitate this steady development by selecting qualified partners and insulating them from the instability

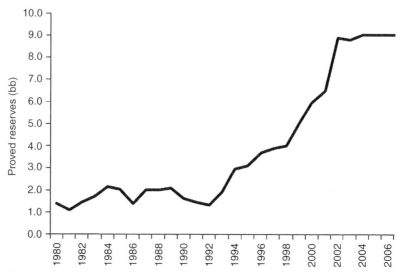

Figure 19.3 Proved reserves.
Source: BP (2008).

and inefficiency that dominates the rest of the economy. The first step in the development of any oil deposit is the selection of operators, and Sonangol is charged with the concessionaire's role of setting block sizes and terms, selecting operating groups, and negotiating formal agreements. The operator-selection process has shifted with the country's needs and opportunities (and with the company's abilities) from sole-source negotiation in the 1970s when the company needed to convince Gulf and others to return to build stability to competitive auctions during the first decade of the 2000s as Sonangol sought to reap the benefits of competition for Angola's much-desired resources.[12]

Though the distribution of rents to political clients of the government has been a key goal for the sector as a whole (and a determining factor in the selection of minority Angolan partners in ownership consortia), Sonangol has not allowed rent seeking to interfere with its commitment to select qualified companies as operators, in large part because the coherent links between the company and the ruling government elite create incentives for Sonangol to maximize the revenue generated by the sector. This has differentiated Sonangol's strategy from the dominant strategy in countries like Nigeria, where exploration and production rights have commonly been awarded as favors to well-connected companies with no technical capabilities.

Beyond Angola's obvious geological advantages, the major reason that Sonangol has been able to attract and hold the interest of capable partners is stability and predictability. The company has been the primary drafter and enforcer of Angola's petroleum legal regime, which has provided predictable mechanisms for the planning of investments and operations, import of goods and equipment, sequencing of payments, conduct of audits, and distribution of physical oil cargos. As will be discussed below, the legal regime features several provisions that provide for a significant portion of the benefits from production to accrue to the government, and disputes over plans and costs are common. But IOC officials who have worked in Angola almost uniformly indicate that Sonangol respects the legal regime and bases arguments within its premises, and they cite the structure that it provides as one of the most important sources of the predictability necessary to make billion-dollar investments. Company officials also mentioned that as Angola prepared a wide-scale revision of the model Production Sharing Agreement and other laws in 2004, consultation with industry officials was frequent and substantive.[13]

Sonangol and IOC officials indicate that the technical skill of top-level Sonangol officials (including board members, operating committee chairs, and the leaders of technical divisions like the Division of Production/DPRO and the Division of Exploration/DEX) is high, which improves the company's ability to anticipate conflicts and manage investments. Although middle managers are sometimes less skilled in the ways of modern oil exploration and production, a young class of technocrats – trained in a variety of fields, with a heavy emphasis on geology, petroleum engineering, and economic and financial management – is rising rapidly within the company.

In effect, Sonangol provides operating companies with a sort of *one-stop shop* that has enabled them to bypass the dysfunction dominating the rest of the Angolan economy.[14] This role includes not only initial facilitation of an investment but also an ongoing role in the operating committee that manages oil projects.[15]

Though Angolan law formally empowers the Ministry of Petroleum (to make concession decisions and oversee operations), Ministry of Finance (to audit revenues and expenditures), and other government agencies, it is rare to hear international oil professionals discuss interactions with any public body other than Sonangol. This arrangement suits external investors well. The 2006 auctions attracted record signature bonuses in excess of $1 billion, and current operators generally express a willingness to pump additional tens of billions into development. As one Western diplomat notes, major world oil companies "are all dying to be here."[16] The enthusiasm derives from a combination of Angola's promising geology and this special, reliable role of Sonangol as the government's agent.

A brief comparison with Nigeria demonstrates the salience of the stable regime that Sonangol has established. Around the same time that Girassol and the other mega-fields were discovered in Angola's deep water in the mid 1990s, discoveries of roughly similar sizes and technical specifications were made off the coast of Nigeria. In Nigeria, as would-be operators were tied up in legal disputes, local companies were unable to meet their technical obligations, and errors and security risks abounded, almost no oil had been produced by the mid 2000s. By contrast Angola, with expert partners and a stable, predictable industry, was able to bring production in its new deep water fields online by the early 2000s and was producing hundreds of thousands of barrels per day by 2005 (McLennan and Williams 2005).

3.2 Steward of the sector charged with maximum delivery of production revenues to the state/ruling elite

To say that Sonangol has created an atmosphere in which private companies have been able to thrive is not equivalent to saying that Angola has given IOCs free rein to allow their priorities to drive sector development. As regulator of Angola's oil industry, Sonangol's interests are different from those of outside investors; it aims to preserve a long production lifespan and ensure that the NOC's key patrons can derive as large a share of the financial benefits as possible without undercutting the incentive for outsiders to invest. One official with extensive experience working closely with Sonangol decision makers describes Sonangol's stewardship priorities as follows:

One thing that's clear is that they are not a commercial company, and we shouldn't expect them to make decisions like a commercial company. They are not there just to make money; they are there to *manage the sector*. Their key goals are both to maximize government revenues from the sector, which is not the same as maximizing the total amount of money it generates,[17] and to use the oil industry as a driver for other industries that can work directly inside, work with, or work completely outside the oil sector.[18]

Sonangol uses two distinct contractual regimes to deliver fiscal benefits to the state. The areas developed in the early stages of the emergence of Angola's oil fields – of which Block 0 is the only significant active area today – are governed by tax-and-royalty concessions. In these fields, Sonangol is a joint venture partner. In Block 0, Sonangol owned 51 percent of the entity as of 1978, and its exploration and production subsidiary has controlled a 41 percent stake (the largest of any of the equity partners) since the concession was renewed in the early 2000s (Sonangol 2007b). In stakes in which it is an equity owner, Sonangol is responsible for meeting its share of costs (though Sonangol costs are commonly carried during exploration) and receives its share of declared dividends.[19]

The second major contractual regime, the production-sharing agreement (PSA), governs all of Angola's major fields except for Block 0 – including all of the deep water offshore blocks that are the frontier for Angola's oil development. PSAs already generate a strong majority of production and of official government revenue from the sector. This share has been increasing in recent years and will represent a growing share of the total in the future as deep water production comes to represent a bigger and bigger portion of Angola's total.[20]

As in all PSA systems, the distinguishing feature of this regime is that most of the country's compensation takes the form of oil that Sonangol receives and sells on international markets, primarily via its trading offices in London, Houston, and Singapore. Sales of this production share represented more than 60 percent of reported PSA revenues in 2008 and more than 70 percent in both 2007 and 2009.[21] To calculate Sonangol's share of oil, the parties first deduct "cost oil" that reimburses expenses incurred in exploration, development, and extraction.[22] The remaining "profit oil" is divided between Sonangol and the operating group according to a progressive rate-of-return-based formula that gives Sonangol a higher share when profits rise. Sonangol's share ranges from as low as 20% (for rates of return under 25%) to 85–90% (for rates of return above 40%) (IMF 2005, p. 9; Wood Mackenzie 2006). Wood Mackenzie asserted in 2006 that Angola's production-sharing formula is one of "the most progressive regimes in the world" and enables Sonangol and the government to capture a heavy share of the benefits in boom times without being confiscatory during periods of low prices or production (Wood Mackenzie 2006).[23] Once the profit oil has been divided and the operating group has sold its share, it pays the government a 50 percent income tax.

As is the case with the tax-and-royalty system governing Block 0, the subsidiary Sonangol Pesquisa e Produção (Sonangol P&P) is an equity partner with 10–20 percent stakes in various PSA operating groups. Sonangol P&P legally owes the government income tax on the earnings it accrues in this role.

Table 19.1 lists the government receipts for recent years, broken down by revenue stream, as reported by the Angolan Ministry of Finance.

The mere existence of government-friendly contractual terms does not, on its own, protect the Angolan state from losing revenue to the profit-maximizing maneuvers of the international partners. Contracts must be monitored, and Sonangol is the lead authority for that activity as well. Although it generally has amicable relationships with its operating partners, several IOCs officials indicate that Sonangol is tougher than its counterparts in other developing-world oil states.[24] Because it has such a central influence on government take in both regimes – in determining the level of profit oil available for sharing under PSAs and in setting deduction levels for PTT and income tax under tax-and-royalty contracts – approval of operating costs is perhaps the most common source of disagreement at the Operating Committee level. Sonangol has to approve operator expenditures in excess of a relatively low threshold and frequently rejects operating group proposals on such issues as the techniques, equipment, or subcontractors selected for technical operations; the deductibility of certain administrative costs; the categorization of expenditures as capex (which favors Sonangol) or opex (which allows operators to deduct more rapidly); and pooling vs. ring-fencing of development areas for cost-recovery purposes.[25]

Beyond cost, Sonangol also sometimes overrides operating-group preference on broader strategic issues facing the sector. One important example of this sort of issue is reservoir management and pace of extraction. Sonangol has hardly been timid about bringing Angola's reserves to production rapidly, but at the margins the company has pushed back on the desires of private partners to pump oil as

Table 19.1. *Reported government receipts*

Year	Barrels exported (m)	Avg. price/ barrel ($/barrel)[a]	Royalties ($m)	Petroleum transactions tax ($m)	Petroleum income tax ($m)	Revenue from sale of Sonangol share of crude ($m)	Total ($m)
2007	433	68	1,503	1,729	6,288	11,774	21,294
2008	588	102	2,026	2,835	13,017	19,244	37,122
2009	657	54	1,335	254	5,154	10,554	17,251

[a] The spreadsheet available on the Ministry of Finance's website as of March 14, 2010, does not provide an average 2007 price for one of the country's minor blocks (which exported fewer than 5 million barrels), and therefore does not provide a total weighted average. The figure listed here for 2007 is thus based on the author's calculations from all of the other blocks, for which an average price is included in the government data.

Source: Ministério das Finanças de Angola (2007, 2008, 2009); author's calculations.

rapidly as possible – especially in times of high prices – which reflects Sonangol's longer time horizon. The company occasionally rejects plans that it believes would risk sacrificing field life or total production potential.[26]

Sonangol's regulatory style is variable. When the company has a different perspective on a management issue than its partners, block chairmen sometimes reject a proposal outright or directly mandate a particular option. At other times, though, they engage in what one Angolan IOC employee calls "organized disorganization" – the strategic delaying of approvals and sending of contradictory signals that box operating partners into a corner and slow the process of operational development.[27] Sonangol officials have also benefited from the fact that staffs at IOCs turn over frequently, while important Sonangol officials often remain in place for decades. "Sometimes, an informal arrangement that has held between Sonangol and a particular member of an IOC staff is dropped, either when that individual is replaced by someone else or even with that individual himself," says an IOC employee. "All of a sudden they'll take an arrangement that both parties know has been going on and say 'where's your letter of approval for that' and they'll no longer allow it. Everything is in writing, and where there is this informal room to maneuver, it will sometimes disappear as quickly as it arrived."[28] IOCs also believe that Sonangol exploits its sector-wide role by seeking to establish management precedents with whichever IOCs is perceived as weakest at a given moment and then apply them to relationships with all companies across the sector.[29] In effect, it ratchets the behavior of the IOCs, which it treats as contractors, toward ever-higher yields for Angola.

One additional core component of Sonangol's ability to deliver a sizable share of oil revenue to the Futungo elite, according to many industry participants and observers, is that the incidence of petty corruption within the company is relatively low, for reasons discussed in more detail in section 4.[30] This contrasts sharply with the endemic problems of employee corruption in many NOCs – notably Nigeria's NNPC.

3.3 Nexus of the ancillary oil economy

In addition to Sonangol's role in managing the oil sector and channeling rents to the Angolan state and Futungo clients, the company is also the key catalyst for an indigenous class of private businesses. Through this "Angolanization" policy, Sonangol directs outside investors to funnel contracts into a vast network of Sonangol affiliates and private Angolan companies while also integrating Angolan professionals into the oil-industry workforce.

The priority accorded to Angolanization comes from two distinct-but-related goals. The first is the development of an indigenous private sector and technocratic class. The civil war and communist economic mismanagement prevented a strong Angolan private sector from developing in the post-independence era. Thus Angola is one of the world's most oil-dependent economies, with oil accounting for approximately 50 percent of GDP and 90 percent of exports (Bellos 2008). The government seeks to use the oil industry, which other than diamonds has been one of the only attractive areas for outside investors, to give Angolan businesses access to capital and to give both businesses and individuals opportunities to gain valuable experience working on technically and managerially challenging projects along-side capable international partners. Aware that oil is a finite resource, the government seeks to use it as a mechanism to stimulate broader capacity building that, in time, could minimize the need for foreign contractors within the oil industry and create a stronger entrepreneurial and technical base for the expansion of the indigenous non-oil economy (Soares de Oliveira 2007a, pp. 605–606; Sonangol Universo 2007; Bellos 2008; Interview with Mangueira 2008).

The second commonly cited motivation behind the focus on local content is that it serves as a means of distributing oil rents among the key clients that the government must placate to keep its hold on power. This logic tracks closely with the analysis in Chapter 2, which explores how national goals arise, first and foremost, from leaders' desires to stay in power. Access to valuable oil contracts and jobs can be tremendously lucrative, and the process for the selection of local partners is not nearly as competitive or transparent as the auctions to select international operators – because Sonangol, in particular, benefits from transparency and competition in its international transactions yet favors exactly the opposite when doling out benefits at home. Almost all of the partners and key officials within companies selected to work in the industry have close personal ties with important figures within Sonangol and the Futungo elite. The Angolan private sector is small and exclusive, which makes it easy for Sonangol to channel benefits that placate key political

Box 19.1 Some key Sonangol subsidiaries and joint ventures

Core oil development and marketing

Sonangol Pesquisa e Produção (P&P) – exploration and production

Sonangol Ltd., Sonusa, and Sonangol Asia – trading offices in London, Houston, and Singapore

Sonangol Distribuidora – downstream unit, including domestic gas stations

Sonamet and Petromar – construction of offshore platforms and other equipment

Sonagas – development and distribution of natural gas

Sonawest – seismic data survey and analysis

Non-core subsidiaries

Sonangol Logística, SONILS, Sonangol Shipping, Sonasurf, and Sonatide – logistical support and other technical services

ESSA – training for oil operations

Mercury Telcom – fixed-line and mobile telephone and internet

SonAir – domestic and international air transportation

AAA – insurance and risk management

supporters and enrich the ruling elite. (Africa Energy Intelligence 2002, 2006, 2007; Hodges 2004, pp. 142–148; Soares de Oliveira 2007a, pp. 608–609; Global Witness 2010).[31]

The particular patronage strategies vary with circumstances. During the war, education and access to employment represented particularly important tools. "From 1997 to 2001, overseas scholarships (almost all of which were given to the children of politically connected families, and many of which were for engineering or other technical degrees involved in oil production) accounted, on average, for 18 percent of total government expenditure on education, more than was spent within the country on technical education (*ensino médio*) and higher education combined" (Hodges 2004, p. 46).[32] After the war the strategies have included many other local components, with special attention devoted to elite-run Angolan oil companies being given rights to participate in operating groups and to contracting for goods and services.

One of Sonangol's tools for managing the ancillary oil economy is its network of subsidiaries. Since 1991, Sonangol has been structured as a holding company in which subsidiaries exist as independent units whose managers "report directly" to the Sonangol Administrative Council (Sonangol 2008a). Sonangol has also entered into a number of joint ventures with foreign companies that supply technical or managerial know-how or access to capital. Sonangol states that its total number of subsidiaries and joint ventures reaches "more than thirty," but the total number of joint ventures is not publicly available and "some estimates are as high as sixty" (Soares de Oliveira 2007a, pp. 603–604; Sonangol 2008b). As the most technically competent organization in the country, Sonangol is seen by the government as the most appropriate manager of these important companies.

Many of the subsidiaries and joint ventures perform services traditionally associated with the integrated oil industry. One of the most high profile of these is Sonangol Pesquisa e Produção (Sonangol P&P), the exploration and production subsidiary. P&P is the largest shareholder in Block 0 (though Chevron remains the operator), a minority equity shareholder in many other operating groups (as well as concessions in Gabon and Equatorial Guinea), and the operator of five onshore/shallow water blocks in Angola.[33] Within Angolan fields, as an equity partner P&P participates in operating group meetings on such issues as planning, expenses, and operations – a role that company officials hope will help P&P build its ambitions to become a larger oil producer. Several other participants in the operating groups have indicated that P&P's priorities in decision-making processes usually track with those of the other equity partners, which is consistent with its role as a profit-sharing participant in the venture. At times, however, conflicts arise between P&P and its parent company. Officials involved in the process say that whatever P&P representatives may say in closed-door contractor group meetings, they never offer firm challenges to the final directives issued by the block chairmen or other parent-company officials.[34]

Besides P&P, Sonangol subsidiaries that help manage Sonangol's core goals include the overseas offices responsible for marketing the company's share of Angolan crude; the supervisor of the country's natural gas industry (Sonagas), which is managing an expanding portfolio of activities including the construction of a multi-billion dollar LNG plant for associated gas (in partnership with Chevron, BP, Total, and Eni); the downstream body responsible for the company's domestic market sales (Sonangol Distruibuidora); and various companies that provide such services to operating oil companies as platform construction (Sonamet, Petromar), logistical support (Sonangol Logistica), shipping (Sonangol Shipping), and seismic data analysis (Sonawest).

Still other subsidiaries drift from the core competency of an oil company, yet reflect Sonangol's broader political and economic roles in Angola. Sonair is a domestic airline and also operates the *Houston Express*, a direct Houston-to-Luanda flight (in collaboration with US-based World Airways), which has become the preferred means of travel to Angola for many US oil companies and diplomats. AAA is a risk management company that initially focused on insurance for the oil industry but has recently expanded to cover other financial sectors as well. Mercury Telcom is a telecommunications company that provides telephone and internet connections to the oil industry and throughout Angola. By most accounts these non-core subsidiaries remain at relatively early levels of development.

Beyond the companies formally incorporated under the umbrella of Sonangol holding, the company maintains a host of informal ties to other Angolan businesses that it helps nourish with opportunities. Most prominent are the Angolan oil companies that are minor equity partners in operating groups, many of which are led or advised by former Sonangol officials. Sonangol awards these shares through a concession process that it manages. Most of these companies are owned by important figures within the Angolan state. Falcon Oil, for example, which has a 10 percent stake in Block 6, and 5 percent holdings in various deep water blocks, is owned by Antonio "Mosquito" Mbakassi, an Angolan businessman believed to have close ties to the family of President dos Santos. Grupo Gema, with 5 percent ownership of block 10/06, is run by several officials who have worked closely with the president, including the former secretary general of his office. The international NGO Global Witness reports that Sociedade de Hidrocarbonetos de Angola, prequalified in late 2007 to bid in oil auctions, included among its shareholders individuals "with the same names" as Sonangol Chairman Vicente, then Minister of Finance Jose Pedro de Morais, and other top government officials. Other companies with ownership interests, including Initial Oil and Somoil, are run by former Sonangol executives (Africa Energy Intelligence 2006; Global

Witness 2009). In addition to the equity participation of Angolan oil companies, IOC officials suggest that Sonangol has also increasingly encouraged them to sign service contracts for a variety of technical, administrative, and equipment needs with particular Angolan providers.[35] By awarding equity participation rights to these well-connected companies, Sonangol is able to bolster the state's patronage networks under the umbrella of local industry development.

Local content and local staffing are important goals of most NOCs that work with international partners, but most international officials who work in Angola indicate that Sonangol is tougher about local content and places more emphasis on it than counterpart companies in other countries. The Petroleum Activities Law dictates that operating groups must procure goods and services from Angolan providers if they are "of the same or approximately the same quality" as is available on international markets and "no more than ten percent" more expensive (Article 27). But in reality, the operating committees and other technical units of Sonangol push operating companies to contract locally at far higher thresholds. In the words of one IOC executive: "They will accept very significant overcosts to ensure the growth of these local contractors. They do it up to a limit that we as IOCs may think is too far. We are perfectly happy to go 10 percent over and even to go a little bit beyond that, but we don't plan on going 50 percent over. But Sonangol will push us to the limit."[36]

Some international partners view this insistence on local content and staffing as an example of Sonangol's inefficiency. In fact, these rules are the result of Sonangol's strategic effort to satisfy the will of its principal – the Angolan state and ruling families. Current and past Sonangol officials say that the government hopes that higher short-term costs for contracting groups (and, therefore, for the government, via cost recovery) will result in longer-term gains as local costs decline and as the economy diversifies.[37] Private operating partners may never benefit from these improvements, which may accrue after they have departed Angola, but the MPLA, which expects to be in power for the long haul, might.

3.4 A state within the state: quasi-sovereign responsibilities

Sonangol's final central role lies in the provision of services that traditionally would be considered to fall under the ambit of the sovereign government. As the most well-respected and best-organized unit in a war-torn country best known for violence, communist policies, and corruption, Sonangol has frequently stepped in at the state's behest. It is the agent for Angola (or its ruling elite) on issues extending far beyond the management of the oil industry, including sovereign debt negotiation and servicing, international relations, wealth management/investment, and various forms of extra-budgetary expenditure that advanced the war effort and the development agenda of President dos Santos and his inner circle. Sonangol's skill has been in performing these regime-stabilizing roles without letting them interfere with sectoral performance and the generation of revenue.

During the war, Sonangol directed money to the government not just through taxes, signature bonuses, and crude sales but by serving as the negotiator and servicer of oil-backed loans.[38] The government's history of defaulting on credit and the perceived risks of theft and mismanagement within the public sector meant that the state faced severe difficulties in accessing credit from private banks, sovereign lenders, and international financial institutions (IFIs). Sonangol, on the other hand, has never defaulted on a loan, and, as a representative of one of the company's overseas trading offices put it, "that gives banks great comfort."[39] Sonangol negotiated the loans (primarily with international banks), which were channeled to government accounts in Angola and abroad. Angola's oil deposits served as collateral, and Sonangol repaid the loans with the delivery of oil shipments to international trading companies that channeled the proceeds into offshore accounts – a routing designed to bolster confidence of the state's creditors. While their maturity was short in duration and the loans required a risk premium, these funds provided a source of large-scale cash infusions that enabled the government to use its long-term oil prospects to fuel short-term spending. Beyond the negotiation, Sonangol has been responsible for much of the day-to-day management of these loan accounts, primarily via its offshore trading subsidiaries (Hodges 2004, pp. 162–164; Reno 2000, p. 225).

Sonangol has served as a key actor in Angola's oil-based international diplomacy. The Angolan government has devoted particular attention over the course of its post-independence history to managing a complex web of commercial and political relationships with governments as varied as Cuba, Nigeria, and the United States. Heaviest attention has been paid in recent years to Angola's multifaceted relationship with

China. Angola has fluctuated between being the biggest and third-biggest supplier of crude oil to China in the past few years. The Chinese government provided Angola with a massive line of credit (reportedly upwards of $11 billion) to finance infrastructure reconstruction. Chinese construction companies have arrived in Angola en masse, the respective governments have formed various official cooperation agreements, other economic ties between the countries have expanded significantly, and the number of Chinese nationals working in Angola has reached almost 50,000. Sonangol has performed several functions in the cultivation of this relationship. Much of the line of credit is oil-backed, so the company is responsible for servicing repayments to China Exim Bank and other entities, in the basic manner described above. Sonangol partnered with Chinese NOC Sinopec and investment company Beiya (now Dayuan) International Development Limited to form Sonangol Sinopec International (SSI), a joint venture that paid a record signature bonus of more than $1 billion for a non-operating 40 percent stake in relinquished areas of the deep water block 18/06 and also controls non-operating stakes ranging from 20 percent to 50 percent in four other Angolan blocks (Vines *et al.* 2009).

In its role as concessionaire, Sonangol was responsible for granting SSI these shares. Most of them were awarded in competitive auctions, though SSI received its 50 percent share in a BP-operated area of Block 18 when Sonangol stepped in to prevent a pending sale of the interest from the previous holder (Shell) to ONGC and directed that the sale be made to SSI instead. Sonangol and Sinopec also engaged in intense negotiations for the construction of a 240,000 bpd refinery in Lobito, a key national development priority, but talks ultimately collapsed (Esau 2006c; Vines *et al.* 2009).

Sonangol also plays an important role in Angola's outreach to other African countries, frequently serving as an advisor to current and would-be allies on the development of nascent petroleum sectors. Among other places, the company has activities in Sao Tome, Cape Verde, Nigeria, Gabon, and Tanzania (Vines *et al.* 2009). These African enterprises serve to bolster Angola's influence across the continent. The company's relationship with Chinese actors has contributed to this African oil diplomacy. In 2009, China Sonangol (30 percent owned by Sonangol, with Sonangol President Vicente on the board of directors) signed agreements for oil acreage with the embattled governments of Guinea and Zimbabwe, deals that were linked to multibillion-dollar minerals-for-infrastructure contracts between these governments and China International Fund, a Hong Kong-based company that has been active in Angola and has close ties to the leadership of both Sonangol and Beiya (Africa Energy Intelligence 2009a, 2009b, 2009c; Oster 2009; Vines *et al.* 2009). The partnership in these troubled African states suggests that Sonangol and its Chinese partners see a comparative advantage in combining expertise in oil management with a willingness to invest heavily in governments that lack broad international support.

Sonangol controls one of the biggest collections of financial assets of any Angolan public body, and with this decade's oil boom it has become a significant investor in assets and companies, both in Angola and overseas. Many of the company's major overseas investments are in the energy sector – it owns 33.4% of Portuguese oil company Galp Energia, a 20% stake in the Gulf LNG Energy of Mississippi, 25% of the interest of Cobalt International Energy in eleven deep water leases in the Gulf of Mexico, and 20% of the Abidjan refinery in Ivory Coast.

Sonangol has also become increasingly invested in banks, acquiring a 49 percent stake in the Angolan affiliate of Portugal's largest listed bank, Millennium BCP in 2008. As of late 2008, the company was believed to be considering the acquisition of additional stakes within a Portuguese banking industry reeling from the global financial crisis, and it continues to seek to broaden its portfolio within the Angolan financial sector (Africa Energy Intelligence 2008; Vicente 2008). Sonangol's investment strategy does not follow the same independent structure as a sovereign wealth fund; rather than simply building a pool of stable financial assets, the company's investment decisions are clearly aimed at affecting the economic health of key Angolan economic sectors.[40] Detailed tracking of the performance of the companies in which Sonangol is investing will be required over time in order to assess whether the company will be as successful in its portfolio strategy as it has been in its other activities.

Like many NOCs, Sonangol is also called upon by the government to provide fuel to domestic consumers at a significantly subsidized rate. This represents a major expenditure and an instance in which the company sacrifices its financial bottom line in order to satisfy political imperatives of the government. The costs of subsidies are growing as domestic consumption expands – a 2010 World Bank report indicates that they represent 4–5 percent of GDP (Hansen-Shino and Soares de Oliveira 2010).

Beyond all of these formal tasks undertaken on the state's behalf, Sonangol has throughout its history served as a convenient vehicle by which the MPLA can avoid the scrutiny given to official government actions. This is particularly evident in the war effort and in the Sonangol-managed patronage scheme – both of which operate off the formal books. Arms purchases represented a recurring type of such activity. As a result of the so-called "Angolagate" scandal, several French government officials and prominent French businessmen (including the son of former French president François Mitterand) were tried and convicted for their roles in supplying Angola with hundreds of millions of dollars worth of weaponry from 1993 to 1998, in violation of a UN embargo. Sonangol was a key player in the deal, allegedly servicing the "loan" via a steady stream of oil payments (Reno 2000, pp. 228–229; Roque 2008). When the negotiations for the deal began, a resurgent UNITA had occupied 70 percent of the Angolan territory, and the MPLA was desperate to get around international sanctions and replenish its war machine.

The Angolagate transactions do not appear to have been unique; Sonangol, it appears, supported other arms purchases via oil payments as well as by awarding concession stakes to companies with links to arms traders (Reno 2000, p. 228; Hodges 2004, p. 161).[41] In 1999, Human Rights Watch quoted the Angolan foreign minister as stating publicly that signature bonus payments made by BP, Amoco, Elf, and Exxon were directly earmarked for the "war effort" (Human Rights Watch 1999).

The non-reported expenditures that Sonangol incurred on the government's behalf – including those for loan servicing, subsidies, arms payments, and other patronage-based activities – were estimated by KPMG's Oil Diagnostic to total $2.1 billion in the year 2000 (Human Rights Watch 2004). A later analysis indicated that in 2005, the total amount of extra-budgetary spending (including debt relief) under the charge of the company was more than $3 billion (World Learning 2006, p. 11). This is not to say that there is no internal accounting of the expenditures that Sonangol undertakes on the government's behalf. Since at least 2002, the company and the Ministry of Finance have engaged in informal arrangements whereby Sonangol deducts such expenditures from the taxes it owes to the government under

Angolan law (World Bank 2005a, pp. 72–74; Interview with Gaspar 2006).

4 Driving factors of Sonangol's performance

There are several reasons why Sonangol has exceeded common expectations of what an NOC in a weak and war-torn country could accomplish, achieving most of the goals set out for it by the government – guiding the efficient expansion of the sector, funneling large shares of the revenue into government accounts, stimulating the ancillary oil economy, supporting the war effort, providing a ready and able tool for the maintenance of patronage systems, and earning the respect of its private partners and foreign governments alike. Angola's geology has played a central role, but four other factors have also been important.

4.1 State–company leadership solidarity

From its earliest days, the leaders of the company and the government leaders at Futungo have enjoyed a relationship of intense trust, forged in the wartime mentality of the early post-independence years and their strong ethno-familial ties.

Sonangol was born into a state of emergency, and its success in protecting and expanding the value of Angola's oil fields was seen as integral to the very survival of the MPLA regime against its domestic and international opponents. The key figures of the CNRIP – which soon morphed into Sonangol itself – had strong identity-based affiliations with President Neto and other leaders; they shared a part-ideological, part-self-interested passion for the role that the MPLA elite should play in the new Angola (Soares de Oliveira 2007a, pp. 598–601). Political decisions were made with a wartime orientation; speed and decisiveness were prized, and consultation was restricted to a small group of trusted advisors. Once the decision was made to vest broad authority over the oil sector in the company, there became effectively no separation between the Sonangol vision and the broader strategy for sector and economic management that the government and ruling families espoused.

Sonangol's founders came from the same background as the presidential inner circle: "the exceedingly small, late colonial world of Luanda-based, mostly mixed-race educated Angolans" (Soares de

Oliveira 2007a, p. 601). The company's first CEO – Percy Freudenthal – was white, but all three of the men who have led Sonangol after he stepped down (a move that Angola analyst Ricardo Soares de Oliveira suggests was precipitated by concerns about his race) have been from the Angolan creole class that dominates the political elite.

As Angolan history has progressed, the elite has used the oil industry to tighten its grip on power and intensify its domination of the economy. Between 1990 and 2000, for example, a study by the Angolan National Statistical Institute reported that the monthly expenditure of the wealthiest 10 percent of Angolans went from nine to twenty-seven times that of the poorest 10 percent. Many believe that the growth of this wealthiest decile is in fact driven by a tiny segment constituting the dominant creole families (Hodges 2004, p. 41). The fact that the in-group is so small also makes it easier to control and limits the risk of individualistic corruption that disrupts the collective purpose (Reno 2000, p. 225).

In contrast with some other NOCs in this book, Sonangol's leadership is stable. It has had just four CEOs in thirty-two years, which helps cement political and social ties between Sonangol and governmental elites. Most observers of the Angolan oil industry indicate that current CEO Manuel Vicente has a direct line of communication with the president and that the two consult frequently on a wide range of issues and share common interests and an intersecting vision for the industry. As one Angolan civil society representative put it, "I cannot imagine Sonangol as being different from the president or envision a scenario in which Sonangol could disagree with the president" (Interview with Calundungo 2006). In short, the company is managed by individuals who have a uniquely well-informed perspective on its principal's needs and who are steeped in its trust.

4.2 Regulatory structure: significant independence on technical and commercial decisions

The strongest evidence of the trust that Sonangol has built with its masters in the government is the wide degree of discretion the company has on technical and management issues. The head of Sonangol formally reports to the Ministry of Petroleum, but in reality Sonangol has always been given tremendous latitude to make all key decisions regarding the sector, including whom to partner with, how to divide and develop fields, and how to promote local economic development (Clarke 2000, pp. 200–201). The international partners interact directly with Sonangol, not the ministry, and Sonangol executives often skip the ministry on their way straight to the presidency for discussions on key political issues.

By vesting Sonangol simultaneously with the roles of oil company and de facto regulator, Angola has gone against conventional international wisdom, which suggests that a strong independent regulator is necessary to maintain efficiency within an NOC.[42] The fathers of the post-independence Angolan oil industry decided early on that the country's physical and human-resource challenges meant it would be virtually impossible to simultaneously vest two bodies with the skills necessary to manage an industry effectively, so they elected to direct all capacity to Sonangol. Angola's parliament was also extremely weak, and through most of the war period other government ministries lacked the knowledge or the political clout to challenge Sonangol's positions on the sector. By bypassing formal bureaucratic control by political bodies and relying upon the informal control mechanisms of the Sonangol–Futungo social network, the state has been able to avoid battles about technical policy or budgeting and the pull of competing interest groups, and Sonangol has been able to act with one voice.

4.3 *Commitment to education and capacity development*

The level of independence given to company leaders might have had disastrous consequences for Sonangol were it not for the company's substantial investment in human capital and professional management. The company's founders recognized at independence that they lacked the skilled cadre of professionals necessary to oversee the industry effectively and immediately began sending wave after wave of Angola's brightest students overseas to study the industry – at first with partners Eni, Sonatrach, and Petrobras; later in Western universities and among the full range of the government's other IOC partners (Soares de Oliveira 2007a). Today, Sonangol still lacks the staff depth of the IOCs and cannot match the expertise of top-tier NOCs such as Petrobras or Statoil. However, it has invested in an ever-expanding pool of geologists, engineers, economists, and financial managers who enable it to engage in well-informed oversight of its international partners and to make long-range strategic plans and investment decisions.

Again, the special relationships between the company and the government have aided this effort to build a highly competent staff. Like many NOCs, Sonangol hires personnel outside of the confines of the formal civil service structure and is able to pay its employees significantly more than ordinary government workers.[43] Sonangol has long recruited talented students from a young age, providing scholarships to those who score highest on standardized tests.[44] These two factors, and the privileged position accorded to the company within the Angolan political system and economy, made Sonangol overwhelmingly the most appealing public sector body in Angola for years.[45] (To be sure, some patronage is also involved in these positions – according to one company employee, for example, Sonangol is pressured to supply scholarships and jobs to the underqualified children of privileged elites.) Despite these challenges, the company's partners say that the steady rise of the company's skills has been undeniable. Alongside that higher competence has come a much higher level of assertiveness. In the words of one IOC official who had a stint in Angola in the 1990s before returning during the past few years, "Ten years ago, we almost never had a situation where Sonangol would disagree with something we proposed. Now, as their management is getting stronger, it's become much more commonplace. Once you have been brave once in rejecting something, it is much easier to be brave a second time."

4.4 Pragmatic reliance on international partners and insulation of operator selection from political patronage

Given the turmoil that engulfed Angola from 1975 to 2002, and the early government's Marxist-Leninist leanings and Iron Curtain alliances, the stability of Sonangol's relationships with private IOCs and leading operational NOCs has been remarkable. The company and its principals decided at the beginning that, given Angola's limitations, the best way for them to have access to the largest, most predictable possible revenue stream was to cast aside ideological and political baggage and rely instead on well-established international companies to find and produce the country's oil. And as Sonangol has managed the sector, it has separated the essential need to support the Futungo's patronage network from its choice of operators and its commitment to maximize revenue from production. It has been consistent in awarding *operating stakes* only to companies qualified to do the work effectively.[46]

Beyond its reliance on Western oil companies, Sonangol has also utilized a network of international consultants on legal, financial, and management matters, which have helped it build a state of the art institutional framework that promotes government interests while preserving profitability for private partners. As such, though Sonangol remains a proud NOC with a dominant role in a post-conflict society, its pragmatic approach to core business has enabled Angola to develop an oil sector into which actors with high international standards can easily adapt.

5 Conclusion: continued evolution and upcoming challenges

Though this chapter does not seek to predict the future or make recommendations about looming management decisions, it bears mentioning briefly that Sonangol continues to evolve, as does the environment in which it operates, and that principal and agent face various challenges as they seek to maintain the company's role as a key vehicle for the government's long-term plans.

Perhaps the most significant challenge lies in the historic volatility of the oil industry, as illustrated by sharp price declines that accompanied the global economic downturn of 2008 and 2009. The government's postwar spending boom came during a time of record high oil prices, and a sustained period of low prices would force it to adjust its ambitious spending plans. Lower oil prices would magnify the financial pain for the Angolan state because not only would gross revenues be smaller but the progressive PSA system would result in a higher percentage of revenues being devoted to cost recovery and partner profits. This could result in additional pressures on Sonangol to deliver money to the state or key clients via other means, which could create pressures for policies that could scare foreign investors or undermine the long-term efficiency and development of the oil sector. Lower long-term oil prices would also change the economic attractiveness of deep water and ultra-deep water fields, which could make it harder for the company to attract sharply pro-government terms in its auctions for new blocks. As world oil prices fell in late 2008 and early 2009, the government's revenue from the sector dropped significantly, from a reported total of $37 billion in 2008 to $17 billion in 2009 (Ministério das Finanças 2008, 2009). A scheduled bid round for ultra-deep water blocks was repeatedly delayed, amid complaints by some IOCs that the terms are not sufficiently appealing for private actors.[47] Oil prices rebounded substantially in 2009 but did not approach the peaks seen before the onset of the global financial crisis, and the dip served as a stern reminder of the fragility of the Angolan economic boom.

A second challenge is Sonangol's role within the ruling Futungo coalition, which may be shifting as other government agencies increase their capacity. Several industry observers and participants suggest that the Ministry of Finance began playing a particularly assertive role within the Futungo in the latter half of the first decade of the 2000s, as its leaders garnered praise inside and outside of Angola for improving the country's macroeconomic standing and increasing the transparency of its finances (including through the publication of monthly oil receipts). Various IOC officials indicate that the Ministry of Finance has begun questioning their costs much more vigorously as part of its verification of their tax payments – a role that was previously left almost exclusively to Sonangol.[48] As one notes, "Sonangol used to be first among equals [within the government], but now MinFin is encroaching on what was Sonangol's exclusive territory." Other reports suggest that the ministry is pushing Sonangol to make more information about its operations and finances public (UNDP 2008, pp. 14–15).

The empowerment of other government bodies vis-à-vis the company will hardly be inexorable or total – a 2008 post-election cabinet shake-up, for example, left it uncertain whether the Ministry of Finance would continue to grow in influence or would begin to recede into the background. But as the postwar Angolan state continues to evolve and the government makes efforts to build capacity beyond the company, it may not enjoy the unparalleled internal power that has been the norm throughout its history. Various reports suggest that the government has a long-term plan to transfer many of Sonangol's duties in the award of licenses back to a more competent and powerful Ministry of Petroleum and to have Sonangol focus on its "core activities" (including an ever-growing Sonangol P&P) and spin off its more distant subsidiaries. Few observers expect these changes to occur in the short term or for the company to cede all of its power over the granting of concessions or the monitoring of partner operations (UNDP 2008, pp. 15–16).

For its part, Sonangol plans to continue its long-term investment in becoming a modern company with broad exposure in international financial and energy markets. The company has announced plans to list some shares on the New York and Johannesburg stock exchanges, though the originally announced 2010 date (Vicente 2008) was not met. It is expected that Sonangol or some of its subsidiaries may be placed among the first businesses traded upon the long-anticipated opening of the Luanda stock exchange. This move toward diversifying the company and making it more open and internationally competitive is being pushed not only by some of its top executives but also by the young generation of technocrats, largely trained in Western universities and companies.[49]

Sonangol continues to seek to become a major player in global oil markets, with a massive increase in high-profile international projects at the end of the 2000s. Perhaps the most dramatic example has been the company's engagement in the effort to reinvigorate production in Iraq. In late 2009, Sonangol won an auction to develop two Iraqi fields, with a targeted total production of more than 200,000 bpd. The fields are located in some of Iraq's most violence-prone regions, suggesting that the company may see a comparative advantage in managing projects amid violence and political tension, where the company's experience of partnering successfully to develop oil amidst political uncertainty will be valuable. Details of the management of the Iraqi fields have not been publicized as of the writing of this chapter, but a statement by the company in early 2010 suggests that it will retain its pragmatic focus in Iraq, by "work[ing] in partnership with foreign companies to explore the reserves" (Sonangol Universo 2010, p. 33).

In addition to its activities in Iraq, the company was reported in late 2009 to be closing in on a deal to develop three oil blocks in Ecuador (Emery 2009) and to be close to a deal to become the leading shareholder in a Brazilian company that owns eleven oil blocks there (Africa Energy Intelligence 2010a). China Sonangol acquired a 4 percent stake in Indonesia's massive Cepu gas field in 2009 (Africa Energy Intelligence 2010b). The company also continues to expand its activity and influence throughout Africa, particularly in frontier states and areas of new activity, with recent investments reported in Guinea, Cote d'Ivoire, Zimbabwe, and the Democratic Republic of Congo, in addition to its long-standing interests elsewhere on the continent.

Sonangol's development into a diversified international company with interests on five continents is the most powerful indicator of the company's dramatic evolution from a tiny outfit in an ostracized state to a powerful global player. In light of the close relationship that the company has always enjoyed with the government, there is reason to believe that these developments represent just the latest step in Sonangol's development as an effective agent of a stronger postwar Angolan government. The company is moving beyond its original role as a closed, narrowly focused manager of the country's oil patrimony into a new life as a modern, market-oriented company that provides funds and security to the state in the context of a broader economic mission. But given that Sonangol's success to date has been based primarily on its tight solidarity with the ruling elite and its limited, pragmatic focus, such an evolution will introduce new challenges into the principal–agent relationship, and the government will have to continue to work to promote the regime's preferred balance of commercial, fiscal, and political concerns.

Notes

I am grateful for the extensive support provided by David Hults, David Victor, Mark Thurber, and Peter Nolan at PESD and by Ricardo Soares de Oliveira, Alex Vines, Indira Campos, Matt Genasci, Juan Carlos Quiroz, and Antoine Heuty. He also wishes to thank the current and former officials of Sonangol, IOCs active in Angola, the Angolan government, Angolan civil society, and international governments and agencies, who were generous with their time and upon whose insights many of the conclusions drawn in this chapter are based. Because of the sensitive nature of the company's role in the Angolan system, many of my interviews were conducted on a not-for-attribution basis. Citations to these individuals in this paper thus note that a particular conclusion was drawn from an interview but do not identify the individual source. The interviews conducted include: Sergio Calundungo (Angola Country Representative, Intermón Oxfam), August 2006, Luanda; Manuel Calunga (DFID), August 2006 and August 2008; Hermenegildo Gaspar (Consultant to Ministry of Finance and former Director Nacional, Ministerio das Finanças, Direcção Nacional de Impostos), August 2006, Luanda; Ricardo Gazel (World Bank), August 2008, Luanda; Tako Koning (Tullow Oil), August 2006, Luanda; Antonio Mangueira (IOG Exploration and former Sonangol official), August 2008, Luanda; Ricardo Soares de Oliveira (Oxford), April 2008, Washington; multiple representatives from various IOCs, August 2006 and August 2008,

Luanda and various international locations; multiple representatives from
international diplomatic missions and international organizations, August
2006 and August 2008, Luanda; multiple representatives from Sonangol
and current and former Angolan government officials, August 2006, March
2008, and August 2008, Luanda and international locations.

1 According to a 2008 statement by Sonangol CEO Manuel Vicente, the
   company employs approximately 8,200 people (Vicente 2008).
2 Though most African NOCs did not try to become fully integrated oil
   companies, many lacked Sonangol's pragmatism and tried to bite off
   larger mandates than they could handle. Examples include Nigeria's
   NNPC and Congo Hydro, which adopted wide swaths of responsibilities and were unable to develop capacity in a targeted way (Chapter 16;
   Soares de Oliveira 2007b).
3 Among the sources that offer more detailed assessments of the impact
   of Angolan government policies are Hodges (2004); Chabal and Vidal
   (2008); and Messiant (2008b).
4 Discussion of the independence movement and the civil war draws
   heavily from several sources, most notably Maier (1996); Guimarães
   (1998); Hodges (2004); Messiant (2008a); Soares de Oliveira (2007a).
5 China also supported UNITA during the 1980s and only established
   relations with the MPLA government in 1983.
6 According to the BP Statistical Review of World Energy June 2009 (BP
   2009a), Angola's oil production went from 13,000 barrels per day in
   1965 to 103,000 bpd in 1970 to 173,000 bpd in 1975.
7 This remains true in the company's formal structure today. The company's Articles of Incorporation, last revised by Decree-Law Number
   19/99 of 1999, dictate that "the guardianship of the activities of
   Sonangol ... accrues to the Ministry of Petroleum."
8 Sonangol's formal authority was further increased in 1978, when rene-
   gotiations with CABGOC and a broad reform of the country's petroleum legal regime gave Sonangol a 51 percent ownership stake in the
   operating fields, vested it with the role of concessionaire in charge of
   the granting of rights over new acreage, and divided the Angolan continental shelf into thirteen blocks that would serve as the basis for the
   large-scale expansion of Sonangol's reach and revenue in the years to
   come (Novaes 2006).
9 Amid the global financial crisis and declines in oil price and production, GDP grew only 2.4 percent in 2009, a dramatic break from the
   postwar boom period (IMF 2011). The risks associated with Angola's
   dependence on volatile oil revenues are discussed in section 5.
10 The plan initially announced was for the 2008 legislative elections to be
   followed the next year by a presidential poll, but as of the finalization

of this chapter in 2011 these plans had been stalled and no presidential election was imminent.

11 Cabinda – the site of Angola's only major onshore production and the operations center for companies extracting in Block 0 and other shallow water fields – has represented a meaningful exception to this general phenomenon. Frustrated by the province's poverty (Cabindans argue that it ranks among the lowest of Angola's provinces in various key human development issues) amid the wealth generated by its oil fields and by the environmental impact of the industry, FLEC fought a low-intensity secessionist war intermittently until a ceasefire in 2006.

12 Auctions that were conducted during the late 2000s (the procedures of which are dictated by the 2004 Petroleum Activities Law) corresponded with international best practice for competitiveness and transparency, as Sonangol has published clear evaluation terms in advance, divulged detailed information about the blocks via data packages and road shows, pre-qualified would-be operators to ensure technical capabilities, and announced bids and results in public (Esau 2006a, 2006b; Sonangol 2005a, 2005b, 2005c, 2006, 2007a). Oil company officials who participated in or witnessed an auction for deep water rights in 2006 commonly indicate that it was world class – one indicated that he felt like "history was being made in the room" (Interview with Koning 2006). The auctions have attracted massive interest from some of the world's largest and most sophisticated IOCs and NOCs – among the companies currently working in Angola are Chevron, Texaco, Statoil, ExxonMobil, BP, Petrobras, Eni, Total, and Sinopec.

The auctions have been heavily criticized in some circles, however, not for the process of selection of operators but for the non-transparent identification of Angolan minority partners, many of which are considered "briefcase companies" that lack the technical or financial capacity to contribute to the development of oil operations but which have strong financial ties to members of the Angolan ruling elite. This strategy of obligating international operating groups to take on politically connected Angolan partners links to the company's patronage-maintenance strategy, discussed in detail below.

Several sources also reported that there is currently speculation in Angola that Sonangol may be moving away from competitive auctions in the award of future interests, and basing decisions increasingly on domestic and international political alliances (Vines *et al.* 2009).

13 Interviews with IOC officials: After the 2004 reforms, the most important legal documents governing the Angolan oil sector include the Petroleum Activities Law, Petroleum Tax Law, Petroleum Customs Law, and Foreign Exchange and Investment Law, as well as the individual

contracts (joint ventures and production-sharing agreements) between the government and individual operating groups.

14 Interviews with IOC officials: In addition to legal predictability, this role has a logistical element, as Sonangol's influence and the skills of its personnel facilitate the importing of equipment, approval of personnel, minimization of delays from petty bureaucratic corruption, and inter-action with Angolan subcontractors and service providers. It also has a political element, as IOCs have called on the company to advocate on their behalf at the highest level of the MPLA inner circle. In recent years, IOC officials suggest that they have called on Sonangol particu-larly to protect their interests against efforts by the Ministry of Finance to alter revenue-collection arrangements.

15 Interviews with IOC officials: Once work on a block is under way, the most frequent form of interaction between Sonangol and international operating companies comes at the level of the Operating Committee, in which representatives from the operator and from Sonangol (usually two from each side) meet regularly (usually weekly) to discuss work plans, budgets, cost approvals, subcontracting, and other central issues related to exploration and production. Committee decisions are osten-sibly made collaboratively, but the committee chair is always a Sonangol representative and has the tiebreaking vote, so operators need Sonangol approval in order to get key decisions through. Sonangol's committee members are advised by a group of technicians with expertise on geol-ogy, data interpretation, finance, drilling, reservoir management, legal structures, and a host of other issues. IOC officials indicate that their most important technical interactions are usually conducted with their counterparts in Sonangol's Production (DPRO) and Exploration (DEX) divisions, which make the formal recommendations that usually form the basis of the Operating Committee decisions. The technicians in these units tend to be well trained and technically sophisticated, and they make decisions both by reviewing proposals made by the operator and by generating their own analysis, depending on the issue.

16 Interview with Western diplomat.

17 As is true in any oil-producing state, there may be instances in which increased government take serves to marginally discourage investment, which may decrease the total revenue generated by the sector at the same time as it increases government take. The goal of increased long-term state control over the sector may also result in a lower total rev-enue generation than a totally private sector-dominated strategy.

18 Interview with IOC official.

19 Block 0 delivers revenue to the government via four direct streams. The first three are to be paid by the JV directly into a treasury account at the

National Bank: a 20 percent per-barrel royalty; a petroleum transaction tax (PTT) of 70 percent of revenue, less operating expenses, amortization of exploration equipment, a per-barrel production premium that differs from block to block, and a 50 percent investment uplift; and a petroleum income tax of 65.75 percent of income (Republic of Angola 2004, Art. 6; IMF 2005, p. 8; Wood Mackenzie 2006). The last item formally should be paid directly by Sonangol: income tax on the company's own share of dividends. The company has not delivered this tax consistently.

20 By the author's calculations based on the Ministry of Finance's figures, the share of production and revenue generated by the traditional tax and royalty concessions declined from 2007 to 2009, representing the following totals (the rest is generated by PSAs) (Ministério das Finanças 2007, 2008, and 2009; my own calculations):

- 2007: 31% of production, 22% of revenue;
- 2008: 18% of production, 17% of revenue;
- 2009: 17% of production, 16% of revenue.

21 According to Ministry of Finance figures and my own calculations, sales of Sonangol shares of PSA oil represented 71% of total PSA revenue in 2007, 63% in 2008, and 73% in 2009 (Ministério das Finanças 2007, 2008, and 2009; my own calculations).

22 Most Angolan PSAs have strict rules on which expenses are reimbursable and they cap the percentage of total oil that is recoverable as cost oil in a given year at 50 percent. (Costs not recovered in a given year can be carried forward to subsequent years: IMF 2005, p. 9.)

23 Sonangol played a major role in developing and negotiating this PSA legal regime. Wood Mackenzie examined one of Angola's PSA's in detail (for the Greater Plutonio field) and found it projected higher revenues for the government than in nine of the fourteen other comparison deep water contracts they studied; moreover, the take from the tax-and-royalty contracts has also been substantial (Kellas 2006).

24 Interviews with IOC officials and one former Angolan government/ IOC official.

25 Interviews with IOC officials and one former Angolan government/ IOC official.

26 Interviews with former Sonangol official Antonio Mangueira and with IOC officials.

27 Interview with IOC official: It is not uncommon for one set of Sonangol officials (DPRO, for example) to indicate approval of a plan or cost, only to have another (say, DEX) make an opposite determination, or for Sonangol officials to say that they plan to make a certain decision, only to reverse course at the last possible second, contending that some other

government office has obligated them to reconsider. Some operating group officials view this as inefficient behavior that limits the productivity of operations. Others, though, recognize it as a tool that Sonangol uses to take advantage of the fact that its value drivers are significantly less time dependent than those of the international operators. "Time matters very much to the international companies," notes the IOC official. "We base all of our calculations on the time value of money, so any delay or disruption of our schedule is very costly. The time value of money doesn't matter to Sonangol – they see delays as just deferring the revenues or the patrimony that will ultimately be theirs no matter what happens ... The company doesn't give you a final decision until the last possible minute before a decision has to be made. That way we [the IOC] don't have time to argue or try to wiggle, and we've got to accept their direction." Several IOC officials also confirmed that the intensified time pressure obligates operating companies to pick their battles and to accept Sonangol standards on issues that they deem non-crucial.

28 Interview with IOC official.

29 Interviews with IOC officials.

30 Interview with Western diplomat; interviews with IOC officials.

31 The interpersonal connections between Sonangol officials and the direct beneficiaries of Angolanization do pose certain challenges to the company, as officials seek to balance their personal financial interests with those of the state. In most cases these interests have been in harmony, and as is noted elsewhere in this chapter individual corruption has not posed a major problem for the company, but the risk of conflict of interest remains and as the company and the structure of the state continue to grow more sophisticated it could prove risky in the future.

32 This elite domination unquestionably spurs resentment on the part of the vast majority of the Angolan population that has lacked access to the spoils of the Futungo system, but to date this resentment has not, in the postwar period, manifested itself in large-scale opposition to MPLA leadership, as the dividends of peace and high growth rates have bought the regime support. This was most dramatically evidenced in the 2008 legislative elections. In the event that the economy takes a serious downturn, it is conceivable that the resentment could have political consequences for the regime.

33 A P&P web page last updated in 2006 states that the production of fields it operates stood at around 82,000 bpd and that it sought to raise its production to approximately 150,000 bpd (Sonangol P&P 2008). Both subsidiary and parent have expansive goals for the company, seeking to deepen its expertise as a field developer and manager and thereby

enhance Sonangol's ability to run more of its production on its own, both within Angola and abroad.

34 Interviews with IOC officials.

35 Interviews with IOC officials.

36 Interview with IOC official.

37 Mangueira, interview with current Sonangol official.

38 The use of oil-backed loans became prominent during the 1990s.

39 Interview with Sonangol official.

40 It may also, it bears noting, serve as a mechanism for the company to increase its independence from the state, by giving Sonangol access to sources of capital not as tightly controlled – or understood – by the rest of the Angolan ruling elite as the domestic oil sector. The issue of possible shifts in the heretofore-close relationship between the company and the rest of the government is discussed in section 5.

41 In addition to arms purchases, Sonangol is widely thought to have served during the war as a ready source of cash for the MPLA to distribute to its key political allies within Angola, for two reasons. First, the company had more direct access to money than any other government agency. Second, in the words of one international organization official with experience in Angola, when there was "something fishy going on, it's easy to do it through Sonangol rather than through the formal channels of government, where things are harder to obscure."

42 Though the lack of an independent regulator has not impeded Sonangol's ability to serve as an effective agent of the ruling regime's interests, some would argue that the presence of a strong regulator might have necessitated more transparency or accountability, and thereby improved the degree to which Angola's oil revenues were used for the benefit of the country's citizenry.

43 Interview with Sonangol official.

44 Interview with IOC official: These scholarships have provided the company with access to the best talent, though some officials within the company also express frustration with the scholarships, arguing that the subjects and courses covered have not provided the best value to the company and that some scholarship recipients have simply used them to live for years overseas without a strong interest in graduating or developing their skills.

45 Interviews with international analysts and Western diplomats.

46 This is not to suggest that all decisions about the award of operating stakes have been entirely devoid of corruption. A former Elf Aquitaine executive testified in 2000 that the company had paid President dos Santos out of a multimillion dollar slush fund in return for privileged access to Angolan oil. My point here is that even if and when the short-

term desire to enhance patronage networks *has* played a role in operator selection, Sonangol has limited the universe of potential operating companies to those with significant financial and technical capabilities.
47 Interview with IOC official.
48 Interviews with IOC officials and international organization official.
49 Interview with Sonangol official.

PART IV

Conclusions and implications

20 | Major conclusions and implications for the future of the oil industry

DAVID G. VICTOR, DAVID R. HULTS, AND
MARK C. THURBER

1 Introduction

Here we return to the central question posed in the Introduction to this book: Why do national oil companies (NOCs) vary in their performance and strategy? In the Introduction we offered three broad hypotheses that might provide answers. NOC performance and strategy might simply reflect the goals and interests of governments. Alternatively, NOC strategy and performance might mainly reflect the quality of state institutions and the associated mechanisms that states use to control their NOCs. Both of these hypotheses suggest that while NOC managers have a role to play, the actual performance and strategy of NOCs depends mainly on their host governments. A third hypothesis suggests that NOC strategy and performance simply reflect the nature of the resources at hand. Where there are large quantities of "easy" oil and gas to be obtained then adequate performance is not difficult to achieve, but when resources are more scarce and difficult to find and tap then there is a bigger premium on organizing the sector for better performance, such as by opening the country's oil and gas industry to outside experts or even fully privatizing the enterprise.

These hypotheses overlap and also leave room for many other factors, including management, to play a role. But they help broadly organize this volume. The three cross-cutting chapters in this volume (Chapters 2–4) looked in detail at each of the broad hypotheses. And case studies (Chapters 5–19) examined strategy and performance empirically for a sample of fifteen of the most important NOCs. Those case studies all followed a common framework, reprinted here from Chapter 1 (see Figure 20.1).

We thank the authors of the case studies for comments and, especially, Francisco Monaldi and Howard Harris for a detailed review of a draft.

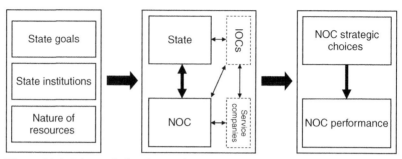

Figure 20.1 Schematic for this study.

Reprinted from this volume's Introduction. The three forces on the left of the schematic lead to choices about the organization of a country's oil sector. That organization sets the mission, functions, and interactions of the NOC. These factors, in turn, help define the strategy and performance of the NOC shown on the right. The cross-cutting studies in this volume correspond to the forces on the left of the schematic: The goals of the state (Chapter 2), the institutions that states use to administer, regulate, and govern their NOCs (Chapter 3), and the influence of geological resources on whether states can choose NOCs or other forms of organization for their oil industry (Chapter 4).

We selected our sample of fifteen NOCs with an eye to diversity across the three main factors that we thought might explain why NOCs vary so widely in their strategy and performance: state goals, the quality of institutions that govern the NOC–state relationship, and the complexity of geological resources. Our contribution to the growing literature on NOCs lies in this scientific approach of selecting a sample of cases that allows us to explore which of these broad hypotheses actually explains how NOCs behave in the real world. In practice, of course, the real world is complicated and even the best scientific research methods are difficult to apply because it is always challenging to nail down the full range of causes and effects at work in any individual case and to compare the lessons from one case study with those from another where the circumstances can be quite different.[1] Thus in setting our sample we erred on the side of selecting companies that were intrinsically important for the world oil and gas markets. That approach raised the odds that whatever we learned in this study would also help explain the global market as fully as possible. Thus our sample of fifteen NOCs covers 46% of all the world's oil production and 56% of total world oil reserves. (We also cover 37% and 46% of gas production and reserves, respectively.)

The rest of this chapter summarizes what we have learned. In section 2 we focus on what explains *performance* of NOCs. In section 3 we examine *strategy*, which has proven much more difficult to measure and explain. And in section 4 we speculate about some ways that our findings might be extended – both to topics that were not in our original research design and to consideration of the future structure of the oil industry.

Throughout this Conclusion, we will make four broad arguments. First, NOCs exist for many reasons, but the most important force at work is the desire by governments to control through direct ownership what is usually the most lucrative source of revenue in the country. While in theory such control is possible without state ownership, in practice the systems for public administration and regulation of private firms are often poorly developed in host governments. This was certainly the case for many governments in the early 1970s, which was the peak period for nationalization of oil companies.

Most NOCs came into existence in the wake of highly visible nationalizations of foreign companies that were politically very popular, and most of these national companies initially worked oil resources that were abundant and relatively straightforward to explore and tap. The fear of losing control over these resources explains why so much Western policy advice – which usually points to privatization – goes unheeded, even when NOCs perform poorly. Most of these governments are stuck in what might be called a "governance trap." They created NOCs (either through nationalization or from the ground up) partly because they did not believe they had governing institutions that were adequate to assert reliable control over private enterprise. And once their NOCs dominated the sector (and most of the state's finances) there was little incentive to create governing institutions that would welcome private enterprise.

Second, we find that there is wide variation in the performance of NOCs. NOCs, in general, appear to perform worse than international oil companies (IOCs) – in some cases, a lot worse. Much of this poor performance reflects special demands and constraints that are placed on NOCs because they are owned by governments that have many objectives beyond just an economically efficient oil industry. In a few extreme cases, NOCs provide a wide array of functions that are far beyond the normal practice of finding and producing oil and gas. Moreover, because NOCs control huge resources these enterprises are often an attractive target for corruption and political patronage, which further undermine performance. We find that the goals that government sets for its NOC – explicitly or otherwise – are the single most important explanator of NOC performance. NOC management also plays a role in performance, but state goals are usually more important.

Third, governments have organized their interactions with their NOCs in very different ways – some aim to control them directly while others create arm's-length systems for regulation and public administration. We find that the most important element of government–NOC interactions is consistency. The worst-performing NOCs tend to exist alongside governments that provide inconsistent and highly variable mandates. Some of the best-performing NOCs are in countries with unified governmental control – an attribute that often correlates with authoritarian rule by a small number of stable elites. This conclusion suggests that reformers should worry less about the particular form of government–NOC interaction and focus, instead, on the credibility and consistency of that interaction.

Fourth, the future for NOCs will probably not look like the past. Today it is fashionable to argue that the oil industry is in the midst of a renationalization and NOCs will become even more dominant in the future. In reality, that trend is not clear – in part because much of what can be nationalized readily is already controlled by NOCs. The more important trend is that the resources that NOCs are tapping have become more complex – partly because oil fields are becoming more complex due to depletion and partly because a growing number of countries are trying to tap natural gas, which is usually more complex than conventional oil to extract, transport, and market. A rift is opening between NOCs that are able to manage such resources internally and those that have lagged behind. Countries on the wrong side of that performance rift are seeing a steep decline in the ability of their state oil firms to tap the country's hydrocarbon wealth. And overall the dominance of NOCs seems poised to decline as a wide array of outside firms – including service companies and IOCs – fill larger niche roles where NOCs used to operate exclusively.

2 Main findings: explaining variations in performance

2.1 Why do NOCs exist (and persist)?

Before turning to the questions of how NOCs behave – their strategy and performance – we must first understand why these companies exist. Our studies point to three forces at work and a fourth force that is often cited as a reason for state control over the oil sector yet, in practice, is less evident.

First has been the fear by host governments that private enterprise was not delivering adequate revenues and other benefits to government. Indeed, outside the Western democracies the history of the oil industry until the 1960s was one seen by locals as foreign exploitation. Major oil producers – some linked to colonial powers and others anchored notably in the United States – were able to exert control over nearly all production because they had nearly cornered the biggest markets where oil products were sold. (And the gas industry, at the time, was almost entirely a local affair. The international gas industry began only in the 1960s and 1970s with a few tightly controlled LNG projects and long-distance pipelines.)[2]

Monopoly control meant that most of the revenues from oil production projects accrued to producers themselves, and as host governments learned more about the real (low) costs of production they understandably wanted a larger share for themselves. They achieved some of that goal when monopoly control eroded – in part because many new smaller oil producers entered the market in the 1960s. But many governments saw a shift to a state-owned oil industry as the best way to obtain the information about production costs and markets as well as the control needed to maximize their share of revenues. This first factor is a timeless problem for any government that relies on other agents to deliver benefits. Ironically, however, the host governments were in the midst of rapidly raising their take from foreign-operated oil operations before the idea of NOCs spread widely. Host governments had already figured out ways to rectify the imbalance of information and power and squeeze out more of the revenues for themselves, such as by changing tax and royalty rules, without needing to resort to state ownership. Thus other factors must be at work to explain why so many countries shifted to national control at the same time.

A second factor is nationalism. Indeed, the oldest NOC studied in this book (Pemex) owes its existence to a highly popular nationalization of foreign oil companies in 1938. Even as Pemex has struggled, today, to stem a steep decline in its oil output, the anniversary of its creation remains a national holiday and the possibility of privatization is politically (and constitutionally) untouchable.

Nationalism arose in complicated ways that were not uniquely tied to oil – the epicenters of Arab nationalism were in Nasser's Egypt (with no appreciable oil) and Kaddafi's Libya (with lots of oil). The Western firms that dominated the region's most lucrative export were highly visible examples of what nationalism hoped to extinguish. The trend toward national control was fully under way by the early 1970s, but the oil embargo – which quickly lifted prices – underscored just how much the host governments thought they would make. The impact of nationalism is most evident in Arab oil companies (see Figure 20.2). Strident Arab nationalism gave little room for organizational forms other than state enterprises. NOCs in the Arab world were first established by the strongest nationalists and then spread rapidly. Nationalizing was popular because it was a highly visible act, and it is not surprising that the governments that were first to nationalize were those with the newest leaders who had risen to power on this platform and also had the most tenuous grip on power and needed to show prompt and visible outcomes from their new policies. As is explained in Chapter 2, when time horizons of leaders are short and constraints on their authority are absent there are strong temptations to exert national control. The benefits of nationalization are immediate while the costs – such as poor performance – arise only much later. Once this logic started to play out it was hard to contain it. In the case study on Saudi Arabia (Chapter 5), for example, it is shown that even though the Saudi government thought (rightly) that its existing production agreements with the Western companies that operated the country's oil fields would be most lucrative for the country, it could not contain popular pressure to nationalize. When Saudi Arabia nationalized it did so relatively slowly and carefully with the goal, largely achieved, of incorporating Western-style management into the increasingly Saudi NOC.

Third is the role of geology and risk. Fourteen of the fifteen NOCs studied in this book were largely created *after* the riskiest part of the

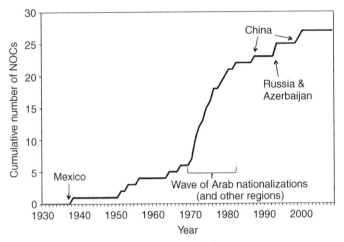

Figure 20.2 The spread of NOCs over time.

Chart shows the cumulative number of NOCs from the 1930s (starting with the nationalization of Pemex in 1938) through the wave of nationalizations inspired by popular Arab nationalism that originated in Libya and Egypt and finally the creation of NOCs after the breakup of the Soviet Union and the reorganization of the Chinese oil industry to create a larger number of semi-independent state-owned oil companies.

oil industry – the initial exploration of virgin territory – was already completed, reserves had been proven, and a basic production system was in place. (Brazil is the only exception.)[3] Once the resources had been found and tapped the roles for technical skill and management of risk capital were much diminished, and that made the decision to nationalize much easier. Chapter 4 shows that when oil operations are at their riskiest (the "frontier"), there is a strong preference for IOCs that can mobilize expertise and spread risks across a large portfolio of global projects. As a basin is developed risks plummet and other forms of industrial organization – such as NOCs – can survive. Chapter 4 also explains that as oil provinces become highly mature, risks rise once again and so does the involvement of industrial players, such as IOCs, that can spread risk across a larger portfolio of projects.[4]

That basic logic explains when and where NOCs can remain dominant. Nonetheless, it can be politically difficult to roll back state control even when geological imperatives seem to warrant it. Examples include Mexico and Kuwait (see Chapters 7 and 8), countries whose gridlocked NOCs perform relatively poorly but where few politically viable modes of industrial organization exist apart from the national enterprise. In such cases NOCs remain dominant but the country's whole oil sector declines.

In only a few cases – such as Petronas, Norway's Statoil, CNPC, and ONGC – have NOCs attempted the forays overseas that would allow them to spread risk across various geographies in an IOC-like manner. Even then, these internationalizing NOCs face severe constraints in developing a truly effective portfolio. With the strong backing of their government, Chinese NOCs (notably CNPC) have been particularly aggressive in trying to lock up oil resources overseas, as detailed in Chapter 9. CNPC and Petronas (in Chapter 18) have been moderately successful in developing resources abroad, although their comparative advantage has derived significantly from their ability to enter countries, such as Sudan, that are off limits to others. (India's ONGC has stumbled badly abroad despite sharing this advantage, see Chapter 17.) Only one of the NOCs that we study in this book – Statoil (Chapter 14) – has a substantial international portfolio that is based mostly on an IOC-like capacity to manage geological and market risks. Other NOCs, notably Petrobras, are in the early stages of developing what could become a similarly international portfolio, but most of the skills and capital at Petrobras are still firmly devoted to its home market. As the political risks surrounding new projects in Brazil rise, Petrobras is likely to find a need to continue to devote most of its attention to managing those risks rather than pursuing an IOC-like worldwide strategy (see Chapter 12).

A fourth rationale often cited by governments as a reason for creating or sustaining an NOC is as a contributor to the nation's industrial base through "forward linkages" (for example, through the supply of cheap, available fuel) and "backward linkages" (for example, by fostering supply chain industries) to the rest of the economy. While this rationale is put forward by many countries that choose NOCs, Norway is the only definitive example in our sample where the NOC has actually served this function in an important way, although many other countries have made major efforts along these lines – such as Saudi Arabia from the 1990s to the present and Pemex today. Such an approach to industrial policy, however, does not require an NOC. Indeed, in many cases, the NOC has actually made it harder for broader, vibrant private sector industries to form. In Abu Dhabi, for example, the presence of the NOC probably impeded the development of gas-based industries due to the NOC's lack of interest and skills in gas supply (see Chapter 11). In the Norwegian case, the development of broader industrial capability was an explicit goal when Statoil was formed; in turn, Statoil has played an important role in nurturing a world-leading supply industry in that country (Chapter 14). Though most countries have found great difficulties in leveraging their NOCs for industrial growth, the Norwegian example shows that it can be possible when conditions are favorable. It further suggests that some of the policies that have been criticized as contributing to inefficiency in the hydrocarbon sector – for example, local content rules – can play a positive role if they help foster value-added industries adjacent to the NOC. Actually implementing such policies effectively is extremely difficult and requires a highly skilled and strategic government.

2.2 *How do NOCs perform?*

Measuring performance has proved to be extremely difficult. Many NOCs are cloaked in secrecy and thus getting an accurate accounting of their activities is challenging or impossible for outsiders. Many governments demand that their NOCs perform a wide array of functions that are far removed or even antithetical to efficient oil and gas operations. Some governments with the richest oil resources set very low depletion rates – in part because they seek to preserve oil riches for future generations – and thus NOCs often look much less effective than IOCs at turning valuable booked assets into actual cash.[5] And NOCs vary in the kinds of geology and market circumstances they confront, which means that simple metrics of performance – such as production costs – are often not comparable across cases. Previous studies have generally ignored these complications, which is understandable since NOCs vary so widely in their circumstances and developing a single metric for comparing performance has proven impossible.

An array of prior studies has already concluded using statistical methods that NOCs are substantially less efficient than IOCs.[6] The case studies that account for most of this book confirm that NOCs on average appear to be less efficient than IOCs. In most of the cases examined in this book where NOCs work alongside IOCs – for example in Abu Dhabi (Chapter 11), India (Chapter 17), and Venezuela (Chapter 10) – IOCs systematically take on riskier projects and appear to earn higher returns. (Brazil and Norway are exceptions, as discussed in Chapters 12 and 14 respectively, as well as in Chapter 4.)

Because no single quantitative or qualitative indicator of oil company performance can account for differences in geology, market position, and the particular roles NOCs fulfill for their governments, we take a multifaceted approach. (For more detail on our rankings and methods see Appendix A.) First, we look at the array of tasks that each NOC performs (Figure 20.3a). Some NOCs work at the geological frontier, where uncertainties are high and capital at risk is large (see Chapter 4). Other NOCs typically work where risks are lower. In each of those settings, NOCs can play roles as operators of hydrocarbon fields and also as the state's formal or de facto manager of other companies – such as IOCs – that find, develop, and produce oil and gas. Nearly all the NOCs in our sample take on significant operational functions. (In a few cases, those roles include overseas operations – for example, China's CNPC, Malaysia's Petronas and Norway's Statoil.) However, for two of the NOCs in this sample (NNPC and Sonangol) the principal functions are management and regulatory in nature, since these NOCs have only minimal operational roles relative to the total scale of oil and gas operations in their respective countries. In a few cases (Petronas is a notable example), NOCs play management and operational roles simultaneously.

Second, we use the case studies to develop a composite ranking of the performance of each NOC relative to an ideal, efficient firm (Figure 20.3b). In making this assessment we focus on the NOC's *principal oil and gas functions* as summarized in Figure 20.3a. For example, we rate Petrobras, among others, highly because in most of its operations it performs as efficiently as the best in the industry. We assess Sonangol's performance highly for the principal role it has played as a frontier and non-frontier manager in assuring stability and production growth over time in Angola; Sonangol, itself, has relatively minor

NOC	Resources and markets			
	Frontier		Non-frontier	
	Operator	*Manager*	*Operator*	*Manager*
ADNOC		X	X	X
CNPC			X	
Gazprom		X	X	
KPC			X	
NIOC	X		X	
NNPC		X		X
ONGC	X		X	
PDVSA		X	X	
Pemex	X		X	
Petrobras	X		X	
Petronas	X	X	X	X
Saudi Aramco			X	
Sonangol		X		X
Sonatrach		X	X	
Statoil	X		X	

Figure 20.3a Functions characteristically undertaken by NOCs in sample.

Chart shows the main functions of each NOC in "frontier" and "non-frontier" settings, where the distinction between the two is a function of risk – the combination of uncertainties and capital requirements described in more detail in Chapter 4. While oil companies are most commonly judged as operators, a number of the NOCs in our sample are tasked with managing their host country's hydrocarbon sector and thus coordinate and regulate the activities of other players (notably IOCs) who actually find and extract the oil and gas and bear the risks of failure and the rewards of success.

The functions that NOCs perform derive from both the roles assigned to them by their governments and the geological opportunities available. Many of the NOCs in our sample have some activities across all four categories (frontier operator, frontier manager, non-frontier operator, non-frontier manager), but we chart only the most characteristic functions for each NOC.

operational roles that are focused on non-frontier fields. (The company is quickly building operational skills, but those will be relevant for the future.) We assign Mexico's Pemex a lower performance rating in part due to its struggles in fulfilling the frontier operational role

Performance	NOCs
High	PDVSA (pre-strikes)
	Petrobras
	Statoil
Upper middle	ADNOC
	CNPC
	Petronas
	Saudi Aramco
	Sonangol
Lower middle	Gazprom
	ONGC
	PDVSA (post-strikes)
	Pemex
	Sonatrach
Low	KPC
	NIOC
	NNPC

Figure 20.3b Composite hydrocarbon performance of NOCs in sample.

Based on the contents of the fifteen case studies, we developed the above composite ranking of the performance of each NOC in its principal hydrocarbon activities in comparison with a hypothetical "ideal" firm performing the same functions. (Appendix A describes the ranking methods in more detail.) Note that this figure (along with Figure 20.3c that follows) offers two rankings for PDVSA because the firm is so different before and after the 2002-2003 strikes and the reorganization by President Chávez that followed.

(deep water exploration) that it controls, even though an ideal organization for the country's hydrocarbon sector would assign that role to much more capable foreign operators. We give Gazprom a similarly low score not just because of its own operational troubles but also due to its role in inhibiting other companies from entering the country's technically complex frontier fields. Appendix A includes a detailed description of how we assigned these scores to each NOC.

Third, while our focus here is on hydrocarbon performance, one of the most challenging aspects of this study has been to account for the fact that NOCs usually have many other non-hydrocarbon tasks set

Level of Burden	Social and Public Goods	Private Goods
High	**Gazprom** *(subsidized domestic gas)* **NIOC** *(fuel subsidies; social programs)* **NNPC** *(fuel subsidies)* **PDVSA (post-strikes)** *(fuel subsidies; social programs)* **Pemex** *(high taxes, spent by government for broad public purposes)*	**NIOC** *(rents to security and police groups that back ruling elites)* **NNPC** *(political patronage; contracts and "lifting licenses" to associates; senior posts as political plums)* **PDVSA (post-strikes)** *(political patronage)*
Upper middle	**CNPC** *(employment)* **KPC** *(employment of Kuwaitis in general)* **Sonatrach** *(high taxes, which government uses to pursue macroeconomic stability goals)*	**Gazprom** *(investments benefiting elites)* **KPC** *(elite employment)* **ONGC** *(nepotism; contract corruption)* **Pemex** *(patronage through unions)* **Sonatrach** *(political patronage)*
Lower middle	**ADNOC** *(training/employment)* **ONGC** *(employment; some CSR)* **PDVSA (pre-strikes)** *(fuel subsidies)* **Petrobras** *(tool for energy self-sufficiency and to supply domestic markets)* **Petronas** *(fuel subsidies; high taxes in Malaysia, spent by government for public purposes)* **Saudi Aramco** *(support diversification of economy and Saudi employment)* **Sonangol** *(fuel subsidies)*	**CNPC** *(senior posts as political plums)* **Petronas** *(private banker and political tool for prime minister)* **Sonangol** *(education and employment for elites)*
Low	**Statoil**	**ADNOC** **PDVSA (pre-strikes)** **Petrobras** **Saudi Aramco** **Statoil**

Figure 20.3c The non-oil burdens on NOCs.

We hypothesize that NOC performance may be affected by the non-hydrocarbon burdens to which it is subject. We distinguish between broad-based burdens (which we call "social and public goods") and burdens that benefit narrowly targeted groups (which we call "private"). Rankings are relative to other NOCs in our sample; examples of burdens (in italics) are our assessment of the main burdens and not an exhaustive list.

by their government owners, and Figure 20.3c ranks the magnitude of those tasks according to whether they are "social and public" (thus affecting a broad base of the population, often providing public goods to the general population) or "private" (thus affecting particular well-defined groups, such as unions or elite populations). The politics of social versus private goods are very different, and we explore that in more detail later.

The rest of this section attempts to explain this variation in performance, starting with the factors that appear to be most important.

2.3 Explaining performance: state goals

The single most important factor in explaining performance of NOCs is the goals that governments set for them. At the outset of this project we asked each of the case study authors to examine four types of goals that governments might set for their NOCs. First is the production of revenues, which is a normal function of oil and gas operators. If resources are spent wisely, revenue production can fuel economic growth – though the linkages between oil wealth and broader developmental goals are hotly debated in the academic literature today.[7] Second is the management of resources and revenues, which most visibly takes the form of the rate of depletion that is allowed for the country's oil and gas resources. Third is regulatory. We expected that some countries would rely on their oil companies to play major roles in the economy and society not only as economic actors but in providing a wide array of functions that governments are normally expected to supply, such as regulation. We knew that NOCs were often the most competent or powerful institutions in the host country and thus we expected the line between government and NOC to be blurry. Fourth is a broad collection of "non-hydrocarbon" functions, such as public works projects and social development activities. Nearly all oil companies – whether owned by governments or by private investors – find themselves building schools and roads and providing an array of local services, but we wanted to know if such functions were an especially large part of what governments expected their NOCs to do.

Some of what we learned we already knew. NOCs, in general, have depletion rates about half those of IOCs – the fifteen NOCs in our sample deplete about 1.5 percent of their reserves in a given year whereas the largest six IOCs have an average depletion rate of about

3 percent.[8] However, using depletion rates to guide comparisons between these types of firms is very difficult and prone to be misleading. Most NOCs obtain their reserves at no cost and thus there is little consequence for not producing; all IOCs, by contrast, pay for their reserves (and often have contracts that forfeit reserves if they are not tapped) and thus face strong incentives to produce promptly.

Even when looking just at NOCs we have learned that depletion rates don't actually reveal much because they reflect many forces at work. One force is the goal of saving valuable resources for future generations. Where the biggest NOCs operate, oil and gas resources are usually the nation's most valuable resources. When governments believe that such resources are scarce then it can be attractive for host governments to save their heritage underground, where it becomes more valuable with time, rather than transform it into cash that might more readily be squandered or be hard to invest wisely. Indeed, in all of the case studies where government was most stable and could set credible long-term policy, national savings through low depletion rates was cited as a major driving force for oil sector policy.

In practice, depletion rates reflect many forces at work.[9] Disentangling them is difficult, and deliberate savings strategies are not the only goal. Depletion rates may be low because the world's largest oil companies are all owned by governments that are part of the OPEC oil cartel. Eight of the fifteen NOCs examined in this book are based in OPEC states. While the influence of OPEC is prone to overstatement, there is no doubt that for some producers – notably lead OPEC member Saudi Arabia and perhaps also Abu Dhabi – production is lower due to cartel-based pricing policy. Thus depletion rates are also much lower. A strategy of saving resources underground is wise if an effective cartel makes those resources more valuable.

In many cases, low depletion rates also simply reflect poor skills. Where NOCs struggle, what might look like effective collusion or a far-sighted savings policy might simply be the inability to produce oil and gas. As shown in the case of Iran NIOC (Chapter 6), the case of Gazprom (Chapter 15), and PDVSA in recent years (Chapter 10), the inability to find and produce more oil and gas is a much more important factor in explaining low depletion rates than any strategy for long-term savings or cartel-linked market manipulation. When we began this study we expected that depletion rates would tell us a lot about government goals and the performance of NOCs, but over

Performance	Non-hydrocarbon burdens			
	High	Upper middle	Lower middle	Low
High			PDVSA (pre-strikes) Petrobras	Statoil
Upper middle			CNPC Petronas Saudi Aramco Sonangol	ADNOC
Lower middle	Gazprom PDVSA (post-strikes) Pemex	Sonatrach	ONGC	
Low	NIOC NNPC	KPC		

Figure 20.4 The impact of non-hydrocarbon functions on performance.

Chart shows our composite rank for performance (same as Figure 20.3b) and the extent to which the NOC is expected to provide a variety of non-hydrocarbon functions (a composite of the two types of burdens reported in Figure 20.3c).

time we found it impractical to disentangle all these different forces at work.[10] Depletion rates are interesting and explored in much more detail in Appendix B, but looking at these rates alone does not reveal very much about the forces at work.

(Looking at depletion rates is additionally complicated by manipulation of official data on booked reserves. Most NOCs do not have independently audited and transparent reserve estimates. Independent audit could lead to radical changes in those estimates as revealed by the experience of Pemex. The Mexican oil giant subjected its reserves to audit according to the rules of the US Securities and Exchange Commission when the company was raising debt on the US market and it was required to cut its official reserves estimate in half.)

Our most important finding about state goals is that the wide array of "non-oil" functions are a major part of what some governments expect from their NOCs with substantial implications for performance. Figure 20.4 plots hydrocarbon performance from Figure 20.3b (vertical axis) against a composite measure of non-oil burdens on the NOC derived from Figure 20.3c (horizontal axis). It suggests a broad correlation. Hydrocarbon performance is highest, not surprisingly, in NOCs whose states allow for a focus on finding and producing oil and gas. There are no top-tier performers who are also responsible for major non-hydrocarbon functions. And the worst performers all have large non-hydrocarbon responsibilities. That correlation is crude, but a close look at the individual cases is supportive. NNPC is one striking example (see Chapter 16). NNPC's efforts to manage the country's oil and gas sector contribute little other than bureaucracy. However, when viewed primarily as a mechanism for patronage, the company is extremely effective. Each approval step provides an opportunity for a gatekeeper to extract benefits for family and associates. Hydrocarbon revenue channeled through NNPC also feeds a larger pyramid of official patronage, with oil funds historically used by politicians at the center to pay off states and help hold the fragile federation together. Mexico offers another instructive case. Today's Pemex is indisputably a poor performer in the hydrocarbon arena, but its troubles stem, in part, from its inability until a few years ago to reinvest its earnings or to precommit earnings to reliably raise adequate debt financing. Instead, Pemex has been used as the single largest supplier of revenues to the Mexican state; only after broader tax reforms that allow the government to tap other sources of income has it been possible to reduce dependence on Pemex a bit (see Chapter 7).

Since state goals play such a large role in explaining NOC performance, why do some governments demand that their NOCs provide a wide array of non-hydrocarbon functions while others are content to let their NOCs focus on finding and producing oil and gas? Our research suggests some preliminary answers to this question. One answer is time horizons. As is explained in Chapter 2, constraints on the power of leaders limit their ability to obtain short-term, private benefits from NOCs. Where such constraints are many, politicians are less able to meddle in the NOC, and the firm is more likely to focus on the long-term task of investing in oil and gas production. Even in the absence of formal checks and balances, leaders facing little political competition as in Angola (see Chapter 19) and Saudi Arabia (see Chapter 5) will also be more likely to seek the larger but longer-term benefits from letting the NOC function as part of an efficient oil industry. The type of regime will also affect the related question of where the benefits from oil are directed. When politics in the country is based on elites and factions – as is often the case in more authoritarian systems of government – then leaders search for ways to channel benefits to those powerful groups. When leaders are democratically elected they search for broad-based and highly visible benefits, such as public works projects. We will return to this puzzle at the end of this chapter and suggest that the time horizons of leaders and the structure of political benefits – whether broad-based or narrowly concentrated – together explain why NOCs vary so much in their performance. But this intriguing hypothesis is more a matter for future research than a clear and unequivocal finding from our study.

2.4 Explaining performance: geology

The second most important factor is geological. We have already seen in Chapter 4 that geology can largely determine whether NOCs exist in the first place. The life cycle of an oil or gas province largely determines the risks involved and the scale of capital investment needed, and NOCs tend to thrive only when the risks are relatively low.

The same line of argument also helps to explain some of the variation in NOC strategy and performance. One of the most important strategic choices that NOCs make concerns their field of operations. Most NOCs work almost exclusively in their home market. But a few move abroad, and geology is one factor that explains why an NOC expands overseas. Of our sample of fifteen NOCs, one-third have significant overseas oil or gas production operations: Petrobras, CNPC, ONGC, Petronas, and Statoil. (In addition, PDVSA has significant downstream operations abroad.) All five moved overseas because of current or expected future scarcity of resources at home. In the case of Petrobras, the company moved abroad – notably to Iraq – before it found substantial resources at home. Not all of these ventures overseas have been successful – ONGC, in particular, has struggled to work in environments where it does not have the special political connections that it enjoys in its home market. Of the five NOCs that moved abroad in the upstream market, only Statoil made the move even as it continued to have access to abundant geological resources at home. This exceptional case (which is now being joined by Petrobras) reflects that Statoil has been able to develop world-class capabilities before geological depletion at home forced it to do so. Even that case, however, aligns with the general rule. As shown in Chapter 14, Statoil's move abroad was also prompted by its managers' recognition that Norwegian resources were finite.[11]

The studies suggest that easy geology allows NOCs to survive with poor performance and difficult geology can force much higher performance. All of the NOCs in this book have seen their geological resources become more challenging over time. In a few cases the change in geological circumstances has been extremely rapid – most evidently in the case of Pemex, which during most of the 1980s through the 1990s had spent virtually nothing on finding new oil resources and in the space of just a few years between 2000 and 2010 found its major oil field in steep decline. About two-thirds of the NOCs in this book have invested to improve their ability to manage these harder circumstances. And about one-third have done little to prepare for the geological troubles that have arrived: NIOC, KPC, Pemex, and Gazprom are all striking for their lack of investment in building new capabilities despite the obvious arrival of geological troubles. (In the case of Pemex the firm is now in the midst of a rapid increase in investment in new technologies and exploration; Gazprom, to a lesser degree, is also increasing its investment.)

Geology is a sorting mechanism. It reveals the challenges that a company will face, but it does not explain why some invest in new capabilities and build new strategic relationships to address their geological challenges and others do not. For that we must turn to other factors. And for those, we look back at government and the incentives that governments create for NOCs to become proficient at finding and producing oil and gas.

2.5 Explaining performance: state–NOC interactions

We started this project with the expectation that the many ways that government administers public policies might explain some of the variation in NOC performance. In essentially every country, state enterprises that require huge amounts of capital and deliver massive revenues are under intense scrutiny by the host governments. Thus we asked each author to focus on "state–NOC" interactions. In the early drafts of these studies the authors concentrated on how government, itself, was organized to make and implement administrative decisions for organizations under its control. That line of research falls within the field of "public administration." In the early drafts of these studies we urged each author to look at all the standard ways that governments make and administer public choices – through the setting and control over budgets, the selection of senior managers, procurement rules and such. Our working hypothesis was that governments would use the tools of public administration to assert control over NOCs in an effort to align the operations of the NOC with government objectives. And we further hypothesized that the NOC would try to escape control. Indeed, as noted in Chapter 3, many earlier studies found that these powerful enterprises often became states within a state. We wanted to understand why some NOCs became autonomous actors and others seemed to follow the opposite path and hewed closely to government objectives.

What we found is that most NOC governance systems don't fit neatly into the public administration scholarship on state control of government agencies. Instead, they are actually a hybrid of public administration and two other activities: regulation and corporate governance. Some governments, like Angola's, treat their NOCs as de facto regulators of the oil sector and other related activities, whereas others, like Norway's, use independent regulators to impose the same set of tax, safety, and environmental regulations on NOCs that private companies face. And partly because many NOCs formed via nationalization, governments often manage their NOCs, at least at a formal level, using corporate governance tools similar to those of their private sector predecessors (voting in shareholder meetings, nominating members of the board of directors, and the like).

NOC governance systems embody this hybrid blend because NOCs are large, complex enterprises with a mix of commercial and noncommercial goals. Their operations and impacts are pervasive, and they exist inside governments that, in most cases, do not have well-developed systems of public administration. A country's NOC isn't just another public agency; it is usually the keystone to the entire system of government and the national economy.

Our studies suggest one central finding about how governments interact with their NOCs. Western analysts have been overly concerned with the particular instruments of state control. When they call for reforms they have in mind an ideal system of public administration, regulation, and governance. That ideal system is patterned on Western liberal democracies that have highly competent public institutions, a strong tradition of administrative law so that decisions are credible and predictable, and where the main decisions of government are highly transparent. The conditions that make that system feasible are difficult to establish. Looking across our sample of fifteen NOCs, those conditions are rare, which partially explains why so many governments have had such difficulty with reforms. Only one of the fifteen NOCs in this book has seen lasting liberal-oriented reforms over the last three decades, and that case (Petrobras) arose in the context of a complete reorganization of the broader Brazilian economy. (Statoil was also exposed to liberalizing reforms over the years including partial privatization in 2001, but unlike Petrobras it was already subject to a relatively open and liberal governing regime at the time of its founding in 1972. PDVSA also initiated liberal reforms in the 1980s and 1990s, but the reform process sharply reversed when President Hugo Chávez came to power.) Nearly all of the countries in our sample of fifteen have undertaken substantial reforms of other state-owned enterprises such as electric utilities and telecommunications – including privatization and schemes to allow private competition or public–private partnerships. But nearly always the reform of large state enterprises is driven by large losses requiring immediate responses that oil and gas companies usually do not incur.[12]

Rather than the particular form of administration, regulation, and corporate governance, what seems to matter much more is a *unified system of control* for the oil and gas sector. Unified control reduces uncertainty, usually creates longer planning time horizons, and allows for much higher NOC performance. In nearly all the cases in this book unified control appears to be a necessary condition for high performance. Even in countries that have pluralistic and dispersed systems of government – such as Norway and Brazil today – the oil and gas industries face highly cohesive and predictable rules under central control, and our studies trace high performance of those NOCs back to that unified system. That matters because it allows, although does not guarantee, that the NOC will be able to plan its operating environment around a stable set of rules, and if those rules are opaque to outsiders or difficult to influence then the NOC will have an even greater advantage in countries where it must compete with other, private enterprises.

In practice, there is no single method for achieving a unified system of control. In some countries, control is integrated around the head of government or a ruling elite. The NOC in Angola, for example, is largely organized to serve the interests of the ruling minority elite (the Futungo), and since few doubt that this elite will retain power the NOC operates according to reliable long-term signals. Sonangol also serves as the leading regulator and planner for the country's oil industry, and thus essentially all private investors see the same reliable signals. In some cases, unified control takes the form of corporate governance, such as in Saudi Arabia or Abu Dhabi where elites that control the NOC's shares play an active role in managing the NOC through shareholder functions. In other countries, unified control arises through institutional agreements, such as the cases of Brazil and Norway already mentioned where government bodies, usually a ministry to set policy and a regulator to oversee the sector, work at arm's length from the NOC.

Looking across the entire sample of NOCs, however, what is striking is that very few of the host governments have typical Western liberal systems for setting and implementing policy at arm's length yet many of these cases have nonetheless been able to create a stable policy environment for their NOCs. In a few cases, the NOCs themselves have boosted stability by integrating their senior managers into the workings of government and government managers have integrated themselves into the NOC. Indeed, one of the hardest tasks for the two countries that have the most independent systems for government control in our sample – Brazil and Norway – was building the capacity inside government to set policy and regulate in a way that did not rely on expertise from the NOC.

Of course, consolidated control doesn't automatically produce good performance. A state can use its extreme influence over the NOC to wreck the company or distract it with goals other than producing oil and gas. The most prominent example from our study is today's PDVSA after the country's rule shifted to Hugo Chávez, but Gazprom is perhaps another example. Nonetheless, it is striking that unified control leads to poor performance only under special circumstances where, as explained in Chapter 2, ruling elites have a strong incentive to respond to short-term pressures. In the case of PDVSA, the destruction of the NOC's capabilities occurred only after political unrest and a massive strike that led to the removal of essentially all of the NOC's management and fractured the relationships that had existed between government and the NOC. An embattled President Chávez turned to the oil company for short term rents that would help him retain power.

In every case in this book where systems for control are more fragmented, poor performance inevitably follows. Some of the poorer performing NOCs in our sample owe their troubles to conflicting and volatile policy signals. Kuwait has had five oil ministers since the country was liberated from Iraqi control in 1991, and a fractious parliament makes it hard to send any reliable signals about oil policy. Similarly, Sonatrach has struggled to find a clear signal as the country has swung between military and democratic rule.

Interestingly, one of the most visible manifestations of fragmented control is the rules that govern procurement. In both Kuwait and Mexico the NOCs are saddled with procurement rules that make it particularly difficult to take risks; NOC managers fear that if risk taking leads to failed projects (as is inevitable) they will be accused of corruption or squandering public funds. When government and the NOC do not trust each other a spiral of suspicion and dysfunctional behavior quickly follows, and inside the NOC the result is a chilling effect on risky, entrepreneurial activities that are essential to good performance.

In addition to this central finding – that unified control is a necessary condition for high performance – the studies also suggest three additional insights and extensions about how states and their NOCs interact.

First, the importance of unified governance helps explain why there are highly competent NOCs in both authoritarian and democratic governments. The type of government matters a lot less than the mechanisms for control. Indeed, our study suggests that open democratic governments have a much harder time creating and sustaining unified control systems because the nature of democracy is to diffuse control and allow for robust political contestation. In democratic countries major transitions in government are often filled with risks for the NOC and in those settings NOCs often shift their focus to the short term and to managing political risks – such as in Brazil and Russia in the 1990s. Brazil has since escaped that political chaos; Russia has not yet fully transitioned to a more stable system of control.

In weak democratic governments – that is, governments that must cater to many diverse interest groups to remain in power – the diverse interests inevitably produce many competing demands on the NOC

that must be managed. In weak democracies it is particularly difficult to create the necessary checks and balances for NOCs (and other
players if the market is open to other firms as well) to have confidence
in government rule. In Norway checks and balances could be established relatively quickly after oil was discovered because most of the
necessary institutions were already in place. In Brazil the transition
took a lot longer; in fact, Petrobras developed much of its expertise in
petroleum during a period of unitary rule by the military that lasted
from the mid 1960s through the mid 1980s. More recently, Petrobras
has been able to thrive in part because it was able to insulate itself
such as by selling shares to outsiders, which has allowed Petrobras
to "tie its hands" and favor commercial decisions in general. In
Malaysia, Petronas has been able to carve out commercial autonomy
during a halting democratic transition by moving most of its frontier
operations overseas where the Malaysian government found it much
harder to intervene in the NOC's decisions. Before Chávez, PDVSA
moved some of its capital investment overseas, such as by purchasing the US refining and marketing giant Citgo, precisely because that
gave the NOC more autonomy. The strategy of moving operations
overseas has proven effective but only up to a point. PDVSA's overseas investments were unable to shield it from withering purges of its
personnel after it crossed Chávez. Political transitions in Malaysia
also yielded uncertainty for Petronas – including through the forced
departure of respected and experienced long-serving Petronas CEO
Hassan Marican.

Second, most of the governments in the fifteen countries we studied
have struggled with the questions of how to elicit information about
the behavior of their NOCs and which types of public administrative
systems, regulation and corporate governance will actually improve
performance of the NOC. These struggles stem back to the creation
of nearly all the NOCs examined in this book: in most countries the
fear that private firms were exploiting the nation's resources led governments to choose an organizational form (NOC) they thought they
could monitor and control more reliably than private enterprise. Yet
in most countries that created an NOC the government soon found
that the NOC could easily become a state within a state. The problem
of control quickly reappeared.

We find that the most important control mechanisms are those
based on extensive monitoring. One of the reasons that market-

oriented reforms are so important (and often resisted so mightily by NOCs) is that they provide an effective means of generating accurate information for the host government that can then use that to regulate the sector more effectively and to administer the NOC. One of the reasons Angola's oil sector performs so well – even though its practice of assigning regulatory functions to the NOC violates nearly all of the conventional wisdom about best practices for organizing an oil sector – is that intense competition through bidding produces prodigious quantities of real-time information about costs and risks for each of the country's oil blocks and the NOC, Sonangol, has become skilled at using that information to manage the sector.

Third, what we have learned about state–NOC interactions also helps to explain why most policy advice has failed to help governments improve the performance of their NOCs. Most policy advice has focused on narrow technical questions on the design of particular administration schemes, but the real causes of NOC underperformance usually lie in the whole system of state–NOC interactions. Fixing that system requires a practical understanding of why governments have chosen the particular methods for overseeing their NOCs and whether other systems for oversight and policy direction are feasible. The fixes are complicated and difficult to organize, which is why many of them arise in the context of much larger reforms of government – such as in Brazil and Russia in the 1990s.

Much policy advice is rooted in an idealized Western model of public administration, regulation, and corporate governance that is not practical in most countries that host the largest NOCs. For example, transparency has been a hallmark of most policy advice. Another fashionable idea that has proved to be misguided without the right context is the need for an autonomous regulator along the lines of the so-called "Norwegian model" (see Chapter 14) – a condition that is hard for most host governments to satisfy. The studies here suggest that it is creating incentives for the provision of detailed operating information to the NOC's government masters rather than broad public transparency that actually matters. Some of the most effective NOCs operate in a context where key authorities have access to extensive information but little of that data is publicly available.

2.6 Explaining performance: management strategy

Finally, does NOC performance perhaps depend on managers? It might seem logical at first blush that the answer must be yes. In fact, we have found that many of the most conspicuous "management failures" in these cases actually derive from other factors at work. For example, the study on Pemex (Chapter 7) shows that the company seems to have made a number of strikingly poor management choices. For example, Pemex owns a large share of the Shell-operated refinery at Deer Park near Houston, Texas. Although that refinery offers experience with world-class operations, Pemex's business strategy does not rotate key personnel through the Deer Park facility and thus it has proved difficult to import lessons about best practices into Pemex's broader operations. But fixing this problem does not merely depend on different management decisions. Rather, it would require changing the system of patronage that leads to high-paying jobs at Mexican-based refineries that are attractive to Pemex's dominant union. The union is well connected to one of Mexico's largest political parties, and thus managers find themselves severely constrained in what they can achieve on the ground. Since the early 1990s Pemex has had highly qualified senior managers, but often the decisions made at the top levels have proved extremely difficult to put into practice throughout the company.

Certainly, of course, managers matter. Selecting the senior management of the NOC at random from the phone book would probably, in time, lead to very poor performance. Our studies suggest, however, that the other factors summarized above – the goals of the state, geology, and the interaction between the state and the NOC – matter a lot more. When those factors are aligned governments do not have a difficult time attracting the best managers, for running the NOC is usually a nation's most prestigious job.

Our studies suggest that the functions of management at an NOC differ from private companies in at least one important respect. Managers of Western oil companies spend most of their time focused on company operations. By contrast, managers at NOCs seem to spend an inordinate amount of time managing political relationships with key stakeholders in government. This focus is hardly surprising since host governments often exert direct control over senior appointments, budgets, and most other key policies of NOCs. In earlier work on the power sector, our research group found that the best state-owned enterprises were usually "dual firms" – that is, firms run by managers who were skilled at running an acceptably efficient enterprise while also managing the political relationships needed to thrive in a state-controlled environment. In our sample of fifteen NOCs, the eight companies that receive our highest rankings for performance – that is "high" and "upper middle" on Figure 20.3b – all are dual firms. From ADNOC to Petrobras to pre-Chávez PDVSA, one of the most important functions of managers has been to curry political favor or maneuver to keep unwelcome political influences at bay.

One of the most important long-term functions of managers is building in-house expertise. When we began our study we heard many analysts claim that NOCs could simply "buy" the technology and expertise they needed on the open market, such as from field service companies. Yet when we looked closely at this proposition we found it was not quite true. The most effective NOCs were those that had substantial in-house expertise; they weren't just buying talent and technologies as needed on the open market.

We found that internal expertise matters for at least three reasons. One is that even if a company plans to contract for expert services it must know how to manage those contracts. Essentially all oil companies – even the most secretive NOCs – rely on outsiders, such as service companies, for some functions. Yet the market for outside services is often opaque, and without in-house expertise an NOC will not know how to evaluate bids or manage its contractors. The idea that an NOC can simply be a shell that contracts its functions is deeply naïve because the most important skill in contracting is knowing what to pay and how to integrate contract services into an overall strategy. The need for internal expertise is high even in countries where NOCs contract with outsiders to perform essentially all services from exploration to production and marketing. Though both NNPC's and Sonangol's operational activities are limited, Sonangol has been more strategic in assimilating the technical expertise of its operational divisions into its contracting and regulatory processes, whereas NNPC's operational subsidiary in the upstream has historically been undervalued by management and is generally disconnected from the rest of what NNPC does. Greater skill in contracting is one reason (among several others) Sonangol has been more effective than NNPC in managing its country's oil sector.

A second reason why expertise matters is that it explains why geology is such an important factor. Companies that work at the geological frontiers can do so because of their in-house expertise and their ability to manage a portfolio of risky, capital-intensive projects. None of the NOCs that we have studied has proved itself able to operate at the technological frontier without having first built up a substantial reservoir of internal expertise. Petronas did not move overseas only because local resources were running scarce; it had also built up a capacity to add value when it bid for overseas oil resources. Petrobras and Statoil display a similar history. One of the first indicators that Pemex and PDVSA would falter was the loss of their most talented staff – in the Pemex case that happened over time as the company stopped investing in its R&D facilities and declined from being one of the most attractive places to work in the country to one of the least well respected by the best-trained and most promising youth. In PDVSA the loss happened almost overnight following a strike by the company and the swift reprisals that followed.

A third reason for the importance of in-house expertise is that highly competent NOCs usually have interesting projects to focus the energies of the most talented employees whereas those that don't soon become sclerotic paper-pushing enterprises. ADNOC has combined a big investment in training for young engineers with a host of new projects that give those graduates something exciting to do. The clarity induced by an operational focus can show up even through performance variation within a single NOC. Employees of the engineering design division of NNPC – one of the few arms of the corporation with a clear technical mission and the capabilities to support it – appear radically more energized and purposeful than those in the other, more bureaucratically oriented parts of the NOC.

In general, we have found that managers have less impact on strategy and performance than we had originally expected. Most performance problems are structural rather than managerial in origin. Managers of the worst-performing NOCs were much more highly constrained than we had originally expected. The troubles at KPC or NIOC stem from their host governments' larger context rather than any particular management scheme. NNPC's profound entanglement in a system of political patronage and broken fuel markets starves its division managers of the resources they would need to build true operational capability. Pemex managers have limited room to maneuver in the face of high taxes, powerful unions, and constitutional and political restrictions on engaging outside firms with needed expertise. In Western business magazines it is common to focus on celebrity managers, and there is no shortage of larger-than-life figures in the history of NOC management. General Geisel at Petrobras, for example, helped insulate his company from political pressure during an era of military rule and set Petrobras on its course of exploring offshore, which twenty years later proved so visionary. (It helped that he came from the same ruling military establishment.) But the cult of celebrity managers is unhelpful in uncovering the real forces that explain performance, for it is usually a string of good managers – along with well-established norms and practices – that is associated with competent NOC performance. And those norms and practices usually are anchored in how the NOC interacts with its host government rather than the genius of its managers.

3 Explaining strategy

We designed this study to explain two aspects of NOC behavior. One, most importantly, was performance. The other was strategy. As shown in Figure 20.1, we aimed to understand what explains strategic choices. Then, in turn, we wanted to understand how those strategies interacted with other factors to explain NOC performance. In other words, "strategy" was both a dependent variable and an intervening variable that helped us explain performance.

We have found it extremely difficult to study strategy systematically. Part of the problem is definitions. For NOCs, "strategy" has at least four different dimensions.[13] First is the question of operatorship. All of the NOCs examined in this book except for two have substantial oil or gas operations, and that was by design since we wanted to draw lessons about NOCs that would help us understand hydrocarbon operations where NOCs were a dominant force. The two exceptions – NNPC and Sonangol – were included to allow some comparisons with other NOCs that performed primarily regulatory and oversight functions.

Figure 20.5 summarizes what we observe about operatorship. Ten NOCs in our sample operate a significantly higher share of their

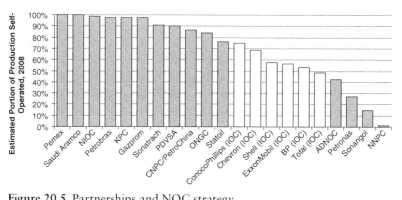

Figure 20.5 Partnerships and NOC strategy.

Chart shows estimated fraction of combined oil and gas working interest production that was self-operated in 2008, including our sample of NOCs as well as six major IOCs. Best efforts were made to include operations of subsidiaries in these estimates.

Data source: derived from Wood Mackenzie (2009a) and Wood Mackenzie (2009b).

own production than the major IOCs shown for comparison. (An eleventh NOC, Statoil, falls just at the upper end of the range of self-operatorship fraction observed among the large IOCs.) A high dependence on self-operatorship means less exposure to best practices. Most of the NOCs with the highest self-operatorship are also poor performers. However, self-operation does not necessarily lead to poor performance, as evident by the high self-operated fraction of some of our sample's best performers such as Saudi Aramco (100 percent self-operated) and Petrobras (over 95 percent self-operated). Both Aramco and Petrobras have been able to achieve high performance with nearly exclusive self-operatorship by investing heavily in in-house technical resources and creating corporate cultures that reward high performance. ADNOC and Malaysia's Petronas are among the relatively few NOCs that have adopted the strategy of working extensively with outside partners to incorporate best practices, leading to low levels of self-operatorship (compared with other NOCs) and high performance.[14] Sonangol and NNPC function mostly as oil sector managers rather than operators, although the former appears serious about developing operational capability.

A second aspect of strategy is the type of resources that the NOC pursues. All of the NOCs in this book have followed what appears to be the most rational strategy: work on the easiest resources first and then move to the frontier later. However, in most cases, that strategy is an artifact of the process of nationalization that produced most NOCs in the first place. (An exception is Pemex, which accidentally found its largest oil field long after the firm was nationalized.) Few countries bother with nationalization until there is something valuable to nationalize. And in oil and gas once the value of a province has been proven the risks decline sharply. Most of the NOCs in this book are only now, today, struggling with the fact that to sustain or expand production they will be required to tap more frontier resources and thus adopt new strategies to take on additional risks. Our studies suggest that one of the best indicators of whether an NOC is preparing to manage those risks is its investment in the technical expertise needed to operate (and manage contracts) for such frontiers.

Third, strategy includes the question of whether to focus entirely within the domestic market or to move overseas. All of the NOCs examined in this book have most of their operations (measured by production) in their home market. As we have already seen, when domestic resources run scarce some of those companies have also branched out overseas, although with mixed results.

We have already discussed the three NOCs that seem to have done well overseas mostly on their own merits (Petronas, Petrobras, and Statoil). CNPC is harder to assess because its efforts to move overseas have had the added boost of the Chinese state – with special funding and development assistance that has helped close special deals, often at inflated prices. And many of CNPC's overseas investments are minority stakes that the firm does not operate. Russia, too, has tried to use its political influence via its state-owned gas company to exert a presence in a few countries of special importance for Russian politics and its gas market, such as Ukraine, Belarus, Romania, Slovenia, and Bulgaria. But that strategy has not worked in markets far beyond the areas where Russia has special leverage. The few other NOCs that have moved overseas have found it much harder to succeed because they bring few skills that overseas markets can't find in other firms – notably IOCs – often at more attractive prices and with more reliable performance. India's ONGC, notably, has floundered outside India. All the other NOCs in this book concentrate at home because they have few other choices and local resources are so rich. In most cases

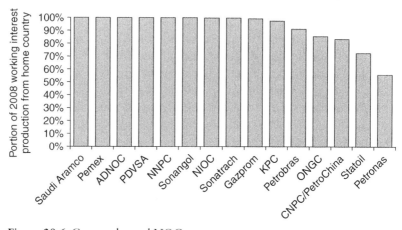

Figure 20.6 Geography and NOC strategy.
Chart shows the percentage of 2008 working interest production (combined oil and gas) that is located in the home country for each of the NOCs in our sample.
Data source: Wood Mackenzie (2009a).

the most valuable asset of the NOC is place-specific: the NOC's political relationship with its host government.

Figure 20.6 provides a snapshot of the internationalization of the NOCs that we are studying. In our sample, Petronas, Statoil, CNPC (including subsidiary PetroChina), ONGC, and Petrobras are the only companies with any significant production coming from abroad. Many of those international opportunities arise in special circumstances where the NOC has a particular advantage.

Finally, a fourth element of NOC strategy is political. If an NOC's most valuable asset is its political relationship with its host government then it would be logical to expect that political strategies would figure prominently in each case study. Indeed, in our original protocol we asked the case study authors to focus on such elements of the NOC's overall strategy. As already indicated, we found that NOC managers spend a disproportionate amount of their time managing political relationships. Yet the impact of this on performance is easy to overstate. The best-performing NOCs were usually the ones that had the most stable political relationships and the least intervention from their political masters. Petronas appears to perform better overseas than at home because the company is a more commercial enterprise abroad where it has less political oversight. Saudi Aramco performs much better than KPC on similar geology because Saudi oversight is more stable and predictable than the volatile Kuwaiti political scene. Norwegian government authorities have intervened at points to check Statoil's power, but the overall policy environment has been stable and interference in commercial decisions rare.

In sum, we were surprised by our findings on strategy. Our study was designed to explain strategic choices and to explain the effect of those choices on performance. As we have indicated, we can explain most strategic choices by looking at the fundamental forces at work in each NOC. But strategic choices, themselves, are not a powerful explanation for performance. Both strategy and performance respond, mainly, to the same underlying fundamental forces such as the goals of the state, the type of geology, and the state–NOC relationship.

4 Some implications for the future

To close, we speculate on three areas where our research may offer insight into the future of the oil industry and the geopolitical relationship between large oil producers and the nations that consume their product. Our aim here is speculation, for we are talking about the future by stretching what we have learned from our systematic examination of the history of the world's most important NOCs.

4.1 Structure of the oil industry

First, what is the future for NOCs? When we began this project the industry was rife with speculation about a swing back to national control. Oil prices were rising and governments were changing the terms of production agreements to keep a larger share of the revenues at home. A few resources that had been in private hands – notably in Russia and Venezuela – were pushed back to national control. And as the financial crisis of 2008–2009 took hold many governments – even in liberal Western market-oriented countries – were asserting much greater national control over the economy, such as in banking. A new era of state control seemed to be on the horizon.

Our studies suggest that, in fact, a swing "back" to NOCs is unlikely. Partly this simply reflects that there is very little left to nationalize. Nearly all of the world's oil patch is already in NOC

hands and has been so for more than three decades. Even in countries where IOCs still operate alongside the NOC – such as Venezuela
– the government has been able to rapidly exert more control through
changes in tax and other provisions (though this trend has ebbed
recently). These tax changes have the effect of increasing revenues
from IOCs through a form of quasi-expropriation that is much more
streamlined than the more disruptive and difficult process of nationalization.[15] Moreover, the 1990s saw substantial liberalization of
the oil industry (and state-owned enterprises generally) – notably
in Latin America outside Mexico – and most of those reforms have
remained intact.[16] Nationalization has prevailed in a few places, such
as Bolivia, Ecuador, and of course Venezuela, and the familiar cycle
of investment and then expropriation has not been extinguished.[17]
Nonetheless, there is no new tide of nationalization and expropriation, and the few particular examples are nothing akin to the broad
nationalizations evident in the 1970s.

In fact, most signs point to more dispersed ownership of oil production. NOCs nearly everywhere are facing the need to manage more
complex and difficult resources, and while many have invested in the
expertise needed to play a more sophisticated role in managing their
oil resources most indications point to more opportunities for non-
NOC players such as the IOCs and the service companies. This is
obviously true in countries that have already opened their oil sectors
to foreign participation. But it is also true in some of the most closed
and secretive (and largest) oil and gas provinces. In Abu Dhabi, for
example, the NOC has pursued a highly effective strategy of controlling production while partnering with outside firms. And as the
country's oil resources have matured the NOC has turned to an even
larger array of outside firms and new business models.

We do not prophesy the end of an NOC era, but we do foresee
NOCs looking outward rather than inward, and that probably fore-
tells a new era for IOCs. Even in Mexico, where the constraints on
outside firms are especially severe, the NOC has been at the forefront
of political and legal efforts to work around the prohibition of foreign
ownership of hydrocarbons that is written into the Mexican constitution. Some of the most interesting opportunities in the oil sector lie in
places such as Abu Dhabi and Angola where the NOC works alongside the most competitive IOCs. To be sure, there will be places where
the swing back to national control looms large, but these are also

in countries where governments seem to be particularly concerned about their grip on power and where nationalism is a potent force for rallying political support, notably Russia and Venezuela. In both countries, the net effect of those political dynamics may be further decline in the oil sector as local firms falter and external firms find the environment too toxic for placing large bets that require a long time horizon to mature.

Perhaps the most interesting area where the dominance of NOCs is particularly tenuous is in gas. In Saudi Arabia, when the government sought to exploit what are probably massive gas resources it turned to outside firms for expertise. (That Saudi Gas Initiative soon faltered in the shadow of Saudi politics, but the same forces that led to the Initiative in the late 1990s have not eased.) Iran, too, finds itself struggling to produce gas even as the country that shares its largest gas field – Qatar – has thrived because it has explicitly turned to outside firms to help with production. And these stories about gas may be just the beginning as news spreads that the world is awash in shale and tight gas – resources that most NOCs, on their own, have not yet been interested in or able to tap. Gas is perhaps likely to feature a smaller NOC role because it poses not just large technical challenges but also the kinds of infrastructure and marketing challenges that led, back in the 1940s and 1950s, the world's largest oil provinces in the Persian Gulf to invite in IOCs to play a central role in developing their oil production industries. Global, integrated production, transportation, and marketing firms are poised to perform better in a globalizing gas industry than national NOC champions.

4.2 NOCs and the price of oil

What can our study say about the price of oil? We have not organized our effort to predict oil prices, and doing so would require a full-blown model of oil supply and demand as well as a lot of hubris since those models don't have a good track record.

However, our study offers some insight into why oil supply curves may remain surprisingly steep and thus so will oil prices until there is response in the form of lower demand. Our study suggests that it is useful to think about the world of NOCs and their host governments along two axes, shown in Figure 20.7. On the vertical axis, put crudely, is the goal of those who control government – do they want

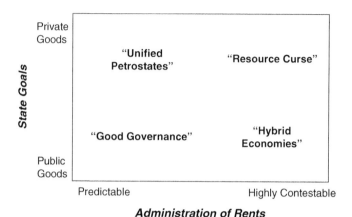

Administration of Rents

Figure 20.7 Goals and administration of the hydrocarbon sector.

In our study we have distinguished public goods (which usually take a long time to produce and are distributed across a broad population) from private goods (which are targeted to particular groups) because those reflect and drive a country's politics. Typically, democracies are anchored in public goods and various forms of client and authoritarian political systems focus on private goods. The administration of rents is an indicator of how a government controls its NOC (and other investors in the hydrocarbon sector). Predictable administrative systems allow for long-term investment in capabilities to find and exploit even the most difficult hydrocarbon resources whereas highly contestable systems favor activities that lead to quick revenues since leaders and managers can't be confident they will be in power for long.

private goods for well-connected elites or broad public goods? On the horizontal axis is the government's administrative capability – its ability to set clear, steady policy for the oil sector so that investors, public or private, can predict where the rents from a project will flow. We have already seen that both of those factors play a big role in the politics of host governments and ultimately in the performance of NOCs.

The matrix corresponds with some important categories of governments, from the unified petrostates such as Saudi Arabia in the upper left to the normal, well-administered democracies in the lower left.[18] And the poorly administered kleptocracies in the upper right lead to the widely discussed "resource curse." In the lower left are hybrids that include fragile, emerging democracies that are notable for good public administration in some areas and dysfunction in others.

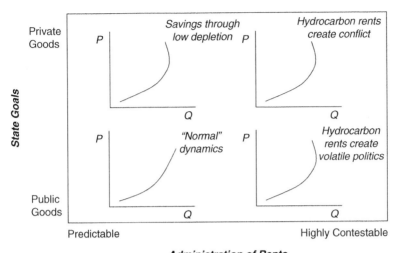

Figure 20.8. Supply curves by type of hydrocarbon politics.
Curves shown here are hypothetical based on the logic described in Figure 20.7.

Oil supply curves probably vary by position in the matrix. What's really interesting here is that higher oil prices don't yield greater supply in most settings. In some, the higher prices give more to fight about, with the result that supply curves rise vertically or even bend backwards. Higher prices lead to greater rents but less physical output and still higher prices until global demand is curtailed and prices abate. Figure 20.8 summarizes our logic in the form of stylized supply curves for the four "types" of host governments. (For sake of brevity, we set aside the effects of OPEC on oil supply, though we acknowledge that OPEC can shift supply inward significantly, at least over the short to medium term.)

Working through the logic in Figure 20.8 may help explain, for example, why the amount of idle Nigerian supply potential climbed sharply as world oil prices rose over the last few years (upper right corner). It's not interesting to bunker and steal oil when it is hard to sell and fetches only $10 a barrel. Poor performance of the NOC also contributes to lesser supply – as in Mexico and Venezuela today, where oil output is on the decline despite both countries' huge endowments in natural resources. In these fragile democracies there are many public demands on oil revenues and higher prices create stronger incentives for politicians to lard additional tasks on the oil company (lower right corner). In the unified petrostates, where time horizons are long and control is much firmer, a different logic plays out with similar outcomes. These states see less of an incentive to produce more oil when prices are high if only because they don't know how to save all that windfall (upper left corner). Sovereign Wealth Funds have blunted that problem by making it easier to invest cash, but our detailed studies show that the main factor explaining when these countries decide to expand output is whether there are rising internal demands to consume and invest the wealth. In well-functioning market systems, such as Norway, higher prices lead to stronger incentives for output (lower left corner).

In a highly speculative way, we have tried to sift all the world's oil resources into these different categories. That is shown in Figure 20.9, and it suggests a simple message: Oil supply curves don't have normal, gradually rising shapes because the politics and the state–NOC relationships in the countries that have the largest oil reserves encourage vertical or backward-bending supply curves. One implication is that the NOC-based oil industry is prone to find itself in what might be called a "supply trap" – that is, a spiral of rising prices and yet strong incentives not to expand output. Another is that high oil prices are usually not helpful to reformers because when prices and earnings rise poor performing NOCs struggle to produce and yet remain dominant supplies stay short and prices rise still further. To drift even further into the realm of speculation we suggest that relief for oil prices will come from the demand side, not supply, because in most of the world demand for oil largely follows normal market response. Demand declines as prices rise.

The propensity for NOCs to find themselves in a supply trap also suggests that frontier oil supplies are likely to come from places where NOCs have a lesser grip on the resource. That means, for example, the tar sands of Canada or the ultra-deep waters off Brazil and West Africa. Looking at the oil industry worldwide it is already clear that if there were optimal depletion of the world's oil resources that production, for a long time, would concentrate on tapping the really cheap resources in the Persian Gulf and the other oil-rich nations. But if those resources are hard to access for reasons rooted in the way they are managed "above ground" then a lot of that oil might never get

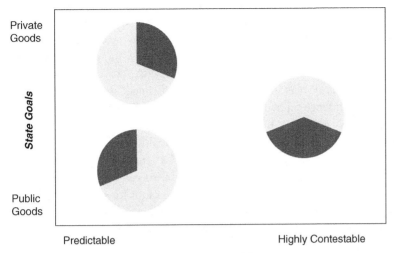

Private
Goods

State Goals

Public
Goods

Predictable   Highly Contestable

Administration of Rents

Figure 20.9 Allocation of world oil production by type of hydrocarbon politics.

Each circle represents a stylized type of political environment. The dark shaded area in each circle represents an estimated proportion of the world's oil production over which the particular political environment holds sway. Estimated from data reported in BP (2010). Perhaps only about 30% of the world's oil production is supplied according to "normal" dynamics in which supplies rise when price increases. The rest is controlled by governments and polities that lead to vertical or backward-bending supply curves.

used. The situation above ground – summarized in Figures 20.8 and 20.9 – explains why there is so much interest in marginal, high-cost supplies. And the fundamental forces, which are political in nature, suggest that will not change soon.

4.3 Geopolitics

Finally, and briefly, we speculate on geopolitics. When this project began there were many worries that state-controlled oil companies would be used as political instruments. Governments, because they controlled NOCs, would turn on and off the taps to satisfy political aims. The canonical cases were Russia's turning off of Europe's gas supply twice – once in 2006 and again in 2009.

We find very little evidence that NOCs are effective geopolitical instruments. (One exception may be Venezuela, where the Chávez government's aggressive oil diplomacy may have extended the country's influence in a few countries in Latin America and the Caribbean. Increased political influence came at great cost, however.) To be sure, there are many reasons why large oil consumers should worry about their dependence on hydrocarbons for which substitutes are not readily and cheaply available. But NOCs aren't one of those reasons. The rarity in the use of NOCs as political tools is striking. The largest political impact of host governments on their NOCs is not in using them as tools for foreign policy. Rather, it is the adverse impact on these companies' ability to find and produce oil, with implications for the world's energy supply and the global economy. The managers at these companies are usually highly aware of this problem and they, along with reformers in government, are usually trying to fix it – mainly by putting government at even greater distance from NOC operations. Actually achieving that outcome, however, has proved very challenging.

Notes

1 Following this scientific approach, we developed a protocol that each case study would follow – thus ensuring that each case examined the three broad hypotheses in a comparable way while, at the same time, addressing other factors that might be at work. The first draft of each of the case studies reflected this protocol and then we edited the text to make it more felicitous to readers – removing most of the rigid superstructure of the protocol but keeping the central arguments in place.

2 For more on the history of the gas industry see Victor et al. (2006).

3 The one clear exception is Brazil, whose NOC was created originally to manage the country's large imports of oil and the refining of crude into useful products. Over time, as explained in Chapter 12, Petrobras assumed a central role in the country's oil production because it already existed and because outside firms assumed that Brazil's oil patch was too small and the risks too large to make much investment in the country. Angola may be a partial exception, because although the NOC in that country was created at a time when risks were high, it initially acted as a regulator for the industry and not as an actual operational company. Only over time did it take on relatively straightforward operational roles as risks subsided.

4 In addition to Chapter 4, for a review of the literature see Hogan and Struzenegger (2010).

5 See also Appendix B. We are mindful that perhaps very few oil producers (notably Saudi Arabia and perhaps Abu Dhabi until recently) have
   low depletion rates that are the result of explicit policy decisions. For
   many governments (perhaps most) low depletion is the result of troubles
   with performance by NOCs and other firms operating in the country.

6 On the theory see, among others, Hartley and Medlock (2008). On the
   evidence see Victor (2007); Wolf and Pollitt (2008).

7 For a sampling of the literature on the so-called "resource curse" afflict-
   ing oil-rich countries, see Humphreys *et al.* (2007); and Brunnschweiler
   and Butte (2008).

8 These rates are computed as working interest combined oil and gas
   production in 2008 as a fraction of oil and gas commercial plus technical reserves as estimated by Wood Mackenzie (2009a). The averages
   provided for our sample of NOCs and for the six largest IOCs (BP,
   Chevron, ConocoPhillips, ExxonMobil, Shell, and Total) are weighted
   by reserves.

9 In the case of Norway, for example, the government consciously weighed
   many factors at the outset of petroleum development in order to decide
   on an acceptable pace of depletion that would balance growth, economic and social adjustment, and environmental concerns. In practice,
   the pace of development in Norway was adjusted in a dynamic way as
   conditions changed, and licensing policy played a much more important role than Statoil in regulating depletion.

10 Victor (2007).

11 Notably, see also Stevens and Mitchell (2008) as it covers some similar
   territory.

12 Among the few exceptions is Russia, which privatized nearly all of its oil
   industry (but kept state control in gas) – in part because oil companies
   were highly profitable and privatization occurred at a time when state
   assets were being reallocated to well-connected elites (Aslund 1995). In
   stable governments such staged fire-sales are much more rare.

13 In this Conclusion we focus on strategy issues that relate to the upstream.
   Indeed, most of this book is focused on the upstream – oil and gas production – because that is where the rents mainly accrue and where the
   political issues are most acute. Individual case studies have also discussed integration strategies that develop downstream capabilities in
   refining and marketing where relevant – for example, the chapter on
   Kuwait (Chapter 8), Venezuela (Chapter 10), and Brazil (Chapter 12).

14 We do not address CNPC in more detail here. Its aggregate numbers
   reflect that it is actually two quite distinct companies – one that dominates its domestic operations and another that has acquired small stakes
   in many overseas operations. See Chapter 9.

15 Manzano and Monaldi (2010).
16 We thank Francisco Monaldi for this point. Also, for a treatment of the issues surrounding the resource nationalism cycle in the Middle East see Stevens (2008a).
17 Notably see Stevens (2008a) and Vivoda (2008) for discussion of the political economy and Chang *et al.* (2009) and Guriev *et al.* (2009) for statistical treatment.
18 Note that Saudi Aramco has little direct burden of dispensing private goods (see Figure 20.3c) even while Saudi Arabia's government maintains what is fundamentally a private goods orientation, with revenues from oil being used to secure the support of elites and help keep the country's leaders in power.

PART V

Appendices

Appendix A: our assessments of NOC performance

DAVID G. VICTOR, DAVID R. HULTS,
AND MARK C. THURBER

Explanation of performance ranking

In this appendix we classify the overall performance of the fifteen
NOCs in our sample into four categories – *high*, *upper middle*, *lower
middle*, and *low*. The assessments are based on the detailed case studies presented in Chapters 5–19. This classification is then used in other
parts of this book, such as the Chapter 3, on how national governments attempt to govern NOCs, as well as the Conclusion that summarizes what we have learned about the factors that explain performance
(Chapter 20). As we describe below, characterizing performance at
the level of the individual firm – especially for firms that are often
secretive and designed to perform many functions – is a necessarily
qualitative and subjective process. Nonetheless, any study that aims to
explain performance must make an effort to measure its quarry. This
Appendix explains what we mean by "performance" and explains our
scoring for each case in the spirit of transparency and debate.

For the purposes of comparing NOCs (and NOCs with IOCs), we
initially sought quantitative metrics. The Introduction (Chapter 1)
summarizes some of the existing quantitative research. Within the
realm of what can be measured quantitatively, existing studies show
that state ownership does in fact have a noticeable effect on standard
performance metrics such as output efficiency, per-barrel operating
cost, investment cost, and net present asset values. However, this kind
of research is difficult to implement because there are no universally
applicable benchmarks for performance comparison between individual companies; the variables that are most interesting to measure are
usually the hardest to quantify.

The question of which quantitative metric or combination of metrics best reflects a given company's overall performance is invariably a subjective one. This problem is particularly acute when NOCs
being compared have fundamentally different roles or are responding

to divergent state objectives. For example, comparing output per employee figures for a sector manager like NNPC with an operator like Statoil is highly misleading. All else being equal, sector management is less labor intensive than full-scale exploration and production. As we have discussed at length throughout this book, some NOCs are established (or encouraged) to perform a wide array of non-hydrocarbon functions, such as social programs, that necessarily divert resources and management talent and incentives within the firm away from core oil and gas operations. The organization of the oil sector derives from a government's goals and capabilities, and in most of the cases in this book that leads governments to assign many functions to its most trusted and capable enterprise – the NOC. Finally, it is clear that any NOC scoring must be handicapped for differences in geology, which, as discussed in Chapter 4, do not lend themselves to any simple quantitative characterization.

Even in cases where quantitative metrics might be suitable indicators, the requisite data may be either unavailable or unreliable. As shown in Appendix B, standard measures such as the speed at which a firm can extract known reserves – the so-called depletion rate – are particularly suspect not just because of difficulties in obtaining reliable reserves data but more fundamentally because maximizing production is not a primary state goal.

In light of the above considerations, we have taken a different approach to assessing overall NOC performance on a firm-by-firm basis. Our approach combines four elements.

First, we assess only performance in the hydrocarbons sector. The focus on hydrocarbon activities allows us to avoid comparing fundamentally incomparable non-hydrocarbon activities, such as channeling rents to elites in Nigeria, protecting unionized jobs in Mexico, and funding populist social missions in Venezuela. We examine these many "non-oil" functions in more detail in the case studies. In the Conclusion, we explicitly assess the relationship between hydrocarbon performance and the other kinds of functions that are expected of NOCs.

Second, we assess the NOC's overall performance in the principal hydrocarbon roles it has assumed. We categorize these roles along two dimensions. Projects to find, develop, or produce hydrocarbons may take place at the frontier, where uncertainties and capital exposure are high (see Chapter 4), or they may be non-frontier in nature, entailing relatively small levels of risk. In either frontier or non-frontier projects, NOCs may engage in hydrocarbon operations themselves, or they may be tasked by their governments with managing private players who actually do the work of finding, developing, and producing oil and gas. The combination of principal roles that an NOC takes on – frontier operator, frontier manager, non-frontier operator, non-frontier manager – is a function both of the opportunities available and of the tasks explicitly or implicitly assigned to the NOC by its government. We rate each company's fulfillment of its principal roles – as summarized in Chapter 20, Figure 20.3a – rather than its capability as a petroleum operator on any absolute scale.

Third, in each case we have imagined a hypothetical case – a capable, ideally efficient firm that would perform the hydrocarbon roles assigned to the NOC in line with the major goals of the government. We have then compared the actual oil sector performance of the NOC (as best we can determine) with that of an ideal firm.[1] This type of counterfactual analysis does not add new information to the detailed analysis of NOCs in each chapter, but it allows for placement of the NOC on a scale according to the extent it approaches ideal firm performance in the hydrocarbon tasks it is given. We stress that this counterfactual analysis is subjective; all we seek is a reasonable holistic assessment of how a given NOC performs in the hydrocarbon activities it is requested and allowed to take on relative to how a world-class company would discharge these functions.

Fourth, where possible, we have asked each case study author to identify benchmarks that the NOC and its host government use to evaluate the firm's performance. We use performance against these benchmarks in our composite rating of performance. The use of benchmarks, alone, is necessarily flawed because often benchmarks are endogenous to performance or are set against wild aspirations. Yet, in practice, we have found that benchmarks are often a subtle measure of what the NOC and its host government think is achievable from reasonably efficient operations. Especially when NOCs fail to meet such goals, it can be a sign of flagging performance.

We use the following performance classification criteria to guide our assessments here:

High Company approaches (though may not entirely meet) the performance of an "ideal firm" in the hydrocarbon tasks it is directed to perform. It is among the most capable players, state-owned or private, that could be envisioned performing these tasks. The company may still experience minor setbacks in its performance, but not to a much greater degree than a best-in-class firm in similar circumstances.

Upper middle Company successfully fulfills its hydrocarbon roles without major problems. However, efficiency may significantly trail that of an ideal firm, or the company may be likely to struggle in addressing emerging challenges such as the production and marketing of gas or the management of complex oil fields.

Lower middle Company broadly fulfills its hydrocarbon role but with some major deficiencies in performance relative to what would be expected of an ideal firm. These can be experienced, for example, as very poor exploration records even given reasonable resource endowments; delays in delivering on key development projects; or substantial, unintentional shortfalls in hydrocarbon production. Nonetheless, the company remains able to execute in some adequate fashion most of the hydrocarbon tasks that it faces. At a very basic level, it can still "do the job" adequately enough that pressures for alternative forms of industrial organization have a hard time gaining political traction.

Low Company has shown very limited ability to fulfill all but the very simplest hydrocarbon tasks before it. Its inability to successfully perform most tasks will tend to put the country's hydrocarbon sector into crisis unless geological endowments are very easy to exploit and resulting revenues significantly exceed the country's needs.

Three important clarifications about our performance assessments are in order. First, these classifications do not imply any statement about the source and cause of any performance deficiency. We leave that task to the individual case studies and the conclusion. *Notably, these performance rankings are not direct measures of managerial performance; in fact, some of the NOCs that we rate especially low in their performance have been run by highly capable top managers.* Indeed, one of the central observations of this study is that NOC performance is often largely determined by factors beyond the control of NOC management, in particular the nature of government goals and the government–NOC relationship itself.

Second, some NOCs face more challenging tasks than others in accordance with geological characteristics and government needs. Comparison against a hypothetical "ideal" performer in the particular tasks that the NOC faces is helpful in such scoring. For example, while any company would be challenged by the current precipitous decline in Mexican hydrocarbon production, the case study on Pemex (Chapter 7) finds that the firm is particularly ill-equipped to respond in suitable fashion (largely due to country-level oil governance issues that have shaped its evolution and capabilities and constrain its current options).

Third, the performance evaluations here are intended to reflect recent NOC performance as of the time of this writing. (The studies are current to 2009 and most are updated with information in 2010 where relevant; however, the period of 2005–2010 was an unusual one in the oil industry with sharply rising prices; thus to assess underlying performance each study has looked to the decade or two before today to complement the current picture.) Where relevant, we have indicated major changes in performance over time – PDVSA before and after the rule of President Chávez is one striking example.

Rankings and an explanation for each follow. The editors prepared these assessments and then edited them in tandem with each case study author – working individually on each case and then allowing each author to compare their rankings with those of the other cases and in a few cases to adjust the rankings.

Performance classifications of NOCs in our sample

Abu Dhabi National Oil Company (ADNOC): upper middle

Rising production with few problems so far based on historically conservative depletion of "easy" oil; effective contracting with partner companies to import capabilities from them and to delegate important operational functions to IOCs; increasingly complex geology may start to challenge technical capabilities.

China National Petroleum Corporation (CNPC): upper middle

Strong technological and R&D capabilities with specialty in management of mature fields; significant operations abroad, especially in places where politically other firms could not operate; financially viable but significantly less efficient than major IOCs due in part to burden of providing employment; excellent financial performance on paper of listed subsidiary PetroChina is misleading due to ubiquitous and opaque financial relationships with CNPC and state.

Gazprom: lower middle

By far the world's largest natural gas producer, with increasingly significant volumes of oil as well. Financial performance and ability to invest profoundly burdened by requirement to sell large volumes of natural gas at very low prices on domestic market; lacks both capital and technology to develop new gas fields that are needed, and efforts to engage IOC partners in Arctic frontier projects have moved very slowly; formal metrics of performance since partial privatization are misleading due to continued pervasive ties to state. Firm has pursued an integration strategy that diverts capital from improved gas operations and works politically to prevent competition from independent gas suppliers.

Kuwait Petroleum Corporation (KPC): low

Unable to hit production goal of 3 million b/d originally targeted for 2004–2005; insufficient technological and managerial capabilities to deal with technical challenges of maturing fields; major accidents in domestic refineries in late 1990s and 2000 to 2005; forced to postpone planned fourth refinery due to ballooning construction costs and dispute over location; unable to develop significant non-associated gas production so far; inefficient operations due in part to pressure to employ and promote Kuwaiti nationals.

National Iranian Oil Company (NIOC): low

Has not returned to anywhere near 6 million b/d production capacity of 1970s; significant production shortfalls relative to OPEC quotas; unable to develop key frontier fields, especially South Pars gas field but also Caspian oil and gas fields.

Nigerian National Petroleum Corporation (NNPC): low

In principal role as de facto oil sector manager via its approval authority over IOCs, NNPC lacks technical capability (and perhaps political support) to truly serve as independent check on IOC activities;

refineries operate at very low utilization factors; upstream subsidiary has not been able to become more than marginal operator of production; gas subsidiary is helpless to build up domestic gas market due in large part to government pricing policy; engineering design subsidiary is relatively competent.

Oil and Natural Gas Corporation Limited (ONGC): lower middle

Oil and gas production has been stagnant overall since 1990s; poor success rate in domestic exploration since 2000, especially at the frontier (deep water blocks); serious field management deficiencies in the 1990s; not very competitive abroad based on technical capabilities, so has instead depended on political positioning to make acquisitions; efforts to move overseas have been largely disastrous.

Petrobras: high

Among world leaders in deep water technology; steadily increasing oil and natural gas production; strong refining capabilities; outstanding exploration results especially massive pre-salt finds in Campos Basin, though that is creating new political pressures to reorganize the oil sector that may degrade long-term capabilities at Petrobras.

Petróleos de Venezuela, S.A. (PDVSA): lower middle

Still able to perform most operations, but production by conservative estimates has dropped 10–15 percent since before 2003 strike, closer to 30 percent if joint ventures with IOCs are excluded; for comparison, incarnation of company before firings and diversion of funding to non-oil purposes under Chávez was highly technologically capable, vertically integrated, and well run – ranked as best-managed NOC by *Petroleum Economist* in 1993, 1995, and 1999.

Petróleos Mexicanos (Pemex): lower middle

Devastating decline in oil production due to Cantarell field depletion without any realistic near-term prospects for replacement; deficient technological capabilities have constrained efforts to engage in crucial deep water exploration in the Gulf of Mexico; development of gas resources has been slow; limited scale of refining operations and poor results despite large domestic needs. Would be ranked "low" except that over the three decades when it produced most of its oil it performed adequately despite many distractions from non-oil tasks assigned to it by the Mexican state, and broad reforms are under way that are likely to improve performance.

Petronas: upper middle

Has effectively replaced its reserves both domestically and internationally through its own exploration efforts as well as its ability as regulator to require IOCs to give it a carried interest in exploration in Malaysia; important domestic and regional gas player with competence in LNG; among most internationalized NOCs, with some significant exploration and production success, most notably in Sudan, but also some disappointments, for example in much of the rest of Africa.

Saudi Aramco: upper middle

World's largest oil producer; reliably meets project targets; under instruction from the Saudi state it has also maintained through most of its history the global swing capacity in oil and used that capacity to manage world prices in ways that benefit Saudi Arabia; downstream the company has surplus refining capacity, which assures ample supply of oil products domestically, but must contend with politically managed prices; the company is highly secretive and thus difficult to gauge its efficiency but cost minimization likely suffers when the company is under pressure to develop projects quickly and when it meets the state-mandated goal of employing Saudi nationals; has had large difficulties building a viable gas industry and mixed experiences in petrochemicals.

Sonangol: upper middle

Primary agent of government in developing and managing stable regime for petroleum administration that has enabled steady growth in reserves and production by means of IOC-led operations in Angola, even through prolonged civil war; predictable regime for partnership with IOCs led to expeditious development of Girassol and other large deep water fields – contrast with NNPC in Nigeria, which was unable to create conditions for IOCs to rapidly bring comparable fields online; has become relatively competent in monitoring IOC contracts and pushing back effectively when in disagreement with operator approach; gradually growing operational capabilities though this role remains secondary for the moment.

Sonatrach: lower middle

Upstream and downstream output have mostly grown over time; significant exploration and production occurs through IOC partnerships as company lags in technology and equipment; tends to perform well enough to meet government needs and targets in high oil price periods but perceived as too inefficient in low price ones, leading to fluctuating incentives for foreign investment but never strong enough sustained incentives to yield a major reorganization of the sector.

Statoil: high

Profitable company with arguably the most arm's-length relationship to its government among NOCs; among world leaders in various technological areas including natural gas processing and transport, production systems for deep water and harsh environments, enhanced oil recovery, heavy oil, carbon capture and storage; moderate success so far in expanding international production; mixed exploration record in recent years.

Notes

1 As research by Wolf (2009) and others, summarized in Chapter 1, describes, performance can be measured as the efficiency of converting inputs (including capital, labor, and resources) to outputs (including production and reserves creation), outputs to financial results (revenues and profits), or, combining both, inputs to financial results. In the holistic approach taken here, we implicitly weigh all of these types of efficiency as documented in the case study assessments. On balance, the case studies weigh output performance most heavily, in part because output performance is easiest to measure, but they consider other notions of performance as well. Our performance characterizations here are the result of a comparison of these subjective, holistic assessments across the sample of NOC cases in this volume.

Appendix B: assessing NOC performance and the role of depletion policy

PAUL STEVENS

The Stanford NOC project is intended to understand how NOCs have developed differently from each other. To this end there has to be comparison between the NOCs. In particular, this concerns their respective performances as oil companies. Measuring the performance of NOCs is difficult and controversial (Stevens 2008c). There are a great many metrics conventionally used. However, one common feature is that many depend either upon reserves or production levels. The implication is that the larger the reserve additions or the increase in production levels the better the performance.

The use of reserves and production data is reinforced for NOCs because they often exhibit extremely poor transparency of financial data commonly available for IOCs.[1] Thus studies that purport to consider NOC behavior are often extremely dependent upon reserve and production data because this is (allegedly) the only consistently available data on NOCs.

This approach view raises two fundamental problems. The first is the controversy that surrounds the accuracy of the reserve figures. This was first triggered in 1987 when OPEC increased its estimates of recoverable reserves during a dispute over how to allocate production quotas. It had been decided to use a formulaic approach. Quotas would be allocated based upon members' population and oil reserves. During the process of deciding how such a formula might be created, five OPEC members increased proven reserves.[2]

Subsequently there have been challenges to reserve numbers in many countries. In the absence of any independent evaluation of reserves there remains doubt over their accuracy. Thus using them as a metric of performance for an NOC is dubious.

However, the second fundamental problem with using reserves and production levels as a performance metric concerns depletion policies. The figures for reserves and production emerge in part as the result of depletion policy. Thus while "low" figures for reserve or

940

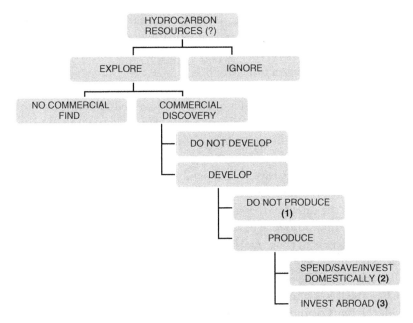

Figure B.1 The depletion choices.

production growth could be a symptom of poor performance by the NOC it could just as well be the result of a deliberate depletion policy by the resource owner. Thus depletion policy becomes central to any evaluation of NOC performance.

Depletion policy emerges from decisions by the owner of the resource in deciding how quickly or slowly to develop it. These choices are stylized in Figure B.1. Outside the United States, the owner of sub-soil hydrocarbons is the state.[3] Thus government decides how much acreage will be available for exploration; what oil-in-place discovered is developed into producing capacity; the rate at which that capacity is produced; and finally how the revenue is deployed.[4]

Ultimately, the key choice arises because oil is an exhaustible resource. The barrel produced today cannot be produced tomorrow and the barrel not produced today can be produced tomorrow. The oil not produced today (option 1 in Figure B.1) will earn a rate of return. If the future price of oil is higher and/or the future costs of producing are lower, this implies a positive rate of return. If prices are lower or costs higher, the rate of return may well be negative. However, it is more complicated than this. If the oil is produced today then the question is what might today's revenue earn as a rate of return compared with the potential rate of return from leaving the oil in the ground? This is why revenue deployment is part of the depletion decision process, as shown in Figure B.1.

Revenues can be deployed domestically as consumption, savings, or investment (option 2 in Figure B.1) or invested abroad through a Sovereign Wealth Fund (SWF) (option 3 in Figure B.1). Deploying revenue domestically will create utility for consumers, savings will earn a rate of interest, and investment in projects will earn a rate of return. The size of these returns will depend on how skillfully the government deploys the revenues – specifically on the government's ability to manage the threat of the "resource curse" (Stevens 2003c). Returns from investing abroad will depend upon the international financial markets, access to those markets, and the competence and honesty of the SWF management (Stevens and Mitchell 2008).

Depletion policies for the major exporters first became an issue when the IOCs dominated upstream oil production in the world outside of the US and the Soviet Union. Almost invariably, the IOCs were operating under "old-style concession agreements" which gave them virtually total managerial freedom (Stevens 1975). This system meant the IOCs effectively set the depletion policy of most oil exporters. This state of affairs came to an end with the nationalizations of the operating joint ventures in the early and mid 1970s. After this point, depletion policy lay firmly in the hands of governments. In the aftermath of the first oil shock of 1973–1974 there was a growing tendency among a number of countries to "leave the oil in the ground."[5] This view of depletion policy was driven by a number of factors. There was a widespread belief that oil prices would rise in the future. For some countries there was a real fear that overseas assets might be exposed to political risk given the growing antipathy between their governments and the US government in particular. Finally, there was the practical problem that in many cases, governments simply lacked the competence and capacity to manage their hydrocarbon reserves following the forced withdrawal of the IOCs. The result was a period of inertia during which governments were effectively forced to try to carry on existing operations. Capacity expansion was simply not a realistic option.

The second oil shock of 1978–1981 initially reinforced the view that oil prices would carry on rising forever and thus the wisdom of not increasing production capacity. Expanding production soon looked even less attractive as oil consumption really did begin to fall in response to both oil shocks of the 1970s.[6] There was an inexorable rise in excess capacity as rising non-OPEC production competed[7] and OPEC was forced to cut back production, for the first time officially, after 1982 to defend prices. In such a context, depletion policy was subsumed to OPEC quotas, although the degree of discipline varied. By contrast, non-OPEC governments in many cases decided to try to expand their oil-producing capacity by encouraging the IOCs to enter and take acreage. Since much of this entry was under the terms of production-sharing contracts, governments in theory had significant control over their depletion policy, but the general attitude of both non-OPEC governments and IOCs was to try to maximize capacity and production as rapidly as possible. In the twelve years following 1978, non-OPEC production outside of the FSU grew by 12.6 million bpd (BP 2008).

Over the course of the 1990s attitudes within some OPEC members towards their depletion rates began to change. The lower prices that followed the price collapse of 1986 created serious macroeconomic problems for many of the OPEC members. They viewed increasing production as a means to restore oil revenues. There was also the issue that OPEC quotas were strongly influenced by capacity levels which created an incentive to increase capacity. In many cases this led the governments to open up their upstream to IOCs. In the fact, by 1998, only Saudi Arabia and Mexico (a non-OPEC state) remained totally off limits to IOC investment.

Following the oil price collapse in 1998, depletion policies began to change yet again. This change related to investment policies (Stevens 2008a), with depletion policies varying depending on whether the oil sector was dominated by the private sector or an NOC. In countries where the NOCs dominated, investment in expanding capacity slowed. This was for several reasons some of which did relate directly to deliberate depletion policy decisions. First there was a growing view after 2000, reminiscent of the 1970s, that oil prices would rise forever. This idea was fueled by the spread of ideas concerning "peak oil" and by the apparently ever-rising prices, albeit with substantial volatility. Thus oil in the ground was seen as increasingly valuable. Several other trends reinforced this. One was the rapidly rising costs of the service companies after 2003, which made exploration, development, and production increasingly expensive. Another was growing concern over the health of the international financial system following the emergence of the subprime mortgage crisis in the US after 2007. Also, the dramatic increase in oil prices gave rise to concern over managing the very much higher oil revenues and avoiding a serious attack of the "resource curse."

At the same time, a principal–agent view of the oil sector began to gain currency among young postgraduate students returning to their native countries (especially to their finance ministries) after having learnt about such ideas and their implications in Western universities. The result has been a growing view, reinforced by many other factors including a number of studies referenced in this volume, that NOCs by their very nature are high-cost, inefficient, and prone to indulging in rent seeking. As a result, NOCs in many cases have been starved of funds with which to operate, seriously constraining their ability to pursue any depletion policy that requires increased capacity and production levels.

In many cases recent years have also seen a revival of "resource nationalism" (Stevens 2008a). This meant that access for IOCs in many cases was restricted, effectively creating another constraint on a government's depletion policy, especially if domestic capacity and competence was limited. Trends toward value-based asset management may also have pushed private company investors to underinvest in expanding production.

For all of the above reasons, it is necessary to be cautious in drawing conclusions about performance from reserves and production data. Growth in either does not necessarily reflect improved NOC performance, nor are declining numbers always a sign of inefficiency. They may simply reflect government preferences in a dynamic oil market.

Notes

1 This of course is not true for NOCs listed on stock exchanges where normally there are strict requirements for reporting financial data.
2 It seems highly likely this was simply done by getting the chief geologists to change the recovery factor on existing fields.
3 In the United States the owner of subsoil hydrocarbons is the landowner, which can be a private individual.
4 This last "choice" may not seem strictly to be part of a depletion policy but as will be seen it is a key issue in the decision process.

5 The analysis that follows inevitably suffers from gross generalization.
6 Between 1980 and 1983, OECD oil consumption fell on average by over 5 percent per year (BP 2008).
7 During 1979–1985 non-OPEC production outside the FSU grew at an annual average rate of 3.8 percent (BP 2008).

References

Abir, Mordechai. 1988. *Saudi Arabia in the Oil Era: Regime and Elites; Conflict and Collaboration.* London: Croom Helm.

Acemoglu, Daron and Simon Johnson. 2005. "Unbundling Institutions." *Journal of Political Economy* 113 (5): 949–995.

Adams, Samuel and Berhanu Mengistu. 2008. "The Political Economy of Privatization in Sub-Saharan Africa." *Social Science Quarterly* 89 (1): 78–94.

Adelaja, Abiodun. 2007. "Nigeria: NNPC–No End to Fuel Scarcity Soon." *Daily Champion*, January 24, accessed April 13, 2011, www.allafrica.com/stories/200701240220.html.

Adelman, Morris A. 1993. *The Economics of Petroleum Supply.* Cambridge: MIT Press.

    1995. *The Genie Out of the Bottle: World Oil Since 1970.* Cambridge: MIT Press.

ADMA-OPCO. 2007. *Annual Review 2007.* Abu Dhabi: ADMA-OPCO.

ADNOC. 1988. *Abu Dhabi National Oil Company: Seventeen Years of Progress (1971–1988).* Abu Dhabi National Oil Company.

    2005. *ADNOC's Five Year Achievements Report: 2000–2004.* Abu Dhabi National Oil Company.

    2006. "The Supreme Petroleum Council (SPC) and Abu Dhabi National Oil Company (ADNOC) Sign Agreements with Exxon Mobil Corporation." ADNOC Press Release, January 1.

    2008a. *ADNOC & Its Group of Companies.* ADNOC Corporate Brochure.

    2008b. "Careers @ ADNOC." ADNOC website, accessed April 13, 2011, www.adnoc.ae/content.aspx?mid=156&tree=.

    2010. "Abu Dhabi National Oil Company – Company Profile." Reference for Business, Company History Index website, accessed October 31, 2010, www.referenceforbusiness.com/history2/92/Abu-Dhabi-National-Oil-Company.html.

Afkhami, Gholam R. 2009. *The Life and Times of the Shah.* Los Angeles: University of California Press.

Africa Confidential. 2006. "Starstruck Starcrest." November 3, accessed April 13, 2011, www.africa-confidential.com/.

Africa Energy Intelligence. 2002. "Angola – Misgivings over Local Ties." *Africa Energy Intelligence* 334.

2006. "Angola – The Local Oil Barons." *Africa Energy Intelligence* 408.

2007. "Angola – Mosquito Seeks to Shed Stakes." *Africa Energy Intelligence* 432.

2008. "Angola – Is Sonangol Africa's First Sovereign Fund?" *Africa Energy Intelligence* 476.

2009a. "China Sonangol Out to Conquer the World." *Africa Energy Intelligence* 607.

2009b. "China Sonangol in Offshore Grab." *Africa Energy Intelligence* 614.

2009c. "State-Owned Companies: Angola/Zimbabwe-Sonangol." *Africa Energy Intelligence* 617.

2010a. "State-Owned Companies: Sonangol." *Africa Energy Intelligence* 621.

2010b. "The World is Sonangol's Oyster." *Africa Energy Intelligence* 623.

African Energy. 2006. "Nigerian Upstream Jitters Following Chukwueke's Sacking and Licence Award Investigations." *African Energy* 105.

Aguilera, Ruth V., Cynthia A. Williams, John M. Conley, and Deborah E. Rupp. 2006. "Corporate Governance and Social Responsibility: A Comparative Analysis of the UK and US." *Corporate Governance: An International Review* 14 (3): 147–158.

Ahima-Young, Victor. 2009. "Nigeria: Minister Plans 18 Boards, Successor Coys for PHCN – Labour." *Vanguard*, January 24, accessed April 13, 2011, www.allafrica.com/stories/200901260700.html.

Ahmad Khan, Sarah. 1994. *Nigeria: The Political Economy of Oil.* Oxford University Press.

Ailemen, Tony. 2010. "Nigeria: Debt Overhang – NNPC Set to Confront FAAC." *Daily Champion*, February 8, accessed April 13, 2011, www.allafrica.com/stories/201002080760.html.

Aissaoui, Ali. 2001. *Algeria: The Political Economy of Oil and Gas.* Oxford University Press.

Akinosho, Toyin. 2011. "Is Nigeria Scaring Off Oil and Gas Investment?" *Africa Oil + Gas Report* 12 (6): 33–35.

Akwaya, Cletus and Okon Bassey. 2004. "Nigeria: Why NEPA Privatisation is Delayed, By BPE." *This Day*, February 6, accessed April 13, 2011, www.allafrica.com/stories/200402060192.html.

Ala, M. A. 1994. "Tārikhcheh-e Naft-e Īrān az Avōkher-e Gharn-e Nuzdahōm Mīlādī tā Kōnun (History of Iran's Oil from the end of the 19th century to the present)." *Anjōman-e Pajuheshgaran-e Īrān (Society of Iranian Researchers)*: 93–138.

Al-Atiqi, Imad. 2005. "Kuwait: Demarcation of Roles and Responsibilities." Presentation to the Good Governance of the National Petroleum Sector workshop, London, UK, September 21–23, Joint Chatham House and CEPMLP project.

Alesina, Alberto and Roberto Perotti. 1996. "Income Distribution, Political Instability, and Investment." *European Economic Review* 40 (6): 1203–1228.

Alike, Ejiofor and Onyebuchi Ezeigbo. 2010. "New Price Regime Approved for Gas; Oil Bid Licensing Expected Next Month." *This Day*, May 28, accessed April 13, 2011, www.thisdayonline.com/nview.php?id=174359.

Al-Kasim, Farouk. 2006. *Managing Petroleum Resources: The 'Norwegian Model' in a Broad Perspective*. Oxford Institute for Energy Studies.

Al Mansouri, Majid, Robert Brett, Yusri Al-Tamimi, Jack Chailer, Patrick Rowe, Maarten Smies, ADNOC. 1998. "Toward 2000: ADNOC's Plans for Health, Safety and Environmental Impact Assessments." Paper No. 49543-MS, Society of Petroleum Engineers.

Al Matroushi, Salem. 2004. "Development of a Competent Workforce for the Oil and Gas Sector." Paper No. 88654, Society of Petroleum Engineers.

Al-Moneef, Majid A. 1998. "International Downstream Integration of National Oil Companies." In *Strategic Positioning in the Oil Industry: Trends and Options*, ed. Paul Stevens, 45–60. Abu Dhabi: The Emirates Center for Strategic Studies and Research.

Al-Sabah, Y. S. F. 1980. *The Oil Economy of Kuwait*. London: Kegan Paul.

Alveal, Edelmira del Carmen. 1993. *Os Desbravadores: A Petrobras e a construcao do Brasil industrial*. Rio de Janeiro: Relume/Dumara. (*in Portuguese*)

Amaize, Emma. 2008. "Ijaw Youth Group Probes NNPC, Mend Claims on $12 Million Fee." *Vanguard*, July 29, accessed April 13, 2011, www.allafrica.com/stories/200807290057.html.

Amuzegar, Jahangir. 1997. "Iran's Economy and the US Sanctions: Lessons from the Iranian Experience." *Middle East Journal* 51 (2): 185–199.

Andrews, Josephine T. and Gabriella R. Montinola. 2004. "Veto Players and the Rule of Law in Emerging Democracies." *Comparative Political Studies* 37 (1): 55–87.

Anglo-Iranian Oil Company (AIOC). 1951. *The Anglo-Iranian Oil Company and Iran: A Description of the Company's Contributions to Iran's Revenue and National Economy and of its Welfare Activities for Employees in Iran*. London: Alfred H. Cooper and Sons.

ANP (Agência Nacional do Petróleo). 2004. *Estimativa da Contribuição do Setor Petróleo ao Produto Interno Bruto no Brasil.* Rio de Janeiro: Nota Técnica ANP. (*in Portuguese*)

APS Review Oil Market Trends. 1999. "Abu Dhabi – The Supreme Petroleum Council." January 25, accessed April 13, 2011, www.allbusiness.com/mining/oil-gas-extraction-crude-petroleum-natural/152238–1.html.

——. 2005. "Venezuela – Spat with Mexico." November 28, accessed April 13, 2011, www.allbusiness.com/mining/oil-gas-extraction-crude-petroleum-natural/841190–1.html.

Arab Petroleum Research Center (APRC). 2008. *Arab Oil and Gas Directory 2008.* Paris: Arab Petroleum Research Center.

Arai, Adriana. 2005. "Mexico Should Sell Some Pemex Units Carlos Slim Says." *Bloomberg,* August 30, accessed April 13, 2011, www.preview.bloomberg.com/apps/news?pid=newsarchive&sid=ai7q0VtVP51o.

Ariweriokuma, Soala. 2009. *The Political Economy of Oil and Gas in Africa: The Case of Nigeria.* New York: Routledge.

Asian Development Bank. 1991. "Report and Recommendation of the President to the Board of Directors on a Proposed Loan and Technical Assistance to India for the Gandhar Field Development Project." October 22.

——. 2001. "Program Performance Audit Report on the Hydrocarbon Sector Program Loan (Loan 1148-IND) in India." January.

Aslund, Anders. 1995. *How Russia Became a Market Economy.* Washington DC: Brookings Institution Press.

——. 1999. "Russia's Collapse." *Foreign Affairs* (September–October).

Associated Press. 2004. "UAE Suggests OPEC Raise Oil Production." *St. Petersburg Times,* May 19, accessed April 13, 2011, www.sptimes.com/2004/05/19/Worldandnation/UAE_suggests_OPEC_rai.shtml.

Astorga, Pablo, Ame R. Berges, and Valpy Fitzgerald. 2005. "The Standard of Living in Latin America During the Twentieth Century." *Economic History Review* 58 (4): 765–796.

Austvik, Ole G. 1991. *Norwegian Gas in the New Europe: How Politics Shape Markets.* Sandvika: Vett & Viten.

Auty, R. M. 1990. *Resource-Based Industrialization: Sowing the Oil in Eight Developing Countries.* Oxford: Clarendon Press.

Azam, Aris. 2008. *The Quintessential Man: The Story of Tan Sri Azizan Zainul Abidin.* Petaling Jaya: Crestime Holding.

Baena, César. 1999a. "The Internationalization Strategy of PDVSA: A Policy-Making Analysis." *SciencesPo* (November).

——. 1999b. *The Policy Process in a Petro-State: An Analysis of PDVSA's (Petróleos de Venezuela SA's) Internationalisation Strategy.* Aldershot: Ashgate.

Baker Hughes. 2008. "International Rotary Rig Count 2008." Baker Hughes website, accessed June 26, 2008, www.investor.shareholder. com/bhi/rig_counts/rc_index.cfm.

Bamberg, James H. 1994. *The History of the British Petroleum Company: The Anglo-Iranian years, 1928–1954*, vol. II. Cambridge University Press.

   2000. *The History of the British Petroleum Company, British Petroleum and Global Oil, 1950–1975: The Challenge of Nationalism*, vol. III. Cambridge University Press.

Banerjee, Sudeshna and Michael Munger. 2004. "Move to Markets? An Empirical Analysis of Privatization in Developing Countries." *Journal of International Development* 16 (2): 213–240.

Barzel, Yoram. 1997. *Economic Analysis of Property Rights*, 2nd edn. New York: Cambridge University Press.

Batley, Richard and George Larbi. 2004. *The Changing Role of Government: The Reform of Public Services in Developing Countries*. Houndsmills: Palgrave Macmillan.

BBC News. 2008. "Landslide for Angola Ruling Party." September 17, accessed March 14, 2010, www.news.bbc.co.uk/2/hi/africa/7620504. stm.

   2009a. "Guide: How Iran is Ruled." June 9, accessed December 7, 2010, www.news.bbc.co.uk/2/hi/middle_east/8051750.stm.

   2009b. "Iraq Oil Contract Goes to Angola's Sonangol." December 30, accessed March 14, 2010, www.news.bbc.co.uk/2/hi/ business/8435151.stm.

Bell, Ruth Greenspan. 2005. "Culture and History Count: Choosing Environmental Tools to Fit Available Institutions and Experience." *Indiana Law Review* 38: 637–669.

Bello, O. 2008. "Political Patronage Dashes Bid to Reduce Diesel Price." *Business Day*, October 6.

Bellos, Alex. 2008. "Money Talks – Interview: Aguinaldo Jaime, Speaking to the Deputy PM." *Sonangol Universo* 18 (Summer): 26–29.

Belton, Catherine and Isabel Gorst. 2010. "Energy: Progress Frozen." *Financial Times*, March 25, accessed April 14, 2011. www. ft.com/cms/s/0/4d9de22c-3847–11df-8420–00144feabdc0. html#axzz1JXTpIyZY.

Bender, Gerald. 1978. *Angola Under the Portuguese: The Myth and the Reality*. Berkeley: University of California Press.

Bentham, R. W. and W. G. R. Smith. 1986. *State Petroleum Corporations: Corporate Forms, Powers and Control*. Dundee: The Centre for Petroleum and Mineral Law Studies, University of Dundee.

Benton, Lauren. 2009. "Not Just a Concept: Institutions and the 'Rule of Law'." *The Journal of Asian Studies* 68: 117–122.

Bermúdez-Lugo, Omayra. 2004. "The Mineral Industry of Angola." In *Minerals Yearbook* vol. III. Washington DC: US Interior Dept., Geological Survey.

Bermúdez Romero, Manuel. 2004. *PDVSA en carne propia: Testimonio del Derrumbe de la Primera Empresa Venezolana.* Caracas: OME Estudios de Mercado y Comunicacion. (*in Spanish*)

Besley, Timothy and Masayuki Kudamatsu. 2008. "Making Autocracy Work." In *Institutions and Economic Performance*, ed. Elhanan Helpman, 452–510. Cambridge: Harvard University Press.

Bevan, David, Paul Collier, and Jan Willem Gunning. 1999. *The Political Economy of Poverty, Equity, and Growth: Nigeria and Indonesia.* New York: Oxford University Press.

Biller, David. 2008. " 'The Problem with PEMEX is It's Just Incredibly Bureaucratic,' " by David Shields. *Business News Americas*, November 7, accessed April 14, 2011, www.energiaadebate.com/Articulos/ Enero2009/imagenes/Biller.pdf

Bindemann, Kirsten. 1999. "Vertical Integration in the Oil Industry: A Review of the Literature." *Journal of Energy Literature* 5 (1).

Birmingham, David. 1995. "Language is Power: Regional Politics in Angola." In *Why Angola Matters: Report of a Conference held at Pembroke College, Cambridge, March 21–22, 1994*, ed. Keith Hart and Joanna Lewis, 91–95. London: James Currey.

Black, Bernard S., Reinier Kraakman, and Anna Tarassova. 2000. "Russian Privatization and Corporate Governance: What Went Wrong?" *Stanford Law Review* 52: 1731–1808.

Blair, John M. 1976. *The Control of Oil.* New York: Pantheon Books.

Boardman, Anthony E. and Aidan R. Vining. 1989. "Ownership and Performance in Competitive Environments: A Comparison of the Performance of Private, Mixed, and State-Owned Enterprises." *Journal of Law and Economics* 32 (1): 1–33.

Bodzin, Steven. 2009. "Ramirez Pumps Cash for Chavez as $40 Crude Imperils Venezuela." *Bloomberg*, February 3, accessed April 14, 2011, www.bloomberg.com/apps/news?pid=newsarchive&sid=arRinmnrGt yE&refer=latin_america.

Boettke, Peter J., Christopher J. Coyne, and Peter T. Leeson. 2008. "Institutional Stickiness and the New Development Economics." *American Journal of Economics and Sociology* 67 (2): 331–358.

Bortolotti, Bernardo, Marcella Fantini, and Domenico Siniscalco. 2001. "Privatisation: Politics, Institutions, and Financial Markets." *Emerging Markets Review* 2 (2): 109–137.

2003. "Privatisation Around the World: Evidence from Panel Data." *Journal of Public Economics* 88 (1–2): 305–332.

Boshcheck, Ralf. 2007. "The Governance of Oil Supply: An Institutional Perspective on NOC Control and the Questions It Poses." *International Journal of Energy Sector Management* 1 (4): 366–389.

Boubakri, Narjess and Jean-Claude Cosset. 1998. "The Financial and Operating Performance of Newly Privatized Firms: Evidence from Developing Countries." *The Journal of Finance* 53 (3): 1081–1110.

Boué, Juan C. 1993. *Venezuela: The Political Economy of Oil.* Oxford University Press.

    2002. "El Programa de Internacionalización de PDVSA: ¿Triunfo Estratégico o Desastre Fiscal?" *Revista Venezoloana de Economía y Ciencias Sociales* 8 (2): 237–282. (*in Spanish*)

    2009. "How Much Oil Has Venezuela Really Been Producing?" *Middle East Economic Survey* 52 (18).

Bowen, J.M. 1991. "25 Years of UK North Sea Exploration." *Geological Society, London, Memoirs 1991* 14: 1–7.

Bowie, Paddy. 2001. *A Vision Realised: The Transformation of a National Oil Corporation.* Kuala Lumpur: Orillia Corp. Sdn Bhd.

BP. "BP in Angola." BP website, accessed January 2, 2009, www.bp.com/ sectiongenericarticle.do?categoryId=427&contentId=2000571.

    2007. *Annual Report and Accounts 2007.* London: BP.

    2008. *Statistical Review of World Energy June 2008.* London: BP.

    2009a. *Statistical Review of World Energy June 2009.* London: BP.

    2009b. *Annual Report and Accounts 2008.* London: BP.

    2010. *Statistical Review of World Energy June 2010.* London: BP.

    2011. *Statistical Review of World Energy June 2011.* London: BP.

Brower, Derek. 2009. "TSGP: A Trans-Saharan Mirage." *Petroleum Economist*, April.

Brown, Anthony C. 1999. *Oil, God, and Gold: The Story of Aramco and the Saudi Kings.* Wilmington: Houghton Mifflin Harcourt.

Brumberg, Daniel and Ariel I. Ahram. 2007. "The National Iranian Oil Company in Iranian Politics." Policy Report. The Baker Institute Energy Forum, *The Changing Role of National Oil Companies in International Energy Markets*, Houston, Texas, Rice University, March 1–2.

Brune, Nancy, Geoffrey Garrett, and Bruce Kogut. 2004. "The International Monetary Fund and the Global Spread of Privatization." *IMF Staff Papers* 51 (2): 1.

Brunnschweiler, Christa N. and Erwin H Butte. 2008. "The Resource Curse Revisited and Revised: A Tale of Paradoxes and Red Herrings." *Journal of Environmental Economics and Management* 55 (3): 248–264.

Bueno de Mesquita, Bruce, Alastair Smith, Randolph Siverson, and James Morrow. 2003. *The Logic of Political Survival.* Cambridge: MIT Press.

Business Monitor International. 2009. *Algeria Oil and Gas Report Q1 2009*. London: BMI.

Business Standard. 2007. "Sharma Formally Appointed ONGC Chief." July 4, accessed April 14, 2011, www.business-standard.com/india/news/sharma-formally-appointed-ongc-chief/25098/on.

2009. "India Can Save $8.3 bn annually on Reliance KG-D6 Gas." July 10, accessed April 14, 2011, www.business-standard.com/india/news/india-can-save-83-bn-annuallyreliance-kg-d6-gas/67326/on.

Butrin, Dmitry. 2007. "Gazprom to Launch Major PR Campaign." *Kommersant*, January 16, accessed April 14, 2011, www.kommersant.com/p734218.

Butt, Gerald. 2001. "Oil and Gas in the UAE." In *United Arab Emirates: A New Perspective*, ed. Ibrahim Al Abed and Peter Hellyer, 231–248. London: Trident Press.

Buxton, Julia. 1999. "Venezuela: Degenerative Democracy." *Democratization* 6 (1): 246–270.

Caiden, Gerald E. 1991. *Administrative Reform Comes of Age*. New York: Walter de Gruyter.

Campodonico, Humberto. 2007. "Gestion Mixta y Privada en la Industria de Hidrocarburos." *Serie Recursos naturales e Infraestructura* n⁰ 122. Santiago de Chile: Cepal, Abril.

Campos, Indira and Alex Vines. 2007. "Angola and China: A Pragmatic Partnership." Paper presented at a CSIS conference, *Prospects for Improving US–China–Africa Cooperation*, London, UK, December 5.

Cárdenas, Cuauhtémoc. 2006. "The Future of US-Mexico Relations." Speech and interview at the Center for Latin American Studies, University of California, Berkeley, March 2.

Carlisle, Tamsin. 2010. "China-Venezuela Oil Deal Bad for Environment." The National Blogs website, April 19, accessed April 14, 2011, www.blogs.thenational.ae/cgi-bin/mt/mt-search.cgi?search=national&IncludeBlogs=67,63,71,70,68,1,18,72,44,55,74,75,40,61,69,59,49,53,48,42,46,65,39,36,64,51,58,47,52,38,60,56,73,45,37,66,43,62,54&limit=10&page=21.

Carneiro, Dionisio D. 1982. "O Terceiro Choque: É Possível Evitar-se a Depressão?" In *Dívida externa, Recessão e Ajuste Estrutural*, ed. Persio Arida. Rio de Janeiro: Paz e Terra. (*in Portuguese*)

Carreón-Rodríguez, Victor G., Armando Jiménez, and Juan Rosellón. 2007. "The Mexican Electricity Sector: Economic, Legal and Political Issues." In *The Political Economy of Power Sector Reform: The Experiences of Five Major Developing Countries*, ed. David Victor and Thomas C. Heller, 175–214. New York: Cambridge University Press.

Castro, Antonio B. and Francisco Pires de Souza. 1985. *A Economia Brasileira em Marcha Forçada*. Rio de Janeiro: Paz e Terra. (*in Portuguese*)

Caves, Douglas W. and Laurits R. Christensen. 1980. "The Relative Efficiency of Public and Private Firms in a Competitive Environment: The Case of Canadian Railroads." *Journal of Political Economy* 88 (5): 958–976.

CBI (Central Bank of the Islamic Republic of Iran) (Bānk-i Markazī-i Īrān). 1975. *Idārah-i Bar- rasīhā-yi Iqtiṣādī: 1338–50 (National Income of Iran: 1959–72)*. Tehran: Bureau of National Accounts (*in Persian*)

   Multiple years. *Economic Report and Balance Sheet*, 1980/81–2008/09. Tehran: Bank Tejarat. (*in Persian*)

Centre for Economics and Management (IFP-School). 2007. *Oil and Gas Exploration and Production: Reserves, Costs, Contracts*. Paris: Editions Technip.

Chabal, Patrick and Nuno Vidal, eds. 2008. *Angola: The Weight of History*. New York: Columbia University Press.

Chang, Ha-Joon. 2008. *Bad Samaritans: The Myth of Free Trade and the Secret History of Capitalism*. New York: Bloomsbury Press.

Chang, Roberto, Constantino Hevia, and Norman Loayza. 2009. "Privatization and Nationalization Cycles." *World Bank*, Policy Research Working Paper No. 5029. doi: 10.1596/1813–9450–5029.

Chevron. 2010. "Nigeria Fact Sheet." Chevron Corporation website, accessed November 23, 2009, www.chevron.com/documents/pdf/nigeriafactsheet.pdf.

Chi-Chang, Teh. 2009. *The Budget: How the Government Is Spending OUR Money*. Kuala Lumpur: Research for Social Advancement.

Chong, Alberto and Florencio Lopez-de-Silanes. 2003. "The Truth About Privatization in Latin America." *Inter-American Development Bank*, Research Network Working Paper No. R-486.

Christensen, Tom and Per Laegreid. 2006. "Regulatory Agencies—The Challenges of Balancing Agency Autonomy and Political Control." *Governance: An International Journal of Policy, Administration, and Institutions* 20 (3): 499–520.

Chukwu, Philip. 2006. "Joint Venture and Production Sharing Contracts." Presentation to *First Nigeria Extractive Industries Transparency Initiative*, Port Harcourt, Nigeria, February.

CIA (Central Intelligence Agency). 2010a. "The World Factbook: Venezuela." CIA website, accessed May 11, 2010, www.cia.gov/library/publications/the-world-factbook/geos/ve.html.

   2010b. "The World Factbook: United Arab Emirates." CIA website, accessed October 25, 2010, www.cia.gov/library/publications/the-world-factbook/geos/ae.html.

CIDCM (Center for International Development and Conflict Management). 2003. *Polity IV Country Reports.* Polity IV Project. University of Maryland, accessed September 14, 2010, www.systemicpeace.org/polity/Nigeria2008.pdf.

Claes, Dag Harald. 2002. "Statoil – Between Nationalisation, Globalisation and Europeanisation." ARENA Working Paper 02/34. Centre for European Studies, University of Oslo, accessed April 14, 2011, www.sv.uio.no/arena/english/research/publications/arena-publications/workingpapers/working-papers2002/wp02_34.htm.

2003. "Globalization and State Oil Companies: The Case of Statoil." *Journal of Energy and Development* 29 (1): 43–64.

Clarke, Duncan. 2000. "Petroleum Prospects and Political Power." In *Angola's War Economy: The Role of Oil and Diamonds*, ed. Jackie Cilliers and Christian Dietrich, 196–218. Pretoria: Institute for Security Studies.

Clarke, George and Robert Cull. 2005. "Bank Privatization in Argentina: A Model of Political Constraints and Differential Outcomes." *Journal of Development Economics* 78 (1): 133–155.

Clarkson, Kenneth W. 1989. "Privatization at the State and Local Level." In *Privatization and State-Owned Enterprises: Lessons from the United States, Great Britain and Canada*, ed. Paul MacAvoy *et al.*, 144–207. Boston: Kluwer Academic.

CNPC (China National Petroleum Corporation). 2003–2007. *Annual Report.* Beijing: CNPC.

Coase, R. H. 1990. *The Firm, the Market and the Law.* University of Chicago Press.

Cockrell, Cathy. 2006. "A Conversation with Cuauhtémoc Cárdenas." *UC Berkeley News*, March 23, accessed June 1, 2010, www.berkeley.edu/news/berkeleyan/2006/03/23_cardenas.shtml.

Cohn, Gabriel. 1968. *Petroleo e Nacionalismo.* São Paulo: Difusão Européia do Livro. (*in Portuguese*)

Collins, Gabe. 2006. "With Oil Companies, Russia Seeking Control Plus Capital." *Oil and Gas Journal* 104 (19): 18–21.

Collins, R., R. Durham, R. Fayek, and W. Zeid. 2008. "Interface Management." Paper No. 117309-MS, Society of Petroleum Engineers.

Comptroller and Auditor General of India. 1996. "Introduction." In *Report of the Comptroller and Auditor General of India on the Union Government No. 1 (Commercial) of 1996*, chapter 1. New Delhi: Government of India.

2001. "Avoidable Expenditure on Creation of Excess Capacity by ONGC Ltd." In *Report of the Comptroller and Auditor General of India on the Union Government*, Review of Activities of Selected Public Sector

Undertakings, Compliance Audit Report No. 4, chapter 6. New Delhi: Government of India.

2008. "Oil and Natural Gas Corporation Limited – Deep Water Exploration." In *Report of the Comptroller and Auditor General of India on the Union Government*, Review of Activities of Selected Public Sector Undertakings, Compliance Audit Report No. 9, chapter 7. New Delhi: Government of India.

Connors, Will. 2009. "Delta Farce: Nigeria's Oil Mess." *The Wall Street Journal*, September 21, accessed September 25, 2010, www.online.wsj.com/article/SB125331370878424233.html.

Coon, Carleton S. 1955. *Operation Bultiste: Promoting Industrial Development in Saudi Arabia*. Leiden: A W Sijthoff's Uitgeversmij.

Coronel, Gustavo. 1983. *The Nationalization of the Venezuelan Oil Industry: From Technocratic Success to Political Failure*. Lexington: Lexington Books.

Costa, Desidério. 2005. "Desidério Costa Remembers." *Sonangol Universo* 5 (Spring): 14–15.

Council of Ministers of Angola. 1999. Decreto No. 19/99 – Law of Public Companies. August 20.

Dadwal, Shebonti R. 1998. "Iran Sets Out to Win Friends in the Arab World." *Strategic Analysis* 22 (2): 263–279.

Daily Trust. 2010. "Nigeria: Kaduna, Warri Refineries Start Production." February 25, accessed September 25, 2010, www.allafrica.com/stories/201002260217.html.

Dam, Kenneth W. 1974. "The Evolution of North Sea Licensing Policy in Britain and Norway." *Journal of Law and Economics* 17 (2): 213–263.

1976. *Oil Resources: Who Gets What How?* University of Chicago Press.

Daniel, Elton L. 2001. *The History of Iran*. Westport: Greenwood.

Darmstadter, Joel. 1971. *Energy in the World Economy: A Statistical Review of Trends in Output, Trade, and Consumption Since 1925*. Baltimore: Johns Hopkins Press.

Davidson, Christopher M. 2006. "After Sheikh Zayed: The Politics of Succession in Abu Dhabi and the UAE." *Middle East Policy* 13 (1): 42–59.

2009. *Abu Dhabi: Oil and Beyond*. New York: Columbia University Press.

Davis, Jeffrey M., Rolando Ossowski, James A. Daniel, and Steven Barnett. 2003. "Stabilization and Savings Funds for Nonrenewable Resources: Experience and Fiscal Policy Implications." In *Fiscal Policy Formulation and Implementation in Oil-Producing Countries*, ed. J. M. Davis, R. Ossowski, and A. Fedelino, 273–315. Washington DC: IMF.

Daya, Ayesha. 2010. "ConocoPhillips Said to Pull Out From Adnoc Shah Gas." *Bloomberg Businessweek*, April 28, accessed April 14, 2011, www.businessweek.com/news/2010–04–28/conocophillips-said-to-pull-out-from-adnoc-shah-gas-update3-.html.

de Araujo, Joao L. and Andre Ghirardi. 1987. "Substitution of Petroleum Products in Brazil: Urgent Issues." *Energy Policy* 15 (1): 22–39.

de Oliveira, Adilson. 1977. "Internationalisation du Capital et Development Economique: L'Industrie Petrolîère au Brésil." Ph.D. Diss., Université de Sciences Sociales, Grenoble, France.

    1991. "Reassessing the Brazilian Alcohol Programme." *Energy Policy* 19 (1): 47–55.

    2007. "The Political Economy of the Brazilian Power Industry Reform." In *The Political Economy of Power Sector Reform*, ed. David Victor and Thomas C. Heller, 31–75. New York: Cambridge University Press.

    2008a. "South Cone Energy Integration: A Look from Brazil." *International Journal of Energy Sector Management* 1 (2): 122–140.

de Oliveira, Adilson. ed. 2008b. "Competitividade Para-Petrolífera Brasileira: Desafios e Oportunidades." Rio de Janeiro: Prominp.

Diamond, Larry. 1988. *Class, Ethnicity, and Democracy in Nigeria: The Failure of the First Republic*. Syracuse University Press.

    1995. "Nigeria: The Uncivic Society and the Descent into Praetorianism." In *Politics in Developing Countries: Comparing Experiences with Democracy* 2nd edn., ed. Larry Diamond, Juan J. Linz, Seymour Martin Lipset, 416–491. Boulder: Lynne Rienner.

Diccionario de la corrupción en Venezuela. 1989. Vol. I, 1959–1979. Caracas: Consorcio de Ediciones Capriles C.A.

Dickson, Prince Charles. 2008. "Nigeria: NEPA Was Privatised in a Haste – Lukman." *Leadership*, February 11, accessed April 14, 2011, www.allafrica.com/stories/200802111353.html.

Dillman Bradford L. 2000. *State and Private Sector in Algeria: The Politics of Rent-Seeking and Failed Development*. Boulder: Westview.

Dinç, I. Serdar and Nandini Gupta. 2011. "The Decision to Privatize: Finance and Politics." *The Journal of Finance* 66 (1): 241–269.

Dirks, Gary. 2006. "Energy Security: China and the World." BP presentation to the *International Symposium on Energy Security: China and the World*, Beijing, China, May 24.

Diwan, Roger. 2007. "The Current Implications of the World Energy Situation for United States Energy Supplies." Presentation at Federal Trade Commission Conference, *Energy Markets in the 21st Century: Competition Policy in Perspective*, Washington DC, April 12.

Dixit, Avinash. 1997. "Power of Incentives in Private Versus Public Organizations." *American Economic Review* 87 (2): 378–382.

2004. *Lawlessness and Economics: Alternative Modes of Governance.* Princeton University Press.

D'León, Milton. 2006. "La 'Revolución Bolivariana' y el mito del 'Socialismo del Siglo XXI (The Bolivarian revolution and the myth of 21st century socialism).'" *Estrategia Internacional* (December 23): 169–206. (*in Spanish*)

Dobbins, Craig, Michael Boehlje, Alan Miller, and Freddie Barnard. 2000. "Financial Performance: Measurement and Analysis." *Purdue Agricultural Economics Report* (March): 14–18.

Domíguez, Jorge. 1982. "Business Nationalism: Latin American National Business Attitudes and Behavior Toward Multinational Enterprises." In *Economic Issues and Political Conflict: US-Latin American Relations,* ed. Jorge Domiguez, 52–58. London: Butterworth Scientific.

DonPedro, Ibiba. 2006. *Oil in the Water: Crude Power and Militancy in the Niger Delta.* Lagos, Nigeria: Foreword Communications Limited.

Downs, Erica S. 2000. *China's Quest for Energy Security.* Santa Monica: RAND.

2004. "The Chinese Energy Security Debate." *China Quarterly* 177: 21–41.

2007a. "China's Quest for Overseas Oil." *Far East Economic Review* (September): 52–56.

2007b. "The Fact and Fiction of Sino-African Energy Relations." *China Security* 3 (3): 42–68.

D'Souza, Juliet and William L. Megginson. 1999. "The Financial and Operating Performance of Privatized Firms During the 1990s." *The Journal of Finance* 54 (4): 1397–1438.

Duncan, Roderick. 2006. "Price or Politics? An Investigation of the Causes of Expropriation." *Australian Journal of Agricultural and Resource Economics* 50 (1): 85–101.

Dunning, Thad. 2008. *Crude Democracy: Natural Resource Wealth and Political Regimes.* New York: Cambridge University Press.

Ebrahimi, S. N., A. Shiroui Khouzani, NIOC, and PEDEC. 2003. "The Contractual Form of Iran's Buy-Back Contracts in Comparison with Production Sharing and Service Contract." Presented at the Middle East Oil Show, Bahrain, Society of Petroleum Engineers, June 9–12.

Economic Bank of Resources of Iran (Bānk-i Tāwsī'ah-i San'atī va Ma'danī-i Īrān). Multiple Volumes. *Annual Report of the Board of Directors to the General Assembly of Shareholders, 1970/71–1977/8.* Tehran: Bureau of National Accounts. (*in Persian*)

Economides, Michael J., Anibal Martínez, and Silvia Puky. 2007. "The History of PDVSA and Venezuela." *Energy Tribune*, January 17, accessed July 9, 2009, www.energytribune.com/articles.cfm?aid=347.

Economist Intelligence Unit. 1982. *Algeria: The Giant Market of North Africa*. London: EIU.

2005. *Algeria Country Report May 2005*. London: EIU.

2008. *Algeria Country Report March 2008*. London: EIU.

2009. Commercially available database containing various economic indicators by country, available at www.eiu.com/ (subscription required).

2010. *Algeria Country Report February 2010*. London: EIU.

Egert, Balazs. 2005. "Equilibrium Exchange Rates in Southeastern Europe, Russia, Ukraine and Turkey: Healthy or (Dutch) Diseased?" *Economic Systems* 29 (2): 205–241.

EGM. 2009a. "Gazprom Delays Start-up of Bovanenkoye by One Year to 2012." June 30, accessed April 14, 2011, www.icis.com/heren/newsindex.aspx?fromdate=01/6/2009&todate=30/06/2009.

2009b. "Focus on Russian Independent Producer Novatek." June 15, accessed April 14, 2011, www.icis.com/heren/newsindex.aspx?fromdate=01/6/2009&todate=30/06/2009&pagenumber=14.

EIA (Energy Information Administration). 2004. "Global Oil Supply Disruptions Since 1951." US Dept. of Energy, EIA website, accessed April 14, 2011, www.eia.doe.gov/security/distable.html.

2007. "Country Analysis Briefs: Venezuela." US Dept. of Energy, EIA website accessed March 29, 2010, www.eia.doe.gov/countries/cab.cfm?fips=VE.

2008a. "Country Analysis Brief: Angola." US Dept. of Energy, EIA website, accessed December 22, 2008, www.eia.doe.gov/cabs/Angola/Oil.html.

2008b. "Country Analysis Briefs: Iran." US Dept. of Energy, EIA website, accessed June 23, 2008, www.eia.doe.gov/emeu/cabs/Iran/Oil.html.

2009a. "Country Analysis Briefs: Venezuela." US Dept. of Energy, EIA website, accessed March 29, 2010, www.eia.doe.gov/countries/cab.cfm?fips=VE.

2009b. "Who are the Major Players Supplying the World Oil Market?" Energy in Brief. US Dept. of Energy, EIA website, accessed September 15, 2010, www.eia.doe.gov/energy_in_brief/world_oil_market.cfm.

2009c. "Russia: Natural Gas." US Dept. of Energy, EIA website, accessed August 6, 2010, www.eia.doe.gov/cabs/Russia/NaturalGas.html.

2010a. "Country Analysis Briefs: Nigeria." US Dept. of Energy, EIA website, accessed July 11, 2010, www.eia.doe.gov/cabs/Nigeria/Oil.html.

2010b. "International Energy Statistics." US Dept. of Energy, EIA website, accessed September 10, 2010, www.tonto.eia.doe.gov/cfapps/ipd-bproject/IEDIndex3.cfm?tid=5&pid=57&aid=6.

2010c. "Country Energy Profiles: United Arab Emirates Energy Profile." US Dept. of Energy, EIA website, accessed May 31, 2010, www.eia.doe.gov/country/country_energy_data.cfm?fips=TC.

Eifert, Benn, Alan Gelb, and Nils B. Tallroth. 2003. "Managing Oil Wealth." *Finance & Development* 40 (1).

Eller, Stacy, Peter Hartley, and Kenneth B. Medlock III. 2007. "Empirical Evidence on the Operational Efficiency of National Oil Companies." Policy Report. The Baker Institute Energy Forum, *The Changing Role of National Oil Companies in International Energy Markets*, Houston, Texas, Rice University, March 1–2.

Elm, Mostafa. 1992. *Oil, Power, and Principle: Iran's Oil Nationalization and Its Aftermath*. Syracuse University Press.

El Mallakh, Ragaei, Øystein Noreng, and Barry W. Poulson. 1984. *Petroleum and Economic Development: The Cases of Mexico and Norway*. Lexington: Lexington Books.

Emery, Alex. 2009. "Sinopec, Angola's Sonangol to Sign Ecuador Oil Contracts." *Bloomberg*, October 22, accessed March 15, 2010, www.bloomberg.com/apps/news?pid=20601089&sid=a4z_qZF4ZUZA.

Emmond, Kenneth. 2005. "Carlos Slim and Mexican Poverty." *Mexidata*, September 12, accessed April 14, 2011, www.mexidata.info/id601.html.

Energy Intelligence. 2006. *Energy Intelligence Top 100: Ranking the World's Oil Companies*. Energy Intelligence Group.

Enright, Michael, Antonio Francés, and Edith Scott Saavedra. 1996. *Venezuela: The Challenge of Competitiveness*. New York: St. Martin's Press.

Entelis, John P. 1986. *Algeria: The Revolution Institutionalized*. Boulder: Westview.

1999. "Sonatrach: The Political Economy of an Algerian State Institution." *The Middle East Journal* 53 (1): 9–27.

Entessar, Nader. 1999. "Iran: Geopolitical Challenges and the Caspian Region." In *Oil and Geopolitics in the Caspian Sea Region*, ed. Michael P. Croissant and Bülent Aras. Westport: Praeger.

Esau, Iain. 2006a. "Eni Bonus Offer Stuns World." *Upstream*, April 13.

2006b. "Angola in New High Bid." *Upstream*, May 12.

2006c. "ONGC Videsh Falls by Wayside in Race for Angola Riches." *Upstream*, April 13.

Esfahani, Hadi S. and M. Hashem Pesaran. 2009. "The Iranian Economy in the Twentieth Century: A Global Perspective." *Iranian Studies* 42 (2): 177–211.

ESMAP (Energy Sector Management Assistance Programme). 2003. "Cross-border Oil and Gas Pipelines: Problems and Prospects." ESMAP technical paper. Washington DC: UNDP/World Bank.

2007. "Investing in Oil in the Middle East and North Africa: Institutions, Incentives and National Oil Companies." ESMAP Report No. 40405–MNA. Washington DC: World Bank.

Espinasa, Ramón. 1996. "Ideología, Marco Institucional y Desarrollo del Sector Petrolero" (Ideology, Institutional Framework and Development of the Petroleum Sector). *Revista Venezolana de Economía y Ciencias Sociales* 2–3(April–September). (*in Spanish*)

2001. "La Economía Política de la Reforma Petrolera." *Economía y Petróleo*, September 10. (*in Spanish*)

2006. "El Auge y el Colapso de PDVSA a los Trienta Años de la Nacionalización." *Revista Venezolana de Economía y Ciencias Sociales* 12(1): 147–182. (*in Spanish*)

Estrin, Saul. 1998. "State Ownership, Corporate Governance and Privatisation." In *Corporate Governance, State-Owned Enterprises and Privatisation*, ed. OECD, 11–32. Paris: OECD.

Europa. 2004. *Regional Surveys of the Worlds: The Middle East and North Africa 2004*, 50th edn. London: Routledge.

Evans, Peter B. 1979. *Dependent Development: The Alliance of Multi-national, State, and Local Capital in Brazil*. Princeton University Press.

Ewing, Richard D. 2005. "Chinese Corporate Governance and Prospects for Reform." *Journal of Contemporary China* 14 (43): 317–338.

ExxonMobil. 2009. *2008 Summary Annual Report*. Irving: ExxonMobil.

Fan, Joseph P. H., T. J. Wong, and Tianyu Zhang. 2007. "Politically Connected CEOs, Corporate Governance, and Post-IPO Performance of China's Newly Partially Privatized Firms." *Journal of Financial Economics* 84 (2): 330–357.

Fantine, J. 1986. "Anais do Seminário: Alternativas para uma Política Energética." CPFL, Campinas/São Paulo. (*in Portuguese*)

Fardmanesh, Mohsen. 1991. "Dutch Disease Economics and Oil Syndrome: An Empirical Study." *World Development* 19 (6): 711–717.

Farmanfarmanian, Manucher and Roxane Farmanfarmaian. 1997. *Blood and Oil: A Prince's Memoir of Iran, from the Shah to the Ayatollah*. New York: Random House.

Fars News. 2008. "Iran to Hike Power Price." July 23, accessed April 14, 2011, www.english.farsnews.com/newstext.php?nn=8705021221.

Fattouh, Bassam. 2008. *North African Oil and Foreign Investment in Changing Market Conditions*. Oxford Institute for Energy Studies.

Faucon, Benoit. 2006. "China Makes Headway in Angola with Multiple Trade Ties." *Dow Jones International News*, November 30.

Feng, Fang, Qian Sun, and Wilson H. S. Tong. 2004. "Do Government-Linked Companies Underperform?" *Journal of Banking & Finance* 28 (10): 2461–2492.

Fernandes, Florestan. 1981. *A Revolução Burguesa no Brasil*. Rio de Janeiro: Zahar. (*in Portuguese*)

Finon, Dominique and Catherine Locatelli. 2008. "Russian and European Gas Interdependence: Could Contractual Trade Channel Geopolitics?" *Energy Policy* 36 (1): 423–442.

Fitch Ratings. 2009. *Fitch Affirms PEMEX's Ratings: Outlook to Stable*. January 26.

Flynn, Norman. 2002. "Explaining New Public Management: The Importance of Context." In *New Public Management: Current Trends and Future Prospects*, ed. Kate McLaughlin, Stephan Osborne, and Ewan Ferlie, 57–76. London: Routledge.

Forbes.com. 2007. "The World's 2,000 Largest Public Companies." *Forbes* Special Report, March 29.

Forrest, Tom. 1986. "The Political Economy of Civil Rule and the Economic Crisis in Nigeria 1979–1984." *Review of African Political Economy* 35: 4–26.

  1995. *Politics and Economic Development in Nigeria*. Boulder: Westview.

Frankel, Francine R. 2005. *India's Political Economy: 1947–2004*, 2nd edn. New Delhi: Oxford University Press.

Frontera Norte Sur. 2006. "Mexicali and San Luis Rio Colorado News." Accessed April 14, 2011, www.nmsu.edu/~frontera/Jan-Dec06/Mexicalinews.html.

Frontier India. 2008. "ONGC and Rocksource Sign Agreement for Partnership in Deepwater Block." September 17, accessed June 25, 2010, www.frontierindia.net/cae/ongc-and-rocksource-sign-agreement-for-partnership-in-deepwater-block/76/.

Furtado, Andre T. and Adriana G. de Freitas. 2000. "The Catch-Up Strategy of Petrobras Through Cooperative R&D." *Journal of Technological Transfer* 25 (1): 23–36.

Furtado, Celso. 1971. *Formação Econômica do Brasil*. São Paulo: Companhia Editora Nacional. (*in Portuguese*)

Furubotn, Eirik G. and Svetozar Pejovich. 1972. "Property Rights and Economic Theory: A Survey of Recent Literature." *Journal of Economic Literature* 10 (4): 1137–1162.

Gandhi, Jennifer and Adam Przeworski. 2007. "Authoritarian Institutions and the Survival of Autocrats." *Comparative Political Studies* 40 (11): 1279–1301.

Gazprom. 2008. IFRS: Consolidated Financial Statements, December 2008, accessed April 14, 2011, www.gazprom.com/f/posts/71/879403/2ifrs. pdf.

2009a. газпром в цифрах, 2004–2008, справочник (*in Russian*), accessed April 14, 2011, www.gazprom.ru/f/posts/51/771468/sr_2008.pdf.

2009b. Добыча газа и нефти (*in Russian*). www.gazprom.ru/production/ extraction.

2010. "Projects." Gazprom website, accessed October 18, 2010, www. gazprom.com/production/projects/deposits/.

Geddes, Barbara. 2003. *Paradigms and Sand Castles: Theory Building and Research Design in Comparative Politics.* Ann Arbor: University of Michigan Press.

Gehlbach, Scott and Phillip Keefer. 2008. "Investment Without Democracy: Ruling-Party Institutionalization and Credible Commitment in Autocracies." Working paper, accessed April 14, 2011, www.users. polisci.wisc.edu/gehlbach/research.html.

Gillies, Alexandra. 2007. "Obasanjo, the Donor Community and Reform Implementation in Nigeria." *The Round Table* 96 (392): 569–586.

2009. "Reforming Corruption Out of Nigerian Oil? Part One: Mapping Corruption Risks in Oil Sector Governance." CMI U4 Brief, February, accessed April 14, 2011, www.u4.no/themes/nrm.

2010. "Oil Sector Reform in Africa: the Case of Nigeria." Ph.D. diss., Dept. of Politics and International Studies, University of Cambridge.

Gilson, Ronald J. 2001. "Globalizing Corporate Governance: Convergence of Form or Function." *American Journal of Comparative Law* 49: 329–357.

Giusti, Luis E. 1999. "La Apertura: The Opening of Venezuela's Oil Industry." *Journal of International Affairs* 53 (1): 117.

Global Witness. 2009. "Private Oil Firm's Shareholders Have Same Names as Top Angolan Government Officials." Global Witness Press Release, April 8.

2010. "Link Between Angolan President's Son-In-Law and State Oil Company Raises Questions About Transparency." Global Witness Press Release, March 15.

Gonzalez, Nathan. 2007. *Engaging Iran: The Rise of a Middle East Powerhouse and America's Strategic Choice.* Westport: Praeger Security International.

González-Páramo, José Manuel and Pablo Hernández De Cos. 2005. "The Impact of Public Ownership and Competition on Productivity." *Kyklos* 58 (4): 495–517.

Gordon, Richard and Thomas Stenvoll. 2007. "Statoil: A Study in Political Entrepreneurship." Policy Report. The Baker Institute Energy Forum, *The Changing Role of National Oil Companies in International Energy Markets*, Houston, Texas, Rice University, March 1–2.

Government of India, Ministry of Finance. 1976. "Foreign Trade and The Balance of Payments." In *Economic Survey 1975–1976*. Union Budget & Economic Survey. New Delhi: Government of India.

Government of India, Ministry of Heavy Industry and Public Enterprises, Department of Public Enterprises. 1997. "Turning Selected PSEs into Global Giants—Restructuring of the Boards—Setting up of a Search Committee for Selection of non-Official Part-Time Directors." In *DPE Guidelines for Administrative Ministries/Departments and Public Sector Enterprises*, chapter 9. New Delhi: Government of India.

Government of India, Ministry of Petroleum & Natural Gas. 2006. *Report of the Committee on Pricing and Taxation of Petroleum Products*. New Delhi: Government of India.

2008. "Several Steps Taken to Enhance Energy Security: Deora, Petroleum Minister Inaugurates International Conference of Society of Petroleum Geophysicists at Hyderabad." Press Release, January 14.

Government of India, Ministry of Petroleum & Natural Gas, Directorate General of Hydrocarbons (DGH). 2007. *Petroleum Exploration and Production Activities*. Annual Report 2006–07. New Delhi: Government of India.

Government of India, Ministry of Petroleum & Natural Gas, Petroleum Planning & Analysis Cell. "Import/Export of Crude & Petroleum Products." Database of Oil Industry Statistics, accessed June 25, 2010, www.ppac.org.in/.

Government of India, Planning Commission. 2006. *Integrated Energy Policy: Report of the Expert Committee*. New Delhi: Government of India.

Grayson, Leslie E. 1981. *National Oil Companies*. Chichester: John Wiley & Sons.

Green, Reginald H. 1995. "Angola Through a Cracked Glass Dimly: Peace, Reconstruction, Rehabilitation, Regionalism." In *Why Angola Matters: Report of a Conference held at Pembroke College, Cambridge, March 21–22, 1994*, ed. Keith Hart and Joanna Lewis, 173–182. London: James Currey.

Grenon, Michel. 1972. *Pour Une Politique de l'Energie*. Belgium: Marbout Université. (*in French*)

1975. *Le Nouveau Petrole*. Paris: Hachette. (*in French*)

Guimarães, Fernando. 1998. *The Origins of the Angolan Civil War: Foreign Intervention and Domestic Political Conflict*. New York: St. Martin's Press.

Guo, Xudong. 2006. "Managing Technological Innovation in State Owned Enterprises: The Case of CNPC." Paper for the IEEE International Conference on Management of Innovation and Technology, Singapore, June 21–23.

Guriev, Sergei, Anton Kolotilin, and Konstantin Sonin. 2011. "Determinants of Nationalization in the Oil Sector: A Theory and Evidence from Panel Data." *The Journal of Law, Economics, and Organization*, 27(2): 301–323.

Haber, Stephen. 2006. "Authoritarian Government." In *The Oxford Handbook of Political Economy*, ed. Barry Weingast and Donald Wittman, 693–707. New York: Oxford University Press.

Haber, Stephen and Victor Menaldo. 2011. "Do Natural Resources Fuel Authoritarianism? A Reappraisal of the Resource Curse." *American Political Science Review* 105: 1–26.

Haber, Stephen, Noel Maurer, and Armando Razo. 2003. "When the Law Does Not Matter: The Rise and Decline of the Mexican Oil Industry." *The Journal of Economic History* 63 (1): 1–32.

Hadenius, Axel and Jan Teorell. 2007. "Pathways from Authoritarianism." *Journal of Democracy* 18 (1): 143–157.

Haggard, Stephan and Robert R. Kaufman. 1995. *The Political Economy of Democratic Transitions*. Princeton University Press.

Haggard, Stephan, Andrew MacIntyre, and Lydia Tiede. 2008. "The Rule of Law and Economic Development." *Annual Review of Political Science* 11: 205–234.

Hahn-Pedersen, Morten. 1999. *A. P. Møller and the Danish Oil*. Copenhagen: Schultz Forlag.

Hallah, Tashikalmah and Francis Okeke. 2008. "Nigeria: NNPC Pays Niger Delta Militants $6 Million Monthly." *Daily Trust*, July 23, accessed September 28, 2010, www.allafrica.com/stories/200807230026. html.

Hallerberg, Mark and Patrik Marier. 2004. "Executive Authority, the Personal Vote, and Budget Discipline in Latin American and Caribbean Countries." *American Journal of Political Science* 48 (3): 571–587.

Hanisch, Tore Jørgen and Gunnar Nerheim. 1992. *Norsk Oljehistorie (Bind 1)* (Norwegian oil history vol. I). Oslo: Norsk Petroleumsforening. (*in Norwegian*)

Hansen, Thorvald Buch, Odd Jan Lange, Håkon Lavik, and Willy Håkon Olsen. 1982. *Olje eventyret: Norsk oljevirksomhet i tekst og bilder*. Oslo: Universitetsforlaget. (*in Norwegian*)

Hansen-Shino, Kjetil and Ricardo Soares de Oliveira. 2010. *The Political Economy of Petroleum Sector Management in Angola*. Washington DC: World Bank.

Hardman, R. F. P. 2003. "Lessons from Oil and Gas Exploration In and Around Britain." *Geological Society, London, Memoirs* 20: 5–16.

Hart Group. 2006a. *Nigerian Extractive Industries Transparency Initiative, Final Report, Combined Executive Summary.* Presented to NEITI, December.

2006b. "Nigerian Extractive Industries Transparency Initiative: Financial Audit – Financial Flows 1999–2004." December.

2006c. "Nigerian Extractive Industries Transparency Initiative: Process Audit – The Process of Marketing Natural Gas." December.

2006d. "Nigerian Extractive Industries Transparency Initiative: Process Audit – Processes for Capital and Operating Expenditure." December.

2006e. "Nigerian Extractive Industries Transparency Initiative: Process Audit 1999–2004: Refineries and Product Importation." December.

2006f. "Nigerian Extractive Industries Transparency Initiative: Physical Audit." December.

2008. "Nigerian Extractive Industries Transparency Initiative: Report on the Financial Audit 2005." October.

Hartley, Peter and Kenneth B. Medlock III. 2008. "A Model of the Operation and Development of a National Oil Company." *Energy Economics* 30 (5): 2459–2485.

Haruna, Godwin. 2007. "Nigeria: A Sale Too Many." *This Day*, July 20, accessed September 28, 2010, www.allafrica.com/stories/200707200430.html.

Hashim, Datuk Ismail. 2004. *The Young Turks of Petronas.* Kuala Lumpur: Malaysia Art Printing Works.

Hausmann, Ricardo. 2003. "Venezuela's Growth Implosion: A Neo-Classical Story?" In *In Search of Prosperity: Analytic Narratives on Economic Growth*, ed. Dani Rodrik, 244–270. Princeton University Press.

Hausmann, Ricardo and Francisco Rodríguez. 2006. "Why Did Venezuelan Growth Collapse?" In *Venezuela: Anatomy of a Collapse*, ed. Ricardo Hausmann and Francisco Rodriguez. Unpublished manuscript.

Hayes, Mark H. 2006. "The Transmed and Maghreb Projects: Gas to Europe from North Africa." In *Natural Gas and Geopolitics: From 1970 to 2040*, ed. David G. Victor, Amy M. Jaffe, and Mark H. Hayes, 49–90. Cambridge University Press.

Heller, C. A. 1980. "The Birth and Growth of the Public Sector and State Enterprises in the Petroleum Industry." In *State Petroleum Enterprises in Developing Countries.* United Nations Symposium on State Petroleum Enterprises in Developing Countries. New York: Pergamon Press.

Heller, Patrick. 2007. "Assessing Petroleum Sector Management in Nigeria and Angola." Paper from the Petroleum Resource Curse Conference at the Center for Democracy, Development, and the Rule of Law, Stanford, California, Stanford University. May.

2009. "The Nigerian Petroleum Industry Bill: Key Upstream Questions for the National Assembly." Analysis Report, Revenue Watch Institute.

Hellinger, Daniel. 2003. "Political Overview: The Breakdown of Puntofijismo and the Rise of Chavismo." In *Venezuelan Politics in the Chávez Era: Class, Polarization, and Conflict*, ed. Steve Ellner and Daniel Hellinger, 27–54. Boulder: Lynne Rienner.

Henisz, Witold. 2000. "The Institutional Environment for Economic Growth." *Economics and Politics* 12 (1): 1–31.

2002. "The Institutional Environment for Infrastructure Investment." *Industrial and Corporate Change* 11 (2): 355–389.

Henisz, Witold and Bennet Zelner. 2001. "The Institutional Environment for Telecommunications Investment." *Journal of Economics & Management Strategy* 10 (1): 123–147.

Henisz, Witold, Bennet Zelner, and Mauro F. Guillén. 2005. "The Worldwide Diffusion of Market-Oriented Infrastructure Reform, 1977–1999." *American Sociological Review* 70 (6): 871–897.

Hen-Tov, Elliot. 2007. "Understanding Iran's New Authoritarianism." *The Washington Quarterly* 30 (1): 163–179.

Hertog, Steffen. 2008. "Petromin: The Slow Death of Statist Oil Development in Saudi Arabia." *Business History* 50 (5): 645–667.

Hertzmark, Donald I. 2007. "Pertamina: Indonesia's State-Owned Oil Company." Policy Report. The Baker Institute Energy Forum, *The Changing Role of National Oil Companies in International Energy Markets*, Houston, Texas, Rice University, March 1–2.

Hilley, John. 2001. *Malaysia: Mahathirism, Hegemony and the New Opposition*. London: Zed Books.

Hirschman, Albert O. 1958. *The Strategy of Economic Development*. New Haven: Yale University Press.

1981. *Essays in Trespassing: Economics to Politics and Beyond*. Cambridge University Press.

Hirst, David. 1966. *Oil and Public Opinion in the Middle East*. New York: Praeger.

Hodges, Tony. 2004. *Angola: Anatomy of an Oil State*. Lysaker: Fridtjof Nansen Institute.

Hogan, William and Federico Struzenegger, eds. 2010. *The Natural Resources Trap*. Cambridge: MIT Press.

Horn, Murray J. 1995. *The Political Economy of Public Administration: Institutional Choice in the Public Sector*. Cambridge University Press.

Houser, Trevor. 2008. "The Roots of Chinese Oil Investment Abroad."
  Asia Policy 5: 141–166.
Howell, Jonathan. 2007. "Privatization of PEMEX." *Law and Business
  Review of the Americas* (Spring): 461–470.
Hubbell, J. W. 2004. "China Industry: President of CNPC Resigns."
  Economist Intelligence Unit (April): 28–29.
Hughes, Owen E. 1998. *Public Management and Administration.* London:
  Macmillan.
Hults, David. 2007. "Petróleos de Venezuela, S.A.: The Right-Hand Man
  of the Government." Working Paper No. 70. Program on Energy and
  Sustainable Development, Stanford University.
Human Rights Watch. 1999. *Angola Unravels – The Rise and Fall of the
  Lusaka Peace Process.* September 13.
  2004. *Some Transparency, No Accountability: The Use of Oil Revenue
  in Angola and Its Impact on Human Rights.* January 12.
Humphreys, Macartan, Jeffrey D. Sachs, and Joseph E. Stiglitz, eds. 2007.
  Escaping the Resource Curse. New York: Columbia University Press.
ICG (International Crisis Group). 2006a. "Fuelling the Niger Delta Crisis."
  Africa Report 118.
  2006b. "The Swamps of Insurgency: Nigeria's Delta Unrest." *Africa
  Report* 115.
IEA (International Energy Agency). 2002. *Russia Energy Survey 2002.*
  Paris: IEA.
  2006a. *Optimizing Russian Natural Gas: Reform and Climate Policy.*
  Paris: IEA.
  2006b. "Upstream Oil: Angola". Accessed April 14, 2011, www.iea.org/
  Textbase/nptable/2006/angola_f12.pdf.
  2008. *World Energy Outlook 2008.* Paris: OECD.
  2009. *World Energy Outlook 2009.* Paris: OECD.
  2010. *IEA Oil Market Report, 12 May 2010.* Paris: OECD.
Igbikiowubo, Hector and Emma Amaize. 2009. "Nigeria: Nation Loses
  N3.74bn Per Day to Niger Delta War." *Vanguard*, June 7, accessed
  April 14, 2011, www.allafrica.com/stories/200906070002.html.
IMF (International Monetary Fund). 2005. *Angola: Selected Issues and
  Statistical Appendix.* IMF Country Report No. 05/125. Washington
  DC: IMF.
  2008. "Islamic Republic of Iran: Selected Issues." IMF Country Report
  No. 08/285. Washington DC: IMF.
  2009a. "IMF Executive Board Concludes 2008 Article IV Consultation
  with Angola." IMF Public Information Notice No. 09/51, April 30.
  2009b. "IMF Executive Board Approves US $1.4 Billion Stand-By
  Arrangement with Angola." IMF Press Release No. 09/425,
  November 23.

2010. "World Economic Outlook Database." World Economic and Financial Surveys. IMF website, accessed October 3, 2010, www.imf. org/external/pubs/ft/weo/2010/01/weodata/index.aspx.

2011. *Angola: Fourth Review Under the Stand-by Arrangement, Request for Waivers of Nonobservance of Performance Criteria, Request for Waivers of Applicability of Performance Criteria, and Request for Modification of Performance Criteria.* IMF Country Report No. 11/51. Washington DC: IMF.

Isine, Ibanga and Chiawo Nwankwo. 2007. "NNPC Spends $1bn on Refineries in Eight Years." *Punch*, January 24, accessed April 14, 2011, www.punchontheweb.com/Article2Print.aspx?theartic=Art20 0701242555679.

Islamic Republic of Iran. 1979. *Constitution of the Islamic Republic of Iran.* Translated by the Embassy of the Islamic Republic of Iran, London.

Islamic Republic of Iran, Ministry of Petroleum. 2008. "National Iranian Oil Company." Ministry of Petroleum website, accessed March 28, 2010, www.mop.ir/subcompanies/nioc/index.asp.

Izundu, Uchenna. 2009a. "OTC: Nigeria Changes Gas-flaring Deadline." *Oil & Gas Journal*, May 18.

2009b. "Oil Companies Slap Nigeria's Petroleum Reform Legislation." *Oil & Gas Journal*, August 10.

Jackson, Mike. 2007. "The Future of Natural Gas in India: A Study of Major Consuming Sectors." Working Paper No. 65. Program on Energy and Sustainable Development, Stanford University.

Jacoby, Neil H. 1974. *Multinational Oil: A Study in Industrial Dynamics.* New York: Macmillan.

Jaffe, Amy M. 2007. "Key Findings." Presentation at The Baker Institute Energy Forum, *The Changing Role of National Oil Companies in International Energy Markets*, Houston, Texas, Rice University, March 1–2.

Jaffe, Amy M. and Jareer Elass. 2007. "Saudi-Aramco: National Flagship with Global Responsibilities." Policy Report. The Baker Institute Energy Forum, *The Changing Role of National Oil Companies in International Energy Markets*, Houston, Texas, Rice University, March 1–2.

Jaidah, Ali M. 1980. "Problems and Prospects of State Petroleum Enterprises in OPEC Countries." In *State Petroleum Enterprises in Developing Countries*. United Nations Symposium on State Petroleum Enterprises in Developing Countries. New York: Pergamon Press.

Jakobson, Linda and Daojiong Zha. 2006. "China and the Worldwide Search for Oil Security." *Asia-Pacific Review* 13 (2): 60–73.

Jensen, Michael C. 1983. "Organization Theory and Methodology." *Accounting Review* 58 (2): 319–339.

　2000. "Value Maximisation and the Corporate Objective Function." *In Breaking the Code of Change*, ed. Michael Beer and Nitin Nohria, 37–58. Cambridge: Harvard Business School.

Jiang, Zemin. 1995. "To Push Forward the Reform of State-owned Enterprises with Steadfast Trust and a Clear Mission." *People's Daily* (translated), July 13.

Jiang, Zhuqing. 2004. "Leaders Held Responsible for Accidents." *China Daily*, April 30, accessed September 15, 2010, www.chinadaily.com. cn/english/doc/2004–04/30/content_327599.htm.

Jin, Khoo Kay. 1992. "The Grand Vision: Mahathir and Modernization." In *Fragmented Vision: Culture and Politics in Contemporary Malaysia*, ed. Joel S. Kahn and Francis L. K. Wah, 62–63. Sydney: Allen & Unwin Pty.

Johnson, Simon, Peter Boone, Alasdair Breach, and Eric Freedman. 2000. "Corporate Governance in the Asian Financial Crisis." *Journal of Financial Economics* 58 (1–2): 141–186.

Jones, Charles I. 1997. "On the Evolution of the World Income Distribution." *Journal of Economic Perspectives* 11 (3): 19–36.

Joshi, Sunjoy and Najeeb Jung. 2008. "Natural Gas in India." In *Natural Gas in Asia: The Challenges of Growth in China, India, Japan and Korea*, 2nd edn., ed. Jonathan Stern, 66–105. Oxford University Press.

Kahn, Joel S. and Francis L. K. Wah, eds. 1992. *Fragmented Vision: Culture and Politics in Contemporary Malaysia*. Sydney: Allen & Unwin Pty.

Kalotay, Kalman. 2008. "Russian Transnationals and International Investment Paradigms." *Research in International Business and Finance* 22 (2): 85–107.

Kalyuzhnova, Yelena and Christian Nygaard. 2008. "State Governance Evolution in Resource-Rich Transition Economies: An Application to Russia and Kazakhstan." *Energy Policy* 36 (6): 1829–1842.

Karl, Terry L. 1997. *The Paradox of Plenty: Oil Booms and Petro-States*. Berkeley: University of California Press.

Karrar-Lewsley, Tahani. 2010. "Conoco to Exit Abu Dhabi Gas Project." *Wall Street Journal*, April 28, accessed April 14, 2011, www.online. wsj.com/article/SB100014240527487044235045752115105908619 20.html.

Karshenas, Massoud. 1990. *Oil, State and Industrialization in Iran*. Cambridge University Press.

Katakey, Rakteem. 2008. "40% 'Peanuts', We Want 100% Hike: PSU Employees." *Business Standard*, March 26, accessed April 14, 2011, www.business-standard.com/india/news/40-%5Cpeanuts%5C-we-want-100-hike-psu-employees/318035/.

Katouzian, Homa. 1981. *The Political Economy of Modern Iran: Despotism and Pseudo-Modernism, 1926–1979*. New York University Press.

Katsouris, Christina. 2008. "Energy Compass: Angola: Sonangol's Strong Hand." *Energy Intelligence*, September 12.

Katzman, Kenneth. 2007. "The Iran Sanctions Act (ISA)." CRS Report for Congress, order code RS 20871, Congressional Research Service.

Kaufmann, Daniel, Aart Kraay, and Massimo Mastruzzi. 1999–2009. *Governance Matters VII: Aggregate and Individual Governance Indicators, 1996–(various years)*. Policy Research Working Paper, The Worldwide Governance Indicators Project. World Bank.

Kaul, H. N. 1991. *K. D. Malaviya and the Evolution of India's Oil Policy*. New Delhi: Allied.

Kay, J. A. and D. J. Thompson. 1986. "Privatisation: A Policy in Search of a Rationale." *The Economic Journal* 96 (381): 18–32.

Keating, Aileen. 2006. *Power, Politics, and the Hidden History of Arabian Oil*. London: Saqi.

Kebede, Rebekah. 2009. "Analysis – PDVSA's Russia, China Oil Alliances Face Hurdles." *Reuters*, October 29, accessed April 14, 2011, www.forexpros.com/news/general-news/analysis-pdvsa%27s-russia,-china-oil-alliances-face-hurdles-98850.

Keddie, N. 2003. *Modern Iran: Roots and Results of Revolution*, 3rd edn. New Haven: Yale University Press.

Keefer, Philip. 2002. "Politics and the Determinants of Banking Crises: The Effects of Political Checks and Balances." In *Banking, Financial Integration, and International Crises*, ed. Leonardo Hernandez and Klaus Schmidt-Hebbel, 85–112. Santiago: Central Bank of Chile.

Keefer, Philip and David Stasavage. 2002. "Checks and Balances, Private Information, and the Credibility of Monetary Commitments." *International Organization* 56 (4): 751–774.

Khajehpour, Bijan. 2001. "Iran's Economy: 20 years after the Islamic Revolution." In *Iran at the Crossroads*, ed. John L. Esposito and R. K. Ramazani, 93–122. New York: Palgrave.

Khan, Kameel. 1985. "Some Legal Considerations on the Role and Structure of State Oil Companies: A Comparative View." *The International and Comparative Law Quarterly* 34 (3): 584–592.

Khanna, Rajvir. 2007. "ONGC, BP Tie-Up For Oil & Gas Exploration." *TopNews.in*, January 9, accessed April 14, 2011, www.topnews.in/ongc-bp-tie-oil-gas-exploration-21264.

Khanna, Tarun, Joe Kogan, and Krishna Palepu. 2006. "Globalization and Similarities in Corporate Governance: A Cross-Country Analysis." *Review of Economics and Statistics* 88 (1): 69–90.

Khoo, Boo Teik. 1995. *Paradoxes of Mahathirism: An Intellectual Biography of Mahathir Mohamad*. Kuala Lumpur: Oxford University Press.

Kim, Younkyoo. 2003. *The Resource Curse in a Post-Communist Regime: Russia in Comparative Perspective*. Aldershot: Ashgate.

Knack, Stephen and Philip Keefer. 1995. "Institutions and Economic Performance: Cross-Country Tests Using Alternative Institutional Measures." *Economics and Politics* 7 (3): 207–227.

Knight, Frank H. 1921. *Risk, Uncertainty, and Profit*. Boston: Houghton Mifflin.

Knudsen, T. W. 1997. "The Gullfaks Field: Applying Tomorrow's Subsea Technology." Paper OTC 8473 presented at The Offshore Technology Conference, Houston, Texas, May 5–8.

Kobrin, Stephen J. 1980. "Foreign Enterprise and Forced Divestment in LDCs." *International Organization* 34 (1): 65–88.

    1984a. "Expropriation as an Attempt to Control Foreign Firms in LDCs: Trends from 1960 to 1979." *International Studies Quarterly* 28 (3): 329–348.

    1984b. "The Nationalisation of Oil Production, 1918–1980." In *Risk and the Political Economy of Resource Development*, ed. David W. Pearce, Horst Siebert, and Ingo Walter, 137. London: Macmillan.

    1985. "Diffusion as an Explanation of Oil Nationalization: Or the Domino Effect Rides Again." *The Journal of Conflict Resolution* 29 (1): 3–32.

Kogut, Bruce and J. Muir Macpherson. 2008. "The Decision to Privatize: Economists and the Construction of Ideas and Policies." In *The Global Diffusion of Markets and Democracy*, ed. Beth A. Simmons, Frank Dobbin, and Geoffrey Garrett, 104–140. New York: Cambridge University Press.

Kole, Stacey R. and J. Harold Mulherin. 1997. "The Government as a Shareholder: A Case from the United States." *Journal of Law and Economics* 40 (1): 1–22.

Kommersant. 2009a. "Европа отвернулась от 'Газпрома'" June 15. (*in Russian*). Accessed September 14, 2010 August 6, 2010, www.kommersant.ru/doc.aspx?fromsearch=4b75b590-cc28–4f40–9264-e61c170f1ec5&docsid=1187320.

    2009b, "К сокращениям подошли по-рабочему" July 14. (*in Russian*). Accessed August 6, 2010, www.kommersant.ru/doc.aspx?DocsID=1203608.

Kramer, Andrew E. 2008. "Gazprom, Once Mighty, Is Reeling." *The New York Times*, December 29, accessed April 14, 2011, www.nytimes.com/2008/12/30/business/worldbusiness/30gazprom.html?ref=worldbusiness.

Kramer, Andrew E. and Steven L. Myers. 2006. "The Business of Russia, Putin's Long Reach: Workers' Paradise Is Rebranded as Kremlin Inc." *The New York Times*, April 24, accessed April 14, 2011, www.nytimes.com/2006/04/24/world/europe/24gazprom.html.

Kretzschmar, Gavin, Magnus Gran-Jansen, and Liliya Sharifzyanova. 2009. "The Ownership Advantage of Resource Hosting." Working Paper, accessed April 14, 2011, www.ssrn.com/abstract=1319494.

Kupolokun, F. M. 2006. "Nigeria and the Future Global Gas Market." Presentation at The Baker Institute Energy Forum, *Nigeria and the Future Global Gas Market*, Houston, Texas, Rice University, May 2.

Lacey, Robert. 1981. *The Kingdom: Arabia & the House of Sa'ud*. San Diego: Harcourt Brace Jovanovich.

Laffont, Jean-Jacques and Jean Tirole. 1991. "Privatization and Incentives." *Journal of Law, Economics, and Organization* 7: 84–105.

1993. *A Theory of Incentives in Procurement and Regulation.* Cambridge: MIT Press.

Lahn, Glada, Valerie Marcel, John Mitchell, Keith Myers, and Paul Stevens. 2007. *Good Governance of the National Petroleum Sector.* The Royal Institute of International Affairs. London: Chatham House.

Lajous, Adrian. 2009. "The Governance of Mexico's Oil Industry." In *No Growth Without Equity? Inequality, Interests, and Competition in Mexico*, ed. Santiago Levy and Michael Walton, 389–426. Hampshire; Palgrave Macmillan; Washington DC: World Bank.

Lane, Jan-Erik. 2005. *Public Administration and Public Management: The Principal–Agent Perspective*. Abingdon: Routledge.

La Porta, Rafael, Florencio Lopez-de-Silanes, Andrei Schleifer, and Robert Vishny. 2002. "Investor Protection and Corporate Valuation." *The Journal of Finance* 57 (3): 1147–1170.

Lavelle, Kathryn C. 2004. *The Politics of Equity Finance in Emerging Markets*. Oxford University Press.

Lei, Tu. 2008. "CNPC May Invest Up to $8.5b to Tap Offshore Oil." *China Daily*, April 3, accessed April 14, 2011, www.chinadaily.com.cn/business/2008–04/03/content_6590513.htm.

Leibenstein, Harvey. 1966. "Allocative Efficiency vs. 'X-Efficiency'." *The American Economic Review* 56 (3): 392–415.

Lemmon, Michael L. and Karl V. Lins. 2003. "Ownership Structure, Corporate Governance, and Firm Value: Evidence from the East Asian Financial Crisis." *The Journal of Finance* 58 (4): 1445–1468.

Lerche, Ian. 1997. *Geological Risk and Uncertainty in Oil Exploration.* London: Academic Press.

Lerche, Ian and James A. MacKay. 1999. *Economic Risk in Hydrocarbon Exploration.* San Diego: Academic Press.

Lerøen, Bjørn Vidar. 2002. *Dråper av svart gull: Statoil 1972–2002.* Stavanger: Statoil. (*in Swedish*)

Lerpold, Lin S. 2000. "Integrating for Success: The BP and Statoil International E&P Alliance." In *International Oil and Gas Ventures: A Business Perspective*, ed. G. E. Kronman, D. B. Felio, and T. E. O'Connor. Tulsa: The American Association of Petroleum Geologists.

Levy, Brian and Pablo Spiller. 1994. "The Institutional Foundations of Regulatory Commitment: A Comparative Analysis of Telecommunications Regulation." *Journal of Law, Economics and Organization* 10 (2): 201–246.

Lewis, Peter M. 2007. *Growing Apart: Oil, Politics, and Economic Change in Indonesia and Nigeria.* Ann Arbor: University of Michigan Press.

Lewis, Steven W. 2007. "Chinese NOCs and World Energy Markets: CNPC, Sinopec, and CNOOC." Policy Report. The Baker Institute Energy Forum, *The Changing Role of National Oil Companies in International Energy Markets*, Houston, Texas, Rice University, March 1–2.

Li, Huijun and Dengkui Wang. 2008. "Analyses of Dynamic Stakeholder Views for CNPC." *Journal of Sustainable Development* 1 (2): 32–39.

Li, Quan. 2009. "Democracy, Autocracy, and Expropriation of Foreign Direct Investment." *Comparative Political Studies* 42 (8): 1098–1127.

Li, Shaomin and Jun Xia. 2007. "The Roles and Performance of State Firms and Non-State Firms in China's Economic Transition." *World Development* 36 (1): 39–54.

Licht, Amir N., Chanan Goldschimdt, and Shalom H. Schwartz. 2007. "Culture Rules: The Foundations of the Rule of Law and Other Forms of Governance." *Journal of Comparative Economics* 35: 659–688.

Lieberthal, Kenneth and Mikkal E. Herberg. 2006. "China's Search for Energy Security: Implications for US Policy." *NBR Analysis* (April).

Lipson, Charles. 1985. *Standing Guard: Protecting Foreign Capital in the Nineteenth and Twentieth Centuries.* Berkeley: University of California Press.

Liu, Qiao. 2006. "Corporate Governance in China: Current Practices, Economic Effects and Institutional Determinants." *CESifo Economic Studies* 52 (2): 415–453.

Locatelli, Catherine. 2006. "The Russian Oil Industry Between Public and Private Governance: Obstacles to International Oil Companies' Investment Strategies." *Energy Policy* 34 (9): 1075–1085.

Lodi, C. F. L. 1993. "Subsídios e Preços de Derivados de petróleo e Álcool no Brasil." In *Revista*. Rio de Janeiro: Petro e Gas. (*in Portuguese*)

Lohmann, Susanne. 1998. "Federalism and Central Bank Independence: The Politics of German Monetary Policy, 1957–92." *World Politics* 50 (3): 401–446.

Longrigg, Stephen H. 1961. *Oil in the Middle East: Its Discovery and Development*, 2nd edn. Oxford University Press.

Lopez, Leslie. 2003. "A Well-Oiled Money Machine." *Far Eastern Economic Review (*March 13): 40–43.

Lucas, Alastair R. 1985. "State Petroleum Corporations: The Legal Relationship with the State." *Journal of Energy and Natural Resources Law* 3: 81–101.

Luxford, Kate. 2003. "Government Reshuffle Ahead of 2004 Election." *World Market Analysis*, May 6.

Ma, Xin and Philip Andrews-Speed. 2006. "The Overseas Activities of China's National Oil Companies: Rationale and Outlook." *Minerals and Energy-Raw Materials Report* 21 (1): 17–30.

Macedo e Silva, A. C. 1985. *Petrobras: A Consolidação do Monopólio Estatal e Empresa Privada*. Campinas: Instituto de Economia-Unicamp. (*in Portuguese*)

Macey, Jonathan R. 2008. *Corporate Governance: Promises Kept, Promises Broken*. Princeton University Press.

Magaloni, Beatriz. 2008. "Credible Power-Sharing and the Longevity of Authoritarian Rule." *Comparative Political Studies* 41 (4): 715–741.

Mahdavy, Hussein. 1970. "The Patterns and Problems of Economic Development in Rentier States: The Case of Iran." In *Studies in Economic History of the Middle East*, ed. M. A. Cook, 428–467. Oxford University Press.

Maier, Karl. 1996. *Angola: Promises and Lies*. Rivonia: William Waterman.

Malaquias, Assis. 2000. "Ethnicity and Conflict in Angola: Prospects for Reconciliation." In *Angola's War Economy: The Role of Oil and Diamonds*, ed. Jackie Cilliers and Christian Dietrich, 95–113. Pretoria: Institute for Security Studies.

Malkin, Elisabeth. 2004a. "Leader of Mexican Energy Monopoly Resigns." *The New York Times*, November 2, accessed April 14, 2011, www.nytimes.com/2004/11/02/business/02pemex.html.

2004b. "Mexico: Pemex May Sell A Stake." *The New York Times*, November 4, accessed April 14, 2011, www.query.nytimes.com/gst/fullpage.html?res=9901E4DA173CF937A35752C1A9629C8B63.

2005. "Mexican President Haggles Over Pemex Reform." *The New York Times*, September 6, accessed April 14, 2011, www.query.nytimes.com/gst/fullpage.html?res=9500E7D81531F935A3575AC0A9639C8B63.

Mallet-Guy Guerra, Sinclair, Karenia Cordova Saez, and Nurco Antonio Bonn. 1993. "Perspectivas y Estrategias para el Gas Natural en la América Latína: Brasil y Venezuela." *Interciencia* 18 (1): 24–28. (*in Spanish*)

Mallin, Chris and Xie Rong. 1998. "The Development of Corporate Governance in China." *Journal of Contemporary China* 7 (17): 33–42.

Manzano, Osmel and Francisco Monaldi. 2008. "The Political Economy of Oil Production in Latin America." *Economia* 9 (1): 59–103.

    2010. "The Political Economy of Oil Contract Renegotiation in Venezuela." In *The Natural Resources Trap*, ed. William Hogan and Federico Struzenegger, 409–466. Cambridge: MIT Press.

Marcano, Christina and Alberto Barrera Tyszka. 2006. *Hugo Chávez: Sin Uniforme*. Caracas: Debate. (*in Spanish*)

Marcel, Valérie. 2006. *Oil Titans: National Oil Companies in the Middle East*. London: Chatham House; Washington DC: Brookings Institution Press.

    2008. "Tomorrow's Big NOC Players." In *Key Issues for Rising National Oil Companies*. Energy & Natural Resources. KPMG International Report, 18–25.

    2009. *The National Oil Company Investment Challenge*. KPMG International Report.

Mares, David R. and Nelson Altamirano. 2007. "Venezuela's PDVSA and World Energy Markets: Corporate Strategies and Political Factors Determining Its Behavior and Influence." Policy Report. The Baker Institute Energy Forum, *The Changing Role of National Oil Companies in International Energy Markets*, Houston, Texas, Rice University, March 1–2.

Marshall, Monty G. and Keith Jaggers. 2000. "Polity IV Project: Political Regime Characteristics and Transitions, 1800–1999, Dataset Users Manual." Polity IV Project. Integrated Network for Societal Conflict Research Program and Center for International Development and Conflict Management, University of Maryland.

Martin, Stephen and David Parker. 1995. "Privatization and Economic Performance Throughout the UK Business Cycle." *Managerial and Decision Economics* 16 (3): 225–237.

Matsuda, Yasuhiko. 1997. "An Island of Excellence: Petróleos de Venezuela and the Political Economy of Technocratic Agency Autonomy." Ph.D. diss., University of Pittsburgh.

Maugeri, Leonardo. 2006. *The Age of Oil: The Mythology, History, and Future of the World's Most Controversial Resource*. Westport: Praeger.

Mazarei Jr., Adnan. 1996. "The Iranian Economy Under the Islamic Republic: Institutional Change and Macroeconomic Performance (1979–1990)." *Cambridge Journal of Economics* 20 (3): 289–314.

McCubbins, Mathew D. and Thomas Schwartz. 1984. "Congressional Oversight Overlooked: Police Patrols versus Fire Alarms." *American Journal of Political Science* 28 (1): 165–179.

McCubbins, Mathew D., Roger G. Noll, and Barry R. Weingast. 1987. "Administrative Procedures as Instruments of Political Control." *Journal of Law, Economics, and Organization* 13 (2): 243–277.

McKinley Jr., James C. and Elisabeth Malkin. 2005. "Accidents Reveal Troubles At Mexico's Oil Monopoly." *The New York Times*, May 15, accessed April 14, 2011, www.nytimes.com/2005/05/15/international/americas/15pemex.html.

McLennan, James and Steward Williams. 2005. "Deepwater Africa Reaches Turning Point." *Oil and Gas Journal* 103 (6): 18–25.

McNally, Christopher A. 2002. "Strange Bedfellows: Communist Party Institutions and New Governance Mechanisms in Chinese State Holding Cooperations." *Business and Politics* 4 (1): 91–115.

McPherson, Charles. 2003. "National Oil Companies: Evolution, Issues, Outlook." In *Fiscal Policy Formulation and Implementation in Oil-Producing Countries*, ed. Jeffrey M. Davis, Rolando Ossowski, Annalisa Fedelino, 184–203. Washington DC: IMF.

Mearsheimer, John J. and Stephen M. Walt. 2003. "An Unnecessary War." *Foreign Policy* 134 (January/February): 50–59.

MEES. 2009a. "GASCO Concession Renewal Terms View as Tough on International Partners." *Middle East Economic Survey* 52 (22): 20.

2009b. "Abu Dhabi Perseveres with Sour Gas Initiative." *Middle East Economic Review* 52 (6): 23.

Megginson, William L. 2005. *The Financial Economics of Privatization.* New York: Oxford University Press.

Megginson, William L., Robert C. Nash, and Matthias van Randenborgh. 1994. "The Financial and Operating Performance of Newly Privatized Firms: An International Empirical Analysis." *Journal of Finance* 49 (2): 403–452.

Megill, Robert E. 1988. *An Introduction to Exploration Economics*, 3rd edn. Tulsa: PennWell.

Mehdudia, Sujay. 2007a. "Process for Selecting ONGC Chief." *The Hindu*, April 13, accessed April 14, 2011, www.hindu.com/2007/04/13/stories/2007041300581400.htm.

2007b. "Panel for Sharma as ONGC Chief." *The Hindu*, June 7, accessed April 14, 2011, www.hindu.com/2007/06/07/stories/2007060714851100.htm.

Messiant, Christine. 1998. "Angola: The Challenge of Statehood." In *History of Central Africa: The Contemporary Years Since 1960*, ed. David Birmingham and Phyllis M. Martin, 131–166. New York: Longman.

2008a. "The Mutation of Hegemonic Domination: Multiparty Politics Without Democracy." In *Angola: The Weight of History*, ed. Patrick Chabal and Nuno Vidal, 93–123. New York: Columbia University Press.

2008b. *L'Angola Postcolonial*. Paris: Karthala.

Metz, Helen C., ed. 1994. *Algeria: A Country Study*. Washington DC: Library of Congress/Federal Research Division.

Middle East Executive Reports. 1992. "New Investment Law for Hydrocarbons Area." *Middle East Executive Reports* 15 (2): 10.

Mikdashi, Zuhayr M., Sherrill Cleland, and Ian Seymour, eds. 1970. *Continuity and Change in the World Oil Industry*. Beirut: Middle East Research and Publishing Center.

Millard, Peter. 2007. "Venezuela Govt Disputes Value of Orinoco Heavy Oil Projects." *Rigzone*, April 24, accessed April 14, 2011, www.rigzone.com/news/article.asp?a_id=44280.

Miller, T. Christian. 2002. "The Struggle for Venezuela's Soul—and Chavez's Ouster." *Los Angeles Times*, December 18, accessed April 14, 2011, www.articles.latimes.com/2002/dec/18/world/fg-venoil18.

Ministério das Finanças de Angola. 2007. Exportações e Receitas de Petróleo, 2007. (*in Portuguese*)

2008. Exportações e Receitas de Petróleo, 2008. (*in Portuguese*)

2009. Exportações e Receitas de Petróleo, 2009. (*in Portuguese*)

Minuto 59. 2009. "Ramírez: 'Con Cero Ingreso Petrólero Nosotros Podemos Trabajar.'" March 3. (*in Spanish*)

Misra, Neha, Ruchika Chawla, Leena Srivastava, and R. K. Pachauri. 2005. *Petroleum Pricing in India: Balancing Efficiency and Equity*. New Delhi: The Energy Resources Institute.

Mitchell, John V. and Paul Stevens. 2008. *Ending Dependence: Hard Choices for Oil-Exporting States*. The Royal Institute of International Affairs. London: Chatham House.

Mitchell, Mark L. and Kenneth Lehn. 1990. "Do Bad Bidders Become Good Targets?" *Journal of Political Economy* 98 (2): 372–398.

Modak, Shrikant. 2002. "Right on Top." *Business India*, September 30– October 13, accessed April 14, 2011, www.ongcindia.com/archives1.asp?fold=archives\oct802&file1=Feature_article&file2=feature_article1.txt.

Moe, Terry M. 1984. "The New Economics of Organization." *American Journal of Political Science* 28 (4): 739–777.

Molchanov, Pavel. 2003. "A Statistical Analysis of OPEC Quota Violations." *Duke Journal of Economics* Special Edition: 2003 Undergraduate Research Symposium, April.

Mommer, Bernard. 2002. *Global Oil and the Nation State.* Oxford University Press.

2004. "Subversive Oil." In *Venezuelan Politics in the Chávez Era: Class, Polarization, and Conflict,* ed. Steve Ellner and Daniel Hellinger, 131–145. Boulder: Lynne Rienner.

Monaldi, Francisco. 2001. "Sunk-Costs, Institutions, and Commitment: Foreign Investment in the Venezuelan Oil Industry." Dept. of Political Science, Stanford University, December, accessed April 14, 2011, www.stanford.edu/class/polisci313/papers/MonaldiFeb04.pdf.

2004. "Inversiones inmovilizadas, instituciones y compromiso gubernamental: Implicaciones sobre la inversión en la industria petrolera Venezolana." *Temas de Coyuntura* (December). (*in Spanish*)

Monaldi, Francisco, Rosa Amelia Gonzelez, Richard Obuchi, and Michael Penfold. 2008. "Political Institutions and Policymaking in Venezuela: The Rise and Collapse of Political Cooperation." In *Policymaking in Latin America: How Politics Shapes Policies,* ed. Ernesto Stein, Mariano Tommasi, Carlos Scartascini, and Pablo Spiller, 371–417. Cambridge: Harvard University Press; Washington DC: Inter-American Development Bank.

Moneycontrol.com. 2006. "ONGC Pumping More Air than Oil: DGH." November 24, accessed April 14, 2011, www.moneycontrol.com/news/business/ongc-pumping-more-air-than-oil-dgh_252758.html.

Moody's Ratings. 2009. "Credit Opinion: Petroleos Mexicanos." *Moody's Investors Service.* December 23.

Moore, Mick and Sheelagh Stewart. 1998. "Corporate Governance for NGOs?" *Development in Practice* 8 (3): 335–342.

Morgan, Bronwen and Karen Yeung. 2007. *An Introduction to Law and Regulation.* Cambridge University Press.

Mouawad, Jad. 2006. "Oil Prices Leap After Attacks in Nigeria." *The New York Times,* February 20, accessed April 14, 2011, www.nytimes.com/2006/02/20/international/africa/20cnd-oil.html.

Muñoz Leos, Raúl. 2006. Pemex en la Encrucijada: Recuento de una Gestión. Mexico DF: Aguilar. (*in Spanish*)

Murillo, Maria Victoria. 2002. "Political Bias in Policy Convergence: Privatization Choices in Latin America." *World Politics* 54 (4): 462–493.

Myers, David J. 2000. "Venezuela: Shaping the 'New Democracy'." In *Latin American Politics and Development,* 5th edn., ed. Howard J. Wiarda and Harvey F. Kline, 259–294. Boulder: Westview.

Myers, Keith and Glada Lahn, eds. 2006. *Good Governance of the National Petroleum Sector.* Interim Report. Chatham House, January.

Myerson, Allen R. 1994. "Kuwait Government to Sell Santa Fe's Petroleum Assets." *New York Times*, November 11, accessed April 14, 2011, www.nytimes.com/1994/11/11/business/kuwaiti-government-to-sell-santa-fe-s-petroleum-assets.html?pagewanted=1/.

Naím, Moisés. 2001. "The Real Story Behind Venezuela's Woes." *Journal of Democracy* 12 (2): 17–31.

Nair, Shanti. 1997. *Islam in Malaysian Foreign Policy.* London: Routledge.

Naji, Kasra. 2008. *Ahmadinejad: The Secret History of Iran's Radical Leader.* Berkeley: University of California Press.

National Iranian Oil Company. 2001–2003. *Financial Reports.* Tehran: Islamic Republic of Iran.

Nawwab, Ismail I., Peter C. Speers, and Paul F. Hoye, eds. 1995. *Saudi Aramco and Its World: Arab and the Middle East*, revised edn. Dhahran: Saudi Arabian Oil Company.

Neff, Jerry M. and Randi Hagemann. 2007. "Environmental Challenges of Heavy Crude Oils: Management of Liquid Wastes." Prepared for Society of Petroleum Engineers, E&P Environmental and Safety Conference, Galveston, Texas, March 5–7.

Nelsen, Brent F. 1991. *The State Offshore: Petroleum, Politics, and State Intervention on the British and Norwegian Continental Shelves.* New York: Praeger.

Newendorp, Paul D. 1975. *Decision Analysis for Petroleum Exploration.* Tulsa: Petroleum Publishing.

Newitt, Malyn. 2008. "Angola in Historical Context." In *Angola: The Weight of History*, ed. Patrick Chabal and Nuno Vidal, 19–92. New York: Columbia University Press.

Nigerian Institute of Social and Economic Research. 2006. *Needs Assessment of Youths Employment in Rivers, Delta, Kaduna, Kano and Plateau States of Nigeria.* Ibadan: Institute of Social and Economic Research.

Nigerian Ministry of Finance and Budget Office of the Federation. 2007. "2008–2010 Medium Term Fiscal Strategy Paper: Executive Brief to the Federal Executive Council," August 15. Abuja: Federal Republic of Nigeria.

  2008. "Fiscal Strategy Paper (Revised Version), Federal Government of Nigeria, 2009–2011." December. Abuja: Federal Republic of Nigeria.

Nigerian Ministry of Finance, Oil and Gas Accounting Unit. 2005. "Margin Allowed under the JV-MOU when the Oil Price Exceeds $30 per Barrel: Government is Entitled to Back Payment." Abuja: Federal Republic of Nigeria.

Nigerian Senate. 2006. *Petroleum Profit Tax Act (PPT) (amendment)*. Senate Bill 282. Abuja: Federal Republic of Nigeria.

Nikansen, William A. 1971. *Bureaucracy and Representative Government*. Chicago: Rand McNally.

1975. "Bureaucrats and Politicians." *Journal of Law and Economics* 18 (3): 617–643.

Nordvik, Frode Martin, Tarjei Moen, and Evy Zenker, eds. 2009. *Facts: The Norwegian Petroleum Sector 2009*. Oslo: Norwegian Ministry of Petroleum and Energy; Stavanger: Norwegian Petroleum Directorate.

Nore, Petter. 1980. "The Transfer of Technology: The Norwegian Case." In *New Policy Imperatives for Energy Producers: Proceedings of the Sixth ICEED International Energy Conference*, ed. Ragaei El Mallakh and Dorothea El Mallakh, 139–158. Boulder: International Research Center for Energy and Economic Development.

2003. "Norsk Hydro's Takeover of Saga Petroleum in 1999." Report No. 73. Power and Democracy Report Series, University of Oslo, August.

Nore, Petter and Terisa Turner. 1980. *Oil and Class Struggle*. London: Zed.

Noreng, Øystein. 1980. *The Oil Industry and Government Strategy in the North Sea*. London: Croom Helm.

Norges Bank. 2009. *The Government Petroleum Fund: Key Figures 2008*. July 6.

North, Douglass C. 1990. *Institutions, Institutional Change, and Economic Performance*. Cambridge University Press.

North, Douglass C. and Barry Weingast. 1989. "Constitutions and Commitment: The Evolution of Institutions Governing Public Choice in Seventeenth-Century England." *The Journal of Economic History* 49 (4): 803–832.

Norwegian Ministry of Finance. 1974. *Parliamentary Report No. 25 (1973–1974)*. Oslo: Norwegian Ministry of Finance.

2009. *Revised National Budget 2009 (Revidert nasjonalbudsjett 2009)*. Oslo: Norwegian Ministry of Finance.

Norwegian Parliament. 1971. *Recommendation No. 294 (1970–1971) from the Storting*. Oslo: Norwegian Parliament.

Norwegian Petroleum Directorate. 2009a. *NPD Fact Pages*. Norwegian Petroleum Directorate website, accessed March 6, 2009, www.factpages.npd.no/factpages/Default.aspx?culture=en.

2009b. *Petroleum Resources on the Norwegian Continental Shelf 2009*. Stavanger: Norwegian Petroleum Directorate.

2010. *NPD Fact Pages*. October 19. www.factpages.npd.no/factpages/Default.aspx?culture=en.

Novaes, Cristina. 2006. "Como Nasceu e Cresceu a Sonangol?" *Ngol Notícias* 105 (July): 21. (*in Portuguese*)

Nwokeji, G. Ugo. 2007. "The Nigerian National Petroleum Corporation and the Development of the Nigerian Oil and Gas Industry: History, Strategies and Current Directions." Policy Report. *The Changing Role of National Oil Companies in International Energy Markets*, Houston, Texas, Rice University, March 1–2.

Nzeshi, Onwuka. 2010. "Nigeria: Gas Flare Deadline Now December 2012." *This Day*, January 14, accessed April 14, 2011, www.allafrica.com/stories/201001140228.html.

Obaid, Nawaf E. 2000. *The Oil Kingdom at 100: Petroleum Policymaking in Saudi Arabia*. Washington DC: Washington Institute for Near-East Policy.

Odell, Peter R. 1986. *Oil and World Power: Background of the Oil Crisis*, 8th edn. New York: Viking Penguin.

Oduniyi, Mike. 2003. "Nigeria: Marginal Field: Major Oil Firms Place Fresh Conditions." *This Day*, April 16, accessed April 14, 2011, www.allafrica.com/stories/200304160012.html.

OECD. 2005. *OECD Guidelines on Corporate Governance of State-Owned Enterprises*. Paris: OECD.

2006. *OECD Economic Survey: Russian Federation 2006*. Paris: OECD.

Office of the US Trade Representative. 2010. *2010 National Trade Estimate Report on Foreign Trade Barriers – Nigeria*. Washington DC: USTR.

Offshore Technology. 2005. "Angola's Girassol Project Underway." September 1, accessed April 14, 2011, www.offshore-technology.com/features/feature602/.

2007. "Rosa Field, Angola." Accessed April 14, 2011, www.offshore-technology.com/projects/Rosaafrica/Rosaafrica5.html.

Oil & Energy Trends. 2007. "UAE's Production Plans May Prove Over-ambitious." March 16.

Oil & Gas Directory. 2007. "Company Profile – Abu Dhabi National Oil Company (ADNOC)." *Oil and Gas Directory – Middle East*.

Oil & Gas Journal. 1988. "Norway's Move to Privatization is a Good Idea That Should Go Further." July 11.

Oil Voice. 2008. "Occidental to Develop Oil and Gas Fields in Abu Dhabi." October 8, accessed April 14, 2011, www.oilvoice.com/n/Occidental_to_Develop_Oil_and_Gas_Fields_in_Abu_Dhabi/e1b9aa1a.aspx.

Olcutt, Martha Brill. 2007. "KazMunaiGas: Kazakhstan's National Oil and Gas Company." Policy Report. The Baker Institute Energy Forum,

The Changing Role of National Oil Companies in International Energy Markets, Houston, Texas, Rice University, March 1–2.

Olson, Mancur. 1993. "Dictatorship, Democracy, and Development." *American Political Science Review* 87 (3): 567–576.

Omorogbe, Yinka. 2003. *Oil and Gas Law in Nigeria*. Lagos: Malthouse Press.

2008. *Why We Have No Energy*. Ibadan University Press.

ONGC. 2005. *Making Tomorrow Brighter, Annual Report 2004–05*. New Delhi: ONGC.

2007. *Exploring Frontiers for the Nation's Energy Security, Annual Report 2006–07*. New Delhi: ONGC.

2008. "ONGC Videsh Limited." In *2007 Fortune Most Admired Companies: Oil and Natural Gas Corporation Limited Annual Report 2007–08*. New Delhi: ONGC.

2009. "ONGC Signs MoU with Weatherford for Enhancing the Production from their Matured Fields." Press Release, February 16.

Onoh, J. K. 1983. *The Nigerian Oil Economy: From Prosperity to Glut*. New York: St. Martin's Press.

Onwuka, Sopuruchi. 2005. "Nigeria: 18 Companies to Emerge from PHCN." *Daily Champion*, July 18, accessed April 14, 2011, www.allafrica.com/stories/200507180840.html.

Oomes, Nienke and Katerina Kalcheva. 2007. "Diagnosing Dutch Disease: Does Russia Have the Symptoms?" Working Paper 07/102. IMF.

OPEC. 2004–2007. *Annual Statistical Bulletin*. Vienna: OPEC.

2007. "OPEC Production Allocations." OPEC website, accessed April 14, 2011, www.opec.org/opec_web/en/data_graphs/335.htm.

2009. *OPEC Annual Statistical Bulletin 2008*. Vienna: OPEC.

2010. *OPEC Annual Statistical Bulletin 2009*. Vienna: OPEC.

Ortega, Daniel and Francisco Rodríguez. 2008. "Freed from Illiteracy? A Closer Look at Venezuela's Misión Robinson Literacy Campaign." *Economic Development and Cultural Change* 57 (1): 1–30.

Oster, Shai. 2009. "China Fund's $7 Billion Deal with Guinea Draws Scrutiny." *The Wall Street Journal*, November 2, accessed April 14, 2011, www.online.wsj.com/article/SB125711859736121663.html.

Otis, John. 2007. "Chávez Wants to Pass Saudis: Venezuela Out to Prove Its Oil Reserves Greater than Any Nation's." *Houston Chronicle*, March 6, accessed April 14, 2011, www.chron.com/CDA/archives/archive.mpl?id=2007_4298910.

Oxford Analytica. 2008. "Mexico's Calderón Attempts Oil Reform." *Forbes.com*, April 11, accessed April 14, 2011, www.forbes.com/2008/04/10/mexico-oil-pemex-cx_0411oxford.html.

Padmanabhan, R. 1998. "A Deal Questioned." *Frontline* 15 (5).

Paris, Francisco. 2006. "Institutional Failure in Venezuela: The Cases of Spending Oil Revenues and the Governance of PDVSA (1975–2005)." Ph.D. diss., London School of Economics and Political Science.

Parra, Francisco. 2004. *Oil Politics: A Modern History of Petroleum.* London: I.B. Tauris.

Parraga, Marianna. 2009. "Chavez's Allies Start Pumping Venezuelan Oil." *Reuters*, September 15, accessed April 14, 2011, www.in.reuters.com/article/idINN149449120090914?pageNumber=1&virtualBrand Channel=0.

 2010. "Nationalized Venezuela Oil Service Firms Await Cash." *Reuters*, March 2, accessed April 14, 2011, www.reuters.com/article/idUSTRE6214TI20100302.

PDVSA (Petróleos de Venezuela, S.A.). 2001, 2002, 2003, 2005a–2006a. *Annual and Transition Report of Foreign Private Issuers.* US Securities and Exchange Commission, filing type 20-F.

 2005b. "Modificación de los convenios operativos acaba con la ilegalidad y la evasión impositiva." PDVSA Press Release. May 25. (*in Spanish*)

 2006b. *Contact with the New PDVSA: A Newsletter about Venezuela's National Oil Industry*, No. 8.

 2007. *Información financiera y operacional al 31 de diciembre de 2006.* (*in Spanish*)

 2008. *PDVSA Financial and Operational Information, December 31, 2007.*

 2009. *PDVSA Informe de Gestión Anual 2008.* (*in Spanish*)

Pearce, David W. 1984. "Introduction and Overview." In *Risk and the Political Economy of Resource Development*, ed. David W. Pearce, Horst Siebert, and Ingo Walter. London: Macmillan.

Pearce, Justin. 2002. "Poverty and War in Cabinda." *BBC News*, October 22, accessed April 14, 2011, www.news.bbc.co.uk/2/hi/programmes/from_our_own_correspondent/2361143.stm.

Pearson, Scott B. 1970. *Petroleum and the Nigerian Economy.* Stanford University Press.

Peltzman, Sam. 1989. "The Control and Performance of State-Owned Enterprises." In *Privatization and State-Owned Enterprises: Lessons from the United States, Great Britain and Canada*, ed. Paul MacAvoy et al., 69–75. Boston: Kluwer Academic.

Pemex. 2010. Pemex company website, accessed February 20. 2010. www.Pemex.com (includes documents from previous years).

Pemex Annual Reports. 2005–2010. Accessed May 10, 2011, www.ri.pemex.com/index.cfm?action=content&sectionID=135&catID=12320.

Pemex Statistical Yearbook. 1999–2011. Accessed May 10, 2011, www.ri.pemex.com/index.cfm?action=content&sectionID=135&catID=12322.

Penfold-Becerra, Michael. 2007. "Clientelism and Social Funds: Evidence from Chávez's Misiones." *Latin American Politics & Society* 49 (4): 63–84.

Penna Marinho, Ilmar. 1970. *Petróleo, Soberania e Desenvolvimento*. Rio de Janeiro: Editora Bloch. (*in Spanish*)

Pereira de Melo, Hildete, Joao Lizardo de Araújo, and Adilson de Oliveira. 1994. "Electricidade no segundo governo Vargas e a crise dos anos 90." In *Vargas e a Crise dos Anos 50*, ed. Angela de Castro Gomes. Rio de Janeiro: Relume Dumara. (*in Portuguese*)

PESD (Program on Energy and Sustainable Development). 2006. "National Oil Companies: Strategy, Performance and Implications for Global Energy Markets." Prospectus, August 15. PESD, Stanford University.

Petras, James F., Morris Morley, and Steven Smith. 1977. *The Nationalization of Venezuelan Oil*. New York: Praeger.

Petrobras. 1955–1965. *Relatórios Anuais de Atividade*. São Paulo: Petrobras.

2011. *2011–2015 Business Plan*. July 22, accessed July 27, 2011, www.petrobras.com.br/ri.

PetroChina. 2008. *2008 Interm Report PetroChina Company Limited*. Beijing: PetroChina.

Petroleum Economist. 1993. "Size and Success Win Votes." June 1.

1995. "A Good Image Wins the Votes: Petroleum/Energy Industries." June 6.

1999. "Best Oil Companies." January 6.

2008. "Gas Exports: LNG Good, Pipeline Poor." May.

2009. "Nigeria: Few Friends for Reform Bill." September.

Petroleum Energy Economist. 2007. "World Energy Atlas 2007 Edition." Petroleum Economist Cartographic.

Petroleum Intelligence Weekly. 2005. "Algeria – After years of fierce debate, the new hydrocarbons law appears to be firmly on track for parliamentary approval in early April, after the powerful UGTA trade union dropped its opposition last month, possibly after receiving government assurances on jobs." March 28.

1986–2009. "Petroleum Intelligence Weekly Ranks World's Top 50 Oil Companies."

Petronas. 1984. *Petronas: A Decade of Growth, 1974–1984*. Kuala Lumpur: Jabatan Hal Ehwal Awam Petronas.

2009a. *Annual Report 2009*. Kuala Lumpur: Petroliam Nasional Berhad.

2009b. *Petronas Group: Financial Results Announcement, Financial Year Ended 31 March 2009*. Financial and Operational Review. Kuala Lumpur: Petroliam Nasional Berhad.

Philip, George. 1982. *Oil and Politics in Latin America: Nationalist Movements and State Companies.* Cambridge University Press.

　　1999. "When Oil Prices Were Low: Petróleos de Venezuela (PdVSA) and Economic Policy-making in Venezuela since 1989." *Bulletin of Latin American Research* 18 (3): 361–376.

Pirani, Simon, ed. 2009. *Russian and CIS Gas Markets and Their Impact on Europe.* Oxford University Press.

Platts Oilgram News. 2008. "Norway Claims $2 Billion from StatoilHydro on Kårstø Expansion." May 1.

Polgreen, Lydia. 2008. "Oil Field Operation Suspended After Attack by Nigerian Rebels." *The New York Times*, June 20, accessed April 15, 2011, www.nytimes.com/2008/06/20/world/africa/20nigeria.html.

Quandt, William B. 1969. *Revolution and Political Leadership: Algeria, 1954–1968.* Cambridge: MIT Press.

Quinlan, Martin. 2007. "New Gas Pipe Quashed." *Petroleum Economist* 74 (12): 21–22.

Radio Free Europe Radio Liberty. 2009. "Let's Drink To Russian Gas." June 8, accessed April 15, 2011, www.rferl.org/content/Lets_Drink_To_Russian_Gas/1749174.html.

Ramírez, Rafael. 2006a. Speech by the Minister of Energy and Petroleum and President of PDVSA, to the National Assembly Plenary on the Model for Mixed Companies, Caracas, Venezuela, March 23.

　　2006b. *Full Sovereignty Over Oil.* Speech of the Venezuelan Minister of Energy and Petroleum during the Third OPEC International Seminar *OPEC in a New Energy Era: Challenges and Opportunities.* September.

Ramm, Hans Henrik. 2009. "The Demise of the Norwegian Diversity Paradigm: Innovation vs Internationalization in the Petroleum Industry." In *Political Economy of Energy in Europe: Forces of Integration and Fragmentation*, ed. Gunnar Fermann, 271–336. Berlin: Berliner Wissenshafts-Verlag.

Randall, Laura. 1993. *The Political Economy of Brazilian Oil.* Westport: Praeger.

　　1987. *The Political Economy of Venezuelan Oil.* New York: Praeger.

Ranis, Gustav. 2003. "Symposium on Infant Industries: A Comment." *Oxford Development Studies* 31 (1): 33–35.

Rediff India Abroad. 2007. "India to Attract $4 bn in Oil Exploration." December 13, accessed April 15, 2011, www.rediff.com/money/2007/dec/13oil.htm.

Red Orbit. 2005. "Market Gives OPEC Opportunity to Improve Oil Reserves Data." July 28, accessed April 15, 2011, www.redorbit.com/news/science/189279/market_gives_opec_opportunity_to_improve_oil_reserves_data/.

Reed, J. 2006. "Angola: In Confident, Expansionary Mode." *Financial Times*, March 1, accessed April 15, 2011, www.ft.com/reports/africaoil2006.

Rego, Jose M., ed. 1986. Inflação Inercial, Teorias sobre Inflação e o Plano Cruzado. Rio de Janeiro: Paz e Terra. (*in Portuguese*)

Reno, William. 2000. "The Real (War) Economy of Angola." In *Angola's War Economy: The Role of Oil and Diamonds*, ed. Jackie Cilliers and Christian Dietrich, 219–236. Pretoria: Institute for Security Studies.

Repsol. 2009. "Repsol Confirms Venezuela's Perla 1X Well as its Largest Ever Gas Find." Repsol Press Release, October 16.

Republic of Angola. 2004. *Petroleum Tax Law – National Assembly Law No. 13/04.*

Reuters. 2009. "Nigeria Minister Says Amnesty Program Working." September 23, accessed April 15, 2011, www.uk.reuters.com/article/idUKN2342225720090923.

Rigobon, Roberto and Dani Rodrik. 2004. "Rule of Law, Democracy, Openness, and Income: Estimating the Interrelationships." NBER Working Paper No. 10570, September.

Rigzone. 2009. "Cobalt, Sonangol Join Forces for Deepwater GOM, Angola Exploration." April 23, accessed April 15, 2011, www.rigzone.com/NEWS/article.asp?a_id=75380.

Rodríguez, Francisco. 2006. "The Anarchy of Numbers: Understanding the Evidence on Venezuelan Economic Growth." Wesleyan Economics Working Paper No. 2006–009, February.

Røed Larsen, Erling. 2006. "Escaping the Resource Curse and the Dutch Disease? When and Why Norway Caught Up with and Forged Ahead of its Neighbors." *American Journal of Economics and Sociology* 65 (3): 605–640.

Roque, Paula. 2008. "The 'Angolagate' Trial: The Political Costs of France's Arms-for-Oil Scandal." *Institute for Security Studies*, November 10, accessed January 3, 2009. www.iss.co.za/pgcontent.php?UID=22557.

Rose, Peter R. 2001. *Risk Analysis and Management of Petroleum Exploration Ventures.* Tulsa: American Association of Petroleum Geologists.

Ross, Michael L. 2001. "Does Oil Hinder Democracy?" *World Politics* 53 (3): 325–361.

Ross, Stephen A. 1973. "The Economic Theory of Agency: The Principal's Problem." *American Economic Review* 63 (12): 134–139.

Ruedy, John. 2005. *Modern Algeria: The Origins and Development of a Nation*, 2nd edn. Bloomington: Indiana University Press.

Russian Energy Strategy. 2003. Энергетическая стратегия России на период до 2020 года (*Russia's Energy Strategy to 2020*). (*in Russian*), accessed August 6, 2010, www.gazprom.ru/documents/strategy.doc.

2008. Энергетическая стратегия России на период до 2030 года (*Russian Energy Strategy to 2030*). (*in Russian*), accessed August 6, 2010, www.inreen.org/node/89.

Rutledge, Ian. 2005. *Addicted to Oil: America's Relentless Drive for Energy Security*. London: I. B. Tauris.

Saeidi, Ali A. 2004. "The Accountability of Para-governmental Organizations *(bonyads)*: The Case of Iranian Foundations." *Iranian Studies* 37 (3): 479–498.

Salehi-Isfahani, D. 2009. "Oil Wealth and Economic Growth in Iran." In *Contemporary Iran: Economy, Society, Politics*, ed. Ali Gheissari, 3–37. New York: Oxford University Press.

Sarmento, Carlos Eduardo and Sergio Lamarao. 2006. *Engenharia da Petrobras: 1972–2005: ontem, hoje e amanhã construindo uma história*. Rio de Janeiro: Petrobras. (*in Portuguese*)

Schwarz, Adam. 1994. *A Nation in Waiting: Indonesia in the 1990s*. Sydney: Allen & Unwin Pty.

Schwarzchild, Maimon. 1986. "Variations on an Enigma: Law in Practice and Law on the Books in the USSR." *Harvard Law Review* 99 (3): 685–702.

Scotch Whisky Association. 2007. *Scotch at a Glance 2007*. London, accessed April 15, 2011, www.scotch-whisky.org.uk/swa/files/ScotchataGlance2007.pdf.

Segal, David. 1988. "The Iran-Iraq War: A Military Analysis." *Foreign Affairs* 66 (5): 946–963.

Seymour, Ian. 1980. *OPEC Instrument of Change*. London: Macmillan.

Shambayati, Hootan. 1994. "The Rentier State, Interest Groups, and the Paradox of Autonomy: State and Business in Turkey and Iran." *Comparative Politics* 26 (3): 307–331.

SHANA. 2008. "Iran's Refining Expansion on Track to Meet Gasoline Deficit." December 13, accessed April 15, 2011, www.shana.ir/137054-en.html.

Sharma, N. C. 2002. "History of Seismic Prospecting In ONGC – A Chronological Sketch of Events." *Geohorizons* (January).

Shaxson, Nicholas. 2009. "Nigeria's Extractive Industries Transparency Initiative: Just a Glorious Audit?" Program Paper. London: Chatham House.

Shehu, Mohammed S. and Hamisu Muhammad. 2010. "Nigeria: NNPC GMD Sacked After 41 Days." *Daily Trust*, May 18, accessed April 15, 2011, www.allafrica.com/stories/201005180958.html.

Shepherd, Rob and James Ball. 2006. "Liquefied Natural Gas from Trinidad and Tobago: The Atlantic LNG Project." In *Natural Gas and Geopolitics: From 1970 to 2040*, ed. David G. Victor, Amy M. Jaffe, and Mark H. Hayes, 268–318. Cambridge University Press.

Shi, Dan. 2005. "Energy Industry in China: Marketization and National Energy Security." *China & World Economy* 13 (4): 21–33.

Shields, David. 2006. *PEMEX: Problems and Policy Options*. Policy Paper No. 4. Berkeley: Center for Latin America Studies, University of California Press.

2009. PEMEX, CFE at a Loss. *The News*, June 5.

Shirley, Mary M. and Patrick Walsh. 2001. "Public Vs. Private Ownership: The Current State of the Debate." Policy Research Working Paper No. 2420. World Bank.

Shosanya, Mohammed. 2010. "Nigeria: As Jonathan Signs Local Content Bill Into Law." *Daily Trust*, April 26, accessed April 15, 2011, www.allafrica.com/stories/201004270637.html.

Silva, Eduardo. 2007. "The Import Substitution Model: Chile in Comparative Perspective." *Latin American Perspectives* 34 (3): 67–90.

Simmons, Matthew R. 2005a. "Proving Proven Reserves are Proven: An Art Form or a Science?" Presentation at SPE GCS Reservoir Study Group Luncheon, Houston, Texas, February 24.

2005b. *Twilight in the Desert: The Coming Saudi Oil Shock and the World Economy*. Hoboken: John Wiley & Sons.

Singh, A. B. and A. Singh. 2004. *Public Sector Reforms in India*. New Delhi: A.P.H.

Sinha, Uttam K. and Shebonti R. Dadwal. 2005. "Equity Oil and India's Energy Security." *Strategic Analysis* 29 (3).

Skancke, Martin. 2003. "Fiscal Policy and Petroleum Fund Management in Norway." In *Fiscal Policy Formulation and Implementation in Oil-Producing Countries*, ed. J. M. Davis, R. Ossowski, and A. Fedelino, 316–338. Washington DC: IMF.

Skocpol, Theda. 1982. "Rentier State and Shi'a Islam in the Iranian Revolution." *Theory and Society* 11 (3): 265–283.

Smith, D. and Michael J. Trebilcock. 2001. "State-owned Enterprises in Less Developed Countries: Privatization and Alternative Reform Strategies." *European Journal of Law and Economics* 12 (3): 217–252.

Smith, Daniel J. 2007. *A Culture of Corruption: Everyday Deception and Popular Discontent in Nigeria*. Princeton University Press.

Smith, Geri. 2001. "Pemex: Still in the Dark Ages." *Business Week*, March 26, accessed April 15, 2011, www.businessweek.com/magazine/content/01_13/b3725173.htm.

2004. "Pemex May Be Turning From Gusher To Black Hole." *BusinessWeek*, December 13, accessed April 15, 2011, www.businessweek.com/magazine/content/04_50/b3912084_mz058.htm.

Soares de Oliveira, Ricardo. 2007a. "Business Success, Angola-Style: Postcolonial Politics and the Rise and Rise of Sonangol." *Journal of Modern African Studies* 45 (4): 595–619.

2007b. *Oil and Politics in the Gulf of Guinea.* London: Hurst and Company.

Sonangol. 2005a. "Comunicado de Imprensa: Programa de Licitação de Novas Concessoes Petrolíferas." *Jornal de Angola*, September 16. (*in Portuguese*)

2005b. "Comunicado de Imprensa." *Jornal de Angola*, October 20. (*in Portuguese*)

2005c. "Anúncio para o Concurso para Novas Concessóes Petrolíferas nos Blocos 1, 5, 6, 26 e Áreas Remanescentes dos Blocos 15, 17, e 18." *Jornal de Angola*, December 15. (*in Portuguese*)

2006. "Comunicado de Imprensa: Alteração dos Termos de Referencia dos Concursos para Novas Concessões Petrolíferas nas Áreas Remanescentes dos Blocos 17 e 18." *Jornal de Angola*, March 21. (*in Portuguese*)

2007a. "Licensing Round 2007/2008." Sonangol website, accessed December 28, 2009, www.sonangol.co.ao/wps/portal/ep/areas/concessionary/infoInvestor.

2007b. "Oil Concessions' Map." Sonangol website, accessed December 30, 2009, www.sonangol.co.ao/wps/portal/ep/areas/concessionary/infoInvestor.

2008a. "Structure–Corporate Organization." Sonangol website, accessed January 2, 2009, www.sonangol.co.ao/wps/portal/ep.

2008b. "History of Sonangol." Sonangol website, accessed January 2, 2009, www.sonangol.co.ao/wps/portal/ep.

Sonangol P&P. 2008. "Goals and Strategy." Sonangol website, accessed January 2, 2009, www.sonangolpp.com/pnpEstrategia_en.shtml.

Sonangol Universo. 2006. "Thirty Years Young." *Sonangol Universo* 9 (Spring): 8–12.

2007. "Win-Win Opportunity." *Sonangol Universo* 14 (Summer): 14–17.

2008. "Sonangol News Briefing." *Sonangol Universo* 17 (Spring): 42–43.

2010. "Sonangol News Briefing." *Sonangol Universo* 25 (March): 32–33.

Sonatrach. 2007. *Sonatrach Annual Report 2007.* Algiers: Sonatrach.

Sosa-Garcia, Rodolfo. "The Historical Oil Rent in the Mexican Economy (1938–2001)." Unpublished manuscript, accessed April 15, 2011, www.papers.ssrn.com/sol3/papers.cfm?abstract_id=938268.

Sosa Pietri, Andrés. 1993. *Petróleo y Poder.* Caracas: Editorial Planeta. (*in Spanish*)

2000. *Quo Vadis Venezuela.* Caracas: Galaxy Group. (*in Spanish*)

Spence, Michael and Richard Zeckhauser. 1971. "Insurance, Information, and Individual Action." *American Economic Review* 61 (2): 380–387.

Standard & Poor's Ratings. 2009. "Oil and Gas: Production & Marketing Industry Survey." Stock Report, New York: Standard & Poor's Corp, March 12.

Stasavage, David. 2003. *Public Debt and the Birth of the Democratic State: France and Great Britain 1688–1789*. New York: Cambridge University Press.

Steinfeld, Edward S. 1998. *Forging Reform in China: The Fate of State-Owned Industry*. Cambridge University Press.

Stepan, Alfred C. 1971. *The Military in Politics: Changing Patterns in Brazil*. Princeton University Press.

Stern, Jonathan P. 2005. *The Future of Russian Gas and Gazprom*. New York: Oxford University Press.

 2009. "Continental European Long-Term Gas Contracts: Is a Transition Away From Oil Product-linked Pricing Inevitable and Imminent?" Oxford Institute for Energy Studies, September.

Stern, Roger. 2007. "The Iranian Petroleum Crisis and United States National Security." *PNAS* 104 (1): 377–382.

Stevens, Paul. 1975. *Joint Ventures in Middle East Oil, 1957–1975*. Beirut: Middle East Economic Consultants.

 1998. "Energy Privatization – Sensitivities and Realities." *Journal of Energy and Development* 23 (1): 1–14.

 2000. "Introduction to the Economics of Energy." In *The Economics of Energy*, vol. I, ed. Paul Stevens, ix–lxvii. Cheltenham: Edward Elgar.

 2003a. "Economists and the Oil Industry: Facts Versus Analysis, The Case of Vertical Integration." In *Energy in a Competitive World*, ed. Lester C. Hunt, 95–101. Cheltenham: Edward Elgar.

 2003b. *National Oil Companies: Good or Bad? A Literature Survey*. Presentation at the National Oil Companies Workshop: Current Roles and Future Prospects. Washington DC, May 27, World Bank.

 2003c. "National Oil Companies: Good or Bad? – A Literature Survey." Working Paper. The Centre for Energy, Petroleum and Mineral Law and Policy Gateway.

 2005. "Oil Markets." *Oxford Review of Economic Policy* 21 (1): 19–42.

 2008a. "National Oil Companies and International Oil Companies in the Middle East: Under the Shadow of Government and the Resource Nationalism Cycle." *The Journal of World Energy Law and Business* 1 (1): 5–30.

2008b. "Kuwait Petroleum Corporation: Searching for Strategy in a Fragmented Oil Sector." Working Paper No. 78. Program on Energy and Sustainable Development, Stanford University.

2008c. *A Methodology for Assessing the Performance of National Oil Companies*. Washington DC: World Bank.

Stevens, Paul and John V. Mitchell. 2008. *Resource Depletion, Dependence and Development: Can Theory Help?* Program Paper. London: Chatham House.

Stocking, George W. 1970. *Middle East Oil: A Study in Political and Economic Controversy*. Nashville: Vanderbilt University Press.

Suberu, Rotimi T. 2001. *Federalism and Ethnic Conflict in Nigeria*. Washington DC: United States Institute of Peace.

Subramanian T. S. 2005. "The Sakhalin Venture." *Frontline* 22 (22), accessed April 15, 2011, www.flonnet.com/fl2222/stories/20051104002810100.htm.

Suleiman, Atef. 1988. "The Oil Experience of the United Arab Emirates and its Legal Framework." *Journal of Energy and Natural Resources* 6 (1): 1–24.

1995. "Certain Aspects of the Gas Experience in the UAE." *Journal of Energy and Natural Resources* 13 (3): 178–198.

Szabo, A. M. 2000. "Energy Industry Drivers/NOCs: The Special Case of Venezuela." Paper to the 21st International Area Conference on National Oil Companies: Trends and Priorities. Boulder: The International Research Center for Energy and Economic Development.

Taghavi, Roshanak. 2008. "Oil Slump Threatens Iran's Plans." *The Wall Street Journal*, November 13, accessed April 15, 2011, www.online.wsj.com/article/SB122651451924321327.html.

Takin, Manouchehr. 2009. "Iran's Oil Century – Reviewing Oil and Gas Operations." *MEES* 52 (1).

TAKREER. 2010. "Ruwais Refinery." TAKREER website, accessed April 14, www.takreer.com/RuwaisRefinery1.aspx.

Tan, Xu and Frank Wolak. 2009. "Does China Underprice Its Oil Consumption?" Working Paper. Department of Economics, Stanford University, February 9.

Taylor, Ian. 2006. "China's Oil Diplomacy in Africa." *International Affairs* 82 (5): 937–959.

Tenev, Stoyan, Chunlin Zhang, and Loup Brefort. 2002. *Corporate Governance and Enterprise Reform in China: Building the Institutions of Modern Markets*. Washington DC: World Bank.

Tetreault, Mary Ann. 1995. *The Kuwait Petroleum Corporation and the Economics of the New World Order*. Westport: Quorum Books.

Thaindian News. 2009. "ONGC Chairman Defends Acqusition of Imperial Energy." January 3, accessed April 15, 2011, www.thaindian.com/newsportal/business/ongc-chairman-defends-acquisition-of-imperial-energy_100137817.html.

Thaler, David E., Alireza Nader, Shahram Chubin, Jerrold D. Green, Charlotte Lynch, and Frederic Wehrey. 2010. *Mullahs, Guards, and Bonyads: An Exploration of Iranian Leadership Dynamics*. Rand National Defense Research Institute. Santa Monica: RAND Corp.

The Economist. 1987. "Statoil: The Mongstad Monster." October 10.

    1989. "Norwegian Crone: Norway Offers an Object Lesson in How Not to Run an Oil Industry." February 18.

    2006. "Oil's Dark Secret." August 12.

    2008a. "Nigeria: Another Deadline Goes Up in Flames." April 5.

    2008b. "Nigeria: Risky Toughness: The Army's Tough Approach to Delta Militants Could End Up Uniting Them." September 18.

    2010. "Hugo Chávez's Venezuela: Feeling the Heat." May 13.

The Financial Express. 2006. "ONGC May Be Denied NELP Blocks." November 23, accessed June 25, 2010, www.financialexpress.com/news/ongc-may-be-denied-nelp-blocks/184656/.

The Hindu. 2008. "44 Blocks Awarded Under NELP VII." November 21, accessed June 25, 2010, www.hindu.com/2008/11/21/stories/2008112158291800.htm.

The Hindu Business Line. 2003. "3 mt Sudan Crude for OVL Annually." March 14, accessed June 25, 2010, www.blonnet.com/2003/03/14/stories/2003031401310500.htm.

The National. 2008. "UAE Keeps OPEC Pledge to Cut Supply." November 3, accessed April 15, 2011, www.thenational.ae/business/energy/uae-keeps-opec-pledge-to-cut-supply.

Thomas, Jonathan and Timothy Worrall. 1994. "Foreign Direct Investment and the Risk of Expropriation." *Review of Economic Studies* 61 (1): 81–108.

Thompson, Fred and L. R. Jones. 1986. "Controllership in the Public Sector." *Journal of Policy Analysis and Management* 5 (3): 547–571.

Thurber, Mark C., David R. Hults, and Patrick R. P. Heller. 2011. "Exporting the 'Norwegian Model': The effect of administrative design on oil sector performance." *Energy Policy* 39(9): 5366–5378.

Tinker-Salas, Miguel. 2005. "Fueling Concern: The Role of Oil in Venezuela." *Harvard International Review* 26 (4).

Tirole, Jean. 1994. "The Internal Organization of Government." *Oxford Economic Papers* 46 (1): 1–29.

Tlemcani, Rachid. 1986. *State and Revolution in Algeria*. Boulder: Westview.

Tofte, Ingebjørg Erlandsen, Tarjei Moen, and Evy Zenker, eds. 2008. *Facts: The Norwegian Petroleum Sector 2008*. Oslo: Norwegian Ministry of Petroleum and Energy; Stavanger: Norwegian Petroleum Directorate.

Tollison, Robert D. 1982. "Rent Seeking: A Survey." *Kyklos* 35 (4): 575–602.

Tomz, Michael and Mark Wright. 2008. "Sovereign Theft: Theory and Evidence About Sovereign Default and Expropriation." Working Paper. Centre for Applied Macroeconomic Analysis, Australian National University.

Toninelli, Pier Angelo. 2000. "The Rise and Fall of Public Enterprise: The Framework." In *The Rise and Fall of State-Owned Enterprise in the Western World*, ed. Pier Angelo Toninelli, 3–24. New York: Cambridge University Press.

Torbat, Akbar E. 2005. "Impacts of the US Trade and Financial Sanctions on Iran." *The World Economy* 28 (3): 407–434.

Torke, James W. 2001. "What Is This Thing Called the Rule of Law?" *Indiana Law Review* 34 (4): 1445–1456.

Trade Arabia. 2010. "Adnoc Awards $5.6bn Deals for Shah Gas Field." May 1, accessed April 15, 2011, www.tradearabia.com/news/ogn_179014.html.

Transparency International. 1999–2009. *Corruption Perceptions Index*. Brussels: Transparency International.

Transparency International and University of Goettingen. 1995–1998. "Corruption Perceptions Index." Brussels: Transparency International and University of Goettingen.

Trebilcock, Michael J. and Ronald J. Daniels. 2008. *Rule of Law Reform and Development: Charting the Fragile Path of Progress*. Cheltenham: Edward Elgar.

Treewater, Evette. 2008. "Venezuela's Hummer Revolution." *Latin Business Chronicle*, March 17, accessed April 15, 2011, www.latin-businesschronicle.com/app/article.aspx?id=2183.

Treisman, Daniel. 1999. *After the Deluge: Regional Crises and Political Consolidation in Russia*. Ann Arbor: University of Michigan Press.

Tsebelis, George. 1995. "Decision Making in Political Systems: Veto Players in Presidentialism, Parliamentarism, Multicameralism and Multipartyism." *British Journal of Political Science* 25 (3): 289–325.

   2002. *Veto Players: How Political Institutions Work*. Princeton University Press.

Tugwell, Franklin. 1975. *The Politics of Oil in Venezuela*. Stanford University Press.

UNDP (United Nations Development Programme). 2008. "Drivers of Change, Angola: Position Paper 1: Strengthening Public Institutions." January. Angola: UNDP.

UNIDO (United Nations Industrial Development Organization). 2004. *SPX News* 2 (2–3). UNIDO Newsletter.

United States Congress. Senate. Committee on Foreign Relations. Subcommittee on International Economic Policy. 1979. *The Future of Saudi Arabian Oil Production*. Staff Report. Washington DC: US Congress.

United States Department of State. 2005. *Country Reports on Human Rights Practices: Kuwait*. Washington DC: Bureau of Democracy, Human Rights, and Labor.

USGS (US Geological Survey). 2000. *USGS World Petroleum Assessment 2000*. Denver: US Dept of Interior.

Úslar Pietri, Arturo. 1936. "Sembrar el petróleo." *Diario Ahora*, July 14. (*in Spanish*)

Uwugiaren, Iyobosa. 2008. "Nigeria: Petrol Corporation Denies Paying Militants." *Leadership*, July 24, accessed April 15, 2011, www.allafrica.com/stories/200807240736.html.

van der Linde, Coby. 2000. *The State and the International Oil Market: Competition and the Changing Ownership of Crude Oil Assets*. Boston: Kluwer Academic.

van Groenendaal, Willem J. H. and Mohammed Mazraati. 2006. "A Critical Review of Iran's Buyback Contracts." *Energy Policy* 34 (18): 3709–3718.

Vanguard. 2006. "Nigeria: NEPA Privatisation in Limbo." April 13, accessed April 15, 2011, www.allafrica.com/stories/200604130192.html.

2009. "Nigeria: Oando – Reaping Benefits of Diversification." November 2, accessed April 15, 2011, www.allafrica.com/stories/200911021747.html.

2010. "Nigerian Content Policy Has Changed the Landscape Significantly, Nwapa." March 2, accessed April 15, 2011, www.allafrica.com/stories/201003020898.html.

Vatikiotis, Michael R. J. 1993. *Indonesian Politics Under Suharto: Order, Development and Pressure for Change*. London: Routledge.

Vernon, Raymond. 1971. *Sovereignty at Bay: The Multinational Spread of US Enterprises*. New York: Basic Books.

Vernon-Wortzel, Heidi and Lawrence H. Wortzel. 1989. "Privatization: Not the Only Answer." *World Development* 17 (5): 633–641.

Vicente, Manuel. 2008. "If We Identify Projects that Are Viable and Profitable...Of Course We Will Take Them On." *Sonangol Universo* 18 (Summer): 40–43.

Victor, David G. and Thomas C. Heller, eds. 2007. *The Political Economy of Power Sector Reform: The Experiences of Five Major Developing Countries*. New York: Cambridge University Press.

Victor, David G., Amy M. Jaffe, and Mark H. Hayes, eds. 2006. *Natural Gas and Geopolitics: From 1970 to 2040.* Cambridge University Press.

Victor, Nadejda M. 2007. "On Measuring the Performance of National Oil Companies (NOCs)." Working Paper No. 64. Program on Energy and Sustainable Development, Stanford University.

2008. "Gazprom: Gas Giant Under Strain." Working Paper No. 71. Program on Energy and Sustainable Development, Stanford University.

Vines, Alex, Nicholas Shaxson, Lisa Rimli, and Chris Heymans. 2005. *Angola–Drivers of Change: An Overview.* London: Chatham House.

Vines, Alex, Lillian Wong, Markus Weimer, and Indira Campos. 2009. *Thirst for African Oil: Asian National Oil Companies in Nigeria and Angola.* London: Chatham House.

Vining, Aidan R. and David L. Weimer. 1990. "Government Supply and Government Production Failure: A Framework Based on Contestability." *Journal of Public Policy* 10 (1): 1–22.

Vitalis, Robert. 2007. *America's Kingdom: Mythmaking on the Saudi Oil Frontier.* Stanford University Press.

Vives, Xavier. 2000. "Corporate Governance: Does It Matter?" In *Corporate Governance: Theoretical and Empirical Perspectives*, ed. Xavier Vives, 1–22. Cambridge University Press.

Vivoda, Vlado. 2008. *The Return of the Obsolescing Bargain and the Decline of Big Oil: A Study of Bargaining in the Contemporary Oil Industry.* Saarbrücken: VDM Verlag Dr. Müller.

von der Mehden, Fred R. and Al Troner. 2007. "Petronas: A National Oil Company with an International Vision." Policy Report. The Baker Institute Energy Forum, *The Changing Role of National Oil Companies in International Energy Markets*, Houston, Texas, Rice University, March 1–2.

von Flatern, Rick. 2006. "Mexico at the Crossroads." *Offshore Engineer*, December, 23–26.

Wainberg, Miranda Ferrell and Michelle Michot Foss. 2007. "Commercial Frameworks for National Oil Companies." Working Paper. Center for Energy Economics, University of Texas at Austin.

Wang, Haijiang H. 1999. *China's Oil Industry and Market.* Oxford: Elsevier Science.

Waterman, Richard W. and Kenneth J. Meier. 1998. "Principal–Agent Models: An Expansion?" *Journal of Public Administration Research and Theory* 8 (2): 173–202.

Watkins, Eric. 2009. "PDVSA, IOCs to Build Two LNG Liquefaction Plants." *Oil & Gas Journal*, March 9.

Weeks, Jessica L. 2008. "Autocratic Audience Costs: Regime Type and Signaling Resolve." *International Organization* 62 (1): 35–64.

Werenfels, Isabelle. 2002. "Obstacles to Privatisation of State-Owned Industries in Algeria: The Political Economy of a Distributive Conflict." *The Journal of North African Studies* 7 (1): 1–28.

2007. *Managing Instability in Algeria: Elites and Political Change Since 1995*. New York: Routledge.

Whalen, Christopher. 2002. "Chávez Revolution May Be in Retreat." *Insight on the News*, April 15, accessed April 15, 2011, www.rcwhalen. com/articles.asp.

Whitford, Andrew B. 2005. "The Pursuit of Political Control by Multiple Principals." *The Journal of Politics* 67 (1): 29–49.

Whittington, Richard. 2001. *What is Strategy – and Does it Matter?* London: Thomson Business.

Williamson, John. 2002. *Did the Washington Consensus Fail?* Speech at the Center for Strategic & International Studies, Washington DC. November 6.

Williamson, Oliver E. 1985. *The Economic Institutions of Capitalism: Firms, Markets, Relational Contracting*. New York: Free Press.

Wilson, Peter. 2008. "Venezuela: Land of 12-Cent Gas." *BusinessWeek. com*, May 23.

Wilson, Woodrow. 1913. *The New Freedom: A Call for the Emancipation of the Generous Energies of a People*. New York: Doubleday.

Wolf, Christian. 2009. "Does Ownership Matter? The Performance and Efficiency of State Oil vs. Private Oil (1987–2006)." *Energy Policy* 37 (7): 2642–2652.

Wolf, Christian and Michael G. Pollitt. 2008. "Privatising National Oil Companies: Assessing the Impact on Firm Performance." EPRG Working Paper 0805. Electricity Policy Research Group, University of Cambridge.

2009. "The Welfare Implications of Oil Privatisation: A Cost-Benefit Analysis of Norway's Statoil." Cambridge Working Paper in Economics No. 0912 and Electricity Policy Research Group Working Paper No. 0905. University of Cambridge and EPRG.

Woodhouse, Erik. 2006. "The Obsolescing Bargain Redux? Foreign Investment in the Electric Power Sector in Developing Countries." *NYU Journal of International Law and Politics* 38: 121–219.

Wood Mackenzie. 2002. "Cabinda Area A (Block 0): Key Facts." *Wood Mackenzie West Africa Upstream Service*, August.

2006. "Angola's E&P Fiscal Regime in a Global Context." Presentation to Angola Petroleum Revenue Management Workshop, Luanda, Angola, May 16.

2009a. *Wood Mackenzie Corporate Analysis Tool*. Wood Mackenzie website, accessed October 11, 2009, www.woodmacresearch.com/cgi-bin/

wmprod/portal/energy/productMicrosite.jsp?productOID=933381. (Wood Mackenzie's Corporate Analysis Tool is a commercially available database, updated quarterly, that contains worldwide asset data for over 2,900 oil and gas companies.)

2009b. *Wood Mackenzie PathFinder Database* (November 2009 update). Wood Mackenzie website, accessed January 18, 2010, www.wood-macresearch.com/cgi-bin/wmprod/portal/energy/productMicrosite. jsp?productOID=664098. (Wood Mackenzie's PathFinder is a commercially-available database, updated quarterly, that contains worldwide exploration and production data for the petroleum industry.)

2009c. "Nigeria Country Overview." *Wood Mackenzie Upstream Service*, October.

2010. "Company Report: Statoil." *Wood Mackenzie Corporate Service*, January.

Woodside, Claire. 2008. "Transparency and the Resource Curse: Evidence from the Case of Nigeria." Paper presented at the 80th Annual Conference of the Canadian Political Science Association, Vancouver, Canada, June 4–6.

World Bank. 2004a. *Nigeria Strategic Gas Plan.* UNDP/World Bank Energy Sector Management Assistance Programme (ESMAP). Washington DC: World Bank.

2004b. *Russian Economic Report, No. 7.* Washington DC: World Bank.

2004c. *Taxation and State Participation in Nigeria's Oil and Gas Sector.* UNDP and World Bank Energy Sector Management Assistance Programme (ESMAP). Washington DC: World Bank.

2005a. *Angola Public Expenditure Management and Financial Accountability. Report No. 29036-AO.* Washington DC: World Bank.

2005b. *Doing Business in 2006: Iran.* International Bank for Reconstruction and Development. Washington DC: World Bank.

2005c. *Russian Federation From Transition to Development: A Country Economic Memorandum for the Russian Federation.* Washington DC: World Bank.

2006a. " Economic Growth in Iran: Opportunities and Constraints." Social and Economic Development Group/MENA Region, Washington DC: World Bank, 29–30.

2006b. *Held by the Visible Hand: The Challenge of SOE Corporate Governance in Emerging Economies.* Washington DC: World Bank.

2007. *Investing in Oil in the Middle East and North Africa: Institutions, Incentives and the National Oil Companies. Board Report No. 40405-MNA.* Washington DC: World Bank.

2008. *A Citizen's Guide to National Oil Companies – Parts A and B.* Washington DC: World Bank Group; Austin: Center for Energy Economics, University of Texas at Austin.

2009. *World Development Indicators 2009.* Washington DC: World Bank.

World Learning. 2006. "Analise Orcamental." August.

Wright, Joseph. 2008. "To Invest or Insure? How Authoritarian Time Horizons Impact Foreign Aid Effectiveness." *Comparative Political Studies* 41 (7): 971–1000.

Xin, Qiu. 2005. "China Overhauls Energy Bureaucracy." *Asia Times*, June 3, accessed April 15, 2011, www.atimes.com/atimes/China/GF03Ad01.html.

Xu, Xiaojie. 2007. "Chinese NOC's Overseas Strategies: Background, Comparison, and Remarks." Policy Report. The Baker Institute Energy Forum, *The Changing Role of National Oil Companies in International Energy Markets*, Houston, Texas, Rice University, March 1–2.

Xu, Yihe. 2004. "China Energy Watch: CNPC Changes Heads, Problems Ahead." *Dow Jones Energy Service*, April 24.

Yar'adua, Abubakar L. 2007. "The Nigerian Gas Master-Plan." Presentation by Managing Director of the Nigerian National Petroleum Corporation to the Gas Stakeholders Forum, Abuja, Nigeria, November 26.

Yergin, Daniel. 1991. *The Prize: The Epic Quest for Oil, Money & Power.* New York: Free Press.

Yuan, Dong Ming. 2007. "China National Petroleum Corporation Case Study." Working Paper translated. Development Research Center of the State Council.

Yusuf, Adeola. 2009. "Nigeria: DPR Begins Enforcement of New Fuel Pump Price." *Daily Independent*, January 27, accessed April 15, 2011, www.allafrica.com/stories/200901270244.html.

2010. "Nigeria: Country Supplies Gas to Ghana Through West Africa Pipeline." *Daily Independent*, March 29, accessed April 15, 2011, www.allafrica.com/stories/201003300148.html.

Zabih, Sepehr. 1982. *The Mossadegh Era: Roots of the Iranian Revolution.* Chicago: Lake View Press.

Zawya. 2010. "ADNOC – Sour Gas Fields Development – Shah Field." Zawya Projects-Projects Monitor, accessed April 29, www.zawya.com/projects/project.cfm/pid020107061032/ADNOC%20-%20Sour%20Gas%20Fields%20Development%20-%20Shah%20Field?cc.

Zhang, Jin. 2004. *Catch-up and Competitiveness in China: The Case of Large Firms in the Oil Industry.* London: Routledge Curzon.

Index

Abacha, Sani, 708
Abdullah Admah Badawi, 829
Abdullah of Saudi Arabia, 188, 189,
    190
Abdullah Salleh, 814, 824–814
Abramovich, Roman, 693
Abu Dhabi
    gas, 488–489
    major projects with international
        involvement, 507
        Dolphin Gas Project, 507–509
        Shah gas field, 509–510
    oil sector history, 482–483
    See also ADGAS; ADNOC;
        GASCO; UAE
ADGAS (Abu Dhabi Gas Liquefaction
    Company Limited), 489
ADNOC (Abu Dhabi National Oil
    Company)
    centralized state authority over, 77
    monitoring-heavy state oversight
        of, 81
    operations and management,
        486–490
    overview, 478–482, 510–512
    performance, 12, 492–494
        ranking, 935
    private sector involvement, 8
    relationship with state, 499–506
    strategy, 490–492, 494–499
Aghazadeh, Gholam Reza, 266
AGIP (Azienda Generale Italiana
    Petroli)
    establishment of, 5
Ahmadinejad, Mahmoud, 255–256,
    262
AIOC (Anglo-Iranian Oil Company),
    240–241, 339
    See also BP
Aiyar, Mani Shankar, 787–788

Al Falih, Khalid, 196, 198
Al Naimi, Ali, 190, 205, 220
Al Otaiba, Mana Saeed, 500–501
Albacora oil field, 533
Algeria
    2005 Hydrocarbons Law, 576,
        577–583
    expropriations, 52–53
    history, 6, 7, 560–561
    nationalization, 181
    natural resources, 564–566
        gas, 566–567
        oil, 567–568
    organization of hydrocarbons sec-
        tor, 568–571
    overview, 557–560, 589–595
    state capacity, 575–577
    state goals, 569–575
    See also Sonatrach
Al-Khalifa, Ali, 354–357, 377
Amoco, Montrose oil field discovery,
    151
Angola
    geology, 849–852
    NOC negotiating on behalf of gov-
        ernment, 70–72
    See also Sonangol
Angolagate scandal, 869
Argentina
    See YPF
Asian premium, 227
associated gas, 331
    ADNOC, 489
    Angola, 863–864
    Gazprom, 656
    KPC, 351
    Nigeria, 710–711
    PDVSA, 440
    Pemex, 308
    Saudi Arabia, 207

Austria, establishment of NOC, 5
Azizan Zainul Abidin, 821–822

Bab oil field, 482
backward linkages, 213
Bandar Abbas refinery project, 277
Bank Bumiputra bailout, 826–827
Barbosa, Horta, 521, 553
Beckett, Angus, 646
benchmarking for performance
    assessment, 192
Benjedid, Chadli, 561–563
Berezovsky, Boris, 693
big contract model (China), 389
BNOC (British National Oil
    Corporation)
  formation, 152–153
  privatization, 153
Bolivia, 1937 nationalization, 145
Bombay High field, 807
  See also Mumbai High field
Bonny LNG terminal, 712
bonyads, Iran, 253, 256
Boumediene, Belkacem, 575–576, 581
Boumediène, Houari, 52–53, 561
Bouteflika, Abdelaziz, 559, 563–564,
    579, 588–589, 590–591
BP
  capacity to take on exploration
    risks during 1970s, 146
  Forties Field discovery, 129–151
  See also AIOC; British Petroleum
Brazil
  aversion to private sector involve-
    ment, 8
  early focus on indigenous technical
    capability, 146
  goals for oil sector, 516, 523, 525
  government control over NOCs,
    74
  stock market listings of NOCs, 71
  See also Petrobras
Brent oil field, 151
British Petroleum, 27
  See also BP
Bu Hasa oil field, 482
bunkering, 712–713

CABGOC (Cabinda Gulf Oil
    Company), 845, 850

Campos Basin, 516, 528–531, 546,
    550
Cantarell oil field, 287, 293, 300,
    313–314, 321–323
Cárdenas, Lázaro, 285–287
Cardoso, Henrique, 535
carried interest, 152
CASOC (California Arabian Standard
    Oil Company), 175–176
  See also Saudi Aramco
CFP (Compagnie Française del
    Pétroles)
  capacity to take on exploration
    risks during 1970s, 146
  establishment of, 5
Chávez, Hugo, 54, 431–435, 442
  fear of the political opposition, 88
  gap between prouncements and pol-
    icy reality, 421
  purge of PVDSA, 418, 419–420,
    434, 456–457
  use of PDVSA to provide social
    functions, 3, 434
Chernomyrdin, Viktor, 661, 662,
    663–658, 664, 693
Chevron, capacity to take on explor-
    ation risks during 1970s, 146
Chicontepec oil field, 316, 323, 333
China
  Company Law, 394–396
  energy demand and consumption,
    385–386
  oil industry
    history, 386–388
    overview, 382–384
  stock market listings of NOCs, 71,
    394
  use of competition between NOCs,
    70–71
  See also CNPC
Ciavaldini, Hector, 432
CNOOC (China National Offshore
    Oil Corporation), 382–383,
    384
CNPC (China National Petroleum
    Corporation)
  disasters, 398
  gas, 385
  history, 387–392
  internationalization, 141, 894

CNPC (*cont.*)
    oil production and reserves,
        384–385
    overview, 379–382, 413
    performance, 380–381
        financial indicators, 406–412
        ranking, 935–936
    privatization, 56
    relationship with PetroChina,
        380–403
    relationship with state, 392
        Communist Party of China
            (CPC), 393
        corporate governance and con-
            trol over senior managers,
            393–401
        overseas activities, 405–406
        subsidies, 405–406
CNRIP (National Commission for
    the Restructuring of the
    Petroleum Sector, Angola),
    845–847
common agency (organizational the-
    ory), 117
competition
    and NOC performance, 90
    between NOCs in China, 70–71
    KPC, 364–367
    ONGC, 778–784
complex agency chain (organizational
    theory), 117
concessions
    Saudi Arabia, details "secret" yet
        published, 219
    to manage risk, 147
corruption
    and Algeria, 559, 575–576
    and Nigeria, 707, 708, 717
    and Pemex, 298, 309, 310
    and Saudi Aramco, 193–194
    and Statoil, 627
    and Venezuela, 441, 442
counter-governance by NOC, 67–68
creation of reserves, 132
Cristóbal Colón project, 440
CVP (Corporación Venezolana del
    Petróleo), 27

Daqing oil fields, 384, 385, 389
D'Arcy, William Knox, 240

Das Island, 489
Deepwater Horizon disaster, 27
Den Norske Stats Oljeselskap AS
    See Statoil
dependent variables, of this study,
    15–17
depletion rate policies, 15
    and oil price, 943–944
depletion rate, as measure of per-
    formance, 900–902, 932,
    940–941, 944
diwaniya, Kuwait, 375
Dolphin Gas Project, 507–509

Eduardo dos Santos, José, 847
Ekofisk oil field, 151, 605–607
Enchova oil field, 530
Evensen, Jens, 605
EXPEC (Exploration and Petroleum
    Engineering Center),
    199–196
exploration risk, 127
    management of, 135
expropriation
    constraints on, 39
    disincentives for, 38–39
    effect of political checks and bal-
        ances, 41–42, 56–57
        case studies, 52–54
        control variables, 46–47
        dependent variables, 43–45
        explanatory variables, 45–46
        research design, 43
        research findings, 48–50
        research methods, 47
    events, 35
    incentives for, 37–38
    literature, 37–39
    overview, 35–37
Exxon
    capacity to take on exploration
        risks during 1970s, 146
    part-ownership of Aramco, 176

Fahd of Saudi Arabia, 183
Falcon Oil, 864
field development risk, 127, 130–132
    management of, 136–137
field redevelopment, 130–132
Fjell, Olav, 602, 609, 627

FLEC (Frente de Libertação do Estado de Cabinda), 837–838
FNLA (Frente Nacional para a Libertação de Angola), 843
Forties Field, 151
forward linkages, 212
France
See CFP
Freudenthal, Percy, 845–846, 871
frontier exploration
future frontiers, 166
risks, 128–129
See also exploration risk
Futungo elite, Angola, 841, 848, 849

Gaidar, Yegor, 662
GALSI (Algeria-Sardinia gas pipeline) project, 567
gas
as harder to produce than oil, 19
See also associated gas
gas flaring
ADNOC, 492, 505
KPC, 335–336, 351
Kuwait, 373
Norway, 642
ONGC, 766
Saudi Arabia, 207
GASCO (Abu Dhabi Gas Industries Limited), 489
Gassco, 624
Gazprom
centralized state authority over, 77
corporate governance, 656
corporate structure, 675–677
domestic holdings, 680–681
establishment of, 7
finances, 677–680
future, 657, 671–672, 692
history
1989–2000 privatization, 661–663
2000–present re-nationalization, 663–657
pre-1989 foundations in the Soviet state, 658–660
informal state governance of, 86
interactions with government, 7–10
international activities, 681–683
non-core activities, 683–685

overview, 655–657, 668–674, 691–692
part-privatization, 55
performance, 655–656
ranking, 936
political functions, 405–406
producing gas rather than oil, 4
regulatory capture, 657, 665
relationship with state, 655
state within a state, 67–68, 662
strategy, 656, 685–686
major projects, 686–691
See also Russia
Gazprom-Media Holding, 684
Geisel, Ernesto, 30, 525–527, 528–529, 554
General Agreement on Participation (New York, October 1972), 180–181, 340–341
geological context, 19–20
and NOC creation, 892–894
and NOC performance, 904–905
geological plays, 129
geological provinces, 129
geopolitics, 925–926
Ghawar oil field, 209
Giusti, Luis, 430
GME (Maghreb-Europe) gas pipeline, 566–567
golden quadrant idea, Saudi Arabia, 184
Good Governance of the National Petroleum Sector (Chatham House Document), 195–196
Gosplan (State Committee for Planning), 693
Government Petroleum Fund, Norway (Government Pension Fund – Global, the Fund), 615–616
Gowon, Yakubu, 706
Groningen gas field, 150
Grupo Gema, 864
Gulf Oil Corporation, capacity to take on exploration risks during 1970s, 146
Gullfaks oil field, 608, 637
Gulnes, Nils, 646

Hacienda (Mexican finance ministry), 296–297

Hassan Marican, 820, 822, 830–831
Hassi Messaoud oil field, 567
Hauge, Jens Christian, 607–608, 619
heavy oil
    CNPC investment in exploitation
        techniques, 410
    geological risk, 167
    Iran, 237–238
    Kuwait, 345, 362
    Pemex, 323
    Venezuela, 420–438, 452
Hertog, Steffen, 11

Imperial Energy, 797
independent variables, of this study,
    17–21
India
    ability to tolerate risks of frontier
        activities, 164
    demand for oil, 768–769
    stock market listings of NOC, 71
    See also ONGC
innovation incentives, to reduce risk,
    137
internationalization, 894
    CNPC, 141, 894
    ONGC, 141, 894
    PDVSA, 427–429
    Petrobras, 4
    Petronas, 141, 894
    Statoil, 4
INTEVEP, 428, 456
investment risk, 127, 134–135
IOCs (International Oil Companies)
    future, 25–26, 165–167, 919–926
    risk management capacity, 138–124
Iran
    1951 nationalization, 179, 257
        market availability risk prevent-
            ing *de facto* control, 148
    buyback scheme, 236–237,
        267–268
    constitution, 247
    expropriations, 53–54
    gas, 239, 275
    geology, 243
    history of oil and gas, 237–244
    Islamic Revolution, 243
    pipeline infrastructure, 238–239
    political system, 245–254

refining capacity, 239, 258–259
resource curse, 234–235
state budgetary control over NOC,
    72
See also NIOC
Iraq, nationalization, 181
Italy
    See AGIP

Jaffe, Amy Myers, 12
Johnsen, Arve, 602, 607–608, 609,
    618–619, 646
joint ventures, to manage risk, 147
Jubail Refinery, 227
Jum'ah, Abdullah, 198–182
Jung, Najeeb, 788

KAFCO (Kuwait Aviation Fuelling
    Company), 372
Kårstø gas processing terminal, 624
Khelil, Chakib, 564, 571, 578, 579,
    589
    See also Algeria, 2005
        Hydrocarbons Law
Khodorkovsky, Mikhail, 693
Khursaniyah field development,
    211–212
KISR (Kuwait Institute for Scientific
    Research), 354
Knight, Frank, *Risk, Uncertainty,
    and Profit*, 125
Knightian uncertainty, 168
KNPC (Kuwait National Petroleum
    Company), 339–341
KOTC (Kuwait Oil Tanker Company),
    356–357, 372
KPC (Kuwait Petroleum Corporation)
    founding law, 341–342
    fragmented state governance of, 79,
        334, 337
    history, 341–345
    Iraq–Kuwait War, 342–343
    organization, 345–347
    overview, 334–339, 368–370
    performance, 12, 335, 344–345,
        347
    fiscal system and, 347–349
    gas, 351–352
    labor-relations, 347, 350–351,
        374

non-core obligations and, 352–353
operational costs, 349
ranking, 936
technical capabilities, 353
procedure-heavy state oversight of, 80
relationship with government, 358–361
Project Kuwait, 336, 361–364, 376
regulation and competition, 364–367
Strategic Management Model, 344
strategy, 354–358
See also KNPC; Kuwait Oil Company
KUFPEC (Kuwait Foreign Petroleum Exploration Company), 355
Ku-Maloob-Zaap oil field, 322
Kupolokun, Funsho, 728
Kuwait
nationalization, 181, 340–341
See also KPC; Kuwait Oil Company
Kuwait Oil Company
establishment of, 6, 339

Lameda, Guaicaipuro, 432, 433
Larsen, Røed, 616–617
Libya, nationalization, 181
Link, Walter, 524–525
Lukoil, 661, 662, 673
Lund, Helge, 602, 609, 626

Magna Reserva project, 454
Mahathir Mohamad, 816–817, 820, 827–829
Malaviya, K. D., 760
Malaysia
oil sector structure, 821–811
See also Petronas
Malaysian Indonesia Shipping Corp., 827–828
Managing Instability in Algeria: Elites and Political Change since 1995 (Werenfels), 558
Mandela, Nelson, 829
Mandini, Robert, 431–432

Manjoon oil field, 833
Manshaus, Karl-Edwin, 646
Marcel, Valérie, 12, 119
Oil Titans: National Oil Companies in the Middle East, 558
Marcellus shale gas project, 625, 634–635
market availability risk, 127–128
precluding nationalization in 1950s, 148
market supply risk, 128
Marlim oil field, 533
Mattei, Enrico, 242
mature provinces, 130
Mbakassi, Antonio Mosquito, 864
MEDGAZ project, 567
Medvedev, Dmitry, 30
Medvezhye gas field, 669–670
Mercury Telecom, 864
Mexico
1938 nationalization, 145, 285, 325
geology, 283
regulatory control of NOCs, 72
state budgetary control over NOC, 72
See also Pemex
Meziane, Mohamed, 575–576
Miller, Aleksei, 664
Mirmoezi, Seyed Mehdi, 255
Mobil
capacity to take on exploration risks during 1970s, 146
part-ownership of Aramco, 176
Mongstad refinery upgrade, 638, 639, 647
Montrose field, 151
Mosaddegh, Mohammad, 180, 241
MPLA (Movimento Popular de Libertação de Angola), 837–838, 843, 844, 845, 847–849
Mumbai High field, 762–765
Muñoz, Raul, 312

Nabucco pipeline, 673
Najib Abdul Razak, 822, 829–831
Nasser, Amin, 200
nationalization, 60, 892
1938 Mexico, 145, 285, 325

nationalization (*cont.*)
  1951 Iran, 179, 257
    market availability risk
      preventing *de facto* control,
      148
  1976 Saudi Arabia, 180–181
  1976 Venezuela, 423–426
  after Six-Day War, June 1967,
    180–181
  death sentence of Dr. Mosaddegh,
    180
  General Agreement on Participation
    (New York, October 1972),
    180–181, 340–341
  Kuwait, 181, 340–341
  risk and state's choice of agent in
    early 1970s, 145–149
  UAE (United Arab Emirates),
    484–486
  See also expropriation
Nazer, Hisham, 182, 183, 184
NCS (Norwegian Continental Shelf),
  646
Neelam fields, 765
Nehru, Jawaharlal, 758
Nejad-Hosseinian, Hadi, 251
NELP, India (New Exploration and
  Licensing Policy), 756,
  767–768
  efforts to inject competition,
    782–784
Nemtsov, Boris, 663
Neto, Agostinho, 847
Neutral Zone (Kuwait/Saudi Arabia),
  339, 372
NIGC (National Iranian Gas
  Company), 243
Nigeria
  corruption, 707, 708, 717
  history, 704
    gas operations, 710–712
    oil operations, 708–710, 712–715
  institutional weakness, 715–718
  political development and oil,
    706–708
  reform prospects, 737–743
  security problems, 712–714
  state–IOC interactions, 718
  See also NNPC
NIOC (National Iranian Oil
  Company)

and sanctions, 235, 236, 237, 263,
  264
establishment of, 5
fragmented state governance of, 79
Iran–Iraq war, 235, 263–264
organizational structure, 243,
  244–245
overview, 234–237, 269–271
performance, 259–261
  external factors, 261–264
  internal factors, 265–269
  ranking, 936
relationship with Iranian State, 68,
  254–259
NIORDC (National Iranian Oil
  Refining and Distribution
  Company), 243
NLNG (Nigeria LNG), 730
NNOC (Nigerian National Oil
  Company), 28, 704, 710
NNPC (Nigerian National Petroleum
  Corporation)
  COMD (Crude Oil Marketing
    Division), 726
  divisions and subsidiaries, 702–701,
    727–731
  Eleme Petrochemicals, 729
  establishment of, 6
  fragmented state governance of, 79
  informal state governance of, 86
  interactions with IOCs, 720–723
  interactions with state, 723–727
  limited capacity to operate as a
    company, 4
  NAPIMS (National Petroleum
    Investment Management
    Services), 721–722
  NETCO (National Engineering
    & Technical Company),
    730–731
  non-hydrocarbon responsibilities,
    903
  overview, 701–704
  patronage, 703–704
  performance, 12, 731
    delivering patronage, 736–737
    developing indigenous techno-
      logical capability, 733–736
    maximizing government revenue
      from hydrocarbons, 731–733
    ranking, 936–937

procedure-heavy state oversight of, 80–64
strategy, 731
NOC governance
and performance
competition, 90
findings, 64–66, 75–87
hypotheses, 64, 75–77
law-based mechanisms, 64, 65, 76–77, 81–87, 91
monitoring-heavy oversight systems, 64, 65, 75–76, 79–81, 89–87, 910–911
overview, 63–93
research methods, 73–74
transparency, 90–91
unified v fragmented control, 64–65, 75, 77–79, 87–89, 907–910
as corporate governance, 69–71
as public administration, 71–72
as regulation, 72
overview, 62–66
principal-agent model, 66–69
NOCs (National Oil Companies)
as misnomer, 3, 4
dominance of, 3, 35
future, 890–891
history, 5–8, 121
interactions with government, 10–11, 20, 890
internal factors, 20–21
literature, 8–13
performance, 895–900
performance factors
geology, 904–905
inhouse expertise, 913–914
management strategy, 912–913
state goals, 900–904
state–NOC interaction, 905–900
reasons for endurance of, 9–10
reasons for forming, 8–9, 889, 891–895
reasons for variance among, 11–13, 887, 889–890
risk management capacity, 139–142
strategy, 915–919
study approach of this book, 13–15, 23–27
case selection, 21–23, 888–889

dependent variables, 15–17
independent variables, 17–21
non-associated gas, 331
non-hydrocarbon responsibilities of NOC, 902–904
Nord Stream pipeline, 688–689
Norsk Hydro, 638–639
Statoil merger, 602–603, 609–610, 625–627
North Sea
approach to risk management by UK and Norway, 149–150
licensing during exploration stages, 150–152
nationalization during lower risk stages, 152–153
Norvik, Harald, 602, 609, 618, 621–623
Norway
early focus on indigenous technical capability, 146
government control over NOCs, 74
history of natural resources development, 604–610
North Sea exploration and development, 149–153
regulatory control of NOCs, 72
state goals, 610–617
Ten Commandments for Norwegian oil sector, 642–643
stock market listings of NOCs, 71, 609
See also Statoil
Norwegian Model, 91–92, 600, 601, 613, 909–911
Novatek, 696
NPC (National Petrochemical Company, Iran), 243
NPD (Norwegian Petroleum Directorate), 613–614, 619
NPM (new public administration), 116

Oando PLC, 735
Obasanjo, Olusegun, 708, 716, 717–718
Odili, Peter, 714
offshore oil development
Brazil, 527–535
Norway, 149–153

oil company model (China), 389–390
oil industry, future structure,
        165–167, 919–921
oil price
    and depletion rate policies,
        943–944
    and nationalizations, 149
    and NOC performance, 20
    and premium on risk minimization,
        133
    and state policy, Algeria, 558
    and state's choice of agent for
        hydrocarbons extraction,
        155, 160–161, 165
    future, 921–925
    influencing without a cartel, 126
    manipulation to maintain petrol-
        eum's dominance, 166–167
oil supply curves, 26
*Oil Titans: National Oil Companies
    in the Middle East* (Marcel),
    558
Omar Mustapha, 830–831
ONGC (Oil and Natural Gas
        Corporation Limited)
    competition, 778–784
    corporatization, 784–785
    engagement with IOCs, 758–760
    exploration, 761–762, 771, 772
        overseas operations, 795–797
    finances, 754–763, 774
        1991 crisis, 765–767
        free cash flow, 793–795
        project management, 774–777
    fragmented state governance of,
        68–79
    governance
        appointment of directors,
            787–788
        corporatization, 784–785
        counterproductive monitoring
            mechanisms, 797–801
        government control and corpor-
            atization, 785
        hiring constraints, 788–789
        multiple vigilance and monitoring
            bodies, 786
        social spending, 789–790
    governance of through law-based
        mechanisms, 85

history
    1947–1970 initial years, 5, 754,
        757–762
    1970–1990 discovery of Mumbai
        High, 762–764
    1991–1998 crisis and reforms,
        764–768
    1999–2008 adapting to new
        rules, 768–777
    internationalization, 141, 894
    overview, 753–757, 801–804
    OVL (ONGC Videsh Limited),
        773–757, 795–797
    performance and strategy, 755,
        772–774, 777–778
    performance ranking, 937
    production plateau, 769–772
    price controls, 790–791
        concessions to oil marketing com-
            panies, 792–793
        pricing of gas from the PMT
            fields, 791–792
    privatization, 55–56
    Russian assistance, 760
OPEC (Organization of the Petroleum
        Exporting Countries), 28
    and nationalizations, 149
    establishment of, 6, 149
    increased proven reserve figures,
        940
    UAE (United Arab Emirates),
        483–484
Operation Bultiste, 180
Orinoco Belt, 428, 429, 434, 437, 454
OSC (oil services companies)
    as not in competition with private
        operating companies, 165
    definitions, 122
    risk management capacity, 142–143
OSF (Oil Stabilization Fund),
        248–252
OVL (ONGC Videsh Limited),
        773–774, 786–795

PABs (Petroleum Administrative
        Bureaus, China), 387,
        389–391, 394
Parliamentary Report No. 25
        (1973–1974 Norway), 611,
        614, 648

Parra-Luzardo, Gastón, 433
PDVSA (Petróleos de Venezuela, S.A.)
  centralized state authority over, 77
  history, 6, 7
    1958–1976 nationalization,
      423–426
    1976–1982 private business
      under government control,
      426–427
    1982–1989 internationalization,
      427–429
    1990–1999 foreign investment,
      429–431
    1999–2003 firmer state control,
      431–433
    2003–today partial
      transformation, 434–435
  informal state governance of,
    68–86
  management strategy, 912
  negotiations with IMF on behalf of
    Venezuelan government, 28
  overview, 418–421, 460–462
  performance, 455
    1976–2002, 455–456
    2003–present, 456–460
    ranking, 937
  pre-Chávez reputation for
    technocratic excellence, 119
  procedure-heavy state oversight of, 80
  relationship with government
    extent of oil reserves and,
      436–437
    extra-heavy crude and, 437–438
    gas and, 439–440
    long investment cycles and,
      438–439
    natural resources and, 435–436
    oil price and, 450
  social functions, 3, 434, 447–449
  state goals, 444
    early Chávez era transition,
      446–447
    later Chávez era expansion,
      447–450
    pre-Chávez era stability,
      444–446
  state within a state, 67–68, 441
    effects on tax policy, 443–444
    weak state institutions, 441–443

strategy, 451
  seeking autonomy, 451–453
  switch to compliance, 453–455
Pemex (Petróleos Mexicanos)
  board composition, 115
  constraints on funding, 140
  corporate structure, 306–307
  employee relations, 309–311
  finances, 299–300
    investment financing, 302–306
    investment priorities, 307–309
    subsidies, 301
    taxes, 300–301
  fragmented state governance of, 79
  gas, 308–309, 314–315
  governance of through law-based
    mechanisms, 85
  history, 5, 7, 284–287
  human capital, 316–318
  interactions with government,
    10–11, 292–293
    Bureaucracy, 295–299
    Congress, 293–295
    Executive, 293
  management dissatisfaction,
    311–313
  nationalism and, 892
  non-hydrocarbon responsibilities,
    903
  overview, 280–284
  performance, 12, 288–292
    ranking, 937–938
  procedure-heavy state oversight of,
    80
  reform prospects, 318–321
  relationships with contractors and
    IOCs, 313–316
  reserves, 321–323
performance
  causal factors, 20–21
    state goals, 900
  definitions, 4
  measures, 15–16, 895
  ranking, 931–933, 934–935
    case study NOCs, 935–939
    category definitions
      high, 933–934
      low, 934
      lower middle, 934
      upper middle, 934

permanent sovereignty over natural
  resources, 178
Petoro, 623
Petrobras
  able to shoulder risks of operating
    in deep water, 158–159
  establishment of, 5, 6
  governance of through law-based
    mechanisms, 80–69
  history, 515–516
    1954–1973 organizing the down-
      stream, 522–527
    1974–1994 developing the off-
      shore, 527–535
    1995–2008 deregulation,
      535–544
    pre-1954 state monopoly,
      519–522
  international nature of, 4
  lobbying, 113
  monitoring-heavy oversight system,
    81
  more aggressive taking risk because
    of state support, 164
  overview, 515–518, 551
  performance, 544–545
    agent's perspective, 548–551
    meeting state goals, 533–535
    principal's perspective, 545–548
    ranking, 937
  political pressures, 141
  privatization, 54–55
  relationship with state, 517–518,
    523–524
  state within a state, 549
  strategy, 517, 518, 543–544
PetroChina, 380–381, 382, 383–384,
  394
  board composition, 396
  relationship with CNPC, 402–403
petroleum provinces, 129
PETROMIN (General Organization
  of Petroleum and Minerals),
  28, 182–184, 204
Petronas (Petroliam Nasional Bhd)
  centralized state authority over, 77
  challenges, 834
  exploration, 818–821
  history, 6, 7, 811–817
  internationalization, 141, 894

monitoring-heavy state oversight of,
  68–81
negotiating on behalf of government, 72
overview, 809–811, 834–835
performance, ranking, 938
relationship with state, 823–824
  Bank Bumiputra bailout,
    826–827
  banker of pet projects, 827–829
  early years, 824–825
  Najib administration, 829–831
  under premier Mahathir
    Mohamad, 825–826
reserves, 818
strategy, 831
  domestic, 831–832
  overseas, 832–834
See also Malaysia
Petronas Carigali, 815–816, 819, 825,
  831–832
Petrossal, 517, 547
Phillips, Ekofisk oil field discovery,
  151
PIC (Petrochemical Industries
  Company, Kuwait), 376
Pidiregas projects, 302–306
PMT (Panna, Mukta, and Tapti) fields
  joint venture, 781–782
  pricing of gas, 791–792
political considerations, and state's
  choice of agent for hydrocarbons extraction, 163–165
political risk, 132
Prasad, N. B., 762
predictive geological modeling, 134
pre-salt, definitions, 553
principal–agent problem, prompting
  NOC formation, 9
privatization
  and performance, 35
  and transition to democracy, 55
  CNPC (China National Petroleum
    Corporation), 56
  effect of political checks and bal-
    ances, 42–43, 57
    case studies, 54–56
    control variables, 46–47
    dependent variables, 43–45
    explanatory variables, 45–46

research design, 43
research findings, 50–52
research methods, 47
events, 35
rationales for, 39–40
profits taxation, introduction by Saudi
Arabia, 177
Project Kuwait, 336, 361–364, 376
PROMOS (PROjet de MOdernisation
de Sonatrach), 563
Proton Cars, 828
proven petroleum provinces, 130
Putin, Vladimir, 664–665
Putrajaya, 828

Rabigh Refinery, 227
Raha, Subir, 787–788
Raja Mohar Raja Badiozaman,
814–824
Ramírez, Rafael, 434, 453
Rastam Hadi, 814, 824
Razak, Abdul, 814
regulatory capture, Gazprom, 657,
665–688
Reiten, Eivind, 626
resource curse, 824, 942
Iran, 234–235
Malaysia, 405–406
Nigeria, 704–705
risk
and state's choice of agent for
hydrocarbons extraction,
121–124, 143–144, 161–163
for the North Sea, 123–153
hypotheses, 154
hypotheses testing, 144–145,
153–161
in ADNOC, 502
in early 1970s nationalizations,
145–149
influence of non-risk factors,
163–165
significance of oil price expectations, 155, 160–161, 165
significance of previous commercial discoveries, 156, 160
significance of water depth,
154–155, 158–159
definitions, 124–125
in petroleum industry, 127–133

risk management, 125
company type and capacity,
137–138
exploration, 135
field development, 136–137
in petroleum industry, 133
International Oil Companies,
138–139
National Oil Companies, 139–142
Oil Service Companies, 142–143
risk taking, not implying risk management, 141
risk tolerance, 126
India, 164
Risk, Uncertainty, and Profit
(Knight), 125
risk-weighting, 124
Rosneft, 661, 662, 665
rule of law, 119
and NOC performance, 91
See also NOC governance, and
performance, law-based
mechanisms
Russia
government control over NOCs, 71
oil and gas sectors
proportion of GDP, 666–668
state involvement, 658–657
stock market listings of NOCs, 71
See also Gazprom

Sabriya gas field, 351–352
Samarec, 405–406
SASAC (State-Owned Assets
Supervision and
Administration Commission,
China), 395
Saud bin Faisal bin Abdul-Aziz, 190
Saudi Arabia
government–IOC relationships and
NOC efficiency, 11
rationale for nationalization, 38,
892
regulatory control of NOCs, 72
See also Saudi Aramco
Saudi Aramco
attempted opening of the upstream,
189–191
board composition, 115
centralized state authority over, 77

Saudi Aramco (*cont.*)
  commercial-type operation, 3
  downstream
    abroad, 205–207
    domestic, 203–205
  establishment of, 6
  financial transparency, 192–193
  future, 217–218
  gas, 207–208
  governance, 195–196
  history, 175–184
  human capital, 179, 196–199,
    214–215
  low-motivated Saudi employees,
    197, 224
  oil marketing, 202–203
  oil production, 201–202
  oil production capacity, 200–201
  oil recovery rates and reserves,
    200–201
  overview, 173–174, 216–217
  performance, 3–13, 208–215
    ranking, 938
  regulation of the oil sector, 187–194
  relationship with government, 174,
    184–187
  strategy, 199–200
Savimbi, Jonas, 844, 845, 848–849
SCPMA/SPC, Saudi Arabia (Supreme
    Council on Petroleum and
    Mineral Affairs/Supreme
    Petroleum Council), 184,
    187–193
secondary oil recovery, 130–132
serial nationalizers, 126
Seven Sisters, 5, 218, 241, 273
SFP (Mexican Ministry of Public
    Administration), 297–298
SFPM (Service for Promotion of
    Mineral Production, Brazil),
    520–521
Shagari, Shehu, 710
Shah gas field, 509–510
Shamsul Azhar Abas, 831
Sharma, R. S., 788
Shell
  Brent oil field discovery, 151
  capacity to take on exploration
    risks during 1970s, 146
  employing local talent, 464

Shonekan, Ernest, 707–708
Shtokman field, 686–687
Shuaiba refinery, 340
Simon, David, 621
Sinochem, 382–383
Sinopec, 382, 384, 390, 392
Sinopec Star Petroleum Co. Ltd., 382
Slavneft, 665
SOCAL (Standard Oil of California),
    agreement with Saudi
    Arabia, 175–176
social functions of an NOC, 7–8
  PDVSA (Petróleos de Venezuela,
    S.A.), 3, 434, 447–449
SOE (state-owned enterprises), 114
Sonair, 864
Sonangol (Sociedade Nacional de
    Combustíveis de Angola)
  centralized state authority
    over, 77
  context
    civil war, 845–847
    conflict and socio-ethnic identity,
      843–844
    evolution of company goals,
      847–849
    geology, 849–852
    quasi-sovereign responsibilities,
      865–870
  core duties, 836–838
  establishment of, 6
  history, 842–843
  informal state governance of, 86
  information disclosure, 842
  overview, 836–842, 874–877
  performance, 12
    ranking, 938–939
  performance factors, 870
    commitment to education and
      capacity development,
      872–873
    independence on technical and
      commercial decisions,
      871–872
    pragmatic reliance on inter-
      national partners, 873–874
    state-company leadership solidar-
      ity, 870–871
  role as regulator, 3
  strategy, 852

as nexus of ancillary oil economy, 860–862, 863–865
stewardship of oil sector, 856–860
to be predictable partner for IOCs, 852–856
subsidiaries, 862, 863–864
Sonangol P&P (Sonangol Pesquisa e Produção), 858, 863
Sonatrach
  gas, 566–560
  history, 6, 7, 561–564
  performance, 583–587
  ranking, 939
  relationship with state, 568
  structure, 569–571
  strategy, 587–589
  See also Algeria
South Pars field, 239, 272
South Stream pipeline, 689–690
SPC
  See SCPMA/SPC, Saudi Arabia; SPC, Kuwait
SPC, Kuwait (Supreme Petroleum Council), 335, 344, 358
Spitsbergen mining accident, 612–613
Star Enterprise, 206
"state within a state"
  Gazprom, 67–68, 662
  PDVSA (Petróleos de Venezuela, S.A.), 67–68, 441
    effects on tax policy, 443–444
    weak state institutions, 441–443
  Petrobras, 549
  Sonangol, 865–870
states
  goals, 17–18
  and NOC performance, 900–904
  motivations, 125–126
  risk tolerance, 126, 164
Statoil (Den Norske Stats Oljeselskap AS)
  able to shoulder risks of operating in deep water, 158–159
  board composition, 114–115
  centralized state authority over, 77
  commercial-type operation, 3
  establishment of, 6, 152, 153–145, 607
  future direction, 640–642

governance of through law-based mechanisms, 85
international nature of, 4
monitoring-heavy oversight by state, 81
Norsk Hydro merger, 602–603, 609–610, 625–627
overview, 599–604
performance, ranking, 939
political pressures, 141, 627, 628
privatization, 55
relationship with state, 602–603, 612–613, 618–628
strategy and performance, 628–640
See also Norway
Statoil–BP Alliance, 621–622
stock market listings of NOCs
  Angola, 841
  Brazil, 71
  China, 71, 394
  India, 71
  Norway, 71, 609
  Russia, 71
Stoltenberg, Jens, 626
strategy, definitions, 4
structured case studies, descriptions, 13–14
Sultan, Nader, 343, 346–347, 349–350, 362
supply trap, 924–925
Supreme Economic Council (Saudi Arabia), 188
Surgutneftegaz, 661, 665
swing producer, Saudi Aramco, 210–211

Tariki, Abdullah, 178
tertiary oil recovery, 132
Texaco
  capacity to take on exploration risks during 1970s, 146
  CASOC joint venture with SOCAL, 176
  part-ownership of Aramco, 176
TME (Trans-Mediterranean) gas pipeline, 566–567
TNK-BP, 665, 673
Troll field, 624
TSGP (Trans-Sahara/Trans-Saharan Gas Pipeline), 567, 712

UN Resolution, 178
UAE (United Arab Emirates)
    formation, 480–481, 485
    nationalization, 484–486
    OPEC membership, 483–484
    See also Abu Dhabi; ADNOC
UK
    BNOC
        formation, 152–153
        privatization, 153
    North Sea exploration and develop-
        ment, 149–153
Umm Niga gas field, 351–352
Umm Shaif oil field, 482–483
UNITA (União Nacional para a
    Independência Total de
    Angola), 843, 844, 845,
    848–838, 849, 852
Urengoyskoye gas field, 669–670
US, import controls prompting cre-
    ation of crude oil trading
    market, 148
Úslar Pietri, Arturo, 423

velayat-e-faqih system, 245–246
Venezuela
    expropriations, 54
    government control over NOCs, 71
    oil sector, pre-PDVSA, 422–423
    private sector involvement, 8
    See also PDVSA
vertical integration, to manage risk,
    147
Vicente, Manuel, 871
Victor, David G., 15

Vision 2020 (Kuwait), 357–358, 361
Vyakhirev, Rem, 664

WAGP (West African Gas Pipeline),
    712
wasta, Kuwait, 375
Werenfels, Isabelle, 592–593, 594
    *Managing Instability in Algeria:
    Elites and Political Change
    since 1995*, 558
West Sole gas field, 151
Willoch, Kåre, 620
Wolf, Christian, 15

Yamal fields, 687–688
Yamani, Ahmed Zaki, 178, 180–181,
    340
Yamburgskoye gas field, 669–670
Yanbu Refinery, 227
Yeltsin, Boris, 661–662, 663
YPF (Yacimientos Petrolíferos
    Fiscales)
    history, 5, 7, 27–28
Yukos, 661, 665
Yuznno-Karsky field, 694

ZADCO (Zakum Development
    Company), 487–488, 493
Zanganeh, Bijan, 255, 258,
    266–267
Zapolyarnoye gas field, 670–671
Zayed bin Sultan Al Nahyan,
    485–486, 490, 500–501
Zenasni, Benamar, 575–576
Zeroual, Liamine, 563